READER'S INDEX
TO

THE
TWENTIETH
CENTURY
VIEWS
LITERARY
CRITICISM
SERIES

VOLUMES 1-100

Prentice-Hall, Inc., *Englewood Cliffs, New Jersey*

Indexes compiled by Robert Mony, Editor, together with Roger Jackson, Elaine Luthy, Carter Ratcliff, Phyllis Derfner, Roy Newbert, Don Wigal, Duskin Shears, Pamela Smith, Paul Pines, and Stephen Book.

©1973 by Prentice-Hall, Inc., Englewood Cliffs, New Jersey. All rights reserved. No part of this book may be reproduced in any form or by any means without permission in writing from the publisher. Library of Congress Catalog Card Number: 72-13287. ISBN: 0-13-753384-5.

10 9 8 7 6 5 4 3 2 1

Prentice-Hall International, Inc. (*London*)
Prentice-Hall of Australia, Pty. Ltd. (*Sydney*)
Prentice-Hall of Canada, Ltd. (*Toronto*)
Prentice-Hall of India Private Limited (*New Delhi*)
Prentice-Hall of Japan, Inc. (*Tokyo*)

CONTENTS

HOW TO USE THIS INDEX   v
AESCHYLUS   1
AUDEN   7
JANE AUSTEN   16
BAUDELAIRE   22
SAMUEL BECKETT   28
THE BEOWULF POET   34
BLAKE   38
BRECHT   45
THE BRONTËS   54
BYRON   60
CAMUS   67
CERVANTES   73
CHEKHOV   78
COLERIDGE   86
CONRAD   93
STEPHEN CRANE   100
E. E. CUMMINGS   109
DANTE   114
DICKENS   120
EMILY DICKINSON   125
JOHN DONNE   132
DOSTOEVSKY   139
DREISER   146
DRYDEN   153
GEORGE ELIOT   160
T. S. ELIOT   165
EMERSON   173
EURIPIDES   179
FAULKNER   184
FIELDING   192
F. SCOTT FITZGERALD   199

FLAUBERT   204
FORSTER   209
ROBERT FROST   215
GIDE   223
GOETHE   231
HARDY   238
HAWTHORNE   244
HEMINGWAY   251
HOMER   256
HOPKINS   261
A. E. HOUSMAN   268
IBSEN   274
HENRY JAMES   280
SAMUEL JOHNSON   286
BEN JONSON   292
KAFKA   298
KEATS   305
D. H. LAWRENCE   311
SINCLAIR LEWIS   318
LORCA   323
ROBERT LOWELL   329
MALRAUX   335
THOMAS MANN   341
MARLOWE   348
ANDREW MARVELL   353
MELVILLE   359
ARTHUR MILLER   364
MILTON: PARADISE LOST   370
THE MODERN AMERICAN
   THEATER   376
MODERN BLACK
   NOVELISTS   383

MODERN BRITISH		STEINBECK	513
DRAMATISTS	390	STENDHAL	519
MOLIERE	398	LAWRENCE STERNE	525
MARIANNE MOORE	406	WALLACE STEVENS	530
O'NEILL	412	STRINDBERG	540
PIRANDELLO	419	SWIFT	547
POE	427	THACKERAY	552
EZRA POUND	434	DYLAN THOMAS	558
PROUST	440	THOREAU	565
RESTORATION DRAMATISTS	446	TOLSTOY	570
SAMUEL RICHARDSON	452	MARK TWAIN	577
EDWIN ARLINGTON		VIRGIL	583
ROBINSON	458	VOLTAIRE	587
SARTRE	465	NATHANAEL WEST	594
SHAKESPEARE: THE		EDITH WHARTON	600
COMEDIES	472	WHITMAN	606
SHAKESPEARE: THE		OSCAR WILDE	613
HISTORIES	478	WILLIAM CARLOS	
SHAKESPEARE: THE		WILLIAMS	619
TRAGEDIES	485	VIRGINIA WOOLF	626
G. B. SHAW	491	YEATS	634
SHELLEY	498	INDEX TO CRITICS	641
SOPHOCLES	503	NUMERICAL LISTING OF	
SPENSER	507	VOLUMES	682

HOW
TO USE
THIS INDEX

This *Reader's Index* provides in one convenient reference work a volume-by-volume guide to the first 100 works in the Twentieth Century Views literary criticism series. An *index to each volume* enables the reader to locate quickly and easily references to particular aspects of an author's life and work, including assessments of each writer's individual works and discussion of such critical topics as style, form, philosophy, etc. Comparisons with other authors in the series may be made by referring to the same topics in the indexes to various other volumes. As a further aid to the reader, the page references for major discussions of important topics are indicated in **boldface type**.

Finally, a master *index to critics* and their contributions to the series as a whole is included, arranged alphabetically by critic. Numbers in **boldface type** indicate the number of the volume in which each article is to be found; the lightface numbers following are the page references within that volume. For example, **65**: 95-98 indicates that the article is to be found on pp. 95-98 of *Faulkner: A Collection of Critical Essays* (book no. 65 in the series). A series listing, giving the volume number of each book followed by the title, is found on p. 682.

AESCHYLUS

A Collection of Critical Essays

Edited by MARSH H. McCALL, JR.

A

Aeneid (Virgil), 110, 175
Aeschylus, 1-9, 13, 17, 20-28, 65, 71-72, 83, 170
  chronology of plays, 5, 13-14
  and Dante, 159
  free will, doctrine of, 102-5
  ideology of, 145-47
  Old Comedy, use of, 156-58
  and Pindar, 9, 24, 26-27, 71-72
  and Pythagoreans, 131-32, 143
  and Shelley, 145-47
  theology of, 8-9, 28, 60, 66, 118-19, 122-23, 140-144, 160-163
Aeschylus, works by:
  Agamemnon, 6, 8, 17, 20, 22-24, 41, 63, 64, 66, **73-77**, 79-84, 85-86, 91-92, 94-96, 99-104, 105, 107-9, 110-19, 152, 154, 163, 164-83
  Choephori, 69-70, 101, 104, 111, 114-15, **119-23**, 152, 154, 159
  Daniad trilogy, 3, 5-6, 17, 28, 63-64, 66-67, 69, 148, 150, 152-54, 156, 158, 160, 162
  Daughters of Danaüs, 5-6, 17, 28, 63, 154, 158, 162
  Diktyoulkoi, 161, 163
  Egyptians, 17, 63, 154, 156
  Eumenides, 7, 15, 17, 18, 21, 23, 27, 60, 63, 79-80, 85, 87-89, 94, 100-103, 111-15, 119, 122, 152-53, 154, 156-59, 162
  Glaucus of Potniae, 18, 29-30

Heliades, 161
Kares è Europe, 161, 163
Laius, 3, 17-18, 155
Net-Haulers, 26
Oedipus, 3, 155
Oresteia, 2, 3, 6-8, 13, 17-19, 64, 65, 67, 70, 77-79, 80, 84, 87-89, 99-104, **106-23**, 143, 145, 148-50, 152-59, 162-63
Persians, 2-3, 7-8, 12-13, 18-19, 21, 26-27, **29-39**, 93, 109-10, 150-151, 161
Phineus, 18, 29-30
Phrygians or Ransoming of Hector, 156
Prometheia, 3, 5, 7-8, 30, 64, 80, **124-47**, 148-50, 152-59, 163
Prometheus Bound, 7-8, 18, 20-21, 25, 27-28, 63, 93, 103-4, **127-35**, 139, 153, 156, 160, 163
Prometheus the Fire-bearer, 18, 29, 30, 139, 153, 154, 156, 158, 163
Prometheus Unbound, 18, **135-39**, 153, 156, 163
Proteus, 6,
Psychostasia, 161
Seven Against Thebes, 3, 4-5, 17-19, 21-22, 28, **40-62**, 94, 150-151, 161
Sphinx, 3, 61
Suppliant Women, 2, 4-6, 15, 17, 20-21, 23-24, 27, 28, **63-72**, 129, 154, 156, 159, 162
Theban trilogy, 3, 17-18, 58-59, 155-56

1

Agamemnon, 6, 8, 17, 20, 22-24, 41,
    63, 64, 66, 73-77, 79-84, 85-86, 91-
    92, 94-96, 99-104, 105, 107-9, 110-
    19, 152, 154, 159, 163, 164-83
    characterization in, 115-19
    conflict, theme of, 73-74
    curse in, 76, 91-92, 94
    imagery, 24-25, 41, 75-76, 82, 110-
        15
    as lyric tragedy, 83-84
    Moira, function of, 99-104
    prose translations of, 178-79
    structure, 22-24, 73-77, 79-84, 85-
        86, 94-99, 110-12, 117-19, 152,
        154, 159, 163
    symbolism, 81, 86, 107-10
    theology, 94-96, 99-105
    translations of, 164-83
Aigyptioi (see *Egyptians*)
Ajax (Sophocles), 13, 151
Alcestis (Euripides), 13, 172
Aldington, Richard, 172
Anaxagoras, 9
Antigone (Sophocles), 4, 128, 151
Antiphonal system, 180
    in *Seven Against Thebes,* 44-45, 48-
        49
Apollodorus, 140
Aristophanes, 41
Aristotle, 11, 93, 104, 106
Arnold, Matthew, 173
Austin, R. G., 175

B

Bacchae (Euripides), 12, 15, 107
Bell, Sir Harold Idris, 174-75
Bergson, Henri, 51
Boileau, Nicolas, 5
Bowra, Sir Maurice, 2, 172
Boyd, H. S., 178
Bridges, Robert, 173
Browning, Robert, 169
Burke, Edmund, 127

C

Childe, Gordon V., 124

Choephori, 69-70, 101, 104, 111, 114-
    15, 119-23, 152, 154, 159
    characterization in, 119-20, 123
    imagery, 111, 114-15, 120-121
    Moira, function of, 101, 104
    structure, 119-23, 152, 154, 159
Chorus:
    in *Agamemnon,* 92, 95
    function of, 15, 20
    in *Suppliant Women,* 5
Cicero, 135
Conington, John, 167-68
Cornford, Francis, 178
Curse, 28, 17-19, 42, 47, 56-61, 76
    in *Agamemnon,* 76
    in *Oresteia,* 90-98
    in *Seven Against Thebes,* 17-19, 47,
        56-61
    in Sophocles, 58-59
Cyclops (Euripides), 92

D

Danaid trilogy, 3, 5-6, 17, 28, 63-64,
    66-67, 69, 148, 150, 152-54, 156,
    158, 160, 162
    dating of, 5, 148, 150
    Daughters of Danaüs, 5-6, 17, 28,
        63, 154, 158, 162
    Egyptians, 28, 63, 154
    structure, 5-6, 63-64, 66-67, 69,
        152-63
    Suppliant Women, 2, 4-6, 15, 17,
        20-21, 23-24, 27, 28, 63-72, 129,
        154, 156, 159, 162
Dante, and Aeschylus, 159
Daughters of Danaüs, 5-6, 17, 28, 63,
    154, 158, 162
    structure, 28, 154, 162
Demokritos, 132
Determinism, theme of, 28
Diktyoulkoi, 161, 163
Diodorus, 140
Diogenes the Cynic, and myth of
    Prometheus, 144-45
Dirge, function of, 60
Divine Comedy (Dante), 159
Doolittle, Hilda, 172

Dryden, John, 164, 165, 170

E

Egyptians, 17, 63
  structure, 154, 156
Electra (Sophocles), 107
Eliot, T. S., 170, 172, 180, 182
Empedokles, 126, 132
Epicurus, 132, 142
Eumenides, 7, 15, 17, 18, 21, 23, 27,
  60, 63, 79-80, 85, 87-89, 94, 100-
  103, 111-15, 119, 122, 152-53, 154,
  156-59, 162
  curse in, 94, 101
  imagery, 88-89, 111-15, 119
  Moira, function of, 100-103
  patriotism in, 27
  structure, 23, 28, 79-80, 87-89, 113-
    15, 122, 152-53, 154, 156-59, 162
  symbolism, 87-88
Euripides, 6, 12, 13-14, 15, 17, 36, 45,
  47, 92, 107, 120, 128, 162, 170, 172
  and Aeschylus, 13-14, 17, 45
"Euripides and Professor Murray"
  (Eliot), 170

F

Family Reunion, The (Eliot), 180, 182
Faust (Goethe), 174
Finley, John H., 5
Fitzgerald, Edward, 168-69, 172
Fraenkel, E., 96, 110, 117, 178-79,
  181
Fragment of a Greek Tragedy (Hous-
  man), 176-77
Free will, theme of, 28
  in *Oresteia,* 90-105

G

Georgics (Virgil), 167
Glaucus of Potniae, 18, 29-30
Goethe, Johann Wolfgang von, 105,
  174
Goheen, Robert F., 6
Gospels, and free will, 93

Green, Peter, 9
Guthrie, W. K. C., 104

H

Hamlet (Shakespeare), 104
Hammond, N. G. L., 6
Heliades (The Daughters of the Sun),
  161
Heraclitus, 16, 53
Herington, C. J., 8
Herodotus, 32, 36, 128, 151, 155
  and Aeschylus, 29-30, 38
Hesiod, 8-9, 125, 141, 145, 153
  and myth of Prometheus, 125, 141,
    145
Hippokrates, 132
Hippolytus (Doolittle tr.), 172
Homer, 8-9, 36, 40, 49, 61-62, 74-75,
  81, 109-10, 152, 156, 173
Hopkins, Gerard Manley, 172, 180
Horace, 149, 175-76
Housman, A. E., 175-77

I

Iliad (Homer), 8, 36, 40, 61-62, 75, 81,
  109-10, 156
Im Westen Nichts Neues (Remarque),
  40
Ionian metre, in *Persians,* 39
Iphigeneia in Aulis (Euripides), 13, 172
Isthmian Odes (Pindar), 72

J

Johnson, Dr. Samuel, 166

K

Kabeiroi, 151-52
Kares ē Europe, 161, 163
Kennedy, Benjamin, 169
Kennedy, James, 166, 169-70
Kitto, H. D. F., 55
Kritias, and the myth of Prometheus,
  141-42, 144

L

Laius, 3, 155
    structure, 17-18
Lattimore, Richard, 172, 173, 180
Leishman, J. B., 172, 173, 175-76
Lewis, Cecil Day, 167, 173, 175
Lewis, Wyndham, 172
Libation Bearers, 6, 17, 22, 23, 25-26,
    78-80, 84-85
    imagery, 25-26
    structure, 23, 79-80, 84-85
    symbolism, 78-79, 86-87
Lloyd-Jones, Hugh, 8, 90-92, 94, 179
Lucas, F. L., 181

M

MacFarlane, John, 174-75
MacNeice, Louis, 169, 172, 173, 174,
    176, 180-182
Mahaffy, J. P., 127
*Mask of Anarchy Written on the Occa-
sion of the Massacre at Manchester*
    (Shelley), 146
Medicean MS of plays, 136
Modernist movement, in translations,
    172-76
"Modes of Translation" (MacFarlane),
    174-75
Moira, concept of, 34, **99-104**, 123,
    135
Moschion, 141-42
Murder in the Cathedral (Eliot), 180,
    182
Murray, A. T., 109
Murray, Gilbert, 3, 8-9, 145, 170-172

N

Natural History (Pliny the Elder), and
    theme of blood, 109-10
Net-Haulers, 26

O

Odes (Horace), 175-76
Oedipus, 3, 155

Oedipus Coloneus (Sophocles), 13, 58,
    172
Oedipus Tyrannus (Sophocles), 58,
    128
Odyssey (Homer), 173
Olympian Odes (Pindar), 71, 72
Oresteia, 2, 3, 6-8, 13, 17-19, 64, 65,
    67, 70, 77-79, 80, 84, 87-89, 99-104,
    106-23, 143, 145, 148-50, 152-59,
    162-63
    Agamemnon, 6, 8, 17, 20, 22-24,
        41, 63, 64, 66, **73-77**, 79-84, 85-
        86, 91-92, 94-96, 99-104, 105,
        107-9, 110-19, 152, 154, 163,
        164-83
    blood, theme of, 110-15
    Choephori, 69-70, 101, 104, 111,
        114-15, **119-23**, 152, 154, 159
    chronology, 148-50
    conflict, theme of, 87-88
    curse, function of, 90-98
    daemonization in, 118
    entanglement, theme of, 77-79
    Eumenides, 7, 15, 17, 18, 21, 23,
        27, 60, 63, 79-80, 85, 87-89, 94,
        100-103, 111-15, 119, 122, 152-
        53, 154, 156-59, 162
    free will, theme of, 90-105
    imagery in, **106-23**
    Moira, concept of, 99-104
    structure, 17-19, 110-11, 113, 115,
        117-21, 152-59, 162-63
    symbolism, 77-79, 87-89, 106-23
    vengeance, theme of, 18-19

P

Papyrus finds, and dating of plays, 4-5,
    26, 29, 63, 148
Paton, W. R., 170
Patriotism, theme of, 2, 26-27, 35-36
Persians, 2-3, 7-8, 12-13, 18-19, 21, 26-
    27, **29-39**, 93, 109-10, 150-151, 161
    free will, concept of, 93
    imagery, 37-38, 109-10
    as a historical play, 29-31
    patriotism, concept of, 26-27, 35-
        36

Persians (continued)
structure, 31-34, 35-39
theology in, 150-151, 161
Persians (Phrynichus), 31
Philemon, and myth of Prometheus, 144
Philoctetes (Sophocles), 13
Phineus, 18, 29-30
Phrygians or Ransoming of Hector, 156
Phrynichus, 31, 36
Picasso, and Aeschylus, 149
Pindar, 9, 24, 26-27, 71-72, 74, 155, 172
Plato, 104, 143-44
Platt, Arthur, 179
Pliny the Elder, 109-10
Poetics (Aristotle), 106
Potter, Robert, 165-66, 167, 169
Pound, Ezra, 172
Prometheia, 3, 5, 7-8, 30, 64, 80, 124-47, 148-50, 152-59, 163
chronology, 148-50
ideology, 124-32, 141
Prometheus Bound, 7-8, 18, 20-21, 25, 27-28, 63, 93, 103-4, 127-35, 139, 153, 156, 160, 163 (*see also* main entry)
Prometheus the Fire-bearer, 18, 29, 30, 139, 153, 154, 156, 158, 163
Prometheus Unbound, 18, 135-39, 153, 156, 163
structure, 126-27, 136, 139-41, 152-59, 163
theology in, 140-143
Prometheus Bound, 7-8, 18, 20-21, 25, 27-28, 63, 93, 103-4, 127-35, 139, 153, 156, 160, 163
characterization, 129-30
imagery, 25
ideology in, 127-28, 131-32, 142
Moira, concept of, 103-4
prophecy and fatalism in, 93
structure, 20-21, 23-24, 27-28, 127-35, 139, 153, 156, 160, 163
Prometheus the Fire-bearer, 18, 29, 30, 139, 153, 154, 156, 158, 163
structure, 153, 156, 158, 163
Prometheus, myth of, 124-27, 141-47

Prometheus Unbound, 18, 135-39, 153, 156, 163
Prometheus Unbound (Shelley), 145
Proteus, 6
Psychostasia, 161
Pyrphoros (*see Prometheus the Fire-bearer*)
Pythagoreans, and Aeschylus, 131-32, 143
Pythian Odes (Pindar), 74, 172

R

Remarque, E. M., 40, 42
Rosenmeyer, Thomas G., 4
Russell, Bertrand, 175

S

Seven Against Thebes, 3, 4-5, 17-19, 21-22, 28, 40-62, 94, 150-151, 161
antiphonal system in, 44-45, 48-49, 61
curse, theme of, 4, 17-19, 42, 47, 56-60, 94
humor in, 51-52
imagery, 41-49, 50-56, 61-62
selection scene in, 45, 47, 49-57
structure, 21-22, 28, 40-62
symbolism, of the shield, 47-48, 51-52, 54-56, 59
theology in, 150-151, 161
Shakespeare, William, 14, 40, 104
Shelley, Percy Bysshe, 127-28, 145-47
Socrates, 173
Sophocles, 4, 5, 6, 13, 17, 30, 47, 58, 75, 107, 120, 128, 149, 151, 172
Sphinx, 3, 61
Staiger, E., 61-62
Stichomythia (*see* Antiphonal system)
Suppliants (Euripides), 128
Suppliants trilogy (*see Danaid* trilogy)
Suppliant Women, 2, 4-6, 15, 17, 20-21, 23-24, 27, 28, 63-72, 129, 154, 156, 159, 162
conflict, theme of, 64-69
imagery, 67, 69-72

Suppliant Women (*continued*)
  structure, 20-21, 23-24, 63-72, 154,
    156, 163
Swinburne, Algernon, 169, 170
Symbolism:
  in *Agamemnon,* 81, 86, 107-10
  in *Eumenides,* 87-88
  in *Libation Bearers,* 78-79, 86-87
  in *Oresteia,* 77-79, 106-23
  in *Seven Against Thebes,* 43-44, 47-
    48, 49, 51-52, 54-56, 59

T

Theban trilogy:
  Laius, 3, 17-18, 155
  Oedipus, 3, 155
  Seven Against Thebes, 3, 4-5, 17-19,
    28, **40-62,** 94, 150-151, 161
  structure, 3, 17-18, 58-59, 155-56
Theogony (Hesiod), 8, 153
Thespis, 1, 10-11
Thomson, George, 7-8, 111, 159
Thucydides, 38, 93

Tragedy:
  characterization, 15-17, 55
  conflict in, 27-28
  historical development of, 10-12
  traditional style of, 14-15, 36-38
Translation, methods of, 174-76, 178-
  83
Trilogy, structure of, 17-19, 59, 152-
  53, 155, 156
Triptolemus (Sophocles), 13

V

Virgil, 110, 167, 175
Voss, J. H., 166-67

W

War, theme of, in *Seven Against Thebes,*
  40-42, 47-48, 51, 59, 60-62
Warner, Rex, 172-73
Woodworth, D. C., 174-75

X

Xenophanes, 161

AUDEN

A Collection of Critical Essays

Edited by MONROE K. SPEARS

A

Adams, Henry, 92
"Address for a Prize Day," 29
Age of Anxiety, 8, 9, 28, 35, 76, 98, 104, 115, 122, 134, 153, 159, 169, 180
"Air de Semiramis" (Valéry), 132
Alleg, M., 100-101
"Allendale," 11
"Alonso to Ferdinand," 92-93
"Annotated Checklist" (Callan), 9
Another Time, 39, 111-13, 114, 121-22, 150, 179
Ariosto, 70
Arnold, Matthew, 174
The Ascent of F.6 (with Isherwood), 1, 32, 71, 179
Ash Wednesday (Eliot), 134
Auden, Wystan Hugh:
  and American Academy of Arts and Letters, 59, 180
  in China, 32, 55, 110
  and Eliot, T. S., 12, 58, 72-75, 78, 105, 127, 128, 133, 134, 161
  and Freudianism, 28, 30, 71, 110, 121, 136, 153
  in Germany, 13, 31, 33, 55, 105
  and Hardy, Thomas, 10, 105, 133
  imagery of 15-25, 34, 62, 81, 107-9, 139
  and Isherwood, Christopher, 7, 11, 12, 13, 26, 32, 55, 67, 85, 86, 134
  and Kierkegaard, Sören, 71, 75, 96, 121, 136, **153-59**, 161, 172
  and Lane, Homer, 13, 136, 153
  and MacNeice, Louis, 32, 54, 128, 172
  and Marxism, 5, 30, 33, 54, 82, 121, 134, 136, 137
  metrical usage of, 48, 93, 114-15, 138, 143, 147, 161, 162, 165, 166-67
  musical understanding of, 6, 10, 48-50, 70
  at Oxford, 3, 26-27, 28, 59, 105, 120, 126, 173
  political views of, 23, 28, 32-33, 34-35, 54, 94, 110-11, 136, 172, 174-76
  religious views of, 3, 6, 10, 28, 29, 30, 31, 35, 41, 45, 52, 87-89, 94-96, 102-3, 120-122, 136, 139, 149-50, **152-59**, **160-71**, 172-73
  scientism of, 6, 10, 28, 60
  and Spain, 32, 33, 55, 110, 172
  and Spender, Stephen, 26, 85, 86, 111, 126, 128, 172
  in the United States, 1, 27, 32, 35, **54-59**, 91, 106, 120, 122, 130, 150, 152, 172
Auden, Wystan Hugh, major works of:
  Age of Anxiety, 8, 9, 28, 35, 76, 98, 104, 115, 122, 134, 153, 159, 169, 180
  Another Time, 39, 111-13, 114, 121-22, 150, 179

Auden, Wystan Hugh (*continued*)
  Ascent of F.6, The (with Isher-
    wood), 1, 32, 71, 179
  Christmas Oratorio, A, 40, 42, 44,
    45, 49-50, 160 (*see also For the
    Time Being*)
  Coal Face (with Britten), 179
  Collected Poetry, 4, 15, 17, 24, 31,
    50, 58, 59, 170, 173, 180
  Collected Shorter Poems, 44, 47,
    111-13, 118, 119, 180
  "Dance of Death, The," 18, 21, 24,
    55, 179
  Dog Beneath the Skin, The (with
    Isherwood), 13, 32, 179
  Double Man, The, 35, 46, 50, 137,
    179 (*see also New Year Letter*)
  Dyer's Hand and Other Essays, The,
    4, 9, 174, 177-78, 180
  Elegy for Young Lovers (with Kall-
    man), 180
  Enchafèd Flood, The, 107, 137,
    169, 180
  Enemies of a Bishop, The (with
    Isherwood), 13
  For the Time Being, 3, 9, 88, 90,
    94, 96, 122, 149, 153, 158, 159,
    160-71, 180 (*see also A Christmas
    Oratorio*)
  Homage to Clio, 123, 138, 139-40,
    150, 173, 180
  "In Praise of Limestone," 46, 48,
    103, 108-9, 150
  Journal of an Airman, 13, 82, 83,
    84, 85
  Letter to Lord Byron, 13, 47, 50,
    68
  New Year Letter, 9, 39-40, 42, 43,
    50, 55, 56, 57, 70, 73-74, 79-80,
    121, 137, 153-57, 158, 159, 179
    (*see also The Double Man*)
  Night Mail (with Britten), 47, 179
  Nones, 46, 47, 49, 98, 101-3, 104,
    132, 135, 138, 150, 170, 173, 180
  Orators, The, 1, 13, 14, 21, 29-30,
    35, 50, 55, 81-82, 83, 84, 85, 86,
    166, 179
  Paul Bunyan (with Britten), 179

  Poems, 1, 58, 60-61, 72, 81, 109
  Poet's Tongue, The (with Garrett),
    179
  Quest, The, 55-56, 57, 107
  Rake's Progress, The (with Stravin-
    sky and Kallman), 44, 107, 108
  Sea and the Mirror, The, 9, 35, 44,
    48, 65, 77, 89, 92, 95, 122-23,
    134, **142-51**, 153, 158, 170
  Selected Poetry, 180
  Shield of Achilles, The, 53, 59, 98-
    101, 138, 141, 150, 173, 180
  (*see also* entries for individual titles)
Auden, Wystan Hugh, works edited by:
  *Faber Book of Modern American
    Verse*, 180
  Oxford Book of Light Verse, 70,
    179
  Oxford Poetry, 105
  Poets of the English Language
    (with Pearson), 180
  Portable Greek Reader, The, 180
  Selected Writings of Sydney Smith,
    180
  *Selections of the Poems of Alfred
    Lord Tennyson, A*, 180
  Viking Book of Aphorisms, The
    (with Kronenberger), 180
  Yale Series of Younger Poets, 180
Auden: An Introductory Essay (Hog-
  gart), 3
Auden Group, The, 1, 7, 26, 110, 172
Augustine, Saint, 103
"Aurore" (Valéry), 132

B

Bacon, Francis, 64
Baden-Powell, R. S. S., 84
Bagehot, Walter, 99
Barker, George, 172
Barzun, Jacques, 180
Baudelaire, Charles, 61
Bayley, John, 6, 7, 8, **60-80**
Beach, Joseph Warren, 4
Beast in the Jungle, The (James), 42
Beethoven, Ludwig van, 70
Benn, Gottfried, 9

Blake, William, 5, 29, 39, 63, 133, 157
Bloomsbury Group, 1, 2, 27, 54
Bogan, Louise, 41, 47
Bontempelli, Massimo, 131
Bottrall, Ronald, 2
Bridge, The (Crane), 158
Bridges, Robert, 14
Britten, Benjamin, 179
Brontë, Emily, 44
Brooks, Cleanth, 7
Browning, Robert, 58-59, 133
"Bryan, Bryan, Bryan, Bryan" (Lindsay), 21
Bucolics, 59, 98, 107, 177
Buried Day, The (Lewis), 7
Burns, Robert, 5, 31
"Burnt Norton" (Eliot), 62-63, 73
Butler, Samuel, 133, 137
Byron, George Gordon, 5, 8, 92, 133, 137

C

Callan, Edward, 9, **152-59**
Calverly, Charles Stuart, 70
Cantos, The (Pound), 158
Cardarelli, Vincenzo, 131
Carlyle, Thomas, 86
"Carter's Funeral, The," 10-11
Catullus, 40
Cervantes, Miguel de, 177
"Chimera, The," 150
Christmas Oratorio, A, 40, 42, 44, 45, 49-50, 160 *(see also For the Time Being)*
Coal Face (with Britten), 179
Cocktail Party, The (Eliot), 129
Coleridge, Samuel Taylor, 142
Collected Poetry, 4, 15, 17, 24, 31, 50, 58, 59, 170, 173, 180
Collected Shorter Poems, 44, 47, 111-13, 118, 119, 180
Collingwood, R. G., 47
"Communist to Others, A," 138
"Composer, The," 47
"Consider if you will how . . . ," 12-13
Cornelia Street Dialogues, 41
Cowley, Malcolm, 143n

Cox, R. G., 3
Crane, Hart, 158
Crashaw, Richard, 96n

D

"Dance of Death, The," 18, 21, 24, 55, 179
D'Annunzio, Gabriele, 131
Dante, 51, 65, 71, 75, 86, 103, 127, 128, 129, 138, 153, 154, 157
Decline and Fall of the Romantic Ideal, The (Lucas), 16
de la Mare, Walter, 89
Dickens, Charles, 6, 8, 65, 80, 127
Dickinson, Emily, 14, 133
Divine Comedy (Dante), 153, 154, 162
Dog Beneath the Skin, The (with Isherwood), 13, 32, 179
Don Giovanni (with Mozart, Kallman), 180
Don Juan (Byron), 92, 137
Donne, John, 8, 173
Double Man, The, 35, 46, 50, 137, 179 *(see also New Year Letter)*
Dover, 1937, 106, 111-13
Dryden, John, 40, 88, 97, 133, 138, 161, 173
"Duet, A," 150
Dulles, John Foster, 50
Dyer's Hand and Other Essays, The, 4, 9, 174, 177-78, 180

E

"East Coker" (Eliot), 73, 74
Easter (Yeats), 114
Eastman, Max, 16
Economist, 92
Edgeworth, Maria, 41
Elegy for Young Lovers (with Kallman), 180
Eliot, George, 80
Eliot, T. S., 2, 5, 7, 17, 27, 69, 130, 132, 158, 162
  and Auden, 27, 58, 74-75, 78, 105, 127-29, 133, 134, 136, 161, 164, 167, 172

Eliot, T. S. (*continued*)
  work of, compared to Auden's, 38,
    41, 62-63, 72-73, 79, 98, 138,
    139, 170, 173
Eliot, T. S., works of:
  Ash Wednesday, 134
  "Burnt Norton," 62-63, 73
  Cocktail Party, The, 129
  "East Coker," 73, 74
  Four Quartets, 74, 96, 170
  Hollow Men, The, 129
  Journey of the Magi, 164
  "Little Gidding," 129
  Murder in the Cathedral, 40
  "Preludes," 76-77
  "Rock, The," 62, 96
  Wasteland, The, 12, 127
Empson, William, 6, 38, 94, 98
Enchafèd Flood, The, 107, 137, 169,
  180
Enemies of a Bishop, The, (with Isher-
  wood), 13
Enoch Arden (Tennyson), 99
"Epithalamion," 44-45, 74

F

*Faber Book of Modern American
  Verse*, 180
"Faces along the bar . . . ," 36
"Fall of Rome, The," 150
Faust, 163
"First Things First," 150
"Fleet Visit," 150
Forster, E. M., 27
For the Time Being, 3, 9, 88, 90, 94,
  122, 149, 153, 158, 159, 160-71, 180
  (*see also A Christmas Oratorio*)
Four Quartets (Eliot), 74, 96, 170
Fraser, G. S., 7, 8, **81-104**
"Free One, A," 110
Freud, Sigmund, 28, 30, 71, 86, 110,
  153, 168, 172
"Freud to Paul: The Stages of Auden's
  Ideology" (Jarrell), 168*n*
Friar, Kimon, 52
"Friday's Child," 123, 150
Frost, Robert, 10, 177-78

G

Garrett, John, 179
Gascoyne, David, 96
Gay, John, 70
Gibbon, Edward, 36
Gide, André, 33
"Gisli the Outlaw," 11
Goethe, Johann Wolfgang von, 65,
  136, 163, 180
Goldsmith, Oliver, 91
Goodbye to Berlin (Isherwood), 105
Graham, W. S., 38
Graves, Robert, 90, 115, 133
Griffin, Howard, 41
Grigson, Geoffrey, 7, 111
Groddeck, 82, 136, 153
Grolier Club, 42

H

Halverson, M., 170
Hardy, Thomas, 8, 10, 40, 98, 105,
  133, 160
Heard, Gerald, 89
Henze, Hans Werner, 180
Herbert, George, 96*n*
Hiawatha (Longfellow), 98
Hitler, Adolf, 96, 110
Hoggart, Richard, 3, 8, 78, 98, **105-24**,
  131
Hollow Men, The (Eliot), 129
Homage to Clio, 123, 138, 139-40,
  150, 173, 180
Homer, 100, 129
Hopkins, Gerard Manley, 14, 93, 99,
  107, 133
"Horae Canonical," 170
Housman, A. E., 65, 68-69
Howard, Brian, 102
Hudibras (Butler), 133, 137
Huxley, Aldous, 89
Ibsen, Henrik, 177
Iliad (Homer), 100
Imagery, in Auden's works, **15-25**, 34,
  62, 81, 107-9, 139
In Memorium (Tennyson), 97
"In Memory of W. B. Yeats," 135

"In Praise of Limestone," 46, 48, 103, 108-9, 150
"In Time of War," 119
Isherwood, Christopher, 6-7, **10-14**, 26, 32, 55, 67, 84, 86, 105, 134, 179
   Ascent of F.6, The (with Auden), 32
   Dog Beneath the Skin, The (with Auden), 13, 32
   Enemies of a Bishop, The (with Auden), 13
   Goodbye to Berlin, 105
   Journey to a War (with Auden), 32, 110, 179
   Lions and Shadows, 7, 67, 84
   On the Frontier (with Auden), 32, 179
   World in the Evening, The, 58
Italian Journey (Goethe), 180
"It's Too Much," 58
Izzo, Carlo, 8-9, **125-41**

J

James, Henry, 28, 42, 46, 53, 133, 145
James, M. R., 74
Jarrell, Randall, 3-4, 168, 174
Johnson, Dr. Samuel, 96
Journal of an Airman, 13, 82, 83, 84, 85
Journey of the Magi (Eliot), 164
Journey to a War (with Isherwood), 32, 110, 179
"Journey to Iceland," 45
Journey to the Centre of the Earth (Verne), 14
Joyce, James, 127, 128, 129, 130
Jung, Carl, 153, 159

K

Kafka, Franz, 5, 133, 170
Kallman, Chester, 180
Keats, John, 8, 38, 63, 64, 72
Keynes, John Maynard, 2
Kierkegaard, Sören, 8, 9, 71, 75, 86, 96, 121, 136, 144, **153-56,** 158-59, 161, 165*n,* 172

Kipling, Rudyard, 58, 84, 87
Kronenberger, Louis, 180

L

"Labyrinth, The," 134
Lane, Homer, 13, 136, 153
Langland, William, 5, 133
"Last Will and Testament" (with MacNeice), 54
Lawrence, D. H., 29, 136, 172
Layard, John, 13, 82, 83
"Lay your sleeping head, my love . . . ," 37, 116
Leavis, F. R., 1, 2, 7, 85
Leopardi, Giacomo, 125
Letters from Iceland (with MacNeice), 32, 54, 179
"Letter to a Wound," 85
Letter to Lord Byron, 13, 47, 50, 68
Levy, Melvin, 160, 170
Lewis, C. Day, 22, 128, 138, 172
Lewis, Sinclair, 92
Lienhardt, R. G., 3
Lindsay, Vachel, 21
Lions and Shadows (Isherwood), 7, 67, 84
Literary Mind, The (Eastman), 16
"Little Gidding" (Eliot), 129
Locksley Hall (Tennyson), 61
Longfellow, Henry Wadsworth, 58-59, 98
Look, Stranger!, 117-18, 179 (*see also On This Island*)
Lucas, F. L., 16
"Lullaby," 115

M

"Macao," 106
Macbeth (Shakespeare), 116, 134, 152, 159
McDowell, F. P. W., 9, **142-51**
MacLeish, Archibald, 17
MacNeice, Louis, 7, 32, 54, 128, 172, 179
Magic Flute, The (with Mozart, Kallman), 180

Making of the Auden Canon, The
   (Beach), 4
Mallarmé, Stéphane, 79, 80
Manchester Guardian, 100
"Many Happy Returns," 49
Marx, Karl, 30, 69, 86, 173
Marxism, 5, 33, 54, 82, 121, 134, 136,
   137
Mayer, Elizabeth, 39, 180
"May with its light behaving . . . ," 117-
   18
"Meditation of Simeon, The," 45, 167-
   68
Melchiori, Signor, 98
Merchant of Venice, The (Shakespeare),
   176
Metrical usage, of Auden, 48, 93, 114-
   15, 138, 143, 147, 161, 162, 165,
   166-67
Milton, John, 96, 157
"Mimesis and Allegory," 71
"Miss Gee," 29
Modern Poetry (Mack, Dean, and Frost,
   eds.), 170
Modern Poetry (MacNeice, ed.), 7
Modern Writer and His World, The
   (Fraser), 8
Montaigne, 50, 159
Montherlant, Henri de, 31
Montale, Eugenio, 132
Moore, Marianne, 8, **39-53**, 92, 93
Mozart, Wolfgang Amadeus, 70, 180
Murder in the Cathedral (Eliot), 40
Murry, John Middleton, 87, 97
"Musée des Beaux Arts," 114
Musical understanding, of Auden, 6,
   10, 48-50, 70
"Music is International," 72
Mussolini, Benito, 110

                        N

Nash, Ogden, 41
Nation, 7
New Bearings in English Poetry
   (Leavis), 2
Newbolt, Henry John, 84
New Statesman, 2

New Verse, 7
New Year Letter, 9, 39-40, 42-43, 50,
   55, 56, 57, 70, 73-74, 79-80, 121,
   152-59 (*see also The Double Man*)
New Yorker. 58, 102
Niebuhr, Reinhold, 121, 150, 161, 172
Nietzsche, Friedrich, 63, 69, 136, 168,
   172
Night Mail (with Britten), 47, 179
Noctambules (Gascoyne), 96
"Nocturne I," 150
Nones, 46, 47, 49, 98, 101-3, 104, 132,
   135, 138, 150, 170, 173, 180
"Novelist, The," 68

                        O

Ode on Intimations of Immortality
   (Wordsworth), 63
"Ode to Gaea," 99
Odyssey (Homer), 61
Oedipus Rex (Sophocles), 152
Ohmann, Richard, 9, 172-78
"Old Man's Road, The," 180
"One Circumlocution," 49
On the Frontier (with Isherwood), 32,
   179
On This Island, 30, 150, 179 (*see also
   Look, Stranger!*)
Orators, The, 1, 13, 14, 21, 29-30, 35,
   50, 55, 81-82, 83, 84, 85, 86, 166,
   179
Orwell, George, 109
Othello (Shakespeare), 177
"Our Bias," 46, 121-22
Owen, Wilfred, 133
Oxford Book of Light Verse, The, 70,
   179
Oxford Poetry, 105

                        P

"Paid on Both Sides: A Charade," 2,
   11, 21, 179
Panzini, Alfredo, 131
Paradise Lost (Milton), 96
Paradox of Oscar Wilde, The (Wood-
   cock), 45n

Pascal, Blaise, 136
Past and Present (Carlyle), 86
Paul Bunyan (with Britten), 179
"Paysage Moralisé," 177
Pearson, Norman Holmes, 180
Pelican Guide to English Literature, 3
"Petition," 15, 94, 110
Picasso, Pablo, 38
Plato, 39, 64
"Please Make Yourself at Home," 58
Poe, Edgar Allan, 53, 65, 79, 126
Poems, 1, 58, 60-61, 72, 81, 109
Poets of the English Language (with
  Pearson, eds.), 180
Poet's Tongue, The (with Garrett), 179
Political views, of Auden, 23, 28, 32-
  33, 34-35, 54, 94, 110-11, 136, 172,
  174-76
Pope, Alexander, 41, 52, 92, 133, 138
Portable Greek Reader, The, 180
Pound, Ezra, 7, 98, 130, 134, 136,
  158
Praz, Mario, 129
"Precious Five," 123
"Preface to Kierkegaard," 156
"Preludes" (Eliot), 76-77
"Prime," 123, 132, 150
"The Prince that Lies," 51
Prologhi (Cardarelli), 131
"Proof, The," 150
"Prophets, The," 121
Purcell, Henry, 88
Purloined Letter, The (Poe), 126

Q

Quest, The, 55-56, 57, 107
Question, La (Alleg), 100

R

Radiguet, Raymond, 63
Raine, Kathleen, 86, 87, 96
Rake's Progress, The (with Stravinsky,
  Kallman), 44, 107, 180
Reflections from Rochester (Empson),
  94
"Reflections in a Forest," 150

Religio Laici (Dryden), 97
Religious Drama (Halverson, ed.), 170
Religious views, of Auden, 3, 6, 10,
  28, 29, 30, 31, 35, 41, 45, 52, 87-89,
  94-96, 102-3, 120-22, 136, 139, 149-
  50, 152-59, 160-71, 172-73
Resurrection, The (Yeats), 168
Rettger, John, 49
Return from the U.S.S.R. (Gide), 33
Riding, Laura, 90, 115, 133
Rilke, Rainer Maria, 79-80, 117, 119,
  131-32, 133
Rimbaud, Arthur, 40, 63
Road to Wigan Pier, The (Orwell), 109
Robinson, Edwin Arlington, 14
"Rock, The" (Eliot), 62, 96
Rousseau, Jean-Jacques, 69

S

"Sabbath," 150
Sartre, Jean-Paul, 65-66, 75-76
Saturday Evening Post, 92
Scientism, of Auden, 6, 10, 28, 60
Scott, Sir Walter, 8
Sea and the Mirror, The, 9, 35, 44, 48,
  65, 77, 89, 92, 95, 122-23, 134, 142-
  51, 153, 158, 170
"Seascape," 115
"Secondary Epic," 150
"Secular Masque" (Dryden), 161
Selected Poetry, 180
Selected Writings of Sydney Smith,
  180
*Selection of the Poems of Alfred Lord
  Tennyson, A*, 180
"September 1, 1939," 114
Sense and Poetry (Sparrow), 16
"Sext," 139
Shakespeare, 39, 40, 69, 89, 90, 129,
  134, 143, 152, 158
Shapiro, Karl, 173
Shaw, George Bernard, 131, 150
Shelley, Percy Bysshe, 7, 63, 69, 125,
  137
Shield of Achilles, The, 53, 59, 98, 98-
  101, 138, 141, 150, 173, 180
Shropshire Lad (Housman), 69

"Since you are going to begin today
. . . ," 30
Skelton, John, 85, 133
"Something is Bound to Happen," 58
"Songs and Other Musical Pieces," 49
"Spain," 106, 110, 179
Sparrow, John, 16
Spears, Monroe K., 160-71
Spectator, 92
Spender, Stephen, 7, 8, 10, 12, 22, 26-
38, 85, 86, 90, 111, 126, 128, 137,
138, 172, 179
Spenser, Edmund, 157
"Squares and Oblongs," 69
Squire, J. C., 26
"Star of the Nativity," 42
Stevens, Wallace, 46
Stravinsky, Igor, 180
"Streams," 139
"Summer Night, 1933, A," 31
Swinburne, Algernon, 59
Sykes Davies, Hugh, 86-87, 94
Symons, Julian, 93-94

T

Tate, Allen, 17
Tempest, The (Shakespeare), 89, 145,
158, 159
"Temptation of St. Joseph, The" 163-
64
Tennyson, Alfred Lord, 59, 61, 63,
67, 97, 99, 106
Testament of Beauty, The (Bridges),
14
Testaments of Villon, 54-55
"This Lunar Beauty," 115
"This One," 115
Thomas, Dylan, 38, 172
Thomas, Edward, 10, 133
Thucydides, 39
Tightrope Walkers, The (Melchiori), 98
Tillich, Paul, 172
Times (London), 92
Tocqueville, Alexis de, 39
Tolstoy, Leo, 65

Townsend, Cecilia, 41
"To You Simply," 49
Trilling, Lionel, 180
Trollope, Anthony, 130
"Truest Poetry is the Most Feigning,
The," 138
Twain, Mark, 92

U

Ulysses (Joyce), 127
"Under Which Lyre," 47
"Unknown Citizen, The," 58

V

Valéry, Paul, 132, 133
Vaughan, Henry, 96n
"Venus Will Now Say a Few Words,"
58
Verne, Jules, 14
Viking Book of Aphorisms, The (with
Kronenberger, eds.), 180
"Vocation," 46
Voltaire, 39, 40, 135, 174
"Voltaire at Ferney," 135

W

Wagner, Richard, 70
"Walk After Dark, A," 150
"Walking Tour, The," 41
"Walks," 140
Warner, Rex, 26, 85, 86, 92
"War Time," 42
Waste Land, The (Eliot), 12, 127
Weil, Simone, 100
Whitman, Walt, 21-22, 130
Wilde, Oscar, 45n
Williams, William Carlos, 161
Wilson, Edmund, 8, 54-59
Winters, Ivor, 104
"Witnesses, The," 134
Woodcock, George, 45n
Woolf, Virginia, 27

Wordsworth, William, 59, 63, 78, 133, 173

World in the Evening, The (Isherwood), 58

World Within World, 7, 126

Y

Yale Series of Younger Poets, 180

Yeats, W. B., 2, 5, 17, 38, 60-62, 63-64, 69, 70, 79, 80, 98, 114, 130, 132, 133, 135, 157, 168, 172, 173

JANE AUSTEN

A Collection of Critical Essays

Edited by IAN WATT

A

Abinger Harvest (Forster), 9
Amelia (Fielding), 129
American, The (James), 151
Arthur Fitzalbini (Brydges), 159, 163-64
Assumption of roles, theme of, 132, 139
Arnold, Matthew, 50
Aspects of the Novel (Forster), 9, 11
Auden, W. H., 11
Augustine, 128
Austen, Cassandra, 15, 156
Austen, Charles, 161
Austen, Edward, 2
Austen, Francis, 161
Austen, George, 6
Austen, Jane:
    aesthetic concerns of, 38, 74
    antagonism toward, 125-26
    artistic development of, 18, 52-61, 97, 176-78
    biographical information, 6, 15-24, 156, 161-62, 172
    and bourgeois morality, 92
    and the British Peerage, 154-65
    caricature, use of, 45-47, 53-54, 170-172
    and character of fathers, 88-89, 103, 137
    Cinderella theme in, 29, 38, 173-79
    and classical tradition, 3, 28, 35, 62, 135
    and contemporary social conventions, 41-42, 121, 175
    and conventions of the novel, 41, 52-61
    critical response to, 1-14, 35, 41, 145
    and deception, theme of, 32
    dialogue, function in work of, 43, 63-65, 71, 73-75, 77-81, 83, 91, 92, 121-22, 141, 169-70
    and eighteenth-century thought, 44-45, 50
    and Gothic novel, 58-61, 174
    juvenilia, 16-18, 45-47, 52-55, 61, 86, 157
    and materialism, 99, 114, 122
    and the modern personality, 138
    and morality, cost of, 124
    novel-reading in works of, 58-61
    and problems of women in society, 117-18, 122
    property and wealth in works of, 12, 77, 79, 84-85, 99-101, 110-11
    religious background, 27, 175
    and rise of the middle class, theme of, 162
    scope of novels, 2, 3, 118-19
    and secular spirituality, 139-40
    self-deception, theme of, 98, 105-6, 108, 116
    and the sentimental novel, 45, 52-61 *passim*

Austen, Jane (*continued*)
  sexual experience, treatment of, 86-
    92, 133
  and Shakespeare, 5, 6, 30, 35, 38
  social and moral assumptions of,
    13, 21, 27, 28, 30, 33, 43, 49,
    70, 77, 98, 104-5, 110, 115-16,
    119, 120, 139, 141-42, 153,
    163-64, 170
  and standards of her class, 119
Austen, Jane, minor works by: (*see
  also juvenilia*)
  Catharine, or the Bower, 54-55, 157
  Collection of Letters, A, 53
  Evelyn, 157
  First Impressions, 52
  Susan, 52
  Three Sisters, The, 54
Austen, Jane, works by:
  Emma, 3, 8, 11, 13, 26, 27, 28, 36,
    38-39, 63, 64, 75, **98-111, 112-23**,
    125, 137, 155, 169, 172, 176,
    177, 178
  Mansfield Park, 11, 13, 14, 28, 30,
    31-32, 36, 37, 64, 109, 124-40,
    141-44, 163, 173, 175-76, 178
  Northanger Abbey, 25, 28, 36, **52-
    61**, 84, 96, 125, 142, 162, 167,
    173, 174, 177
  Persuasion, 22, 23, 28, 30, **32-34**,
    36, 37, 39, 130, 137, 139, 141,
    145-53, 155, 161, 162, 168, 177-
    79
  Pride and Prejudice, 3, 4, 7, 11, 12,
    13, 16, 18, 26, 27, 29, 36, 37, 39,
    52, **62-75**, 76-97, 109, 124, 127,
    128, 129, 134, 135, 137, 141,
    155, 160, 162, 173, 174, 175,177
  Sense and Sensibility, 7, 11, 13, 26,
    28, 36, 39, **41-51**, 52, 55, 84, 96,
    109, 125, 156, 162, 173, 174, 177
  Watsons, The, 19, 21, 155, 173
Austen-Leigh, James, E., 6, 23
Autobiography (Brydges), 159, 163

B

Bailey, John, 145
Barrett, Eaton Stannard, 60

Barrett, Eaton Stannard, 60
Belinda (Edgeworth), 55, 61
  61
Blake, William, 128
Bloomsbury Group, 8
Blower, Elizabeth, 60
Bradley, A. C., 10
British Critic, The, 43
British Peerage, The, 154-65
Brontë, Charlotte, 4, 29, 31, 156
Brontë, Emily, 19, 156
Brower, Reuben, 12
Brydges, James, 156
Brydges, Sir Samuel Egerton, 157, 159,
  163-64
Burke, Edmund, 165
Burney, Fanny, 54, 57, 59, 156, 157
Byron, Lord, 3

C

Camilla (Burney), 57, 59
Carlyle, Thomas, 4
Castle of Otranto, The (Walpole), 60
Catharine, or the Bower, 54-55, 157
Cecil, Lord David, 28
Cecilia (Burney), 90, 96, 155
Cervantes, Miguel de, 7
Chapman, John Jay, 68
Chapman, R. W., 8, 10, 11, 12, 50,
  125, 155
Choice and free will, theme of, 86, 89-
  90, 95-97
Cinderella theme, 29, 38, 173-74, 176-
  79
    in *Emma*, 176-78
    and the idealized mother, 177-79
    in *Mansfield Park*, 173, 175-76, 178
    in *Northanger Abbey*, 173-74
    in *Persuasion*, 178-79
    in *Pride and Prejudice*, 173
    in *Sense and Sensibility*, 173-74
    in *The Watsons*, 173
Coleridge, Samuel, 35
Coleridge, Sara, 3
Collection of Letters, A, 53
Collins, Arthur, 157-59 *passim*

Comedy, 22, 26-28, 33, 35, 36, 42, 61
Complexity of character, 77-97 *passim*,
    113
    and free will, 86, 95-96
    in *Pride and Prejudice*, 77, 90, 94-
        95, 83, 86, 89
    vs. simplicity, 77, 80, 82, 84, 85,
        87, 95
Cowper, William, 45, 165
"Crapy Cornelia" (James), 135

D

Daiches, David, 11
Deception, theme of, 32
Dewey, John, 139
Dialogue, function of, 1, 43, 63-65, 71,
    73-75, 79-81, 83, 91, 92, 121-22,
    141, 169-70
Dickens, Charles, 35, 129
Donne, John, 44
Dudley, Robert, 158
Duty, concept of, 129
    in *Mansfield Park*, 130-32
    in *Persuasion*, 151

E

Edgeworth, Maria, 55, 61
Edinburgh Magazine, 3
Electra theme, 11
    in *Mansfield Park*, 29
    in *Persuasion*, 29
"Elegiac Verses" (Wordsworth), 136
Eliot, George, 131
Eliot, T. S., 44, 49, 139
Emma, 3, 8, 11, 13, 26, 27, 36, **38-39**,
    63, 64, 75, **98-111**, **112-23**, 125, 137,
    155, 169, 172, 176, 177, 178
    and economics of marriage, 101, 111
    and marriage, theme of, 112-13,
        117, 118
    and paternal relationships, theme
        of, 38-39
    and property values, 99
    protégées in, 39, 105, 107, 123
    and self-deception, theme of, 98

and social class, 119-23
    thematic structure of, 105-11
    and undeception, 28
Ethics (Dewey), 139
Evalina (Burney), 38
Evangelical Movement, 37, 134
Evelyn, 157

F

Family relationships, theme of, 39-40
"Fiction and the 'Matrix of Analogy'"
    (Schorer), 12
Fielding, Henry, 7, 75, 129
First Impressions, 52
Following the Equator (Twain), 6-7
Forster, E. M., 35, 41, 139
Fountain, The, (Morgan), 154
Freud, Sigmund, 11

G

Garrod, H. W., 10, 28, 126-27
Gentlemen Prefer Blondes (Loos), 38
Gide, André, 139
Goldsmith, Oliver, 164
Gone with the Wind (Mitchell), 38
Gorer, Geoffrey, 11
Gothic novel, 59-60
Greene, D. J., 12

H

Hamlet, 38
Hegel, G. W. F., 139
Herbert, George, 44
Heroine (Barrett), 60
Hobbes, Thomas, 44
Holmes, Justice O. W., 38
Hulme, T. E., 129
Hutcheson, Francis, 44

I

Insincerity, theme of, 133
Impersonation (*see also* Assumption
    of roles), 132
    in *Mansfield Park*, 133, 136

Idler, 28
Impregnable Women, The, (Linklater),
166
Irony, 33, 62-75, **76-97,** 138, 142
in *Emma,* 103-5
and malice, 125
as a method of comprehension,
124
in *Northanger Abbey,* 96
as organizing principle, 86
in *Pride and Prejudice,* 63, 65-75
as self-defense, 88, 96
in *Sense and Sensibility,* 96

J

James, Henry, 8, 9, 24, 34, 37, 70,
129, 139, 151
*Jane Austen: Irony as Defense and
Discovery* (Mudrick), 12
"Jane Austen, Karl Marx, and the
Aristocratic Dance" (Daiches), 11
*Jane Austen's Letters to her Sister
Cassandra and Others,* 2, 93, 101,
159, 167
"Janeites, The" (Kipling), 10
Jenkins, Elizabeth, 172
Johnson, Samuel, 29, 30, 34, 165
Jonathan Wild (Fielding), 112
Jonson, Ben, 35
Joyce, James, 50, 139
Juvenilia:
Catharine, or the Bower, 54-55,
157
Collection of Letters, A, 53-54
Evelyn, 157
Love and Friendship, 16-18, 45-
47, 52, 86
Three Sisters, The, 54

K

Kipling, Rudyard, 10, 34
Kotzebue, August von, 32, 132
Kronenberger, Louis, 145

L

Language, 43-44, 63-67, 74-75, **99-
101,** 115
Lascelles, Mary, 11, 86
Law, William, 27
Lawrence, D. H., 133, 139
Leavis, F. R., 8
Leavis, Q. D., 36, 90, 112, 143
"Lesson of Balzac, The" (James), 7-8
"Letter to Lord Byron, Part I" (Au-
den), 11-12
Lewes, George Henry, 4, 5
Linklater, Eric, 166
Little Dorrit (Dickens), 130
Locke, John, 44
Love, theme of, 33, 75, 83, 145, 150
Love and Friendship, 16-18, 45-47, 52,
86
Lovers' Vows (Kotzebue), 32, 132,
143

M

Macaulay, Thomas, 4, 5, 35
Macbeth, 17
Mackenzie, Henry, 45
McKillop, Alan D., 12
Man of Feeling (Mackenzie), 45
Mansfield, Katherine, 8, 9
Mansfield Park, 11, 13, 14, 28, 30, **31-
32,** 36, 37, 64, 109, **124-40, 141-44,**
163, 173, 175-76, 178
and Christian virtue, 129
and concept of duty, 130-132
and conventional virtues, 175
and discrediting of irony, 125, 135
ordination, theme of, 129-30
and problem of identity, 132-36
passim, 139
and rejection of sensibility, 136
and social coercion, 126
and social stasis, 127
Maria (Blower), 60
Marriage, theme of, 77-79, 84
and economics, 46, 84-85
in *Emma,* 112-13, 117-18
in *Pride and Prejudice,* 84

Marriage of Figaro, The, 127
Marx, Karl, 11
Mary, Queen of Scots, 18
Mead, George, 132
Memoir of Jane Austen, A (Austen-Leigh), 6
Meredith, George, 42
Metaphor, use of, 98-99, 111
Middlemarch (Eliot), 130
Milton, John, 128
Molière, 28, 35
Moore, George, 35
Moral Life and the Ethical Life, The (Vivas), 153
Moral values, 1, 21, 27, 32, 33-34, 43, 47, 49, 70, 74, 82, 84, 86-87, 92, 98, 100, 105, 107, 110, 115, 116, 119, 124, 129-31, 133-34, 138-40, 153, 164, 170, 172
More, Hannah, 114
Morgan, Charles, 154
Mozart, W. A., 127, 145
Much Ado about Nothing, 75
Mudrick, Marvin, 12, 49
Muir, Edwin, 11
Myers, F. W. H., 131
"Myth in Jane Austen" (Gorer), 11

N

Natural benevolence, doctrine of, 44-45
Newman, Cardinal, 5
Nietzsche, Friedrich, 139
Northanger Abbey, 25, 28, 36, **52-61,** 84, 96, 125, 142, 162, 167, 173, 174, 177
  and Cinderella theme, 173
  and novelistic conventions, 55-61
  and novel-reading, 58

P

Paris Review, 9
Passage to India, A (Forster), 9
Persuasion, 22, 23, 28, 30, **32-34,** 36, 37, 39, 130, 137, 139, 141, 145-53, 155, 161, 162, 168, 177-79
  and conflict between love and duty, 151
  and conflict between love and prudence, 145, 150-51
Peerage of England, The (Collins), 157
Pitt, William, 160, 161-62, 165
Plato, 132
Plot structure, 101
  in *Emma,* 101-5, 112-13
Pollock, Sir Frederick, 38
Pope, Alexander, 62, 70
"Prayer for His Daughter" (Yeats), 137
Pride, theme of, 43, 72, 90, 91, 107, 108, 110, 116, 119
Pride and Prejudice, 3, 4, 7, 11, 12, 13, 16, 18, 26, 27, 29, 36, 37, 39, 52, **62-75, 76-97,** 109, 124, 127, 128, 129, 134, 135, 137, 141, 155, 160, 162, 169, 173, 174, 175, 177
  dialogue, function in, 71
  ironic vision in, 77
  language in, 63-66, 74
  literary design of, 74
  and powerlessness, theme of, 82
  variety of tone in, 67
Prince Regent, the, 21, 175
Profession, choice of, 129-30, 133
Property and wealth, importance of, 12, 46, 77, 79, 84-85, 99-101, 110-11
Proust, Marcel, 9, 24, 139

Q

Quarterly Review, 3, 10

R

Radcliffe, Mrs. Ann, 59, 60
Rambler, 28
"Resolution and Independence" (Wordsworth), 131
Richardson, Samuel, 54, 57, 59
Romantic movement, 44-45
Room with a View (Forster), 9
Rousseau, Jean Jacques, 44

S

Satire, 22, 58-61, 168-69
  as self-preservation, 170-171
Schorer, Mark, 12
Scott, Sir Walter, 3, 4, 5, 35, 163, 165
Scrutiny, 36
Self-deception, theme of, 27-32
  in *Emma*, 98-102
Self-knowledge, theme of, 27-33
Sense and Sensibility, 7, 11, 13, 26,
  28, 36, 39, 41-51, 52, 55, 84, 96,
  109, 125, 156, 162, 173, 174, 177
  and the resolution of contraries, 51
Sensibility, theme of, 44, 46, 48, 49-
  51, 52, 125, 136
Sentimental Journey, The (Sterne), 45
Sentimental novel, 45, 52-61 *passim*
*Serious Call to a Devout and Holy Life,
  A* (Law), 27
Seymour, Beatrice Kean, 166
Shaftesbury, Lord, 44
Shakespeare, William, 4, 5, 6, 7, 30,
  35, 38
Shelley, Percy B., 3
Simpson, Richard, 5-6, 10
Sincerity, concept of, 50, 138-39
Sir Charles Grandison (Richardson),
  54, 59
Smith, Charlotte, 55, 56
Social values, 119-21, 122, 127, 137,
  154, 162, 165, 168
Southey, Robert, 3, 35
Speaking of Jane Austen (Stern and
  Kaye-Smith), 35-40 *passim*
Speculations (Hulme), 129
Staël, Madame de, 1
Sterne, Laurence, 45, 53
Structure of the Novel, The (Muir), 11
Style, 12, 42, 51, 62-75 *passim*, 98-
  101, 110, 115, 134-36
Stylistic devices, 53-54, 63-75, 77, 93,
  100, 101-8, 113, 168-69, 171
  in *Mansfield Park*, 135-39
  and morality, 110, 134-35
  in *Pride and Prejudice*, 62-75
Susan, 52

T

Tabula rasa, theory of, 44
Tennyson, Alfred Lord, 6
Thematic structure, 105
  in *Emma*, 105-10
  and symbolic relationships, 106-8
Three Sisters, The, 54
"Tintern Abbey" (Wordsworth), 131
Tolstoi, Leo, 27
Toynbee, Philip, 13-14
Tom Jones (Fielding), 59, 75
Trilling, Lionel, 13
Twain, Mark, 6, 7, 9, 126

U

Udolpho (Radcliffe), 59

V

Vivas, Eliseo, 153
Vulgarity, concept of, 138-39

W

Walpole, Horace, 4
Watsons, The, 19, 21, 155, 173
Wealth and social rank, 90
Weather as a dramatic device, 37, 111
Whately, Archbishop Richard, 4, 5
What Maisie Knew (James), 37
Wings of the Dove, The (James), 129
Wit, 20-21, 62-67
Woolf, Virginia, 8, 9, 35
Wordsworth, William, 3, 131
Wuthering Heights (Brontë), 38

Y

Yeats, W. B., 137, 139
Young, Stark, 35

BAUDELAIRE

A Collection of Critical Essays
Edited by HENRI PEYRE

A

"A celle qui est trop gaie," 73-74, 76, 159-60
Adventures of J. Gordon Pym, The (Poe), 14
"Advice to Young Writers," 47
Aeschylus, 5
Africa (Petrarch), 84
Album (Valéry), 29
Alexandrine, in French prosody, 98
"Allégorie," 177
"Ame du vin, L'," 114-15
"A mon frère revenant d'Italie" (Musset), 127
Appreciations (Pater), 24
Approximations (du Bos), 3
Arnold, Matthew, 26, 27
Artificial Paradises, 1, 35, 82-83, 84, 132-48
Art romantique, L', 86, 97
"Aube spirituelle, L'," 59, 159, 176
Auerbach, Erich, 4
"Au lecteur," 119
"Avéc tes vetements," 88

B

"Balcon, Le," 87, 113, 122, 124
Balzac, Honoré, 20, 21, 24, 26, 95
Bandy, Walter T., 2
Banville, Théodore de, 27, 68, 92
Baudelaire, Charles:

Christian aspects of, 30-37, 48-53, 163-69
classicism of, 12-13, 25-29, 119-21
as a critic, 12-13, 18, 19-21
dandyism of, 96-98, 102, 167-68
and Dante, 67, 70-71, 74-75, 81-84, 106, 151, 175
and Daubrun, Marie, 68-72
and decadence, historical and literary, 94-97
and drugs, 136, 142-43, 171-72, 173
and Duval, Jeanne, 32, **86-93**, 107-8, 177
eroticism of, 156-62
and Hugo, 8, 10-12, 98, 111-14, 118, 120-21, 170, 175
last years, 61-66
and love, theme of, 54-61, 121-23
originality of, 40-41, 154-55
and original sin, 32, 50-53, **132-48**
and Petrarch, 67, 70, 72, 82-84, 175
and Poe, 8, **13-16**, 22, 171, 174
psychology of, 94-109, 132-48
as a romantic, 9-12, 13, **19-24**, 96-97
and Sabatier, Mme., 3-4, **56-61**, 73-82, 159-60, 174-77
satanism of, 25, 51-52, 98, 132-48, 173-74
sympathy for the poor, 105-6, 114, 118-19
and Vigny, 110, 112-13, 125-26, 174

Baudelaire, Charles (*continued*)
will, paralysis of, **43-48**, 106-8, 142-
46
and women, idealization of, 3-4,
67-85
Baudelaire, Charles, works by:
Art romantique, L', 86, 97
Fanfarlo, 34
Fleurs du mal, Les, 1-2, 7-18, 32-
37, 86-93, **149-69**, 170-77 (*see
also* main entry)
Fusées, 54, 63-64, 87, 89, 93
Journals, 103, 108, 175
Letters to His Mother, 38, 41, 46
Mon coeur mis à nu, 22, 31, 34, 39,
45, 63, **64-66**, 165n
Paradis artificiels, Les, 1, 35, 82-83,
84, **132-48**
"Philosophic Art," 6
*Projets de préface pour une édition
nouvelle*, 163n
Salon de 1846, 20, 86
*Spleen de Paris, Le (Petits poèmes
en prose)*, 37, 44-45, 82, 103-5
(*see also* either titles of individual
poems or first lines)
"Béatrice, La," 84
"Beauté, La," 166
"Bénédiction," 26, 133, 164, 172
Benjamin, Walter, 2
"Bernica, La" (Leconte de Lisle), 131
Beyle, Marie Henri (pseud. Stendhal),
22, 26, 41, 96, 107
"Bijoux, Les," 87, 88, 89-90, 124-25
Blake, William, 24
Boileau, Nicolas, 170
"Booz endormi" (Hugo), 110-13
Bourget, Paul, 42-43
Bowra, C. M., 5
Byron, George Gordon, 26

C

"Cadre, Le," 91
Cahiers de la quinzaine (Péguy), 37
Camus, Albert, 25
Canzoniere (Petrarch), 72, 82, 84

Catullus, 5
Cézanne, Paul, 98, 154
"Chagrins d'enfant," 84
"Chambre double, La," 171-72
"Chant d'automne," 23, 106, 117
"Charogne, Une," 90, 124
"Chat, Le," 88
"Chevelure, La," 88, 122
Christian aspects, of Baudelaire's work,
30-37, 48-53, 163-69
Cid, Le (Corneille), 121
Classicism, in Baudelaire's work, 12-13,
25-29, 119-21
Claudel, Paul, 22, 34, 36
"Colère de Samson, La" (Vigny), 112,
125-26
Coleridge, Samuel Taylor, 24
"Confession," 80-81, 159, 175
Confessions (Rousseau), 164
*Confessions of an English Opium Eater,
The* (De Quincy), 96
Constant, Benjamin, 22, 41
Contemplations (Hugo), 121
Corde d'airain (Hugo), 11
Corneille, Pierre, 121
Countries of the Mind (Murry), 4
"Coup de Dés, Le" (Mallarmé), 25
Coupe et les lèvres, La (Musset), 129
Creative Experiment, The (Bowra), 5
Crime and Punishment (Dostoevsky),
107
Criticism, Baudelaire's, 12-13, 18, 19-21
Croce, Benedetto, 2
"Cynge, Le," 116-17, 130

D

Dandyism, in Baudelaire's work, 96-
98, 102, 167-68
D'Annunzio, Gabriele, 7
Dante, 67, 70-71, 74-75, 81-84, 106,
151, 169, 175
Daubrun, Marie, poems to, 68-72
Daumier, 18, 20
da Vinci, Leonardo, 42-43
De Baudelaire au surréalisme (Ray-
mond), 2

Decadence, historical and literary, in Baudelaire's work, 94-97

"Déjà," 104

Delacroix, Eugène, 18, 20, 24, 26, 28

"De Profundis Clamavi," 53, 91-92

De Quincy, Thomas, 96, 171, 174

Desbordes-Valmore, Marceline, 128

"Destruction," 23-24

Dieu (Hugo), 11

Divina Commedia (Dante), 83

Doctor Faustus (Mann), 156

Donne, John, 5

Dostoevsky, Feodor, 96, 107-8, 114

Drugs, evocation of, 136, 142-43, 171-72, 173

du Bos, Charles, 3, 4

Duval, Jeanne, 32, **86-93**, 107-8, 177

E

École des Muses, L' (Gilson), 3

Eliot, T. S., 2, 4, 21, 25, 168

"Eloa" (Vigny), 174

Emerson, Ralph Waldo, 20

Eroticism, in Baudelaire's work, 156-62

"Espoir en Dieu, L'" (Musset), 127

Études (Rivière), 2

Eupalinos (Valéry), 114

Evil, theme of (*see* Satanism)

F

Fanfarlo, 34

"Fantôme, Un," 91

Fauré, Gabriel, 117

"Femmes damnées," 120, 121, 123, 162

"Fin de la journée, La," 172

Fin de Satan (Hugo), 11

"Flacon, Le," 159

"Flambeau vivant, Le," 32, 81, 159, 176

Flaubert, Gustave, 9, 23, 26, 53, 97, 129, 154, 169

Fleurs du mal, Les, 1-2, **7-18**, 32-37, 86-93, 149-69, 170-77 *(see also* either titles of individual poems or first lines)

and Baudelaire's life, 38-66

Christian aspects of, 30-37, 48-53, 163-69

critical reception, 1-2, 168-69, 170

Daubrun, Marie, poems to, 68-72

death, theme of, 172-73

Duval, Jeanne, poems to, 32, **86-93**, 107-8, 177

evil, theme of, 25, 51-52, 98, 132-48, 173-74

imagery in, 5-6, 86-93, **98-104**, 149-54

lesbianism, evocation of, 123-27

Sabatier, Mme., poems to, 3-4, **56-61**, 73-82, 159-60, 174-77

symbolism *vs.* realism in, 149-69

"Fontaine aux lianes, La" (Leconte de Lisle), 129-30

France, Anatole, 123

"Franciscae meae laudes," 81

For Lancelot Andrewes (Eliot), 4

Fusées, 54, 63-64, 87, 89, 93

G

Gautier, Théophile, 1, 9, 45, 107, 168, 171, 176

George, Stefan, 7

Gide, André, 2, 21, 168

Gilson, Étienne, 3

Goethe, Johann Wolfgang von, 20, 21, 25, 28, 35, 43

Guys, Constantin, 18, 48

H

Hardy, Thomas, 98

"Harmonie du soir," 159, 176-77

Herrick, Robert, 5

Hölderlin, Friedrich, 22

Hommes, Femmes (Verlaine), 123

Horace, 120

"Horreur sympathique, L'," 173

Hugo, Victor, 8, 10-12, 20, 21, 24, 26, 27, 98, 111-14, 118, 120-21, 170, 175

"Hurleurs, Les" (Leconte de Lisle), 152n

Huxley, Aldous, 2
"Hymne," 75-76, 159
"Hymne à la Beauté," 166

I

Igitur (Mallarmé), 25
"Illusion suprême, L'" (Leconte de Lisle), 130
Imagery, in *Les Fleurs du mal*, 5-6, **98-104**
  in "Jeanne Duval" poems, 86-93
  in "Spleen," 149-54
"Imprévu, L'," 114, 115
Ingres, Jean, 18, 26
In Memoriam (Tennyson), 27
Intérieurs (Thibaudet), 2
"Invitation au voyage," 33
"Irrémédiable, L', " 174
"Irréparable, L'," 68, 109

J

"J'aime le souvenir des ces époques nues," 163*n*
"Je n'ai pas oublié," 161*n*
"Je t'adore à l'égal," 162
"Je te donne ces vers," 92, 156-57
Jeune Parque (Valéry), 29
Jocelyn (Lamartine), 27
Journal (du Bos), 3
Journals, 103, 108, 175
Jung, C. G., 21

K

Kassner, Rudolf, 49
Keats, John, 24
Kierkegaard, Sören, 22

L

La Fontaine, Jean, 5
Laforgue, Jules, 1
Lamartine, Alphonse de, 8, 27, 170, 175
Leconte de Lisle, Charles, 9, 16, 23, 76, **128-31**, 152*n*, 168

Légende de Sainte Julien l'Hospitalier (Flaubert), 127
Légende des Siècles, La (Hugo), 11
Lemaître, Jules, 32
Lesbianism, evocation of, 123-27
"Lesbos," 123-24, 125, 126
Leopardi, Conte Giacomo, 5
Letters to His Mother, 38, 41, 46
"Levrier de Magnus, Le" (Leconte de Lisle), 129
Ligeia (Poe), 14
Lohengrin (Wagner), 18
Love, theme of, in *Les Fleurs du mal*, 54-61, 121-23

M

Madame Bovary (Flaubert), 97
"Mademoiselle Bistouri," 108
"Maison du Berger, La" (Vigny), 113
Mallarmé, Stéphane, 1, 2, 18, 22, 25, 29, 168
Manet, Edouard, 18
Mann, Thomas, 156, 168
"Martyre, Une," 122, 124
Mauriac, François, 3
"Mauvais moine, Le," 154-55
"Maya, La" (Leconte de Lisle), 130
Meditation on the Life of Baudelaire (du Bos), 3
Meistersinger, Die (Wagner), 116
Meredith, George, 27
Mérimée, Prosper, 22, 96
Michaux, Henri, 25
Michelet, Jules, 21
Modern Love (Meredith), 27
Mon coeur mis à nu, 22, 31, 34, 39, 45, 63, **64-66**, 165*n*
Mon Faust (Valéry), 29
Montaigne, Michel de, 21, 166-67
Montherlant, Henri de, 21
Moquet, M. J., 81-82
Morgan, Charles, 69, 77
"Mort des pauvres, La," 114
"Mort des amants, La," 172
"Mort des artistes, La," 165-67, 172
"Mort joyeaux, Le," 172

Murry, John Middleton, 4
Musset, Alfred de, 8, 23, 26, 76, 123,
    128-29, 175
Mystery of the Rue Morgue, The (Poe),
    14

N

"Nanouna" (Musset), 127
Nerval, Gerard de, 22, 25
Nietzsche, Friedrich, 36, 95, 96
"Nuit que j'étais, Une," 122
"Nuits" (Musset), 127

O

Orientales (Hugo), 27
Original sin, doctrine of, 32, 50-53,
    132-48

P

Paradis artificial, Les, 1, 35, 82-83, 84,
    132-48
"Parfum exotique," 88, 89
Parnassus, poets of, 9, 16, 26, 127-30
Pascal, Blaise, 27, 31, 33, 36, 40, 66,
    170-71
Pater, Walter, 24
Paul, Saint, 50
Péguy, Charles, 37
Pensées (Pascal), 43, 170
"Petites Vieilles, Les," 115
Petits essais de psychologie religieuse
    (Mauriac), 3
*Petits poèmes en prose (Le Spleen de
    Paris),* 37, 44-45, 82, 103-5
Petrarch, Francesco, 67, 70, 72, 82-84,
    175
"Phares, Les," 120
Phèdre (Racine), 119
"Philosophic Art," 6
"Pipe, La," 116
Poe, Edgar Allan, 8, 13-16, 22, 171,
    174
Poèmes d'amour de Baudelaire
    (Royère), 161*n*, 164*n*
Poésie et profondeur (Richard), 2

Poetic Principle, The (Poe), 15
Poor, Baudelaire's sympathy for, 105-
    6, 114, 118-19
"Port, Le," 104
"Portrait, Le," 91
Portrait in a Mirror (Morgan), 69, 77
"Position of Baudelaire" (Valéry), 2
Possessed, The (Dostoevsky), 107
Poulet, Georges, 4
Pretexts (Gide), 2
Prévost, Jean, 5
*Projets de préface pour une édition
    nouvelle,* 163*n*
Proust, Marcel, 4, 168
Pushkin, Aleksander, 5

Q

"Que diras-tu ce soir," 81, 159-60

R

Racine, Jean, 7, 27, 119-20
"Ravine Saint-Gilles, La" (Leconte de
    Lisle), 131
Raymond, Marcel, 2
"Rebelle, Le," 173
"Recueillement," 17, 106, 120-21
"Reniement de Saint-Pierre, Le," 163
"Rêve d'un curieux, Le," 167, 172
"Rêve parisien," 98-99, 163, 171-72
"Réversibilité," 81, 159-60, 176
"Revolt," 25
Richard, Jean-Pierre, 2
Rilke, Rainer Maria, 168
Rimbaud, Arthur, 1, 18, 25, 34, 36
    154, 168
Rivière, Jacques, 2, 27
"Rolla" (Musset), 127
Romanticism, in Baudelaire's thought,
    9-12, 13, 19-24
    vs. realism, 96-97
Rousseau, Jean-Jacques, 164
Royère, Jean, 161*n*, 164*n*

S

Sabatier, Mme., poems to, 3-4, 56-61,

Sabatier, Mme., poems to, (*continued*)
  159-60, 174-77
Sagesse (Verlaine), 36
Sainte-Beuve, Charles, 9, 42, 123, 170
St. John Perse, 22
Salon de 1846, 20, 86
Sartre, Jean-Paul, 3, 25, 164
Satanism, theme of, 25, 51-52, 98,
  132-48, 173-74
"Semper eadem," 159
"Serpent qui danse, Le," 88-89
Soirées (De Maistre), 50-51
"Solitudes, Les" (Sully-Prudhomme),
  127-28
"Sonnet d'automne," 163n
Sophocles, 5
"Spleen" ("Quand le ciel"), 149-54,
  174
*Spleen de Paris, Le (Petits poèmes en
  prose)*, 37, 44-45, 82, 103-5
"Spleen et ideal," 46
"Squelette laboureur, Le," 172
Stendhal (*see* Beyle, Marie Henri)
Sully-Prudhomme, René, 127-28
Swinburne, Algernon, 7
Symbolists, 127-30
Symons, Arthur, 107

T

"Tableaux parisiens," 24
Taine, Hippolyte, 37, 127
Tannhäuser (Wagner), 18, 116
Tell-Tale Heart, The (Poe), 14
"Ténèbres, Les," 90-91
Tennyson, Alfred, 27
Theocritus, 5
Thibaudet, Albert, 1-2
Toussenel, Alphonse, 51-52
"Tout entière," 76, 81, 159

Trionfi (Petrarch), 84
Tristan and Isolde (Wagner), 116
Turnell, Martin, 2

U

Unconscious in Psychological Life, The
  (Jung), 21

V

Valéry, Paul, 2, 19, 22, 28-29, 43, 114
"Vampire, Le," 90
Van Gogh, Vincent, 154
Verlaine, Paul, 1, 5, 18, 36, 106, 123
"Veuves, Les," 105-6
"Vie antérieure, La," 122
Vigny, Alfred de, 5, 8, 20, 26, 110,
  112-13, 125-26, 174
Villon, François, 37
Vita Nuova (Dante), 82
"Voyage, Le," 33-34, 116, 119, 172-73
"Voyage à Cythère, Un," 6, 51, 120

W

Wagner, Richard, 18, 67, 116
Watts-Dunton, Theodore, 24
Will, paralysis of, in Baudelaire's life,
  43-48, 106-8, 142-46
Women, idealization of, 67-85

Y

Yeats, W. B., 22
"Yeux de pauvres, Les," 105

Z

Zola, Émile, 154

SAMUEL BECKETT

A Collection of Critical Essays
Edited by MARTIN ESSLIN

A

Act without Words, 136, 137
Aesop, 140
"Alba," 26, 27
Aldington, Richard, 25
Al-Haqq, 20
All That Fall, 50, 51, 90, 91, 137, 138
Anders, Günther, 14
Apollinaire, Guillaume, 23-24
Archimedes, 58
Aristotle, 174
Artaud, Antonin, 167
"Ascension," 30, 31
Ash-Wednesday (Eliot), 28
As You Like It (Shakespeare), 85
Augustine, Saint, 4, 126
Aurélia (Nerval), 80

B

Baillet, Adrien, 25
Bateau ivre, Le (Rimbaud), 23
Baudelaire, Charles, 88
Beckett, Samuel:
    biographical information, 1-2, 11, 23-25, 27
    critical response to, 1-2, 12-14
    and Descartes, 53-61, 169-77 *passim*
    esthetics of, 1-2, 4, 30, 62, 92, 106, 153
    and the French language, 91
    and Kierkegaard, 5-8
    moral vision of, 4, 83, 125-26, 132, 168
    parody in, 8, 77-91 *passim*, 99-100, 112, 114
    women in works of, 138-39
Beckett, Samuel, works by:
    Act without Words, 136, 137
    "Alba," 26, 27
    All That Fall, 50, 51, 90, 91, 137, 138
    "Ascension," 30, 31
    "Calmant, Le," 53, 55, 161, 166
    Cascando, 3, 4, 29, 30
    "Dante and the Lobster," 29, 38
    "Dieppe," 31
    "Ding Dong," 40
    "Dortmunder," 29
    "Draff," 40
    Dream of Fair to Middling Women, 27
    "Echo's Bones," 27, 30
    Echo's Bones and Other Precipitates, 26
    Embers, 90, 91
    "End, The," 78, 83
    Endgame (Fin de Partie), 1, 7, 29, 43, 49-50, 52, 78, 83, 86, 113, 115, 132-39, 154, 157, 158-59, 170
    "Enueg," 23, 26, 27, 28
    "Expelled, The ("Expulsé, L'")," 36, 53, 83
    "First Love," 169

Beckett, Samuel, works by (*continued*)
"For Future Reference," 26
From an Abandoned Work, 90, 91
"From the Only Poet to a Shining
Whore," 25
"Gnome," 27
Happy Days, 12, 50, 53, 167, 170,
173, 175, 177
How It Is (Comment c'est), 7, 12,
24, 39, 42, 44, 45, 50, 51, 95,
106, 167, 173-74, 177
Krapp's Last Tape, 90, 91, 105,
152
"Malacoda," 27
Malone Dies (Malone meurt), 29,
36, 46-47, 59, 83, 90, 95, 98, 105,
130, 153, 155
Mercier et Camier, 170-71
Molloy, 8, 33, 36, 42, 46, 77, 78,
80, 81, 84, 87, 91, 95, 105, 153,
166
More Pricks Than Kicks, 12, 29, 38,
40, 42
"Mort de A. D.," 31
"Mouche, La (Fly, The)," 30
Murphy, 4, 29, 33, 35-36, 41, 90,
153, 154, 155, 170, 174
Play, 7, 12
Poems in English, 162
Project I, 2
Proust, 3
"Rue de Vaugirard," 31
"Saint-Lô," 31
"Sanies," 27, 28
"Serena," 26, 27, 28, 29, 30
Stories and Texts for Nothing, 30,
77, 79-80, 81, 83, 84, 85, 90, 104,
105, 158, 173
"Three Dialogues," 24, 25
Unnamable, The (Innommable, L'),
4, 29, 36, 42-43, 47, 59, 77, 78,
80, 81, 82, 85, 101, 105, 115,
153, 155, 169, 173
"Vulture, The," 29, 31
*Waiting for Godot (En attendant
Godot)*, 1, 4, 7, 8, 12, 37, 41, 42,
46, 47, 49, 109, 111, 115, 120-
32, 133-38 *passim*, **140-51**, 158,

160, 162-64, 167, 170, 171
Watt, 15, 31, 41, 47, 48-49, **62-76**,
78, 91, 174
"Wet Night, A," 39, 40
"Whoroscope," 25, 27, 169
Bergson, Henri, 84
Berkeley, Bishop George, 2, 4
Biblical references, 25, 26, 28-30, 71
Blanchot, Maurice, 104
Boëthius, 161
Bonnard, 18, 19
Borges, J. L., 103
Bosch, Hieronymous, 71, 76
Botticelli, 40, 43
Bouvard et Pécuchet (Flaubert), 61
Brecht, Bertolt, 86, 87, 120, 140
Brentano, Clemens, 106
Breton, André, 24
Bunyan, John, 77
Byron, George Gordon, Lord, 149

C

"Calmant, Le," 53, 55, 161, 166
Camus, Albert, 176
Carroll, Lewis, 112
Cascando, 3, 4, 29, 30
Castle, The (Kafka), 145
"Chanson de mal-aime" (Apollinaire),
24
Chaplin, Charlie, 142, 151
Chateaubriand, F. R. de, 91
Christianity, references to, 10, 29, 30,
71, 76, 77, 95-96, 99, 102, 105, 106,
125, 126, 131
Cicero, 8
Coat, Tal, 16-17, 18, 19
Concluding Unscientific Postscript
(Kierkegaard), 5, 6, 7, 8
Consciousness, 9-10
Crowder, Henry, 25
Cruelty, 44, 78, 82, 120, 122
Cunard, Nancy, 25

D

Dante, 25, 26, 29, 37, 38, 39, 40, 41,
43, 46, 47, 157

"Dante and the Lobster," 29, 38
Death, theme of, 9, 97, 100, 101, 105,
    115-25, 153, 155, 161
Decay, theme of, 7, 34, 36, 52, 59,
    72, 85, 96-97, 105, 108, 111, 113,
    115, 122, 127, 171
Defoe, Daniel, 28
Democritus, 28
De Motu Cordis (Harvey), 25
Descartes, René, 25, 41, 53, 54, 56,
    57, 59, 61, 153, 169, 170, 171, 172,
    174, 176, 177
Devlin, Denis, 24
"Dieppe," 31
"Ding Dong," 40
Diogenes, 83
Discourse on Method (Descartes), 177
Divine Comedy (Dante), 37, 40
Doeblin, A., 141, 142
"Dortmunder," 29
Dostoevsky, F., 118
"Draff," 40
Dream of Fair to Middling Women, 27
Duthuit, Georges, 2, 62

E

"Echo's Bones," 27, 30
Echo's Bones and Other Precipitates,
    26
Either/Or (Kierkegaard), 8
Eliot, T. S., 25
Eluard, Paul, 24, 30
Embers, 90, 91
Encylopaedia Brittanica, 46
"End, The," 78, 83
Endgame (Fin de Partie), 1, 7, 29, 43,
    49-50, 52, 78, 83, 86, 113, 115, 132-
    39, 154, 157, 158-59, 170
Enlightenment, 61
"Enueg," 23, 26, 27, 28
Estang, Luc, 77
Ethics (Geulincx), 170, 171, 172
Euclid, 55
European Caravan, The, 26
Evergreen Review, 3
Existentialism, 4, 5, 6, 118, 127, 174,
    175, 176

Expiation, theme of, 81, 82, 85, 86,
    152, 156, 166
"Expelled, The" ("Expulsé, L'"), 36,
    53, 83
Expression, artist's obligation for, 2-3,
    9, 10, 14, 19, 20, 98, 156, 167

F

Faust (Goethe), 8
Finnegans Wake (Joyce), 48
"First Love," 169
Fleurs de Tarbes, Les, 36
Fontaine, 36
Fordham, M., 137
"For Future Reference," 26
Forgetting, theme of, 31, 34
Form, 11, 12
Freud, Sigmund, 18, 55
From an Abandoned Work, 90, 91
"From the Only Poet to a Shining
    Whore," 25
Fursey, Saint, 37

G

Games, 9, 11, 49, 68, 86-87, 134, 147-
    49, 159
"Garden of the Forking Paths, The"
    (Borges), 103
Geulincx, Arnold, 170, 171, 172
"Gnome," 27
Godwi (Brentano), 106
Goethe, J. W. von, 8, 27, 29, 149
Goncharov, I. A., 44
Gorgias of Lentini, 46-47, 48
Guggenheim, Peggy, 30
Guilt, theme of, 44, 77, 83, 85

H

Handicaps, prevalence of, 43, 50, 53,
    57, 60, 93, 98, 109, 163, 171
Happy Days, 12, 50, 53, 167, 170, 173,
    175, 177
Hardy, Thomas, 79
Harvey, William, 25
"Harzreise im Winter" (Goethe), 29

Hegel, F., 104, 146, 149, 150
Heidegger, Martin, 5, 6, 108, 118, 136, 144, 145, 169, 174, 175, 176, 177
Henry IV, 25
Henry-Music, 25
"Hiawatha" (Longfellow), 27
Hölderlin, J. C. F., 31, 118, 145
Horace, 12
How It Is (Comment c'est), 7, 12, 24, 39, 42, 44, 45, 50, 51, 95, 106, 167, 173-74, 177
  "After Pim," 44
  "Before Pim," 44
  "With Pim," 44

I

Ibsen, Henrik, 149
Ideology, rejection of, 4, 8, 10, 92, 125, 132, 135-36
Illuminations (Rimbaud), 23
Imagery, 11, 26-27, 32, 83-85, 88, 91, 96-97, 102, 105, 134, 137, 173
Images, recurrent, 43, 95
  armchair, 84, 170
  bicycle, 34, 43, 52-61 *passim,* 85, 94, 98, 108, 171
  hat, 52, 84, 93, 99, 100, 112, 114
Indifference, theme of, 31, 40, 69
Inferno (Dante), 26, 29, 41

J

Jarry, A., 82, 83, 86, 112
Jaspers, Karl, 118, 119
Journal of the Plague Year (Defoe), 28
Jouve, Pierre-Jean, 23
Joyce, James, 10, 27, 33, 47, 48, 79, 88, 91, 130
Jung, Carl, 79, 117, 118, 128, 129, 130, 131, 132, 137

K

Kafka, Franz, 5, 34, 77, 83, 84, 87, 90, 118, 141, 145, 146
Kandinsky, V., 21
Kant, Immanuel, 18, 141

Keaton, Buster, 2
Kierkegaard, Sören, 5, 6, 7, 8, 13, 14, 118, 119
Kleist, Heinrich von, 141
Krapp's Last Tape, 90, 91, 105, 152

L

La Fontaine, 140
Language (*see also* Speech), 10, 26, 28, 30-31, 34, 35, 46, 47, 48, 50, 63-64, 67, 90-91, 92, 102, 104-6, 155-56, 160-61, 166-67, 175, 177
Lautréamont, Comte de, 36
Leonardo, 18
Lichtenberg, 36
Lives of the Irish Saints (O'Hanlon), 37
Logical Positivism, 63, 174
Longfellow, Henry Wadsworth, 27
Love Song of J. Alfred Prufrock, The (Eliot), 28
Luke, Saint, 20

M

"Malacoda," 27
Malebranche, Nicolas, 173
Malone Dies (Malone meurt), 29, 36, 46-47, 59, 83, 90, 95, 98, 105, 130, 153, 155
Marie Antoinette, 85
Martial de Brives, 153
Marx, Karl, 149
Masson, A., 17-19
Master-servant relationship, 78, 120, 123, 130-33, 149-50
Matisse, 16-17, 18
Meaning, man's need for, 78, 79, 104, 122-23, 125, 144-45
Meditation II (Descartes), 172
Meditation VI (Descartes), 53, 171
Melville, Herman, 43-44, 77
Mercier et Camier, 170-71
"Message of the Dead King" (Kafka), 145
Metamorphoses (Ovid), 30
Method, 11, 33-35, 82, 110-11, 124, 129, 162

Metman, Eva, 14
Michaux, Henri, 82, 90
Milton, John, 81
Minnesingers, 26
Molloy, 8, 33, 36, 42, 46, 77, 78, 80,
   81, 84, 87, 91, 95, 105, 153, 166
Mondrian, P., 21
Monologue, use of (*see also* Speech),
   80, 120, 172-73, 175-76
More Pricks Than Kicks, 12, 29, 38,
   40, 42
Morse, J. Mitchell, 24
"Mort de A. D.," 31
Morungen, Heinrich von, 26
"Mouche, La ("Fly, The")," 30
Mouches, Les (Sartre), 149
Mozart, W. A., 148
Murphy, 4, 29, 33, 35-36, 41, 90, 153,
   154, 155, 170, 174
Mylius, 131
Mythological references, 30, 96-97, 125

N

Names, significance of, 48-50, 72, 73-74
Narrative devices, 33, 35, 48, 53-59,
   72-73, 80, 101-2, 105, 140-51, 162-
   63
Nathan, George Jean, 117
"Nemt, frowe, disen kranz" (Vogel-
   weide), 26
Nerval, Gérard de, 80
Neumann, E., 132
New Review, The, 26
Newton, Isaac, 52, 53, 57
Nietzsche, F. W., 118, 119

O

Occasionalists, 170, 172, 173, 174
O'Neill, Eugene, 117
Ovid, 30

P

Paradiso (Dante), 25
Parody, 8, 77-91 *passim*, 99-100, 112,
   114

Pascal, Blaise, 86
Phaenomenologie des Geistes (Hegel),
   149
Plato, 55, 155, 167
Play, 7, 12
Poems in English, 162
Portrait of the Artist as a Young Man
   (Joyce), 79
Predestination, idea of, 77, 84
Priestley, J. B., 167
Project I, 2
Protagoras, 159
Proust, Marcel, 3, 6, 12, 81, 88, 122,
   124, 131, 152, 156, 161
Purgatorio (Dante), 38-39, 40
Pythagorus, 21

Q

Quest, theme of, 34, 36, 43-44, 47, 62,
   64-67, 70, 72-73, 81, 83, 93-94, 96,
   98, 101, 107, 115, 155, 176

R

Reality, nature of, 6-9, 34, 47-48, 75-
   76, 78-79, 82, 88, 102, 105, 148
Return of Fursey, The (Wall), 37
Rilke, R. M., 118, 145
Rimbaud, Arthur, 23
Rossetti, D. G., 39
"Rue de Vaugirard," 31

S

Saint Genet (Sartre), 118
"Saint-Lô," 31
"Sanies," 27, 28
Sartre, Jean-Paul, 5, 6, 118, 123, 149,
   169, 176, 177
Sayers, Dorothy, 38
Schärf, Rivkah, 128
Schneider, Alan, 1, 2, 136
Schopenhauer, Arthur, 3
Self, nature of, 4, 7, 80, 84, 153, 154,
   166-67, 169, 174, 176
Self-perception, theme of, 3, 6, 7, 10,
   66, 80, 92, 101-2, 124, 153

Sennett, Mack, 83
"Serena," 26, 27, 28, 29, 30
Shakespeare, William, 55
Shelley, P. B., 149
Silence, search for, 81, 85, 87, 93, 102, 104, 107
Socrates, 169
Solitude, theme of, 31, 58, 78, 80, 87, 88-89, 91, 123, 141
Sordello, 42
"Spaziergang, Der" (Hölderlin), 31
Speech, 4, 24, 46-47, 64, 66-67, 72, 80, 85, 87, 92-93, 94, 98-99, 100-105, 109, 112, 155
Stages on Life's Way (Kierkegaard), 8
Stasis, theme of, 35, 38-41 *passim*, 43, 79, 81, 90, 121, 148
Sterne, Laurence, 84, 87
Stories and Texts for Nothing, 30, 77, 79-80, 81, 83, 84, 85, 90, 104, 105, 158, 173
Strindberg, August, 143
Style, 28, 90, 99
Stylistic devices, 10-11, 24, 26, 28-32, 45, 48, 73, 76
Suffering, inevitability of, 72, 83, 85, 88, 89, 120, 126, 127
Surrealism, 11, 23, 24, 31
Swift, Jonathan, 50, 88,
Symbols, 23, 39, 74-75, 78, 81, 83, 88, 90, 135
Symbolists, 23

T

"Three Dialogues," 24, 25
Threepenny Opera (Brecht), 140
Timaeus (Plato), 167
Time, theme of, 25, 78-79, 82, 87-88, 104, 112, 114, 146-51, 152
Tractatus Logico-Philosophicus (Wittgenstein), 74-75, 174
Transition, 24, 62
Tristram Shandy (Sterne), 84
Troubadours, 26

U

Ulysses (Joyce), 130

Unanimistes, 23
Unfortunate Fursey, The (Wall), 37
Unnamable, The (Innommable, L'), 4, 29, 36, 42-43, 47, 59, 77, 78, 80, 81, 82, 85, 101, 105, 115, 153, 155, 169, 173

V

Valéry, Paul, 24, 43
Velde, Bram van, 19-21
Vermischte Gedichte (Goethe), 29
Vielé-Griffin, Francis, 23
Village Voice, 1
Virgil, 29, 40
Vogelweide, Walther von der, 26
"Vulture, The," 29, 31

W

Waiting for Godot (En attendant Godot), 1, 4, 7, 8, 12, 37, 41, 42, 46, 47, 49, 109, 111, 115, **120-32**, 133-38 *passim*, **140-51**. 158, 160, 162-64, 167, 170, 171
Waley, Arthur, 26
Wall, Mervyn, 37
Waste Land, The (Eliot), 28
Watt, 15, 31, 41, 47, 48-49, **62-76**, 78, 91, 174
"Wet Night, A," 39, 40
"Whoroscope," 25, 27, 169
Wittgenstein, Ludwig, 74-75, 174-75, 176
Woolf, Virginia, 88
Wordsworth, William, 42
Wren, Sir Christopher, 28

X

Xenien (Goethe), 27

Z

Zen Buddhism, 10
Zeno, 159
"Zone" (Apollinaire), 24

THE BEOWULF POET

A Collection of Critical Essays
Edited by DONALD K. FRY

A

Addy, S. O., 137
Aeneid (Virgil), 29, 32*n*, 157
Alcuin, 21
Aldhelm, 73, 95, 103
Alexandria Quartet (Durrell), 2
Alfred the Great, 95*n*, 131*n*, 136
Allegory, in *Beowulf*, 68-75
Andreas, 17, 99, 104, 121
Apocryphal Gospel of St. Matthew and St. Andrew, 104
Archaeology, and *Beowulf*, 114-40
Arminius, 87
Arnold, Matthew, 1
Art of Beowulf, The (Brodeur), 158
Augustine, Saint, 68, 95
Author of *Beowulf*, 1-2, 35*n*
Azarias, 99

B

Bateman, J., 114
Bede, 73, 75*n*, 85, 96*n*, 132
Beowulf:
   and the *Aeneid*, 29
   and allegory, 68-75
   and archaeology, 114-40
   author of, 1-2, 35*n*
   characterization in, 1-3
   and *Christ and Satan*, 97-102
   chronology of, 171
   death in, 23, 43, 81

diction of, 2, 5, 85-86, 141-53
dramatic audience in, 76-82
dramatic technique of, 1, 4
errors in, 35*n*, 51-52
as history, 9-41 *passim* (*see also* Archaeology)
imagery in, 3, 155-66
mythology in, 20-41
narrative technique of, 1, 4 (*see also* Oral poetry)
and the *Odyssey*, 29, 168
oral poetry and, **83-110**
plot of, 13-14, 18, 76-82
point of view in, **154-66**
religion in, 12, 23-39, 41-56, **68-75**, 95-104
structure of, 1-2, 5, 14, **34-38, 57-65**, 85-86, 141-53
style of, 18, **57-65**
themes of, 2, 5-6, 14, 18, 23, 58-65, 154-66
Beowulf and the Heroic Age (Chambers), 16, 23
"*Beowulf*: The Monsters and the Critics" (Tolkien), *ix*, 1, 8-56, 57*n*, 76*n*
"Beowolf" (Wilbur), 7, 66-67
Bête Humaine, La (Zola), 156-57
Blomfield, Joan, 2, 57
Bonjour, Adrien, 76*n*, 154*n*
Bosworth, Joseph, 8
Bowra, Cecil Maurice, 84, 104*n*
Brodeur, Arthur G., *ix*, 5, 158-62

Bruckner, W., 69*n*

C

Caedman, 52, 85, 96, 103
Chadwick, H. M., 72*n*
Chambers, R. W., *ix*, 9*n*, 14-16, 20, 21*n*, 30*n*
Characterization in *Beowulf*, 1-3
Chaucer, Geoffrey, 1
Christ and Satan, 97-102, 111-13
Chronology, of *Beowulf*, 171
Claudian, 73
Clubb, M. D., 101-2
Cockayne, Oswald, 8
Coifi, 75
Conrad, Joseph, 165
Constantine, 118
Cooper, Lane, 103
Creed, Robert P., 95*n*, 141, 154
Crowne, David K., 154
Cynewulf, 17, 94, 100*n*, 103-4, 118

D

Daniel, 99
Dark Ages, The (Ker), 13-14, 25
Death, in *Beowulf*, 23, 43, 81
Deutschbein, M., 72*n*
Diamond, Robert E., 100*n*, 103*n*
Diction, of *Beowulf*, 2, 5, 85-86, 141-53
Dramatic audience, in *Beowulf*, 76-82
Dramatic technique, of *Beowulf*, 1, 4
Dream of the Rood, The, 100, 156
Durrell, Lawrence, 2

E

Elene, 94, 99
Errors, in *Beowulf*, 35*n*, 51-52
Exodus, 99

F

Fadlan, Ibn, 115

Folk-tale and History in Beowulf (Girvan), 16
Forssner, T., 69*n*
Förstemann, E., 70*n*
Fowler, Roger, 152
Fry, Donald K., 1, 153

G

Garnett, James M., 171
Genesis, 32, 145*n*, 150, 156, 164
Germania (Tacitus), 86
Girvan, R., 12, 16, 20, 73, 118, 129
Goethe, Johann Wolfgang von, 142
Greenfield, Stanley B., *ix*, 152, 154*n*
Gregory the Great, 68
Guthlac, 17

H

Harrison, James A., 171
Hawkes, C. F. C., 140*n*
History, *Beowulf* as, 9-41 *passim* (*see also* Archaeology)
Homer, 29*n*, 143, 154, 167
Hulbert, J. R., 76*n*

I

Iliad (Homer), 84*n*, 88, 154
Imagery, in *Beowulf*, 3, 155-66

J

Jones, P. F., 79
Judith, 26*n*, 47*n*, 88*n*, 99, 156
Juliana, 99, 104*n*

K

Kail, J., 104*n*
Kemble, John M., 171
Ker, W. P., 13-14, 18*n*, 25, 140
Klaeber, F., *ix*, 34, 60-61, 65*n*, 76*n*, 79, 81, 88*n*, 97*n*, 100*n*, 104*n*, 128, 138*n*, 146*n*, 158

Krapp, George P., 102, 164*n*

L

Lawrence, R. F., 152
Levin, Harry T., 164
Liestøl, A., 124*n*, 126
Lindqvist, 115*n*, 116*n*
Lord, Albert Bates, 83*n*, 84-107 *passim*, 155
Lord of the Rings, The (Tolkien), 6

M

Magoun, Francis Peabody, Jr., 83, 141*n*, 143*n*, 154
Malone, Kemp, *ix*, 70, 74*n*, 75*n*
Martianus Capella, 68
Milton, John, 17
Mossé, Fernand, 104*n*
Mustanoja, Tauno F., 155
Mythology, and *Beowulf*, 20-41

N

Narrative technique of *Beowulf*, 1, 4
(*see also* Oral poetry)
Nerman, Birger, 10

O

Odyssey (Homer), 29, 84*n*, 88, 168
Ogilvy, J. D. A., 73
Olrik, A., 71*n*, 72
Olson, O. L., 72*n*
Oral poetry, and *Beowulf*, 83-110

P

Panzer, F., 72*n*
Parry, Milman, 83-107 *passim*, 141, 143, 154*n*
Paulinus, 75, 95
Pfeilstucker, Suse, 130, 134, 135*n*, 137, 139*n*
Plot of *Beowulf*, 13-14, 18, 76-82

Poesis, Wanley, 9
Point of view, in *Beowulf*, **154-66**
Pope, John Collins, *ix*, 91*n*, 142*n*
Power of Blackness, The (Levin), 164
Prudentius, 68, 72-74
Psychomachia (Prudentius), 72

Q

Quirk, Randolph, 105

R

Religion and *Beowulf*, 12, 23-39, 41-56, **68-75**, 95-104

S

Saint-Exupéry, Antoine de, 165
Sievers, Eduard, 104*n*, 106*n*
Schaar, Claes, 104*n*
Schücking, L. L., 68, 73
Sedulius, 68, 73
Sisam, K., *ix*
Solomon and Saturn, 121
Speratus, 21
Sprachschatz (Grein-Köhler-Holthausen), 152
Stevick, Robert D., 151
Stjerna, K., 115*n*, 116-17, 125*n*, 129*n*
Strong, Archibald, 10, 18*n*
Structure, of *Beowulf*, 1-2, 5, 14, 34-38, 57-65, 85-86, 141-53
Style of *Beowulf*, 18, **57-65**

T

Tacitus, Cornelius, 85-86
Themes of *Beowulf*, 2, 5-6, 14, 18, 23, 58-65, 154-66
Thorkelin, Grimur Jonsson, *ix*, 9, 171
Timmer, Benno J., 107*n*
Tolkien, J. R. R., *ix*, 1-2, 8, 57*n*, 60, 76*n*

BLAKE

A Collection of Critical Essays

Edited by NORTHROP FRYE

A

Abrams, M. H., 65
Adams, Hazard, 4
Advancement of Learning, The
  (Bacon), 147
"Ah! Sun-Flower," 56-64
  illustration to, 51
All Religions are One, illustrations to,
  127
America, 4, 89-90, 96, 101, 152
  illustrations to, 92, 122, 124, 125,
  133-34
American Revolution, Blake's theories
  on the, 88-90
Archetypal figures, in *Songs of Inno-
  cence and Experience*, 65-78
"Artist," Blake's concept of, 26
Auguries of Innocence, 37-38, 45, 82-
  83

B

Bacon, Sir Francis, 144, 145, **147**, 151
"Bard," Blake's concept of, 30-31, 35-
  36
Bard, The (Gray), 143, 160-61
Bardism (*see* Druidism)
Bateson, F. W., 32, 35, 45
Biblical references:
  in *Europe*, 136, 138, 139-40
  in *Four Zoas, The*, 109-13, 115-16
  in "Golden Net, The," 87
  in the illustrations, 55, 124

in *Songs of Innocence and Experience*, 12, 25-28, 30-31, 68, 70-71
Blake, William:
  and Bacon, Sir Francis, 144, 145,
    147, 151
  "Bard," concept of, 30-31, 35-36
  critical studies of, 1-7
  and Christianity, 24-28, 30-31, 73,
    107, 125-26, 150, 165-66
  and Coleridge, 76-77
  cyclical recurrence, doctrine of,
    163-70
  and Deism, 24, 116, **149-53**, 167
  and Druidism, 156-78
  economic freedom, theories of, 89-
    91, 100-101
  and the French Revolution, 88-90,
    131-32, 134-35, 151-53
  God, concept of, 30-31, 174-75
  and Greek mythology, 57, 58-62
  as an illustrator, 4, 45-55, 68, 69,
    119-26, 127-41
  and Keats, 75-76, 78
  and Locke, 145-46, 147, 151, 154-
    55
  macrocosm and microcosm, inter-
    changeability of, 79-85
  and Milton, 25, 27, 54, 138, 143
  neoclassicism, rejection of, 142-55
  Newtonian science, rejection of,
    29, 31, 139, 145, **147-49**
  and Ovid, 3, 58-59, 60, 66-67
  persona of, 2, 35-36, 42-43
  pre-romantic influences on, 142-46

Blake, William (*continued*)
  radicalism of, 119-20, 131-32, 134-
    35, **147-48, 150-53**
  and Romanticism, 73-78, 144
  sexual freedom, theory of, 133
  and slavery, works on, 88-103
  and Spenser, 44, 67-68, 75, 77,
    125, 143
  and Voltaire, 145, 147, 148, 150,
    151-53
  and Wagner, 123, 124
  and Wordsworth, 73-74, 90-91,
    143
Blake, William, works by: (*see also*
titles of individual works)
  All Religions are One, 127
  America, 4, 89-90, 96, 101, 152
  Auguries of Innocence, 37-38, 45,
    82-83
  Book of Ahania, The, 109
  Book of Los, The, 121, 122
  Book of Thel, The, 59, 121-22, 127-
    32
  Book of Urizen, The, 50, 52, 54,
    112, 117, 122, 124
  "Crystal Cabinet, The," 72, 79-85
  Europe, 54, 82, 96n, 122, 124, 125,
    136-41, 148
  Four Zoas, The, 4, 59, 69, 91, **104-
    18,** 122
  French Revolution, The, 132, 133n,
    147
  Gates of Paradise, The, 29, 40, 49-
    50, 51, 53, 133, 144
  "Golden Net, The," 85-87
  Island in the Moon, An, 41, 120,
    129-30
  Jerusalem, 10, 24-25, 40n, 81, 83-
    84, 85, 105, 122-23, 124-25, 149,
    151, 152, 162-66, 170-74, 177-
    78
  Lambeth Books, 135-41
  Marriage of Heaven and Hell, The,
    9, 69, 70, 122, 124, 132-33, 147,
    175, 178
  Mental Traveller, The, 29, 50, 72,
    79, 80-81, 84, 112, 164
  Milton, 26-27, 31, 33-34, 38, 105,

118, 122, 144, 149, **153-54,** 164,
  166, 169-71
  Poetical Sketches, 23, 71, 143
  Songs of Innocence and Experience,
    8-14, 15-22, 23-31, 32-55, 56-64,
    65-78, 127-32
  Song of Los, 103, 151
  There is no Natural Religion, 53,
    127
  Tiriel, 120-21, 152
  Visions of the Daughters of Albion,
    30, 57, 59, 62, 84, 89-103, 121-
    22, 133
Bloom, Harold, 4
Blunt, Sir Anthony, 4
Bodkin, Maud, 65
Book of Ahania, The, 109
Book of Los, The, Blake's illustrations
  to, 121, 122
Book of Job, illustrations to,
  49
Book of Thel, The, 59, 121-22
  illustrations to, 127-32
Book of Urizen, The, 112, 117
  illustrations to, 50, 52, 54, 122,
    124
Bowra, C. M., 57
*Brewer's Dictionary of Phrase and
  Fable,* 60-61
Burke, Edmund, 91, 97, 101
Burns, Robert, 44
Butts, Thomas, 137
Byron, George Gordon, 143

C

Chatterton, Thomas, 143
Chayes, Irene, 3
"Chimney Sweeper, The," 14
  and child labor laws, 15-22
*Chimney Sweeper's Friend and Climb-
  ing Boy's Album, The* (Montgomery),
  18
"Christabel" (Coleridge), 76-77
Christianity, and Blake's thought, 24-
  28, 30-31, 150, 165-66
  in Blake's symbology, 73
  and Druidism, 157-58, 162

Christianity, and Blake's thought
   (*continued*)
     in *Four Zoas, The,* 107
     in the prophetic writings, 125-26
"Clod and the Pebble, The," 14
Coleridge, Samuel Taylor, 76-77
Collins, William, 109, 143
Color, use of, in the illuminated works,
   98*n*, 123, 129, 137
Confessions (Rousseau), 152
Cowper, William, 90
"Cruelty," 14
"Crystal Cabinet, The," 72, 79-85
     and *Jerusalem,* 83-84
Cyclical recurrence, doctrine of, 163-
   70

D

Damon, S. Foster, 1, 32, 33-34, 35,
   45, 49, 91
Dante Alighieri, 70, 71
Davies, Edward, 156, 158*n*
Deism:
   Blake's rejection of, 24, 116, **149-53**
   and Druidism, 167-68
Descartes, René, 148
Descriptive Catalogue, A, and Druid-
   ism, 156-57, 160, 167
"Design" (Frost), 45
Divine Comedy, The (Dante), illustra-
   tions to, 70, 71
"Divine Image, The," illustrations to,
   121
Dostoevsky, Feodor, 43-44
"Dream, A," 74
Druidism, and Blake's thought, 156-78
   and Christianity, 157-58, 162
   and *Four Zoas, The,* 164-67, 174,
     176-77
   and Greek mythology, 158-61
   history of, 158-60
   in *Jerusalem,* 156, 158*n*, 159*n*, 160,
     162-66, 170-74, 177-78
Dryden, John, 145-46

E

"Earth's Answer," 14, 24, 30, 35, 69
"Echoing, Green, The," illustration to,
   129-30
Eckhart, Meister Johannes, 113
Economic freedom, theories of, 89-91,
   100-101
Ellis, E. J., 56-57, 126
Empirical rationalism, Blake's rejec-
   tion of, 144-46, 147-48
Englishman's Flora, The (Grigson), 60
Engraving methods, in the illuminated
   works, 123, 127-29, 137
Enlightenment, Blake's rejection of the,
   142-55
Erdman, David V., 2-3, 84-85
Europe, 82, 96*n*, 140, 148
   Biblical references in, 136, 138,
     139-40
   illustrations to, 54, 122, 124, 125,
     136-41
"Eve of St. Agnes, The" (Keats), 75-76,
   78

F

Faerie Queene, The (Spenser), 44
   and *Songs of Innocence and Experi-
     ence,* 67-68, 75, 77
Fearful Symmetry (Frye), 23
Fisher, Peter F., 5, 84
"Fly, The," 32-55
   illustration to, 45-51
   and *Milton,* 35-36
   Shakespearean references in, 37-38,
     40*n*
"Fly, The" (Shapiro), 45
Four Zoas, The, 4, 59, 69, 91, **104-18**,
   122
   Biblical references in, 109-13, 115-
     16
   and Druidism, 164-67, 174, 176-77
   as Freudian allegory, 113-14
   sexual freedom, theme of, 108-9

Four Zoas, The (*continued*)
  and *Songs of Innocence and Experience*, 107, 108
  and *Visions of the Daughters of Albion*, 102, 103
French Revolution, Blake's theories on, 88-90, 131-32, 134-35, 151-53
French Revolution, The, 132, 133*n*, 147
Freud, Sigmund, 6
Freudian allegory, in *The Four Zoas*, 113-14
Frost, Robert, 45
Frye, Northrop, 4, 23, 65, 104, 109

G

"Garden of Love, The," 14
Gates of Paradise, The, 29, 40, 144
  and "Fly, The," 51*n*-52*n*, 53
  illustrations to, 49-50, 51, 53, 133
Gibbon, Edward, 152
Gleckner, Robert F., 2, 19, 43*n*
God, Blake's concept of, 30-31, 174-75
Godwin, William, 131-32, 135
"Golden Net, The," 85-87
Grant, John E., 2
Gray, Thomas, 43, 44, 46*n*, 52, 143, 144, 160-61
Greek mythology:
  in "Ah! Sun-Flower," 57, 58-62
  and Druidism, 158-61
  in *Songs of Innocence and Experience*, 65-78
"Grey Monk, The," 135
Grigson, Geoffrey, 60
Guyon, Mme., 150

H

Hagstrum, Jean H., 5
Hamlet (Shakespeare), 63*n*
Harper, G. M., 57
Hayley, William, 147, 152

Hervey, James, 150
"Holy Thursday," 11-14, 40*n*
  illustration to, 121, 130
Hood, Thomas, 18
"Human Abstract, The," 14, 43*n*
"Human Brain, The," 14
Hume, David, 145
"Humility," 14

I

Illustration, 119-26, 127-41
  to *America*, 122, 124, 125, 133-34
  Biblical references in, 55
  to *Book of Los, The*, 121, 122
  to *Book of Thel, The*, 127-32
  to *Book of Urizen*, 122, 124
  color, use of, 98*n*, 123, 129, 137
  to *Divine Comedy, The* (Dante), 70, 71
  engraving methods, 4, 123, 127-29
  to *Europe*, 122, 124, 125, 136-41
  to "Fly, The," 45-51
  to *Gates of Paradise, The*, 133
  to *Island in the Moon, An*, 129-30
  to *Jerusalem*, 52-53, 54, 122-23, 124-25
  to *Macbeth* (Shakespeare), 138, 139
  to *Marriage of Heaven and Hell, The*, 122, 124
  to *Night Thoughts* (Young), 53, 122, 149
  to "Ode on the Spring" (Gray), 43, 44, 46*n*, 52
  of slave conditions, 92-93, 97-98
  to *Songs of Innocence and Experience*, 68, 69, 121, 127-32, 134
  to *Visions of the Daughters of Albion*, 121-22, 133
  words and design, relation between, 121-26, 130-31
"Il Penseroso" (Milton), Blake's illustrations to, 54
Imagery, in the illuminated works, 45-55 (*see also* Symbolism)

"Infant Joy," illustration to, 121, 134
"Infant Sorrow," 40*n*, 84
  illustration to, 49
"Introduction," to *Songs of Experience,* 12, 35
  illustration to, 49
  symbolism of, 24-31
"Introduction," to *Songs of Innocence,* illustration to, 130
Island in the Moon, An, 41, 120
  illustrations to, 129-30

J

Jerusalem, 10, 24-25, 40*n*, 81, 83-84, 85, 105, 149, 151, 152, 164
  Druidism in, 156, 158*n*, 159*n*, 160, 162-66, 170-74, 177-78
  illustrations to, 122-23, 124-25
Johnson, Joseph, 92
Johnson, Dr. Samuel, 142, 146
Jung, C. G., 66

K

Keats, John, 75-76, 78
Keith, William J., 3
Kerényi, C., 66
King Lear (Shakespeare), 37-38
Kirschbaum, Leo, 32, 33-35, 37-44

L

La Fayette, Marquis de, 151
"L'Allegro" (Milton), Blake's illustrations to, 54
Lamb, Charles, 18
"Lamb, The," illustration to, 48
Lambeth Books, 135-41
"Laughing Song," illustration to, 130
"Little Black Boy, The," 19-20, 90, 98
"Little Girl Found, The," 40*n*, 66, 71, 72
"Little Girl Lost, A," 68, 69
  illustration to, 54
"Little Girl Lost, The," 66, 68-70, 72-73

"Little Vagabond, The," 11, 14, 35
Locke, John, Blake's rejection of, 139, 145-46, 147, 151, 154-55
"Lucy Gray" (Wordsworth), 73-74, 78

M

Macbeth (Shakespeare), 58
  Blake's illustrations to, 138, 139
Macpherson, James, 96, 143
Macrocosm and microcosm, in "The Crystal Cabinet," 79-85
Malory, Thomas, 177
Margoliouth, H. M., 105, 113
Marriage of Heaven and Hell, The, 9, 69, 70, 132-33, 147
  and Druidism, 175, 178
  illustrations to, 122, 124
"Mary," 23
Maxims of the Saints (Guyon), 150
Meditations Among the Tombs (Hervey), 150
Mental Traveller, The, 29, 72, 79, 80-81, 84, 112, 164
  illustration to, 50
Metamorphoses (Ovid), 3, 66-67
  and "Ah! Sun-Flower," 57, 58-59, 60
Midsummer Night's Dream, A (Shakespeare), 138
Milton, 26-27, 31, 33-34, 38, 105, 118, 122, 144, 149, 153-54, 164, 166, 169, 171
  and Druidism, 156, 159, 164, 166, 169-71, 176
  and "Fly, The," 35-36
  illustrations to, 55
Milton, John, 25, 27, 138
"Mock on, Mock on," 83
Montgomery, James, 18
Morris, William, 119-20
Morte d'Arthur (Malory), 177
"Muiopotmos" (Spenser), 44
Mutabilitie Cantoes (Spenser), 125
"My Pretty Rose Tree," 8-9, 14
  illustration to, 54
"My Spectre around me," 79-87

N

*Narrative, of a five Years' expedition
. . .* (Stedman), Blake's illustrations
to, 92-93, 97-98
Natural law, concept of, 28
Natural religion (*see* Druidism)
Negro's Complaint, The (Cowper), 90
Neoclassicism, Blake's rejection of,
142-55
Newtonian science, Blake's rejection
of, 29, 31, 139, 145, 147-49
Nietzsche, Friedrich, 6
"Night," 72
Night Thoughts (Young), Blake's illus-
trations to, 53, 122, 149
Nurmi, Martin K., 2-3
"Nurses Song," illustration to, 49, 50

O

"Ode for Music on St. Cecilia's Day"
(Pope), 61
Ode on the Poetical Character (Col-
lins), 109
"Ode on the Spring" (Gray), Blake's
illustration to, 43, 44, 46*n*, 52
Oithona (Macpherson), 96
Opuscules spirituels (Guyon), 150
Ovid, 3, 57, 58-59, 60, 66-67

P

Paine, Thomas, 101, 131-32, 147, 151
Painting and poetry (*see* Words and de-
sign, relation between)
Paradise Lost (Milton), 25, 138
Persephone, myth of:
in "Ah! Sun-Flower," 59-62
in *Songs of Innocence and Experi-
ence*, 66-73, 76-78
Perspective, principle of, in "The Crys-
tal Cabinet," 79-85
Poetical Sketches, 23, 71, 143
"Poison Tree, A," 35
illustration to, 48
Pope, Alexander, 61, 144, 146

Pre-romantic influences, in Blake's
thought, 142-46
Proverbs of Hell (see *Marriage of
Heaven and Hell, The*)
Pythagoreans and Druidism, 158-59,
163

R

Radicalism, in Blake's thought, 119-20,
131-32, 134-35, **147-48, 150-153**
Rasselas (Johnson), 142
Ready and Easy Way, The (Milton), 27
Reynolds, Sir Joshua, 142, 155
Rights of Man, The (Paine), 101
Romantic Imagination, The (Bowra),
57
Romanticism, in *Songs of Innocence
and Experience*, 73-78
Rousseau, Jean-Jacques, 150, 151-52

S

"School Boy, The," 35
illustration to, 134
Schorer, Mark, 14, 150
Shapiro, Karl, 45
Sexual freedom, theory of, 133
in *Four Zoas, The*, 108-9
in *Visions of the Daughters of Al-
bion*, 89-91
Sexual symbolism, in "The Crystal
Cabinet," 80-82, 86-87
Shakespearean references:
in "Ah! Sun-Flower," 58, 60, 63*n*
in "Fly, The," 37-38, 40*n*
in the illuminated works, 138
"Sick Rose, The," illustration to, 134
Sion, Llewelyn, 157, 161
Slavery, theme of, 88-103
in *Visions of the Daughters of Al-
bion*, 90-103
"Smile, The," 23
Song of Los, The, 103, 151
Songs of Innocence and Experience,
8-14, 15-22, 23-31, 32-55, 56-64, 65-
78 (*see also* titles of individual poems)

Songs of Innocence and Experience
  (*continued*)
    "Ah! Sun-Flower," 56-64
    archetypal figures in, 65-78
    Biblical references in, 12, 25-28,
      30-31, 68, 70-71
    child labor laws, and "The Chimney
      Sweeper," 15-22
    "Fly, The," 32-55
    and *Four Zoas, The,* 107, 108
    Greek mythology in, 65-78
    illustrations to, 45-55, 121, 127-32,
      134
    "Introduction," to *Songs of Experi-
      ence,* 24-31
    persona in, 2, 35-36, 42-43
    points of view in, 2, 8-14
    Shakespearean references in, 58, 60,
      63*n*
    sources of, 57-62
    symbolism in, 8-14, 23-31
"Soul," Blake's concept of, 28
Spenser, Edmund, 44, 67-68, 75, 77,
  125, 143
Stedman, Captain J. G., 92-96
Sterne, Laurence, 38
Stevens, Wallace, 105
Stukeley, William, 156, 159
Swedenborg, Emanuel, 142, 153
Sweet Meat Has Sour Sauce (Cowper),
  90
Swift, Jonathan, 144, 146
Symbolism:
    in "Ah! Sun-Flower," 56-64
    in *Four Zoas, The,* 104-18
    in the illuminated works, 45-55
    sexual, 80-82, 86-87, 89-91
    in *Songs of Innocence and Experi-
      ence,* 23-31

T

Tale of a Tub, A (Swift), 146
Taylor, Thomas, 57, 61, 62, 66-67, 71
There is no Natural Religion, illustra-
  tions to, 53, 127
Thomas, Dylan, 45
Thomson, James, 143, 148
Tiriel, 120-121, 152

"To a Mouse" (Burns), 44
Treatise on Tolerance (Voltaire), 152
Tristram Shandy (Sterne), 38
"Tyger, The," 35, 40*n*
    illustration to, 48, 51

V

Vala (see *Four Zoas, The*)
Vindication of the Rights of Men
  (Wollstonecraft), 100, 101
Vindication of the Rights of Women
  (Wollstonecraft), 90
Visions of the Daughters of Albion,
  30, 57, 59, 62, 84
    and *Four Zoas, The,* 102, 103
    illustrations to, 121-22, 133
    sexual symbolism in, 89-91
    slavery, theme of, 90-103
Voltaire, François, 145, 147, 148, 150,
  151-53

W

Wagner, Richard, 123, 124
Warton, Joseph, 143
Warton, Thomas, 143
Wedgwood, Thomas, 90
Whitman, Walt, 6
Wicksteed, Joseph, 8, 21, 32, 45
    on Blake's pictorial symbolism, 50,
      51, 55
Wilberforce, William, 95, 96*n,* 97
*William Blake: His Philosophy and
  Symbols* (Damon), 1
"William Bond," 23
Williams, Edward, 157-78 *passim*
Winter's Tale, The (Shakespeare), 60
Wollstonecraft, Mary, 90, 100, 101,
  135, 136
Words and design, relation between, in
  illuminated works, 121-26, 130-131
Wordsworth, William, 73-74, 90-91, 143
Works of William Blake (Yeats and
  Ellis), illustrations to, 126
Wright, Thomas, 8

Y

Yeats, William Butler, 56-57, 126
Young, Edward, 53, 122, 143, 149

BRECHT

A Collection of Critical Essays

Edited by PETER DEMETZ

A

Aesthetic distance, **59-85**, 88-89
  and characterization, 76-78
  and dramatic structure, 60-62, 64,
    67
  and Expressionism, 60-62, 64, 67
  and stage construction, 79-83
  and stage directions, 66-75
A la recherche du temps perdu
  (Proust), 65
"Alienation Effect in the Acting Art of
  the Chinese, The," 108
Alienation, theme of, 3-4, 56, 108-9,
  111-12, 120-21, 140, 142
Ansermet, Ernest, 158
Antheil, Georges, 160, 170
Apollinaire, Guillaume, 5, 59, 62-63,
  81
Apollonio, Mario, 73
Arendt, Hannah, 1
Aristotelian theater, 24, 78, 113-15,
  128-29, **133-34**
  (*see also* Formalism; Traditional
    theater)
Aristotle, 14, 122-23, 129, 131
"Art and the Proletariat" (Bogdanov),
  87
"Art as Artifice" (Shklovsky), 108
Auden, W. H., 11

B

Baal, 2, 8, 12, 14, 53, 137, 152,

157, 175, 181-82
Baby in the Bar (Grosz), 159
Baden Cantata of Acquiescence, The,
  10
Ballad of Paragraph 218, 28
Ballad of the Dead Soldier, 18, 19
"Ballad of the Pirates," 177, 178
Balzac, Honoré, 102, 103
Barth, Karl, 115
Bartholomew Fair (Jonson), 71
Bartók, Béla, 170
Baudelaire, Charles, 175
Beaumont, Francis, 71-72
Beckett, Samuel, 51, 135, 182
Beggar's Opera (Gay), 162, 181
*Belphégor. Essai sur l'esthetique de la
  présente société française* (Benda),
  60-61, 60n
Benda, Julien, 60-61, 60n
Benn, Gottfried, 1, 2, 48, 113
Bergson, Henri, 61, 65, 70
Bernstein, Leonard, 170
Blitzstein, Marc, 170
Boeuf sur le toit (Milhaud), 158
Bogdanov, A., 87, 90
Borchardt, Rudolf, 49
Bornemann, Ernest, 9, 173
Bourgeois, references to, 20, 21, 45,
  46, 58, 86, 89, 94-96, 101-2, 110-12,
  119, 173
Brecht, Bertold:
  and aesthetic distance, **59-85**, 88-89
  and Aristotelian theater, 24, 78,
    113-15, 128-29, **133-34**

Brecht, Bertold (*continued*)
  biographical information, 16-29,
    30-42, 106, 117, 173-74
  and capitalism, 27, 52, 55, 58, 95,
    98, 109, 129, 136, 143-45, 177
  and Chinese theater, 77-78, 108,
    180-81
  and communism, 22, 23, 26, 28,
    32-33, 34-36, 40-41, 52, 54, 57,
    58, 87, 112, 127, 132, 133, 135-
    37, 151, 166 (*see also* Marxism)
  and Dessau, Paul, 157, 168-69
  as director, 19, 56
  and Eisler, Hanns, 28, 32, 33, 34,
    38-39, 41, 157, 164, 166-68
  and epic theater, 3-10, 23, 24, 25,
    29, 47, 53, 75-77, 90-91, 99, 105,
    106, 112, 122, 124, 126, 133-34,
    138, 141, 146-50, 152 (*see also*
    Theater)
  and Japanese theater, 34, 36, 106,
    179
  and Pirandello, Luigi, 5, 54-55, 59,
    60, 63, 64, 68-70, 73, 74, 106,
    135
  and Piscator, Erwin, 3, 77, 81, 86-
    96, 106
  revolution, theme of, 19, 25, 28,
    33, 86-89, 95, 109, 132
  science and technology, influences
    of, 83, 92, 110, 115, 117-23, 138,
    139
  socialist realism, 5, 44, 50, 97-105,
    108-16, 151
  and traditional theater, 101-2, 106-
    7, 124, 149
  and Weill, Kurt, 23, 157, 159, 160,
    161-64, 165-67, 169
Brecht, Bertold, works by:
  PLAYS AND LIBRETTOS
    Baal, 2, 8, 12, 14, 53, 137, 152,
      157, 175, 181-82
    Baden Cantata of Aquiescence, The,
      10
    Ballad of Paragraph 218, 28
    Ballad of the Dead Soldiers, 18, 19
    "Ballad of the Pirates," 177, 178
    Caucasian Chalk Circle, The, 2, 14,
      15, 125, 136-37, 139, 151-56,
      168-69, 181
    Condemnation of Lucullus, The,
      157, 169
    Days of the Commune, 55, 111-12,
      182
    Drums in the Night, 8-9, 19, 37,
      157, 175
    Edward II, 157
    Faust II, 57
    "Forward, We've Not Forgotten,"
      41-42
    Galileo, 3, 11-12, 45, 56, 117-26,
      127, 168, 181
    Good Woman of Setzuan, The, 13,
      14, 47, 55-56, 77, 125, 127-31,
      134-37, 139, 152, 165, 180
    Hangmen Also Die (film), 32, 167
    Happy End, 157, 163
    He Who Says No, 115, 179
    He Who Says Yes, 115, 165, 166,
      179
    "In Praise of Learning," 38
    In the Swamp, 9, 51, 52-53, 55, 57,
      137, 138, 176
    Kuhle Wampe (film), 167
    Lehrstücke, 76-78, 157, 161, 164-
      65, 166, 178-79
    Lindbergh's Flight, 164, 165, 178-
      79
    "Liturgy of Breath," 49
    Lullabies for Proletarian Mothers,
      28
    Maid of Orleans, The, 57
    Man's a Man, A, 9, 19, 20-21, 27,
      53-57, 99, 106, 107, 114, 127,
      139, 157, 165, 177
    *Master Puntila and His Servant
      Matti*, 13, 53, 74, 127, 131-35,
      152, 180
    Measures Taken, The, 10, 19, 26,
      28, 34, 37, 43-45, 133, 135-37,
      138, 139, 166, 179
    Mother Courage, 13-15, 19, 25, 26,
      56, 75, 127, 134, 138-50, 151,
      166-67, 168-69, 180
    Private Life of the Master Race, The,
      11, 33, 44, 56, 138

Brecht, Bertold, works by: (*continued*)
  Private Tutor, The, 56
  Resistible Rise of Arturo Ui, The,
    11, 57, 138
  Rise and Fall of the City of Ma-
    hagonny, The, 9-10, 52, 56, 106-7,
    157, 158, 160, 161, 162-63, 165
  Roundheads and the Peakheads,
    The, 10-11, 28, 100, 108, 138,
    167, 181
  Saint Joan of the Stockyards, 10,
    26, 27, 49, 57-58, 138, 176
  Schweik in World War II, 53, 138,
    140, 165, 181
  Señora Carrar's Rifles, 11
  Seven Deadly Sins, The, 52, 55-56,
    127, 166
  Simone Machard, 167
  "Solidarity Song," 28, 167
  "Song of the Great Capitulation,"
    141-43
  "Song of the Wise and Good," 141-
    43
  Threepenny Opera, The, 7, 9, 19,
    23, 27, 45, 106, 128, 137, 141-42,
    157, 162-64, 167, 170, 175, 176
  OTHER WORKS
  "Alienation Effect in the Acting Art
    of the Chinese, The," 108
  Buckow Elegies, 2
  "Burial of the Agitator in a Zinc
    Coffin, The," 44, 56
  Domestic Breviary, 48, 161, 175,
    177-78
  "Forgotten Glories of the Giant
    City of New York," 177
  "Jew, a Misfortune for the People,
    The," 44
  "Little Description of a New Tech-
    nique of Acting, A," 108-9, 110
  Little Organon for the Theater, 4,
    7, 107, 110-11, 113-15, 116, 121,
    138
  "On the Range and Variety of the
    Realist Way of Writing," 103
  On Unrhymed Verse with Irregular
    Rhythms, 180
  "Socialist Realism in the Theater," 97

  Strassenszene, Die, 75
  Threepenny Novel, The, 1
  What is Formalism?" 103
Brik, Ossip, 21
Britten, Benjamin, 169
Brout (Régis), 70-71
Büchner, Georg, 6-7, 14, 19, 20, 53,
  62, 175
Buckow Elegies, 2
Bullough, Edward, 60
"Burial of the Agitator in a Zinc Cof-
  fin, The," 44, 56
Burkard, Heinrich, 159

C

Camus, Albert, 135
Candide (Voltaire), 104
Cangiullo, Francesco, 63
Capitalism, references to, 27, 52, 55,
  58, 95, 98, 109, 129, 136, 143-45,
  177
Caramel Mou (Milhaud), 158
Catholicism, references to, 40, 45, 121-
  23
Caucasian Chalk Circle, The, 2, 14, 15,
  125, 136-37, 139, 151-56, 168-69,
  181
Caudwell, Christopher, 58
Céline, F., 48
Characterization, 26, 47, 57-58, 75-78,
  127-37 (*see also* Split characters)
  in *Caucasian Chalk Circle, The,* 151-
    56
  in *Galileo,* 117-26
  in *Mother Courage,* 139-46
Chinese theater, 77-78, 108, 180-
  81
"Christophe Colomb" (Claudel), 106
Ciascuno a suo modo (Pirandello), 64
Claudel, Paul, 5, 106, 159, 160
Cocardes (Cocteau), 160
Cocteau, Jean, 62-63, 75, 157, 158,
  160
Communism, references to, 22, 23, 26,
  28, 32-33, 33-36, 40-41, 52, 54, 57,
  58, 87, 112, 127, 132, 133, 135-37,
  151, 166 (*see also* Marxism)

Condemnation of Lucullus, The, 157,
169
Coq et l'harlequin, Le (Cocteau), 158
Cradle Will Rock, The (Blitzstein),
170

D

Dante, 15, 179
Danton's Death (Büchner), 175
Days of the Commune, 55, 111-12,
182
Dead Souls (Gogol), 26
Deathwatch (Genet), 52
Dehumanization, theme of, 17-22, 48,
148
Dessau, Paul, 157, 168-69
Dickens, Charles, 103, 176
Diderot, Denis, 3, 104, 105
Dilthey, Wilhelm, 62, 78
Döblin, 91, 106, 165
Domestic Breviary, 48, 161, 175, 177-
78
Dos Passos, John, 91
Down in the Valley (Weill), 169
Drums in the Night, 8-9, 19, 37, 157,
175
Duino Elegies (Rilke), 11
Dürrenmatt, Friedrich, 6, 83

E

Edward II, 157
Edward II (Marlowe), 181
Eisler, Hanns, 28, 32, 33, 34, 38-39,
41, 157, 164, 166-68
Eliot, T. S., 2, 10, 15, 109, 115, 182
Emperor's Coolie, The (Plivier), 93
Enfant et les sortilèges, L' (Ravel), 159
Enlevement de l'Europe, L' (Milhaud),
160
Epic theater, 3-10, 23, 24, 25, 29, 47,
53, 75-77, 90-91, 99, 105, 106, 112,
122, 124, 126, 133-34, 138, 141,
146-50, 152
Erpenbeck, Fritz, 1
*Essai sur les données immediates de la
conscience* (Bergson), 61

Esslin, Martin, 1, 3, 10, 13, 55, 127
Every Man out of His Humour (Jonson), 71
Expressionism, 5-6, 53, 54, 86, 177-78
and aesthetic distance, 60-62, 64,
67
and dramatic structure, 61-62, 64

F

Fancy Free (Bernstein), 170
Fascism, references to, 16, 18-19, 21,
26, 116 (*see also* Nazi Party)
Faulkner, William, 74
Faust (Goethe), 102
Faust II, 57
Fergusson, Francis, 70
Feuchtwanger, Lion, 18, 183
Fielding, Henry, 60, 84
Flags (Paquet), 5, 90-91, 92
Fletcher, John, 71-72
"Forgotten Glories of the Giant City
of New York," 177
Formalism, in theater, 92, 102-3, 108
(*see also* Aristotelian theater; Tradi-
tional theater)
"Forward, We've Not Forgotten," 41-
42
Forzane, Giovacchino, 77
Freud, Sigmund, 128
Fröken Julie (Strindberg), 62

G

Galbraith, John Kenneth, 55
Galileo, 3, 11-12, 45, 56, 117-26, 127,
168, 181
Gay, John, 162, 176, 181
Genet, Jean, 52-53, 135
George, Stefan, 2, 172
Gershwin, George, 159, 169-70
Gestiefelte Kater, Der (Tieck), 72
Gherardi, Gherardo, 64
Gide, André, 11, 70, 164
Glass Menagerie, The (Williams), 74
Goethe, Johann Wolfgang von, 19, 49,
57, 62, 65, 101-2, 104, 105, 174
Gogol, Nikolai, 26

Goldoni, Carlo, 83, 114
Goll, Ivan, 62-63, 64n
Good Woman of Setzuan, The, 13, 14, 47, 55-56, 77, 125, 127-31, 134-37, 139, 152, 165, 180
Gorky, Maxim, 10, 25, 38, 58, 75, 103
Götz von Berlichingen (Goethe), 62
Gregor, Joseph, 74
Gropius, Walter, 81
Grosz, Wilhelm, 159, 169
Grüne Kakadu, Der (Schnitzler), 69
Gulliver's Travels (Swift), 102, 104

H

Hamburgische Dramaturgie (Lessing), 105
Hangmen Also Die, 32, 167
Happy End, 157, 163
Hauptmann, Gerhardt, 7, 14, 164, 172
Hauser, Arnold, 64
Hebbel, Friedrich, 46, 78
Hegel, Georg, 1, 109, 110
Heidegger, Martin, 116
Heine, Heinrich, 43, 179
He Who Says No, 115, 179
He Who Says Yes, 115, 165, 166 179
Hindemith, Paul, 115, 157, 159, 160-161, 162, 163, 164, 166
Hin und Züruck (Hindemith), 160
Histoire du soldat, L' (Stravinsky), 106, 158, 159, 169
Hitler, Adolf, 10, 28, 31, 33, 35, 44, 49, 57, 108, 138, 181
Hoppenot, Henri, 160
Hurray, We Live (Toller), 92

I

Ibsen, Henrik, 60, 62
Illusion and Reality (Caudwell), 58
"In Praise of Learning," 38
In Spite of Everything (Piscator), 88-89, 90, 93, 94
In the Swamp, 9, 51, 52-53, 55, 57, 137, 138
Ionesco, Eugene, 135

J

James, William, 65
Japanese theater, 34, 36, 106, 179
Jazzband (Grosz), 159
Jazz Percussion Tutor (Seiber), 159
"Jew, a Misfortune for the People, The," 44
Johst, Hanns, 72
Jonny Spielt Auf (Křenek), 159
Jonson, Ben, 71
Journalistic theater, 77, 89-91
Joyce, James, 91, 182

K

Kaiser, Georg, 55
Kantorowicz, Alfred, 34
Kapital, Das (Marx), 99
King Lear (Shakespeare), 56
Kipling, Rudyard, 161, 175-76
Knight of the Burning Pestle, The (Beaumont and Fletcher), 71-72
Kommerell, Max, 113-14
Kornfeld, Paul, 67
Kraus, Karl, 77
Křenek, Ernst, 159, 163, 169
Kuhle Wampe, 167

L

Lambert, Constant, 166
Lawrence, D. H., 58, 175
Lehmann, Wilhelm, 1
Lehrstücke, 76-78, 157, 161, 164-65, 166, 178-79
Lenin, V. I., 23, 27, 28, 29, 35, 38, 89
Lenja, Lotte, 162
Lessing, Gotthold, 14, 78, 104, 105
Lettere d'amore (Gherardi), 64
Letzten Tage der Menschheit, Die (Kraus), 77
Lindbergh's Flight, 164, 165, 178-79
"Little Description of a New Technique of Acting, A," 108-9, 110
Little Organon for the Theater, 4, 7, 107, 110-11, 113-15, 116, 121, 138
"Liturgy of Breath," 49

London, Jack, 176
Lukács, Georg, 1, 5
Lullabies for Proletarian Mothers, 28
Luther, Martin, 2, 19, 173

M

Macbeth (Shakespeare), 133
Machines agricoles (Milhaud), 160
Magnetic Lady (Jonson), 71
Mahler, Gustav, 158
Maid of Orleans, The, 57
Maid of Orleans, The (Shiller), 26
Major Barbara (Shaw), 57, 58
Mamelles de Tirésias, Les (Apollinaire),
    62, 62n, 81
Manifesto del teatro futurista sintetiro
    (Marinetti), 63
Mann, Thomas, 65, 80n, 81n, 84, 171
Man's a Man, A, 9, 19, 20-21, 27, 53-
    57, 99, 106, 107, 114, 127, 139, 157,
    165, 177
Maria (Obey), 74
Mariés de la Tour Eiffel, Les (Cocteau),
    62, 75, 158
Marinetti, F. T., 63
Marlowe, Christopher, 181
Master Puntila and His Servant Matti,
    13, 53, 74, 127, 131-35, 152, 180
Mavra (Stravinsky), 158, 169
Marxism, references to, 52, 83, 91, 99,
    109, 110, 119, 120, 124-25, 132,
    138-39, 179 (*see also* Communism)
Marx, Karl, 17, 23, 38, 52, 57, 99,
    109, 110, 131
Mayakovsky, V., 103
Mayer, Hans, 142
Measure for Measure (Shakespeare),
    100, 181
Measures Taken, The, 10, 19, 26, 28,
    35, 37, 43-45, 133, 135-37, 138,
    139, 166, 179
Melchinger, Siegfried, 66, 75, 77, 83
Meyerhold, 5, 6, 20, 94-95
Milhaud, Darius, 106, 158, 159, 160-
    61, 170
Molière, 78n, 83, 134-35
Mother (Gorky), 10, 25, 38, 75

Mother Courage, 13-15, 19, 25, 26, 56,
    75, 127, 134, 138-50, 151, 166-67,
    168-69, 180
Music, in Brecht's theater, 19, 114,
    141-42
    folk, influence of, 152
    jazz (rag), influence of, 157-70
Mussolini, Benito, 63, 77

N

Nazi Party, 11, 45, 56 (*see also* Fas-
    cism)
Neue Rheinische Zeitung (Marx), 23
New Model of the Universe, A,
    (Ouspensky), 65
Nietzsche, Friedrich, 59, 156
Nihilism, 53, 137
Noces, Les (Stravinsky), 166

O

Obey, André, 74
Oedipus (Sophocles), 133, 136-37
One Touch of Venus (Weill), 169
"On the Range and Variety of the
    Realist Way of Writing," 103
On the Theory of Prose (Shklovsky),
    108
*On Unrhymed Verse with Irregular
    Rhythms,* 180
Orff, Carl, 161
Ours et la lune, L' (Claudel), 159
Our Town (Wilder), 63, 74
Ouspensky, P. D., 65
"Over All the Peaks Lies Peace"
    (Goethe), 49

P

Parody, 49, 57-58, 100-102, 178, 181
Paquet, Alfons, 5, 90-91, 92, 106
Paradoxe sur le Comédien (Diderot),
    105
*Party Organization and Party Litera-
    ture* (Lenin), 89
Peau de chagrin, La (Balzac), 102
Peer Gynt (Ibsen), 62

Perret, Auguste, 82
Piano-Rag-Music (Stravinsky), 158
Pierrot Lunaire (Schönberg), 158
Pirandello, Luigi, 5, 54-55, 59, 60, 63, 64, 68-70, 73, 74, 106, 135
Piscator, Erwin, 3, 77, 81, **86-96**, 106
Plato, 76
Plivier, Theodor, 93
Poetics (Aristotle), 115
Political Theater, The (Piscator), 90
Porter, Cole, 158-59
Pound, Ezra, 2, 43, 182
Priestley, J. B., 64, 65
Princess of Babylon (Voltaire), 104
Prinzessin auf der Erbse (Toch), 160
Private Life of the Master Race, The, 11, 33, 44, 56, 138
Private Tutor, The, 56
Proletarian theater, 86-96
Proletariat, references to, 20, 26, 28, 29, 50, 58, **86-96**
Proust, Marcel, 65

Q

Questa sera si recita a soggetto (Pirandello), 68-69, 74
"Qu'est-ce que la littérature" (Sartre), 48

R

Ragtime (Stravinsky), 158
Rasputin (Tolstoy), 90, 93
Ravel, Maurice, 159
Régis, Léon, 70
Renard, Le (Stravinsky), 158, 169
Resistible Rise of Auturo Ui, The, 11, 57, 138
Revolution, theme of, 19, 25, 28, 33, 86-89, 95, 109, 132
Rhapsody in Blue (Gershwin), 159
Rilke, Rainer Maria, 2, 11, 172
Rimbaud, Arthur, 53, 56, 175
Rise and Fall of the City of Mahagonny, The, 9-10, 52, 56, 106-7, 157, 158, 160, 161, 162-63, 165
Robbers, The (Schiller), 94

Rogonosetz (Meyerhold), 20
Roi Bombance, Le (Marinetti), 63
Roundheads and the Peakheads, The, 10-11, 28, 100, 108, 138, 167, 181
Rousseau, Jean-Jacques, 131

S

Sachs, Hans, 174
Saint Joan of the Stockyards, 10, 26, 27, 49, 57-58, 138, 176
Saint Joan (Shaw), 57, 58, 75
Sartre, Jean-Paul, 48, 66n, 171
Satie, Eric, 158, 160
Schiller, Friedrich von, 4, 26, 57, 65, 66, 83, 94, 101-2, 105, 115, 174
Schlegel, Friedrich, 59, 72
Schlösser, R., 72-73
Schneider, Reinhold, 85
Schnitzler, Arthur, 69-70, 69n, 75, 135
Schönberg, Arnold, 158, 166
Schopenhauer, Arthur, 109
Schüller, Herman, 86
Schulwerk (Orff), 161
Schumacher, Ernst, 5, 6, 58
Schweik in World War II, 53, 138, 140, 165, 181
Science and technology, influences of, 83, 92, 139
  in *Galileo*, 117-23
  in *Little Organon for the Theater*, 110, 115, 138
Seiber, Matyas, 159
Sei personaggi (Pirandello), 64, 73
Señora Carrar's Rifles, 11
Seven Deadly Sins, The, 52, 55-56, 127, 166
Shakespeare, William, 56, 57, 83, 100-102, 133, 175, 179, 181
Shaw, Bernard, 57, 58, 75
Shelley, Percy B., 15, 109
Shklovsky, Victor, 7, 108-9
Simone Machard, 167
Sinclair, Upton, 176
Skin of Our Teeth, The (Wilder), 64, 73
Social injustice, theme of, 16, 21-22, 44, 100, 109

Socialist realism, 5, 44, 50, **97-105,**
    108-16, 151
"Socialist Realism in the Theater," 97
Socrates, 23
"Solidarity Song," 28, 167
"Song of the Great Capitulation," 141-
    43
"Song of the Wise and Good," 141-43
Sophocles, 133, 136-37
Spender, Stephen, 11
Split Characters: (*see also* Characteriza-
    tion)
    in *Good Woman of Setzuan, The,*
        127-31, 134-37
    in *Master Puntila and His Servant
        Matti,* 131-35
    in *Measures Taken, The,* 133, 135-
        37
Sprung über den Schatten (Křenek),
    159
Stanislavsky, 5, 6, 75, 92
Staple of News, The (Jonson), 71
Strauss, Richard, 158
Stravinsky, Igor, 10, 157-58, 106, 160,
    162, 168, 169, 170
Strassenszene, Die, 75
Strindberg, August, 5, 60, 62
Strobel, Heinrich, 160-161, 164-65
Success (Feuchtwanger), 18
Swift, Jonathan, 102, 103, 104, 176
Syntax and dialect, problems of, 1,
    171-74

T

Tai Yang Awakens (Wolf), 93
Tale of a Tub (Swift), 104
Tempo der Zeit (Eisler), 164
Theater:
    Aristotelian, 24, 78, 113-15, 128-
        29, 133-34
    Chinese, 77-78, 108, 180-181
    epic, **3-10,** 23, 24, 25, 29, 47, 53,
        75-77, 90-91, 99, 105, 106, 112,
        122, 124, 126, 133-34, 138, 141,
        146-50, 152

Formalism in, 92, 102-3, 108
    Japanese, 34, 36, 106, 179
    journalistic, 77, 89-91
    proletarian, 86-96
    traditional, 101-2, 106-7, 124, 149
Threepenny Novel, The, 1
Threepenny Opera, The, 7, 9, 19, 23,
    27, 45, 106, 128, 137, 141-42, 157,
    162-64, 167, 170, 175, 176
Tieck, Ludwig, 72
Till Damaskus (Strindberg), 62
Time and the Conways (Priestley), 64
Toch, Ernst, 160, 165
Tolstoy, Alexei, 90, 93
Tolstoy, Leo, 77, 103
Totalitarianism, theme of, 43-45
Traditional theater, 101-2, 124, 149
    (*see also* Aristotelian theater; Formal-
    ism)
Transatlantic (Antheil), 170
Tretiakov, Sergy, 10, 37
Trumpets and Drums (Wagner-Regeny),
    168

U

Unüberwindlichen, Die (Kraus), 77

V

Verkehrte Welt, Die (Tieck), 72
Verlaine, Paul, 175
Villon, François, 161, 175, 177, 179
Voltaire, 17, 103, 104, 179

W

Wagner-Regeny, Rudolf, 157, 161,
    168
Waiting for Godot (Beckett), 182
War and Peace, (Tolstoy), 77
Webern, Anton, 166
Wedekind, Frank, 75, 106, 175
Weill, Kurt, 23, 157, 159, 160, 161-64,
    165-67, 169

Wekwerth, Manfred, 111-13
Werfel, Franz, 62
What is Formalism?, 103
What is Proletarian Literature?
  (Bogdanov), 87
Wiéner, Jean, 158
Wilder, Thornton, 6, 63, 64, 73,
  74
Willett, John, 10, 108
Williams, Tennessee, 74

Wolf, Friedrich, 93
Woolf, Virginia, 62n
Woyzek (Büchner), 6-7, 62,
  175

Z

Zauberberg, Der (Mann), 65
Zaubermacht (Weill), 161
Zech, Paul, 106

THE BRONTËS

A Collection of Critical Essays

Edited by IAN GREGOR

A

Agnes Grey (A. Brontë), 157
Allen, Walter, 114-15
Allott, Miriam, 57*n*
Angrian stories (C. Brontë), 24, 97, 99,
    135, 138-39, 140-41, 147
Arnold, Matthew, 1, 171
Auden, W. H., 78, 157
Austen, Jane, 12, 50, 76-80, 95, 98
"Aye, there it is" (E. Brontë), 167,
    168-70

B

Barthes, Roland, 171
Bell, Acton, 157 (*see also* Brontë,
    Anne)
Bell, Currer, 157 (*see also* Brontë,
    Charlotte)
Bell, Ellis, 157 (*see also* Brontë,
    Emily)
Benson, A. C., 19
British law, in *Wuthering Heights*, 12-15
Brontë, Anne:
    Agnes Grey, 157
    "Gondal poems," 157
Brontë, Brandwell, 20-21, 159
Brontë, Charlotte:
    and Austen, Jane, 76-80, 98
    and Brontë, Emily, 2-3, 19-33, 44-
        47, 57-58, 85-86
    duty, theme of, 20, 24-25, 137-56

family influence, 20-21
and imagination, 137-56
love, theme of, 78-85, 102-4
sexuality, theme of, 21-22, 23-25,
    83-84, 96-98, 100-101, 116, 142-
    43
societal themes of, 26, 101
and Southey, Robert, 137-40
Brontë, Charlotte, works by:
    Angrian stories, 24, 97, 99, 135,
        138-39, 140-141, 147
    Jane Eyre, 1, 2, 19-20, 21, 23-25,
        26-29, 33, **76-85**, 87, 95, 98-101,
        105, 106, **110-36**, 141-43, 152,
        155, 167
    Preface to *Wuthering Heights*, 45-
        47, 53, 57-58
    Professor, The, 96-97, 106, 141-42
    Roe Head journal, 139
    Shirley, 101-5, 106, 140
    Villette, 1, 97, 98, 105-8, **143-56**
Brontë, Emily:
    and Brontë, Charlotte, 2-3, **19-33**,
        44-47, 57-58, 85-86
    childhood, theme of, 31-33, 65-66,
        161, 164-65
    evil, theme of, 29, 41, 51, 54-58
    family influence, 20-21
    and imagination, 157-72
    love, theme of, 32-33, 41-42, 51-53,
        61-64, **85-95**
    revenge, theme of, 8, 35, 42, 53, 60-
        61, 64-65, 73-74, 92-93

Brontë, Emily (*continued*)
  will power, theme of, 30, 35-36,
    42-43, 165-66
Brontë, Emily, works by:
  "Aye, there it is," 167, 168-70
  "Butterfly, The," 40-41
  "Cold in the Earth," 168
  "Day Is Done, The," 167
  "Death, That Struck When I Was
    Most Confiding," 168
  "Enough of Thought, Philosopher,"
    168
  "Fall, leaves, fall," 167
  Gondal poems, 31, 42-43, 68, 157-
    60, 166, 170-172
  "Heavy Hangs the Raindrop," 157,
    168
  "How Beautiful the Earth Is Still,"
    168
  "How Clear She Shines," 167-68
  "How still, how happy," 167
  "If grief for grief can touch thee,"
    167
  "In Summer's Mellow Midnight,"
    167
  "In the Dungeon Crypts," 168
  "I See Around Me Tombstones
    Grey," 167
  "Linnet in the Rocky Dells, The,"
    168
  "Little while, a little while, A," 167
  "Night is darkening round me, The,"
    157, 167
  "Night Wind, The," 163
  "No Coward Soul," 168
  "Often Rebuked," 168
  "O, Thy Bright Eyes," 168
  "Philosopher's Conclusion, The,"
    68
  "Prisoner, The," 22-23
  "Sacred watcher, wave thy bells,"
    167
  "Shall earth no more inspire thee?,"
    163
  "Silent Is the House," 168
  "Stars," 166-67
  "Tis Moonlight," 167

"Well Hast Thou Spoken," 168
"When Weary with the Long Day's
  Care," 168
Wuthering Heights, 3-6, 7-18, 19,
  20, 21, 25, 26, 28, 29-33, 34-43,
  44-58, 59-75, 76, 77-78, 80, 85-
  95, 113, 117, 118, 159, 160, 165,
  167, 171
Brontë, Patrick, 20-21
Brontës: Charlotte and Emily, The
  (Hinkley), 158*n*
"Brontës, or, Myth Domesticated, The"
  (Chase), 113
Brontë Society, 19
"Butterfly, The" (E. Brontë), 40-41

C

Cecil, David, 3, 67, 68, 70, 114
Character analysis:
  in *Jane Eyre*, 80-85, 89-101, 111-36
  in *Professor, The*, 96-98
  in *Shirley*, 101-5
  in *Villette*, 105-8, 143-56
  in *Wuthering Heights*, 3-5, 34-43,
    44-58, 59-75, 85-94
*Charlotte Brontë: A Psychological
  Study* (Langbridge), 20
"Charlotte Brontë, Reason and the
  Moon" (Heilman), 131
Chase, Richard, 3, 113, 125
Childhood, theme of, in Emily Brontë,
  31-33, 65-66, 161, 164-65
Christabel (Coleridge), 121, 121*n*
Christianity, references to, 21, 83, 84-
  85, 89, 91, 94, 111, 112, 116, 127-
  29, 153-54
Colby, Robert, 149*n*
"Cold in the Earth" (E. Brontë), 168
Coleridge, Samuel, 106, 121, 121*n*,
  164
Conrad, Joseph, 116
Cosmos et l'imagination, Le (Tuzet),
  164
Critical controversy, over *Wuthering
  Heights*, 29, 44-58

D

"Day Is Done, The" (E. Brontë), 167
"Death, That Struck When I Was Most
  Confiding" (E. Brontë), 168
Defoe, Daniel, 99
Degré Zéro de l'Ecriture, Le (Barthes),
  171
Dickens, Charles, 19, 50, 64
Dickinson, Emily, 159-60

E

Ego Dominuus Tuus (Yeats), 171
Eliot, George, 12
Eliot, T. S., 1-2, 115n, 171
Emma (Austen), 76, 94
"Enough of Thought, Philosopher"
  (E. Brontë), 168
Evil, theme of, in _Wuthering Heights_,
  29, 41, 51, 54-58

F

"Fall, leaves, fall" (E. Brontë), 167
Faust (Goethe), 27
Felix Holt (Eliot), 12
Fiedler, Leslie, 108
Flint, F. Cudworth, 108
"Fresh Approach to _Wuthering Heights_,
  A" (Q. D. Leavis), 5
Freud, Sigmund, 21, 23, 27

G

Garrod, W. H., 44-45
Gaskell, Mrs., 117
Genesis of Wuthering Heights (Visick),
  61
Goethe, Johann Wolfgang von, 27
Gondal poems (E. Brontë), 31, 42-43,
  68, 157-60, 166, 170-172
Gondal's Queen (Ratchford), 158n
Gothic Quest, The (Summers), 97
Gothic tradition, 4, 23, 89
  in _Jane Eyre_, 98-101
  in _Professor, The_, 96-98
  in _Shirley_, 101-5

  in _Villette_, 105-8
Graves, Robert, 132
Great Expectations (Dickens), 64

H

Hafley, James, 46
Hamlet (Shakespeare), 4
Hazlitt, William, 165-66
"Heavy Hangs the Raindrop"
  (E. Brontë), 157, 168
Heidegger, Martin, 88
Heilman, Robert, 131-33
Hinkley, Laura, 158n
History of British Birds (Bewick), 80,
  118-19, 123, 124n, 132
"How Beautiful the Earth Is Still"
  (E. Brontë), 168
"How Clear She Shines" (E. Brontë),
  168
"How still, how happy" (E. Brontë),
  168

I

"If Grief for Grief Can Touch Thee"
  (E. Brontë), 167
Imagery: (_see also_ Metaphor; Symbol-
  ism)
  of the book, in _Wuthering Heights_,
    34-43
  of the four elements, in _Jane Eyre_,
    116-36
  of the mythical hero, 26-30, 113-14
Imagination:
  and Brontë, Charlotte, 137-56
  and Brontë, Emily, 157-72
"In Summer's Mellow Midnight"
  (E. Brontë), 167
"In the Dungeon Crypts" (E. Brontë),
  168
Invisible Poet, The (Kenner), 171
"I See Around Me Tombstones Grey"
  (E. Brontë), 167

J

James, Henry, 143, 153, 167

Jane Eyre (C. Brontë), 1, 2, 19-20, 21, 23-25, 26-29, 33, **76-85**, 87, 95, 98-101, 105, 106, **110-36**, 141-43, 152, 155, 167
  character analysis in, 80-85, 98-101, 111-36
  Gothic tradition in, 98-101
  imagery in, 26-28, 113-14, **116-36**
  metaphor in, 79-85, 94-95
  structure of, 80-85, 100
  symbolism in, 23-25, 98-99
  will power, theme of, 25, 27
  and *Wuthering Heights*, 2-3, 19-33, 85-86, 95, 113, 117, 118, 167
Joyce, James, 116

K

Keats, John, 29, 166, 170
Kenner, Hugh, 171
Kettle, Arnold, 4, 59-60
"Kubla Khan" (Coleridge), 106

L

Langbridge, Rosamond, 20-21
Lawrence, D. H., 88, 93, 100, 131
Leavis, Q. D., 5, 86*n*
Lectures on Modern Idealism (Royce), 171
Lectures on the English Poets (Hazlitt), 166
"Lesson of Balzac" (James), 167
"Linnet in the Rocky Dells, The" (E. Brontë), 168
"Little while, a little while, A" (E. Brontë), 167
Love, theme of:
  in *Jane Eyre*, 32-33, **78-85**
  in *Shirley*, 102-4
  in *Wuthering Heights*, 32-33, 41-42, 51-53, 61-64, **85-95**

M

Mansfield Park (Austen), 79, 94
Marlowe, Christopher, 57
Marmion (Scott), 110

Marxist themes, in *Wuthering Heights*, 60-61
Medea (Euripides), 65
Metamorphoses du cerele, Les (Poulet), 163
Metaphor, in *Jane Eyre*, 79-85, 94-95
  (*see also* Imagery; Symbolism)

N

"Night is darkening round me, The" (E. Brontë), 157, 167
Night Rider (Warren), 101
"Night Wind, The" (E. Brontë), 163
Nineteenth Century Minor Poets (Auden), 157
"No Coward Soul" (E. Brontë), 168
Note on Charlotte Brontë (Swinburne), 19

O

"Ode to a Nightingale" (Keats), 170
"Often Rebuked" (E. Brontë), 168
Old Curiosity Shop, The (Dickens), 50
Orley Farm (Trollope), 12
"O Thy Bright Eyes" (E. Brontë), 168

P

Pamela (Richardson), 19, 78-79
Paradise Lost (Milton), 80
Persuasion (Austen), 76, 95
"Philosopher's Conclusion, The" (E. Brontë), 68
Plot outline, of *Wuthering Heights*, 7-9, 15-18, 47-50 (*see also* Structure)
Plot symmetry, in *Wuthering Heights*, 9-12 (*see also* Structure)
Poems (Arnold), 172
Poulet, George, 163
Preface to *Wuthering Heights* (C. Brontë), 45-47, 53, 57-58
"Prisoner, The" (E. Brontë), 22-23
"Prisoner, The" (Rochelle), 166
Professor, The (C. Brontë), 96-98, 106, 141-42
  character analysis in, 96-98

Professor, The (*continued*)
  Gothic tradition in, 96-98
  realism in, 141-42
Proust, Marcel, 171-72
Puritanism, references to, 20, 28, 96,
  114

R

Ratchford, Fanny, 24, 138, 139, 158n
Read, Herbert, 28-29
Realism, in *The Professor*, 141-42
Revenge, theme of, in *Wuthering
  Heights*, 8, 35, 42, 53, 60-61, 64-65,
  73-74, 92-93
Richardson, Samuel, 19, 97, 108
Roe Head journal (C. Brontë), 139
Romanticism, aspects of:
  in Brontë, Charlotte, 19-20, 95,
    110-14, 121-22, 133, 135
  in Brontë, Emily, 19-20, 50, 95,
    163, 168-69
Royce, Josiah, 171
Ruskin, John, 115n

S

"Sacred watcher wave thy bells"
  (E. Brontë), 167
Sanditon (Austen), 50
Sartre, Jean-Paul, 92
Scott, Walter, 110
Sexual themes:
  in *Jane Eyre*, 21-22, 23-25, 83-84,
    100-101, 116
  in *Professor, The*, 96-98
  in *Wuthering Heights*, 21-22, 25-26
Shakespeare, William, 4, 160, 165-66,
  171-72
"Shall Earth No More Inspire Thee?"
  (E. Brontë), 163
Shannon, E. F., 47, 50n, 74
Shirley (C. Brontë), 101-5, 106, 140
  character analysis in, 101-5
  Gothic tradition in, 101-5
"Silent Is the House" (E. Brontë), 168
Societal themes, in Charlotte Brontë,
  26, 101

Sophocles, 29
Southey, Robert, 137-39, 140
"Stars" (E. Brontë), 166-67
Study of History 1933-38, A (Toyn-
  bee), 27
Structure:
  of *Jane Eyre*, 80-85, 100
  of *Wuthering Heights*, 7-**18**, 71-72
    (*see also* Plot outline; Plot sym-
    metry)
Summers, Montague, 97, 106, 108
Supernatural themes, in *Wuthering
  Heights*, 67-70
Surrealism:
  in *Jane Eyre*, 99
  in *Villette*, 106-7
Swinburne, Algernon, 19, 21
Symbolism, in *Jane Eyre*, 23-25, 98-99
  (*see also* Imagery; Metaphor)

T

Thackeray, William Makepeace, 19
Tillotson, Kathleen, 119n
Tillyard, E. M. W., 116
"'Tis Moonlight" (E. Brontë), 167
Toynbee, A. J., 27
Trollope, Anthony, 12
Tuzet, Hélène, 164

V

Van Ghent, Dorothy, 34, 39-40, 65-66,
  67, 70, 74, 119n
Victorianism, of the Brontës, 20, 27,
  32-33, 142
Villette (C. Brontë), 1, 97, 98, 105-8,
  143-56
  character analysis in, 105-8, **143-56**
  Gothic tradition in, 105-8
  surrealism in, 106-7
Visick, Mary, 61
Vision, A (Yeats), 171

W

Ward, Mrs. Humphrey, 19
Warren, Robert P., 101

Watson, Melvin, 50
"Well Hast Thou Spoken" (E. Brontë), 168
West, Rebecca, 21
"When Weary with the Long Day's Care" (E. Brontë), 168
White Goddess, The (Graves), 132
Williams, W. S., 54
Will power, theme of:
  in *Jane Eyre*, 25, 27, 30
  in *Wuthering Heights*, 30, 35-36, 42-43, 165-66
Wilson, Edmund, 108
Women in Love (Lawrence), 131
Woodhouse, Richard, 166
Woolf, Virginia, 32
Wordsworth, William, 6, 19, 30-31, 166
Wuthering Heights (E. Brontë), 1, 2, 3-6, 7-18, 19, 20, 21, 25, 26, 28, 29-33, 34-43, 44-58, 59-75, 76, 77-78, 80, 85-95, 113, 117, 118, 159, 160, 165, 167, 171
  and British law, 12-15

character analysis in, 34-43, 44-58, 59-75, 85-94
critical controversy over, 29, **44-58**
evil, theme of, 29, 41, 51, 54-58
imagery in, 34-43
and *Jane Eyre*, 2-3, **19-33**, 85-86, 95, 113, 117, 118, 167
love, theme of, 32-33, 41-42, 51-53, 61-64, **85-95**
Marxist themes in, 60-61
plot outline of, 7-9, 15-18, 47-50
plot symmetry in, 9-12
revenge, theme of, 8, 35, 42, 53, 60-61, 64-65, 73-74, 92-93
structure of, 7-18, 71-72
supernatural themes in, 67-70
will power, theme of, 30, 35-36, 42-43, 165-66
"*Wuthering Heights* and the Critics" (Watson), 50

Y

Yeats, W. B., 171-72

BYRON

A Collection of Critical Essays

Edited by PAUL WEST

A

Ancient Mariner, The (Coleridge), 32, 33, 39
Antony, Marc, 77
Ariosto, 29
Arnold, Matthew, 4, 144
Arnold, Thomas, 142
Auden, W. H., 92
Aurevilly, Barbey d', 45
Austen, Jane, 170

B

Ball, Patricia, 8
Bartholomew Fair (Jonson), 62
Baudelaire, Charles, 3
Bayley, John, 10
Beatty, James, 161
Bell, Clive, 142
Beppo, 9-10, 54, **65-82**, 88, 108, 118, 139, 167
Berkeley, Bishop, 102
Berlioz, Hector, 146
Biblical references, 7, 10, 28, 32, 33, 37, 38, 39, 44, 51-53, 63, 84, 86, 102
Bismarck, Otto von, 156
Blackstone, Bernard, 7
Blake, William, 4, 31, 37
Blessington, Lady, 45, 142
Boone, Daniel, 103, 106
Bos, Charles du, 7, 44-45
Boswell, James, 159

Bounty, 34
Bride of Abydos, The, 20, 21, 32
Browning, Elizabeth B., 165
Browning, Robert, 15, 16, 162
Burke, Edmund, 89
Burnet, Bishop, 93
Burns, Robert, 9, 85, 88, 162
Byron, Ada, 48
Byron, Mrs. Catherine Gordon, 145, 160, 162
Byron, George Gordon, Lord:
   and animals, 17, 21, 24, 35, 57
   and Augustanism, 8, 83, 92, 93, 127, 131, 161, 166, 169
   autobiographical aspects of works, 1-5, 10-13, 15-16, 34, 44-45, 53-55, 69, 88-92, 101-4, 107, 160-61, 162, 166
   biographical information, 11, 42, 45-47, 65, 138-44 *passim*, 145-50, 152-53, 158, 160
   biographies of, 11-13, 138-44, 157
   and Byronism, 2, 6, 36, 42-45, 48, 161
   and Chateaubriand, 42-44, 48
   and Coleridge, 32-33
   and comedy, 3, 9, 12, 13, 14, 85, 88, 119
   as dramatist, 5, **50-64**
   and epic style, 64, 122, 123, 130, 136, 137
   and homosexuality, 11, 158
   internationalism of, 3, 25, 118, 119, 140, 141, 144, **151-56**, 165-69

Byron, George Gordon, Lord (*continued*)

and Italian literary models, 88, 136, 148, 166

married life of, 46-48, 139, 141

and Milton, influence of, 36-39, 61

nature in works of, 17-21, 22, 26-30, 31-40, 137 (*see also* Imagery)

political and social beliefs, 2, 13, 15, 16, 25-26, 85-87, 93, 97, 100, 103, 107, 118, 119-20, 133, 141-42, 151-56 *passim*, 165-69

and Pope, influence of, 10, 17, 21, 83-86, 93, 123, 131

and Restoration writers, 8, 9, 93

and Romanticism, 3, 11, 12, 43, 54, 81-92, 105-6, 146, 154, 156, 163

and Satanism, 5, 7, 10, 12, 42-49, 145, 152, 153-54

and sister, Augusta, 12, 46-48, 153, 161

Byron, George Gordon, Lord, works by:

Beppo, 9-10, 54, **65-82**, 88, 108, 118, 139, 167

Bride of Abydos, The, 20, 21, 32

Cain, 7, 51, 153

Childe Harold's Pilgrimage, 6-7, 13, 16, **22-30**, 31, 42-43, 60, 65, 91-92, 125, 139, 141, 147, 152, 163-65

Corsair, The, 6, **18-21**, 27, 29, 32, 44, 145, 154

Curse of Minerva, The, 65

Deformed Transformed, The, 50, 51, 55, 56, 57, 60, 62

Don Juan, 4, 5-8, 9, 10, 12, 13, 29, 31, 32, **36-41**, 55, 60, 64, 66, 71, 83, **89-95**, **96-112**, **113-21**, 122-37, 139, 148-49, 155, 167-69

"Egotism," 65

English Bards and Scotch Reviewers, 65, 102, 147

"Farewell to Malta," 65

Giaour, The, 16-18, 20, 21, 22

Heaven and Earth, 7, 45, 50, 52

Hebrew Melodies, 158

Hints from Horace, 65

Hours of Idleness, 161

Island, The, 29, 31, **32-36**, 38

Lara, 20, 21, 31

"Lines to Mr. Hodgson, Written on Board the Lisbon Packet," 65

Manfred, 4, 18, 47-48, 51-53, 62, 65, 154, 155

Marino Faliero, 58-59, 60-62, 63

Mazeppa, 21, 31

Parisina, 28

Prisoner of Chillon, The, 21

"Queries to Casuists," 65

Sardanapalus, 51, 58, 60, 62, 63-64

Siege of Corinth, The, 2

"Song for the Luddites," 166

"Stanzas Written in Passing the Ambracian Gulf," 31

Two Foscari, The, 51, 52, 55, 62

Vision of Judgment, The, 8, 9, 31, **83-87**, 88, 148

Waltz, The, 65-66

Werner, 51, 56, 60, 62

Byron and Goethe (Mazzini), 4

Byron as Skeptic and Believer (Marjarum), 5

Byron: The Last Journey (Nicolson), 142

C

Caesar, Julius, 26

Cain, 7, 51, 153

Calvinism, 140, 153, 158

Camus, Albert, 6

Candide (Voltaire), 8

Canterbury Tales (Lee), 51

Carlyle, Thomas, 12, 155

Castelnau, 122

Castlereagh, Viscount, 103, 110, 132

Cenci, The (Shelley), 64

Chamfort, N. S. R., 45

Chateaubriand, F. R., Vicomte de, 42-44, 48

Chaucer, Geoffrey, 12, 15, 42, 119

Childe Harold's Pilgrimage, 6-7, 13, 16,

Childe Harold's Pilgrimage, (*continued*)
22-30, 31, 42-43, 60, 65, 91-92, 125,
139, 141, 147, 152, 163-65
Claremont, Claire (Jane), 141, 166
Clausewitz, Karl von, 154
Coleridge, Samuel T., 15, 28, 31, 32,
74, 83, 90, 106, 107
Confessions (Rousseau), 159
Congress of Vienna, 13, 165
Connolly, Cyril, 150
Conrad, Joseph, 54
Convergence of the Twain, The
(Hardy), 39
Corsair, The, 6, **18-21**, 27, 29, 32, 44,
145, 154
Cowper, William, 75
Crabbe, George, 19, 89
Crane, Hart, 169
Curse of Minerva, The, 65
Cuvier, Baron L. C. F., 105

D

Decameron (Boccaccio), 42
Deffand, Madame du, 142
Deformed Transformed, The, 50, 51,
55, 56, 57, 60, 62
Dejection: an Ode (Coleridge), 90
Diaboliques (d'Aurevilly), 45
Diogenes, 12
Don Juan, 4, 5, 8, 9, 10, 12, 13, 29,
31, 32, **36-41**, 55, 60, 64, 66, 71, 83,
89-95, **96-112**, **113-21**, **122-37**, 139,
148-49, 155, 167-69
Donne, John, 1, 4
Dowden, Edward, 157
Dryden, John, 4, 8, 83, 87, 93, 164,
165, 169
Dumas, Alexandre Davy, 48-49
Dunbar, William, 8, 9, 12
Dynasts, The (Hardy), 22

E

Ecclesiastes, 102
Edinburgh Review, 90
"Egotism," 65

Elegy Written in a Country Churchyard
(Gray), 27
Eliot, T. S., 2, 8, 9, 165
Eloisa to Abelard (Pope), 18
Eminent Victorians (Strachey), 142
English Bards and Scotch Reviewers,
65, 102, 147
Epaminondas, 103
Escarpit, Robert, 1
Essai sur la littérature anglaise
(Chateaubriand), 42
Ezzelino, 12, 154

F

Fall, theme of, 10, **31-46**, 131, 137
(*see also* Guilt and retribution)
"Farewell to Malta," 65
Fatal Man, theme of, 7, 44-49 (*see also*
Satanism)
Faustus (Marlowe), 18
Fichte, J. G., 154
Folk figures, 11, 37, 42
Fox, Charles J., 89
French Revolution, 118
Frere, John Hookham, 65, 166
Frye, Northrop, 4, 5

G

Galileo, 103
Gardner, Helen, 10, 11
Genseric, 12, 154
George III, 83-85, 87, 148
George IV, 88
Giaour, The, **16-18**, 20, 21, 22
Gide, André, 53
Gifford, William, 73
Goethe, J. W. von, 3, 64, 96, 144, 155
Gray, Mary, 158
Gray, Thomas, 22, 27
Guedella, Philip, 142
Guiccioli, Countess Teresa, 95, 138,
140, 155
Guilt and retribution, theme of, **31-46**,
52 (*see also* Fall, theme of)

H

Hamlet, 22
Hanover royalty, 84, 85, 87, 120
Hardy, Thomas, 22, 37, 39
Haydn, Franz J., 108
Hazlitt, William, 8, 94
Heaven and Earth, 7, 45, 50, 52
Hebrew Melodies, 158
Heine, Heinrich, 92, 146, 154, 155
Herzen, T., 4
Hewlett, Maurice, 11, 138
Highet, Gilbert, 2
Hints from Horace, 65
His Very Self and Voice (ed., Lovell),
    157
Histoire de la nouvelle russie (Castel-
    nau), 122
Hobhouse, John Cam, 73, 138, 139,
    141, 158
"Holy Willie's Prayer" (Burns), 162
Horace, 90, 91
Hours of Idleness, 161
Hugo, Victor, 5

I

Imagery, 5, 21, 26-30 *passim,* 31-46,
    64, 79, 94, 105, 108, 111, 117, 120,
    127, 132, 137, 149, 164
In Memoriam (Tennyson), 93
Irene (Johnson), 64
Island, The, 29, 31, 32-36, 38
Itinéraire (Chateaubriand), 42

J

Jeffers, Robinson, 13-14
Jeffrey, Lord Francis, 106
Johnson, Samuel, 25, 64
Jonson, Ben, 12, 56, 57, 64

K

Keats, John, 2, 3, 15, 64, 95, 106, 145,
    148, 169
Kennedy, Dr. James, 93

Kingsley, Charles, 11
Knight, G. Wilson, 5-7, 95, 161
Kubla Khan (Coleridge), 28, 38

L

Laclos, P. C. de, 10
"To a Lady Who Presented to the Au-
    thor a Lock of Hair," 161
Lamartine, 146
Lamb, Charles, 11
Language, 17, 18, 20-21, 23-25, 29,
    55-56, 61-64, 72-82 *passim,* 108-9,
    117-18, 130-31, 132-33, 165
Lara, 20, 21, 31
Lawrence, D. H., 15, 16
"On Leaving Newstead Abbey,"
    152
Leavis, F. R., 8, 9
Le Bonheur dans le crime (d'Aurevilly),
    45
Leigh, Augusta Byron, 12, 46-48, 161
Leigh, Medora, 47
Leonidas, 103
Leopardi, Giacomo, 94, 146
Les Natchez (Chateaubriand), 43
*Letters and Journals of Lord Byron,
    with Notices of His Life* (Moore),
    138, 157
Lewis, M. G., 5
*Life and Letters of Anne Isabella, Lady
    Noel Byron, The* (Mayne), 46
"Lines to Mr. Hodgson, Written on
    Board the Lisbon Packet," 65
Locke, John, 103
Lord Byron's Correspondence (ed.,
    J. Murray), 138
Lovell, E. J., Jr., 157
Lucretius, 57

M

Macbeth, 20-22
Machiavelli, 148-49
Mailer, Norman, 2
Malthus, Thomas, 93

Manfred, 4, 18, 47-48, 51-53, 62, 65, 154, 155
Mann, Thomas, 3
Manning, Cardinal, 142
Marchand, Leslie, 13, 113, 157-58, 159, 161, 169
Marino, G., 44
Marino Faliero, 58-59, 60-62, 63
Marjarum, E. W., 5
Marlowe, Christopher, 16
Maurois, André, 11, 45
Marx, Karl, 151
Mayne, Ethel Colburn, 45, 46
Mazeppa, 21, 31
Mazzini, 4
Melbourne, Lady, 46, 139, 143
Mémoires d'outre-tombe (Chateaubriand), 42
Metamorphoses (Ovid), 53
Mickiewicz, Adam, 5
Milbanke, Annabella (Lady Byron), 46-49, 139, 141
Milton, John, 7, 10, 15, 16, 19, 28, 32, 36, 38, 39, 43, 44, 61, 103, 120, 123
Missolonghi, 13, 55, 169
Monk, The (Lewis), 5
Monks and Giants (Frere), 166
Moore, John, 46
Moore, Thomas, 88, 157, 159, 161
Mozart, Wolfgang A., 108
Murray, John, 3, 50, 65, 73, 113, 115
Musset, Alfred de, 92, 146, 155
My Past and Thoughts (Herzen), 4
Mythological references, 7, 11, 25, 33, 34, 39, 51, 54, 72, 88, 110, 114, 120, 122, 123, 132, 135

N

Napoleon, 94, 140, 152, 154, 155, 156
"Narrative of the Mutiny and Seizure of the Bounty, in the South Seas, in 1789" (Bligh), 31
Nicolson, Harold, 11, 142-44

Nietzsche, F. W., 12, 153-54, 156
Nightingale, Florence, 142
Nodier, Charles, 48

O

Otho the Great (Keats), 64
Ovid, 53

P

Paradise Lost (Milton), 37
Parisina, 28
Pater, Walter, 4
Peacock, Thomas L., 170
Peter Grimes (Crabbe), 19
Pigot, Elizabeth, 159-60
Pilate, Pontius, 102
Pitt, William, 85
Political Career of Lord Byron, The (Raymond), 141
Pope, Alexander, 3, 6, 9, 10, 16, 17, 19, 21, 27, 83, 84, 85, 86, 92, 93, 95, 123, 131, 156
Pratt, Willis W., 113, 115
Praz, Mario, 1, 7
Prelude, The (Wordsworth), 92, 159
Prisoner of Chillon, The, 21
Prometheus (Shelley), 141
Proust, Marcel, 10
Pushkin, Alexander, 5, 146
Pythagoras, 103

Q

Quarterly, 90
Queen Victoria (Strachey), 144
Quennell, Peter, 11
"Queries to Casuists," 65

R

Racine, 142
Radcliffe, Mrs. Ann, 5, 7, 44
Räuber, Die (Schiller), 48, 49

Raymond, Dora Neill, 141-42, 143, 144
Regency, 2, 8, 86, 92
René (Chateaubriand), 42, 48
Restoration, 8
Revolt of Islam, The (Shelley), 33
Richardson, Samuel, 10
Ridenour, George, 9, 10
Robson, W. W., 8, 9
Rochester, Earl of, 8, 9, 93
Rogers, Samuel, 46
Romilly, Sir Samuel, 76-77
Rousseau, Jean-Jacques, 5, 85, 156, 159
Ruskin, John, 24
Russell, Bertrand, 1, 12
Ryleyeu, Kondraty, 165

S

Sainte-Beuve, C. A., 43
Sappho, 114
Sardanapalus, 51, 58, 60, 62, 63-64
Satire, 9, 36, 69, **83-87**, 98, 100, 104, 118-19, 147-49, 161, 162, 166, 169
Schiller, Friedrich, 48, 49
Scott, Sir Walter, 3, 22, 102, 106, 161
Shakespeare, William, 1, 2, 9, 12, 15, 16, 21, 22, 24, 27, 28, 29, 56, 102, 145
Sheldon, William, 150
Shelley, Mary, 113
Shelley, Percy B., 3, 15, 16, 22, 33, 41, 64, 105, 106, 141, 153, 157, 170
Sheridan, Richard B., 89
Shirley, James, 58
Sidney, Sir Philip, 165
Siege of Corinth, The, 21
Smith, Sydney, 146
Socrates, 103
"Song for the Luddites," 166
Sorrows of Werther, The (Goethe), 155
Southey, Robert, 3, 87, 93, 103, 107, 110, 148
Spengler, Oswald, 146
Spenser, Sidney, 135

"Stanzas Written in Passing the Ambracian Gulf," 31
Steffan, Guy, 9, 113, 115, 116, 118, 134
Stendhal, 140, 154, 159
Stowe, Harriet Beecher, 161
Strachey, Lytton, 11, 142-43, 144
Style, 3, 9, 10, 27, 92-95, 123
Style of Don Juan, The (Ridenour), 10
Stylistic devices, 10, 24, 56, 57-60, 63-64, 65, 66-67, 71-82 *passim*, 84, 90, 96, 99, 104, 107-12 *passim*, 114-18, 123-24, 127, **128-34**, 135-37
Swift, Jonathan, 12, 120
Swinburne, A. C., 8
Symons, Arthur, 1, 2, 3

T

Tasso, 44
Tempest, The (Shakespeare), 2
Tennyson, Alfred, Lord, 64, 93, 143, 145
Tess of the D'Urbervilles (Hardy), 15
Thurber, James, 63
Timon of Athens (Shakespeare), 27
Tolstoy, Leo, 154
Tourneur, Cyril, 58
Trapped Man, theme of, 7, 50-64 *passim*
Tristram Shandy (Sterne), 8
Twentieth Century, The, 8
Two Foscari, The, 51, 52, 55, 62

U

Ubu Roi (Jarry), 62
Under Western Eyes (Conrad), 54

V

Vauvenargues, Marquis de, 45
Versification, 9-10, 108, 115, 123-31, 164-65
Vision of Judgment, The, 8, 9, 31, **83-87**, 88, 148

W

Wain, John, 12, 13
Waiting for Godot (Beckett), 62
Waltz, The, 65-66
Wanderer, theme of, 32
War and Peace (Tolstoy), 154
Washington, George, 103, 104, 155
Waterloo, 22-23, 154
Webster, Daniel, 147
Webster, Lady Frances, 138
Wellington, Duke of, 88, 103, 110,
  168-69
Werner, 51, 56, 60, 62
Whistlecraft (Frere), 65, 166

Wilberforce, William, 76-77, 88, 103-4
Wilkes, John, 87, 88
Wilson, Edmund, 11, 13
Wordsworth, William, 3, 15, 27, 28,
  31, 92, 93, 103, 106, 110, 148, 159,
  170
Wuthering Heights (Brontë), 18

Y

Yeats, William B., 4

Z

Zeluco (Moore), 46

CAMUS

A Collection of Critical Essays
Edited by GERMAINE BRÉE

A

Abbas, Ferhat, 43
Absurd, theme of, 9, 14, 59, 60-61, 67-
68, 72, 77-78, 81, 86, 94-96, 108-21
passim, 138, 149, 174
Actuelles, 24-25, 46, 52, 55-56, 69,
72, 82 (see also *Resistance, Rebellion,
and Death*)
"Adulterous Woman, The," 152, 155,
158, 165
Algeria, 11-13, 24, 26-30, 38-47, 82,
86-87, 135, 165-66
Allegory, 87, 90, 91, 146-47
"Artist and His Time, The," 25
"Artist at Work, The," 152-53, 155
Aspects mystiques de la Rome paienne
(Carcopino), 67
Atheism, 68-70
and Christianity, 61
as a humanism, 18
and socialism, 54-55
Auden, W. H., 140-41
Authentic action, concept of, 77, 81

B

Bad faith, theme of, 14, 38, 76-77,
103, 160
and suicide, 61
"Ballad of Billie Potts" (Warren), 170
Balzac, Honoré, 94
Beauvoir, Simone de, 78, 79, 80, 81
Being and Nothingness (Sartre), 73, 79

Benito Cereno (Melville), 147
Bentley, Eric, 171
Bergson, Henri, 74, 118-19
Bernard, Jean-Jacques, 115
Beyle, Marie Henri (*pseud.* Stendhal),
94-96, 102
Blum-Violette Project, 40, 42
Book of Pilgrimage (Rilke), 64
Bourdet, Claude, 83-84

C

Caligula, 8, 9, 23, 39, 57, 60, 67, 88,
89, 102-4, 154, 161, 172
Camus, Albert:
and Algeria, 11-13, 24, 26-30, 38-
47, 82, 86-87, 135, 165-66
American response toward, 16-19,
20-23
atheism of, 18, 61, 54-55, 68-70
British response toward, 85-91
and Christianity, 29, 33, **48-58**, 62,
68-70, 90, 100-101
and Communism, 15, 31-37, 40-41
ethics of, 17, **71-83**, 98-101, **122-31**,
173-75
existentialism of, 66, 71-72, 77-80,
83-84
and Gide, 76-77, 83, 92, 93, 102,
115, 154, 170
and Hemingway, 16-18, 116, 119,
148
journalism, 8, 11-12, 23-24, 26-30,
41-47, 72, 89

Camus, Albert (*continued*)
  and Melville, 17, 147, 163
  nature, influence of, 86-87, 91 (*see also* Imagery)
  and Nazism, 14-15, 17, 28, 33
  paganism of, 65-70, 87, 132-34
  and Sartre, 2, 4-5, 13, 27, **31-37**, 56, 59, 68, 72, 73-74, **76-80**, 83, 170, **173-75**
  and Stendhal, 94-96, 102
  theater work, 8, 86, 102-7, 154, 170-172
  and Tolstoy, 33, 102, 145, 163
Camus, Albert, works by:
  Actuelles, 24-25, 46, 52, 55-56, 69, 72, 82 (*see also Resistance, Rebellion, and Death*)
  "Adulterous Woman, The," 152, 155, 158, 165
  "Artist and His Time, The," 25
  "Artist at Work, The," 152-53, 155
  Caligula, 8, 9, 23, 39, 57, 60, 67, 88, 89, 102-4, 154, 161, 172
  Cross Purpose, 60
  Envers et l'endroit, L' (Betwixt and Between), 5, 38-39, 60, 72, 73, 74, 83, 86, 132, 154, 158, 167-68
  Eté, L' (Summer), 38, 157
  "Exil d'Hélène" (Helen's Exile), 68, 70
  Exile and the Kingdom, 9, 38-39, 63, 65, 70, **152-56**, 158
  Fall, The, 8-9, 15, 38, 45, 63-64, 65, 68, 70, 83, 152, 153-54, 155, **157-69**, 172, 173
  "Growing Stone, The," 152, 166-67
  "Guest, The," 152, 156, 165
  Just Assassins, The, 43, 57, 90-91, 140, 171, 172
  Letters to a German Friend, 58, 61, 89
  "Minotaur, The," 39, 60, 132-34, 149
  Misunderstanding, The, 23, 57, 88-89, 104-7, 138-40, 171
  Myth of Sisyphus, The, 13-23, 60-61, 62, 72, 88, 106-7, **108-21** *passim*, 138, 149

Noces (Nuptials), 12, 38, 48, 60, 66, 69, 74, 75, 80, 86-87, 132-34, 149, 165
"Notebooks," 6, 9
Plague, The, 38, 39, 57, 65, 68, 75-76, 83, 90, 98-101, 140, **145-51**, 152, 153-54, 158
"Portrait d'un élu" (Portrait of a Chosen One), 70
"Prometheus in Hell," 149
Rebel, The, 31-37, 49-50, 54-56, 64, 72, 73, 76, 78, 80, 81, 89, 154, 158, 161
"Renegade, The," 166, 168, 172
Requiem for a Nun (Faulkner), 69, 154
Resistance, Rebellion, and Death, 24, 26-30, 58, 69
"Silent Men, The," 152, 155, 164-65
State of Siege, 57, 90, 140, 142-44, 171
Stranger, The, 6-7, 13, 15, 23, 38, 57, 60-61, 65, 72, 74-75, 88-89, **92-98**, **108-21**, 141, 152, 154, 165, 171
"Summer in Algiers," 39, 165
"Camus and the Problem of Clean Hands" (Bourdet), 83-84
Candide (Voltaire), 121
Carcopino, Jérôme, 67
Chonez, Claudine, 68
Christianity, 29, 33, 48-58, 62, 68-70, 90, 100-101
  Hellenic elements in, 51-52, 53
  and Marxism, 54-56
Clio, Dialogue of History and of the Pagan Soul (Péguy), 65
Clurman, Harold, 170
Cocteau, Jean, 162, 170
Colonialism, in Algeria, 38-47
Communism, 15, 31-37 (*see also* Marxism)
  in Algeria, 40-41
Conquerors, The (Malraux), 94
Corneille, Pierre, 105, 106
Counterfeiters, The (Gide), 115
Cross Purpose, 60
Crucible, The (Miller), 172

D

Death:
   imagery of, 93-94
   immanence of, 75-76
Death in the Afternoon (Hemingway),
   116
Defoe, Daniel, 145, 146
Descartes, René, 119, 154
Dostoevsky, Feodor, 68, 102, 106,
   111, 146, 157, 163
Drama (*see* titles of individual works;
   Theater, Camus's work in)
Drama of Atheistic Humanism, The
   (de Lubac), 66
Drucker, Peter, 85-86
du Gard, Roger Martin, 64, 158

E

Einstein, Albert, 86
Eliot, T. S., 65
Enchafèd Flood, The (Auden), 140-
   141
Envers et l'endroit, L' (Betwixt and
   Between), 5, 38-39, 60, 72-74, 83,
   86, 132, 154, 158, 167-68
Epicureanism, Camus's early, 67-68
Eté, L' (Summer), 38, 157
Ethics, of Camus, 98-101, 173-75
Ethics, of Camus, 98-101, 173-75
   philosophical basis of, 71-83
   in *The Stranger*, 122-31
"Exil d' Hélène" (Helen's Exile), 68,
   70
Exile and the Kingdom, 9, 38-39, 63,
   65, 70, 152-56, 158
Existentialism, 33, 59, 66, 71-73, 83-
   84
   and Christianity, 68-70
Existentialism is a Humanism (Sartre),
   77, 78

F

Fall, The, 8-9, 15, 38, 45, 63-64, 65,
   68, 70, 83, 152, 153-54, 155, 157-69,
   172, 173

Faulkner, William, 16, 17, 18, 65, 69
Festugière, Fr., 70
Flaubert, Gustave, and Camus's rebels,
   102
Flies, The (Sartre), 78, 79, 170
For an Ethic of Ambiguity (de Beau-
   voir), 78, 79
Four Quartets (Eliot), 65
Fraisse, Simone, 67
Freud, Sigmund, 86
Fruits of the Earth (Gide), 66

G

Gide, André, 20, 66, 76-77, 83, 92, 93,
   102, 115, 154, 170
Giraudoux, Jean, 170
"Graveyard by the Sea" (Valéry), 73
Greene, Graham, 63
Grenier, Roger, 24
"Growing Stone, The," 152, 166-67
"Guest, The," 152, 156, 165
Gulliver's Travels (Swift), 118

H

Hawthorne, Nathaniel, 147
Hedonism, of Camus, 76-77
Hegel, Friedrich, 32, 33
Heidegger, Martin, 109, 115
Hellenism, of Camus, 39, 60, 67
   and Christianity, 51-52, 53
Hemingway, Ernest, 16-18, 116, 119,
   148
"Historical task," and *The Rebel*, 32
Humanism, of Camus, 48-58 *passim*
Hume, David, 56, 118

I

Ibsen, Henrik, 171
Idiot, The (Dostoevsky), 111
Imagery:
   of death, 93-94, 114
   of the sea, 38-39, 66, 88, 140-44
   of the sun, 38-39, 66, 73-74, 88,
      132-40, 166

Immoralist, The (Gide), 93
Indochina, French policy in, 34, 43
Ingénu, L' (Voltaire), 118
Ionesco, Eugène, 82

J

James, Henry, 170
Jaspers, Karl, 72, 109
Jeanson, Francis, 34
Journalism, 8, 11-12, 23-24, 26-30,
   41-47, 72, 89
Just Assassins, The, 43, 57, 90-91, 140,
   171, 172

K

Kabylia, 41-42
Kafka, Franz, influence of, 68, 102,
   116, 147-48
Kapital, Das (Marx), 32
Kessouz, Aziz, 43, 45
Kierkegaard, Sören, 58, 106, 109, 115
Killers, The (Ionesco), 82

L

Lawrence, D. H., 87
"Letter to the Editor of *Les Temps
   Modernes*," 34-35
Letters to a German Friend, 58, 61, 89
Lévi-Strauss, Claude, 21-22
Leynaud, René, 25, 28
Limitations, concept of, 80-82
Locroix, Jean, 70
Love, in *The Stranger*, 74, 113
Lubac, Henri de, 66
Lucretius, and Camus, 67-68

M

Maisoneul, M. de., 45
Malraux, André, 65, 77-78, 83, 86, 93,
   94, 96, 145, 148
   Conquerors, The, 94
   Man's Fate, 76, 77-78
   Man's Hope, 71, 76, 148

Walnut Trees of Altenburg, The,
   145
Marcel, Gabriel, 102
Marxism, 32, 33, 34-35, 97-98
   and Christianity, 54-56
Maupassant, Guy de, 146
Mauriac, François, 24, 63, 69
Melville, Herman, 17, 147, 163
Mendès-France, Pierre, 24
Merleau-Ponty, Maurice, 79, 109
Micromégas (Voltaire), 118
Miller, Arthur, 172
"Minotaur, The," 39, 60, 132-34, 149
Misunderstanding, The, 23, 57, 88-89,
   104-7, 138-40, 171
Mitterand, François, 24
Montherlant, Henri de, 66, 96
Morocco, French policy in, 43
Motchane, Léon, 22
Murder in the Cathedral (Eliot), 65
Myth of Sisyphus, The, 13, 23, 60-61,
   62, 72, 88, 106-7, 108-21 *passim*,
   138, 149

N

Nature, influence of, 86-87, 91 (*see
   also* Imagery)
Nausea (Sartre), 73, 77
Nazism, 14-15, 17, 28, 33
Neo-realism, in *The Stranger*, 118-21
Nietzsche, Friedrich, 70, 80, 94-98,
   109, 161
Nihilism, theme of, 14, 32, 59, 85-86,
   91
Nobel Prize, 59, 158, 170
Noces (Nuptials), 12, 38, 48, 60, 66,
   69, 74, 75, 80, 86-87, 132-34, 149,
   165
No Exit (Sartre), 170
"Notebooks," 6, 9

O

Old Man and the Sea, The (Hemingway), 17
Orwell, George, 27

P

Paganism, in Camus's work, 65-70, 87, 132-34
Pascal, Blaise, 65, 106, 109, 110
Paulhan, Jean, 115
Péguy, Charles, 7, 60-65 *passim*
Pensée patiente, La (Motchane), 21
"Permanence de la Grèce," (Festugière), 70
Phenomenology, 72-74
Plague, The, 38, 39, 57, 65, 68, 75-76, 83, 90, 98-101, 140, 145-51, 152, 153-54, 158
    allegory in, 146-47
    and American society, 17-18
    Christian themes in, 50-51, 52-53
    sea imagery in, 141-42
    Sisyphian character in, 61-62
Plotinus, Camus's interest in, 74
Ponge, Francis, 81
"Portrait d'un élu" (Portrait of a Chosen One), 70
Possessed, The (Dostoevsky), 157, 163
Present perfect tense, in *The Stranger*, 119
Prisoner of Altona, The (Sartre), 161-62
"Prometheus in Hell," 149

R

Rameau's Nephew (Diderot), 9
Realism, in *The Plague*, 146-47 (*see also* Neo-realism)
Rebel, The, 31-37, 49-50, 54-56, 64, 72, 73, 76, 78, 80, 81, 89, 154, 158, 161
    Christ, significance of, 51-52, 53-56
    Sisyphian character in, 61-62
    revolt, theme of, 62-63
Red and the Black, The (Stendhal), 94
Red Gloves (Sartre), 77
"Reflections on the Guillotine," 24
Renard, Jules, 115, 120
Reprieve, The (Sartre), 145

Requiem for a Nun (Camus-Faulkner), 69, 154
Resistance, Rebellion, and Death, 24, 26-30, 58, 69
Revolt, theme of, 7, 9, 32, 55-56, 61, 68-69, 72, 80-82, 88, 89, 149, 174
    in Algeria, 38-47
    in *Caligula*, 102-4
    in *The Misunderstanding*, 104-7
    and Nietzschean ethics, 95-98
    in *The Rebel*, 62-63, 81
Rilke, Rainer Maria, 64
Rimbaud, Arthur, 32, 68
Roblès, Emmanuel, 8
Rolland, Romain, 44

S

Sade, Marquis de, and nihilism, 32
Saint-Exupéry, Antoine de, 98
Sartre, Jean-Paul, 7, 17, 27, 56, 59, 68, 72, 73-74, 76-80, 81, 83, 145, 161-62, 170
    Being and Nothingness, 73, 79
    and Camus, 2, 4-5, 13, 27, 31-37, 56, 59, 68, 72, 73-74, 76-80, 83, 170, 173-75
    and Communism, 35-37
    Existentialism is a Humanism, 77, 78
    Flies, The, 78, 79, 170
    Nausea, 73, 77
    No Exit, 170
    Prisoner of Altona, The, 161-62
    Red Gloves, 77
    Reprieve, The, 145
    Wall, The, 75
Scarlet Letter, The (Hawthorne), 147
Sea imagery, 38-39, 66, 88, 140-44
Sens de l'Athéisme moderne, Le (Locroix), 70
Sensory impressions, importance of, 93, 112
Sétif Rebellion, 42-43
Sickness, and Camus's sensibility, 60
Silence of the Sea, The ("Vercors"), 21
"Silent Men, The," 152, 155, 164-65

Sisyphus, metaphor of, 61 (see also
  Myth of Sisyphus, The)
Socialism, and atheism, 54-55
Stalinism, and Camus, 33, 34
State of Siege, 57, 90, 140, 142-44,
  171
Stranger, The, 6-7, 13, 15, 23, 38, 57,
  60-61, 65, 72, 74-75, 88-89, 92-98,
  108-21, 141, 152, 154, 165, 171
  dialogue in, 120-21
  ethics in, 122-31
  first-person narrator in, 92-93
  structure of, 119-21
  style of, 116-17
  sun imagery in, 136-38
Strindberg, August, 171
Structure du Comportement, La
  (Merleau-Ponty), 109
Suicide, and bad faith, 61
"Summer in Algiers," 39, 165
Sun imagery, 38-39, 66, 73-74, 88,
  132-40, 166
Swift, Jonathan, 118

T

Tertullian, and Camus, 67, 70

Theater, Camus's work in, 8, 86, 102-
  7, 154, **170-172** (*see also* titles of
  individual works)
Tolstoy, Leo, 33, 102, 145, 163
Trial, The (Kafka), 147
Tunisia, French policy in, 34, 43

V

Valéry, Paul, 73, 74, 86, 120
Voltaire, François, 118, 121, 148

W

Wall, The (Sartre), 75
Walnut Trees of Altenburg (Malraux),
  145
Warren, Robert Penn, 170
Will to power, theme of, 94-97,
  104
Wright, Richard, 20

Z

Zadig (Voltaire), 121
Zola, Émile, 146

CERVANTES

A Collection of Critical Essays

Edited by LOWRY NELSON, JR.

A

Adventures of Huckleberry Finn, The (Clemens), 11, 41
Adventures of Tom Sawyer, The (Clemens), 41
Aeneid (Virgil), 164
Alemán, Mateo, 135, 145
Amadis de Gaula, 4, 5, 41, 42, 43, 126
Ancient Poetic Philosophy (Heliodorus), 163
Anti-Romance, or The Wayward Shepherd (Sorel), 48
Antonio the Spanish Barbarian, 165, 166
Apuleius, 60, 61
Araucana (Ercilla), 167
Arcadia (Sannazaro), 133
Ariosto, 25, 38, 91, 118
Avellandea, 8, 43, 92, 129, 135, 152
Azorín, 165

B

Balzac, Honoré, 55, 89
Bandello, 133
Basque Imposter, The, 156, 159
Baudelaire, Charles, 31
Bédier, Joseph, 84
Bergson, Henri, 45
Beyle, Marie Henri (*pseud.* Stendhal), 11
Boccaccio, 62, 132

Bouvard et Pécuchet (Flaubert), 86
Burlador de Sevilla, El (Molina), 3
Byron, George Gordon, 12, 124

C

Calderón, 28, 47, 135, 139
Canterbury Tales, The (Chaucer), 31, 44
Carolingian legends, 22-23
Carroll, Lewis (*see* Dodgson, Charles Lutwidge)
Castiglione, 126
Castro, Américo, 90, 119, 120, 143, 161
Cave of Salamanca, The, 154, 156, 159, 161
Celestina, La, 3, 121
Cervantes, Miguel de:
    and the absurd, use of, 26-27, 38
    and Apuleius, 58-62
    and artistic freedom, 66-68
    and the Baroque, 28, 86-87
    and his contemporaries, 153
    contemporary ideas about, 30
    and the Counter-Reformation, 91-92, 131
    as dramatist, 14
    and Flaubert, 89, 95
    and the Greco-Roman novel, 58-61
    and Heliodorus, 163-64, 165
    humor of, 28, 57, 96
    idealism of, 10, 107, 108
    irony, use of, 10, 17, 27, 40, 43,

Cervantes, Miguel de, (*continued*)
    55, 128, 129, 152
  life of, 2, 13-16, 31, 35
  literary techniques of, 7, 29, 39,
    42, 55, 92, 94-95, 96, 121-22,
    123, 145, 166
  and Montaigne, 28, 119
  philosophy of, 10, 27-28, 31, 97
  and the picaresque mode, 18, 42,
    137-51
  poetry of, 14
  and Rabelais, 85-86
  and the Romantics, 55-56
  and Shakespeare, 1, 2, 10, 27, 87,
    119
  and the Spanish character, 54, 96-
    97, 119, 126-27
  and Tatius, 60
Cervantes, Miguel de, works by:
  Basque Imposter, The, 156, 159
  Cave of Salamanca, The, 154, 156,
    159, 161
  Choosing a Councilman in Daganzo,
    155
  Colloquy of the Dogs, The, 40, 137,
    143, 144-45, 147, 168
  Curioso Impertinente, 129
  Deceitful Marriage, The, 11, 143-45
  Desdichado, El, 35
  Divorce-Court Judge, The, 155,
    159, 161
  Don Quixote, **49-72, 73-81, 82-98,**
    99-122, 162-63
  Eight Plays and Eight Interludes
    (see *Interludes*)
  Exemplary Novels, 11, 15, 44, 91,
    137, 143, 145
  Galatea, La, 2, 5, 10, 11, 14, 35,
    87, 129, 152
  Hawk-Eyed Sentinel, The, 155
  Illustrious Kitchen Maid, The
    148-51
  Interludes, 3, 152-61
  Jealous Old Husband, The, 156,
    159-61
  Journey to Parnassus, 2
  Manuel de Sousa Coutinho or the
    enamoured Portuguese, 166

  Novel and Colloquy that Took Place
    Between Cipión and Berganza,
    140-147
  Renato and Eusebia, 165, 167
  Rinconete and Cortadillo, 11, 41,
    129, 137, 145, 147-48, 168
  Rutilio the Italian Dancer, 166
  Siege of Numantia, The, 152, 154
  Talaveran Wanton, The, 167-68
  Trabajos de Persiles y Sigismunda,
    Los, 10, 129-30, 152, 162-66
  Trampagos: the Pimp Who Lost His
    Moll, 156, 159, 161
  Transila or jus primae noctis, 166
  Wonder Show, The, 156, 159-60
Chaplin, Charlie, 30, 111
Charles V, 165
Chateaubriand, François de, 86
Chaucer, Geoffrey, 10, 44
Chekhov, Anton, 10
Chivalry, novels of, 4-7, 15-19, 102-3,
    111-12, 114, 124-28, 132-33, 145
  theme of, 18, 76-77, 124-28, 158
Choosing a Councilman in Daganzo,
    155
Cinzio Giraldi, 167
Clark, Sir Kenneth, 136
Clemens, Samuel, 11
Coeur Simple, Un (Flaubert), 95
Cohen, J. M., 1
Colloquy of the Dogs, The, 40, 137,
    143, 144-45, 147, 168
Confessions of Felix Krull, The
    (Mann), 42
Corneille, Pierre, 129, 135
Counterfeiters, The (Gide), 42, 135
Counter-Reformation, influence of, on
    Cervantes, 91-92, 131
Cueva, Juan de la, 153
Curioso Impertinente, 129

D

Dante, 1, 88-90, 113
Decameron, The (Boccaccio), 132,
    162
Deceitful Marriage, The, 11, 143-45
Delicado, Francisco, 133

Descartes, René, 31, 91, 97
Desdichado, El, 35
Discours de la Méthode (Descartes), 91
Divorce-Court Judge, The, 155, 159, 161
Dodgson, Charles Lutwidge, 135
Don Quixote, 49-72, 73-81, 82-98, 98-122, 162-63
  and the Baroque, 28
  characterization in, 19-21, 77-78
  Christian themes in, 75-76
  and *The Golden Ass* (Apuleius), 58-62
  and the Greco-Roman novel, 58-61
  and the hero, concept of, 73-81
  illusion in, 9, 18-19, 34-39, 42-44, 55-56, 83-84, 92-95, 102, 104, 108, 115, 129
  imagery in, 61
  irony in, 17, 20, 27, 43, 55, 113, 128, 129, 135
  madness, theme of, 15-19, 77-78, 95, 110-16, 120-122, 125-26
  and Montaigne, 28
  and the *Novel and Colloquy that Took Place Between Cipión and Berganza,* 140-142, 144, 145
  parody in, 38, 42, 44, 48, 87-88, 120, 124, 127
  pastoral themes in, 128
  and the picaresque mode, 18, 42, 137-44, 150
  plagarism of, 52-53
  political satire in, 65
  psychology in, 39-41
  snobbery, theme of, 79-80
  and the Spanish character, 54, 96-97, 119
  structure of, 6-7, 127
  and women, idealization of, 79
  world view in, 83
Dostoevski, Fyodor, 108, 110

E

Eclogues (Garcilaso), 133
Eight Plays and Eight Interludes (see *Interludes*)

Entwistle, W. S., 121
Erasmus, 27, 28, 40, 97
Ercilla, 129, 167
Ethiopic History (Heliodorus), 132
Eugénie Grandet (Balzac), 89
Everyman in His Humour (Jonson), 87
Exemplary Novels, 11, 15, 44, 91, 137, 143, 145

F

Faulkner, William, 89, 90
Female Quixote (Lennox), 124
Fernández-Guerra, Don Luis, 165
Fielding, Henry, 3, 11, 48
Flaubert, Gustave, 10, 11, 86, 89, 95, 121
Francis, Saint, 86-87

G

Galatea, La, 2, 5, 10, 14, 35, 87, 129, 152
Galdós, Perez, 135
Garcilaso, 133
Gautier, Théophile, 136
Gide, André, 42, 135
Goethe, Johann Wolfgang von, 50, 52, 64, 86, 92, 97
Golden Ass, The (Apuleius), 58
Goncharov, Ivan, 50
Gran teatro del mundo, El (Calderón), 135
Greene, Robert, 40
Guzmán de Alfarache (Alemán), 133, 138, 139-40, 141, 145, 147, 149

H

Hardy, Thomas, 10
Hawk-Eyed Sentinel, The, 155
Heine, Heinrich, 48
Heliodorus, 132-33, 163-64, 165
Hero, the concept of in *Don Quixote,* 73-81
History of Leucippe and Cleitophon (Tatius), 60
Hoffmann, E. T. A. 55

Hofmannsthal, Hugo von, 67
Homer, 163
Humor, 51-52, 54
  gracia, 22, 26-27
Humours, doctrine of, 87

I

Ibsen, Henrik, 10
Idiot, The (Dostoevski), 108
Il faut etre ivre (Baudelaire), 31
Illusion Comique (Cornéille), 135
Illusion and reality, theme of, 88-90, 139-47
  in *Don Quixote*, 9, 18-19, 31, 34-39, 42-44, 55-56, 83-84, 92-95, 102, 104, 108, 129, 135
  in *Interludes*, 156-61
Illustrious Kitchen Maid, The, 148-51
Imagery, Greco-Roman in *Don Quixote*, 61
Interludes, 3, 152-61
Irony, theme of, 10, 40, 152
  in *Don Quixote*, 17, 20, 27, 43, 55, 113, 128, 129, 135
Isherwood, Christopher, 133

J

James, Henry, 42
Jealous Old Husband, The, 156, 159-61
Jonson, Ben, 87
Journey to Parnassus, 2
Joyce, James, 125

K

Kafka, Franz, 10
Kant, Immanuel, 89
Kerenyi, Karl, 60
Kierkergaard, Sören, 97
Knight Errant, The (*see* Chivalry, theme of)

L

Lafayette, Mme. de, 3
La Rochefoucauld, 36

Lazarillo de Tormes, 3, 41, 42, 137, 139
Lennox, Mrs., 124
López, Alonso ("El Pinciano"), 163
Loyola, Saint Ignatius, 125
Lozana andaluza, La, (Delicado), 133
Lucan, 167
Lucian, 40

M

Madame Bovary (Flaubert), 11, 86, 89
Madariaga, Salvador de, 7, 18, 20
Madness, theme of (see *Don Quixote*)
Magnus, Olaus, 164
Malkiel, María Rosa Lida de, 92
Malraux, André, 48
Mann, Thomas, 10, 42, 89, 93
Manuel de Sousa Coutinho or the enamoured Portuguese, 166
Melville, Herman, 11, 92
Meninas, Las (Velasquez), 135-36
Moby Dick (Melville), 11
Molière, 86
Montaigne, Michel de, 28, 31, 87, 119
Montesquieu, Charles, 89

N

Nerval, Gérard de, 35
Nietzsche, Friedrich, 63, 86
No hay más fortuna que Dios (Calderón), 135
Northanger Abbey (Austen), 48
Novel and Colloquy that Took Place Between Cipión and Berganza and *Don Quixote*, 140-142, 144-45
Novel, genre of:
  chivalric, 15-16, 85, 124-26, 128, 132, 145
  in England, 29, 31
  Greco-Roman (Heliodoran), 10, 60, 132-33
  and the modern novel, 3, 9, 11, 137
  origin of, 88-89
  pastoral, 14, 142, 144
  psychological, 25-29
  in Russia, 31
  in Spain, 83

O

Oblamov (Goncharov), 50
Orlando Furioso (Ariosto), 18, 36
Ortega y Gasset, José, 4, 9

P

Parody, technique of, in *Don Quixote*,
  38, 42, 44, 48, 87-88, 120, 124, 127
Pascal, Blaise. 36, 64, 97
Pastoral (*see* Novel, genre of)
Paul, Saint, 86
Pedro de Urdemalas, 3
Philip II, 14, 17
Philip III, 64
Picaresque, mode of, in *Don Quixote*,
  18, 42, 137-44, 150
Picasso, Pablo, 136
Pirandello, Luigi, 135
Princesse de Clèves (La Fayette), 3
Proust, Marcel, 89
Putnam, Samuel, 1

R

Rabelais, 40, 85-86, 90
Rape of Lucrece, The (Shakespeare), 2
Reality (*see* Illusion and reality, theme
  of)
Red and the Black, The, (Beyle), 11
Renato and Eusebia, 165
Rinconete and Cortadillo, 11, 41, 129,
  137, 145, 147-48, 168
Rohde, Erwin, 60
Rojas, Ricardo, 154
Rousseau, Jean-Jacques, 86
Rueda, Lope de, 14, 152
Rutilio the Italian Dancer, 166
Royal Commentaries (Vega el Inca),
  164

S

Sannazaro, 133
Scaliger, Joseph T., 134
Scott, Sir Walter, 45-46
Seneca, 167

Shakespeare, William, 1, 2, 10, 27, 39,
  47, 87, 111, 119
Shelton, Thomas, 1, 34, 40
Siege of Numantia, The, 152, 154
Soneto de Repente (Lope de Vega),
  135
Sophocles, 4
Sorel, Charles, 48
Starkie, Walter, 1
Stendhal (*see* Beyle, Marie Henri)
Sterne, Laurence, 92

T

Talaveran Wanton, The, 167-68
Tatius, Achilleus, 60, 164
Through the Looking Glass (Dodgson),
  135
Tieck, Ludwig, 12, 51, 58
Timoneda, Juan de, 153
Tolstoy, Leo, 42, 89
Tom Jones (Fielding), 3, 11
Trabajos de Persiles y Sigismunda, Los,
  10, 129-30, 152, 162-66
*Trampagos: the Pimp Who Lost His
  Moll*, 156, 159, 161
Transila or jus primae noctis, 166
Twain, Mark (*see* Clemens, Samuel)

U

Umoristi, Academy of, 87
Unamuno, Miguel de, 4, 9, 85, 96-97,
  125, 129, 135

V

Valéry, Paul, 90
Vega, Lope de, 3, 14, 15, 135
Vega el Inca, Garcilaso de la, 164, 166
Velasquez, Diego Rodriquez,
  135-36
Venus and Adonis (Shakespeare), 2
Vicente, Gil, 153
Virgil, 134, 163, 165

W

Wagner, Richard, 49
War and Peace (Tolstoy), 43
Wonder Show, The, 156, 159-60

CHEKHOV

A Collection of Critical Essays

Edited by ROBERT LOUIS JACKSON

A

"About Love," 24
Action, in Chekhov's drama, 69, 85-
    87, 120, 179, 179n
"Agafya," 52-53, 189-90
Aleksandrinsky Theatre, 67, 93
Aleksandrov, B. I., 14-15
Aleksandrovich, Yu., 8
Andreevich, S., 8
Animality, in Chekhov's works, 34-36,
    38-39
Anna Karenina (Tolstoy), 16, 26, 53,
    61, 168
"Anna on the Neck," 42, 43-44
Annensky, I. F., 53
"Anonymous Story, An," 11-12, 57,
    105n
"Ariadne," 35, 42, 43
Aristotle, 148
Arnold, Matthew, 179
"At Home," 57
"Attack of Nerves, An," 33, 34-35, 52,
    57
"At the Mill," 28
At the Monastery (Yartsev), 62-63
Aveugles, Les (Maeterlinck), 55-56

B

Balukhaty, S. D., 14, 18-19, 55, 70, 71
Balzac, Honoré de, 47
Banality, theme of, in Chekhov's
    drama, 74-80, 85-86, 122-23,
    132-33, 178, 204
Batyushkov, F. D., 7, 13
Beethoven, Ludwig van, 48
"Beggar, The," 24
Bel-Ami (Maupassant), 39
Berdnikov, G., 19
Berdynaev, N., 5
Bernard, Claude, 11, 33, 159
Bête humaine (Zola), 38
"Betrothed, The," 12, 104
"Bishop, The," 58
"Bobok" (Dostoevsky), 8
Boborykin, P. D., 8, 21
"Boring Story, A," 3-4, 8, 9, 10, 41,
    50, 54, 57, 186, 192-93
Bourget, Paul, 26, 32
Brothers Karamazov, The
    (Dostoevsky), 16
Browning, Robert, 186
Bulgakov, S., 8
Bunin, Ivan, 1n, 4, 13, 36, 39
Butler, Samuel, 184

C

Carmen (Mérimée), 159
Cervantes, Miguel de, 159
Chekhov, Al. P., 90-91
Chekhov, Anton:
    aesthetics of, 4-7, 8
    character of, 1-2, 9, 29-30, 179-80,
        182-83, 187-88, 195-205
    and his characters, 1-2, 9, 11, 177,
        181, 183, 188-89, 191

Chekhov, Anton: (*continued*)
  and comedy, 136-37, 144, 145,
    146, 175-77, 179
  contemporary criticism of, 1, 3-4,
    8-10, 12-13, 25, 50-53, 60, 69-
    72, 92-93, 94, 95-96
  contribution of, 27-29, 48
  critical reputation of, 2-4, 8, 12, 49,
    175-78, 183
  and Darwin, 11, 33, 36-37, 48
  dramatic innovations of, 71-72, 75,
    88-91
  dramaturgy of, **69-87**, 119
  and Flaubert, 17, 36, 39, **42-47**
  French influence on, 36-47
  and Gorky, 2, 7, 13, 20, 25, 30, 49,
    50-51, 109, 117, 184, **195-205**
  on himself, 4-5, 6-7, 28, 180
  as humorist, 22-23, 54-55, 175,
    177-78, 179, 203
  as impressionist, 4, 17-18, 27, **53-
    61**, 65
  as incipient writer, 22-23
  literary antecedents of, 21-22
  literary innovations of, 27-29, 50-
    51, 60
  literary objectivity of, 28-29, 44
  and lyric drama, 29, 62-68, 69-71
  and Maupassant, 8, 17, 36, **39-47**,
    52, 191
  and modernism, 179, 182
  and naturalism, **32-48**, 71-72, 73,
    178, 182
  and negativism, 1-2, 4, 8-9, 12-13,
    15, 17, 44, 55, 182, 184
  and Nemirovich-Danchenko, 19, 69,
    72, 121, 133-35, 146, 159,
    161-63, 164, 172
  philosophy of, 2, 9-10
  and rationalism, 6-7
  and realism, 49, 50-51, **55-60**, 70-
    87, 148, 152, 156, 159, 160, 164,
    165, 177
  and religion, 7-8, 11
  and Russian life, 7, 23-27, 29-31
  and Russian literature, **49-61**
  and science, 11, 25-26, 32-34,
    181-82

  and the short-story form, 27-29,
    40, 45, 190
  social consciousness of, 4-6
  Soviet criticism of, 2-3, 4, 8, **13-16**
  and Stanislavsky, 14*n*, 18, 19, 69,
    121-35, 146, 159, 166, 170, 173,
    176, 177, 180-181
  and symbolism, 45-46, 60
  and Tolstoy, 21, 24, 33, 36, 39, 52,
    53, 54, 55, 61, 186, 190-191
  and tragedy, 175-76, 179
  on his work, 23, 24, 27, 28, 38, 40,
    44, 49-50, 51, 65-66, 72-73, 86,
    88-89, 90, 91-92, 93, 96-97, 136,
    137, 144-46, 166, 168, 169, 171,
    173-74
  and Zola, 11, 17, 36, **37-39**, 42, 45,
    47
Chekhov, Anton, works by: (*see also*
  titles of individual works)
  DRAMA
    Cherry Orchard, The, 8, 18-19, 46,
      56, 59, 64-65, 66-67, 68, 76-77,
      81-82, 83-84, 85, 105, **136-46**,
      147-60, **165-74**, 176, 177, 179*n*,
      204
    Ivanov, 8, 19, 81, **88-98**
    Seagull, The, 9, 11, 12, 19, 34, 35,
      52, 63, 65-66, 67, 72-73, 76, 78,
      79, 81-82, 83-84, 85-86, **99-111**,
      121, 122, 123, 133, 164, 176,
      177, 181
    Three Sisters, The, 8, 12-13, 14,
      14*n*, 15, 19, 41, 42, 60, 76, 78,
      81-82, 83-84, 86, 105-6, **121-35**,
      136, 143, 145, 150, 152, 164-65,
      168, 169-70, 172, 177, 178, 180,
      181, 183, 204
    Uncle Vanya, 19, 52, 68, 76, 78-79,
      81-82, 83-84, 85, 86, **112-20**, 121,
      122, 123, 145, 164, 165, 166,
      170, 177, 178
    Wood Demon, The, 72, 76, 81
  ESSAY
    Island of Sakhalin, 45
  STORIES
    "About Love," 24
    "Agafya," 52-53, 189-90

Chekhov, Anton, works by:
  STORIES (*continued*)
    "Anna on the Neck," 42, 43-44
    "Anonymous Story, An," 11-12,
      57, 105*n*
    "Ariadne," 35, 42, 43
    "At Home," 57
    "Attack of Nerves, An," 33, 34-35,
      52, 57
    "At the Mill," 28
    "Beggar, The," 24
    "Betrothed, The," 104
    "Bishop, The," 58
    "Boring Story, A," 3-4, 8, 9, 10, 41,
      54, 57, 186, 192-93
    "Conspirator, The," 199
    "Cossack, The," 56
    "Darling, The," 178
    "Daughter of Albion," 203
    "Doctor's Visit, A," 56
    "Dreams," 52-53
    "Duel, The," 12, 56, 61, 188-89
    "Gamekeeper, The," 52
    Gloomy People, 51
    "Good People," 24
    "Gooseberries, 2, 24, 30-31
    "House with a Mezzanine, The," 36
    "In the Cart," 59-61
    "In the Ravine," 30, 35, 39, 48
    In the Twilight, 51
    "Lady with the Pet Dog, The," 12,
      35, 57
    "Man in a Shell," 24, 114
    "Man in the Case, The," 60
    "Meeting, The," 24
    "Murder, The," 35-36, 57, 58
    "My Life," 35, 36, 54, 56
    "Nameday Party, The," 33, 57
    "Peasants, The," 39, 52, 178, 179
    "She Yawned," 58
    "Steppe, The," 45, 54, 60
    "Story of Mrs. N. N., The," 58
    "Student, The," 7
    "Teacher of Literature," 57
    "Three Years," 40-41, 54, 57-58
    "Trivial Incident, A," 10
    "Typhus," 10, 28
    "Vanka," 28

    "Verochka," 56
    "Ward No. 6," 178, 179
    "Wife, The," 58
    "Woman's Kingdom, A," 57, 58,
      104-5, 105*n*
    "Work of Art, A," 175
  VAUDEVILLE
    On the Harmful Effects of Tobacco,
      136-37
Chekhov, M. P., 92-93
Chernyshevsky, N. G., 16
Cherry Orchard, The, 8, 18-19, 56, 59,
    136-46, 147-60, 176, 177, 179*n*
  banality, theme of, 76-77, 85, 204
  chance, theme of, 105
  characterization in, 137
  Chekhov on, 136, 137, 144-46,
    166, 173-74
  as comedy, 136-37, 144, 145, 146
  composition of, 137-41, 151-56
  conflict in, 81-82, 83-84
  dialogue in, 141-43, 144
  intonation and rhythm in, 142-43,
    165-74
  Moscow Art Theatre production of,
    64-65, 66-67, 68, 146, 173-74
  plot in, 140-141, 144, 147-51
  and *Purgatorio* (Dante), 156-58
  Stanislavsky's direction of, 146
  symbolism in, 46
Chizhevsky, Dmitri, 9, 17-18
Chukovsky, Kornei, 2
Cocteau, Jean, 151
Comedy, in Chekhov's drama, 136-37,
    144, 145, 146, 175-77, 179
Conflict, in Chekhov's drama, 80-87
"Conspirator, The," 199
Constant, Benjamin, 185
Copeau, Jacques, 159
"Cossack, The," 56

D

Dante, 150, 156-58
"Darling, The," 178
Darwin, Charles, 11, 33, 36-37, 48, 61
"Daughter of Albion," 203
Dead Souls (Gogol), 24

Derman, A., 14
Diaghilev, S. P., 7
Docteur Pascal, Le (Zola), 37
"Doctor's Visit, A," 56
Dostoevsky, Feodor, 2, 3, 4, 5, 6, 7, 8, 9, 11, 12, 16, 21, 23, 27, 47, 51, 106, 111, 177, 185
Dramatic innovations, in Chekhov's works, 71-72, 75, 88-91
Dramaturgy, of Chekhov, 69-87, 119
"Dreams," 52-53
"Dreary Story, A," 3*n*
Duality, in Chekhov's works, 2, 175-83
du Bos, Charles, 8, 10, 20
"Duel, The," 12, 56, 61, 188-89

E

Ehrenburg, Ilya, 15
Eichenbaum, Boris, 17
Eliot, George, 186-87
Eliot, T. S., 156
Ennui, theme of (*see* Banality, theme of)
Eugene Onegin (Pushkin), 26
Existentialisme est un humanisme, L' (Sartre), 104

F

Fathers and Sons (Turgenev), 34
Fergusson, Francis, 19-20
Fet, A. A., 51, 53, 60
Flaubert, Gustave, 17, 36, 39, 42-47
Fofanov, K., 53
From the Past (Nemirovich-Danchenko), 133

G

"Gamekeeper, The," 52
Garshin, V., 21, 50, 61
Gassner, John, 20
Ghosts (Ibsen), 147, 150
Gloomy People, 51
Goethe, Johann Wolfgang von, 26, 32, 187
Gogol, N. V., 24

"Good People," 24
"Gooseberries," 2, 24, 30-31
Gorky, Maxim, 2, 7, 13, 20, 25, 49, 109, 117, 150, 184
    on Chekhov, 25, 30, 50-51, 180, 195-205
Grigorovich, Dmitri, 50, 52-53, 54
Grippius, Zinaida, 8
Grossman, Leonid, 13, 17

H

Hagen, Uta, 181
Hamlet (Shakespeare), 100, 108, 109, 159
Hardy, Thomas, 189, 192
Hauptmann, Gerhart, 68
Heartbreak House (Shaw), 176
Hedda Gabler (Ibsen), 173
Hellman, Lillian, 180
Histrionic art, of Chekhov, 62-68, 121-35, 156-60, 161-71
Horla, Le (Maupassant), 41-42
"House with a Mezzanine, The," 36
Humor, in Chekhov's works, 22-23, 54-55, 175, 177-78, 179, 203

I

Ibsen, Henrik, 147, 149, 150, 155, 156, 160, 173, 182
Impressionism, in Chekhov's works, 4, 17-18, 53-61, 65
"In the Cart," 59-60
"In the Ravine," 30, 35, 39, 48
In the Twilight, 51
Intonation and rhythm, in Chekhov's drama, 142-43, 161-74
Intruse, L' (Maeterlinck), 56
Island of Sakhalin, 45
Ivanov, 8, 19, 88-98
    banality, theme of, 79
    Chekhov on, 88-89, 90, 91-92, 93, 96-97
    conflict in, 81
    contemporary criticism of, 92-93, 94, 95-96
    dramatic innovation in, 88-91

Ivanov, (continued)
  plot in, 91-95
  revisions of, 93-94
  structure of, 96
Izmailov, A., 13

J

James, Henry, 149
Jones, Robert Edmond, 152
Julius Caesar (Shakespeare), 66

K

Karamzin, N. M., 6
Knipper, Olga, 131, 137, 162, 165,
  166, 168, 169, 170-171
Korolenko, V. G., 13, 23, 24, 27, 59
Korsh Theatre, 88, 92
Kreutzer Sonata, The (Tolstoy), 33
Kuprin, A. I., 28, 39
Kurdyumov, M., 10-11

L

"Lady with the Pet Dog, The," 12, 35,
  57
Laforgue, Jules, 157
Lensky, A., 72
Leskov, N. S., 6, 17, 22, 23, 51
Lessing, Gotthold, 16
Let's Settle It Among Ourselves
  (Ostrovsky), 77
Levitan, Isaac, 34
Literary innovations, of Chekhov, 27-
  29, 50-51, 60
Literary objectivity, in Chekhov's
  works, 28-29, 44
Logan, Joshua, 176
Lourdes (Zola), 37
Lower Depths, The (Gorky), 109
Lunacharsky, A. V., 4, 8, 12-13, 13-
  14, 15
Lunt, Alfred, 176
Lyricism, in Chekhov's drama, 29, 62-
  68, 69-71

M

Madame Bovary (Flaubert), 42
Maeterlinck, Maurice, 55-56, 65
Magarshak, David, 176
Mamin-Sibiryak, D., 49
"Man in a Shell," 24, 114
"Man in the Case, The," 60
Mann, Thomas, 16
Mariés de la Tour Eiffel, Les
  (Cocteau), 151
Marx, Karl, 155
Maupassant, Guy de, 8, 17, 36, 39-47,
  52, 150, 191
"Meeting, The," 24
Meininger company, 62, 62*n*, 67-68
Merezhkovsky, D. S., 2, 4, 7, 8, 50
Mérimée, Prosper, 159
Meyerhold, V., 18, 162, 165, 173
Mikhailovsky, N. K., 3-4, 8
Mirsky, D. S., 8, 11
Mont-Oriol (Maupassant), 39, 45-46
Moscow Art Theatre, 19, 56, 62-68,
  121, 133, 146, 159, 161, 166, 170,
  176, 177, 181
Motivation, in Chekhov's works, 55-58
"Murder, The," 35-36, 57, 58
Music, in Chekhov's drama, 114-15,
  153
"My Life," 35, 36, 54, 56
My Life in Art (Stanislavsky), 181

N

Nadson, S., 49
"Nameday Party, The," 33, 57
Nana (Zola), 37
Naturalism, in Chekhov's works, 32-48,
  71-72, 73
Negativism, in Chekhov's works, 1-2,
  4, 8-9, 12-13, 15, 17, 44, 55
Nekrasov, N. A., 4
Nemirovich-Danchenko, V. I., 19, 69,
  72, 121, 133-35, 159, 161-63, 164,
  172
"Neutral Tones" (Hardy), 189

New Project, A (Nemirovich-Dan-
chenko), 161-63, 164
Nietzsche, Friedrich, 5, 16, 61
Nilsson, Nils Åke, 20
Notes from the Underground
(Dostoevsky), 6

O

"Ode to the West Wind" (Shelley), 188
Odets, Clifford, 159
On the Harmful Effects of Tobacco,
136-37
Opochinin, E. N., 2
Ostrovsky, A. N., 3, 21, 73, 77
Ovsyaniko-Kulikovsky, D. N., 5, 7, 13

P

Page d'amour, Une (Zola), 38
"Peasants, The," 39, 52, 178, 179
Pisemsky, A., 17, 22
Plato, 19, 109, 110
Pleshcheev, A. N., 4, 7, 88, 162
Plot, in Chekhov's drama, 70, 178
in *Cherry Orchard, The,* 140-141,
144, 147-51
in *Ivanov,* 91-95
Pope, Alexander, 63
Pre-Chekhovian drama, 74-75, 83
Proust, Marcel, 185
Przhevalsky, N. M., 29
Purgatorio (Dante), 150, 156-58
Pushkin, Alexander, 6, 25, 26, 165
Pushkin Prize, 52

R

Realism, in Chekhov's works, 49, 50-
51, 55-60, 70-87, 148, 152, 156,
159, 160, 164, 165, 177
Reinhardt, Max, 159
Resurrection (Tolstoy), 55
Return of the Native, The (Hardy),
189
Rod, Edouard, 32

Roskin, A., 14
Rossolimo, G., 26
Rougon-Macquart, Les (Zola), 38-39
Rudin (Turgenev), 96
Russian literature, and Chekhov, 49-61

S

Saint Francis of Assisi, 48
Salammbô (Flaubert), 44
Saltykov-Shchedrin, N., 3, 4, 21, 23,
90
Sartre, Jean-Paul, 104
Schloezer, Boris de, 192-93
Schluck und Jau (Hauptmann), 68
Schopenhauer, Arthur, 63
Seagull, The, 9, 10, 12, 19, 34, 35, 99-
111, 121, 122, 123, 133, 150, 152,
164, 176, 177, 181
art as theme in, 99, 111
banality, theme of, 76, 78, 79, 85-
86, 122
Chekhov on, 65-66, 72-73
conflict in, 81-82, 83-84
love as theme in, 108
Moscow Art Theatre production of,
63, 65-66, 67
Tolstoy on, 52
Shakespeare, William, 12, 34, 100,
152, 160
Shapir, N., 55
Shaw, G. B., 155, 176, 178
Shelley, Percy Bysshe, 186, 188
Shestov, Leon, 8-10
"She Yawned," 58
Short-story form, in Chekhov's works,
27-29, 40, 45, 190
Sienkiewicz, Henryk, 45
Skaftymov, A., 14, 18, 19, 93
Sobolev, Yu., 14
Socrates, 110
Sodom and Gomorrah (Proust), 185
Soloviev, Vladimir, 7, 50
Sophocles, 12, 150, 155, 179
Soviet criticism, of Chekhov's works,
2-3, 4, 8, 13-16

Stanislavsky, K. S., 14*n*, 18, 19, 56,
    66, 69, 121-35, 146, 159, 161, 166,
    170, 173, 176, 177, 180-181
Stendahl, 185
"Steppe, The," 45, 54, 60
"Story of Mrs. N. N., The," 58
Stroeva, M. N., 19
"Student, The," 7
Suvorin, A. S., 1, 13, 29, 37, 49, 52,
    55, 72, 73, 89, 91, 93, 96, 97, 180
Symbolism, in Chekhov's works,
    45-46, 60
Symphonie Pastorale (Delannoy and
    Aurenche), 159

T

"Teacher of Literature," 57
Terre, La (Zola), 39
Theatre Guild, 176, 181
Themes, in Chekhov's works:
    anguish, 4, 14, 136, 144
    art, 99, 111
    banality, 74-80, 85-86, 122-23,
        132-33, 178, 204
    beauty and its destruction, 112
    chance, 10-12, 56-57, 59, 104-6
    character versus fate, 2, 19, 104-7
    love, 108
    tragedy, 10, 12, 12*n*
Thérèse Raquin (Zola), 37, 38
Three Sisters, The, 8, 12-13, 14, 14*n*,
    15, 19, 41, 42, 60, 121-35, 136, 145,
    164-65, 177, 178, 180, 181, 183,
    191
    banality, theme of, 76, 78, 86,
        122-23, 132-33, 178, 204
    chance as theme in, 105-6
    Chekhov on, 131, 168, 169
    conflict in, 81-82, 83-84
    intonation and rhythm in, 143,
        144, 164-65, 168, 169-70, 172
    Nemirovich-Danchenko's direction
        of, 133-35, 172
    Stanislavsky's direction of,
        121-35

"Three Years," 40-41, 54, 57-58
Tolstoy, Leo, 4, 6, 16, 21, 23, 24, 25-
    26, 29, 33, 36, 39, 51, 52, 53, 54,
    55, 61, 163-64, 165, 168, 184, 186,
    190-191, 192
    on Chekhov, 27, 52, 53, 54
Tragedy, in Chekhov's drama, 175-76,
    179
"Trivial Incident, A," 10
Turgenev, I. S., 3, 4, 6, 16, 21, 23, 27,
    34, 53-54, 96, 110, 162
"Typhus," 11, 28

U

Uncle Vanya, 19, 68, 112-20, 121,
    122, 123, 143, 164, 165, 177, 178
    banality, theme of, 76, 78-79, 85,
        86, 122, 178
    beauty and its destruction, theme
        of, 112
    Chekhov on, 86, 168, 171
    conflict in, 81-82, 83-84
    Gorky on, 117
    intonation and rhythm in, 164,
        165, 166, 170
    Tolstoy on, 52
Und Pippa tanzt! (Hauptmann), 68
Uspensky, Gleb, 21, 23

V

"Vanka," 28
"Verochka," 56
Vie, Une (Maupassant), 41
Vildrac, Charles, 159
Voltaire, 63
Volzhsky, V., 8

W

Wagner, Richard, 155, 173
War and Peace (Tolstoy), 26, 33, 163
"Ward No. 6," 178, 179
Waste Land, The (Eliot), 156
"Wife, The," 58

COLERIDGE
A Collection of Critical Essays
Edited by KATHLEEN COBURN

A

Abrams, M. H., 11
Aids to Reflection, 4, 23, 30, 166-67
Aloneness, theme of, in *The Rime of the Ancient Mariner,* 35-40
Ancient Mariner, The (see *Rime of the Ancient Mariner, The*)
Anima Poetae, 2, 24, 38, 40, 45, 163, 170
Archetypal Patterns in Poetry (Bodkin), 62-64
Archetypal symbols, 113-14
  in *The Rime of the Ancient Mariner,* 62-64
Auerbach, Erich, 116-17
Autobiography (Hunt), 12

B

Babbitt, Irving, 3, 175
Beaumont, Francis, 105-6
Beeley, Harold, 29
Beer, J. B., 66
Beres, David, 59-60
Berkeley, George, 19, 67, 165
Bibliography of Coleridge (Wise), 4
Biographia Literaria, 3-4, 15-16, 22, 23, 28-29, 31, 48, 77, 95, 97, **104-11,** **126-36,** 169, 170, 177
  and Coleridge's childhood, 12
  Imagination, doctrine of, 28-29
  imagination and fancy, theory of, 104-6, **128-36,** 168, 170

Blake, William, 113-14, 121, 172
"Blind Highland Boy, The" (Wordsworth), 135
Bodkin, Maud, 62-64
Boehme, Jakob, 97
Bolman, Frederick, 104
Bowles, William Lisle, 131-33
Bowyer, James, 131

C

Calleo, David, 10
Carlyle, Thomas, 24, 49-50
Chambers, E. K., 5
Chester, John, 18
Christabel, 7, 26, 60, 71, 176
"Christ's Hospital Five-and-Thirty Years Ago" (Lamb), 12
Coleridge, Berkeley, 17, 18
Coleridge, David Hartley, 14, 21, 22
Coleridge, Luke, 12
Coleridge, Samuel Taylor:
  biography of, 12-24
  and Bowles, William Lisle, 131-33
  as a critic, 3, 94-111, **125-36**
  on dreams and the poetic process, 41, 72-73
  early critics of, 2-7
  economic theories, 142-51
  and empirical rationalism, 163-65
  and existentialism, 108-10
  and Fricker, Sarah, 13
  and German philosophy, 97-100, 134, **162-68**

Coleridge, Samuel Taylor (*continued*)
  and Hartley, David, 19, 67, 97, 133,
    163-64
  historical theories, 152-60
  imagination and fancy, theory of,
    103-6, **128-36, 168-69**
  Imagination and Understanding,
    doctrine of, 28-29, 45-48, 165-68
  and Kant, Immanuel, 8, 96, 98,
    102-3, 137-38, 162-68, 171
  and Kierkegaard, Sören, 96, 108-9,
    110-11, 164, 175
  and Lamb, Charles, 9, 12, 14, 17,
    31, 32, 40, 86, 96
  language, theory of, 107-8
  and Locke, John, 19, 97, 98
  and Malthus, Thomas, 145-51
  and Milton, John, 137-41
  neoclassic concepts of, 126-28
  and Pantisocracy, 13, 143
  and opium addiction, 19, 21, 22,
    23, 26-27, 42*n*, 47*n*
  as a philosopher, 28, 95-100, 133-
    34
  political thought, 29-30, 75-76,
    137-41
  religious beliefs, 71, 75-77
  romantic egotism of, 79-81
  Romanticism of, 123-24, 137
  and Schelling, Friedrich von, 98-
    100, 103, 104, 108-9, 177
  on Shakespeare, 101-2, 105-6, 130
  and Southey, Robert, 10, 12-13, 17,
    18, 21
  and Steuart, Sir James, 142-43, 148,
    149-50
  symbolism, theory of, 112-22
  and *Watchman, The,* 13
  and Wordsworth, William, 5, 10-11,
    14-23, 31, 32, 44, 79, 103, 125-
    36, 172-73, 176
Coleridge, Samuel Taylor, works by:
POETRY
  Christabel, 7, 26, 60, 71, 176
  "Constancy to an Ideal Object," 27
  "Dejection: An Ode," 12, 19, 37,
    48, 54, 58, 78, 95, 162, 171-72,
    173

"Eolian Harp, The," 13, 67, 75, **78-
  87**
"Epitaph," 23
"Fears in Solitude," 17, 78, 84
"France: An Ode," 17
"Frost at Midnight," 12, 17, 18, 36-
  37, 78, 84
"Knight's Tomb, The," 26
Kubla Khan, 7, 18, 43, 73, **88-93,**
  176
"Life," 81
"Nightingale, The," 17, 33-34, 78
"Pains of Sleep, The," 47, 54-56,
  74-75
"Phantom and Fact," 23-24, 27
"Psyche," 27
"Quae Nocent Docent," 25
"Reflections on having left a Place
  of Retirement," 78, 84, 85-86
"Religious Musings," 163
Rime of the Ancient Mariner, The,
  7, 26, **32-50, 51-64, 65-77,** 174-75,
  176
"Self-Knowledge," 24
"Sunset, A," 26
"This Lime Tree Bower My Prison,"
  14, 78, 86
"Time, Real and Imaginary," 26
"Tombless Epitaph, A," 26
"To a Gentleman," 78
"To a Young Friend," 42
"To Two Sisters," 22
"To William Wordsworth," 21, 172
"Work without Hope," 39
"Youth and Age," 23-24, 38
DRAMA
Remorse, 16, 22
Zapolya, 23
PROSE
Aids to Reflection, 4, 23, 30, 166-
  67
Anima Poetae, 2, 24, 38, 40, 45,
  163, 170
Biographia Literaria, 3-4, 15-16, 22,
  23, 28-29, 31, 48, 77, 95, 97, **104-
  11, 126-36,** 169, 170, 177
Confessions of an Inquiring Spirit,
  30

Coleridge, Samuel Taylor, works by:
PROSE (*continued*)
    *Constitution of the Church and
    State, The*, 152-53, 157-60
    "Essay on Method," 26
    Friend, The, 4, 10, 21-23, 25, 26,
    30, 150
    *Hints towards the Formation of a
    More Comprehensive Theory of
    Life*, 178
    Lay Sermons, 10, 23, 142-51
    Letters, 5, 33, 34, 37, 39-41, 42,
    46, 49, 75-76, 95, 132-33
    *On the Principles of Genial Criti-
    cism Concerning the Fine Arts*, 22
    Philosophical Lectures, 164-65,
    173-74
    Statesman's Manual, The, 23, 112-
    13, 121, 140, 177
    Table Talk, 2, 26
    Treatise on Method, 4, 23
"Coleridge and Asra" (Raysor), 4-5
"Coleridge and *Remorse*" (Yura), 8
*Coleridge and the Broad Church Move-
ment* (Sanders), 6
"Coleridge and the Stream of Con-
sciousness" (Takahashi), 8
Coleridge as Philosopher (Muirhead),
4, 5
Coleridgeiana (Wise), 4
Coleridge in Logic and Learning (Sny-
der), 4
Coleridge on Imagination (Richards),
2, 3
"Coleridge's Critical Terminology"
(Isaacs), 6
Coleridge: Vingt-Cinq Poems (D'Hang-
est), 6
Confessions of an Inquiring Spirit, 30
"Constancy to an Ideal Object," 27
Constitutional History (Hallam), 159
*Constitution of the Church and State,
The*, 152-53, 157-60
Conversation poems, heart-beat rhy-
thm in, 78-87
"Cooper's Hill," (Denham), 131-32
Criticism, Coleridge's major works of,
3, 94-111, 125-36 (*see also Bio-*

graphia Literaria; Friend, The)
Critique of Judgment (Kant), 99
"Cycle of Joy and Dejection in the
Poetry of Coleridge" (Yamanouchi),
8

D

Darwin, Erasmus, 131
Davy, Sir Humphrey, 163
Death of Wallenstein, The (Schiller),
18
"Dejection: An Ode," 12, 19, 37, 48,
54, 58, 78, 95, 162, 171-72, 173
Denham, Sir John, 131-32
Depression, theme of, in *The Rime of
the Ancient Mariner*, 53-60
De Quincey, Thomas, 25, 145
D'Hangest, Germain, 6
"Dream, a vision, and a poem, A"
(Beres), 59-60
Dreams and the poetic process, 72-73
Dryden, John, 100

E

Economic theories, in *Lay Sermons*,
142-51
Edmund Oliver (Lloyd), 17
Eliot, T. S., 1-2, 114
Emmet, Dorothy, 11
Empirical rationalism, in Coleridge's
thought, 163-65
Encylopaedia Metropolitana, 4
"Eolian Harp, The," 13, 67, 75, 78-87
    imagery in, 82-83
    romantic egotism in, 79-81
"Epitaph," 23
"Essay on Method," 26
Evans, Mary, 13
Existentialism, and Coleridge's thought,
8, 108-10

F

Fairchild, H. N., 69-70
"Fears in Solitude," 17, 78, 84

"Female Vagrant, The" (Wordsworth), 133
Fichte, Johann Gottlieb, 98, 99, 104
Fletcher, John, 105-6
Fox, George, 172
"France: An Ode," 17
Freudian interpretation, of *The Rime of the Ancient Mariner*, 59-62
Fricker, Edith, 13
Fricker, Sarah, 13
Friend, The, 4, 10, 21-23, 25, 26, 150
criticism, theories, of, 101-2, 109-10
"Frost at Midnight," 12, 17, 18, 36-37, 78, 84

G

German philosophy, and Coleridge's thought, 97-100, 134, **162-68**
Gillman, James, 23
Goethe, Johann Wolfgang von, 98
Gose, Elliott B., 66
Griggs, E. L., 5

H

Hallam, Henry, 159
Harper, G. M., 84, 85
Hartley, David, 19, 67, 97, 133, 163-64
Hazlitt, William, on Coleridge, 16, 40, 80
Herbert, George, 118, 119-20
Hints towards the Formation of a more Comprehensive Theory of Life, 178
Historical theories, in *Lay Sermons*, 152-60
House, Humphrey, 3
Hume, David, 97, 98, 140, 156, 159
Hunt, Leigh, 12
Hutchinson, Sara, 18, 21

I

Imagery:
in "The Eolian Harp," 82-83
in *The Rime of the Ancient Mariner*, 65-66

Imagination:
and fancy, theory of, 103-6, **128-36, 168-69**
theories of, 168-78
theme of, in *The Rime of the Ancient Mariner*, 45-48
and Understanding, doctrine of, 28-29, 45-48, 165-68
Inquiry into the Principles of Political Oeconomy (Steuart), 142
Isaacs, J. J., 6
Isolation, theme of, in *The Rime of the Ancient Mariner*, 53-60

J

Johnson, Dr. Samuel, 100-101, 131
Jungian interpretation, of *The Rime of the Ancient Mariner*, 62-63

K

Kant, Immanuel, 8, 96, 98, 102-3, 137-38, 162-68, 171
Keats, John, 124
Keynes, John Maynard, 150
Kierkegaard, Sören, 96, 108-9, 110-11, 164, 175
Kingdom of Christ, The (Maurice), 6
Kubla Khan, 7, 18, 27, 43, 73, 88-93, 176
Miltonic influences in, 88, 90, 91, 92
sound patterns in, 88-93

L

Lamb, Charles, 9, 12, 14, 17, 31, 32, 40, 86, 96
Langer, Susanne, 120
Language, Coleridge's theory of, 107-8
Law, William, 97
Lay Sermons, 10, 23, 142-51
and Coleridge's historical theories, 152-60
Leibnitz, Gottfried Wilhelm von, 99
Lessing, Gotthold Ephraim, 98

Letters, 5
  and *The Rime of the Ancient Mari-*
    ner, 33, 34, 37, 39-41, 42, 46, 49
  Imagination and fancy, theory of,
    132-33
  poetry, theories on, 95
  religious beliefs, 75-76
Lewis, C. Day, 178
"Life," 81
Life-in-Death, theme of, in *The Rime
  of the Ancient Mariner*, 34-35, 57
Lloyd, Charles, 17, 25
Locke, John, 19, 97, 98
Lowes, J. Livingston, 2-3, 5, 44, 51-53,
  66, 71-72, 170
Lycidas (Milton), 88, 91
Lyrical Ballads, 103
  Preface to (Wordsworth), 15, 17,
    125, 127

M

Malthus, Thomas, 145-51
"Man" (Herbert), 119-20
Maritain, Jacques, 116
Maurice, F. D., 6
Mesmer, Franz, 104
Metaphysics, Coleridge's preoccupa-
  tion with, 94-100 (*see also* German
  philosophy)
Mill, James, 154, 155
Mill, John Stuart, 2, 96, 145
Milton, John, 137-41
Miltonic influences, in *Kubla Khan*, 88,
  90, 91, 92
Mimesis (Auerbach), 116-17
Montagu, Basil, 22
Moon-sun imagery, in *The Rime of the
  Ancient Mariner*, 65-66
Morgan, John, 22
Muirhead, J. H., 4, 5
My First Acquaintance with Poets
  (Hazlitt), 16

N

Napoleon Bonaparte, 137, 139

Neoclassicism, in Coleridge's thought,
  126-28
"Nightingale, The," 17, 33-34, 78
Nineteenth Century and After, The
  (Babbitt), 3

O

Ode on the Intimations of Immortality
  (Wordsworth), 172-73
Ode to a Nightingale (Keats), 124
*On the Principles of Genial Criticism
  Concerning the Fine Arts*, 22
Opium, Coleridge's addiction to, 19,
  21, 22, 23, 26-27, 42n, 47n
"Osorio" (see *Remorse*)

P

"Pains of Sleep, The," 47, 54-56, 74-75
Pantisocracy, 13, 143
"Phantom and Fact," 23-24, 27
Philosophical Lectures, 164-65, 173-74
Piccolomini, The (Schiller), 18
Plato, 19, 97, 165, 168
Plotinus, 12, 19
"Poem of Pure Imagination, A" (War-
  ren), 65-77 *passim*
Political thought, 75-76, 137-41
  in *The Friend*, 29-30
*Political Thought of Samuel Taylor
  Coleridge* (White), 6
*Political Tracts of Wordsworth, Cole-
  ridge and Shelley* (White), 6
Poole, Thomas, 13-14, 24
Pottle, Frederick, 65
Preface to the *Lyrical Ballads* (Words-
  worth), 15, 17, 125, 127
Prelude, The (Wordsworth), 18, 21
Priestley, Joseph, 67
Principles of Political Economy (Mal-
  thus), 147-48, 150
"Psyche," 27
Psychoanalytic interpretations, of *The
  Rime of the Ancient Mariner*, 59-62
Puritanical elements, in *The Rime of
  the Ancient Mariner*, 70-71

Q

"Quae Nocent Docent," 25

R

Raysor, T. M., 4-5, 103, 105
Read, Herbert, 2, 164
Reflections on having left a Place of Retirement, 78, 84, 85-86
Religious beliefs, in *The Rime of the Ancient Mariner,* 71, 75-77
Religious Musings, 163
Remorse, 16, 22
Ricardo, David, 144, 145-46, 148-49, 150, 151
Richards, I. A., 2, 3, 164
Rime of the Ancient Mariner, The, 7, 26, 32-50, 51-64, 65-77, 174-75, 176
    aloneness, theme of, 35-40
    creative imagination, theme of, 45-48
    depression, theme of, 53-60
    isolation, theme of, 53-60
    Life-in-Death, theme of, 34-35, 57
    as a personal allegory, 33-50, 72-77
    psychoanalytic interpretations of, 59-62
    puritanical elements in, 70-71
    sacramental vision in, 65-67, 69, 72
    sentimentalism in, 71-72
    sources of, 2-3
    symbolism in, 37, 43-46
"River Duddon, The" (Wordsworth), 15-16
Road to Xanadu, The (Lowes), 2-3, 5, 51-53, 66, 71-72, 170
Robbins, Lionel, 151
Robinson, Crabb, 167
Romanticism, in Coleridge's works, 123-24, 137
Romantic egotism, in "The Eolian Harp," 79-81

S

Sacramental vision, in *The Rime of the*

Ancient Mariner, 65-67, 69, 72
Saintsbury, George, 3
Sanders, C. R., 6
Sartre, Jean-Paul, 108
Schelling, Friedrich von, 98-100, 103, 104, 108-9, 123, 177
Schiller, Friedrich von, 18
Schlegel, August Wilhelm, 98
Schlegel, Friedrich, 98
Scienza Nuova (Vico), 96
"Self-Knowledge," 24
Sentimentalism, in *The Rime of the Ancient Mariner,* 71-72
Shakespeare, William, 101-2, 105-6, 119-20, 130
Snyder, Alice, 4
Sound patterns, in *Kubla Khan,* 88-93
Southey, Robert, 10, 12-13, 17, 18, 21
Statesman's Manual, The, 23, 112-13, 121, 140, 177
Steiner, F. G., 80
Steuart, Sir James, 142-43, 148, 149-50
Strachey, Lytton, 3-4
"Structure of Romantic Nature Imagery, The" (Wimsatt), 133
"Sunset, A," 26
Symbolism:
    archetypal, 62-64, 113-14
    theory of, 112-22
    in *The Rime of the Ancient Mariner,* 37, 43-46

T

Table Talk, 2, 26
Takahashi, Yasunari, 8
"This Lime Tree Bower My Prison," 14, 78, 86
Tillich, Paul, 118
"Time, Real and Imaginary," 26
"To a Gentleman," 78
"To a Young Friend," 42
"Tombless Epitaph, A," 26
"To Two Sisters," 22
"To William Wordsworth," 21, 172

Traherne, Thomas, 119-20
Treatise on Method, 4, 23
Two Lake Poets, A Catalogue (Wise),
  4
"Tyger, The" (Blake), 113-14

V

Voltaire, 12, 97

W

Walsh, William, 115
Warren, Robert Penn, 65-77 *passim*
Warton, Thomas, 100
Watchman, The, 13
Wedgwood, John, 17
Wedgewood, Josiah, 16-17, 21, 22
Wedgwood, Thomas, 16-17, 21
White, R. J., 6, 10
Whitehead, Alfred North, 170

Willey, Basil, 164
Wimsatt, W. K., 133
Winter's Tale, The (Shakespeare), 119-
  20
Wise, T. J., 4
Wittgenstein, Ludwig, 172
Wordsworth, William, 2, 5, 10-11, 14-
  23, 31, 32, 44, 79, 103, 125-36,
  172-73, 176
Works of Love, The (Kierkegaard), 175
"Work without Hope," 39

Y

Yamanouchi, Asanari, 8
"Yew Trees" (Wordsworth), 135
"Youth and Age," 23-24, 38
Yura, Kimiosha, 8

Z

Zapolya, 23

CONRAD

A Collection of Critical Essays
Edited by MARVIN MUDRICK

A

Alexander II, 123
Alexander III, 123
Almayer's Folly, 6, 17, 69, 73, 111,
116, 127
"Amy Foster," 4, 73
"Anarchist, An," 119, 120, 125
Ancient Mariner, The (Coleridge), 31
Anthony and Cleopatra (Shakespeare),
165
Aquinas, Saint Thomas, 27
Arrow of Gold, The, 10, 116, 161
"Autocracy and War," 99, 119, 139
Azeff (Russian double agent), 123-25

B

Baines, Jocelyn, 2, 4, 9, 11
Bakunin, Mikhail, 121, 122
Balzac, Honoré, 123, 133
"Bear, The" (Faulkner), 17
Beerbohm, Max, 5, 13-15
Benito Cereno (Melville), 30
Beyle, Marie Henri (*pseud.* Stendhal),
129, 133, 135, 142
Billy Budd (Melville), 77
"Black Mate, The," 179
Blackwood, William, 111-13
Blanco, General Guzman, 85
Bobrowska, Ewelina, 126
Bobrowski, Tadeusz, 126, 138
Bolshevik Revolution, 124, 127
Booth, William Stone, 83

Bouvard et Pécuchet (Flaubert), 7
Bowen, Elizabeth, 161-62
Bradbrook, M. C., 128
Brothers Karamazov, The (Dostoevsky),
128, 140
Bulwer-Lytton, Edward, 165
Burtzeff, V. L., 124

C

Cadence, concept of, 170-172
Calvin, John, 121
Camus, Albert, 117, 135, 143
Chance, 1, 2, 10, 23, 37, 116, 120,
130, 132, 145-48, 150, 152, 160
chance, function of, 145-46
characterization, 160-165
evil and the individual, theme of,
146-48, 150
Characterization:
in *Chance*, 160-165
in "End of the Tether, The," 63-66
in "Falk," 69-70
in *Heart of Darkness*, 42-43
in *Lord Jim*, 57-60
in *Nostromo*, 87-88, 90-97
in *Rescue, The*, 154-61
in "Rescuer, The," 153-55, 157-58,
161
Children of the Sea, The (see *Nigger of
the Narcissus," The*)
Coleridge, Samuel Taylor, 31
Communist Manifesto (Marx), 122
Conrad, Borys, 120

Conrad, Joseph:
  action and negation, theme of, 73,
    118
  artistic development (*see also* Con-
    rad: life of), 111-15, 119-20, 126,
    137, 138
  and Blackwood, William, 111-13
  cadence, concept of, 170-172
  chance, function of, 145-50, 151-52
  chronology of works, 116-17
  death and love, theme of, 151-53
  detachment, use of, 136
  and Dostoevsky, Fyodor, 41-42, 44,
    61, 117, 119, 128-29, 139-41
  double plot, concept of, 38
  evil and the individual, theme of,
    66-69, 70-73, 131-35, 146-53
  fate, theme of (*see also* Conrad: evil
    and the individual, theme of), 143-
    44
  guilt, denial of, 165
  imagination of, 86-87, 115, 120
  as innovator, 37-44
  instinct, concept of, 81
  irony, use of, 103-5, 107-9, 120
  and James, Henry, 43-44
  and Kafka, Franz, 41-42, 44, 117
  language, concept of, 175-77
  life of, 1-2, 100-101, 111-15, 119-
    20, 125-26, 137, 138
  morality, concept of, 41, 62, 72,
    77, 126, 135, 141, 144, 152, 163
  misogyny of, 163
  parallel characters, function of, 158-
    60
  pessimism of, 61-62, 69, 100, 126,
    134, 137, 142
  and Poland, 99-100, 112, 114, 117,
    128, 136-39, 142
  and political concepts, 98-101, 114-
    15, 116, 119, 127, 135-36, 141-43
  psychological concepts, 23-24, 25,
    72-73
  religion and scepticism, theme of,
    65
  and revolution, theme of, 122-25
  and Russia, 112, 123, 125-27, 128,
    136-37, 139-42, 144

and social values, 71, 73
structure, concept of, 172-74
style, 3-4, 28-34, 38-41, 130-131,
  143-44, 167-70
and Turgenev, Ivan, 140-141
and women, 162-65
Conrad, Joseph, works by:
  Almayer's Folly, 6, 17, 69, 73, 111,
    116, 127
  "Amy Foster," 4, 73
  "Anarchist, An," 119, 120, 125
  Arrow of Gold, The, 10, 116, 161
  "Autocracy and War," 99, 119, 139
  "Black Mate, The," 179
  Chance, 1, 2, 10, 23, 37, 116, 120,
    130, 132, 145-48, 150, 152, 160
  Children of the Sea (see *Nigger of
    the "Narcissus," The*)
  "Duel, The," 119
  "End of the Tether, The," 63-66, 73
  "Falk," 66, 69-70, 73, 111
  "Gaspar Ruiz," 119
  Heart of Darkness, 2, 4-6, 10, 11,
    27, **38-58**, 60-61, 63, 66, 71, 73,
    86, 114, 116, 129, 132, 144, 148,
    170
  "Il Conde," 119
  "Informer, The," 119, 120, 125
  "Lagoon, The," 5, 10, 32
  Lord Jim, 2, 4, 10, 23, 29, 32, 37,
    55-62, 63, 66-68, 73, 79, 86, 90,
    111, 112, 116, 118-20, 129, 132,
    133, 144, 145, 147-48, 158
  Mirror of the Sea, The, 119
  Nigger of the "Narcissus," The, 4, 6,
    10, **17-36**, 37, 38, 66, 71, 112,
    113, 116, 127, 146
  Nostromo, 2, 4, 8, 9-10, 32, 37, **83-
    101**, 115, 116, 119, 120, 129, 132,
    135-36, 144, 145, 160, 175-76
  Outcast of the Islands, An, 6, 7, 66,
    71, 73, 152
  "Outpost of Progress, An," 10, 11,
    114
  "Planter of Malata, The," 152-53
  "Prince Roman," 142
  Razumov, 118
  Rescue, The, 10, 111, 114, 116,

Conrad, Joseph, works by (*continued*)
119, 120, 132, 145, 153, 154-61
"Rescuer, The," 153-55, 157-59, 161
"Return, The," 72, 158
Romance (Conrad and Ford), 1,
176
Rover, The, 10, 116, 177
Secret Agent, The, 4, 8, 37, 59,
103-10, 115, 116, 117, 119, 120,
121-22, 125, 136, 144, 161, 173
"Secret Sharer, The," 4, 18, 22, 27,
75-82, 129, 132, 144, 146, 148-50,
159
Shadow Line, The, 4, 5, 116, 148-51
Typhoon, 3, 5, 6, 10, 29, 37, 38, 41-
42, 66-70, 73, 111, 116, 135
Under Western Eyes, 2, 4, 8, 37,
111-44
Victory, 1, 2, 10, 37, 73, 116, 120,
129, 132, 144, 145, 148, 150-152,
156, 162
Youth, 5, 55, 71, 73, 112, 116
Crime and Punishment (Dostoevsky),
8, 61, 117, 129
Curle, Richard, 84, 89

D

Darkness at Noon (Koestler), 117, 129
Das Kapital (Marx), 122
Death of the Heart (Bowen), 162
Dostoevsky Fyodor, 2, 8, 9, 41-42, 44,
61, 117, 119, 122, 128, 133, 135,
139-41, 142, 144
Douglas, Norman, 130
Dreiser, Theodore, 163
"Duel, The," 119

E

Eastwick, Edward B., 84-86
Éducation Sentimentale, L' (Flaubert),
7
"End of the Tether, The," 63-66, 73,
113
characterization, 63-66
evil and the individual, theme of,
63-64

vision, theme of, 65-66
Evil and the individual, theme of:
in *Chance*, 146-48, 150
in "End of the Tether, The," 63-64
in "Falk," 70
in *Heart of Darkness*, 43-44, 66
in *Lord Jim*, 147
in "Secret Sharer, The," 148-50
in *Shadow Line, The*, 148-50
in *Typhoon*, 66-70
in *Under Western Eyes*, 131-35
in *Victory*, 148, 150

F

"Falk," 66, 69-70, 73, 111
characterization, 69-70
evil and the individual, theme of, 70
pessimism in, 61-62, 69
Faulkner, William, 17, 18, 20
"Feast, The" (Beerbohm), 13-15
Flaubert, Gustave, 7, 8, 72, 73, 168,
177
Ford, Ford Madox, 1, 118, 119, 122
Forster, E. M., 2, 128, 129
France, Anatole, 98, 174
Frazer, Sir George James, 45-50 *passim*,
53
Freud, Sigmund, 27

G

Galsworthy, John, 84, 114, 130, 131
Garnett, Constance, 114, 122, 140
Garnett, Edward, 113, 114, 122, 140
"Gaspar Ruiz," 119
Gide, André, 118, 133, 134
Golden Bough, The (Frazer), 45-46
Graham, Cunningham, 84, 88, 142,
171
Great Soviet Encyclopedia, 117
Greene, Graham, 117, 121
Guerard, Albert, 5, 37, 45, 50, 75

H

Hamblen, Herbert (*pseud.* Williams,
Frederick Benton), 83

Hardy, Thomas, 163
Heart of Darkness, 2, 4-6, 10, 11, 27,
    38-58, 60-61, 63, 66, 71, 73, 86, 114,
    116, 129, 132, 144, 148, 170
    characterization, 42-43
    evil and the individual, theme of, 43-
        44, 66
    man-god concept, 45-49 *passim*
    morality in, 42, 44, 53
    pessimism in, 61-62
    psychological aspects of, 49, 53-54
    style of, 38-41, 170
    symbolism in, 40-42
    "unspeakable rites," meaning of,
        45-54
Hemingway, Ernest, 18, 143
Henry, O. (*see* Porter, William Sydney)
Herzen, Alexander, 121
Hewitt, Douglas, 86
Hudson, W. H., 169
Humières, Robert d', 24

I

"Il Conde," 119
"Informer, The," 119, 120, 125

J

James, Henry, 7, 10, 25, 37, 43-44,
    121-22, 125, 129, 131, 135, 165, 171
Jung, Carl Gustav, 4, 10, 17, 27

K

Kafka, Franz, 41-42, 44, 117
Kipling, Rudyard, 41
Kliszczewski, Spiridion, 142
Koestler, Arthur, 117, 129, 135
Korzeniowski, Appollo Nalęcz, 125-2⁶
Kropotkin, Prince Peter, 121, 122

L

"Lagoon, The," 5, 10, 32
Language, concept of, 175-77
Lawrence, D. H., 129
Leavis, F. R., 4, 9, 41, 54, 118, 151

Lenin, V. I., 121
Log of the "Cutty Sark," The (Lub-
    bock), 76, 80
Lopez, Francisco Solano, 85
Lord Jim, 2, 4, 10, 23, 29, 32, 37, 55-
    62, 63, 66-68, 73, 79, 86, 90, 111,
    112, 116, 118-20, 129, 132, 133,
    144, 145, 147-48, 158
    chance, function of, 147-48
    characterization, 57-60
    evil and the individual, theme of,
        147
    pessimism in, 61-62
    plot summary, 55-57
Lubbock, Basil, 76, 80

M

Malraux, André, 135, 142
Mann, Thomas, 129, 133
Markham, Sir Clements, 85
Marx, Karl, 122
Masterman, George Frederick, 84-85,
    86
Maupassant, Guy de, 7, 168, 172
Melville, Herman, 11, 22, 24, 25, 30,
    77, 133
Mirror of the Sea, The, 119
Moby Dick (Melville), 25
Molière, 171
Moral themes, of Conrad, 41, 62, 72
    77, 126, 135, 141, 144, 152, 163
Moser, Thomas, 5
Most, Johann, 122
Much Ado About Nothing (Shakes-
    peare), 105-6

N

Napoleon Bonaparte, 120
Nation, Carrie, 164
Nigger of the "Narcissus," The, 4, 6, 10,
    17-36, 37, 38, 66, 71, 112, 113, 116,
    127, 146
    clichés in, 33
    contrast, themes of, 34
    criticism, types of, 17-19
    death, theme of, 30

Nigger of the "Narcissus," The (continued)
  grace, theme of, 19-20
  point of view, function of, 21-22
  as a psychological novel, 25-28
  solidarity, theme of, 21
  structure, 34-36
  style, 28-34
  symbolism, 20, 22, 24-28, 31
1984 (Orwell), 117
Nostromo, 2, 4, 8, 9-10, 32, 37, 83-101, 115, 116, 119, 120, 129, 132, 135-36, 144, 145, 160, 175-76
  action, theme of, 93
  characterization, 87-88, 90-97
  greed, theme of, 90-93
  historical sources, 83-86
  human behavior, themes of, 89-90
  language, use of, 175-76
  moral conflict, theme of, 94-97
  pessimism in, 97, 100
  political themes of, 86-87, 98-101
  structure, 87-90
  symbolism, 92
  vision, theme of, 87

O

Old Man and the Sea, The (Hemingway), 18
On Many Seas: the Life and Exploits of a Yankee Sailor (Hamblen), 83
Orwell, George, 117, 129, 135
Outcast of the Islands, An, 6, 7, 66, 67, 71, 73, 152
"Outpost of Progress, An," 10, 11, 114

P

Parallel characters, concept of:
  in *Rescue, The*, 158-60
  in "Rescuer, The," 158-59
  in "Secret Sharer, The," 75-82
Pasternak, Boris, 128, 135, 143
Pelham (Bulwer-Lytton), 165
Pessimism:
  of Conrad, 61-62, 69, 100, 126, 134, 137, 142

  in "Falk," 61-62, 69
  in *Heart of Darkness*, 61-62
  in *Lord Jim*, 61-62
  in *Nostromo*, 97, 100
  in *Under Western Eyes*, 134
Philosophy, concept of, 174-75
Pimenova, E., 117
"Planter of Malata, The," 152-53
Plehve, Viatscheslav Konstantinovitch, 123, 125
Poe, Edgar Allen, 41
Political themes:
  in *Nostromo*, 86-87, 98-101
  in *Under Western Eyes*, 135-36, 141-43
Porter, William Sydney (*pseud.* O. Henry), 172
Possessed, The (Dostoevsky), 117, 129
"Prince Roman," 142
Princess Casamassima (James), 122, 125
Pritchett, V. S., 118, 132
Progression d'Effet, concept of, 175

R

Racine, Jean Baptiste, 171
Razumov, 118
Red Badge of Courage, The (Crane), 17
Religion and scepticism, theme of in "End of the Tether, The," 65
Rescue, The, 10, 111, 114, 116, 119, 120, 132, 145, 153, 154-61
  characterization, 154-61
  parallel characters, concept of, 158-60
"Rescuer, The," 153-55, 157-59, 161
  characterization, 153-55, 157-58, 161
  parallel characters, concept of, 158-59
"Return, The," 72, 158
Revolution, theme of:
  in *Secret Agent, The*, 117, 121-22
  in *Under Western Eyes*, 117, 122, 124-25
Ribiera, Antonia, 85
Romance (Conrad and Ford), 1, 176

Rothenstein, William, 114
Rover, The, 10, 116, 177
Rudin (Turgenev), 122
Russian influences, on Conrad, 112,
   123, 125-27, 128, 136-37, 139-42
   144

S

Sartre, Jean-Paul, 117, 135
Schopenhauer, Arthur, 69, 73
Secret Agent, The, 4, 8, 37, 59, **103-**
   10, 115, 116, 117, 119, 120, 121-22,
   125, 136, 144, 161, 173
   comedy in, 105-6
   failure, theme of, 107
   historical sources, 120, 121-22, 125
   irony, 103-9, 120
   police, theme of, 108-9
   revolution, theme of, 117, 121-22
   structure, 103-10, 173
   symbolism in, 103-4
"Secret Sharer, The," 4, 18, 22, 27, 75-
   82, 129, 132, 144, 146, 148-50, 159
   evil and the individual, theme of,
      148-50
   historical sources, 76-77, 80
   initiation ritual, theme of, 81-82
   luck, theme of, 78
   moral conflict, theme of, 77-78, 79,
      81
   parallel characters, concept of, 75-
      82
   structure, 76-78
Serge, Victor, 117
Sergei, Grand Duke, 124
Seven Eventful Years in Paraguay
   (Masterman), 84-85
Shadow Line, The, 4, 5, 116, 148-51
   evil and individual, theme of, 148-
      50
   work, concept of, 151
Shakespeare, William, 4, 105-6, 165
Silone, Ignazio, 135
Smoke (Turgenev), 122
"Socialist Revolutionary" Party, 122
Stendhal (*see* Beyle, Marie Henri)
Structure, concept of 172-74

Style:
   concept of, 167-70
   in *Heart of Darkness,* 38-41, 170
   in *Nigger of the "Narcissus," The,*
      28-34
   in *Typhoon,* 3-4, 41-42
   in *Under Western Eyes,* 130-131
Success (Graham), 171
Swinburne, Algernon, 5
Symbolism:
   in *Heart of Darkness,* 40-42
   in *Nigger of the "Narcissus," The,*
      20, 22, 24-28, 31
   in *Nostromo,* 92
   in *Secret Agent, The,* 103-4
   psychological, 24-28
   in *Typhoon,* 66-67
Symons, Arthur, 18

T

Tchekhov, Anton, 172
Tobin, Agnes, 121
Tolstoy, Count Lev Nikolaevich, 86-
   87, 128, 142
Trial, The (Kafka), 117
"Trial by Water" (Young), 18
Trilling, Lionel, 54, 122
Trotsky, Leon, 121
Turgenev, Ivan, 117, 122, 128, 133,
   135, 140-141, 142
Turn of the Screw, The (James), 25,
   43-44
Typhoon, 3, 5, 6, 10, 29, 37, 38, 41-
   42, **66-70,** 73, 111, 116, 135
   evil and the individual, theme of,
      66-70
   irony, 68-69
   structure, 66-69
   style, 3-4, 41-42
   symbolism, 66-67
   vision, theme of, 66, 67-68

U

Under Western Eyes, 2, 4, 8, 37, 38,
   111-44
   and Europe, 117, 144

Under Western Eyes (continued)
  evil and the individual, theme of,
    131-35
  fate, theme of (*see also* evil and the
    individual, theme of), 143-44
  as historical novel, 116-17, 144
  historical sources, 121, 123-25
  pessimism in, 134
  political concepts in, 135-36, 141-
    43
  revolution, theme of, 117, 122,
    124-25
  and Russia, 117, 123, 127-28
  Russian life, theme of, 117, 118,
    129, 139-42, 144
  structure, 118-19, 129-34, 143-44
  style, 130-131, 134-35, 143-44
  title, meaning of, 128

V

Venezuela (Eastwick), 85-86
Victory, 1, 2, 10, 37, 73, 116, 120,
  129, 132, 144, 145, 148, 150-152,
  156, 162

  action and negation, theme of, 73
  evil and the individual, theme of,
    148, 150
  love, concept of, 151
Virgin Soil (Turgenev), 117, 122
Voltaire, François, 121

W

War and Peace (Tolstoy), 86-87
Warren, Robert Penn, 25, 99
Wells, H. G., 114
Williams, Frederick Benton (*see* Ham-
  blen, Herbert Elliot)

Y

Young, Vernon, 18, 22, 24, 25
Youth, 5, 55, 71, 73, 112, 116

Z

Zabel, Morton, 4, 25, 37, 146

STEPHEN CRANE

A Collection of Critical Essays

Edited by MAURICE BASSAN

A

Active Service, 6
Adams, Henry, 8
Adams, Samuel Hopkins, 22
Adventures of Huckleberry Finn, The
  (Clemens), 52, 165
Aeneid (Virgil), 147
Alcman, 149
Aldrich, Thomas Bailey, 1, 166, 170,
  173
"Alpine Idyll, An" (Hemingway), 55
"A man adrift on a slim spar," 29, 38,
  59, 60
"A man feared that he might find an
  assassin," 33-35, 60
"A man said to the universe," 60
"A man saw a ball of gold in the sky,"
  36, 60
Ambassadors, The (James), 45
Anderson, Sherwood, 9, 28, 36, 167
Anderson, Warren D., 5
"A newspaper is a collection of half-
  injustices," 60
"Angel Child, The," 170-171
Animism:
  concept of, 31-32
  in *Red Badge of Courage, The,* 147-
  49
Anna Karenina (Tolstoy), 64
"Appreciation" (Garnett), 30
Archer, William, 81
Arnold, Matthew, 44
"A row of thick pillars," 144

Austen, Jane, 43
"A youth in apparel that glittered,"
  57-58, 60
"Ay, workman, make me a dream," 37

B

Bad Seed, The (March), 165
Barrie, J. M., 122
Bartleby the Scrivener (Melville), 158
"Battle Hymn, The," 60
Baudelaire, Charles, 3
Beardsley, Aubrey, 13
Beckett, Samuel, 4
Beer, Thomas, 9, 23, 38, 69, 78
Being a Boy (Warner), 166
Belasco, David, 24
Bernanos, Georges, 85
Berryman, John, 5, 9, 10, 23, 59, 118,
  148-49, 164
Bierce, Ambrose, 46, 87
Billy Budd (Melville), 162
Black Riders and Other Lines, The, 3-
  4, 15, 30-31, 35-36, 91, 101-3
  Christian influence in, 3-4, 101-3
  sinister mountains, theme of, 101-2
  style, 35-36
Blackmur, R. P., 33
"Black riders came from the sea," 60
"Blue Battalions, The," 60, 62
"Blue Hotel, The," 7, 20, 24, 25, 28,
  41, 44, 49, 51, 54-55, 59, 73, 74-77,
  94, 104, 154-64, 171
  characterization, 76-77

"Blue Hotel, The" (*continued*)
   and Hemingway, Ernest, 54-55
   homosexuality in, 161-64
   man and Nature, theme of, 104
   meaningless decorum, theme of,
      74-77
   psychological concepts in, 154-64
   structure, 75-76
   style, 54-55
   symbolic meaning in, 24
"Bonheur, Le" (Maupassant), 14
"Bottles and bottles and bottles," 60
Boy's Town, A (Howells), 166
"Bride Comes to Yellow Sky, The," 7,
   20, 29, 44, 49, 59, 73, 74-75, 94
   meaningless decorum, theme of,
      74-75
   structure, 74-75
Bridge, The (Hart Crane), 64
Brontë, Emily, 29
Brooks, Van Wyck, 86

C

Cady, Edwin H., 10
Camus, Albert, 25, 151, 152
Cantos, The (Pound), 63, 64
Cather, Willa, 2, 9, 28
Characterization:
   in "Blue Hotel, The," 76-77
   in Crane's art, 48-49
   in *Maggie: A Girl of the Streets*,
      114-16
Chekhov, Anton, 46, 85
"Clan of No-Name, The," 28, 44
Clark, Dora, 107
"Clean Well-Lighted Place, A" (Hemingway), plot summary, 55
Clemens, Samuel (*pseud.* Twain, Mark),
   1, 2, 5, 10, 28, 44, 52, 64, 165
Colvert, James B., 7
Comedian as the Letter C, The
   (Stevens), 64, 65
Congreve, William, 43
Conrad, Joseph, 5, 6, 9, 28, 47, 81,
   85, 91-92, 93
Court of Boyville, The (White), 166

Crane, Cora, 19-21, 23
Crane, Hart, 38, 64
Crane, Reverend Jonathan T., 103
Crane, Mary Helen, 103
Crane, Stephen:
   and American culture, 67-69
   animism, use of, 31-32, 147-49
   artistic development, 24-26, 52-53,
      82-83
   artistic sources, 30-31, 36
   career of, 1-8, 12-24
   and Cather, Willa, 12-17
   color, use of, 48
   critical attitudes to, 22-24, 29-32
   and Expressionism, 94
   and French Symbolists, 60-62
   and Greek comedy, 40
   and Hemingway, Ernest, 52-56
   and Homer, 146-49
   and Imagists, 62-64
   and Impressionism, 47-48, 80, 82,
      85-94
   literary influence of, 28
   man and Nature, theme of, 5, 7, 95,
      96, 99, 104-5
   and money problems, 18-22
   moral codes, theme of, 116-17
   and Naturalism, 80-83, 91, 94
   and Norris, Frank, 68-69
   pessimism in art of, 8-9, 141-45
   and Poe, Edgar Allan, 64-65
   and poetic tradition, 57-66
   poetry, concept of, 64-65
   psychological concepts in works of,
      23, 154-64
   religious influence on, 1-2, 3-4, 8, 9,
      36, 102-5
   social behavior, theme of, 3, 112-17,
      165-76
   structure, concept of, 45-46, 50
   style, development of, 35, 36-38,
      42-48, 57-60, 65
   symbolism, concept of, 24, 60-62
Crane, Stephen, works by:
POETRY
   "A man adrift on a slim spar," 29,
      38, 59, 60

Crane, Stephen, works by (*continued*)
  "A man said to the universe," 60
  "A man saw a ball of gold in the
    sky," 36, 60
  "A newspaper is a collection of half-
    injustices," 60
  "A row of thick pillars," 144
  "Ay, workman, make me a dream,"
    37
  "A youth in apparel that glittered,"
    57-58, 60
  "Battle Hymn, The," 60
  Black Riders and Other Lines, The,
    3-4, 15, 30-31, 35-36, 91, 101-3,
  "Black riders came from the sea,"
    60
  "Blue Battalions, The," 60, 62
  "Bottles and bottles and bottles,"
    60
  "Do not weep, maiden, for war is
    kind," 29, 32, 33-35, 37, 60, 62
  "Each small gleam was a voice," 60
  "Fast rode the knight," 60
  "Forth went the candid man," 60
  "I explain the silvered passing of a
    ship at night," 60
  "In heaven/Some little blades of
    grass," 60
  "In the night/Grey heavy clouds
    muffled the valleys," 62
  "I saw a man pursuing the horizon,"
    32-33, 60
  "'It was wrong to do this,' said the
    angel," 60
  "Once a man clambering to the
    housetops," 102
  "Once I saw mountains angry," 29,
    101
  "On the horizon the peaks assem-
    bled," 32-33, 58-59, 60, 101
  "The hard hills tore my flesh," 101
  "The patent of a lord," 60
  "There exists the eternal fact of
    conflict," 60
  "There was one I met upon the
    road," 60
  "The trees in the garden rained
    flowers," 60
  "The wayfarer,/Perceiving the path-
    way to truth," 57, 60
  "'Think as I think,' said a man," 61
  "To the maiden/The sea was a blue
    meadow," 38, 60
  "What says the sea, little shell?" 61
  "When a people reach the top of a
    hill," 102
PROSE
Active Service, 6
  "Angel Child, The," 170-171
  "Blue Hotel, The," 7, 20, 24, 25,
    28, 41, 44, 49, 51, 54-55, 59, 73,
    74-77, 94, 104, **154-64**, 171
  "Bride Comes to Yellow Sky, The,"
    7, 20, 29, 44, 49, 59, 73, 74-75,
    94
  "Clan of No-Name, The," 28, 44
  "Dark Brown Dog, A," 29
  "Death and the Child," 7, 8, 10, 28,
    29
  "End of the Battle, The," 28
  "Episode of War, An," 28, 55, 71,
    94
  "Experiment in Luxury, An," 3
  "Experiment in Misery, An," 3, 29,
    86, 118-22
  "Five White Mice, The," 44, **157-60**,
    164
  George's Mother, 3, 10, 29, 59, 94,
    100
  "His New Mittens," 94
  "Horses—One Dash," 44
  "Illusion in Red and White, An,"
    29, 94
  "Kicking Twelfth, The," 44
  "Knife, The," 94
  "Little Pilgrimage, A," 175-76
  Little Regiment, The, 6, 29, 168
  "Lover and the Telltale, The," 173-
    75
  "Lynx-Hunting," 171-73
  Maggie: A Girl of the Streets, 2, 3,
    4, 5, 10, 20, 25, 28, 40, 41, 44,
    46, 49, 59, 83-86, 107-9, **110-17**,
    118

Crane, Stephen, works by (*continued*)
"Men in the Storm," 24, 86
"Mesmeric Mountain, The," 100, 105
Monster, The, 7, 10, 28, 44, 49, 59, 73-74, 94, 151, 167-68
"Mystery of Heroism, A," 28, 47, 70-71, 78, 94
"Ominous Baby, An," 3
"Open Boat, The," 7, 20, 28, 29, 41, 42, 44, 49, 50, 54-55, 59, 94, 100, 104-5, 122, 144, 150-153, 168
"Pace of Youth, The," 29
"Price of the Harness, The," 28, 156-57, 59
Red Badge of Courage, The, 3, 4, 5, 6, 8, 10, 13, 15, 16, 18, 19, 20, 24, 25, 28, 30, 40-41, 42, 44, 46, 49, 51, 54, 58, 59, 69-73, 78, 87-93, **95-105**, 116, 118, 123-26, 141-45, 146-49, 154-59, 161-62, 172
"Reluctant Voyagers, The," 29
"Shame," 29
Sullivan County Sketches, 2, 44, 59, 82, 100
Third Violet, The, 6
"Three Miraculous Soldiers," 29
"Upturned Face, The," 24, 28, 71-72, 94
"Veteran, The," 29
"Virtue in War," 28
Whilomville Stories, 7, 165-76
Wounds in the Rain, 8
"Crazy Jane" (Yeats), 64
Criticism and Fiction (Howells), 82, 83
Crouse, Nellie, 6
Crumbling Idols (Garland), 83-84

D

"Dark Brown Dog, A," 29
Davis, Richard Harding, 68
"Death and the Child," 7, 8, 10, 28, 29
Débâcle, La (Zola), 126
Defoe, Daniel, 44
Dickens, Charles, 42, 44, 108
Dickinson, Emily, 32, 33, 36, 91
"Do not weep, maiden, for war is

kind," 29, 32, 33-35, 37, 60, 62
Doolittle, Hilda, 36, 63
Dostoevsky, Fyodor, 25-26, 51
Dreams (Schreiner), 36
Dreiser, Theodore, 1, 22, 28, 47, 116
Dryden, John, 43, 44
Dubliners (Joyce), 85

E

"Each small gleam was a voice," 60
Education of Henry Adams, The, 8
Eliot, George, 42
Eliot, T. S., 37, 62, 63, 64
Emerson, Ralph Waldo, 28, 31, 66, 77
"End of the Battle, The," 28
"Episode of War, An," 28, 55, 71, 94
Essay of Dramatic Poesy (Dryden), 43
Euripides, 149
"Experiment in Luxury, An," 3
"Experiment in Misery, An," 3, 29, 86, 118-22
    imagery in, 120-122
    man and Nature, theme of, 121-22
    structure, 118-22
Existentialism, in "The Open Boat," 150-153

F

"Fast rode the knight," 60
Fathers and Sons (Turgenev), 120
Faulkner, William, 8, 10
Fifth Column, The (Hemingway), 55
Fitzgerald, F. Scott, 6, 8, 28
"Five White Mice, The," 44, **157-60**, 164
Flaubert, Gustave, 5
Fletcher, John, 63
Fleurs du mal, Les (Baudelaire), 3
Flower, B. O., 2
Follett, Wilson, 9
Ford, Ford Madox, 6, 54, 91, 92
"Forth went the candid man," 60
Four Quartets (Eliot), 64
Frederic, Harold, 45
French Symbolists and Crane, 60-62
Freud, Sigmund, 23

Friday Nights (Garnett), 30
Frost, Robert, 32
Fryckstedt, Olov, W., 10

G

Garland, Hamlin, 2, 13, 25, **82-84**, 86,
  107, 109, 120
Garnett, Edward, 16, 19, 30, 39, 47,
  86, 91, 118
Gautier, Théophile, 83
George's Mother, 3, 10, 29, 59, 94,
  100
Gilder, Richard Watson, 1
Gissing, George, 81
Goethe, Johann Wolfgang von, 28
Golding, William, 165, 166, 174
Grant, Ulysses S., 18
Graves, Robert, 35, 37
Gray, Thomas, 42
Green Hills of Africa, The (Heming-
  way), 54
Gullason, Thomas A., 10

H

Hale, Edward Everett, 166
Hamlet (Shakespeare), 14
Hardy, Thomas, 43, 45-46, 81
Hawthorne, Nathaniel, 1, 22, 24, 44,
  45, 51, 77
Hearst, William Randolph, 19-20, 106
Hemingway, Ernest, 5, 8, 10, 25, 28,
  30, **52-56**, 65, 163-64
Henley, W. E., 36
Henry, O. (*see* Porter, William)
Hergesheimer, Joseph, 9
High Wind in Jamaica (Hughes), 165
Hill, Eldon C., 84
Hilliard, John N., 84
"His New Mittens," 94
Hoffman, Daniel, 9, 10, 144
Hoffman, F. J., 8
*Holiness the Birthright of All God's
  Children* (Jonathan Crane), 103
Homer, 5, 146-49
Homosexuality, concept of, in "Blue
  Hotel, The," 161-64

"Horses—One Dash," 44
Howells, William Dean, 1, 2, 5, 13, 17,
  36, 47, **82-83**, 108, 117, 122, 166,
  167, 170
Hughes, Richard, 165

I

Ibsen, Henrik, 22
"I explain the silvered passing of a ship
  at night," 60
Iliad (Homer), 146-49
"Illusion in Red and White, An," 29,
  94
Imagery:
  in *Maggie: A Girl of the Streets*,
    108-9, 111-12
  in *Red Badge of Courage, The*, 4,
    99-100, 142-43
Imagism, concept of, 62-64
Impressionism:
  concept of, 47-48, 80-86
  and Conrad, Joseph, 91-92, 93
  in *Maggie: A Girl of the Streets*, 84-
    86
  in *Red Badge of Courage, The*, 88-
    93
"In heaven/Some little blades of grass,"
  60
"In the night/Grey heavy clouds muf-
  fled the valleys," 62, 102
Irony:
  concept of, 30, 39-41
  in *Maggie: A Girl of the Streets*,
    110-11, 115-17
  in *Red Badge of Courage, The*, 95,
    96, 98
"I saw a man pursuing the horizon,"
  32-33, 60
"'It was wrong to do this,' said the
  angel," 60

J

James, Henry, 6, 17, 24, 44, 45-46, 51,
  81, 86
Jefferson, Thomas, 44
Jennie Gerhardt (Dreiser), 116

Johnson, Samuel, 27, 43, 44
Joyce, James, 45, 85

K

Kazantzakis, Nikos, 149
Keats, John, 2, 5, 10, 42, 43
"Kicking Twelfth, The," 44
"Killers, The" (Hemingway), 55, 163-64
Kipling, Rudyard, 2, 25, 44, 45-46, 81, 82
"Knife, The," 94

L

La Fontaine, Jean, 63
Lanier, Sidney, 63
Lawrence, T. E., 28
Lewis, Sinclair, 28
Lewisohn, Ludwig, 118
Liebling, A. J., 6
"Little Pilgrimage, A," social behavior, theme of, 175-76
Little Regiment, The 6, 29, 168
"Lodger, The" (Dostoevski), 26
Lombardo, Agostino, 88
London, Jack, 45
Lord Arthur Savile's Crime (Wilde), 108
Lord of the Flies (Golding), 165, 166, 174
"Lover and the Telltale, The," parody of adults, theme of, 173-75
Lowell, Amy, 9
Lucretius, 39
"Lynx-Hunting," plot summary, 171-73

M

Macbeth (Shakespeare), 14, 158
MacLeish, Archibald, 64
Maggie: A Girl of the Streets, 2, 3, 4, 5, 10, 20, 25, 28, 40, 41, 44, 46, 49, 59, 83-86, 107-9, **110-17**, 118
    characterization, 114-16
    imagery, 108-9, 111-12

and Impressionism, 84-86
    irony in, 110-11, 115-16
    moral codes, theme of, 116-17
    and Naturalism, 83-85, 110-17
    social behavior, theme of, 3, 112-17
    social conditions, theme of, 110, 111, 117
    style, 110-11
    subjective projection in, 107-9
Main-Travelled Roads (Garland), 83
Mallarmé, Stéphane, 60-61
Mansfield, Katherine, 85
March, William, 165
"Master and Man" (Tolstoy), 51
Maupassant, Guy de, 13-14, 16, 46, 50, 83
Melville, Herman, 3, 6, 22, 44, 158, 162
Men, Women and Boats (Starett), 54
"Men in the Storm," 24, 86
Mencken, H. L., 9, 45, 46
Meredith, George, 17, 42
"Mesmeric Mountain, The," 100, 105
Moby Dick (Melville), 3, 22
Monster, The, 7, 10, 28, 44, 49, 59, 73-74, 94, 151, 167-68
    meaningless decorum, theme of, 73-74
Montaigne, Michel de, 39
Moore, George, 81
Moore, Marianne, 63
Mozart, Wolfgang Amadeus, 51
Munroe, Lily Brandon, 82
"Mystery of Heroism, A," 28, 41, 94
    isolation, theme of, 78
    meaningless decorum, theme of, 70-71, 78

N

Nana (Zola), 64
Naturalism:
    concept of, 80-83, 91
    in *Maggie: A Girl of the Streets*, 83-85, 110-17
New England Boyhood, A (Hale), 166
Nigger of the "Narcissus," The (Conrad), 91

Norris, Frank, 47, 68-69
Nouvelle histoire de Mouchette, La (Bernanos), 85

O

O'Connor, William Van, 118
Odyssey (Homer), 146
Odyssey, The: A Modern Sequel (Kazantzakis), 149
Oliver, Arthur, 86-87
"Ominous Baby, An," 3
"Once a man clambering to the housetops," 102
"Once I saw mountains angry," 29, 101
"On the horizon the peaks assembled," 32-33, 58-59, 60, 101
"Open Boat, The," 7, 20, 28, 29, 41, 42, 44, 49, 50, 54-55, 59, 94, 100, 104-5, 122, 144, 150-153, 168
   and existentialism, 150-53
   indifferent universe, theme of, 7, 144, 150-152
   man and Nature, theme of, 104-5
   style, 42, 50, 54-55, 59
Ovid, 63

P

"Pace of Youth, The," 29
Parrington, Vernon, 118
Pater, Walter, 81
Paterson (Williams), 63, 64
Pearson, Hesketh, 108
Peck, George W., 166, 170
Peck, Bishop Jesse Truesdell, 103
Peck's Bad Boy and His Pa (Peck), 166
Penrod (Tarkington), 166
People, Yes, The (Sandburg), 64
Perosa, Sergio, 10
Pessimism:
   in Crane's art, 8-9
   in *Red Badge of Courage, The,* 141-45
Pinker, James B., 20-21
Poe, Edgar Allan, 2, 9, 14, 17, 22, 37, 45, 46, 50, 64, 65
"Poet, The" (Emerson), 66

Poetry, Crane's concept of, 64-65
Poetry of Stephen Crane, The (Hoffman), 9
Porter, William (*pseud.* O. Henry), 45, 46
Pound, Ezra, 32, 36, 62, 63
"Price of the Harness, The," 28, 156-57, 159
Psychological concepts:
   in "Blue Hotel, The," 154-64
   in *Red Badge of Courage, The,* 154-59, 161-62
Pulitzer, Joseph, 106

R

Red Badge of Courage, The, 3-6, 8, 10, 13, 15, 16, 18, 19, 20, 24, 25, 28, 30, 40-41, 42, 44, 46, 49, 51, 54, 59, 69-73, 78, 87-93, **95-105,** 116, 118, 123-26, 141-45, 146-49, 154-59, 161-62, 172
   animism, concept of, 147-49
   critical response to, 123-24
   fear, theme of, 87-88, 125-26
   and Homer, 146-49
   imagery in, 4, 99-100, 142-43
   and Impressionism, 88-93
   incongruity and the unknown, theme of, 70, 72-73
   indifferent universe, theme of, 143-45
   irony in, 95-96, 98
   isolation, theme of, 72, 78
   man and Nature, theme of, 141-42, 144
   meaningless decorum, theme of, 70-71, 72, 78
   plot summary, 70, 100-101
   point of view, 95-96
   psychological concepts in, 154-59, 161-62
   sinister mountains, theme of, 99-100, 104-5
   structure, 124-26
Religion, influence of, 1-2, 3-4, 8, 9, 36
"Reluctant Voyagers, The," 29

Remords, Georges, 10
Rimbaud, Arthur, 43
Robinson, Edwin Arlington, 1, 32
Roman experimental, Le (Zola), 81
Roosevelt, Theodore, 69

S

Saintsbury, George, 39
Sandburg, Carl, 28, 36, 63, 64
Sartre, Jean-Paul, 25, 151, 153
Schreiner, Olive, 28, 36
Sevastopol (Tolstoy), 48, 51
Shakespeare, William, 14, 42, 43, 44,
  51, 158, 162
"Shame," 29
Shaw, George Bernard, 81
Sister Carrie (Dreiser), 116
Solomon, Eric, 6, 10
Stallman, R. W., 9, 10, 23-24, 25, 58,
  118
Starett, Vincent, 53-54
Stedman, E. C., 64
Stendhal, 45
Stephen Crane (Berryman), 9
Stephen Crane (Cady), 10
Stephen Crane: An Omnibus (Stall-
  man), 9, 24, 118
*Stephen Crane: From Parody to Real-
  ism* (Solomon), 10
Stephen Crane in England (Solomon),
  6
Stevens, Wallace, 63, 64, 65
Story of a Bad Boy, The (Aldrich),
  166
Stranger, The (Camus), 152
Structure:
  in "Blue Hotel, The," 75-76
  in "Bride Comes to Yellow Sky,
    The," 74-75
  concept of, 45-46, 50
  in "Experiment in Misery, An,"
    118-22
  in *Monster, The*, 73-74
  in *Red Badge of Courage, The*, 124-
    26
Style:
  in "A youth in apparel that glit-

  tered," 57-58
  in *Black Riders, The*, 35-36
  in "Blue Hotel, The," 54-55
  concept of, 35, 36-38, 42-45,
    57-60, 65
  in *Maggie: A Girl of the Streets*,
    110-11
  in "On the Horizon the peaks
    assembled," 58-59
  in "Open Boat, The," 42, 50, 54-55,
    59
Sullivan County Sketches, 2, 44, 59,
  82, 100
Swift, Jonathan, 42
Symbolism:
  in "Blue Hotel, The," 24
  concept of, 60-62
Symons, Arthur, 81

T

Tacitus, 45
Tarkington, Booth, 166, 167, 173
Taylor, Cora, 107
Tess of the d'Urbervilles (Hardy), 45
Thackeray, William Makepeace, 42
"The hard hills tore my flesh," 101
"The patent of a lord," 60
"There exists the eternal fact of con-
  flict," 60
"There was one I met upon the road,"
  60
"The trees in the garden rained
  flowers," 60
"The wayfarer,/Perceiving the pathway
  to truth," as allegory, 57, 60
"'Think as I think,' said a man," 61
Third Violet, The, 6
Thomson, J. A. K., 39
Thoreau, Henry David, 77
"Three Miraculous Soldiers," 29
Tindall, William York, 60, 62
"To the maiden/The sea was a blue
  meadow," 38, 60
Tolstoy, Leo, 5, 17, 22, 28, 51, 64, 83,
  87
Trilling, Lionel, 10
Trudeau, Doctor Edward Livingston, 20

Turgenev, Ivan, 120
Twain, Mark (*see* Clemens, Samuel)

U

Under the Wheel (Garland), 120
"Upturned Face, The," 24, 28, 71-72,
  94

V

Valéry, Paul, 37
Vergil, 147, 149
"Veteran, The," 29
"Virtue in War," 28
Voyages (Hart Crane), 38

W

Walcutt, Charles C., 86
War and Peace (Tolstoy), 64, 126
Warner, Charles Dudley, 166
Washington, George, 27
Waste Land, The (Eliot), 64
Webster, John, 38
Weiss, Daniel, 9
Wells, H. G., 5, 29-30, 49, 77, 81
Wharton, Edith, 8

What Must I Do to be Saved? (Bishop
  Jesse Peck), 103
"What says the sea, little shell?" 61
"When a people reach the top of a
  hill," 102
Whilomville Stories, social behavior,
  theme of, 7, **165-76**
White Devil, The (Webster), 38
White, William Allen, 166, 170
Whitman, Walt, 28, 36, 63
Wilde, Oscar, 81, 108
Williams, William Carlos, 63, 64
Winesburg, Ohio (Anderson), 167
Wordsworth, William, 39
Work of Stephen Crane, The (Follett),
  9
Wounds in the Rain, 8
Wuthering Heights (Brontë), 29
Wyatt, Edith, 63
Wyndham, George, 49, 124

Y

Yeats, William Butler, 64
Young, Philip, 8

Z

Ziff, Larzer, 4
Zola, Émile, 5, 81, 83

E. E. CUMMINGS

A Collection of Critical Essays

Edited by NORMAN FRIEDMAN

A

Abstraction, Cummings's use of, 23-24, 29-30, 37
Adams, Robert Martin, 2
Adding Machine, The (Rice), 153
Adventures in Value, 11
After the Lost Generation (Aldrich), 40
Aiken, Conrad, 133
Aldrich, John, 40
Allen, Charles, 80
Alsberg, Henry, 133
"Amores," 82, 88
& (AND), 64, 73, 89
"Animals, The" (Muir), 54
Anthropos: or the Future of Art, 62
"anyone lived in a pretty how town," 23, 68
Aristophanes, 158
"as any (men's hells having wrestled with)," 96-97
Ash Wednesday (Eliot), 5
"a thrown a/-way It," 117-18
Atkinson, Brooks, 135
Auden, W. H., 3, 4, 5, 34, 54, 154

B

Barzun, Jacques, 135
Baum, S. V., 3, 13
"being to timelessness as it's to time," 8-10
Belasco, David, 134
Bentley, Eric, 141

Billy Budd (Melville), 47
"! blac/ k/ agains/ t," 118
Blackmur, R. P., 2, 13, 72, 82-83, 92-93, 107-8
Blake, William, 47
Brooks, Van Wyck, 44
"Buffalo Bill," 76, 86
Burke, Kenneth, 1, 37, 124
Burns, Robert, 83

C

Camino Real (T. Williams), 154
Campion, Thomas, 34, 57
Cantos, The (Pound), 5
"Chansons Innocentes," 87
Chirico, Giorgio de, 20
Chuang Tzu, 7, 11
Cline, Patricia, 11, 13
Coblentz, Stanton A., 2
Cocteau, Jean, 154
Coleridge, Samuel Taylor, 47
Collected Poems, 1923-1954, 31, 62, 64-65, 67, 88 *(see also* titles of individual poems)
    typographical innovations in, 107-20 *passim*
"come, gaze with me upon this dome," 175-76
"conceive a man, should he have anything," 20
"Cool Web, The" (Graves), 54
Cowley, Malcom, 32-34
Cozzens, James Gould, 47

Crane, Hart, 5
Crashaw, Richard, 83
Cummings, E. E.:
    abstraction, use of, 23-24, 29-30,
        37
    and Bunyan, John, 121-32
    critical reputation of, 1-3, 60
    and the Dada Movement, 42-43,
        136, 138, 143
    and expressionism, 29, 134
    linguistic innovations of, 4, 12, 17-
        18, 22-26, 36, 53-56, 76-77, **80-
        99, 105-20** *passim*
    love poetry, 3-4, 8-11, 20-27, 44,
        51-52, 62, 64, 67, 68-70, 102-3
    metonymy, use of, 92-98
    vs. New Criticism, 2-4, 6, 9-12, 81
    paradox, use of, 47, 48-49, 83
    personality of, 100-103
    Platonism of, 62-63
    and Pound, Ezra, 4, 5
    rhyme, use of, 108
    rhythm, use of, 96-97
    and the Romantic tradition, 47-48
    satire, use of, 4, 12, 68, 70, 121-32
    social and political views, 27, 37-42,
        50-51, 52
    transcendence, theme of, 3-4, 6-7,
        12, 25-26, 28-29, **47-50**, 61-70
    typographical innovations, 4, 5, 17-
        18, 24-25, 36, 54-55, 56, 71-72,
        76, 79, **104-20**
    and Yeats, W. B., 48-54
Cummings, E. E., works by:
    Adventures in Value, 11
    & (AND), 64, 73, 89
    Anthropos: or the Future of Art, 62
    Collected Poems, 1923-1954, 31,
        62, 64-65, 67, 88 (*see also* titles of
        individual poems)
    *E. E. Cummings: A Miscellany Re-
        vised*, 17, 28, 48, 49, 51
    Eimi, 13, 16, 18-20, 41-42, 105,
        156-67, 172
    Enormous Room, The, 13, 17, 40-
        41, 63-64, 102, 139, 161-63
    50 POEMS, 13, 20-21, 68, 75-78,
        91, 95

    XLI POEMS, 85, 89, 118
    Him, 13, 61, 65-66, **133-55**, 164
    is 5, 56, 172
    i: Six Nonlectures, 13, 35, 49, 60,
        79, **168-71**, 172-76
    95 poems, 7-8, 56, 58, 60, 68, 69
    no thanks, 20, 22, 26, 84
    1 X 1 (One times One), 21, 26, 62,
        82, 90, 94, 96-98 (*see also* titles of
        individual poems)
    Santa Claus, 20, 29
    73 poems, 68, 69
    Tulips and Chimneys, 64, 71, 81-82,
        104-5, 106
    Vanity Fair essays, 63
    ViVa, 62, 64, 67, 71-74
    XAIPÉ, 40, 106, 117-18

D

Dada, influence of, in Cummings' work,
    42-43, 136, 138, 143
Damon, S. Foster, 133
Dante Alighieri, 19, 66, 158
"death (having lost) put on his uni-
    verse," 21
Death in Venice (Mann), 47
Defoe, Daniel, 122
Deutsch, Babette, 92
"Dialogue of Self and Soul" (Yeats), 48
Dickens, Charles, 47, 168
"dive for dreams," 7-8
"does yesterday's perfection seem not
    quite," 20
Dos Passos, John, 121-22, 153
Dowson, Ernest, 57
Dupee, F. W., 14

E

Eastman, Max, 2
E. E. Cummings (Marks), 14
*E. E. Cummings: A Miscellany Re-
    vised*, 17, 28, 48, 49, 51
Eimi, 13, 16, 18-20, 41-42, 105, **156-
    67**, 172
    and *The Divine Comedy*, 19, 66,
        158

Eimi (continued)
   transcendence, theme of, 66-67
   typographical innovations in, 110-
      11, 113, 156
Eliot, T. S., 2, 3, 5, 11, 25, 34, 43, 44,
   54
Emerson, Ralph Waldo, 170, 171
Emperor Jones, The (O'Neill), 153
Enormous Room, The, 13, 17, 40-41,
   63-64, 102, 139, 161-63
   critical reception of, 121-22
   linguistic innovations in, 105
   and *The Pilgrim's Progress,* 121-32
"Epithalamion," 88
Expressionism, in Cummings' work,
   29, 134

F

50 POEMS, 13, 20-21, 68, 75-78, 91,
   95
   linguistic innovations in, 85
   typographical innovations in, 118-
      20
Fitch, Eugene, 134
XLI POEMS, 85, 89, 118
"Forward to *Krazy Kat,*" 9, 10, 28, 49,
   51
Four Quartets (Eliot), 5
Frank, Waldo, 133
Frankenberg, Lloyd, 2, 8, 20
Freud, Sigmund, 63
Frost, Robert, 5, 12, 54

G

Garbage Man, The (Dos Passos), 153
"Gaston Lachaise," 48, 52
Gide, André, 44
Graves, Robert, 1, 13, 54, 107
Great God Brown, The (O'Neill), 146,
   153
"Guerre, La," 86-87
Gulliver's Travels (Swift), 131-32

H

Haines, George, 3, 13

Hairy Ape, The (O'Neill), 153
Hammond, Percy, 135
Hawthorne, Nathaniel, 95
Heine, Heinrich, 159
Hemingway, Ernest, 44
Herne, James A., 134
Herrick, Robert, 57
Him, 13, 61, 64, 65-66, 133-55, 164
   critical reception of, 133-36
Hoffman, F. J., 80
Hopkins, Gerard Manley, 47
"how dark and single, where he ends,
   the earth," 20
Hulme, T. E., 2, 54, 55

I

Inferno (Dante), 19, 66, 158
is 5, 56, 172 (*see also* titles of individual poems)
i:Six Nonlectures, 13, 35, 49, 60, 79,
   168-71, 172-76
"i thank You God for most this amaz-
   ing," 174-75

J

James, William, 169
"Jehovah buried, Satan dead," 21
John, Saint, 27
Journal de Guerre (Malaquais), 41
Journal of the Plague Year (Defoe),
   122
Joyce, James, 44

K

Kazin, Alfred, 13, 121-22
Keats, John, 53, 71
Koestler, Arthur, 41
"kumrads die because they're told," 21

L

Lamb, D. K., 121
Landor, W. S., 57
Lawrence, D. H., 5, 51

"Lay your sleeping head, my love"
  (Auden), 4
Light, James, 134
Little Magazine, The (Allen and Hoff-
  man), 80
Lindsay, Vachel, 172-73
Linguistic innovations, in Cummings'
  work, 4, 12, 17-18, 22-26, 36, 53-56,
  76-77, **80-99, 105-20** *passim*
Logan, John, 3
"love is a place," 21
"Love Song of J. Alfred Prufrock, The"
  (Eliot), 5

M

MacNeice, Louis, 1, 154
Magic-Maker, The (Norman), 14
Malaquais, Jean, 41
Mann, Thomas, 44, 47
Marks, Barry, 14
Marvell, Andrew, 73, 83
Masson, P. L., 121
Matthiessen, F. O., 2
Maurer, Robert E., 3, 13
Melville, Herman, 47
Metonymy, Cummings' use of, 92-98
Miller, Henry, 47
Mills, Ralph J. Jr., 3
Monroe, Harriet, 104-5
Moore, Marianne, 1, 5, 11, 24-25, 106,
  107
Morison, Samuel Eliot, 33
"mortals)," 24-26, 27
Muir, Edwin, 54
Munson, Gorham, 107, 108
"my father moved through dooms of
  love," 68, 91, 160, 170

N

Nathan, George Jean, 135
New Criticism, 2-4, 6, 9-12, 81
95 poems, 7-8, 56, 58, 60, 68, 69
  typographical innovations in, 110
Norman, Charles, 14
"Notes on E. E. Cummings' Language"
  (Blackmur), 72, 82-83, 92-93, 107-8

"Notes Toward a Supreme Fiction"
  (Stevens), 30
no thanks, 20, 22, 26, 84

O

"Of Nicolette," 88
O'Neill, Eugene, 146, 153
"one's not half two. It's two are halves
  of one," 7, 27, 62, 98
1 X 1 (One times One), 21, 26, 62, 82,
  90, 94, 96-98 (*see also* titles of individual poems)
  linguistic innovations in, 84
"Orientale," 88
"o sweet spontaneous," 7

P

Paradox, Cummings' use of, 47, 48-49,
  83
Pater, Walter, 57
Picasso, Pablo, 44
"Plaisirs du Poète, Les" (Chirico), 20
Plato, 62-63
"POEM, OR BEAUTY HURTS MR.
  VINAL," 35, 127
Pound, Ezra, 1, 2, 4, 5, 11, 34, 43, 54
Priestley, J. B., 154
Prior, Matthew, 57
"Puella Mea," 88, 89

R

Ransom, John Crowe, 1
"reason let others give and realness
  bring," 21
Redman, Ben Ray, 121-22
Rhyme, Cummings' use of, 108
Rhythm, Cummings' use of, 96-97
Rice, Elmer, 153
Richards, I. A., 2
Riding, Laura, 107
Romantic influences, in Cummings'
  work, 47-48, 62
"Rose-Cheeked Laura" (Campion), 34
Rosenfeld, Paul, 2, 133
Rossetti, D. G., 80, 81

Roucke, Maurice, 164
Royce, Josiah, 80, 169

S

Santa Claus, 20, 29
Satire, in Cummings' works, 4, 12, 68, 70, 121-32 (*see also* Social and political views)
Scum of the Earth (Koestler), 41
Selected Letters of E. E. Cummings (Dupee and Stade, eds.), 14
73 poems, 68, 69 (*see also* titles of individual poems)
Shapiro, Karl, 40
Shaw, George Bernard, 47, 53, 138
"she being Brand/ -new," 175
Shelley, Percy Bysshe, 83
Silone, I., 44
"since feeling is first," 7
Smith, David E., 13
Social and political views, in Cummings' works, 27, 37-42, 50-51, 52 (*see also* Satire)
"sometimes/ in)Spring," 37
"somewhere i have never travelled, gladly beyond," 4, 62, 67
Sparrow, John, 2
Spencer, Theodore, 2
Stade, George, 14
Stein, Gertrude, 41
Stevens, Wallace, 3, 5, 30, 54
"stinging/ gold swarms/ upon the spires," 107
Stravinsky, Igor, 44
Strindberg, August, 154
Surrey, Earl of, 83
Survey of Modernist Poetry, A (Graves and Riding), 107
Swift, Jonathan, 122, 131-32
Swinburne, Algernon, 71, 83
Symposium (Plato), 62
"Syrinx" (Munson), 107, 108

T

Taggard, Genevieve, 133
Tao Te Ching, 67
"ta/ ppin/ g/ toe," 115-17
Tate, Allen, 1, 13, 31, 59

"Their Lonely Betters" (Auden), 54
"this mind made war," 21
Thoreau, Henry David, 170, 171
Three Centuries of Harvard (Morison), 33
Transcendence, theme of, in Cummings' works, 3-4, 6-7, 12, 25-26, 28-29, 47-50, 61-70
Tulips and Chimneys, 64, 71, 81-82, 104-5, 106
  linguistic innovations in, 86, 87-89
Twain, Mark, 168
Typographical innovations, in Cummings' works, 4, 5, 17-18, 24-25, 36, 54-55, 56, 71-72, 76, 79, **104-20**

V

Vanity Fair essays, 63
ViVa, 62, 64, 67, 71-74
  linguistic innovations in, 84
"voices to voices, lip to lip," 7
Von Abele, Rudolf, 3

W

Warren, Robert Penn, 1
Waste Land, The (Eliot), 5
Watson, Barbara, 3, 13
"what if a much of a which of a wind," 7, 97
Wilder, Thornton, 154
Williams, Tennessee, 154
Williams, William Carlos, 1, 2, 13, 36
Wilson Edmund, 1, 88-89, 133
Winchell, Walter, 135
Winter, Yvor, 2
Woollcott, Alexander, 135
Wordsworth, William, 47, 83
"worshipping Same," 21
Wouk, Herman, 47

X

XAIPE, 40, 106, 117-18

Y

Yeats, William Butler, 5, 12, 48, 54
"yes is a pleasant country," 26

DANTE

A Collection of Critical Essays

Edited by JOHN FRECCERO

A

Aeneid, 78-79
Albert, Saint, 45
Albertus Magnus, 42, 127-28
"Al cor gentil ripara sempre amore"
 (Guinicelli), 67
Allegory, 21-22, 23-24, 29, 103-9, 122-
 23, 126, 175
Ambrose, Saint, 127
"Anaphoric Hymnal Style" (Hatzfeld),
 96
Angeles, Juan de los, 168
Anna Karenina (Tolstoy), 74, 75
Apocalypse, 127-29, 132, 136
Arezzo, Guittone d', 29, 33
Ariosto, 82
Aristotle, 26, 27, 40, 44, 45, 46, 47,
 50, 144, 145
Arius, 156
Arnold of Villanova, 134
Around the Moon (Verne), 19
Around the Sun (Verne), 19
Augustine, Saint, 5, 6, 7, 42, 110, 146,
 156
Auriol, Pierre, 154
Averroës, 41, 42, 43

B

Banquet (Plato), 74
Barbi, Michele, 147
Beatrice, 2, 3, 4, 5, 8, 23, 25, 31, 45,
 51, 56, 70n, 72, 109, 110, 116, 122,
132, 134, 136, 137, 139, 140, 144,
170, 171, 172, 174, 175, 176
 analogy to Christ, 138
 as Divine grace, 22, 50
 as wisdom, 52
"Beginnings of Political Thought in
 Florence, The" (Rubinstein), 144
Beleth, John, 124
Bellamy, Ralph, 19
Bernard, Saint, 58, 160
Bérulle, Cardinal De, 164
Bettinelli, 15
Boccaccio, 12, 82
Boethius, 45, 152
Böhme, Jakob, 160, 166
Bonaventure, Saint, 152-53, 157, 158,
 163
Boniface VIII, Pope, 148, 150
Bonilla, Alonso de, 165
*Book of the Twenty-four Philosophers,
 The*, 151, 152, 157
Book on the Antichrist (William of St.
 Amour), 130
Born, Bertrand de, 36
Bornelh, Guiraut de, 36
Bouelles, Charles de, 166, 168
Bouterweck, F., 14, 15
Bruno, Giordano, 158, 166, 167

C

Cabbala, 165
Cacciaguida, 70n, 143, 144
Caetani, Pope, 150

Campanella, 166
Can Grande, 44, 103, 106, 112
Casale, Ubértino da, 129
Casella, 107, 113
Casini, 85
Cato, 107
Cavalcanti, Guido, 26
Christian doctrine (*see also* Theology),
    3-6, 10-12, 26-27, 40-41, 49, 82, 109-
    12, 123, 125-36, 151-52
Chronica de Origine Civitatis, 144
Cicero, 45
Cino da Pistoija, 26, 29, 38
Commedia, 1, 4, 8, 9, 10, 12, 14, 23,
    26, 29, 34, 36, 39, 40, 43, 44, 46, 56,
    69, 75, 84, 102, 107, 129, 141, 143,
    153, 156, 158, 160, 163, 170
    allegory in, 21-22, 103-6, 108-9
    as *exemplum*, 3-7, 170-77
    structure, 10, 15-22, 97, 103, 128-
    29, 139, 170-77
Confessions (Rousseau), 24
Confessions (St. Augustine), 5
Consolation of Philosophy (Boethius),
    45
Contini, Gianfranco, 4
Conversion, 4-5, 102-6, 112
Convivio, 8, 20, 23, 28-29, 35-37, 43-
    50 *passim*, 53, 141, 144-46, 150,
    174, 175
Corneille, 98
Counter-Reformation, 10, 39, 164
Cousin, Victor, 49
Crashaw, Richard, 164
Croce, Benedetto, 1, 14, 15-20 *passim*,
    33, 36n, 96
Cudworth, Ralph, 168
Cusanus, Nicolaus, 158, 166

D

Daniel, Arnaut, 36, 69
D'Annunzio, Gabriele, 34, 74
Dante Alighieri:
    biographical information, 24-25,
    46, 141-45, 148, 150
    exile of, 46, 142, 149
    and Florence, 46, 98

and Italian lyric poetry, 25, 28-34
and politics, 46, 141-50
and vision-literature, 25-26
world-view of, 11-13, 39-42, 43-60
Dante Alighieri, works by:
    "Allora dico che la mia lingua parlò
    quasi come per se stessa mossa,"
    35
    "Amor da che convien," 37
    "Amore e il cor gentil sono una
    cosa," 67
    "Amore lo mira con pietà," 33
    Canzoniere, 38
    Commedia, 1, 4, 8, 9, 10, 12, 14-20
    passim, 23, 26, 29, 34, 36, 39, 40,
    43, 44, 46, 56, 69, 75, 84, 102,
    103, 106, 107, 129, 139, 141, 143,
    153, 156, 158, 160, 163, 170, 173,
    175, 176
    Inferno, 3, 4, 6, 8, 26, 29, 34, 61-
    77, 78-101, 102, 106, 129, 131-
    32, 137, 140, 143
    Purgatorio, 2, 7, 8, 31, 49, 56,
    57, 66, 68, 69, 102-21, 122-40
    passim, 143, 173
    Paradiso, 2, 7, 8, 26, 50-60 *pas-
    sim*, 109, 139, 141-43, 149,
    153-54, 171, 172, 175, 176
    Convivio, 8, 20, 23, 28-29, 35, 37,
    43-50 *passim*, 53, 141, 144-46,
    150, 174, 175
    "De gli ochhi de la mia donna," 32
    De Monarchia, 8, 20, 41, 43, 44,
    145, 146
    De Vulgari Eloquentia, 8, 20, 23,
    29, 31, 36, 71, 142
    "Doglia mi reca," 34, 36, 37
    "Due donne in cima de la mente
    mia," 35
    "Le dolce rime," 35
    "Lisetta," 33
    Montanina, 37, 38
    "Poscia ch'Amor," 34
    "Prendo vergogne, onde mi ven
    pesanza," 33
    "Sonar bracchetti," 32
    Stony Verses, 8, 36
    "Tre Donne," 37
    "Un dì si venne a me Malinconia," 33

Dante Alighieri, works by: (*continued*)
   Vita Nuova, 8, 20, 23-27, 28, 30,
     35, 36, 44, 45, 50, 67, 90, 154,
     170, 175, 176
   "Voi che 'ntendendo," 35
"Dante and Peter de Vinea" (Olschki),
   96, 99
De Anima (Aristotle), 45
Del Rio, Martin, 39
De Monarchia, 8, 20, 41, 43, 44, 145,
   146
De Sanctis, Francesco, 14, 71, 72*n*, 73,
   74, 75, 83, 87, 88, 91, 96
Deuteronomy, 120
De Vulgari Eloquentia, 8, 20, 23, 29,
   31, 36, 71, 142
Dionysius the Areopagite, 158
Disquisitiones Magicae (Del Rio), 39
Divine Comedy, (see Commedia)
Divine Justice, 97
Dolce stil nuovo, 28-36, 67
Donati, Forese, 8, 37
D'Ovidio, Francesco, 76-77, 79, 80*n*,
   82, 87, 88, 92, 97
Durandus, William, 124

E

Eckhart, Master, 157, 158, 159, 165
Eliot, T. S., 1, 2, 32
Ercole, Francesco, 147
Estetica (Croce), 18
Ethics (Aristotle), 46
Exodus, 102-21 *passim*

F

Farinata, 6, 17, 142
Ficino, Marsilio, 166-68 *passim*
"Figure," 103-6, 112-13, 116, 119,
   120, 130
Flaubert, Gustave, 76
Fludd, Robert, 166
Folguet de Marseilles, 36
Francesca da Rimini (*see also* Paolo
   and Francesca), 2, 17, **61-77**
Francesca da Rimini (D'Annunzio),
   74-75

Frederick II, 34
Friendship, theme of, 30-32, 46-47, 49

G

Ganymede, 117, 120
George, Stefan, 9
Gerson, Jean, 155
Gesta Florentinorum (Sanzanome), 144
Ghibellines, 141, 142-43, 148
Giacomo da Sant'Andrea, 86*n*, 88, 97
Gilson, Etienne, 43, 44
Girard, René, 6
Glaucus, 2
Gospel of St. John, 156
Gourmont, Remy de, 25
Grandgent, C. H., 78, 79, 94
Gregory, Saint, 105, 106, 107, 121
Gregory VII, 146
Grèves, Philippe de, 162
"Grief brings me daring" (*see* "Doglia
   mi reca")
Griffon, 122, 127, 137
Grosseteste, Robert, 165
Guelfs, 46, 142-43, 146, 148
Guinicelli, Guido, 26, 67, 68
Guyon, Madame, 159

H

Harphius, Henricus, 159
Henry IV, 146
Henry of Harclay, 135

I

"I am ashamed and become downcast"
   (*see* "Prendo vergogne")
"Il canto di Piero delle Vigne"
   (D'Ovidio), 96
Imagery, 23-25, 26, 49, 53, 56, 107-9,
   117, 122, 124-40, 151-69, 170-76
Incarnation, 6, 7, 110, 136, 160-62
Inferno, 3, 4, 6, 8, 26, 29, 34, 61-77,
   78-101, 102, 106, 129, 131-32, 137,
   140, 143
*In the Glorious Epiphanie of Our Lord
   God* (Crashaw), 164

Isaiah, 121
Itinerarium Mentis (St. Bonaventure), 158

J

Jacopone, 19
Jerome, Saint, 134
Joachim of Flora, 131
John Scotus Erigena, 42, 154, 165
Journey to the Center of the Earth (Verne), 19
Julian, Lady, 174

K

Kepler, Johann, 166

L

La Boderie, 166
Lancelot du Lac, 73
Lancelot romance, 61-74
Landino, Cristoforo, 156
Language, 40, 62-65, 69-72, 78-101
Latini, Brunetto, 100, 144
Le Chevalier de la Charrette, 73
Leibniz, G. W., 166
Le jour n'est pas plus pur que le fond de mon coeur (Racine), 92
Leonardo da Vinci, 158
Letter to Can Grande, 103, 112
Liber de Causis, 45, 54
Lille, Alain de, 160
"Lisetta," 33
Lombard, Peter, 133
Lombardo, Marco, 142
Looking Backward (Bellamy), 19
Love, 32-38, 40-41, 45-46, 54-59, 67-68, 74-77, 171
"Love is one with the gentle heart" (*see* "Amore e il cor gentil sono una cosa")
"Love looks upon him with pity" (*see* "Amore lo mira")
"Love, since I must grieve" (*see* "Amor da che convien")

Lucia, Saint, 116, 118, 119, 120, 121
Lukács, György, 7
Luther, Martin, 39
Lyell, Charles, 28

M

Madame Bovary (Flaubert), 76
Malherbe, 95
Mammotrectus (Marchesini), 124
Manzoni, Alessandro, 39, 49, 50
Marchesini, John, 124
Martello, Carlo, 142, 143, 145, 146
Medieval philosophy, 10, 39-42, 151-69
Metamorphoses (Ovid), 79, 136
Metamorphosis, 79-82
Meung, Jean de, 161, 162
Mimesis, 9-13, 112
Montanina, 37, 38
Moralia (St. Gregory), 105, 106
More, Henry, 167
"My Lady's Eyes" (*see* "De gli ochhi de la mia donna")

N

Neri, Ferdinando, 38
Nicolas of Lyra, 134, 135
Nicomachean Ethics (Aristotle), 45
Novati, Francesco, 91, 92

O

Olivi, Peter John, 129, 132
Olschki, L., 96, 99, 100
"One day melancholy came to me" (*see* "Un di si venne a me Malinconia")
Orcagna, 11
Ovid, 79, 80, 81, 136

P

Paolo and Francesca 17, 61-77, 95, 96
Paracelsus, 167
Paradiso, 2, 7, 8, 26, 50-60 *passim*,

Paradiso, (continued)
   109, 139, 141-43, 149, 153-54, 171,
   172, 175, 176
Parmenides, 152
Patrizzi, 166
Pelletier du Mans, 166
Peter of Auvergne, 135
Petrarch, 10, 11, 12, 13, 28, 29
Phaedrus (Plato), 40
Pico della Mirandola, 166, 168
Pier della Vigna, 34, 78-101 *passim*
"Piero delle Vigne" (De Sanctis), 96
Pirandello, Luigi, 1
Plato, 4, 26, 29, 40, 43, 74
Plotinus, 152, 165
Poggioli, Renato, 2
Poiret, Pierre, 160
Politics (Aristotle), 145
Prelude, The (Wordsworth), 170
Proclus, 155
Provençal poetry, 26, 29-31, 36, 38,
   67-69, 117
Purgatorio, 2, 7, 8, 31, 49, 56, 57, 66,
   68, 69, **102-21**, 122-40 *passim*, 143,
   173
Pythagoras, 47

Q

Quidort, John of Paris, 130, 135

R

Racine, 92, 95
Ramus, Pierre, 166
Reformation, 10
Renaissance, 1, 11, 111, 166, 167
Republic (Plato), 40
Richard of St. Victor, 41
Roman de la Rose (Meung), 160-61
Romanic Review, 99
Ronsard, 166
Rose, elle a vécu ce que vivent les roses
   (Malherbe), 95
Rosmini, 40
Rousseau, Jean-Jacques, 24
Rubinstein, Nicolai, 144

Rudolph of Habsburg, 148

S

Salve Regina, 113
Santa Maria Novella, 11
Scheffler, Johann, 164
Scholasticism, 10, 40, 59, 149
Scipio, 45
Shakespeare, 27
Shepherd of Hermas, 23
Sicard of Cremona, 124
Sicilian School, 29, 38
"Since love" (*see* "Poscia ch'Amor")
Singleton, Charles, 3, 138
Socrates, 40
"So I say that my tongue was moved
   as by itself" (*see* "Allora dico che la
   mia lingua")
Sordello, 36, 117
Spitzer, Leo, 4
Statius, 2, 5, 113
Sterry, Peter, 159
Stony Verses, 8, 36
Style (see also *Dolce stil nuovo*), 28-32,
   88-101
Stylistic devices, 28-38, 62-73, 79,
   88-101
Summa Theologica (Aquinas), 52, 54
Suso, Heinrich, 157

T

Te lucis ante, 114
Terrena, Guido, 135
Theologia mystica (Harphius), 159
Theology, 1-7, 10-12, 27, 53-55, 59,
   102, 110-12, 139-40, 151-69
Thibaudet, Albert, 76
Thomas Aquinas, 10, 27, 39, 42, 43,
   45, 52, 53, 54, 144, 145, 154
"Three Ladies" (*see* "Tre Donne")
Timaeus (Plato), 161
Tolstoy, Leo, 74, 75
Torraca, F., 87
Traditio, 122n, 124, 125, 129, 135, 137

"Tradizione e poesia" (Schiaffini),
   90-91
Traherne, Thomas, 169
*Treatise Concerning the Time of the
   Coming of the Antichrist* (Arnold of
   Villanova), 134
Treatise on the Antichrist (Quidort),
   130
Truth, 45-49, 52-54, 56-60, 175-76
"Two Ladies uppermost in my Mind"
   (*see* "Due donne in cima de la mente
   mia")
Tyard, Pontus de, 166

V

Venturi, Leonello, 85
Verne, Jules, 19
Victorinus, Marius, 156
Villani, Giovanni, 144
Virgil, 2, 3, 5, 34, 56, 68, 80, 81, 83,
   84, 86, 87, 95, 97, 100, 102, 103,
107, 112, 113, 116, 117, 119, 131,
   138, 139, 176
Vita Nuova, 8, 20, 23-27, 28, 30, 35,
   36, 44, 45, 50, 67, 90, 154, 170, 175,
   176
Vossler, Karl, 14, 15, 16, 87, 91, 92,
   97

W

"Whether the Advent of Christ can be
   Known through Astronomy" (Henry
   of Harclay), 135
William of St. Amour, 130-31, 132,
   135, 136
Wordsworth, William, 170

Y

"You Intelligences who Move" (*see*
   "Voi che 'ntendendo")
Yves de Paris, 166

DICKENS

A Collection of Critical Essays

Edited by MARTIN PRICE

A

Ambassadors, The (James), 39
Anna Karenina (Tolstoy), 7, 68
Arnold, Matthew, 149
Auden, W. H., 71
Austen, Jane, 39, 55, 64

B

Balzac, Honoré, 27, 65, 152n
Barnaby Rudge, 107, 136
Beadnell, Maria, 155-56
Beggars Opera, The (Gay), 89
Bennett, Arnold, 65
Blake, William, 11, 70
Bleak House, 9, 33, 94, **135-46**, 147, 156
    characterization, 25, 26
    dramatic devices, 30, 148
    satire, use of, 2, 12
Brecht, Bertolt, 1
Brothers Karamazov, The (Dostoevsky), 152
Browne, Sir Thomas, 117
Bunyan, John, 39, 157
Burckhardt, Jacob, 153
Burnett, Fanny Dickens, 130

C

Cather, Willa, 66
Caves du Vatican, Les (Gide), 84
Cervantes, Miguel de, 68, 69

Chamisso, Adelbert von, 42
Characterization, in Dickens's novels, 2-6, 8-9, 63-64, 68-69, 119, 120, 137
    child characters, 16-17, 19, 29, 33, 36-37, 88, 125, 128-30, 153
    child-woman characters, 20, 63, 125
    contrast, use of, 4-6, 42-44, 46, 49-51, 52-53, 55, 161-63
    criminals, 26, 32, 33-38, 87, 90-94, 159
    dialogue, use of, 60-61, 96
    heroes and heroines, 16-23, 119, 123
    techniques of, 26, 61, 96
    villains, 62-63, 79, 84, 151-52
Chesterton, G. K., 83, 94
Christmas Carol, A, 41, 43-45
Clarissa (Richardson), 84
Collins, Wilkie:
    and conversion, theme of, 40
    influence of, on Dickens, 57, 62, 64n
    No Name, 62
    Woman in White, 64n
Conrad, Joseph, 42
Counterfeiters, The (Gide), 59

D

Daily News, 115
Daniel Deronda (Eliot), 39, 43, 55, 56
Dante, 55, 157
Das Kapital (Marx), 1

David Copperfield, 48, 88, 107, 115, 129
  autobiographical nature of, 130, 167
  education, theme of, 19-20, 41, 138
  symbolism, use of, 32, 176
Death in Venice (Mann), 84
Defoe, Daniel, 39, 56*n*
Dickens, Charles: (*see also* main entry for starred items)
  and America, 97, 100-101, 104-10 *passim,* 117
  and Austen, Jane, 39, 64
  and Beadnell, Maria, 155
  and Blake, William, 11, 70
  characterization in novels of (*see* Characterization)
  and Collins, Wilkie, 40, 62, 64*n*
  and *Daily News,* 115
  and Eliot, George,* 1, 7, 39-40, 43, 44, 51, 55-57, 63
  family of, 87, 149, 153-54
  and Forster, John,* 25, 89, 97, 103, 104, 115, 117, 119, 130*n*
  and Galsworthy, John, 61
  in Italy, 104
  and James, Henry,* 1, 39-41 *passim,* 51, 55, 56, 60-62, 64, 66, 99, 147
  as poet, 9, **58-67,** 135, 158, 168
  religious implications of his work, 2, 11, 30, 69-71, 111, 156-57
  sexual life of, 1, 18, 155-56
  and Shakespeare, William,* 1, 7, 60, 90, 92, 95, 97, 99, 140
  sister of, 130
  as social critic, 13-14, 17, 18-19, 33, 91-93, 106-7, 115, 118, 126, 130-32, 134, 135, 147-51
  style in novels of (*see* Style)
  in Switzerland, 115
  and Ternan, Ellen, 1
  themes in novels of (*see* Themes)
  and Wordsworth, William, 44
  working methods of, 102-3, 115-16
Dickens, Charles, works of: (*see also* main entries for starred items)

Barnaby Rudge, 107, 136
*Bleak House,** 2, 9, 12, 25, 26, 30, 33, 94, 135-46, 147, 148, 156
Christmas Carol, A, 41, 43-45
*David Copperfield,** 19-20, 32, 41, 48, 88, 107, 115, 129, 130, 138, 167, 176
*Dombey and Son,** 9, 10, 21, 62, 64, **115-34,** 176
Edwin Drood, 90, 92
*Great Expectations,** 3-4, 9, 17, 27, 32, 35, 36, 41, 51, 61, 63, 90, 136, 138, 145, **158-68**
*Hard Times,** 9, 25, 28, 41, 49, 95
*Little Dorrit,** 1, 4-6, 9, 10-11, 26, 30, 31, 33, 34, 41, 50, 67, 94, 138, 146, **147-57**
*Martin Chuzzlewit,** 12, 24-38 *passim,* 59-60, **97-114,** 115, 116-18
Nicholas Nickleby, 62-63, 126, 130
Old Curiosity Shop, The, 126, 128
Oliver Twist, 61, **83-96,** 107, 126, 128, 144
*Our Mutual Friend,** 1, 6, 9, 12, 22, 41, 53, 92, 94, 144, 147, 148, 149*n,* 156, **169-77**
*Pickwick Papers, The,** 6, 19, 26, 64, **68-82,** 83, 104, 136
Sketches by Boz, 91
Tale of Two Cities, A, 13, 42, 61
"Dickens and the Double" (Lane), 42*n*
Dickens: The Dreamer's Stance (Stoehr), 13
Diderot, Denis, 84
Divine Comedy, The (Dante), 157
Dombey and Son, 9, **115-34**
  characterization, 62, 64
  symbolism, 10, 176
Don Quixote (Cervantes), 68
Dostoevsky, Fyodor, 1, 42, 56*n*
  Dickens's influence on, 63, 92-93, 152
Doyle, Sir Arthur Conan, 68
Drama of Duncan Parrenness (Kipling), 42

E

Edwin Drood, 90, 92
Eliot, George:
  Daniel Deronda, 39, 43, 55, 56
  and Dickens, their work compared,
    1, 40, 41, 44, 51, 57, 63
  Felix Holt, 55
  Middlemarch, 7, 40
Eliot, T. S., 1
Emma (Austen), 39
"Erscheinung" (Chamisso), 42

F

Felix Holt (Eliot), 55
Felton, C. C., 102
Fiedler, Leslie, 105
Fielding, Henry, 57, 89
Firbank, Ronald, 71
Fitzgerald, Edward, 130n
Flaubert, Gustave, 90
Ford, George, 8, 11
Forster, E. M., 163
Forster, John, 2, 89, 115, 117
  Dickens's letters to, 25, 103, 119
  influence of, on Dickens, 97, 104,
    130n
Forsyte Saga, The (Galsworthy), 61
Freud, Sigmund, 149-50

G

Galsworthy, John, 61
Gay, John, 89, 96
Gide, André, 59, 84
Great Expectations, 9, 32, 35, 61, 138,
  156-68
  characterization, 3-4, 63, 145
  ending, 17, 90
  plot structure, 51, 63, 136
  transformation and conversion,
    theme of, 27, 36, 41
Greene, Robert, 40

H

Haggard, Rider, 68

Hard Times, 9, 28, 95
  characterization, 25, 49
  transformation and conversion,
    theme of, 41, 49
Hardy, Thomas, 95
Harvey, W. J., 8
Heart of Darkness (Conrad), 106
Hitler, Adolf, 70
Hogarth, Mary, 124n
Hogarth, William, 2, 96
House, Humphry, 15, 44, 56n
Hutton, R. H., 63n

I

Idiot, The (Dostoevsky), 63
Introductory Letters on Psychoanaly-
  sis (Freud), 149

J

James, Henry, 17, 86, 139, 140
  as critic of Dickens's work, 60-62,
    66, 147
  and Dickens, their work compared,
    1, 39-41 *passim,* 51, 55, 56, 64,
    99
  and the novel, 135, 136
James, William, 39, 55n
Johnson, Edgar, 15, 149n
Jonathan Wild (Fielding), 89
Jonson, Ben, 40
Joyce, James, 99, 100, 101

K

Kafka, Franz, 1, 67
Keats, John, 11, 62, 110
Kierkegaard, Sören, 38
King Lear (Shakespeare), 7, 123, 152
Kipling, Rudyard, 42, 83

L

Lane, Lauriat, 42
Langland, William, 157
Lawrence, D. H., 94, 95

Leavis, F. R., 15, 95
Lewes, G. H., 56n
Little Dorrit, 9, **147-57**
  characterization, 4-6, 26
  crime, theme of, 26, 33
  imagery, 10-11, 30, 31, 34, 67
  narrative style, 138, 146
  social criticism, 1, 94
  transformation and conversion,
    theme of, 41, 50
"London" (Blake), 11
Lytton, Bulwer, 90, 167

M

"Macabre Dickens, The" (House), 56n
Macbeth (Shakespeare), 100
McCarthy, Mary, 3
Marcus, Steven, 11
Markheim (Stevenson), 42
Martin Chuzzlewit, 24-38 *passim*, **97-114**, 115
  design of, 59-60, 116-118
  satire, use of, 12, 42
  transformation and conversion,
    theme of, 39, 40, 41, 42
Masson, David, 2
Measure for Measure (Shakespeare), 7
Melville, Herman, 87, 154
Meredith, George, 39
Middlemarch (Eliot), 40
Miller, J. Hillis, 12, 15
Milton, John, 99
Modest Proposal, A (Swift), 2
Molière, 34
Muir, Edwin, 63, 64, 65

N

Nausée, La (Sartre), 28
Nicholas Nickleby, 62-63, 126, 130
Nietzsche, Friedrich, 68
Nightingale, Florence, 59
No Name (Collins), 62
"Novel Démeublé, The," (Cather), 66

O

Old Curiosity Shop, The, 126, 128
Old Wives Tale, The (Bennett), 65
Oliver Twist, 61, **83-96**, 107, 126, 128, 144
Orwell, George, 15, 60, 168
Our Mutual Friend, 1, 9, 12, 144, 147, **169-77**
  characterization, 6, 22, 92, 156
  imagery, 94, 148, 149n
  transformation and conversion,
    theme of, 41, 53

P

Palmer, Samuel, 14-15
Pater, Walter H., 58
Père Goriot (Balzac), 65
Pickwick Papers, The, **68-82**, 83, 104
  characterization, 6, 19, 26
  plot structure, 64, 136
Piers Plowman (Langland), 157
Pilgrim's Progress (Bunyan), 157
Poe, Edgar Allan, 42, 55
Pope, Alexander, 5

R

Racine, Jean Baptiste, 140
Richardson, Samuel, 84
Richard III (Shakespeare), 100
Robinson Crusoe (Defoe), 39
Rossetti, Christina, 162

S

Sartre, Jean-Paul, 28
Shakespeare, William, 40, 147
  characterization, 60, 68
  and Dickens, their work compared,
    1, 7, 90, 92, 95, 99, 140
  influence of, on Dickens, 60, 97
  Macbeth, 100
  Measure for Measure, 7
  Richard III, 100
Shaw, George Bernard, 1, 15, 148

She (Haggard), 68
Sketches by Boz, 91
Smollett, Tobias, 57
Songs of Innocence (Blake), 11
Stevenson, Robert Louis, 42, 55
Stoehr, Taylor, 13
Structure of the Novel (Muir), 63
Style, in Dickens's novels:
  comedy, use of, 2, 3, 6, 12, 24, 25,
    29, 57*n*, 61-63, 102, 104-5, 110,
    114, 118
  coincidence, role of, 7-9, 31, 42,
    135, 143-45
  dialogue, role of, 59-61, 104, 111,
    116, 118
  fantasy, use of, 3-4, 6, 125-26,
    158-59, 161, 166
  language, use of, 11-13, 29, 97-102,
    135, 174-75
  narrative techniques, 58-67, 73, 85-
    86, 89-90, 97, **135-40**
  satire, use of, 1, 2, 3, 12, 57, 88,
    110, 145
  symbolism, use of, 25-34, 95,
    126-27, 148-49
Swift, Jonathan, 2

T

Tale of Two Cities, A, 13, 42, 61
Tartuffe (Molière), 34
Ternan, Ellen, 1
Thackeray, William Makepeace, 17,
  130*n*, 131
  as critic of Dickens, 18, 83
Themes, in Dickens's novels:
  corruption, 141, 154
  freedom, 10-11, 102, 146

imprisonment, 5-6, 148-50
love, 10, 17, 38, **39-57**, 124, 153,
  166
money and wealth, 9, 14, 43-45, 53-
  54, 71-72, 79-80, 131-33, 152,
  169-77
murder, 90-94, 123, 169
pride, 117, 119, 121
redemption, 21, 22, 36-38
selfishness, 9-10, 40, 46-47, 117
sexuality, 17-18, 20-23
transformation and conversion, 4,
  19, 27, 36, **39-57**
Thomas, Dylan, 100
Tillotson, Kathleen, 10, 41
Tocqueville, Alexis de, 100
Tolstoy, Leo, 39, 68
To the Lighthouse (Woolf), 163
Tourneur, Cyril, 40
Trilling, Lionel, 5
Twain, Mark, 167
"Two Scrooges, The" (Wilson), 56*n*
Tymms, Ralph, 42

U

Ulysses (Joyce), 100, 101

W

Waste Land, The (Eliot), 1
Wilde, Oscar, 61, 71
William Wilson (Poe), 42
Wilson, Edmund, 15, 23, 56*n*, 87, 94
Wodehouse, P. G., 71
Woman in White, The (Collins), 64*n*
Woolf, Virginia, 163
Wordsworth, William, 44, 149

EMILY DICKINSON

A Collection of Critical Essays
Edited by RICHARD B. SEWALL

A

Adams, Elizabeth, 5
Aiken, Conrad, 2, 19
Alden, John, 43
American Dictionary of the English Language (Webster), 144
Ancestors' Brocades (Bingham), 52
Anderson, Charles R., 4
Anthon, Kate, 110
Arnold, Matthew, 23, 24, 45
Atlantic Monthly, 9
Auden, W. H., 118, 144

B

Baudelaire, Charles, 49, 87
Bay Psalm Book, The, 145
Beecher, Henry Ward, 168, 169
Beethoven, Ludwig van, 79, 103
Behn, Mrs. Aphra, 120
Berkeley, George, 109
Bianchi, Martha Dickinson, 2, 10, 19, 102
Bingham, Millicent Todd, 2
Blackmur, R. P., 4, 7, 117, 119, 120, 122
Blake, William, 10, 121, 124, 138, 139, 140, 143, 151
Blessed Damosel (D. G. Rossetti), 48
Bogan, Louise, 4, 5
Boileau, Nicolas, 119
Bolts of Melody, 2
Boltwood, Mrs. Lucius, 169

Bowles, Samuel, 5, 10, 110, 168, 169, 171, 173, 174, 176
Bowles, Mrs. Samuel, 143, 169
Bowra, C. M., 139
"Brahma" (Emerson), 104
Brontë, Charlotte, 113
Brontë, Emily, 138, 140
Brook Farm, 12
Browne, Sir Thomas, 106-7
Browning, Elizabeth B., 11, 120
Browning, Robert, 11, 45, 47
Bryant, W. C., 112, 113
Bunyan, John, 84
Burns, Robert, 103
Byron, George Gordon, Lord, 45

C

"Cannibalism in the cars" (Twain), 41
Cannon, W. B., 79
Capsule of the Mind (Ward), 6
Cazamian, L., 41
Channing, Ellery, 169
Channing, William Ellery, 169
"Chariot, The," 26
Chase, Richard, 143
Christian Psalmody (Watts), 70, 99, 118
Coleridge, S. T., 45, 119, 139
Courtship of Miles Standish, The (Longfellow), 42-43
Cowley, William, 17
Crowell, Mary Warner, 173

D

Dante, 47, 83, 138
"Days" (Emerson), 106
"Diagnosis of the Bible, by a boy," 107
Dickinson, Edward, 9, 110, 158
Dickinson, Emily:
   artistic development, 3, 52-54,
     101-4, 137, 141, 144-49 *passim*
   biographical information, 2, 5-6, 9-
     15 *passim*, 19, 82, 85-86, 93, 97-
     100, 109-14, 160, 162-77
   New England background, impor-
     tance of, 12, 17-21, 25, 27, 31,
     39-40, 106, 118-19, 147, 156,
     159
   religious background, 12, 13, 25,
     27, 39, 45, 106-8, 116, 127-30,
     135, 139-43, 145
Dickinson, Emily, works by:
   "Chariot, The," 26
   "Diagnosis of the Bible, by a boy,"
     107
   "Drowning," 13
   Juvenilia, 6
   "Single Hound, The," 13
Dickinson, Emily, works by: (index of
  first lines)
   "A bird came down the walk," 124
   "A charm invests a face," 68
   "A clock stopped," 114
   "A drunkard cannot meet a cork,"
     158
   "A dying tiger moaned for drink,"
     91-92
   "A light exists in spring," 36-37
   "A little overflowing word," 55
   "A nearness to tremendousness,"
     51-52
   "A route of evanescence," 153
   "A solemn thing it was I said," 151
   "A still volcano, life," 62
   "A word dropped careless on a
     page," 56
   "A word is dead," 54
   "Abraham to kill him," 158
   "All circumstances are the frame,"
     84

"Alone and in a circumstance," 60
"Although I put away his life," 47-
  48
"An awful tempest mashed the air,"
  112
"As imperceptibly as grief," 37
"At half-past three a single bird," 7,
  30-31, 92, 152
"Because I could not stop for
  death," 21, 32-33, 90-91, 123, 125
"Bee! I'm expecting you," 163
"Best things dwell out of sight," 64
"Could any mortal lip divine," 56
"Dare you see a soul at the white
  heat," 47
"Did the harebell loose her girdle,"
  68
"Don't put up my thread and
  needle," 49
"Dust is the only secret," 157
"Elysium is as far to," 82
"Experiment escorts us last," 172
"Faith bleats to understand," 145
"Faith is a fine invention," 147
"Farther in summer than the birds,"
  35-36, 38
"Forever cherished be the tree," 50
"Give little anguish," 65
"Glee! the great storm is over," 49
"Go slow my soul to feed thyself,"
  171
"God is a distant, stately lover," 42
"Good night! which put the candle
  out," 50
"Gratitude is not to mention," 66
"Great streets of silence led away,"
  31
"Growth of man like growth of
  nature," 63-64
"Had we our senses," 49
"He fumbles at your soul," 83
"How many times these low feet
  staggered," 114
"I am ashamed, I hide," 48
"I can wade grief," 156
"I could suffice for Him," 58
"I died for beauty, but was scarce,"
  14

Dickinson, Emily, works by: (index of
first lines) (*continued*)
"I dreaded that first robin so," 119
"I fear a man of scanty speech," 59
"I found the phrase to every
thought," 66
"I got so I could hear his name,"
55-56, 94
"I have not told my garden yet,"
57-58
"I heard a fly buzz when I died," 90
"I like to see it lap the miles," 6, 7,
28-29
"I never lost as much but twice," 74
"I never saw a moor," 105
"I never told the buried gold," 73
"I started early, took my dog," 29-
30, 125
"I stepped from plank to plank," 49
"I taste a liquor never brewed," 76
"I was the slightest in the house,"
49
"If I could tell how glad I was," 64
"If I shouldn't be alive," 114
"If it had no pencil," 174
"If your nerve deny you," 116
"I'm sorry for the dead today," 114
"I'm 'wife', I've finished that," 75,
175
"Is it too late to touch you, dear,"
173
"It dropped so low in my regard,"
121
"It might be lonelier," 120
"It was not death, for I stood up,"
115
"Just lost, when I was saved," 74-75
"Lay this laurel on the one," 14,
155
"Lightly stepped a yellow star," 43,
159
"Many a phrase has the English
language," 57
"Me from myself to banish," 49
"Mine by the royal seal," 145
"Much madness is divinest sense,"
7, 86

"My best acquaintances are those,"
61
"My friend must be a bird," 173
"My life closed twice before its
close," 14
"My life had stood, a loaded gun,"
142
"Nature the gentlest mother is," 77
"Of all the souls that stand create,"
116, 134
"Of God we ask one favor," 159,
166
"On such a night or such a night,"
114
"One and One are One," 60
"Our little secrets slink away," 62
"Our share of night to bear," 151
"Publication is the auction," 129
"Rearrange a wife's affections," 7,
84
"Safe in their alabaster chambers,"
114
"Sang from the heart, Sire," 48
"'Shall I take thee?' the poet said,"
53
"She bore it till the simple veins,"
156
"Some work for immortality," 78
"Speech is a symptom of affection,"
64
"Step lightly on this narrow spot,"
57
"Success is counted sweetest," 131
"Superiority to fate," 60
"Tell all the truth but tell it slant,"
148
"The Bible is an antique volume,"
52, 107
"The body grows outside," 49
"The future never spoke," 62
"The hills in purple syllables," 57
"The last night that she lived," 34,
124
"The missing all prevented me," 85,
136
"The mountains grow unnoticed,"
93

Dickinson, Emily, works by: (index of
  first lines) (*continued*)
  "The reticent volcano keeps," 61
  "The riddle that we guess," 172
  "The show is not the show," 118
  "The soul selects her own society,"
    95
  "The soul's superior instants," 96
  "The way I read a letter's thus," 48,
    94-95
  "There came a day at summer's
    full," 171
  "There is a word," 55
  "There is no silence in the earth so
    silent," 64
  "There's a certain slant of light,"
    37-38, 115
  "There's something quieter than
    sleep," 26
  "They say that time assuages," 122
  "They shut me up in prose," 149
  "Those dying then," 129
  "'Tis little I could care for pearls,"
    135
  "'Tis not that dying hurts us so,"
    105
  "'Tis whiter than an Indian pipe,"
    58
  "To disappear enhances," 133
  "To help our bleaker parts," 104
  "To lose, if one can find again," 48-
    49
  "To make one's toilette after
    death," 154
  "To tell the beauty would
    decrease," 69
  "Too happy time dissolves itself,"
    172
  "Too much of proof affronts be-
    lief," 108, 135
  "'Twas just this time last year I
    died," 49
  "'Twas the old road through pain,"
    102, 114
  "'Twas warm at first, like us," 34-35
  "Undue significance a starving man
    attaches," 130
  "Water is taught by thirst," 121, 131
  "We pass and she abides," 62
  "We thirst at first, 'tis nature's act,"
    133
  "Wert thou but ill," 48
  "Who is the east," 91
  "Why make it doubt, it hurts it so,"
    174
  "Within my garden rides a bird,"
    153
  "Your thoughts don't have words
    every day," 54
Dickinson, Lavinia, 41, 160, 170, 176
Dickinson, Susan Gilbert, 110, 129,
  171
Dickinson, William Austin, 110, 111
Dickinson Collection, 89
Dobson, Austin, 123
Donne, John, 7, 16, 17, 21, 23, 25,
  121, 124, 160
"Drowning," 13

E

Edwards, Jonathan, 20
Eliot, George, 113
Eliot, T. S., 7, 138, 140, 146
Emerson, Ralph Waldo, 12, 13, 17, 18,
  20, 27, 106, 111, 112, 139, 141, 147,
  148, 149, 168-69
*Emily Dickinson, An Interpretive
  Biography* (Johnson), 2, 4, 80, 82,
  85, 96-100
Emily Dickinson, A Revelation (Bing-
  ham), 5
*Emily Dickinson's Home: Letters of
  Edward Dickinson and his Family,
  with Documentation and Comment*
  (Bingham), 2, 109-10
Emmons, Henry Vaughan, 5, 167
Essays (Emerson), 104, 106
Explicator, 4

F

Family Library of Poetry and Song
  (Bryant), 112

Franklin, Benjamin, 148
From Baudelaire to Surrealism (Raymond), 87
Frost, Robert, 7, 136, 157

G

Gascoigne, George, 38
Gide, André, 85-86
Gilbert, Susan, 5, 110, 167
Gilded Age, 18
Gospel of St. John, 51
Graves, John, 5, 168
Greville, Fulke, 38

H

"Hamatreya" (Emerson), 104, 106
Hardy, Thomas, 27, 29, 92, 117, 124
Harvard edition of poems, 1, 3, 4, 6, 78, 80, 81, 86, 87, 88, 93, 95, 101-16 *passim*, 137, 141, 157
Haven, Mrs. Joseph, 168
Hawthorne, Nathaniel, 11, 17, 18, 20, 27, 106, 115
Heine, Heinrich, 139
Herbert, George, 23, 29, 138
Herrick, Robert, 81, 83
Higginson, T. W., 9, 10, 11, 25, 26, 47, 82, 101, 106, 111, 112, 120, 121, 127, 140, 141, 144, 149, 160-61, 162, 163, 167, 168, 169, 170-76 *passim*
Higginson, Mrs. T. W., 162, 169, 175
Hölderlin, J. C. F., 139
Holland, J. G., 171
Holland, Mrs. J. G., 168, 170-171
Holmes, O. W., 18
Homer, 119
Hopkins, Gerard Manley, 103, 124, 133, 138, 146
House of the Seven Gables, The (Hawthorne), 11
Howe, Julia Ward, 111
Hugo, Victor, 139
"Humble Bee, The" (Emerson), 106

Humphrey, Jane, 5
Humphrey, Leonard, 5, 110
Huxley, T. H., 23

I

Indicator, 167
Introduction to Emily Dickinson (Wells), 2

J

Jackson, Helen Hunt, 10, 110, 129, 164, 165, 166, 168-70 *passim*, 176
James, Henry, 12, 20, 21, 103
James, William, 81
John of the Cross, Saint, 138
Johnson, Thomas H., 1, 2, 78, 80, 81, 82, 86-89 *passim*, 93, 95, 101, 102, 103, 105, 137, 141, 157
Jonson, Ben, 29, 124
Juvenilia, 6

K

Keats, John, 45, 124, 138, 139

L

Laforgue, Jules, 86
Language, 48, **51-69**, 79, 89, 100, 122-26, 146-49, 150-153, 160, 173-77
"Lapis Lazuli" (Yeats), 157
Leaves of Grass (Whitman), 11
Lermontov, Mikhail, 139
Letters of Emily Dickinson, The (ed. Johnson and Ward), 1, 9, 10, 137, 140
Letters of Ralph Waldo Emerson, The (ed. Rusk), 104
Leyda, Jay, 2, 5
Longfellow, Henry Wadsworth, 18, 26, 49
Loomis, Eben J., 165-66, 169
Lord, Judge Otis, 5, 166, 168, 169
Lowell, James Russell, 18, 26

Lyke-Wake Dirge, The (anon.), 125

M

MacLeish, Archibald, 4
Mallarmé, Stéphane, 142
Manchester Guardian, 10
Mansfield Park (Austen), 120
Masque of Poets, A (ed. Jackson), 10
Mather, Cotton, 17, 20, 25, 27
Melville, Herman, 11, 17, 31, 40, 145
"Merlin" (Emerson), 149
Miller, Joaquin, 11
Milton, John, 23, 72, 83, 146
"Mithridates" (Emerson), 106
Moby Dick (Melville), 11
Mount Holyoke Seminary, 128-29
Mozart, Wolfgang A., 103

N

Newton, Benjamin, 5, 110
Niles, Thomas, 170
Norcross, Frances, 42, 168, 169, 173
Norcross, Joel, 166
Norcross, Louisa, 42, 168, 169, 173
"Nuptiall Song on Sir Clipseby Crew
    and His Lady" (Herrick), 81

O

On the Death of Dean Swift (Swift),
    49
Over-Soul, 18

P

Parnassus (Emerson), 112
"Phoenix and the Turtle, The"
    (Shakespeare), 79
Poe, E. A., 11, 18, 87, 98, 113, 143
Poems (Emerson), 104, 149
Poems: First Series (ed. Todd and Hig-
    ginson), 14
Poems: Second Series (ed. Higginson
    and Todd), 10, 14
Poets of America (Cheever), 113

Pollitt, Josephine, 19
Pope, Alexander, 16, 119
Poulter's Measure, 38
Pound, Ezra, 146, 157
Priam, 18
*Psalms, Hymns, and Spiritual Songs,
    The* (Watts), 70-71
Pyrrhus, 18

R

Ramona (Jackson), 168
Ransom, John Crowe, 1, 7
Raymond, Marcel, 87
Reeves, James, 4
Renaissance, 146
Representative Men (Emerson), 162
Restoration, 21, 46
Revelations, 106, 115
Richardson, Samuel, 48
Rilke, Rainer Maria, 81, 83, 143, 160
Rimbaud, Arthur, 141
Romanticism, **45-50**, 138-40
Root, Abiah, 129
Rossetti, Christina, 9
Rusk, R. L., 104
Ruskin, John, 106

S

Sanborn, Franklin B., 169
Sappho, 47
Saturday Club, 112
Scarlet Letter, The (Hawthorne), 11
Scott, Sir Walter, 45, 118
Shakespeare, 5, 24, 25, 27, 118, 119,
    125, 126, 141, 145, 146, 166, 176
Shelley, Percy B., 25, 45, 47, 119,
    138, 139
Sidney, Sir Philip, 38
"Single Hound, The," 13
Single Hound, The (ed. Bianchi), 10, 28
Siris (Berkeley), 109
Skelton, John, 124
Slater, Samuel, 17
Springfield Republican, 10, 110, 113,
    160, 168

Stairway of Surprise (Anderson), 4
Standish, Miles, 43
Stylistic devices, 13, 15, 22, 26, 28-29, 32, 34, 36, 49, 75, 77, **78-87**, 89, 90-93, 102, 122-26, 145-49, **150-54** 159-61
"Success," 10
Surrey, Henry Howard, Earl of, 38
Sweetser, Catherine, 169
Swinburne, A. C., 45
Swift, Jonathan, 49

T

Taggard, Genevieve, 19
Tanto gentile e tanto onesta (Dante), 83
Tate, Allen, 2, 5, 8, 33, 35, 106, 119, 120, 125
Tempest, The (Shakespeare), 125
Tennyson, Alfred, Lord, 23, 24, 45, 47, 172
Thackrey, Donald, 2
"Thantopsis" (Bryant), 113
Themes, major:
    death, 14-15, 20-22, 26, 30, 32-33, 34, 42, 57, 58, 60, 63, 90, 113-16, 124-26, 156
    immortality, 20, 22, 31, 50, 66-67, 78, 96, 105, 134, 157
    nature, 10, 13, 20-21, 35, 48-49, 61, 62, 63, 77, 93, 112, 116, 124, 132, 133
    privation, 35, 74, 81, 84-85, 104, 115, 130-133, 135-36, 155-56, 158
    silence, 61-65, 66, 69
    soul, 33-34, 60, 93, 95, 96, 116
    words, 53, 54, 55, 56, 57, 58, 59, 62, 63, 66, 142
"There is a Land of Pure Delight" (Watts), 104-5
This Was a Poet (Whicher), 2
Thoreau, Henry David, 11, 12, 112, 169
Todd, Mabel Loomis, 101, 163, 169, 170, 176
Toscanini, Arturo, 80
Traherne, Thomas, 132
Tramp Abroad, A (Twain), 44
Transcendentalism, 12, 139

Twain, Mark, 41, 44

U

Underhill, Evelyn, 137
Unpublished Poems of Emily Dickinson (Bianchi and Hampson), 105
"Uriel" (Emerson), 148

V

Vaughan, Henry, 23, 138
Versification, 15, 28-29, 38-39, 70-77, 99, 104-5, 151
Very, Jones, 32
Villon, François, 25
Virgil, 119

W

Wadsworth, Rev. Charles, 5, 110, 168
Walden (Thoreau), 11
Ward, Theodora, 1, 6
Warren, Austin, 1, 2, 3
Warren, Robert Penn, 18
Watts, Isaac, 70, 71, 99, 104-5, 127
Webster, Noah, 144, 169
Wells, Henry, 2
Wesley, John, 84
Whicher, George F., 2, 128, 129, 173
Whitman, Walt, 11, 27, 98, 104, 112, 147
Whitney, Maria, 169
Whitney, William Dwight, 169
Wilbur, Richard, 4, 153
Williams, Oscar, 86
Winters, Yvor, 2, 4, 6-7, 122
Woman's Journal, The (Phelps), 170
Women of Trachis, The (trans. Pound), 157
Wordsworth, William, 97, 138, 139
Wuthering Heights (Brontë), 120

Y

Years and Hours of Emily Dickinson, The (Leyda), 2
Yeats, W. B., 7, 97, 117, 157

JOHN DONNE

A Collection of Critical Essays

Edited by HELEN GARDNER

A

Addison, Joseph, 3, 35
"Air and Angels," 12, 79, **171-79**
Allegory of Love (Lewis), 9
Alma, or the Progress of the Mind
  (Prior), 16
Amores (Ovid), 27
Anatomy of the World, An, 17, 67, 87,
  154-61, 162, 165, 166, 169 *(see also*
  First Anniversary, The)
Anglicanism *(see* Religious beliefs, in
  the Divine Poems)
Anniversaries (see First Anniversary,
  The; Second Anniversary, The)
"Anniversary, The," 31-32, 33, 34, 50,
  93
"Apparition, The," 28, 94
  dramatic elements in, 37-38
Arezzo, Guittone d', 69
Astraea Redux (Dryden), 18
Astronomy, metaphors of, in *The First*
  Anniversary, 158-60
Astrophel and Stella (Sidney), 42-43,
  68, 124n
Audi Filia (Avila), 163
Augustine, Saint, 170
Avila, Juan de, 163

B

Baudelaire, Charles, 5
Bedford, Countess of, 18, 149
Bembo, Cardinal, 25

Bennett, Joan, 9, 11
Bernard, Saint, doctrines of, in the
  Anniversaries, 156, 159, 163-70
  passim
Biathanatos, 125, 137, 138
Book of Common Prayer, The, 156
"Bracelet, The," 28
Brahe, Tycho, 68
"Break of Day," 39-40
Brooke, Rupert, 5-6
Brooks, Cleanth, 9
Browne, Sir Thomas, 137
Browning, Robert, 6-7, 30, 31, 50-51,
  73
Bruno, Giordano, 70n
Burns, Robert, 29-30, 31, 32
Business of Criticism, The (Gardner),
  11
Byron, George Gordon, 4

C

"Calm, The," 2, 18
"Canonization, The," 20, 33, 42-46,
  50-51, 80, 122
  paradox in, 100-108
  satire in, 43-44
Carew, Thomas, 2, 97-98, 111, 116
Castara (Habington), 34
Catullus, 29-30, 31, 32, 94
Cavalcanti, Guido, 23, 65
Chambers, E. K., 5
Chapman, George, 66-67, 71-72, 86
"Character of a Dunce, The," 137-38

Cleveland, John, 3
Coffin, Charles Monroe, 166
Coleridge, Samuel Taylor, 4, 34, 106-7, 142
Colin Clout's Come Home Again (Spenser), 62
"Come into the garden, Maude" (Browning), 50
"Community," 84
"Contre les Pétrarquistes" (Du Bellay), 71
Copernicus, Nicolaus, 68
"Corona, La," 123-33 *passim*
Coronation, The (Dryden), 18
Coryat, Thomas, 110
Cowley, Abraham, 111, 112-13
Crashaw, Richard, 58, 65, 99, 115, 117
Crofts, J. E. V., 1, 9
"Cross, The," 76, 94, 123
Crudities (Coryat), 110

D

"Damp, The," 47
Dante, 14, 23-24, 26, 33, 65
Danvers, Magdalen, 149
"Definition of Love, The" (Marvell), 117
De Quincey, Thomas, 4
Devereux, Robert, 28, 57
Digby, Kenelm, 34
Divine Poems, 4, 14, 18-19, 37n, 58, 74-76, 123-36 and *Songs and Sonnets,* 134-36
Donne, John:
    and Browning, Robert, 6-7, 30, 31, 50-51, 73
    and Chapman, George, 66-67, 71-72, 86
    and his contemporaries, 61-76, 97-99, 109-22, 126-29, 137
    and Dante, 14, 23-24, 26, 33, 65
    and Drayton, Michael, 29, 68
    and Dryden, John, 18, 45, 83, 112-13, 116
    early criticism of, 1-2
    and Egerton, Sir Thomas, 33, 81

    eighteenth-century views of, 14-16, 83-84
    and Elizabeth I, 78-79, 81
    and Elizabethan love poetry, 26-29, 32-33, 62-64, 113-15, 173
    and Herbert, George, 11, 86, 99, 116-17, 122, 135-36
    and Horace, 38-39, 117-21
    and Jonson, Ben, 2, 34, 37n, 67, 110-22, 154
    and Marlowe, Christopher, 27, 66, 71-72
    and Marvell, Andrew, 34, 98-99, 117
    and the medieval love poets, 23-24, 32-34, 65, 90, 93
    and medieval philosophy, 68-71, 116
    and Michelangelo, 74-76
    and Milton, John, 28, 35, 38, 79, 112-14, 137
    and More, Anne, 5, 81
    nineteenth-century views of, 4-5
    and Ovid, 27-28, 29, 124n
    and the Petrarchan tradition, 24-25, 26, 64-71, 97, 103, 115, 152, 154-55, 156, 164, 168, 173, 175
    poetic techniques of, 85-86, 124-25, 131-32
    religious beliefs, 123-36, 147-48, 152-70 (*see also* main entry)
    scientific interests of, 10, 68, 158-60
    seventeenth-century influences on, 77-89, 109-22
    and Shakespeare, William, 27, 29, 33, 40, 64, 66, 71-72, 106, 107-8, 113, 115
    and Sidney, Sir Philip, 27, 28, 33, 42-43, 64, 68-69, 71, 124-25
    and Spenser, Edmund, 9, 18, 27, 28, 33, 113, 114-15, 173
    thought and sensibility of, 86-89
    "Wit" of, 2-4, 6-12, 23, 85-86, 96, 116, 172-73, 175-79
    and women, conception of, 79-82
    (*see also* Donne, and the Petrarchan tradition)

Donne, John, works by:
  editions of, 2-3, 5
  POETRY
    Divine Poems, 4, 14, 18-19, 37*n*, 58,
      74-76, 123-36
    Elegies, 14, 18, 31, 35, 36*n*, 37*n*,
      92, 94
    Epithalamions, 18, 33, 38, 149
    Epistles, 18, 37*n*, 95, 117-18
    First Anniversary, The, 72-73, 95,
      110, **152-60**
    "Holy Sonnets," 37*n*, 58, 74-76, 93,
      128-32, 133, 135, 146
    Satires, 2, 3, 5, 14, 15-16, 38, 77-
      79, 131
    Second Anniversary, The, 5, 17-18,
      84, 87, 95, 110, **160-170**
    Songs and Sonnets, 4, **19-22**, 31-32,
      52-60, **61-72**, 79-81, 83-86, 88-
      89, 92-95, 116-17, 134-36 (*see
      also* main entry)
  PROSE
    Bianthanatos, 125, 137, 138
    "Character of a Dunce, The,"
      137-38
    Essays in Divinity, 137, 138, 167,
      170
    Ignatius his Conclave, 137, 138
    Paradoxes and Problems, 138, 142,
      166
    Pseudo-Martyr, 125, 138
    Sermons, 10-11, 37*n*, 82, 130, 134,
      137-51 (*see also* main entry)
Donne, Lucy, 149
Donne the Craftsman (Legouis), 8
Dramatic elements in *Songs and Son-
  nets*, 116-17
Drayton, Michael, 29, 68, 114
"Dream, The, 20, 22, 48-50, 63-65
Drummond of Hawthornden, William,
  111-12
Drury, Elizabeth, 110
  and the *Anniversaries*, 152-55, 157,
    160, 166
Drury, Sir Robert, 152
Dryden, John, 3, 7, 15, 18, 45, 83,
  112-13, 116
Du Bellay, Guillaume, 71

E

"Ectasy, The," 8, 22, 33-34, 50, 70,
  92-93, 177
Egerton, Sir Thomas, 33, 81
Eighteenth-century views, of Donne's
  works, 14-16, 83-84
Elegies, 14, 18, 31, 35, 36*n*, 37*n*, 92,
  94
Eliot, T. S., 1, 6-8, 9, 11, 65-66, 171
Elizabeth I, 78-79, 81
Elizabethan love poetry, influence of,
  on Donne's works, 26-29, 32-33, 62-
  64, 113-15, 173
Empson, William, 9, 155, 174
England's Helicon, 113
Epistles, 18, 37*n*, 95, 117-18
Epithalamions, 18, 33, 38, 149
Essay of Dramatick Poesy (Dryden), 3
Essays in Divinity, 137, 138, 167, 170
Essex (*see* Devereux, Robert)
Every Man in His Humour (Jonson),
  113

F

Faerie Queene, The (Spenser), 28, 114,
  173
"Fever, The," 72-73, 93
First Anniversary, The, 72-73, 95, 110,
  152-60
  scientific imagery in, 86
"Flea, The," 47-48
"Funeral, The," 88

G

Galilei, Galileo, 68
Gardner, Helen, 11
Georgics (Virgil), 120
Gilson, Etienne, 163, 165, 168
"Good Friday, Riding Westward," 130,
  132-33
"Good-morrow, The," 40-41, 93, 122,
  175
Gorges, Sir Arthur, 62-63
Gosse, Edmund, 5, 12, 28
Grierson, Sir Herbert, 1, 2, 5, 6, 8, 9,

Grierson, Sir Herbert (*continued*)
  53, 125, 129
Guinizelli, Guido, 65

H

Habington, William, 34
Hall, Joseph, 16
Hebrew poetry, influence of, in the
  Sermons, 138-40
Herbert, George, 11, 86, 99, 116-17,
  122, 135-36
Herbert of Cherbury, Edward, 6
Hero and Leander (Marlowe), 33
"Heroic Stanzas" (Dryden), 45
Herrick, Robert, 34, 115, 120
"His Picture," 28-29
Holmes, Elizabeth, 65, 67
"Holy Sonnets," 37n, 58, 74-76, 93,
  128-32, 133, 135, 146
Hooker, Richard, 137
Horace, 15, 38-39, 117-21
"Horatian Ode, An" (Marvell), 117
Hughes, Merritt Y., 10, 70n
Hunt, Leigh, 4
"Hymns," 129-30, 133, 134

I

Ignatius his Conclave, 137, 138
Imagery, 26-27
  in "Air and Angels," 171-79
  in "Canonization, The," 44-45,
    101-9
  scientific in *Songs and Sonnets*, 85-
    86
  in *Second Anniversary, The*, 164
  in the *Sermons*, 144-47
  in "Valedicton, A: of Weeping,"
    53-60
"Indifferent, The," 20, 80, 94
Interior Castle (St. Teresa), 170
Irony, use of, in the *Sermons*, 143-44

J

Johnson, Dr. Samuel, 3-4, 14, 135,
  145, 171, 173

Jonson, Ben, 2, 34, 37n, 67, 110-22,
  154
Juvenal, 15

K

Keats, John, 108
Kepler, Johannes, 68
Keynes, Geoffrey, 6

L

Lachrymae Lachrymarum, Donne's
  poetry in, 110
Lamb, Charles, 4
"Lamentations of Jeremy, The," 18-
  19, 132
"Last Ride Together, The" (Browning),
  50
"Lecture upon the Shadow, A," 94
Legouis, Pierre, 8
Leishman, J. B., 10
Letters (see *Epistles*)
Lewis, C. S., 1, 9
Life and Letters of John Donne
  (Gosse), 5
Life of Cowley (Johnson), 3
"Litany, The," 19, 125-29, 130
Lovelace, Richard, 97, 98, 111
"Lovers' infiniteness," 69, 122
"Love's Alchemy," 79, 80
"Love's Deity," 177
"Love's Exchange," 80
"Love's Usury," 94
Lowell, James Russell, 5
Luther, Martin, 91-92

M

McCarthy, Desmond, 6
Marlowe, Christopher, 27, 33, 66, 71-
  72
Marston, John, 16
Martz, Louis L., 11
Marvell, Andrew, 34, 98-99, 117
Massingham, H. J., 38
Medieval love poets, influence of, on
  Donne's works, 23-24, 32-34, 65, 90,

Medieval love poets, influence of, on Donne's works (*continued*) 93 (*see also* Petrarchan tradition)

Medieval philosophy, in Donne's works, 68-71, 116

"Message, The," 20

Metamorphoses (Ovid), 114

Metaphor (*see* Imagery)

Metaphysical poetry, 3-4, 6-8, 65 (*see also* Imagery; "Wit," in Donne's works)

Metaphysical Poetry, Donne to Butler (Grierson), 6

"Metaphysical Poets, The" (Eliot), 6-7

"Metempsychosis" (see *Progress of the Soul, The*)

Michelangelo Buonaroti, 74-76

Milton, John, 1, 7, 28, 35, 79, 112-14, 137

Monarch of Wit, The (Leishman), 10

More, Anne, 5, 81

More, Sir Thomas, 91-92

"My Last Duchess" (Browning), 50

N

"Negative Love," 83

New Criticism, and Donne's poetry, 9

Nineteenth-century views, of Donne's works, 4-5

"Nocturnal on St. Lucy's Day, A," 32

Norton, Charles Eliot, 5

O

Of the Progress of the Soul, 16, **160-170** (see also *Second Anniversary, The*)

Old Testament sources, in Donne's *Sermons*, 139-40, 148-51

Ovid, 27-28, 29, 114, 124*n*

P

Paracelsus, Philippus, 68

Paradise Lost (Milton), 79

Paradox:

in "Canonization, The," 100-108

in the *Sermons*, 142-43

in *Songs and Sonnets*, 116-17

Paradoxes and Problems, 138, 142, 166

"Perfume, The," 28

Persius, 15, 78

Petrarch, Francesco (*see* Petrarchan tradition, in Donne's works)

Petrarchan tradition, in Donne's works, 24-25, 26, 64-71, 97, 103, 115, 152, 154-55, 156, 164, 168, 173, 175 (*see also* Medieval love poets, influences of, on Donne's works)

"Phoenix and the Turtle, The" (Shakespeare), 107-8

Poetic techniques, 85-86, 124-25, 131-32 (*see also* Imagery; "Wit," in Donne's works)

Poly-olbion (Drayton), 114

Pope, Alexander, 3, 14-16, 35, 84, 121

Pound, Ezra, 172

Praz, Mario, 8, 46

"Primrose, being at Montgomery Castle, The," 85

Private Memoirs (Digby), 34

Progress of the Soul, The ("Metempsychosis"), 81-82, 95 (see also *Second Anniversary, The*)

"Prohibition, The," 31, 46-47

Pseudo-Martyr, 125, 138

Puritanism, in the seventeenth century, 91-92

R

Raleigh, Sir Walter, 28, 77

Rape of Lucrece, The (Shakespeare), 113, 114

Rape of the Lock, The (Pope), 35

"Relic, The," 22, 84

Religious beliefs, Donne's:

in the *Anniversaries*, 152-70

in the Divine Poems, 123-36

in the *Sermons*, 147-48

Rochester, Earl of (*see* Wilmot, John)

Roman Catholicism, in the seventeenth century, 91-92 (*see also* Religious beliefs, in the Divine Poems)
Romeo and Juliet (Shakespeare), 106
Ronsard, Pierre de, 25, 68

S

Saintsbury, George, 5
Sannazaro, 64, 72
Sappho, 29-30
Satire, in "The Canonization," 43-44
Satires, 2, 3, 5, 14, 15-16, 38, 77-79, 131
Sasso Panfilo, 68
Schoell, F. L., 67
Science, Donne's interest in, 10, 68, 158-60
Scourge of Villany, The (Marston), 16
Secentismo e Marinismo in Inghilterra (Praz), 8
Second Anniversary, The, 5, 17-18, 84, 87, 95, 110, **160-170**
Sermons, 10-11, 37*n*, 82, 130, 134, 137-51
    and Hebrew poetry, 138-40
    imagery in, 144-47
    irony and paradox in, 142-44
    Old Testament sources of, 139-40, 148-51
Seventeenth-century influences, on Donne's works, 77-89, 109-22
Shakespeare, William, 27, 29, 33, 40, 64, 71-72, 106, 107-8, 113, 115
Sidney, Sir Philip, 25, 27, 28, 33, 42-43, 63, 64, 68-69, 71, 124-25
Simpson, Evelyn, 11
Sitwell, Sir Osbert, 150
Smith, A. J., 11-12
"Song" ("Goe, and catche a fallinge starre"), 20, 94
"Song" ("Sweetest love, I do not goe"), 39, 41-42, 93
Songs and Sonnets, 4, **19-22**, 31-32, **52-60**, **61-72**, 79-81, 83-86, 88-89, 92-95, 116-17, 134-36 (*see also* titles of individual poems)

"Air and Angels," 171-79
"Canonization, The," 100-108
contemporary influences on, 61-72
and the Divine Poems, 134-36
dramatic elements in, 36-51, 116-17
imagery in, 85-86
paradox in, 100-108
"Valediction, A: of Weeping," 52-60
Sonnet form, Donne's use of, 124-25, 131-32
Southampton, Earl of, 28
Spenser, Edmund, 9, 18, 27, 28, 33, 62, 112, 113, 114-15, 173
Speroni, Sperone, 177-78
"Storm, The," 18
Suckling, Sir John, 97, 111, 115
"Sun Rising, The," 40

T

Table-talk (Luther), 91-92
Taylor, Jeremy, 137
"Tears of Peace" (Chapman), 67
Temple, The (Herbert), 86
Tennyson, Alfred, 114
Teresa, Saint, 170
Theatrical metaphors, in *Songs and Sonnets*, 37-38
"To His Coy Mistress" (Marvell), 98-99, 117
"To Laura in Death" (Petrarch), 154-55
"To Lucasta, going beyond the Seas" (Lovelace), 97, 98
"Too Late" (Browning), 50
"To Sir Robert Wroth" (Jonson), 119-21
"To the World: a farewell" (Jonson), 119
Tourneur, Cyril, 67
Transformed Metamorphosis (Tourneur), 67
Troilus and Cressida (Shakespeare), 66
Tuve, Rosemond, 10, 174

U

"Undertaking, The," 92

V

"Valediction, A: forbidding Mourning," 39, 92
"Valediction, A: of my Name in the Window," 39
"Valediction, A: of the Book," 39
"Valediction, A: of Weeping," 39, 52-60, 89
Vaughan, Henry, 115, 117, 122
Venus and Adonis (Shakespeare), 33, 113, 114
Virgidemiarum (Hall), 16
Virgil, 120
Volpone (Jonson), 115

W

Walton, Izaac, 4-5
Watson, Thomas, 61-62

Webster, John, 67, 126-29
"Weeper, The" (Crashaw), 65
"When thou, poor Excommunicant" (Carew), 97-98
"Will, The," 149
Wilmot, John, Earl of Rochester, 34
"Wit," in Donne's works, 2-4, 6-12, 23, 85-86, 96, 116
   in "Air and Angels," 172-73, 175-79
   and verse form, 85-86
"Woman's Constancy," 94
Women, Donne's conception of, 79-82
   (see also Petrarchan tradition, in Donne's works)
Wordsworth, William, 134-35
Wyatt, Sir Thomas, 69-70

Y

Yeats, William Butler, 6

DOSTOEVSKY

A Collection of Critical Essays
Edited by RENÉ WELLEK

A

Acis and Galathea (Lorrain), 158
Aksakov, Sergei, 54
Alexander the Great, 34
Alexander II, 37, 67
Alexander III, 59
American Tragedy, An (Dreiser), 13
Anna Karenina (Tolstoy), 147, 152
Antichrist, Der (Nietzche), 36
Apokalypse der deutschen Seele
  (Balthasar), 9
Araktcheyev, Alexis, 33
Archimedes, 150
Aristotle, 74

B

Bakhtin, M. M., 5
Bakunin, Mikhail, 33
Balthasar, Hans Urs von, 9
Balzac, Honoré de, 7, 28-31, 33, 114,
  147-50, 154
Baring, Maurice, 11
Barth, Karl, 8
Bauer, Bruno, 122
Belinsky, Vissarion, 1, 112, 131
Bennett, Arnold, 11
Bentham, Jeremy, 50
Berdyaev, Nikolai, 5, 12, 73, 133, 135,
  143, 159, 163, 169-70
Bergson, Henri, 18
Bernard, Claude, 76, 81, 87, 88
Beyle, Marie Henri (*pseud.* Stendhal),

29, 61, 147-48
Blackmur, R. P., 14, 56
Blake, William, 13
Blick ins Chaos (Hesse), 10
"Bobok," 8
Bonaparte, Napoleon, 21, 29, 34, 147-
  48
Bradley, Francis Herbert, 84
Brandes, Georg, 3
Bronze Horseman, The (Pushkin), 30
*Brothers Karamazov: Novelistic Tech-
  nique, The* (Matlaw), 14
Brothers Karamazov, The, 2, 4, 9, 10,
  11, 13, 40-41, **75-88**, 90-97, 98, 102,
  107-8, 117, 121-22, 124, 126-27,
  137, 141, 151, 154, 159, 166, 169
  characterization, 40-41, 75-79, 87-
    88
  double personality, theme of,
    121-22
  and ethical rationalism, 126-27
  human destiny, theme of, 87-89
  and human nature, concept of, 90-
    97
  and Jesus, 90-97
  and the liberal, concept of, 75-76
  parricide, theme of, 107-8
  religious aspects of, 80-86
  and the Spanish Inquisition, 93-94,
    97
  and the unconscious, concept of,
    76-78 (*see also* double personality,
    theme of)
Bruck, Arthur Möller, van den, 9

Bryusov, Valeri, 5
Bukharev, Archimandrite, 142
Bulgakov, Mikhail, 143
Byron, George Gordon, 168

C

Caesar, Julius, 34, 85, 93, 95
Camus, Albert, 8, 49
Carlyle, Thomas, 69
Carr, E. H., 12, 13
Carus, Carl, 7
Catechism of the Revolutionist
   (Nechaev), 60
Cervantes, Miguel de, 6, 44-45, 70
Characters of Dostoevsky (Curle), 12
Chekhov, Anton, 147
Chernov, Viktor, 113
Chernyshevsky, Nikolay, 28, 53, 134,
   139
Chizhevsky, Dmitri, 5-6
Claudel, Paul, 7
Conrad Joseph, 10
Cook, Albert, 14
Creation and Discovery (Vivas), 14
Crime and Punishment, 2-4, 10, 11, 13,
   16-38, 83, 116, 139, 148-49, 153,
   160, 169
   and Balzac, Honoré de, 148-49
   characterization, 24-27
   development of, 23-26
   and French literature, 28-30
   and Hegel, Georg, 33-34
   indeterminate characterization,
      concept of, 21-22
   narrative technique of, 16-19
   political aspects of, 34-37
   realism of, 27-28
   and Saint Petersburg, 30-33
   self-motivation, theme of, 19-23
   time, concept of, 17-18
"Cruel Talent, A" (Mikhailovsky), 2
Curle, Richard, 12
Custine, Marquis de, 32

D

Dante, 6, 153

Dark Forest, The (Walpole), 12
Dead Souls, The (Gogol), 112
Defense de l'Occident (Massis), 8
Defoe, Daniel, 153
Devil in Dr. Faustus, The (Leverkühn),
   10
Dewey, John, 81, 87, 88
Diary of a Writer, The, 113, 123, 131,
   136-37, 139, 143, 163
Dickens, Charles, 7, 10, 24, 28, 31,
   114, 153
Dobrolyubov, Nikolay, 1, 28, 123
Dolinin, A. A., 4
Donne, John, 162, 170
Don Quixote (Cervantes), 44, 70
Dostoevsky (Gide), 7
Dostoevsky (Mochulsky), 6
Dostoevsky (Zander), 6
"Dostoevsky and Dickens" (Futrell), 13
Dostoevsky and His Creation (Lavrin),
   12
Dostoevsky and Nietzche (Shestov), 3
Dostoevsky, Andrey, 102
Dostoevsky, Fyodor:
   anthropology of, 132-38
   antirationalism of, 79-80, 83, 87-89
   and Balzac, Honoré de, 28-30, 147-
      50
   critical attitudes toward, 1-15
   and the double personality, concept
      of, 112-29
   and epilepsy, 100-108
   and ethical rationalism, 124-29
   and freedom, concept of, 135-38,
      140, 143-44
   and Freud, Sigmund, 76-78
   and gambling, concept of, 108-11
   literary influence of, 8-10, 12-13
   metaphysical development, in works
      of, 165-71
   mysticism of, 162-65
   philosophy of, 71-74, 122-29, 138-
      45
   politics of, 55-57, 59-70
   psychology of, 98-111
   realism of, 152-55
   and religion, 72-73, 80-86, 130-132,
      138, 142-45

Dostoevsky, Fyodor: (*continued*)
and the Roman Catholic Church,
163-64
and the Russian "Enlightenment,"
123-24
and Saint Petersburg, 153-55
and self-knowledge, theme of,
149-52
and sense experience, use of, 160-
161
and the slavophiles, 54-55
and solitude, theme of, 150-152,
154-58
and Western literature, 155-56
Doestoevsky, Fyodor, works by:
"Bobok," 8
Brothers Karamazov, The, 2, 4, 9,
10, 11, 13, 40-41, 75-88, 90-97,
98, 102, 107-8, 117, 121-22, 124,
126-27, 137, 141, 151, 154, 159,
166, 169
Crime and Punishment, 2-4, 10, 11,
13, 16-38, 83, 116, 139, 148-49,
153, 160, 169
Diary of a Writer, The, 113, 123,
131, 136-37, 139, 143, 163
Double, The, 1, 112-16, 124
"Dream of a Ridiculous Man," 137
Drunkards, The, 24
Eternal Husband, The, 7
Faint Heart, The, 116
"Fragment of Novel Shchedroda-
rov," 123-24
Gambler, The, 13, 152
Grand Inquisitor, The, 2, 9, 12, 14,
123, 138, 143
House of the Dead, The, 10, 136,
152
Idiot, The, 16, 39-52, 83, 136, 150-
151, 157, 159-60, 162-64, 166-68
Insulted and the Injured, The, 1, 3,
10, 25, 26, 153
Landlady, The, 24, 114
Mr. Prokharchin, 116
Notes from the Underground, 3, 37,
83, 88-89, 134-35, 139, 150, 153
Petersburg Chronicle, The, 116
Poor People, 1, 10, 25

Possessed, The, 2, 4, 11, 56, 57-70,
71-73, 81, 83, 117-21, 123, 124,
137-38, 141-43, 150-151, 154,
160-161, 165, 167-69
Raw Youth, A, 16, 57, 117, 137,
150, 152
White Nights, 24, 116
"Winter Notes on Summer Impressions," 140
"Dostoevsky—in Moderation" (Mann),
6-7
Dostoevsky, Mikhail, 34, 112-13
Dostoevsky, The Making of a Novelist
(Simmons), 13
Dostoevsky's World-view (Prager), 8
Double personality, theme of:
in *Brothers Karamazov, The,* 76-78,
121-22 (see also *Brothers Karamazov, The,* unconscious, concept
of)
in *Double, The,* 112-16
in *Idiot, The,* 42-46
in *Possessed, The,* 117-21
Double, The, 1, 112-16, 124
development of, 112-13
double personality, theme of,
112-16
"Dream of a Ridiculous Man," 137
Dreiser, Theodore, 13
Drunkards, The, 24

E

Eliot, T. S., 57
Emerson, Ralph Waldo, 147
Ernst, Max, 9
Essays on Russian Novelists (Phelps),
11
Eternal Husband, The, 7
Euclid, 121
Eugenie Grandet (Balzac), 147
Evgeni Onegin (Pushkin), 147

F

Faint Heart, The, 116
Fall, The (Camus), 49
Faulkner, William, 13

Faust (Goethe), 159
Feuerbach, Ludwig Andreas, 122, 128
Fichte, Immanuel, 125-26, 128
Flaubert, Gustave, 154
Fourier, François, 57, 87, 139
"Fragment of a Novel Shchedrodarov,"
    123-24
Frank, Joseph, 14
Freedom and the Tragic Life (Ivanov),
    5
Freud, Sigmund, 9, 71, 72, 74, 76-78,
    103
Futrell, Michael H., 13
Fyodor Dostoevsky (Murry), 11
Fyodorov, N. F., 140

G

Galsworthy, John, 10
Gambler, The, 13, 152
Garnett, Constance, 10, 16
Gibian, George, 14
Gide, André, 7
Gissing, George, 10
Gnostics, 164
Goethe, Johann, 147, 149, 159
Gogol, Nikolai, 10, 30, 54, 112, 114,
    124, 144
Goncharov, Ivan, 27
Goncourt, Edmond de, 155
Gorky, Maxim, 4, 154
Grand Inquisitor, The, 2, 9, 12, 14,
    123, 138, 143
Griboyedov, Aleksandr, 54
Grigoryev, A., 141, 143
Grossman, Leonid, 4
*Grundlegung zu einer Metaphysik der
    Sitten* (Kant), 125
Guardini, Romano, 8

H

Hamlet (Shakespeare), 107
Hauser, Arnold, 31, 70
Hegel, Georg, 7, 33-34, 122-23, 125,
    128
Hehn, Victor, 2
Heidegger, Martin, 123

Helmholtz, Hermann, 100
Hennequin, Emile, 3
Herder, Johann, 143
Hero of Our Time, A (Lermontov), 62
Herzen, Alexander, 33, 55, 134, 143
Hesse, Herman, 10
*History of Nineteenth Century Litera-
    ture* (Saintsbury), 10
History of Russian Literature (Mirsky),
    12
History of Russian Philosophy (Zen-
    kovsky), 6
Hoffman, E. T. A., 7, 28, 114
Homer, 123
Homme revolté, L' (Camus), 8
House of the Dead, The, 10, 136, 152
Howe, Irving, 14
Hugo, Victor, 7, 138
Huis clos (Sartre), 8
Huneker, James, 13
Huxley, Aldous, 12

I

Ibsen, Henrik, 7, 147, 154
Idiot, The, 16, 39-52, 83, 136, 150-
    151, 157, 159-60, 162-64, 166-68
    characterization, 40-52, 166-67
    and *Don Quixote* (Cervantes),
        44-45
    double personality, theme of, 42-46
    mysticism in, 162-64
Impressions of Russia (Brandes), 3
Insulted and the Injured, The, 1, 3, 10,
    25, 26, 153
Ivanov, Vyacheslav, 5, 12
Ivory Apes and Peacocks (Huneker),
    13

J

Jackson, Robert L., 14
James, Henry, 10, 14, 66, 71
Jarrett-Kerr, Martin, 13
Jesus, 37, 40, 85, 90-97
John of the Cross, Saint, 163
Justification of the Good? (Solovyov),
    140

K

Kafka, Franz, 10, 72
Kant, Immanuel, 125-26, 128, 137
Kavelin, Konstantin, 134, 139
Khomyakov, Aleksei, 32
Kierkegaard, Sören, 64, 72, 80, 88, 122-24, 126
Krieger, Murray, 14

L

Landlady, The, 24, 114
Landmarks in Russian Literature (Baring), 11
Lauth, Reinhard, 8
Lavrin, Janko, 12
Lavrov, Pëtr, 134
Lawrence, D. H., 11-12
Leiden des Jungen Werthers, Die (Goethe), 149
Lenin, V. I., 22, 92, 94
Leonov, Leonid, 5
Lermontov, Mikhail, 12, 62
Leskov, Nikolai, 54
Leverkühn, Adrian, 10
Life of Dostoevsky (Nötzell), 8
Lorrain, Claude, 158
Loyola, Ignatius, 60
Lukács, Georg, 4, 29

M

Maceina, Antanas, 8
Machiavelli, Niccolò, 60
Maikov, Apolloni Nikolaevich, 157
Maistre, Joseph de, 33
Malraux, André, 8
Malte Laurids Brigge (Rilke), 9
Manichaeans, 164
Mann, Thomas, 6-7, 10, 43
Mansfield, Katherine, 12
Markheim (Stevenson), 10
Marvell, Andrew, 162
"Marx-Dostoevsky Duel, The" (Moravia), 35
Marx, Karl, 4, 6, 14, 35, 57, 69, 87, 123, 144

Massis, Henri, 8
Matlaw, Ralph, 14
Mauriac, François, 8
McCullers, Carson, 13
Meaning of Fiction, The (Cook), 14
Merezhkovsky, Dmitri, 3, 11
Mikhailovsky, Nikolay, 2, 134, 143
Milton, John, 6, 83
Mirsky, D. S., 11, 12
Mochulsky, Konstantin, 6, 17
Moll Flanders (Defoe), 153
Moore, George, 10
Moravia, Alberto, 35
Mr. Prokharchin, 116
Murry, Middleton, 11-12, 13, 90
Mussolini, Benito, 92
My Past and My Thoughts (Herzen), 33
Myth of Sisyphus, The (Camus), 8

N

Natorp, Paul, 8
Nechaev, Sergey, 60-61, 66
Nicholas I, 124
Nicholas II, 67
Nietzsche, Friedrich, 3, 7, 34, 36, 62, 65, 69, 77, 88, 123-26, 128
Nose, The (Gogol), 112
Notes from the Underground, 3, 37, 83, 88-89, 134-35, 139, 150, 153
Notzel, Karl, 8

O

Oedipus Rex (Sophocles), 107
Outsider, The (Wilson), 13
"Overcoat, The" (Gogol), 30, 112

P

Pascal, Blaise, 6
Paul, Saint, 57
Péguy, Charles, 7
Père Goriot, Le (Balzac), 29-30, 148
Petersburg Chronicle, The, 116
Peter the Great, 32

Phelps, William Lyon,
    10-11
Philippe, Charles-Louis, 8
Philosophie Dostojewskis, Die (Lauth),
    8
Philosophy of History (Hegel), 34
Phoenix and the Spider, The (Poggioli),
    14
Pisarev, Dmitri, 1-2, 28
Poggioli, Renato, 14
Point Counter Point (Huxley), 12
Politics and the Novel (Howe), 14
Poor People, 1, 10, 25
Possessed, The, 2, 4, 11, 56, 57-70, 71-
    73, 81, 83, 117-21, 123, 124, 137-38,
    141-43, 150-151, 154, 160-161, 165,
    167-69
    characterization, 62-70, 168-69
    double personality, theme of,
        117-21
    historical sources of, 60-61
    politics of, 59-70
    Russian society, theme of, 58-59
Prager, Hans, 8
Praz, Mario, 13
Prisonnière, La (Proust), 8
Problems of Dostoevsky's Writings
    (Bakhtin), 5
Proust, Marcel, 7-8, 16, 155
Pugachev, Emelian, 33
Pushkin, Aleksander, 12, 30, 123, 143,
    147

R

Rahv, Philip, 14, 57
Raphael, 69
Raw Youth, A, 16, 57, 117, 137, 150,
    152
Reil, Johann, 7
Richardson, Samuel, 149
Rilke, Rainer Maria, 9
Rivière, Jacques, 7
Rolland, Romain, 7
Roman russe, Le (Vogué), 2, 10
Rousseau, Jean Jacques, 29, 57, 137,
    139, 149
Rozanov, V. V., 2, 123

S

Saintsbury, George, 10
Saint-Simon, Claude Henri, 57
Sanctuary (Faulkner), 13
Sand, George, 57, 139
Sartre, Jean Paul, 8
Saurat, Denis, 8
Savage, D. S., 13
Schelling, Friedrich, 7, 143
Schiller, Johann, 24, 128, 141
Schnitzler, Arthur, 156
Schopenhauer, Arthur, 88
Secret City, The (Walpole), 12
Shakespeare, William, 2, 69, 76, 98,
    107, 161, 170
Shestov, Leo, 3, 11, 12, 132
Simmel, Georg, 125
Simmons, E. J., 13, 80
Smoke (Turgenev), 58
Soirées de St. Pétersburg (Maistre), 33
Solovyov, Vladimir, 2, 140, 144
Sophocles, 107
Spenser, Herbert, 45
Spinoza, Baruch, 86
Stalin, Joseph, 4, 67
Steiner, George, 14
Stendhal (Beyle, Marie Henri), 29, 61,
    147-48
Steppenwolf (Hesse), 10
Stevenson, Robert Louis, 10
Stirner, Max, 122, 126, 128
Studies in Literature and Belief
    (Jarrett-Kerr), 13
Suarez, André, 8
Sue, Marie Joseph, 28
Suslova, Appolinaria, 2
Swift, Jonathan, 58

T

"Theme of the Double, The" (Chizhev-
    sky), 6
Thurneysen, Eduard, 8
Tillich, Paul, 123, 128
Tolstoy and Dostoevsky (Merezhkov-
    sky), 3
Tolstoy, Leo N., 2, 4, 7, 10, 11, 12,

Tolstoy, Leo N., (*continued*)
14, 27, 54, 147, 152-55
*Tolstoy or Dostoevsky: An Essay in
the Old Criticism* (Steiner), 14
Totem and Taboo (Freud), 103
Tragic Vision, The (Krieger), 14
Traversi, Derek, 13
Troilus and Cressida (Shakespeare),
161
Turgenev, Ivan, 2, 10, 11, 13, 27, 54,
55, 58, 153

U

Underground Man in Russian Literature
(Jackson), 14

V

Verwirrung der Gefühle, Die (Zweig),
109
"Vierundzwanzig Stunden aus dem
Leben einer Frau" (Zweig),
109-10
Vivas, Eliseo, 14, 41
Vogué, Count Melchoir de, 2, 10,
13

W

Walpole, Hugh, 12
Wassermann, Jacob, 10
"Wer denkt abstrakt?" (Hegel), 125
Werfel, Franz, 10
White Nights, 24, 116
Wilde, Oscar, 10
Wilson, Colin, 13
"Winter Notes on Summer Impres-
sions," 140
Women in Love (Lawrence), 12
World View of Dostoevsky, The
(Berdyaev), 5

Y

Yarmolinsky, Avrahm, 13

Z

Zadonsky, Tikhon, 7
Zander, L. A., 6
Zenkovsky, V. V., 6
Zhelyabov, Andrey, 36-37
Zola, Émile, 2
Zweig, Stefan, 109-10

DREISER

A Collection of Critical Essays

Edited by JOHN LYDENBERG

A

Addams, Dr. Jane, 76
"Advance of the English Novel, The"
  (Phelps), 73-74
Alden, Henry Mills, 58
Allen, James Lane, 78
*American Literary Naturalism: The
  Divided Stream* (Walcutt), 9
American Renaissance (Matthiessen),
  90
American Scholar, The, 171
American Tragedy, An, 3, 5, 8, 9, 16,
  30, 33, 34, 50, 93, 120-122, 128,
  131-40, 143, **145-52**, 154, 155-56,
  164, **165-70**, 172-73
  determinism and free-will, theme
    of, 121, 133, 138-40, 149-50
  morality in, 168-73
  naturalism in, 51, 145, 148, 151
  sex in, 50, 51, 133-34, 136-37,
    150-151, 165-67
  success in, 147-49
  transcendentalism in, 151-52
Anderson, Sherwood, 5, 12, 15, 24, 51
Anna Karenina (Tolstoy), 155
"Apparition of Mrs. Veal, The" (De
  Foe), 71
Aristotle, 97
Aristophanes, 73
Armour, Philip, 43
Atlantic Monthly, 60, 78
Atherton, Gertrude, 15
Austin, Mary, 15

Author's League of America, 78

B

Balzac, Honoré de, 66, 91, 109, 130,
  153
"Barbaric Naturalism of Mr. Dreiser,
  The" (Sherman), 8
Batuta, Ibn, 59
Beard, Charles Austin, 89
Bellow, Saul, 17, 156
Belasco, David, 15
Bennett, Arnold, 16, 76, 78
Berryman, John, 6
Billings, Josh, 73
Blade, 53
Bohemian, The, 46
Boni and Liveright, 60
Book About Myself, A, 28, 108
  determinism and free-will, theme
    of, 106
Bourne, Randolph, 8, 135
Boysen, H. H., 61
Boynton, H. W., 74
Brisbane, Arthur, 41
Brooks, Van Wyck, 15, 74
Brown, Grace, 132
Brustein, Robert, 153
Bryan, W. J., 61
Bulwark, The, 9, 17, 34, 53, **93-95**
  determinism and free-will, theme
    of, 102
  naturalism in, 126-28
  realism in, 90

Bulwark, The (continued)
  religion in, 94, 126-28
Bunyan, John, 64-65
Burgum, Edwin Berry, 90
Butterick magazines, 45, 62, 72
C
Carnegie, A. 44
Cather, Willa, 6
Century, The, 56, 78
Chambers, Robert W., 74
Chicago Globe, 40
Churchill, Winston, 78
Clift, Montgomery, 165
communism, 16, 17, 33-34, 105, 142
Communist Party, the, 34, 95, 153
Conrad, Joseph, 79, 97, 138, 148
Cowley, Malcolm, 8, 20
Crack-up, The, (Fitzgerald), 4
Crane, Stephen, 18, 24, 29, 45, 48, 51, 61, 111
Crawford, Marion, 74

D
Damnation of Theron Ware, The
  (Frederic), 61
Darrow, Clarence, 50
Darwin, Charles, 66
Davis, David Brion, 14
Davis, Richard Harding, 74
Dawn, 5
De Foe, Daniel, 71
Deland, Margret, 74
Delineator, The, 22, 24, 46
Dell, Floyd, 31
Determinism and free-will, theme of,
  97-98, 105-22, 143, 145, 166-70
  in *An American Tragedy*, 121, 133,
    138-40, 149-50
  in *The Bulwark*, 102
  in *The "Genius"*, 106, 119-20
  in *Hey, Rub-a-Dub-Dub; A Book of
    the Mystery and Terror and Won-
    der of Life*, 107
  in *Jennie Gerhardt*, 117
  in *Sister Carrie*, 111-13, 117
  in *The Stoic*, 125-26
Dickens, Charles, 156
Dos Passos, John, 6, 35, 170

Doubleday, Frank, 8, 13, 15, 58
Doubleday, Page & Co., 58, 59
Dream of Success (Lynn), 7
Dreiser, Theodore:
  anti-Semitism of, 16, 142, 163
  and Balzac, Honoré de, 66, 91, 109,
    130, 153
  and Bunyan, John, 64-65
  childhood of, 24, 37-39, 129, 154
  and communism, 16, 17, 33-34,
    105, 142
  and the Communist Party, 34, 95,
    153
  and Conrad, Joseph, 79, 97, 138,
    148
  and Crane, Stephen, 18, 24, 29, 45,
    48, 51, 61, 111
  determinism and free-will, theme
    of, 97-98, 102, 105-22, 106, 107,
    111-13, 117, 119-20, 124, 125-26,
    133, 138-40, 143, 145, 149-50,
    166-70
  and Durkheim, Emile, 143
  and Edison, T. A., 43, 44
  and Emerson, R. W., 28, 91, 104,
    153
  and Farrell, J. T., 16
  and Faulkner, William, 51
  and Fitzgerald, F. Scott, 4-5, 6, 144
  and Flaubert, Gustave, 57, 75, 147,
    170
  and Hardy, Thomas, 14, 112, 131
  and Hawthorne, N., 91, 153, 155
  and Howells, William Dean, 18, 24,
    29, 30, 35, 43, 60, 64
  and James, Henry, 1, 12, 14, 18, 29,
    30, 64, 87, 88-90, 141, 146, 148,
    156
  as journalist, 22, 24, 27, 32, 40-43
  and Lewis, Sinclair, 6, 16, 35, 55
  and Marden, Orison S., 43, 44
  materialism in, 4, 59
  money, theme of, 37, 74-76, 99,
    165
  morality in, 1-3, 5, 8, 9, 15, 25, 67,
    69-70, 73-81, 88, 92-95, 96-103,
    107-22, 156-61, 168-73
  naturalism in, 1, 3, 5, 8, 9, 14, 19,

Dreiser, Theodore (*continued*)
  20, 51, 56, 57, 61-62, **63-72**, 74-
  75, 102, 104, 105, 108-9, 111,
  116, 120-121, 125, 128, 145, 148,
  151, 154, 170
and Nietzsche, F., 75, 79, 80, 116,
  117, 120
Nobel Prize speech of, 16
and Norris, Frank, 4, 8, 12, 30, 35,
  56, 58, 59, 60, 61
religion in, 94, 126-28
in Russia, 16, 33
sex, theme of, 37, **45-51**, 52, 67,
  70-71, 74-76, 77, 82-83, 84, 100-
  101, 108, 141, 150-151, **158-61**,
  165-67
and Spencer, Herbert, 107, 108, 130
success, theme of, 4, 6, 7, 37, **38-44**,
  52, 98-100, **129-33**, 144, 147-49
and Thoreau, H. D., 1, 24, 28, 91
transcendentalism in, 1, 9, 19, 104,
  105, 151-52
and Twain, Mark, 24, 29, 45, 61,
  73, 74, 170, 171-73
and Whitman, W., 19, 24, 30, 87,
  153
and Zola, Émile, 1, 4, 30, 56, 59,
  66, 72, 75, 108, 113, 130, 131,
  170
Dreiser, Theodore, works by:
  American Tragedy, An, 3, 5, 8, 9,
  16, 30, 33, 34, 50, 93, 120-122,
  128, **131-40**, 143, **145-52**, 154,
  155-56, 164, **165-70**, 172-73
  Book About Myself, A, 28, 106,
  108
  Bulwark, The, 9, 17, 34, 53, 90,
  93-95, 102, 126-28
  Dawn, 5
  Financier, The, 3, 30, 64, 67, 71,
  74-76, 79, 84, 116-20, 121, 130-
  131, 141, 143
  "Genius", The, 4, 46, 51, 52, 64,
  68, 71, 76-78, 79, 119-20, 121-22,
  130-131
  *Hey, Rub-a-Dub-Dub; A Book of
  the Mystery and Terror and Wonder of Life,* 107, 108
  Hoosier Holiday, A, 78, 81, 84
  Jennie Gerhardt, 12, 20, 29, 49, 62,
  64, 69, 76, 92-93, 113-15, 117-18,
  128, 131-32, 143
  Sister Carrie, 1, 7, 8, 9, 12, 13-14,
  18, **56-62**, 64, 76, 100, **108-13**,
  117-18, 127, 131-32, 141, 153,
  154-62
  Stoic, The, 9, 17, 30, 34, 116, 122,
  124-26
  Titan, The, 3, 30, 64, 68, 71, 76,
  79, 84, **116-20**, **121-24**, 130-131,
  141
  Traveler At Forty, A, 4, 6, 32
Dreiser, John Paul, 37
Dresser, Paul, 25, 41, 47, 53, 62,
  129-30, 154
Dudley, Dorothy, 51, 57
Dumas, Alexander, 75
Durkheim, Emile, 143

E

Edison, T. A., 43, 44
Education of Henry Adams, The, 62
Eisenstein, Sergei, 16
Elias, Robert, 95
Eliot, George, 69
Eliot, T. S., 30, 146, 171
Emerson, R. W., 28, 91, 104, 153
"Essays on Modern Novelists"
  (Twain), 73
*Ev'ry Month. The Woman's Magazine
  of Literature & Popular Music,* 41-43

F

Farrell, James T., 16, 142
Faulkner, William, 51
"Feast of St. Friend, The" (Bennett),
  76
Ficke, Arthur Davidson, 81
Fiedler, Leslie, 7, 167
Field, Marshall, 43
Financier, The, 3, 30, 64, 79, 84,
  116-20, 121, 141, 143
  money, theme of, 71, 74-76
  morality in, 67, 118-19

Financier, The, (continued)
  naturalism in, 116
  sex, theme of, 71, **74-76**
  success, theme of, 130-131
Fitzgerald, F. Scott, 4-5, 6, 144
Flaubert, Gustave, 57, 75, 147, 170
Ford, Ford Madox, 16
Frederic, Harold, 29, 61
Freide, D., 5
Freud, S., 82
Fuller, Henry B., 61

G

Garland, Hamlin, 29, 35, 61
"Genius", The, 4, 52, 64, 68, 71, **76-78**, 79, 81, 121-22
  determinism and free-will, theme
    of, 106, 119-20
  morality in, 76-77, 119-20
  sex, theme of, 46, 51, 77, 83
  success, theme of, 103, 130-131
George, W. L., 78
Gilette, Chester, 132
Gilman, Lawrence, 78
Globe-Democrat, 40, 53
Globe, 53
Goethe, Johann Wolfgang von, 153
Great Tradition, The (Hicks), 89
Grosset and Dunlop, 59

H

Halleck, Ruben Post, 74
Holley, Marietta, 74
Hamilton, Clayton, 78
Harben, Will N., 74
Hardy, Thomas, 14, 112, 131
Harper & Brothers, 58, 59
Harper's Magazine, 58, 60
Harper's Monthly, 60
Harrison, Henry Sydnor, 74
Harvey, Colonel, 60
Hawthorne, N., 24, 91, 153, 155
"Heart of Darkness" (Conrad), 97
Hemingway, E., 6, 17
Henry, Arthur, 28, 53, 56
Henry, O., 74

Herne, James A., 61
Herrick, Robert, 30, 35
Hey, Rub-a-Dub-Dub; A Book of the Mystery and Terror and Wonder of Life,
  determinism and free-will, theme
    of, 107
  sex, theme of, 108
Hicks, Granville, 89, 90
Hiss, Alger, 17
"History of American Literature, A"
  (Halleck), 74
"History of American Literature Since 1870" (Pattee), 74
Holmes, O. W., 73
Hoosier Holiday, A, 78, 81, 84
Hope, Anthony, 43
Horses and Men (Anderson), 5, 24
Howe, I., 9, 29
Howells, W. D., 18, 24, 29, 30, 35, 43, 60, 64
Huckleberry Finn (Twain), 71-73
Huneker, James, 78
Huxley, T. H., 130

I

"Introduction to American Literature, An" (Pancoast), 74
Irving, Washington, 73
Ishmael, 22, 35

J

Jackson, Charles, 91
James, Henry, 1, 12, 14, 18, 29, 30, 64, 87, **88-90**, 141, 146, 148, 156
Jennie Gerhardt, 12, 20, 29, 62, 64, 92-93, **113-15**, 117-18, 128, 131-32, 143
  determinism and free-will, theme
    of, 117
  money, theme of, 76
  morality in, 69, 70, 113, 118
  sex, theme of, 49, 70, 76, 93, 100-101
  success, theme of, 103
Julius Caesar (Shakespeare), 138

K

Kazin, A., 7, 142, 163, 164
Kipling, R., 79

L

Lanier, Henry, 58
Lawrence, D. H., 51
Leaves of Grass (Whitman), 1
Leavis, F. R., 166
Lewis, Sinclair, 6, 16, 35, 55
Libby, Laura Jean, 45
Liberal Imagination, The (Trilling), 163
Lindsay, Vachel, 84
Liverwright, Horace, 54
London, Jack, 1, 116
Lord Jim (Conrad), 138
Lowell, Amy, 73, 81
Lynn, K., 7
Lyon, Harris Merton, 81

M

Mackaye, Percy, 78
Madame Bovary (Flaubert), 155
Maggie (Crane), 18, 30
Mann, Thomas, 91
Marden, Orison S., 43, 44
Marx, Leo, 171-73
Masters, Edgar Lee, 81, 153
Materialism, in Dreiser's works, 4, 59
    (*see also* Money, theme of)
Matthiessen, F. O., 17, 90, 94, 159,
    164,165
McCullagh, Joseph B., 53
McTeague (Norris), 56-58
Melville, H., 22, 24, 48
Memoirs of an American Citizen, The
    (Herrick), 30
Mencken, H. L., 1, 4, 8, 14, 15, 16, 23,
    46, 155
Meredith, G., 69
Mizener, A., 5
Moers, Ellen, 9
Moliére, 73
Money, theme of, 37, 74-76, 75, 99,
    165

Moore, George, 75
Morality, in Dreiser's works, 1, 2, 3, 5,
    8, 9, 15, 25, 67, 69-70, 73-81, 88,
    92-95, 96-103, 107-22, 156-61, 168-
    73
More, Paul Elmer, 16, 18
Morgan, J. P., 60
"Mr. Eliot, Mr. Trilling and Huckleberry
    Finn" (Leo Marx), 171
Muckraking, 29
"My Gal Sal" (Dresser), 25, 130
My Life with Dreiser (Richardson), 22

N

Naturalism, in Dreiser's works, 1, 3, 5,
    8, 9, 14, 19, 20, 51, 56, 57, 61-62,
    63-72, 74-75, 102, 104, 105, 108-9,
    111, 116, 120-121, 125, 128, 145,
    148, 151, 154, 170
Nation, The, 81
Nasby, Petroleum V., 73
New Republic, 78
New York Times Book Review, 90
New York World, 40, 42
Nietzsche, F., 75, 79, 80, 116, 117, 120
Nobel Prize, 16, 55
Norris, Frank, 4, 8, 12, 30, 35, 56, 58,
    59, 60, 61

O

Octopus, The (Norris), 56
Oppenheim, James, 54
Ouida, 45

P

Page, Walter Hines, 58
Pancoast, Henry S., 74
Parrington, V. L., 88, 90, 95
Pattee, Fred Lewis, 74
Phelps, William Lyon, 16, 73-74
Phillips, David Graham, 35
Pierre (Melville), 48
Pit, The (Norris), 61
"Plain Man and His Wife, The" (Ben-
    nett), 76
Poe, Edgar Allan, 24

Pot-Bouille (Zola), 75
Pound, Ezra, 15
Pushing to the Front, or, Success under Difficulties (Marden), 43

R

Rabelais, François, 73
Rahv, Philip, 146
"Reality in America" (Trilling), 18
Red Badge of Courage, The (Crane), 1
Reed, John, 15
Return of the Native (Hardy), 112
Richardson, Helen, 22, 73
Rise of American Civilization, The (Beard), 89
Rives, Amelie, 74
Rosenberg, Bernard, 143

S

Samuels, Charles Thomas, 9
Santayana, George, 90, 152
Scarlet Letter, The (Hawthorne), 154
Scribner's Magazine, 56
Sea Wolf, The (London), 116
Self-Help (Smiles), 39
Seven Arts, The (Brooks), 74
Sex, theme of, 37, **45-51**, 52, 67, 70-71, **74-76**, 77, 82-83, 84, 100-101, 108, 141, 150, 151, **158-61**, **165-67**
Shakespeare, 138
Sherman, Stewart, 5, 8, 15, 30, **74-76**
Shore Acres (Herne), 61
Sister Carrie, 1, 7, 8, 9, 12, 13-14, 18, 23, 28, 29, 30, 44, 47-49, 52, 53, 54, **56-62**, 64, **108-13**, 117-18, 127, 153, **154-62**
   determinism and free-will, theme of, 111-13, 117
   morality in, 110-13, 118, 156, 161
   naturalism in, 14, 111
   sex, theme of, 47-48, 67, 83, 100, 141, **158-61**
   success, theme of, 131-32
   transcendentalism in, 110
Smiles, Samuel, 39
Smith, F. Hopkinson, 74

Spencer, Herbert, 107, 108, 130
Spinoza, Baruch, 152
Stall, Dr. Sylvanus, 77
Steffens, Lincoln, 25, 72
Steinbeck, John, 35
Stevens, George, 165
Stoic, The, 9, 17, 30, 34, 116, 122, **124-26**
   determinism and free-will, theme of, 125-26
   transcendentalism in, 126
Success, theme of, 4, 6, 7, 37, 38-44, 52, **98-100**, 129-33, 144, **147-49**
Sumner, John S., 8, 15
Sumner, William Graham, 165

T

Tarkington, Booth, 78
Taylor, Elizabeth, 165
Tess of the d'Urbervilles (Hardy), 14, 131
Thackeray, W. M., 69
Thoreau, H. D., 1, 24, 28, 91
Titan, The, 3, 30, 64, 68, 79, 84, 116-20, 121-24, 141
   money, theme of, 71, 76
   morality in, 118-19
   naturalism in, 116
   sex, theme of, 71, 76
   success, theme of, 130-131
   transcendentalism in, 122-23
Transcendentalism, in Dreiser's works, 1, 9, 19, 104, 105, 151-52
Traveler at Forty, A, 4, 6, 32
Trilling, Lionel, 8, 18, 31, 135, 142, 163, 164, 165, 170, 171-73
Trollope, A., 69
Twain, Mark, 24, 29, 45, 61, 73, 74, 170, 171-73

V

Vivas, Eliseo, 19, 163

W

Walcutt, Charles, 9

Wallace, Lew, 74
Walpole, Hugh, 78
Ward, Artemus, 73
Warren, Robert Penn, 9, 155, 165,
    171, 172-73
Welles, H. G., 75, 78
Wharton, Edith, 29
Whitman, Walt, 19, 24, 30, 87, 153
Who's Who in America, 27, 43, 155
Willen, Gerald, 9
Wilson, Augusta E., 74
Wilson, Woodrow, 76

Wister, Owen, 74
Woolf, Virginia, 156
World, 57

Y

Yerkes, Charles T., 116

Z

Zola, Émile, 1, 4, 30, 56, 59, 66, 72,
    75, 108, 113, 130, 131, 170

DRYDEN

A Collection of Critical Essays
Edited by BERNARD N. SCHILLING

A

Absalom and Achitophel, 4, 5-6, 9, 45, 49, 51, 66-67, 68, 86, 117, 118-21, 123-24, 126
Addison, Joseph, 12, 50, 52, 53
Adonais (Shelley), 137
Aeneid (Virgil), 56, 59, 177
Alcander (Pope), 43
Alexander's Feast, 12, 65, 151, **156-64**
All for Love, 14, 58, 61-62, 63, 70, **86-94, 95-114,** 117
American, The (James), 142
Anglicanism, references to, 26, 48-49, 126
Annus Mirabilis, 49, 66, 86, 146
Anthony and Cleopatra (Shakespeare), 63, 91, 92, 95
Apology for the Discourse of Humane Reason, An (Warren), 129
Aristotle, 48, 71, 72-73, 74, 81, 144
Arnold, Matthew, 1, 2, 3, 11, 44, 116, 136
At a Solemn Musick (Milton), 65, 136
Astraea Redux, 45
Augustanism, references to, 2, 3, 50, 52, 53, 58, 60, 116, 136 (*see also* Classicism; Neoclassicism)
Aureng-Zebe, 14-15, 25-26, 45, 61, 62-63, 64, 87, 98

B

Bacon, Francis, 147

Beljame, Alexander, 49
Benson, A. C., 19
Biblical references, 5-6, 45, 47-51, 119-23, 176, 177-78, 180 (*see also* Anglicanism; Catholicism)
Biographical information, 4-5, 19, 20-21, 35-36, 39-42, 125-26, 165-66
Blake, William, 56
Blank verse, Dryden's use of, 56-57, 61-62, 93-94, 98-99
Boileau, Nicolas, 49-50
Boyle, Robert, 133-34
Bredvold, Louis, 4-5
Brower, Reuben, 4, 5
Burns, Robert, 117-18
Butler, Samuel, 50
Byron, George Gordon, 8

C

Campion, Thomas, 65
Camus, Albert, 166
Carew, Thomas, 48
Carlyle, Thomas, 145
Case, John, 157-58
Catholicism, references to, 5, 26, 27, 121
Catullus, 53
Chapman, George, 24, 59
Charleton, Dr., 71-85
Charron, Pierre, 27, 30
Chaucer, Geoffrey, 11, 44, 160, 174-76, 179, 180
Christie, W. D., 1-2

Churchill, Charles, 8
Cicero, 25
Classicism: (*see also* Augustanism;
  Neoclassicism)
    British, 2, 115, 141, 144-45, 172,
    174
    Continental, 44
    Greco-Roman, 48, 49, 50-51, 57,
    144-45, 177-78, 180
Clemens, Samuel, 10
Clifford, James, 2
Clifford, Martin, 128-29
Coleridge, Samuel Taylor, 115, 116,
  120
Congreve, William, 5, 29, 36, 87, 147,
  168, 169-73
Conquest of Granada, The, 56-57, 61,
  87, 88, 89, 146-47
Coriolanus (Shakespeare), 88
Corneille, Pierre, 15, 90
Cowley, Abraham, 10, 12, 43, 45, 52,
  65, 66, 136, 137, 158
Cowper, William, 8, 56
Crabbe, George, 8
Crashaw, Richard, 53, 65
Critical evaluation, of Dryden:
    in the eighteenth century, 6-7, 44,
    56, 135, 149, 155, 163
    in the nineteenth century, 1-3, 8-
    12, 16, 18-19, 136
Cromwell, Oliver, 31, 73-74, 81, 126,
  153

D

Dante Alighieri, 18, 59, 60
Davies, Sir John, 136, 139, 140, 146
Defense of an Essay of Dramatic Poesy,
  A, 22, 41, 86-87
Defence of Poetry (Shelley), 145
Defoe, Daniel, 39
Deism, references to, 28, 130, 141
Denham, John, 8, 24, 44, 53
Descartes, René, 130, 132
Discourse Concerning the Original and
  Progress of Satire, A, 19-20, 66, 68
Divine Comedy (Dante), 59
Dobrée, Bonamy, 17

Donne, John, 44, 56, 57, 59, 115, 116
Don Sebastian, 87
Dryden, John:
    biographical information, 4-5, 19,
    20-21, 35-36, 39-42, 125-26,
    165-66
    blank verse, use of, 56-57, 61-62,
    93-94, 98-99
    Classicism, influences of, 2, 44, 48,
    49, 50-51, 57, 115, 141, 144-45,
    172, 174, 177-78, 180
    Elizabethans, comparison with, 14,
    56, 57, 60, 63, 70, 91, 115-16,
    117, 141, 147, 168 (*see also*
    Renaissance)
    epic genre, use of, 22-23, 43, 45, 47,
    50-51, 121-23, 145
    European influences on, 43-54, 90-
    91
    heroic couplet, use of, 4, 45, 56, 58-
    59, 61, 65-66, 69, 74-75, 87, 98-
    99, 116
    heroic genre, use of, 22, 44, 45, 46,
    47, 51, 57, 61-62, 68, 87-94, 95-
    114, 121-24, 146-48
    and Johnson, Samuel, 2, 6-7, 8, 17,
    23-24, 26, 43, 44, 51, 52, 56, 57,
    58, 69, 149, 155, 163
    Metaphysical influences, 44-45, 52,
    56, 57, 58, 60, 65, 84, 115, 175,
    180
    and Milton, John, 11, 12, 15, 23,
    43, 44, 45, 49, 50-51, 52, 53, 56,
    57, 58, 65, 66, 115, 122-23, 127,
    142, 145, 166, 174, 180
    monarchy, influences of, 6, 20-21,
    51, 71-85, 121-23, 166-67, 170
    parody, use of, 10, 46-48, 49, 51
    philosophy, influences of, 22-23,
    27-30, **127-35**
    as poetic innovator, 4, 17, 45-47,
    55-56
    and Pope, Alexander, 2, 3, 5, 8, 11,
    12, 43-44, 52-54, 56, 58, 59,
    115-16, 120, 121-22, 135, 144,
    145, 148, 172-73
    prosaic verse, criticism of, 10-11, 45-
    46, 49, 62-64, 99-100, 136

Dryden, John: (*continued*)
  Restoration, influence of the, 40,
    44, 45, 49, 51, 53, **71-85**, 87, 90-
    91, 95, 119, 142, 147, 149, 168
  satire, use of, 9-10, 44-45, 46-52,
    58, 64-65, 66-70, 121-22
  and Shakespeare, William, 11, 44,
    45, 53, 56, 57, 58, 59, 61, 63, 87,
    88, 90, 91, 92, 93, 95, 108, 147
  as translator, 13, 14, 68, 166
  and Virgil, 23, 43, 44, 45, 47, 50,
    53, 56, 90, 144, 145, 174-75, 176,
    177-78, 179, 180
  wit, use of, 15, 44, 63, 67, 68-69,
    118-19, 121, 155, 167-71
Dryden, John, works by:
PLAYS
  All for Love, 14, 58, 61-62, 63, 70,
    86-94, 95-114, 117
  Aureng-Zebe, 14-15, 25-26, 45, 61,
    62-63, 64, 87, 98
  Conquest of Granada, The, 56-57,
    61, 87, 88, 89, 146-47
  Don Sebastian, 87
  Indian Emperor, The, 87, 89
  Limberham, 64
  Love Triumphant, 65, 167
  Marriage-a-la-Mode, 64
  Rival Ladies, The, 63
  *State of Innocence and Fall of Man,
    The* (opera), 13, 127
  Tyrannic Love, 87, 89
POETRY
  Absalom and Achitophel, 4, 5-6, 9,
    45, 49, 51, 66-67, 68, 86, 117,
    118-21, 123-24, 126
  Alexander's Feast, 12, 65, 151,
    156-64
  Annus Mirabilis, 49, 66, 86, 146
  Astraea Redux, 45
  *Elegy Upon the Death of the Lord
    Hastings*, 66, 84
  Evening's Love, An, 27
  Fables, 147, 173-80
  Hind and the Panther, The, 26, 66,
    121, 165-66
  Mac Flecknoe, 4, 9, 10, 33, 42, 49,
    66-68, 121-24, 126

  Medall, The, 51, 66-67
  Ode on Anne Killigrew, 65, 116,
    136-48, 149-51
  "On the Death of Mr. Purcell,"
    151-52
  Religio Laici, 18, 26, 27, 66, **125-35**
  "Song for St. Cecilia's Day," 65,
    149, 152-56
  Sylvae, 26-27
  "To my Dear Friend Mr. Congreve,"
    166-73
  "To my Honour'd Friend, Dr.
    Charleton," 71-85
  "To my Honour'd Kinsman, John
    Driden," 167
PROSE
  *Defense of an Essay of Dramatic
    Poesy, A*, 41, 86-87
  *Discourse Concerning the Original
    and Progress of Satire, A*, 19-20,
    66, 68
  Duke of Guise, The, 20-21
  Essay of Dramatic Poesy, An, 26, 27
  Of Heroique Plays, 42
  Vindication, 20
Dryden and His Poetry (Nicoll), 1
Duchess of Malfi, The (Webster), 89
Duke of Guise, The, 20, 21
Dunciad (Pope), 53, 121-22, 172

E

*Elegy Upon the Death of the Lord
  Hastings*, 66, 84
Eliot, T. S., 2, 3, 5, 17, 86, 116
Elizabethans, influence of, on Dryden,
  14, 56, 57, 60, 63, 70, 91, 115-16,
  117, 141, 147, 168 (*see also* Renais-
  sance)
Epic genre, Dryden's use of, 22-23, 43,
  45, 47, 50-51, 121-23, 145 (*see also*
  Heroic genre)
Epicurus, 130, 131-32
Epistle to Dr. Arbuthnot (Pope), 12
Epistle to the Tories (Shadwell?), 34-35
Essay of Dramatic Poesy, An, 26, 27
Essay on Criticism (Pope), 145
Etherege, George, 87, 169-70

Evening's Love, An, 27

F

Fables, 147, 173-80
Faulkner, William, 90
Fletcher, John, 87
Ford, John, 87-88
Forster, E. M., 134

G

Georgics (Virgil), 144
Goldsmith, Oliver, 8
Gray, Thomas, 8, 23, 52, 65
Grierson, Sir Herbert, 116
Gulliver's Travels (Swift), 3

H

Hamlet (Shakespeare), 89
Hazlitt, William, 11-12
Henry VI (Shakespeare), 147
Henryson, Robert, 136, 139
Heroic couplet, 4, 45, 56, 58-59, 61,
   65-66, 69, 74-75, 87, 98-99, 116
Heroic genre: (*see also* Epic genre)
   in plays, 45, 46, 49, 61-62, 87-94,
      95-114, 121-24
   in poetry, 22, 44, 51, 57, 68, 121-24
Herrick, Robert, 66
Hind and the Panther, The, 26, 66,
   121, 165-66
Hobbes, Thomas, 26, 28, 30, 87, 129,
   132-33
Hollander, John, 5
Homer, 25, 43, 44, 47, 145, 174-75,
   176, 179, 180
Homer (Chapman), 24
Horace, 14, 24, 44, 45, 47, 53, 68,
   139, 144
Howard, Robert, 71-72
Hulme, T. E., 2, 115

I

Ibsen, Henrik, 91

Imagery: (*see also* Metaphor)
   in *Absalom and Achitophel,* 50
   in *Alexander's Feast,* 159-63
   in *All for Love,* 62-63, 98-113
   in *Annus Mirabilis,* 66
   in *Fables,* 173-80
   in "To my Dear Friend Mr. Con-
      greve," 167-72
   in "Song for St. Cecilia's Day,"
      152-56
Indian Emperor, The, 87, 89
*Intellectual Milieu of John Dryden,
   The,* (Bredvold), 4-5

J

James, Henry, 142
*John Dryden: Some Biographical Facts
   and Problems* (Osborn), 2
Johnson, Samuel, 2, 6-7, 8, 17, 23-24,
   26, 43, 44, 51, 52, 56, 57, 58, 69,
   149, 155, 163
Jones, Inigo, 72, 82-83, 84
Jonson, Ben, 8, 12, 16, 45-46, 48, 87,
   88, 92, 136, 144, 155
Juvenal, 24, 66-67, 68, 69-70, 174

K

Keats, John, 8
King Lear (Shakespeare), 89
Knight's Tale, The (Chaucer), 175,
   176, 179

L

Landor, Walter Savage, 18
La Rochefoucauld, 133
Last Instructions to a Painter (Marvell),
   51
Leavis, F. R., 44, 115
Lectures on Dryden (Verrall), 2
Lee, Nathaniel, 13
Leviathan (Hobbes), 132
Lewis, C. S., 1
Life of John Dryden, The (Ward), 5
Limberham, 64

Locke, John, 133
Love Triumphant, 65, 167
Lubbock, Allan, 17-18
Lucretius, 13, 18, 24, 26-27, 29, 60, 131
Lukács, George, 88
Luttrell, Narcissus, 31-32, 34
Lycidas (Milton), 137

M

Macbeth (Shakespeare), 108
Macdonald, Hugh, 34
Mac Flecknoe 4, 9, 10, 33, 42, 49, 66-68, 121-24, 126
Mackenzie, George, 24
Mack, Maynard, 121
Mallarmé, Stephane, 12
Malone, Kemp, 19, 31
Malory, Thomas, 147
Marlowe, Christopher, 8, 59, 87-88
Marriage-a-la-Mode, 64
Marvell, Andrew, 44, 45, 49, 51-52, 65, 66, 153
Masterbuilder, The (Ibsen), 91
Mayakovsky, Vladimir, 55
Maxims (La Rochefoucauld), 133
Medall, The, 51, 66-67, 126
Medal of John Baynes, The (Shadwell?), 5, 31-34, 42
Memoir (Christie), 1-2
Metaphor, 115-24 (*see also* Imagery)
  in *Absalom and Achitophel,* 117-21, 123-24
  in *Mac Flecknoe,* 121-24
Metaphysical influences, 44-45, 52, 56, 57, 58, 60, 65, 84, 115, 175, 180
Milton, John, 11, 12, 15, 23, 43, 44, 45, 49, 50-51, 52, 53, 56, 57, 58, 65, 66, 115, 122-23, 127, 142, 145, 166, 174, 180
Miner, Earl, 5-6
Montaigne, Michel de, 25, 27, 30
Moral Essays (Pope), 53-54
Morgan, Edwin, 4, 5
Musicks Duell (Crashaw), 65

N

Neoclassicism, 50, 90, 144, 149 (*see also* Augustanism; Classicism)
Nicoll, Allardyce, 1
Noyes, George, 2
Nun's Priest Tale, The (Chaucer), 160

O

Ode on Anne Killigrew, 65, 116, 136-48, 149-51
Ode on Cromwell (Marvell), 51-52
Odes (Gray), 52
Oedipus (Sophocles), 87, 91
Of Heroique Plays, 42
Oldham, John, 8, 152
"On the Death of Mr. Purcell," 151-52
On Time (Milton), 136-37
Orchestra (Davies), 136, 139, 146
Osborn, James, 2, 5
Ovid, 14, 43, 53

P

Paradise Lost (Milton), 13, 45, 59, 122-23, 127, 142
Parody, 10, 46-48, 49, 51
Pascal, Blaise, 30
Pastorals (Pope), 53
Pater, Walter, 11
Persius, 24, 66-67, 69, 70
Philips, Katherine, 59
Phillips, Ambrose, 8
Philosophy, Dryden's interest in, 22-23, 27-30, 127-35
Plato, 23, 27, 48, 161, 175, 176
Plutarch, 130-131, 160, 161
Poe, Edgar Allan, 8
Poetry of John Dryden, The (Van Doran), 2-3
Pollio (Virgil), 176, 177-78
Pope, Alexander, 2, 3, 5, 8, 11, 12, 43-44, 52-54, 56, 58, 59, 115-16, 120, 121-22, 135, 144, 145, 148, 172-73
Pope and his Contemporaries (Mack), 121

Praise of Musicke, The (Case), 157-58
Prosaic verse, in Dryden, 10-11, 45-46,
    49, 62-64, 99-100, 136

R

Racine, Jean, 15
Rape of the Lock (Pope), 53, 67, 116
Rapin, Paul de, 50
Reason of Church Government
    (Milton), 145
Rehearsal, The (Villiers), 31, 36-39
Religio Laici, 18, 26, 27, 66, **125-35**
Renaissance, influence of, 22, 44-47,
    52, 140, 170, (*see also* Elizabethans)
Restoration, influence of:
    historical, 40, **71-85**
    stylistic, 44, 45, 49, 51, 53, 87, 90-
        91, 95, 119, 142, 147, 149, 168
Review, The (Defoe), 39
Richards, I. A., 117-18
Rival Ladies, The, 63
Romanticism, references to, 2, 55,
    115-16
Rymer, Thomas, 143

S

Saintsbury, George, 1, 4, 19, 126
Samson Agonistes (Milton), 91
Santayana, George, 167
Sappho, 137
Sartre, Jean-Paul, 88
Satire, 9-10, 44-45, 46-52, 58, 64-65,
    66-70, 121-22
Satyr against Mankind, A (Wilmot),
    133
Schilling, Bernard, 120*n*
Scott, Walter, 1, 19, 173
Settle, Elkanah, 9, 22-23
Shadwell, Thomas, 9, **31-42**, 121-24
Shakespeare, William, 11, 44, 45, 53,
    56, 57, 58, 59, 61, 63, 87, 88, 90,
    91, 92, 93, 95, 108, 147
Shelley, Percy Bysshe, 9, 67, 115, 145
Shepherd's Calendar, The (Spenser),
    137

Short View of Tragedy, A (Rymer),
    143
Sidney, Sir Philip, 22
Socrates, 27
"Song for St. Cecilia's Day," 65, 149,
    152-56
Sophocles, 87
Southerne, Thomas, 169-70
Spenser, Edmund, 11, 22, 43, 44, 53,
    136, 137
Spinoza, Baruch, 132-33
State of Innocence and Fall of Man,
    The, 13, 127
"Study of Poetry, The" (Arnold), 2
Swift, Jonathan, 3, 70
Swinburne, Arnold, 15
Sylvae, 26-27
Sylvester, Josuah, 45

T

Tamburlaine (Marlowe), 87-88
Tennyson, Alfred, 115
Tenth Satyr of Juvenal, The (Shad-
    well), 32-33
Testament of Cresseid (Henryson), 136
Thackeray, William Makepeace, 3
Thomson, James, 141
Thorn-Drury, George, 31-34
Tintern Abbey (Wordsworth), 116
Tillyard, E. M. W., 5, 150, 151
Tis Pity She's a Whore (Ford), 87-88
"To my Dear Friend Mr. Congreve,"
    166-73
"To my Honour'd Friend, Dr. Charle-
    ton," 71-85
"To my Honour'd Kinsman, John
    Driden," 167
Tractatus Theologico-Politicus
    (Spinoza), 132-33
Tragedies of the Last Age, The
    (Rymer), 143
Treatise of Humane Reason, A (Clif-
    ford), 128-29
Troilus and Cressida (Shakespeare),
    87
Tyrannic Love, 87, 89

V

Van Doren, Mark, 2-3, 5, 8, 10, 14, 45, 116, 137, 152, 155, 173
Verrall, A. W., 2
Villiers, George, 2nd Duke of Buckingham, 9, 39, 125, 128, 129, 134
Villon, François, 11
Vindication, 20
Virgil, 23, 43, 44, 45, 47, 50, 53, 56, 90, 144, 145, 174-75, 176, 177-78, 179, 180

W

Waller, Edmund, 8, 24, 44, 45, 56
Ward, Charles, 5

Warren, Albertus, 129
Warren, Austin, 134
Wasserman, Earl, 5
Waste Land, The (Eliot), 116
Way of the World, The (Congreve), 87, 147
Wilmot, John, 53, 133
Wit, in Dryden, 15, 44, 63, 67, 68-69, 118-19, 121, 155, 167-71
Wordsworth, William, 8, 18, 56, 69n, 115
Wright, David, 7, 181
Wycherley, William, 87, 169-70

Y

Yeats, W. B., 176

GEORGE ELIOT

A Collection of Critical Essays

Edited by GEORGE R. CREEGER

A

Adam Bede, 1, 5, 37, 38, 41, 47, 56,
    70, **86-106**, 110, 142, 147, 162
    and Feuerbach, influence on, 80-85
    maturity, theme of, 93-94, 105
    regeneration, theme of, 99, 102-3
    suffering in, 92, 99, 101-3, 106
"Amos Barton," 44, 71
Allbutt, Clifford, 13
Allott, Miriam, 37
Analogy, as unifying principle, 66-76
    passim, 124-25, 128, 129, 132-34
Arnold, Matthew, 120, 121
Austen, Jane, 163, 176

B

Balzac, Honoré de, 163, 169
"Belles Lettres," 26
Bennett, Joan, 80, 153
Blackwood, John, 1, 66, 70, 110
Blackwood's Magazine, 56, 142, 146
Bodichon, Madame, 12, 22
Bray, C. H., 11, 142
Bullett, Gerald, 80
Burke, Edmund, 41
Byron, George Gordon, Lord, 4

C

Carlyle, Jane, 1
Carlyle, Thomas, 3, 11, 68
Carroll, David, 73, 75

Chapman, John, 142
Christian Theism (Hennell), 11
Coleridge, S. T., 61, 62, 63
"College Breakfast-Party, A," 19
Collins, Wilkie, 166
Comte, August, 11, 50, 51, 79, 109,
    110, 112, 113, 114, 115, 116, 117,
    118, 121, 156
Cornhill, 142
Cross, J. W., 3, 38, 154

D

Daniel Deronda, 2, 5, 7, 37, 38, 44, 49,
    50, 51, 53, 54, 60, 64, 66, 68, 70,
    71, 74, 77, 125, 142, 143, 158, 159,
    162, 163, 164, 165
    and duty, 150-151, 153
    and individual and society, conflict
        between, 2, 125, 140
Darwin, Charles, 14, 79
Defense of Poetry, A (Shelley), 76
Determinism, 108-13, 115, 117
Dickens, Charles, 1, 150
Diderot, Denis, 156
Disenchantment, theme of, 55-65, 97-
    98
Dostoevsky, F., 3
Double Méprise, La (Mérimée), 176
Duty, theme of, 6, 42, 50-53

E

Edinburgh Review, 66

Egoism, theme of, 4-6, 26-29, 64, 90, 96-98, 112, 117-19, 122, 135, 136, 137, 144

Eighteenth Century Background, The (Willey), 41n

Eliot, George:
biographical information, 11-13, 38, 63-64, 142, 155-57, 159
and Christianity, break with, 11-13, 18-19, 39, 156
conservatism of, 2, 5, 14, 38-41
Englishness of, 2-3
and moral order, 12-19, 35-36, 47
as philosopher, 80-85, 147
quest for values, 29-36, 54, 123
and social connectedness, importance of, 14-19, 116, 124-30, 137, 140

Eliot, George, works by:
Adam Bede, 1, 5, 37, 38, 41, 47, 56, 70, **86-106**, 110, 142, 147, 162
"Amos Barton," 44, 71
"Belles Lettres," 26
"College Breakfast-Party, A," 19
Daniel Deronda, 2, 5, 7, 37, 38, 44, 49-54 *passim*, 60, 64, 66, 68, 70, 71, 74, 77, 125, 140, 142, 143, 150-151, 153, 158, 159, 162-65 *passim*
Felix Holt, 1, 37, 39, 44, 47, 48, 51, 58-59, 65-66, 73, **124-40**, 142, 143, 157, 159, 171
"Mr. Gilfil's Love Story," 45, 71-72
Impressions of Theophratus Such, 17
"Janet's Repentance," 44, 47, 55, 125
Legend of Jubal and Other Poems, The, 19
"Lifted Veil, The," 56-57
Middlemarch, 2, 36-39 *passim*, 44, 45, 47, 48, 49, 59-60, 64, 65, 66, 68, 69, 71-74 *passim*, 77, 80, **141-60**, 165, 175
Mill on the Floss, The, 37, 38, 44, 45, 47-48, 57, 64, 71, 107-23, 142, 162

"Notes on Form in Art," 67-70 *passim*, 74-76
"Notes on 'The Spanish Gypsy'," 19
Romola, 17, 36-38, 41-44, 51, 57-58, 72, 73, 124, 125, 142, 143, 159
Scenes of Clerical Life, 1, 7, 37, 142
Silas Marner, 37, 38, 44, 48, 62, 72, 120, 142
Spanish Gypsy, The, 16, 46, 51-52, 142
"Versification," 69-70
"Empedocles on Etna" (Arnold), 120
Essays of George Eliot (ed. Pinney), 16, 18
Essence of Christianity, The (Feuerbach), 21-23, 24-25, 28, 80-82, 94n, 102-3, 105n
Ethics (Spinoza), 142
Evans, Mary Ann (*see also* George Eliot), 142, 155-56
Evans, Robert, 142
Evolution and Ethics and Other Essays (Huxley), 14
Excursion, The (Wordsworth), 41n

F

Faulkner, William, 84
Feeling, authority of, 41-45, 49-50, 88-90, 101, 117, 120
Felix Holt, 1, 37, 39, 44, 47, 48, 51, 58-59, 65, 66, 73, **124-40**, 142, 143, 157, 159, 171
imagery in, 130-131, 138-39
individual and society, conflict between, 124-28, 130, 137
regeneration, theme of, 125, 135, 139
renunciation, theme of, 132
Ferguson, Suzanne, 75
Feuerbach, L. A., 11, 13, 21, 22, 23, 24, 28, 35, 40, 79-85 *passim*, 94n, 102-3, 109, 110, 112, 113, 114, 115, 116, 117, 118, 121, 122, 123
Fiction, theory of, 7-8, 67-78

Fielding, Henry, 149-50
Flaubert, Gustave, 2, 143, 160

G

General View of Positivism, A
   (Comte), 50
George Eliot Letters, The (ed. Haight),
   141
*George Eliot's Life as related in her
   Letters and Journals* (Cross), 38, 55,
   61, 64, 154
"Mr. Gilfil's Love Story," 45, 71-72
Gluck, Christoph von, 7
Great Tradition, The (Leavis), 66, 141

H

Haight, Gordon S., 154
Hamlet, 146
Hardy, Barbara, 75, 80
Harrison, Frederic, 1
Harvey, W. J., 80
Hawthorne, Nathaniel, 176
Hegel, G. W. F., 3
Heine, Heinrich, 4
Hemingway, Ernest, 84
Hennell, Charles C., 11, 22, 79, 142
Hennell, Sara, 12, 55, 63, 64
Houdon, B., 7
Huxley, T. H., 14, 79

I

Imagery, 47-48, 55-65 *passim*, 70, 82-
   84, 86-87, 94-99, 102, 106, 110,
   130-131, 134, 138-40, 144, 148-51
   in *Felix Holt*, 130-131, 138-39
   in *Middlemarch*, 59-60, 64, 65,
      144-50
   in *Romola*, 57-58
Impressions of Theophrastus Such, 17
In Memoriam (Tennyson), 26
*Inquiry Concerning the Origin of
   Christianity, An* (Hennell), 22n
Isaacs, Neil, 80

J

James, Henry, 1, 2, 9, 66, 77, 84, 103,
   159
"Janet's Repentance," 44, 47, 55, 125
   and past, importance of, 44
Joyce, James, 9, 74

K

Keats, John, 63

L

Leavis, F. R., 2, 37, 66, 71, 74, 107,
   141, 145, 159
Legend of Jubal and Other Poems, The,
   19
Levine, George, 79, 80, 84
Lewes, George Henry, 1, 3, 11, 14, 15,
   16, 69, 79, 114, 142, 160
Life of Jesus, The (Strauss), 22n, 142
"Lifted Veil, The," 56-57

M

Main, Alexander, 36
Mallock, W. H., 18
Marx, Karl, 3
Maturity, concept of, 83, 93-94, 103,
   105
Melville, Herman, 3
Mérimée, Prosper, 176
"Michael" (Wordsworth), 45
Middlemarch, 2, 36-39 *passim*, 45, 47,
   48, 49, 66, 68, 69, 71-74, 77, 80,
   141-60, 165, 175
   author as commentator in, 145,
      147-50, 154-60
   imagery in, 59-60, 64, 65, 144-50
   and past, importance of, 44
   self-deception in, 150-153
Mill, J. S., 3, 11, 79, 80, 118

Mill on the Floss, The, 37, 38, 44, 45, 47-48, 64, 71, **107-23**, 142, 162
  determinism in, 108-13, 116-17
  and past, importance of, 47
  renunciation, theme of, 44, 57, 119
  rootedness, theme of, 44-45
  suffering in, 110, 117, 120
Modern Painters, III (Ruskin), 69, 70
Morley, John, 14-15

N

Napoleon, 143
Natural History of German Life (Riehl), 40
Newcomes, The (Thackeray), 163
Newman, Cardinal, 61
Nineteenth-Century Studies (Willey), 38
"Notes on Form in Art," 67-70 *passim,* 74-76
"Notes on 'The Spanish Gypsy'," 19
Novels of George Eliot, The (Thale), 77

O

Oldtown Folks (Stowe), 157
On the Eve (Turgenev), 168

P

Paris, Bernard, 79, 80, 113*n*, 114*n*
Past, importance to present of, 40-44, 46-51, 109-13, 116-17
Père Goriot (Balzac), 169
Poems (Arnold), 120
Ponsonby, Mrs., 13, 32, 33
Positivism, 11, 17-18, 19-21, 61, 156
Prelude, The (Wordsworth), 46-47, 141
Pride and Prejudice (Austen), 163
Problems of Life and Mind: First Series (Lewes), 15
Proust, Marcel, 2

R

Reform Bill, 39, 143, 153

Regeneration, theme of, 7, 99, 102, 110, 130-131, 135
"Religion in the Novels of George Eliot" (Svaglic), 33
"Religion of Humanity" (Paris), 79
Renunciation, theme of, 57, 119, 132, 138
Romola, 17, 51, 72, 73, 124, 125, 142, 143, 159
  and feeling, authority of, 41-44
  imagery in, 57-58
  suffering, importance of, 36
Rootedness, theme of, 41, 44-46, 48, 112
Ruskin, John, 69, 70, 76

S

Sand, George, 163, 166
Savonarola, 42, 58
Scenes of Clerical Life, 1, 7, 37, 142
Scott, Sir Walter, 41
Sentimental Education (Flaubert), 143
Sewell, Anna, 174
Shakespeare, 165
Shelley, Percy B., 76
Silas Marner, 37, 38, 44, 48, 62, 72, 120, 142
Spanish Gypsy, The, 16, 142
  and duty, 51-52
  and past, importance of, 46
Spencer, Herbert, 11, 14, 79
Spinoza, B., 11, 22, 142
Stephen, Leslie, 155, 159
Sterne, Laurence, 9
Stowe, Harriet Beecher, 157
Strauss, D. F., 22, 40, 79, 142
Study of Psychology, The (Lewes), 16
Stump, Reva, 80
Suffering, value of, 6, 7, 36, 83, 92, 99, 101-3, 106, 110, 117, 120
Svaglic, Martin, 33

T

Technique, 8-9, 70-78, 86-90, 144, 148, 151

Tennyson, Alfred, Lord, 26
Thackeray, William M., 150, 163, 176
Thale, Jerome, 77
Theological-Political Tractate
   (Spinoza), 22
Tolstoy, Leo, 2, 31, 143, 160
Tom Jones (Fielding), 150
Tradition, importance of, 16, 116,
   118, 156
Turgenev, Ivan, 168

U

Ulysses (Joyce), 74

V

"Versification," 69-70
Victorian Studies, 79n

W

War and Peace (Tolstoy), 143
Westminster Review, 40, 69, 142
Willey, Basil, 38, 79
Woolf, Virginia, 2, 160
Wordsworth, William, 11, 40, 41, 45,
   46, 47, 53, 54, 61, 62, 63, 141

Y

Yonge, Charlotte, 174
Young, Edward, 18

T. S. ELIOT

A Collection of Critical Essays

Edited by HUGH KENNER

A

Acharnians, The (Aristophanes), 180
Adonais (Shelley), 56
Aiken, Conrad, 2, 17
Alcestis (Euripides), 170, 177-80,
   183-84
Aldington, Richard, 34
Alice in Wonderland (Dodgson), 8, 67,
   68-69
Allegory, in *Murder in the Cathedral*,
   162-63
Analogical perception, in *The Cocktail
   Party*, 182-83
Analogy:
   in "Love Song of J. Alfred Pruf-
      rock, The," 59-91
   in *Waste Land, The*, 61-64
"Analysis and Comparison," 2
Anglo-Catholicism, in *Ash Wednesday*,
   129-35
Anglo-Saxon locutions, in *Murder in
   the Cathedral*, 162
"Animula," 105
Antony and Cleopatra (Shakespeare),
   171
Appearance and Reality (Bradley),
   39-57
Aristophanes, 180
Aristotle, 136
Arnold, Matthew, 39, 136, 140
Arrowsmith, William, 175, 177, 178
Ash Wednesday, 13, 23, 24, 53, 106-7,
   111, 129-35, 139, 141, 201

irony in, 132-33
rhythm and imagery in, 134-35
and *Waste Land, The*, 131-33
Augustine, Saint, 60, 98
Autobiography (Lear), 67

B

Babbitt, Irving, 136
Baudelaire, Charles, 74-76, 90, 99, 102,
   131, 137, 141
Beaumont, Francis, 21
Becket (Tennyson), 156-60, 166
Beckett, Samuel, 7
Bell, Clive, 2
Bergson, Henri, 40, 55, 197
Betjeman, John, 2
Biographia Literaria (Coleridge), 136
Bird in Flight (Brancusi), 55
Blackmur, R. P., 6-7, 12, 13
Blake, William, 156
Book of Common Prayer, The, 141
Bowles, William Lisle, 37
Bradley, Francis Herbert, 6, 38-57
Brancusi, Constantin, 55
Browning, Robert, 6, 38, 45, 47
"Burbank with a Baedeker," 77-78, 90
"Burial of the Dead" (*The Waste Land*),
   94, 96, 100-102
"Burnt Norton" (*Four Quartets*), 8, 13,
   26, 54, 70, 80, 106-9, 112, 116-19,
   198-99, 200
Byron, George Gordon, 47,
   156

C

Carroll, Lewis (*see* Dodgson, Charles Lutwidge)
Chapman, George, 45
"Charles Whibley," 138-39
Chorus, function of, in *Murder in the Cathedral,* 158-62, 166-67
Christian themes:
  in *Cocktail Party, The,* 174-77
  in *Four Quartets,* 111-12, 122-23
Cocktail Party, The, 13, 50, 68, 71, 155, 170-172, **173-86**, 188-89
  and *Alcestis* (Euripides), 170, 177-80, 183-84
  analogical perception, 182-83
  Christian themes in, 174-77
  comic elements in, 173-74, 179-80, 184-85
  imagery in, 174-78
  manichean elements in, 182-83
Coghill, Neville, 2
Coleridge, Samuel Taylor, 37, 136
Comic elements, in *The Cocktail Party,* 173-74, 179-80, 184-85
Confessions (St. Augustine), 98
Confidential Clerk, The, 68, 71, 188
Conrad, Joseph, 52, 136, 137
"Cooking Egg, A," 68, 90
Coriolan, 13, 14, 114-16
Coriolanus (Shakespeare), 171
Coup de Dés, Un, (Mallarmé), 66
"Cousin Nancy," 18
Cowper, William, 37
Crane, Hart, 18, 197
Criterion, The, Eliot's associates on, 34
Criticism, Eliot's, 2-3, **136-48**, 149-51
  conversational order in, 138-39
  and Eliot's poetry, 139-41

D

Dante Alighieri, 67, 98, 99, 111, 137-38, 141
Davie, Donald, 13-14
"Death by Water" (*The Waste Land*), 101-2

Death, reconciliation to, in "Little Gidding," 127-28
"Deserted House, The" (Tennyson), 78
Dickens, Charles, 47
"Difficulties of a Statesman," 116
Dodgson, Charles Lutwidge (*pseud.* Lewis Carroll), 8, **66-72**
Donne, John, 38, 48, 140
Donoghue, Denis, 13
Drama, 12-13, **155-72**, **173-86**, 187-91
  (*see also* titles of individual works)
Dramatic monologue, in Eliot's early poetry, 21-33
Dryden, John, 141, 150
"Dry Salvages, The" (*Four Quartets*), 26, 68, 71, 112, 120-123, 192-200

E

"Early London Environment" (Lewis), 5-6
"East Coker" (*Four Quartets*), 19, 25-26, 49, 53, 70, 71, 78, 119-20, 198, 199-200
Eastman, Max, 201
Egoist, The, and Eliot's early work, 34
Elder Statesman, The, 13, 189-91
"Eliot's Moral Dialectic" (Kenner), 198-200
Eliot, Thomas Stearns:
  Anglo-Catholicism of, 129-35
  and Baudelaire, 74-76, 90, 99, 102, 131, 137, 141
  and Bradley, 6, **36-57**
  as a critic, 2-3, **136-48**, 149-51
  and Dodgson (Lewis Carroll), 7, **66-72**
  dramatic works, 12-13, **155-72**, **173-86**, 187-91
  early career, 1, 17-18, **28-35**, 38-39
  early poetry, 20-22, 104-5
  late poetry, 12-13, 106-9, 110-24
  narrative voice, in poetry, 3-4, 21-23
  as a Nonsense poet, 7, **66-72**
  objective correlative, theory of, 144-46
  personality of, 152-54
  and Pound, 5, 20, **28-35**, 141, **149-51**

Eliot, Thomas Stearns (*continued*)
  and Tennyson, 10, 38, **75-85,**
    156-60, 166
  and Whitman, 10, 73-74, 193,
    196-97, 200
  on writing poetry, 152-53
Eliot, Thomas Stearns, works by:
  POETRY
  "Animula," 105
  Ash Wednesday, 13, 23, 24, 53,
    106-7, 111, 129-35, 139, 141, 201
  "Burbank with a Baedeker," 77-78,
    90
  "Cooking Egg, A," 68, 90
  Coriolan, 13, 114-16
  "Cousin Nancy," 18
  "Difficulties of a Statesman," 116
  "Figlia che Piange, La," 53
  Four Quartets, 14, 23, 24-27, 53-
    54, 106-9, 110-12, **116-24,** 192-
    205 (*see also* main entry)
  "Fragment of an Agon," 90
  "Gerontion," 13, 21-23, 31, 36-37,
    71, 78-79, 81, 91, 203
  "Hippopotamus, The," 139
  Hollow Men, The, 23, 33-34, 49,
    104
  "Hysteria," 68
  "Lines for an Old Man," 66
  "Love Song of J. Alfred Prufrock,
    The," **36-58,** 68, 81-82, 91
  "Marina," 112-14
  "Mr. Apollinax," 68
  *Old Possums' Book of Practical
    Cats,* 67, 68
  Poems, 20-22
  "Portrait of a Lady," 42-43, 46, 68,
    81
  "Preludes," 31, 105
  Prufrock and Other Observations, 5,
    20-22, 34
  "Rhapsody on a Windy Night," 31,
    105-6
  "Rock, The," Choruses from, 22,
    75, 80, 105
  "Song for Simeon, A," 13
  Sweeney Agonistes, 68, 176

  "Sweeney Among the Nightingales,"
    106
  "Sweeney Erect," 20-21
  "Triumphal March," 13, 14, 114-16
  Waste Land, The, 7-10, 23, 37, 47-
    48, 67, **89-103,** 104, 131-32, 173
    (*see also* main entry)
  DRAMA
  Cocktail Party, The, 13, 50, 68, 71,
    155, 170-172, **173-86,** 188-89
  Confidential Clerk, The, 68, 71,
    188
  Elder Statesman, The, 13, **189-91**
  Family Reunion, The, 52, 68, 82,
    111, 155, 170, 173, 184-85, 186
  Murder in the Cathedral, 12-13, 68,
    155-72, 173, 181-82, 188
  CRITICISM
  "Analysis and Comparison," 2
  "Baudelaire," 75
  "Charles Whibley," 138-39
  "Dante," 67, 137-38, 141
  "Experience and the Objects of
    Knowledge in the Philosophy of
    F. H. Bradley," 38, 39
  Ezra Pound, his Metric and Poetry,
    5
  "Frontiers of Criticism, The," 16,
    19
  "Function of Criticism, The," 3
  "Lancelot Andrewes," 139
  "Leibniz's Monads and Bradley's
    Finite Centers," 39
  "Hamlet and His Problems," 144-45,
    171
  *Notes Towards the Definition of
    Culture,* 139
  On Poetry and Poets, 13-14
  "Poetry and Drama," 177
  "Tradition and Individual Talent,"
    19-20, 46, 48, 143-44, 199, 204
  *Use of Poetry and the Use of Criti-
    cism, The,* 10
  "Whitman and Tennyson," 73
Elizabethans, Eliot's essays on, 140-
  141
Emerson, Ralph Waldo, 197

Emotion, and poetic expression,
145-46
Empson, William, 2, 6, 71
Ennui, L' (Baudelaire), 102
Ethical Studies (Bradley), 39
Euripides, 59, 170, 177-80, 183-84
"Experience and the Objects of Knowl-
edge in the Philosophy of F. H. Brad-
ley," 38, 39
Ezra Pound, his Metric and Poetry, 5

F

Family Reunion, The, 52, 68, 82, 111,
155, 170, 173, 184-85, 186
"Fatima" (Tennyson), 79
Feeling, and poetic expression, 145
Fergusson, Francis, 173, 181-82
Fertility themes, in *The Waste Land*,
93-99
"Figlia che Piange, La," 53
Finite centers, Bradley's doctrine of,
50-51
"Fire Sermon, The" (*The Waste Land*),
102-3, 132-33
Fitzgerald, F. Scott, 48-49
Fletcher, Gould, 34
Fletcher, John, 21
Fleurs du Mal, Les (Baudelaire), 74-76
Ford, Ford Madox, 30-32, 34
Four Quartets, 14, 23, 24-27, 53-64,
106-9, 110-12, **116-24**, **192-205**
Bradley's influence on, 53-54
"Burnt Norton," 8, 13, 26, 54, 70,
106-9, 112, **116-19**, 198-99, 200
Christian themes in, 111-12, 122-
23
"Dry Salvages, The," 26, 28, 71,
112, **120-123**, **192-200**
"East Coker," 19, 25-26, 49, 53, 70,
71, 78, 119-20, 198, 199-200
language of, 201-5
"Little Gidding," 24-25, 66, 70, 78,
80, **125-28**, 139, 198-99, 200
natural phenomena in, 25-26
Nonsense techniques in, 67, 69-71
parody, in "The Dry Salvages,"

197-200, 204
philosophical method of, 116-19
as post-symbolist poetry, 202-5
structure of, 197-200
"Fragments of an Agon," 90
Frazer, Sir James, 56, 62
Free will vs. conditioning, in Eliot's
plays, 155-56
Freud, Sigmund, 57, 155
From Ritual to Romance (Weston), 89,
92-94, 98-99, 103
"Frontiers of Criticism, The," 16, 19
Frost, Robert, 59
"Function of Criticism, The," 3

G

"Game of Chess, A" (*The Waste Land*),
95, 100-101, 174
Gardner, Helen, 192-93, 195-96
Genetic Fallacy, and sources to *The
Waste Land*, 9-11
"Gerontion," 13, 21-23, 31, 36-37, 71,
78-79, 81, 91, 203
dramatic monologue in, 21-23
Golden Bough, The (Frazer), 94, 102
Gourmont, Rémy de, 136
Graves, Robert, 195, 201
Great Gatsby, The (Fitzgerald), 48-49
Greek tragedy:
and *Cocktail Party, The*, 170, 177-
80, 183-84
and *Murder in the Cathedral*, 158-60
Guiness, Alec, 188

H

"Hamlet and His Problems," 144-45,
171
Harding, D. W., 8, 12, 111, 121
Heart of Darkness (Conrad), 52
Heilman, Robert B., 177-79, 180, 183
Herbert, George, 140
"Hippopotamus, The," 139
History of the Royal Society (Sprat),
43
Hollow Men, The, 23, 33-34, 49, 104

Housman, A. E., 43
Hueffer (see Ford, Ford Madox)
Hunt, Violet, 31
Hunting of the Snark, The (Dodgson),
  66, 68, 71
Huxley, Aldous, 16
"Hysteria," 68

I

Illuminative Way, The (St. John of the
  Cross), 176
Imagery:
  in Ash Wednesday, 134-35
  in Cocktail Party, The, 174-78
  in Four Quartets, 116-18, 122
  in Waste Land, The, 89-103
Imagism, of Ezra Pound, 20
"Immediate experience," Bradley's
  doctrine of, 6, 39, 42-45
Impersonality, in Eliot's poetry, 91-92,
  203-4
Incantatory elements, in Eliot's
  poetry, 36-38
Inferno, The (Dante), and The Waste
  Land, 7
In Memoriam (Tennyson), 75-76, 82-
  84
"In the Hope of Straightening Things
  Out" (Blackmur), 12

J

Jacobean elements, in Eliot's early
  poetry, 21-22
James, Henry, 56
John of the Cross, Saint, 176, 198
Johnson, Samuel, 130
Jonson, Ben, 45, 140, 141, 150
Joyce, James, 33, 34

K

Keats, John, 14, 156
Kenner, Hugh, 198-200
King Lear (Shakespeare), 157
Krutch, Joseph Wood, 132

L

"Lady of Shalott, The" (Tennyson), 78
Laforgue, Jules, 46-47, 48, 90
"Lancelot Andrewes," 139
Larisch, Countess Marie, 86-88
Lawrence, D. H., 197
Lear, Edward, 67
Leaves of Grass (Whitman), 74
Leavis, F. R., 11-12, 13, 201
Leggat, Alison, 188
"Leibniz's Monads and Bradley's
  Finite Centers," 39
Lewis, Wyndham, 3, 5-6, 17, 197
"Lines for an Old Man," 66
"Little Gidding," 24-25, 66, 70, 78, 80,
  125-28, 139, 198-99, 200
London Vortex, in Eliot's early career,
  4
"Lotos-Eaters, The" (Tennyson), 78
"Love Song of J. Alfred Prufrock,
  The," 36-58, 59-61, 68, 81-82, 91
Lycidas (Milton), 204
Lynch, William, 182-83

M

Macbeth (Shakespeare), 157
McLuhan, Marshall, 37-38
Mallarmé, Stéphane, 66-67
Maid's Tragedy, The (Beaumont and
  Fletcher), 21
Manichean elements, in The Cocktail
  Party, 182-83
Matthiessen, F. O., 17
"Mariana" (Tennyson), 78-80
"Marina," 112-14
Marvell, Andrew, 140
Marx, Karl, 57
Maud (Tennyson), 76-77
Measure for Measure (Shakespeare),
  180
Melville, Herman, 197
"Mermaid, The" (Tennyson), 81
"Merman, The" (Tennyson), 81
Metaphysical poets, Eliot's essays on,
  140-141
Milton, John, 137, 140, 150, 204

Mizener, Arthur, 4-5, 13
Moby Dick (Melville), 197
Morley, Felix, 2
Morris, George L. K., 9-10
"Mr. Apollinax," 68
Mr. Weston's Good Wine (Powys), 90
Murder in the Cathedral, 12-13, 68,
   155-72, 173, 181-82, 188
   and *Becket* (Tennyson), 156-60,
     166
   chorus, function of, 158-62, 166-67
   and Greek tragedy, 158-60
"Musgrave Ritual," in *Murder in the
   Cathedral,* 163, 170
Musgrove, S., 9, 10-11, 196-97, 198
My Past (Larisch), as a source of *The
   Waste Land,* 86-88

N

Nonsense techniques, in Eliot's poetry,
   7, 66-72
"Notes," to *The Waste Land,* 103
   (see also Waste Land, The, sources
   of)
*Notes Towards the Definition of Cul-
   ture,* 139

O

Objective correlative, theory of,
   144-46
"Ode to a Nightingale" (Keats), 14
"Ode to Memory" (Tennyson), 80
"Ode to the West Wind" (Shelley), 45
Old Possum's Book of Practical Cats,
   67, 68
On Poetry and Poets, 13-14
Order, Eliot's concern with, 137, 143
Othello (Shakespeare), 157

P

Parody, in "The Dry Salvages," 197-
   200, 204
Pascal, Blaise, 23, 137, 139, 181
Pater, Walter, 136
Paul, David, 178

Pensées (Pascal), 23, 181
Peter, John, 12-13
Poems, 20-22
Poetics (Aristotle), 136
"Poetry and Drama," 177
"Poetry of *Four Quartets,* The"
   (Thorlby), 202-4
"Portrait of a Lady," 42-43, 46, 68, 81
Post-symbolist poetry, in *Four
   Quartets,* 202-5
Pound, Ezra, 5, 20, 136, 140, 141
   and Eliot, 5, 20, **28-35,** 149-51
Powys, T. F., 90
Preface (Wordsworth), 136
"Preludes," 31, 105
Principia Mathematica (Whitehead and
   Russell), 56
Proust, Marcel, 153-54
Prufrock and Other Observations, 5,
   20-22, 34

Q

Quiller-Couch, Sir Arthur, 1

R

Racine, Jean, 150
Rajan, B., 192-93, 194, 196, 197, 201
Ransom, John Crowe, 204
"Rhapsody on a Windy Night," 31,
   105-6
Rhythm, in *Ash Wednesday,* 134-35
Richards, I. A., 40, 136, 142-43
"Rock, The," Choruses from, 22, 75,
   80, 105
Romeo and Juliet (Shakespeare), 156
Rousseau, Jean Jacques, 55
Russell, Bertrand, 56

S

"Sailing to Byzantium" (Yeats), 14
Santayana, George, 56, 136
Satire, in *Coriolan* poems, 114-16
Schopenhauer, Arthur, 48
"Sea-Fairies, The" (Tennyson), 78, 81

Sensibility, and poetic expression, 146-47
Seventeenth Century Background, The (Willey), 62-63
Sewell, Elizabeth, 7, 58
Sexual themes, in *The Waste Land,* 90-92
Shakespeare, Dorothy, 30
Shakespeare, William, 38, 41-42, 49, 145, 156-57, 180, 187-88
Shelley, Percy Bysshe, 45, 56, 58-59, 137, 140, 156
"Sisters, The" (Tennyson), 77-78
"Song for Simeon, A," 13
"Song of the Open Road" (Whitman), 196
"Song of the Sisters, The" (Tennyson), 78
Sophocles, 59
Spiritual values, and tradition, in "Little Gidding," 125-27
"Stopping by Woods on a Snowy Evening" (Frost), 59
"Style of the Master, The" (Empson), 6
Sweeney Agonistes, 68, 176
"Sweeney Among the Nightingales," 106
"Sweeney Erect," 20-21
Swinburne, Algernon, 45-46, 136, 140
Sylvie and Bruno (Dodgson), 66-67, 69, 71

T

Table Talk (Coleridge), 137
Tarot pack, function of, in *The Waste Land,* 92-94, 101-2
Tate, Allen, 12, 18
Tempest, The (Shakespeare), 180
Tennyson, Alfred, 10, 37, 38, 45
    Becket and *Murder in the Cathedral,* 156-60, 166
    and Eliot, 38, 75-85
Thorlby, Anthony, 202-4
Time, processes of, in "Little Gidding," 127-28

Tourneur, Cyril, 140
"Tradition and Individual Talent," 19-20, 46, 48, 143-44, 199, 204
Tradition, Eliot's concern with, 137, 143-44
Trilling, Lionel, 180-181
Tristan und Isolde (Wagner), 87, 101
"Triumphal March," 13, 14, 114-16
T. S. Eliot and Walt Whitman (Musgrove), 196

U

Use of Poetry and the Use of Criticism, The, 10

V

Valéry, Paul, 58
Vegetation themes, in *The Waste Land,* 93-99
Vorticism, in Eliot's early career, 5

W

Wagner, Richard, 87, 101
Waste Land, The, 7-10, 23, 37, 47-48, 61-64, 67, 79-85, 89-103, 104, 131-33, 173
    analogy in, 61-64
    and *Ash Wednesday,* 131-33
    "Burial of the Dead," 94, 96, 100-102
    compression of experience in, 99-102
    critical reception of, 16-17, 23
    "Death by Water," 63-64, 101-2
    fertility and vegetation themes in, 93-99
    "Fire Sermon, The," 102-3, 132-33
    "Game of Chess, A," 95, 100-101, 174
    Nonsense techniques in, 68-69
    "Notes," 103
    sexual themes in, 90-92
    sources of, 9-10, 86-88, 92-94

Waste Land, The, (continued)
   Tennysonian influences in, 79-85
   "What the Thunder Said," 93-94,
     98-99, 100, 102
Weaver, Harriet, 34
Webster, John, 102, 140
Weston, Jessie, 62, 89-99, 103, 141
"What the Thunder Said" (*The Waste
   Land*), 93-94, 98-99, 100, 102
Whitehead, Alfred North, 56
"Whitman and Tennyson," 73

Whitman, Walt, 10, 73-74, 196-97, 200
Willey, Basil, 62-63
Wilson, Edmund, 22, 133
Wimsatt, W. K., 184-85
"Wind Sprang Up, The" (Tennyson), 80
Winters, Yvor, 197
Wordsworth, William, 47, 136, 156

Y

Yeats, William Butler, 14, 63, 197

EMERSON

A Collection of Critical Essays

Edited by MILTON R. KONVITZ
and STEPHEN E. WHICHER

A

Adams, Henry, 39, 44
Adams, John, 95
AE (*see* Russell, George)
Aesthetics, Emerson's theories on,
 108-20, 137-38, 144-47, 149-53
 (*see also* Perception and knowledge)
Alcott, Bronson, 2-3, 90, 118, 124
Aldridge, John, 45
Amaury of Bene, 131, 132
American Scholar, The, 42-43, 66, 67-
 68
American society, Emerson's criticisms
 of, 2-3, (*see also* Capitalism)
Antigone (Sophocles), 4-5
"Aristocracy," 73
Aristotle, 109, 114, 115, 162
Arnold, Matthew, 1, 153
"Art," 81
Augustine, Saint, 54-55, 56, 127, 128,
 176

B

Baudelaire, Charles, 57
Bellamy, Edward, 97
Bhagavad-Gita, 56, 178
Birrell, Augustine, 1
Boehme, Jacob, 125
"Brahma," 14, 138
Braun, Rev. Henry A., 167
Brihadaranyaka Upanishad, 56
Brook Farm, 63, 96

Brownson, Orestes A., 77
Burke, Edmund, 114
Byron, George Gordon, 75-76, 79

C

Calvin, John, 123
Capitalism, Emerson's theories on, 91-
 93, 96-99
Carlyle, Thomas, 57, 73, 77, 80, 105,
 115, 123, 125
Carnegie, Andrew, 98
Channing, William Ellery, 95
"Circles," 160-161
City of God, The (St. Augustine), 54-
 55, 56
Clemens, S. L., 39
Coleridge, Samuel Taylor, 110-11, 125,
 139, 141, 171, 173, 177
Conduct of Life, The, 43, 51-52, 57,
 58
"Conservative, The," 69
Cooper, James Fenimore, 80, 83, 105
Cranch, Christopher, 159, 167
Crater, The (Cooper), 80
Croce, Benedetto, 109, 111-12
Cromwell, Oliver, 79, 115
"Culture," 73

D

"Days," 103-5, 107
Democracy, Emerson's concept of,
 72-84 (*see also* Progressive tradition)

Democracy in America (Tocqueville),
   86-88, 93
Descartes, René, 163
Dewey, John, on Emerson, 24-30
Dialectical method, in Emerson's
   thought, 154-57
Dickens, Charles, 123
Dickinson, Emily, 39
Dionysius the Areopagite, 125, 131
Divinity School Address, 53-54, 169

E

Eckhart, Meister Johannes, 125-26
Education, Emerson's theory of, 3
Edwards, Jonathan, 101, 127, 132
Eliot, T. S., 9, 10, 46
Emerson, Mary Moody, 124
Emerson, Ralph Waldo:
   aesthetic theories of, **108-20**, 137-
      38, 144-47, 149-53 (*see also*
      Emerson: perception and knowl-
      edge)
   and Alcott, Bronson, 2-3, 90, 118,
      124
   on American socity, 2-3
   on capitalism, 91-93, 96-99
   and Carlyle, Thomas, 57, 73, 77,
      80, 105, 115, 123, 125
   and Coleridge, Samuel Taylor, 110,
      111, 125, 139, 141, 171, 173, 177
   democracy, concept of, 72-84
   and Dewey, John, 24-30
   dialectical method of, 154-57
   and English Romanticism, 64-65,
      66, 73, 75-76, 79, 110, 111, 129,
      139, 141
   and evil, problem of, 3, 16-17, 36-
      37, 47-50, 52-59, 91, 122-23,
      127-28
   and Frost, Robert, 12-17
   and Fuller, Margaret, 63, 76, 103,
      107, 112, 118, 156, 165
   genius, doctrine of, 64-65, 74-82
      117-19
   and the German transcendentalists,
      28, 32-34, 73, 137
   and Goethe, Johann Wolfgang von,

      75, 76, 79, 112, 113, 119
   and Hawthorne, Nathaniel, 47, 53,
      88, 101
   and Hindu philosophy, 53-54, 56,
      178
   on history, the meaning of, 8-10
   individual, doctrine of the, 20-23,
      88-89, 93, 95-96
   and James, Henry, 47, 60, 64
   and James, William, 18-23, 160
   language, theory of, 144-47, 149-57
   life of, 41, 50-51, 60-71, 72
   and man, ideal view of, 4-8, 41-42
   and Melville, Herman, 47, 50, 52,
      88, 101, 106, 136, 147, 153-57
   as a minister, 60-71
   mysticism of, 35-36, 115, 125-33,
      168-71
   on Napoleon Bonaparte, 75, 76-77,
      79, 82, 83, 90, 93
   Nature, theory of, 5-6, 140-141,
      143, 171-73
   and Neo-Platonism, 54-55, 56, 66-
      67, 109-11, 115-17, 131
   optimism of, 50-54, 91, 98, 122,
      128-29
   Oversoul, doctrine of the, 35-36, 56,
      95, 129-31, 138-39, 176
   and Parker, Theodore, 63, 73, 91,
      95, 124
   perception and knowledge, theory
      of, 140-147, 158-78
   and Plato, 4, 6, 27, 29, 54-55, 56,
      104, 106, 175
   and Plotinus, 54, 55, 125, 127, 129
   poetry of, 13-17, 44, **100-107**
   and the progressive tradition, 85-99
      (*see also* Emerson: democracy,
      concept of)
   and Puritanism, 37-38, 44, 60-62,
      122-23, 126-30
   religious views of, 3-4, 38, (*see also*
      Emerson: Oversoul, doctrine of
      the)
   Scholar, concept of the, 67-71, 92
   self-reliance, doctrine of, 62-65, 88,
      129-31
   and Swedenborg, Emanuel, 12-13,

Emerson, Ralph Waldo (*continued*)
52, 116, 125, 128
symbolism, theory of, 136, 138,
143 (*see also* Emerson: perception and knowledge, theory of)
and Thoreau, Henry David, 86, 93-
94, 95, 96, 100, 112, 153, 160,
174
transcendentalism of, 68-71, 73-
74, 88-89, 92, 94-95, 124
and Unitarianism, 17, 37-38, 62,
63-64, 68-69, 101, 124
vision, theory of, 158-78
and Whitman, Walt, 75, 86, 88, 95,
100, 101-2, 136, 161
Emerson, Ralph Waldo, works by:
PROSE
American Scholar, The, 42-43, 66,
67-68
"Aristocracy," 73
"Art," 81
"Circles," 160-161
"Culture," 73
Conduct of Life, The, 43, 51-52,
57, 58
"Conservative, The," 69
Divinity School Address, 53-54, 169
"English Traits," 126, 134
Essays (*see* titles of individual
essays)
Experience, 40, 42, 101, 160
"Fate," 51-52, 57, 58
"Genius," 81
"Intellect," 81, 168-69
"Inspiration," 172-73
Journals, 61, 63-71, 73, 75, 76, 77,
81, 82, 110, 112, 114, 123-24,
127-30, 132, 135, 140, 158-78
passim
"Manners," 73
"Man of Letters, The," 66
"Man the Reformer," 66
"Method of Nature, The," 59
"Miracle of Our Being, The," 169-70
"Miracles," 169
Nature, 2, 80, 108, 109, 137, 140-
141, 145, 159, 166
"New England Reformers," 58

"Oversoul, The," 52
"Politics," 83
"Power," 90
"Prudence," 47
Representative Men, 8-9, 12, 77-78,
80-83, 90, 93, 109
"Scholar, The," 66
Self-Reliance, 40-41, 43-44, 81, 116
Society and Solitude, 113-14
"Spiritual Laws," 172
"Times, The," 62, 66
"Tragic, The," 40, 44, 48-49, 51
"Transcendentalist, The," 70-71
"Trifles," 165
"Wealth," 90
"Works and Days," 104, 175
"Worship," 172
POETRY
"Brahma," 14, 138
"Days," 103-5, 107
"May-Day," 104
"Monadnock," 13
"Ode to William Ellery Channing,"
44
"Saadi," 104
"Threnody," 44, 174
"World-Soul, The," 44
Emmet, Dorothy, 160
English Romanticism, in Emerson's
thought, 64-65, 66, 73, 75-76, 110,
111, 129, 139, 141
"English Traits," 126, 134
Erigena, John Scotus, 125, 131
Essays (*see* titles of individual essays)
Evil, problem of, and Emerson's
thought, 3, 16-17, 36-37, 47-50, 52-
59, 91, 122-23, 127-28
Experience, 40, 42, 101, 160

F

"Fate," 51-52, 57, 58
Faulkner, William, 39
Flaubert, Gustave, 112
Frost, Robert, 1-2, 39
on Emerson, 12-17
Fuller, Margaret, 63, 76, 103, 107,
112, 118, 156, 165

G

Gay, R. M., 63
"Genius," 81
Genius, Emerson's doctrine of the,
  64-65, **74-82**, 117-19
German transcendentalists, influence
  of, on Emerson's thought, 28, 32-34,
  73, 137
Gide, André, 57
Goethe, Johann Wolfgang von, 75, 76,
  79, 112, 113, 119

H

Hawthorne, Nathaniel, 47, 53, 88,
  101, 136
Herschel, Sir John, 166
Hindu philosophy, influence of, on
  Emerson's thought, 53-54, 56,
  178
Holmes, Oliver Wendell, 1, 72,
  119
Home as Found (Cooper), 80
Hume, David, 163

I

Ibsen, Henrik, 41
Individual, Emerson's doctrine of the,
  20-23, 88-89, 93, 95-96
"Inspiration," 172-73
"Intellect," 81, 168-69

J

Jackson, Andrew, 72, 73, 75-78
Jackson, Lydia, 163
James, Henry, 39, 47, 60, 64
James, William, 160
  on Emerson, 18-23
Jaspers, Karl, 57
Jeffers, Robinson, 44
Jefferson, Thomas, 95
Johnson, Dr. Samuel, 52
Journals, 61, **63-71**, 73, 75, 76, 77, 81,
  82, 110, 112, 114, 123-24, 127-30,
  132, 135, 140, 158-78 *passim*

K

Kant, Immauel, 137, 163
Keats, John, 119
Kepler, Johannes, 6
Kierkegaard, Sören, 56, 59

L

Language, Emerson's theory of,
  144-47, 149-57
Lawrence, D. H., 46
Leaves of Grass (Whitman), 75
Lincoln, Abraham, 78, 79, 81-82, 83
Looking Backward (Bellamy), 97
Lowell, Amy, 13
Luther, Martin, 123, 125

M

Man, Emerson's ideal view of, 4-8, 41-
  42
Manicheans, 54
"Manners," 73
"Man of Letters, The," 66
"Man the Reformer," 66
"May-Day," 104
Mazzini, Giuseppe, 97
Melville, Herman, 39, 47, 50, 52, 88,
  101, 106, 136, 147, 153-57
"Method of Nature, The," 59
Michelangelo, 111, 113, 116
Milton, John, 2, 116
Ministry, Emerson's vocation in the,
  60-71
"Miracle of Our Being, The," 169-70
"Miracles," 169
"Monadnock," 13
Morris, William, 97-98
Mysticism, in Emerson's thought, 35-
  36, 115, 125-33, 168-71

N

Napoleon Bonaparte, 75, 76-77, 79,
  82, 83, 90, 93
Nature, 2, 80, 108, 109, 137, 140-141,
  145, 159, 166

Nature, Emerson's theory of, 5-6, 140-141, 143, 171-73

Neo-Platonism, in Emerson's thought, 54-55, 56, 66-67, 109-11, 115-17, 131

"New England Reformers," 58

Newton, Sir Isaac, 173, 177

Nietzsche, Friedrich, 57

Norris, Frank, 44

Norton, Andrews, 75, 76, 124

O

"Ode to William Ellery Channing," 44

Optimism, in Emerson's thought, 50-54, 91, 98, 122, 128-29

Ortega y Gasset, José, 161-63

Oversoul, Emerson's doctrine of the, 35-36, 56, 95, 129-31, 138-39, 176

"Oversoul, The," 52

P

Parker, Theodore, 63, 73, 91, 95, 124

Partial Portraits (Henry James), 60, 64

Perception and knowledge, Emerson's theory of, 140-147, 158-78

Phaedrus (Plato), 6

Pierce, Franklin, 83

Pierre (Melville), 101

Pioneers, The (Cooper), 80

Pitt, William, 114

Plato, 4, 6, 27, 29, 54-55, 56, 104, 106, 175

Plotinus, 54, 55, 125, 127, 129

Poe, Edgar Allan, 39, 108-9, 111, 114, 115, 119, 136

"Politics," 83

"Power," 90

Proclus, 27

Progressive tradition, Emerson's involvement in, 85-99 (*see also* Democracy)

"Prudence," 47

Puritanism, influence of, 37-38, 44, 60-62, 122-23, 126-30

R

Rationalism (*see* Perception and knowledge, Emerson's theory of)

Reed, Sampson, 159

Representative Men, 8-9, 12, 77-78, 80-83, 90, 93, 109

Ripley, George, 73

Rousseau, Jean-Jacques, 117-18

Russell, George, 46-47

S

"Saadi," 104

Sandburg, Carl, 44

Santayana, George, on Emerson, 31-38

Schelling, Friedrich von, 125

Schlegel, Friedrich von, 110

Schleiermacher, Friedrich, 10

Scholar, Emerson's concept of the, 67-71, 92

"Scholar, The," 66

Self-Reliance, 40-41, 43-44, 81, 116

Self-reliance, Emerson's doctrine of, 62-65, 88, 129-31

Shakespeare, William, 109, 114, 119-20

Shelley, Percy Bysshe, 109

Society and Solitude, 113-14

Socrates, 4, 6

Sophocles, 4-5, 174

"Spiritual Laws," 172

Steinbeck, John, 44

Swedenborg, Emanuel, 12-13, 52, 116, 125, 128

Symbolism, Emerson's theory of, 136, 138, 143 (*see also* Perception and knowledge, Emerson's theory of)

T

Tauler, Johannes, 125, 131

Thomas Aquinas, Saint, 57, 127

Thoreau, Henry David, 39, 44, 86, 93-94, 95, 96, 100, 112, 153, 160, 174

"Threnody," 44, 174
"Times, The," 66
Tocqueville, Alexis de, 86-88, 93
"Tragic, The," 40, 44, 48-49, 51
Transcendentalism, in New England,
    69-71, 73-74, 88-89, 92, 94-95, 124
"Transcendentalist, The," 70-71
"Trifles," 165
Twain, Mark (*see* Clemens, S. L.)
Twilight of Idols, The (Nietzsche), 57

U

Unitarianism, 17, 37-38, 62, 63-64, 68-
    69, 101, 124 (*see also* Puritanism)
Upanishads, The, 56

V

Van Buren, Martin, 77
Van Doren, Mark, 40

Very, Jones, 75
Vishnu Purana, 56
Vision, Emerson's theory of, 158-78
Voltaire, 52

W

Ward, Lester, 97
Ware, Henry, 124
"Wealth," 90
Webster, Daniel, 114
Whitehead, Alfred North, 141
Whitman, Walt, 39, 44, 75, 77, 78, 86,
    88, 95, 100, 101-2, 136, 161
Wordsworth, William, 73, 114, 141
"Works and Days," 104, 175
"World-Soul, The," 44
"Worship," 172

Y

Yeats, W. B., 40, 46-47

EURIPIDES

A Collection of Critical Essays

Edited by ERICH SEGAL

A

Aeschylus, 1, 9, 12, 14, 18, 29, 30, 32, 33, 37, 41, 54, 81, 91, 128, 132-34, 139, 143, 144-45, 147, 151, 153
Agamemnon (Aeschylus), 81, 91, 139, 140, 151
Ajax (Sophocles), 20, 152
Albee, Edward, 10
Alcestis, 1, 2-3, 5-6, 11, 19, 36, **51-69,** 164
  action of, 53, 55
  characterization, 56-59, 61-62
  death, theme of, 55-59, 61-63, 66-69
  deus ex machina in, 5-6, 19
  dissonance, concept of, 17-18
  house and repayment, themes of, 54-55, 56, 58, 60-61, 66
  logos and *ergon,* theme of, 17
  as mystery play, 68-69
  myth of, 51-52, 66
  plot summary, 55-67
  prologue summary, 53-55
  structure, 51-53, 59-60, 63
Anaxagoras, 37
Andromache, 19, 140
Andromeda, 1
Anouilh, Jean, 75-76, 79, 89
Antigone (Sophocles), 2, 7, 130
Antilogiai (Protagoras), 6
Apology (Plato), 57
Aristophanes, 1, 9, 11-12, 15, 39, 66, 133, 140, 146, 148-49

Aristotle, 1-2, 5-6, 8, 9, 16-17, 22, **74-76,** 77, 78, 85, 87, **90-91,** 100-101, 146, 152, 155, 158, 164

B

Bacchae, 1, 7-8, 10, 22, 24, 28, 39-41, 50, **150-70**
  bestialization of man, theme of, 155-58, 160
  characterization, 155-56, 164-67
  chorus, function of, 159-61
  destruction of Pentheus, meaning of, 163-70
  Dionysus, description of, 154-57, 161-62
  double nature of man, theme of, 155
  hybris, concept of, 162
  imagery of beasts in, 156-57
  philosophical aspects of, 151-53, 158-59
  political aspects of, 164-65
  psychological meaning in, 157-58, 167-69
  refrain, function of, 158
  religious influence of, 39-40, 41
  sparagmos, concept of, 162-63
  symbolism of the hunt, 162
Bacchylides, 67-68
Bald Soprano, The (Ionesco), 128
Beckett, Samuel, 128-29
Birds (Aristophanes), 11, 140
Blood Wedding (Lorca), 10

179

Brecht, Bertoldt, 18, 30
Brooks, Van Wyck, 150

C

Characterization:
  in *Alcestis*, 56-59, 61
  in *Bacchae*, 155-56, 164-67
  in *Hippolytus*, 90-91, 92
  in *Medea*, 79, 83-85
  in *Orestes*, 143-44
  in *Trojan Women*, 121-22
Children of Heracles, 45
Choephoroi (Aeschylus), 132, 139-40
Cocktail Party, The (Eliot), 10
Cohen, Morris, 19
Confidential Clerk, The (Eliot), 10
Corinthians, I (Paul, Saint), 10
Corneille, Pierre, 75, 84, 86, 88
Cornford, Francis, 32
Cratinus, 12

D

Democritus, 71
Desire Under the Elms (O'Neill), 10
Deus ex machina:
  in *Alcestis*, 5-6, 19
  in Euripides' works, 3-6, 19-20
  in *Medea*, 74-75
Dionysus, description of, 154-57
Dissonance:
  in Euripides' works, 17-21, 23
  in *Orestes*, 132-33, 140-141, 146
Drama, Greek:
  and cultural crisis, theme of, 13-16,
    27-28
  purpose of, 14, 20
  religious influence of, 39
  ritualistic interpretation of, 32-33
  and theater of ideas, concept of,
    13-14, 27-29

E

Electra, 42, 50, 139, 140, 142-43
Electra (Sophocles), 41, 132-33, 139,
  143

Eliot, T. S., 10
Eumenides (Aeschylus), 54, 132-34,
  144-45, 147
Euripides:
  and Anouilh, Jean, 75-76, 79, 89
  and Aristophanes, 11-12
  classicists' attitudes toward, 29-33
  commonplace language, use of,
    128-29
  critique of social tradition, 18-20
  and cultural revolution, 14-15, 27-
    29, 31-32, 128-29
  deus ex machina, uses of, 3, 5, 6,
    19-20, 74-75
  and Dionysus, function of, 154-57
  dissonance, concept of, 17-21, 23,
    132-33, 140, 146
  dramatic influence of, 10-11
  and fallible gods, theme of, 43-48
  life of, 9-10, 12
  morality of characters, 23-24
  and paradox, theme of, 2-7
  and Plato, 27-29
  realism of, 9, 17-20, 28-29, 41-42,
    44-45, 152-53
  religious beliefs of, 37-41, 45-50
  and Sophocles, 7-8
  staging technique of, 8-9, 115
  and theater of ideas, concepts of,
    13-33
  "theos," concept of, 34-36, 40-42
  and traditional drama, 2-3, 8-9,
    20-23
Euripides, works by:
  Alcestis, 1-3, 5-6, 11, 19, 36, **51-69**,
    164
  Andromache, 19, 140
  Andromeda, 1
  Bacchae, 1, 7-8, 10, 22, 24, 28, 39-
    41, 50, **150-70**
  Children of Heracles, 45
  Electra, 42, 50, 139, 140, 142-43
  Hecuba, 17, 28, 50, 139
  Helen, 1, 4, 6
  Heracles, 2, 4-5, 6, 17, 19, 22, 36,
    40, 43-44, 45-47, 49, 50
  Heraclidae, 23, 140
  Hippolytus, 3-4, 8, 10, 16, 24, 36,

Euripides, works by: (*continued*)
39-41, 48-50, **90-114**, 140
Ion, 10, 140, 151, 157
Iphigenia at Aulis, 2, 43
Iphigenia in Tauris, 19-20, 42
Medea, 5, 10, 22, 24-27, 29, 41, 50,
70-89
Orestes, 6, 42, 43, **132-49**
Peliades, 9
Phoenician Women, 44
Rhesus, 9
Troades (see Orestes)
Trojan Women, 1, 2, 8, 19, 40, 43,
44, 49, 50, **115-27**, 128-31, 135,
142

F

Faust (Goethe), 86, 153
Finley, John, 31
Freud, Sigmund, 8
Fritz, Kurt von, 83
Frogs (Aristophanes), 1, 9, 133, 140,
146, 148-49

G

Goethe, Johann von, 33, 74, 86, 153

H

Harrison, Jane, 32
Havelock, Eric, 10
Hebbel, Friedrich, 29
Hecuba, 17, 28, 50, 139
Hegel, Georg, 7
Helen, 1, 4, 6
Heracles, 2, 4-5, 6, 17, 19, 22, 36, 40,
43-44, 45-47, 49, 50
deus ex machina in, 4-5
fallible gods, theme of, 45-47
loneliness, theme of, 22
Heraclidae, 23, 140
Heraclitus, 71
Herodotus, 7, 126
Hesiod, 14
Hippolytus, 3-4, 8, 10, 16, 24, 36, 39-
41, 48-50, 90-114, 140

characterization, 90-92, 101-8
determinism, theme of, 91
and divine law, concept of, 108-10,
112-14
"escape ode," theme of, 3-4
free will, theme of, 91-92, 93, 110
imagery of being thrown, 8, 109-10
irrational order, theme of, 16
meaningless choice, theme of,
101-2, 108, 110-11
and myth, function of, 111
mythic truth of, 48-49
plot summary, 92-100
religious belief, theme of, 106-8
religious influence of, 39-40
speech or silence, theme of, 92-101,
103-4
symbolism of Artemis and Aphro-
dite, 111-12
"theos" and man, theme of, 40-41
Homer, 34, 35, 36, 71, 72, 76, 78, 85,
118, 120, 121, 125, 126, 140-41

I

Ibsen, Henrik, 6, 18, 30
Iliad (Homer), 34, 71-72, 85,
118, 120, 121, 125, 126, 140-41
Imagery:
in *Bacchae*, 156-57, 161-62
in *Hippolytus*, 8, 109-10
in *Orestes*, 140-41
Ion, 10, 140, 151, 157
Ionesco, Eugene, 20, 128-29
Iphigenia at Aulis, 2, 43
Iphigenia in Tauris, 19-20, 42

J

Jaeger, Werner, 11, 15, 29
James, Henry, 14

K

King Lear (Shakespeare), 1
Kitto, H. D. F., 12
Knox, Bernard,
8

L

Lesky, Albin, 5
Longinus, 9
Lorca, García, 10

M

Macbeth (Shakespeare), 37
Mann, Thomas, 33
Measure for Measure (Shakespeare), 23
Medea, 5, 10, 22, 24-27, 29, 41, 50,
    70-89
    agon of Jason and Medea, meaning
        of, 26-27
    and Anouilh, Jean, 75-76, 79, 89
    Aristotle's criticism of, 74-76, 78,
        85, 87
    characterization, 79, 83-85
    children, theme of, 87-89
    deus ex machina in, 74-75
    homelessness, theme of, 84
    infanticide, theme of, 72, 80-81,
        83-84, 88
    physis against *nomos*, theme of, 24,
        25-26
    plight of women, theme of, 81-82,
        85
    plot summary, 78-80, 82-83, 87-88
    psychological interpretations of,
        24-27, 70-74
    regret, theme of, 79-80
    revenge and inevitability, theme of,
        72-74, 88
    structure, 74-81
    as theater of ideas, 25-26
    and traditional myth, 80
Menander, 10, 128
Müller, Max, 166
Murray, Gilbert, 3, 32

N

Nietzsche, Friedrich, 1, 23, 32, 33

O

Odyssey (Homer), 78, 120, 126

Oedipus at Colonus (Sophocles), 40
Oedipus Rex (Sophocles), 11, 87, 90,
    152
O'Neill, Eugene, 10
Oresteia (Aeschylus), 9, 41, 91, 151
Orestes, 6, 42, 43, 132-49
    and Aristophanes' *Frogs*, 148-49
    characterization, 143-44
    civil justice, theme of, 143-45
    death, theme of, 135-37
    dissonance, function of, 132-33,
        140-141, 146
    human survival, theme of, 148
    illusion, theme of, 138-40
    imagery of beasts in, 140-141
    monody of Helen, 141
    moral conflict, theme of, 136-38
    passion, concept of, 146
    plot summary, 132-48
    politics of, 145-47
    revenge, theme of, 142-43, 146
    and Sophocles' *Electra*, 132-33
    style, 140-142
    and traditional myth, 133-34, 138,
        143, 146-48
Ovid, 12
Oxbow Incident (Brooks), 150

P

Paideia (Jaeger), 15
Parian Marble, 9
Paul, Saint, 10
Peliades, 9
Pericles, 28
Persians (Aeschylus), 81
Phaedo (Plato), 153
Phaedrus (Plato), 152, 155
Philemon, 10
Philoctetes (Sophocles), 11, 140
Phoenician Women, 44
Phrynichus, 59
Pindar, 150
Pirandello, Luigi, 6
Plato, 27-29, 36, 57, 71, 151-53, 155,
    165, 168
Plautus, 10
Plutarch, 11

Poetics (Aristotle), 1-2, 74-76, 85, 86
Politics (Aristotle), 100-101
Procrustes, 1
Prometheus Bound (Aeschylus), 153
Protagoras, 6
Pythagoreans, 155

R

Reality, Greek concept of, 152-53
Religion, Olympian concept of, 36-37
Renan, Ernest, 131
Rhesus, 9

S

Sappho, 158-59
Sartre, Jean-Paul, 30, **128-31**
Schadewaldt, Wolfgang, 70
Schegel, August Wilhelm von, 1
Schiller, Johann von, 29
Seneca, 8, 10, 75
Shakespeare, William, 1, 18, 23, 30,
  37
Shaw, George Bernard, 18
Socrates, 12, 94, 151, 152
Sophocles, 1, 2, 5, 7-8, 9, 11, 12, 14,
  15, 18, 20, 30, 33, 40, 41, 78, 87,
  90-91, 121, 130, 132-33, 139, 143,
  151, 152
Strohm, Hans, 76, 77
Symbolism:
  in *Bacchae*, 162
  in *Hippolytus*, 111-12
  in *Trojan Women*, 125
Symposium (Plato), 151

T

Tempest, The (Shakespeare), 1
Terence, 10
Theetetus (Plato), 151
Themistocles, 107
Theramenes, 133
Thesmophoriazusae (Aristophanes), 11
Thucydides, **15-16**, 18, 31, 107, 146,
  165, 168

Tiny Alice (Albee), 10
Trachiniae (Sophocles), 11
Tragedy, concept of, 1-2, 90-91,
  153-54
Troades (see Orestes)
Trojan Women, 1, 2, 8, 19, 40, 43, 44,
  49, 50, **115-27**, 128-31, 135, 142
  adaptation by Sartre, Jean-Paul,
    128-31
  characterization, 121-22
  cynicism in, 120
  divine intervention, theme of,
    116-17
  gods rebuked in, 43
  irrational order, theme of, 127
  monody of Hecuba, 117-18
  moral ambiguities of, 123, 125-27
  nihilism in, 131
  parody in, 119, 121
  plight of women, theme of, 121-23
  plot summary, 115-27
  political meaning of, 130
  prologue summary, 115-17
  religious meaning of, 131
  staging of, 8, 115
  symbolism of values in, 125

V

Vellacott, Phillip, 157

W

Waiting for Godot (Beckett), 128
Who's Afraid of Virginia Woolf?
  (Albee), 10
Winter's Tale, The (Shakespeare), 1

X

Xenophanes, 37

Z

Zürcher, W., 72-73

FAULKNER

A Collection of Critical Essays

Edited by ROBERT PENN WARREN

A

Abinger Harvest (Forster), 14

Absalom, Absalom! 13, 26-27, 29, 34, 36, 37-39, 41, 42, 46, 49-51, 53, 55-56, 60, 66-67, 70-72, 95, 102, **175-85, 186-203,** 205-6, 227, 230, 257, 259-60, 262, 275, 276, 280, 282 289-90, 296
   characterization, 60, 187-94, 201
   and the detective story genre, 196-99
   historical aspects of, 184-85, 194-97
   innocence, concept of, 186-93
   miscegenation, theme of, 182-83
   morality, theme of, 26-27, 183-84
   plot summary, 37-38, 175-82
   religious symbolism in, 70-72
   society, symbolism of, 38-39
   sociological aspects of, 193-94, 259-60
   structure, 175-78
   style of, 289-90

Adventures of Huckleberry Finn, The (Twain), 44, 149, 214-15

Aeneid (Vergil), 211

Aiken, Conrad, 20

Alanus de Insulis, 27, 66

Aldington, Richard, 8

Allen, Hervey, 277

"All the Dead Pilots," 59

America Amara (Cecchi), 206

American Tragedy, An (Dreiser), 255

Anderson, Sherwood, 95-96, 221

Anna Karenina (Tolstoy), 104

Anthony Adverse (Allen), 277

Aristotle, 12, 163, 164, 275

As I Lay Dying, 1, 7, 27, 32, 34, 41, 43, 49-50, 55, 106, 161, 205, 274, 275, 285, 293

Aspects du roman americain (Coindreau), 76

Aymé, Marcel, 293-94

B

Babbitt (Lewis), 106

Baldwin, James, 258

Balzac, Honoré de, 35, 52, **73-77,** 225, 273

Barbusse, Henri, 8

Barnes, Djuna, 32

Baudelaire, Charles, 5, 274

Beard, Charles Austin, 184

"Bear, The," 42, **208-18,** 220, 249, 257, 260-61, 263, 275, 293
   the hero, theme of, 208-18
   and the life of Christ, 211, 217-18
   and magic weapons, theme of, 216-17
   morality, theme of, 209-10, 214-17
   negro, concept of, 260-261, 263
   plot summary, 209-13
   structure, 211-14

Beck, Warren, 20

Becker, Carl Lotus, 184

Bernanos, Georges, 205

Biblical references, 70-71, 77, 182,

Biblical references, (*continued*)
184, 193, 204, 206, 208-9, 217-18,
239-40, 246-48, 293-94
Billy Budd (Melville), 209
Bleak House (Dickens), 231-32
Bobbsey Twins, The (Hope), 9
Bowling, Lawrence, 22
Boynton, Percy, 9
Bradley, F. H., 76
Breit, Harvey, 186
Bridge, Horatio, 45
Brothers Karamazoff, The (Dostoevsky), 273, 294
Brown, Charles Brockden, 44
Buber, Martin, 183
Butterfield, Herbert, 184
Byron, George, 191

C

Caldwell, Erskine, 9
Camus, Albert, 11, 18, 149, 160, 205, 295
Castle, The (Kafka), 69
Cecchi, Emilio, 206
Chance or Destiny: Turning Points in American History (Handlin), 184
Chapman, John Jay, 281
Charlotte Temple (Rowson), 286
Chartreuse de Parme (Stendhal), 72-73
Christianity and History (Butterfield), 184
Citizen Tom Paine (Fast), 10
Claudel, Paul, 205
Coindreau, Maurice, 76, 97
Coiners, The, 87
Collins, Carvell, 290-291
Comédie Humaine, La (Balzac), 35, 75
"Conflict of Convictions, The" (Melville), 11
Conrad, Joseph, 5, 11, 14, 82, 166, 211, 221
Coolidge, Calvin, 6, 254
Cooper, James Fenimore, 208
Cowley, Malcolm, 10, 15, 67, 75, 104-5
Crane, Stephen, 44, 238
Crane, Hart, 5

Création chez Stendhal, La (Prévost), 72
"Crisis of Barbarism, The" (Cecchi), 206
Crockett, David, 44

D

Dante, 28, 253
Davenport, Marcia, 9
"Delta Autumn," 265-66, 268
Diable et le Bon Dieu, Le (Sartre), 205
Dickens, Charles, 231-32, 274, 286
Divina Commedia (Dante), 28
Doctor Martino, 35, 75
Dos Passos, John, 8, 19, 77, 85, 88, 91, 154, 250, 281
Dostoevsky, Fyodor, 5, 11, 32, 72, 81, 166, 172, 246, 273, 278, 286, 294
Dreiser, Theodore, 254-55

E

"Edge of Order: The Pattern of Faulkner's Rhetoric, The" (Slatoff), 15
Electra (Sophocles), 28
Eliot, T. S., 5, 11, 17, 19, 26, 73, 77, 123, 157, 183, 186, 238, 269
Ellison, Ralph, 258
Emerson, Ralph Waldo, 149, 215, 281
Emmanuel, Pierre, 291-92
"Evening Sun, That," 35, 94, 97, 296

F

Fable, A, 16-17, 152-53, 156, 159, 209, 238-42, 243-50, 275
  historical aspects of, 238-39
  plot summary, 239-40, 246-47
  religious aspects of, 239-40, 246-49
  style of, 240-42
Fadiman, Clifton, 13, 227, 289-90
Farewell to Arms, A (Hemingway), 122
Fast, Howard, 10
"Fathers and Sons" (Hemingway), 287
Faulkner, William:
  and American GI's, 10-12
  and Anderson, Sherwood, 95-96

Faulkner, William: (*continued*)
  and Balzac, Honoré de, 73-77
  and civil-rights, 222-25, 276
  colloquialisms, in works of, 58-60
  critics' attitudes toward, 6-22,
    204-7
  destiny, concept of, 81-86
  and the detective story genre,
    196-99
  and Frost, Robert, 2-3
  genealogies, in works of, 296-302
  and Hawthorne, Nathaniel, 44-45
  historical aspects, in works of, 5-6
  interrelated themes, in works of,
    34-37
  and italics, use of, 99-100
  and James, Henry, 47, 49-52
  life of, 2-10
  and the middle class, 244-45, 293
  and miscegenation, theme of,
    261-64
  misogyny, in works of, 182-83,
    281-83, 284-88
  narrative technique of, 82-84, 91-
    92, 99-101, 161-62, 220-22
  politics of, 16-19, 249-50, 280-81
  and Proust, Marcel, 81-82, 90-91,
    122-24
  realism of, 1-2, 61, 124-25
  religious symbolism, in works of,
    69-72
  and social reform, 8-10, 269-71
  and Southern literature, 4-5
  and stream-of-consciousness writing,
    63-65
  style of, 12-13, 15, 42-45, 46-52,
    53-64, 123-24, 240-42, 276-77,
    294-95
  subjective projection, in works of,
    72-74
  time, concept of, 67-69, 75-78, 79-
    86, 87-93, 122-23, 267-69
  traditionalism of, 28-30
  tragedy, concept of, 163-67, 170-
    174
  works of, as mythology, 23-33, 39-
    41, 124-26
Faulkner, William, works by:

Absalom, Absalom! 13, 26-27, 29,
  34, 36, 37-39, 41, 42, 46, 49-51,
  53, 55-56, 60, 66-67, 70-72, 95,
  102, **175-85, 186-203,** 205-6, 227,
  230, 257, 259-60, 262, 275, 276,
  280, 282, 289-90, 296
"All the Dead Pilots," 59
"Bear, The," 42, **208-18,** 220, 249,
  257, 260-261, 263, 275, 293
Coiners, The, 87
"Delta Autumn," 265-66, 268
Doctor Martino, 35, 75
"Evening Sun, That," 35, 94, 97,
  296
Fable, A, 16-17, 152-53, 156, 159,
  209, **238-42,** 243-50, 275
"Fire and the Hearth, The," 262-63,
  265
Go Down Moses, 10, 35, 36, 41, 42,
  67, 208, 224-25
Hamlet, The, 5, 12, 21, 35-36, 41,
  42, 44, 54, 55-57, 208, 256, 275,
  282-83, 284-85
Intruder in the Dust, 17, **219-25,**
  227-30, 260-61, 263, 270, 297
Knight's Gambit, 297
Light in August, 3, 14, 29-30, 34-
  35, 40-42, 49, 50, 54, 55, 67, 69,
  70, 80, 81, 83-86, 124, **147-62,**
  163-74, 205, 207, 221, 243, 259,
  263, 275, 277-78, 279, 281, 284-
  85, 293
"Lizards in Jamshyd's Courtyard,"
  35
"Long Hot Summer, The" (screen-
  play), 288
Mansion, The, 282, 283, 297
"Miss Zilphia Gant," 35
Mosquitoes, 30, 54, 55, 66, 282,
  285
"Old Man," 41, 42, 44
"Old People, The," 264
"Pantaloon in Black," 261, 263
Pylon, 30, 32, 49, 55, 57, 60, 66-
  67, 68, 71, 72, 219, 243, 277,
  282, 295
Red Leaves, 243, 263
Reivers, The, 275, 299, 302

Faulkner, William, works by: (*continued*)
  Requiem for a Nun, 127-28, 205, 209, 268, 288, 298-99
  "Rose for Emily, A," 10
  Sanctuary, 1, 6, 12, 28-29, 32, 34-35, 40, 44, 49-50, 54, 58-59, 67-69, 70-72, 76, 80-84, 127-36, 137-46, 161, 219, 272-74, 275, 277, 279, 282-83, 285-86, 290-91, 293, 295
  Sartoris, 3, 7, 24-26, 34-35, 44, 53, 54, 68, 89, 96, 134, 161, 251-52, 277, 279, 299
  Soldier's Pay, 1, 25, 54, 66, 96, 238, 251, 279, 282, 285
  Sound and the Fury, The, 1, 5, 7, 10, 22, 25-26, 34-36, 42, 49-51, 53, 54, 63, 67, 68, 77, 79-81, 87-90, 94-121, 122, 161, 184, 193, 200, 205-6, 226, 243, 251-58, 269, 275, 278-79, 281, 293
  "Spotted Horses," 12, 42, 56, 243
  "There Was a Queen," 24-25, 35
  "These Thirteen," 1, 35, 75
  Town, The, 288, 297
  "Turn About," 238
  Unvanquished, The, 23-24, 32, 35, 41, 54, 56, 59, 252, 298-99
  "Was," 257
  "Wash," 66-67, 283
  Wild Palms, The, 12, 23, 31-32, 35, 47, 49-50, 55, 56, 66, 69, 76, 77, 257, 263, 275, 282
Fiedler, Leslie A., 284-88
Finnegan's Wake (Joyce), 9, 241
"Fire and the Hearth, The," 262-63, 265
Fitzgerald, F. Scott, 12, 149, 275, 284
Flaubert, Gustave, 18, 19, 29, 221-22, 244, 275
Fletcher, John Gould, 1
Flint, R. W., 293
Ford, Ford Madox, 8, 275
Forster, E. M., 14
Freud, Sigmund, 40
Frost, Robert, 2-3, 19

G

Geismar, Maxwell, 227, 278-81
Georgia Scenes (Longstreet), 44
Gide, André, 91, 205
Glasgow, Ellen, 4
Go Down Moses, 10, 35, 36, 41, 42, 67, 208, 224-25
Golden Bowl, The (James), 51
Gone With the Wind (Mitchell), 277
Grapes of Wrath, The (Steinbeck), 10
Great Hatred, The (Samuels), 280
Greene, Graham, 276-77

H

Hamlet (Shakespeare), 166
Hamlet, The, 5, 12, 21, 35-36, 41, 42, 44, 54, 55-57, 208, 256, 275, 282-83, 284-85
Hamsun, Knut (*see* Pedersen, Knut)
Handlin, Oscar, 184
Handy, W. C., 94
Hardy, Thomas, 156
Harrison, Jane, 164
Hawthorne, Nathaniel, 18, 28, 39, 42, 44-45, 215, 238, 254
Hegel, Georg, 245
Heidegger, Martin, 92-93
Hemingway, Ernest, 8, 12, 19, 30, 44, 64-65, 122, 149, 166, 221, 238, 250, 275, 281, 284-85, 287
Hildegard of Bingen, Sister, 27
Histoire des Treize, l' (Balzac), 66
History and Human Relations (Butterfield), 184
Hitler, Adolf, 10
Hoffman, Frederick J., 22
Homer, 216
Hope, Laura L., 9
Housman, A. E., 252
Howe, Irving, 154, 258, 263, 281-83
Huxley, Aldous, 30, 254

I

Illusions perdues (Balzac), 273

In Dubious Battle (Steinbeck), 10
In the Cage (James), 50
Intruder in the Dust, 17, **219-25**,
    227-30, 260-61, 263, 270, 297
    and civil-rights, theme of, 222-25,
        228-30, 231-33
    morality, theme of, 219-20
    plot summary, 227-29
    point of view, 233-37
"Irresponsibles, The" (MacLeish), 8

J

James, Henry, 5, 18, 42, 44, 47, **49-
    52**, 73, 76, 186, 222, 244, 254, 275,
    286
Jonson, Ben, 294
Joyce, James, 5, 9, 64-65, 77, 91, 102,
    105-6, 122-25, 157, 200, 207, 221-
    22, 238, 241, 271, 275

K

Kafka, Franz, 11, 69, 166
Kazin, Alfred, 13-15, 16, 19
Keats, John, 102
Kierkegaard, Sören, 292
Knight's Gambit, 297
Knox, Barnard, 165

L

Lardner, Ring, 281
Lawrence, D. H., 103, 244, 249, 273,
    294
Leavis, F. R., 277-78
Lewis, Sinclair, 60, 105-6
Lewis, Wyndham, 15-16, 19, 47
Life on the Mississippi (Twain), 149
Light in August, 3, 14, 29-30, 34-35,
    40-42, 49, 50, 54, 55, 67, 69, 70, 80,
    81, 83-86, 124, **147-62**, 163-74, 205,
    207, 221, 243, 259, 263, 275, 277-
    78, 279, 281, 284-85, 293
    characterization, 150-56, 166-73,
        259
    destiny, concept of, 81, 84-86

    existentialism in, 166-67
    guilt, theme of, 157-58
    imagery of the South in, 148-50
    narrative technique of, 277-78
    and *Oedipus Rex* (Sophocles),
        164-67
    the past, theme of, 159-61
    plot summary, 147-49
    racism, theme of, 150-52
    stillness, theme of, 153-59
    terror, theme of, 172-73
    traditionalism, theme of, 29-30
    and tragedy, concept of, 163-67,
        170-74
Lincoln, Abraham, 224
Lindegren, Erik, 207
*Literary Career of William Faulkner,
    The* (Meriwether), 299
"Lizards in Jamshyd's Courtyard," 35
"Long Hot Summer, The" (screenplay),
    288
Longstreet, Augustus, 44
Look Homeward Angel (Wolfe), 122

M

Macaulay, Thomas, 46
Macbeth (Shakespeare), 95, 107, 119,
    166-67, 173, 187, 194
Machiavelli, Niccolò, 183
MacLeish, Archibald, 8
Madame Bovary (Flaubert), 18
Magny, C.-E., 206
Main Street (Lewis), 60
Mallarmé, Stéphane, 67
Malraux, André, 13, 72, 76, 81, 84,
    205, 272-74
Mann, Thomas, 123, 124
Mansion, The, 282, 283, 297
Man Who Died, The (Lawrence), 249
Man Who Knew Coolidge, The
    (Lewis), 106
Man Without a Way (Lindegren), 207
Martin of Tours, Saint, 216
Marx, Karl, 7, 19, 184
Matthew, Saint, 70, 248
Mauriac, François, 205, 292, 293

Melville, Herman, 5, 11, 18, 44, 209, 214, 254, 283, 287, 294
Men Without Art (Lewis), 15
Meriwether, James, 99, 299
Milton, John, 11, 39
"Miss Zilphia Gant," 35
Mitchell, Margaret, 277
Moby Dick (Melville), 18, 214, 294
"Moralist with a Corn-Cob, The" (Lewis), 15
Mosquitoes, 30, 54, 55, 66, 282, 285

N

Nathan, Monique, 12
Nesbit, E., 224
Nietzsche, Freidrich, 172, 274
Noces (Camus), 149
Nostromo (Conrad), 211
Notes of a Son and Brother (James), 76

O

"Ode to a Grecian Urn" (Keats), 102
O'Donnell, George Marion, 10, 20
Odyssey, The (Homer), 216
Oedipus Rex (Sophocles), 164-67, 187, 194
O'Faolain, Sean, 15-16, 19
O'Hara, John, 77
"Old Man," 41, 42, 44
"Old People, The," 264
On Native Ground (Kazin), 13-14
Othello (Shakespeare), 166

P

"Pantaloon in Black," 261, 263
Paradise Lost (Milton), 11, 39
Past Recaptured, The (Proust), 82
Pedersen, Knut, 280
Picasso, Pablo, 124-25
Plaisirs et Les Jours, Les (Proust), 91
Plato, 6, 75, 78
Podhoretz, Norman, 16-19, 293
Poe, Edgar Allan, 12, 44, 273
Portable Faulkner, The (Cowley), 10,
36, 75, 104-5
Portrait of a Lady, The (James), 18
"Post-War Writers and Pre-War Readers" (MacLeish), 8
Pouillon, Jean, 67
Pound, Ezra, 5, 9, 19, 123
Prevóst, Jean, 72
Propos de Littérature (Alain), 66
Proust, Marcel, 5, 11, 12, 19, 67, 76-77, **81-82**, 86, 90-91, 122-23, 221, 275
Pylon, 30, 32, 49, 55, 57, 60, 66-67, 68, 71, 72, 219, 243, 277, 282, 295

R

Racine, Jean Baptiste, 84
Rainbow, The (Lawrence), 103
Randolph, A. Philip, 9
Ransom, John Crowe, 294-95
Rebel, The (Camus), 205
Red and the Black, The (Stendhal), 245
Red Leaves, 243, 263
Reivers, The, 275, 299, 302
Remarque, Erich, 8
Remembrance of Things Past (Proust), 18, 122
Requiem for a Nun, 127-28, 205, 209, 268, 288, 298-99
Resurrection (Tolstoy), 241
Robinson, James Harvey, 184
Roosevelt, Eleanor, 9
"Rose for Emily, A," 10
Roth, Russell, 19
Rowson, Susanna, 286

S

Saint-Exupéry, Antoine de, 205
"Saint Louis Blues" (Handy), 94
Saltykov, Mikhail, 274
Samuels, Maurice, 280
Sanctuary, 1, 6, 12, 28-29, 32, 34-35, 40, 44, 49-50, 54, 58-59, 67-69, 70-72, 76, 80-84, **127-36, 137-46**, 161, 219, 272-74, 275, 277, 279, 282-83, 285-86, 290-91, 293, 295

Sanctuary, (continued)
   characterization, 132-36, 141-43
   colloquialisms in, 58-59
   historical sources of, 290-91
   morality, theme of, 128-33
   plot summary, 128-36, 140-41
   psychological aspects of, 138-46
   religious symbolism of, 70-72
   sexual impotence, theme of, 140,
     142-45
   structure, 28-29, 49-50, 82-84
   time, concept of, 68-69
   violence, theme of, 127-28
Sartoris, 3, 7, 24-26, 34-35, 44, 53,
   54, 68, 89, 96, 134, 161, 251-52,
   277, 279, 299
Sartre, Jean-Paul, 67-69, 72, 84, 125,
   205-6, 267
Scarlet Letter, The (Hawthorne), 18,
   39
Schlesinger, Arthur M., 193
Shakespeare, William, 18, 61, 95, 107,
   166-67, 173, 187, 194, 221, 294
Shchedrin, N. (*see* Saltykov, Mikhail)
Silone, Ignazio, 207
Slatoff, Walter J., 15
Smith, Lillian, 9
Socrates, 74
Soldier's Pay, 1, 25, 54, 66, 96, 238,
   251, 279, 282, 285
Sophocles, 10, 28, 164-67, 187, 194,
   276
Sound and the Fury, The, 1, 5, 7, 10,
   22, 25-26, 34-36, 42, 49-51, 53, 54,
   63, 67, 68, 77, 79-81, 87-90, 94-121,
   122, 161, 184, 193, 200, 205-6, 226,
   243, 251-58, 269, 275, 278-79, 281,
   293
   characterization, 101-7, 257-58
   conflict, theme of, 114-21
   development of, 96-101, 106
   formalized tradition, theme of, 25-
     26
   mirror symbolism in, 109-21
   modernism, concept of, 253-57
   morality, theme of, 105-8, 112-14
   shadow symbolism in, 115-17
   structure, 111-12, 120-21, 252-53

   time, concept of, 79-81, 87-90,
     122-23
   twilight symbolism in, 94-95
Spinoza, Baruch, 86
"Spotted Horses," 12, 42, 56, 243
Stalin, Joseph, 10, 229
Stein, Gertrude, 277
Steinbeck, John, 9, 10
Stendhal, 72-73, 77, 244-45, 275
Strange Fruit (Smith), 9
Stribling, T. S., 4
Sun Also Rises, The (Hemingway), 64
Symbolism:
   in *Absalom, Absalom!* 38-39, 70-72
   religious, in Faulkner's works, 69-
     72
   in *Sanctuary*, 70-72
   in *Sound and the Fury, The*, 94-95,
     109-21

T

Tate, Allen, 274-76
Temple, Minny, 286
"There Was a Queen," 24-25, 35
These Thirteen, 1, 35, 75
Thibaudet, Albert, 12
Thoreau, Henry David, 149
Three Decades of Faulkner Criticism
   (Hoffman and Vickery), 22
Timaeus (Plato), 75, 78
Time, concept of:
   in *Light in August*, 80-81
   in *Sanctuary*, 68-69, 81
   in *Sound and Fury, The*, 79-81, 87-
     90, 122-23
Tolstoy, Leo N., 104, 126, 241
Town, The, 288, 297
Trial, The (Kafka), 69
Troilus and Cressida (Shakespeare),
   18
"Turn About," 238
Twain, Mark, 5, 44, 208, 254
*Twelve Original Essays on Great
   Americans* (Kazin), 14
Two Decades of Faulkner Criticism
   (Hoffman and Vickery), 22
Typee (Melville), 287

U

Ulysses (Joyce), 64, 77, 122, 241
Unvanquished, The, 23-24, 32, 35, 41,
  54, 56, 59, 252, 298-99

V

Valley of Decision, The (Davenport), 9
Veblen, Thorstein, 188
Vergil, 211
Vickery, Olga, 22

W

Walden, or Life in the Woods
  (Thoreau), 149
Warren, Robert Penn, 166
"Was," 257
"Wash," 66-67, 283
Wasson, Ben, 99

Waste Land, The (Eliot), 77, 175, 269
Webster, John, 32, 209
Weil, Simone, 159
Welty, Eudora, 292
What Maisie Knew (James), 51
Whitman, Walt, 9
Wild Palms, The, 12, 23, 31-32, 35, 47,
  49-50, 55, 56, 66, 69, 76, 77, 257,
  263, 275, 282
Wilson, Edmund, 270
Winesburg, Ohio (Anderson), 95-96
Wolfe, Thomas, 9, 12, 122
Woolf, Virginia, 91, 123

Y

Yeats, William Butler, 5, 11

Z

Zola, Émile, 254

FIELDING

A Collection of Critical Essays
Edited by RONALD PAULSON

A

Addison, Joseph, 29, 31
Aeneid (Virgil), 167
Aeschylus, 63, 64
Affectation, theme of, 35, 56, 61
Alchemist, The, (Jonson), 105-6
Alexander, The Great, 71
Allegory, Fielding's use of, 38, 40, 41, 43-44, 85
Allen, Ralph, 119
Amelia, 3, 13, 19, 79, 146-57, 163
  good nature, theme of, 173
  humours, doctrine of, 148-49
  irony in, 163-64, 166
  satire in, 63, 170
  and *Tom Jones,* 91, 125, 128, 158, 163-66, 174-75
Anarchism, theme of, 2, 80
Apology for the Life of Mr. Colley Cibber (Cibber), 36, 46, 48
Apology for the Life of Mrs. Shamela Andrews (*see Shamela*)
Aristotle, 110, 115, 117-18, 119
Ars Poetica (Horace), 160
Austen, Jane, 10, 115
Author's Farce, The; and the Pleasures of the Town, 13
  burlesque in, 39-40
  farce in, 26-27, 39
  mock-heroic in, 27-28

B

Bach, J. S., 126
Barbauld, Mrs., 46, 121
Battle of the Books, The (Swift), 43
Beggar's Opera, The (Gay), 3, 41, 72
Bentley, Dr. Richard, 46
Bergson, Henri, 58
Berkeley, George, 13
Blake, William, 126
Boileau, Nicolas, 71
Bolingbroke, Sir Henry, 128
Bond, Richmond P., 25
Boswell, James, 99, 117
Bouvard et Pécuchet (Flaubert), 71
Bradshaigh, Lady, 46
Bunyan, John, 43, 133-34
Burlesque, 4, 6, 30
  in *The Author's Farce,* 39-40
  in *The Grub-Street Opera,* 50
  in *Shamela,* 50-51
  in *The Tragedy of Tragedies,* 26, 40, 50
Butler, Samuel, 12, 16
Byron, George Gordon, 80

C

Caesar, 71
Caligula, 43
Calvinism, 128-29
Cervantes, Miguel de, 6, 7, 20-21, 30,

Cervantes, Miguel de, (*continued*) 41, 43-44, 54, 61, 147
Champion, The, 29, 33, 35, 36, 37-38, 39, 43-44, 73
Chaplin, Charlie, 62
Charles I, 73
Charles VII, 73
Charles XII, 38, 72
Chastity, theme of:
    in *Joseph Andrews,* 59-60, 62, 64-67, 138
    in *Pamela* (Richardson), 53
    in *Tom Jones,* 129
Chaucer, Geoffrey, 2
Chesterfield, Lord, 144, 157
Christianity, in Fielding's works, 1-2, 13, 34, 127-28, 134, 151-52
Cibber, Colley, 36, 43, 46-48
Cicero, 31
City Lights (Chaplin), 62
Clarissa (Richardson), 52, 98-105, 107, 110-12, 115, 121
Claudian, 147, 151, 153, 164
Clemens, Samuel A., 130
Coffee-House Politician, The, 37, 39
Coleridge, S. T., 54, 74, 80, 105, 109, 114
Conrad, Joseph, 36
Conyers, Dr. Middleton, 46
Coolidge, John S., 4
Cooper, Anthony Ashley, 1, 6, 9
Covent Garden Journal, The, 3, 36, 89, 147
Crane, R. S., 121
Cross, Wilbur, 1, 5, 45, 176

D

Dampier, Thomas, 47
Dante, 43
David Copperfield (Dickens), 20
Decline and Fall of the Roman Empire, The (Gibbon), 125
Defoe, Daniel, 71, 74, 106, 112, 115, 121-22, 165
De Quincey, Thomas, 60
Dickens, Charles, 20, 57, 114
Digeon, Aurélion, 1, 17, 60, 160

Dobson, Austin, 45
Don Quixote (Cervantes), 7, 30, 41, 43, 54
Don Quixote in England, 37
Dudden, F. H., 136, 137
Dunciad, The (Pope), 40, 51

E

"Editor to Himself, The," 49
Edwards, Thomas, 120
Empson, William, 2, 7
Epictetus, 31
"Epistle Dedicatory" (Middleton), 46-47
Essay Concerning Human Understanding (Locke), 36
"Essay on Conversation," 39
"Essay on Man" (Pope), 71, 149
Existentialism, theme of, 2
Euclid, 125

F

Fable of the Bees, The (Mandeville), 71
Faerie Queene (Spenser), 141
Fair Haven (Butler), 14
Fairy tale, the, 133-34
Farce, 25-26, 28-30
    in *The Author's Farce,* 26-27, 39
    in *The Lottery,* 28
    in *Pasquin,* 26-27, 41-42
    in *The Tragedy of Tragedies,* 26-27, 40
Fathers, or the Good-Natur'd Man, The, 38
Fielding, Henry:
    and Cervantes, 20-21, 30, 41, 43-44, 54, 61
    Christianity of, 1-2, 13, 34, 127-28, 134
    and classical tradition, 5
    and Cibber, Colley, 36, 43, 46-47
    and the clergy, 48-49
    Conservatism of, 106-7
    and Defoe, 74, 106, 112, 115
    and Dickens, 20, 57, 114

Fielding, Henry: (*continued*)
  as dramatist, 3, 13, 23, 25, 30-32,
    53-54, 84, 136, 160
  and Johnson, Samuel, 2-3, 56, 98-
    100, 113, 115, 118, 122, 125, 128
  and Lucian, 43-44
  as magistrate, 121-22, 130, 140,
    143-44, 145, 166, 176
  modern view of, 1-3, 9-11, 123-26
    132-33, 138, 145
  and Molière, 21-22, 28
  poetry of, 38
  and Pope, Alexander, 2-3, 47
  and Richardson, Samuel, 2-5, 7, 9,
    17, 44-46, 51, 98-100, 105-8,
    115-17, 119, 128, 133, 138, 143
  and Shakespeare, William, 23-24
  and Smollett, Tobias, 114
  and Swift, Jonathan, 2-3, 5, 6, 12-
    16, 19, 31, 41, 43-44, 117
Fielding, Henry, works by:
  JOURNALS AND ESSAYS
  "Essay on Conversation," 39
  Journal of a Voyage to Lisbon,
    121, 147
  Miscellanies, The, 38, 39, 69
  "On the Knowledge of the Char-
    acters of Men," 39, 94
  NOVELS
  Amelia, 3, 13, 19, 63, 79, 91, 113,
    116, 125, 128, **146-58**, 163-66,
    170, 173-75
  Jonathan Wild, 4, 6-7, 13-20, 36,
    39, 40, 44, **69-80**, 84, 86, 160
  Joseph Andrews, 4-5, 9, 10, 26,
    28, 39, 49, **52-58**, **59-68**, 74, 84,
    89-90, 92, 125, 128, 129-30,
    137-38, 160
  Shamela, 4, **45-51**, 90, 128
  Tom Jones, 7-8, 24, 53, 55-56, 79,
    81-83, **84-88**, **89-97**, **98-112**, 115,
    124-28, 128-30, 134-35, 139,
    141-42, 144-45, 158, **160-66**,
    174-75
  PLAYS
  *Author's Farce; and the Pleasures of
    the Town, The,* 13, 26-28, 39-40

Coffee-House Politician, The, 37, 39
Don Quixote in England, 37
*Fathers, or the Good Natur'd Man,
  The,* 38
Grub-Street Opera, The, 25, 39, 50
*Historical Register for the Year
  1736, The,* 42-43
*Journey From This World to the
  Next, The,* 40
Letter Writers, The, 32
Lottery, The, 28
Love in Several Masques, 31
Modern Husband, The, 39
Pasquin, 13, 26-27, 41-42
Rehearsal, The, 26
Tom Thumb, 13, 25, 40
Tragedy of Tragedies, The, 26-27,
  39-40, 50
  POEMS
  "Editor to Himself, The," 49
  "Of Good-Nature," 38
  "Of True Greatness," 39
  "Opposition: a Vision, The," 73
Flaubert, Gustave, 71, 136
Ford, F. M., 117, 120, 134-36
French Revolution, 143

G

Gay, John, 3, 41
Gibbon, Edward, 12, 16, 125
Gide, André, 2, 10
Good nature, theme of, 37-39, 89,
  168
  in *Amelia,* 173
  in *Jonathan Wild,* 38
  in *Joseph Andrews,* 63
  in "Of Good-Nature," 38
  in *Tom Jones,* 81, 92, 94-97, 116,
    128-30, 144-45
"Great Man," theme of the, 6-7, 38-40,
  71-76, 78-80
Greene, Robert, 69
Grub Street, 40
Grub-Street Opera, The, 25, 39, 50
Guzman d'Alfarache (Le Sage),
  69

H

Handel, George Fredrick, 126
Hardwicke, Lord Chancellor, 119
Hawkins, Sir John, 125, 128
Hemingway, Ernest, 51
*Historical Register for the Year 1736,
   The,* 42-43
Hobbes, Thomas, 61, 128
Homer, 3, 56, 119
Horace, 29, 146, 160
Humours, doctrine of, 25, 30-35, 160
   in *Amelia,* 148-49
   in *Joseph Andrews,* 9
   in *The Letter Writers,* 32
   in *Tom Jones,* 85
Humphreys, A. R., 5
Hypocrisy, theme of, 2, 19, 128
   in *Jonathan Wild,* 71, 78
   in *Joseph Andrews,* 13, 55-56, 61,
      65
   in *Shamela,* 51
   in *Tom Jones,* 23, 82, 95

I

Iliad, The (Homer), 71
Inchbald, Mrs., 87
Irony, use of, 4-9, 17-24
   in *Amelia,* 163-64, 166
   in *Jonathan Wild,* 13-16, 39, 69, 71-
      72, 76-79
   in *Joseph Andrews,* 58, 67
   in *Tom Jones,* 7, 87, 112, 124-28,
      134-35, 141-42, 144-45
   in *The Tragedy of Tragedies,* 40

J

James, Henry, 88, 120, 121
Jesus, 13, 31
John, Lord Hervey, 46
Johnson, Samuel, 2-3, 13, 56, 98-100,
   108, 113, 115, 118, 122, 128, 157
Jonathan Wild, 4, 14-20, 36, 40, 44,
   69-80, 84, 160
   "great man," theme of, 6-7, 73-76,
      78-80

hypocrisy, theme of, 71, 78
   irony in, 13-16, 39, 69, 71-72, 76-
      79
   mock-heroic in, 6-7, 18, 20
   picaresque in, 77
   satire in, 79
   and *Tom Jones,* 86
Joseph Andrews, 4-5, 7, 10, 26, 36,
   44, 49, 52-58, 59-68, 74, 77, 84, 89,
   125, 128, 137-38, 160
   affectation, theme of, 35, 56, 61
   chastity, theme of, 59-60, 62, 64-
      67, 138
   humours, doctrine of, 9
   hypocrisy, theme of, 13, 55-56, 61,
      65
   irony in, 58, 67
   mock-heroic in, 20, 28, 56, 58
   and *Pamela* (Richardson), 52-58,
      60-61, 89-90, 129-30
   picaresque in, 55, 59
   satire in, 26, 28, 92
Journal of a Voyage to Lisbon, 121,
   147
*Journey From This World to the Next,
   The,* 40
Joyce, James, 10, 148

K

Kettle, Arnold, 2
Keyber, Conny, 45-46
Keystone Cops, The, 62

L

Leavis, F. R., 2, 9
Le Blance, Abbé, 69
Le Sage, Alain René, 69, 70, 165
Letter Writers, The, 32
Lewis, C. S., 29
Life of Cicero (Middleton), 46, 48
Life of Jonathan Wild, The (Defoe), 71
Life of Jonathan Wilde, The (anon.),
   70
*Lives of the Most Remarkable Crimi-
   nals* (anon.), 17
Locke, John, 36-37, 165

Lottery, The, 28
Louis XIV, 38, 72
Love in Several Masques, 31
Lucian, 43-44, 122
Lyttleton, George, 119

M

Macbeth (Shakespeare), 60
McKillop, Alan D., 45
Mack, Maynard, 4, 10
Mandeville, Bernard, 71
Marivaux, Pierre, 71
Merchant of Venice, The
    (Shakespeare), 23
Meredith, George, 57, 120
Methodism, 49
Middleton, Dr. Conyers, 46-47
Milton, John, 19, 168
Miscellanies, The, 38, 69
Miser, The (Molière), 28
Mock Doctor, The (Molière), 28
Mock-heroic, 6, 30
    in *The Author's Farce,* 27-28
    in *Jonathan Wild,* 6-7, 18, 20
    in *Joseph Andrews,* 20, 28, 56, 58
    in *Pasquin,* 41-42
    in *Tom Jones,* 20, 24, 113
    in *Tom Thumb,* 40
Modern Husband, The, 39
Molière, 21-22, 28, 76, 81
Moll Flanders (Defoe), 106
Montagu, Lady Mary Whortley, 108,
    133
More, Hannah, 115
Murry, John Middleton, 2, 123, 137

N

Nakedness, theme of, 62
    in *Joseph Andrews,* 60, 62-63, 65-
    67
    in *Tom Jones,* 62, 141
Nash, Thomas, 69
Nature and Art (Inchbald), 87
Newgate Garland (Swift), 71
Newton, Sir Isaac, 19
Novels of Fielding, The (Digeon), 17

O

Odyssey, The (Homer), 10, 147
Oedipus (Sophocles), 56, 105-6
"Of Good-Nature," 38
"Of True Greatness," 39
Oliver Twist (Dickens), 20
"On the Knowledge of the Characters
    of Men," 39, 94
"Opposition: a Vision, The," 73

P

Pamela; or, Virtue Rewarded (Richard-
    son), 45-46, 48-49, 50, 65, 90
    theme of chastity in, 53
    and *Joseph Andrews,* 52-58, 60-61,
    89-90, 109-30
    satire in, 92
Paradise Lost (Milton), 159
Pascal, Blaise, 73, 80
Pastourelle, genre of the, 113
Pasquin, 13
    farce in, 26-27, 41-42
    mock-heroic in, 41-42
    satire in, 27
Picaresque, the, 3, 69
    in *Jonathan Wild,* 77
    in *Joseph Andrews,* 55, 59
    in *Tom Jones,* 121
Plato, 62, 64
Pleasures of the Town (*see The*
    Author's Farce)
Plotinus, 109
Pope, Alexander, 2-3, 47, 49, 71, 107,
    149, 157
Priestley, J. B., 9
Proust, Marcel, 115, 127, 135

Q

"Quixotism," 37, 41, 54

R

Ranby, John, 119
Realism:
    of Fielding, 4-8, 10-11, 35-36, 85,

Realism: (*continued*)
91-92, 159-60, 165
of Richardson, 4-7, 99, 102-5,
121-22
Redinger, Dr. R. V., 43
Rehearsal, The, 26
Richardson, Samuel, 48-49, 52-54, 72
and Fielding, 2-5, 7, 9, 17, 44-46,
51, 98-100, 105-8, 110-12,
115-17, 119, 128, 133, 138, 143
Roderick Random (Smollett), 115,
157
Rogers, Winifield H., 4
Romanticism, 126
Rousseau, Jean Jacques, 87

S

Saintsbury, George, 131, 139
Satire, 31, 71
in *Amelia,* 63, 170
in *Jonathan Wild,* 79
in *Pamela* (Richardson), 92
in *Pasquin,* 27
in *Shamela,* 50-51
in *Tom Jones,* 106, 139
in *Tom Thumb,* 40
Scarron, Paul, 21, 72, 147
Scott, Sir Walter, 80, 158
Shaftesbury, Earl of (*see* Cooper,
Anthony Ashley)
Shakespeare, 19, 23-24, 56, 121
Shamela, 4, 45-51, 90, 128
burlesque in, 50-51
theme of hypocrisy in, 51
satire in, 50-51
and *Tom Jones,* 51
Shaw, George Bernard, 12, 80
Shelley, Percy Bysshe, 126
Short Account, A (Whitefield), 49
Sidney, Sir Philip, 21
Simonides, 146
Slocock, Dr. Benjamin, 48
Smollett, Tobias, 114, 157
Sophocles, 106
Spectator, The (Addison and Steele),
17, 29

Spilka, Mark, 10
Steele, Richard, 29, 31
Stephan, Sir Leslie, 12, 117
Sterne, Lawrence, 115
Suetonius, 43
*Survey of Sixteenth-Century Litera-
ture* (Lewis), 129
Swift, Jonathan, 43, 80
and Fielding, 2-3, 5, 6, 12-16, 19,
31, 41, 43-44, 117

T

Tartuffe, (Molière), 76
Thackeray, W. M., 10, 174
Thrale, Mrs., 99
Tom Jones, 2, 7-8, 10, 24, 36, 44, 53,
55-56, 63, 79, **81-83, 84-88, 89-97,**
98-112, 160-66
and *Amelia,* 91, 125, 128, 158,
163-66, 174-75
chastity, theme of, 129
and *Clarissa* (Richardson),
98-105, 110-12, 115
good nature, theme of, 81, 92, 94-
97, 116, 128-30, 144-45
humours, doctrine of the, 85
hypocrisy, theme of, 23, 82, 95
irony in, 112, 124-28, 134-35,
141-42, 144-45
mock-heroic in, 20, 24, 113
and *Oedipus* (Sophocles), 105-6
picaresque in, 121
realism in, 7-8, 10
satire in, 106, 139
and *Shamela,* 51
Tom Thumb, 13, 25, 40
Torrents of Spring (Hemingway),
51
Tragedy of Tragedies, The, 39-40
burlesque in, 26, 40, 50
farce in, 26-27, 40
irony in, 40
Trapp, Dr. Joseph, 49
Trollope, Anthony, 120
Twain, Mark (*see* Clemens,
Samuel A.)

U

Ulysses (Joyce), 10
"Upholsterer, The" (Addison), 32
Unprofessional Essays (Murry), 123, 137

V

Virgil, 3, 147
Voltaire, 38

W

Walpole, Horace, 45
Walpole, Robert, 15, 17, 29, 41, 47, 48, 73
Whitefield, George, 49
Wild, Jonathan, 15, 17-18, 69-71, 74-75
Woods, Charles B., 45
Work, James A., 1
Wit, in Fielding's works, 29, 40, 89

F. SCOTT FITZGERALD

A Collection of Critical Essays

Edited by ARTHUR MIZENER

A

"Absolution," 150-51, 154, 164
"Afternoon of an Author," 168
Anthony, Saint, 71
Arthur, Chester A., 5

B

"Babylon Revisited," 69, 155
Balzac, Honoré, de, 15, 16
Barzun, Jacques, 127
Baudelaire, Charles, 24
Beardsley, Aubrey, 75
Beautiful and Damned, The, 1, 9, 21, 33-35, 37, 41, 45, 82, 83, 84
Beerbohm, Max, 84
Bellow, Saul, 112
Billy Budd (Melville), 22
Bishop, John Peale, 2, 60, 78, 79, 106-7
Boswell, James, 4
Brooks, Van Wyck, 101, 103
Brothers Karamazov, The (Dostoevsky), 16
Broun, Heywood, 6
Burnam, Tom, 3
Butler, Samuel, 17, 79
Byron, George Gordon, 16, 28, 73

C

Cabell, James Branch, 5, 71
Camus, Albert, 26

Chamberlain, John, 2
Clemens, Samuel (pseud. Mark Twain), 25, 28, 109
Col. David Crockett's Exploits and Adventures in Texas, 128
Columbus, Christopher, 46, 49
Comstock, Anthony, 5
Conrad, Joseph, 21, 61
Coolidge, Calvin, 5
Cowley, Malcom, 2, 3, 4, 74
Crack-Up, The, 2, 3, 11, 16, 20, 23-24, 25, 26, 27-28, 31, 54-55, 57-60, 61, 62, 63, 64, 73, 146-48, 154
Crane, Stephen, 63, 64, 71
Crèvecoeur, Michel, 48
Crockett, Davy, 128, 131
Cronin, A. J., 135

D

"Dalyrimple Goes Wrong," 45
Dante Alighieri, 27
Death in the Afternoon (Hemingway), 28
"Design in Plaster," 163
"Diamond as Big as the Ritz, The," 3, 45, 76, 84
Dickens, Charles, 15
Disenchanted, The (Schulberg), 3, 109
Dos Passos, John, 2, 6, 61-62, 71
Dostoevsky, Feodor, 24, 28
Dreiser, Theodore, 71
Dr. Faustus (Jonson), 92

E

El Greco, 22
Eliot, T. S., 6, 21, 112, 113, 162
Emerson, Ralph Waldo, 48, 93

F

Farewell to Arms, A (Hemingway), 8
Farnol, Jeffrey, 5
Far Side of Paradise, The (Mizener), 73
Faulkner, William, 6, 25, 31, 71
Fiedler, Leslie, 3
Fitzgerald, F. Scott:
    and the absurd, 26-27, 30
    and American culture, 13, 24, 27-
        28, 33-37, 41-42, 43-56
    and the American Dream, 20-21,
        35, 49, 55-56, 99-103
    asceticism of, 15-16
    and his audience, 3, 70-72, 74-75
    career of, 11-19, 20-24, 25-31, 32-
        42, 43-56, 57-63, 64-69, 70-76
    and his contemporaries, 1-3
    and his daughter, 17
    failure of, 20-24, 33, 55, 71
    as hero, 11-12, 19, 27, 64-65
    in Hollywood, 39, 40, 41, 52, 61,
        64, 66, 67, 68
    idealism of, 16
    irony of, 43, 46, 52, 53, 59-60, 68,
        73, 74, 83, 164, 168
    and the Jazz Age, 13, 35, 77
    late work of, 143-45, 146-56,
        157-68
    and Lewis, Sinclair, 82-83
    life of, 58, 61-63, 65-69, 72-73, 82-
        85, 146-49
    and the Lost Generation, 45, 46,
        48-49
    and love, theme of, 12-13
    and Mackenzie, Compton, 80, 83
    maturity of, 157
    morality of, 12-13, 18, 21, 43, 57-
        59, 78, 84-85, 88, 103, 106, 108
    and nostalgia, function of, 25-31,
        59, 71
    realism of, 60-63

    religious background of, 23-24, 71
    revolt of, 79, 81
    romanticism of, 43, 44-45, 66, 73,
        78, 90
    significance of, 146-56
    and social class, 14-15
    style of, 81-84
    success of, 20-24
    and suicide, 27
    symbolism of, 45
Fitzgerald, F. Scott, works by:
    "Absolution," 150-51, 154, 164
    "Afternoon of an Author," 168
    "Babylon Revisited, 69, 155
    Beautiful and Damned, The, 1, 9,
        21, 33-35, 37, 41, 45, 82, 83, 84
    Crack-Up, The, 2, 3, 11, 16, 20, 23-
        24, 25, 26, 27-28, 31, 54-55, 57-
        60, 61, 62, 63, 64, 73, 146-48,
        154
    "Dalyrimple Goes Wrong," 45
    "Design in Plaster," 163
    "Diamond as Big as the Ritz, The,"
        3, 45, 76, 84
    Flappers and Philosophers, 3
    Great Gatsby, The, 1, 2, 3, 4, 10,
        13, 17-19, 21-22, 25, 28, 30, 31,
        35-37, 41, 45, 46-50, 53, 60-63,
        64, 69, 72, 75, 99-103, 104-11
        112-24, 143, 150, 154-55, 159,
        161, 164
    "I Didn't Get Over," 163
    "Infidelity," 4
    Last Tycoon, The, 2, 3-4, 22-23,
        39-41, 61-62, 69, 72, 73, 75, 153,
        162-68
    "Long Way Out," 163
    "Lost Decade, The," 163
    "May Day," 8, 23, 45, 49
    Notebooks, 3, 56
    "News of Paris," 163
    "Offshore Pirate, The," 45
    "Outside the Cabinet-Maker's," 3,
        159-60
    "Popular Girl, The," 3
    "Rich Boy, The," 23
    "Sensible Thing, The," 158-59
    Tender Is the Night, 1, 2, 3, 22, 30,

Fitzgerald, F. Scott, works by (*Tender Is the Night*) (*continued*)
37-41, 50-54, **143-45**, **148-53**, 150,
This Side of Paradise, 1, 2, 6, **20-21**,
32-34, 41, 53, 58, 65, 72, 75-76,
77-79, **86-91**, 146, 153
"Vegetable, The," 84
Fitzgerald, Zelda (*see* Sayre, Zelda)
Flappers and Philosophers, 3
Flaubert, Gustave, 22
Four Quartets (Eliot), 102
Francis of Assisi, Saint, 28
Franklin, Benjamin, 44, 50
Freud, Sigmund, 41, 154
Fussell, Edmund, 3

G

Goethe, Johann Wolfgang, 11, 15, 16, 28
Graves, Robert, 155
Great Gatsby, The, 1, 2, 3, 4, 10, 13,
17-19, 21-22, 25, 28, 30, 31, **35-37**,
41, 45, 46, 53, 60, 64, 69, 72, 75,
104-11, **112-24**, 143, 150, **154-55**,
159, 161, 164
    allegory in, 99-103
    and the American Dream, 17, 21,
        36, 46-50, 125-41
    irony in, 36, 49, 50, 105, 107, 108,
        113, 114, 115, 120
    money, theme of, 22, 149
    morality in, 120, 122
    realism of, 60-63
    and *Tender Is the Night*, 149-53
    symbolism in, 105-8, 110-11, 113-
        15, 122, 123, 134, 136, 140, 153
Great Good Place, The (James), 130
Griswold, Rufus W., 72

H

Harbor, The (Poole), 81
Harding, Dennis, 2
Harding, Warren G., 5, 41, 43
Hardy, Thomas, 59, 83
Hart, Laurence, 12, 59
Held Jr., John, 72

Hemingway, Ernest, 1, 2, 4, 5, 6, 10,
14, 24, 25, 28-29, 41, 62, 71, 72, 75,
108-9

I

"I Didn't Get Over," 163
"Infidelity," 4
"Invite with Gilded Edges, An" (Weir), 57

J

James, Henry, 15, 21, 29, 86, 87, 130
Jazz Age, The, 8
Jefferson, Thomas, 126
John of the Cross, Saint, 16
Johnson, Dr. Samuel, 4, 168
Jonson, Ben, 92
Joyce, James, 24, 72
Jurgen (Cabell), 5

K

Kazin, Alfred, 91
Keats, John, 16, 27, 43, 80
Kierkegaard, Sören, 55, 147
King, Ginevra, 72
Kipling, Rudyard, 61, 67

L

Landon, Alfred, 8
Lardner, Ring, 74
Last Tycoon, The, 2, 3-4, 39-41, 61-62,
69, 72, 73, 75, 153, 162-68
    and the American Dream, 40
    and Hollywood, 22-23
Leon, Ponce de, 44, 48, 50
Letters from an American Farmer
    (Crèvecoeur), 48
Lewis, Sinclair, 6, 82
Lincoln, Abraham, 5, 167, 168
Longfellow, Henry Wadsworth, 93
"Long Way Out, The," 163
Lord Jim (Conrad), 106
"Lost Decade, The,"
    163

Lowell, James Russell, 93
Lubbock, Percy, 86, 87

M

Mackenzie, Compton, 80, 83
Main Street (Sinclair), 82
Manet, Edouard, 132
Mankiewicz, Joe, 72
Mann, Thomas, 24
Marx, Leo, 112
"May Day," 8, 23, 45, 49
Mencken, H. L., 2, 4, 5, 7-8, 83
Milton, John, 12
Mizener, Arthur, 39, 70, 74, 108, 146, 150, 153, 157
Morgan, J. P., 28, 69
"Myths for Materialists" (Barzun), 127

N

"News of Paris," 163
Notebooks, 3, 56
Notes from Underground (Dostoevsky), 28

O

Ober, Harold, 3, 68
Oedipus Rex (Sophocles), 71
"Offshore Pirate, The," 45
Olson, George, 5
"Outside the Cabinet-Maker's," 3, 159-60

P

Paradise Lost (Milton), 92
Paterson, Isabel, 2
Pegler, Westbrook, 2, 57
Perkins, Maxwell, 102, 103
Poe, Edgar Allan, 71, 72
Poole, Ernest, 81
"Popular Girl, The," 3
Porter, Cole, 12, 59

Portrait of the Artist as a Young Man, A (Joyce), 73
Proust, Marcel, 13

Q

Quennell, Peter, 2

R

Racine, Jean, 11
Red Badge of Courage, The (Crane), 22
Renan, Ernest, 79
"Rich Boy, The," 23
Rimbaud, Arthur, 28
Rogers, Richard, 12, 59
Rogers, Will, 165
Roosevelt, Franklin, 8
Rosenfeld, Paul, 88
Ryan, General J. A., 65

S

Sacco-Vanzetti Case, 8
Salinger, J. D., 112
Savage, D. S., 3
Sayre, Zelda, 58, 61, 73, 74, 109, 146, 149, 154, 156
Schulberg, Budd, 2, 3, 68, 71, 72, 109
Season in Hell, A (Rimbaud), 28
"Sensible Thing, The," 158-59
Shakespeare, William, 15
Shaw, G. B., 16, 28, 82, 83
Shelley, Percy Bysshe, 16
Sinister Street (Mackenzie), 80, 87
Sorrows of Young Werther, The (Goethe), 16
Stein, Gertrude, 6
Steinbeck, John, 70, 71
Stendahl, 16, 66
Stephan Hero (Joyce), 73
Sun Also Rises, The (Hemingway), 4, 5, 30

T

Temple, Shirley, 69
Tender Is the Night, 1, 2, 13, 22, 30,
  40, 41, 61, 64, 72, 74, 75, 112,
  143-45, 150, **151-53**
    and the American Dream, 50-54
    and *The Great Gatsby,* 149-53
    irony in, 39, 53
    neurosis, theme of, 37-39
    religion, theme of, 51, 52, 54
    romanticism in, 51, 53
    symbolism in, 150, 153
Tennyson, Alfred, 70
This Side of Paradise, 1, 2, 6, 16, **20-
  21**, **32-34**, 41, 58, 65, 72, 146, 153
    and the Jazz Age, 77-79
    money, theme of, 75-76
    structure of, 86-91
    symbolism in, 153
Thoreau, Henry David, 48
Thurber, James, 2
Tolstoy, Leo, 24
Trilling, Lionel, 2, 3, 4, 110, 157
Troy, William, 3
Twain, Mark (*see* Clemens, Samuel)

V

Van Gogh, Vincent, 27

"Vegetable, The," 84
Voltaire, 15, 79

W

Wanger, Walter, 68
Wanning, Andrews, 3
Washington, George, 5
Waste Land, The (Eliot), 6, 18, 113,
  136
Weir, Charles, 57
Wells, H. G., 83, 87
Wescott, Glenway, 2, 10, 77,
  157
What is Man? (Clemens), 28
Wheeler, Wayne B., 5
Whiteman, Paul, 5
Wilson, Edmund, 2, 11, 16, 20, 21,
  39, 64, 79, 87, 91, 107, 164
Wine of the Puritans, The (Brooks),
  101
Wolfe, Thomas, 25, 31, 38
Woolf, Virginia, 20
Wordsworth, William,
  16, 27

Y

Yeats, W. B., 13-14, 15

FLAUBERT

A Collection of Critical Essays

Edited by RAYMOND GIRAUD

A

A la recherche du temps perdu
(Proust), 73
American Credo (Mencken and
Nathan), 65
Anti-bourgeois sentiments, in Flau-
bert's works, 10-11, 61, 65, 138-39,
142-43, 152-53
Argent, L', (Zola), 111
Assassinat du Pont-Rouge, L' (Bar-
bara), 90
Aurevilly, Jules d', 90

B

Ballad of Billie Potts, The (Warren), 62
Balzac, Honoré, 34, 36, 65, 89-90,
117, 119, 130, 135, 139, 140, 142,
149, 158, 171
Barbara, Charles, 90
Baudelaire, Charles, 4, 7, 9, 13, 14, 16,
58, 98, 153, 172
on *Madame Bovary*, 88-96
Boileau, Nicolas, 135
Bopp, Leon, 123
Bossu (Feval), 90
Bouche d'Ombre (Hugo), 43
Bouilhet, Louis, 5, 14, 16, 18, 59, 71-
72
Bourget, Paul, 2, 147
Bouvard et Pécuchet, 3, 57-58, **64-72**
Burke, Kenneth, 85

C

Camus, Albert, 62
Candidat, Le, 59, 65, 66
Candide (Voltaire), 70
Cervantes, Miguel de, 113
Champfleury (*pseud.* Fleury-Husson),
90
Characterization:
in *Madame Bovary*, 92-94, 109-10,
114-22, 138-40
in *Salammbô*, 146-49
Characters, Flaubert's involvement
with, 9-11, 13-20
Chateaubriand, François René, 146
Château de coeurs, Le, 64
Chevalier, Ernest, 5, 71
Coeur simple, Un, 58, **62-64**
Colet, Louise, 5, 14n-15n, 41, 59, 77,
82, 97-98, 121-22, 163-64
Confessions (Rousseau), 136
Conrad, Joseph, 98
Correspondance, 3-4, 5, 14n-15n, 29-
32, 36, 37, 39, 41, 60, 73, 136,
163-64
on hallucinatory experience, 75-77,
79, 82-84, 86-87
on *Madame Bovary*, 47-49, 55, 97-
98, 122, 130
on *Salammbô*, 142-43
on sensory perception, 21-22, 26,
45
Cousin Pons, Le (Balzac), 65

D

Daudet, Léon, 2, 58
De l'Intelligence . . . (Taine), 75-76
Demorest, D. L., 44-45, 50, 75
Dernières Chansons (Bouilhet), Flaubert's Preface to, 5, 71-72
Derniers vers (Laforgue), 99
Dictionnaire des idées reçues, 65, 69
Diderot, Denis, 4
Don Quixote (Cervantes), 113
Du Camp, Maxine, 5, 18
Dumesnil, René, 70, 75

E

Éducation sentimentale, L', 1, 10-11, 26-27, 28, 31, 33, 34, 44, 46, 57, 71, 126, 143, **154-73**
  hallucinatory experience in, 166-67
  imagery in, 162-64, 171-72
  and *Madame Bovary*, 154-55
  structure of, 165-73
Eliot, T. S., 99
Engels, Friedrich, 150
Ensorcelée, L' (d'Aurevilly), 90
Être et le néant, L' (Sartre), 8-9
Exercices de style (Queneau), 2

F

Faux-Monnayeurs, Les (Gide), 112-13
Feval, Paul, 90
Finnegans Wake (Joyce), 64, 70
Flaubert, Gustave:
  aesthetics of, 1-3, 6-7, 98
  anti-bourgeois sentiments of, 10-11, 61, 65, 138-39, 142-43, 152-53
  and Balzac, Honoré, 34, 36, 65, 89-90, 117, 119, 130, 135, 139, 140, 142, 149, 158, 171
  and Baudelaire, Charles, 4, 7, 9, 13, 14, 16, 58, **88-96**, 98, 153, 172
  and Bouilhet, Louis, 5, 14, 16, 18, 59, 71-72
  and his characters, 9-11, 13-20
  and Colet, Louise, 5, 14n-15n, 41, 59, 77, 82, 97-98, 121-22, 163-64
  critical reputation of, 1-3
  fictional techniques of, 123-31
  and Hugo, Victor, 36, 43, 51, 63, 171, 172
  influence of, 98-99
  and James, Henry, 2, 74, 98, 120, 169
  life of, 4-5, 15-16, 58
  psychology and thought of, **21-35**, **36-56**, 136-37, 139-40
  and realism, 8, 13-14, 19-20, 62-63, 86, 91-92, 135
  and Romanticism, 21-22, 86, 110
  and Sainte-Beuve, Charles, 114, 141-42, 144-46, 148-49, 152
  and Sand, George, 59-60, 61, 62, 72
  and Scott, Sir Walter, 147, 151
  and Stendhal, 73, 74, 111, 135, 139
  style of, 10, 121-23
  and Taine, Hippolyte, 75-77, 79, 82, 83, 86, 114, 150-51
  and Turgenev, Ivan, 59, 68, 69-70, 154
  and Zola, Émile, 8, 57, 58, 72, 74, 86, 98, 101, 111, 113, 141, 149, 150, 153, 171
Flaubert, Gustave, works by: (*see also* titles of individual works)
  Bouvard et Pécuchet, 3, 57-58, **64-72**
  Candidat, Le, 59, 65, 66
  Château de coeurs, Le, 64
  Coeur simple, Un, 58, 62-64
  Correspondance, 3-4, 5, 14n-15n, 21-22, 26, 29-32, 36, 37, 39, 41, 45, 47-48, 49, 55, 60, 73, 97-98, 122, 130, 136, 163-64
  Dictionnaire des idées reçues, 65, 69
  Éducation sentimentale, L', 1, 10-11, 26-27, 28, 31, 33, 34, 44, 46, 57, 71, 126, 143, **154-73**
  Hérodias, 57, 58, 62
  Légende de Saint Julien l'hospitalier, La, 58, 61-62
  Madame Bovary, 7-9, 11-12, **17-20**, 24-25, 27-28, 39, **41-56**, 57-74 *passim*, **77-86**, **97-111**, **112-31**, **132-40**

Flaubert, Gustave, works by: (*continued*)
   Memoirs d'un fou, 26, 164,
      165
   Novembre, 24, 29, 31, 40, 123,
      164, 165
   Par les champs et par les grèves, 22,
      23, 24, 123
   Salammbô, 4, 8, 9, 12, 30, 42-43,
      50, 57, 58, 61, **141-53**
   Tentation de Saint Antoine, La, 5,
      12, 14, 18, 19-30, 22-24, 32-34,
      37-39, 41, 46, 57
   Trois Contes, 12, 28, 58, **61-64**
   Voyage en Pyrénées et en Corse,
      21, 23, 24
Fleurs du mal, Les (Baudelaire),
   58
Fossiles (Bouilhet), 71
France, Anatole, 8
Frank, Joseph, 79

G

Gautier, Théophile, 4, 6, 7
Germinie Lacerteux (Goncourt
   brothers), 62
Gide, André, 1, 7, 60, 72, 112-13
Gilbert, Pierre, 2
Gommes, Les (Robbe-Grillet), 112
Goncourt brothers, 7, 8, 16, 43, 57,
   58, 61, 62, 72, 113
Gosse, Edmund, 2

H

Hallucinatory experience:
   in *Éducation sentimentale, L',*
      166-67
   in *Madame Bovary,* 77-86, 107-8
Héloïse (Barbara), 90
Hérodias, 57, 58, 62
Histoire du roman moderne (Marill-
   Albérès), 7-8
Holy Sinner, The (Mann), 62
Hugo, Victor, 36, 43, 51, 63, 171,
   172
Huysmans, J. K., 113

I

Imagery (*see also* Symbolism):
   in *Éducation sentimentale, L',*
      162-64, 171-72
   in *Madame Bovary,* 45-52, 53-56
   in *Salammbô,* 50

J

Jalousie, La (Robbe-Grillet), 112
James, Henry, 2, 74, 98, 120, 169
James, William, 87
Jarry, Alfred, 66
Joyce, James, 60, 64, 74, 98

L

La Bruyère, Jean, 135
Laforgue, Jules, 99
Lamartine, Alphonse de, 4
Leconte de Lisle, Charles, 121
*Légende de Saint Julien l'hospitalier,
   La,* 58, 61-62
Lettres de Dupuis et Cotonet (Musset),
   65-66
Loti, Pierre, 8
Lukács, Georg, 9

M

Madame Bovary, 7-9, 11-12, **17-20,**
   24-25, 27-28, 39, **41-56,** 57-75 *passim,* **77-86, 97-111, 112-31, 132-40**
   anti-bourgeois sentiments in,
      138-39
   and *Coeur simple, Un,* 62-63
   characterization in, 92-94, 109-10,
      114-22, 138-40
   contemporary reception of, 88-96
   and *Éducation sentimentale, L',*
      154-55
   and Flaubert's personality, 17-20
   hallucinatory experience in, 77-86,
      107-8
   imagery in, 45-52, 53-56
   point of view in, 114-22, 129-30,
      133-35

realism in, 85-86, 91-92, 135
Madame Bovary (*continued*)
   and *Salammbô*, 143-44, 145-46
   structure of, 101-8
   symbolism in, 98-111, 123-31
   and *Tentation de Saint Antoine, La,*
     95-96
Malentendu, Le (Camus), 62
Mallarmé, Stéphane, 3, 4, 7
Malraux, André, 2
Mann, Thomas, 62
Marill-Albérès, René, 7-8
Marx, Karl, 150
Maupassant, Guy de, 7, 8, 37
Mauriac, François, 117
Memoirs d'un fou, 26, 164, 165
Mencken, H. L., 65
Misérables, Les (Hugo), 51
Moore, George, 113
Musset, Alfred de, 4, 65-66
Mystère de Londres, Le (Feval), 90

N

Nathan, George Jean, 65
Nietzsche, Friedrich, 150, 153
Novembre, 24, 29, 31, 40, 123, 164,
   165

O

Origin of the Family, The (Engels),
   150

P

Par les champs et par les grèves, 22,
   23, 24, 123
Poe, Edgar Allan, 4, 89
Point of view, in *Madame Bovary,*
   114-22, 129-30, 133-35
Polite Conversation (Swift), 65
Portrait d'un inconnu (Sarraute), 112
Port Royal (Sainte-Beuve), 142
Poulet, Georges, 82, 84, 123
Pound, Ezra, 63, 64
Proust, Marcel, 2, 73, 74, 98, 99

Q

Queneau, Raymond, 3, 70
"Qu'est-ce que la littérature?" (Sartre),
   7-9

R

Rabelais, François, 36
Realism, 8, 13-14, 19-20
   in *Coeur simple, Un,* 62-63
   in *Madame Bovary,* 85-86, 91-92,
     135
   in *Salammbô,* 152-53
Richard, Jean-Pierre, 3, 10, 122
Robbe-Grillet, Alain, 112, 119
Romanticism, 21-22, 86, 110
Rousseau, Jean-Jacques, 136
Rousset, Jean, 9

S

Sainte-Beuve, Charles, 114, 141-42,
   144-46, 148-49, 152
Salammbô, 4, 8, 9, 12, 30, 42-43, 57,
   58, 61, **141-53**
   characterization in, 146-49
   imagery in, 50
   realism in, 152-53
Sand, George, 59-60, 61, 62, 72
Sarraute, Nathalie, 112
Sartre, Jean-Paul, 7-9, 57, 97, 112, 117
Schlésinger, Elisa, 59
Scott, Sir Walter, 147, 151
Soulié, Frédéric, 90
Spitzer, Leo, 83
Stein, Gertrude, 64
Stendhal, 73, 74, 111, 135, 139
Suarez, André, 2
Sue, Eugène, 90
Swift, Jonathan, 65, 71
Symbolism (*see also* Imagery):
   in *Éducation sentimentale, L',*
     162-64, 171-72
   in *Madame Bovary,* 98-111,
     123-31

T

Taine, Hippolyte, 75-77, 79, 82, 83,
   86, 114, 150-51
Tentation de Saint Antoine, La,
   5, 12, 14, 18, 22-24, 29-30, 32-
   34, 37-39, 41, 46, 57
   and *Madame Bovary,* 95-96
Thibaudet, Albert, 1, 12, 76, 85, 99,
   111, 171
Three Lives (Stein), 64
Trilling, Lionel, 70, 76
Trois Contes, 12, 28, 58, **61-64**
Turgenev, Ivan, 59, 68, 69-70,
   154

U

Ubu roi (Jarry), 66
Ulysses (Joyce), 64

V

Valéry, Paul, 2, 7, 73
Vieille Maîtresse (D'Aurevilly), 90
Voltaire, 70
Voyage en Pyrénées et en Corse, 21,
   23, 24

W

Wagner, Richard, 150
Warren, Robert Penn, 62
Waste Land, The (Eliot), 99
Woolf, Virginia, 98, 113

Z

Zola, Émile, 8, 57, 58, 72, 74, 86, 98,
   101, 111, 113, 141, 149, 150, 153,
   171

FORSTER

A Collection of Critical Essays
Edited by MALCOLM BRADBURY

A

A la recherche du temps perdu (Proust), 50
Abinger Harvest, 46, 50, 164, 164n, 167
Achievement of E. M. Forster, The (Beer), 11
Alexandria: A History and a Guide, 23
Allen, Glen O., 164n, 171-72, 172n
Allen, Walter, 2
Ambassadors, The (James), 97
Anderson, Sherwood, 72, 78-79
Anna Karenina (Tolstoy), 26n
Appropriate Form, The (Hardy), 3
Arnold, Mathew, 51, 75, 112, 113, 115, 116
Art and Order: A Study of E. M. Forster (Wilde), 12
"Art for Art's Sake," 163n
Art of E. M. Forster, The (Oliver), 11
Aspects of the Novel, 2, 8, 11, 12, 22, 25, 36, 46, 49, 97, 104, 142
Athenaeum, 150
Auden, W. H., 89
Austen, Jane, 2, 8, 34, 35, 49, 51, 99, 101, 114
Awkward Age, The (James), 48

B

Balzac, Honoré de, 146
Beer, J. B., 11, 171

Beethoven, L. V., 70, 78, 108, 135, 138, 154-55, 157-58
Belgion, Montgomery, 7
Bell, Clive, 5
Bennett, Arnold, 37, 89
Bergson, Henri, 83
Bhagavad Gita, 164n
Billy Budd (Melville), 97
Blake, William, 80, 114
Bloomsbury group, 1, 4, 5, 9, 46
Bourgh, Lady Catherine de, 51
Bowen, Elizabeth, 71
Brooks, Van Wyck, 72
Brown, E. K., 7, 9
Browne, Sir Thomas, 51
Browning, Robert, 113
Burke, Edmund, 75, 80
Burra, Peter, 6, 7, 8, 9, 69, 71
Butler, Samuel, 1, 2, 16, 49, 78, 98, 98n, 101, 112

C

Carpenter, Edward, 1, 115
Carlyle, Thomas, 51, 110, 112, 113
Catcher in the Rye, The (Salinger), 137
Cecil, Lord David, 128
Celestial Omnibus, The, 22, 34-36, 38, 51
"Characteristics" (Carlyle), 110
Chartism (Carlyle), 110
Chaucer, Geoffrey, 105

Clara Hopgood (Rutherford), 113*n*

Clough, Arthur, 113, 116

Concise Cambridge History of England, The, 71

Conflict, Forster's use of, 28-30, 31

Connolly, Cyril, 71

Conrad, Joseph, 1, 36, 49, 86, 89

Crews, Frederick C., 164*n*

Criterion, The, 7

D

Dante Alighieri, 51, 52, 78

Darwin, Charles, 115

Death of the Moth and Other Essays, The (Woolf), 9

Dickens, Charles, 23, 71, 73, 111, 112

Dickinson, Goldsworthy Lowes, 50, 166

Dickinson, Lowes, 54, 99

Dostoevsky, Fyodor, 49

"Double vision," Forster's use of, 48*n*, 99, 128

Dover Beach (Arnold), 115

Dream of John Ball, A (Morris), 111

Dreiser, Theodore, 72, 87

E

Egoist, The (Meredith), 35, 36, 102, 103

Eliot, T. S., 7, 85

Emerson, Ralph W., 115

E. M. Forster (Gransden), 11

E. M. Forster (Trilling), 10

E. M. Forster: The Perils of Humanism (Crews), 11

"Emperor Babur, The," 164

English Novel, The (Allen), 2

Erasmus, 78, 112, 158

Erewhon (Butler), 98, 112

Essay on Comedy (Meredith), 101

Esther Waters (Moore), 144, 146

Eternal Moment, The, 22

"Ethan Brand" (Hawthorne), 88

F

Fathers and Sons (Turgenev), 159

Faux-Monnayeurs, Les (Gide), 49

Fielding, Henry, 1, 71, 72, 99

Forster, E. M.:
  aesthetic principals of, 2
  and Austen, Jane, 2, 8, 34-35, 49, 51, 99, 101, 114
  and Beethoven, L. V., 70, 78, 108, 135, 138, 154-55, 157-58
  biographical information, 7, 8, 22, 27, 77-78
  and the Bloomsbury group, 1, 5, 9, 46
  and Butler, Samuel, 1, 2, 16, 49, 78, 98, 98*n*, 101, 112
  and Cambridge, 1, 40, 59
  and Carpenter, Edward, 1, 115
  Catholic critique of, 3, 13, 13*n*
  and conflict, use of, in works by, 28-30, 31
  and Connolly, Cyril, 71
  and Conrad, Joseph, 1, 36, 49, 86, 89
  and his contemporaries, 1
  early criticism of, 1, 6, 7
  and Dickens, Charles, 23, 71, 73, 111, 112
  and Dickinson, Lowes, 54, 99
  and "double vision," use of, 48*n*, 99, 128
  and experimentalism, 6
  and Holt, Lee E., 2
  and Ibsen, Henrik, 16
  and Isherwood, Christopher, 71
  and James, Henry, 36, 48-49, 52, 71, 73, 82, 91, 138
  and Lawrence, D. H., 1-2, 6, 8, 35-36, 38, 61, 75, 77
  Leit-motif, use of 7, 26, 27, 64, 142
  and liberalism, 2-4, 8, 10, 13, 46, 56-57, 67, 68, **71-80**, 106, 130
    (*see also* main entry)
  literary influences on, 2, 4, 35, 36, 49, 71, 77-78, 98, 98*n*, 101, 158

Forster, E. M. (*continued*):
and Macaulay, Rose, 6, 8, 34, 55,
57-58, 71
and Mann, Thomas, 4
Marxist critique of, 3, 13, 13*n*, 46
and Meredith, George, 1-2, 8, 35-
36, 71, 73, 101-4, 115
musical composition, use of, 27, 28
and Myers, L. H., 45-46
plot development, 24-26
and Proust, Marcel, 2, 49-50
recent criticism of, 2, 3, 10, 12, 13
and religious view of life, 81
reputation of, 1, 7, 16, 71
and rhythm, use of, 3, 7, 9, 11, 12,
26, 27, **144-59**
and Richards, I. A., 6, 7, 71
and Rutherford, Mark, 1, 113, 113*n*
social comedy, in works of, 6, 28,
30, 57, 123, 128-29, 130, 138
(*see also* main entry)
and survival, theme of, 18-19
and symbolism, use of, 3, 6, 10, 12,
18, 22, 26, 27, 41, 42, 60, 62, 65,
67, **90-95**, 96, 97, 125, 127, 128,
135, 144, 146-52 (*see also* main
entry)
and the Victorian intellectual tradition, 3
and violence, use of, 24, 25, 28, 35,
75, 165 (*see also* main entry)
and Woolf, Virginia, 1-3, 5-6, 9, 21,
22, 24, 26, 31, 49, 71, 91, 129
Forster, E. M., works by:
BIOGRAPHY
Goldsworthy Lowes Dickinson, 50,
166
ESSAYS
Abinger Harvest, 46, 50, 164, 164*n*,
167
"Art for Art's Sake," 163*n*
Aspects of the Novel, 2, 8, 11, 12,
22, 25, 36, 46, 49, 97, 104, 142
"Emperor Babur, The," 164
"Hymn Before Action," 164*n*
"Liberty in England," 50*n*
"Mohammed Iqbal," 166
"My Wood," 50*n*

"Pan," 167
"Syed Ross Masood," 160*n*
Two Cheers for Democracy, 97, 98,
113, 163*n*, 166
What I Believe, 57, 112, 114, 158
NOVELS
Howards End, 2, 4, 5, 8, 12, 14, 18,
19, 20, 23, 27, 28, 31, 32, 36, 40,
43, 50, 64, 65, 69, 70, 77, 81, 85,
98*n*, 108, 111, 113, 113*n*, 114,
115, 116, 128-43, 146 (*see also*
main entry)
Longest Journey, The, 7, 8, 18, 22,
26, 27, 28, 31, 36, 37, 38, 40, 57,
58, 59, 60, 61, 62, 64, 66, 76, 80,
84, 101, 103, 104, 106, 114, 115,
117-27
Passage to India, A, 2, 4, 5, 7, 8, 9,
12, 13, 14, 16-19, 23, 25, 26, 27,
28, 43, 47, 69, 70, 71, 73, 77, 83,
90, 92, 95, 98*n*, 104-5, 108, 113,
116, 127, 143, **144-59**, **161-74**
(*see also* main entry)
Room with a View, A, 8, 18, 26,
27, 28, 34, 35, 36, 52, 57, 58, 59,
69, 76, 82, 98*n*, 99, 100, 103,
104, 106, 115
Where Angels Fear to Tread, 8, 15,
16, 17, 18, 19, 25, 28, 34, 35, 36,
37, 52, 57, 59, 61, 75, 84, 102,
106 (*see also* main entry)
SHORT STORIES
Celestial Omnibus, The, 22, 34, 35,
36, 38, 51
Eternal Moment, The, 22
Other Kingdom, 36
HISTORICAL SKETCHES
Alexandria: A History and a Guide,
23
Notes on the State of Egypt, 23
Pharos and Pharillon, 17
Forum, The, 7
Four Quartets (Eliot), 85
Fry, Roger, 5, 90

G

Galsworthy, John, 37, 89

Gibbon, Edward, 112
Gide, André, 49, 91
Goethe, Johann Wolfgang von, 54, 78
Goldsworthy Lowes Dickinson, 50, 166
Gransden, K. W., 11
Gulliver's Travels (Swift), 98

H

Hard Times (Dickens), 111
Hardy, Barbara, 3
Hardy, Thomas, 49, 89
Hawthorne, Nathaniel, 73, 88
Hemingway, Ernest, 49
Henry IV, Part I (Shakespeare), 32
Hindu and Buddhist Monuments, Northern Circle (Mysore Archaeological Department), 151, 152
Hinduism, in *A Passage to India*, 161-67, 164n, 171-72
Hoare, Dorothy, 6, 8
Holt, Lee Elbert, 2
Horne, E. A., 169n
Howards End, 2, 4, 5, 8, 12, 14, 18, 19, 20, 23, 27, 28, 31, 32, 36, 40, 43, 50, 64, 65, 69, 70, 77, 81, 85, 98n, 108, 111, 113-16, 113n, **128-43**, 146
    theme of survival in, 19
Hoy, Cyrus, 130
Hume, David, 83
Huxley, Aldous, 49
"Hymn Before Action," 164n

I

Ibsen, Henrik, 16
"In Harmony with Nature" (Arnold), 115
In Memoriam (Tennyson), 115
Inge, W. R., 113
Isherwood, Christopher, 71

J

James, Henry, 36, 48, 52, 59, 71, 73, 82, 91, 138

Johnson, Dr. Samuel, 75
Joyce, James, 1, 3, 6, 49, 89

K

Keats, John, 110, 114
Kermode, Frank, 3, 12

L

Lamb, Charles, 52
Last Puritan, The (Santayana), 51
Lawrence, D. H., 1, 2, 6, 8, 35, 36, 38, 61, 75, 77
Lear of the Steppes, A (Turgenev), 146
Leavis, F. R., 2, 5, 7, 8, 9, 10, 129
Leit-motif, Forster's use of, 7, 26, 27, 64, 142
Liberalism, 2-4, 8, 10, 13, 46, 56-57, 67, 68, **71-80**, 106, 130
    in *Howards End*, 67, 68, 130
"Liberty in England," 50n
Little Dorrit (Dickens), 128
Longest Journey, The, 7, 8, 17, 22, 26-28, 31, 36-38, 40, 57-62, 64, 66, 76, 80, 84, 101, 103-4, 106, 114-15, **117-27**

M

MacCarthy, Desmond, 134
Macaulay, Rose, 6, 8, 34, 55, 57, 58, 71
Magic Mountain, The (Mann), 133
Mann, Thomas, 4
Marriages, The (James), 36
Mansfield, Katherine, 6
Maugham, Somerset, 89
McConkey, James, 11, 99, 164n, 172
Meredith, George, 1, 2, 8, 35, 36, 71, 73, 101-4, 115
Milton, John, 75
"Mohammed Iqbal," 166
Montaigne, Michel de, 72, 78, 112, 158
Moore, George E., 48, 94, 114n, 134, 146
Morris William, 110-111

Moses, 158
Murry, Middleton, 90
Musical composition, Forster's use of, 27, 28
"My Wood," 50n
Myers, L. H., 45-46
Mysore Archaeological Department, 151-52

N

"Nature of Gothic, The" (Ruskin), 110
News from Nowhere (Morris), 111
Nietzsche, Friedrich, 77
Nineteenth Century and After, The (Burra), 7
Notes on the State of Egypt, 23
Novels of E. M. Forster, The (McConkey), 11
"Novels of E. M. Forster, The," (Woolf), 9

O

Old Wives Tale, The (Bennet), 158
Oliver, H. J., 11
O'Neill, Eugene, 72
Ordeal of Richard Feveral, The (Meredith), 103
Othello (Shakespeare), 86
Other Kingdom, 36
Our Mutual Friend (Dickens), 77

P

"Pan," 167
Paris Review, 165
Passage to India, A, 2, 4, 5, 7-9, 12-14, 16-19, 23, 25-28, 43, 47, 69-71, 73, 77, 83, 90, 92, 95, 98n, 104-5, 108, 113, 116, 127, 143, **144-59**, 161-74
   Hinduism in, 161-67, 164n, 171, 172
Past and Present (Carlyle), 110
Paul, Saint, 158
Père Goriot, Le (Balzac), 146
Pharos and Pharillon, 17
Plato, 77, 130

Plot development, Forster's use of, 24-26
Point Counterpoint (Huxley), 49
Portrait of a Lady, The (James), 36
Powys, T. F., 51
Prelude, The (Wordsworth), 115
Princess Casamassima, The (James), 77
Principia Ethica (Moore), 1, 94, 114n, 134
Protestantism (Inge), 113
Proust, Marcel, 2, 49, 50

R

Rhythm, Forster's use of, 3, 7, 9, 11, 12, 26, 27, **144-59**
   in *Aspects of the Novel*, 11, 12
   in *Passage to India, A*, 7, **144-59**
Rhythm in the Novel (Brown), 9
Richards, I. A., 6, 7, 71
Room with a View, A, 8, 18, 26-28, 34-36, 52, 57-59, 69, 82, 98n, 99-100, 103, 104, 106, 115
Ruskin, John, 16, 110, 111, 112
Russell, Bertrand, 91
Rutherford, Mark (William Hale White), 1, 113, 113n

S

Santayana, George, 50, 54
Sartor Resartus, (Carlyle), 110
"Scholar Gipsy, The" (Arnold), 112
Schumann, Robert, 79
Secret Sharer, The (Conrad), 86
Shakespeare, William, 29, 32, 86
Shanks, Edward, 6
Shaw, G. B., 16
Shelley, P. B., 52, 78, 115
"Signs of the Times" (Carlyle), 110
Smollet, Tobias, 99
Social Comedy, Forster's use of, 6, 28, 30, 57, 123, 128-30, 138
   in *Howards End*, 128-29, 130, 138
   in *Longest Journey, The*, 123
   in *Passage to India, A*, 30
Some Studies in the Modern Novel (Hoare), 8

Steinbeck, John, 72
Stendhal, 72
Stephen, Fitzjames, 75
Sterne, Laurence, 97
Stones of Venice, The (Ruskin),
    110
Strachey, Lytton, 5, 46, 77
Survival, theme of, in Forster's work,
    18-19
"Syed Ross Masood," 160*n*
Swift, Jonathan, 72, 98
Symbolism, Forster's use of, 3, 6, 10,
    12, 18, 22, 26, 27, 41, 42, 60, 62,
    65, 67, 90-95, 96, 97, 125, 127, 128,
    135, 142, 144, 146-52
    in *Celestial Omnibus, The*, 22
    in *Eternal Moment, The*, 22
    in *Howards End*, 18, 41, 42, 65,
        67, 128, 135, 142
    in *Longest Journey, The*, 60, 62,
        125, 127
    in *Passage to India, A*, 144, 146-52

T

Tennyson, Alfred, 113
Thackeray, W. M., 52
Tolstoy, Leo, 52, 77
Tom Jones (Fielding), 128
Towards Democracy (Carpenter), 115
Trilling, Lionel, 1, 2, 4, 10, 117-19,
    166, 171
Tristram Shandy (Sterne), 97
Troilus and Criseyde (Chaucer), 105
Turgenev, Ivan, 146, 159
Two Cheers for Democracy, 97, 98,
    113, 163*n*, 166

U

Ulysses (Joyce), 49

V

Valéry, Paul, 91
Vanity Fair (Thackeray), 158
Violence, Forster's use of, 24, 25, 28,
    35, 75, 165
    in *Passage to India, A*, 165
    in *Where Angels Fear to Tread*,
        35, 75
Voltaire, 112

W

Waiting for Godot (Beckett), 113
War and Peace (Tolstoy), 158
Warren, Austin, 7, 9, 10
Waves, The (Woolf), 31, 49
Way of all Flesh, The (Butler), 98
Wells, H. G., 16, 36, 91
What I Believe, 57, 112, 114, 158
Where Angels Fear to Tread, 8, 15-19,
    25, 28, 34-37, 52, 57, 59, 61, 75, 84,
    102, 106
    theme of survival in, 18-19
White, Gertrude, 171
Whitehead, Alfred N., 83
Whitman, Walt, 10, 159
Wilde, Alan, 12
Winter's Tale, The (Shakespeare), 73
Woolf, Virginia, 1, 2, 3, 5, 6, 9, 21, 22,
    24, 26, 31, 49, 71, 91, 129
"Woods of Westermain, The" (Mere-
    dith), 115
Wordsworth, William, 115
Writings of E. M. Forster, The
    (Macaulay), 8, 34

Z

Zabel, Morton, 7, 9
Zola, Émile, 87, 89

ROBERT FROST

A Collection of Critical Essays
Edited by JAMES M. COX

A

Abercrombie, Lascelles, 16, 39, 187
Acton, Lord, 116
Adams, Henry, 49-50, 72
Adams, J. Donald, 9, 151, 152, 153
Aiken, Conrad, 44
Alexander the Great, 118
"Altarwise by Owl-Light" (Thomas),
  126-27
"American Scene, The" (James), 54
"Among School Children" (Yeats), 166
Amphitryon 38 (Giraudoux), 120
Arnold, Matthew, 84, 179
Ash Wednesday (Eliot), 12, 48, 169
Atlantic Monthly, The, 152
Auden, W. H., 17, 47, 83, 152, 171,
  172, 173, 189, 191
Augustine, St., 103

B

Babbitt, Irving, 129
Bacon, Francis, 180
Baker, Howard, 81
Baudelaire, Charles, 125
Benét, Stephen Vincent, 36
"Biglow Papers, The" (J. R. Lowell),
  39
Blackmur, R. P., 164
Blake, William, 70-71, 87, 142
Bogan, Louise, 159-60, 167
Boy's Will, A, 2, 3, 6, 39, 48, 49, 53,
  131, 139, 143, 159, 185

Bridges, Robert, 81
Brogan, Denis, 174
Brooke, Rupert, 39
Brooks, Cleanth, 182-83
Brooks, Van Wyck, 44
Brown, Charles Brockden, 44
Brown, John, 42
Browning, Robert, 170
Bryant, William Cullen, 90
Burnett, Whit, 2
"Burnt Norton" (Eliot), 168, 182

C

Carpenter, Frederic I., 171-72
Celtic Twilight, The (Yeats), 1
Charlemagne, 74
Chase, Richard, 175
Chaucer, Geoffrey, 160
Chew, Samuel, 188
Cocktail Party, The (Eliot), 169
Coleridge, Samuel T., 179
Collected Poems (1939), 6, 67
Collected Poems (Yeats), 161, 173
"Collected Poems of Robert Frost,
  The" (Carpenter), 172
Complete Poems, 2, 13, 85, 117, 161,
  165-66
Confucius, 136
Conrad, Joseph, 1
Cook, Reginald, 139
Coriolanus (Shakespeare), 196
Corneille, Pierre, 105
Cowley, Malcolm, 7, 8

Cox, Sidney, 5
Crane, Hart, 60, 64, 77, 81
Crane, Stephen, 1
Crashaw, Richard, 60
Cummings, E. E., 71, 84, 191, 195
Cunningham, J. V., 81-82

D

Dante Alighieri, 97
"Dawn, The" (Yeats), 161
"Delight in Disorder" (Herrick), 126
Democritus, 149
De Rerum Natura (Lucretius), 129
Desire under the Elms (O'Neill), 51
"Dialogue of Self and Soul, A"
    (Yeats), 95
Dickinson, Emily, 1
Divine Comedy, 183
Donne, John, 105, 126-27
Dos Passos, John, 44
Dostoevsky, F., 40

E

"Easter 1916" (Yeats), 161
Edwards, Jonathan, 71
Einstein, Albert, 124, 178
"Elegy" (Gray), 87
Eliot, T. S., 1, 4, 5, 8, 10, 11, 12, 13,
    31, 34, 47, 48, 54, 55, 71, 72, 83,
    124, 125, 129, 160, 168, 169, 170,
    171, 172, 173, 180, 182, 183, 184,
    186, 189, 195, 196
Emerson, Ralph W., 1, 6, 7, 27, 30, 31, 32,
    33, 38, 42, 58, 60, 61, 66, 82, 128
Empson, William, 87
Engle, Paul, 17
Epicurus, 121
"Essay on Man, An" (Pope), 170, 179
"Eros Turannos" (Robinson), 63
Ethan Frome (Wharton), 51
Euclid, 127
Exodus, 192

F

Faulkner, William, 1, 44

Fire and Ice (Thompson), 6
Fitzgerald, F. S., 1
Fourierism, 38
Four Quartets (Eliot), 12, 48, 173
Frazer, James, 183
Freud, Sigmund, 152
Frost, Robert:
    biographical information, 1, 3, 39,
        41-42, 46-48
    critical reception of, 5-11, 36-38
    and modern literature, 1, 3-5, 83-
        84, 177-97 *passim*
    and nature, 7, 8, 23, 48, 49, 55, 78,
        106-8, 114-15, 117, 121, 138-50,
        177-78, 184-85
    and science, 178-84, 187
    theory of poetry, 16-35, 124-37
        passim, 166-76
Frost, Robert, works by:
    "Acquainted with the Night," 37,
        56, 79, 81, 97, 159, 195
    "After Apple-Picking," 85, 188, 196
    "All Revelation," 134
    "Answer, An," 101
    "Atmosphere," 102
    "Ax-Helve, The," 29, 148
    "Bear, The," 64, 65, 72, 111-12,
        130, 141, 149, 161
    "Bearer of Evil Tidings, The," 61,
        63
    "Beech," 10, 37, 102, 193, 195
    "Bereft," 177
    "Birches," 28, 47, 56, 85, 115
    "Black Cottage, The," 40-41, 52,
        94-95, 100
    "Blueberries," 52
    "Bond and Free," 132
    Boy's Will, A, 2, 3, 6, 39, 48, 49,
        53, 131, 139, 143, 159, 185
    "Brook in the City, A," 56
    "Brown's Descent," 146
    "Build Soil," 5, 42, 43, 56, 66-67,
        68, 117, 143
    "Canis Major," 195
    "Case for Jefferson, A," 168
    "Census-Taker," 146
    Collected Poems (1939), 6, 67
    "Come In," 37, 80

Frost, Robert, works by: (*continued*)
  Complete Poems, 2, 13, 85, 117,
    161, 165-66
  "Considerable Speck, A," 140-41,
    149
  "Constant Symbol, The," 124, 128
  "Cow in Apple Time," 37
  "Death of the Hired Man, The," 37,
    51, 176
  "Departmental," 140-41
  "Desert Places," 100
  "Design," 88-89, 157, 189
  "Devotion," 170
  "Directive," 56, 159, 167, 168,
    196-97
  "Discovery of the Madeiras, The,"
    80, 159, 168
  "Dust of Snow," 102, 139
  "Egg and the Machine, The,"
    67-68
  "Empty Threat, An," 102, 159
  "Etherealizing," 135, 168
  "Fear, The," 50, 51, 100, 176
  "Figure a Poem Makes, The," 2,
    124, 166, 168
  "Fire and Ice," 37
  "For Once, Then, Something," 24,
    25-26, 102, 141
  "Fountain, a Bottle, a Donkey's Ear
    and Some Books, A," 102
  "From Plane to Plane," 114
  Further Range, A, 37, 61, 65, 79,
    130, 134, 142, 159
  "Gathering Leaves," 102
  "Generations of Men, The," 52
  "Ghost House," 185
  "Gift Outright, The," 9, 95
  "Going for Water," 53-54
  "Grindstone, The," 37
  "Happiness Makes Up in Height,"
    53, 56
  "Hill Wife, The," 50, 56, 61, 63,
    102, 146
  "Home Burial," 50, 51, 52, 100,
    120, 170, 176
  "Housekeeper, The," 50
  "Hundred Collars, A," 51
  "Hyla Brook," 185

"I Could Give All to Time," 80, 95-
  96
"Importer, An," 168
"In a Disused Graveyard," 100-101
"Ingenuities of Debt, The," 102
"In Hardwood Groves," 102
"In Time of Cloudburst," 139
"Into My Own," 28
"Investment, The," 102
"I Will Sing You One-O," 133, 195
"Last Mowing, The," 77-78, 81-82
"Lesson for Today, The," 74-75,
  126, 134, 138, 145
"Line-Storm Song, A," 185
"Lone Striker, A," 113-14
"Loose Mountain (Telescopic), A,"
  134
"Lost Follower, The," 161
"Lost in Heaven," 134
"Lovely Shall Be Choosers, The,"
  100, 171
"Lucretius Versus the Lake Poets,"
  121
Masque of Mercy, A, 110, 119, 120,
  142, 149-50, 161, 162, 168,
  170
Masque of Reason, A, 69, 70-73
  79, 110, 119-20, 142, 143, 161
"Mending Wall," 4, 47, 52, 85, 147
"Minor Bird, A," 139
"Moon Compasses," 102, 134, 170
"Most of It, The," 81, 91-93, 159,
  178
"Mountain Interval," 39
Mountain Interval, 61, 159
"Mowing," 188
"My Butterfly," 1
"My November Guest," 185
"Need of Being Versed in Country
  Things, The," 102-3
"Neither Out Far Nor In Deep," 25,
  37, 85-86, 157, 159, 190
"Never Again Would Birds' Song Be
  the Same," 80
"New Hampshire," 116
New Hampshire, 5, 123, 132, 133,
  159
North of Boston, 2, 3, 4, 14, 16,

Frost, Robert, works by: (*North of Boston*), (*continued*)
  49, 51, 52, 53, 55, 56, 71, 159, 168, 172, 174, 185, 187
  "Now Close the Windows," 37, 56
  "October," 56
  "Old Barn at the Bottom of the Fogs, The," 96
  "Old Man's Winter Night, An," 50, 56, 85, 196
  "Once By the Pacific," 177
  "On Going Unnoticed," 77
  "Onset, The," 185
  "Our Hold on the Planet," 134, 139
  "Oven Bird, The," 56, 102, 185
  "Passing Glimpse, A," 141
  "Pasture, The," 2, 13, 37, 102, 170
  "Pauper Witch of Grafton, The," 98-99, 171
  "Poetry and the School," 124
  "Provide Provide," 87-88, 102
  "Putting in the Seed," 12
  "Rabbit Hunter, The," 80
  "Range-Finding," 101-2
  "Riders," 107
  "Road Not Taken, The," 61, 63, 77, 169
  "Roadside Stand, The," 56, 116
  "Rose Pogonias," 123
  "Runaway, The," 102, 195
  "Sand Dunes," 64
  Selected Poems (1936), 17
  "Self-Seeker," 171
  "Serious Step Lightly Taken, A," 63
  "Servant to Servants, A" 50, 51, 99-100, 146, 159, 176
  "Silken Tent, The," 128
  "Snow," 159
  "Sound of the Trees, The," 37, 61, 62-63
  "Span of Life, The," 101
  "Spring Pools," 56, 78, 81
  "Stars," 131, 159
  "Star-Splitter, The," 133, 140, 177
  Steeple Bush, 56, 74, 79, 110, 111, 114, 118, 136, 161
  "Steeple on the House, A," 119

"Stopping by Woods on a Snowy Evening," 12, 22, 37, 44, 56, 102
"Strong Are Saying Nothing, The," 141
"Subverted Flower, The," 41, 98, 159
"Telephone, The," 102
"There are Roughly Zones," 143
"Time Out," 97-98, 140
"Times Table, The," 75-76
"To Earthward," 37, 56, 100
"To a Moth Seen in Winter," 96, 184
"To a Thinker," 63, 161
"Tree at My Window," 37, 77, 115, 140
"Trespass," 147
"Trial By Existence, The," 143, 144, 175
"Triple Bronze," 145
"Two Look at Two," 138-39, 171
"Two Tramps in Mud Time," 41-42, 140, 188
"Vindictives, The," 79, 80, 81
"West-Running Brook," 8, 29, 69, 106-10 *passim*, 171
West-Running Brook, 5, 64, 67-68, 78, 130, 133, 159
"White-Tailed Hornet, The," 65, 128, 131, 149
"Willful Homing," 37
"Wish to Comply, A," 119, 136
"Witch of Coös, The," 37, 100, 141
Witness Tree, A, 6, 25, 37, 53, 63, 79, 80, 110, 111, 114, 134, 159, 193
"Wood-Pile, The," 185
Fugitive Slave Law, 42
Further Range, A, 37, 61, 65, 79, 130, 134, 142, 159

G

Georgian poets, 187-88
German Romanticism, 38
Gibson, W. W., 16, 39, 187
Gilded Age, 9

Giraudoux, Jean, 120
Goethe, J. W. von, 104
Gray, Thomas, 87
Greville, Fulke, 60
Guest, Edgar, 46

H

Hackluyt, Richard, 80
Hadamard, J., 124
Hamlet (Shakespeare), 196
Hardy, Thomas, 98, 103
Harte, Bret, 68
Hawthorne, Nathaniel, 1, 38, 42, 44
Hemingway, Ernest, 1, 39, 44
Herrick, Robert, 63, 74, 123, 126, 133
Hesse, Mary, 129-30
Hillyer, Robert, 16
Hinduism, 38
Hobbes, Thomas, 180
"Hollow Men, The" (Eliot), 31
Homer, 96
Hooker, Richard, 64
Horace, 74, 123
Housman, A. E., 85-86
Hovey, Richard, 16
Howells, William Dean, 4

I

Independent, 1
In Memoriam (Tennyson), 179-80
"In Memory of Eva Gore-Booth and Con Markievicz" (Yeats), 168
Imagists, 16, 172, 180

J

James, Henry, 1, 44, 54-55
Jarrell, Randall, 8-9, 195
Jeans, Sir James, 133
"Jeat Ring Sent, A" (Donne), 127
Jones, Lewellyn, 143
Jonson, Ben, 59, 60, 64, 123
Journals (Kierkegaard), 46
Joyce, James, 1

K

Kekulé von Stradonitz, F. A., 124
Kierkegaard, Sören, 46

L

Laforgue, Jules, 71, 72
Langer, Susanne, 8, 126, 128, 131
Lanier, Sidney, 35
"Lapis Lazuli" (Yeats), 161
Last Poems (Yeats), 161
Lawrence, D. H., 1, 152, 156, 157, 189
"Leda and the Swan" (Yeats), 166
Lewis, C. Day, 17
Lowell, Amy, 5, 16
Lucretius, 121, 129
"Lycidas" (Milton), 167
Lynen, John F., 10, 11, 14
Lyrical Ballads (Wordsworth), 129

M

Macbeth, 89
Machiavelli, 118
MacLeish, Archibald, 16
Mallarmé, Stéphane, 125
Man on His Nature (Sherrington), 135
Markievicz, Constance, 161
"Maruja" (Hart), 68
Marvell, Andrew, 102
Masque of Mercy, A, 110, 119, 120, 142, 149-50, 161, 162, 168, 170
Masque of Reason, A, 69, 70-73, 79, 110, 119-20, 142, 143, 161
Maxwell, J. C., 130
Melville, Herman, 1, 44, 90
Millikan, Robert, 119, 136
Milton, John, 32, 60, 160, 167, 170, 186
Modern Poetry and the Tradition (Brooks), 183
Molière, 59
Monroe, Harriet, 16
Montaigne, 38, 109

Montgomery, Marion, 8
Moore, Marianne, 83, 84, 103
Mourning Becomes Electra
   (O'Neill), 51
Muir, Edwin, 5, 17
Munson, Gorham, 5, 38

N

Napier, John, 8
Neff, Emery, 152-53
New Criticism, 5
New Deal, 5
New England, 2, 3, 4, 5, 7, 8, 10, 14,
   23, 38, 39, 40, 41, 44, 45, 49, 50,
   51, 52, 54, 55, 56, 71, 77, 85, 105,
   118, 121, 174, 186, 188
New England Primer, The, 193, 194
New Hampshire, 5, 123, 132, 133, 159
New Republic, 16
Newton, Isaac, 178
New York Times Book Review, The,
   151-52
"Night-Piece to Julia" (Herrick), 63
"Nineteen Hundred and Nineteen"
   (Yeats), 166, 168
Nitchie, George W., 9-11 *passim*
North of Boston, 2, 3, 4, 14, 16, 49,
   51, 52, 53, 55, 56, 71, 159, 168,
   172, 174, 185, 187

O

"Ode on Intimations of Immortality"
   (Wordsworth), 144
O'Donnell, W. G., 8
"On a House Shaken by the Land
   Agitation" (Yeats), 161
O'Neill, Eugene, 51

P

Parrington, V. L., 174, 175
Partisan Review, 155
Pascal, Blaise, 38
Pastoral Art of Robert Frost, The

(Lynen), 10, 11, 14
"Penal Colony, The" (Kafka), 90
Pericles, 118
"Piano que baise une main frêle, Le"
   (Verlaine), 78
Pinkerton Academy, 161
Plato, 149
Poe, E. A., 28, 35, 44, 125
Poems (Yeats), 1
Poetry, 16, 142
Poincaré, J. H., 124
Pope, Alexander, 127, 170, 179, 186
Pound, Ezra, 1, 4, 11, 16, 64, 71, 81,
   124, 174, 180, 186
"Prayer for My Daughter, A" (Yeats),
   161
Prelude, The (Wordsworth), 140, 179
Puritan heritage, 32-33, 41, 71

R

Racine, Jean, 38, 59
Ransom, John Crowe, 16, 20
"Raven, The" (Poe), 125
Recognition of Robert Frost (ed.
   Thornton), 5, 36
Red Badge of Courage, The (Crane), 1
Renaissance, 178, 186
Rilke, Rainer Maria, 83, 88
Robinson, Edwin Arlington, 16, 30,
   36, 63, 77, 161
Rochester, Earl of, 61-62
Romanticism, 58, 59, 65, 68, 71, 72,
   77, 78, 82, 179, 180, 181
Roosevelt, Franklin, 5, 66
Rousseau, Jean-Jacques, 38

S

"Sailing to Byzantium" (Yeats), 71,
   162, 166
Saturday Review, The, 83, 152
"Science and the Human Imagination"
   (Hesse), 129-30
Science and the Modern World
   (Whitehead), 178

"Second Coming, The" (Yeats), 79,
   164
Selected Poems (1936), 17
"September 1, 1939" (Auden), 173
Sergeant, Elizabeth S., 13
Shakespeare, 12, 32, 59, 88, 170, 183
Sherrington, Sir Charles, 135
"Skipper Ireson's Ride" (Whittier), 39
Smith, Adam, 116
"Snowman, The" (Stevens), 100
Socrates, 65
Spender, Stephen, 171
Spenser, Edmund, 160, 170
Steeple Bush, 56, 74, 79, 110, 111,
   114, 118, 136, 161
Stendhal, 102
Stevens, Wallace, 10, 11, 13, 83, 100,
   171, 173, 191
Strindberg, August, 89
Structure, 3, 18, 19-20, 31-33, 43, 70,
   75, 86, 133
   dramatic narrative, 7, 26-27, 63
   pastoral, 10, 59, 66-67, 183-87,
      196-97
Style, 14, 20, 56, 75, 96, 192-93, 195
Stylistic devices, 2-3, 10, 12, 13-14,
   17, 21, 22-23, 24-30, 34-35, 56, 59,
   71-72, 77, 80-81, 87, 95, 105,
   128-31, 183, 187
Sufism, 38
Swift, Jonathan, 82
Synge, John Millington, 56
Symbolists, 18, 48, 180, 181, 182,
   184, 196
Symbols, 28, 43, 55, 69, 79, 81, 86,
   130, 183, 188, 193-94

T

Tempest, The (Shakespeare), 183
Tennyson, Alfred Lord, 179, 180
Themes, major, 91, 118, 168
   alienation, 52
   man's limitations, 91-93, 103,
      109-12
   moral choice and will, 61, 175-76

transience, 55, 91-93
Thomas Aquinas, 62, 64, 65
Thomas, Dylan, 10, 99, 126-27, 128,
   191-92, 193, 194, 195
Thomas, Edward, 16, 39, 162
Thompson, Lawrance, 6
Thoreau, H. D., 7, 38, 42, 67, 68, 82
Thornton, Richard, 5
"To a Water-Fowl" (Bryant), 90
Torrence, Ridgely, 162
"Tower, The" (Yeats), 161, 166
Tower, The (Yeats), 166
Trilling, Lionel, 9, 160, 174, 175,
   189-90
Twain, Mark, 1, 9
"Two Songs from a Play" (Yeats),
   162-63, 166

U

"Under Ben Bulben" (Yeats), 161

V

Valéry, Paul, 125
Van Doren, Mark, 5
Verlaine, Paul, 78
Voltaire, 38
Vision, A (Yeats), 164, 165,
   166
"Vision of Sir Launfal, The," 42

W

Wagner, Richard, 183
Waste Land, The (Eliot), 5, 12, 34,
   48, 84, 125, 182, 183
Watts, Harold, 7, 8
Weeks, Edward, 152
Wertheimer, L., 124
West-Running Brook, 5, 64, 67-68, 78,
   130, 133, 159
Wharton, Edith, 51
Whitehead, Alfred North, 164, 178,
   182

Whitman, Walt, 1, 7, 44, 52, 60, 66, 191
Whittier, John G., 9
Wilde, Oscar, 172
William the Silent, 65
Williams, William Carlos, 191
Winters, Yvor, 7, 8, 126, 134
Witness Tree, A, 6, 25, 37, 53, 63, 79, 80, 110, 111, 114, 134, 159, 193

Wordsworth, William, 6, 8, 125, 127, 128, 129, 138, 139, 140, 141, 144, 146, 147, 160, 186

Y

Yeats, W. B., 1, 10, 11, 47, 71, 79, 105, 123, 124, 160-61, 162, 163, 164, 165, 167, 168, 170, 171, 173, 180, 182, 186, 189, 191

GIDE

A Collection of Critical Essays

Edited by DAVID LITTLEJOHN

A

Adler, A., 143, 147, 154
Ainsi soit-il (*see also Journal 1939-1949*), 141, 153
    homosexuality, theme of, 141
Alibert, François-Paul, 5
Amiel, 136, 137, 158, 159
Amyntas, 21, 132
    homosexuality, theme of, 132
Ancient Mariner, The (Coleridge), 65
"André Gide et l'opinion en France de 1890 à 1950" (Lafille), 14
Arbousse-Bastide, M., 137-38
Armance (Stendhal), 59
Asceticism, theme of, in *Porte étroite, La*, 96-111
As You Like It (Shakespeare), 113
Atheism, 7, 17, 18
Autobiography, Gide's use of, 8, 9-10, 24, 49-62, 152-53
    in *Cahiers et les poésies d'André Walter, Les*, 76
    in *Faux-Monnayeurs, Les*, 76
    in *Immoraliste, L'*, 74, 80
    in *Isabelle*, 74
    in *Journal 1889-1939*, 50-52, 74
    in *Porte étroite, La*, 10, 74, 95, 107-8
    in *Si le grain ne meurt*, 11, 74, 129-30
    in *Symphonie pastorale, La*, 74, 81

B

Balzac, H., 78, 83, 153
Barrère, J. B., 13
Barrès, M., 22, 24, 25
Bastide, Roger, 6
Baudelaire, Charles, 5, 66, 133, 148
Beraud, Henri, 2, 3
Biran, Maine de, 154
Blake, William, 112, 118, 121
Blanchot, Maurice, 6, 9, 10, 12
Bonaventura, Saint, 17
Bossuet, J. B., 20
Bourget, Paul, 24, 159
Brecht, B., 10
Brée, Germaine, 6, 8, 9, 11, **109-10**

C

Cahiers et les poésies d'André Walter, Les, 63, 153
    autobiography, Gide's use of, 76
    homosexuality, theme of, 67, 132
Caillois, Roger, 48
Calmette, Germain, 13
Camus, Albert, 5, 48
Carnets d'Egypte, Les, (*see also Journal 1939-1949*), 153
Carpenter, E., 148
Caves du Vatican, Les (*see also Lafcadio's Adventures*), 50, 66, 77
    irony in, 74

Caves du Vatican, Les (continued)
   morality in, 46
Chants de Maldoror, Les (Lautréa-
   mont), 52, 66
Chateaubriand, F., 21, 24, 46, 85
Classicism, Gide's use of, **37-48, 60-62,**
   77
   in *Journal 1889-1939*, **53-56,** 59
   in *Thesée*, 37-39
Claudel, Paul, 6, 20, 24, 26, 27, 32, 93
"Colloque de l'Altenburg" (Malraux),
   47
Communism, 3, 16, **42-43,** 57
Confessions (Rousseau), 21, **130-31**
Confession d'une jeune fille, La,
   (Proust), 141
Constant, B., 154
Copeau, Jaques, 20, 26
Copée, François, 55
Corydon, 3, 15, 22
   homosexuality, theme of, 134, 135,
      136-37, 142, 144, 160
Cotnam, Jaques, 13
*Counterfeiters, The (see Faux-
   Monneyeurs, Les)*

D

Delay, Jean, 6, 8, 12, **158-59**
Demarest, Albert, 145
Development, in Gide's works, 79-92
Dickens, Charles, 153
Discours sur l'origine de l'inégalité
   (Rousseau), 135
Dostoevsky, F., 78, 153
Douglas, Lord Alfred, 146, 149
DuBos, Charles, 20, 21, 26, 32, 147
Dupouey, M., 20, 26

E

Envers du Journal de Gide, L' (Rim-
   baud), 155
Esprit non prévenu, Un, 79-83
   method in, **79-81**
Estève, Claude-Louis, 5
Etiemble, René, 6, 14

*Et nunc manet in te (see also Journal
   1939-1949)*, 10, 95, 107, 111, 130,
   134, 153

F

Faux-Monnayeurs, Les, 1, 3, 9, 10,
   24, 50, 73, **76-77, 78-79, 112-28,**
   153-54
   autobiography, Gide's use of, 76
   homosexuality, theme of, 117, 134,
      150, 161
   irony in, 127
   morality in, 46, **119-22**
   organization of, 122-27
   religion in, 28
   sexuality in, 116-18
Fernandez, Ramon, 5, 47
Flaubert, G., 84, 153
Fontanin, Daniel de, 5
Forster, E. M., 10
Freud, S., 116, 135, 136, **138-39,**
   141-42, 148, 150
Fusées (Baudelaire), 133

G

Galsworthy, J., 116
Gard, Roger Martin du, 2, 3, 6, 8, 10,
   116
Gautier, T., 24
Ghéon, Henri, 1, 20, 26, 32
Gide, André:
   and Amiel, 136, 137, 158, 159
   asceticism, theme of, 96-110
   autobiography, Gide's use of, 8,
      9-10, 11, 24, 49-62, 74, 76, 80,
      81, 95, **107-8, 129-30, 152-53**
   and Balzac, H., 78, 83, 153
   and Baudelaire, C., 5, 66, 133, 148
   and Blake, William, 112, 118, 121
   and Brecht, B., 10
   and Camus, Albert, 5, 48
   and Chateaubriand, F., 21, 24, 46,
      85
   childhood of, 7, **139-43, 158-59**
   classicism, use of, **37-48, 53-56,**

Gide, André (*continued*)
59, 60-62, 77
and Claudel, Paul, 6, 20, 24, 26,
27, 32, 93
and communism, 3, 16, 42-43, 57
and Dickens, Charles, 153
and Dostoevsky, F., 78, 153
and Douglas, Lord Alfred, 146, 149
and Flaubert, G., 84, 153
and Forster, E. M., 10
and Freud, S., 116, 135, 136,
138-39, 141-42, 148, 150
and Galsworthy, J., 116
and Gide, Madeleine, 10, 31-32, 34,
95, 105, 107-8, 129-30, 139-50,
151, 155-56
and Giradoux, J., 25
and Goethe, J. W., 7, 41, 42,
134-35
and Hegel, G. W. F., 15, 18
homosexuality, theme of, 7, 11, 12,
16, 19, 23, 27-28, 66-72, 117,
129-51, 160, 161
humanism in, 15-18, 37-43
iconoclasm of, 2-3, 15-18, 22-24
immorality, theme of, 2-3, 30-35
influence of, 5, 6, 9, 12-13, 24-25,
43-48
irony in, 73-79, 93-94, 127
and Jammes, Francis, 1, 20, 24, 26
and Jarry, A., 51
journal intime, use of, 154-57,
159-62
and Joyce, James, 1, 128
and Jung, C. G., 148
and Keats, J., 5
and Kierkegaard, S., 15
and LaFayette, Madame de, 94
and Lautréamont, Comte de, 50
and Loti, P., 137
and Louÿs, P., 139, 145, 157-58
and Maeterlink, M., 71
and Mallarmé, S., 57, 63
and Malraux, A., 5, 39, 47, 52
and Mann, T., 1, 116
marriage of, 8, 10, 31-32, 34, 95,
105, 107-8, 129-30, 139, 151

and Marx, K., 15, 57
and Maupassant, Guy de, 78
and Mauriac, Claude, 6, 8, 33
and Mauriac, François, 7
and Meredith, G., 116
and Montaigne, M. de, 141
morality, theme of, 4, 5, 7, 10, 11,
12, 23, 41-43, 46, 49, 55-58,
119-22, 163
naturalism, use of, 84-85
and Nietzsche, F., 21, 42, 137, 139
and the Nobel Prize, 4, 6, 20, 23,
24
and Novalis, 64, 70
organization in works of, (*see also*
"Recits"), 87-91, 122-27
and Pascal, B., 19, 20, 28, 38, 54-
55
and Poe, E. A., 65-66
polarity, use of, 39-43, 45-48, 49,
60-62, 74-77, 94
politics of, 3, 4, 5, 16
and Proust, Marcel, 1, 44, 45, 118,
127-28, 141, 148
and Racine, J., 21, 32, 55
religion, theme of, 4, 7, 19-29, 30-
35, 41-43, 93-94, 162
and Rimbaud, Arthur, 55, 66, 138
and Rochefoucauld, La, 145
Roman Catholic Index of Forbidden Books, proscribed by, 4-6,
12, 30
romanticism in, 77-79
and Rousseau, J. J., 21, 24, 38, 43,
130-131, 135, 137
sexuality, theme of (*see also* Homosexuality), 4, 7, 11, 12, 96-97,
116-18, 129-31
and Shakespeare, 21, 113, 148
and Spartacus, 22, 23
and Stekel, W., 150
and Stendhal, 5, 59
surrealism, use of, 65
symbolism, use of, 63-64, 65, 67
and Valéry, Paul, 23
and Verlaine, Paul, 44, 53-54
and Vinci, Leonardo da, 138, 148

Gide, André (*continued*)
  and Wilde, Oscar, 23, 145, 146, 147
  and Zola, 83
Gide, André, works by (*see also* main
  entries for titles):
  CORRESPONDENCE
    *Letters de Charles DuBos et Re-
      sponses d'André Gide,* 156
  JOURNALS
    Journal 1880-1939 (includes
      Numquid et tu . . .), 1, 2, 6, 7-8,
      9, 21, 22, 23, 24, 26, 28, 36, 38,
      39-40, 41-43, 46, 47, 49, 50-52,
      53-60, 74, 94, 99, 110-111, 141,
      152-63
    Journal 1939-1949, 3, 10, 15, 21,
      24, 26, 28, 36, 67-68, 74, 83, 95,
      107, 111, 129-33, 134, 142-43,
      149, 153, 160, 161
  OUVRES LYRIQUES
    Nourritures terrestres, Les, 1, 2, 9,
      21, 39, 40, 43, 50, 64, 73, 76,
      126
    Retour de l'Enfant Prodique, Le,
      26, 28
    Tentative amoureuse, La, 50
    Thesée, 36-42, 46
    Traite de Narcisse, Le, 148
  RECITS
    Immoraliste, L', 9, 19, 21, 24, 39-
      40, 50, 73, 74-77, 80, 84, 85, 87,
      88-91, 93-94, 111, 117, 130, 134
    Isabelle, 73, 74, 76, 77-78, 85-87,
      88, 90
    Porte étroite, La, 1, 6, 9, 10, 11,
      24, 39-40, 50, 73-77, 83-84, 85,
      87-88, 88-89, 93-111, 113, 153
    Symphonie pastorale, La, 50, 73,
      74, 76, 81, 85, 88, 91
  ROMANS
    Faux-Monnayeurs, Les, 1, 3, 9, 10,
      24, 28, 46, 50, 73, 76-77, 78-79,
      112-28, 134, 150, 153-54
    Voyage d'Urien, Le, 11, 36, 63-72,
      132, 144
  SOTIES
    Caves du Vatican, Les, 46, 50, 66,
      74, 77

    Paludes, 9, 64, 66, 74, 76, 85
    Promethée mal enchâine, Le, 66,
      74, 76
  THÉÂTRE
    Roi Candaule, Le, 76
    Saül, 76
  OTHER
    Amyntas, 21, 132
    *Cahiers et les poésies d'André
      Walter, Les,* 63, 67, 76, 132, 153
    Corydon, 3, 15, 22, 134, 135,
      136-37, 142, 144, 160
    Esprit non prévenu, Un, 79-83
    Retour de l'U.R.S.S., 3, 5
Gide, Madeleine, 10, 31-32, 34, 95,
  105, 107-8, 129-30, 139, 150,
  151, 155-56
Girard, Alain, 9
Giraudoux, J., 25
Goethe, J. W. V., 7, 41, 42, 134, 135
Gosse, Edmund, 1
Green, Julien, 28
Guerard, Albert, 6, 11, 12, 13

H

Hegel, F., 15, 18
Hervé, Gustave, 23
Homosexuality, theme of (*see also*
  Sexuality), 7, 12, 16, 19, 23, 129-51
  in *Ainsi soit-il,* 141
  in *Amyntas,* 132
  in *Cahiers et les poésies d' André
    Walter, Les,* 67, 132
  in *Corydon,* 134, 135, 136-37, 142,
    144, 160
  in *Faux-Monnayeurs, Les,* 117, 134,
    150, 161
  in *Immoraliste, L',* 130, 134
  in *Journal 1889-1939,* 141
  in *Porte étroite, La,* 11
  in *Si le grain ne meurt,* 67-68,
    129-31, 132-33, 142-43, 144, 161
  in *Retour de l'Enfant Prodique, Le,*
    27-28
  in *Voyage d'Urien, Le,* 11, 66-72,
    132, 144
Hoy, Peter, 13

Humanism, of Gide, 15-18, 37-43
Hytier, Jean, 4, 5, 11, 13

I

Iconoclasm, of Gide, 2-3, 15-18, 22-24
Immoraliste, L', 9, 19, 21, 24, 50, 73,
  84, 111, 117
  autobiography in, 74, 80
  homosexuality, theme of, 130, 134
  naturalism in, 85
  organization of, 87, **88-91**
  polarity in, **39-40, 74-77, 94**
  religion, theme of, **93-94**
Immorality in Gide, question of, 2-3,
  30-35
Impressions d'Afrique (Roussel), 66
Ireland, G. W., 13
Irony, in works of, **73-79, 93-94,** 127
Isabelle, 73
  autobiography in, 74
  irony in, 76
  naturalism in, 85-87
  organization of, 88
  polarity in, 74, 90
  romanticism in, 77-78

J

Jammes, Francis, 1, 20, 24, 26, 32, 54
Jarry, A., 51
Jeunesse d'André Gide, Le, (Delay),
  158
Journal (Amiel), 159
Journal 1889-1939, 1, 2, 6, **7-8,** 9, 21,
  22, 23, 24, 28, 36, 38, **39-40,** 47, 49,
  53-60, 99, **110-111, 152-63**
  autobiography in, **50-52,** 74
  classicism in, **53-56,** 59
  homosexuality, theme of, 141
  morality, theme of, 46, **55-58**
  Numquid et tu, 20, 21, 26, 155
  polarity in, 60, 94
  religion, theme of, **41-43**
Journal 1939-1949:
  Ainsi soit-il, 141, 153
  Carnets d'Egypte, Les, 153
  Et nunc manet in te, 10, 95,

  107, 111, 130, 134, 153
Retour du Tchad, Le, 153
Si le grain ne meurt, 3, 15, 21, 24,
  26, 36, **67-68,** 74, 83, 129-31,
  132-33, 142-43, 149, 158, 160,
  161
Journal intime, 154-57, 159-62
Joyce, James, 1, 128
Jung, C. G., 148

K

Keats, J., 5
Kierkegaard, S., 15
Knecht, Loring D., 6, 11, 12

L

LaFayette, Madame de, 94
*Lafcadio's Adventures (see Caves du
  Vatican, Les)*
Lafille, Pierre, 4, 6, 13
Laforgue, Jules, 66
Lautréamont, Comte de, 50
Lehrlinge zu Sais (Novalis), 64, **70-71**
*Lettres de Charles DuBos et Responses
  d'André Gide,* 156
Lévy, Jacques, 6
Loti, P., 137
Louÿs, P., 139, 145, **157-58**

M

McLaren, James C., 14
Maeterlink, M., 71
Magic Mountain, The (Mann), 116
Magny, Claude-Edmond, 6
Mallarmé, S., 57, 63
Malraux, André, 5, 39, 47, 52
Mann, Thomas, 1, 116
Manon Lescaut (Prévost), 73
Marriage, of Gide *(see also* Gide,
  Madeleine), 8, 10, **31-32,** 34, 95, 105,
  107-8, 129-30, 139, 151
Marini, Marinus, 30
Martin, Claude, 13
Marx, Karl, 15, 57
Massis, Henri, 2, 3

Maupassant, Guy de, 78
Mauriac, Claude, 6, 8, 33
Mauriac, François, 7
Mémoires d'outre-tombe (Chateau-
    briand), 21, 46, 85
Menasce, Jean de, 20
Mercure de France, 1
Meredith, G., 116
Monde, Le, 1
Montaigne, M. de, 141
Morality, theme of (*see also*
    Immorality, theme of), 4, 5, 7, 10,
    11, 12, 23, **41-43,** 46, 49, 55-58,
    119-22, 163
Moutote, Daniel, 13

N

Nadja (Breton), 52
Naturalism, Gide's use of, 84-85
Nietzsche, F., 21, 42, 137, 139
Nobel Prize, 4, 6, 20, 23, 24
Nourritures terrestres, Les, 1, 2, 9, 21,
    43, 50, 64, 73, 126
    polarity in, 39, 40, 76
Nouvelle Revue Francaise, 2, 6, 21
Novalis, 64, 70
Numquid et tu (*see also Journal 1889-
    1938*), 20, 155
    religion, theme of, 21, 26

O

O'Brien, Justin, 6
Organization, in Gide's works (*see also*
    "Recits"), 87-91, 122-25

P

Paludes, 9, 64, 66
    irony in, 74
    naturalism in, 85
    polarity in, 76
Pascal, B., 19, 20, 28, 38, **54-55**
Phèdre (Pradon), 55
Phèdre (Racine), 55
Picon, Gaeton, 6, 7, **12-13**
Pius XII, 30

Plato, 148
Poe, E. A., **65-66**
Polarity, Gide's use of, **39-43, 45-48,**
    49, **60-62**
    in *Immoraliste, L'*, **39-40,** 74-77, 94
    in *Isabelle,* 74, 90
    in *Journal 1889-1939,* 60, 94
    in *Nourritures terrestres, Les,* 39-
        40, 76
    in *Paludes,* 76
    in *Porte étroite, La,* **39-40,** 74-77, 94
    in *Promethée mal enchâine, Le,* 76
    in *Saül,* 76
    in *Symphonie pastorale, La,* 74
    in *Thesée,* 39-40
Politics, 3, 4, 5, 16
Porte étroite, La, 1, 6, 9, 24, 50, 73-
    77, **83-84, 93-111,** 113
    autobiography, Gide's use of, 10,
        74, 95, **107-8**
    asceticism, theme of, 96-111
    homosexuality, theme of, 11
    naturalism in, 85
    organization of, 87-89
    polarity in, **39-40,** 74-77, 94
    sexuality, theme of, 96-97, 110
Princess de Clèves, La (Madame de
    Lafayette), 73
Promethée mal enchâine, Le, 66
    irony in, 74
    polarity in, 76
Proust, Marcel, 1, 44, 45, 118, **127-28,**
    141, 148
Pruner, MM, 14

R

Racine, J., 21, 32, 55
Rambaud, H., 155
"Recits," **73-92**
    classicism, Gide's use of, 77
    irony in, 73-91
    organization of, 87-91
    method in, 79-92
    romanticism in, **77-78**
    and "Soties," 74
    style in, 87-91
Régnier, H. de, 24, 139

Religion, theme of, 4, 7, 19-29, 30-35, 162
in *Faux-Monnayeurs, Les,* 28
in *Immoraliste, L',* 93-94
in *Journal 1889-1939,* 41-43
in *Numquid et tu,* 21, 26
in *Retour de l'Enfant Prodique, Le,* 26-27
in *Si le grain ne meurt,* 26, 28
Renan, E., 22, 25
René (Chateaubriand)
Retour de l'Enfant Prodique, Le, 26-28
homosexuality, theme of, 27-28
religion, theme of, 26-27
Retour de l'U.R.S.S., 3, 5
Retour du Tchad, Le, 153
Rimbaud, Arthur, 55, 66, 138
Rivière, Jacques, 4, 14
Rochefoucauld, La, 145
Roi Candaule, Le, 76
Romains, Jules, 25
Roman Catholic Index of Forbidden Books, 4-6, 12, 30
Romanticism, in works of, 77-79
Rougemont, Denis de, 144
Rousseau, J. J., 21, 24, 38, 43, 130-131, 135, 137
Roussel, M., 66

S

Sartre, J., 5, 7, 12-13, 39
Saül, 76
Schlumberger, Jean, 6
Schlegel, F., 148
Sexuality, theme of (*see also* Homosexuality), 4, 7, 11, 12, 129-31
in *Faux-Monnayeurs, Les,* 116-18
in *Porte étroite, La,* 96-97, 110
Shakespeare, William, 21, 113, 148
Si le grain ne meurt, 3, 21, 24, 36, 83, 158, 160
autobiography, Gide's use of, 74, 111, 129-30

homosexuality, theme of, 67-68, 129-31, 132-33, 142-43, 149, 161
religion, theme of, 26, 28
Singlin, M., 19
Souday, Paul, 1
Spartacus, 22, 23
Starkie, Enid, 6
Stekel, W., 150
Stendhal, 5, 59
Serres Chaudes (Maeterlink), 71
Strauss, G., 13
Surrealism, Gide's use of, 65
Symbolism, Gide's use of, 63-64, 65, 67
Symphonie pastorale, La, 50, 73
autobiography, Gide's use of, 74, 78
irony in, 76, 91
naturalism in, 85
organization of, 88
polarity in, 74

T

Temps, Le, 1
Tentative amoureuse, La, 50
Thesée, 36-42, 46
Thibault, Les (du Gard), 2-3
Traite de Narcisse, Le, 148

U

Ulysses (Joyce), 128

V

Valéry, Paul, 44, 53-54
Verlaine, Paul, 23
Vickner, Carl, 14
Vinci, Leonardo da, 138, 148
Voyage au Congo, 3, 15, 153
Voyage d'Urien, Le, 36, 63
homosexuality, theme of, 11, 66-72, 132, 144
surrealism in, 65

GOETHE

A Collection of Critical Essays
Edited by VICTOR LANGE

A

Aeschylus, 100
Aesthetics, Goethe's concepts of,
  119-20, 124-27
Agathon (Wieland), 75
Allwill (Jacobi), 75
Analyse und Synthese, 172
"An den Mond," 55
Anschauung, Goethe's concept of,
  123-24, 166
Arber, Agnes, 116, 123
Aristotle, 116
Arnold, Matthew, 2

B

Balzac, Honoré de, 66, 97, 124-25
Bedenken und Ergebung, 167-68
Belsazer, 18
Blake, William, 5
Blank verse, Goethe's use of, 18
"Blümlein Wunderschön," 18-19
Boccaccio, Giovanni, 66
Botany, Goethe's interest in, 147,
  153, 165
Browne, Sir Thomas, 120
"Brautnacht," 23
"Braut von Korinth, Die," 19
Bruno, Giordano, 119
Buff, Charlotte, 27, 68
Burke, Kenneth, 113

C

Canova, Antonio, 102
Cervantes, Miguel de, 66
Cicero, 150
Clavigo, 20-21
Coleridge, Samuel Taylor, 121, 171
Comédie Humaine (Balzac), 124-25
Conrad, Joseph, 66
Contributions to Morphology, 121,
  122-23, 146, 173
Cooper, Anthony Ashley, 55, 119
Cooper, James Fenimore, 66
Critique of Judgment (Kant), 151
Critique of Pure Reason (Kant),
  151

D

Darwin, Charles, 146, 154
David, Jacques Louis, 102
Defoe, Daniel, 97
Dichtung und Wahrheit, 8-9, 26-27, 66,
  67, 72, 170, 177
Diderot, Denis, 78
Dilthey, Wilhelm, 35
Discours en l'honneur de Goethe
  (Valéry), 166
Doctor Faustus (Mann), 141-43
Drama, Goethe's work in, 6-7, 33-49,
  (*see also* titles of individual
  works)

E

Eckermann, J. P., 75, 77, 163, 174
Egmont, 35-36, 44
Elective Affinities, The, 7, 58, 97
Eliot, T. S., 2, 60
Emerson, Ralph Waldo, 2
Essai sur les Fictions (Staël), 77
Eumenides (Aeschylus), 100
Euripides, 52
"Experiment as a Mediator between Object and Subject," 149

F

Fairley, Barker, 4, 5, 8
Faust, 6-7, 12, 17, 19, 34, 43, 44-45, 65, 103-4, 127, 129, 130, 164, 174 *(see also Urfaust)*
  and *Iphigenie auf Tauris*, 54-55, 61-62
  meter, Goethe's use of, 19, 20
  symbolism in, 45
Faust II, 45-46, 65, **99-109**, **132-44**
  and *Doctor Faustus* (Mann), 141-43
  and Greek tragedy, 100, 102-3, 106, 108-9
  irony in, 105-8
  magic in, 139-40
  man, Goethe's conception of, 136-37
  and *Mon Faust* (Valéry), 140-41
  moral complexities of, 134-35
  rococo influences in, 104-6
Faust (Lessing), 134-35
Fénelon, François de La Mothe-, 66
Fichte, Johann Gottlieb, 149, 151
Fictional techniques, in Goethe's works, 65-85, 78-79, 82
Flaubert, Gustave, 117
Folk-poetry, Goethe's use of, 18-19
Form, Goethe's conception of, **110-31**, 151-52, **161-78**
Fourier, François, 93

G

Gabriele (Schopenhauer), 79
Galilei, Galileo, 155
Gauss, Karl Friedrich, 154
Geology, Goethe's interest in, 146-47, 153
"Gerontion" (Eliot), 60
Gide, André, 117
Goethe, Johann Wolfgang von:
  aesthetic concepts of, 119-20, 124-27
  Anschauung, concept of, 123-24, 166
  and Buff, Charlotte, 27, 68
  as a critic, 5-6, 77-79, 82
  drama of, 6-7, **33-49** (*see also* titles of individual works)
  and Eckermann, J. P., 75, 77, 163, 174
  fictional techniques of, 65-85, 78-79, 82
  form, conception of, 110-31, 151-52, 161-78
  and Greek culture, influence of, 78-79, 100, 102-3, 106, 108-9, 119, 150-51
  and Herder, Johann Gottfried von, 5, 17, 18, 46, 66, 70, 119
  historical place of, 1-3
  intellectual development of, 119-21, 161-78
  and Klopstock, Friedrich Gottfried, 23-24, 69-70, 71, 113
  and Lessing, Gotthold, 18, 34, 42, 46, 71, 132-35
  and Neoplatonism, 120-21
  and Newton, Sir Isaac, 116, 135-36, 147, 155, 156-59
  poetry of, 5-6, 8, **10-25**, 128-31, 161-78 *passim*
  and rococo tradition, 104-6
  and Romanticism, 5, 94-95, 120
  and Schiller, J. C. F. von, 6, 18, 19, 20-21, 22-23, 34, 46, 47-48, 50-51, 75-77, 78, 84, 97, 124,

Goethe, Johann Wolfgang von:
and Schiller, J. C. F. von, (continued)
   126, 149, 151, 172
and Schlegel, Friedrich von, 74-75,
   88-89, 90
scientific interests of, 3, 110-31,
   145-60, 162-69, 172-73
and Shakespeare, 14-15, 19, 22, 34,
   35, 42, 47, 48, 71, 88, 104, 119,
   174
as a social critic, 86-98
and Staël, Mme. de, 30, 77
and Stein, Charlotte von, 18, 35, 37
and Sterne, Laurence, 66, 70
and the *Sturm und Drang* movement, 34, 35, 48, 120
and symbolism, theory of, 6, 78-
   79, 82
and Winckelmann, J. J., 46, 102,
   126
Goethe, Johann Wolfgang von, works
   by: (*see also* main entries for individual works)
VERSE DRAMA
   Belsazer, 18
   Clavigo, 20-21
   Egmont, 35-36, 44
   Faust, 6-7, 12, 17, 19, 34, 43, 44-
      45, 65, 103-4, 127, 129, 130,
      164, 174
   Faust II, 45-46, 65, **99-109, 132-44**
   Götz von Berlichingen, 21, 34, 35,
      44, 174
   Iphigenie auf Tauris, 6, 17-18, 21,
      34, 35, **36-38,** 44-45, **50-64**
   Natürliche Tochter, Die, 6, 34, 45
   Pandora, 45-46
   Torquato Tasso, 6, 12, 18, 34, 36,
      38-42, 43-44, 86, 127, 130
   Urfaust, 21, 45, 174
FICTION
   Elective Affinities, The, 7, 58, 97
   Hermann und Dorothea, 21, 22,
      173
   Märchen, Das, 77-78
   Novelle, 66

Roman in Briefen (1772), 170
Sorrows of Young Werther, The,
   11-12, 21-22, **26-32, 67-71,** 72,
   75, 81, 86, 87, 130, 170, 172, 174
*Unterhaltungen der deutschen
   Ausgewanderten*, 77
Wahlverwandtschaften, Die, 21-22,
   65, **79-82,** 83
Wilhelm Meisters Lehrjahre, 73-76,
   86-98, 125
*Wilhelm Meisters Theatricalische
   Sendung*, 71-73, 76, 86, 87, 88, 96
Wilhelm Meisters Wanderjahre, 7, 8,
   65, 82-84
POETRY (*see also* titles of individual
   poems)
   "Trilogie der Leidenschaft," 11-13,
      19-20, 130, 169
   "Um Mitternacht," 16, 175-76
   West-Östlicher Divan, 8, 13, 16-17,
      84, 170, 177-78
ESSAYS
   Analyse und Synthese, 172
   Bedenken und Ergebung, 167-68
   "Experiment as a Mediator between
      Object and Subject," 149
   Nachlese zu Aristoteles Poetik, 79
   "Über epische und dramatische
      Dichtung," 77
SCIENTIFIC WRITINGS
   Contributions to Morphology, 121,
      122-23, 146, 173
   Lectures in Comparative Anatomy,
      121
   Metamorphosis of Plants, The, 147
   "On Mathematics and its Abuse,"
      154-55
   Theory of Chromatics, 77, 147,
      155, **156-59,** 169
   Vorwort zur Morphologie, 166-67
OTHER WORKS
   Dichtung und Wahrheit, 8-9, 26-27,
      66, 67, 72, 170, 177
   Italienische Reise, 66
   Kampagne in Frankreich, 66
   Maximen und Reflexionen, 6, 110-
      31 *passim*

234

Goethe, Johann Wolfgang von, works
by: (OTHER WORKS) (*continued*)
  Sammler und die Seinigen, Der, 66
  Self-portrait (1797), 162-63
  Von deutscher Baukunst, 164
Goldsmith, Oliver, 28-29, 71, 129
"Göttliche, Das," 56
"Gott und die Bajadere, Der," 19
Götz von Berlichingen, 21, 34, 35, 44,
  174
"Grant me a summer and an autumn"
  (Hölderlin), 15
Greek culture, influence of, on
  Goethe's works, 78-79, 100, 102-3,
  106, 108-9, 119, 150-51
Grillparzer, Franz, 47

H

Hardenberg, Friedrich von (Novalis),
  95
"Harzreise im Winter," 16
Hawthorne, Nathaniel, 64
Hegel, Friedrich, 94
"Heidenröslein," 18
Heine, Heinrich, 19
Heisenberg, Werner, 157
Heraclitus, 128
Herder, Johann Gottfried von, 5, 17,
  18, 46, 66, 70, 119
Hermann und Dorothea, 21, 22, 173
Helmholtz, Hermann von, 157
Hofmannsthal, Hugo von, 46, 128
Hölderlin, Friedrich, 15
Homer, 71, 102
Horace, 14
Hugo, Victor, 17
Humboldt, Wilhelm von, 117

I

Ibsen, Henrik, 47
Iliad (Homer), 102
Ingres, Jean Auguste, 102
Iphigenia among the Taurians
  (Euripides), 52
Iphigenie auf Tauris, 6, 17-18, 21, 34,
  35, **36-38,** 44-45, **50-64**

and *Faust,* 54-55, 61-62
Greek sources of, 51-52, 102-3
meter, use of, 17-18
"Parzenleid, Das," 60-61
Irony:
  in *Faust* II, 105-8
  in *Sorrows of Young Werther, The,*
    70-71
Irving, Washington, 66
Italienische Reise, 66

J

Jacobi, Friedrich Heinrich, 75, 149,
  152
James, Henry, 66
James, William, 3
Jaspers, Karl, 2

K

Kabale und Liebe (Schiller), 21
Kafka, Franz, 64
Kampagne in Frankreich, 66
Kant, Immanuel, 94, 150, 151
Keats, John, 129
Kepler, Johannes, 155
Klinger, Friedrich M. von, 75
Klopstock, Friedrich Gottfried, 23-33,
  69-70, 71, 113
"König in Thule," 18

L

Lamarck, Jean Baptiste, 153-54
La Roche, Sophie, 68
Lavater, Johann Kasper, 69
Lectures on Comparative Anatomy,
  121
Lehrjahre (see Wilhelm Meisters Lehr-
  jahre)
Le Sage, Alain, 97
Lessing, Gotthold Ephraim, 18, 34, 42,
  46, 71, 132-35
Lewes, G. H., 4
"Libelle, Die," 173
Liber Basiorum (Secundus), 131
Life of Goethe, The (Lewes), 4

M

Macpherson, James, 71
Magic, in *Faust* II, 139-40
Man, Goethe's conception of, in
  Faust II, 136-37
Mann, Thomas, 141-43
Märchen, Das, 77-78
Marienbad Elegies (see "Trilogie der
  Leidenschaft")
Marmontel, Jean François, 66
Mathematics, Goethe's interest in,
  154-56
Maximen und Reflexionen, 6, 110-
  31 *passim*
Melville, Herman, 66
Mercier, Louis Sébastien, 120
"Metamorphose der Tiere," 169
Metamorphoses (Ovid), 137
Metamorphosis of Plants, The, 116,
  147
Meter, Goethe's use of, 17-20
Milton, John, 17
Mineralogy, Goethe's interest in,
  146-47
Mon Faust (Valéry), 140-41
Müller, Günther, 115
Müller, Johannes, 153

N

Nachlese zu Aristoteles Poetik, 79
Nathan der Weise (Lessing), 34
Natürliche Tochter, Die, 6, 34, 45
Neoplatonism, in Goethe's thought,
  120-21
Neveu de Rameau, Le (Diderot), 78
Newton, Sir Isaac, 116, 135-36, 147,
  155, 156-59
"Nicht mehr auf Seidenblatt," 170
Nietzsche, Friedrich, 115
Nouvel essai sur l'art dramatique
  (Mercier), 120
Nouvelle Héloïse, La, 28, 69
Novalis *(see* Hardenberg, Friedrich
  von)
Novelle, 66

O

Oken, Lorenz, 146, 155
"On Mathematics and its Abuse,"
  154-55
*On Naïve and Sentimental Poetical
  Composition* (Schiller), 149
Optics (Newton), 147, 159
Ovid, 137

P

Pandora, 45-46
"Parzenlied, Das" (*Iphigenie auf
  Tauris*), 60-61
Phenomenology (Hegel), 94
Philosophische Studie, 173
Physics, Goethe's interest in, 155, 157
Plato, 150-51
Plotinus, 119, 120
Poetry, Goethe's, 5-6, 8, **10-25,**
  128-31, 161-78 *passim (see also*
  titles of individual poems)
  blank verse, Goethe's use of, 18
  as confession, 10-17
  folk-poetry, 18-19
  meter, 17-20
*Poetry and Truth (see Dichtung und
  Wahrheit)*
Prévost, Abbé, 66

Q

"Quand tu seras bien vieille" (Ronsard), 15

R

Racine, Jean, 34, 42, 44, 47, 48
"Reineke Fuchs," 87
Richardson, Samuel, 28, 66, 68, 71
Ritterdrama, 48
Rococo influences, in *Faust* II, 104-6
Roman in Briefen (1772), 170
Romanticism, influence of, on
  Goethe's work, 5, 94-95, 120 *(see
  also Sturm und Drang* movement)

Römische Elegien, 173
Ronsard, Pierre de, 15
Rousseau, Jean-Jacques, 10, 28, 46,
    66, 69, 71
Rührstück, 48

S

Saint-Hilaire, Geoffroy, 125
Sammler und die Seinigen, Der, 66
Schiller, J. C. F. von, 6, 18, 19, 20-21,
    22-23, 34, 46, 47-48, 50-51, 75-77,
    78, 84, 97, 124, 126, 149, 151, 172
Schlegel, Friedrich von, 74-75, 88-89,
    90
Schopenhauer, Johanna, 79
Science, Goethe's interest in, 3, 110-
    31, 145-60, 162-69, 172-73
Scienza Nuova (Vico), 119
Scott, Sir Walter, 66
Secundus, Johannes, 131
Self-portrait (1797), 162-63
"Selige Sehnsucht," 169
Shaftesbury, Earl of (*see* Cooper,
    Anthony Ashley)
Shakespeare, William, 14-15, 19, 22,
    34, 35, 42, 47, 48, 71, 88, 104, 119,
    174
Shelley, Percy Bysshe, 120
Sherrington, Sir Charles, 116
Simmel, Georg, 19-20
Social criticism, in *Wilhelm Meisters
    Lehrjahre*, 86-98
Sorrows of Young Werther, The, 11-
    12, 21-22, 26-32, 67-71, 72, 75, 81,
    86, 87, 130, 170, 172, 174
    ironic techniques in, 70-71
    and *Tristram Shandy*, 70
Spinoza, Baruch, 82, 90, 148, 150,
    151, 173
Staël, Mme. de, 30, 77
Staiger, Emil, 5
Stein, Charlotte von, 18, 35, 37
Stendhal, 66, 97
Sterne, Laurence, 28-29, 66, 70
Sturm und Drang movement, 34, 35,
    48, 120

Symbolism:
    Goethe's theory of, 6, 78-79, 82
    in the poetic dramas, 42-43

T

"Tagebuch" (1810), 16
Theory of Chromatics, 77, 147, 155,
    156-59, 169
Thompson, D'Arcy, 114
Torquato Tasso, 6, 12, 18, 34, 36, **38-
    42**, 43-44, 86, 127, 130
"Trilogie der Leidenschaft," 11-13, 19-
    20, 130, 169
Tristram Shandy (Sterne), 70
Troll, Wilhelm, 115

U

"Über epische und dramatische
    Dichtung," 77
"Um Mitternacht," 16, 175-76
*Unterhaltungen der deutschen Aus-
    gewanderten*, 77
Urfaust, 21, 45, 174
"Urworte Orphisch," 169

V

Valéry, Paul, 117, 140-41, 166
"Vermächtnis," 176
"Versunken," 16
Vesalius, Andreas, 145, 154
Vicar of Wakefield, The (Goldsmith),
    129
Vico, Giovanni, 119
Vogelweide, Walther von der, 23
Voltaire, 3, 46, 66
Von deutscher Baukunst, 164
Vorwort zur Morphologie, 166-67

W

Wahlverwandtschaften, Die, 21-22,
    65, **79-82**, 83
Wallenstein (Schiller), 47

Weizsächer, Viktor von, 115
Werner, A. G., 146
Werther (see Sorrows of Young
   Werther, The)
West-Östlicher Divan, 8, 13, 16-17,
   84, 170, 177-78
Wieland, Christoph Martin, 68
Wien, Wilhelm, 157
Wilhelm Meisters Lehrjahre, 73-76,
   86-98, 125
Wilhelm Meisters Theatralische Send-
   ung, 71-73, 76, 86, 87, 88, 96
Wilhelm Meisters Wanderjahre, 7, 8,
   65, 82-84

Winckelmann, J. J., 46, 102,
   126
Willemer, Marianne von, 13-14
Wordsworth, William, 23

Y

Young, J. Z., 114

Z

"Zauberlehring, Der," 144
Ziehen, Theodor, 149

HARDY

A Collection of Critical Essays

Edited by ALBERT J. GUERARD

A

Aesthetics, Hardy's principles of, 27-45
After Strange Gods (Eliot), 30
Alienation, theme of, 4, 120, 143-59
Alvarez, A., 8
"Ancient to Ancients, An," 27
Anna Karenina (Tolstoy), 113
"At Waking," 148
Auden, W. H., 26, 146

B

Bacon, Francis, 30, 38
Ballad forms influence of, on Hardy's works, 13-19
Barnes, William, 20, 44
Barren Ground (Glasgow), 21
Baudelaire, Charles, 26
Benét, Stephen V., 18
Blackmore, Richard, 20
Blackmur, R. P., 146, 147
Blake, William, 143, 151, 156, 157, 158
"Bride-Night Fire, The" (ballad), 14
Brontë, Emily, 3
Browning, Robert, 27, 141
Butler, Samuel, 35

C

Cabell, James B., 11
Cantos, The (Pound), 160

Chakravarty, Amiya, 36
Chapman, Frank, 40
Characterization, Hardy's technique of, 19-23, 46-51, 63-70, 71-76 (*see also* titles of individual works)
Chew, Samuel, 17
Christian beliefs, in Hardy's works, 128-29, 131-32
Coleridge, Samuel, 31, 132-33
"Comedian as the Letter C, The" (Stevens), 160
Comte, Auguste, 35
Conrad, Joseph, 3, 4-5, 8, 38, 63, 116
Corbière, Tristan, 26
Crabbe, George, 4

D

Dante Alighieri, 123
"Darkling Thrush, The," 43, **151-54**
Darwin, Charles, 6, 35, 36, 38, 100, 110, 127
Davidson, Donald, 3
Desperate Remedies, 3, 48, 49
characterization in, 46
"Devil and Daniel Webster" (Benét), 18
Dickens, Charles, 38
"Distracted Preacher, The," 69
Donne, John, 141
"Dream-Follower, The," 158-59
Dreiser, Theodore, 127
"Drizzling Easter Morning, A," 131-32, 133, 134
Dynasts, The, 6, 10, 14, 34, 35, 38,

Dynasts, The, (continued)
39, 124, 126, 132-33, 139, 147, 157,
160-74
    characterization in, 165-66
    Freudian analogies in, 36
    imagery in, 169-70

E

Early Life of Thomas Hardy, The
(Hardy), 13, 161, 163
Egoist, The (Meredith), 77-78
Eliot, George, 7
Eliot, T. S., 11, 26, 30, 136, 160
Ellis, Havelock, 7
Exideuil, Pierre d', 36

F

*Famous Tragedy of the Queen of
Cornwall, The,* 162
Far From the Madding Crowd, 7, 15,
16, 21, 48, 91, 104
    characterization in, 64, 65-67
Fate and chance, in *The Mayor of
Casterbridge,* 95-97 (*see also* Pessi-
mism and fatalism)
Faulkner, William, 5
Few Crusted Characters, A, 15, 16
"Fiddler of the Reels, The," 69
Flaubert, Gustave, 3, 15, 26, 42
"For Conscience' Sake," 69

G

Galilei, Galileo, 38
Georgia Scenes (Longstreet), 12
Gide, André, 3
Gifford, Emily Lavinia, 2
Glasgow, Ellen, 21
"God-Forgotten," 147
"God's Funeral," 125-26
Goldsmith, Oliver, 30
Greek tragedy, and *The Mayor of
Casterbridge,* 4, 91-92, 96, 98, 100,
101, 102, 104, 109
Group of Noble Dames, A,
15, 68

H

Hamlet (Shakespeare), 3, 50, 105, 109
Hand of Ethelberta, The, 3, 15, 48, 67
"Hap," 164
Hardy, Thomas:
    aesthetic principles of, 27-45
    alienation, theme of, 4, 120,
        143-59
    and ballad forms, 13-19
    career of, 1-2, 27
    characterization, technique of, 19-
        23, 46-51, 63-70, 71-76
    Christian beliefs of, 128-29, 131-32
    contemporary reception of, 7-8, 11,
        24-25, 113
    on critics, 10-11, 27, 40, 132
    and Darwin, Charles, 35, 36, 38,
        127
    and Eliot, T. S., 11, 26, 30
    and James, Henry, 28, 29, 40
    and Meredith, George, 11, 29-30,
        39, 40, 77-78
    narrative technique of, 15-19
    pessimism and fatalism of, 3, 5-6,
        18-19, 34, 50, 85-87, 143-44,
        157
    philosophical beliefs of, 123-34,
        164-68, 171-74
    realism of, 3-4, 30-33, 41-43
    rural and urban society, conflict
        between, 5-6, 52-53, 101-9
    and Schopenhauer, Arthur, 35, 36-
        37, 139
    and the supernatural, 18, 86, 88-89,
        96, 161
    on tragedy, 33, 50-51
    as a transitional writer, 3, 12, 25-26
    and Wordsworth, William, 143,
        146, 147, 151, 153, 156, 157,
        158
    and Wessex, 5, 15, 21, 44, 52
Hardy, Thomas, works by:
FICTION
    Desperate Remedies, 3, 48, 49
    Far From the Madding Crowd, 7,
        15, 16, 21, 48, 91, 104
    Few Crusted Characters, A, 15, 16

Hardy, Thomas, works by:
(FICTION), (*continued*)
  Group of Noble Dames, A, 15, 68
  Hand of Ethelberta, The, 3, 15, 48, 67
  Jude the Obscure, 1-2, 3, 7, 15, 33, 34-35, 52, 57, 63, 91, 96, 97, 100, 104, 109, 110, 111, 113-22, 162
  Laodicean, The, 3, 15
  Mayor of Casterbridge, The, 2, 3-4, 5, 7, 15, 16, 19, 31, 39, 40, 46, 48, 53, 54, 56, 83, **91-112**
  Pair of Blue Eyes, A, 43, 49, 63, 64
  Return of the Native, The, 7, 8, 15, 16, 18, 39, 42, 48, 53-55, 83, 91-92, 96, 100, 104, 139, 162
  Tess of the D'Urbervilles, 1, 2, 6, 7, 15, 17, 18, 30, 32, 39, 53, 57, 77-90, 96, 97, 104, 109, 110-11, 113
  Trumpet-Major, The, 12, 15, 48, 104
  Two on a Tower, 39, 47, 48, 49, 130
  Under the Greenwood Tree, 6, 15, 16, 21, 48, 104
  Well-Beloved, The, 1n
  Wessex Tales, 68-69
  Woodlanders, The, 15, 16-17, 22, 47, 49, 57-58, 91
POETRY, 1-3, 6, 8, 14-15, 27, 29, 43-45, **123-24**, **135-42**, **143-59**, **160-74** (*see also* titles of individual poems)
  "Darkling Thrush, The," 43, **151-54**
  Dynasts, The, 6, 10, 14, 34, 35, 38, 39, 124, 126, 132-33, 139, 147, 157, **160-74**
  Late Lyrics and Earlier, 40, 132
  Moments of Vision, 33
  Time's Laughingstocks, 2
ESSAYS
  "Profitable Reading of Fiction, The," 40-41, 42
  "Science of Fiction, The," 41
Hawthorne, Nathaniel, 3

"He Abjures Love," 43
Hegel, Friedrich, 97
Holland, Norman, 8
Holloway, John, 1-2, 6
Hopkins, Gerard Manley, 44
Hopkins, R. Thurston, 14
Hugo, Victor, 38
Huxley, T. H., 6, 127

I

Ibsen, Henrik, 52
Imagery, in *The Dynasts,* 169-70
"Impercipient, The," 154-56, 157
"In a Waiting Room," 156
"In a Whispering Gallery," 157-58
"I Say I'll Seek Her," 44
Isolation (*see* Alienation, theme of)

J

James, Henry, 3, 7, 25, 28, 29, 38, 40
Jeffers, Robinson, 127
Joyce, James, 3, 8, 26, 160
Jude the Obscure, 1-2, 3, 7, 15, 33, 34-35, 52, 57, 63, 91, 96, 97, 100, 104, 109, 110, 111, 113-22, 162
  alienation, theme of, 120
  characterization in, 71-76
  contemporary reception of, 113
  rural and urban society, conflict between, 56
  sexual themes in, 116-18
  and Shakespearean tragedy, 115

K

Kafka, Franz, 3, 8
Keats, John, 27, 151, 152
King Lear (Shakespeare), 3, 50, 92, 115
Krutch, Joseph Wood, 127

L

Laforgue, Jules, 26
Laodicean, The, 3, 15

Laodicean, The, (*continued*)
  characterization in, 46, 47
Late Lyrics and Earlier, 40, 132
Later Years of Thomas Hardy, The
  (Hardy), 10, 13
Lawrence, D. H., 4, 114, 116-17
Lee, Vernon, 40
Locke, John, 38
Longstreet, Augustus Baldwin, 12
Lorna Doone (Blackmore), 20
Lucretius, 123
Lyell, Charles, 38

M

Macaulay, T. B., 30
Macbeth (Shakespeare), 50
MacLeish, Archibald, 127
"Mad Judy," 143-44
"Man He Killed, The," 144-45
Mann, Thomas, 37
"Masked Face, The," 129-30, 133
Mayor of Casterbridge, The, 2, 3-4, 5,
  7, 15, 16, 19, 31, 39, 40, 46, 48, 53,
  54, 56, 83, 91-112
  characterization in, 58-60
  fate and chance in, 95-97
  rural and urban society, conflict
    between, 101-9
  tragedy in, 91-112
Measure for Measure (Shakespeare),
  105
Melville, Herman, 3
Meredith, George, 11, 29-30, 39, 40,
  77-78
"Midnight on the Great Western,"
  156-57
Milton, John, 174
Modern Temper, The (Krutch), 127
"Mollie Vaughn" (ballad), 14, 18
Moments of Vision, 33
Montaigne, Michel de, 38
Moore, George, 25, 26, 130
Morgan, Charles, 10, 40
"Moth-Signal, The," 173
Murry, J. Middleton, 128, 129

N

Narrative techniques, in Hardy's
  works, 15-19
Newbolt, Henry, 39
Newton, Sir Isaac, 38
"New Year's Eve," 147
Nietzsche, Friedrich, 36, 127
"Night in the Old Home," 150

O

"Ode to a Nightingale" (Keats), 152
"Ode to the West Wind" (Shelley),
  150
Oedipus Rex (Sophocles), 4, 92, 109
"Old Furniture," 149
"Old Neighbor and the New, The,"
  149
"On a Fine Morning," 158-59
"On the Western Circuit," 69
Origin of Species, The (Darwin), 35
"Oxen, The," 126, 128-29, 134

P

Pair of Blue Eyes, A, 43, 49, 63, 64
Paradise Lost (Milton), 174
Paradiso (Dante), 123
Pater, Walter, 42
Paterson, John, 8
"Paying Calls," 149
Pessimism and fatalism, in Hardy's
  works, 3, 5-6, 18-19, 34, 50, 85-87,
  143-44, 157
Philosophical beliefs, in Hardy's
  works, 123-24, 164-68, 171-74
Philosophy of the Unconscious, The
  (Von Hartmann), 6, 35
"Places," 148-49
"Plaint to Man, A," 125
Poetry, 1-3, 6, 8, 14-15, 27, 29, 43-
  45, 123-24, 135-42, 143-59, 160-
  74 (*see also* titles of individual
  poems)
Pope, Alexander, 141

Pound, Ezra, 26, 160
Pound, Louise, 18
"Profitable Reading of Fiction, The,"
    40-41, 42
Proust, Marcel, 3, 8, 26, 38, 147-48

R

Ransom, John Crowe, 131, 146
Realism, Hardy's use of, 3-4, 30-33,
    41-43
Return of the Native, The, 7, 8, 15,
    16, 18, 39, 42, 48, 53-55, 83, 91-92,
    96, 100, 104, 139, 162
    characterization in, 21-22, 64-65
Reverberator, The (James), 28
Richards, I. A., 30, 41-42, 127-28
Rural and urban society, conflict
    between, 5-6, 52-53, 101-9 (*see also*
    titles of individual works)
Russell, Bertrand, 127

S

"Satires of Circumstance," 173
Schopenhauer, Arthur, 5, 6, 35, 36-
    37, 127, 139
"Schreckhorn, The," 43
Science and Poetry (Richards), 30, 41-
    42, 127-28
"Science of Fiction, The," 41
Secret Sharer, The (Conrad), 116
Shakespeare, William, 3, 50, 92, 105,
    115, 141
Shakespearean tragedy, in *The Mayor
    of Casterbridge*, 91-92, 95, 97, 98,
    99, 100, 102, 104, 105, 106, 109
Shaw, George Bernard, 35, 127
Shelley, Percy Bysshe, 27, 150, 151,
    156
"Sigh, The," 148
"Something that Saved Him, The," 43
"Sons's Veto, The," 69
Sophocles, 4, 92, 97
Spencer, Herbert, 6, 35
Spinoza, Baruch de, 139

Stallman, Robert, W., 8
Stevens, Wallace, 160
Study of Thomas Hardy, A
    (Lawrence), 114, 116-17
"Sundial on a Wet Day, The," 142
Supernatural, Hardy's use of the, 18,
    86, 88-89, 96, 161
Swift, Jonathan, 144, 146
Swinburne, Algernon, 27, 110

T

Tennyson, Alfred, 27, 139
Tess of the D'Urbervilles, 1, 2, 6, 7,
    15, 17, 18, 30, 32, 39, 53, 57, 77-
    90, 96, 97, 104, 109, 110, 111, 113
    alienation, theme of, 55
    characterization in, 22, 67-68
    rural and urban society, conflict
        between, 55-56
    structure of, 60-62
Thomas, Edward, 136
Thomas Hardy's Dorset (Hopkins), 14
Thus Spake Zarathustra (Nietzsche),
    36
Time's Laughingstocks, 2
"To a Skylark" (Shelley), 152
Tolstoy, Leo, 113
"To Meet or Otherwise," 43
Tragedy, Hardy's concern with, 33,
    50-51 (*see also* Greek tragedy;
    Shakespearean tragedy)
Trollope, Anthony, 38
Trumpet-Major, The, 12, 15, 48, 104
Turgenev, Ivan, 38
Two on a Tower, 39, 47, 48, 49, 130

U

Ulysses (Joyce), 160
Under the Greenwood Tree, 6, 15, 16,
    21, 48, 104

V

Valéry, Paul, 26

Van Doren, Mark, 127
Van Ghent, Dorothy, 8
"Veteris Vestigia Flammae," 44
"Voices from Things Growing," 43
Von Hartmann, Eduard, 6, 35, 127

W

Waste Land, The (Eliot), 160
Weber, Carl, 33
Well-Beloved, The, 1n
Wessex, Hardy's involvement with, 5,
  12, 21, 44, 52
Wessex Tales, 68-69
Wordsworth, William, 5, 100, 143,
  147, 151, 153, 156, 157, 158

Woodlanders, The, 15, 16-17, 22, 47,
  49, 57-58, 91
  characterization in, 67
Woolf, Virginia, 25

Y

"Year's Awakening, The," 150-51
Yeats, William Butler, 26
"Young Man's Exhortation, A," 158-59

Z

Zabel, Morton Dauwen, 3
Zola, Émile, 15, 41, 113

HAWTHORNE

A Collection of Critical Essays

Edited by A. N. KAUL

A

Adams, Henry, 23
Aeschylus, 152
Allegory, Hawthorne's use of, 3, 4, 11-24, 30, 65-66, 93 (*see also* Symbolism)
    in *Blithdale Romance, The,* 22, 174-75
    in *Marble Faun, The,* 70-71
    in *Scarlet Letter, The,* 17-22, 26, 70, 174-75
American literary tradition, Hawthorne's influence, 1, 3-5, 27-28, 43, 57, 62-63, 72-76, 78-79, 83-84, 139-40, 142-43, 153-55, 158-59
American Notebooks, The, 64
American People, The (Parks), 25-26
American Prose Masters (Brownell), 4
American Renaissance (Matthiessen), 27
Ames, William, 12-13
Ancestral Footsteps, The, 11
Anderson, Hans, 61
Anderson, Maxwell, 76
Anderson, Quentin, 27
Andrews, Charles M., 13, 15-16, 18-19
Anna Karenina (Tolstoy), 28, 29, 45, 50, 51
Aristophanes, 152
"Artist of the Beautiful, The," 3, 26, 61, 62, 78, 79, **99-110**
Arvin, Newton, 5

Askew, Melvin, 112
Austen, Jane, 28

B

"Bartleby the Scrivener" (Melville), 170
Baudelaire, Charles, 71
Benito Cereno (Melville), 23, 48
Biblical allusions, in Hawthorne:
    in *Marble Faun, The,* 77-78, 85, 165-69
    in "Roger Malvin's Burial," 119-20
    in *Scarlet Letter, The,* 47-48
Billy Budd (Melville), 48, 81
Biographical Information, of Hawthorne, 1, 11-12, 123-25, 137-38, 154, 164-65, 167-68
"Birthmark, The," 11, 80, 86, 93-95, 97, 108
Blake, William, 43, 62, 109
Blithedale Romance, The, 3, 7, 8-9, 11, 21, 26, 28, 29, 30, 42, 43, 47, 51, 52, 64, 65, 69-70, 75, 78, 106, 110, 151, 172
    allegory in, 22, 174-75
    character analysis of, 53-61, 153-63
    communalism, theme of, 53-61, 65, 153-63
Boynton, Percy, 23
Bradford, William, 30, 153, 155
Brook Farm, 52, 65, 128, 138, 141, 153, 154, 158
Brownell, W. C., 4

Bryant, William Cullen, 12
Bunyan, John, 26, 27, 30, 34, 35, 36, 52
Bushnell, Horace, 82
Byron, George Gordon, 103

C

Calvinism, references to, 12-13, 20, 37, 68 (*see also* Puritanism)
"Canal Boat, The," 133
"Canterbury Pilgrims, The," 60
Castaway, The (Cowper), 37-38
Catholicism, references to, 12, 13, 14, 30, 31-32, 34, 44, 170
"Celestial Railroad, The," 62, 77, 172
Cervantes, Miguel de, 90, 152
Channing, W. E., 16, 78, 128
Character analysis:
    in *Blithedale Romance, The,* 53-61, 153-63
    in *House of Seven Gables, The,* 141-52
    in *Marble Faun, The,* 69-71, 82-85, 166-75
    in *Scarlet Letter, The,* 17-22, 67-69, 127, **130-40**
Chekhov, Anton, 150
Cherry, F. N., 90-91
Cherry Orchard, The (Chekhov), 150
Clemens, Samuel, 158
Coleridge, Samuel Taylor, 37-38, 103
Communalism, theme of, 53-61, 65, 153-63
Conrad, Joseph, 47, 62
Cooper, James Fenimore, 1, 73, 74, 75-76, 80, 162, 163
Cowper, William, 37-38
Crabbe, George, 46
Crews, Frederick C., 6

D

Dante, 2, 96, 137, 152, 169
Davidson, E. H., 28*n*
Deedes, C. N., 63
"Devil in Manuscript, The," 61

Dickens, Charles, 8-9
Dickinson, Emily, 12
Doliver Romance, The, 11, 24
Dombey and Son (Dickens), 8
Dos Passos, John, 59
Dreiser, Theodore, 28, 63, 158
Dr. Grimshaw's Secret, 11, 84
"Drowne's Wooden Image," 129

E

"Earth's Holocaust," 73, 154, 172
Edwards, Jonathan, 14, 16, 17, 74, 76, 86
Eliot, George, 47, 51
Eliot, T. S., 4, 5, 6, 7, 81
Emerson, Ralph Waldo, 12, 16-17, 23, 74, 76, 79, 80, 128, 137, 149, 160
Endecott, John, 18-19
"Endicott and the Red Cross," 26, 30, 34, 43, 45, 46, 130
Engels, Friedrich, 152
Episcopalianism, references to, 30-31, 49
"Ethan Brand," 108
Ethics, theme of, 43-45, 66-67, 111-12, **123-28**
Europeans, The (James), 16, 48, 63

F

Faerie Queen, The (Spenser), 30
Fanshaw: A Tale, 133
Faust, (Goethe), 35
Foster, Frank, 15, 16
Fourier, François, 153-54
Freud, Sigmund, 6, 96, 115

G

"Genius of Nathaniel Hawthorne, The" (Trollope), 3
"Gentle Boy, The," 108, 130
Gide, André, 3, 78
Goddard, H. C., 98
God's Promise to His Plantation (Mather), 13
Goethe, Johann Wolfgang von, 35

246

Gothic tradition, in Hawthorne, 2, 31,
  37, 81, 84, 86
Granville-Barker, H., 152
"Gray Champion, The," 26, 30, 43,
  62
"Great Carbuncle, The," 106, 134
Guilt, theme of:
  in *Marble Faun, The,* 164-65,
    169-70, 175
  in "Roger Malvin's Burial," 112-19,
    121-22, 165
  in *Scarlet Letter, The,* 130, 137,
    138

H

Hardy, Thomas, 51
Hawthorne (James), 4, 47
"Hawthorne Aspect, The" (Eliot), 4
Hawthorne, Julian, 97, 150
Hawthorne's Last Phase (Davidson),
  28n
Hawthorne, Nathaniel:
  allegory, use of, 3, 4, 11-24, 26, 30,
    65-66, 70-71, 93, 174-75
  American literary tradition, influ-
    ence on, 1, 3-5, 27-28, 43, 57, 62-
    63, 72-76, 78-79, 83-84, 139-40,
    142-43, 153-55, 158-59
  Biblical allusions, use of, 47-48, 73-
    74, 77-78, 85, 119-20, 165-69
  biographical information, 1, 11-12,
    123-25, 137-38, 154, 164-65,
    167-68
  communalism, theme of, 53-61, 65,
    153-63
  and Cooper, James Fenimore, 1, 73,
    74, 75-76, 80, 162, 163
  and Emerson, Ralph Waldo, 12, 16-
    17, 23, 74, 76, 79, 80, 128, 137,
    149, 160
  ethics, theme of, 43-45, 66-67,
    111-12, 123-28
  gothic tradition in, 2, 37, 81, 84,
    86
  guilt, theme of, 112-19, 121-22, 130,
    137, 138, 164-65, 169-70, 175
  historical themes of, 2, 4, 6-10, 18-

  20, 24, 30-35, 58-60, 82-83,
    123-28, 141-45, 150-51, 152,
    153-55, 165
  imagination, Hawthorne's concep-
    tion of, 65-66, 69-70, 101-5, 109,
    123-28, 138, 175
  and James, Henry, 2, 4-5, 6, 16, 21,
    26, 29, 47, 48, 52, 59, 61, 62, 76,
    80, 82, 92, 98, 129, 134, 138,
    139, 142, 143, 145, 162, 174
  materialism, theme of, 3, 9-10, 52-
    63, 99-110, 123-28, 143-45,
    155-59, 162
  and Melville, Herman, 4, 5, 12, 14,
    21, 23, 27, 47-48, 57, 61, 62, 66,
    76, 79, 98, 145, 146, 148-49, 152,
    155, 170
  poetic qualities, of prose, 17, 23,
    26, 27, 28, 29, 34-38, 43-63, 77
  as psychological novelist, 2-3, 4, 7,
    27, 36-37, 47, 51-52, 67-68,
    111-19, 160-61, 175
  Puritanism, influences of, 6, 9, 12,
    13-21, 24, 30-35, 49, 60, 67-68,
    74, 83, 90, 109, 126-27, 132,
    137-38, 141, 153-55, 159, 160-61,
    173
  Romance, Hawthorne's conception
    of, 64-66, 123-28, 141-43, 147-48,
    152, 158
  sin, theme of, 2, 12-20, 24, 36-37,
    46, 67-68, 73, 85, 91-93, 97, 105,
    113, 118-19, 132, 137, 160, 162,
    164-67, 169-70, 175
  supernatural, theme of, 35-38, 89-
    91, 117, 121, 135-36
  symbolism, use of, 3, 4, 27, 30-34,
    43-44, 61-62, 67-70, 79-80, 88-
    89, 96-98, 119, 142-45, 160, 168,
    169-70, 174-75
Hawthorne, Nathaniel, works by:
NOVELS
Ancestral Footstep, The, 11
Blithedale Romance, The, 3, 7, 8-9,
  11, 21, 22, 26, 28, 29, 30, 42, 43,
  47, 51, 52, 53-61, 64, 65, 69-70,
  75, 78, 106, 110, 151, 153-63,
  172, 174-75

Hawthorne, Nathaniel, works by
(NOVELS), (*continued*)
Dolliver Romance, The, 11, 24
Dr. Grimshaw's Secret, 11, 84
Fanshaw: A Tale, 133
House of the Seven Gables, The, 5,
7, 11, 20, 21, 52, 64, 69, 78, 83,
126, 128, **141-52**, 158, 161, 165,
172
Marble Faun, The, 11, 20-21, 22,
64, 69-71, 72, 77-78, 80-85, 105,
136, 142-43, **164-76**
Mosses from an Old Manse, 28
Our Old Home, 133
Scarlet Letter, The, 1-2, 3-4, 5, 6-7,
11, 14, 17-22, 24, 26, 27, 28, 29,
30, 31, 34, 35, 36, 38, **43-52**, 53,
61, 63, 66-69, 72-74, 82-83, 105,
109, 123-28, **129-40**, 141, 153,
154, 172
Septimius Felton, 11, 23, 108
Snow Image, The, 2-3, 26, 27, 61-
62
SHORT STORIES AND SKETCHES
American Notebooks, The, 64
"Artist of the Beautiful, The," 3,
26, 61, 62, 78, 79, **99-110**
"Birthmark, The," 11, 80, 86, 93-
95, 97, 108
"Canal Boat, The," 133
"Canterbury Pilgrims, The,"
60
"Celestial Railroad, The," 62, 77,
172
"Devil in Manuscript, The," 61
"Drowne's Wooden Image," 129
"Earth's Holocaust," 73, 154, 172
"Endicott and the Red Cross," 26,
30, 34, 43, 45, 46, 130
"Ethan Brand," 108
"Gentle Boy, The," 108, 130
"Gray Champion, The," 26, 30, 43,
62
"Great Carbuncle, The," 106, 134
"Hollow of the Three Hills, The,"
172
"Main Street," 26, 35, 45, 62
"Maypole of Merry Mount, The,"
26, **29-35**, 42, 43, 44-45, 47, 55,
60, 109, 110
"Minister's Black Veil, The," 11, 45,
49, 86, 92-93, 97-98
"Mr. Higginbotham's Catastrophe,"
11, 63, 88
"My Kinsman Major Molineux," 26,
27, 30, 35, 38-42, 43, 53, 59, 164,
165
"New Adam and Eve, The," 17, 20,
73, 77
"Old News," 26, 28, 38
"Prophetic Pictures, The," 78, 110
"Rapaccini's Daughter," 45, 86, 95-
97, 108, 164-65
"Roger Malvin's Burial," 6, 77,
111-22, 165
Seven Tales of My Native Land,
28
"Shaker Bridal, The," 60-61
Twice Told Tales, 62, 65
"Wives of the Dead, The," 86, 87-
89, 98, 134
"Young Goodman Brown," 11, 26,
35-38, 45, 49-50, 62, 86, 87, 89-
92, 97, 164-65
Hemingway, Ernest, 76
"Henry James and the New Jerusalem"
(Anderson), 27
Hero, The (Raglan), 43
Historical themes, 4, 18-20, 58-60,
165
in *Blithedale Romance, The,* 7-9,
153-55
in *House of the Seven Gables, The,*
141-45, 150-51, 152
in "Maypole of Merry Mount, The,"
30-35
in *Scarlet Letter, The,* 2, 6, 24, 82-
83, 123-28
"Hollow of Three Hills, The," 172
Holmes, Oliver Wendell, 5, 12
Homer, 131, 134
House of the Seven Gables, The, 5, 7,
11, 20, 21, 52, 64, 69, 78, 83, 126,
128, **141-52**, 158, 161, 165, 172
historical themes in, 141-45,
150-51, 152

House of the Seven Gables, The, (continued)
  materialism, theme of, 143-45
Howe, Irving, 3
Howells, William Dean, 125
Huckleberry Finn (Clemens), 158

I

Imagination, Hawthorne's conception
  of, 65-66, 69-70, 101-5, 109, **123-28,**
  138, 175
Israel Porter (Melville), 48

J

James, Henry, 2, 4-5, 6, 16, 21, 26, 29,
  47, 48, 52, 59, 61, 62, 76, 80, 82, 92,
  98, 129, 134, 138, 139, 142, 143,
  145, 162, 174
Johnson, Samuel, 26
Joyce, James, 37, 78

K

Kant, Immanuel, 86
Keats, John, 52, 103
Knight, G. Wilson, 27

L

"Labyrinth, The" (Deedes), 63
Lawrence, D. H., 3, 50, 62, 75, 82,
  133, 150-51
Leavis, Q. D., 1, 90, 154
Levin, David, 91
Levin, Harry, 88, 90, 92, 93, 112, 113
Lewis, Sinclair, 150
Longfellow, Henry Wadsworth, 5, 128
Lowell, James Russell, 142

M

Macbeth (Shakespeare), 35
"Main Street," 26, 35, 45, 62
Male, R. R., 90, 96
Mann, Thomas, 80

Marble Faun, The, 11, 20-21, 22, 64,
  69-71, 72, 77-78, 80-85, 105, 136,
  142-43, **164-76**
Mardi (Melville), 23
Martin Chuzzlewit (Dickens), 8-9
Materialism, theme of, 3, 9-10
  in "Artist of the Beautiful, The,"
    99-110
  in *Blithedale Romance, The,* **52-63,**
    155-59, 162
  in *House of the Seven Gables, The,*
    143-45
  in *Scarlet Letter, The,* 123-28
Mather, Cotton, 13-14, 44-45
Matthiessen, F. O., 5, 27
"Maule's Curse, or Hawthorne and the
  Problem of Allegory" (Winters),
  26
Mauriac, François, 3
"Maypole of Merry Mount, The," 26,
  29-35, 42, 43, 44-45, 47, 55, 60, 109,
  110
Measure for Measure (Shakespeare), 29
Melville, Herman, 4, 5, 12, 14, 21, 23,
  27, 47-48, 57, 61, 62, 66, 76, 79, 98,
  145, 146, 148-49, 152, 155, 170
Merton, Thomas, 30
Mervyn, Arthur, 74
Michelangelo, 138
Milton, John, 27, 34-35, 62
"Minister's Black Veil, The," 11, 45,
  49, 86, 92-93, 97-98
Moby Dick (Melville), 23, 89, 93, 94
Mosses from an Old Manse, 28
"Mr. Higginbotham's Catastrophy," 11,
  63, 88
"My Kinsman Major Molineux," 26,
  27, 30, 35, 38-42, 43, 53, 59, 164,
  165

N

"New Adam and Eve, The," 17, 20, 73,
  77
New England Canaan (Merton), 30
"New England Reformers" (Emerson),
  160
Nostromo (Conrad), 53

Novelas ejemplares (Cervantes), 90

O

"Old News," 26, 28, 38
Our Old Home, 133

P

Parker, Theodore, 73
Parkes, H. B., 12-13, 25-26, 28
Peabody, Sophia, 12, 86, 150, 154,
 164, 167, 173
Pierre (Melville), 23, 147
Pilgrim's Progress, The (Bunyan), 28,
 30, 35, 99
Poe, Edgar Allan, 11-12, 23, 61, 76,
 92, 93
Politics and the Novel (Howe), 3
Powys, T. F., 49
"Prophetic Pictures, The," 78, 110
Psychological novel, Hawthorne's influence on, 2-3, 4, 7, 27, 36-37, 47,
 51-52, 67-68, 111-19, 160-61, 175
Puritanism, influences of, 12, 13-21,
 24, 83, 90, 141, 173 (*see also* Calvinism)
 in *Blithedale Romance, The*, 9, 60,
  153-55, 159, 160-61
 in "Maypole of Merry Mount, The,"
  30-35, 49, 109
 in *Scarlet Letter, The*, 6, 67-68, 74,
  109, 126-27, 132, 137-38

R

"Rapaccini's Daughter," 45, 86, 95-97,
 108, 164-65
Resurrection (Tolstoy), 29
Rime of the Ancient Mariner, The
 (Coleridge), 37-38
"Roger Malvin's Burial," 6, 77, 111-22,
 165
Romance, Hawthorne's conception of,
 64-66, 123-28, 141-43, 147-48, 152,
 158
Rosenberry, E. H., 95
Rourke, Constance, 136

S

Sartre, Jean Paul, 94
Scarlet Letter, The, 1-2, 3-4, 5, 6-7, 11,
 14, 17-22, 24, 26, 27, 28, 29, 30, 31,
 34, 35, 36, 38, 43-52, 53, 61, 63, 66-
 69, 72-74, 82-83, 105, 109, 123-28,
 129-40, 141, 153, 154, 172
 character analysis, 17-22, 67-68,
  45-52, 127-28, 130-36, 139-40
 Puritan influences, 6, 67-68, 74,
  109, 126-27, 132, 137-38
 symbolism in, 13-14, 17-18, 44, 46-
  49, 69-70, 74-75, 130-31, 139
Schneider, H. W., 13-14
Scott, Walter, 52, 63
Septimius Felton, 11, 23, 108
Seven Tales of My Native Land, 28
"Shaker Bridal, The," 60-61
Shakespeare, William, 27, 29, 35, 47,
 52, 62, 63, 155
Shelley, Percy Bysshe, 103
Sin, theme of, 2, 12-20, 24, 36-37, 67-
 68, 91-93, 97, 113, 118-19, 160, 162,
 164
 in *Marble Faun, The*, 85, 105, 165-
  67, 169-70, 175
 in *Scarlet Letter, The*, 46, 67-68,
  73, 105, 132, 137
 in "Young Goodman Brown," 36-
  37, 91-92
Sister Carrie (Dreiser), 158
Snow Image, The, 2-3, 26, 27, 61-62
Spenser, Edmund, 27, 30, 62
"Spirit of Place, The" (Lawrence), 3-4
Stedman, E. C., 5
Stewart, Randall, 5, 25
Studies in Classic American Literature
 (Lawrence), 3
Swift, Jonathan, 46, 56
Symbolism, 3, 4, 27, 61-62, 79-80, 96-
 98, 119, 160 (*see also* Allegory)
 in *House of the Seven Gables, The*,
  142-45
 in *Marble Faun, The*, 168, 169-70,
  174-75
 in "Maypole of Merry Mount, The,"
  30-34

Symbolism (*continued*)
  in *Scarlet Letter, The*, 13-14, 17-
    18, 44, 46-49, 67-70, 74-75,
    130-31, 139
  in "Wives of the Dead, The," 88-
    89
Symbols, analysis of:
  armory, 17-18, 32-33, 43-44, 48
  custom house, 66-67
  forest, 36-37, 57, 74-75, 120-22
  labyrinth, 49, 51, 52-53, 63,
    171-72, 175
  rose, 31, 35, 46-48, 51
  scarlet letter A, 13-14, 67-68,
    130-31, 139

T

Tate, Allen, 79, 80, 92
Tess of the D'Urbervilles (Hardy), 51
Thompson, W. R., 119, 120
Thoreau, Henry, 74, 79, 128, 145
"Tiger" (Blake), 109
Tocqueville, Alexis de, 83
Tolstoy, Leo, 29, 45, 47, 50, 150
Transcendentalism, references to, 16,
  79-80, 103, 137, 147
Trollope, Anthony, 3, 4, 64, 65, 70,
  149-50
Turner, Arlin, 88, 112, 113
"Turn of the Screw" (James), 87, 92,
  96, 98
Twice Told Tales, 62, 65

U

Ulysses (Joyce), 37

Unitarianism, references to, 16, 17
U. S. A. (Dos Passos), 59

V

Van Doren, Mark, 88, 89, 92, 96, 112,
  113, 161-62
Veblen, Thorstein, 150
Very, Jones, 20
Village, The (Crabbe), 46

W

Waggoner, Hyatt, 96, 115
Wandering Willie's Tale (Scott), 63
War and Peace (Tolstoy), 150
Warrcn, A., 89, 96
Waste Land, The (Eliot), 151
What Happened in Salem? (Levin), 91
Whittier, John, 12
Wilson, E., 98
Wings of the Dove, The (James), 59
Winter's Tale (Shakespeare), 63
Winters, Yvor, 26, 52
"Wives of the Dead, The," 86, 87-89,
  98, 134
Wolfe, Thomas, 63
Women in Love (Lawrence), 53
Woodberry, G. E., 84, 93, 96
Wordsworth, William, 103

Y

"Young Goodman Brown," 11, 26, 35-
  38, 45, 49-50, 62, 86, 87, 89-92, 97,
  164-65

HEMINGWAY

A Collection of Critical Essays

Edited by ROBERT P. WEEKS

A

Across the River and Into the Trees,
13, 18, 63, 82, 84, 86, 102, 110,
122, 157-58, 166*n*, 176
"After the Storm," 79
American Claimant (Twain), 81
Anderson, Sherwood, 44, 72, 76
Auden, W. H., 15

B

"Battler, The," 84, **99-102**, 107
Baudelaire, Charles Pierre, 28
Benét, Stephen Vincent, 23
"Big Two-Hearted River," 41, 48, 50,
81, 91, 96, 104-7, 110, 131-32
Browning, Robert, 37

C

"Capital of the World, The," 12, 15
Cervantes, Miguel de, 73
"Champs d'Honneur," 64
Characterization, 1-8, 12-16, 54, 77,
118-19
Chartreuse de Parme (Stendhal), 84
"Clean, Well-Lighted Place, A," 12, 15,
53, 73, 112-13
Coleridge, Samuel Taylor, 75
Conrad, Joseph, 49
Cooper, James Fenimore, 76, 79
"Cross Country Snow," 82, 87, 103,
109

Cummings, E. E., 85

D

Dark Laughter (Anderson), 72
Daudet, Alphonse, 28
Death, theme of, 11, 13-16, 40-44, 46,
48-51, 54, 63, 65, 80, 83-84, 87,
122-26, 133*n*
    in *Across the River and Into the
    Trees,* 13
    in "The Capital of the World," 15
    in *A Farewell to Arms,* 13-14, 63,
    145
    in *For Whom the Bell Tolls,* 13, 46,
    157
    in *In Our Time,* 48-49, 95-111
    in "Indian Camp," 83, 87
    in "The Killers," 16, 48
    in "The Short Happy Life of Francis
    Macomber," 149
    in "The Snows of Kilimanjaro," 46,
    80, 122-26
    in *The Sun Also Rises,* 127-38
    in *To Have and Have Not,* 13, 48
Death in the Afternoon, 1*n*, 44, 48,
55, 56, 69-70, 72-75, 98, 103, 121,
141, 153-54, 164-65, 175
Dickens, Charles, 80
Dietrich, Marlene, 20, 22, 24-26
"Doctor and the Doctor's Wife, The,"
97-98
Don Quixote (Cervantes), 73
Donne, John, 67-68, 155

251

Dreiser, Theodore, 40

E

Eliot, T. S., 7, 49-50, 72, 77, 127, 169, 174
Emerson, Ralph Waldo, 50-51
"End of Something, The," 98-99

F

Faerie Queene, The (Spenser), 56, 74
Farewell to Arms, A, 6, 11, 13-14, 18, 24, 36, 41, 45-46, 48, 52-53, **56-63,** 65-66, 72, 77-78, 82n, 87, 102-3, 109, 125, 130, **139-43,** 152, 154n, 160, 172, 175
"Fathers and Sons," 74, 80, 87
Faulkner, William, 3, 169, 174
Fielding, Henry, 72-73
Fifth Column and the First Forty-Nine Stories, The, 14, 176
"Fifty Grand," 80, 84
Fitzgerald, Scott, 28, 31, 85-86, 88, 121
Flaubert, Gustave, 28
For Whom the Bell Tolls, 10, 11, 13, 43, 45-46, 48-49, 52-55, 67-69, 74, 77, 85-86, 90, 95, 98, 142, 155-56, 164n, 176
Ford, Ford Madox, 44

G

"Gambler, the Nun, and the Radio, The," 73
Gide, André, 7, 28
Goethe, Johann Wolfgang von, 159
Green Hills of Africa, The, 47, 72, 80, 85, 103, 118-19, 122, 125, 154, 176
Guest, Winston, 32-33

H

Hawthorne, Nathaniel, 7, 40, 46, 51, 55, 169, 174
Hemingway, Ernest:
    and Anderson, Sherwood, 44, 72, 76
    and Dietrich, Marlene, 20, 22, 24-26
    and Eliot, T. S., 49-50, 72, 77
    and Fitzgerald, Scott, 28, 31, 85-86, 88, 121
    and Hawthorne, Nathaniel, 7, 40, 46, 51, 55, 169, 174
    life of, 7-11, 17-39, 43-47, **175-76**
    and Melville, Herman, 7, 16, 40, 51, 55, 88-89, 158, 169, 174
    and Poe, Edgar Allan, 7, 40, 51, 55, 88
    poetry of, 64, 85
    and Scribner, Charles, 34, 37-38
    and Stein, Gertrude, 44, 77-78, 81, 149, 170
    style of, 1-7, 15-16, **72-85,** 105, **169-74**
    and Tolstoy, Leo, 16, 23, 154, 158, 173
    and Twain, Mark, 10, 76, 79
Hemingway, Ernest, works by: *(see also* titles of individual works)
    Across the River and Into the Trees, 13, 18, 63, 82, 84, 86, 102, 110, 122, 157-58, 166n, 176
    "After the Storm," 79
    "Battler, The," 84, **99-102,** 107
    "Big Two-Hearted River," 41, 48, 50, 81, 91, 96, **104-7,** 110, 131-32
    "Capital of the World, The," 12, 15
    "Champs d'Honneur," 64
    "Clean, Well-Lighted Place, A," 12, 15, 53, 73, 112-13
    "Cross Country Snow," 82, 87, 103, 109
    Death in the Afternoon, 1n, 44, 48, 55, 56, 69-70, 72-75, 98, 103, 121, 141, 153-54, 164-65, 175
    "Doctor and the Doctor's Wife, The," 97-98
    "End of Something, The," 98-99
    Farewell to Arms, A, 6, 11, 13-14, 18, 24, 36, 41, 45-46, 48, 52-53, 56-63, 65-66, 72, 77-78, 82n, 87, 102-3, 109, 125, 130, **139-43,** 152, 160, 164n, 172, 175
    "Fathers and Sons," 74, 80, 87

Hemingway, Ernest, works by:
(*continued*)
  *Fifth Column and the First Forty-
    Nine Stories, The,* 14, 176
  "Fifty Grand," 80, 84
  For Whom the Bell Tolls, 10, 11,
    13, 43, 45-46, 48-49, 52-55, 67-
    69, 74, 77, 85-86, 90, 95, 98,
    142, 155-56, 164*n*, 176
  "Gambler, the Nun, and the Radio,
    The," 73
  Green Hills of Africa, The, 47, 72,
    80, 85, 103, 118-19, 122, 125,
    154, 176
  "In Another Country," 23, 72, 78
  In Our Time, 45, 48, 52, 64, 78,
    81, **93-111,** 139, 141, 159, 175
  "Indian Camp," 83, 87, **96-98,** 101
  "Killers, The," 12, 15-16, 48, 55,
    77, 82, 98, 107-8, 114-17
  "Light of the World, The," 77, 108
  Men at War, 154, 176
  Men Without Women, 4, 86-92,
    107, 175
  "Mother of a Queen, The," 76
  "Mr. and Mrs. Elliot," 95
  "My Old Man," 82, 175
  "Natural History of the Dead, A,"
    142
  "Notes on Dangerous Game,"
    118-21
  "Now I Lay Me," 23, 41-42, 91
  Old Man and the Sea, The, 6, 10,
    12-13, 15, 52-56, 64, 70, 136,
    158-59, **161-68,** 173, 176
  "Old Man at the Bridge," 14, 16,
    156
  "One Reader Writes," 74
  "Open Boat, The," 148
  "Out of Season," 175
  "Short, Happy Life of Francis
    Macomber, The," 73, 82, **118-21,**
    126, 136, 141, 147, 149, 154
  "Snows of Kilimanjaro, The," 46,
    48, 75, 80, 88, 95, 118-19,
    122-26, 154
  "Soldier's Home," 82
  Sun Also Rises, The, 6, 41, 45, 49,

    53, 56-57, 73, 82, 84, 89-91,
    102-3, 121, 124, **127-39,** 141,
    160, 163, 166-67, 173, 175
  "Ten Indians," 107
  Three Stories and Ten Poems, 175
  "Three-Day Blow, The," 98-99
  To Have and Have Not, 13, 48, 72,
    76, 82, 86, 103, 121, 154-55, 172,
    176
  "Today is Friday," 54, 84, 164-65*n*
  Torrents of Spring, The, 48, 72,
    175
  "Undefeated, The," 70, 73, 141,
    147, 161
  "Up in Michigan," 81, 86, 95, 175
  "Valentine," 4
  "Way You'll Never Be, A," 23, 80,
    109-10
  "Wine of Wyoming," 81
  Winner Take Nothing, 54, 84, 107,
    175
Huckleberry Finn (Twain), 76
Hudson, W. H., 129
Huxley, Aldous, 2, 82

I

"In Another Country," 23, 72, 78
In Our Time, 45, 48, 52, 64, 78, 81,
  93-111, 139, 141, 159, 175
"Indian Camp," 83, 87, **96-98,** 101
Irony, 7, 64-71, 112-13, 117, 119
  in "A Clean, Well-Lighted Place,"
    112-13
  in *Death in the Afternoon,* 69-70
  in *A Farewell to Arms,* 65-66, 77,
    150
  in *For Whom the Bell Tolls,* 67-69
  in *The Green Hills of Africa,* 119
  in *In Our Time,* 64, 95-111
  in "The Killers," 117
  in *The Old Man and the Sea,* 64, 70
  in "The Short, Happy Life of Fran-
    cis Macomber," 121
  in "The Snows of Kilimanjaro,"
    119, 123-26
  in *The Sun Also Rises,*
    73

J

James, Henry, 122-23, 139, 174
Jew of Malta (Marlowe), 72
Jonson, Ben, 74
Joyce, James, 3, 7, 75, 80, 169, 172

K

Kafka, Franz, 7, 55, 135
"Killers, The," 12, 15-16, 48,
    55, 77, 82, 97, 107-8, 114-17
Kipling, Rudyard, 169

L

Lardner, Ring, 76
Lawrence, D. H., 7, 127
Lewis, Sinclair, 169, 174
"Light of the World, The," 77, 108
Liveright, Horace, 95
London, Jack, 40, 76
Lorca, Garcia, 83
Lyrical Ballads (Wordsworth), 75

M

Magny, Claude-Edmonde, 7, 80
Malraux, André, 84
Mann, Thomas, 31, 159
Marble Faun, The (Hawthorne), 46
Marlowe, Christopher, 72
Marvell, Andrew, 145
Maugham, W. Somerset, 23
Maupassant, Guy de, 23, 28
Meine Zeit (Mann), 159
Melville, Herman, 7, 16, 40, 51, 55,
    88-89, 158, 169, 174
Men at War, 154, 176
Men Without Women, 4, 86-92, 107,
    175
"Mother of a Queen, The," 76
"Mr. and Mrs. Elliot," 95
"My Old Man," 82, 175

N

"Natural History of the Dead, A," 142

"Notes on Dangerous Game," 118-21
"Now I Lay Me," 23, 41-42, 91

O

O'Faolain, Sean, 2-5
Ogden, C. K., 78
Old Man and the Sea, The, 6, 10, 12-
    13, 15, 52-56, 64, 70, 136, 158-59,
    161-68, 173, 176
"Old Man at the Bridge," 14, 16, 156
"One Reader Writes," 74
O'Neill, Eugene, 169
"Open Boat, The," 148
"Out of Season," 175

P

Pilgrim's Progress, The (Bunyan), 56
Poe, Edgar Allan, 7, 40, 51, 55, 88
Pound, Ezra, 44
Proust, Marcel, 7, 80

R

Red Badge of Courage, The (Crane),
    85
Religion, 3-4, 37, 47-50, 53-54, 84,
    161-68
    in *Across the River and Into the
        Trees*, 166n
    in "A Clean, Well-Lighted Place,"
        53, 73
    in *Death in the Afternoon*, 164
    in *A Farewell to Arms*, 140-45
        164n
    in *For Whom the Bell Tolls*, 49, 53,
        164n
    in *The Old Man and the Sea*, 53-54,
        161-68
    in *The Sun Also Rises*, 163-67
    in "Today is Friday," 54, 84-85,
        164n
Reynolds, Joshua, 36
Rimbaud, Arthur, 28
Richardson, Samuel, 72
Robinson, Edwin Arlington, 169
Runyon, Damon, 80

S

Sartre, Jean-Paul, 84
Savage, D. S., 2
Schorer, Mark, 83
Schwartz, Delmore, 3
Scribner, Charles, 34, 37-38, 175
Shakespeare, William, works of, 9, 63, 117, 121
Shaw, George Bernard, 30
"Short, Happy Life of Francis Macomber, The," 73, 82, **118-21**, 126, 136, 141, 147, 149, 154
"Snows of Kilimanjaro, The," 46, 48, 75, 80, 88, 95, 118-19, **122-26**, 154
"Soldier's Home," 82
Stein, Gertrude, 44, 77, 78, 81, 149, 170
Stendhal, 23, 28, 84
Sun Also Rises, The, 6, 41, 45, 49, 53, 56-57, 73, 82, 84, 89-91, 102-3, 121, 124, **127-39**, 141, 160, 163, 166-67, 173, 175
Symbolism, 7, 10, 46, 52-63
   in "Across the River and Into the Trees," 63
   in *Death in the Afternoon,* 56
   in *A Farewell to Arms,* 56-63
   in *For Whom the Bell Tolls,* 46, 55
   in "The Killers," 55
   in *The Old Man and the Sea,* **55-56,** 161-68
   in "The Snows of Kilimanjaro," 46, 122-26
   in *The Sun Also Rises,* 56-57

T

"Ten Indians," 107
Thoreau, Henry David, 173
Three Stories and Ten Poems, 175
"Three-Day Blow, The," 98-99

To Have and Have Not, 13, 48, 72, 76, 82, 86, 103, 121, 154-55, 172, 176
"Today is Friday," 54, 84, 164n
Tolstoy, Leo, 16, 23, 154, 158, 173
Torrents of Spring, The, 48, 72, 175
Trollope, Anthony, 50, 51
Turgenev, Ivan, 23
Twain, Mark, 10, 76, 79, 81, 169
Typee (Melville), 88

U

"Undefeated, The," 70, 73, 141, 147, 161
"Up in Michigan," 81, 86, 95, 175

V

"Valentine," 4
Valéry, Paul Ambroise, 28
Verga, Giovanni, 158

W

War and Peace (Tolstoy), 85
Waste Land, The (Eliot), 49
"Way You'll Never Be, A," 23, 80, 109-10
Whitman, Walt, 75
"Wine of Wyoming," 81
Winner Take Nothing, 54, 84, 107, 175
Woolf, Virginia, 3
Wordsworth, William, 7, 75, 141

Y

Yeats, William Butler, 7

Z

Zola, Émile, 6, 56

HOMER

A Collection of Critical Essays
Edited by GEORGE STEINER
and ROBERT FAGLES

A

Adapa, 96-97
Aeneid (Virgil), 17, 133, 161
Aeschylus, 146
Agias, 74
Aithiopis (Arctinus), 74
Ajax (Sophocles), 129
Alembert, Jean d', 87
Ancient Mariner, The (Coleridge), 164
Anna Karenina (Tolstoy), 89, 100-1
Apollonius, 64
Arctinus of Miletus, 74
Aristotle, 68, 94, 137, 171
Arnold, Matthew, 146, 160-61, 170
Arthur, King, 85
Auden, W. H., 163

B

Bach, J. S., 17
Bacon, Francis, 2
Balzac, Honoré, 88, 156
Beerbohm, Max, 162
Bees, mythology of, 94-96
Bentley, Richard, 161
Bérard, Victor, 11
Bible, 1-2, 23-37, 77, 93-94, 135
"Bird and the Fish, The" (fable), 78
Bloody Mary, 145
Bogan, Zachary, 11
Bonaparte, Napoleon, 124
Book of Common Prayer, The, 143

Browning, Robert, 147
Buddha, 96
Budge, E. Wallis, 93
Butcher, Samuel Henry, 161
Butler, Samuel, 12, 161, 164, 165
Byron, George Gordon, 83, 133

C

Calvin, John, 145
Cantos (Pound), 169-72
Cervantes, Miguel de, 83, 85
Cézanne, Paul, 88
Chapman, George, 160-61, 164-65, 172
Chaucer, Geoffrey, 144
Childe Harold's Pilgrimage (Byron), 133
Cicero, 135
Cinaethon, 74
Cohen, Marcel, 94
Coleridge, Samuel Taylor, 164
Columbus, Christopher, 83-84
Cuchulain, 124
Cypria (Stasinus), 74

D

Dante, 3, 10, 81-85, 132, 140, 143
Daumier, Honoré, 81
Dead Sea scrolls, 1, 2
Defoe, Daniel, 86
Dickens, Charles, 141

Divina Commedia (Dante), 10, 81-85, 140, 143

Don Giovanni (Mozart), 12

Don Juan (Byron), 83

Don Quixote (Cervantes), 83, 85

Dostoevsky, Fyodor, 141, 156

Dow, Sterling, 70-71

E

E Document, 77

Egyptian Book of the Dead (ed. Budge), 93

Eliot, T. S., 119

Epic Cycle, the, and Homer, 74-75, 77

Epigonoi, 74

Ericson, Leif, 84

Eugammon of Cyrene, 74

Euripides, 130, 146

"Evangeline" (Longfellow), 142-43

F

Faust (Goethe), 83, 140, 156-57

Fitzgerald, Robert, 162, 163-65, 167, 172

Flaubert, Gustave, 156

Flying Dutchman (Wagner), 81-83

Formulaic method, concept of, 40, 54-55, 61, 62-65

Freud, Sigmund, 2

G

Genèse de l'Odyssée (Germain), 10

Germain, Gabriel, 10

Gervinus, Georg, 15

Gilgamesh, Epic of, 10, 77, 93

Glory (Montaigne), 135

Goethe, Johann Wolfgang von, 21, 83, 140, 156

Goncourt, Edmond, 87, 88

Goncourt, Jules, 87, 88

Graf, Arturo, 132

Graves, Robert, 12, 162, 165-67, 169, 172

H

Hamlet (Shakespeare), 130, 143, 156-57

Hardy, Thomas, 141

Henry III of France, 17

Hesiod, 77

Homer:

and Arnold, Matthew, 160-61

and the Bible, 23-27, 93-94

and biblical characterizations, 26-28

and digression, concept of, 20-21

and enjambment, concept of, 64-65

and the Epic Cycle, 74-75, 77

and Fate, concept of, 51-52

and the formulaic method, concept of, 40, 54-55, 61, 62-65

and Graves, Robert, 165-67, 169

and Joyce, James, 167-69

and Lawrence, T. E., 161-65

and legend, concept of, 32-34

and literacy, 69-71, 73-78

and oral composition, tests for, 62-68

and oral tradition, 62-78

and poetry, concept of, 86-89

and Pound, Ezra, 169-72

realism of, 28-37, 140-47

and Shakespeare, William, 15-16

style of, 19-37, 153-55

and Virgil, 17-18

and Yugoslav poetry, 62-65, 71-72

Homer, works by:

Epigonoi, 74

Hymn to Hermes, 95

Iliad, 2-14, 15, 21, 31, 40-55, 66-68, 71-78, 100-4, 107, 122-38, 140-46, 148-49, 153-55, 160, 166

Odyssey, 1-14, 15, 17, 19-37, 54-55, 68, 71-78, 81-85, 91-97, 106-21, 122-38, 140, 148-51, 153-55, 156-57, 160-72

Thebaid, 74

Homer and the Heroic Tradition (Whitman), 6, 74-75

Homer's Daughter (Graves), 165-67
Homerus Hebraizon (Bogan), 11
Housman, A. E., 2
Hugo, Victor, 141
Hymn to Hermes, 95

I

Iliad, 2-14, 15, 21, 31, 40-55, 66-68,
71-78, 100-4, 107, 122-38, 140-46,
148-49, 153-55, 160, 166
and the assembly, theme of, 66-67
authorship of, 2-3, 5-14, 140,
148-49
beauty, theme of, 102-4
and the blinding storm, theme of,
58-61
cowardice, theme of, 129-32
eagles, symbolism of, 45-46
eating, theme of, 124-27
fallen city, theme of, 3-4
Fate, concept of, 51-52
fire imagery in, 41-55
fire, symbolism of, 41-44, 46-55
and the formulaic method, concept
of, 40, 54-55, 61
funeral pyres, theme of, 42-44
and the hero, concept of, 122-38
historical aspects of, 3-14, 71-78
intellectual curiosity, theme of,
132-33
lightning, symbolism of, 44-48
and Mycenae, 4-5, 9-10
nature imagery in, 55-56
oratory, theme of, 128-29
original sin, theme of, 100-3
sea imagery in, 55-56
stars, symbolism of, 52-53
style of, 153-55
Theomachia, theme of, 49-51, 55-
56
water, symbolism of, 49-52, 55-56
Ilias Mikra (Lesches), 74
Imagery:
of fire, in the *Iliad*, 41-55
of nature, in the *Iliad*, 55-61

of the sea, in the *Iliad*, 55-56

J

James, Henry, 17
Jamyn, Amadis, 17
J Document, 77
Jesus, 1-2, 97
Joyce, James, 10, 11, 137, 162, 165,
167-69, 172

K

Kazantzakis, Nikos, 10, 132, 170
Keats, John, 144, 147, 160, 165, 172
King Lear (Shakespeare), 140, 143
Kitchener, Horatio Herbert, 157
Knox, Ronald, 145
Kramer, S. N., 77, 93

L

Lang, Andrew, 161
Langdon, Stephen, 93
Laocoön (Lessing), 87
"Lapis Lazuli" (Yeats), 8
Lawrence, T. E., 9, 12, 14, 161-65,
167, 169, 171
Lesches, 74
Lessing, Gotthold, 87-89
Linear B, and pre-Homeric literacy, 5,
70-71
Literacy, pre-Homeric, 69-71, 75-78
Longfellow, Henry Wadsworth, 142-43
Lord, Albert B., 5
Lucian, 83

M

Macbeth (Shakespeare), 143
Machiavelli, Niccoló, 129
Malinowski, Bronislaw, 133
Mann, Thomas, 141
Marlowe, Christopher, 1, 2
Marriage of Figaro, The (Mozart), 12

Medea (Seneca), 84
Milton, John, 140, 143, 145, 147
"Minoan Writing" (Dow), 70-71
Montaigne, Michel de, 135
Morgann, Maurice, 1
Morris, William, 154
"Mother of Hermes! and still youthful
    Maia!" (Keats), 144
Mozart, Wolfgang Amadeus, 12
Münchausen, Baron Karl Friedrich, 83
Murder in the Cathedral (Eliot), 119
Murray, Gilbert, 2
Myres, Sir John L., 5

N

Nana (Zola), 86-87
Nietzsche, Friedrich, 101, 104
Nineveh, library of, 77
Nippur, clay tablet of, 93
Nostoi (Agais), 74
Notopoulos, J. A., 75-76

O

Odyssey, 1-14, 15, 17, 19-37, 54-55,
    68, 71-78, 81-85, 91-97, **106-21**,
    122-38, 140, 148-51, 153-55,
    156-57, 160-172
    authorship of, 1-3, 5-14, 140,
        148-51
    and bees, mythology of, 94-96
    and the Bible, 93-94
    birth, theme of, 110-11
    characterization, 135-38
    cowardice, theme of, 129-32
    and the *Divina Commedia* (Dante),
        81-85
    eating, theme of, 125-27
    and the formulaic method, concept
        of, 54-55
    and the hero, concept of, 122-38
    historical aspects of, 3-14, 71-78,
        93-94
    and *Homer's Daughter* (Graves),
        165-67
    identity search, theme of, 106-21

intellectual curiosity, theme of,
    132-35
and Joyce, James, 156-57, 167-69
literary adaptations of, 165-72
and Mycenae, 4-5, 9-10
Odysseus, meaning of the name,
    106-21
oratory, theme of, 128-29
pain, theme of, 107-9, 114-21
and Pound, Ezra, 169-72
and the sirens, nature of, 91-97,
    98-99
style of, 11-12, 19-37, 153-55
sources of, 10-11
temptation, theme of, 92-94
translations of, 160-65
trouble, theme of, 110-21
and *Ulysses* (Joyce), 167-69
Oidipodeia (Cinaethon), 74
On Translating Homer (Arnold), 160
Oral composition, tests for, 62-68
Othello (Shakespeare), 143
Oxford, Earl of, 2

P

Page, Denis, 12
Paradise Lost (Milton), 140
Parry, Milman, 5, 63, 65, 69
Paul, Saint, 31
Pentateuch, 14, 93
Philostrates, 95
"Pickax and the Plow, The" (fable), 78
Pindar, 95
Pisistratean Recension, 7
Plato, 126
Pliny, 33
Pope, Alexander, 160-65, 171-72
Porter, H. N., 108
Pound, Ezra, 162-63, 165, 169-72
Powys, A. R., 147
Powys, John Cowper, 9, 12
Prolegomena ad Homerum (Wolf), 2

R

Read, Forrest, Jr., 171

Redwood-Anderson, J., 142, 145
Rembrandt, 88
Renan, Joseph, 2
Robinson Crusoe (Defoe), 86
Rogers, Bruce, 162
Rouse, William Henry, 161, 164, 169

S

Sack of Ilium (Arctinus), 74
Sargon II, 77
Schiller, Johann, 21, 26
Schliemann, Heinrich, 1
Scott, Sir Walter, 88, 141, 154
Seneca, 10, 84
Septuagint, 94
Seven Pillars of Wisdom, The (Law-rence), 162
Shakespeare, William, 1-3, 8, 11, 15-16, 130, 143, 145, 147, 156-57
Shaw, George Bernard, 11
"Silver and Bronze" (fable), 78
Singer of Tales, The (Lord), 5
Sirens, nature of, 91-97, 98-99
Solomon, King, 11
Sophocles, 129, 146-47
Spenser, Herbert, 144
Sphinx, the, 92
Stasinus of Cyprus, 74
Stevens, Wallace, 172
Sumerian Mythology (Kramer), 77
Symbolism:
    of eagles, in the *Iliad*, 45-46
    of fire, in the *Iliad*, 41-44, 46-55
    of lightning, in the *Iliad*, 44-48
    of stars, in the *Iliad*, 52-53
    of water, in the *Iliad*, 49-52, 55-56

T

Telegonia (Eugammon), 74
Tempest, The (Shakespeare), 143
Tennyson, Alfred, 132, 172
Thebaid, 74
Theomachia, 49-51, 55-56
Thrones (Pound), 170-71
Titian, Vecellio, 88

Titus Andronicus (Shakespeare), 3
Tolstoy, Leo N., 8, 88-89, 100-1, 156
Trajan, 33
"Tree and the Reed, The" (fable), 78

U

Ulysses (Joyce), 11, 137, 167-69

V

Varro, Marcus Terrentius, 83
Ventris, Michael, 1, 5
Vera Historia (Lucian), 83
Vergil, 17-18, 64, 82, 145, 161, 164
Vie de Jésus (Renan), 2

W

Wagner, Richard, 81-83
Wallace, Edgar, 17
War and Peace (Tolstoy), 8
"Warrior as an Oral Poet: A Case His-tory, The" (Notopoulos), 75-76
Webster, T. B. L., 5
Weil, Simone, 9
Wellhausen, Julius, 3
Wellington, 1st Duke of, 124
Whitman, Cedric, H., 2, 6, 11-12, 74-76
Whitman, Walt, 171
Wilamowitz-Moellendorff, Ulrich von, 3
Wilson, Edmund, 1
Wolf, Friedrich, 2
Woolf, Virginia, 166
Wordsworth, William, 143-44

Y

Yeats, William Butler, 8, 17-18

Z

Zola, Émile, 86-87, 88
Zoroaster, 96

HOPKINS

A Collection of Critical Essays
Edited by GEOFFREY H. HARTMAN

A

Aesthetics, Hopkins's theories of, 89-
116, 136-37 (*see also* Poetry;
Rhyme; Sprung rhythm; "Instress"
and "inscape")
"Afterwards" (Hardy), 49-50
"Ah! Sun-flower" (Blake), 32
Akenside, Mark, 153
Alphonsus Rodriguez, Saint, 86
Ambassadors, The (James), 132, 135,
140-41
"Andromeda," 67-69, 168
Anglo-Saxon, Hopkins's interest in,
93, 157-59, 173-75
Annus Mirabilis (Dryden), 176
Aquinas, Saint Thomas, 112, 113
Aristotle, 4, 124, 126
Arnold, Matthew, 32, 111
"As Kingfishers Catch Fire," 83, 114,
125-26
Auden, W. H., 148

B

Bachelard, Gaston, 10
Barnes, William, 174-76
Baudelaire, Charles, 61, 65-66, 80
Beerbohm, Max, 134
Beowulf, 173
Blake, William, 32, 62, 155
"Blessed Damozel, The" (D. G.
Rossetti), 13
Bridges, Robert, 1, 3, 4, 7, 12, **18-21,**
35-36, 39-40, 45, 57-60, 64, 66, 99,
144-45, 173, 174, 175
Browning, Robert, 11, 12-13, 14, 97,
133, 156, 175
"Bugler's First Communion, The," 74,
132-33, 173, 176-77
Bull John, 176
Burkhardt, Sigurd, 2
Burns, Robert, 155, 174
Byrd, William, 176
Byron, George Gordon, 155

C

"Caged Skylark, The," 83
"Candle Indoors, The," 35
Canning, George, 157
Cantos, The (Pound), 63
Carlyle, Thomas, 90
"Carrion Comfort," 6, 10, 34-35, 87,
121-22, 166
Catholicism, doctrines of, in Hopkins's
work, 2-3, 4-5, 11, 67-68, 80-83, 89,
110-16, 168-69
Chesterton, G. K., 61-62, 171
"Church Monuments," (Herbert), 48
Cocteau, Jean, 70
Coleridge, Samuel Taylor, 49, 62
"Come Up from the Fields Father"
(Whitman), 145
Comus (Milton), 154
Confession, A (Tolstoy), 150
"Convent Threshold, The" (C. Ros-
setti), 13

"Course of a Particular, The"
   (Stevens), 164-66
Crashaw, Richard, 12, 13, 46
Cynewulf, 173

D

Dante Alighieri, 81
Delius, Frederick, 176
Democratic Vistas (Whitman), 150
Devlin, Christopher, 112
Diatonism and chromatism, Hopkins's
   principle of, 90-92, 137
Dickens, Charles, 139, 140
"Dirge, A" (Shelley), 155
Dixon, Richard Watson, 3, 95, 173,
   174
Dodgson, Charles Lutwidge, 60
Dolmetsch, Arnold, 176
Donne, John, 24, 37, 38-39, 48, 81,
   88, 153, 154, 168
Douglas, Gavin, 153
Dowland, John, 176
"Down in the depth of mine
   iniquity" (Greville), 48
Dryden, John, 154, 176
Duino Elegies (Rilke), 76-77
"Duns Scotus's Oxford," 48-49, 55

E

"Elegy Written in a Country Church-
   yard" (Gray), 159
Eliot, T. S., 24, 80, 147, 148, 152,
   173
Emerson, Ralph Waldo, 140, 144
Empson, William, 1, 30, 66
Engels, Friedrich, 150
English, Past and Present (Trench),
   174
Enoch Arden (Tennyson), 7
"Expérience Mystique et Philosophie,
   L'" (Maritain), 82

F

"Fairy, The" (Blake), 155
"Felix Randall," 11, **58-60**, 74, 171

"Flower, The" (Herbert), 124
Freeman, E. A., 174
Froude, Hurrell, 170
Furnivall, F. J., 174
Fusées (Baudelaire), 65-66

G

Gardner, W. H., 14, 64-65, 66-67
Gérard, Albert, 62
*Gerard Manley Hopkins, Priest and
   Poet* (Pick), 50-51
"God's Grandeur," 8, 46-47, 120, 123
Golden Bowl, The (James), 135
Googe, Barnabe, 42, 44
Gosse, Edmund, 174
Grammar of Assent, The (Newman),
   170
Graves, Robert, 34
Gray, Thomas, 159, 171
Greene, Robert, 44
Greville, Fulke, 48
Guardini, Romano, 14

H

"Habit of Perfection, The," 172
Haecceitas, Scotus's concept of, 94-95,
   170
Hardy, Thomas, 49-50, 174
"Harry Ploughman," 95, 120, 134-35,
   145, 168, 171
Hemingway, Ernest, 148
"Henry Purcell," 11, 81, 85, 106-7
Heraclitus, 124
Herbert, George, 48, 124
Herrick, Robert, 2, 160-62
Heuser, Alan, 67-68
History of English Prosody (Saints-
   bury), 153
Holst, Gustav, 176
Holy Sonnet I (Donne), 38-39, 48
Hopkins, Gerard Manley:
   aesthetic theories of, 89-116,
      136-37
   and Anglo-Saxon, interest in, 93,
      157-59, 173-75
   and Bridges, Robert, 1, 3, 4, 7, 12,

Hopkins, Gerard Manley: and
Bridges, Robert (*continued*)
18-21, 35-36, 39-40, 45, 57-60,
64, 66, 95, 144-45, 173, 174,
175
and Browning, Robert, 11, 12-13,
14, 97, 133, 156, 175
and Catholicism, doctrines of, 2-3,
4-5, 11, 67-68, 80-83, 89, 110-
16, 168-69
contemporary misunderstanding of,
17-27, 35-36, 70
and Crashaw, Richard, 12, 13, 46
diatonism and chromatism, principles of, 90-92, 137
and imitation, theory of, 5-6, 10-
11, 13, 115-16
as an innovator, 21-36, 59, 60-63
"inscape" and "instress," theory of,
7-8, 53, 64-67, 72, 81-82, 91-98,
105-6, 108-10, 141-42, 147, 171-
72, 175-77
and James, Henry, 131-43
linguistic researches of, 92-93, 95,
172-75
mannerism of, 1, 8, 138-43
and meditation, influence of, 4-5,
79, 82
music, theory of, 90, 93-94, 104-5,
106, 137, 146, 176
obscurity of, 41-56, 72-73
and Parmenides, 2, 10, 107-10
and Pater, Walter, 90-91, 136-37,
169
poetry, theory of, 84-116
rhyme, theory and use of, 90-98,
106, 115-16, 119-20
and Romanticism, 2, 3, 26, 54, 62-
63, 172
and Ruskin, John, 169-70
and Scotus, Duns, 10, 93-95, 111-
13, 170-71
and Shakespeare, 22-24, 88, 154
and Spenserian tradition, 1, 151-54
sprung rhythm, use of, 9, **42-45**,
134, 144, 145, **151-59**
and Tennyson, Alfred, 7, 24, 133,
146

and the Victorian age, 60-61,
156-58, 174
vocative style of, 6-7
and Welsh poetry, 93, 173-74
and Whitman, Walt, 2, **144-50**
and Yeats, William Butler, 1, 2, 4,
24
Hopkins, Gerard Manley, works by:
POETRY
"Andromeda," 67-69, 168
"As Kingfishers Catch Fire," 83,
114, 125-26
"Bugler's First Communion, The,"
74, 132-33, 173, 176-77
"Caged Skylark, The," 83
"Candle Indoors, The," 35
"Carrion Comfort," 6, 10, 34-35,
87, 121-22, 166
"Duns Scotus's Oxford," 48-49, 55
"Felix Randall," 11, 58-60, 74, 171
"God's Grandeur," 8, 46-47, 120,
123
"Habit of Perfection, The," 172
"Harry Ploughman," 95, 120,
134-35, 145, 168, 171
"Henry Purcell," 11, 81, 85, 106-7
"Hurrahing in Harvest," 5, 48,
114-15, 122*n*, 141
"Leaden Echo and the Golden
Echo, The," 12, 25-26, 86, 119,
137, 144-45
"Lines for a Picture of St. Doro-
thea," 13
"Loss of the Eurydice, The," 74,
127, 171
"May Magnificat, The," 114
"My own heart let me have more
pity on," 34
"Nature is a Heraclitean Fire, That,"
11, 87, 124, 126, 159, 176
"Nondum," 7
"No worst, there is none," 40-46,
54, 83
"Pied Beauty," 31, 48, 83, 99-104
"Ribblesdale," 10, 124
"Sea and the Skylark, The," 48, 135
"Spelt from Sybil's Leaves," 8-10,
30-33, 87-88, 176

Hopkins, Gerard Manley, works by,
  POETRY (*continued*)
  "Spring," 48, 123
  "Spring and Fall," 162-64
  "Starlight Night, The," 47, 114
  "Terrible" sonnets, 33-34 (*see also*
    titles and first lines of individual
    poems)
  "The fine delight that fathers
    thought," 35-36
  "Tom's Garland," 134, 149, 168,
    176
  "To what serves Mortal Beauty?"
    147
  "Vision of Mermaids, A," 13
  "Windhover, The," 2, 5, 8, 11, 29-
    30, 48, **49-56**, 76-79, 81, **83-88**,
    117-30, 140
  "Wreck of the Deutschland, The,"
    5-6, 11, 26-29, 81, 83, 84, 86,
    89, 127, 168, 171, 172, 176
  PROSE
  Journals and Papers, 89-110 *pas-
    sim,* 123, 129
  Letters to Robert Bridges, 93-94, 95,
    105-6, 111, 114
  Note-Books, 66-67, 170, 172, 173
  "On the Origin of Beauty," 136
  "Probable Future of Metaphysics,
    The," 90-91
  Sermons and Devotional Writings,
    90, 100
"Hurrahing in Harvest," 5, 48, 114-15,
  122*n,* 141

I

Imitation, theory of, and Hopkins's
  work, 5-6, 10-11, 13, 115-16
Induction, The (Sackville), 153
"Inscape" and "instress," Hopkins's
  theory of, 7-8, 53, 64-67, 72, 81-82,
  91-98, 105-6, 108-10, 141-42, 147,
  171-72, 175-77

J

James, Henry, 131-43

Johnson, Dr. Samuel, 170
Jonson, Ben, 47, 153
Journals and Papers, 89-110 *passim,*
  123, 129

K

Keats, John, 49, 155-56, 168, 172
Kilmer, Joyce, 80

L

Laforgue, Jules, 63, 80
Lahey, G. F., 17-18
"Leaden Echo and the Golden Echo,
  The," 12, 25-26, 86, 119, 137,
  144-45
Lear, Edward, 60
Leaves of Grass (Whitman), 144
Leavis, F. R., 1
Lectures on the English Language
  (Marsh), 173
Lee, Sir Sidney, 153
Letters to Robert Bridges, 93-94, 95,
  105-6, 111, 114
"Lines for a Picture of St. Dorothea,"
  13
Linguistic research, Hopkins's interest
  in, 92-93, 95, **172-75**
"London Snow" (Bridges), 57-60
"Loss of the Eurydice, The," 74, 127,
  171
"Low Barometer" (Bridges), 39-40, 45
Loyola, Saint Ignatius, 4-5, 51

M

McLuhan, H. M., 15, 46, 49, 51-52,
  53-54, 55, 56, 65
Mallarmé, Stéphane, 4
Malraux, André, 148
Mannerism, elements of, in Hopkins's
  work, 1, 8, 138-43
Marsh, George P., 173
Maritan, Jacques, 82
Marius the Epicurean (Pater), 138-39
Marvell, Andrew, 120
Mathiessen, F. O., 2

Maurice, F. D., 174
"May Magnificat, The," 114
Meditational techniques, and Hopkins's work, 4-5, 79, 82
Melchiori, Giorgio, 1
Meredith, George, 132
Meter (*see* Sprung rhythm)
Miller, J. Hillis, 2, 15
Milton, John, 22, 23, 24, 120, 144, 146, 151, 154, 168-69, 173
Mizener, Arthur, 46
Modern Painters (Ruskin), 169
Morris, William, 146
Moore, Sturge, 25
Murry, Middleton, 26
Music, Hopkins's theory of, 90, 93-94, 104-5, 106, 137, 146, 176
"Music's Duell" (Crashaw), 12
"My own heart let me have more pity on," 34

N

"Nature is a Heraclitean Fire, That," 11, 8, 124, 126, 159, 176
Newman, John Henry Cardinal, 90, 169, 170
New Poets from Old: A Study in Literary Genetics (Wells), 173
Nietzsche, Friedrich, 110-11
"Nondum," 7
Note-Books, 66-67, 170, 172, 173
"No worst, there is none," 40-46, 54, 83
    diacritical analysis, 42-45

O

"Ode on a Grecian Urn" (Keats), 156
"Ode on Melancholy" (Keats), 155-56
"On the Origin of Beauty," 136
Oxford Book of Sixteenth Century Verse, The, 44
Oxoniense (Scotus), 112

P

Parmenides, 2, 10, 107-10

Parnassian style, Hopkins's rejection of, 7-8, 13
Pater, Walter, 63, 90-91, 136-39, 169
Patmore, Coventry, 3, 12, 13-14, 66, 95, 174
Paul, Saint, 11, 78, 82, 84, 111
Peters, W. A. M., 141
Philo Judaeus, 82
Pick, John, 50-51, 54, 55
"Pied Beauty," 31, 48, 83, 99-104
Piers Plowman, 173
Pindar, 13
Poe, Edgar Allan, 63
Poems of Rural Life (Barnes), 176
Poetry, Hopkins's theory of, 84-116
    (*see also* Aesthetics; Rhyme; Sprung rhythm; "Instress" and "inscape")
Pope, Alexander, 11, 155
Portrait of a Lady, The (James), 134
Pound, Ezra, 63, 65, 80, 173
"Prayer to Trinity, A" (Stanyhurst), 157
"Probable Future of Metaphysics, The," 90-91
Purcell, Henry, 146

Q

Queen Mab (Shelley), 155

R

Ransom, John Crowe, 59
Renaissance, The (Pater), 169
Reverberator, The (James), 136
Reynolds, Sir Joshua, 170
Rhyme, Hopkins's theory and use of, 90-98, 106, 115-16, 119-20
"Ribblesdale," 10, 124
Richards, I. A., 1, 20, 30
Riding, Laura, 34
Rilke, Rainer Maria, 76-77
Rimbaud, Arthur, 61
Ring and the Book, The (Browning), 156
Romanticism, influence of, on Hopkins's work, 2, 3, 26, 54, 62-63, 172
Rossetti, Christina, 13

Rossetti, Dante Gabriel, 13
Ruggles, Eleanor, 52-53, 54, 55, 56
Ruskin, John, 169-70

S

Saintsbury, George, 151, 152-53
Sackville, Thomas, 153
Samson Agonistes (Milton), 154, 168, 173
School-Mistress, The (Shenstone), 153
"School of Giorgione, The" (Pater), 63
Scotus, Duns, 10, 93-95, 111-13, 170-171
"Sea and the Skylark, The," 48, 135
Sermons and Devotional Writings, 90, 100
Seven Types of Ambiguity (Empson), 30, 66
Shakespeare, William, 22-24, 88, 154
Shelley, Percy Bysshe, 54, 120, 155
Shenstone, William, 153
Shepheardes Calendar, The (Spenser), 151
Sherman, Stuart Pratt, 137
Skelton, John, 153
Southey, Robert, 155, 157
"Spelt from Sybil's Leaves," 8-10, 30-33, 87-88, 176
    diacritical analysis of, 8-10
Spenserian tradition, influence of, on Hopkins's work, 1, 151-54
"Spirit that Form'd this Scene" (Whitman), 145
"Spring," 48, 123
"Spring and Fall," 162-64
Sprung rhythm, 9, 42-45, 134, 144, 145
    sources of, 151-59
Stanyhurst, Richard, 157
"Starlight Night, The," 47, 114
Stevens, Wallace, 2, 4, 164-66
Stress (*see* Sprung rhythm)
Style and Beauty in Literature (Moore), 25
Survey of Modernist Poetry, A (Riding and Graves), 34
Swinburne, Algernon, 12, 20, 133, 144

T

Taylor, Jeremy, 82-83
Tennyson, Alfred, 7, 24, 133, 146, 157
"Terrible" sonnets, 33-34 (*see also* titles or first lines of individual poems)
Thalaba (Southey), 155
"The fine delight that fathers thought," 35-36
Thompson, Francis, 80
Thomson, James, 154
"Thou hast made me" (Donne), 47-48
"To a Louse" (Burns), 155
"To a Skylark" (Shelley), 54
"To Daffodils" (Herrick), 160-62
To Heaven (Jonson), 47
Tolstoy, Leo, 150
"Tom's Garland," 134, 149, 168, 176
"To the Man-of-War Bird" (Whitman), 145
"To what serves Mortal Beauty?" 147
"Tramp and Strike Questions, The" (Whitman), 148
Trench, R. C., 174
Tristan und Isolde (Wagner), 137

U

Unknown Eros, The (Patmore), 13-14

V

Valéry Paul,, 3, 4
Vaughan, Henry, 124
Verlaine, Paul, 61
Victorian age, influence of, 60-61, 156-58, 174
"Vision of Mermaids, A," 13
Vocative style, in Hopkins's works, 6-7

W

Wagner, Richard, 137
Wain, John, 2, 15
Waller, Edmund, 152
Ward, Alan, 93

Warren, Austin, 2, 69-70

Wells, Henry, 173

Welsh poetry, Hopkins's interest in, 93, 173-74

Whitman, Walt, 2, **144-50**

Williams, Charles, 22

Williams Vaughan, 176

"Windhover, The," 2, 5, 8, 11, 29-30, 48, **49-56**, **76-79**, 81, 83-88, 117-30, 140

    assonance and alliteration in, 117-18

    and "inscape," theory of, 53, 77-78

    rhythm in, 119

Wings of the Dove, The (James), 137-38, 142

Winters, Yvor, 2, 3, 15

Wordsworth, William, 2, 49, 120, 144

"Wreck of the Deutschland, The," 5-6, 11, 26-29, 81, 83, 84, 89, 127, 168, 171, 172, 176

    syntax of, 133-34

Y

Yeats, William Butler, 1, 2, 4, 24, 62

"Yes: in the sea of life enisled" (Arnold), 32

A. E. HOUSMAN

A Collection of Critical Essays

Edited by CHRISTOPHER RICKS

A

"A. E. H." (Amis), 13
"A. E. Housman" (Auden), 11, 143
Across the River and into the Trees
(Hemingway), 66
Additional Poems
   i ("Atys"), 126
   vi, 128*n*
   ix, 118-19
   xvii, 33
   xviii, 33, 128*n*
Aeneid (Virgil), 43, 100
Aeschylus, 17, 41
Amis, Kingsley, 3, 13
Anacreon, 43
"Ancient Mariner, The" (Coleridge),
133
*Application of Thought to Textual
Criticism,* 148
Arcades (Milton), 116
Arnold, Matthew, 15, 17, 21, 89, 124,
133, 146, 151, 149, 156, 158-59
Astronomica (Manilius), 131
Astrophel and Other Poems (Swin-
burne), 133
"Atys" (*Additional Poems,* 1), 126
Auden, W. H., 3-5, 11, 143, 159*n*

B

Bacchae (Euripides), 28
Bacon, Francis, 152
Bailey, D. R. Shackleton, 161-62

"Ballad of Reading Goal, The"
(Wilde), 133
Barrack Room Ballads (Kipling), 137
Baudelaire, Charles, 124, 128
"Bear, The" (Faulkner), 79
Belloc, Hilaire, 36-37
Bentley, Richard, 17, 21-22, 29, 50,
147*n*, 148-49, 154, 156, 159, 160
Betjeman, John, 3
Blake, William, 110
"Brendon Hill" (*A Shropshire Lad,*
xxi), 71-73, 126
Brontë, Emily, 44
Brooks, Cleanth, 6, 91, 95, 110
Browning, Robert, 31, 97, 159

C

Callimachus, 150
Carmen Seculare (Horace), 36
"Carpenter's Son, The" (*A Shrop-
shire Lad,* xlvii), 94, 173
Carroll, Lewis, 24, 27, 117
Catullus, Gaius Valerius, 35, 43
Catullus (Schulze), 133
Cantos (Pound), 103-4
Chesterton, G. K., 1
Cicero, 134, 150
Collins, William, 92, 110
Crane, Stephen, 90
"Culprit, The" (*Last Poems,* xiv), 2,
49, 126, 128*n*

Cymbeline (Shakespeare), 45

D

Daniel, Samuel, 110-11, 122
Dante, 21
Darrow, Clarence, 2
Darwin, Charles, 78
"Day of Battle, The" (*A Shropshire Lad*, lvi), 173
Degas, Hilaire, 131
Dickinson, Emily, 119
Dodgson, Charles (*pseud.* Lewis Carroll), 24
Donne, John, 68
"Dover Beach" (Arnold), 89
Dreiser, Theodore, 155
Dryden, John, 145
Duino Elegies (Rilke), 127

E

"Eight O'Clock" (*Last Poems*, xv), 66-67, 118
"1887" (*A Shropshire Lad*, i), 36, 94-95, 132
Eliot, T. S., 1, 3, 5, 49, 105, 155
Empson, William, 1-3, 6, 120
"Epitaph on an Army of Mercenaries" (*Last Poems*, xxxvii), 63-64, **89-91**, 95
Euripides, 17, 28, 43

F

"Far in a Western Brookland" (*A Shropshire Lad*, lii), 126
"Far known to sea and shore" (*More Poems*, xliv), 126
"Farewell" (de la Mare), 135-37
Faulkner, William, 63-66
FitzGerald, Edward, 3, 24-25, 129
Frost, Robert, 79-80, 88, 99, 155

G

Garrod, H. W., 1, 4, 110, 117
Gibran, Kahlil, 3

Gentlemen Prefer Blondes (Loos), 155
Goethe, Johann Wolfgang von, 21, 151, 156, 159
Gow, A. S. F., 19, 23-24
Gray, Thomas, 24-25, 35, 38, 40, 50, 130
"Grenadier" (*Last Poems*, v), 92

H

Haber, Tom Burns, 164-75
Hardy, Thomas, 79, 124, 155
Haunted Palace, The (Poe), 155, 157-58
Heine, Heinrich, 25, 36, 41, 43, 62, 124, 133
Heinsius, Nicholaus, 156, 160
Hemingway, Ernest, 63-66
Herbert, George, 118
Hölderlin, Friedrich, 34
"How sleep the brave" (Collins), 92
Homer, 17, 41, 48-49, 150
Housman, Alfred Edward:
  and Auden, 4-5
  and Bailey, 161-62
  and the Bible, 93-99, 133
  and Faulkner, 63-66
  and Frost, 79-80, 155
  and Heine, 62, 125, 133
  and Hemingway, 63-66
  and Kipling, 37, 76
  and Latin poets, 17-22 *passim*, 38-50 *passim*, 43, 48-49, 132-36 *passim*, 144 (*see also* individual poets)
  and Lawrence, 23, 42
  and Leopardi, 44, 48
  life of, 33, 138-41, 143, 177
  and Manilius, 16, 19, 21-23, 28, 131-32, 135, 154, 160, 162
  and Millay, 3, 155
  and Milton, 93-100, 115, 155
  personality of, 6-8, 128-32, 135
  and Poe, 155, 157-58
  poems about, 3, 11-13
  and religion, 32-34, 37, 106, 141
  and Shakespeare, 62, 113, 125, 133, 155, 158

Housman, Alfred Edward: (*continued*)
  and Stevenson, 133
  and Swift, 6-8, 21-22
  themes of, 37, 63
  and Wordsworth, 30-31, 78, 83,
    110
  and Yeats, 9, 103, 128
Housman, Alfred Edward, works by:
  (*see also* titles of individual works)
  Additional Poems
    i ("Atys"), 126
    vi, 128n
    ix, 118-19
    xviii, 33, 128n
  *Application of Thought to Textual
    Criticism*, 148
  Introductory Lecture, 14, 148, 155,
    157, 159
  Last Poems, 2, 37-40, 44, 130, 167
    v ("Grenadier"), 92
    vi ("Lancer"), 92
    vii ("In valleys green and still"), 126
    ix, 39, 65, 141
    x, 65
    xi ("Yonder see the morning
      blink"), 126
    xii ("The Laws of God"), 126
    xiv ("The Culprit"), 2, 49, 126,
      128n
    xv ("Eight O'Clock"), 66-67, 118
    xx ("The night is freezing fast"),
      29-30, 68-70
    xxvii, 118
    xxxii ("Epitaph on an army of
      mercenaries"), 63-64, 89-91, 95
    xxxviii, 38
    xl, 37, 80-83, 137
    xli, 38, 40
  More Poems, 2
    vi ("I to my perils"), 107-8, 126
    xxiii, 52-56,
    xxviii, 128n
    xxi, 131
    xxxii ("With seed the sowers scat-
      ter"), 57, 126, 140
    xxxiv, 138
    xliv ("Far known to sea and
      shore"), 126

  xlvi ("The land of Biscay"), 127
  Name and Nature of Poetry, The, 1,
    62, 107-22, 148, 154, 156-57, 167
  Poems of Terence Hearsay (*see A
    Shropshire Lad*)
  Poet's Defence, The, 127
  Shropshire Lad, A, 1-3, 17, 19, 23,
    36-39, 73-80, 123, 132-33, 139-44,
    155, 167
    i ("1887"), 36, 94-95, 132
    ii, 37
    iv ("Reveille"), 36, 137, 143
    viii, 130
    ix, 143
    x, 38, 137n
    xii, 143
    xiv, 143
    xv, 128n
    xvi, 57-61, 139-40
    xix ("To an athlete dying young"),
      126, 141, 143-44
    xxi ("Brendon Hill"), 71-73, 126
    xxii, 63, 92
    xxiv ("Say, lad, have you things to
      do"), 126
    xxvii ("Is my team ploughing"), 36,
      126
    xxviii ("The Welsh Marches"), 126
    xxx ("Others, I am not the first"),
      126, 142
    xxxi ("On Wenlock Edge"), 126,
      144
    xxxii, 143
    xxxiii, 68
    xxxiv, 36
    xxxv ("On the idle hill of sum-
      mer"), 99-100
    xxxvii, 37
    xl, 144-45
    xlii ("The Merry Guide"), 126
    xliii ("The Immortal Part"), 70,
      126
    xliv, 128n
    xlv, 128n
    xlvii ("The Carpenter's Son"), 94
      173
    xlvii, 141
    xlix ("Think no more, lad"), 126

Housman, Alfred Edward, works by:
(*Shropshire Lad, A*), (*continued*)
  lii ("Far in a western brookland"),
    126
  liv ("With rue my heart"), 38-39,
    126, 143
  lxi ("Hughley Steeple"), 126, 143
  lxii, 37, 49, 134, 143,
    lxiii, 132
Housman, Laurence, 33, 117, 119,
  130, 138, 158, 163-65, 174
Hugh Selwyn Mauberley (Pound), 156
"Hughley Steeple" (*A Shropshire Lad,*
  lxi), 126, 143
Huxley, Thomas, 78
Hyperion (Keats), 119

I

"I to my perils" (*More Poems,* vi),
  107-8, 126
Ibis (Ovid), 154
Idiot's Delight (Sherwood), 86
"Immortal Part, The" (*A Shropshire
Lad,* xliii), 70, 126
"In Memoriam" (Tennyson), 97
"In valleys green and still" (*Last
Poems,* vii), 126
Introductory Lecture, 14, 148, 155,
  157, 159
Iphigenia in Tauris (Euripides), 43
Irony, 62-84 *passim,* 92-105 *passim,*
  125
"Is my team ploughing" (*A Shrop-
shire Lad,* xxvii), 36, 126

J

Jarrell, Randall, 3, 6, 107, 119-20,
  140*n*
Jonson, Ben, 3
Juvenal, 18, 21-22, 132, 134, 144,
  154

K

Keats, John, 79, 119
"King and No King" (Yeats), 100-3

Kipling, Rudyard, 36-37, 137-38

L

"Lancer" (*Last Poems,* vi), 92
"Land of Biscay, The" (*More Poems,*
  xlvi), 126
Last Poems, 2, 37-40, 44, 130, 167
  (*for individual poems see* works by
  A. E. Housman)
Latin poets, 17-22 *passim,* 38-50
  passim, 132-36 *passim,* 144 (*see also*
  individual names)
Lawrence, Thomas Edward, 23-24, 42,
  127
"Laws of God, The" (*Last Poems,* xii),
  126
Lear, Edward, 116-17
Lectures on Translating Homer
  (Arnold), 15
Leopardi, Giacomo, 44, 48, 124
Lessing, Gotthold, 151, 156
Lewis, Sinclair, 154-55
Locksley Hall (Tennyson), 121
Longfellow, Henry Wadsworth, 97
Lowell, James Russell, 97
Lucan, 19, 132, 144, 154, 172
Lucretius, 41

M

Macbeth (Shakespeare), 112
McGinley, Phyllis, 88
Mallarmé, Stephane, 131
Manilius, Marcus, 16, 19, 21-23, 28,
  131-32, 135, 154, 160, 162
Mare, de la, 135-37
Martial, 134
Mayakovsky, Vladimir, 105
Measure for Measure (Shakespeare),
  113-14, 122
Meredith, George, 1
"Merry Guide, The" (*A Shropshire
Lad,* xlii), 126
Millay, Edna St. Vincent, 3, 155
Milton, John, 15-16, 28, 87, 92-100,
  115-16, 118, 131, 155
"Mr. Housman's Message" (Pound), 12

More Poems, 2 (*for individual poems see* works by A. E. Housman)

N

Name and Nature of Poetry, The, 1, 62, **107-22**, 148, 154, 156-57, 167
Nash, Ogden, 88
Newbolt, Henry John, 37
Newton, Isaac, 18, 160
"Night is freezing fast, The" (*Last Poems,* xx), 29-30, **68-70**

O

"Ode to a Nightingale" (Keats), 79
"Ode to the Cuckoo" (Logan or Bruce), 111
Odes (Horace), 36
"On the idle hill of summer" (*A Shropshire Lad,* xxxv), 99-100
"On Wenlock Edge" (*A Shropshire Lad,* xxxi), 126, 144
"Once to Every Man and Nation" (Lowell), 97
Orwell, George, 4-5, 106
"Others, I am not the first" (*A Shropshire Lad,* xxx), 126, 142
Ovid, 18, 154

P

Paradise Lost (Milton), 16, 29, 93-94, 98-100
Pascal, Blaise, 124
Pater, Walter, 24, 27, 134
"Paul Revere" (Longfellow), 97
Phaedrus (Plato), 45
Phalaris, 150
"Pied Piper of Hamelin, The" (Browning), 97
Pindar, 43
Plato, 45
Platt, Arthur, 156-59
Playboy of the Western World, The (Synge), 42
Pliny the Elder, 86
Poe, Edgar Allan, 158

Poems of Terence Hearsay (*see A Shropshire Lad*)
Poet's Defence, The, 127
Pope, Alexander, 20, 87, 92, 146
Porson, Richard, 17, 148, 160
Pound, Ezra, 3, 9, 12, 103-4, 156
Propertius, Sextus, 19, 22, 28, 142

R

Raleigh, Walter, 35, 156
Rape of the Lock, The (Pope), 92
Redgrove, Peter, 110
Religion, 32-34, 37, 93-99, 106, 133, 141
"Reveille" (*A Shropshire Lad,* iv), 36, 137, 143
"Revenge, The" (Tennyson), 97
Rilke, Rainer Maria, 127-28
Rousseau, Henri (Le Douanier), 152
Rubáiyát of Omar Khayyám (FitzGerald), 3

S

"Say, lad, have you things to do" (*A Shropshire Lad,* xxiv), 126
Scaliger, Julius Caesar, 21-22, 156, 160
Seven Pillars of Wisdom (Lawrence), 23
Shakespeare, William, 16, 45, 62, 125, 133, 155, 158
Shapiro, Karl, 97-105
Shelley, Percy Bysshe, 5, 87
Shaw, George Bernard, 146
Shropshire Lad, A, 1-3, 17, 19, 23, 36-39, **73-80**, 123, 132-33, 139-44, 155, 167 (*for individual poems see* works by A. E. Housman)
Simonides, 91
Sitwell, Edith, 1
Socrates, 32, 34, 45
"Sonne, The" (Herbert), 118
Sparrow, John, 1, 5, 138
Spenser, Edmund, 111
Stevenson, Robert Louis, 133

"Stopping by Woods on a Snowy
Evening" (Frost), 80
Sun Also Rises, The (Hemingway),
65, 79
Swift, Jonathan, 6-8, 21-22
Swinburne, Algernon Charles, 22, 133

T

Tale of Balen, A (Swinburne), 133
Tennyson, Alfred, 3, 31, 97, 113, 115,
121
Terence, 41
Theocritus, 41, 46, 48
"Think no more, lad" (*A Shropshire
Lad*, xlix), 126
"To an athlete dying young" (*A
Shropshire Lad*, xix), 126, 141,
143-44
Triple Thinkers, The (Wilson), 109
Twain, Mark, 155

U

"Ulysses" (Tennyson), 113
"Ulysses and the Siren" (Daniel),
122
*Use of Poetry and the Use of Criticism,
The* (Eliot), 5

V

Valéry, Paul, 155
Verlaine, Paul, 124
Villon, François, 124
Virgil, 18, 36, 41, 43, 46, 48-49, 155

W

Waste Land, The (Eliot), 40
"Welsh Marches, The" (*A Shropshire
Lad*, xxviii), 126
Whitman, Walt, 87
Wilamowitz-Moellendorff, Ulrich von,
17
Wilson, Edmund, 6, 106, 109, 146
"With rue my heart" (*A Shropshire
Lad*, liv), 38-39, 126, 143
"With seed the sowers scatter" (*More
Poems*, xxxii), 57, 126, 140
Wordsworth, William, 30-31, 78, 83,
110
Wordsworth's Grave (Watson), 155

Y

Yeats, William Butler, 1, 9, 42, 49,
100-3, 128, 133
"Yonder see the morning blink" (*Last
Poems*, xi), 126

IBSEN

A Collection of Critical Essays

Edited by ROLF FJELDE

A

Adler, Alfred, 6
Aeschylus, 92
Amiel, Henri Frédéric, 83-84
Andreev, Leonid, 116
Archer, William, 115
Arup, Jens, 6
As You Like It (Shakespeare), 30,
   42-43

B

Beethoven, Ludwig van, 9, 176
Bentley, Eric, 1-2, 10, 137
Bergen National Theatre, 29, 30, 31-35
Björnson, Björnstjerne, 1, 45, 81, 156
Brand, 2, 3, 4, 10, 17, 52-62, 92n, 96,
   99, 159, 169, 171, 172, 173, 174,
   177
   art as theme in, 55
   dramaturgy of, 96-97
   idealism in, 52, 56-57, 62
   paradox in, 56-62
   radicalism in, 14-15
   realism in, 56-62
   self-realization, theme of, 6, 12, 56-
      60
   Shakespeare's influence on, 49-50,
      51
   symbolism in, 57-62, 98
   tragedy in, 97
   truth as theme in, 23-24, 26, 56,
      58

Brandes, Georg, 84, 86, 174
Brecht, Bertolt, 1n, 11-12, 16
Brieux, Eugène, 109, 116
Bröchner, Hans, 84
Brustein, Robert, 4
Bruun, Christopher, 54, 55
Bull, Francis, 45-46
Bull, Ole, 30, 42

C

Casino Theatre, Copenhagen, 30
Caspari, C. P., 83
Cassirer, Ernst, 9
Catiline, 14, 17, 30, 42, 45, 46, 47,
   50-51
   dramaturgy of, 33, 34, 35
   Shakespeare's influence on, 94
Cervantes, 145
Christiana Theatre, 29, 35, 43
Coriolanus (Shakespeare), 49-50

D

Dahl, J. C., 31
Dalgard, Olav, 46, 47
Dance of Death (Strindberg),
   169
Dante Alighieri, 175
Darwin, Charles, 3n, 82-83
Deer, Irving, 6
Descent of Man (Darwin), 82-83
Doll's House, A, 2, 6, 14, 99-108, 109,

Doll's House, A (*continued*)
110, 118, 129, 140-57 *passim*, 171,
172, 175
dramaturgy of, 38-39, 100-108
as tragedy, 99-108
truth, theme of, 25

E

Egils Saga, 48
Ehrhard, Auguste, 131
Eliot, T. S., 1, 137-38
Emerson, Ralph Waldo, 173
Emperor and Galilean, 7-8, 14, 21, 53,
80-90
dramaturgy of, 37, 98-99
historical process, theme of, 7-8,
80-90
myth in, 8-9
Enemy of the People, An, 16, 17, 140,
156, 171
radicalism in, 15, 171
Shakespeare's influence on, 50,
51
truth, theme of, 20-21, 22
Enemy of the People, An (Miller), 15-
16
Engels, Friedrich, 12

F

Feast at Solhaug, The, 45
dramaturgy of, 35, 36, 94
Shakespeare's influence on, 48, 51,
94
Fergusson, Francis, 5
Fisher, Ruth, 12
For Self-Examination (Kierkegaard),
118
Forster, E. M., 10
Frankl, Viktor, 6
Freud, Sigmund, 6, 68, 122

G

Garborg, Arne, 80
Gauntlet, A (Björnson), 45
Ghosts, 17, 32, **109-19**, 140-57 *passim*,
169, 170, 171, 177
dramaturgy of, 110-19
and Greek tragedy, 111, 113, 114
morality in, 110
radicalism in, 14, 15, 171
realism in, 112, 116, 118, 119
self-realization, theme of, 13
symbolism in, 112, 116-17, 119
as tragedy, 111-19
truth as theme in, 22-23, 25-26, 27
Gide, André, 15

Goethe, Johann Wolfgang von, 1, 3, 9,
18, 41-42, 85, 141, 142, 157
Greek tragedy, 1, 2, 111, 113, 114
Grillparzer, Franz, 18
Groddeck, Georg, 6
Grosse, Edmund, 46, 50, 131

H

Haakon's Hall, 43
Haeckel, Ernst, 83
Hamlet (Shakespeare), 30, 31, 42, 43,
47, 115, 138
Hartmann, Eduard von, 82
Hauptmann, Gerhart, 16
Hawthorne, Nathaniel, 170
Hebbel, Christian Friedrich, 7
Hedda Gabler, 2, 6, 14, **131-38**, 140-67
passim, 159, 172, 175, 177
dramaturgy of, 36, 132-38
myth in, 9
self-realization, theme of, 132-38
symbolism in, 131-38
as tragedy, 138
truth, theme of, 26-27
Heiberg, J. L., 30, 46
Hertz, Henrik, 30, 45
Hettner, Hermann, 7, 31, 44, 46
Holberg, Ludwig, 30, 42
Holinshed, Raphael, 48
Hostrup, Jens Christian, 30-31

I

Ibsen, Henrik:
and art, 55, 55*n*, 62, 149-50, 155-56,
162-64

Ibsen, Henrik (*continued*)
  and Brecht, 1*n*, 11-12, 16
  and his characters, 50-51, 95,
    145-46
  contribution of, 1-10
  correspondence of, 1, 20-22, 31,
    32, 53, 54, 139, 152, 156-57, 160
  critical reputation of, 1-10, 11-12,
    80-81
  dramatic aims of, 3-10
  dramaturgy of, 4-5, **33-40, 41-51**,
    94-108, 132-38, 167-68
  and form, 4-5
  and Greek tragedy, 1, 2, 111, 113,
    114
  and the historical process, 3, 7-8,
    80-90
  and idealism, 52, 56-57
  and illusion, 120-30
  life of, 3, 29-33, 53-55
  and the Marxist theory of drama,
    1*n*, 11-12, 116
  and morality, 3, 110
  and myth, 8-10
  and the naturalistic style, 4, 8, 32,
    34, **37-40**, 131, 157
  and the Norse sagas, 48, 94
  and Oehlenschläger, 33, 42
  producer's notebooks of, 32-33
  and psychological insight, 5-7, 13,
    63-97, 130*n*
  radicalism of, **3-10**, 11, **14-16**, 20,
    139-40, 170-71
  and realism, 56-62, 108, 112, 116,
    118, 119, 174
  as a romantic, 174-78
  and Schiller, 3, 33, 42, 46
  and Scribe, 5, 30, 31, 46, 47, 93,
    94-95, 96, 98, 99, 109
  and self-realization, theme of, 2-3,
    6-7, 12-14, 17, 19, 21, 44-45, **56-**
    60, 120-30, 132-38, 141-43, 149
  and Shakespeare, 2, 5, 9, 30, 31, 33,
    41-51, 93-94, 96, 103*n*, 115, 145
  and society, 10, 93, 96, 139-41,
    155-57
  as stage craftsman, **29-40**
  and Strindberg, 4, 5-6, 29, 130*n*,
    169

  and symbolism, 35, 57-62, 108,
    112, 116-17, 119, 121, 127-28,
    131-38, 167-68
  and tragedy, **91-108**, **109-19**, 138
  and "Tragic Muse, The," 1, 2, 4, 7,
    8
  and the theme of truth, **3-10, 18-**
    28, 54-62 *passim*, 109
  and the role of women, 50-51, 132,
    132*n*, **152-55**
Ibsen, Henrik, works by:
  DRAMA (*see also* listings of individual
  titles)
    Brand, 2, 3, 4, 6, 10, 12, 14-15, 17,
      23-24, 26, 49-50, 51, **52-62**, 92*n*,
      96, 97-98, 99, 159, 169, 171, 172,
      173, 174, 177
    Catiline, 14, 17, 30, 33, 34, 35, 42,
      45, 46, 47, 50-51, 94
    Doll's House, A, 2, 6, 14, 25, 38-39,
      99-108, 109, 110, 118, 129, 140-
      57 *passim*, 171, 172, 175
    Emperor and Galilean, 7-8, 8-9, 14,
      21, 37, 53, **80-90**, 98-99
    Enemy of the People, An, 15, 16,
      17, 20-21, 22, 50, 51, 140, 156,
      171
    Feast at Solhaug, The, 35, 36, 45,
      48, 51, 94
    Ghosts, 13, 14, 15, 17, 22-23, 25-
      26, 27, 32, **109-19**, 140-57 *passim*,
      169, 170, 171, 177
    Hedda Gabler, 2, 6, 9, 14, 26-27, 36,
      131-38, 140-57 *passim*, 159, 172,
      175, 177
    John Gabriel Borkman, 14, 29, 36,
      39, 50, 51, 123, 140-57 *passim*,
      158-68, 175, 177
    Lady from the Sea, The, 9, 36, 118,
      140-57 *passim*, **158-68**, 169, 172,
      175, 177
    Lady Inger of Östraat, 34, 35-36,
      37, 46-47, 94
    League of Youth, The, 8, 15, 32,
      37-38, 92*n*, 98, 99, 174
    Little Eyolf, 27-28, 36, 123, 140-57
      passim, **158-68**, 172, 175, 177
    Love's Comedy, 32, 53, 92*n*, 95-96,
      98

Ibsen, Henrik, works by (DRAMA),
(*continued*)
   Master Builder, The, 2, 28, 39, 55n,
     123, 140-57 *passim*, **158-68**, 172,
     175, 176-77
   Midsummer Eve, 31, 33, 34, 35, 36,
     46, 92n, 94
   Olaf Liljekrans, 36
   Peer Gynt, 2, 5, 6-7, 10, 14, 17, 26,
     43, **63-79**, 98, 105, 138, 169-70,
     171, 174, 177, 178
   Pillars of Society, The, 14, 36, 37-
     38, 51, 99, 140-57 *passim*, 170,
     171
   Pretenders, The, 29, 48-49, 51, 53,
     96
   Ptarmigan of Justedal, The, 35
   Rosmersholm, 2, 9, 22-23, 27-28,
     36, 39, 51, 120, 123, **124-27**, 128,
     130n, 140-57 *passim*, 169, 172,
     175, 177
   Vikings at Helgeland, The, 35, 36,
     48, 51, 94-95, 97
   Warrior's Barrow, The, 30, 33, 35,
     42, 94
   When We Dead Awaken, 3, 8, 17,
     28, 36, 55n, 123, 140-57 *passim*,
     158-68, 175, 177
   Wild Duck, The, 9, 12, 13, 17, 23,
     24-25, 32, 34, 39-40, 45, 51, 118,
     120-24, 128, 130, 130n, 140-57
     passim, 171, 174, 176
  ESSAYS
   *On the Importance of Knowledge of
     Oneself*, 6
   "Shakespeare and His Influence on
     Nordic Art," 41-42, 45
  POETRY
   Haakon's Hall, 43
   "In the Picture Gallery," 55n
   "On the Fells," 55n
   "On the Vidde," 170
"In the Picture Gallery," 55n
Iphigenie (Goethe), 18

J

James, Henry, 2, 112, 117

Jarry, Alfred, 6
John Gabriel Borkman, 14, 29, 123,
  140-57 *passim*, **158-68**, 175, 177
  art, as theme of, 162-64
  dramaturgy of, 36, 39, 167
  Shakespeare's influence on, 50
    51
Johnson, Gisle, 83
Jonson, Ben, 1
Julian the Apostate, 81-90
Julius Caesar (Shakespeare), 49
Jung, C. G., 158, 160, 161, 162, 166

K

Kierkegaard, Sören, 6, 8, 61n, 96, 118,
  119
King Lear (Shakespeare), 30, 42, 43,
  48-49, 50, 103n
King Richard III (Shakespeare), 31, 43,
  47, 50
Koht, Halvdan, 5, 109

L

Laading, Hermann, 31-32
Lady from the Sea, The, 27, 118, 120,
  127-30, 130n, 140-57 *passim*, 169,
  172, 175, 177
  dramaturgy of, 36, 167
  illusion in, 127-30
  myth in, 9
  self-realization, as theme of, 127-30
  symbolism in, 127-28
  truth as theme in, 27
Lady Inger of Östraat:
  dramaturgy of, 34, 35-36, 37,
    94
  Scribe's influence on, 94
  Shakespeare's influence on, 46-47,
    94
Laube, Heinrich, 37
Laxdoela (saga), 48
League of Youth, The, 8, 15, 32, 92n,
  99, 174
  dramaturgy of, 37-38, 98
  Scribe's influence on, 98
Lee, Jeanette, 131

Lessing, Gotthold, 139
Lewis, C. S., 85
Little Eyolf, 123, 140-57 *passim,*
  158-68, 172, 175, 177
  dramaturgy of, 36, 167
  truth, as theme of, 27-28
Love's Comedy, 32, 53, 55n, 92n,
  98
  art as theme in, 55n
  dramaturgy of, 95-96
Lowenthal, Leo, 6, 8

M

Macbeth (Shakespeare), 46-47, 48, 50
"Main Currents of Nineteenth Century
  Literature" (Brandes), 84
Marx, Karl, 12
Marxist theory of drama, 1n, 11-12
Massnahme, Die (Brecht), 12, 16
Master and Apprentice (Hostrup), 30-
  31
Master Builder, The, 2, 123, 140-57
  passim, **158-68,** 172, 175, 176-77
  art, theme of, 55n, 162-64
  dramaturgy of, 39, 167
  truth, theme of, 28
May, Rollo, 6
Mayerson, Caroline, 9
Meininger company, 29, 37
Merchant of Venice, The
  (Shakespeare), 50
Midsummer Eve, 31, 92n
  dramaturgy of, 33, 34, 35, 36
  Shakespeare's influence on, 46, 94
Midsummer Night's Dream, A (Shake-
  speare), 31, 43, 46
Miller, Arthur, 15-16
Moderne Drama, Das (Hettner), 31, 44
Molière, 1, 141, 142, 143
Motifs, in Ibsen's works, 139-57

N

Natürliche Schöpfungsgeschichte
  (Haeckel), 83
Northam, John, 5

O

Oedipus Rex (Sophocles), 111, 138
Oedipus Tyrannus (Sophocles), 103n
Oehlenschläger, Adam, 30, 33, 42
Olaf Liljekrans, 36
  dramaturgy of, 36, 94
  Shakespeare's influence on, 94
"On the Fells," 55n
*On the Importance of Knowledge of
  Oneself,* 6
"On the Vidde," 170
Othello (Shakespeare), 48, 50
Overskou, Thomas, 31, 32

P

Peer Gynt, 2, 5, 10, 17, 43, **63-79,** 98,
  105, 138, 169-70, 171, 174, 177, 178
  myth in, 8
  psychological insight in, 63-79
  self-realization, theme of, 6-7, 14,
    76-79
  truth, theme of, 26
"Phenomenology of the Spirit in Fairy
  Tales" (Jung), 158
Pillars of Society, The, 14, 51, 99,
  140-57 *passim,* 170, 171
  dramaturgy of, 36, 37-38
Pretenders, The, 29, 53
  dramaturgy of, 96
  Scribe's influence on, 96
  Shakespeare's influence on, 48-49,
    51, 96
Ptarmigan of Justedal, The, 35

R

Racine, Jean, 115
Raphael, Robert, 10
Raüber, Die (Schiller), 42
Riesman, David, 14
Ring of the Nibelungs, The (Wagner),
  63-64, 73
Romantische Schule, Die (Hettner), 31
Romeo and Juliet (Shakespeare), 30,
  42
Rosmersholm, 2, 36, 51, 120, 123,

Rosmersholm (*continued*)
  124-27, 128, 130n, 140-51 *passim*,
    169, 172, 175, 177
  dramaturgy of, 39
  illusion in, 120, 124-27
  myth in, 9
  truth, theme of, 22-23, 27-28
Royal Court Theatre, Copenhagen, 30-
  31, 42
Royal Theatre, Copenhagen, 30-31

S

Schechner, Richard, 9
Schiller, Johann Christoph von, 3, 33,
  42, 46
Schnitzler, Arthur, 1n
Schopenhauer, Arthur, 82
Scott, Walter, 85
Scribe, Eugène, 5, 30, 31, 46, 47, 93,
  94-95, 96, 98, 99, 109
Shakespeare, William, 1, 2, 5, 9, 17,
  30, 31, 33, **41-51**, 92, 93-94, 96,
  103n, 115, 145
"Shakespeare and His Influence on
  Nordic Art," 41-42, 45
Shaw, G. B., 52-53, 57, 116, 126, 177,
  178
Sophocles, 103n, 111, 115
Stace, W. T., 10
Steiner, George, 9
Strindberg, August, 4, 5-6, 29, 130n,
  169
Svend Dyring's House (Hertz), 45
Svendsen, Paulus, 7

T

Tennant, P. F. D., 5
Themes, in Ibsen's works:
  art, 55, 55n, 62, 149-50, 162-64
  historical process, 7-8, 80-90
  idealism, 52, 56-57, 62
  illusion, 120-30
  radicalism, 14-16, 170-71
  self-realization, 2-3, 6-7, 12-14, 17,
    19, 21, 44-45, **56-60**, 76-79,
    120-30, 132-38

tragedy, **91-108**, **109-19**, 138
truth, **3-10**, **18-28**, 54-62 *passim*
Thoreau, Henry David, 173
Tieck, Ludwig, 37
Trilling, Lionel, 12

V

Vikings at Helgeland, The:
  dramaturgy of, 35, 36, 94-95, 97
  Scribe's influence on, 95
  Shakespeare's influence on, 48, 51
Volsung saga, 48

W

Wagner, Richard, 9, 63-64, 68, 73, 119
Warrior's Barrow, The, 30, 42
  dramaturgy of, 33, 35
  Shakespeare's influence on, 94
Weh dem, der lügt (Grillparzer), 18
Wergeland, Henrik, 42, 45, 85
When We Dead Awaken, 3, 8, 17, 123,
  140-57 *passim*, **158-68**, 175, 177
  art, theme of, 55n, 149-50, 162-64
  dramaturgy of, 36, 167-68
  symbolism in, 167-68
  truth, theme of, 28
Whitman, Walt, 173
Wild Duck, The, 17, 32, 51, 118,
  120-24, 128, 130, 130n, 140-57
  passim, 171, 174, 176
  dramaturgy of, 34, 39-40
  illusion in, 120-24
  myth in, 9
  self-realization, theme of, 12, 13,
    120-24
  symbolism in, 121
  truth, theme of, 23, 24-25, 45
Williams, Tennessee, 130n
Woerner, Roman, 48, 49, 130n
Wordsworth, William, 10, 177

Z

Zola, Émile, 4
Zucher, A. E.,
  49-50

HENRY JAMES

A Collection of Critical Essays

Edited by LEON EDEL

A

Abbey, Edwin, 147
Adams, Henry, 150
AE (*see* Russell, George)
Aeschylus, 28
Allston, Washington, 142
"Altar of the Dead, The," 26, 47, 177
Ambassadors, The, 9, 12, **37-46,** 57,
  65, 67, 69, 72-78, 86, 96, 100, 120,
  127, 151
American, The, 30, 67, 112, 113, 114,
  118, 121, 128, 143
American Scene, The, 33, 139
America's Coming of Age (Brooks), 71
Anderson, Quentin, 8, 9
Antony and Cleopatra (Shakespeare),
  25
Apes of God, The (Lewis), 110
Artistic genius, theme of, 18, 146-49
"Aspern Papers, The," 25, 65, 172
Atlantic, 79
Augier, Émile, 124
Austen, Jane, 114
Awkward Age, The, 65, 97, 98, 113,
  114, 125, 149

B

Bacon, Sir Francis, 8
Balzac, Honoré de, 9, 33, 34, 66, 104
Baudelaire, Charles, 79, 105
Beach, Joseph Warren, 6
Beard, Charles, 5

Beard, Mary, 5
"Beast in the Jungle, The," 172, 177
Beaumont, Joseph, 128
"Beldonald Holbein, The," 151
Bennett, Arnold, 60, 61
Benson, A. C., 126
Bernini, 145
Better Sort, The, 178
Blackmur, R. P., 6, 9
Bocaccio, 173
Boon (Wells), 80
Bosanquet, Theodora, 94
Bostonians, The, 57, 65, 113, 146
Bourget, Paul, 126
Bronzino, 128
Brooks, Van Wyck, 3, 4, 6, 9-10, 63-71
  passim, 80, 81, 83, 84, 92
Brownell, W. C., 142
Browning, Robert, 65
"Bundle of Letters, A," 29
Burr, A. R., 118

C

Cabell, James Branch, 89
Cantwell, Robert, 4
Chapman, John Jay, 59
Chaucer, Geoffrey, 173
Confidence, 174n
Conrad, Joseph, 111, 112, 123, 157
Conscience, importance of, 15, 25, 81
Courbet, Gustave, 167
"Covering End," 149
Crane, Stephen, 123

Curie, Pierre, 30

D

Daily News, 24
"Daisy Miller," 119, 123, 172
D'Annunzio, Gabriele, 89
Dante, 71
Daumier, Honoré, 148
Davies, W. H., 103
"Death of the Lion, The," 25
Defoe, Daniel, 73
Degas, 131
Dickens, Charles, 19, 62, 66, 104
Donne, John, 106
Dostoevsky, F., 56, 59, 60, 62, 119,
    156, 160
Dreiser, Theodore, 89
Duchess of Malfi (Webster), 106-7
Dumas, Alexandre, 36
Du Maurier, George, 148
Dupee, F. W., 8

E

Edgar, Pelham, 6
Education Sentimentale, L' (Flaubert),
    29
Eliot, George, 94, 131
Eliot, T. S., 6, 7, 60, 79
Elliott, Gertrude, 26
Embarrassments, 177
Emerson, R. W., 136
Europeans, The, 113, 114
Evan Harrington (Meredith), 73

F

Fadiman, Clifton, 6
Fiction, theory of, 2, 31, **84-90**, 95,
    173-74
"Figure in the Carpet, The," 25, 178
Flaubert, Gustave, 29, 31, 32, 88, 104,
    114
Forbes-Robertson, Ian, 22, 23, 26
Ford, Ford Madox, 61, 123
Form, importance of, 31, 33-36, 85,
    86, 97

Fourierism, 157
France, Anatole, 76
Frank, Waldo, 57
"Friends of the Friends, The," 49, 50

G

Galsworthy, John, 101
Gavarni, 148
Geismar, Maxwell, 4
Gide, André, 88
Giotto, 142
Glasgow, Ellen, 59
Goethe, J. W. von, 1
Golden Bowl, The, 2, 24, 36, 57, 60,
    65, 68, 69, 106, 112, 118, 121, 127,
    130, 132, 134, 135, 136, 144, 152,
    177
Goncourt, Edmond, 88, 144
Goncourt, Jules, 88, 144
Gorgias (Plato), 127
Goya, 131
"Great Good Place, The," 47-48
Great Tradition, The (Leavis), 57

H

Hardy, Thomas, 59, 66, 92, 94, 111
Harland, Henry, 123
Harper's, 79, 147
Hawthorne, Nathaniel, 5, 58, 66, 123,
    127, 132, 136, 140, 141, 144, 155,
    165
Hedda (Ibsen), 124, 125
Henley, W. E., 29
Henry James: Man and Author
    (Edgar), 6
Herrick, Robert, 59
High Bid, The, 22, 26
Hoare, Dorothy, 7
Hound and Horn, 6
Howells, W. D., 32, 33, 69, 82, 123,
    148, 178

I

Ibsen, Henrik, 123, 124, 125
In the American Jungle (Frank), 57

Ivory Tower, The, 56, 110, 111, 119, 127, 130, 137, 154

J

James, Alice, 117, 118, 119, 157
James Family, The (Matthiessen), 7
James, Garth Wilkinson, 118
James, Henry:
  artistic development of, 55-56, 147-55, 174-79 *passim*
  biographical information, 27, 63, 83, 115-19 *passim*, 123-24, 156-57
  and civilization, importance of in works, 9, 25, 28, 93, 140, 143, 150
  and evil, sense of, 111-22 *passim*, 135-37
  expatriation of, 1, 3, 57-62, 63-69, 80, 82-84, 92, 143
  international theme, in works of, 27-30, 108, 113, 175-77
  and moral values, 18, 31, 66-68, 81-82, 89-91, 106, 108-10, 112, 138, 143-44, 178-79
  point of view, importance of, **37-46**
  romanticism of, 56, 95, 136
  and supernatural, **47-54**, 178-79
  works of art, in the work of, 1, **139-55**
James, Henry, works by:
  "Altar of the Dead, The," 26, 47, 177
  Ambassadors, The, 9, 12, **37-46**, 57, 65, 67, 69, **72-78,** 86
  American, The, 30, 67, 112, 113, 114, 118, 121, 128, 143
  American Scene, The, 33, 139
  "Aspern Papers, The," 25, 65, 172
  Awkward Age, The, 65, 97, 98, 113, 114, 125, 149
  "Beast in the Jungle, The," 172, 177
  "Beldonald Holbein, The," 151
  Better Sort, The, 178
  Bostonians, The, 57, 65, 113, 146
  "Bundle of Letters, A," 29

Confidence, 174n
"Covering End," 149
"Daisy Miller," 119, 123, 172
"Death of the Lion, The," 25
Embarassments, 177
Europeans, The, 113, 114
"Figure in the Carpet, The," 25, 178
"Friends of the Friends, The," 49, 50
Golden Bowl, The, 2, 24, 36, 57, 60, 65, 68, 69, 106, 112, 118, 121, 127, 130, 132, 134, 135, 136, 144, 152, 177
"Great Good Place, The," 47-48
High Bid, The, 22, 26
Ivory Tower, The, 56, 110, 111, 119, 127, 130, 137, 154
"Jolly Corner, The," 120
"Lesson of the Master, The," 25
"Liar, The," 147
Little Tour in France, A, 145
"Madonna of the Future, The," 142
"Middle Years, The," 25
"Mrs. Temperley," 147
"New England Winter, A," 146
Notes of a Son and Brother, 8, 116
Other House, The, 97
Outcry, The, 97
"Owen Wingrave," 50
Passionate Pilgrim and Other Tales, A, 173
"Pension Beaurepas, The," 119
Portrait of a Lady, The, 24, 57, 67, 75, 80, 95, 112, 143, 145, 149, 159
Portraits of Places, 145
Princess Casamassima, The, 95, 110, **157-71**
"Real Thing, The," 149
Reverberator, The, 174
Roderick Hudson, 80, 143
"Round of Visits, A," 119
Sacred Fount, The, 36, 69, 112, 149
Sense of the Past, The, 56, 128, 131, 133, 154, 155
Small Boy and Others, A, 116, 120
Soft Side, The, 177, 178

James, Henry, works by: (*continued*)
  "Special Type, The," 151
  Spoils of Poynton, The, 69, 75, 88, 95, 96, 97, 120, 123, 149
  Terminations, 177
  "Tone of Time, The," 151
  Tragic Muse, The, 28, 95, 110, 113, 148
  Transatlantic Sketches, 145
  "Traveling Companions," 141
  "Turn of the Screw, The," 2, 9, 28, 53, 69, 117, 149, 172, 174, 178
  Two Magics, The, 26, 149
  Washington Square, 57, 114
  Watch and Ward, 174n
  What Maisie Knew, 65, 68, 77, 97, 98, 149
  Wings of the Dove, The, 24, 36, 50, 57, 65, 67, 69, 77, 94, 96, 98, 99, 110, 115, 124, 125, 127, 151, 155
James, Henry, Sr., 63, 116, 124
James, Robertson, 118
James, William, 6, 57, 58, 92, 116, 117, 118, 124
Jerome, Jerome, 22
Johnson, Samuel, 2
"Jolly Corner, The," 120
Joyce, James, 6, 60, 103, 104
Jude the Obscure (Hardy), 111

K

Kazin, Alfred, 9
Kenton, Edna, 6
Kenyon Review, 139
King, Henry, 128

L

La Farge, John, 141
Lamb, Charles, 24
Lawrence, D. H., 61, 119, 165
Leavis, F. R., 9, 57, 59
Legend of the Master, The (Nowell-Smith), 8
Leonardo da Vinci, 141
"Lesson of the Master, The," 25

Lewes, G. H., 131
Lewis, Sinclair, 70
Lewis, Wyndham, 61, 103, 110
"Liar, The," 147
Little Tour in France, A, 145
Loti, Pierre, 34, 36
Lowell, James, Russell, 136
Lubbock, Percy, 7, 35, 60, 96, 111

M

MacCarthy, Desmond, 58, 119
Mackenzie, Compton, 35
"Madonna of the Future, The," 142
Maeterlinck, Maurice, 123, 124, 125
Major Phase, The (Matthiessen), 7
Mallarmé, Stéphane, 86
Mare, Walter de la, 103
Marble Faun, The (Hawthorne), 140
Marivaux, 1
Marxism, 4, 10, 105, 119-20
Master Builder (Ibsen), 124, 125
Matthiessen, F. O., 7, 8, 139, 140, 149
Maugham, Somerset, 58, 61
Melville, Herman, 5
Memling, 128
Meredith, George, 37, 65, 73
Method, 24-25, 34-36, **37-46**, 74-78, 86-91 *passim*, **95-101**, 104-7, 162-65
"Middle Years, The," 25
Millet, Frank, 147
Molière, 66, 124
Monet, Claude, 146
Moral order, importance of, 18, 31, 66-68, 87-88, 90-91, 137, 150-151
More, Paul Elmer, 59, 61
"Mrs. Temperley," 147
Murdock, Kenneth, 7

N

Newcomes, The (Thackeray), 85
"New England Winter, A," 146
New York Edition, 6, 128, 173
Norton, C. E., 136, 149
Notebooks (Hawthorne), 141
Notebooks of Henry James, The, (ed. Matthiessen and Murdock), 7

Notes of a Son and Brother, 8, 116
Nowell-Smith, Simon, 8

O

Ordeal of Mark Twain, The (Brooks),
  63, 71
Other House, The, 97
Outcry, The, 97
"Owen Wingrave," 50

P

Parrington, Vernon, 4
Parsons, Alfred, 147
Passing of the Third-Floor Back, The
  (Jerome), 22
Passionate Pilgrim and Other Tales, A,
  173
Pater, Walter, 123, 140
"Pension Beaurepas, The," 119
Perkins, Maxwell, 6
Perry, Ralph Barton, 6, 7
Personal relations, importance of, 67-
  68, 81-82, 93, 126-27, 166, 174-75
Phaedrus (Plato), 127
Phillips, Le Roy, 6
Picture of Dorian Gray, The (Wilde),
  155
Pilgrimage of Henry James, The
  (Brooks), 6, 63, 64, 80, 92
Plato, 71, 127
Poe, E. A., 5
Portrait of a Lady, The, 24, 57, 67,
  75, 80, 95, 112, 143, 145, 149, 159
Portraits of Places, 145
Pound, Ezra, 2, 6, 60, 79, 103
Prefaces, 35, 84, 115
Princess Casamassima, The, 95, 110,
  157-71
Proust, Marcel, 4, 104

Q

Queen Victoria (Strachey), 71
Question of Henry James, The
  (Dupee), 8

R

Racine, 1, 66, 124, 125, 126
Radcliffe, Mrs. Ann, 49
Rahv, Philip, 6
Raphael, 141, 142, 149
"Real Thing, The," 149
Renoir, Pierre A., 146
Renunciation, theme of, 14-17,
  168-69, 175
Republic, 127
Reverberator, The, 174
Richards, I. A., 102
Richelieu, Duc de, 110
Rise of American Civilization, The
  (Beard), 4
Roderick Hudson, 80, 143
Rosenfeld, Paul, 61
Roughead, William, 126
"Round of Visits, A," 119
Russell, George (*pseud.* AE), 59, 61

S

Sacred Fount, The, 36, 69, 112, 149
Sardou, Victorien, 124
Sargent, John Singer, 147, 148
Scarlet Letter, The (Hawthorne), 132,
  144
Schapiro, Meyer, 167
Secret Agent, The (Conrad), 112
Sense of the Past, The, 56, 128, 131,
  133, 154, 155
Shakespeare, William, 1, 8, 24, 66, 71,
  79, 122
Shaw, G. B., 4, 18-22 *passim*
Small Boy and Others, A, 116, 120
Soft Side, The, 177, 178
"Special Type, The," 151
Spoils of Poynton, The, 69, 75, 88, 95,
  96, 97, 120, 123, 149
Stein, Gertrude, 60
Stevenson, R. L., 123, 148, 172
Story, William Wetmore, 60, 142, 147
Strachey, Lytton, 71
Sturgis, Howard, 126
Style, 3-4, 12-14, 23-26, 51-54, 59, 85,
  94-95, 99-101, 104, 174-79

Stylistic devices, 42-43, 55, 68, 72, 77, 97, 100-1, 124-32, 137, 154-55, 163, 174-79
Subject, importance of, 31-33, 35, 83, 96, 108
Swedenborgianism, 8, 121-22
Symbols, 8, 9, 104, 123-38, 144-45, 153-54

T

Tempest, The (Shakespeare), 125
Temple, Mary, 98, 115, 116
Terminations, 177
Thackeray, William M., 33, 37, 104
Thaïs (France), 72
Thought and Character of William James, The (Perry), 7
Times, 27
Tintoretto, 145
Titian, 128, 145
Tolstoi, Leo, 34, 59, 62, 66, 71, 85, 104, 119
"Tone of Time, The," 151
Tono Bungay (Wells), 73
Toulouse-Lautrec, 131
Tragic Muse, The, 28, 95, 110, 113, 148
Transatlantic Sketches, 145
"Traveling Companions," 141
Trilling, Lionel, 9, 161, 169
Trois Mousquetaires, Les (Dumas), 85
Trollope, Anthony, 59, 73
Turgenev, Ivan, 58, 64
Turner, J. M. W., 116
"Turn of the Screw, The," 2, 9, 28, 53, 69, 117, 149, 172, 174, 178
Twain, Mark, 70, 71, 84

Two Magics, The, 26, 149

V

Van Eyck, 128
Velasquez, 147
Veronese, 128, 145

W

Walkley, A. B., 23
War and Peace (Tolstoi), 85
Ward, Mrs. Humphry, 34, 100
Warren, Austin, 139-40
Washington Square, 57, 114
Waste Land, The (Eliot), 102, 103
Watch and Ward, 174n
Webster, John, 106, 107
Wells, H. G., 4, 33, 35, 36, 73, 79, 80, 85, 93, 94
Wharton, Edith, 6, 60, 126
What Maisie Knew, 65, 68, 77, 97, 98, 149
Whitman, Walt, 5, 83
Wilde, Oscar, 123
Wilder, Thornton, 89
Wilson, Edmund, 6, 10
Wings of the Dove, The, 24, 36, 50, 57, 65, 67, 69, 77, 94, 96, 98, 99, 110, 115, 124, 125, 127, 151, 155

Y

Yeats, William Butler, 1
Yellow Book, 123

Z

Zabel, Morton, 9
Zola, Émile, 88-89

SAMUEL JOHNSON

A Collection of Critical Essays

Edited by DONALD J. GREENE

A

Abrams, M. H., 58, 127
Account of the Commemoration of Handel (Burney), Johnson's Dedication to, 175
Achievement of Samuel Johnson, The, (Bate), 7, 61, 154
Adam, R. B., 48, 49
Adventurer, The, Johnson's contributions to, 42-43
Age of Johnson, The, 51
Akenside, Mark, 161
Antony and Cleopatra (Shakespeare), Johnson's comments on, 129
Aristotle, 99, 160
Arnold, Matthew, 86, 87
Artificial Bastard, The: A Biography of Richard Savage (Tracy), 60
Atkins, J. W. H., 103
Augustan language, Johnson's use of, 70-88

B

Babbitt, Irving, 158-59
Bailey, John, 51
Bailey, Nathan, 55
Balderston, Katharine, 17, 51
Baretti, Giuseppe, 67
Bate, Walter Jackson, 7, 58, 61, 154
Bentham, Jeremy, 171
Bentley, Richard, 64
Berkeley, George, 36, 57

Blake, William, 97
Books and Characters (Strachey), 58
Boswell, James, 11-12, 17, 21, 27, 30, 31, 32, 34, 42, 47-48, 60, 62, 63-65, 67, 109, 110, 173, 174, 176
  archives of, 49, 52
Bradley, A. C., 82
Bridges, Robert, 58
Bronson, Bertrand, 19, 56
Brown, Stuart G., 56, 57, 58
Burney, Fanny, 30, 174
Butler, Samuel, 130
Butt, John, 124
Byng, Adm. John, 42
Byron, George Gordon, 46

C

"Canonization, The" (Donne), 101
Carlyle, Thomas, 174
Castaway, The (Cowper), 77
Chambers, Ephraim, 121-22
Chapman, R. W., 6-7, 49, 52-53
Cheke, Sir John, 117
Clifford, James L., 22, 60
Coleridge, Samuel Taylor, 158-59
Collection of Poems (Dodsley, ed.), Johnson's revisions for, 177
Collins, J. Churton, 58
Collins, William, Johnson's *Life* of, 67
Comus (Milton), 74, 75, 76, 128
Congreve, William, Johnson's *Life* of, 81-82
"Cooper's Hill" (Denham), 90

Cowley, Abraham, Johnson's *Life* of, 59, 79, 87, 94-97, 137
Cowper, William, 77
Crabbe, George, 77
Criticism, Johnson's works of, 4-5, 13, 58-60, 70-88, 89-101, 102-13 *(see also Lives of the Poets)*
Cymbeline (Shakespeare), Johnson's comments on, 126

D

Dante Alighieri, 117
Davis, Bertram H., 60
De Anima (Aristotle), 160
Debates in Parliament, 145
Dedications and Prefaces, 52, 172-78
Deism, Johnson's rejection of, 158-71
Denham, Sir John, Johnson's *Life* of, 74, 75, 90-91, 92, 94
De Quincey, Thomas, 58
Dialogues Concerning Natural Religion (Hume), 171
Diaries, Prayers, and Annals, 61
Dictionary, 6, 18, 55, 103, 106, 114-23, 125-36 *passim*, 173, 174
   and the French Academy, 114-15
   Plan of, 114, 115, 141, 175
Diderot, Denis, 168
Doctor Johnson: A Study in Eighteenth Century Humanism (Houston), 51
Dr. Johnson and Fanny Burney (Tinker), 51
Dr. Johnson and His Circle (Bailey), 51
Dr. Johnson and the English Law (McAdam), 61
Dr. Johnson's Dictionary (Kolb), 61
Dodd, William, 42
Dodsley, Robert, 173, 177
Donne, John, 87, 91-92, 95, 96, 97, 100-1
Dryden, John, 56, 67, 87, 101, 131-32
   Johnson's *Life* of, 67, 74, 129

E

Elegy Written in a Country Church-
yard (Gray), 86-87
Eliot, T. S., 4, 54
Enneads (Plotinus), 160, 161, 162
Essay Concerning Human Understanding (Locke), 161
"Essay on Epitaphs," 67-68
Evelina (Burney), 30
"Extasie, The" (Donne), 100-1

F

Fielding, Henry, 21
Franklin, Benjamin, 50
Free Inquiry into the Nature and Origin of Evil (Jenyns), 159, 163-66, 170-71
Freud, Sigmund, 145-50, 154-55
Further Thoughts on Agriculture, 56

G

Gateways to Literature (Matthews), 48
Gissing, Algernon, 50
Goldsmith, Oliver, 68, 73, 77
Grange, Kathleen M., 61
Gray, Thomas, 58-59, 77
   Johnson's *Life* of, 85-87
Greene, Donald J., 62

H

Hagstrum, Jean H., 7
Hallett, H. F., 57
Harding, D. W., 78
Hazen, Allen T., 53, 61
Henry V (Shakespeare), Johnson's comments on, 133
Henry VI (Shakespeare), Johnson's comments on, 133
Henry VIII (Shakespeare), Johnson's comments on, 129, 133
Hemlow, Joyce, 60-61
Hill, G. B., 49, 53, 56
Hilles, F. W., 60
History of Fanny Burney, The (Hemlow), 60-61
Housman, A. E., 67
Houston, Percy H., 51

Hudibras (Butler), 130
Hume, David, 36, 39, 56, 57, 171
Hyde, Donald, 49, 52

I

Idler, The, 27, 43, 53, 55, 105
   Christian beliefs in, 168-69
   psychological perceptions in, 150-
     51, 152
Imagery, scientific, in *The Rambler,*
   138-48
Irene, 54, 80, 97
Isham, Col. Ralph, 49

J

James, Robert, 52
Jenyns, Soame, 159, 163-66, 170-71
Johnson, Charles F., 125-26
Johnson, Michael (father), 22, 23-24,
   26, 33-34
Johnson, Sarah (mother), 22-29
Johnson, Samuel:
   and Augustan language, 70-88
   biographical information, 15-17,
     22-29
   biographies of, 50-52
   and Boswell, James, 11-12, 17, 21,
     27, 30, 31, 32, 34, 42, 47-48, 62,
     63-65, 67, 109, 110, 173, 174,
     176
   Christian beliefs of, 166-71
   critical writings, 4-5, 13, 58-60,
     70-88, 89-101, 102-13 (*see also*
     Lives of the Poets, The)
   and deism, 158-71
   and Donne, John, 91-92, 95, 96, 97,
     100-1
   and Dryden, John, 70, 74
   as an editor, 104
   and Freud, Sigmund, 149-50,
     154-55
   linguistic theories of, 115-23
   and Locke, John, 94-95
   on the Metaphysical poets, 89-101
   misconceptions about, 1-3, 15, 21,
     39, 46-48

   nineteenth-century views of, 46-48,
     58, 59
   and the patronage system, 173-78
   personality of, 5, 16-18, 30-34, 42
   philosophical and moral beliefs, 20-
     21, **35-45**, 53, **158-71**
   poetry of, 4, 14, 54, 63-69, **80-81**,
     106
   political beliefs, 3, 18-20, 34-35,
     38-45, 55-57
   and Pope, Alexander, 92, 124
   psychoanalytical perceptions of,
     149-57
   and Rousseau, Jean-Jacques, 21, 39-
     41, 42, 159, 168
   scientific imagery of, 138-48
   on social issues, 39-45, 56, 165,
     168-69
   and Thrale, Mrs., 25, 28, 48, 49, 51,
     63, 67, 68, 156-57, 175, 176
Johnson, Samuel, works by:
   Debates in Parliament, 145
   Dedications and Prefaces, 52,
     172-78
   Diaries, Prayers and Annals, 61
   Dictionary, 6, 18, 55, 103, 106,
     114-23, 125-36 *passim,* 173-74
   editions of, 48-50, 52-53, 60-61, 63
   Further Thoughts on Agriculture,
     56
   Idler, The, 27, 43, 53, 55, 105,
     150-51, 152, 168-69
   Irene, 54, 80, 97
   Journey to the Western Islands of
     Scotland, 49, 50
   Letters, 52-53
   Lives of the Poets, The, 13, 49, 53,
     58-59, 66-67, 89-101, 103, 105,
     111, 124, 125, 128, 173 (*see*
     main entry)
   London, 14, 37-38, 52
   Marmor Norfolciense, 18, 56
   Notes to Shakespeare, 124-37 (*see*
     also Preface to Shakespeare)
   Poems, 4, 14, 54, **63-69**, 80-81,
     106
   Prayers and Meditations, 21
   Preface to Shakespeare, 13, 21, 33,

Johnson, Samuel, works by: (Preface to Shakespeare) (*continued*) 76-79, 82-86, 102-3, 105, 108, 111-12, 124-25, 165 (*see also* Notes to Shakespeare)
  Rambler, The, 29, 44, 53, 55, 83-84, 105, **138-48**, 151, 152-56
  Rasselas, 40-41, 47, 55, 79
  Taxation No Tyranny, 19, 34-35, 56, 166
  Vanity of Human Wishes, The, 4, 14, 52, 54, 64, 68-69, 80-81, 164, 177
  Vindication of the Licensers of the Stage, 18
Johnson Agonistes (Bronson), 19
Johnson Before Boswell (Davis), 60
Johnsonian Gleanings (Reade), 5, 15n, 50
Johnsonian Miscellanies (Hill), 49
Journey to the Western Islands of Scotland, 49, 50

K

Ker, W. P., 106
King, Henry, 161-62
King John (Shakespeare), Johnson's comments on, 130, 132, 133, 134
King Lear (Shakespeare), Johnson's comments on, 21, 33, 108
Kolb, Gwin J., 61
Krutch, Joseph Wood, 7, 11-14, 51, 56, 58

L

Laithwaite, Percy, 50
Langton, Bennet, 26
Laski, Harold J., 171
Leavis, F. R., 58-59, 125
Lewis, Nöel, 59-60
Lewis, Wyndham, 48
Liebert, Herman W., 52
Life of Johnson, The (Boswell), 11-12, 27, 30-31, 32, 34, 41-42, 47-48, 62, 173, 174, 176
  editions of, 49-50

Linguistic theory, and the *Dictionary*, 115-23
Lives of the Poets, The, 13, 49, 53, 58-59, 66-67, 89-101, 103, 105, 111, 124, 125, 128, 173
  Collins, 67
  Congreve, 81-82
  Cowley, 59, 79, 87, 94-97, 137
  Denham, 74, 75, 90-91, 92, 94
  Dryden, 67, 74, 129
  Gray, 58-59, 85-87
  Milton, 72-74, 75-76
  Pope, 64, 74, 83, 109-10
  Savage, 29, 108, 112
  Swift, 59, 88
  Waller, 74-75, 92-93
Lloyd, William, 119
Locke, John, 94-95, 161
London, 14, 37-38, 52
Longinus, 97
Lovejoy, A. O., 161
Love's Labour's Lost (Shakespeare), Johnson's comments on, 136
"Lycidas" (Milton), 59, 67, 74, 75-76, 129, 131

M

McAdam, E. L., 61
Macaulay, T. B., 3, 11, 158
  on Johnson, 46-47
Macbeth (Shakespeare), Johnson's comments on, 33, 106-7, 127, 130, 132
McNulty, J. B., 59
Macpherson, James, 31
Mandeville, Bernard, 165
Marmor Norfolciense, 18, 56
Martin, Benjamin, 117-18
Matthews, Brander, 48
Measure for Measure (Shakespeare), Johnson's comments on, 129
Medicinal Dictionary (James), 52
Metaphysical poets, Johnson's views on, 89-101
Metaphysics (Aristotle), 160
Middendorf, John H., 61
Milton, John, 59, 67, 128, 129, 131

Milton, John, (*continued*)
  Johnson's *Life* of, 72-74, 75-76
Modern Temper, The (Krutch), 14
Mossé, Fernand, 119
Mossner, Ernest, 57

N

Namier, Sir Lewis, 4
Newton, A. Edward, 48, 49
"Nocturnall upon S. Lucie's Day, A"
  (Donne), 91
Notes to Shakespeare, 124-27 (*see also*
  Preface to Shakespeare)
Noyes, Alfred, 54, 59

O

"Of Wit" (Cowley), 96
"On the Death of Mr. Levet," 65-66,
  67
Osgood, Charles G., 53-54

P

Pageant of Letters, The (Noyes), 54
Paradise Lost (Milton), 73
Patronage system, Johnson's involve-
  ment with, 173-78
Perilous Balance, The (Watkins), 51
Phillips, Claudy, 68
Philosophical and moral beliefs, in
  Johnson's works, 20-21, 35-45, 53,
  158-71
Physico-grammatical Essay (Martin),
  117-18, 121-22
Piozzi, Mrs. (*see* Thrale, Mrs.)
Pleasures of the Imagination, The
  (Akenside), 161
Plotinus, 160, 161, 162
Poe, Edgar Allan, 93, 100
Poems, 4, 14, 54, 63-69, 80-81, 106
Poetics (Aristotle), 99
Poetry as a Means of Grace (Osgood),
  53-54
Political beliefs, in Johnson's works, 3,
  18-20, 34-35, 38-45, 55-57
Politics of Samuel Johnson, The
  (Greene), 62

Pope, Alexander, 47, 77, 79, 84, 92,
  124
  Johnson's *Life* of, 64, 74, 83,
    109-10
Pope's Taste in Shakespeare (Butt),
  124
Porter, Lucy, 26-27, 28
Portraits by Sir Joshua Reynolds
  (Hilles), 60
Pottle, Frederick A., 49, 58
Powell, L. F., 6-7, 49, 50
Prayers and Meditations, 21
Preface to Shakespeare, 13, 21, 33,
  76-79, 82-86, 102-3, 105, 108,
  111-12, 124-25, 165 (*see also* Notes
  to Shakespeare)
Prelude, The (Wordsworth), 101
"Prologues," 66
*Proposals for Printing the Dramatick
  Works of William Shakespeare*, 102
Psychoanalytical perceptions, in John-
  son's works, 149-57

Q

Quinlan, Maurice, 50

R

Raleigh, Sir Walter, 51, 102, 110
Rambler, The, 29, 44, 53, 55, 83-84,
  105
  psychoanalytic perceptions in, 151,
    152-56
  scientific imagery in, 138-48
Rasselas, 40-41, 47, 55, 79
  psychoanalytic perceptions in, 150
Reade, Aleyn Lyell, 5, 15, 50, 51
Reynolds, Sir Joshua, 38, 174, 175
Richardson, Samuel, 21, 45
Rochester, Earl of (*see* Wilmot, John)
Rousseau, Jean-Jacques, 21, 39-41, 42,
  159, 168

S

Sainte-Beuve, Charles, 106

Samuel Johnson (Krutch), 7, 11-14, 51, 58

Samuel Johnson's Literary Criticism (Hagstrum), 7

Sargeaunt, John, 56

Savage, Richard, Johnson's *Life* of, 18, 29, 108, 112

Scott, Geoffrey, 49

Scott, Sir Walter, 46, 54, 68

Seasons, The (Thomson), 161

Second Greatest Man, The (Lewis), 59-60

Seven Discourses (Reynolds), 174, 175

Shakespeare, William, 21, 33, 106-7, 108, 126, 127, 130, 132 (*see also* titles of individual plays)

Shelley, Percy Bysshe, 106

Six Essays on Johnson (Raleigh), 51

Sledd, James H., 61

Smith, D. Nichol, 51, 52, 54, 55, 58, 131

Social issues, Johnson's thought on, 39-45, 56, 165, 168-69

"Song to David," 63

Steevens, George, 36

Stendhal, 106

Stephen, Leslie, 34, 50

Sterne, Laurence, 21

Strachey, Lytton, 58, 107

Swift, Jonathan, 47, 56, 122
  Johnson's *Life* of, 88

Symons, Julian, 59

T

Taxation No Tyranny, 19, 34-35, 56, 166

Thomson, James, 161

Thrale, Mrs., 25, 28, 48, 49, 51, 63, 67, 68, 156-57, 175, 176

Timon of Athens (Shakespeare),

Johnson's comments on, 130, 136

Tinker, Chauncey, 11, 48, 51

Tooke, Horne, 121

Toryism (*see* Johnson: political beliefs)

Tour to the Hebrides (see Journey to the Western Islands of Scotland)

Tracy, C. R., 60

Turner, William, 122

U

"Upon the Feast of St. Simon and St. Jude," 63, 66

V

Valéry, Paul, 100

Vanity of Human Wishes, The, 4, 14, 52, 54, 64, 68-69, 80-81, 177

View of the Internal Evidence of the Christian Religion, A (Jenyns), 159

Vindication of the Licensers of the Stage, 18

Voltaire, 39, 161

Vulliamy, C. E., 50-51

W

Waller, Edmund, Johnson's *Life* of, 74-75, 92-93

Watkins, W. B. C., 51

Webster, Noah, 121

Wilmot, John, Earl of Rochester, 87

Wilson, J. Dover, 82

Wimsatt, W. K., 55, 119

Winters, Yvor, 5

Wordsworth, William, 101, 106

Y

Young Sam Johnson (Clifford), 60

BEN JONSON

A Collection of Critical Essays

Edited by JONAS A. BARISH

A

Acharnians, The (Aristophanes), 106, 118

Alchemist, The, 15, 18, 20, 24, 27, 32, 38, 49, 50-51, 55, 61-65, 70-71, 79-80, **106-20,** 175

Anthony and Cleopatra (Shakespeare), 2, 47

Aretino, Pietro, 136

Aristophanes, 15, 58, 63, 83, 146

Aristotle, 40-41, 106, 161, 167

Art of Poetry (Horace), 55

L'Avare (Molière), 116

B

Bacon, Francis, 34, 42, 153

Bartholomew Fair, 1n, 18, 20, 48-50, 55-56, 63, 65, 71-72, 74, 78-79, 89, 122, 134, **141-46,** 175

Baudelaire, Charles, 12

Beaumont, Francis, 14, 20, 123

Bellum Catilinae (Sallust), 148-51

Bergson, Henri, 56, 106

Boileau-Despréaux, Nicolas, 40

Boswell, James, 5

Brandt, Sebastian, 45, 86

Brome, Richard, 21

Bunyan, John, 32, 33n

C

Campion, Thomas, 168

Carroll, Lewis, 73

Castiglione, Baldassare, 45, 89n

Catiline, 8-9, 15-18, 69-71, 73, **147-59**

Catullus, Gaius Valerius, 34, 44

Cervantes, 45

Chapman, George, 41, 47

Characterization, 7, 10-12, 18, 21, 25, 40-41, 48, 52-58, 62, 67-72, 78-81, 85-92, 107-9, 121

Chaucer, Geoffrey, 50

Cicero, 148

Coleridge, Samuel Taylor, 7-8, 35

Colman, George, 131-32

Comus (Milton), 23

Conversations, 3, 30n, 32n

Coriolanus (Shakespeare), 47, 123, 156

Corneille, Pierre, 40

Country Wife, The, 49

Courtier (Castiglione), 89

"Coy Mistress" (Marvell), 37

Cynthia's Revels, 64, 66, 68, 70, 89

D

Dante, 14, 171

Davies, John, 84

Dead Souls (Gogol), 73-74

Dedekind, Friedrich, 45

Dekker, Thomas, 41, 47, 78, 87, 123

Demeter (Tennyson), 73

Devil Is an Ass, The, 18, 30-32, 34, 36-38, 45, 64, 67

Dickens, Charles, 21, 72

Dio Cassius, 148, 151, 154, 155n

Discoveries, 27, 34, 42, 50, 83, 136
D'Israeli, Isaac, 3, 7*n*
Donne, John, 9-10, 14, 20, 37, 39,
  41-42, 74
Dowden, Edward, 54
Drummond, William, 3, 40, 49, 52, 57,
  69, 74, 83*n*, 175
Dryden, John, 1, 4, 9, 11, 14, 24, 43,
  50, 57, 62, 79, 132-33, 135
Durantinus, Constantius Felicius, 148,
  151

E

Eastward Ho, 46, 51, 175
"Ectasy, The" (Donne), 59
Elegy, 72
Eliot, T. S., 9-11, 37, 45-46, 52, 61-
  62, 76, 77*n*, 79, 133-34
Entertainment at Fenchurch, 164
Epicene, or The Silent Woman, 2, 15,
  17-18, 20, 36, 48-50, 56, 62, 64-66,
  72, 79, **121-41**, 146, 175
Erasmus, Desiderius, 45
Ethics (Aristotle), 167
Euripides, 15
Every Man In His Humour, 2, 18, 22,
  49-50, 67, 72, **75-83**, 85, 174
Every Man Out of His Humour, 10, 41,
  55, 65-66, 76, **82-92**

F

Faery Prince, The, 162
Famous Voyage, The, 71
Firbank, Ronald, 73
Flaubert, Gustave, 18, 70
Fleay, F. G., 87-88
Fletcher, John, 14, 20
Florio, John, 101
Ford, John, 3-4, 78
Forest, The, 42
Freud, Sigmund, 63, 106

G

"Gamblers" (Gogol), 115
Ghosts (Ibsen), 83

Gifford, William, 2*n*, 3*n*, 4*n*, 5, 8, 30,
  35, 38*n*, 60, 71-72, 80
Gilbert and Sullivan, 118
Gogol, Nikolai Vasilievich, 73-74, 115
Gordon, D. J., 172-73
Greene, Robert, 92*n*

H

Hamlet (Shakespeare), 17, 85
Heinsius, Daniel, 42
Henry IV (Shakespeare), 30, 108
Henry V (Shakespeare), 28*n*
Henry VIII (Shakespeare), 2
Henslowe, Philip, 175
Herford, C. H., 9-10, 60, 136*n*, 137,
  146
Hero and Leander (Marlowe), 54, 72
Herrick, Robert, 44
Heywood, Thomas, 41, 147
Histriomastix (Marston), 87
Hopkins, Gerard Manley, 39
Horace, 34-38, 40, 44, 55
Hulme, T. E., 8-9
Huxley, Aldous, 72
Hymenaei, 165*n*, 168-69

I

Ibsen, Sigurd, 83
In Memoriam (Tennyson), 72
Inspector General, The (Gogol), 73

J

Jew of Malta, The (Marlowe), 18, 27,
  46
Johnson, Samuel, 43, 107
Jones, Inigo, 53, 60, 165, 173, 176
Jonson, Ben:
  and Aristophanes, 146
  and Carroll, 73
  and Chaucer, 50-51
  and Firbank, 73
  and Gifford, 5
  and Gogol, 73-74
  influence of, 72
  and Joyce, 73-74

Jonson, Ben: (*continued*)
  life of, 1, 12, 42-43, 68-69, 74,
    175-76
  and Marlowe, 19, 52, 72
  and Massinger, 77
  and Milton, 72
  and Molière, 17
  personality of, 63-74
  as poet, 6-9, 18-19, 57
  and Shakespeare, 1-8, 11-15, 40-41,
    53-54, 58-59, 62, 67, 74, 77, 85,
    102, 155-59
  and Shaw, 76
  and Swift, 17
  style of, **40-59**
  and Tennyson, 72
Jonson, Ben, works by: (*see also* titles
  of individual works)
  Alchemist, The, 15, 18, 20, 24, 27,
    32, 38, 49, 50-51, 55, 61-65, 70-
    71, 79-80, 89, **106-20**, 175
  Bartholomew Fair, 1n, 18, 20, 48-
    50, 55-56, 63, 65, 71-72, 74,
    78-79, 89, 122, 134, **141-46**, 175
  Catiline, 8, 9, 15-18, 69-71, 73,
    147-59
  Conversations, 3, 30n, 32n
  Country Wife, The, 49
  Cynthia's Revels, 64, 66, 68, 70, 89
  Devil Is an Ass, The, 18, 30-32, 34,
    36-38, 45, 49, 64, 67
  Discoveries, 27, 34, 42, 50, 83, 136
  Eastward Ho, 46, 51, 175
  Elegy, 72
  Entertainment at Fenchurch, 164
  Epicene, or The Silent Woman, 2
    15, 17-18, 20, 36, 48-50, 56, 62,
    64-66, 72, 79, **121-41**, 146, 175
  Every Man In His Humour, 2, 18,
    22, 49-50, 67, 72, **75-83**, 85, 174
  Every Man Out of His Humour, 10,
    41, 55, 65-66, 76, **82-92**
  Faery Prince, The, 162
  Famous Voyage, The, 71
  Forest, The, 42
  Hymenaei, 165n, 168-69
  Lethe, 163-64
  Love Freed, 163

  Love Restored, 162, 167
  Love's Triumph, 166
  Magnetic Lady, The, 30
  Mandragola, 49
  Masque of Beauty, The, 172
  Masque of Blackness, The, 23, 165,
    167, 169, 172
  Masque of Queens, The, 58, 161-62,
    166, 168n
  Mercury Vindicated, 32, 162-63
  New Inn, The, 1n, 55
  News from the New World, 171-72
  Oberon, 162, 169-70
  "Ode to Himself," 1n
  Pleasure Reconciled to Virtue, 164
  Poetaster, The, 8, 16, 49, 66, 71,
    74, 87
  Sad Shepherd, The, 44
  Sejanus, 7, **25-31**, 35, 38, 42, 47,
    50, 63, 70-71, 147-48, 154,
    156-58
  Silent Woman, The (see Epicene)
  Staple of News, The, 33, 48, 52, 55,
    68, 81, 126
  Timber, 42
  Turcaret, 49
  Underwoods, 42, 72
  Vision of Delight, The, 54, 57, 68,
    73, 170
  Volpone, 8, 15, 18-20, 24-25, 27,
    29, 32, 36, 45-46, 48, 50-51, 55,
    61-73, 79, **93-105**, 175
  Works, 42, 75, 147, 175
Joyce, James, 73-74
Julius Caesar (Shakespeare), 156
Juvenal, 136

K

Kant, Immanuel, 106
Keats, John, 6, 30
King Lear (Shakespeare), 2, 158
Kipling, Rudyard, 62

L

Lethe, 163-64
Leviathan (Hobbes), 46

Levin, Harry, 61, 70, 80n, 94n, 121
Lodge, Thomas, 84
Lords Maske (Campion), 168
Love Freed, 163
Love Restored, 162, 167
Love's Triumph, 166

M

Macbeth (Shakespeare), 15
Macklin, Charles, 3-5
Magnetic Lady, The, 30
Malone, Edmund, 4-5, 14
Mandeville, Bernard, 52
Mandragola, 49
Marescalco, Il (Aretino), 136
Marivaux, Pierre, 21
Marlowe, Christopher, 19, 21-22, 27,
   41, 45-46, 52, 59, 61
Marston, John, 18, 47, 74, 84, 87
Marvell, Andrew, 9, 37
Marx brothers, 63
Masque of Beauty, The, 172
Masque of Blackness, The, 23, 165,
   167, 169, 172
Masque of Queens, The, 58, 161-62,
   166, 168n
Masques, 14, 23, 52, 54, 60, 68, 74,
   160-74
Massinger, Philip, 77
Médecin malgré lui, Le (Molière), 111,
   119
Menander, 83, 146
Merchant of Venice, The
   (Shakespeare), 15, 20
Mercury Vindicated, 32, 162-63
Merry Wives of Windsor, The
   (Shakespeare), 78
Middleton, George, 20, 30n, 41
Midsummer Night's Dream, A
   (Shakespeare), 108, 113, 127
Milton, John, 23, 72
Misanthrope, Le (Molière), 108, 116
Molière, 17-18, 21-22, 56, 63, 92, 108,
   111, 113, 116, 119
Money (Hoarding), theme of, 51, 58,
   64-69
   in Volpone, 71

More, Thomas, 46
Much Ado About Nothing
   (Shakespeare), 90

N

Nashe, Thomas, 41, 92n
New Inn, The, 1n, 55
News from the New World, 171-72

O

Oberon, 162, 169-70
"Ode to Himself," 1n
Oedipus (Sophocles), 112, 118
Old Wives' Tale (Peele), 127
O'Neill, Eugene, 41
Othello (Shakespeare), 46
Ovid, 64, 136

P

Peele, George, 92n, 127
Peer Gynt (Ibsen), 83
Pericles (Shakespeare), 1
Pilgrim's Progress, The (Bunyan), 32n
Plautus, 45, 83, 89n, 146
Pleasure Reconciled to Virtue, 164
Plots of Jonson's plays, 88-105, 133
Plutarch, 59, 148, 151-52, 154
Poetaster, The, 8, 16, 49, 66, 71, 74,
   87
Polybius, 149
Pope, Alexander, 9, 43, 45, 79
Portrait of the Artist, A (Joyce), 74
Pound, Ezra, 34
Précieuses ridicules, Les (Molière), 113
Propertius (Pound), 34
Purcell, Henry, 56

Q

Quiller-Couch, Arthur, 30n
Quintilian, 42

R

Rabelais, François, 17, 45, 58

Realism, 6-7, 72, 88
  in *Bartholomew Fair*, 50, 78
  in *Every Man in His Humour*, 78-79
Richard II (Shakespeare), 156
Roaring Girl (Dekker), 78
Ronsard, Pierre de, 44
Rousseau, Jean-Jacques, 52

S

Sackton, Alexander, 121
Sacred Wood, The (Eliot), 27, 61, 76
Sad Shepherd, The, 44
Saint-Evremond, 40
Saintsbury, George, 68
Sallust, 148-51
Sarte, Jean-Paul, 12
Satire, 17, 22, 58-59, 78-79, 84
  in *The Devil Is an Ass*, 31
Schlegel, A. W., 6
Sejanus, 7, 25-31, 35, 38, 42, 47, 50, 63, 70-71, 147-48, 154, 156-58
Seneca, 42, 45, 47, 64
Sex, in Jonson's plays, 50, 67-71
  in *Epicene*, 121-28
Shakespeare, William, 18, 23, 27, 40, 47, 78, 123 (*see also* individual works)
  and Dante, 15
  and Jonson, 1-8, 11-15, 40-41, 53-54, 58-59, 62, 67, 74, 77, 85, 102, 155-59
  and Shaw, 61-62
  and Sophocles, 4
Shaw, George Bernard, 61, 76
Shelley, Percy Bysshe, 6
Ship of Fools, The (Brandt), 85
Shoemaker's Holiday (Dekker), 78
Silent Woman, The (see Epicene)
Simpson, Percy and Evelyn, 9-10, 60, 75, 123, 136n, 137, 146
Skelton, John, 39
Small, R. A., 87-88
Smith, Gregory, 14, 20-22
Southwark Fair (Hogarth), 63
Spanish Tragedy, The (Kyd), 41
Spenser, Edmund, 56, 59

Spurgeon, Caroline, 58
Staple of News, The, 33, 48, 52, 55, 68, 81, 126
Suetonius, 34, 154, 155n
Swift, Jonathan, 17, 59, 72, 79
Swinburne, Algernon Charles, 7-8, 14, 60, 71
Symbolism, 11, 133-46
Symonds, John Addington, 6

T

Tacitus, 34
Tale of a Tub, A (Swift), 72
Tamburlaine (Marlowe), 16, 26
Taming of the Shrew (Shakespeare), 67, 82
Tartuffe (Molière), 116
Tempest, The (Shakespeare), 1-2, 15, 46
Tennyson, Alfred, 72
Terence, 45, 120, 134, 146
Theophrastus, 86
Timber, 42
Tourneur, Cyril, 20-21
Townsend, Freda L., 93n, 133-34, 136
Trick to Catch the Old One, A (Middleton), 136
Turcaret, 49
Twelfth Night (Shakespeare), 90, 136

U

Underwoods, 42, 72
Utopia (More), 46

V

Vision of Delight, The, 54, 57, 68, 73, 170
Volpone, 8, 15, 18-20, 24-25, 27, 29, 32, 36, 45-46, 48, 50-51, 55, **61-73**, 79, **93-105**, 175
Vossius, Gerhard Johannes, 42

W

Webster, John, 11, 14, 20, 41, 61

Wilson, Edmund, 11-12
Winter's Tale, The (Shakespeare),
 2, 123
Witch of Edmonton, The (Rowley),
 15
Woman Hater, The (Beaumont),
 123
Works, 42, 75, 147, 175

Worlde of Wordes (Florio), 101
Worthies (Fuller), 121
Wound and the Bow, The (Wilson),
 12

Z

Zweig, Stefan, 71

KAFKA

A Collection of Critical Essays

Edited by RONALD GRAY

A

Ackermann, Paul Kurt, 174
Aggadit Bereshit IX, 159
Albrecht, Erich A., 170
Alger, Horatio, 123
Alice in Wonderland (Carroll), 87
Also Sprach Zarathustra (Nietzsche), 105
America, 2, 4, 15, 17, 34, 49-50, 128, 131, 141, 174, 175
Anders, Günther, 167
Archimedes, 172
Arendt, Hannah, 169
Auden, W. H., 62, 165, 172
Augustine, Saint, 2
Axel's Castle (Wilson), 78

B

Balzac, Honoré de, 170
Bauer, Felice, 68-69, 70
Beckett, Samuel, 10
"Before the Law" ("Vor dem Gesetz"), 125, 131, 171
Beissner, Friedrich, 2, 163, 173
Benn, Gottfried, 11
Bense, Max, 167
Beschreibung einer Form (Versuch über Franz Kafka) (Walser), 177
Bible, Holy, 29, 59, 106, 111, 118, 158, 160-62
Bierce, Ambrose, 78

Big Two-Hearted River (Hemingway), 80
Blumfeld, an Elderly Bachelor (Blumfeld, ein älterer Junggeselle), 141, 171
Böckmann, Paul, 29
Bordeaux, Henri, 153
Bouvard et Pécuchet (Flaubert), 9, 95
Braybrooke, Neville, 176
Brecht, Bertolt, 10
Brod, Max, 1, 3, 15, 17, 25, 34, 68, 88, 91-95, 102, 117, 131, 134, 135, 142-43, 164-65, 167, 170, 173-74, 177
Brunner, Emil, 157
Buber, Martin, 6
Bucket Rider, The (Der Kübelreiter), 176
Bunyan, John, 8, 41-42, 45, 96, 102, 114
Burgum, Edwin Berry, 167
Burrow, The (Der Bau), 141, 171, 176

C

Calvin, John, 95
Camus, Albert, 2, 3, 5, 165, 166
Carouges, Michel, 166
Carroll, Lewis (*see* Dodgson, Charles)
Castle, The, 2, 5, 7, 8, 15, 17, 26, 33, 34, 35, 37-44, 46-50, 61, 70-72, 88, 91, 92, 94, 95, **101-120,** 125, 126-27,

Castle, The (continued)
128-31, 137, 139-42, 148, 150-54,
158-59, 170, 173-74
allegory in, 111-15
characterization, 70-72
existentialism in, 151-54
and *Fear and Trembling* (Kierkegaard), 117-18
Gnostic dogma in, 116, 118-20
humor in, 37-41
Manichean dogma in, 116, 118-20,
122
narrative technique of, 128-29, 131
papers, symbolism of, 126-27
and *Pilgrim's Progress* (Bunyan), 41-
42, 102, 114
plot summary, 37-38, 112-13
romantic love, theme of, 115-16
structure of, 173-74
style of, 42-44
and symbolism, concept of, 106-10
theological aspects of, 116-22
world-view in, 139-40
Catherine of Siena, Saint, 62
Cervantes, Miguel de, 155
Chaplin, Charles Spenser, 3, 170
Chekhov, Alexander, 77
Chekhov, Anton, 2, 77-78
Claudius Matthias, 27-28
Country Doctor, A (Ein Landartz), 30,
127, 170, 176
Crane, Stephen, 78
Crossbreed, A (Eine Kreuzung), 16

D

Dante, 62, 96
Darwin, Charles, 105
Dauvin, R., 166
David Copperfield (Dickens), 175
Day of the Locust, The (West), 89
Dead Souls (Gogol), 86
Death in Venice (Mann), 176
Demetz, Peter, 170, 175
Dickens, Charles, 66-67, 123, 124, 170,
175
Dodgson, Charles (*pseud.* Carroll,
Lewis), 87, 124

Donne, John, 49
Don Quixote (Cervantes), 155
Dos Passos, John, 47
Dostoevsky, Fyodor, 86, 123, 141,
170
Duino Elegies (Rilke), 101

E

Eckermann, Johann, 110
"Economy of Chaos, The" (Weiss),
165
Eisner, Pavel, 168
Eliot, T. S., 7, 47
Emrich, Wilhelm, 57, 172, 176
Emunah, concept of, 6, 161-62
*Ermordung einer Puppe namens Franz
Kafka, Die* (Brod), 167
Erzähler Franz Kafka, Der (Beissner),
173

F

"Faith and Vocation" (Savage), 165
Farewell to Arms, A (Hemingway), 77
Faust (Goethe), 1, 107, 155
Fear and Trembling (Kierkegaard),
117-18, 130
Flaubert, Gustave, 9, 34, 68, 95, 170
Flores, Angel, 92, 175, 176
Francis of Sales, Saint, 62
Franklin, Benjamin, 123
Franz Kafka (Emrich), 176
Franz Kafka: A Biography (Brod), 91,
143
"Franz Kafka, an American Bibliogra-
phy" (Jonas), 175
*Franz Kafka, eine Betrachtung seines
Werkes* (Reiss), 169
Franz Kafka, eine Bibliographie (Hem-
merle), 176
*Franz Kafka, eine Biographie seiner
Jugend* (Wagenbach), 176
Franz Kafka, Pro und Contra (Anders),
167
Franz Kafka als wegweisende Gestalt
(Brod), 164
Franz Kafka and Prague (Eisner), 168

Franz Kafka et les lettres francaises:
  1928-1955 (Goth), 176
Franz Kafka Inferno (Kaiser), 168
Franz Kafkas Glauben und Lehre
  (Brod), 164
Franz Kafka Today (eds. Flores and
  Swander), 176
Freud, Sigmund, 85, 134, 141, 168-69,
  175
Fromm, Erich, 169
Frozen Sea, The (Neider), 168
Fuchs, Rudolf, 167

G

Giant Mole, The, 141
Gide, André, 33
Give It Up! (Gib's Auf!), 171
Gnostics, 3, 7, 116, 118-20, 160
Goethe, Johann, 1, 9, 62, 107, 109,
  155, 176
Gogol Nikolai, 85-90, 92, 96, 170
Goncharov, Ivan, 86
Goodman, Paul, 92, 169
Gordon, Caroline, 2, 4
Goth, Maja, 176
Grandmother, The (Nemcová), 170
Gravier, Maurice, 170
Gray, Ronald, 176
Great Wall of China, The, 30, 33, 91,
  95, 141
Grillparzer, Franz, 109
Gulliver's Travels (Swift), 128

H

Hamlet (Shakespeare), 1
Hard Times (Dickens), 66
Hawthorne, Nathaniel, 76, 80, 123,
  128
Hegel, Georg, 113
Heidegger, Martin, 167
Heller, Erich, 3-4, 7, 9, 165-66
Hemingway, Ernest, 75, 77-83
Hemmerle, Rudolf, 176
"He," Notes from the Year 1920, 46-
  47
Herman und Dorothea (Goethe), 176

Heselhaus, Clemens, 172
Hesse, Hermann, 15, 33
Hintz, Victor, 166
"History of Critical Writing on Kafka,
  A" (Ackermann), 174
History of Form in German Literature
  (Böckmann), 29
Hitler, Adolf, 91
Hoffman, Frederick T., 169
Hölderlin, Friedrich, 22, 30, 109
"Homecoming," 21, 27, 30
Homer, 29
Hunger-Artist, The (Ein Hunger-
  künstler), 47, 171, 176
Hunter Gracchus, The, 81-83
Husserl, Edmund, 175
Huxley, Aldous, 33

I

Imperial Message, An (Eine kaiser-
  liche Botschaft), 30-31, 171
Inspector General, The (Gogol), 86
Interior Castle (Teresa), 8
Investigations of a Dog (Forschungen
  eines Hundes), 46, 95, 141, 176

J

James, Henry, 80, 82-83
James, William, 145
Janouch, Gustav, 164
Jesenská, Milena, 18-20, 23
Jesus, 79, 81-83, 106-8, 130, 157-61
Jewett, Sarah Orne, 78
John, Saint, 160
John of the Cross, Saint, 131
Jolles, André, 172
Jonas, Klaus W., 175
Josephine the Singer, or the Mouse
  Folk (Josefine, die Sängerin, oder Das
  Volk der Mäuse), 141, 171
Joyce, James, 47, 92, 103
"Judgement, The," 23-25, 141

K

Kafka, Franz:

Kafka, Franz (*continued*)
  and the absurd, concept of, 147-50
  and allegory, concept of, 106-7,
    130-31
  aphorisms of, 34-36
  artistic development of, 17-20
  and Bunyan, John, 41-42
  critics' interpretations of, 101-6,
    133-37, 163-77
  and Dickens, Charles, 66-67
  dream-like inner life, use of,
    23-26
  empiricism of, 142-46
  and evil, 61-63, 67, 99-106
  and existentialism, 145, 151-55
  and Gogol, Nikolai, 85-90, 96
  and Hemingway, Ernest, 80-83
  and hierarchy, theme of, 124-25
  humor of, 37-41
  and Kierekegaard, Sören, 134-37,
    141-45, 151-53
  literary acceptance of, 15-19, 33-
    34
  narrative technique of, 45-51, 65-
    67, 70-73, 128-31
  and Naturalism, 80-83
  and Nietzsche, Friedrich, 104-6
  and Paulinism, concept of, 157-62
  personality of, 62-73, 92-94
  religion of, 36-37, 41-43, 102-5
  and symbolism, concept of, 106-10
  and teleological problems, 45-51
  and the unsuccessful arrival, theme
    of, 19-22
  wordless quality, in works of, 27-31
  world-view of, 123-27, 136-46
Kafka, Franz, works by:
  America, 2, 4, 15, 17, 34, 49-50,
    128, 131, 141, 174, 175
  "Before the Law" ("Vor dem
    Gesetz"), 125, 131, 171
  Blumfeld, an Elderly Bachelor
    (*Blumfeld, ein älterer Junggeselle*),
    141, 171
  Bucket Rider, The (*Der Kübelreiter*),
    176
  Burrow, The (*Der Bau*), 141, 171,
    176

Castle, The, 2, 5, 7, 8, 15, 17, 26,
  33, 34, 35, 37-44, 46-50, 61, 70-
  72, 88, 91, 92, 94, 95, **101-20**,
  125, 126-27, 128-31, 137, 139-42,
  148, 150-54, 158-59, 170, 173-74
Country Doctor, A (*Ein Landartz*),
  30, 127, 170, 176
Crossbreed, A (*Eine Kreuzung*),
  16
Giant Mole, The, 141
Give It Up! (*Gib's Auf!*), 171
Great Wall of China, The, 30, 33,
  91, 95, 141
"*He*," *Notes from the Year 1920*,
  46-47
"Homecoming," 21, 27, 30
Hunger-Artist, The (*Ein Hunger-
  künstler*), 47, 171, 176
Hunter Gracchus, The, 81-83
Imperial Message, An (*Eine kaiser-
  liche Botschaft*), 30-31, 171
Investigations of a Dog (*For-
  schungen eines Hundes*), 46, 95,
  141, 176
*Josephine the Singer, or the Mouse
  Folk* (*Josefine, die Sängerin, oder
  Das Volk der Mäuse*), 141, 171
"Judgement, The," 23-25, 141
Letters to Milena (*Briefe an Milena*),
  171
Little Woman, A (*Eine kleine Frau*),
  171
Metamorphosis, The (*Die Verwand-
  lung*), 2, 5, 7, 8, **53-59**, 85-89, 91,
  94, 127, 141, 148-49, 171, 176
My Neighbor (*Der Nachbar*), 176
"On the Tram," 70, 72
Penal Colony, The (*In der Straf-
  kolonie*), 61, 141, 171
Problems of Our Laws, The, 141
Report to the Academy, A (*Ein
  Bericht für eine Akademie*), 171
"Stoker, The," 124, 131
Trial, The, 2, 3-4, 5, 7, 8, 15, 17,
  18, 34, 35, 43, 49-50, 61, 86, 88,
  91, 92, 94, 95, 123,126-27, 128,
  130, 131, 137-42, 147-54, 159,
  166, 168, 174

Kafka, Franz, works by (*continued*)
  "Up in the Gallery" ("Auf der
    Galerie"), 64-65, 69, 171
"Kafka and Kierkegaard" (Wahl),
  165
Kafka ou le mystère juif (Nemeth),
  166
Kafka ou l'irréducible espoir (Roche-
  fort), 166
Kafka Problem, The (ed. Flores), 92,
  165
Kafka's Castle (Gray), 176
"Kafkas Erzählformen" (Heselhaus),
  172
Kafka's Prayer (Goodman), 169
Kaiser, Helmut, 168
Kassner, Rudolf, 170
Kelly, John, 165
Kierkegaard, Sören, 9, 34, 36, 45, 94,
  117-18, 127, 130, 134-37, 141-46,
  151-53, 160, 169
Killers,The (Hemingway), 80, 82
Kingdom of Love, The (Brod), 34
Kleist, Ewald van, 109
Klopstock, Friedrich, 29

L

Leibniz, Gottfried, 143
Lerner, Max, 167
Lessing, Gotthold, 170
Letters to Milena (*Briefe an Milena*),
  171
Lewis, Sinclair, 75-76
Little Woman, A (*Eine kleine Frau*),
  171
Loyola, Saint Ignatius, 62
Lukács, Georg, 10-11
Luke, F. D., 171
Luther, Martin, 108

M

Magny, C. -E., 136-37
Main Street (Lewis), 75-76
Malraux, André, 153
"Man" (Claudius), 28-29
Manhattan Transfer (Dos Passos), 47

Manicheans, 7, 116, 118-20, 122
Mann, Thomas, 11, 15, 33, 109, 127,
  175, 176
Marcion, 160
Marie Donadieu (Philippe), 19
Martini, Fritz, 172-73
Marx, Karl, 95
Maupassant, Guy de, 82-83
Mediator, The (Brunner), 157
Meidinger-Geise, Ilse, 170
Melville, Herman, 86
Metamorphosis, The (*Die Verwand-
  lung*), 2, 5, 7, 8, 53-59, 85-89, 91, 94,
  127, 141, 148-49, 171, 176
  hidden meaning in, 53-59
  and *The Nose* (Gogol), 85-89
  plot summary, 53-56
Mirandola, Pico della, 108
Mühlberger, Josef, 167
Muir, Edwin, 1, 3, 51, 102, 106, 114,
  165
Muir, Willa, 51, 102
Muschg, Walter, 167
Musil, Alois, 175
My Neighbor (*Der Nachbar*), 176

N

Neale, John Mason, 129-30
Neider, Charles, 5, 168-69
Nemcová, Bozena, 170
Nemeth, André, 166
Newton, Isaac, 109
Nietzsche, Friedrich, 3, 104-6, 109,
  122, 149, 154
Norris, Frank, 78
Nose, The (Gogol), 85-89

O

Oliver Twist (Dickens), 124
Olsen, Regina, 152
"On the Tram," 70, 72
"Overcoat, The" (Gogol), 86

P

Parry, Idris, 170

Pascal, Blaise, 6, 34, 170
Paul, Saint, 157-62
Penal Colony, The (*In der Straf-kolonie*), 61, 141, 171
Peter, Saint, 160
Pfeiffer, Johannes, 5
Philippe, Charles Louis, 19
Pilgrim's Progress (Bunyan), 41-42, 96, 102, 114, 130
Pit and the Pendulum, The (Poe), 61
Plato, 99, 127, 142
Plotinus, 151
Poe, Edgar Allan, 4, 61-62, 76-78, 86, 92, 96, 123
Politzer, Heinz, 17, 163, 171, 174, 175
Pongs, Hermann, 167
"Probleme und Problematik der Kafka-Forschung" (Politzer), 174
Problem of Our Laws, The, 141
Proust, Marcel, 43, 92, 123, 151

R

Rabelais, Francois, 144
Rahv, Phillip, 137
Read, Herbert, 33
Reed, Eugene, 172
Reiss, H. S., 8, 169
Report to the Academy, A (*Ein Bericht für eine Akademie*), 171
Republic (Plato), 99
Richards, I. A., 135, 136
Rilke, Rainer Maria, 9, 26, 89-90, 101, 107, 175
Rimbaud, Arthur, 62
Rochefort, Robert, 166

S

Salinger, J. D., 10
Salter, Georg, 123
Sappho (Grillparzer), 109
Savage, D. S., 92, 96, 165
Scarlet Letter, The (Hawthorne), 128
Schaufelberger, Fritz, 172
Schiller, Johann, 17
Schoeps, Hans Joachim, 165

Schopenhauer, Arthur, 9, 143
Sennett, Mack, 3, 124
Seypel, Joachim, 169
Shakespeare, William, 1, 45, 62, 103
Spann, Meno, 176
Spender, Stephen, 132
Spinoza, Baruch, 86
Stalin, Joseph, 11
Steer, A., 167
"Stoker, The," 124, 131
Strindberg, August, 170
Struktur von Kafkas "Der Prozess" (Uyttersprot), 173
Swander, Homer, 176
Swift, Jonathan, 43, 128, 144, 170

T

Talmud, 68, 130
Tasso (Goethe), 9, 109
Tauber, Herbert, 165
Tedlock, E. W., 175
Teresa, Saint, 8, 131, 176
Theorie Kafkas (Bense), 167
Thorlby, A. K., 167
Today is Friday (Hemingway), 79, 82
Tolstoy, Leo N., 78, 86
Tonio Kröger (Mann), 109
"Tragedy of Faithlessness, The" (Schoeps), 165
Trial, The, 2, 3-4, 5, 7, 8, 15, 17, 18, 34, 35, 43, 49-50, 61, 86, 88, 91, 92, 94, 95, 123, 126-27, 128, 130, 131, 137-42, 147-54, 159, 166, 168, 174
and the absurd, concept of, 147-48, 150
existentialism in, 151-54
guilt, theme of, 137-39
world-view in, 137-42
"*Trial* and the Theology of Crisis, The" (Kelly), 165
Turgenev, Ivan, 78, 170
"Twice-Told Tales" (Hawthorne), 76

U

Ulshöfer, Robert, 176
Ulysses (Joyce), 47

Unamuno, Miguel de, 11, 145
Undefeated, The (Hemingway), 80
"Up in the Gallery" ("Auf der Galerie"), 64-65, 69, 171
Ur-Geräusch (Primal Sound) (Rilke), 89
Uyttersprot, Herman, 4, 173-74

V

Verzweiflung und Erlosung im Werk Franz Kafkas (Brod), 177
Vietta, Egon, 167
Vigny, Alfred de, 170
Vivas, Eliseo, 5, 9

W

Wagenbach, Klaus, 176
Wagnis der Sprache, Das (Martini), 172
Wahl, Jean, 165
Walker, Augusta, 176
Walpole, Hugh, 33
Walser, Martin, 177

Wanderer, Der (Hölderlin), 22
Wandering Jew, the, 62
Warner, Rex, 170
Warren, Austin, 2, 5, 80, 169
Waste Land, The (Eliot), 47
Weil, Simone, 62
Weiss, T., 165
Werfel, Franz, 175
West, Nathanael, 86, 89
West, Rebecca, 33
Whitman, Walt, 123
Wilde, Oscar, 85
Will to Power, The (Nietzsche), 105
Wilson, Edmund, 4, 78, 169
Winkler, R. O. C., 2
Wittgenstein, Ludwig, 9
"World of Franz Kafka, The" (Heller), 165

Y

Yeats, William Butler, 11

Z

Zwingli, Ulrich, 108

KEATS

A Collection of Critical Essays
Edited by WALTER JACKSON BATE

A

Abbey, Richard, 1, 39
Alastor (Shelley), 18, 19, 39
Aleman, Mateo, 62
Alfred, King, 15, 17
Allegory in Keats's works, 16, 22, 25, 74, 91
"After dark vapours," 108, 159
Anatomy of Melancholy, The (Burton), 78-79, 82-83, 87, 88
Apostrophe, Keats's use of, 110, 124
Arabian Nights, The, 33
Archaeologia Graeca (Potter), 26, 29, 30
Arnold, Matthew, 27, 165
Ariosto, Lodovico, 90
As You Like It (Shakespeare), 96

B

Bacon, Sir Francis, 56
Bailey, Benjamin, 11, 19, 55, 61, 62, 73, 82
"Bards of Passion and of Mirth," 141
Barnes, Barnabe, 24
Beattie, James, 14
"Belle Dame sans Merci, La," 4, 87, 89, 110, 143, 147
Blake, William, 13, 95, 97, 101
Boccaccio, Giovanni, 48
Botticelli, Alessandro, 22
Brawne, Frances (Fanny), 1, 23, 29, 39, 108

"Bright Star," 109, 127
Brown, Charles, 31, 56
Brown, Leonard, 20
Browne, William, 21, 26
Burke, Kenneth, 114
Burton, Robert, 28, 78-79, 82-83, 87, 88
Bush, Douglas, 6, 71
Byron, George Gordon, 1, 13
"Byzantium" (Yeats), 97

C

"Canonization, The" (Donne), 80
Celtic Researches (Davies), 33
Chapman, George, 16, 17, 21, 33
Characters of Shakespeare's Plays (Hazlitt), 67
Chaucer, Geoffrey, 23, 53, 62, 78, 90
"Christabel" (Coleridge), 28
Christianity, in Keats's works, 36, 83, 168-69
Clarissa (Richardson), 79, 81
Clarke, Charles Cowden, 15, 60
Classical tradition, in Keats's works, 14-27 *passim*, 29-31, 33, 34, 91-99, 109, 143, 165, 169
Claude (*see* Lorrain, Claude)
Coleridge, Samuel Taylor, 6, 13, 56, 94
Collins, William, 14, 96
Colvin, Sir Sidney, 6, 22
Comus (Milton), 25, 31
"Credences of Summer" (Stevens), 97

Cymbeline (Shakespeare), 79

D

Dante Alighieri, 5, 33
Davies, Edward, 33
"Death on a Pale Horse" (West), 51
Dilke, Charles, 56-57, 130
Disinterestedness, doctrine of, 59, 64
Donne, John, 80
Dryden, John, 1, 4, 14, 28, 146

E

Edinburgh Review, The, 52
"Egotistical sublime," doctrine of the, 23, 66
Einfühlung (*see* Empathy)
Elegaic Stanzas (Wordsworth), 153
Elgin Marbles, 26, 32, 54
Eliot, T. S., 3, 6
Elizabethan literature, 16-17, 22, 24, 26, 33
Empathy, doctrine of, 63, 119-24, 129-30, 135-36
Endymion, 4, 19, 23-28 *passim*, 31, 57, 61, 67, 68, 75, 89, 104, 119-21, 125-26, 141, 152, 159
  myth, use of, 15, 17-18, 114, 138
  style of, 18, 32, 42, 44, 47
  symbol, use of, 18-23, 38, 108, 122
Epipsychidion (Shelley), 21
Essay on the Principles of Human Action (Hazlitt), 62-63
"Esthétique du Mal (Stevens), 100
Eve of St. Mark, The, 4, 87
Eve of St. Agnes, The, 4, 39, 43, 46, 55, 68, 71-90
Excursion, The (Wordsworth), 16, 18, 34, 36, 94

F

Fall of Hyperion, The, 4, 24, 31, 33, 40, 62, 88, 96, 101, 104-5, 148, 152, 161-69
  symbol, use of, 39
Flaubert, Gustave, 71, 136

Fletcher, John, 21
"Four Seasons," 29
French Revolution, 34
From Classic to Romantic (Bate), 63
Frost, Robert, 3

G

Garrod, H. W., 7
Gebir (Landor), 32
Gibbon, Edward, 59
"God of the Meridian," 89
Godwin, William, 35
Gray, Thomas, 14
"Gypsy, The" (Wordsworth), 11

H

Hamlet (Shakespeare), 85
Haydon, Benjamin Robert, 54, 56, 86
Hazlitt, William, 27, 32, 52-53, 61, 62-65
Henry VI (Shakespeare), 54
Hesiod, 33
Hessey, J. A., 86
Hobbes, Thomas, 62-64
Homer, 5, 113
Homer (Chapman), 17, 33, 60
Houghton, Lord, 5
Hunt, Leigh, 1, 7, 33, 60, 78
Hyginus, 33
"Hymn to Pan," 21, 24
Hyperbole, Keats's use of, 109
Hyperion, 4, 11, 14, 17, 23, 24, 31-39, 44-48, 55, 60, 108, 150, **161-69**
  symbol, use of, 166

I

Imagination, theme of, 51-52, 63-67, 72-74, 92-98, 105, 107, 119-21, 130, 143-44, 147-48, 151, 164, 168
Imagists, The, 3
"Imitation of Spenser," 159
"In drear-nighted December," 159
Indicator, The, 33
Inferno, The (Dante), 86
"Intensity," doctrine of, 53-55, 159, 160

Irony, in Keats's works, 75, 84, 99, 101, 110, 134

Isabella, 42, 47, 49, 68, 165

"I Stood Tip-toe," 15, 16, 17, 38-39

Italian sonnet, the, 136

J

Jacobean literature, 26

Johnson, Samuel, 2

Jonson, Ben, 14, 21

K

Kean, Edmund, 51, 53

Keats, George, 15, 23, 39, 55, 56, 67, 155

Keats, Georgiana (Mrs. George), 153

Keats, John:
  allegory, use of, 16, 22, 25, 91
  apostrophe, use of, 110, 124
  and Ariosto, Lodovico, 90
  and Bailey, Benjamin, 55, 61, 62, 73
  and Blake, William, 13, 95
  and Boccaccio, Giovanni, 48
  and Brawne, Frances (Fanny), 1, 23, 29, 39, 108
  and Burton, Robert, 78-79, 82-83, 87, 88
  caricature, use of, 146
  and Chaucer, Geoffrey, 53, 62, 78, 90
  and Christianity, 36, 83, 168-69
  and classical tradition, 14-27 *passim,* 29-31, 33, 34, 91-99, 109, 143, 165
  and Coleridge, Samuel Taylor, 13, 56, 94
  and Collins, William, 14, 94
  critical reputation of, 1-2, 5-8
  and "disinterestedness," doctrine of, 59, 64
  and Dryden, John, 14, 28, 146
  and "the egotistical sublime," doctrine of, 23, 66
  and Elizabethan literature, 16-17, 22, 24, 26, 33
  and empathy, doctrine of, 63, 119-24, 129-30, 135-36
  and Haydon, Benjamin Robert, 54, 56, 86
  and Hazlitt, William, 27, 32, 52-53, 61, 62-65
  and Hunt, Leigh, 17, 33, 60, 78
  hyperbole, use of, 109
  and imagination, theme of, 51-52, 66-67, 72-74, 92-98, 105, 107, 119-21, 130, 143-44, 147-48, 151, 164, 168
  and *The Inferno* (Dante), 86
  influence of, 3
  and "intensity," doctrine of, 53-55, 159, 160
  irony, use of, 75, 84, 99, 101, 110, 134
  the Italian sonnet, use of, 136
  and Jacobean literature, 26
  and Keats, George, 15, 23, 39, 55, 56, 67, 155
  and Keats, Georgiana (Mrs. George), 153
  and Keats, Tom, 23, 55, 56, 67
  and Landor, Walter Savage, 32
  legend, use of, 38
  life of, 1-3, 23, 39, 165
  and Lorrain, Claude, 26, 53
  and Mathew, Felton, 60
  and Melville, Herman, 83
  metaphor, use of, 42, 97, 107
  and Milton, John, 3, 5, 23-25, 31-35, 54, 60, 61, 78, 94, 101, 145
  myth, use of, 14-15, 18, 21, 144
  and nature, theme of, 15, 38, 97-98, 100-1
  and "negative capability," doctrine of, 20, 23, **51-68,** 130
  oxymoron, use of, 95, 114-38 *passim*
  pathetic fallacy, use of, 129
  periphrasis, use of, 134, 145
  personification, use of, 124, 135
  Platonism of, 20-21, 26
  and Proust, Marcel, 49
  and Reynolds, John Hamilton, 54, 58-60, 74, 83, 89

Keats, John: (*continued*)
  and Romanticism, 22, 24, 28-29,
    90, 98, 164-65, 169
  satire, use of, 145
  and Shakespeare, William, 3, 17,
    19, 22, 23, 52, 54, 55, 60, 89, 96,
    144, 160, 166-68
  and Shelley, Percy Bysshe, 1, 12,
    13, 18, 19, 22, 23, 25, 26, 32, 34,
    35, 97, 103, 165
  simile, use of, 74
  and "soul-making," doctrine of, 95
  and Spenser, Edmund, 16, 21, 23,
    27, 34, 100-1
  and Stevens, Wallace, 97, 98, 100-
    1
  and the sublime, 51
  synesthesia, use of, **41-50**, 107
  and Taylor, John, 19-66, 81
  and Titian, 53
  and West, Benjamin, 51, 52
  and Woodhouse, Richard, 66, 81,
    82, 86, 120
  and Wordsworth, William, 1, 11, 12,
    13, 21-22, 23, 24, 34, 35, 39, 58,
    94-96, 101, 153, 168
  and Yeats, W. B., 3, 96-97,
    101
Keats, John, works by:
  "After dark vapours," 108, 159
  "Bards of Passion and of Mirth,"
    141
  "Belle Dame sans Merci, La," 4, 87,
    89, 110, 143, 147
  "Bright Star," 109, 127
  Endymion, 15-28 *passim*, 31, 32,
    38, 42, 44, 47, 57, 61, 68, 75, 89,
    104, 108, 114, 119-21, 125-26,
    141, 152, 159
  Eve of St. Agnes, The, 4, 39, 43,
    46, 55, 68, **71-90**
  Eve of St. Mark, The, 4, 87
  Fall of Hyperion, The, 4, 24, 31,
    33, 39, 40, 62, 88, 96, 101, 104-5,
    148, 152, **161-69**
  "Four Seasons," 29
  "God of the Meridian," 89
  Hyperion, 4, 11, 14, 17, 23, 24,

    31-39, 44-48, 55, 60, 108, 150,
    161-69
  "Imitation of Spenser," 159
  "In drear-nighted December," 159
  Isabella, 42, 47, 49, 68, 165
  "I Stood Tiptoe," 15, 16, 17, 38-39
  Lamia, 4, 27-31, 39, 45, 88-89,
    104-5, 113, **143-53**
  "Ode on a Grecian Urn," 25, 26,
    88, 97, 103, 110, **113-41**, 143,
    147-48, 151, 157, 159
  "Ode on Melancholy," 86, 98-101,
    105
  "Ode to a Nightingale," 25-26, 48-
    50, 88-89, 98, 100, **103-11**, 123,
    139, 143, 146, 156
  "Ode to Apollo," 14
  "Ode to Maia," 24, 27
  "Ode to Psyche," 5, 11, 25, 48, **91-
    98**
  "Ode to Sorrow," 21
  "On Edmund Kean as a
    Shakespearean Actor" (review), 53
  "To Autumn," 24, 40, 97, 107,
    155-60
  "To George Felton Mathew," 14-15
  "To Homer," 113
  "To J. H. Reynolds, Esq.," 89
  "To My Brother George," 152
  "What the Thrush Said," 59
  "Where's the Poet," 61
  "Why did I laugh," 108
  "Written in Disgust of Vulgar
    Superstition," 83
Keats, Tom, 23, 55, 56, 67
King Lear (Shakespeare), 52, 67, 89,
  166-68
Kingston, John, 56
Kosciusko, Tadeo, 17

L

Lamb, Charles, 29
Lamia, 4, 27-31, 39, 45, 88-89, 104-5,
  113, **143-53**
  symbol, use of, 143-46, 149, 151
Landor, Walter Savage, 32
Lawrence, D. H., 29

Lectures on the English Poets
  (Hazlitt), 28, 65
Legend, Keats's use of, 38
Locke, John, 63
Lorrain, Claude, 26, 53
"Lovely Maya" (Barnes), 24
Lowell, Amy, 3, 6, 20, 85
Lowell, James Russell, 3

M

Marston, John, 21
"Material sublime," doctrine of the,
  16, 26
Mathew, Felton, 60
Melville, Herman, 83
Metaphor, Keats's use of, 42, 97, 107
Milton, John, 3, 5, 23-25, 31-35, 54,
  60, 61, 78, 94, 101, 145
Morris, William, 29
Myth, 17, 96
  Keats's use of, 14-15, 17-18, 21, 23,
    114, 138, 144

N

Nature, theme of, in Keats's works, 15,
  38, 97-98, 100-1
"Negative capability," doctrine of, 20,
  23, 51-68, 130
Nostalgia, in Keats's works, 27

O

Oberon (Wieland), 78
"Ode on a Grecian Urn," 25, 26, 88,
  97, 103, 110, 113-41, 143, 147-48,
  151, 157, 159
  symbol, use of, 103, 110, 114,
    117-18, 121-24, 126, 132, 135-36
"Ode on Melancholy," 86, 98-101, 105
"Ode on the Poetical Character"
  (Collins), 94, 96
"Ode to a Nightingale," 25-26, 48-50,
  88-89, 98, 100, 103-11, 123, 139,
  143, 146, 156
  symbol, use of, 25-26, 103-6, 108,
    110-11

"Ode to Apollo," 14
"Ode to Maia," 24, 27
"Ode to Psyche," 5, 11, 25, 48, 91-98
"Ode to Sorrow," 21
"On Edmund Kean as a Dramatic
  Actor" (review by Keats), 53
"On Gusto" (Hazlitt), 52
"On Shakespeare and Milton (Hazlitt),
  63
Ovid, 23, 26, 33
Ovid (Sandys), 23, 26, 33
Oxymoron, Keats's use of, 95, 114-38
  passim

P

Paradise Lost (Milton), 31, 61, 78, 81,
  145, 159
Pathetic fallacy, Keats's use of, 129
Peacock, Thomas Love, 28
Periphrasis, Keats's use of, 134, 145
Personification, Keats's use of, 124,
  135
Petrarch, 17
Platonism, in Keats's works, 20-21, 26
Plutarch, 32
Pope, Alexander, 1, 82, 146
Potter, John, 26, 29, 30
Prelude, The (Wordsworth), 34, 168
Pre-Raphaelites, the, 3, 5
Prometheus Unbound (Shelley), 165
Proust, Marcel, 49

Q

Queen and huntress (Jonson), 14

R

Rape of the Lock (Pope), 82
Recluse, The (Wordsworth), 94
Reynolds, John Hamilton, 54, 58-60,
  74, 83, 89
Rice, James, 62
Richardson, Samuel, 79, 81
"Rock, The" (Stevens), 100
Romanticism, 22, 24, 28-29, 90, 98,
  164-65, 169

Romeo and Juliet (Shakespeare), 75
Ronsard, Pierre de, 33
Rossetti, William Michael, 26
Rogue, The; or, the Life of Guzman de Alfarache (Aleman), 62

S

"Sailing to Byzantium" (Yeats), 96
Sandys, George, 16, 21, 26, 33
Satire, in Keats's works, 145
Severn, Joseph, 24, 61, 62
Shakespeare, William, 3, 17, 19, 22, 23, 52, 54, 55, 60, 89, 96, 144, 160, 166-68
Shelley, Percy Bysshe, 1, 12, 13, 18, 19, 22, 23, 25, 26, 32, 34, 35, 97, 103, 165
Sidney, Sir Philip, 26
Simile, Keats's use of, 74
"Sleep and Poetry," 16-18, 21, 39, 54, 104, 141, 159, 166
Smith, Adam, 63
Smith, Horace, 55
"Soul-making," doctrine of, 95
Sotheby, William, 78
Southey, Robert, 32
Spenser, Edmund, 16, 21, 23, 27, 34, 100-1
Stevens, Wallace, 97, 98, 100-1
Sublime, the, theme of, 51
"Sunday Morning" (Stevens), 97, 100
Swann's Way (Proust), 49
Swift, Jonathan, 58
Symbol, 16, 58
   in *Endymion*, 18-23, 38, 108, 122
   in *The Fall of Hyperion*, 39
   in *Hyperion*, 166
   in *Lamia*, 143-46, 149, 151
   in "Ode on a Grecian Urn," 103, 110, 114, 117-18, 121-24, 126, 132, 135-36, 139
   in "Ode to a Nightingale," 25-26, 103-6, 108, 110-11
Synesthesia, Keats's use of, 41-50, 107

T

Taylor, John, 19, 66, 81

Tell, William, 15
Tennyson, Alfred Lord, 3, 5
Theodore and Honoria (Dryden), 28
Theory of Moral Sentiments (Smith), 63
Thomson, James, 14
"Tintern Abbey" (Wordsworth), 16, 95
Titian, 53
"To Autumn," 24, 40, 97, 107, **155-60**
"To Evening" (Collins), 14
"To George Felton Mathew," 14-15
"To Homer," 113
"To J. H. Reynolds, Esq.," 89
"To My Brother George," 152
Troilus and Criseyde (Chaucer), 78
Turner, J. M. W., 22

V

Vathek (Beckford), 33
Venus and Adonis (Shakespeare), 17
Virgil, 22, 32, 33
Voltaire, 59

W

Wasserman, Earl, 144
West, Benjamin, 51, 52
"What the Thrush Said," 59
"Where's the Poet," 61
Whitman, Walt, 3
"Why did I laugh," 108
Wieland, C. M., 78
Woodhouse, Richard, 66, 81, 82, 86, 120
Wordsworth, William, 1, 11, 12, 13, 21-22, 23, 24, 34, 35, 39, 58, 94-96, 101, 153, 168
"Written in Disgust of Vulgar Superstition," 83

Y

Yeats, W. B., 3, 96-97, 101

D. H. LAWRENCE

A Collection of Critical Essays

Edited by MARK SPILKA

A

Aaron's Rod, 61, 62, 63, 70, 101-2, 104, 116
Achievement of D. H. Lawrence, The (ed. Moore and Hoffman), 6
Adam Bede (Eliot), 20
Aldington, Richard, 138, 143
"Almond Blossom," 137-38, 141
Altitude, 144
Alvarez, A., 11, 138
Amis, Kingsley, 9
Anna Karenina (Tolstoy), 39
"Art and Morality," 161
Assorted Articles, 154
Attila, 62
Austen, Jane, 3, 4, 20, 29, 31

B

Balzac, Honoré de, 15, 31, 156
Barrie, J. M., 156
Bates, H. E., 10-11
"Bavarian Gentians," 71, 141
Beerbohm, Max, 130
Bennett, Arnold, 33, 155
Bertocci, Angelo, 4
Betjeman, John, 130
Beyond the Mexique Bay (Huxley), 70
Biographia Literaria (Coleridge), 128
Birds, Beasts and Flowers, 136-39
Bismarck, O. E. L. von, 62
Blackmur, R. P., 2, 11, 12, 127, 128,
129, 131, 132, 133, 135, 136, 137, 140
Blake, William, 127, 130, 131, 139, 152
"Blind Man, The," 11, 13, **112-16**
Blutbrüderschaft, 10, 14, 69
Boy in the Bush, The, 116
Braine, John, 9
Brontë, Charlotte, 156, 157
Brontë, Emily, 21, 31
Brook Kerith, The (Moore), 106
Brooks, Cleanth, 2
Brown, Curtis, 157
Burnet, John, 139
Burns, Robert, 127, 153, 155
Byron, George Gordon Lord, 133, 134, 138

C

Captain's Doll, The, 4, **95-97**
Carlyle, Thomas, 162-63, 168, 172
Carswell, Catherine, 142
Carswell, Donald, 155
Censorship, 32-33
Chambers, Jessie, 135
Chance (Conrad), 32, 51
Chaucer, Geoffrey, 31, 33
Chekhov, Anton, 152
Christianity, influence of, 13, 99, 101-11, 112, 124-25, 159
"Climbing Down Pisgah," 163
Cobbett, William, 170
Coleridge, S. T., 128, 129, 169

Colette, 33
Collected Letters of D. H. Lawrence
    (ed. Moore), 6
Collected Poems, 127, 128, 131
Collier's Friday Night, A, 143-44
Collings, Ernest, 120
Community, theme of, 9, 25, 27, 34,
    36, 37, 39-40, 47, 62, 115, 167-69,
    173
Conrad, Joseph, 3, 4, 8, 15, 29, 32, 51,
    54, 60, 155
Cooper, James Fenimore, 62, 160, 161
Cowper, William, 133
Crane, Hart, 12
Crèvecoeur, M. G. J. de, 159-60, 161
Crime and Punishment (Dostoevsky),
    117
Culture and Society (Williams), 9

D

Dana, Richard Henry, 160, 161
D'Annunzio, Gabriele, 66
Dante, 133, 151
Dark Sun, The (Hough), 6
"Daughters of the Vicar," 4
David, 142, 149
Davis, Robert Gorham, 119
Defoe, Daniel, 30, 40
"Democracy," 164, 169, 170, 171,
    172
"Descent in Darkness: The Myth of
    The Plumed Serpent" (Kessler), 69
*D. H. Lawrence: A Composite Biogra-
    phy* (Nehls), 5
*D. H. Lawrence: The Failure and the
    Triumph of Art* (Vivas), 10
D. H. Lawrence: Novelist (Leavis), 10
D. H. Lawrence: A Personal Record
    (Chambers), 135
D. H. Lawrence and Human Existence
    (Jarrett-Kerr), 65
D. H. Lawrence Miscellany, A, (ed.
    Moore), 6
*D. H. Lawrence's Letters to Bertrand
    Russell* (ed. Moore), 6
Dialogues (Plato), 68
Dickens, Charles, 29, 31, 40, 78, 156

"Doe at Evening, A," 134
Don Juan (Byron), 138
Donne, John, 138
Dos Passos, John, 155
Dostoevsky, F., 15, 27, 29, 31, 40, 49,
    51, 152, 155, 157, 159
Dubliners (Joyce), 32

E

Early Greek Philosophy (Burnet), 139
Eliot, George, 3, 20, 29, 30, 31, 157
Eliot, T. S., 2, 12, 67, 138, 151, 157,
    159
Emerson, Ralph Waldo, 153
"Elysium," 134
Engel, Monroe, 13
*English Novel: Form and Function,
    The* (Van Ghent), 8
Escaped Cock, The, 70, 71, 99,
    106
"Evening Walk, The" (Wordsworth),
    131

F

Fall of Hyperion, The (Keats), 140
"Fannie and Annie," 67
Fantasia of the Unconscious, The,
    127
Fantazius Mallare (Hecht), 157
Faulkner, William, 1, 161
Fergusson, Francis, 13, 15, 17
Fielding, Henry, 20, 29, 31, 78
First Lady Chatterley, The, 81
Five Stages of Greek Religion (Mur-
    ray), 139
Flame, The (D'Annunzio), 66
Flaubert, Gustave, 30, 31, 158
Ford, Ford Madox, 32
Form, 2, 4, 6, 8, 51-52, 54-57, 72-73,
    75-76, 99-100, 109, 112-16 *passim,*
    129-41 *passim*
Forster, E. M., 58
Foster, Richard, 9, 14
Fox, The, 4, 66, 93-95, 100
Franklin, Benjamin, 159,
    161

G

Galdós, Benito Pérez, 30
Galsworthy, John, 33, 152, 154, 155, 174
Garnett, Edward, 38, 158
Gide, André, 151
Gissing, George, 153
Goebbels, 63
Goethe, J. W. von, 157
Gogol, N. V., 154
Gordon, Caroline, 29, 119
Grand Inquisitor, The (Dostoevsky), 135, 159
Great Tradition, The (Leavis), 3
Green, Martin, 9
Greene, Graham, 29
Gregory, Horace, 13

H

Hadrian the Seventh (Rolfe), 153
Hamlet, 14
Hardy, Thomas, 10, 21, 29, 54, 56, 130, 136, 155, 156, 160, 161
Hawthorne, Nathaniel, 29, 30, 62, 156, 157, 160, 161
Hecht, Ben, 157
Hemingway, Ernest, 155
Hoffman, Frederick, 115-16
Homer, 153
Homosexuality, 10, 47
Horace, 128
Hough, Graham, 6, 10, 11, 12, 13, 33
Huxley, Aldous, 13, 70, 152

I

Idiot, The (Dostoevsky), 39
Imagery, 8, 12, 17, 18, 19, 21, 32, 43, 55-56, 82
In Our Time (Hemingway), 155
"Insouciance," 70
Intelligent Heart, The (Moore), 6

J

James, Henry, 3, 8, 15, 29, 30, 32, 50, 54

Jane Eyre (Brontë), 42
Jarrett-Kerr, Martin, 7, 65, 67
Johnson, Samuel, 128, 151
Joyce, James, 1, 29, 32, 115, 157
Jude the Obscure (Hardy), 56

K

Kafka, Franz, 1
Kangaroo, 61, 62, 64, 69, 70, 116
Keats, John, 129, 131, 140
Kessler, Jascha, 69
Knopf, Alfred, 61
Kreutzer Sonata (Tolstoy), 61

L

Ladybird, The, 68, **96-97**, 100
Lady Chatterley's Lover, 1, 4, 7, 9, 13, 23, 26, 32, 33, 46, 57, 60, 66, 68, 70, 71, **72-92**, 104, 110, 112, 113, 143, 145, 149, 155, 157, 164, 173
Language, 22-23, 42, 58-59, 135
Language as Gesture (Blackmur), 127
"Last Laugh, The," 67
Lawrence, D. H.:
    biographical information, 3, 70, 165, 168-69
    and Christianity, 13, 99, 101-11 *passim*, 112, 124-25, 159
    literary criticism of, 151-61
    moral vision of, 9-10, 16, 59-60, 61, 75, 151-61 *passim*, 162-74
    and nature, 20, 22, 76-77, 84, 94, 96, 107, 131-32, 134-41 *passim*
Lawrence, D. H., works by:
    Aaron's Rod, 61, 62, 63, 70, 101-2, 104, 116
    "Almond Blossom," 137-38, 141
    Altitude, 144
    "Art and Morality," 161
    Assorted Articles, 154
    "Bavarian Gentians," 71, 141
    Birds, Beasts and Flowers, 136-39
    "Blind Man, The," 11, 13, 112-16
    Boy in the Bush, The, 116
    Captain's Doll, The, 4, **95-97**
    "Climbing Down Pisgah," 163

Lawrence, D. H., works by: (*con-tinued*)
  Collected Poems, 127, 128, 131
  Collier's Friday Night, A, 143-44
  David, 142, 149
  "Daughters of the Vicar," 4
  "Democracy," 164, 169, 170, 171, 172
  "Doe at Evening, A," 134
  "Elysium," 134
  Escaped Cock, The, 70, 71, 99, 106
  "Fannie and Annie," 67
  Fantasia of the Unconscious, The, 127
  First Lady Chatterley, The, 81
  Fox, The, 4, 66, 93-95, 100
  "Insouciance," 70
  Kangaroo, 61, 62, 64, 69, 70, 116
  Ladybird, The, 68, **96-97**, 100
  Lady Chatterley's Lover, 1, 4, 7, 9, 13, 23, 26, 32, 33, 46, 57, 60, 66, 68, 70, 71, **72-92**, 104, 110, 112, 113, 143, 145, 149, 155, 157, 164, 173
  "Last Laugh, The," 67
  Look! We Have Come Through!, 133-35
  Lost Girl, The, 62, 73, 74, 76, 85, 116
  Lovely Lady, The, 68
  "Love on the Farm," 131-32
  "Manifesto," 134
  Man Who Died, The, 4, 9, 13, 60, 70, 99-100, 101-11, 130
  Married Man, The, 144-45
  "Men Must Work and Women as Well," 121
  Merry-Go-Round, 144, 145
  "Modern Prayer," 139
  "Morality and the Novel," 154
  "New Heaven and New Earth," 134
  New Poems, 128-29
  Noah, 149
  "Nottingham and the Mining Country," 163, 164, 165, 167
  "Novel, The," 68
  "Odour of Chrysanthemums," 146

"Piano," 132-33
Plumed Serpent, The, 4, 13, 61-71, 74, 75, 103, 104, 110, 116, 148, 149, 155
"Pornography and Obscenity," **122-26**, 157, 161
"Prussian Officer, The," 11, 93
Rainbow, The, 4, 6, 9, 11, 13, **29-49**, 51, 61, 64, 67, 68, 70, 71, 75, 100, 102, 112, 113, 114, 116, 130, 173
Reflections on the Death of a Porcupine, 68
"Rocking-Horse Winner, The," **117-26**
St. Mawr, 4, 66, **97-99**, 130, 173
"Sex versus Loveliness," 174
"Snake," 136-37, 141
Sons and Lovers, 4, 6, 8, 9, 13, **15-28**, 38, 39, 66, 70, 71, 103, 112, 116, 133, 144, 168
"State of Funk, The," 174
Studies in Classic American Literature, 151, 153, 158-61 *passim*, 172
"Study of Thomas Hardy," 161
"Surgery for the Novel—or a Bomb," 157
"Things," 155
Touch and Go, 143, **146-49**, 150
Virgin and the Gypsy, The, 4
"Wages," 138-39
White Peacock, The, 91, 92
"Why the Novel Matters," 154
Widowing of Mrs. Holroyd, The, 142, 145, 150
Women in Love, 4, 6, 7, 9, 10, 11, 38, 39, 45, 46, **50-60**, 61, 64, 66, 68, 69, 70, 75, 101, 112, 113, 116, 130, 143, 147, 148, 150, 173
"Lawrence and Expressive Form" (Blackmur), 127
Leavis, F. R., 2-3, 4, 5, 9, 10, 13, 14, 29, 30, 32. 45, 68, 143, 161, 168
Lewis, C. S., 110
Liebestod (Wagner), 86
Life force, idea of, 18, 19, 21, 22, 24

Life and Works of D. H. Lawrence
(Moore), 5, 6
"Ligeia" (Poe), 160
"Lines on his Mother's Picture"
(Cowper), 133
Look! We Have Come Through!
133-35
Lost Girl, The, 62, 73, 74, 76, 85, 116
Love, theme of, 9, 56, 57, 101-3
Love Ethic of D. H. Lawrence, The
(Spilka), 9
Lovely Lady, The, 68
"Love on the Farm," 131-32
Lowell, Amy, 133, 134
Luhan, Mabel Dodge, 70

M

Magic Mountain, The (Mann), 62
Magnus, Maurice, 50
Malraux, André, 26-27
Manhattan Transfer (Dos Passos), 155
"Manifesto," 134
Mann, Thomas, 1, 28, 62, 152, 157
Man Who Died, The, 4, 9, 13, 60, 70,
99-100, **101-11,** 130
Marble Faun, The (Hawthorne), 152
Marinetti, E. F. T., 51-52
Married Man, The, 144-45
Marsh, Edward, 128, 129
Marvell, Andrew, 138
Mastro-Don Gesualdo (Verga), 156
Matthiessen, F. O., 160
Melville, Herman, 65, 153, 160-61
Memoirs of the Foreign Legion
(Magnus), 50
"Men Must Work and Women as Well,"
121
Merry-Go-Round, 144, 145
Middlemarch (Eliot), 30, 60
Miller, James E., Jr., 11
Milton, John, 127, 128, 151, 159
Mirror for Anglo-Saxons, A (Green), 9
Moby Dick (Melville), 62
Modern Poetry and the Tradition
(Brooks), 2
"Modern Prayer," 139
Modes of Thought (Whitehead), 79

Moll Flanders (Defoe), 29
Moore, George, 106
Moore, Harry T., 5, 6, 9, 13, 144, 148
Monroe, Harriet, 156
"Morality and the Novel," 154
Morris, William, 170, 171, 172
Moynahan, Julian, 9, 13
Mudrick, Marvin, 9, 13
Murray, Gilbert, 139
Murry, John Middleton, 63, 96, 118,
156
Myers, Neil, 12
Mythological references, 18, 65, 68-69,
89, 108, 109, 140

N

"Nature Alive" (Whitehead), 79
Nehls, Edward, 5
New Bearings in English Poetry
(Leavis), 2
New Criticism, 1, 2, 3, 4, 6, 9, 10, 13,
117
"New Heaven and New Earth," 134
New Poems, 128-29
Nietzsche, F. W., 62
Noah, 149
Noguche, Yone, 128
"Nottingham and the Mining Country,"
163, 164, 165, 167
"Novel, The," 68
"Novel as Dramatic Poem, The"
(Leavis), 4

O

"Odour of Chrysanthemums," 146

P

Palmer, Samuel, 127
Pamela (Richardson), 30
Paradise Lost (Milton), 159
"Piano," 132-33
Pierre (Melville), 61
Pinker, J. B., 158
Pinto, Vivian de Sola, 11, 13
Plato, 68

Plumed Serpent, The, 4, 13, 61-71, 74, 75, 103, 104, 110, 116, 148, 149, 155

Poe, E. A., 62, 123, 157, 160, 161

Poetical Sketches (Blake), 131

Poetry, 156

"Poor Susan" (Wordsworth), 133

Pope, Alexander, 127, 128

"Pornography and Obscenity," 122-26, 157, 161

Porter, Katherine Anne, 13

Portrait of the Artist as a Young Man, A (Joyce), 39

Portrait of a Lady, The (James), 50

Possessorship, theme of, 8, 17, 25-26, 170-171

Poste Restante: A Lawrence Travel Calendar (Moore), 6

Pound, Ezra, 12, 134, 151

Power, theme of, 101-4

Pride and Prejudice (Austen), 20

Prometheus Unbound (Shelley), 95

Proust, Marcel, 1, 152, 157

"Prussian Officer, The," 11, 93

R

Rainbow, The, 4, 6, 9, 11, 13, **29-49**, 51, 61, 64, 67, 68, 70, 71, 75, 100, 102, 112, 113, 114, 116, 130, 173

Rank, J. Arthur, 117

Read, Sir Herbert, 134

Red and the Black, The (Stendhal), 39

Reflections on the Death of a Porcupine, 68

Renewal, theme of, 42, 48, 87, 97, 106, 110, 154, 160

"Resolution and Independence" (Wordsworth), 130

Revaluation: Tradition and Development in English Poetry (Leavis), 2

Richardson, Dorothy, 157

Richards, I. A., 2

Richardson, Samuel, 29, 30, 152

Riders to the Sea (Synge), 145

Rilke, Rainer Maria, 28

"Rocking-Horse Winner, The," 117-26

Rolfe, Frederick, 153, 154

Romola (Eliot), 61

S

St. Mawr, 4, 66, **97-99**, 130, 173

Sartor Resartus (Carlyle), 61

Scarlet Letter, The (Hawthorne), 152

Schorer, Mark, 6-7, 10, 11, 13, 39, 143, 148

Scrutiny, 3, 4

Sex, Literature and Censorship (ed. Moore), 6

Sexuality, theme of, 19, 27, 33-49, 66-69, 74, 79, 84-92, 94, 109, 114-15, 117-26 *passim*

"Sex versus Loveliness," 174

Shakespeare, William, 31, 127, 142, 153

Shapiro, Karl, 11

Shaw, G. B., 151, 155

Shelley, P. B., 99, 129, 151, 153, 159

Sillitoe, Alan, 9

Skelton, John, 127

Slote, Bernice, 11

Smollett, Tobias, 78

"Snake," 136-37, 141

Snodgrass, W. D., 9, 11, 13

Son of Woman (Murry), 62

Songs of Experience (Blake), 130

Sons and Lovers, 4, 6, 8, 9, 13, **15-28** 38, 39, 66, 70, 71, 103, 112, 116, 133, 144, 168

Spender, Stephen, 8, 15, 28, 50

"State of Funk, The," 174

Stendhal, 15, 29, 31

Sterne, Laurence, 29

Strindberg, August, 157

Studies in Classic American Literature, 151, 153, 158-61 *passim*, 172

"Study of Thomas Hardy," 161

Style, 16, 32-33, 42, 50-51, 58-60, 67, 93-100 *passim*, 152

"Surgery for the Novel—or a Bomb," 157

Swift, Jonathan, 151

Symbols, 4, 7-8, 10, 11, 17, 20, 24, 25, 45, 68-69, 108, 117

Synge, J. M., 142, 153

T

Tate, Allen, 119
Technique, 5, 6, 8, 9, 11, 15, 38-39,
  58-59, 93, 95-97, 135, 137-39,
  144-45, 149, 157-58
"Technique as Discovery" (Schorer),
  6, 7
Tennyson, Alfred Lord, 127
Thackeray, W. M., 29
Themes, major, 5, 55
  Being, 18, 19, 21, 22, 24, 55, 72,
    76-77, 78, 83-92, 115
  Death, 7, 10, 12, 22, 28, 51, 53,
    55-57, 77, 79-84 *passim*, 93,
    155-57
  Selfhood, 5, 8, 9, 17, 21, 24, 53,
    60, 83, 101, 170, 174
  Will, 8, 17, 25-26, 55, 57, 67, 74,
    79-83, 96-97, 103-4, 121, 125,
    147, 163-64
"Things," 155
Thomas, Dylan, 12
Thoreau, H. D., 89, 151, 161
Thus Spake Zarathustra (Nietzsche), 61
Tindall, William York, 4, 68
Tolstoy, Leo, 29, 30, 31, 51, 155,
  157, 160
Tom Jones (Fielding), 20
Touch and Go, 143, **146-49**, 150
Trilling, Diana, 13
Tristram Shandy (Sterne), 30
Tristan und Isolde (Wagner), 86
True Voice of Feeling, The (Read),
  134n
Turgenev, Ivan, 30, 51
Twain, Mark, 154

U

Ulysses (Joyce), 32, 33
Understanding Poetry (Brooks and
  Warren), 2

V

Van Ghent, Dorothy, 8-9, 13
Verga, Giovanni, 153, 155, 160
Virgin and the Gypsy, The, 4
Vita Nuova (Dante), 133
Vivas, Eliseo, 4, 10, 12, 68
Voltaire, 151

W

"Wages," 138-39
Wagner, Richard, 86
Warren, Robert Penn, 2
Waterman, Arthur, 14
Waves, The (Woolf), 53
Weaver, R., 161
Wells, H. G., 152, 156
Well-Wrought Urn, The (Brooks), 2
West, Anthony, 13
Whitehead, A. N., 79
White Peacock, The, 91, 92
Whitman, Walt, 12, 62, 128, 134, 136,
  138, 153, 155, 160, 161
"Why Not Read Lawrence Too?"
  (Moore), 5
"Why the Novel Matters," 154
Widowing of Mrs. Holroyd, The, 142,
  145, 150
Wildi, Max, 13
Williams, Raymond, 9, 14
Wings of the Dove (James), 60
Winters, Yvor, 2
Women in Love, 4, 6, 7, 9, 10, 11, 38,
  39, 45, 46, **50-60**, 61, 64, 66, 68, 69,
  70, 75, 101, 112, 113, 116, 130,
  143, 147, 148, 150, 173
Woolf, Virginia, 53
Woolsey, Judge, 32
Wordsworth, William, 128, 130, 131,
  133, 135, 136, 141
Wuthering Heights (Brontë), 21, 30

SINCLAIR LEWIS

A Collection of Critical Essays

Edited by MARK SCHORER

A

Adams, Henry, 107
Ade, George, 116
American Humor (Rourke), 121
American Tragedy, An (Dreiser), 144
Anderson, Margaret, 19, 112, 153
Anderson, Sherwood, 3, 27, 53, 69,
  102, 111, **119-28**, 136, 144
Angela Is Twenty-Two, 168
Ann Vickers, 7, 115-17, 127, 160,
  168
Arrowsmith, 1-5, 33-36, 39, 52, 62-
  70, 73-78, 81-82, 84, 88-89, 93-94,
  97, 104-5, 114-15, 123-25, 147-49,
  151, 159, 163-65, 168

B

Babbitt, 1, 3, **20-26**, 28, 30, 33-34, 36-
  37, 40, 44, 50, 52, **62-70**, 73-82, 84-
  86, 88-91, 93, 100, 103-5, 111,
  114-16, 120, 128, 140, 144-52,
  159-65, 167
Balzac, Honoré de, 87, 112
Bennett, Arnold, 140, 151
Bethel Merriday, 7, 129-30, 136, 160,
  167
Billings, Josh, 32
Bok, Edward W., 19
Brooks, Van Wyck, 8, 144, 153
Broun, Heywood, 155
Bulwark, The (Dreiser),
  144

C

Cabell, James Branch, 105
Caldwell, Erskine, 152
Cantwell, Robert, 7, 49, 60
Carlyle, Thomas, 69
Carman, Bliss, 153
Cass Timberlane, 7, 48, **132-42**, 144,
  160, 169
Cather, Willa, 29n, 130, 136, 144
Characterization, 14, 59, 74-83, 111,
  116-18, **121-28**, 144-45, 156-65
  in *Arrowsmith*, 62-70, 81-82, 88-89
  in *Babbitt*, 20-34 *passim*, 62-70,
    103-4, 116, 149-50
  in *Bethel Merriday*, 130
  in *It Can't Happen Here*, 108-10
  in *Main Street*, 62-70, 102-3
  in *The Trail of the Hawk*, 14
  in *World So Wide*, 8
Churchill, Charles, 62
Clemens, S. L. (*pseud.* Mark Twain),
  32, 44, 95, 152, 162
Cooper, Fenimore, 64
Crane, Stephen, 121, 148, 152

D

Darrow, Clarence, 68
Defoe, Daniel, 31
Dell, Floyd, 119-20
Dickens, Charles, 12n, 40, 103, 106,
  162
Dickinson, Emily, 107

Dodge, Mabel, 153
Dodsworth, 1, 5-6, 8, 52, 98, 100-1,
    105, 115-16, 127, 144, 147-49, 151,
    157, 160, 168
Dos Passos, John, 136, 152
Dostoevski, Feodor, 106
Dreiser, Theodore, 2, 102, 111, 120-
    121, 136, 144, 162
Dunne, Finley Peter, 102
Dunsany, Lord, 19

E

Eliot, T. S., 8, 144, 153
Elmer Gantry, 1, 4-6, 36-38, **39-45**,
    52-61, 73-78, 81-82, 92-94, 104,
    107, 114, 126-27, 144, 147, 151,
    156, 159, 164-65, 168
Emerson, Ralph Waldo, 17, 69
"Eve of St. Agnes, The" (Keats), 51

F

Farrell, James Thomas, 152
Faulkner, William, 124, 152-53
Fiedler, Leslie, 53
Fitzgerald, F. S., 152-53, 162
Flaubert, Gustave, 148
Ford, Ford Madox, 5, 100
Forster, E. M., 5
Francis of Assisi, Saint, 69
Free Air, 15, 78, 80, 102, 113, 156-58,
    164, 167
Freud, Sigmund, 153
Frost, Robert, 6, 102, 105, 107

G

Gale, Zona, 120-21
Galsworthy, John, 161
Geismar, Maxwell, 2-3, 7, 10, 60,
    129
Gideon Planish, 7, 130-36, 140, 160
    169
God-Seeker, The, 8, 169
Gogh, Vincent van, 106
Great Gatsby, The (Fitzgerald),
    162

H

Harcourt, Alfred, 154-55
Hawthorne, Nathaniel, 107, 148, 152
Hearst, William Randolph, 152
Hemingway, Ernest, 152-53
Hergesheimer, Joseph, 105
Herrick, Robert, 69, 102
Hike and the Aeroplane, 11
Hovey, Richard, 153
Howells, William Dean, 119-20,
    152
Humor, 32-34, 121, 152, 162

I

In Our Time (Hemingway), 153
Innocents, The, 12n, 113, 167
It Can't Happen Here, 7, **108-10**, 115,
    124, 127, 135n, 144, 147, 160, 168
Ivanhoe, (Scott), 155

J

James, Henry, 5, 105, 107, 126
    148, 152
Jayhawker, The (Lewis and Lewis),
    130n
Jeffers, Robinson, 105
Job, The, 2, 12-15, 78-79, 81, 102,
    113, 144, 154-55, 158
Joyce, James, 153

K

Karlfeldt, Erik Axel, 155
Kazin, Alfred, 7, 162-63
Keats, John, 51
Kingsblood Royal, 8, 135n, 144, 160
Krutch, Joseph Wood, 4, 9

L

Lady Chatterley's Lover (Lawrence),
    46
Lardner, Ring, 27, 120-21, 150, 162
Lawrence, D. H., 46, 49, 59, 61
Levin, Jack, T., 8

Lewis, Dorothy Thompson, 7, 168
Lewis, Grace Hegger, 153, 155-56,
   161, 167
Lewis, Harry Sinclair
   and Anderson, Sherwood, 53,
      119-28, 136
   and Cather, Willa, 136
   and Defoe, Daniel, 31
   and Dickens, Charles, 40, 106, 162
   and Dos Passos, John, 136
   and Dreiser, Theodore, 136, 144
   and Faulkner, William, 124
   and Flaubert, Gastone, 148
   and James, Henry, 105
   life of, 8, 113, 123, 145, 150-51
      155-57, 167-69
   and Mencken, H. L., 32, 154
   and the Nobel Prize in literature, 6,
      102-7, 112, 119, 148, 152, 155,
      168
   and Shaw, G. B., 156
   and Sinclair, Upton, 111-12, 114
   and Voltaire, 4
   and Wells, H. G., 99, 161
   and Wolfe, Thomas, 144
   and Zola, Émile, 33
Lewis, Harry Sinclair, works by: (*see
   also* titles of individual works)
   Angela Is Twenty-Two, 168
   Ann Vickers, 7, 115-17, 127, 160,
      168
   Arrowsmith, 1-5, 33-36, 39, 52,
      62-70, 73-78, 81-82, 84, 88-89,
      93-94, 97, 104-5, 114-15, 123-25,
      147-49, 151, 159, 163-65, 168
   Babbitt, 1, 3, 20-26, 28, 30, 33-34,
      36-37, 40, 44, 50, 52, 62-70, 73-
      82, 84-86, 88-91, 93, 100, 103-5,
      111, 114-16, 120, 128, 140,
      144-52, 159-65, 167
   Bethel Merriday, 7, 129-30, 136,
      160, 167
   Cass Timberlane, 7, 48, 132-42,
      144, 160, 169
   Dodsworth, 1, 5-6, 8, 52, 98, 100-
      1, 105, 115-16, 127, 144,
      147-49, 151, 157, 160, 168
   Elmer Gantry, 1, 4-6, 36-38, 39-45,

      52-61, 73-78, 81-82, 92-94, 104,
      107, 114, 126-27, 144, 147, 151,
      156, 159, 164-65, 168
   Free Air, 15, 78, 80, 102, 113,
      156-58, 164, 167
   Gideon Planish, 7, 130-36, 140
      160, 169
   God-Seeker, The, 8, 169
   Hike and the Aeroplane, 11
   Innocents, The, 12n, 113, 167
   It Can't Happen Here, 7, 108-10,
      115, 124, 127, 135n, 144, 147,
      160, 168
   Jayhawker, The (Lewis and Lewis),
      130n
   Job, The, 2, 12-15, 78-79, 81, 102,
      113, 144, 154-55, 158
   Kingsblood Royal, 8, 135n, 144,
      160
   Main Street, 1-4, 17-22, 23, 29-31,
      33, 36-37, 62-70, 73, 76, 78, 80,
      84, 86, 88, 93, 95, 99, 102-5,
      111-16, 119, 122-25, 128, 133,
      140, 144-52, 154-63, 167
   Man Who Knew Coolidge, The, 104,
      116, 126-27, 143, 157, 159, 164
   Mantrap, 4, 36-45, 104, 115
   Martin Arrowsmith (see
      Arrowsmith)
   "Miracle Forsooth, A," 155
   Our Mr. Wrenn, 1, 11-13, 15, 78-79,
      144, 155-57
   Prodigal Parents, The, 7, 127, 137,
      143, 160
   Saturday Evening Post, short
      stories in, 111, 115, 151, 156
   Selected Short Stories, 15n
   Trail of the Hawk, The, 2, 10-15,
      78, 81, 115, 154
   Village Virus, The (see *Main Street*)
   Work of Art, 7, 111, 115-17,
      127
   World So Wide, 8, 143-45, 157,
      160
Lewisohn, Ludwig, 156
Lindsay, Vachel, 112, 153
Lippmann, Walter, 5, 22, 109
London, Jack, 69

Long, Huey, 108-9
Love and Mr. Lewisham (Wells), 99
Lovett, Robert Morss, 4

M

McCarthy, Mary, 165
McHarg, Lloyd, 157
Mackaye, Percy, 19
Madame Bovary (Flaubert), 148
Main Street, 1-4, **17-22**, 23, **29-31**,
    33, 36-37, 62-70, 73, 76, 78, 80, 84,
    86, 88, 93, 95, 99, 102-5, 111-16,
    119, 122-25, 128, 133, 140, 144-52,
    154-63, 167
Man Who Knew Coolidge, The, 104,
    116, 126-27, 143, 157, 159, 164
Mantrap, 4, **36-45**, 104, 115
Marriage (Wells), 140
Martin Arrowsmith (see Arrowsmith)
Masters, Edgar Lee, 119, 121, 153-54
Melville, Herman, 106-7, 148, 152
Mencken, H. L., 3-5, 20, 32, 48, 52,
    73, 91, 116, 119, 147, 154, 164
Michelangelo, 69
Millay, Edna, 153-54
"Miracle Forsooth, A," 155
Monroe, Harriet, 153
Moon-Calf (Dell), 119
More, Paul Elmer, 102
Morris, William, 69
Mueller, Max, 87
Mumford, Lewis, 6, 102

N

Nicholson, Meredith, 2
Nietzsche, Friedrich, 19
Nobel Prize in literature, 6, 102-7, 112,
    119, 148, 152, 155, 168
Norris, Frank, 46, 59, 61, 102,
    119-21

O

O'Neill, Eugene, 102, 144, 153
On Native Grounds (Kazin), 7

Our Mr. Wrenn, 1, 11-13, 15, 78-79,
    144, 155-57

P

Parrington, V. L., 4-5
Phelps, William Lyon, 155
Pope, Alexander, 62
Pound, Ezra, 153
Prejudices (Mencken), 119
Pride and Prejudice (Austen), 150
Pritchett, V. S., 8
Prodigal Parents, The, 7, 127, 137,
    143, 160
Public Opinion (Lippmann), 22

R

Rabelais, François, 87
Rahv, Philip, 8
Ransom, John Crowe, 8
Realism, 2, 15*n*, 120, 162
    in *Babbitt*, 33-34, 150
    in *The Job*, 13
Religion, 49, 92-94, 156, 163-64 (*see
    also Elmer Gantry*)
Ripley, George, 69
Robinson, E. A., 102
Rosenfeld, Paul, 27
Rourke, Constance, 3, 121
Rousseau, Jean Jacques, 68
Ruskin, John, 69

S

Sandburg, Carl, 17, 153
Sanger, Margaret, 19
Satire, 2, 5, 15*n*, 41-45, 63, 71, 102,
    105-6, 123-24, 160-61
    in *Babbitt*, 3
    in *Elmer Gantry*, 4, 41-45, 74
    in *Main Street*, 123
Saturday Evening Post, short stories
    in, 111, 115, 151, 156
Schorer, Mark, 46, 164
Selected Short Stories,
    15*n*

Shaw, George Bernard, 19, 156
Sherman, Stuart Pratt, 4
Sinclair, Upton, 69, 102, 111-12,
    114, 156
Sister Carrie (Dreiser), 119, 144
Sitwell family, 153
Soldiers' Pay (Faulkner), 153
Song of the Lark, The (Cather), 131n
Spoon River Anthology (Masters),
    119, 154
Stein, Gertrude, 120, 153-54
Steinbeck, John, 152
Stevens, Wallace, 153

T

Tar (Anderson), 119
Tarkington, Booth, 2, 163
Tate, Allen, 8
Tennyson, Alfred, 52
These Twain (Bennett), 140
This Side of Paradise (Fitzgerald),
    152-53, 162
Thoreau, Henry David, 87, 107
Three Lives (Stein), 153
Tolstoi, Leo, 106
Trail of the Hawk, The, 2, 10-15, 78,
    81, 115, 154
Trilling, Diana, 7
Twain, Mark (*see* Clemens, S. L.)

U

Uncle Tom's Cabin (Stowe), 93

V

Van Doren, Carl, 119, 148, 154
Van Dyke, Henry, 112
Village Virus, The (see Main Street)

Voltaire, 45

W

Walpole, Hugh, 152, 161
Ward, Artemus, 32, 162
Warren, Dale, 8
Wells, H. G., 23, 88, 99, 140, 151, 161
West, Rebecca, 3-4, 9, 22
Wharton, Edith, 120, 152
Whipple, T. K., 4-5, 9, 49-50, 113-14,
    124
White, William Allen, 53
Whitman, Walt, 17, 26
Wilson, Edmund, 7
Wolfe, Thomas, 130, 144, 152, 157,
    163
Work of Art, 7, 111, 115-17, 127
Web and the Rock, The (Wolfe),
    130n
Winesburg, Ohio (Anderson), 119,
    122
With Love from Gracie (G. Lewis),
    155, 161, 162n
World So Wide, 8, 143-45, 157, 160

Y

Yankee at the Court of King Arthur, A
    (Clemens), 43
Yeats, William Butler, 153
You Can't Go Home Again (Wolfe),
    157, 163

Z

Zola, Émile, 112
Zweig, Arnold, 155

LORCA

A Collection of Critical Essays

Edited by MANUEL DURÁN

A

"Abandoned Church," 112-13, 122
Aeneid, The (Virgil), 120, 132
Alberti, Rafael, 5, 43, 48, 52, 131-32
Alfonzo X, 19
Alonso, Dámaso, 1
"Another Dream," 100
Apollinaire, Guillaume, 6, 65-66
Arabic influences, on Lorca's work,
 84, 93-95
Arp, Jean, 1
Ash-Wednesday (Eliot), 114-15
Aub, Max, 53
Ayala, Pérez de, 33

B

"Back from a Walk," 109, 118-19
"Ballad of a Day in July, The," 39
"Ballad of Thanár and Amnón," 84-85,
 137
"Ballad of the Civil Guard, The," 23,
 101
"Ballad of the Little Square, The,"
 71
"Ballad of the Summoned Man, The,"
 138
Ballads of Coral Gables (Jiménez), 2
Baudelaire, Charles, 75, 117
Bécquer, Gustavo, 51, 131
Benavente, Jacinte, 11
Berenguer, General, 11
Bergamin, José, 33

Bergson, Henri, 157
Bitter Oleander (see Blood Wedding)
"Blind Panorama of New York," 120-
 21, 122, 124
Blood Wedding, 12, 47, 54, 55, 101,
 138, **148-52,** 168, 173
Book of Good Love, The (Ruiz), 19-
 20, 24
Book of Poems, 3, 6, 28, 32, **65-70,**
 73-77
 nursery songs in, 38-41
Book of Songs, 6, 32, 44, 58
Borrow, George, 134
Brancusi, Constantin, 1
Brenan, Gerald, 1
Breton, André, 1
Brickell, Herschel, 4
Buñuel, Luis, 3, 33

C

Calderón, Pedro, 12, 48, 90
Camões, Luis Vaz de, 73
Camp, Jean, 59
Camus, Albert, 14
"Canción oriental," 71-73
Canedo, Enreque Diéz, 142
Cantar de Mio Cid, 18, 19, 23, 24
Canto a Teresa (Espronceda), 74
Carducci, Enotrio, 132
Castillejo, Cristóbal de, 21
Cervantes, Miguel de, 10, 132, 170
Chabás, Juan, 12
Chekhov, Anton, 147-48, 174

Cherry Orchard, The (Chekhov), 147
Chirico, Giorgio de, 1
"Christmas on the Hudson," 109
Cocteau, Jean, 1, 172
Color, Lorca's use of, 57-64 (*see also*
   Imagery)
Conrad, Joseph, 118, 122
Contemplado, El (Salinas), 2
Copeau, Jacques, 173
Couffon, Claude, 1
Crow, John A., 7-8, 9
"Crucifixion," 123-24, 126
"Cry to Rome," 116, 126-29

D

Dali, Salvador, 1, 8, 33, 57, 63-64, 75,
   86-87, 88
Dama boba, La (Vega), 12
D'Annunzio, Gabriele, 151
Darío, Rubén, 5, 29, 30, 71, 74
Dark Night of the Soul (St. John of
   the Cross), 67, 73
Death, theme of, in Lorca's works,
   60-61, 71-73, 76-77, 100-7
   in *Gypsy Ballads*, 137-38
   in *Poet in New York*, 91
De Falla, Manuel, 3, 12, 27, 28, 46,
   47, 62
Desnos, Robert, 1
Diego, Gerardo, 3, 5, 6, 8, 28, 53,
   65
Diván at the Tamarit, The, 93-95
Domaine espagnol (Larbaud), 57
Doña Rosita the Spinster, 145, 146-48,
   152, 173
   humor in, 158-59, 160, 164, 165
Don Juan Tenorio (Zorrilla), 105
"Double Poem of Lake Edem,"
   117-18
Douces grenades entrouvertes
   (Valéry), 71
Drama, Lorca's works of, 9-13, 47-48,
   53-55, 140-54, 167-75 (*see also*
   titles of individual plays)
Drayton, Michael, 68
Dudgeon, Patrick,
   47

E

Echegaray, José, 11
Eddington, Sir Arthur, 3
El Cid (see Cantar de Mio Cid)
"Elegy to Lady Joan the Mad,"
   73
Eliot, T. S., 108, 110, 114-16, 118-19,
   122-23, 167, 171, 172
Eluard, Paul, 1, 57
Espronceda, José de, 74

F

"Fable and Round of the Three
   Friends," 119
"Faithless Wife, The," 23, 24-25, 32,
   75, 83-84
Family Reunion, The (Eliot), 171
First Songs, 6
Folklore, Lorca's use of, 85
Frame of Don Cristóbal The, 143,
   144
   humor in, 158, 160, 163, 165
Franco, Francisco, 13, 30, 49
Frazer, Sir James, 119-20, 127-28

G

Galdós, Pérez, 30
Gallo, 1, 3
Garcilaso de la Vega, 42
Gasch, Sebastián, 4
Gauguin, Paul, 134
Gautier, Théophile, 58
Georgics (Virgil), 67
Gili, J. L., 41
Golden Bough, The (Frazer), 119-20,
   127-28
Gómez de la Serna, Ramón, 6-7, 57
Góngora, Luis de, 22-23, 42, 43, 51,
   53, 67, 71, 83
Goya, Francisco, 51
Greco, El, 21, 22, 23, 51, 105-6
Gris, Juan, 1
Guillén, Jorge, 5, 13, 14-15, 111,
   131
Guillén, Nicolás, 34

Gypsy Ballads, 3, 5, 6, 31-32, 36-38, 70-71, 130-39, 141, 148, 156, 171
  color, Lorca's use of, 58-59
  death, theme of, 137-38
  and folklore, 85
  themes of, 80-86, 89

H

Heart of Darkness, The (Conrad), 122
"Heaven Alive," 114, 118, 123
Heidegger, Martin, 103
Herrera, Fernando de, 21, 22
Hollow Men, The (Eliot), 110
House of Bernarda Alba, The, 14, 47, 54, 101-2, 153-54, 168, 174
Huidobro, Vicente, 8
Humor, in Lorca's dramas, 155-66
Huxley, Aldous, 67

I

Ibsen, Henrik, 174
If Five Years Pass, 144, 145, 152, 158
Imagery, in Lorca's work, 6-7, 42-43, 75
  in *Poet in New York,* 109-29
Impeccable Nude, The (Salinas), 2
Irving, Washington, 134

J

Jacob, Max, 6
Janés, Benjamín, 70
Jealous Old Man, The (Cervantes), 170
"Jewish Cemetery," 123
Jiménez, Don Alberto, 33
Jiménez, Juan Ramón, 2, 5, 6, 29, 30, 33, 43, 47, 52, 59, 80
John of the Cross, Saint, 67, 73, 114

K

Keats, John, 43
"King of Harlem," 109, 116-17, 126

L

La Barraca, 12, 48, 167-68
Lament for the Death of a Bull-fighter, 10, 23-24, 48-49, 60, 77-78, 95-100, 107, 148
"Landscape of the Urinating Multitudes," 109
"Landscape of the Vomiting Multitudes," 109
Langer, Suzanne K., 133
Larbaud, Valery, 57
Larrea, Juan, 8
Lautréamont, Comte de, 75
Le Corusier, 1
León, Fray Luis de, 21, 51
"Little Boy Stanton," 113
"Little Girl Drowned in the Well," 113, 119-20
"Lluvia," 78-79
Lorca, Federica García:
  Arabic influences on, 84, 93-95
  color, use of, 57-64 (*see also* Imagery)
  cosmopolitanism of, 1-2
  and Dali, Salvador, 1, 8, 33, 57, 63-64, 75, 86-87, 88
  and Darío, Rubén, 5, 29
  death, theme of, 60-61, 71-73, 76-77, 91, 100-7, 137-38
  and De Falla, Manuel, 3, 12, 46, 47, 62
  drama, 9-13, 47-48, 53-55, **140-54,** 167-75
  and Eliot, T. S., 108, 110, 114-16, 118-19, 122-23, 167, 171, 172
  folklore, use of, 85
  humor of, in drama, 155-66
  imagery of, 6-7, 42-43, 75, **109-29**
  and Jiménez, Juan Ramón, 5, 6, 29, 33, 43
  and *La Barraca,* 12, 48, 167-68
  life of, 2-5, 9-10, 32-33
  meter, use of, 19, 31
  myth, use of, 132-34, 172-73
  as a nature poet, 66-70
  in New York, 9-10, 33, 108-9, 156-57

Lorca, Federica García: (*continued*)
  nursery songs, use of, 34-36, 38-41
  on poetry, 5-10, 45-47, 61-62, 65
  political beliefs of, 13-14
  religious and mystical themes, 88-
    91, 93, 113-14, 123-24
  reputation of, 13-15
  and Rilke, Rainer Maria, 103-4,
    106, 107
  and the Spanish Civil War, 1, 3, 4,
    11, 13
  and Spanish poetry, history of,
    18-26
  and Surrealism, 2, 5, 6, 8-9, 33,
    144-46
  translations of, 41-42
  and Vega, Lope de, 1, 12, 48, 151
  and Whitman, Walt, 33, 92-93, 116,
    125-26
Lorca, Federica García, works by:
POETRY (*see also* titles of individual
poems)
  Book of Poems, 3, 6, 28, 32, **65-70**,
    73-77
  Book of Songs, 6, 32, 44, 58
  Diván at the Tamarit, The, 93-95
  First Songs, 6
  Gypsy Ballads, 3, 5, 6, 31-32, 36-
    38, 70-71, 130-39, 141, 148
    156, 171
  *Lament for the Death of a Bull-
    fighter*, 10, 23-24, 48-49, 60, 77-
    78, **95-100**, 107, 148
  Odes, 6, 7-8, 74-75, 86-89, 92-93,
    95, 124-26
  Poem of the Cante Jondo, The, 6,
    11, 32, 44-45, 59, 62, 78-79, 89,
    148
  Poet in New York, 5, 8-10, 33, **89-
    93**, **108-29**
DRAMA
  Blood Wedding, 12, 47, 54, 55, 101,
    138, 148-52, 168, 173
  Doña Rosita the Spinster, 145, 146-
    48, 152, 173
  Frame of Don Cristóbal, The, 143,
    144
  House of Bernarda Alba, The,

  14, 47, 54, 101-2, 153-54, 168,
    174
  If Five Years Pass, 144, 145, 152,
    158
  Love of Don Perlimplin, The, 10,
    12, 143, 144, 152, 168-75
  Love the Sorcerer, 12
  *Maiden, the Sailor, and the Student,
    The*, 159
  Mariana Pineda, 3, 10, 12, 47, 132,
    140-42, 146, 152, 162
  Public, The, 144-45, 158
  Puppets of Cachiporra, The, 144,
    157-58, 159, 160, 161-62, 165
  Shoemaker's Prodigious Wife, The,
    10, 11-12, 143-44
  Spell of the Butterfly, The, 10, 11,
    140, 157, 159, 161
  Walk of Buster Keaton, The, 161,
    164
  Yerma, 54, 101, 138, 152-53, 154,
    173
Lord Jim (Conrad), 118
Love in the Western World (Rouge-
  mont), 170
Love of Don Perlimplin, The, 10, 12,
  143, 144, 152, **168-75**
  myth in, 172-73
  plot summary, 168-70
Love the Sorcerer, 12
Lowell, Amy, 6
Loyola, Saint Ignatius, 73
Lusiads, The (Camões), 73

M

Machado, Antonio, 29, 30-31, 33, 52
Madariaga, Salvador de, 20
Maeterlinck, Maurice, 151
*Maiden, the Sailor, and the Student,
  The*, 159
"Mañana," 78
Mariana Pineda, 3, 10, 12, 47, 132,
  140-42, 146, 152, 162
"Marina" (Eliot), 119
Maritain, Jacques, 1
"Martyrdom of Saint Olalla, The," 137
Mayakovsky, Vladimir, 13, 14

Mena, Juan de, 20, 21, 22, 25
Merimée, Prosper, 134
Mesa, Enrique de, 29, 33
Meter, Lorca's use of, 19, 31
Midsummer Night's Dream, A
(Shakespeare), 68
Milton, John, 132
Miró, Joan, 1
Molière, 10
Murder in the Cathedral (Eliot), 171
Myth, Lorca's use of, 132-34
    in *Love of Don Perlimplin, The,*
    172-73

N

Neruda, Pablo, 4, 13-14
New York, Lorca's visit to, 9-10, 33,
    108-9, 156-57
"1910, Interlude," 110-11, 113, 116,
    122
"Nocturne of the Void," 112
Nursery songs, Lorca's use of, 34-36,
    38-41
Nymphidia (Drayton), 68

O

Odes, 6, 7-8, 74-75, 92-93, 95, 124-26
    religious and mystical themes,
    88-89
"Ode to Salvador Dali," 31, 86-87, 95
"Ode to the Most Holy Eucharist,"
    87-89
"Ode to the West Wind" (Shelley), 74
"Ode to Walt Whitman," 59-60, 92-93,
    124-26
"Office and Denunciation," 7, 109,
    116, 117, 120-25 *passim*
Ortega y Gasset, José, 63

P

Paradise Lost (Milton), 132
"Pattern and Paradise of Negroes,"
    113-14, 118
Picasso, Pablo, 1, 60
Poem of the Cante Jondo, 6, 11,

32, 44-45, 59, 62, 78-79, 89, 148
Poesias selectas castellanas (Quintana),
    21-22
Poet in New York, 5, 8-10, 33, 86,
    89-93
    death, theme of, 91
    religious and mystical themes, 90-
    91, 93, 113-14, 123-24
    symbolism and allegory in, 108-29
Poetry, Lorca's view on, 5-10, 45-47,
    61-62, 65
"Preciosa and the Wind," 23, 137
"Prológo," 75
Public, The, 144-45, 158
Puppets of Cachiporra, The, 144,
    157-58, 159, 160, 161-62, 165

Q

Quevedo, Francisco, 51, 104-5
Quintana, Manuel José, 21-22

R

Reinhardt, Max, 173
Religious and mystical themes, in
    Lorca's work, 88-91, 93, 113-14,
    123-24
    in *Odes,* 88-89
    in *Poet in New York,* 90-91, 93,
    113-14, 123-24
Resurrection, The (Yeats), 124
Reverdy, Pierre, 1, 6
Revista de Occidente, 63-64
"Reyerta," 2
Reyes, Alfonso, 33
Riders to the Sea (Synge), 47
Rilke, Rainer Maria, 103-4, 106, 107
Rio, Angel del, 108
Rios, Fernando de los, 3, 11
Rivas-Cherif theater group, 10, 12
Rivera, Primo de, 11
"Romance de la Guardia Civil
"Española," 23, 101
"Romances históricos," 23
Rosales, Luis, 4
Rougemont, Denis de, 170, 173
"Ruin," 114-16, 121

Ruiz, Juan, 19-20, 24

S

Saint Maurice (El Greco), 105-6
Salazar, Adolfo, 153
Salinas, Pedro, 2, 5, 33, 156
Sánchez, Roberto, 173, 174
Schonberg, Jean-Louis, 1, 3-4, 10
Secret Life (Dali), 8
Shakespeare, William, 68, 103, 113,
   119, 125
Shaw, G. B., 157
Shelley, Percy Bysshe, 43, 74
Shoemaker's Prodigious Wife, The,
   10, 11-12, 143-44
   humor in, 158, 160, 161, 162-63,
   164-66
Simmel, Georg, 103
"Somnambulist Ballad," 101, 138
"Song for the Moon," 76-77
Sotelo, Calvo, 4
Spanish Civil War, 1, 3, 4, 11, 13
Spanish poetry, Lorca's place in his-
   tory of, 18-26
Spell of the Butterfly, The, 140, 157,
   159, 161
Spender, Stephen, 41
"Spring Song," 71
Steinbeck, John, 13, 14
Stravinsky, Igor, 1, 12
Surrealism, influence of, on Lorca's
   work, 2, 5, 6, 8-9, 33, 144-46
Synge, J. M., 47

T

Tempest, The (Shakespeare), 113, 119
Teresa, Saint, 21, 22, 23, 25, 73
Thompson, Francis, 43
Three Sisters (Chekhov), 147
Toriada, La (Villalón), 48
Torre, Guillermo de, 30, 33
Tragic Sense of Life, The (Unamuno),
   152
Translation, of Lorca's work, 41-42
Tríptico del sacrificio (Torre), 30

Tzara, Tristan, 1

U

Unamuno, Miguel de, 21, 23, 30, 140,
   152
"Unsleeping City," 109, 123

V

Valéry, Paul, 3, 71
Valle-Inclán, Ramón de, 29, 54, 151
Vega, Lope de, 1, 12, 18, 48, 51-52,
   54, 140, 151
Velasquez, Rodríguez, 106
Vicente, Gil, 140
Villa, Moreno, 33, 43
Villalón, Francisco, 48
Virgil, 67, 120, 132
Vivar, Rodrigo Díaz de, 18

W

Walk of Buster Keaton, The, 161, 164
Waste Land, The (Eliot), 108, 110-29
   passim
Whitman, Walt, 33, 92-93, 116, 125-26
Wordsworth, William, 66-67

X

Xavier, Saint Francis, 73
Xirgu, Margarita, 11, 12, 47

Y

Yeats, William Butler, 124, 167, 171,
   175
Yerma, 54, 101, 138, 152-53, 154, 173
"Your Childhood in Menton," 111-12,
   113, 116, 119, 121, 122, 125

Z

Zalamea, Jorge, 5-6, 61
Zorrilla, José, 105, 140

ROBERT LOWELL

A Collection of Critical Essays

Edited by THOMAS PARKINSON

A

"Adonais" (Shelley), 63, 64, 70
"Aeneas at Washington" (Tate), 79
Aeschylus, 25-26
"After Surprising Conversions," 47,
 51, 57-58, 59, 117
Albee, Edward, 11
Alspach, Russell, 6
Alvarez, A., 152
"Am letzten Tage des Jahres" (Droste-
 Hülshoff), 133
"Among School Children" (Yeats),
 146
"Arethusa" (Shelley), 4
"Armadillo, The" (Bishop), 133
"Armageddon" (Ransom), 84
"As a Plane Tree by the Water," 55,
 59, 114
"At a Bible House," 58, 59
"At the Indian Killer's Grave," 21,
 46, 83-85
Auden, W. H., 40, 55, 143

B

Barker, George, 122
Baudelaire, Charles, 5, 55, 74, 87-88,
 93, 94, 97-98
 Lowell's translations of, 153-54,
 163-65
Beddoes, Thomas Lovell, 125
Bellow, Saul, 19
Benito Cereno (Lowell), 135-42

Bernard, Saint, 39
Berryman, John, 134, 148
"Between the Porch and Altar," 22, 41,
 46, 59
 as a confessional poem, 115-16
"Beyond the Alps," 89-91, 126
Biographical information, on Lowell,
 12, 28, 74-77
Bishop, Elizabeth, 13, 19-20, 30, 125,
 128, 133
Blackmur, R. P., 14, 80
"Blind Leading the Blind, The," 47
Bogan, Louise, 86
"Boston Nativity, The," 79
Bridge, The (Crane), 122
Bridges, Robert, 15
"Brod und Wein" (Hölderlin), 133
Brooks, Cleanth, 2
Brown, Harry, 27
Browning, Robert, 18, 34
"Buenos Aires," 96

C

Calvinism, Lowell's views on, 55, 58,
 62, 79-80
Canti, I (Leopardi), 165-66
Cantos, The (Pound), 154-55
Cape Cod (Thoreau), 70, 71
Cathay (Pound), 159
Catholic Art and Culture (Watkins),
 72-73
Catullus, 26, 27
"Castaway, The" (Cowper), 125

329

"Charles the Fifth and the Peasant, 1790," 58

Chatterton, Thomas, 125

Chekhov, Anton, 22, 35, 128

"Children of Light," 58, 60, 67, 114, 115

"Christ for Sale," 78

"Christmas at Black Rock," 43, 60, 61

"Christmas Eve Under Hooker's Statue," 41, 61, 67

"Cistercians in Germany, The," 21

Cobbett, William, 55

Cocteau, Jean, 103

Coleridge, Samuel Taylor, 125

"Colloquy in Black Rock," 45, 46, 66, 114, 117

"Commander Lowell," 18-19

"Concord," 50, 80

Confessional poetry, in Lowell's work, 113-23, 124-30, 143-51

Coriolanus (Schwartz), 31

Crane, Hart, 15, 21, 22, 31-32, 82, 88, 113, 122, 125

Crashaw, Richard, 55, 58

"Crucifix, The," 50, 61

Cowper, William, 125

Creeley, Robert, 2-3

"Cynge, Le" (Baudelaire), 98, 162

D

"Dandelion Girls, The," 74

Dante Alighieri, 55, 56, 154

"David and Bathsheba in the Public Garden," 99, 105

Dawson, Christopher, 36

"Dead in Europe, The," 116

"Dea Roma," 41, 50

"Death from Cancer," 36, 47

"Death of a Son" (Silkin), 125

"Death of the Sheriff, The," 41, 46, 85, 117

Dickinson, Emily, 113

Don Giovanni (Mozart), 96

Donne, John, 5, 150

Drayton, Michael, 16, 17, 36

Dream Songs (Berryman), 148

Drew, Elizabeth, 15

Droste-Hülshoff, Annette von, 133

"Drunken Fisherman, The," 15, 39, 41, 46, 47, 50, 114

Dryden, John, 154

"Dry Salvages, The" (Eliot), 83

"Dunbarton," 49

Duncan, Robert, 1, 4, 5

Dupee, F. W., 80

E

Eberhart, Richard, 15, 75

Edwards, Jonathan, 16, 17, 55, 58

Elegies (Rukeyser), 122

Eliot, T. S., 14, 24, 31, 32, 33-34, 36, 55, 81, 83, 88, 110, 113-14, 122, 128, 143

Ellmann, Richard, 5-6

Empson, William, 15

"Exile's Return, The," 40, 47, 80-81

"Eye and Tooth," 97

F

"Falling Asleep over the Aeneid," 99, 101, 105

"Fat Man in the Mirror, The," 99, 104

Fearing, Kenneth, 122-23

"First Sunday in Lent, The," 61

Ford, Ford Madox, 25, 28, 29, 120

"Ford Madox Ford," 111

For the Union Dead, 143-51

"For the Union Dead," 93, 98

Four Quartets (Eliot), 34, 128

Frost, Robert, 75, 95, 102
    Lowell's views on, 27-28, 33-35

G

"Gerontion" (Eliot), 24

"Ghost, The," 17, 58, 59, 85, 117

Goethe, Johann Wolfgang von, 103

Graves, Robert, 30

"Green Light" (Fearing), 122-23

Grene, David, 156

H

"Hälfte des Lebens" (Hölderlin), 125
Hardwick, Elizabeth, 12, 86
Hawthorne, Nathaniel, 55
Herbert, George, 150
"Her Dead Brother," 99, 104, 117
History of England, The (Macaulay), 21
Hölderlin, Friedrich, 125, 133
Homer, 26, 93, 152, 153, 157-58
Hooker, Thomas, 55
Hopkins, Gerard Manley, 14, 51
Horace, 26
Hugh Selwyn Mauberley (Pound), 122
Hulme, T. E., 55
Hyperion (Keats), 27-28

I

Iliad (Homer), 26, 93, 152, 153, 157-58
Imitations, 94, 152-70
Inferno (Dante), 154
"In Memory of Arthur Winslow," 49, 68, 80
"In the Cage," 51, 89

J

Jarrell, Randall, 14, 23, 55-56, 59, 75, 129-30
John of the Cross, Saint, 130, 131
Johnson, Lyndon B., 149
Johnson, Dr. Samuel 152-53, 154, 158
Jonson, Ben, 163
Joyce, James, 32
Juvenal, 26, 158

K

"Katherine's Dream," 17, 18, 43, 59
Kay, George, 169
Keats, John, 27-28
Kenyon College, 12, 14, 75, 77
"Killing of Lykaon, The," 93, 157-58
Kittel, Charles, 4

Knight, Walter, 4
Kunitz, Stanley, 23, 30

L

Laforgue, Jules, 20, 55
Land of Unlikeness, 12, 16, 21-22, 29, 43, 48-50, 76-80, 114
  Christian symbolism in, 36-37
  Latin poetry, Lowell's interest in, 25-27, 159, 162-63
Lattimore, Richmond, 152
Lawrence, D. H., 10, 115
Leopardi, Giacomo, 165-66
Levertov, Denise, 1
Lewis, R. W. B., 3, 5
"Lice-Hunters, The," 95
"Lied des Idioten, Das" (Rilke), 25
Life Studies, 9, 18-21, 88-98, 110-12, 117-23
  "Skunk Hour," 124-30, 131-34
Lindsay, Vachel, 125
Li Po, 158
Logue, Christopher, 157
Lord Weary's Castle, 12, 16, 17, 23, 40-47, 49-52, 53-62, 80-85, 106, 114-17
  "Quaker Graveyard in Nantucket, The," 63-73
"Love Song of J. Alfred Prufrock, The" (Eliot), 122
Lowell, Amy, 28
Lowell, Harriet, 12
Lowell, James Russell, 28, 75
Lowell, Robert:
  and Baudelaire, Charles, 5, 55, 74, 87-88, 93, 94, 97-98, 153-54, 163-65
  and Calvinism, 55, 58, 62, 79-80
  as a confessional poet, 113-23, 124-30, 143-51
  on contemporary poets, 30-35
  on critics, 14
  on Frost, Robert, 27-28, 33-35
  on Latin poetry, 25-27, 159, 162-63
  life of, 12, 28, 74-77
  on literary quarterlies, 29-30

Lowell, Robert: (*continued*)
  and Melville, Herman, 135-42
  on poetic technique, 17-23, 131-34
  on Pound, Ezra, 24-25, 26
  and Ransom, John Crowe, 12, 25,
    28, 75, 76, 81, 84, 88, 97, 134
  and Rilke, Rainer Maria, 5, 25, 54,
    55, 81-82, 93, 94
  and Roman Catholicism, 8-9, 29,
    36-37, 38-39, 42, 45-46, 53, 59-
    62, 76, 116, 149
  and Tate, Allen, 14, 15, 16-17, 23,
    28, 31-32, 75, 76, 79, 81, 82, 83,
    88, 148-49
  on teaching, 13-14
  and Thomas, Dylan, 113, 114,
    121
  as a translator, 9, 25-27, 92-95,
    152-70
  on writing, 13-14 (*see also* Lowell:
    on poetic technique)
Lowell, Robert, works by:
POETRY (*see also* titles of individual
poems)
  For the Union Dead, 143-51
  Imitations, 94, 152-70
  Land of Unlikeness, 12, 16, 21-22,
    29, 43, 48-50, 76-80, 114
  Life Studies, 9, 18-21, **88-98**, **110-
    12**, 117-23
  Lord Weary's Castle, 12, 16, 17, 23,
    40-47, **49-52**, **53-62**, 80-85, 106,
    114-17
  Mills of the Kavanaughs, The, 12,
    85-88, **99-102**, **104-5**, **106-9**, 117,
    143
DRAMA
  Benito Cereno, 135-42
  Prometheus Bound, 9
"Lycidas" (Milton), and "The Quaker
  Graveyard," 63-73 *passim*, 83

M

Macaulay, Thomas, 21
Macleish, Archibald, 143
"Mad Negro Soldier Confined at
  Munich, A," 116, 119-20, 121

Mailer, Norman, 11
Mandelstam, Osip, 156-57
"Man-Moth, The" (Bishop), 20
Mann, Thomas, 81
March of Literature, The (Ford), 29
Marvell, Andrew, 19, 26, 163
"Mary Winslow," 47
Mather, Cotton, 55
Mayakovsky, Vladimir, 125
Melville, Herman, 55, 64, 71, 72,
  116-17, 135-42
"Memories of West Street," 91
Merton, Thomas, 51-52
Millett, Frederick, 3, 5
Mills of the Kavanaughs, The, 12, **85-
  88**, **99-103**, **104-5**, **106-9**, 117, 143
  poetic techniques in, 106-7
  Roman Catholicism in, 9
  symbolism in, 109
Milton, John, 63-73 *passim*, 83, 87,
  155
Mizener, Arthur, 80
Moby Dick (Melville), 71, 72, 116-17
Monroe, Harriet, 27
Montale, Eugenio, Lowell's transla-
  tions of, 166-69
Moore, Marianne, 31-32
Moore, Merrill, 28
"Mother Marie Therese," 99-101, 105
Mozart, Wolfgang Amadeus, 96
"Mr. Edwards and the Spider," 47, 51,
  59, 117
"My Last Duchess" (Browning), 18

N

"Napoleon Crosses the Berezina," 50
Near the Ocean, 152
"Necrological" (Ransom), 84
"New Year's Day," 47, 51, 59
"Night Sweat," 97
Nims, J. F., 80, 134
"91 Revere Street," 110, 117,
  121
North of Boston (Frost), 34,
  35
"North Sea Undertaker's Complaint,
  The," 56-57

O

O'Conner, Flannery, 23
"Ode to an Urn" (Crane), 22
"Ode to the Confederate Dead"
(Tate), 83
Oedipus Rex (Sophocles), translations
of, 155-56
O'Hara, Frank, 1

P

Paradise Lost (Milton), 87
Parker, Frank, 15
15
"Park Street Cemetery, The,"
79, 80
Pasternak, Boris, 25
Phaedra (Lowell), 166
Picasso, Pablo, 32
"Pigeons, The," 94
Pisan Cantos, The (Pound), 24-25
Plath, Sylvia, 144
Poe, Edgar Allan, 125
Poetic techniques:
    Lowell's views on, 17-23, 131-34
    in *Mills of the Kavanaughs, The*,
    106-7
Pope, Alexander, 153, 158
Pound, Ezra, 55, 88, 110, 113-14, 122,
149
    Lowell's views on, 24-25, 26
    as a translator, 152, 153, 154-55,
    158-59, 163
Powers, J. F., 23
Prometheus Bound (Lowell), 9
Propertius, Sextus, 25, 26, 54, 59, 85,
158
Purgatorio (Dante), 56

Q

"Quaker Graveyard in Nantucket,
The," 42, 43, 46, 51, 55, 59, **63-73**,
82-83, 128
    as a confessional poem, 116-17
    and "Lycidas" (Milton), 63-73
    passim, 83

R

Ransom, John Crowe, 12, 25, 28, 75,
76, 81, 84, 88, 97, 129, 134
"Rebellion," 41, 51, 117
Richards, I. A., 2, 14
Rilke, Rainer Maria, 5, 25, 54, 55,
81-82, 93, 94, 125
Rimbaud, Arthur, 25, 54, 81, 93, 94-
95
"River Roses" (Lawrence), 115
Roethke, Theodore, 30-31, 129
Roman Catholicism, Lowell's involve-
ment with, 8-9, 29, 36-37, 38-39, 42,
45-46, 53, 59-62, 76, 116, 149
Roth, William, 5
Rukeyser, Muriel, 38, 122

S

"Salem," 50, 58, 59, 80
Salinger, J. D., 19
Santayana, George, 120
"Satan's Confession," 36
Schönberg, Arnold, 32
Schwartz, Delmore, 31, 120
Seafarer, The (Pound), 159
"Servante au grand coeur, La" (Baude-
laire), 163-65
Seven Types of Ambiguity (Empson),
15
"Severed Head, The," 147
Sexton, Ann, 144, 149
Shapiro, Karl, 30
Shelley, Percy Bysshe, 4, 26, 63, 64,
70
Shenandoah (Schwartz), 31
Silkin, Jon, 125
"Skunk Hour," 92, 118, 121-22,
124-30, 131-34
"Slough of Despond, The," 50, 117
Smart, Christopher, 125
Snodgrass, W. D., 20, 149
Snyder, Gary, 1, 148
"Soldier, The," 56, 57
Sophocles, 25-26, 155-56
Stafford, Jean, 76, 86
Stark, John, 74

Steiner, George, 155, 166
Stevens, Wallace, 163
"Suicidal Nightmare, A," 36
Swift, Jonathan, 125, 126
Symbolism, in *The Mills of the Kava-*
naughs, 109
Symons, Arthur, 163

T

Tate, Allen, 14, 15, 16-17, 23, 28, 31-
32, 44, 75, 76, 79, 81, 82, 83, 88,
148-49
Taylor, Peter, 75
Teaching, Lowell's views on, 13-14
Teasdale, Sara, 125
Testament, Le (Villon), 159
"Thanksgiving's Over," 86, 99, 117
Thomas, Dylan, 15, 113, 114, 121,
125, 143
Thoreau, Henry David, 64, 65, 70, 71,
72
Tolstoy, Leo, 17, 112
Tonio Kröger (Mann), 81
"'To Speak of Woe That Is in Mar-
riage,'" 27, 121
Translation, Lowell's skill in, 9, 25-27,
92-95, 152-70
True Confessions of George Barker,
The, 122

V

Valéry, Paul, 54, 81
Villon, François, 153, 159-60
159-60
Virgil, 26, 27, 55, 86, 155

"Virginian Voyages, The" (Drayton),
16, 36
"Visits to St. Elizabeth's" (Bishop),
125
"Voyage à Cythère, Un" (Baudelaire),
88
"Voyages" (Crane), 32

W

Wade, Allan, 6
"Waking in the Blue," 91
War and Peace (Tolstoy), 112
Waste Land, The (Eliot), 34
Watkins, E. I., 72-73
W. B. Yeats, the Man and the Masks
(Ellmann), 6
Werfel, Franz, 86, 99, 104
"Where the Rainbow Ends," 41-42,
46, 59, 61, 71, 81
Whitman, Walt, 4, 82, 113
Wilbur, Richard, 1, 134
Williams, William Carlos, 4, 27, 32, 75,
144
Wilson, Edmund, 155
Winslow, Edward, 74
Winters, Yvor, 14, 15, 57
"Words for Hart Crane," 121
Wordsworth, William, 125
"Work Without Hope" (Coleridge),
125

Y

Yarmolinsky, Avrahm, 157
Yeats, William Butler, 5, 6, 10, 23,
116, 146

MALRAUX

A Collection of Critical Essays

Edited by R. W. B. LEWIS

A

Action, theme of, 4, 7, 94, 96,
  114-16, 161
    in *Le Condition Humaine*, 103,
      166
    in *L'Espoir*, 143
Aeschylus, 169
Aesthetic of the Cinema, 114
*Aftermath of the Absolute (see Voix
  du Silence, Les)*
Alain (*see* Chartier, Emile)
Also Sprach Zarathustra (Nietzsche),
  90
"Appeal for Those in Indochina,"
  100
Aragon, Louis, 108
Aristotle, 6
Aurevilly, Barbey d', 169

B

Balzac, Honoré de, 87, 105, 124,
  127n, 168-69, 172
Battle-Pieces (Melville), 6
Baudelaire, Charles, 123, 151, 168
Berdyaev, Nicolai, 71
Bergson, Henri, 72, 93
Bernanos, Georges, 124, 164
Birth of Tragedy, The (Nietzsche), 90
Blum, Léon, 15
Brothers Karamazov, The
  (Dostoevsky), 30, 44, 168
Burnham, James, 112-13

C

Camus, Albert, 9, 71
Cervantes, Miguel de, 50, 61
Cézanne, Paul, 94, 115, 156, 158
Characterization, 4, 6-8, 24, 27-28,
  44n, 73, 94, 103-5, 119, 121-23, 127,
  131n, 137-39, 144-46, 162, 165, 168,
  171-73
    in *Le Condition Humaine*, 12-23
    in *Les Conquérants*, 12-23
    in *L'Espoir*, 64-70, 141-43
    in *Les Noyers de l'Alterburg*, 72-85,
      110-12
    in *Les Temps du Mépris*, 110
Chartier, Emile (*pseud.* Alain), 132
Chauveau, Léopold, 91-92
Chiang Kai-shek, 18, 22-23, 29, 35-60
  passim, 103, 120
Cimetière Marin, Le (Valéry), 66
Civilization as Conquest and Destiny,
  91
Coleridge, Samuel Taylor, 67
Communism, 3, 20-24, 42n, 72, 88,
  106-13, 117, 170
Condition Humaine, La (Man's Fate),
  1, 3-7, 9, **26-60**, 61-62, 72-73, 77,
  86-88, 94, 96, 101-6, 117-20, 122,
  129-30, 135, 138-39, 166, 175, 179
Conquérants, Les (The Conquerors),
  1-6, **12-30**, 33-34, 40-41, 50-53, 57,
  62, 65-66, 70, 86-89, 94, 98-99,
  101-2, 119-22, 126, 128-30, 135,
  138-39, 162, 166, 172, 175, 179

Corneille, Pierre, 123
*Création Artistique, La (The Creative
    Act) (see Psychologie de l'Art, La)*
*Creative Process, The (see Voix du
    Silence, Les)*
Critique of Judgement, The (Kant),
    85
Critique of Pure Reason, The (Kant),
    85

D

*Days of Contempt (see Temps du
    Mépris, Le)*
*Days of Wrath (see Temps du Mépris,
    Le)*
Death, theme of, 61-62, 71, 92, 137,
    165
    in *Le Condition Humaine,* 42, 58,
        72, 119, 135, 146
    in *Les Noyers de l'Altenburg,* 71,
        82, 88, 137, 141
    in *Le Temps du Mépris,* 70
Debray, Pierre, 88, 91
Defoe, Daniel, 50, 61
De Gaulle, Charles, 96, 112-13,
    145-46, 162, 176
Dickens, Charles, 164, 168, 172
Dilthey, Wilhelm, 101
Dostoevsky, Feodor, 42, 44-45, 50, 61,
    105, 123, 144, 163, 168-69, 172
Dreyfus case, 87
Drôle de jeu (Vailland), 139, 142
"D'une Jeunesse Européene," 180

E

Eliot, T. S., 10, 133
Éluard, Paul, 121
Eroticism, 89, 127, 172
Espoir, L' (Man's Hope), 1, 3-6, 8-9,
    42, 50, 64-70, 73, 87, 105-6, 110,
    119, 122-24, 128-29, 134-36, 138-39,
    141-43, 161-62, 166, 172, 179

F

Faulkner, William, 9, 164

Flanner, Janet, 175
Flaubert, Gustave, 6, 52, 173
Fontamara (Silone), 2
Forster, E. M., 27

G

Gandhi, Mohandas K., 22
Gide, André, 25, 49, 135-36, 138,
    164, 171
Goethe, Johann Wolfgang von, 164,
    167
Gogh, Vincent van, 115, 160
Golden Bowl, The (James), 5
Gone With the Wind (Mitchell), 168
Goya, Francisco de, 8, 10, 62, 80, 91,
    94, 115, 144, 153, 156, 160
Groethuysen, Bernard, 49, 101

H

Hegel, Georg Wilhelm Friedrich,
    149-50, 159
Heidegger, Martin, 63, 71-72, 85,
    101
Herriot, Édouard, 15
"Homme et la culture artistique, L',"
    88n
Hoog, Armand, 1-2, 86, 145
Hugo, Victor, 163
Huxley, Aldous, 26

I

Idiot, The (Dostoevsky), 45, 169
Illuminations (Rimbaud), 120
*Imaginary Museum, The (see Musée
    Imaginaire)*
Immoraliste, L' (Gide), 136
Irony, 169
    in *L'Espoir,* 66
    in *Le Temps du Mépris,* 64

J

James, Henry, 5
Jaspers, Karl, 71

Journal (Gide), 49
Joyce, James, 133, 144*n*

K

Kant, Immanuel, 85
Kierkegaard, Sören, 72, 77, 96
Koestler, Arthur, 3

L

"Laclos," 180
Laclos, Choderlos de, 105, 164
Lafayette, Comtesse de, 135
"Lawrence and the Demon of the
    Absolute," 180
Lawrence, T. E., 76, 112
Lemaître, Frédérick, 169
Lenin, Nikolai, 22, 90
Liaisons dangereuses, Les (Laclos),
    121, 127
Lunes en Papier, 97, 167, 179
*Lutte avec l'Ange, La (see Noyers de
    l'Altenburg, Les)*

M

Magny, Claude-Edmonde, 6, 8, 56,
    117
Malraux, Clara, 44*n*
Malraux, George-André
    and the Absurd, 2, 55
    and art, 1-2, 9, 70, 83, 88-89, 101,
        108, 114-15, 126, 145, 147-60,
        173 (see also *Psychologie de
        l'Art, La*)
    and Balzac, Honoré de, 168-69
    and "Berger," 74, 86, 176
    and Burnham, 112-13
    and Communism, 3, 20-24, 42*n*, 72,
        88, 106-13, 117, 170
    and Dostoevsky, Feodor, 44-45, 144,
        168-69
    and Existentialism, 2, 71-72, 85,
        96
    and de Gaulle, Charles, 96, 112-13,
        145-46, 162, 176
    and Gide, André, 49, 164, 171

and Goya, 62, 144, 160 (*see also
    Saturne*)
and Groethuysen, 49, 101
influence of, 2-11
and Lawrence, D. H. 76, 112
life of, 10, 30, 49, 86, 88-89, 96,
    108-9, 162-63, 175-76
and "Möllberg," 88
and Racine, 25
and religion, 2, 55-56, 77, 79, 85,
    94, 96, 98, 115, 124, 127, 131-33,
    139, 146, 157, 167, 170
and Rimbaud, Arthur, 120
and Spengler, Oswald, 78, 91
and Stendhal, 99, 105
themes of, 2, 33, 57, 83, 165 (*see
    also* Action)
and Tolstoy, Leo, 99, 105
Malraux, George-André, works by:
    (*see also* titles of individual works)
    Aesthetic of the Cinema, 114
    "Appeal for Those in Indochina,"
        100
    "Chapitre inédit de la Condition
        humaine, Un," 46-47
    *Civilization as Conquest and Des-
        tiny,* 91
    *Condition Humaine, La (Man's
        Fate),* 1, 3-7, 9, 26-60, 61-62, 72-
        73, 77, 86-88, 94, 96, 101-6,
        117-20, 122, 129-30, 135, 138-39,
        166, 175, 179
    Conquérants, Les (The Conquerors),
        1-6, 12-30, 33-34, 40-41, 50-53,
        57, 62, 65-66, 70, 86-89, 94, 98-
        99, 101-2, 119-22, 126, 128-30,
        135, 138-39, 162, 166, 172, 175,
        179
    "D'une Jeunesse Européene," 180
    Espoir, L' (Man's Hope), 1, 3-6, 8-9,
        42, 50, 64-70, 73, 87, 105-6, 110,
        119, 122-24, 128-29, 134-36,
        138-39, 141-43, 161-62, 166, 172,
        179
    "Homme et la culture artistique, L'"
        88*n*
    "Laclos,"
        180

Malraux, George-André, works by:
(*continued*)
"Lawrence and the Demon of the
Absolute," 180
Lunes en Papier, 97, 167, 179
*Métamorphose des Dieux, La
(The Metamorphosis of the Gods)*,
73, 180
*Musée Imaginaire, Le (Museum
without Walls or The Imaginary
Museum)*, (Part I of *La Psycholo-
gie de l'Art*), 1, 87, 96, 101, 115,
121, 124-26, 128, 131, 148, 158,
179-80
*Noyers de l'Altenburg, Les (The
Walnut Trees of the Altenburg)*,
1, 4, 7, 9-10, 48, 56, 68, 70-71,
72-95, 99-100, 110-12, 122, 124,
130-31, 135-37, 141, 145-46,
162, 164-66, 170-72, 179
"On Certain Young Europeans,"
98
"Préface" (to *L'Amant de Lady
Chatterley*), 180
"Préface" (to *Sanctuaire*), 121, 180
*Psychologie de l'Art, La (The
Psychology of Art)*, 10, 62, 88-90,
94, 121, **147-60**, 165, 179-80
Royaume Farfelu, 97, 179
Saturne (Saturn, an Essay on Goya),
179
*Temps du Mépris, Le (Days of
Wrath)*, 1, 6, 50, **61-64**, **67-70**,
87-88, 97, 107, 110, 123, 131,
135, 138, 145, 165, 170, 173, 179
*Tentation de l'Occident, La (The
Temptation of the West)*, 2, 72,
88-89, 97, 120, 128-31, 136-37,
141, 146, 166, 179
Voie Royale, La (The Royal Way),
1, 4, 6, 34, 40, 44, 51, 62, 87,
100-1, 112, 118, 125, 135,
138, 162, 165, 172, 179
*Voix du Silence, Les (The Voices of
Silence)*, 10, 89-90, 94, 164-67,
180
Mann, Thomas,
78

Man's Fate (see *Condition Humaine,
La*)
Man's Hope (see *Espoir, L'*)
Marcel, Gabriel, 117
Marion de Lorme (Hugo), 163
Marx, Karl, 93
Mauriac, Claude, 117*n*, 133, 140-41
Melville, Herman, 6
*Métamorphose des Dieux, La (The
Metamorphosis of the Gods)*, 73,
180
*Métamorphoses of Apollo, The (see
Voix du Silence, Les*)
*Métamorphosis of the Gods, The (see
Métamorphose des Dieux, La)*
Miserables, Les (Hugo), 127*n*
*Monnaie de l'Absolu, La (The Twilight
of the Absolute)*, (see *Psychologie
de l'Art, La)*
Monnier, Henri, 168
Morand, Paul, 30
*Museum without Walls (see Musée
Imaginaire, Le)*
1, 87, 96, 101, 115, 121, 124-26,
128, 131, 148, 158, 179-80
My Life (Trotsky), 21

N

Nausée, La (Sartre), 85
Nietzsche, Friedrich, 90, 93-94, 97,
141, 162, 164-65, 173
Notes from Underground
(Dostoevsky), 45
*Noyers de l'Altenburg, Les (The Wal-
nut Trees of the Altenburg)*, 1, 4, 7,
9-10, 48, 56, 68, 70-71, 72-95, 99-
100, 110-12, 122, 124, 130-31, 135-
37, 141, 145-46, 162, 164-66, 170-
72, 179

O

"On Certain Young Europeans," 98

P

Passage to India, A (Forster), 27

Péguy, Charles, 93
Picon, Gaëtan, 8, 123, 130, 135, 145, 161
Poetics (Aristotle), 6
Poincaré, Jules Henri, 15
Portrait of the Artist (Joyce), 144
Possessed, The (Dostoevski), 168
Poussin, Nicolas, 158
"Préface" (to L'Amant de Lady Chatterley), 180
"Préface" (to Sanctuaire), 121, 180
Proust, Marcel, 6, 87, 135, 168
Psychologie de l'Art, La (The Psychology of Art), 10, 62, 88-90, 94, 121, 147-60, 165, 179-80

R

Rabouilleuse, La (Balzac), 168
Racine, Jean Baptiste, 25
Religion, 2, 77, 85, 94, 96, 98, 115, 124, 127, 131-33, 139, 146, 157, 170
   in Le Condition Humaine, 55-56
   in Les Conquérants, 89
   in Les Noyers de l'Altenburg, 79
   in Les Voix du Silence, 167
Rimbaud, Arthur, 120
Royal Way, The (see Voie Royale, La)
Royaume Farfelu, 97, 179

S

Sartre, Jean-Paul, 71-72, 85, 135-36, 139-40, 145
Saturne (Saturn, an Essay on Goya), 179
Shakespeare, William, 164, 168-70
Silone, Ignazio, 2-3, 9
Spengler, Oswald, 78, 81, 91
Stalin, Josef, 103, 108
Stendhal, 98-99, 105, 140, 164, 173
Storm in Shanghai (see Condition Humaine, La)
Struggle with the Angels, The (see Lutte avec l'Ange, La)
Sue, Eugène, 127n
Symbolism, 2

in L'Espoir, 67
in Les Noyers de l'Altenburg, 82, 92, 111-12, 170
in Le Temps du Mépris, 67

T

Temps du Mépris, Le (Days of Wrath), 1, 6, 50, 61-64, 67-70, 87-88, 97, 107, 110, 123, 131, 135, 138, 145, 165, 170, 173, 179
Temps Retrouvé, Les (Proust), 168
Tentation de l'Occident, La (The Temptation of the West), 2, 72, 88-89, 97, 120, 128-31, 136-37, 141, 146, 166, 179
Thibaudet, Albert, 78
Thorez, Maurice, 108
Tolstoy, Leo, 99, 105, 164, 172
Trotsky, Leon, 2-3, 5, 7, 9-10, 12, 20-24, 26-30, 109, 165
Twilight of the Absolute, The (see Monnaie de l'Absolu, La)

U

Ulysses (Joyce), 133
Uomini e no (Vittorini), 132

V

Vailland, Roger, 139, 142
Valéry, Paul, 66, 93-94, 147-48
Voices of Silence, The (see Voix du Silence, Les)
Voie Royale, La (The Royal Way), 1, 4, 6, 34, 40, 44, 51, 62, 87, 100-1, 112, 118, 125, 135, 138, 162, 165, 172, 179
Voix du Silence, Les (The Voices of Silence), 10, 89-90, 94, 164-67, 180
Voltaire, 105

W

Walnut Trees of the Altenburg, The (see Noyers de l'Altenburg, Les)

War and Peace (Tolstoy), 98, 168
Waste Land, The (Eliot), 133
Wordsworth, William, 84
Wuthering Heights (Brontë), 30

Z

Zola, Émile, 168

THOMAS MANN

A Collection of Critical Essays

Edited by HENRY HATFIELD

A

Alice in Wonderland (Dodgson), 68
Andreas-Salomé, Lou, 2
Anna Karenina (Tolstoy), 13
"Apocalypse" (Dürer), 116
Aquinas, Saint Thomas, 129
Archimedes, 165
Aristotle, 15, 105
"Asking for an Inner View of Goethe" (Gasset), 155
"Aspects of Contradiction: On Recent Criticism of Thomas Mann" (Blume), 2
Augustine, Saint, 129
Aus dem Leben eines Taugenichts (Eichendorff), 88

B

Bach, Johann, 20, 130
Balzac, Honoré, 157
Bang, Hermann, 111
Beethoven, Ludwig, 119, 127, 129, 132
Beloved Returns: Lotte in Weimar, The, 114, 124, 157, 160
Bergson, Henri, 68
Bible, Holy, 99-107 *passim*
Bismarck-Schonhausen, Prince Otto, 126, 132
Bizet, Alexandre, 88
Blume, Bernhard, 2, 4

Blunck, Hans, 168
Boehlich, Walter, 162
Bonaparte, Napoleon, 132
Bouvard et Pécuchet (Flaubert), 65
Brock, Erich, 163
Bruckner, Anton, 127
Buddenbrooks, 2, 4, 7-21, 31, 44, 63, 73, 83, 86-87, 110, 112-13, 117, 124-25, 143, 163, 167, 171
    autobiographical aspects of, 10-11, 14, 16
    death, theme of, 16-18
    decadence, theme of, 13-17
    and European literature, 10-13
    historical aspects of, 13-15
    and the leitmotif, use of, 18-21
Burckhardt, Jacob, 130
Byron, George Gordon, 50, 133

C

Camus, Albert, 109
Carlyle, Thomas, 125
Carroll, Lewis (*see* Dodgson, Charles)
Cervantes, Miguel de, 74, 104
Chaucer, Geoffrey, 96, 104
Cocteau, Jean, 147
Confessions of Felix Krull, Confidence Man, 3, 70, 73, 113, 133-54, 158, 165-66, 171
    the artist, theme of, 145-51
    autobiographical aspects of, 141-45
    belief and fulfillment, theme of, 152-54

Confessions of Felix Krull, Confidence Man (*continued*)
  and the Faustus myth, 139-42
  and the picaresque tradition, 133-54
  psychological aspects of, 137-39
  and the rogue (picaro), concept of, 134-39
Conrad, M. G., 12
Critobolus, 50
Curtius, Ernst Robert, 167

D

Dante, 81, 135
Darwin, Charles, 14, 87
Death in Venice, 2, 45, **46-61**, 63, 67, 83, 86, 88, 90, 110, 112-13
  characterization, 51-61
  irony in, 47-48
  myth and reality in, 46-61
  psychological symbolism in, 55-60
  style, 49-61
Debussy, Claude, 88
Defoe, Daniel, 136
Demetz, Peter, 5
Dichtung und Wahrheit (Goethe), 142
Dickens, Charles, 21, 157
Dilettante, The, 111
Ditters von Dittersdorf, Karl, 172
Doctor Faustus, 3, 5, 65, 73, 75, 110, 114-28, 133, 144, 160, 162-64, 168, 171
  autobiographical aspects of, 117-19
  and German character, 116-17, 121, 123-30
  and Luther, Martin, 123-31 *passim*
  political aspects of, 125-32
  and the Reformation, 128-32
  and theology, theme of, 119-22, 124-30
Doctor Faustus, The World Without Transcendence (Holthusen), 3
Dodgson, Charles (*pseud.* Lewis Carroll), 68
Don Giovanni (Mozart), 128

Don Juan (Byron), 133
Dostoevsky, Fyodor, 141
"Dostoevsky-within Limits," 63
Dryden, John, 62
Du Bos, Charles, 165
Dürer, Albrecht, 116, 131

E

Eichendorff, Joseph von, 88, 126, 129, 155
Einstein, Albert, 68
Either-Or (Kierkegaard), 128
Eliot, T. S., 10, 33-34
Elmer Gantry (Lewis), 136
Emrich, Wilhelm, 161
Entstehung des Doktor Faustus, Die, 140
Étranger, L' (Camus), 109

F

Family at Gilje, The (Lie), 12
Faust (Goethe), 82, 114, 164
Faust (Valéry), 119
Faux-Monnayeurs (Gide), 109
Fichte, Johann, 70
Fidelio (Beethoven), 132
Fielding, Henry, 141
Fiorenza, 47, 111
Flaubert, Gustave, 65
Flying Dutchman (Wagner), 89-90
Fontane, Theodor, 11
Forster, E. M., 85
Forsyte Saga (Galsworthy), 10
"Freedom of a Christian Man" (Luther), 131
Freud, Sigmund, 85, 129
Friedrich, Caspar David, 129

G

Galsworthy, John (*pseud.* John Sinjohn), 10
Garman and Worse (Kielland), 12
Gasset, Ortega y, 155
Gautier, Théophile, 111
Geibel, Emanuel, 163

George, Stefan, 2
German Poetry (Grenzmann), 168
"Germany and the Germans," 160
Gide, André, 3, 109
Ginzberg, Louis, 104
Gladius Dei, 47, 111
Goethe, Johann, 6, 11, 23, 25, 62, 67,
69, 71-74, 81, 82, 87, 91, 93, 114-15,
121, 123-24, 127, 129-30, 141-42,
145, 155-58, 162-64, 170
Goncourt, Edmond, 11, 12-13
Goncourt, Jules, 11, 12-13
Gounod, Charles, 88
Grass, Günter, 4
Grenzmann, Wilhelm, 168
Gronicka, André von, 2, 13

H

Hamlet (Shakespeare), 98
Hamsun, Knut (*see* Pedersen, Knut)
Händel, Georg Friedrich, 130
Hardenberg, Friedrich von (*pseud.*
Novalis), 72, 86, 92, 155
Harris, Frank, 5
Hatfield, Henry, 143
Hauptmann, Gerhart, 91, 117
Haydn, Joseph, 172
Hegel, Georg, 70, 72, 131
Heidegger, Martin, 68
Heilman, Robert B., 3
Heine, Heinrich, 14, 33, 168
Helbling, Carl, 172
Heller, Erich, 2-3
Hitler, Adolf, 5, 132, 157
Hofmannsthal, Hugo von, 161
Hölderlin, Friedrich, 121, 129, 155
Holthusen, Hans Egon, 1, 3, 160-65,
168
Holy Bible, 99-107 *passim*
Holy Sinner, The, 133
Homer, 59-60
Horace, 148
"Humor and Irony," 4, 170-72

I

Ibsen, Henrik, 12, 41, 45, 117

Idiot, The (Dostoevsky), 141
Iphigenie auf Tauris (Goethe), 114
Irony:
in *Death in Venice*, 47-48
in *The Magic Mountain*, 67, 93-
95
in *Tonio Kröger*, 28-29
in Mann's works, 112-14, 170-71

J

Jancke, Oskar, 170, 172
Jesus, 114
Joseph and His Brothers, 3, 5, 13, 20,
47, 54, 63, 65, 75, 81, 96-108, 114,
140, 171
and the Bible, 99-107
comic aspects of, 96-108
narrative technique of, 102-6
Joyce James, 65, 109, 141, 151

K

Kafka, Franz, 3, 109, 156, 161, 168
Kahler, Erich, 3
Kant, Immanuel, 4, 121, 129, 132
Kayser, Wolfgang, 4
Kerényi, Karl, 46
Keyserling, Eduard, 111
Kielland, Alexander, 11-12
Kierkegaard, Sören, 95, 126, 128-29,
155
Kleist, Heinrich von, 116, 121-22,
155
"Knight, Death and Devil" (Dürer),
131
Kolbenheyer, Erwin, 168
Koran, 104
Krupp, Alfred, 126
Kunz, Joseph, 168

L

Lawrence, D. H., 3, 111
Legends of the Jews (Ginzberg), 104
Leibniz, Gottfried, 124
Leitmotif, concept of:
in *Buddenbrooks*, 18-21, 31

Leitmotif, concept of (*continued*)
   in *Tonio Kröger*, 31-33
Lessing, Gotthold, 2, 129
Levin, Harry, 65
Lewis, Sinclair, 136
Lie, Jonas, 11-12
Lisle, Leconte de, 111
Little Gidding (Eliot), 33-34
Little Herr Friedemann, 111
Little Lizzie, 47, 111
Lucinde (Schlegel), 74
Lukács, Georg, 1
Luther, Martin, 3, 63, 70, 119, 123-31
   passim

M

Magic Mountain, The, 2, 5, 13, 20, 30,
   62-95, 97, 110, 111-13, 114-15, 133,
   144, 157-58, 160, 168
   death, theme of, 88-91
   disease, theme of, 86-88
   eternal recurrence, theme of,
     79-81
   formlessness, theme of, 66-67, 77-
     78
   and German romanticism, 70-76,
     85-87
   irony in, 67, 93-95
   realism in, 82-85
   and Relativity, theory of, 68
   and scientific knowledge, 75-76
   style, 69-76
   time, theme of, 67-68
Maid of Orleans (Schiller), 37
Manet, Edouard, 19
Mann, Heinrich, 11, 13, 44
Mann ohne Eigenschaften (Musil), 109
Mann, Thomas:
   and the artist and society, theme
     of, 109-15
   artistic development of, 109-13,
     115
   and comedy, concept of, 97-107
   and direct experience, function of,
     162-63
   and European literature, influence
     of, 10-13

   and German romanticism, 70-76,
     85-87
   humor, in works of, 171-72
   irony, in works of, 112-14, 170-71
   and the leitmotif, use of, 18-21,
     30-33
   and morality, 165-67
   and music, concept of, 124-32
   narrative technique of, 7-9, 18-21,
     30-33, 102-6
   negative criticism of, 155-69
   and the picaresque tradition, 133-54
   and poetry, concept of, 167-68
   politics of, 130-32, 156-59
   and Schlegel Friedrich, 70-76, 84-
     86, 88, 91-92
   style of, 62-67, 69-76
   and theology, 163-65
   and truth, concept of, 160-61
Mann, Thomas, works by:
   *Beloved Returns: Lotte in Weimar,
     The*, 114, 124, 157, 160
   Buddenbrooks, 2, 4, 7-21, 31, 44,
     63, 73, 83, 86-87, 110, 112-13,
     117, 124-25, 143, 163, 167, 171
   *Confessions of Felix Krull, Confi-
     dence Man*, 3, 70, 73, 113, 133-54,
     158, 165-66, 171
   Death in Venice, 2, 45, 46-61, 63,
     67, 83, 86, 88, 90, 110, 112-13
   Dilettante, The, 111
   Doctor Faustus, 3, 5, 65, 73, 75,
     110, 114-28, 133, 144, 160,
     162-64, 168, 171
   "Dostoevsky-within Limits," 63
   *Entstehung des Doktor Faustus,
     Die*, 140
   Fiorenza, 47, 111
   "Germany and the Germans," 160
   Gladius Dei, 47, 111
   Holy Sinner, The, 133
   "Humor and Irony," 4, 170-72
   Joseph and His Brothers, 3, 5, 13,
     20, 47, 54, 63, 65, 75, 81, 96-
     108, 114, 140, 171
   Little Herr Friedemann, 111
   Little Lizzie, 47,
     111

Mann, Thomas, works by (*continued*)
Magic Mountain, The, 2, 5, 13, 20,
30, 62-95, 97, 110, 111-13,
114-15, 133, 144, 157-58, 160,
168
Mario and the Magician, 113
Reflections of a Nonpolitical Man,
88, 91, 124-25, 127, 156, 160,
165
Romandichtung und Mythologie,
47
Royal Highness, 2, 35-45, 47, 113
"Royal Highness, On," 35
"Sketch of My Life," 48-49, 142
Table of the Law, The, 85
Theme of the Joseph Novels, The,
47-48
Tonio Kröger, 2, 17, 20, 22-34, 36,
38, 40-41, 45, 83, 110, 112-13,
115-16, 157
Transposed Heads, The, 133
Tristan, 111, 124
Wardrobe, The, 47, 111
Way to the Churchyard, The, 111,
112
Weary Hour, A, 15
Mann, Viktor, 14
Mario and the Magician, 113
Marlowe, Christopher, 76, 124
Marx, Karl, 1, 131-32, 135
Mautner, Franz, 2
Mazzini, Giuseppe, 130
Medici, Giovanni de, 130
Merezhkovski, Dmitri, 13
Moll Flanders (Defoe), 136
Molo, Walter von, 156
Mörike, Eduard, 129
Moses, 85
Mozart, Wolfgang Amadeus, 127-29
Münzer, Thomas, 130
Muschg, Walter, 167
Musil, Robert, 3, 5, 109, 161

N

Nadler, Joseph, 168
Nausée (Sartre), 109
Neider, Charles, 1, 5

Newton, Isaac, 70
Nietzsche, Friedrich, 3, 14, 16, 33, 39,
43, 50, 63, 80, 87, 93, 111, 118, 125,
129-31, 160-61, 168
Novalis (*see* Hardenberg, Friedrich
von)

O

Odyssey (Homer), 59-60

P

Paeschke, Hans, 162
Palestrina (Pfitzner), 125
Pascal, Blaise, 124, 129
Pedersen, Knut (*pseud.* Knut Hamsun),
3, 111
Pfitzner, Hans, 125
Phaedros, 50
Platen, August, 50, 86
Plato, 62, 71, 84, 105
Poe, Edgar Allan, 79
Poémes Barbares (Lisle), 111
Proust, Marcel, 3, 68, 89, 96, 109
Puppet Show (Kleist), 116, 121-22

R

Rahn, Felix, 165
Reflections of a Nonpolitical Man, 88,
91, 124-25, 127, 156, 160, 164
Remembrance of Things Past (Proust),
96, 109
Rembrandt, 81
Renée Mauperin (Goncourt), 12-13
Reuter, Fritz, 171
Rilke, Rainer Maria, 1, 2, 156
Ring des Nibelungen, Der (Wagner),
10, 63
Robespierre, Maximilien de, 132
Rohde, Erwin, 130
Romandichtung und Mythologie,
47
Roosevelt, Franklin, 98
Rosenberg, Alfred, 132
Rougon Macquart, "Histoire d'une
famille sous l'Empire" (Zola), 12

Royal Highness, 2, **35-45**, 47, 113
  artistic renunciation, theme of,
    38-41
  autobiographical aspects of, 35-37,
    42-45
  representative achievement, theme
    of, 42-45
  symbolic existence, theme of, 35-
    45
"*Royal Highness,* On," 35
Rubens, Peter, 90
Rychner, Max, 156, 165

S

Santayana, George, 155
Sartre, Jean Paul, 109
Savonarola, Girolamo, 111
Schiller, Johann, 3, 4, 15, 33, 35, 121,
  124, 129, 132
Schlegel, Friedrich, 2-3, 62, 67, 68,
  70-76, 84-86, 88, 91-92
Schopenhauer, Arthur, 10, 16-17, 33,
  58, 87, 113, 124, 160, 171
Schubert, Franz, 88, 93, 129
Sebastian, Saint, 58
Segantini, Giovanni, 8
Shakespeare, William, 5, 10, 65, 74,
  98, 133
Silva-Bruhns, Julia Da, 11
Simenon, Georges, 141
Sinjohn, John (*see* Galsworthy, John)
"Sketch of my Life," 48-49, 142
Socrates, 50, 58
Sonneman, Ulrich, 157-60
Spengler, Oswald, 3, 72, 111
Spontaneous and Sentimentive Poetry
  (Schiller), 33
Staiger, Emil, 4
Stature of Thomas Mann, The (Neider),
  1, 5
Stein, Baron Heindrich von, 132
Storm, Theodor, 11, 33
Strauss, Johann, 127

T

Table of the Law, The, 85

Tales of Two Countries (Kielland),
  12
Taming of the Shrew (Shakespeare),
  133
Theme of the Joseph Novels, The, 47-
  48
Thiess, Frank, 168
"Thomas Mann and Politics" (Rychner),
  156
"Thomas Mann oder Mass und An-
  spruch" (Sonnemann), 157-60
Tin Drum, The (Grass), 4
Tirpitz, Grand Admiral von, 125
Tolstoy, Leo N., 11, 13, 115
Tonio Kröger, 2, 17, 20, 22-34, 36, 38,
  40-41, 45, 83, 110, 112-13, 115-16,
  157
  awareness, theme of, 22-26
  irony in, 28-29
  leitmotif in, 31-33
  structure, 26-28
  style, 28-30
Torquato Tasso (Goethe), 25, 114
Transposed Heads, The, 133
Tristan, 111, 124
Trotzky, Leon, 15
Turgenev, Ivan, 29
Two Friends (Kielland), 12

U

Uhland, Johann Ludwig, 132
Ulysses (Joyce), 65, 109

V

Valéry, Paul, 119, 124
Van Doren, Mark, 3
"Variations on Picaresque" (Heilman),
  3
Venable, Vernon, 2, 55
Verdi, Giuseppe, 88

W

Wackenroder, Wilhelm, 164
Wagner, Richard, 10, 31, 33, 50, 63,
  86, 89-90, 115, 125, 127, 157, 171

Wardrobe, The, 47, 111
Warren, Robert Penn, 1
Way to the Churchyard, The, 111, 112
Weary Hour, A, 15
Weber, Max, 14
Weber, Werner, 172
Weigand, Herman, 2, 66

Wellek, René, 1
Wilhelm Meisters Wanderjahre (Goethe), 67, 71-74, 142, 155, 157
Wilkinson, E. M., 2

Z

Zola, Émile, 11, 12

MARLOWE

A Collection of Critical Essays

Edited by CLIFFORD LEECH

A

Admiral's Men, The, 3, 128
Aeneid, The (Virgil), 16, 17, 169
Aeschylus, 24, 31, 37
Agrippa, Cornelius, 92
Alchemist, The (Jonson), 20
Aldritch, Simon, 163, 166
Alexander, 61
Alexander, Sir William, 90
Alleyn, Edward, 3, 19, 128
Amores (Ovid), 117
Anatomy of Melancholy, The
  (Burton), 66
Andromeda Liberata (Chapman), 64
Arania, The (Du Bartas), 65
Arden of Feversham (anon.), 20
Aretino, Pietro, 20
Aristotle, 57
Arte of Englishe Poesie (Puttenham),
  90
As You Like It (Shakespeare), 26
Atheism, doctrine of, 159-66
Atheist's Tragedy, The (Tourneur), 22
Aubrey, John, 40
Augustine, Saint, 31, 114-16, 118,
  119

B

Bacon, Francis, 34-35
Baines, Richard, 4, 6, 159-66 *passim*
"Bait, The" (Donne), 25
Baldwin, William, 67

Barnes, Barnabe, 65
Barrie, J. M., 16
Battenhouse, Roy W., 4
Beard, Thomas, 164, 168
Beaumont, Francis, 22-23
Bevington, David M., 9
Blake, William, 5, 113
Brecht, Berthold, 11
Bridges, Robert, 24
Brockbank, J. P., 5
Burbage, Richard, 19
Burton, Robert, 36, 37, 66

C

Caesar's Revenge (anon.), 64
Cambises (Preston), 7
Camden, William, 37
Chapman, George, 5, 21-22, 28, 57-58,
  64, 65, 67, 68, 71
Charlemagne, 36
Charles V, 49
Charron, Pierre, 61, 62
Cholmly, Richard, 4, 160, 164-66
Christ, 82
Christianity, doctrines of, 159-66
  passim
Churchyard, Thomas, 119
City of God, The (St. Augustine), 118
Compleat Angler, The (Walton), 25
Comus (Milton), 23
Confessions (St. Augustine), 114, 115
Congreve, William, 34
Conrad, Joseph, 26, 36

Cornford, F. M., 33
Cornwallis, William, 59
Cortes, Hernando, 56
Creech, Thomas, 34

D

Dante, 17, 28, 63
Defence of Poesie (Sidney), 63
Dekker, Thomas, 20, 25
De Quincey, Thomas, 55
De Sapientia Veterum (Bacon), 34-35
Dickens, Charles, 16
Dido, Queen of Carthage, 1, 2, 9, 29,
   113, 137, **168-72**, 173, 174
Discoveries (see Timber)
*Divine Century of Spirituall Sonnets,
   A* (Barnes), 65
Doctor Faustus, 1-11 *passim*, 14-16,
   23, 24, 31, 32, **92-107**, 108-11,
   112-19, 121, 125, 137, 142, 143,
   145, 157, 168, 178
Donne, John, 25, 32
Dora (Tennyson), 15
Drake, Sir Francis, 43
Drayton, Michael, 28, 34, 68, 131
Dryden, John, 71, 72
Du Bartas, Guillaume, 61, 65
Duchess of Malfi, The (Webster), 7

E

Edward II, 1, 2, 5, 8, 10, 11, 16, 19,
   120, 124-27, 128, 130-37, 138-43,
   168, 172
Elegies (Ovid), 10
Eliot, T. S., 5, 20, 34, 120, 144,
   167, 169
Elizabeth I, 19, 30
Ellis-Fermor, Una, 5, 167
Endymion (Keats), 24
*English Literature in the Sixteenth
   Century* (Lewis), 167
Epicurus, 34
Euripides, 69, 108, 109

F

Faerie Queene, The (Spenser), 13, 65

Faithful Shepherdess, The (Fletcher),
   23
Father, The (Stindberg), 108
Faust (Goethe), 31, 105
Feuchtwanger, L., 11
Fineux, Thomas, 165, 166
Flaubert, Gustave, 33
Fletcher, John, 22-23
Freud, Sigmund, 26, 28

G

Gent, P. F., 92
Gilbert, Sir Humphrey, 37
Globe Theatre, The, 19
Goethe, Johann Wolfgang von, 24, 28,
   31, 105, 119
Gorboduc (Norton and Sackville), 141
Greene, Robert, 18, 25, 67
Greg, W. W., 2, 4, 114, 116, 145
Greville, Fulke, 58, 59, 63, 66, 109
Gyllius, Petrus, 54

H

Hakluyt, Richard, 36, 37, 40, 52
Hamlet (Shakespeare), 32
Hardy, Thomas, 33
Hartwell, Abraham, 48
Harvey, Gabriel, 90
Henry IV (Shakespeare), 3, 5, 18, 19
Henry V (Shakespeare), 19
Henry VI (Shakespeare), 11, 128
Henslowe, Philip, 25, 144-45
Hercules Furens (Seneca), 87
Hercules Oetaeus (Seneca), 87
Hero and Leander (Chapman), 65
Hero and Leander, 5, 10, 21, 27-28,
   167, 168, **174-78**
Herrick, Robert, 25
Heywood, Thomas, 2, 30
Hierarchy of the Blessed Angels (Hey-
   wood), 30-31
Holinshed, Raphael, 130, 131, 135
Holland, Philemon, 54, 57
Homer, 63, 68, 81

I

Iliad, The (Homer), 81
Ion (Plato), 63, 66

J

James I, 19, 65
Jew of Malta, The, 1, 2, 5, 10, 11, 16,
    22, 55, 120-26, 138, 144-58, 168,
    178
Job, Book of, 121
John, Saint, 31
Jones, Richard, 167
Jonson, Ben, 1, 5, 20-21, 125, 168
Joyce, James, 34
Julius Caesar (Shakespeare), 3

K

Keats, John, 23, 24, 56
King Lear (Shakespeare), 7
Knight of the Burning Pestle, The
    (Beaumont and Fletcher), 22
Kocher, Paul H., 4
Kyd, Thomas, 4, 6, 12, 15, 115,
    122-23

L

L'Allegro (Milton), 23
Lamb, Charles, 29, 136, 137
Lawrence, D. H., 5, 119
Le Roy, Louis, 69
Lessing, Gotthold, 24
Levin, Henry, 5
Lewis, C. S., 167
Lives (Plutarch), 58
Lluyd, Humphrey, 37, 40
Lord Chamberlain's Men, the,
    11
Lucan, 10, 34, 90
Lucretius, 34
Lyly, John, 18

M

Macbeth (Shakespeare), 5
Machiavelli, Niccoló, 27, 120, 123,

124, 125, 126, 133, 134, 148, 153
Mirror for Magistrates, A (Ferrers,
    Baldwin, and Sackville), 58
Mallarmé, Stéphane, 33
Mann, Thomas, 33
Maps, Marlowe's use of, 36-56
Marlowe, Christopher:
    and Aeschylus, 31, 37
    and Baines, Richard, 4, 6, 159-66
        passim
    and Beaumont, Francis, 22-23
    and Chapman, George, 21-22, 28
    critical reputation of, 1, 3-11
    and Drayton, Michael, 28
    and Euripides, 109
    and Fletcher, John, 22-23
    and Herrick, Robert, 25
    influence of, 18-26
    and Jonson, Ben, 20-21
    and Keats, John, 23, 24
    and Kyd, Thomas, 122-23
    and Lamb, Charles, 29
    life of, 2, 156-66
    and Lucretius, 34
    and Machiavelli, Niccoló, 27, 120
        123, 124, 125, 126, 133, 134,
        148, 153
    maps, use of, 36-56
    and Marston, John, 22
    and Massinger, Philip, 22
    and Milton, John, 15, 23-24
    and Raleigh, Sir Walter, 21, 25,
        164-66
    and Seneca, 69, 72, 87-88
    and Shakespeare, 1, 3, 7-13 *passim,*
        19-20, 54, 55, 79, 89, 118, 127,
        128, 132, 137, 139, 142-43, 168
    and Spenser, Edmund, 13-15, 63
    texts of, 2
    and Tourneur, Cyril, 22, 125
    as translator, 10
    and Virgil, 169
    and Webster, John, 5, 7, 22, 79,
        125
Marlowe, Christopher, works by:
    Dido, Queen of Carthage, 1, 2, 9,
        29, 113, 128, 137, 168-72, 173,
        174

Marlowe, Christopher, works by:
(*continued*)
  Doctor Faustus, 1-11 *passim*, 14-
    16, 23, 24, 31, 92-107, 108-
    11, 112-19, 121, 125, 137,
    142, 143, 145, 157, 168, 178
  Edward II, 1, 2, 5, 8, 10, 11, 16,
    19, 120, 124-27, 128, 130-37,
    138-43, 168, 172
  Hero and Leander, 5, 10, 21, 27-
    28, 167, 168, 174-78
  Jew of Malta, The, 1, 2, 5, 10, 11,
    12, 16, 55, 120-26, 138, 144-58,
    168, 178
  Massacre at Paris, The, 1, 2, 9-11,
    21, 28, 128-30, 137, 145, 168,
    172-74
  "Passionate Shepherd, The," 23,
    24-25
  Tamburlaine, 1-11 *passim*, 13-15,
    18-20, 24, 27, 36, 41-56, 57-68,
    69-91, 113, 117, 120-23, 126,
    143-45, 147, 158, 167-68, 174
Marlowe Society, The, 1
Marston, John, 22
Massacre at Paris, The, 1, 2, 9-11, 21,
  28, 128-30, 137, 145, 168, 172-74
Massinger, Philip, 22
Mercator, Geradus, 37
Medea (Euripides), 108
Mermaid Tavern, The, 23
Merry Wives of Windsor, The
  (Shakespeare), 25
Middleton, Thomas, 129
Milton, John, 12, 15, 23-24, 40, 112
Miss Julia (Strindberg), 108
Montaigne, Michel, 33
Mulcaster, Richard, 37
Murray, Dr. Henry A., 29

N

Nashe, Thomas, 20, 25, 57,
  161
New Way to Pay Old Debts, A
  (Massinger), 22
Nicholay, Nicolas, 54
Nicolson, Marjorie, 32
Nietzsche, Friedrich, 31

"Nymph's Reply to the Shepherd,
  The" (Raleigh), 25

O

Odyssey, The (Homer), 66
Old Fortunatus (Dekker), 20
Oration (Pico), 112
Ortelius, Abraham, 37, 40-47, 52
Ovid, 10, 34, 117, 133
Oxinden, Henry, 163, 165

P

Paradise Lost (Milton), 23
Paradise Regained (Milton), 24
Parsons, Robert, 165-66
Pascal, Blaise, 31
"Passionate Shepherd, The," 23, 24-25
Peele, George, 14
Pembroke's Men, 128
Pericles (Shakespeare), 2
Phaedrus (Plato), 66
Pharsala (Lucan), 90
Philaster (Beaumont and Fletcher),
  22
Pico della Mirandola, Giovanni, 112
Pierce Penniless (Nashe), 161
Plato, 57, 63, 65, 66
Pliny, 54
Plotinus, 58
Plutarch, 48, 57, 58
Pollaiuolo, Antonio, 69
Praz, Mario, 29, 69
Preston, Thomas, 7
Principal Navigations (Hakluyt), 37
Prometheus Bound (Aeschylus), 31
Prose pour des Esseintes (Mallarmé),
  33
Punch, 16
Puttenham, Richard, 90, 91
Pythagoras, 118

R

Racine, Jean, 28
Raleigh, Sir Walter, 21, 25, 26, 40,
  160, 164-66

Return from Parnassus, The (anon.),
  25
Richard II (Shakespeare), 132, 135,
  137, 142
Richard III (Shakespeare), 17, 130,
  135, 139
Richards, I. A., 31
Rogers, Daniel, 37

S

Sad Shepherd, The (Jonson), 21
Samson Agonistes (Milton), 24
Sanuto, Livio, 42
"Scholler-like Shepheard, The"
  (Nashe), 25
Seaton, Ethel, 4
Sejanus (Jonson), 21
Seneca, 69, 72, 74, 87-88
Shakespeare, William, 1, 2, 23, 53,
  113, 130, 135
    and Marlowe, Christopher, 1, 3, 7-
      13 *passim*, 19-20, 54, 55, 79, 89,
      118, 127, 128, 132, 137, 139,
      142-43, 168
Shore's Wife (Churchyard), 119
Sidney, Sir Philip, 26, 32, 63
Smith, Henry, 67
Socrates, 58
Song of Solomon, The, 113
Sophocles, 69, 111
Spanish Tragedy, The (Kyd), 115,
  122-23
Spengler, Oswald, 33
Spenser, Edmund, 13-15, 63
Stoics, the, 57
Stow, Jogn, 135
Strindberg, August, 108
Surrey, Henry Howard, 12, 15
Swift, Jonathan, 42
Swinburne, A. C., 12, 55

T

Tamburlaine, 1-11 *passim*, 24, 27,
  57-68, 69-91, 113, 117, 126, 143,

147, 158, 167-68, 174
  influence of, 18-20, 24
  and *The Jew of Malta*, 120-23,
    144-45, 147, 158
  maps, use of, 36, 41-56
Taming of a Shrew, The (Shakespeare),
  20
Tears of Peace (Chapman), 58
Tennyson, Alfred Lord, 12, 15
Testament of Beauty, The (Bridges),
  24
Theatre of Gods judgements (Beard),
  164
Theatrum Orbis Terrarum (Ortelius),
  37, 40-47 *passim*
*Timber, or Discoveries made upon
  Men and Matter* (Jonson), 20
Timon of Athens (Shakespeare), 2
"To Phyllis, to Love and Live with
  Him" (Herrick), 25
Tourneur, Cyril, 22, 125
*Tragedy of Dido (see Dido, Queen of
  Carthage)*
*Tragedy of Doctor Faustus (see
  Doctor Faustus)*
Treatise on Monarchy, A (Greville), 63
Troades, The (Euripides), 108, 109

V

Valéry, Paul, 33
Virgil, 17, 169
Volpone (Jonson), 15, 16, 20, 168

W

Waith, Eugene M., 7
Walton, Izaak, 25
Webbe, Edward, 136
Webster, John, 5-7, 22, 79, 125,
  129
Woman in the Moon, The
  (Lyly), 18
Women of Trachis, The
  (Sophocles), 81

ANDREW MARVELL

A Collection of Critical Essays

Edited by GEORGE deFOREST LORD

A

"Absalom and Achitophel" (Dryden), 12, 87, 166, 173

Account of the Growth of Popery and Arbitrary Government in England, An, 15

Aeneid (Virgil), 57, 125

Ailmer, John, 147, 150

Alexander the Great, 34

"Ametus and Thestylis making Hayropes," 83-84

Annus Mirabilis (Dryden), 11, 12, 166, 169, 170, 172, 174

Antony and Cleopatra (Shakespeare), 6

Aristophanes, 78

Augustine, Saint, 82, 104-5

Ayloffe, John, 9

B

Baudelaire, Charles, 18

"Bearded Oaks" (Warren), 43

"Bermudas, The," 16, 49-50, 56, 121

Blake, William, 109, 118, 137

Bradbrook, M. C., 13-14

Brooks, Cleanth, 3, 6, 17, 34, 85

Brown, Robert, 154

Browning, Robert, 19, 28

Bunyan, John, 137

Busenello, Giovanni Francesco, 165

Bush, Douglas, 6, 35, 85

Butler, Samuel, 165, 174

C

Caesar, Augustus, 91-93, 98-100

Caesar, Julius, 87-89, 92, 151

Caesar, Octavian, 5, 89, 92, 93

Calvin, John, 161

Campion, Thomas, 42

Carroll, Lewis (*see* Dodgson, Charles Lutwidge)

Case, John, 34

Castiglione, Baldassare, 82

Catullus, 20, 21

"Character of Holland," 7

Charles I, 4, 70, 87, 89, 90, 92, 96, 163

Charles II, 2, 9, 11-13, 20, 57, 68, 70, 71, 73, 146, 154, 163, 166, 170, 172

"Clarinden's House-Warming," 29

Cleveland, John, 21

"Clorinda and Damon," 31, 47, 56, 74

Coleridge, Samuel Taylor, 25

Collins, William, 26-27

Commager, Steele, 5, 6, 57

Compleat Angler, The (Walton), 138

Comus (Milton), 19

Confessions (St. Augustine), 104

Conrad, Joseph, 129

"Contemplateur, Le" (Saint-Amant), 108-9

Coolidge, J. S., 5, 6, 17, 57

Cooper, Sir Anthony Ashley, 12, 146

"Cooper's Hill" (Denham), 71, 131, 150

"Coronet, The," 16, 54, 56, 57

Cowley, Abraham, 19, 21, 111
Crashaw, Richard, 15, 75, 111
Cromwell, Henry, 146
Cromwell, Oliver, 57, 60, 63, 66-70,
   85, 88, 89, 92, 96-98, 172
   and Marvell, 2, 5-8, **32-38**, 41, 50,
   58-59, 122, **143-64**
Cromwell, Richard, 68

D

"Damon the Mower," 47, 48-49
Dante Alighieri, 82, 109, 122
"Daphnis and Chloe," 16
"Definition of Love, A," 16, 17, 56,
   74-84
Denham, John, 71
"Dialogue between the Resolved Soul
   and Created Pleasure, A," 50, 74-75
Dodgson, Charles Lutwidge (*pseud.*
   Lewis Carroll), 123, 129
Donne, John, 3, 15, 19, 21, 30, 56, 74,
   82, 84, 116
Drayton, Michael, 5, 37
Dryden, John, 3, 10, 19, 26, 87
   and Marvell, **10-15**, 16, 26-27, 169,
   170, 172-74
Duchess of York (*see* Hyde, Anne)

E

Eliot, T. S., 1, 3, 6, 16, 17, 42, 55, 122
Empson, William, 3, 6, 17
Enneads (Plotinus), 79
"Epistle to Burlington" (Pope), 122

F

Faerie Queene, The (Spenser), 120
Fairfax, Lady Isabel, 31
Fairfax, Maria, **60-65**, 124-27, 138-40
Fairfax, Thomas, 37, **60-65**, 121, 122,
   124, 126-30, 132, 134, 136
Fairfax, William, 131
"Fair Singer, The," 32
"First Anniversary, The," 7, 17, 32,
   36, 38, **65-69**, 71, **143-64**
Flaubert, Gustave, 131

"Fleckno, or an English Priest of
   Rome," 30
Flecknoe, Richard, 5
Frazer, James George, 140

G

"Gallery, The," 42
"Garden, The," 17, 45, 46, 57, 59-60,
   63, 74, **101-7**, **109-19** *passim,* 121,
   131
Garlan, Augustine, 146
Gautier, Théophile, 19
George III, 2
Georgics, The (Virgil), 17, 122, 128
Gray, Thomas, 27
"Great Good Place, The" (James), 120
Grierson, Sir Herbert, 1

H

Haley, K. D. H., 9
Hall, John, 147
Hall, Joseph, 30
Hall, Thomas, 156
Hardy, Thomas, 19
Hartman, Geoffrey, 17
Herbert, George, 2, 48
   and Marvell, 15, 54, 80
*History of the Parliament of England,
   The* (May), 86
Hollander, John, 17
Horace, 21, 71, 143
   and Marvell, 5-7, 16, 61, 85-100,
   121
"Horatian Ode, An," 5-7, 13, 17, 19,
   25, 27, 34, 36, 50, 57, **58-69**, 108,
   153, 160, 170
Huckleberry Finn (Twain), 138
Hudibras (Butler), 165
Hunton, Samuel, 150
Hyde, Anne, 166

I

"Il Penseroso" (Milton), 21
"Instructions to a Painter" (Wallace),
   69, 165, 170

"Invitation au Voyage" (Baudelaire), 31

J

James II, 29
James, Henry, 120
Jonson, Ben, 43-44
    and Marvell, 3, 19, 25, 61, 122

K

Kabbala, the, 118
Keats, John, 2, 16, 19, 21, 28
Kiligrew, Anne, 171
Kneller, Sir Godfrey, 166

L

Landor, Walter Savage, 19
"L'Allegro" (Milton), 21
"Last Instructions to a Painter," 8, 11, 12, 17, 57-58, 69-72, 165-74
Leavis, F. R., 3, 7, 17
Legouis, Pierre, 1
Leishman, J. B., 6, 15
Lely, Sir Peter, 168, 170
Life and Death of Jason, The (Morris), 24
Louis XIV, 9
Lovelace, Richard, 5, 7
Lucan, 87, 88, 96, 97
    and Marvell, 87-90, 92, 93
Lucasta (Lovelace), 5
Lucretius, 20
"Lycidas" (Milton), 46-47

M

Mac Flecknoe (Dryden), 5
Machiavelli, Niccoló, 57
MacLeish, Archibald, 42, 43
Margoliouth, H. M., 1, 3
Marlowe, Christopher, 19
Marvell, Andrew, works by:
    and Collins, William, 26-27
    critical reputation of, 2, 3-4

Cromwell, Oliver, 2, 5-8, 32-38, 41, 50, 58-59, 122, 142-64
    and Donne, John, 3, 15, 19, 21, 30
    and Dryden, John, 10-15, 16, 26-27, 169, 170, 172-74
    and Fairfax, Maria, 60-65
    and Fairfax, Thomas, 37, 60-55, 121, 122, 124, 126-30, 132, 134
    and Gray, Thomas, 27
    Herbert, George, 15, 54, 80
    and Horace, 5-7, 16, 60, 85-100, 121
    Jonson, Ben, 3, 19, 25, 61, 122
    life of, 2, 4-15, 20, 55-75, 143-64
    and Lucan, 87-90, 92, 93
    and May, Tom, 7, 86-87, 92
    and Milton, John, 8-10, 26-27, 46-47, 54
    and modern poetry, 18-19, 22, 25-26, 42-43
    and neo-Platonism, 78-84, 119, 134-35, 137
    and Parker, Samuel, 9, 91
    and Paul, Saint, 101-19
    and Saint-Amant, Antoine-Girard de, 108-9
    and Shakespeare, William, 5-6
    and Virgil, 61, 116, 122, 134
    Account of the Growth of Popery and Arbitrary Government in England, 15
    "Ametus and Thestylis making Hay-ropes," 83-84
    "Bermudas, The," 16, 49-50, 56, 121
    "Character of Holland," 7
    "Clarinden's House-Warming," 29
    "Clorinda and Damon," 31, 47, 56, 74
    "Coronet, The," 16, 54, 56, 57
    "Damon the Mower," 47, 48-49
    "Daphnis and Chloe," 16
    "Definition of Love, A," 16, 17, 56, 74-84
    "Dialogue between The Resolved Soul and Created Pleasure, A," 50, 74-75

Marvell, Andrew, works by:
    (*continued*)
    "Fair Singer, The," 32
    "First Anniversary, The," 7, 17,
        32, 36, 38, **65-69**, 71, **143-64**
    "Fleckno, or an English Priest of
        Rome," 30
    "Gallery, The," 42
    "Garden, The," 17, 45, 46, 57, 59-
        60, 63, 74, **101-7**, **109-19**, 121,
        131
    "Horatian Ode, An," 5-7, 13, 17, 19,
        25, 27, 34, 36, 50, 57, **58-69**,
        108, 153, 160, 170
    "Last Instructions to a Painter," 8,
        11, 12, 17, 57-58, 69-72, **165-74**
    "Mourning," 16
    "Mower Against Gardens, The,"
        36, 46
    "Mower's Song, The," 47-48, 107-8,
        114-17
    "Mower to the Glo-Worms, The,"
        49
    "Musicks Empire," 29, 36, **37-41**
    "Nymph and the Faun, The," 24,
        27
    "Nymph complaining for the Death
        of her Faun, The," 121
    "On a Drop of Dew," 121
    "On the Victory obtained by
        Blake," 7
    "Picture of Little T. C. in a Prospect
        of Flowers," 121
    "Rehearsal Transpos'd, The," 9, 11,
        13, 14, 84, 91
    "Second Advice to a Painter, The,"
        69, 71-72
    "Statue in Stocks-Market, The,"
        170-71
    "Third Advice to a Painter, The,"
        69, 72
    "Thyris and Dorinda," 7, 31
    "To His Coy Mistress," 16, 50
    "Tom May's Death," 7, 86-87, 94
    "Two Songs at the Marriage of the
        Lord Fauconberg and the Lady
        Mary Cromwell," 7

Upon Appleton House, 8, 16, 17,
    32, 40, 43, **44-50**, **60-65**, 67, 108,
    113, 115, 120-42, 170
"Upon the Death of O. C.," 7, 67-
    69
"Upon the Hill and Grove at Bill-
    borow," 44
"Marvell, Mary," 2
May, Tom, 7, 86-87, 92
Melville, Herman, 129
Milton, John, 2, 19, 20, 26, 75, 116,
    118, 121
    and Marvell, 8-10, 26-27, 46-47,
        54
Morris, William, 24
"Mourning," 16
"Mower Against Gardens, The," 36,
    46
"Mower's Song, The," 47-48, 107-8,
    114-17
"Mower to the Glo-Worms, The," 49
"Musicks Empire," 29, 36, **37-41**

N

"Negative capability," doctrine of, 16
Neo-Platonism, **78-84**, 102, 105, 119,
    134-35, 137
"Nymph and the Faun, The," 24, 27
"Nymph complaining for the Death of
    her Faun, The," 121
"Nymph's Song to Hylas, The"
    (Morris), 24

O

"Ode on a Grecian Urn" (Keats), 16
Odyssey (Homer), 17
Of Government and Obedience (Hall),
    147
O'Loughlin, Michael, 17
"On a Drop of Dew," 121
"On Mr. Milton's *Paradise Lost*"
    (Dryden), 10
"On the Victory obtained by Blake,"
    7
Ovid, 106

P

Paradise Lost (Milton), 10, 58, 138
Paradiso (Dante), 24
"Parallel of Poetry and Painting, The,"
   (Dryden), 171, 172
Parker, Samuel, 9, 91
Paul, Saint, **101-19**
Petrarch, 78, 116
Pico della Mirandola, Giovanni, 79
"Picture of Little T. C. in a Prospect
   of Flowers," 121
Plato, 78
Plotinus, 79, 82, 134
Plutarch, 165
Poe, Edgar Allan, 25
"Poly-Olbion" (Drayton), 39
Pope, Alexander, 3, 11, 19, 81, 122
Praise of Music, The (Case), 34
*Prospective of the Naval Truimph of the
   Venitians* (Busenello), 165

R

"Rehearsal Transpos'd, The," 9, 11,
   13, 14, 84, 91
"Religio Laici" (Dryden), 10, 11,
   13
Richard II (Shakespeare), 61
Rochester, Earl of (*see* Wilmot, John)
Rogers, John, 152
Royal Society, The, 2

S

Saint-Amant, Antoine-Girard de,
   108-9
St. John, Oliver, 7
Scoles, Percy, 30
"Second Advice to a Painter, The,"
   69, 71-72
Shaftesbury, Earl of (*see* Cooper,
   Anthony Ashley)
Shakespeare, William, 5-6, 19
Shelley, Percy Bysshe, 19, 28
Socrates, 78
"Solitude, La" (Saint-Amant), 108-9

Song of Songs, The, 17
Southwell, Robert, 75
Spurnstowe, William, 155
"Statue in Stocks-Market, The,"
   170-71
Summers, Joseph, 17
Swift, Jonathan, 10, 19
Symposium, The (Plato), 78, 81

T

Tale of a Tub, A (Swift), 10
Tennyson, Alfred Lord, 19
"Third Advice to a Painter, The," 69,
   72
Thomas Aquinas, Saint, 105, 111
Thomas, M. G. Lloyd, 13-14
"Thyris and Dorina," 7, 31
Timaeus (Plato), 80
"To His Coy Mistress," 16, 50
Toliver, Harold, 17
"Tom May's Death," 7, 86-87, 94
"To Penhurst" (Jonson), 122
"To the Memory of Sir Lucius Cary
   and Sir Henry Morison" (Jonson),
   44
"Two Songs at the Marriage of the
   Lord Fauconberg and the Lady Mary
   Cromwell," 7

U

Upon Appleton House, 8, 16, 17, 32,
   40, 43, **44-50**, **60-65**, 67, 108, 113,
   115, 120-42, 170
"Upon Nothing" (Wilmot),
   75
"Upon the Death of O. C.,"
   7, 67-69
"Upon the Hill and Grove at
   Bill-borow," 44

V

Van Dyck, Sir Antony,
   168

Vaughan, Henry, 15, 45
Virgil, 6, 12, 128
   and Marvell, 61, 116, 122, 134
Vita Nuova, Una (Dante), 25

W

Wallace, John M., 8, 17
Waller, Edmund, 69
Warren, Robert Penn,
   43

Wilmot, John, Earl of Rochester, 75
Wordsworth, William, 2, 19, 28
Wortley, Sir Francis, 150
"Wreath, A" (Herbert), 54
Wyatt, Thomas, 74

Y

Yeats, W. B., 19, 55
"You, Andrew Marvell" (Mac Leish),
   43

MELVILLE

A Collection of Critical Essays

Edited by RICHARD CHASE

A

Adams, Henry, 168
Adams, John Quincy, 91, 92, 94, 107, 108
Adventures of Huckleberry Finn, The (Twain), 143
Aeneid, The (Virgil), 54
Age of Innocence, The (Wharton), 57
"America," 151, 152
American, The (James), 122
Ames, Nathaniel, 35-36
Aristotle, 65
Arnold, Matthew, 10
Arthur Gordon Pym (Poe), 29
As I Lay Dying (Faulkner), 57
"At Melville's Tomb" (Crane, H.), 156

B

Balzac, Honoré de, 28
Barnum, P. T., 55
"Bartleby the Scrivener," 4, 113, 122, 143
"Battle of Stone River, Tennessee, The," 153
Battle-Pieces, 2, 148, 152-53, 154, 155, 167
Baudelaire, Charles, 28
"Benito Cereno," 4, **116-24**, 163
"Big Bear of Arkansas, The" (Thorpe), 130

Bigelow Papers, The (Lowell), 138
Billy Budd, 2, 4, 7, 9-10, 76, 95, 116, **156-68**
"Birthmark, The" (Hawthorne), 159
Blake, William, 73, 157
Bleak House (Dickens), 28
Blithedale Romance, The (Hawthorne), 127
Brontë, Emily, 88
Brown, Brockdon, 27
Browne, Sir Thomas, 69
Bryant, William Cullen, 1
Byron, George Gordon, Lord, 70, 158

C

Cabell, James Branch, 2
Calvinism, 2, 23, 68, 70-71, 93, 160, 167
Camoëns, Luiz Vaz de, 50
Candide (Voltaire), 142
Carlyle, Thomas, 22
"Celestial Railroad, The" (Hawthorne), 127
Channing, Ellery, 89
Chapman, John Jay, 168
Christianity, doctrines of, 7, 14, 23-24, **56-61**, **66-74**, **92-110**, 131, 141-42, 154-55, 157-58, **162-68**
Civilization and Its Discontents (Freud), 70
Clarel, 10, 146, 148, 154-55
Coleridge, Samuel Taylor, 86

"College Colonel, The," 150, 151
Comédié Humaine, La (Balzac),
  85
"Coming Storm, The," 154
"Commemorative of a Naval Victory,"
  151
Confidence Man, The, 5, 9, 76, 94,
  106, 125-143, 166, 167
Connecticut Yankee, A (Twain), 22
"Conflict of Conviction, The," 148-49,
  150, 152
Conrad, Joseph, 11
Cooper, Anthony Ashley, 127
Cooper, James Fenimore, 1, 5, 6, 8,
  53, 93, 108, 110, 113, 114
Crane, Hart, 156

D

Dana, Richard Henry, 32, 34-35, 53,
  88
Dante, Alighieri, 76, 78, 90, 103
David Copperfield (Dickens), 27
Defoe, Daniel, 29
Democratic Vistas (Whitman), 2
Dickens, Charles, 4, 22
Divine Comedy, The (Dante), 103
Doctor Faustus (Marlowe), 89
Don Quixote (Cervantes), 129, 142
Dostoyevsky, Fyodor, 4, 19, 28, 159
Duchess of Malfi, The (Marlowe),
  89

E

Edwards, Jonathan, 167
Eliot, T. S., 24
Emblems (Quarles), 33
Emerson, Ralph Waldo, 1, 23,
  58, 128, 138
Endymion (Keats), 22
Engels, Friedrich, 22

F

"Fable for Critics, A" (Emerson), 138
Faulkner, William, 56
Flaubert, Gustave, 32, 78, 85

Ford, John, 88
Franklin, Benjamin, 10, 54
Freud, Sigmund, 64, 68, 69, 70
"Fruit of Travel Long Ago," 144

G

Gargantua and Pantagruel (Rabelais),
  142
Gide, André, 25
Goethe, Johann Wolfgang von, 46,
  67
Grant, Ulysses S., 143
Greeley, Horace, 1
Gulliver's Travels (Swift), 3, 142

H

Hamlet (Shakespeare), 76
Hardy, Thomas, 153
Hawthorne, Nathaniel, 1, 2, 5-8, 45,
  58, 62, 66, 67, 77, 82, 88, 93-94,
  110, 113-14, 119, 123, 126-27, 143,
  158-59, 167
Henry V (Shakespeare), 158
Hobbes, Thomas, 69
Hogarth, William, 28
Holmes, Oliver Wendell, 77
Homer, 50
Hopkins, Gerard Manley, 87

I

Iliad, The (Homer), 54
"In a Bye-Canal," 145-46
"In a Church in Padua," 148
Israel Potter, 10, 132-33

J

"Jack Roy," 146-47
Jackson, Andrew, 54
James, Henry, 5, 6, 27, 78, 79, 84,
  85, 93, 110, 113, 114, 122
Jefferson, Thomas, 108
"Jimmy Rose," 130
Jew of Malta, The (Marlowe), 89

John Marr and Other Sailors, 146
Jones, John Paul, 10
Jonson, Ben, 9
Jung, Carl, 64

K

Kafka, Franz, 4, 33
Keats, John, 69, 168
King Lear (Shakespeare), 50, 77, 78, 88, 167

L

"Lake, The," 155
Lawrence, D. H., 8, 24, 100
Life on the Mississippi (Twain), 130
Longfellow, Henry Wadsworth, 77
Lowell, James Russell, 138
Lucian, 70

M

Macbeth (Shakespeare), 50, 167
"Maldive Shark, The," 151, 155
Maldoror (Lautréamont), 102
"Malvern Hill," 152
Mann, Thomas, 29
Marble Faun, The (Hawthorne), 27, 158
"March into Virginia, The," 147-48, 149, 150, 154
Mardi, 2, 8-9, 21-25, 30, 31, 33, 38, 50, 84, 153, 158
Mariner's Sketches, A (Ames), 35-36
Marlowe, Christopher, 88-89
Marvell, Andrew, 146
Melville, Herman:
  and Arnold, Matthew, 10
  and Blake, William, 73, 157
  and Cabell, James Branch, 2
  Calvinism, 2, 23, 68, 70-71, 93, 160, 167
  and Camoëns, Luiz Vaz de, 50
  and Christianity, doctrines of, 7, 14, 23-24, 56-61, 66-74, 92-110, 131, 141-42, 154-55, 157-58, 162-68

  and Conrad, Joseph, 11
  and Cooper, James Fenimore, 1, 5, 6, 8, 53, 93, 108, 110, 113, 114
  critical reputation of, 1-10, 62-66, 75-77, 116
  and Dana, Richard Henry, 32, 34-35, 53, 88
  and Dante Alighieri, 76, 78, 90, 103
  and Defoe, Daniel, 29
  and Dickens, Charles, 4, 22
  and Dostoyevsky, Fyodor, 4, 19, 28, 159
  and Dryden, John, 158
  and Emerson, Ralph Waldo, 1, 23, 58, 128, 138
  and Gordon, George, Lord Byron, 158
  and Hardy, Thomas, 153
  and Hawthorne, Nathaniel, 1, 2, 5-8, 45, 50, 58, 62, 66, 67, 77, 82, 88, 93-94, 110, 113-14, 119, 123, 126-27, 143, 158-59, 167
  and Homer, 50
  and Hopkins, Gerard Manley, 87
  influence of, 75
  and James, Henry, 5, 6, 27, 78, 84, 85, 93, 110, 113, 114, 122
  and Jonson, Ben, 9
  life of, 3-4, 21-22, 31-32, 35, 49
  and Kafka, Franz, 4, 33
  and Lowell, James Russell, 138
  and Mann, Thomas, 29
  and Milton, John, 67
  and Molière, 9
  and Poe, Edgar Allan, 1, 5, 29, 35
  as poet, **144-55**
  and Radcliffe, Ann, 87
  and Schopenhauer, Arthur, 157-58
  and Shakespeare, 2, 35, 42, 50, 157, 158, 167, 168
  and Shelley, Percy Bysshe, 158
  and Smollett, Tobias, 53
  and Thorpe, Thomas Bangs, 130
  and Twain, Mark, 5, 130, 143
  and Virgil, 50
  and Whitman, Walt, 2, 51, 58

Melville, Herman, works by:
NOVELS AND STORIES
"Bartleby the Scrivener," 4, 113,
122, 143
"Benito Cereno," 4, 116-24, 163
Billy Budd, 2, 4, 7, 9-10, 76, 95,
116, **156-68**
Confidence Man, The, 5, 9, 76, 94,
106, **125-43**, 166, 167
Israel Potter, 10, 132-33
Mardi, 2, 8-9, 21-25, 30, 31, 33, 38,
50, 84, 153, 158
Moby-Dick, 1, 3, 5-9, 36, **39-48, 49-
61, 62-74, 75-88, 94-115**, 116,
124-26, 128, 133, 134, 142, 149,
154, 158, 161, 164, 165, 167
Omoo, 3, 11, 12, 18-19, 25-26, 30,
31, 139
Pierre, 4, 5, 8, 9, 19, 68, 71-72, 74,
75-76, 81, **82-90**, 94, 103, 106,
110, 111-14, 125, 157, 158, 164,
166
Redburne, 9, 21, 25, 26-31, 35, 37,
111, 158, 161
Typee, 3, 7-8, 11, 12, 14-18, 25,
26, 30, 31, 49, 71, 84, 123, 157,
158
White-Jacket, 9, 18, 21, 25, **31-38**,
69, 84, 111, 160, 166
POETRY
"America," 151, 152
"Battle of Stone River, Tennessee,
The," 153
Battle-Pieces, 2, 148, 152-53, 154,
155, 167
Clarel, 10, 146, 148, 154-55
"College Colonel, The," 150, 151
"Coming Storm, The," 154
"Commemorative of a Naval Vic-
tory," 151
"Conflict of Convictions, The,"
148-49, 150, 152
"Fruit of Travel Long Ago," 144
"In a Bye-Canal," 145-46
"In a Church in Padua," 148
"Jack Roy," 146-47
"Jimmy Rose," 130
John Marr and Other Sailors, 146

"Lake, The," 155
"Maldive Shark, The," 151, 155
"Malvern Hill," 152
"March into Virginia, The," 147-48,
149, 150, 154
"On the Slain Collegians," 149
"Portent, The," 148
"Requiem for Soldiers Lost in
Ocean Transports, A," 152
"Shilo, A Requiem," 147, 151-52
"Swamp-Angel, The," 154
Merchant of Venice, The
(Shakespeare), 78
Milton, John, 67
Moby Dick, 1, 3, 5-9, 36, **39-48, 49-61,
62-74, 75-88, 94-115**, 116, 124-26,
128, 133, 134, 142, 149, 154, 158,
161, 163, 164, 165, 167
allegory in, 44-48, 50, 53, 59-61,
63-74, 80-81, 84, **95-114**
and "Benito Cereno," 124
Christianity, doctrines of, 66-74,
92-114
as epic, 53-56
evil, theme of, 43-44, **66-74, 94-
114**
and *King Lear* (Shakespeare),
88
and nature, theme of, 39, 45-48,
60-61, 64-65
prose style of, 36, 39, 41, 42, 50,
51-53, 81, **84-88**
Molière, 9
Montaigne, Michel de, 78
Mosses from An Old Manse (Hawthorne), 62

N

Nietzsche, Friedrich, 70

O

Odyssey, The (Homer), 54
Omoo, 3, 11, 12, 18-19, 25-26, 30, 31,
139
"On the Slain Collegians," 149
Ormond (Brown), 27

Othello (Shakespeare), 78
Our Mutual Friend (Dickens), 28

P

Paradise Lost (Milton), 54, 67, 158
Pierre, 4, 5, 8, 9, 19, 68, 75-76, 81,
 82-90, 94, 103, 106, 110, 111-14,
 125, 157, 164, 166
Pilgrim's Progress (Bunyan), 80, 127
Plato, 78, 129, 138, 160
Plutarch, 35
Poe, Edgar Allan, 1, 5, 29, 35, 88
"Portent, The," 148

Q

Quarles, Francis, 33

R

Rabelais, François, 25
Radcliffe, Ann, 87
"Rappaccini's Daughter" (Hawthorne),
 119
Redburne, 9, 21, 25, 26-31, 35, 37,
 111, 158, 161
"Requiem for Soldiers Lost in Ocean
 Transports, A," 152
Roderick Random (Smollett), 36

S

Scarlet Letter, The (Hawthorne), 53
Schiller, Friedrich, 27
Schopenhauer, Arthur, 157-58
Sea Lions, The (Cooper, J. F.), 93
Shaftesbury, Earl of (*see* Cooper,
 Anthony Ashley)
Shakespeare, William, 2, 35, 42, 50,
 78, 157, 158, 167, 168
Shaw, Elizabeth, 22
Shelley, Percy Bysshe, 70, 158
"Shilo, A Requiem," 147, 151-52
Smollett, Tobias, 37, 53

*State of Innocence, and Fall of Man,
 The* (Dryden), 158
Studies in Pessimism (Schopen-
 hauer), 158
"Swamp-Angel, The," 154
Swift, Jonathan, 25
Swinburne, A. C., 11

T

Tamburlaine (Marlowe), 88
Thoreau, Henry David, 22, 138
Thorpe, Thomas Bangs, 130
"To His Coy Mistress" (Marvell), 146
Tolstoy, Leo, 22
Turgenev, Ivan, 85
Twain, Mark, 5, 77, 130, 143
Two Years before the Mast (Dana), 32
Typee, 3, 7-8, 11, 12, 14-18, 25, 26,
 30, 31, 49, 71, 84, 123, 157, 158

U

Ulysses (Joyce), 28
Uncle Tom's Cabin (Stowe), 23
Urn Burial (Browne), 89

V

Virgil, 50
Vita Nuova, La (Dante), 80
Voltaire, 70
Voyages (Delano), 117

W

Washington, George, 54
Wharton, Edith, 57
What is Man? (Twain), 143
White-Jacket, 9, 18, 21, 25, 31-38, 69,
 84, 111, 160, 166
Whitman, Walt, 1-3, 51, 58
Whitney, Eli, 107
Whittier, John Greenleaf, 77
Wilson, Edmund, 62

ARTHUR MILLER

A Collection of Critical Essays
Edited by ROBERT W. CORRIGAN

A

Actors, in Miller's productions, 4n, 42

Aeschylus, 56

After the Fall, 2, **10-15**, 23, **46-51**, 95, 109, 124, 131, **137-42**, 143, 145, 147-48, 150-52, 165, 166-67
  and *Crucible, The*, 47
  and *Death of a Salesman*, 141-42
  identity crisis in, 138-40
  and *Incident at Vichy*, 11, 13-15, 55, 139-40
  Miller on, 10n, 11n, 47, 48, 49, 56
  morality in, 166-67
  responsibility crisis in, 10-15
  Semitism in, 48, 49, 50, 55
  sexuality in, 47

Albee, Edward, 1

All My Sons, 1, 27-29, 30, 32, 52, 60, 82, 96, **132-41**, 144, 145, **146-48**, 165
  and *Death of a Salesman*, 71-76
  identity crisis in, 2-3, 132-33
  Miller on, 3, 63, 72-73
  sexuality in, 6
  tragedy in, 85-87, 90

American Legion, 32

Anderson, Maxwell, 81

ANTA Washington Square Theatre, 152-53

Arendt, Hannah, 8

Aronson, Boris, 153

Arts and Humanities Act, 25

Auden, W. H., 91

Awake and Sing! (Odets), 103n, 146

B

Babbitt (Lewis), 75-76, 76n

Beckett, Samuel, 123-24

Bentley, Elizabeth, 120

Bentley, Eric, 66

Bergson, Henri, 165

Betti, Ugo, 21

Billy Budd (Melville), 127-28

Blacks, The (Genet), 124

Brecht, Bertolt, 61, 63, 64, 98, 123, 132

"Bridge to a Savage World," 41, 136

Brothers Karamazov, The (Dostoevsky), 126

Budenz, Louis, 120

C

Camus, Albert, 70

Carnegie, Dale, 103

Catholic Veterans, 32

Chambers, Whittaker, 120

Children's Hour, The (Hellman), 118

Clift, Montgomery, 42

Clurman, Harold, 24, 144, 152-64

Columbia Pictures, 150

Community, Miller's attitude towards, 3-4, 23-24, 28, 32

Crucible, The, 28, 33-38, 60-67
  passim, 76, 78, 82, 108, 111-21,
  125-30, 132-41, 147-48, 149, 166
  and *After the Fall,* 47
  and *Billy Budd* (Melville), 127-28
  identity crisis in, 2, 134-36
  Miller on, 61, 63, 66, 88, 89,
    125-29 *passim*
  sexuality in, 6, 114
  and *Sorcières de Salem, Les*
    (Sartre), 36-37
  tragedy in, 87-89

D

Death of a Salesman, 1, 16, 25, 29-33,
  38, 41, 60-67 *passim,* 82, 95-109,
  113-16, 118, 124-35, 132-42, 145,
  146-47, 151, 165-66, 167-68
  and *After the Fall,* 141-42
  and *All My Sons,* 71-76
  and *Death of the Hired Man, The*
    (Frost), 106-7
  expressionism in, 74-76, 98-101
  identity crisis in, 2, 132-34
  Miller on, 5n, 61, 62, 64-65, 73-75,
    87, 100-102, 108n, 136
  realism in, 96-101
  Semitism in, 26
  sexuality in, 114
  tragedy in, 86-90
Death of the Hired Man, The (Frost),
  106-7
Desire under the Elms (O'Neill), 98
Disputed Questions (Merton), 9n,
  15
Doll's House, A (Ibsen), 82
Dostoevsky, Fedor, 126-27, 129
Drama Critics Circle, 144
Drama from Ibsen to Eliot (Williams),
  73
Dramatic aims, of Miller, 22, 41-42,
  59-67, 77, 125-26, 132
Dreiser, Theodore, 27, 32

E

8½ (Fellini), 48, 138

Eliot, T. S., 83
Enemy of the People, An (Ibsen), 82,
  96
Enemy of the People, An (Miller), 2,
  21
Erikson, Erik, 2, 10
Everyman (Anon.), 109
Expressionism, in *Death of a Salesman,*
  74-76, 98-101

F

"Family in Modern Drama, The," 56
Family, Miller's attitude towards the,
  7, 15n, 105-6, 145-47, 150
Father, The (Strindberg), 105-6
Federal Theatre, 24, 144
Fellini, Federico, 48, 138
Fiedler, Leslie, 26, 42
Fitzgerald, F. Scott, 50
Focus, 26, 132, 144
Fried, Walter, 144
Frost, Robert, 106-7

G

Gable, Clark, 42, 46
Galsworthy, John, 85
Gambler, The (Betti), 21
Gas (Kaiser), 56
Gassner, John, 65
Genet, Jean, 123-24
Glass Menagerie, The (Williams), 1
Glenn, John, 128
Goes, Albrecht, 70
Group Theatre, 144

H

Hairy Ape, The (O'Neill), 56
Hamlet (Shakespeare), 83, 124
Hawthorne, Nathaniel, 52, 112,
  125-26
Hedda Gabler (Ibsen), 97
Hellman, Lillian, 118
Hemingway, Ernest, 43, 44
Hiss, Alger, 116-17, 120-21
Hogan, Robert, 46

Hook, The, 150
Hoover, Herbert, 144
Hopwood Prize, Jule and Avery, 144
House Un-American Activities Committee, 25, 35
How Not to Write a Play (Kerr), 63
Human Condition, The (Arendt), 8*n*
Huston, John, 42, 44, 46

I

Ibsen Henrik, 21, 28, 60, 71-73, 82, 84, 85, 86, 97-98, 100, 168
Identity crisis, 2-6, 9-10, 12, **131-42**
   in *After the Fall,* 138-40
   in *All My Sons,* 2-3, 132-33
   in *Crucible, The,* 2, 134-36
   in *Death of a Salesman,* 2, 132-34
   in *Incident at Vichy,* 132, 137-40
   in *View from the Bridge, A,* 2-3, 135-36, 138
I Don't Need You Anymore (short stories), 132
Incident at Vichy, 2, 11, **13-15,** 23, 35, **52-57,** 131, 132, **137-42,** 165
   and *After the Fall,* 11, 13-15, 55, 139-40
   director's notes on, 152-64
   identity crisis in, 132, 137-40
   Miller on, 140
   responsibility crisis in, 11, 13-15
   Semitism in, 13-15
Inge, William, 136
Inside of His Head, The, (original title of *Death of a Salesman*), 62, 74, 102, 141
Introduction to *A View from the Bridge,* 38, 123
Introduction to *The Collected Plays,* 3, 5, 57, **59-67,** 72-75, 77, 87, 89, 92-93, 95-96, 108*n,* 109, 123-29 *passim,* 136
Ionesco, Eugène, 64

J

James, Henry, 112
Johnson, Lyndon, 24

K

Kafka, Franz, 124, 128
Kaiser, Georg, 56
Kazan, Elia, 99, 144, 150, 154
Kerr, Walter, 63
King Lear (Shakespeare), 83
Krapp's Last Tape (Beckett), 124
Krutch, Joseph Wood, 81

L

Last Year at Marienbad (Robbe-Grillet), 124
Lattimore, Owen, 116
League of Youth, The (Ibsen), 71
Levin, Harry, 56
Lewis, Sinclair, 75-76, 76*n*
Liberalism, 24-25, 32, 66
   in *Crucible, The,* 111-21, 130
Lincoln Center Repertory Theatre, 23, 131, 143
Long Day's Journey into Night, A (O'Neill), 131
Lucas, F. L., 81

M

Macbeth (Shakespeare), 83
McCarthy, Joseph, 37-38, 116, 118, 125, 134
McCarthyism, 33, 63, 88, 125, 147
McCarthy trials, 24, 35, 50
Male Animal, The (Nugent and Thurber), 118
Man Who Had All the Luck, The, 2, 27, 144, 145, 148
Melville, Herman, 112, 127-28
Memory of Two Mondays, A, 2, 3, 76, 78, 148-49
   Miller on, 60

Merton, Thomas, 9n, 15
Mielziner, Jo, 98
Miller, Arthur:
  and Beckett, Samuel, 123-24
  and Brecht, Bertolt, 61, 63, 64, 98,
    123, 132
  and Clurman, Harold, 24, 144,
    152-64
  and the community, 3-4, 23-24,
    28, 32
  critical reputation of, 1-2, 23, 131
  and Dostoevsky, Fedor, 126-27,
    129
  dramatic aims of, 22, 41-42, 59-
    67, 77, 125-26, 132
  and expressionism, 74-76, 98-101
  and the family, 7, 15n, 105-6,
    145-47, 150
  and Fellini, Federico, 48, 138
  and Frost, Robert, 106-7
  and Genet, Jean, 123-24
  and Hemingway, Ernest, 43, 44
  and the House Un-American Activi-
    ties Committee, 25, 35
  and Ibsen, Henrik, 21, 28, 60, 71-
    73, 82, 84, 85, 86, 97-98, 100,
    168
  and identity crisis, 2-6, 9-10, 12,
    132-42
  and Lewis, Sinclair, 75-76, 76n
  and liberalism, 24-25, 32, 66,
    111-21, 130
  life of, 24-26, 143-46, 149-50
  and Melville, Herman, 127-28
  and Monroe, Marilyn, 5-7, 42, 46,
    48, 49, 149-50
  and morality, 21-22, 27-29, 42, 47-
    48, 56-57, 64-67, 84-85, 145-47,
    164-68
  and Odets, Clifford, 103n, 115-16,
    146
  and O'Neill, Eugene, 1, 26, 47, 48,
    50, 52, 98, 131
  as a political dramatist, 23-57, 63,
    82, 102-4, 111-12, 125-26,
    147

  and realism, 60-61, 69-79, 96-101,
    165
  and Sartre, Jean-Paul, 37-38
  and Semitism, 4, 4n, 26, 42, 48, 49,
    50, 52-56, 144
  and sexuality, 6-7, 47, 114, 147-48,
    149
  and Shaw, G. B., 82, 85, 164-65
  and social responsibility, 21-22
    35, 41-42, 69-70, 71-72, 73, 82,
    84, 85-86
  and tragedy, 4-5, 26, 32-33, 81-93,
    123-24
  and Williams, Tennessee, 1, 6, 7,
    25, 26
  on his works (*see also* titles of indi-
    vidual works), 3, 5n, 10n, 11n,
    16, 16n, 38, 41, 44, 47, 48, 49,
    56, 57, 59-67, 72-77, 87, 89, 90,
    92-93, 100-102, 108n, 123-29
    passim, 136, 140, 143
Miller, Arthur, works by (*see also*
  titles of individual works):
  DRAMA
    After the Fall, 2, 10-15, 23, 46-51,
      95, 109, 131, 137-42, 143, 145,
      147-48, 150-52, 165, 166-67
    All My Sons, 1, 2-3, 27-29, 30, 32,
      52, 60, 71-76, 82, 85-87, 90, 96,
      132-41, 144, 145, 146-48, 165
    Crucible, The, 2, 6, 28, 33-38, 47,
      60-67 *passim*, 76, 78, 82, 87-89,
      108, 111-21, 125-30, 132-41,
      147-48, 149, 166
    Death of a Salesman, 1, 2, 5n, 16,
      29-33, 38, 41, 60-67 *passim*, 71-
      76, 82, 86-90, 95-109, 113-16,
      118, 124-25, 132-42, 145, 146-47,
      151, 165-66, 167-68
    Enemy of the People, An, 2,
      21
    Incident at Vichy, 2, 11, 13-15, 23,
      35, 52-57, 131, 132, 137-42,
      152-64, 165
    Man Who Had All the Luck, The,
      2, 27

Miller, Arthur, works by (DRAMA)
  (*continued*)
  Memory of Two Mondays, A, 2, 3,
    60, 76, 78, 148-49
  Price, The, 2, 13, 15-21, 165,
    167-68
  View from the Bridge, A, 2-3, 6,
    38-41, 60, 62-63, 77-79, 89-92,
    132, 135-36, 138, 149, 166
  ESSAYS
  "Bridge to a Savage World," 41,
    136
  "Family in Modern Drama, The,"
    56
  Foreword to *After the Fall,* 10*n*, 11*n*
  Introduction to *A View from the
    Bridge,* 38, 123
  Introduction to *The Collected
    Plays,* 3, 5, 57, 59-67, 72-75,
    77, 87, 89, 92-93, 95-96, 108*n*,
    109, 123-39 *passim,* 136
  "On Social Plays," 132
  "Our Guilt for the World's Evil,"
    140
  "Playwright and the Atomic
    World, The," 42
  "Shadow of the Gods, The," 26
  Situation Normal, 26, 136, 144
  "Tragedy and the Common Man,"
    32, 84-87, 90
  FICTION
  Focus (novel), 26, 132, 144
  I Don't Need You Anymore (short
    stories), 132
  SCREENPLAYS
  Hook, The, 150
  Misfits, The, 2, 3, 5-9, 12-13, 42-46,
    49, 136, 149-50
Miller, Inge Morath, 150
Miller, Mary Slattery, 149
Misfits, The, 2, 3, 5-9, 12-13, 42-46,
    19, 136, 149-50
  as a *pivitol* work 5-9
  Miller on, 44
  responsibility crisis in, 7-9, 12-13,
    42-43
  sexuality in, 6-7

Monroe, Marilyn, 5-7, 42, 46, 48, 49,
    149-50
Morality, 2-22, 42, 47-48, 64-47, 84-
    85, 145-47, 164-68
  in *After the Fall,* 166-67
  in *All My Sons,* 27-29
  in *Price, The,* 167-88

N

Night of the Iguana, The (Williams),
    7
Nugent, Eliott, 118

O

Odets, Clifford, 103*n*, 115-16, 146
Oedipus Rex (Sophocles), 109, 124
O'Neill, Eugene, 1, 26, 47, 48, 50, 52,
    56, 98, 131
"On Social Plays," 132
Othello (Shakespeare), 83
"Our Guilt for the World's Evil," 140
Our Town (Wilder), 1

P

PEN (Poets, Essayists and
    Novelists), 24
Pillars of Society (Ibsen), 71, 72
Pirandello, Luigi, 64
Plays Unpleasant, Preface to (Shaw),
    82
"Playwright and the Atomic World,
    The," 42
Political dramatist, Miller as, 23-57,
    63, 82, 102-4, 111-12, 125-26, 147
Popkin, Henry, 4*n*
Possessed, The (Dostoevsky), 126
Powers of Blackness, The (Levin), 56
Price, The, 2, 13, 15-21, 165, 167-68
  Miller on, 16, 16*n*
  morality in, 167-68
  responsibility crisis in, 13, 15-21
  Semitism in, 20
Prometheus Bound (Aeschylus), 56
Pyle, Ernie, 144

R

Rascoe, Burton, 144
Realism, 60-61, **69-79**, 165
  in *Death of a Salesman*, 96-101
Responsibility crisis, **10-22**
  in *After the Fall*, 10-15
  in *Incident at Vichy*, 11, 13-15
  in *Misfits, The*, 7-9, 12-13, 42-43
  in *Price, The*, 13, 15-21
Riders to the Sea (Synge), 86
Roosevelt, Franklin, 144
Rosenberg, Julius and Ethel, 116-17,
  120-21
Rosmersholm (Ibsen), 71
Ross, David, 142

S

Sartre, Jean-Paul, 37-38, 55
Scarlet Letter, The (Hawthorne),
  125-26
Semitism, 4, 4n, 26
  in *After the Fall*, 48, 49, 50, 55
  in *Death of a Salesman*, 26
  in *Focus*, 26, 144
  in *Incident at Vichy*, 13-15, 52-56
  in *Misfits, The*, 42
  in *Price, The*, 20
Sexuality, 6-7
  in *After the Fall*, 47
  in *All My Sons*, 6
  in *Crucible, The*, 6, 114, 148
  in *Death of a Salesman*, 114, 147-48
  in *Misfits, The*, 6-7
  in *View from the Bridge*, A, 6, 148,
  149
"Shadow of the Gods, The," 26
Shakespeare, William, 83, 98, 124
Shaw, George Bernard, 82, 85, 164-64
Situation Normal, 26, 136, 144
Social responsibility, 21-22, 35, 41-42,
  69-70, 73, 82, 84
  in *All My Sons*, 71-72, 85-86
Sophocles, 109, 124
Sorcières de Salem, Les (Sartre),
  37-38
Strindberg, August, 105-6

Synge, John Millington, 86

T

Theatre Guild National Award, 25
Theatre Guild's Bureau of New Plays,
  144
Thurber, James, 118
Tolstoy, Leo, 124, 144
Tragedy, 4-5, 26, 32-33, **81-93**,
  123-24
  in *All My Sons*, 85-87, 90
  in *Crucible, The*, 87-89
  in *Death of a Salesman*, 86-90
  in *View from the Bridge*, A, 89-92
Tragedy (Lucas), 81
"Tragedy and the Common Man," 32,
  84-87, 90
Trial, The (Kafka), 124

V

View from the Bridge, A, **38-41**, 60,
  62-63, 77-79, 132, 135-36, 138, 149,
  166
  identity crisis in, 2-3, 135-36, 138
  Miller on, 3, 38, 41, 90
  sexuality in, 6
  tragedy in, 89-92

W

Waiting for Lefty (Odets), 115
War and Peace (Tolstoy), 124, 144
Ward, Steven, 103
Weales, Gerald, 46
Whitehead, Robert, 154
Who's Afraid of Virginia Woolf?
  (Albee), 1
Widowers' Houses (Shaw), 82
Wilder, Thornton, 1
Williams, Raymond, 73
Williams, Tennessee, 1, 6, 7, 25, 26

Y

You Can Never Tell (Shaw), 164-65
Young Man Luther (Erikson), 2

MILTON: PARADISE LOST

A Collection of Critical Essays

Edited by LOUIS L. MARTZ

A

Adam, character analysis, 33, 38, 111, 116-20, 131, 132-33, 135-39, **157-72**, 176-82, **182-205**
Addison, Joseph, 1, 167, 183, 185, 189, 193, 196
Aeneid (Virgil), 62, 70, 105, 109-10, 111, 118, 148, 192
Allegro, L', 14, 38
Aquinas, Saint Thomas, 144-45
Aristotle, 49, 52*n*
Arnold, Matthew, 2-3
Artificiality, of Milton's style, 3-5, 14-16, 71-73, 75
Augustine, Saint, 194

B

Becket, Thomas à, 36
Beethoven, Ludwig van, 150
Bembo, Pietro, 64
Bentley, Richard, 19-20, **22-35**, 37-39, 185
Bernardus, 43
Biblical influences, 17, 32, 34-35, 101, 105, **187-202**
Blake, William, 6-7, 17, 111, 119, 144-45
Blank verse, Milton's use of, 22, 61-76
Blindness, of Milton, 13, 16, 53-54, 129
Bodkin, Maud, 46

Bunyan, John, 30, 164
Bush, Douglas, 9
Butler, Samuel, 2

C

Carducci, Giosuè, 62
Chapman, George, 48
Character analysis:
    Adam, 33, 38, 111, 116-20, 131, 132-33, 135-39, **157-72**, 176-82, **185-205**
    Eve, 32-35, 36-38, 116-20, 132-33, 136-39, **156-72**, 176-82, 185-90
    Satan, 4-5, 6-9, 27-32, **77-99**, 100-8, 111-20, 126-32, 139-46, 149-55, 160-61, 168, 174-77
Chaucer, Geoffrey, 138
City of God (Augustine), 194
Classical influences, in *Paradise Lost*, 32-34, 36-37, 105-7
Coleridge, Samuel Taylor, 36, 40, 102
Comus, 2, 102, 146
Copernicus, 22
Counterplot, Milton's use of, 5, 100-8
Crane, Hart, 11
Creation, Milton's conception analyzed, 9, 121-47

D

Dante Alighieri, 3, 15-16, 35, 64, 75,

Dante Alighieri (*continued*)
110, 122, 124-25, 133, 145, 146
De Doctrina, 166
Defence of Poetry, A (Shelley), 7
Della Casa, Giovanni, 64-67, 69-70, 75
Diction, as stylistic technique, 3, 6, 54, 57-60, 62-76, (*see also* Syntax)
Divine Comedy, The (Dante), 110
Doctor Faustus (Marlowe), 144
Donne, John, 44, 51, 53, 60
Dryden, John, 12, 16
Dry Salvages (Eliot), 55

E

Eighteenth century, comparisons with, 12-13, 16, 21, 61-62, 185, 189, 193
Eliot, T. S., 1-2, 3, 51, 55, 56, 110, 112, 160
Empson, William, 1, 4-5, 6, 7, 93
Epic form, Milton's use of, 3-4, 6, 40-41, 46, 53, 54, 60, 61-76, 90-91, 103, 109-11, 117, 142n, 148, 152-54
Essay on Man (Pope), 36
Eve, character analysis, 32-35, 36-38, 116-20, 132-33, 136-39, 156-72, 176-82, 185-90
Evil, theme of, 7-8, 101-2, 103-5, 111-12, 114-15, 186

F

Finnegans Wake (Joyce), 124
Freud, Sigmund, 46

G

Galateo (Della Casa), 75
Galileo, 43, 102-4
Georgics (Virgil), 70
Gerusalemme Liberata (Tasso), 74-75
Giorno, Il (Parini), 62, 70
Grand style, of Milton, 4-5, 61-63, 71-76
Grierson, Herbert, 82, 146n

H

Hamlet (Shakespeare), 178
Handel, George Frederick, 45
Hanford, James, 90n, 178
Hartman, Geoffrey, 5, 9
Hazlitt, William, 7-9
Hero and Leander (Marlowe), 48
History of Italian Literature (De Sanctis), 74
Hitler, Adolf, 114-15
Homer, 8, 15, 24, 31, 40, 109
Hooker, Thomas, 44, 113
Horace, 91n
Huxley, Aldous, 115

I

Imagery, function of, 3, 5, 8, 13-14, 25-26, 46-48, 57-60, 61-76, 100-8, 126-31, 142-43 (*see also* Metaphor; Simile)
"Is the Devil an Ass?" (Musgrove), 91n
Italia Liberata (Trissino), 62
Italian, influence of, 6, 30, 61-76
Ivory Tower, The (James), 15

J

James, D. G., 50
James, Henry, 14, 15
Johnson, Samuel, 1, 2, 10, 38, 75, 105, 148, 184
Joyce, James, 16, 17-18, 124, 125-26, 141

K

Knolles, Richard, 115

L

Landor, Walter Savage, 115
Latini, Brunetto, 62n
Latin, influence of, 4, 6, 43, 44-45, 72-73, 76
Leavis, F. R., 3, 4, 56-57

Lenzoni, Carlo, 62-63
Lewis, C. S., 1, 3-4, 79-80, 83-85, 90,
   98-99, 109, 144*n*, 169, 183-84
Lucan, 153-54
Lycidas, 17

M

Macbeth (Shakespeare), 13, 85*n*, 89,
   111, 112, 115, 116, 141
Mahood, M. M., 123-24, 128-29
Marlowe, Christopher, 17, 36, 48*n*,
   144, 144*n*
Marriage of Heaven and Hell, The
   (Blake), 6-7
Metaphor, analysis of, 21, 148-55
   (*see also* Imagery; Simile)
Michelangelo, 89, 122, 134
Milton and Wordsworth (Grierson),
   146*n*
Milton, John:
   and Addison, Joseph, 1, 167, 183,
      185, 189, 193, 196
   artificiality, of style, 3-5, 14-16,
      71-73, 75
   and Bentley, Richard, 19-20, **22-35,**
      37-39, 185
   and Blake, William, 6-7, 17, 111,
      119, 144-45
   blank verse, history of, 22, 61-76
   blindness, influence of, 13, 16,
      53-54, 129
   and Dante Alighieri, 3, 15-16, 35,
      64, 75, 110, 122, 124-25, 133,
      145, 146
   diction, as stylistic technique, 3, 6,
      54, 57-60, **62-76**
   and Eliot, T. S., 1-2, 3, 51, 55, 56,
      110, 112, 160
   grand style, discussion of, 4-5, 61-
      63, 71-76
   and Homer, 8, 15, 24, 31, 40, 109
   Italian, influence of, 6, 30, 61-76
   and Johnson, Samuel, 1, 2, 10, 38,
      75, 105, 148, 184
   Latin, influence of, 4, 6, 43, 44-45,
      72-73, 76
   and Lewis, C. S., 1, 3-4, 79-80, 83-

      85, 90, 98-99, 109, 144*n*, 169,
      183-84
   music, influence of, 13-14, 16, 43,
      104, 134-35, 150
   puns, use of, 22-25, 26, 43, 71-75
   and Puritanism, 109, 110, 113-14,
      117, 119, 135
   rhetoric, use of, 15-17, 58-59, 70-
      71, 79-80, 186
   ritual, as stylistic technique, 3-4,
      40-41, 53, 54-55, 142
   and Shakespeare, William, 13-14,
      15-17, 44, 111-12, 114-15, 116,
      117, 138, 144*n*
   and sonnet form, 61, 64-70, 74*n*
   and Spenser, Edmund, 2, 43, 44,
      102-3, 138, 146, 166
   syntax, stylistic use of, 14, 23-27,
      44-45, 56-60, **61-76**
   and Virgil, 3, 6, 31, 37, 39, 40, 62,
      63, 105, 106-7, 109-10, 111-12,
      184
Milton, John, works by:
   Allegro, L', 14, 38
   Comus, 2, 102, 146
   De Doctrina, 166
   Lycidas, 17
   Ode on Christ's Nativity, 121
   Paradise Lost:
      Adam, character analysis, 33, 38,
         111, 116-20, 131, 132-33,
         135-39, **157-72,** 176-82, **185-
         205**
      Biblical influences, 17, 32, 34-
         35, 101, 105, **187-202**
      classical influences, 32-34, 36-37,
         105-7
      epic form of, 3-4, 6, 40-41, 46,
         53, 54, 60, **61-76,** 90-91, 103,
         109-11, 117, 142*n*, 148, 152-54
      Eve, character analysis, 32-35,
         36-38, 116-20, 132-33, 136-39,
         156-72, 176-82, 185-90
      evil, theme of, 7-8, 101-2, 103-5,
         111-12, 114-15, 186
      imagery, analysis of, 3, 5, 8, 13-
         14, 25-26, 46-48, 57-60, **61-76,**
         100-8, 126-31, 142-43

Milton, John, works by: (*continued*)
  Paradise Lost: (*continued*)
    metaphor, Milton's use of, 21,
      148-55
    Paradise, analysis of, 9-10, 46-
      48, 138, 152, 175-76
    pride, them of, 8, 10-11, 34, 77-
      99, 110-11, 167
    rebellion, theme of, 8, 77-99,
      110-11, 112-13, 142-44, 149-
      50, 167
    Satan, character analysis, 4-5,
      6-9, 27-32, 77-99, 100-108,
      111-20, 126-32, 139-46, 149-
      55, 160-61, 168, 174-77
    simile, Milton's use of, 4, 5, 9,
      41-43, 47, 100, 102-8, 126-31,
      173-74
    sin, theme of, 34-37, 58-59, 82-
      83, 101-2, 138-44, 156-59,
      168-69, 174-76, 186-87, 194,
      201-2
    symbolism in, 107, 110-11, 113,
      132-33, 144, 146, 150, 151-52,
      175
  Paradise Regained, 72, 103, 119,
    146
  Penseroso, Il, 14
  Samson Agonistes, 53, 54, 177
  Vacation Exercise, A, 121
Milton's God (Empson), 7, 19n
Mondo Creato (Tasso), 62, 68-69, 71,
  73-74
Music, influence of, 13-14, 16, 43,
  104, 134-35, 150
Myers, L. H., 165

N

Newton, Thomas, 177-78
"Note on the Verse of John Milton,
  A" (Eliot), 2, 3

O

Ode on Christ's Nativity, 121
Odyssey (Homer), 118
Othello (Shakespeare), 122, 165

Ovid, 34, 43, 62n

P

Paradise Lost:
  Adam, character analysis, 33, 38,
    111, 116-20, 131, 132-33, 135-39,
    157-72, 176-82, **185-205**
  Biblical influences, 17, 32, 34-35,
    101, 105, **187-202**
  classical influences, 32-34, 36-37,
    105-7
  epic form of, 3-4, 6, 40-41, 46, 53,
    54, 60, **61-76**, 90-91, 103, 109-11,
    117, 142n, 148, 152-54
  Eve, character analysis, 32-35, 36-
    38, 116-20, 132-33, 136-39, 156-
    72, 176-82, 185-90
  evil, theme of, 7-8, 101-2, 103-5,
    111-12, 114-15, 186
  imagery, analysis of, 3, 5, 8, 13-14,
    25-26, 46-48, 57-60, **61-76**, 100-
    108, 126-31, 142-43
  metaphor, Milton's use of, 21,
    148-55
  paradise, analysis of, 9-10, 46-48,
    138, 152, 175-76
  pride, theme of, 8, 10-11, 34, 77-
    99, 110-11, 167
  rebellion, theme of, 8, 77-99,
    110-11, 112-13, 142-44, 149-50,
    167
  Satan, character analysis, 4-5, 6-9,
    27-32, 77-99, 100-108, 111-20,
    126-32, 139-46, 149-55, 160-61,
    168, 174-77
  simile, Milton's use of, 4, 5, 9, 41-
    43, 47, 100, 102-8, 126-31,
    173-74
  sin, theme of, 34-37, 58-59, 82-83,
    101-2, 138-44, 156-59, 168-69,
    174-76, 186-87, 194, 201-2
  symbolism in, 107, 110-11, 113,
    132-33, 144, 146, 150, 151-52,
    175
Paradise Regained, 72, 103, 119, 146
Paradise Within, The (Martz), 9
Parini, Giuseppe, 62, 70

Parody, Milton's use of, 9, 173-75
Peacham, Henry, 58
Pearce, Zachery, 19-20, 21, 22-26, 31, 34, 36, 37
Penseroso, Il, 14
Petrarch, 64, 74n, 75
Pliny, 43
Pope, Alexander, 5-6, 12, 56, 73
Pound, Ezra, 2, 12
Preface to Paradise Lost, A (Lewis), 183-84
Pride, theme of, 8, 10-11, 34, 77-99, 110-11, 167
Prince, F. T., 1, 6
Prometheus Unbound (Shelley), 114
Proust, Emile, 141
Puns, Milton's use of, 22-25, 26, 43, 71-75
Puritanism, references to, 109, 110, 113-14, 117, 119, 135
Puttenham, George, 58

R

Rajan, B., 1, 5
Raleigh, Walter, 20, 30, 156, 159, 178
Rebellion, theme of, 8, 77-99, 110-11, 112-13, 142-44, 149-50, 167
Rhetoric, Milton's use of, 15-17, 58-59, 70-71, 79-80, 186
Richards, I. A., 50
Rime of the Ancient Mariner, The (Coleridge), 178
Ritual, as stylistic technique, 3-4, 40-41, 53, 54-55, 142
Romanticism, comparisons with, 6-7, 62, 112, 115, 119
Rousseau, Jean Jacques, 136

S

Samson Agonistes, 53, 54, 177
Satan, character analysis, 4-5, 6-9, 27-32, 77-99, 100-108, 111-20, 126-32, 139-46, 149-55, 160-61, 168, 174-77
Saurat, M., 85n
Shakespeare, William, 13-14, 15-17,

44, 111-12, 114-15, 116, 117, 138, 144n
Shaw, Bernard, 85
Shelley, Percy Bysshe, 7, 111, 114
Simile, Milton's use of, 4, 5, 9, 41-43, 47, 100, 102-8, 126-31, 173-74 (*see also* Imagery; Metaphor)
Sin, theme of, 34-37, 58-59, 82-83, 101-2, 138-44, 156-59, 168-69, 174-76, 186-87, 194, 201-2
Sitwell, Edith, 2
Socrates, 113
Sonnet form, Milton's use of, 61, 64-70, 74n
Spenser, Edmund, 2, 43, 44, 102-3, 138, 146, 166
Statius, 153-54
Stein, Arnold, 9
Summers, Joseph, 10
Swift, Jonathan, 126
Symbolism, in *Paradise Lost*, 110-11, 150, 151-52
 of God, 113
 of Moon, 107, 132-33
 of Satan, 144, 146, 175
Syntax, as stylistic technique, 14, 23-27, 44-45, 56-60, **61-76** (*see also* Diction)

T

Taming of the Shrew, The (Shakespeare), 117
Tasso, 61, 68-69, 71, 73-76
Tennyson, Alfred, 136
Tillyard, E. M. W., 10
Trissino, Giovanni, 62
Turner, Paul, 171n

U

Ulysses (Joyce), 16

V

Vacation Exercise, A, 121
Virgil, 3, 6, 31, 37, 39, 40, 62, 63, 105, 106-7, 109-10, 111-12, 184

THE MODERN AMERICAN THEATER

A Collection of Critical Essays

Edited by ALVIN B. KERNAN

A

Abbey Theatre, The, 16
Actors Studio, The, 131, 149, 150
Adams, Henry, 9
Aeschylus, 1, 6, 19
Albee, Edward, 11, 16, 26, **80-89**, **99-103**, 112, 114, 116
Albee, Edward, works by:
  American Dream, The, 82, 84, 87, 90, 100
  Ballad of the Sad Cafe, The, 101, 102
  Death of Bessie Smith, The, 81, 82 84
  Tiny Alice, 80, 81, **84-85**, **93-96**, 98
  Who's Afraid of Virginia Woolf? 80-82, 84, 85, **90-93**, **96-97**, **100-3**, 116
  Zoo Story, The, 1, **13-14**, 32, 86-87, **88-89**, **99-100**
All My Sons (Miller), 35, 36-37
American Dream, The (Albee), 82, 84, 87, 90, 100
Anderson, Maxwell, 34
Andorra (Frisch), 137, 139-40
And the Sea Shall Give Up Its Dead (Wilder), 55
Angel That Troubled the Waters, The (Wilder), 45, 54, 68
Aristophanes, 1, 66, 67
Arms and the Man (Shaw), 23
Aronson, Boris, 139
Arrabel, Hernando, 26, 170
Artaud, Antonin, 165, 166, 168
As You Like It (Shakespeare), 62

Axel's Castle (Wilson), 156

B

Balcony, The (Genet), 5, 162, 170
Bald Soprano, The (Ionesco), 52
Ballad of the Sad Cafe, The (Albee), 101, 102
Balm in Gilead and Other Plays (Wilson), 118
Bancroft, Anne, 147-48
Bankhead, Tallulah, 64
Barr, Richard, 114
Barrie, J. M., 54
Barrymore, Lionel, 152
Bauhaus, The, 161
Beckett, Samuel, 15, 26, 66, 78, 116, 137, 157-59, **165-75** *passim*
Beckett, Samuel, works by:
  Endgame, 173
  Krapp's Last Tape, 170
  Waiting for Godot, 137, 167, 168
Bed, The (Heide), 117
Beiderbecke, Bix, 42
Ben Hur (Wallace), 56
Bentley, Eric, 149, 161, 164, 165
Bergman, Ingemar, 140
Berliner Ensemble, The, 16
Bernhardt, Sarah, 42, 150
Blacks, The (Genet), 167, 173
Blau, Herbert, 119
Bloedow, Eldine, 120
Bloedow, Jerry, 120
Blood Wedding (Lorca), 30-31

Bolt, Robert, 21
Brecht, Bertolt, 14, 16, 26, 53, 58, 95, 116, 135, **141-49**, 153, 157-59, 165, 171, 174
Brecht, Bertolt, works by:
  Exceptions to the Rule, 141
  Galileo, 95
  Measures Taken, The, 141
  Mother Courage, **141-49**
Bridge of San Luis Rey, The, 49, 54
Broadway:
  as a market, 104, 108, 109-10
  playwrights of, 106-7
  producers of, 105-6
  reviewers of, 107-8
Brustein, Robert, 135, 162, 164, 166
Büchner, Georg, 162
Bucholz, Horst, 140
Burrows, Abe, 106, 108
Bus Stop (Inge), 70, 72, 73, 75, 76

C

Cafe Cino, 114, 115
Callas, Maria, 144
Camino Real (Williams), 35, 42-43, 53
Camus, Albert, 172
Candida (Shaw), 53
Candida (Wilder), 46
Candide (Voltaire), 119
Caretaker, The (Pinter), 175
Carmines, Rev. Alvin, 120
Cézanne, Paul, 163
Chaikin, Joseph, 118
Chairs, The (Ionesco), 16, 32
Chaplin, Charlie, 129
Chayefsky, Paddy, 157
Chekhov, Anton, 14, 24, 26, 27, 32, 39, 77, 98, 157, 158, 164, 171, 175
Cherry Orchard, The (Chekhov), 24-25, 27, 30
Chicago (Shepard), 116
Cino, Joe, 114
Cocteau, Jean, 15, 26, 165, 168
Come Back, Little Sheba (Inge), 70, 72-75
Congreve, William, 53, 67

Connolly, Cyril, 36
Cook, Ralph, 120
Corneille, Pierre, 1
Cornelia Street Coffeehouse, 114
Crucible, The (Miller), 35, 38-39

D

Dark at the Top of the Stairs, The (Inge), **70-79**
Darwin, Charles, 28-29
Davis, Audrey, 120
Day Well Spent, A (Oxenford), 62
Death of a Salesman (Miller), 1, 35-38, 72
Death of Bessie Smith, The (Albee), 81, 82, 84, 90, 97
Demetz, Peter, 144
Devils of Loudun, The (Huxley), 39
Dewhurst, Colleen, 101
Doctor Faustus (Mann), 159
Dostoevsky, Fydor, 163
Drake, Alfred, 140
Dream Play, A (Strindberg), 167
Duse, Elenora, 42, 150

E

Eliot, T. S., 15, 21
Elizabeth I, 14
Elizabethan theatre (*see* Theatre, Elizabethan)
Emperor and Galilean (Ibsen), 16
Endgame (Beckett), 173
Enemy of the People, An (Ibsen), 38
Esslin, Martin, 145, 148, 172
Euripides, 6, 19
Everyman (anon.), 57
Exceptions and the Rule, The (Brecht), 141

F

Falcone, Richard, 118
Feldman, Peter, 118
Fergusson, Francis, 17-18, 132, 134-35

Field, Betty, 152
Flight Into Egypt, The (Wilder),
    55-56, 57, 58
Fonda, Jane, 153
Ford, Henry, 8-9
Foster, Paul, 118
Freud, Sigmund, 15, 29
Frisch, Max, 139
Fry, Christopher, 15

G

Gazzara, Ben, 152-53
Galileo (Brecht), 95
Genet, Jean, 5, 26, 98, 116, 157-59,
    161-62, 165, 167, 170-174
Genet, Jean, works by:
    Balcony, The, 5, 162, 170
    Blacks, The, 167, 173
    Our Lady of the Flowers, 98
Ghosts (Ibsen), 28, 30, 31
Gibbs, Walcott, 137
Gide, André, 158
Giehse, Therese, 148
Giraudoux, Jean, 165
Glass Menagerie, The (Williams), 35,
    40
Goodman, Paul, 120
Griffith, Hugh, 140
Guicharnaud, Jacques, 168
Guthrie, Tyrone, 65, 158

H

Hagen, Uta, 101
Hamlet (Shakespeare), 63, 137
Hammerstein, Oscar, Jr., 71, 78
Hammett, Dashiell, 158
Happenings, 121-30
*Happy Journey from Trenton to
    Camden* (Wilder), 45-46, 57
Hardware Poets Playhouse, 115, 120
Harris, Julie, 71
Hay, David, 140, 153
Hegel, G. F. W., 144
Heide, Robert, 117
Hellman, Lillian, 139, 157
Hemingway, Ernest, 156

Hill, Arthur, 101
Hingle, Pat, 152
Hogarth, William, 64
Horne, Geoffrey, 149, 153

I

Ibsen, Henrik, 14, 16, 24, 26, 27, 32,
    34, 35, 38, 58, 78, 157-66 *passim*,
    171, 175
Ibsen, Henrik, works by:
    Emperor and Galilean, 16
    Enemy of the People, An, 38
    Ghosts, 28, 30, 31
    When We Dead Awaken, 159
Iceman Cometh, The (O'Neill), 92
Inge, William, 70-79, 139, 157
Inge, William, works by:
    Come Back, Little Sheba, 70,
        72-75
    Dark at the Top of the Stairs, The,
        70-79
    Picnic, 70, 72, 73, 75
Ionesco, Eugène, 15, 16, 26, 52, 66,
    78, 100, 116, **158-68** *passim*, 170,
    172, 173
Ionesco, Eugène, works by:
    Bald Soprano, The, 52
    Chairs, The, 16, 32
    Jack, 173
    Submission, The, 173
Irving, Henry, 140

J

Jack (Ionesco), 173
James I, 14
James, Henry, 109, 134
Jefferson, Thomas, 9
Johnson, Lyndon, 132
Jones, Leroi, 116
Jonson, Ben, 66, 67
Joyce, James, 159

K

Kazan, Elia, 36, 37, 40, 42, 71-72,
    132, 150, 158, 159

Kennedy, John F., 132
Kerr, Walter, 137, 161
King Lear (Shakespeare), 35, 137
Kingsley, Sidney, 157
Kleist, Heinrich von, 162
Koch, Kenneth, 170
Kornfeld, Lawrence, 120
Kortner, Fritz, 139
Krapp's Last Tape (Beckett), 170

L

Lahr, Bert, 137
La Mama-Experimental Theatre Club,
  114, 115, 118
Langham, Michael, 139
Lawrence, D. H., 35, 40
Lawson, John Howard, 58
Levin, Peter, 120
Lewis, Sinclair, 139
Lincoln Center Repertory Theater,
  150
Living Theatre, The, 134
Long Christmas Dinner, The (Wilder),
  45, 56, 57
Long Day's Journey Into Night, A
  (O'Neill), 1
Long Revolution, The (R. Williams),
  133
Lorca, Garcia, 15, 30, 35, 157
Lorenzo (Richardson), 140-141
Louis XIV, 1, 14
Love and How to Cure It (Wilder), 46,
  56
Love's Labour's Lost (Shakespeare),
  140
Luther, Martin, 2
Luther (Osborne), 2

M

McCoy, Horace, 158
Magnani, Anna, 41, 42
Mains Sales, Les (Sartre), 105
Man and Superman (Shaw), 77
Man for All Seasons, A (Bolt), 21
Man Who Had All the Luck, The
  (Miller), 36

Mann, Thomas, 159
Mansfield, Jayne, 74
Marcus, Steve, 139
Marechal, Judith, 111, 112
Mary Rose (Barrie), 54
Marx, Karl, 14, 29, 142, 163
Matchmaker, The (Wilder), 50, 65-66,
  67
Measure Taken, The (Brecht), 141
Mee, Charles L., Jr., 11
Merchant of Yonkers, The (Wilder),
  49-50, 62-65
Miller, Arthur, 26, **34-40**, 42-44, 70,
  78, 81, 157, 158
Miller, Arthur, works by:
  All My Sons, 35, 36-37
  Death of a Salesman, 1, 35-38, 72
  Man Who Had All the Luck, The,
    36
Miss Julie (Strindberg), 166-67
Molière, 1, 66, 104, 135
More, Thomas, 21
Moscow Art Theatre, 16, 131
Mother Courage (Brecht), 141-49
Mourning Becomes Electra (O'Neill),
  16
Music Man, The (Willson), 71

N

Nabokov, Vladimir, 159
Nestroy, Johann, 62
Nietzsche, Friedrich, 163
Night of the Iguana, The (Williams),
  173

O

O'Casey, Sean, 15, 171
Odets, Clifford, 34
Oedipus at Colonos (Sophocles), 7
Oedipus the King (Sophocles), 7
Off-Broadway, 111-12, **113-20**
Oklahoma! (Rogers and Hammerstein),
  71
O'Neill, Eugene, 10, 15, 26, 34, 53,
  58, 68, 78, 92, 116, **149-53**,
  157-58

O'Neill, Eugene, works by:
  Iceman Cometh, The, 92
  Long Day's Journey Into Night, A,
    1
  Mourning Becomes Electra, 16
  Strange Interlude, 149-53, 154
Open Theatre Workshop, 118
Oresteia (Aeschylus), 1, 6, 19
Osborne, John, 21
Our Lady of the Flowers (Genet), 98
Our Town (Wilder), 46-47, 49, 50, 53,
  54, 59-62, 63, 65
Oxenford, John, 62

P

Page, Geraldine, 149, 152, 153
Patrick, Robert, 114
Penn, Arthur, 140
Picasso, Pablo, 155, 159, 163
Picnic (Inge), 70, 72, 73, 75
Pilgrim's Progress (Bunyan), 168
Pinero, Arthur Wing, 53
Pinter, Harold, 174, 175
Pirandello, Luigi, 4, 5, 14, 17, 26, 27,
  158-60, 164, 165
Pisthetainos (Aristophanes), 67
Plato, 6, 8
Plautus, 1
Playwright as Thinker, The (Bentley),
  161-62
Pollock, Jackson, 155, 159
Pope, Alexander, 145
Poppe, Nils, 140
Prince, William, 152, 153
Pullman Car Hiawatha (Wilder), 45,
  57, 58, 64-65

Q

Queens of France (Wilder), 56
Quintero, José, 149, 159

R

Racine, Jean, 1
Regelson, Bill, 118
Reinhardt, Max, 49, 63

Republic, The (Plato), 6
Rice, Elmer, 34
Richardson, Jack, 112, 139, 140-141,
  170
Rimbaud, Arthur, 163
Rivers, Larry, 114
Robbins, Jerome, 147, 148
Rodgers, Richard, 71, 78
Rose Tattoo, The (Williams), 41-42

S

Saint Joan (Shaw), 38
Sand Box, The (Albee), 16, 81, 84
Sarraute, Natalie, 168
Sartre, Jean Paul, 15, 26, 105, 165
Schneider, Daniel, 37
Seneca, 1
Seventh Seal, The (Bergman), 140
Shakespeare, William, 5, 32, 53, 64,
  78, 88, 137, 171
Shakespeare, William, works by:
  As You Like It, 62
  Hamlet, 63, 137
  King Lear, 35, 37
  Love's Labour's Lost, 140
  Taming of the Shrew, The, 76
  Tempest, The, 87, 88, 137
Shaw, George Bernard, 14, 15, 23, 24,
  26, 43, 53, 66, 77, 158, 164, 165,
  171
Shaw, George Bernard, works by:
  Arms and the Man, 23
  Candida, 53
  Man and Superman, 77
  Saint Joan, 38
Shepard, Sam, 116
Sherwood, Robert E., 157
Ship of Fools (Porter), 156
Six Characters In Search of an Author
  (Pirandello), 13, 26-27, 156, 158
Skin of Our Teeth, The (Wilder), 1, 49,
  50, 53, 63, 64, 109
Socrates, 6-8
Sophocles, 1, 6, 19, 104
Stern, David, 118
Stevens, Wallace, 159
Stewart, Ellen, 119

Strange Interlude (O'Neill), 149-53, 154

Strasberg, Lee, 131, 149, 154

Stravinsky, Igor, 159, 163

Streetcar Named Desire, A (Williams), 1, 30, 35-36, 40-41

Strindberg, August, 15, 16, 24, 26, 27, 58, 158, 162, 166-67, 171

Strindberg, August, works by:
   Dream Play, A, 167
   Miss Julie, 166-67
   To Damascus, 16

Submission, The (Ionesco), 173

Such Things Happen Only in Books (Wilder), 56

Summer and Smoke (Williams), 41

Sutherland, Joan, 140

Symposium, The (Plato), 7

T

Taming of the Shrew, The (Shakespeare), 76

Tardieu, Jean, 161

Tempest, The (Shakespeare), 87, 88, 137

Terence, 1

Theater, Elizabethan, 3, 12, 16, 21-22, 28, 31-32, 53

Theater, French, 3

Theater Genesis, 115, 120

Theater, Greek, 3, 6-8, 21-22, 67
   character in, 31
   stage design, 19-20

Theater, modern, 12-33
   alienation in, 12-14
   expressionism in, 25-28, 32
   influences on, 14-15
   and Marxism, 14
   naturalism in, 14
   and the plastic arts, 160-61
   realism in, 23-25, 26-28, 32
   stage design, **16-19**, 20-21, 22

Theater of Revolt, The, 162

Theater of the Absurd, The (Esslin), 171, 172

Theater of the Absurd Repertory Company, 170

Tiny Alice (Albee), 80, 81, 84-85, **93-96**, 98

Tocqueville, Alexis de, 9

To Damascus (Strindberg), 16

Todd, Mike, 129

Toilet, The (Jones), 116

Tolstoy, Leo, 136

Tone, Franchot, 152

Tynan, Kenneth, 140, 143

V

Volpone (Jonson), 67

Voltaire, 119

W

Wagner, Richard, 162

Waiting for Godot (Beckett), 137, 167, 168

Warhol, Andy, 114

Weales, Gerald, 111

Weaver, Fritz, 140

When We Dead Awaken (Ibsen), 159

Whitehead, Robert, 133

Whiteman, Paul, 42

Who's Afraid of Virginia Woolf? (Albee), 80-82, 84, 85, **90-93**, **96-97**, **100-103**, 116

Wiegel, Helene, 148

Wilder, Clinton, 114

Wilder, Thornton, 14, **45-51**, **52-69**, 109

Wilder, Thornton, works by:
   Angel That Troubled the Waters, The, 45, 54, 68
   Bridge of San Luis Rey, The, 49, 54
   Candida, 46
   Flight Into Egypt, The, 55-56, 57, 58
   Happy Journey from Trenton to Camden, 45-46, 57
   Long Christmas Dinner, The, 45, 56, 57
   Love and How to Cure It, 46, 56
   Matchmaker, The, 50, 65-66, 67

Wilder, Thornton, works by:
(*continued*)
  Merchant of Yonkers, The, 49-50,
    62-65
  Our Town, 46-47, 49, 50, 53, 54,
    59-62, 63, 65
  Pullman Car Hiawatha, 45, 57, 58,
    64-65
  Queens of France, 56
  Skin of Our Teeth, The, 1, 49, 50,
    53, 63, 64, 109
  Such Things Happen Only in Books,
    56
  Woman of Andros, The, 54
Williams, Raymond, 133
Williams, Tennessee, 15, 26, 34-36,
  39-44, 53-54, 70, 72, 74, 76, 116,
  139, 157, 158, 173
Williams, Tennessee, works by:
  Camino Real, 35, 42-43, 53
  Glass Menagerie, The, 35, 40
  Night of the Iguana, The, 173

Rose Tattoo, The, 41-42
Streetcar Named Desire, A, 1, 30,
  35-36, 40-41, 42, 72
Summer and Smoke, 41
You Touched Me (Williams and
  Windham), 40
Willson, Meredith, 71
Wilson, Lanford, 117-18
Woman of Andros, The (Wilder), 54
Wright, Teresa, 72

Y

Yeats, W. B., 15, 31
You Touched Me (Williams and Windham), 40

Z

Zola, Émile, 163
Zoo Story, The (Albee), 1, **13-14**, 32,
  84, 86-87, **88-89**, 90-100

MODERN BLACK NOVELISTS

A Collection of Critical Essays

Edited by M. G. COOKE

A

Abrahams, Peter, 25
Abruquah, Joseph, 6, 7-8
Achebe, Chinua, 4, 5-6, 9, **122-31**
Achebe, Chinua, works by:
   Arrow of God, 128-31
   Man of the People, A, 4, 5-6
   No Longer at Ease, 126-28
   Things Fall Apart, 6, 122-26
Adventures of Augie March, The
   (Bellow), 51, 64
African Child, The (Laye), 7, 8,
   133-34, 135, 142-43
African Image, The (Mphahlele), 129
"Alas Poor Richard" (Baldwin), 103
Allen, Samuel, 24, 25
Amen Corner, The (Baldwin), 100
American Negro Writer and His Roots,
   The (AMSAC), 25
American Society of African Culture
   (AMSAC), 24, 25, 26, 28
American Tragedy, An (Dreiser),
   5
Amis, Kingsley, 7
"And Hickman Arrives" (Ellison),
   78
Anna Karenina (Tolstoy), 128
Anthony, Michael, 159-61
Area of Darkness, An (Naipaul), 171
Arendt, Hannah, 129
Armstrong, Louis, 47, 54
Arrow of God (Achebe), 128-31
Art nègre, L', 14

Aswell, Ed, 100
"At the Stelling" (Hearne), 39
Autobiography of Malcolm X, The,
   7
Aventure ambiguë, L' (Kane), 106,
   114-17, 118
Azikiwe, Dr. Nnamdi, 27

B

Balandier, G., 16*n*, 22
Baldwin, David, 100
Baldwin, James, 2, 9, 11, 21, 57, 59,
   64, **88-104**
   adolescence of, 100
   and Wright, Richard, 98, 100-103
Baldwin, James, works by:
   "Alas, Poor Richard," 103
   Amen Corner, The, 100
   "Crying Holy," 100
   "Down at the Cross," 100
   "Everybody's Protest Novel," 2, 98,
     101
   Fire Next Time, The, 95, 99, 100
   Go Tell It on the Mountain, 2,
     88-104
   "In My Father's House," 100
   Nobody Knows My Name, 21,
     21*n*
Banana Bottom (McKay), **198-209**
Banda, Dr. Hastings, 27
Bandstand, 29
Banjo (McKay), **188-98**, 206
"Bantu Philosophy" (Temple), 19

Barbados, 25, 148, 155
Baudelaire, Charles, 26
Baumbach, Jonathan, 11
Bellow, Saul, 2, 51, 64
Beti, Mongo, 133, 136-39, 140-41
Beti, Mongo, works by:
  Mission terminée, 138-39
  Pauvre Christ de Bomba, Le,
    136-38, 140
  Roi miraculé, Le, 138-39
  Ville cruelle, 139
Bigsby, C. W. E., 10
Big Time Buck White (Tuotti), 3
Black Boy (Wright), 80, 133
"Black Boys and Native Sons" (Howe),
  57
Black Jacobins, The (James), 40-41
Black Lightning (Mais), 151
Black Muslims, 21, 98
Black Thunder (Bontemps), 10
Blade Among the Boys (Nzekwu), 105,
  111-14, 118, 121
Bleak House (Dickens), 42
Bone, Robert, 11, 98
Bontemps, Arna, 10
Bowles, Paul, 83
Brathwaite, L. Edward, 10, 11
Brazil, 32
Brighter Sun, A (Selvon), 150
Brothers Karamazov, The (Dostoev-
  sky), 80
Brown, John, 52
Buber, Martin, 31

C

Cameroon Republic, 133, 137, 139
Campanella, Roy, 57, 58
Camus, Albert, 5, 64, 83
Capitalism and Slavery (Williams),
  40
Catcher in the Rye, The (Salinger),
  64
Catechist, The (Abruquah), 7-8
Césaire, Aimé, 24, 25-36
Children of Sisyphus (Patterson), 9
Christmas Story (Naipual), 169
Cleaver, Eldridge, 7, 10

Columbus, Christopher, 147
Communist Party, 46, 66
"Concord Hymn" (Emerson), 52
Confessions of Nat Turner, The
  (Styron), 3, 10
Conrad, Joseph, 7, 46
Corentyne Thunder (Mittelholzer),
  149
Crime and Punishment (Dostoevsky),
  81, 82, 84
"Crying Holy" (Baldwin), 100

D

Dahomey, 15, 25
Damas, Léon, 14
Damico, James, 3
Dante, Alighieri, 35-36
Dark Child, The (see *African Child,
  The*)
Davis, Arthur, 26
Dawes, Neville, 207
Dawson, William, 46
Deer Park, The (Mailer), 85
Dickens, Charles, 42
Diop, Alioune, 13, 16, 24
Diop, Cheikh-Anta, 13-14
Dissent, 57
Dostoevsky, Fedor, 5, 46, 80, 81, 82,
  84
"Down at the Cross" (Baldwin), 100
Dramouss (Laye), 136
Dreiser, Theodore, 3, 5
Du Bois, W. E. B., 2, 191

E

Ebony, 28-29
Egypt, 13-14
Eight Men (Wright), 79
Einstein, Albert, 61
Either/Or (Kierkegaard), 81
Ekwensi, Cyprian, 105, 109-11,
  118-19, 121
Eliot, George, 128
Eliot, T. S., 35, 42, 46, 53
Ellison, Ralph, 2, 3, 4, 5, 6-7, 9, 11,
  45-63, 64-78, 80, 103

Ellison, Ralph (*continued*)
  and American Negro culture, 60-63
  background of, 45-47
  and Howe, Irving, 59, 103
  and literature, 51-56, 77-78
  and music, 47-51
  and politics, 56-60
Ellison, Ralph, works by:
  "And Hickman Arrives," 78
  Invisible Man, 2, 4, 5, 6, 7, 9, 45, 50, 51, **64-78**, 80
  Shadow and Act, 45-63 *passim*
Emerson, Ralph Waldo, 52, 55, 59, 61
Enfant noir, L' (*see African Child, The*)
English in the West Indies, The (Froude), 167
Etranger, L' (Camus), 83
Etre et le néant, L' (Sartre), 84
Euripides, 123
"Everybody's Protest Novel" (Baldwin), 2, 98, 101

F

Fabre, Michel, 11
Fanon, Frantz, 16
Far Journey of Oudin, The (Harris), 178, 179, **183-84**
Faulkner, William, 2, 3, 34, 53, 64, 78
Fetchit, Stepin, 3, 29
Fire Next Time, The (Baldwin), 95, 99, 100
First Congress of Negro Writers and Artists, 15
Flaubert, Gustave, 128
Ford, Jesse Hill, 3
Foster, Stephen, 62
Freedom Movement, 57
Froude, Anthony, 167

G

Gandhi, Mahatma, 196
Garvey, Marcus, 12, 195
Genet, Jean, 83

Gide, André, 178
Gift of Black Folk, The (Du Bois), 2
God Who Failed, The (Wright et al.), 83
Go Tell It on the Mountain (Baldwin), 2, **88-104**
Great White Hope, The (Sackler), 3
Guinea, 133
Guyana, 32, 150, 177-78, 185, 186

H

Haiti, 15, 40-41
Happersberger, Lucien, 102
Harris, Wilson, 4, 5, 6, 9, 11, **177-87**
Harris, Wilson, works by:
  Far Journey of Oudin, The, 178, 179, **183-84**
  Palace of the Peacock, The, 4, 178-79, **180-83**, 186
  Secret Ladder, The, 178, **185-87**
  Tradition and the West Indian Novel, 179
  Tumatumari, 5
  Whole Armour, The, 178, 179, **184-86**
Hawthorne, Nathaniel, 51
Hayden, Robert, 2
Hazoumé, Paul, 15
Hearne, John, 11, 38-39
Heart of Darkness (Conrad), 7
Hegel, Friedrich, 39
Hemingway, Ernest, 50, 53
Henderson and the Rain King (Bellow), 2
Hill, J. Newton, 28
Himes, Chester, 102
Hobbema, 177
Homer, 59
Home to Harlem (McKay), **188-98**, 208
Hopkins, Gerard Manley, 42
House for Mr. Biswas, A (Naipaul), 37-38, 163, 166, **170-75**, 206
Howe, Irving, 45, 57-58, 59, 103
Huckleberry Finn (Twain), 51

I

"Idiom in African Art, The" (Hill), 28
Ikenga, Patrick, 119
"In My Father's House" (Baldwin), 100
In the Castle of My Skin (Lamming), 155-59
Invisible Man (Ellison), 2, 4, 5, 6, 7, 9, 45, 50, 51, 64-78, 80
Irele, Abiola, 11
Islands (Brathwaite), 10

J

Jackson, Mahalia, 50
Jacobson, Dan, 129
Jagua Nana (Ekwensi), 105, 109-11, 118-19, 121
Jahn, Janheinz, 11
Jamaica, 12, 21, 25, 147-49, 151-52
James, C. L. R., 40-41, 180
Jefferson, Thomas, 6
Jones, Emma Berdis, 100
Joyce, James, 9, 34, 42, 53, 61, 64, 78
July, Robert W., 11

K

Kafka, Franz, 42, 64, 78, 142
Kane, Cheikh Amidou, 106, 114-17, 118, 119, 120, 121
Kierkegaard, Sören, 81, 85

L

La Guma, Alex, 106-9, 118, 119, 121
Lamming, George, 25, 36-38, 155-59, 162, 163, 165, 169, 204, 209
Last Enchantment, The (Dawes), 207
Lawrence, D. H., 8, 188-89
Laye, Camara, 2, 4, 6, 7, 8, 9, 133-36, 139-40, 142-46
Laye, Camara, works by:
    African Child, The, 7, 8, 133-34, 135, 142-43
Dramouss, 136
    Radiance of the King, The, 2, 4, 133-34, 142, 143-46
Leadbelly, 47
Leopard, The (Reid), 43
Lévy-Bruhl, Lucien, 18, 18n, 19
Lewis, Wyndham, 42
Liberation of Lord Byron, The (Ford), 3
Long Dream, The (Wright), 80
Lowry, Malcolm, 35

M

Macaulay, Jeannette, 11
McCullers, Carson, 64
McKay, Claude, 11-12, 188-209
McKay, Claude, works by:
    Banana Bottom, 198-209
    Banjo, 188-98, 206
    Home to Harlem, 188-98, 208
Madame Bovary (Flaubert), 128
Mailer, Norman, 5, 83, 85
Mais, Roger, 43, 151
Malagasy, 15, 24
Malamud, Bernard, 7
Malcolm X, 7, 10
Malraux, André, 47
Mann, Thomas, 54, 167
Man of the People, A (Achebe), 4, 5-6
Man Who Lived Underground, The (Wright), 79-80, 86
Marlowe, Christopher, 81
Marxism, 16, 20n
Masks (Brathwaite), 10
Mboya, Tom, 27
Melville, Herman, 3, 54, 64
Member of the Wedding, A (McCullers), 64
Michelangelo, 6
Middlemarch (Eliot), 128
Middle Passage, The (Naipaul), 163, 164-65, 166-70, 171, 175
Miguel Street (Naipaul), 163
Mission terminée (Beti), 138-39
Mittelholzer, Edgar, 40, 149, 152-54, 155, 156
Monde noir, Le, 14

Monod, Theodore, 14
Moore, Gerard, 10
Morning at the Office, A (Mittel-
holzer), 152-54, 156
Mozart, Wolfgang Amadeus, 6
Mphahele, Ezekiel, 9, 10, 11, 128,
129
Mr. Sammler's Planet (Bellow), 2
*Mr. Stone and the Knight's Com-
panion* (Naipaul), 162
Mystic Masseur, The (Naipaul), 9,
151, 163, 164, 165

N

Naipaul, V. S., 9, 37-38, 40, 149-51,
162-76, 181, 199, 206, 209
Naipaul, V. S., works by:
Area of Darkness, An, 171
Christmas Story, 169
House for Mr. Biswas, A, 37-38,
163, 166, **170-75**, 206
Middle Passage, The, 163, 164-65,
166-70, 171, 175
Miguel Street, 163, 165-66, 175
*Mr. Stone and the Knight's Com-
panion*, 162
Mystic Masseur, The, 9, 151, 163,
164, 165
Suffrage of Elvira, The, 151, 163-64
National Fiction Award, 45, 51
Nations nègres et culture (Diop),
13-14
Native Son (Wright), 2, 4, 5, 80, 98
Nausea (Sartre), 84
Négritude, 10, 11-12, **13-23**, **24-29**,
61, 120, 121, 134
    and the African presence, 21-23,
    61, 120, 121
    and politics and race, 16-17
    Sénghor's attitude towards, 17-21
New Day (Reid), 147-49, 151, 152
New Leader, The, 45, 57
Nietzsche, Friedrich, 81, 85
Nigeria, 105, 109-14 *passim*, 118,
120, 122, 127
Nkrumah, Kwame, 27
Noble Savage, The, 78

Nobody Knows My Name (Baldwin),
21, 21*n*
No Longer at Ease (Achebe), **126-28**
Notes from the Underground
(Dostoevsky), 80
Nyerere, Julius, 27
Nzekwu, Onuora, 105, 111-14, 118,
119, 120-21

O

Ode: Intimations of Immortality
(Wordsworth), 8
Of Age and Innocence (Lamming),
36-37
O'Hara, John, 7
"Open Road, The" (Whitman), 52
Orwell, George, 83
Outsider, The (Wright), 2, **80-87**

P

Palace of the Peacock, The (Harris),
4, 178-79, **180-83**, 186
Parker, Charlie, 47
Paris Review, 45
"Passage to India" (Whitman), 52
Patterson, Orlando, 9
Paul, Emmanuel, 15
Pauvre Christ de Bomba, Le (Beti),
136-38, 140
Picasso, Pablo, 48
Plato, 25
Pleasures of Exile, The (Lamming),
162
Porter, Hal, 34
Porterfield, Gordon, 3
*Premier Congrès des Ecrivains et
Artistes Noirs*, 102
Présence africaine, 14, 105, 133
Poe, Edgar Allan, 42
Pound, Ezra, 42
Proust, Marcel, 34

Q

Quality of Violence, A (Salkey),
151

R

Rabemananjara, Jacques, 15, 24
Radiance of the King, The (Laye),
  2, 4, 133-34, 142, **143-46**
Ramchand, Kenneth, 11
Ramsaran, J. A., 142
Ras Tafarians, 21
Reid, V. S., 43, 147-49, 151, 152
Rights of Passage (Brathwaite),
  10
Robeson, Paul, 158
Robinson, Jackie, 57, 58
Rohlehr, Gordon, 11
Roi miraculé, Le (Beti), 138-39
Rushing, Jimmy, 47, 50
Ruskin, John, 42

S

Sackler, Howard, 3
Salinger, J. D., 64
Salkey, Andrew, 39, 151
Sartre, Jean-Paul, 24, 81, 83, 84,
  85
Saturday Review, The, 45
Scarlet Letter, The (Hawthorne), 51
Seasons of Adventure (Lamming),
  204, 209
Secret Ladder, The (Harris), 178,
  185-87
"Self Reliance" (Emerson), 52
Selvon, Samuel, 4, 5, 6, 9, 40, 150,
  151
Senegal, 114, 143
Sénghor, Leopold Sédar, 17-21, 24,
  25, 27, 28, 141, 143, 195
Sepia, 29
Serge, Victor, 59
Shadow and Act (Ellison), 45-63
  passim
Simbi and the Satyr of the Dark Jungle
  (Tutuola), 4
Simon, Claude, 35
Smith, Bessie, 47
SNCC, 56
Society of African Culture, 24
Soul on Ice (Cleaver), 7

Souls of the Black Folk, The (Du
  Bois), 2
South Africa, Republic of, 25, 28, 106,
  108-9, 118, 119, 121, 132
Stein, Gertrude, 53
Stowe, Harriet Beecher, 100, 101
Styron, William, 3, 10
Suffrage of Elvira, The (Naipaul), 151,
  163-64

T

Tacitus, 167
Teilhard de Chardin, Pierre, 20
Temple, Fr., 19
Things Fall Apart (Achebe), 6, **122-26**
Thomas, L.-V., 22
Thoreau, Henry David, 52
Tibble, Anne, 11
Tolstoy, Leo, 128
Toomer, Jean, 48
Toussaint L'Ouverture, 40-41
Tradition and the West Indian Novel
  (Harris), 179
Trial of A. Lincoln, The (Damico),
  3
Trinidad, 149-51, 152, 154, 157, 159,
  163, 164, 166-70, 171, 172, 175
Tumatumari (Harris), 5
Tuotti, James, 3
Turn Again Tiger (Selvon), 4, 5, 6
Tuskegee Institute, 46
Tutuola, Amos, 4, 35
Twain, Mark, 51, 54

U

Uncle Tom's Cabin (Stowe), 100,
  101
Under the Volcano (Lowry), 35
Universal Nigger, The (Porterfield),
  3

V

Vesey, Paul, 24
Ville cruelle (Beti), 138

W

Walk in the Night, A (La Guma), 106-9, 118, 119
Waste Land, The (Eliot), 46
Waugh, Evelyn, 7
West, Nathanael, 64
West Indian Stories (ed. Andrew Salkey), 39
White, Patrick, 34
Whitehead, Alfred North, 31
Whitman, Walt, 52, 53
Whole Armour, The (Harris), 178, 179, 184-86
Widmer, Kingsley, 11
Williams, Eric, 40
Williams, William Carlos, 45
Wirth, Louis, 17n
Wordsworth, William, 8

Wright, Richard, 1, 2, 3, 4, 5, 6, 9, 11, 12, 25, 46, 57, 58, 59, 64, 79-87, 98, 100-103, 133
Wright, Richard, works by:
 Black Boy, 80, 133
 Eight Men, 79
 Long Dream, The, 80
 Man Who Lived Underground, The, 79-80, 86
 Native Son, 2, 4, 5, 80, 98
 Outsider, The, 2, 80-87

Y

Year in San Fernando, The (Anthony), 159-61
Yeats, William Butler, 53, 177
Yerby, Frank, 26

MODERN
BRITISH
DRAMATISTS

A Collection of Critical Essays

Edited by

JOHN RUSSELL BROWN

A

Adamov, Arthur, 58, 68
Albee, Edward, 68
All Fall Down (Arden), 85
All that Fall (Beckett), 34
Amedee (Ionesco), 138
Anderson, Lindsay, 166
Anniversary Waltz, The (Chodorov), 16
Anouilh, Jean, 15, 31
Arden, John, 2, 4, 7, 8, 32, 36, 38-46, 84-97, 98-103, 104-16, 165, 168
  and Brecht, 87-88, 105
  and his characters, 84
  dramatic aims of, 7, 8
  dramatic attitude of, 83-84, 89-90
  and dramatic device, 88, 94, 98-103
  and illusion versus naturalism, 98-103, 105-6
  and purity, theme of, 107-16
  as socio-political dramatist, 7, 84, 105-16
Arden, John, works by:
  All Fall Down, 85
  Armstrong's Last Goodnight, 114-16
  Christmas Play, A, 93
  Happy Haven, The, 84, 85, 91, 93-96, 102, 108-9
  Ironhand, 97
  Left-Handed Liberty, 104, 107, 112

  Life of Man, The, 85
  Live Like Pigs, 3, 32, 84, 87-90, 91, 93, 101-2, 104-5, 109-12
  Serjeant Musgrave's Dance, 36, 38-46, 84, 90-93, 101, 102, 104, 112-14, 115
  Soldier, Soldier, 87-90, 93
  Waters of Babylon, The, 84, 85-87, 88, 90, 96
  Wet Fish, 96-97
  Workhouse Donkey, The, 3, 7
Aristophanes, 39
Armstrong's Last Goodnight (Arden), 114-16
Arrabal, Fernando, 68
Artaud, Antonin, 140-41, 167
Ashcroft, Peggy, 16, 22
Auden, W. H., 29
Aymé, Marcel, 15

B

Bagnold, Enid, 17, 19
Bald Prima Donna, The (Ionesco), 15, 58
Banbury Nose, The (Ustinov), 18
Beckett, Samuel, 15, 17, 34, 58-70, 124, 131-32, 138, 140, 143, 153, 167
Before the Monday (Cooper), 24, 25
Behan, Brendan, 33, 39
Bernard, Jean-Jacques, 139
Betti, Ugo, 15
Billetdoux, François, 141

Birthday Party, The (Pinter), 11, **38-46**, 67, 126-27, 129-30, 131, 136, 138, 142-43, 147, 148-49, 151, 161
Blow Your Own Trumpet (Ustinov), 18
Bolt, Robert, 35, 141
Bond, Edward, 2, 3
Bond Honoured, A (Osborne), 10
Bost, Pierre, 16
Boy Friend, The (Wilson), 16
Brecht, Bertolt, 9, 15, 31, 32-33, 36, 72, 81, 87-88, 100, 101, 118-19, 167, 168, 170
Brook, Peter, 4, 16, 21
Browning Version, The (Rattigan), 18
Bruce, Lenny, 167
Buccaneer, The (Wilson), 16
Buñuel, Luis, 41
Burnt Flowerbed, The (Betti), 15
Bury, John, 1

C

Cannan, Denis, 4, 16, 19-21, 25
Captain Carvallo (Cannan), 16, 20
Caretaker, The (Pinter), 11, 67-68, 122, 128-29, 135, 136, 140, 143, 149, 161
Caucasian Chalk Circle, The (Brecht), 36
Chalk Garden, The (Bagnold), 17
Chaplin, Charles, 63
Charley's Aunt (Thomas), 16
Chekhov, Anton, 19, 77, 78, 124-26, 132, 137, 139-40, 143, 149
Chicken Soup with Barley (Wesker), 12, 75, 79, 168-69
Chin-Chin (Billetdoux), 141
Chips with Everything (Wesker), 3, 7, 12-13, 81-82, 168
Christmas Play, A (Arden), 93
Christopher Columbus (MacNeice), 18
Civilization and Its Discontents (Freud), 106
Clements, John, 16
Cocktail Party, The (Eliot), 18
Codron, Michael, 17

Collection, The (Pinter), 3, 11, 123, 127, 128, 129, 130-31, 132, 134-35, 138-39, 142, 147
Coming, Sir! (Marlowe), 76
Complaisant Lover, The (Greene), 19
Conditions of Agreement (Whiting), 21
Confidential Clerk, The (Eliot), 18
Cooper, Giles, 24-25
Counsellor-at-Law (Rice), 74
Count of Clerembard, The (Aymé), 15
Coward, Noel, 16, 165
Cranko, John, 17
Cranks (Cranko), 17
Creditors (Strindberg), 40
Cregan, David, 2
Crucible, The (Miller), 17
Curtmantle (Fry), 16

D

Dance of Death (Strindberg), 40
Dark is Light Enough, The (Fry), 16, 18
Darkling Child (Merwin and Milroy), 17
Dark Tower, The (MacNeice), 18
Day by the Sea, A (Hunter), 19
Deep Blue Sea, The (Rattigan), 18
Delaney, Shelagh, 32, 33, 34, 39, 165
Devils, The (Whiting), 17, 23, 35
Devils of Loudon, The (Huxley), 23
Dexter, John, 82
Doll's House, The (Ibsen), 40, 149
Down and Out in Paris and London (Orwell), 76
Dramatic device, in Pinter's works:
  gesture as, 136-42, 150
  humor as, 128-32
  levels of consciousness as, 132-35, 142-43
  menace as, 122, 126
  rhythm as, 127-28, 150
Dumb Waiter, The (Pinter), 11, 34, 126, 143, 149
Duncan, Ronald, 18

Dwarfs, The (Pinter), 124, 129, 130
Dyer, Edward, 4

E

Elder Statesman, The (Eliot), 30
Eliot, T. S., 7, 18, 30, 33, 38
Elizabethan theatre, 5-7, 10
Empty Chair, The (Ustinov), 19
Encore Reader, The, 166-68
Endgame (Beckett), 65
Enemy of the People, An (Ibsen), 34
Entertainer, The (Osborne), 32, 117, 118
Epitaph for George Dillon (Osborne), 9, 118, 169
Evans, Dame Edith, 18, 19
Everything in the Garden (Cooper), 25
Eye Witness (Whiting), 23

F

Family Reunion, The (Eliot), 16, 30
Father, The (Strindberg), 40
Feydeau, Georges, 15
Flowering Cherry (Bolt), 141
Forster, E. M., 73
Four Seasons (Wesker), 3, 13
Fregonese, Hugo, 92
Freud, Sigmund, 106, 126, 128, 131, 143
Fry, Christopher, 2, 16, 18, 21, 30, 33, 38, 165

G

Galileo (Brecht), 36
Gates of Summer, The (Whiting), 23
Genet, Jean, 41, 68, 167
Germinal (Zola), 110
Ghosts (Ibsen), 28, 39, 149, 150
Gielgud, Sir John, 18, 19, 22
Gigi (Loos), 16
Giraudoux, Jean, 31
Goethe, Johann Wolfgang von, 97
Goetz von Berlichingen (Goethe), 97

Good Soldier Schweik, The (MacColl), 17
Gorky, Maxim, 76, 78
Greene, Graham, 2, 16, 19
Guthrie, Tyrone, 21

H

Haigh, Kenneth, 134
Hall, Peter, 134
Hamlet (Shakespeare), 5, 6, 16, 48, 52-53
Happy Days (Beckett), 131
Happy Haven, The (Arden), 84, 85, 91, **93-96**, 102, **108-9**
Hašek, Jaroslav, 17
Herbert, Jocelyn, 1
Hitchcock, Alfred, 3, 122, 126
Hochwalder, Fritz, 15
Hole, The (Simpson), 123
Homecoming, The (Pinter), 11, **145-63**
Hordern, Michael, 134
Hostage, The (Behan), 33
Hotel Paradiso (Feydeau), 15
House by the Lake, The (Mills), 16
House of Regrets (Ustinov), 18
Howerd, Frankie, 16
Hunter, N. C., 19
Huxley, Aldous, 23

·I

Ibsen, Henrik, 27, 28, 34, 39, 40, 48, 49, 60, 144, 149-50
Iceman Cometh, The (O'Neill), 76
I'm Talking About Jerusalem (Wesker), 79
Inadmissable Evidence (Osborne), 9-10, 169
Indifferent Shepherd, The (Ustinov), 18
Invasion, L' (Adamov), 58
Ionesco, Eugène, 15, 31, 34, 58, 68, 138, 153, 167
Ironhand (Arden), 97
Isherwood, Christopher, 29

J

Jellicoe, Ann, 3, 4, 41, 137, 165
Johnson, Samuel, 100
Jokes and Their Relation to the Unconscious (Freud), 128
Joyce, James, 153

K

Kafka, Franz, 63, 65, 153
Kahler,Erich, 160
Kenny, Sean, 1
Kerr, Walter, 147
Kidders, The (Stewart), 41
King, Norman, 16
King Lear (Shakespeare), 6, 16
Kitchen, The (Wesker), 12, 13, 33, 34, 74-79, 141
"Kitchen-sink" drama, 2, 34, 66, 71, 72
Knack, The (Jellicoe), 3
Kops, Bernard, 33
Krapp's Last Tape (Beckett), 65

L

Lady's Not For Burning, The (Fry), 18
Last Joke, The (Bagnold), 19
Laurel and Hardy, 63
Left-Handed Liberty (Arden), 104, 107, 112
Lesson, The (Ionesco), 15
Life of Man, The (Arden), 85
Likely Tale, A (Savory), 16
Littlewood, Joan, 39
Live Like Pigs (Arden), 3, 32, 84, 87-90, 91, 93, 101-2, 104-5, 109-12
Living Room, The (Greene), 19
Livings, Henry, 3, 4
Look Back in Anger (Osborne), 9, 17, 23, 31, 33, 34, 39, 45-46, 47-57, 117, 118, 136, 141
Lope de Vega, 10
Lord Chamberlain, 2-3
Losey, Joseph, 167

Love of Four Colonels, The (Ustinov), 18
Lover, The (Pinter), 11, 130, 142, 143
Lower Depths, The (Gorky), 76
Luther (Osborne), 9, 36, 117-21

M

MacColl, Ewan, 17
MacNeice, Louis, 18
Mailer, Norman, 121
Malone Dies (Beckett), 65
Man for All Seasons, A (Bolt), 35
Marat/Sade (Weiss), 102
Marching Song (Whiting), 17, 22-23
Martine (Bernard), 139
Master Builder, The (Ibsen), 149
Mathry Beacon (Cooper), 24, 25
Max (Cannan), 20
Men in White (Kingsley), 74
Merwin, W. S., 17
Method acting, 133-35, 143-44
Miller, Arthur, 17, 28, 72, 167
Milroy, Dido, 17
Misalliance (Shaw), 16, 40
Misery Me! (Cannan), 20
Moment of Truth, The (Ustinov), 19
Morley, Christopher, 1
Mortimer, John, 17
Mr. Kettle and Mrs. Moon (Priestley), 16
Mrs. Warren's Profession (Shaw), 39, 40
Much Ado About Nothing (Shakespeare), 16
Mulberry Bush, The (Wilson), 17
Murder in the Cathedral (Eliot), 30
Murray, Barbara, 134

N

Never Get Out (Cooper), 24
New drama, discussed generally, 1-9, 16, 19-25, 31-37, 38-46, 71-72, 140-42, 164-70
  and American drama of the Thirties, 165, 169-70

New drama, *(continued)*
  antecedents of, 15-25, 26-31, 36-37
  appraisal of, 38-39, 71-72
  labels given, 2
  naturalism in, 34-35
  shock in, 2-3
  as social drama, 32-34, 39, 165-67, 168
  subjects of, 3
  violence in, 38-46
New dramatists, discussed generally, 1-9, 164-70
  appraisal of, 4-5, 165, 168
  dialogue of, 8
  dramatic aims of, 7-9, 14
  dramaturgy of, 9-14
  and Elizabethan dramatists, 5-7, 10
  social consciousness of, 7-9
  theatre training of, 3-4
New Tenant, The (Ionesco), 15, 138
Nicholson, Norman, 18
Nina (Roussin), 15
No Why (Whiting), 23

O

O'Casey, Sean, 29, 33
Old Man of the Mountains (Nicholson), 18
Olivier, Sir Lawrence, 18, 101
"On Building the House" (Wesker), 8
O'Neill, Eugene, 73, 76, 78
Ortega y Gasset, José, 104
Orton, Joe, 2, 4
Orwell, George, 76
Osborne, John, 2, 3, 8, 9-10, 15, 17, 23, 31-32, 33, 34, 36, 39, 45-46, 47-57, 79, 117-21, 136, 141, 165, 166, 169
  appraisal of, 120-121, 169
  and Brecht, 9, 118-19
  and his characters, 48-49
  dramatic aims of, 8
  dramaturgy of, 9
  and social realism, 50, 56-57

Osborne, John, works by:
  Bond Honoured, A, 10
  Entertainer, The, 32, 117, 118
  Epitaph for George Dillon, 9, 118, 169
  Inadmissable Evidence, 9-10, 169
  Look Back in Anger, 9, 17, 23, 33, 34, 39, 45-46, 47-57, 117, 118, 136, 141
  Luther, 9, 36, 117-21
  Patriot For Me, A, 10
  Plays For England, 10
  World of Paul Slickey, The, 117, 118, 120, 166
Othello (Shakespeare), 101
Owen, Alun, 175

P

Pajama Game, The (Abbott and Bissell), 16
Paris Not So Gay (Ustinov), 19
Part of the View (Cooper), 24
Patriot For Me, A (Osborne), 10
Penny for a Song, A (Whiting), 21, 22, 85
Phoenix Too Frequent, A (Fry), 18
Pillars of Society (Ibsen), 149
Pinter, Harold, 2, 3, 4, 8, 9-12, 17, 34, 38-46, 65-70, 84, 122-44, 145-63, 165, 168
  and allegory, 66-67
  Beckett's influence on, 65, 66, 124, 131, 153
  and Chekhov, 124-26, 132, 137, 139-40, 143, 149
  contribution of, 68
  dialogue of, 8, 66, 68, 69, 122-44, 150-51
  and dramatic action, 150-52
  dramatic aims of, 8
  and dramatic device (*see also* main entry), 126-35, 142-43, 150
  dramaturgy of, 10-12
  and the family, 145-63
  and Ibsen, 149-50
  and the Judaic tradition, 152-57, 160

Pinter Harold, (*continued*)
  philosophy of, 69-70
  and realism, 66, 67
  and Shakespeare, 153, 154, 157-60, 162-63
  and the titles of his plays, 145, 148-49
  and triviality, use of, 124-33, 143, 145-46, 147, 150
Pinter, Harold, works by:
  Birthday Party, The, 11, **38-46**, 67, 126-27, 129-30, 131, 136, 138, 142-43, 147, 148-49, 151, 161
  Caretaker, The, 11, 67-68, 122, 128-29, 135, 136, 140, 143, 149, 161
  Collection, The, 3, 11, 123, 127-28, 129, 130-31, 132, 134-35, 138-39, 142, 147
  Dumb Waiter, The, 11, 34, 126, 143, 149
  Dwarfs, The, 124, 129, 130
  Homecoming, The, 11, **145-63**
  Lover, The, 11, 130, 142, 143
  Pumpkin Eater, 128
  Room, The, 3, 11, 66-67, 123, 143, 150-51
  Servant, The, 128
  Slight Ache, A, 143, 147
Plain and Fancy (Stein and Glickman), 16
Plays For England (Osborne), 10
Potting Shed, The (Greene), 19
Power and the Glory, The (Bost-Cannan), 16
Priestley, J. B., 2, 7
Proust, Marcel, 63, 153
Psychopathology of Everyday Life, The (Freud), 126, 128, 131
Pumpkin Eater (Pinter), 128

Q

Queen and the Rebels, The (Betti), 15
Queen of Air and Darkness, The (MacNeice), 18
Qui est là (Tardieu), 58

R

Raid, The (Fregonese), 92
Rainmaker, The (Nash), 16
Raisin in the Sun, A (Hansberry), 40
Rattigan, Terence, 16, 18, 60, 137, 165
Redgrave, Sir Micheal, 19
Reed, Henry, 24
Resounding Tinkle (Simpson), 2-3
Return of General Forefinger, The (Cooper), 24-25
Return to Naples (Reed), 24
Richardson, Sir Ralph, 19
Ridler, Anne, 18
Rivals, The (Sheridan), 16
Robson, Flora, 16
Romanoff and Juliet (Ustinov), 16, 19
Room, The (Pinter), 3, 11, 66-67, 123, 143, 150-51
Ronane, John, 134
Roots (Wesker), 39, 46, 73-74, 75, 79-80, 100, 101
Rose Tattoo, The (Williams), 141
Rosmersholm (Ibsen), 150
Roussin, André, 15

S

Saint Joan (Shaw), 23
Saint's Day (Whiting), 16-17, 21-22, **38-46**
Salad Days (Slade), 16
Samson Agonistes (Milton), 85
Sartre, Jean-Paul, 7, 31, 63, 72
Saved (Bond), 3
Savory, Gerald, 16
Scofield, Paul, 16
Seagull, The (Chekhov), 139
Separate Tables (Rattigan), 16, 137
Serjeant Musgrave's Dance (Arden), 36, **38-46**, 84, **90-93**, **98-100**, 101, 102, 104, **112-14**, 115
Servant, The (Pinter), 128
Shadow Factory, The (Ridler), 18
Shadow of a Doubt, The (King), 16

Shakespeare, William, 5-7, 8, 12, 16, 35, 48, 52-53, 72, 100, 101, 144, 153, 154, 157-60, 162-63
Shaw, G. B., 23, 34, 39, 40, 71, 80, 170
Simpson, N. F., 2-3, 68, 123
Slight Ache, A (Pinter), 143, 147
Soldier, Soldier (Arden), 87-90, 93
Sophocles, 149
South Sea Bubble (Coward), 16
Sport of My Mad Mother (Jellicoe), 41, 137
Stanislavsky, K. S., 133
Sterne, Laurence, 126
Stewart, Donald Ogden, 41
Streets of Pompeii (Reed), 24
Strindberg, August, 40, 143
Strong Are Lonely, The (Hockwalder), 15
Stronger, The (Strindberg), 40
Summertime (Betti), 15
Sweeney Agonistes (Eliot), 30
Swift, Jonathan, 63, 121
Synge, John Millington, 33

T

Tardieu, Jean, 58
Taste of Honey, A (Delaney), 32, 33, 34
Theatre and Its Double, The (Artaud), 140-41
Theatre of the Absurd, 2, 58, 68, 149
Their Very Own and Golden City (Wesker), 3, 13
Third Man, The (Greene), 19
This Way to the Tomb (Duncan), 18
Thorndike, Dame Sybil, 19
Threepenny Opera, The (Brecht), 15
Three Sisters, The (Chekhov), 124-26, 137
Touch of the Sun, A (Hunter), 19
Tower and the Abyss, The (Kahler), 160
Troilus and Cressida (Shakespeare), 153, 157-60, 162-63
Tynan, Kenneth, 167

U

Uncle Vanya (Chekhov), 77, 139-40
Unman (Cooper), 24
Unnamable, The (Beckett), 65
US (Cannan), 4
Ustinov, Peter, 16, 18-19

V

Venus Observed (Fry), 18
Very Great Man Indeed, A (Reed), 24
Victims of Duty (Ionesco), 138
View from the Bridge, A (Miller), 28

W

Waiting for Godot (Beckett), 15, 17, 34, 58-63, 68, 132, 138, 140
Wajda, Andrezej, 41
Walk in the Desert, A (Whiting), 21
Wallach, Eli, 167
Waltz of the Toreadors, The (Anouilh), 15
Waters of Babylon, The (Arden), 84, 85-87, 88, 90, 96
Waters of the Moon (Hunter), 19
Wesker, Arnold, 2, 3, 4, 7, 8, 9, 12-14, 33, 34, 39, 46, 71-82, 100, 101, 141, 165, 166, 168-69
  appraisal of, 168-69
  dramatic aims of, 7, 81
  dramaturgy of, 12-14, 75-79
  social consciousness of, 7, 73
Wesker, Arnold, works by:
  Chicken Soup with Barley, 12, 75, 79
  Chips with Everything, 3, 7, 12-13, 81-82
  Four Seasons, 3, 13
  I'm Talking About Jerusalem, 79
  Kitchen, The, 12, 13, 33, 34, 74-79, 141
  "On Building the House," 8
  Roots, 39, 46, 73-74, 75, 79-80, 100, 101

Wesker, Arnold, works by:
  (*continued*)
    Their Very Own and Golden City,
      3, 13
West Side Story (Laurents), 82
Wet Fish (Arden), 96-97
Who's Your Father (Cannan), 20
Wild Duck, The (Ibsen), 16, 49
Wilde, Oscar, 17
Williams, Tennessee, 141
Wilson, Angus, 2, 17
Wilson, Sandy, 16
Without the Grail (Cooper), 24, 25
Wittering and Zigo (Cooper), 24
Women, The (Boothe), 74
Wood, Charles, 2, 3, 4

Workhouse Donkey, The (Arden),
  3, 7
World of Paul Slickey, The (Osborne),
  117, 118, 120, 166
Wymark, Olwen, 1
Wynyard, Diana, 19

Y

Yeats, William Butler, 31
You and Your Wife (Cannan), 20

Z

Zola, Émile, 110

MOLIÈRE

A Collection of Critical Essays
Edited by JACQUES
GUICHARNAUD

A

Adam, Antoine, 105, 106
All's Well That Ends Well (Shakespeare), 111
Amants magnifiques, Les, 148
Amour médecin, L', 7, 35, 64, 112, 132, 133, 136, 152-53
Amphitryon, 7, 57, 59, 70, 76, 88, 117, 131, 133, 134-35, 147
Andromaque (Racine), 76, 77-78, 122
Anouilh, Jean, 4
Aretino, Pietro, 27
Ariosto, Ludovico, 156
Aristotle, 22
Arnavon, Jacques, 13, 95-96, 106, 108
Art poétique, L' (Boileau), 153
Assoucy, Charles d', 2
Attinger, G., 17
Aubignac, L'Abbé d', 55
Aurelia (*see* Bianchi, Brigida)
Avare, L', 7, 8, 10-11, 19, 20, 21, 25, 27, 31, 33, 36, 41, 43-44, 56, 57, 58, 64, 67, 71, 72, 73, 74, 75, 76, 100, 111, 129, 135, 139, 155-59
  antibourgeois sentiment in, 64, 67
  comic hero in, 71, 72, 73, 74, 75, 76, 111, 157-59
  dialogue in, 33, 41, 43-44
  greed, theme of, 155-57
  love, theme of, 10, 11, 67, 157
  plot in, 20, 21
  props in, 36, 155
  the romanesque in, 10-11, 155

B

Bailly, Auguste, 111, 121, 123, 135
Ballet des incompatibles, Le, 52
Balourd, Doctor, 16, 18
Balzac, Honoré de, 54, 70
Baudelaire, Charles, 117
Baumal, Francis, 122
Bayle, Pierre, 86
Beauchamp, 147
Beaumarchais, Pierre Augustin de, 10, 20
Beckett, Samuel, 5
Béjart, Madeleine, 2
Belle invisible, La (Boisrobert), 21
Belle plaideuse, La (Boisrobert), 156
Bénichou, Paul, 116, 119, 123
Bensérade, Isaac de, 6
Bergson, Henri, 52, 106, 109, 131, 133
Bianchi, Brigida, 16
Biancolelli, Dominique, 16, 17, 18, 28
Bogerhoff, 111
Boileau, Nicolas, 9, 19, 28, 60, 62n 63, 63n, 64, 148, 151, 153, 154, 156
Bourgeois gentilhomme, Le, 11, 18, 19, 27, 30, 32, 33, 35, 37, 51, 52, 56, 58, 59, 62, 63, 63n, 69, 70, 71, 74, 75, 76, 87, 100, 111, 117, 139, 147, 148

Bourgeois gentilhomme, Le
(*continued*)
  antiaristocratic sentiment in, 62-63
  antibourgeois sentiment in, 62-63,
    70
  Colbert as protagonist in, 147
  comic hero in, 64, 70, 71, 74, 75,
    76, 111
  dialogue in, 32, 33
Bray, René, 2, 3, 13, 35
Briguelle, 18
Britannicus (Racine), 76, 77
Brossette, 19
Brunetière, 60
Bruno, Giordano, 151
Busoni, 153

C

Cabale des Dévots, La, 139, 139*n*
Cairncross, John, 115
Candelaio, Il (Bruno), 151
Celestina, La (Rojas), 156
Chalussay, Le Boulanger de, 15, 17
Chapelain, Jean, 59
Chapelle, 1
Chaplin, Charles, 36, 38, 137, 148-49,
  170-72
Chappuzeau, S., 16
Chauveau, 31
Cid, Le (Corneille), 4
Cinna (Corneille), 122
City Lights (Chaplin), 171
Colbert, Jean Baptiste, 144, 146, 147
Comedia de figuron, 23*n*
Comédie-Française, La, 21
Compagnard, Le (Gillet de la Tesson-
  nerie), 22-23
Comtesse d'Escarbagnas, La, 11, 37,
  68, 75
  antiaristocratic sentiment in, 68
  comic hero in, 75
Conti, Armand de Bourbon, prince of,
  2
Copeau, Jacques, 13, 29, 37
Corneille, Pierre, 1, 4, 20, 21, 22, 23,
  27, 28, 52, 97*n*, 119-23, 127, 145,
  146

Corneille, Thomas, 23*n*
Critique de l'École des femmes, La,
  19, 68, 156
Cuvier, Le (old French farce), 27
Cyrano de Bergerac, 52

D

Dangeville, 152
De Cive (Hobbes), 86
Dépit amoureux, Le, 21
Descartes, René, 8, 9, 51, 122, 124
Desmarets, Jean, 23*n*
Despois, Eugène, 114
Despréaux (*see* Boileau, Nicolas)
Diderot, Denis, 60, 82-84, 100
Discours sceptiques (Sorbière),
  86
Dom Juan, ou le Festin de Pierre, 7, 8,
  9, 10, 13, 21, 24, 30, 31, 32, 33-34,
  36, 37, 52, 56, 57, 58, 60, 69, 70,
  73, 75-76, 77, 79-89, 90-102, 103-10,
  111, 112, 117-28, 129, 130, 131,
  132, 133, 134, 135, 136, 140, 142,
  144, 145, 151
  anthropocentrism, theme of, 125
  as comedy, 96, 103-10
  comic hero in, 69, 70, 73, 75-76,
    77, 104-10, 112
  convention, theme of, 93-102, 119
  dialogue in, 33-34, 96
  as experimental drama, 9
  fâcheux in, 108-10
  hypocrisy, theme of, 102, 103, 118,
    124-27
  libertinism, theme of, 80, 83-87, 88,
    103, 107, 119
  love, theme of, 79, 87, 90-93, 118
  morality in, 83-89, 100, 119,
    124-25
  myth in, 79-82, 86-87, 88, 105-6
  plot in, 21
  props in, 36, 37
  as satire, 103-4
Don Japhet (Scarron), 22
Donneau de Visé, Jean, 15, 16, 17, 30,
  136
Doolittle, James, 118

Dorimond (Nicholas Drouin), 107
Dostoevsky, Fedor, 54
Dubreuil, 152
Du Croisy, M. and Mme. Philibert
  Gassot, 14
Dufresne company, 16
Dullin, Charles, 10, 13
Du Parc, Monsieur (*see* Gros René)
Dussane, Beatrix, 12

E

École des femmes, L', 3-6, 7, 8, 9, 11,
  12, 19, 20, 25, 26, 27, 36-37, 41,
  50, 51, 52-53, 56, 58, 66, 66n, 67,
  69, 72, 73, 74, 75, 77, 87, 88, 110,
  111, 112-13, 117, 129, 130, 134,
  135, 171, 172
    antibourgeois sentiment in, 66,
      66n, 67
    as comedy of substance, 3-6
    as comedy of will, 50, 51
    comic hero in, 69, 72, 73, 74, 75,
      77, 111, 112
    dialogue in, 41
    influence of, 4
    innovations in, 4-6
    love, theme of, 66, 66n, 67
    plot in, 20
    props in, 36-37
    realism in, 5-6
    universalities in, 5
École des maris, L', 6, 24n, 51, 64-65,
  66, 72, 73, 74, 87, 167
    antibourgeois sentiment in, 64-65,
      66
    comic hero in, 72, 73, 74
    love as theme in, 64-65, 66
Élomire hypocondre (Chalussay), 15,
  17
Emery, Léon, 120
Esprit follet, L' (D'Ouville), 21
Esprit géométrique, L', 48
Esprits, Les (Larivey), 156
Essay on Human Understanding
  (Locke), 86
Étourdi, L', 3, 6, 21,
  57

F

Fâcheux, Les, 21, 66n, 138
Faguet, 60
Femmes savantes, Les, 9-10, 11, 20,
  21, 30, 37, 51, 58, 60, 61-62, 73,
  74, 75, 88, 130, 134, 160, 171, 172
    antibourgeois sentiment in, 60, 61-
      62
    comic hero in, 73, 74, 75
    plot in, 20, 21
Fénelon, François, 25
Fernandez, Ramon, 112, 120
Festin de Pierre, Le (Dorimond),
  107
Festin de Pierre, Le (Villiers), 106,
  107, 109
Fiorelli, Tiberio (Scaramouche), 16,
  17, 18, 21, 28, 31
Flaubert, Gustave, 114
Fourberies de Scapin, Les, 10, 11, 13,
  30, 37-39, 41, 42-43, 54, 56, 57, 107,
  112, 133, 147, **148-49**, **150-54**
    as *commedia dell'arte*, 38, 148-49,
      151-54
    dialogue in, 38, 41, 42-43
    gesture in, 38
    mask in, 38, 152-54
    props in, 37, 39

G

Galantries du duc d'Ossone, Les
  (Mairet), 21
Gassendi, Pierre, 9, 83
Gaultier-Garguille, 16, 18
Georges Dandin, ou le mari confondu,
  7, 9, 11, 19, 20, 26, 27, 32, 33, 40,
  57, 58, 62-63, 68, 76, 87, 88, 117,
  133, 148
    antiaristocratic sentiment in, 62-63,
      68
    antibourgeois sentiment in, 62-63
    dialogue in, 33, 40
    plot in, 20
Georges le Veau (old French farce),
  27
Gillet de la Tessonnerie, 22-23

Gold Rush, The (Chaplin), 171
Grand divertissement royal de Versailles, Le (Molière *et al*), 117
Great Dictator, The (Chaplin), 172
Grimarest, 1, 15
Gros-Guillaume, 16, 18, 28
Gros-René (René Berthelot), 2, 17, 170
Guillot-Gorju, 18, 24, 28

H

Hamlet (Shakespeare), 105
Harlequin (*see* Biancolelli, Dominique)
Hernani (Hugo), 4
Hobbes, Thomas, 86
Horace, 22
Hôtel du Bourgogne company, 2, 14, 15, 16, 18
Hôtel de Marais company, 2
Hubert, J. D., 4
Hugo, Victor, 4

I

Illusion comique, L' (Corneille), 22
Illustre Théâtre, 2, 16
Importance of Being Earnest, The (Wilde), 126
Impromptu at Versailles, L', 119, 121, 123, 133, 143, 144
Ionesco, Eugène, 4, 5

J

Jalousie du Barbouillé, La, 32, 171
Jarry, Alfred, 4
Jasinski, René, 13, 132
Jekels, Ludwig, 131-32, 133
Jodelet, 17, 18
Jodelet (Scarron), 22
Jouvet, Louis, 12, 37, 56, 58, 142

K

Kean, Edmund, 137

Kid, The (Chaplin), 171

L

La Bruyère, Jean de, 8, 25, 142
Lafayette, Madame de, 147
Lagrange, Charles, 3, 136, 170
Lancaster, Henry, 114-15, 120
Lanson, Gustave, 13, 172
Larivey, Pierre de, 156
Le Brun, Charles, 18
Lettres écrites à un provincial (Pascal), 105
Lettre sur L'Imposteur, La, 137
Leviathan, The (Hobbes), 86
Limelight (Chaplin), 137, 171
Livre abominable, Le, 139
Locatelli, Dominique (Trivelin), 16, 17, 18, 21
Locke, John, 86
Loret, J., 107
Louis XIV, 60, 63, 68, 114, 134, 135, 144-47
Lucretius, 107
Luillier, 83
Lully, Jean Baptiste, 11, 147

M

Mabel's Busy Day (Chaplin), 170
Macbeth (Shakespeare), 55, 105
Machiavelli, Niccolò, 27
Mairet, Jean de, 21
Maître étourdi, Le (Quinault), 21
Maître Minim étudiant (old French farce), 27
Malade imaginaire, Le, 11, 12, 18, 19, 21, 30, 35, 37, 45, 47, 56, 57, 58, 76, 77, 100, 108, 112, 113, 117, 133, 148, **160-69**
  comic hero in, 76, 77
  command and obedience, theme of, 160-63
  dialogue in, 45, 47
  pleasure, theme of, 165-67
Malraux, André, 105

Mariage de Figaro, Le (Beaumarchais), 10
Mariage forcé, Le, 21, 24, 35, 64, 117
Marivaux, Pierre, 119, 130
Masquerade, The (Chaplin), 170
Matamore, 18
Mauriac, François, 7, 54, 136, 140
Mazarin, Cardinal, 17
Measure for Measure (Shakespeare), 111
Médecin malgré lui, Le, 7, 19, 24, 41, 45, 133
Médicin volant, Le, 24, 171
Mélicerte, 7
Mémoire des décorateurs de l'Hôtel de Bourgogne, La, 36
Menteur, Le (Corneille), 21, 22, 27
Mesnard, Paul, 114, 153, 154
Michaut, Gustave, 12, 103, 105, 107, 114, 115, 116, 120, 125, 127
Mignard, Pierre, 19
Misanthrope, Le, 7, 8, 9, 10, 11, 13, 19, 20-21, 21-22, 25, 25n, 27, 30, 31, 32, 35-36, 37, 38, 41-42, 44, 47-48, 51, 52, 53, 54, 55-56, 57, 58, 59, 69, 73, 76, 77, 97, 110, 111, 112, 120, 121, 125-36, **128-31**, 132, 133, 134, **136-46**, 148, 151, 167, 171
  comic hero in, 69, 73, 76, 77, 112, 140-42
  dialogue in, 41-42, 44, 47-48
  as experimental drama, 9
  fâcheux in, 137-39, 140, 141
  man vs. society, theme of, 129-31
  mask in, 35-36, 137, 139-40
  plot in, 20-21, 21-22
  as satire, 130, 132-33, 143-46
Moland, Louis, 150, 151
Molière (Jean-Baptiste Poquelin):
  as actor, 1-3, 9, 12, **14-19**, 31
  and the aristocracy, attitude towards, 62-63, 68, 70, 143-46
  audience response to, 4-6, 7, 8, 10, 19, 30-31, 69
  and Boileau, Nicolas, 9, 19, 28, 60, 62n, 63, 63n, 64, 148, 151, 153, 154, 156

  and the bourgeoisie, attitude towards, 5-6, **60-68**, 70
  and Chaplin, Charles, 36, 38, 137, 148-49, **170-72**
  and comedy, 3, 7-9, 10, 11, **20-28**, 29-39, 54, 58-59, 63-64, 69-70, **103-10**, 122, 130, 132-35, 137, 145
  and comedy of character, 8, 22, 23
  and comedy of the *fâcheux,* 37, 108-10, **137-39**, 140, 141
  and comedy of intrigue, 4
  and comedy of passion, 8-9
  and comedy of reason, 58
  and comedy of substance, 3-6, 117
  and comedy of will, 50-53
  and the *comique grotesque,* 117, 132-33, 135
  and the *comique significatif,* 117, 132-33, 135
  and *commedia dell'arte,* 16-19, 23-25, 26, 35, 38, 142, 148, **150-54**
  and *commedia sostenuta,* 30, 38
  and Corneille, 1, 20, 22, 23, 27, 28, 52, 97n, **119-23**, 127, 145, 146
  and court entertainment, 6-7, 11, 59, 63, 132-35, **144-47**
  critical reputation of, 12-13, 27-28, 29, 60
  and dialogue, use of, 27, **32-34**, 37, 38, **40-49**
  dramatic career of, 2-12, 143-49
  and farce, 3-6, 7, 10, 13, 18-19, 20-28, 29-39, 154
  and gesture, use of, 15, **18-19**, 30-32, 37, 38-39
  and his characters, 8-9, 22-26, 27, **56-58**, 63-64, 67-68, **69-78**, 102, **111-13**, **136-49**
  and illusion, 9, 10, 55-59
  innovations of, 3-6, 9
  and irony, use of, 47-48
  life of, 1, 9, 11-12
  and mask, use of, 4-5, 10, 11, 23-26, 27, **34-36**, 37, 39, 54, 56, 112, 137, **139-40**, 141, 148, **152-54**
  and morality, 29, **87-89**, 100, 125

Molière (Jean-Baptiste Poquelin)
(*continued*)
    and naturalism, 13, 18, 31, 60, 122,
        132-34
    and noise, use of, 18, 32
    and old French farce, 26-27
    personality of, 2, 9, 14-16
    philosophy of, 87-89
    and the play of consent, 8, 10, 11
    and plot, use of, 20-22
    and props, use of, 18-19, 36-37, 38-
        39, 155
    and Racine, 1, 8, 9, 28, 52, 60, 69,
        76, 77-78, 120-23, 146
    and realism, 5-6, 6*n*, 7, 29, 57,
        156
    and relationship, use of, 26
    and the romanesque, 4, 7, 10, 11,
        155
    and satire, 103-4, 115, 116, 117,
        122, 132-35, 143-46
Molière, works by (*see also* individual
    listings for works marked by asterisk):
    Amants magnifiques, Les, 148
    Amour médecin, L', 7, 35, 64, 112,
        132, 133, 136, 152-53
    Amphitryon, 7, 57, 59, 70, 76, 88,
        117, 131, 133, 134-35, 147
    Avare, L',* 7, 8, 19, 20, 21, 25, 27,
        31, 33, 36, 41, 43-44, 56, 57, 58,
        64, 67, 71, 72, 73, 74, 75, 76,
        100, 111, 129, 135, 139, 155-59
    Ballet des incompatibles, Le,
        52
    Bourgeois gentilhomme, Le,* 11,
        18, 19, 27, 30, 32, 33, 35, 37, 51,
        52, 56, 58, 59, 62, 63, 63*n*, 69,
        70, 71, 74, 75, 76, 87, 100, 117,
        139, 147, 148
    Comtesse d'Escarbagnas, La,* 11,
        37, 68, 75
    Critique de l'École des femmes, La,
        19, 68, 156
    Dépit amoureux, Le, 21
    *Dom Garcie de Navarre, ou le prince
        jaloux*, 25, 25*n*, 66*n*, 120-23, 145
    Dom Juan, ou le festin de Pierre,*
        7, 8, 9, 10, 13, 21, 24, 30, 31, 32,

        52, 56, 57, 58, 60, 69, 70, 73, 75-
        76, 77, 79-89, 90-102, 103-10,
        111, 112, 117-28, 129, 130, 131,
        132, 133, 134, 135, 136, 140,
        142, 144, 145, 148, 151
    École des femmes, L',* 3-6, 7, 8, 9,
        11, 12, 19, 20, 25, 26, 27, 36-37,
        41, 50, 51, 52-53, 56, 58, 66, 66*n*,
        67, 69, 72, 73, 74, 75, 77, 87, 88,
        110, 111, 112-13, 117, 129, 130,
        134, 135, 171, 172
    École des maris, L',* 6, 24*n*, 51, 64-
        65, 66, 72, 73, 74, 87, 167
    Étourdi, L', 3, 6, 21, 57
    Fâcheux, Les, 21, 66*n*, 138
    Femmes savantes, Les,* 9-10, 11,
        20, 21, 30, 37, 51, 58, 60, 61-62,
        73, 74, 75, 88, 130, 134, 160,
        171, 172
    Fourberies de Scapin, Les,* 10, 11,
        13, 30, 37-39, 41, 42-43, 54, 56,
        57, 107, 112, 133, 147, 148-49,
        150-54
    *Georges Dandin, ou le mari con-
        fondu*,* 7, 9, 11, 19, 20, 26, 27,
        32, 33, 40, 57, 58, 62-63, 68, 76,
        87, 88, 117, 133, 148
    Impromptu de Versailles, L', 119,
        121, 123, 133, 143, 144
    Jalousie du Barbouillé, La, 32,
        171
    Malade imaginaire, Le,* 11, 12, 18,
        19, 21, 30, 35, 37, 45, 47, 56, 57,
        58, 76, 77, 100, 108, 112, 113,
        117, 133, 148, 160-69
    Mariage forcé, Le, 21, 24, 35, 64,
        117
    Médecin malgré lui, Le, 7, 19, 24,
        41, 45, 133
    Médecin volant, Le, 24, 171
    Mélicerte, 7
    Misanthrope, Le,* 7, 8, 9, 10, 11,
        13, 19, 25, 25*n*, 27, 30, 31, 32,
        35-36, 37, 38, 41-42, 44, 47-48,
        51, 52, 53, 54, 55-56, 57, 58, 59,
        69, 73, 76, 77, 97, 110, 111, 112,
        120, 121, 125-26, 128-31, 132,
        133, 134, 136-46, 151, 167, 171

Molière, works by:
(*continued*)
  Monsieur de Pourceaugnac, 18,
    19, 21, 27, 33, 37, 56, 58, 68,
    148
  Précieuse ridicules, Les,* 5, 6, 9,
    18, 19, 21, 23, 25*n*, 51, 69, 70-
    71, 74, 75, 87, 172
  Princesse d'Élide, La, 7, 117, 132,
    148
  Psyché, (with Corneille), 11, 59,
    152
  Sganarelle, ou le cocu imaginaire,
    19, 21, 23, 64-65, 66
  Sicilien, ou l'amour peintre, Le,
    7, 19
  Tartuffe, ou l'imposteur,* 7, 8, 9,
    10, 11, 20, 21, 25, 26, 27, 30, 31,
    33, 35, 38, 42, 43, 44, 45-47, 48-
    49, 51, 52, 56-57, 58, 69, 71, 72-
    73, 74, 76, 84, 87, 88, 102, 105,
    110, 111, 112, **113-17**, 118, 123,
    124, 125, 127, 128, 130, 131,
    132, 133, 134, 135, 136, 139,
    142, 144, 145, 146, 148, 151
Monsieur de Pourceaugnac, 18, 19, 21,
  27, 33, 37, 56, 58, 68, 148
Monsieur Verdoux (Chaplin),
  172
Montaigne, 88
Montfleury, 1, 15, 16, 17
Montpensier, Mlle de, 62
Moore, Will G., 13, 56, 57, 103, 127
Moreto y Cabaña, Agustín, 27
Morin, Simon, 105, 107
Mornet, 115
Mouhy, Chevalier de, 153

N

Neufvilleaine, 18-19, 31
Neveu de Rameau, Le (Diderot), 82,
  100

O

Othello (Shakespeare), 120
Ouville, Antoine d', 21

P

Palais Royal, 14, 147, 150, 152
Pantalon, 16, 18
Parasite, Le (Tristran), 22
Pascal, Blaise, 11, 105, 134
Patin, Gui, 152
Pédant joué, Le, (Cyrano de Bergerac),
  22
Pernet qui va à l'école (old French
  farce), 27
Phèdre (Racine), 69
Pilgrim, The (Chaplin), 171
Pionvana, La (Ruzzante), 151
Plaisirs de l'île enchantée, Les
  (Molière *et al.*), 117, 146
Pleasant Nights (Straparola), 153
Poisson, 18
Poisson, Mlle, 14
Polichinelle, 18
Pont aux ânes, Le (old French farce),
  27
Poulaille, Henri, 119
Poussin, Nicolas, 18
Précieuses ridicules, Les, 5, 6, 9, 18,
  19, 21, 23, 25*n*, 34, 51, 60, 61-62,
  69, 70-71, 74, 75, 87, 172
  antibourgeois sentiment in, 60,
    61-62, 70
  comic hero in, 69, 70-71, 74, 75
  mask in, 34
Princesse d'Élide, La, 7, 117, 132,
  148
Psyché (Molière and Corneille), 11, 59,
  152

Q

Quinault, Philippe, 21

R

Rabelais, François, 60
Racine, Jean, 1, 8, 9, 28, 52, 60, 69,
  76, 77-78, 120-23, 146
Rapin, Père René, 59
Recueil, Le (Montpensier), 62
Remerciement au Roy, Le, 146

Rojas, Francisco de, 27, 156
Romano, Danilo, 108
Ronsard, Pierre de, 24n
Rotrou, Jean de, 21, 27
Rousseau, Jean-Jacques, 74n, 132
Royal Grove, The (Ronsard), 24n
Ruzzante, 151

S

Sainte-Beuve, Charles Augustin, 26
Sardou, Victorien, 20
Sartre, Jean-Paul, 5, 161
Satire X (Boileau), 61, 62n, 64n
Scala, Flaminio, 151
Scaramouche (*see* Fiorelli, Tiberio)
Scarron, Paul, 7, 22, 23n, 27
Scribe, Eugène, 20
Scudéry, Madeleine de, 62, 90
Sennett, Mack, 7, 170, 171
Sertorius (Corneille), 50
Sévigné, Marie de, 163
Sganarelle, ou le cocu imaginaire, 19,
    21, 23, 64-65, 66
Shakespeare, William, 54, 55, 105
Shoulder Arms (Chaplin), 171
Sicilien, ou l'amour peintre, Le, 7,
    19
Simon, Alfred, 13
Soeur, La (Rotrou), 21
Somaise, 16, 18
Sorbière, 86
Stendhal, 70, 81
Straparola, Giovanni, Francesco, 153
Sunny Side, The (Chaplin), 171
Supplement au Voyage de Bouganville,
    Le (Diderot), 82-84
Suppositi, I (Ariosto), 156

T

Tabarin, 16, 151
Tablettes dramatiques (de Mouhy),
    153
Tartuffe, ou l'imposteur, 7, 8, 9, 10,
    11, 19, 20, 21, 25, 26, 27, 30, 31,
    33, 35, 38, 43, 44, 45-47, 48-49, 51,
    52, 56-57, 58, 69, 71, 72-73, 74, 76,

84, 87, 88, 102, 105, 110, 111, 112,
    113-17, 118, 123, 124, 125, 127,
    128, 130, 131, 132, 133, 134, 135,
    136, 139, 142, 144, 145, 146,
    148, 151
  comic hero in, 69, 71, 72-73, 74,
    76, 77, 112
  dialogue in, 33, 42, 43, 44, 45-47,
    48-49
  plot in, 20, 21
  as satire, 116, 117
  structure of, 113-17
Terence, 22, 151
Théâtre-Française, 18, 155
Torelli, Giacomo, 147
Tristan L 'Hermite, 22, 23n
Trivelin (*see* Locatelli, Dominique)
Troilus and Cressida (Shakespeare),
    111
Turlupin, 16, 18

U

Ubu Roi (Jarry), 4

V

Valéry, Paul, 70
Varda, Agnès, 36
Vedel Valdeman, 1, 6n, 57
Vengeance des Marquis, La (De Visé),
    14, 15-16
Veuillot, 88
Vie de Monsieur de Molière, La
    (Grimarest), 1
Vieux-Colombier, 37
Villiers, Claude Deschamps de, 106,
    107, 109
Visionaries, Les (Desmarets), 23n

W

Waiting for Godot (Beckett), 5
Wilde, Oscar, 126

Z

Zorilla, José, 80

MARIANNE MOORE

A Collection of Critical Essays

Edited by CHARLES TOMLINSON

A

ABC of Reading (Pound), 163
"Adam's Curse" (Yeats), 168
Aiken, Conrad, 150, 157
American speech, Moore's use of,
  172-78 (*see also* Vocabulary)
Analogy, use of, in "Nevertheless,"
  156-57
"Arctic Ox, The," 165
"Armour's Undermining Modesty,"
  123-24, 145, 146
  prosody of, 149
Auden, W. H., 121, 127-28
Augustine, Saint, 131
Autobiography (Williams), 26

B

Bacon, Sir Francis, 126, 129
Barnes, William, 174
Baxter, Richard, 83
Beach, Sylvia, 25
Beloof, Robert, 8-9
Besitz und Gemeingut (Brandes),
  128
Biographical information, on Moore,
  16-17, 20-45
"Bird-Witted," 5-6, 99
  prosody of, 161-63
Bishop, Elizabeth, 30
"Black Earth" (*see* "Melancthon")
Blake, William, 17, 21, 26
"Blue Bug," 165

Bodenheim, Maxwell, 18
Bogan, Louise, 37, 127
"Bowls," 145
Boyle, Kay, 40
Brandes, Georg, 128
Brontë, Emily, 172
Broom, 20, 40
Browning, Robert, 46
"Buffalo, The," 32, 164
"Bulwarked against Fate," 155
Burke, Kenneth, 39
"By Disposition of Angels,"
  146

C

Caesar, Julius, 166
Caldwell, Erskine, 117
"Camellia Sabrina," 160, 161, 164
Cantos, The (Pound), 83-84, 128
"Carnegie Hall: Rescued," 163-64
Cato, Marcus, 102
"Charity overcoming Envy," 166
Cicero, 131
Cocteau, Jean, 128
Cohen, Gustav, 41
Coleridge, Samuel Taylor, 69
Collected Poems, 114-24, 160
Collected Poems, 1921-31 (Williams),
  1-2
Complete Poems, The, 14-15
Congreve, William, 76
Connolly, Cyril, 32
Counter-Statement (Burke), 39

Cowley, Malcom, 143
Craig, Gordon, 17
Crane, Hart, 38-39, 40-41
Crapsey, Adelaide, 7-8
Criticism, Moore's works of,
  125-33
"Critics and Connoisseurs," 58, 100
  rhyme, use of, 159-60
Cummings, E. E., 74, 127, 128, 145,
  150

D

Daniel, Arnaut, 163
Dante Alighieri, 76
De Doctrina Christiana (St. Augustine),
  131
Defoe, Daniel, 166
Dial, The, Moore's involvement with,
  35-39, 61, 93, 128-29
Dickinson, Emily, 20, 86, 156
  and Marianne Moore, 172-78
Dodge, Mabel, 21
Donne, John, 170
Doolittle, Hilda (H.D.), 20, 27, 61-62
Drayton, Michael, 76
Dryden, John, 139, 170
Duncan, Robert, 12

E

"Elephants," 155
Eliot, T. S., 1, 10, 14, 15, 18, 20, 21,
  39, 46, 85, 102, 127, 129, 131, 138,
  145, 151-52, 154, 168, 175
Empson, William, 165
Engel, Monroe, 143
"England," 82, 158
"Enough," 12
Euphues (Lyly), 107
Ezra Pound (Norman), 31

F

Fables (La Fontaine), Moore's transla-
  tions of, 29, 34-35, 134-43
"Face, A," 31-32, 145, 146
"Feed Me Also River God," 14

"Feeling and Precision," 130
"First Anniversary, The" (Donne),
  170
"Fish" (Lawrence), 5
"Fish, The," 93-94
  prosody of, 147-48
Five Great Philosophies (Hyde), 83
Form, in Moore's poetry (*see* Syllabic
  verse form)
"Four Quartz Crystal Clocks," 2, 10,
  88-89, 95, 141
Free verse, Moore's use of, 9-10,
  145-46
"Frigate Pelican, The," 5
  revision of, 161, 164
Frost, Robert, 40, 42

G

Ghil, René, 17
"Granite and Steel," 165
"Grave, A," 2, 9, 19, 103-4, 145, 163
Grosz, George, 37

H

Hardy, Thomas, 17
Hawthorne, Nathaniel, 86
H.D. (*see* Doolittle, Hilda)
"He 'Digesteth Harde Yron'," 104-5,
  107-11
Hellman, Lillian, 23
"He Made this Screen," 14
"Hero, The," 8, 80
  prosody of, 148-49
"His Shield," 123, 146
Holmans, A. M., 10, 77
"Hometown Piece for Messrs. Alston
  and Reese," 12
Hopkins, Gerard Manley, 74, 132,
  174
"Humble Animal, The" (Jarrell), 144
"Humility, Concentration, and Gusto,"
  130
Humor, in Moore's works, 2-3
Hyde, W. D.,
  83

I

"Icosasphere, The," 145
"Ideas of the Meaning of Form"
   (Duncan), 12
Imagism, 61-63, 88, 101-3
"In Distrust of Merits," 13-14, 155
   prosody of, 146, 148
Infernal Machine, The (Cocteau),
   128
Inferno (Dante), 76
"In the Days of Prismatic Colour,"
   100, 150-51
"In the Public Garden," 12
"In This Age of Hard Trying, Non-
   chalance is Good, and," 100

J

James, Henry, 17, 30, 31, 86, 89-90,
   127, 129, 132, 166, 167, 172, 177
Jammes, Francis, 30
Jarrell, Randall, 144
Jeffers, Robinson, 20
"Jerboa, The," 3-4, 63, 94, 141
Johnson, Samuel, 3, 30
*Journey to the Western Islands of
   Scotland* (Johnson), 3
"Jubilate Agno" (Smart), 166

K

Keats, John, 82
"Keeping Their World Large," 13
Kreymborg, Alfred, 17, 20, 26-27,
   41

L

"Labours of Hercules, The," 82, 145
La Fontaine, Jean, 29, 34-35, 134-43
Laforgue, Jules, 17, 46
Landor, Walter Savage, 166, 167
Language, Moore's use of (*see* Vocabu-
   lary; American speech)
Lawrence, D. H., 5, 85, 128
Levin, Harry, 35, 39, 143
Lewis, H. D., 107

Like a Bulwark, 152, 161
Lord, Gertrude, 26
Lowell, Robert, 1, 7
Loy, Mina, 46, 112
Lycidas (Milton), 82
Lyly, John, 107

M

Marianne Moore Reader, A, 160-161,
   167, 169
"Marriage," 9, 10-11, 48, 54, 57, 63,
   84-85, 92-93, 95*n*-96*n*, 120-121,
   122, 145, 176
McAlmon, Robert, 26
Mc Avoy, Thomas, 165
"Melancthon," 14, 72, 96-97, 141-42
   syllabic verse form of, 8
Melville, Herman, 86
Milton, John, 82
"Mind is an Enchanting Thing, The,"
   116
"Monkey Puzzle, The," 79, 93,
   145
"Monkeys, The," 82, 83, 100, 141
Monroe, Harriet, 17, 20, 26-27
Moore, Marianne:
   and American speech, 172-78
      (*see also* Vocabulary)
   biographical information, 16-17,
      20-45
   on Hart Crane, 38-39, 40-41
   as a critic, 125-33
   critical reputation of, 114-16
   and *The Dial,* 35-39, 61, 93,
      128-29
   and Dickinson, Emily, 54, 86, 156,
      172-78
   and Eliot, T. S., 1, 10, 14, 15, 18,
      21, 39, 85, 102, 127, 129, 131,
      145, 151-52, 154, 168, 175
   free verse, use of, 9-10, 145-46
   on her own work, 27-30
   humor, in works of, 2-3
   and Imagism, 61-63, 88, 101-3
   and James, Henry, 17, 30, 31, 86,
      89-90, 127, 129, 132, 166, 172,
      177

Moore, Marianne (*continued*)
    and Kreymborg, Alfred, 17, 20,
        26-27, 41
    as an Objectivist poet, 88-100
    and Pound, Ezra, 1, 6, 10, 14, 20,
        25, 30, 31, 39, 41-42, 83-84, 128,
        129, 137, 145, 163
    rhyme, use of, 63-64, 80-81, 105-6,
        146, 154, 159-60
    rhythm, use of, 49, 147
    and scientific observation, 2-4, 44,
        62, 88-89, 165-66, 169
    and Stevens, Wallace, 41, 45, 127,
        129, 131, 133, 157, 166, 175
    syllabic verse form, use of, 7-9, 17,
        28, 33-34, 63-64, 74, 81, 83, 105,
        144-49, 154, 159-64
    as a translator, 134-43
    understatement, use of, 77-79
    vocabulary, use of, 49-50, 56, 57-
        58, 98, 166, 176-77 (*see also*
        American speech)
    and Williams, William Carlos, 1-2,
        10, 20, 26, 41, 45, 88, 126, 127,
        129, 133, 151, 152, 154, 157,
        166, 171
    working methods of, 33-34
    and Yeats, W. B., 1, 71, 128, 165,
        168, 170, 175
Moore, Marianne, works by: (*see also*
    titles of individual poems)
    Collected Poems, 114-24, 160
    Complete Poems, The, 14-15
    Fables (La Fontaine), 29, 34-35,
        134-43
    Like a Bulwark, 152, 161
    Marianne Moore Reader, A, 160-
        161, 167, 169
    Nevertheless, 152
    O To Be a Dragon, 152, 161
    Poems, 48-51
    Predilections, 125-33
    Selected Poems, 60-65, 66-86,
        87-100, 152
    Tell Me, Tell Me, 165-67
    What Are Years, 87-100 *passim*,
        152
Munson, Gorham, 15

Murray, Gilbert, 138
"My Apish Cousins" (*see* "Monkeys,
    The")

N

Nevertheless, 152
"Nevertheless," 123
    analogy, use of, 156-57
"New York," 116, 145, 158, 163,
    166
"Nine Nectarines," 81, 123
    revision of, 164
Norman, Charles, 31
"No Swan So Fine," 154
Notes of a Son and Brother (James),
    167
"Novices," 68, 100, 145

O

Objectivism, in Moore's works, 88-100
Observations (see *Selected Poems*)
"Octopus, An," 2, 11, 63, 82, 83-84,
    95, 96n, 145
"Ode to Mrs. Anne Killigrew" (Dray-
    ton), 170
"Old Tiger," 14, 18-19
"On Poetic Truth" (Lewis), 107-111
    passim
On the Making of Gardens (Sitwell),
    128
Others, 20, 26, 29, 40-41, 56
O To Be a Dragon, 152, 161

P

"Pangolin, The," 99, 141, 164
    revision of, 169-71
"Paper Nautilus, The," 4-5, 100
"Parting, The" (Drayton), 76
"Part of a Novel, Part of a Poem, Part
    of a Play," 84
"Past is the Present, The," 67-70, 100
Pavlova, Anna, 129-30
"People's Surroundings," 89, 145
"Picking and Choosing," 100, 153

Pierre (Melville), 86
Plato, 108, 109
Pliny the Elder, 102
"Plumet Basilisk, The," 82, 94, 155,
   160-161
Poe, Edgar Allan, 55, 86
Poems, 48-51
Poetry (magazine), 20
"Poetry," 14, 58, 70-74, 84, 100,
   152-53, 161
Pope, Alexander, 46, 63, 139
Pound, Ezra, 1, 6, 10, 14, 20, 25, 30,
   31, 39, 41-42, 83-84, 128, 129, 137,
   145, 163
Predilections, 125-33
Prior, Matthew, 10, 77
"Propriety," 12-13, 116

Q

Queneau, Raymond, 41

R

"Radical," 14
Ransom, John Crowe, 20
Rhyme, Moore's use of, 63-64, 80-81,
   105-6, 146, 154, 159-60
Rhythm, Moore's use of, 49, 147
Richards, I. A., 69, 170
Ridge, Lola, 36, 40
Roebling, John, 165

S

Saintsbury, George, 32, 36, 128
Saint's Everlasting Rest, The (Baxter),
   83
Sarett, Lew, 40
Scientific observation, in Moore's
   works, 2-4, 44, 62, 88-89, 165-66,
   169 (*see also* Objectivism)
"Sea Unicorns and Land Unicorns,"
   63, 95n-96n, 145
Selected Poems, 60-65, 66-86, 87-100,
   152
Shakespeare, William, 76
"Silence," 9, 10, 75-79, 145

Sitwell, Sir George, 128
Smart, Christopher, 166
"Smooth Gnarled Crape Myrtle," 97
"Snakes, Mongooses, Snake-Charmers
   and the Like," 145
"Sojourn in the Whale," 92, 93, 95
"Spenser's Ireland," 90-91, 93, 95
"Sphinx" (Wilde), 64
Spirit of Romance, The (Pound), 31,
   42
"Staff of Aesculapius, The," 166
Stanza form (*see* Syllabic verse form)
"Steeple-Jack, The," 6, 79-80, 116,
   155, 175
   revisions of, 161, 164
Stein, Gertrude, 169
Stevens, Wallace, 41, 45, 81, 127, 129,
   131, 133, 157, 166, 175
"Student, The," 93-94
"Sun," 167-68
"Sycamore, The," 170
Syllabic verse form, in Moore's works,
   7-9, 17, 28, 33-34, 63-64, 74, 81, 83,
   105, 144-49, 154, 159-64

T

"Talisman, The," 14, 61-62
Tate, Allen, 174
"Teach, Stir the Mind, Afford Enjoy-
   ment," 131
Teal, John J., 165
Tell Me, Tell Me, 165-71
Thayer, Scofield, 36
"There's been a Death, in the Opposite
   House" (Dickinson), 175
Thoreau, Henry David, 174
"Those Various Scalpels," 49, 74
   prosody of, 145
"To a Prize Bird," 14
"To a Snail," 98
"To a Steam Roller," 2
Tolstoy, Leo, 71
"Tom Fool at Jamaica," 11, 155, 156
Translation, Moore's work in, 134-43
"Triad" (Crapsey), 7-8
"Two Women,The" (Willis), 55

U

"Under Sirius" (Auden), 121
Understatement, Moore's use of, 77-
    79

V

"Veracities and Verities," 145
"Virginia Brittania," 9, 160
    prosody of, 146
Vocabulary, in Moore's works, 45-50,
    56, 57-58, 98, 166, 176-77 (*see also*
    American speech)

W

"Walking Sticks and Paper-Weights
    and Water-Marks," 100
Way of the World, The (Congreve), 76
Wescott, Glenway, 48, 56
What Are Years, 87-100 *passim,* 152

"What Are Years," 92, 116, 118, 123,
    156
"When I Buy Pictures," 100, 115, 145,
    153
Whitman, Walt, 20
Wilde, Oscar, 64
Wilson, Edmund, 95
"William Blake and the Imagination"
    (Yeats), 71
Williams, William Carlos, 1-2, 10, 20,
    26, 41, 45, 88, 126, 129, 133, 151,
    152, 154, 157, 166, 171
Willis, Nathaniel, 55
Wolfe, Thomas, 117
"Wood Weasel, The," 146
Wright, Elizur, 137
Wylie, Elinor, 40

Y

Yeats, W. B., 1, 71, 128, 165, 168,
    170, 175

O'NEILL

A Collection of Critical Essays
Edited by JOHN GASSNER

A

Abbott, George, 110
Abortion, 12
Ah, Wilderness!, 6, 13, 50-51, 95, 124, 126, 169, 171
All God's Chillun Got Wings, 13, 19, 29, 35, 60, 71, 125
Ancient Mariner, The (Coleridge), 31, 32
Ancient Mariner, The, 29
 use of masks in, 31-32
Anderson, Maxwell, 124
Anna Christie, 3, 6, 12, 13, 19, 23, 28, **62-71**, 95, 110, 142, 147-48, 160n, 170
Anthony and Cleopatra (Shakespeare), 26
Antoine, André, 27
Aristotle, 19
Asides, in O'Neill's works, 3, 17, 161, 168
 in *Dynamo*, 155
 in *Strange Interlude*, 44, 47, 154

B

Before Breakfast, 106
Benchley, Robert, 4, 12
Bentley, Eric, 5, 53
Bernstein, Henry, 27
Beyond the Horizon, 3, 13, 19, 37, 56, 63, 65, 67, 68, 70, 106, 144, 145-47, 164

Birth of Tragedy, The (Nietzsche), 74, 78, 79
Boulton, Agnes, 130n
Bound East for Cardiff, 32-33, 64, 68, 106, 143, 145, 146, 147
Broun, Heywood, 11, 12
Buried treasure, as motif in O'Neill's works, 14-15
Burnett, Whit, 36

C

Camus, Albert, 55, 122
Candida (Shaw), 46
Carlyle, Thomas, 18
Chekhov, Anton, 144
Chiaramonte, Nicola, 56
Chorus, in O'Neill's works, 3, 94
Chris Christophersen, 62-67, 148
Clurman, Harold, 111
Coleridge, Samuel, 31, 32
Comus (Milton), 99
Contrast, as device in O'Neill's works, 23
Cook, George Cram, 2
Count of Monte Cristo, The (Dumas), as influence on O'Neill's works, 7-22, 53
Craig, Gordon, 3, 30

D

Days Without End, 13, 21-22, 29, 33-34, 56, 95, 112, 114, 144, 158-59,

Days Without End, (*continued*), 160, 161, 164, 168, 169
  use of religion in, 34, 43, 50-51, 144
Death, O'Neill's dramatic preoccupation with, 111-23 *passim*
Death of a Salesman (Miller), 124
Desire Under the Elms, 3, 11, 12, 13, 15, 16, 17-18, 19, 20, 36, 50, 54, 57-61, 71, 106, 110n, 125, 136, 142, 143-44, 152-53, 154, 164, 168, 169, 171
  and *Phèdre* (Racine), 57, 59
De Voto, Bernard, 12n
Dialects, O'Neill's use of, 3, 18, 92
Dialogue, O'Neill's use of, 3, 4-5, 23-25, 28
Diff'rent, 13, 17, 19, 106, 110n
Dostoevsky, Fydor, 9, 90
Dramatic devices, in O'Neill's works (*see also* listings of each device), 12, **142-64**
  asides, 3, 17, 31, 44, 47, 154, 155, 161, 168
  chorus, 3, 93
  contrast, 23
  duality, 44
  masks, 17, 29-41, 44-45, 153-58, 161, 168
  repetition, 17-18, 23, 25, 48, 50, 90, 116
  revelation, 21-22, 33-41
  soliloquy, 17, 154, 155, 168
  sound effects, 2, 33, 35, 149
  trilogy, 3, 84
Dramatic inventiveness, in O'Neill's works, 3, 4, 29-41
Dramatic motifs, in O'Neill's works:
  buried treasure, 14-15
  family mysteries, 15-16
  family oppression, 16
  happy drunks, 16
  locales, 16, 146-48
  revenge, 12
  suffering and aging, 20
Dramatic movement, in O'Neill's works, 25-28
Dream Play, The (Strindberg), 3

Duality, in *Days Without End*, 44
Dumas, Alexandre (*père*), 7-22
Dynamo, 12, 13, 19, 21, 22, 43, 56, 95, 114, 142, 155-56, 160n, 168

E

Education of Henry Adams, The (Adams), 21
Eliot, T. S., 55
Emperor Jones, The, 2, 3, 15, 17, 18, 19, 23, 28, 55, 67, 70, 95, 106, 124, 148-49, 150, 170, 171
  sound effects in, 2, 35
  symbolism in, 35
Engel, Edwin A., 121-22
Ervine, St. John, 4

F

Family mysteries, as motif in O'Neill's work, 15-16
Family oppression, as motif in O'Neill's work, 16
  in *Desire Under the Elms*, 58
Farrell, James T., 125
Fergusson, Francis, 54
First Man, The, 13, 19, 20-21, 23, 28
Fitzgerald, F. Scott, 135
Flower, Robin, 128
Ford, John, 111
Fountain, The, 13, 15, 18, 19, 20, 29, 35-36, 38, 74, 80, 106, 142, 150-51, 152, 153, 155, 159, 164
French Revolution (Carlyle), 18
Freud, Sigmund, 3, 5, 42, 97, 115-18, 120, 158, 168

G

Gas (Kaiser), 150
Gassner, John, 111
Geddes, Virgil, 4
Ghosts (Ibsen), 114
Ghost Sonata, The (Strindberg), 3, 155
Glaspell, Susan, 2

Gold, 15, 19, 110
Goncourt brothers, 26
Gorky, Maxim, 90, 99-109
Great God Brown, The, 3, 12, 13, 15, 19, 34, 36-37, 38, 44-46, 50, 54, 56, 60, 73-74, 81, 95, 106, 144, 159, 164
  use of masks in, 30-31, 32, 37, 44-45, 153-56
Greek drama, and O'Neill, 1, 38, 55, 57-61, **82-88**, 96-98, 112-23 passim, 126, 156-58, 168

H

Hairy Ape, The, 3, 12, 13, 19, 23, 28, 55, 68, 69, 70, 72, 74, 106, 124, 143, 149, 170, 171
  use of masks in, 29, 32
Happy drunks, as motif in O'Neill's works, 16
Hardy, Thomas, 138
Hauptmann, Gerhart, 26, 27
Hedda Gabler (Ibsen), 46
Heidegger, Martin, 122
Hirschfeld, Kurt, 89, 90, 91
Hughie, 13, 22, 111

I

Ibsen, Henrik, 19, 25, 27, 42-43, 46, 50, 52-53, 55, 93, 114, 118
Iceman Cometh, The, 4, 5, 6, 9, 13, 16, 17, 18, 22, 34, 37-38, 40, 56, **89-95**, 110, 111, 112, **160-64**, 165, 168, 169, 170
  Freudian influence on, 115-18
  and Lower Depths, The (Gorky), 99-109
  realism and illusion in, 93-94, 100, 104, 106-7, 115-18
Ile, 110

J

James, Henry, 52, 53
Jeffers, Robinson, 98

Jones, Robert Edmond, 2, 3, 30, 87, 90
Joyce, James, 36, 125, 128, 130, 131, 137, 138, 141
Jung, Carl, 3, 158, 168

K

Kaiser, Georg, 150
Kenton, Edna, 53
Kierkegaard, Sören, 122
Krutch, Joseph Wood, 4, 89, 111

L

Language, O'Neill's use of, 4-5, 18, 54, 55, 111, 120
Lao-tse, 72
Lazarus Laughed, 3, 13, 18, 19, 29, 36, 38, 56, **72-81**, 95, 106, 114, 124, 142, 144, 151-52, 153, 155, 164
Lewis, C. S., 56
Lewis, Sinclair, 138
Lewisohn, Ludwig, 55
Light, James, 31
Locales, as motif in O'Neill's works, 16
Long Day's Journey into Night, A, 4, 9, 13, 18, 19, 22, 34, **37-41**, 54, 56, 65, 70, 110, 110n, 111, 112-14, 119, 120-21, **124-41**, 144, **160-64**, 166, 168, 169, 170, 171
  as autobiography, 8, 121, 124-41 passim, 143
Long Voyage Home, The, 64, 110n, 160n
Lower Depths, The (Gorky), 99-109

M

McCarthy, Mary, 4, 53, 115
MacGowan, Kenneth, 2, 3, 30, 31
Maeterlinck, Maurice, 44
Marco Millions, 13, 19, 29, 106, 108, 110n, 124, 143
Marx, Karl, 138, 168
Masks, in O'Neill's works, 17, 29-41, 153-58, 161, 168

Masks, in O'Neill's works, (*continued*)
in *Ancient Mariner, The,*
31-32
in *Great God Brown, The,* 29, 30-
31, 32, 37, 44-45, 153-56
in *Hairy Ape, The,* 29, 32
in *Lazarus Laughed,* 29, 32
Melville, Herman, 120
"Memoranda on Masks," 29-30, 31, 38
Miller, Arthur, 124, 138
Milton, John, 99
Moby Dick (Melville), 120
Moeller, Philip, 87
Moon for the Misbegotten, A, 6, 13,
19, 22, 54, 66, 110, 114, 126, 129,
132, 136, 137, **160-64,** 166, 168,
169
Moon of the Caribbees, 145, 146
Moore, George, 130
More Stately Mansions, 111
Mourning Becomes Electra, 3, 5, 12,
13, 18, 19, 38, 43, 49-51, 55, 57,
60, 61, **82-88,** 96-98, 106, 112, 115,
124, 144, 156-58, 159, 160, 168,
169, 170, 171
Myth, in *Desire Under the Elms,* 57-61

N

Napoleon, as tutelary figure in
O'Neill's works, 14
Nathan, George Jean, 5, 63*n*, 89, 111,
142
Nietzsche, Friedrich, 9, 11, 30, 36,
70-71, **72-81,** 132
Nobel Prize, 2

O

O'Casey, Sean, 131, 165
O'Connor, Edwin, 125
Odyssey, The (Homer), 99, 108-9
O'Faolain, Sean, 127
Ole Davil, The, 62, 68-70
O'Neill, Ella, 8
O'Neill, Eugene:
and comedy, 90-91, 124, 126
contribution of, 1-6, 95, **165-71**

and *Count of Monte Cristo, The*
(Dumas), **7-22,** 53
critical reputation of, 1-6, 10, 18,
21, 53-56, 57, 81, 89-98, 99,
110-12, 124, 142, **165-71**
and death, dramatic preoccupation
with, 111-23 *passim*
and dialects, use of, 3, 18, 92
and dialogue, use of, 3, 4-5, 23-25,
28
dramatic aims of, 2, 5, 31, 35-36,
44, 94, 142, 145
and dramatic device (*see also* Main
entry), 2, 3, 12, 17-18, 23, 25,
29-41, 44-45, 47, 48, 50, 84, 90,
93, 116, 142-64 *passim,* 168
and dramatic inventiveness, 3, 4,
29-41, 142-64
and dramatic motifs (*see also* Main
entry), 12, 14-16, 20, 146-48
and Elizabethan drama, 13, 17, 111,
154
and his family,
2, 7-11
Freudian influence on, 3, 42, 43,
97, 112, **115-18,** 158, 168
and Gorky, 90, **99-109**
and Greek drama, 1, 38, 55, 57-61,
82-88, 96-98, 112-23 *passim,* 126,
156-58, 168
and his heritage, 124-41
and Ibsen, Henrik, 19, 25, 42-43,
46, 50, 52-53, 55, 93, 118
and language, use of, 4-5, 18, 54,
55, 111, 120
and Nietzsche, Friedrich, 9, 11, 30,
36, 70-71, **72-81,** 132
philosophy of, 42-43, 45-46, 58-59,
72-81
and poetry, 2, 18, 45
and realism, 3, 4, 38, 93-94, 100,
104, 106-7, 171
and religion, 34, 43, 50-51*n,* 57-61,
74-81, 119, 168
and rhythm, use of, 17-22
and Schopenhauer, Arthur, 72, 78-
79, 117
sea plays of, 63-71, 145-48, 170

O'Neill, Eugene: (continued)
  and sexuality, use of, 97, 136-37
  and Strindberg, August, 1, 3, 5, 9,
    25, 52, 90, 114-15, 155, 168,
    169, 171
  and symbolism, 3, 35, 57-58,
    142-64 passim, 171
  tragic drama of, 57-61, 111-12
O'Neill, Eugene, works by: (see also
  titles of individual works)
  Abortion, 12
  Ah, Wilderness!, 6, 13, 50-51, 95,
    124, 126, 169, 171
  All God's Chillun Got Wings, 13,
    19, 29, 35, 60, 71, 125
  Ancient Mariner, The, 29, 31-32
  Anna Christie, 3, 12, 13, 19, 23,
    28, 62-71, 95, 110, 142, 147-48,
    160n, 170
  Before Breakfast, 106
  Beyond the Horizon, 3, 13, 19, 37,
    56, 63, 65, 67, 68, 70, 106, 144,
    145-47, 164
  Bound East for Cardiff, 32-33,
    64, 68, 106, 143, 145, 146,
    147
  Chris Christophersen, 62-67, 148
  Days Without End, 13, 21-22, 29,
    33-34, 43, 50-51, 56, 95, 112,
    114, 144, 158-59, 160, 161, 164,
    168, 169
  Desire Under the Elms, 3, 11, 12,
    13, 15, 16, 17-18, 19, 20, 36, 50,
    54, 57-61, 71, 106, 110n, 125,
    136, 142, 143-44, 152-53, 154,
    164, 168, 169, 171
  Diff'rent, 13, 17, 19, 106, 110n
  Dynamo, 12, 13, 19, 21, 22, 43,
    53, 95, 114, 142, 155-56, 160n,
    168
  Emperor Jones, The, 2, 3, 12, 15,
    17, 18, 19, 23, 28, 35, 55, 95,
    106, 124, 148-49, 150, 170,
    171
  First Man, The, 13, 19, 20-21, 23,
    28
  Fountain, The, 13, 15, 18, 19, 20,
    29, 35-36, 38, 74, 76, 80, 106,
    142, 150-51, 152, 153, 155,
    159, 164
  Gold, 15, 19, 110
  Great God Brown, The, 3, 12, 13,
    15, 19, 29, 30-31, 32, 34, 36-37,
    38, 44-46, 50, 54, 56, 60, 73-74,
    81, 95, 106, 144, 153-56, 159,
    164
  Hairy Ape, The, 3, 12, 13, 19, 23,
    28, 29, 32, 55, 68, 69, 70, 72, 74,
    106, 124, 143, 149, 170, 171
  Hughie, 13, 22, 111
  Iceman Cometh, The, 4, 5, 6, 9, 13,
    16, 17, 18, 22, 34, 37-38, 40, 56,
    89-95, 99-109, 110, 111, 112,
    115-18, 160-64, 165, 167, 168,
    169, 170, 171
  Ile, 110
  Lazarus Laughed, 3, 13, 18, 19, 29,
    32, 36, 38, 56, 72-81, 95, 106,
    114, 124, 142, 144, 151-52, 153,
    155, 164
  Long Day's Journey into Night, A,
    4, 8, 9, 13, 18, 19, 22, 34, 37-41,
    54, 56, 65, 70, 110, 110n, 111,
    112-14, 119, 120-21, 124-41,
    144, 160-64, 166, 168, 169,
    170, 171
  Long Voyage Home, The, 64, 110n,
    160n
  Marco Millions, 13, 19, 29, 106,
    108, 110n, 124, 143
  "Memoranda on Masks," 29-30, 31,
    38
  Moon for the Misbegotten, A, 6,
    13, 19, 22, 54, 66, 110, 114, 126,
    129, 132, 136, 137, 160-64, 166,
    168, 169
  Moon of the Caribbees, 145,
    146
  More Stately Mansions, 111
  Mourning Becomes Electra, 3, 5, 12,
    13, 18, 19, 38, 43, 49-51, 55, 57,
    60, 61, 82-88, 96-98, 106, 112,
    115, 124, 144, 156-58, 159, 160,
    168, 169, 170, 171
  Ole Davil, The, 62, 68-70
  Rope, The, 12, 106

O'Neill, Eugene, works by:
(*continued*)
  Sniper, The, 12
  Strange Interlude, 3, 5, 12, 13, 15,
    16, 19, 20, 44, 47-49, 50, 54,
    55, 71, 74, 106, 110n, 115, 136,
    144, 154, 155-56, 169
  Straw, The, 13, 19, 106, 147
  Thirst, 11
  Touch of the Poet, A, 12, 13, 14,
    16, 22, 110, 111, 112, 114,
    118-19, 121, **160-64**, 166,
    171
  Welded, 13
  Where the Cross Is Made, 14, 15,
    110
O'Neill, James, 2, 7-11, 20, 53,
  126-27
Otto, Ted, 90, 91

P

Paul, Saint, 122-23
Phèdre, (Racine), 57, 59
Philosophy, of O'Neill, 42, 45-46,
  58-59
  in *Lazarus Laughed,* **72-81**
Pinero, Sir Arthur, 27
Pirandello, Luigi, 94
Provincetown Players, 2, 3, 11, 30, 31,
  53, 67, 166

Q

Quintero, José, 54, 116

R

Racine, Jean, 57, 59
Realism, in O'Neill's works, 3, 4, 38,
  171
Realism and illusion, in *Iceman
  Cometh, The,* 93-94, 100, 104,
  106-7, 115-18
Reinhardt, Max, 3, 23
Religion, in O'Neill's works, 34, 43,
  50-51, 119, 168
  in *Days Without End,* 34

  in *Desire Under the Elms,*
    57-61
  in *Great God Brown, The,*
    73-74
  in *Lazarus Laughed,* 74-81
Repetition, as device in O'Neill's
  works, 25
  in *Desire Under the Elms,* 17-18
  in *Diff'rent,* 17
  in *Great God Brown, The,* 50
  in *Hairy Ape, The,* 23
  in *Iceman Cometh, The,* 17, 90,
    116
  in *Mourning Becomes Electra,* 50
  in *Strange Interlude,* 48, 50
Revelation, as device in O'Neill's
  works, 21-22, 33-41
  in *All God's Chillun Got Wings,* 35
  in *Fountain, The,* 35-36
Revenge, as motif in O'Neill's works,
  12
Rhythm, O'Neill's use of, 17-22
Rope, The, 12, 106
Rousseau, Jean Jacques, 56

S

Sardou, Victorien, 26-27, 53
Sartre, Jean-Paul, 122
Schopenhauer, Arthur, 72, 78-79, 117
Scribe, Eugène, 26, 53
Sea plays, of O'Neill, 63-71, 145-48,
  170
Shakespeare, William, 19, 24, 25, 26,
  82, 111, 112
Shaw, G. B., 4, 42, 46, 75n, 114, 126,
  130, 138, 139
Sniper, The, 12
Soliloquy, in O'Neill's works, 17, 154,
  155, 168
Sound effects:
  in *Bound East for Cardiff,* 32-33
  in *Emperor Jones, The,* 2, 35, 149
Stevenson, Robert Louis, 15
Strange Interlude, 3, 5, 12, 13, 15, 16,
  19, 20, 44, 47-49, 50, 54, 55, 71, 75,
  106, 110n, 115, 136, 144, 154,
  155-56, 169

Strange Interlude (*continued*),
   asides in, 44, 47, 154
   and *Hedda Gabler* (Ibsen), 46
Straw, The, 13, 19, 106, 147
Strindberg, August, 1, 3, 5, 9, 25, 26,
   27, 52, 90, 114-15, 155, 168, 169,
   171
Studs Lonigan (Farrell), 125
Suffering and aging, as motif in
   O'Neill's works, 20
Swinburne, Algernon, 18
Symbolism, in O'Neill's works, 3, 35,
   57-58, 142-64 *passim*, 171
Synge, John Millington, 3, 130

T

Theatre Guild, 2, 90, 94
Thirst, 11
This Is My Best (Burnett), 36
Thus Spake Zarathustra (Nietzsche),
   30, 36, 74, 76, 79
Tillich, Paul, 122
Touch of the Poet, A, 12, 13, 14, 16,
   22, 110, 111, 112, 114, 118-19, 121,
   160-64, 166, 171
Toynbee, Arnold, 141
Tragic drama, and O'Neill, 57-61,
   111-12
Treasure Island (Stevenson), 15
Trilling, Lionel, 89
Trilogy, as device in O'Neill's work,
   3, 84
Tristan und Isolde (Wagner), 120
Twilight of the Idols, The (Nietzsche),
   76

Tynan, Kenneth, 37

U

Ulysses (Joyce), 36, 125, 128, 137,
   138, 141

V

Vaughan, Stuart, 54
Villiers de l'Isle-Adam, Comte de, 27
Von Wiegand, Charmion, 49

W

Wagner, Richard, 120
Webster, John, 111
Wedekind, Frank, 5
Welded, 13
When We Dead Awaken (Ibsen), 43
Where the Cross Is Made, 14, 15, 110
Whitman, Robert F., 5
Wild Duck, The (Ibsen), 27, 118
Wilde, Oscar, 130
Williams, Tennessee, 111
Winterset (Anderson), 124

Y

Yeats, William Butler, 126, 130, 139
Young, Stark, 52, 55, 89

Z

Zola, Émile, 27
Zorach, William, 11

PIRANDELLO

A Collection of Critical Essays
Edited by GLAUCO CAMBON

A

Abba, Marta, 2, 80, 104, 156
Abel, Lionel, 144
Adamov, Arthur, 56-58, 59, 60
Albee, Edward, 133
All for the Best, 20, 32
All'uscita (see *At the Exit*)
Amédée (Ionesco), 59
Anouilh, Jean, 43-51, 56, 64, 133
Antigone (Anouilh), 45
Antonelli, Luigi, 108
Ardèle (Anouilh), 46-47
Artaud, Antonin, 57
As Well as Before, Better than Before,
   20, 25, 32
As You Desire Me, 109
At the Exit, 25
Autre Alexandre, L' (Libéraki),
   60

B

Baccolo, Luigi, 7
Balcony, The (Genet), 149
Baroque theatre, 37, 41
"Bat, The," 27
Beckett, Samuel, 56, 58, 59, 60,
   133
Bentley, Eric, 8, 112, 115, 156*n*, 157
Bergson, Henri, 7, 24, 137
*Berretto a sonagli, Il (see Cap and
   Bells)*
Betti, Ugo, 65, 149

Bishop, Thomas, 7
Blacks, The (Genet), 149
Bonnes, Les (Genet), 63
Brecht, Bertolt, 2, 120, 133, 150,
   151
Brée, Germaine, 60
Brustein, Robert, 7, 8
Büchner, Georg, 58
Burnt Norton (Eliot), 107
"By Himself," 22

C

Calderon de la Barca, Pedro, 9
Caligula (Camus), 55-56
Call to Order (Cocteau), 36
Camus, Albert, 54-56, 133
"Candelora" (*see* "Candlemas")
"Candlemas," 21
"Canta l'epistola" (*see* "Sing the
   Epistle")
Cantatrice chauve, La (Ionesco), 59
Cap and Bells, 3, 6-7, 20, 25, 32, 33,
   164-65
Cappiddazzu Pays for All, 20, 70
Castris, A. L. de, 6, 8
Cervantes, Miguel de, 9
Chaises, Les (Ionesco), 59
Chekhov, Anton, 38, 41, 133
Chiarelli, Luigi, 108, 164*n*
*Ciascuno a suo modo (see Each in His
   Own Way)*
Clothing the Naked (see Naked)
Clouard, Henri, 50

Cocteau, Jean, 36, 42, 64
Colombe (Anouilh), 45
*Come prima, meglio di prima (see
     As Well as Before, Better than
     Before)*
Commedia dell'arte, 12, 17, 39, 113,
     118, 124
Coscienza di Zeno, La (Svevo), 98n
*Cosi é (se vi pare)(see It Is So, if You
     Think So)*
Counterfeiters, The (Gide), 6,
     90
Crémieux, Benjamin, 138, 153n
Croce, Benedetto, 5-6, 8, 17, 94

D

D'Annunzio, Gabriele, 2, 104, 105,
     106, 110n
Dante Alighieri, 38, 41
"Da sè *(see* "By Himself")
Deputy, The (Hochhuth), 150
*Devil and the Good Lord, The (see
     Diable et le Bon Dieu, Le)*
Diable et le Bon Dieu, Le (Sartre), 51,
     53-54, 150
Dialogue on Dramatic Poetry (Eliot),
     36
Diana and Tuda, 73-75, 79, 110, 122,
     125
Double Inconstance, La (Marivaux),
     48
"Dovere del medico, Il" *(see*
     "Physician's Duty, The")
Dressing the Naked (see Naked)
Dr. Faustus (Mann), 90
"Dry Salvages" (Eliot), 70
Dumas, Alexandre *(fils),* 139

E

Each in His Own Way, 1, 71, 75, 77,
     106n, 107, 109, 110, 113, 113n,
     124, 125, 127, 142-48, 150-52,
     155, 156, 159, 167, 172
Each in His Role, 20, 25, 46, 111,
     118, 154, 155
"Either of One or of No One," 83

Eliot, T. S., 36, 42, 70, 107-8
Elizabethan theatre, 41, 111, 126
En attendant Godot (Beckett),
     56
Enrico IV (see Henry IV)
Erma bifronte (see Two-faced Herma)
Esclusa, L' (see Outcast, The)
*Essays on the Immediate Data of Con-
     sciousness* (Bergson), 137

F

Fabbri, Diego, 65
Fable of the Changeling, The, 80
Faulkner, William, 6
*Favola del figlio cambiato, La (see
     Fable of the Changeling, The)*
"Feather," 27
Felix Krull (Mann), 5
Fergusson, Francis, 8, 128
Filippo, Eduardo de, 65
Fin de partie (Beckett), 56
"First Wedding Night," 22-23
Fog (Unamuno), 28n
French drama, influence of Pirandello
     on, 7, 43-65
     of Adamov, Arthur, 56-58, 59,
          60
     of Anouilh, Jean, 43-51, 64, 133
     of Beckett, Samuel, 56, 58, 59, 60,
          133
     of Camus, Albert, 54-56, 133
     of Cocteau, Jean, 64
     of Genet, Jean, 63, 133, 149
     of Giraudoux, Jean, 43, 133
     of Ionesco, Eugène, 59-60, 64, 133
     of Libéraki, Marguerite, 60
     of Neveux, Georges, 60-64
     of Sartre, Jean-Paul, 51-54, 55, 133
Frye, Northrop, 113
*Fu Mattia Pascal, Il (see Late Mattia
     Pascal, The)*

G

Galileo (Brecht), 150
Garibaldi, Giuseppe, 4
Gelber, Jack, 133

Genet, Jean, 63, 133, 149-50
Gherardi, Gherardo, 65
Ghosts (Ibsen), 38
Gide, André, 1, 5, 6, 70, 90
Giganti della Montagna, I (see Moun-
    tain Giants, The)
Giraudoux, Jean, 43, 50, 133
Giuoco dele parti, Il (see Each in His
    Role)
Goetz, Kurt, 64
Gorgias, 7
Gozzi, Carlo, 17
Grafting, The, 20, 32
Gramsci, Antonio, 8
Grande et la petite manoeuvre, La
    (Adamov), 57, 58

H

Hamlet (Shakespeare), 7, 69, 71, 109,
    132, 137
Henry IV, 3, 7, 11-13, 20, 31, 33, 43
    45, 50, 52, 55, 116-21, 126, 131,
    137, 156, 156n, 157
Herman, William, 7
Homme révolté, L' (Camus), 54
Howe, Irving, 163
Huis clos (Sartre), 52-53, 61
Humor, 1, 8, 21, 108, 111, 139n,
    156

I

Ibsen, Henrik, 38, 41, 64, 104, 105,
    133, 136
"If," 27
"Illustre estinto, L'" (see "Illustrious
    Deceased, The")
"Illustrious Deceased, The," 23
I'm Dreaming, but Am I?, 98n
Innesto, L' (see Grafting, The)
In the Jungle of Cities (Brecht), 120
Invasion, L' (Adamov), 58
Invitation au château, L' (Anouilh),
    49
Ionesco, Eugène, 59-60, 64, 133
It Can't Be Serious, 20, 22, 141, 142,
    143, 144

It Is So, if You Think So (It's True
    if It Seems So to You), 3, 15-18, 19,
    32, 58, 83-90, 107, 114-16, 137n,
    153n
It's Only a Joke (see It Can't Be
    Serious)

J

Janner, Arminio, 8
Jones, Robert Edmond, 11
Joyce, James, 4, 5, 142
Juliette (Neveux), 60, 62

K

Kafka, Franz, 1, 142
Kant, Immanuel, 23
Kleist, Heinrich von, 58
Krakatos, László, 64

L

Late Mattia Pascal, The, 3, 5, 19, 20,
    23, 91-95, 96n, 109
Lazarus, 80, 104, 106, 122
Lazzaro (see Lazarus)
Leo, Ulrich, 8
Léocadia (Anouilh), 49, 50
Libéraki, Marguerite, 60
License, The, 20
Life I Gave You, The, 20
Liolà, 6, 46
Livingston, Arthur, 11, 16
Lorca, Federico García, 42, 106
Lumie di Sicilia (see Sicilian
    Limes)

M

Ma Chance et ma chanson (Neveux),
    60, 62
Mains sales, Les (Sartre), 53, 54
Mallarmé, Stéphane, 6, 150
Man, Beast and Virture, 6, 20, 22,
    83
Man Is Man (Brecht), 149
Mann, Thomas, 5, 90

Ma non è una cosa seria (see It Can't
Be Serious)
Martini, Fausto, 108
Maschere nude (see Naked Masks)
Mask and the Face, The (Chiarelli),
108, 164n
Metatheatre (Abel), 144
Miller, Arthur, 64
Molière, 111
Mondrian, Piet, 68
Morts sans sépulture (Sartre), 53
Mouches, Les (Sartre), 52
Mountain Giants, The, 3, 7, 80-81,
104, 106
"Mrs. Frola and Her Son-in-Law, Mr.
Ponza," 83-90
Mrs. Morli, One and Two, 45
Murder in the Cathedral (Eliot),
107
Musco, Angelo, 2
Musil, Robert, 142
Musset, Alfred de, 50
Myth, in Pirandello's works, 7, 80-81,
106

N

Naked, 20, 25, 30, 32, 45, 156,
157-58, 160-63, 165, 168-69,
170-72
Naked Life, 23
Naked Masks, 23, 155-56
Nardelli, Federico, 1
Nekrassov (Sartre), 54
"Nenè and Nini," 22
Nerval, Gérard de, 50
Neveux, Georges, 60-64
New Colony, The,
80, 105, 106
New Theatre and Old, 156
Nietzsche, Friedrich, 104n
1984 (Orwell), 57
Nobel Prize, 121n
No Exit (See Huis clos)
Notebooks of Serafina Gubbio,
Cameraman, The, 6, 80, **95-102**
Nuova colonia, La (see
New Colony, The)

O

"O di uno o di nessuno" (*see* "Either
of One or of No One")
Old and the Young, The, 3, 4-5, 6, 9,
19, 24, 25
O'Neill, Eugene, 133
One, No One, and a Hundred Thou-
sand, 6, 19, 24, 136
Orwell, George, 57
Other People's Points of View, 20, 27-28
Our Lord of the Ship, 77
Outcast, The, 169

P

Parodie, La (Adamov), 58, 59
Patente, La (see License, The)
Pauvre Bitos (Anouilh), 45-46
Pêcheur d'ombres, Le (Sarment), 43
Pensaci, Giacomino, (see, Think It
Over, Giacomino!)
"Physician's Duty, The," 22
Piacere dell'onestà, Il (see Pleasure of
Honesty, The)
Pinter, Harold, 133
"Pipistrello, Il" (*see* "Bat, The")
Pirandello, Antonietta, 2, 157, 163,
163n, 165
Pirandello, Luigi:
  and the audience, 1, 7, 68, 69, 76-
  77, **146-49**, 152
  and his characters, 16-17, 25-26,
  107, 159-60
  and commedia dell'arte, 12, 17, 39,
  113, 118, 124
  contribution of, 33-34, 41-42, 64-
  65, 133
  critical reputation of, 7-8, 105
  and "cubist" drama, 6, 67-71
  and drama of revolt, 103-33
  dramaturgy of, 13, 16-18, 27-31,
  36, 41, 67-71, 76-78, 106-7, 116,
  135-39, 142, 154
  and existential drama, 7, 51-54, 56,
  104, 112-13, 127, 133
  and experimental drama, 6-7, 9, 30-
  31, 106, 110n, 126-27, 133

Pirandello, Luigi: (*continued*)
  and French drama (*see* main entry),
    7, **43-65**, 106, 133, 149
  and humor, 1, 2, 3, 22
  life of, 2
  and morality, 25-26
  and myth, 7, 80-81, 106
  as novelist, 4-6, 8-9, 33, **91-102**
  philosophy of, 3, 20-34, 105-12,
    122
  and Racine, 37, 39, 40
  and realism, 6, 27, 37-39, 40-41,
    125, 143-44, 149
  and Shakespeare, 7, 8, 9, 13, 64,
    69, 71, 109, 132, 136-37
  and Shaw, G. B., 35, 38, 39, 40,
    41, 105, 106, 107, 133
  and the short-story form, 33, **83-
    90**, 137n
  as a Sicilian, 3-5, 17-18, 33, 106,
    112, 153
  social consciousness of, 8, 9, 105,
    109, 112, 115-16
  and theatre of the absurd, 55, 56,
    57-58, 59-60, 145-46
  and theatre of the grotesque, 108,
    115-16
  and theatre of the looking glass,
    109, 111, 145, 166
  and tragedy, 39-40
Pirandello, works by:
DRAMA
  All for the Best, 20, 32
  *As Well as Before, Better than
    Before*, 1, 20, 25, 32
  As You Desire Me, 109
  At the Exit, 25
  Cap and Bells, 3, 6-7, 20, 25, 32,
    33, 164-65
  Cappiddazzu Pays for All,
    20, 77
  Clothing the Naked (*see Naked*)
  Diana and Tuda, 73-75, 79, 110,
    122, 125
  Dressing the Naked (*see Naked*)
  Each in His Own Way, 1, 71, 75,
    77, 106n, 107, 109, 110, 113,
    113n, 124, 125, 127, **142-48**,

    150-52, 155, 156, 159, 167,
    172
  Each in His Role, 20, 25, 46, 111,
    128, 154, 155
  Fable of the Changeling, The,
    80
  Grafting, The, 20, 32
  Henry IV, 3, 7, **11-13**, 20, 31, 33,
    43-45, 50, 52, 55, **116-21**, 131,
    137, 156, 156n, 157
  It Can't Be Serious, 20, 22, 141,
    142, 143, 144
  *It Is So, if You Think So (It's True
    if It Seems So to You)*, 3, **15-18**,
    19, 32, 58, **83-90**, 107, **114-16**,
    137n, 153n
  Lazarus, 80, 104, 106, 125
  License, The, 20
  Life I Gave You, The, 20
  Liolà, 6, 46
  Man, Beast and Virtue, 6, 20, 22,
    83
  Mountain Giants, The, 3, 7, 80-81,
    104, 106
  Mrs. Morli, One and Two, 45
  Naked, 20, 25, 30, 32, 45, 156,
    157-58, 160-63, 165, 168-69,
    170-72
  Naked Masks, 23, 155-56
  New Colony, The, 80, 105, 106
  Other People's Points of View,
    20, 27-28
  Our Lord of the Ship, 77
  Pleasure of Honesty, The, 20, 32,
    63, 111, 153n
  *Right You Are if You Think You
    Are* (*see It is So, If you Think So*)
  Rules of the Game, The (*see Each
    in His Role*)
  Sicilian Limes, 20
  *Six Characters in Search of an
    Author* (*see also* main entry), 1, 6,
    20, 25, 27, **28-31**, 31n, 32, 33,
    35-42, 48, 53, 61, 62, 63-64, 77,
    81, 105, 123, 123n, 125, 126,
    127-32, 136, 137, 137n, 138, 139,
    144-45, 148-49, 153-55, 156, 157,
    158-59, 165-67, 172

Pirandello, Luigi, works by: DRAMA
(*continued*)
   Think It Over, Giacomino!, 20, 22,
    32
   To Find Oneself, 3, **78-80**, 123
   Tonight We Improvise, 48, **75-78**,
    104, 124, 125, 127, 137*n*, 142,
    155, 156, 159, 167-68, 172
   When Someone is Somebody, 2,
    103-4, 109
  ESSAYS
   Humor, 1, 8, 21, 108, 111, 139*n*,
    156
   New Theatre and Old, 156
   Preface to *Six Characters in Search*
    of an Author, 36, 37, 39, 122,
    156
  NOVELS
   Late Mattia Pascal, The, 3, 5, 19,
    20, 23, 33, **91-95**, 96*n*, 109
   Notebooks of Serafino Gubbio,
    Cameraman, The, 6, 80, **95-102**
   Old and the Young, The, 3, 4-5, 6,
    9, 19, 24, 25
   One, No One and a Hundred Thou-
    sand, 6, 19, 24, 136
   Outcast, The, 169
   Shoot! (see Notebooks of Serafino
    Gubbio, Cameraman, The)
  SCENARIO
   I'm Dreaming, but Am I?,
    98*n*
  SHORT STORIES
   "Bat, The," 27
   "By Himself," 22
   "Candlemas," 21
   "Either of One or of No One,"
    83
   "Feather," 27
   "First Wedding Night," 22-23
   "If," 27
   "Illustrious Deceased, The," 23
   "Mrs. Frola and Her Son-in-Law,
    Mr. Ponza," 83-90
   Naked Life, 23
   "Nenè and Nini," 22
   "Physician's Duty, The," 22
   "Reality of Dreams, The," 27

   "Remedy: Geography, The," 27
   "Sing the Epistle," 22
   "Tragedy of a Character, The," 28
   "Train Whistled, The," 27
   "Trap, The," 21
   "Triplet," 159
   Two-faced Herma, 22
Pitoëff, Georges, 64, 153, 154
"Piuma" (*see* "Feather")
Plainte contre inconnu (Neveux), 60-
  61, 62
Plautus, 18
Pleasure of Honesty, The, 20, 32, 63,
  111, 153*n*
Portrait of the Artist as a Young Man,
  A (Joyce), 5
Preface to *Six Characters in Search of*
  an Author, 36, 37, 39, 122, 156
"Prima notte" (*see* "First Wedding
  Night")
Professeur Taranne, Le (Adamov),
  58
Proust, Marcel, 1
Purgatory (Yeats), 123, 123*n*

Q

Quaderni di Serafino Gubbio, opera-
  tore, I (see Notebooks of Serafino
  Gubbio, Cameraman, The)
Quando si è qualcuno (see When Some-
  one is Somebody)
Questa sera si recita a soggetto (see
  Tonight We Improvise)

R

Racine, Jean, 37, 39, 40
Ragione degli altri, La (see Other
  People's Point of View)
"Reality of Dream, The," 27
"Realtà del sogno, La" (*see* "Reality
  of Dream, The")
"Remedy: Geography, The," 27
Rendezvous de Senlis, Le (Anouilh),
  49-50
Répétition, La (Anouilh), 47-48
Rice, Elmer, 64

Right You Are if You Think You Are (see It Is So, If You Think So)

"Rimedio: La geografia" (*see* "Remedy: Geography, The")

Rizzo, Gino, 141-52

Rules of the Game, The (see Each in His Role)

S

Sagra del Signore della Nave, La (see Our Lord of the Ship)

"Sailing to Byzantium" (Yeats), 117

Salinari, Carlo, 8

Sarment, Jean, 43

Sartre, Jean-Paul, 51-54, 55, 133, 150

Sauvage, La (Anouilh), 45

Screens, The (Genet), 149

"Se . . . " (*see* "If")

Sei personaggi in cerca d'autore (see Six Characters in Search of an Author)

Seneca, 18

Shakespeare, William, 6, 7, 8, 9, 13, 64, 69, 71, 109, 132, 136-37

Shaw, G. B., 35, 38, 39, 40, 41, 105, 106, 107, 133

Shoot! (see Notebooks of Serafino Gubbio, Cameraman, The)

Schopenhauer, Arthur, 7

Sicilian Limes, 20

Siegfried (Giraudoux), 43

Si gira (see Notebooks of Serafina Gubbio, Cameraman, The)

"Signora Frola e il signor Ponza, suo genero, La" (*see* "Mrs. Frola and Her Son-in-Law, Mr. Ponza")

Signora Morli, una e due, La (See Mrs. Morli, One and Two)

"Sing the Epistle," 22

Sinicropi, Giovanni, 8

Six Characters in Search of an Author, 1, 6, 20, 25, 27, **28-31**, 31*n*, 32, 33, **35-42**, 48, 53, 61, 62, 63-64, **67-70**, 77, 81, 105, 123, 123*n*, 125, 126, **127-32**, 136, 137, 137*n*, 138, 139, 144-45, 148-49, 153-55, 156, 157, 158-59, 165-67, 172

as "cubist" drama, 6, 67-70

epiphany as theme in, 30, 37, 39, 61

first performance of, 1, 6

identity as theme in, 6, 20, 67, 136

interpretations of, 36-37

life *vs.* form as theme in, 6, 28-31, 31*n*, 36-38, 40, 52-53, 68, 127-32, 136, 137, 138, 139, 145

plot of, 35-36, 39, 41, 67-68

realism in, 37-39, 40-41

Socrates, 7

Sogno (ma forse no) (see I'm Dreaming, but Am I?)

Squarzina, Luigi, 141-52

Starkie, Walter, 4

Stevens, Wallace, 6

Strindberg, August, 58, 133, 149

Svevo, Italo, 98*n*

Synge, John Millington, 106

Sypher, Wylie, 6

T

Teatro nuovo e teatro vecchio (see New Theatre and Old)

Tempest, The (Shakespeare), 7

"Terzetto" (*see* "Triplet")

Theatre of the absurd, 55, 56, 57-58, 59-60

Themes, in Pirandello's works:
communication, 6, 58, 131, 146

epiphany, 30, 37, 39, 61

existentialism, 51-54

identity, 6, 7, 9, 44, 46-47, 67, 108-12, 135-36

life *vs.* form (reality *vs.* illusion, appearance, fiction; Nature *vs.* Art; time *vs.* timelessness; face *vs.* mask; change *vs.* immutability), 6, 7, 8, 13, 15, 17, **19-34**, 36-38, 40, 50, 52-63 *passim*, 68, 71, 73-81, 86, **103-33**, **135-39**, 143, 143*n*, 144, 145

Think It Over, Giocomino!, 20, 22, 32

Thomas Aquinas, Saint, 17

Tilgher, Adriano, 3, 7, 8, 143

To Clothe the Naked (*see Naked*)
To Find Oneself, 3, 78-80, 123
Tonight We Improvise, 48, 75-78, 104, 124, 125, 127, 137n, 142, 155, 156, 159, 167-68, 172
Tonio Kröger (Mann), 5
Tous contre tous (Adamov), 57, 58
"Tragedia di un personaggio, La" (*see* "Tragedy of a Character, The")
"Tragedy of a Character, The," 28
"Train Whistled, The," 27
"Trap, The," 21
"Trappola, La" (*see* "Trap, The")
"Treno ha fischiato, Il" (*see* "Train Whistled, The")
"Triplet," 159
Tristan und Isolde (Wagner), 39
Trovarsi (*see To Find Oneself*)
Tutto per bene (*see All for the Best*)
Two-faced Herma, 22

U

Umorismo, L' (*see Humor*)
Unamuno, Miguel de, 28n, 64
Uno, nessuno e centomila (*see One, No One and a Hundred Thousand*)
Uomo, la bestia e la virtu, L' (*see Man, Beast and Virtue*)

V

Valéry, Paul, 6
Valse des toréadors, La (Anouilh), 46, 47

Vecchi e i giovanni, I, (*see Old and the Young, The*)
Verga, Giovanni, 33, 106, 163
Vestire gli ignudi (*see Naked*)
Vico, Giovanni Battista, 17
Viola, Cesare, 65
Vita che ti diedi, La (*see Life I gave You, The*)
Vita Nuda, La (*see Naked Life*)
Vittorini, Domenico, 109, 110n, 126
Volupte de l'honneur, La (*see Pleasure of Honesty, The*)
Voyage de Thésée, Le (Neveux), 61-62
Voyageur sans bagage, Le (Anouilh), 43-45

W

Wagner, Richard, 39, 41
Waste Land, The (Eliot), 40
Weiss, Auréliu, 7
When Someone Is Somebody, 2, 103-4, 109
Whitehead, Alfred North, 69
Wilder, Thornton, 64, 133
Wycherly, William, 111

Y

Y'avait un prisonnier (Anouilh), 48
Yeats, William Butler, 42
Young, Stark, 8

Z

Zamore (Neveux), 62-63

POE

A Collection of Critical Essays
Edited by ROBERT REGAN

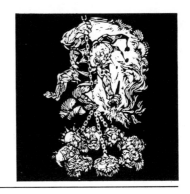

*Conti the Discarded; with other Tales
    and Fancies* (Chorley), 19
Cooke, John Estes, 38
Cooke, Philip Pendleton, 61-62, 63
Cooper, James Fenimore, 12
Crime and Punishment (Dostoyevsky),
    8

D

Damon, S. Foster, 153
Dante Alighieri, 11, 46, 50
d'Aurevilly, Barbey, 67
Davidson, Edward H., 135, 148-49,
    154, 165
Da Vinci, Leonardo, 67
De Causis Linguae Hebreae (Leescher),
    156
Defoe, Daniel, 16, 47
De La Mare, Walter, 5
*Deliverances of the Children of Israel,
    The* (Vondel), 160
"Descent into the Maelström," 47, 89-
    90, 95
"Devil in the Belfrey, The," 68, 79-83,
    84, 86, 88, 91, 94
Dickens, Charles, 18-19
Dickinson, Emily, 12
"Domain of Arnheim, The," 113,
    163
Dostoyevsky, Fyodor, 8
"Dream Land," 114-15, 175
"Duc de l'Omelette, The," 112
Dunciad, The, 138

E

Edgar Allan Poe: A Critical Biography
    (Quinn), 2
Edgar Allan Poe: A Study in Genius
    (Krutch), 173
*Edgar Allan Poe: His Life, Letters, and
    Opinions* (Ingram), 1
"Eldorado," 7
"Eleanora," 145
Eliot, T. S., 2, 4, 40, 49, 66, 164,
    172
Emerson, Ralph Waldo, 65, 156, 177

Erotic Motive in Literature, The
    (Mordell), 134-35
Essays (Emerson), 65
"Eulalie," 31
Eureka, 11, 13, 38-39, 45-46, 49, 68,
    71, 74, 92, **121-24**, 126, 128, **129-33**,
    143, 177
Evans, Augusta, 38
Evidence of Prophesy (Keith),
    161
Excursion, The (Wordsworth), 126

F

Fable for Critics, A (Lowell), 162
"Facts Concerning the Recent Carnival
    of Crime in Connecticut" (Twain),
    9
"Facts in the Case of Monsieur Valde-
    mar, The," 42
"Fall of the House of Usher, The," 9,
    10-11, 38, 42, 43-45, 76, 87-89, 108,
    121-33, 176
Fleurs du Mal, Les (Baudelaire), 64,
    146
Foerster, Norman, 137, 138
"For Annie," 7
"Four Beasts in One; or The Homo-
    camelleopard," 8
Freeman, John, 5, 6
French Poets and Novelists (James),
    147
Freud, Sigmund, 63, 73, 148

G

George Balcomb (Tucker), 162
Georgia Scenes (Longstreet), 16
*Girlhood of Shakespeare's Heroines,
    The* (Clarke), 3
Glasgow, Ellen, 40
Gide, André, 67
Gilfillan, George, 1
Goethe, Johann Wolfgang von,
    37
"Gold Bug, The," 8, 69, 97, 113, 161
Golden Bowl, The (James), 9, 147
Greeley, Horace, 145-46

Griswold, R. W., 1, 2, 20, 146

H

Hamilton, Clayton, 51-52
"Haunted Palace, The," 31, 104-7
Hawthorne, Nathaniel, 3, 20, 40, 65, 98, 143, 161, 176-77
Hazlitt, William, 3
Hoffman, E. T. A., 76
Holmes, Oliver Wendell, 65
Homer, 29, 98
Hood, Thomas, 18, 102
"Hop-Frog," 97, 112, 162
Howells, William Dean, 8
Huckleberry Finn (Twain), 9, 12, 165
Huxley, Aldous, 7, 48, 164
Huysmans, J. K., 67

I

Iliad, The (Homer), 98
"Imp of the Perverse, The," 9
Inferno, The (Dante), 46
Ingram, J. H., 1, 2
Ingram, Susan, 40-41
"Israfel," 175

J

Jaloux, Edmond, 67, 73
James, Henry, 2, 9, 56, 66, 147, 148, 152-53
Johnson, Samuel, 5
"Jolly Crone, The" (James), 9
"Journal of Julius Rodman, The," 161-62

K

Keats, John, 18
Keith, Alexander, 161
Kemble, Fanny, 162
Kennedy, J. P., 20
Kepler, Johannes, 177

"King Pest," 100, 116
Krutch, Joseph Wood, 41, 73, 135

L

La Fontaine, Jean de, 31
Lafitte (Ingraham), 162
Laforgue, Jules, 37
Lalla Rookh (Moore), 18
Lang, Andrew, 27, 29
Lawrence, D. H., 42, 143, 173
Leibnitz, Gottfried Wilhelm von, 116-17
Lemaitre, Jules, 67
"Lenore," 25
Levin, Harry, 137, 138, 149, 161
Life and Works of Edgar Allan Poe: A Psycho-Analytic Interpretation (Bonaparte), 72-75, 173
"Ligeia," 38, 43, 47-48, 51-63, 89, 112, 113, 114, 166-67, 175-76
Longfellow, Henry Wadsworth, 65
"Loss of Breath," 74, 135
Lowell, James Russell, 7, 20-21, 38, 162, 165, 174
Ludolphus, Job, 158

M

Mabbott, T. O., 162
"Mad Tryst of Sir Lancelot Channing, The," 38, 130
Mallarmé, Stéphane, 2, 31, 66, 67, 68, 71
"Man That Was Used Up, The," 74, 97
Manual of the Art of Fiction (Hamilton), 52
"Ms. Found in a Bottle," 90-92, 99, 100, 103, 150-51, 152, 160
Marginalia, 6-7, 38
"Marie Roget," 162
Marvell, Andrew, 18
"Masque of the Red Death, The," 85-87, 88, 94, 95, 112, 118-19, 134-44
Matthiessen, F. O., 153
Melville, Herman, 40, 98, 148, 154, 160-61, 163

"Metzingerstein," 100
Milton, John, 6, 33-34, 166
Mind of Poe and Other Studies, The
  (Campbell), 136
Moby Dick (Melville), 9, 148
Moore, George, 5-6
Moore, Thomas, 18
Mordell, Albert, 134-35, 138
More, Paul Elmer, 66, 172
Moréas, Jean, 68
"Morella," 38, 51, 61
"Murders in the Rue Morgue, The," 8,
  75, 162, 176
Mysteries of Udolpho, The (Radcliffe),
  19
"Mystification," 99

N

Narrative of Arthur Gordon Pym, The,
  9-10, 47, 76-77, **145-63**
Natural History (Pliny), 158
Nautical Reminiscences (Ames), 146
Nerval, Gerard de, 71
Newton, Isaac, 177
Nicols, Mrs. Gove, 20

O

Odyssey, The (Homer), 28
Old Saint Paul's (Ainsworth), 136
"Oval Portrait, The," 112

P

Paradise Lost (Milton), 25
Paulding, James Kirke, 145, 163
"Philosophy of Composition, The,"
  22, 34-35, 62, 63, 99, 142, 173, 175,
  177-78
"Philosophy of Furniture, The," 112
"Pit and the Pendulum, The," **94-97,**
  113
Plato, 68
Pliny, 150, 158
Poe, Edgar Allan:
  allegory, use of, 134, 135, 137,
    138, 146
  architectural imagery of, **104-20**
  and Baudelaire, Charles, 68, 68-72
  beauty, theme of, 23-25, 26, 28
  clock, theme of, **79-97**
  consciousness, theme of, 165,
    166-78
  critical reputation of, 1-2, **64-78,**
    164-65, 172-74
  criticism of, 2-4, **15-30**, 46-47, 49,
    172-73
  and Greek drama, 17
  Hebrew, use of, 155-57
  and Hoffman, E. T. A., 76
  irony of, 165
  madness of, 46, 74
  and Mallarmé, Stéphane, 67
  morality of, 29-30, 134, 135
  poetry, theories of, **4-8**, 24-26,
    101-2, 177-78
  solecisms of, 32
  as stylist, **164-67**
  symbolism of, 51, 54, 55, 98-100,
    102
  vampires, theme of, 42
  water, theme of, 76
  women, idealization of, 41
Poe, Edgar Allan, works by:
  *Al Aaraaf, Tamerlane, and Minor
    Poems*, 7, 55, 175
  "Angel of the Odd, The," 9
  "Assignation, The," 112-16
  "Bells, The," 31
  "Berenice," 51, 97, 149
  "Black Cat, The," 94, 97, 169-71
  "Bridal Ballad, The," 37
  "Business Man, The," 97
  "Cask of Amontillado, The," 97,
    138, 168-69, 170
  "City in the Sea," 31, 76,
    174
  "Descent into the Maelström," 47,
    89-90, 95
  "Devil in the Belfrey, The," 68,
    79-83, 84, 86, 88, 91, 94
  "Domain of Arnheim, The," 113,
    163
  "Dream Land," 114-15, 175
  "Duc de l'Omelette, The," 112

Poe, Edgar Allan, works by
(*continued*):
  "Eldorado," 7
  "Eleanora," 145
  "Eulalie," 31
  Eureka, 11, 13, 38-39, 45-46, 49,
    68, 71, 74, 92, 121-24, 126, 128,
    129, 130, 131, 132-33, 143, 177
  "Facts in the Case of Monsieur
    Valdemar, The," 42
  "Fall of the House of Usher, The,"
    9, 10-11, 38, 42, 43-45, 76, 87-89,
    108, **121-33**, 176
  "Four Beasts in One; or The Homo-
    camelleopard," 8
  "For Annie," 7
  "Gold Bug, The," 8, 69, 97, 113,
    161
  "Haunted Palace, The," 31, 104-7
  "Hop-Frog," 97, 112, 162
  "Imp of the Perverse, The," 9
  "Israfel," 175
  "Journal of Julius Rodman, The,"
    161-62
  "King Pest," 100, 116
  "Lenore," 25
  "Ligeia," 38, 43, 47-48, **51-63**, 89,
    112, 113, 114, 166-67, 175-76
  "Loss of Breath," 74, 135
  "Mad Tryst of Sir Lancelot Chan-
    ning, The," 38, 130
  "Man That Was Used Up, The," 74,
    97
  "Ms. Found in a Bottle," 90-92, 99,
    100, 103, 150-51, 152, 160
  Marginalia, 6-7, 38
  "Marie Roget," 162
  "Masque of the Red Death, The,"
    85-87, 88, 94, 95, 112, 118-19,
    134-44
  "Metzingerstein," 100
  "Morella," 38, 51, 61
  "Murders in the Rue Morgue, The,"
    8, 75, 162, 176
  "Mystification," 99
  *Narrative of Arthur Gordon Pym,
    The*, 9-10, 47, 76-77, **145-63**
  "Oval Portrait, The," 112

"Philosophy of Composition, The,"
    22, 34-35, 62, 63, 99, 142, 173,
    175, 177-78
  "Philosophy of Furniture, The,"
    112
  "Pit and the Pendulum, The," **94-
    97**, 113
  "Poetic Principle, The," 22, 172,
    177
  "Premature Burial, The," 97
  "Purloined Letter, The," 68, 75,
    176
  "Rationale of Verse, The," 46-47,
    172
  "Raven, The," 4-5, 7, 15, 31, 34-35,
    52, 62, 83-84, 91, 142-43, 175,
    177-78
  "Scythe of Time, The," 84-85, 86,
    95
  "Shadow—A Parable," 97
  "Silence—A Fable," 97
  "Siope—A Fable," 158
  "Sleeper, The," 175
  "System of Dr. Tarr and Mr. Fether,
    The," 117-18, 119, 162
  Tales of the Folio Club, 145
  *Tales of the Grotesque and the
    Arabesque*, 72
  "Tell-Tale Heart, The," 8, 42, 92-
    94, 97, 167, 169, 170
  "Thule," 37
  "To Helen," 4, 7, 31, 175
  "To One in Paradise," 5
  "Ulalume," 7, 28, 31, 32, 36,
    76
  "Unparalleled Adventures of Hans
    Pfall, The," 97
  "Valley of Unrest, The," 7
  "William Wilson," 9, 38, 47, 48, 71,
    135, 167-68, 170, 176
"Poetic Principle, The," 22, 172, 177
Pope, Alexander, 6, 138
Power of Blackness, The (Levin), 149
"Premature Burial, The," 97
Prometheus Bound (Aeschylus), 29
Psychoanalyse du feu, La (Bachelard),
    76
"Purloined Letter, The," 68, 75, 176

Q

Quinn, Arthur H., 2, 136-37, 149-50
Quinn, Patrick F., 8, 45-46, 148,
    153-54

R

Racine, Jean, 36
Radcliffe, Ann, 146
Raleigh, Sir Walter, 9
Randolph, John, 41
"Rationale of Verse, The," 46-47,
    172
"Raven, The," 4-5, 7, 15, 31, 34-35,
    52, 62, 83-84, 91, 142-43, 175,
    177-78
Rein, David M., 135-36
Reynolds, Jeremiah N., 152
Rimbaud, Arthur, 67, 161
Robinson Crusoe (Defoe), 16, 146
Robinson, Edwin Arlington, 98
Rochester, John Wilmot, Earl of, 5
Roe, E. P., 38

S

Sainte-Beuve, Charles, 64, 67, 70, 77,
    146
Samain, Albert, 68
Santayana, George, 116
Sartre, Jean Paul, 161
Seaborn, Adam, 151-52
Scarlet Letter, The (Hawthorne), 65
"Scythe of Time, The," 84-85, 86, 95
"Shadow—A Parable," 97
Shakespeare, William, 3-4, 29, 40, 68,
    136
Shanks, Edward, 153
Shaw, G. B., 2, 12
Shelley, Percy Bysshe, 18, 147
Sheppard Lee (Bird), 162
Sigourney, Mrs. L. H., 15
"Silence—A Fable," 97
"Siope—A Fable," 158
Sitwell, Edith, 173
Slavery in the United States (Pauld-
    ing), 163

"Sleeper, The," 175
Songs of Experience (Blake), 6
Songs of Innocence (Blake), 6
Stephens, John L., 161
Stoddard, R. H., 42
Stoker, Bram, 45
Stovall, Floyd, 8, 164-65
Studies in Classic American Literature
    (Lawrence), 173
Swinburne, A. C., 66
Symmes, John Clewes, 151-52
Symzonia: A Voyage of Discovery
    (Seaborn), 151
"System of Dr. Tarr and Mr. Fether,
    The," 117-18, 119, 162

T

Tales of the Folio Club, 145
*Tales of the Grotesque and the
    Arabesque*, 72
Tate, Allen, 66, 164, 173-74
"Tell-Tale Heart, The," 8, 42, 92-94,
    97, 167, 169, 170
Tempest, The (Shakespeare), 136
Tennyson, Alfred Lord, 18
Terre et les rêveries du repos, La
    (Bachelard), 72
Thoreau, Henry, 151
Thorp, Willard, 136
"Thule," 37
"To Helen," 4, 7, 31, 175
"Tombeau d'Edgar Poe, La"
    (Mallarmé), 67
Tom Sawyer (Twain), 8
"To One in Paradise," 5
Trollope, Madame, 162
"Turn of the Screw, The" (James),
    9, 152
Turner, Nat, 163
Twain, Mark, 8-9, 12, 98
Twice Told Tales (Hawthorne), 3, 143,
    176-77

U

"Ulalume," 7, 28, 31, 32, 36,
    76

"Unparalleled Adventures of Hans Pfall, The," 97

V

Valéry, Paul, 2, 31, 38, 45, 67, 71, 154, 174, 177
"Valley of Unrest, The," 7
"Vanity of Human Wishes, The" (Johnson), 7
Verlaine, Paul, 67

W

Walden (Thoreau), 151
Welby, Amelia, 25
Weld, Theodore, 163

What is Poetry (Wheelock), 6
Wheelock, John Hall, 6
Whitman, Sarah Helen, 62
Whitman, Walt, 12, 65, 147-48, 173
Whittier, John Greenleaf, 65
Wilbur, Richard, 11
Williams, William Carlos, 2
"William Wilson," 9, 38, 47, 48, 81, 135, 167-68, 170, 176
Willis, N. P., 136
Winters, Yvor, 2, 48, 66, 164, 173
Winwar, Frances, 137
Wordsworth, William, 4, 176

Z

"Zingendorf" (Sigourney), 15

EZRA POUND

A Collection of Critical Essays

Edited by WALTER SUTTON

A

ABC of Reading, 164
Abelard, Peter, 101-2
Adams, John, 7, 64, 72, 94, 111, 167
Aestheticism, in Pound's work, 30-32, 34
"Age Demanded, The," 36
Aiken, Conrad, 17-18
"Alba," 122, 153-54
Aldington, Richard, 80, 121, 128
Ambassadors, The (James), 51
Antheil, Georges, 139
Apollonius of Tyana, 173, 175
"April," 122
Aristotle, 21
"Art, L', 1910," 121, 122
Auden, W. H., 10, 158

B

Babbitt, Irving, 3, 7-8
Bach, J. S., 139, 140
Backward Glance, A (Whitman), 107
Bartók, Béla, 139
"Bath Tub, The," 123
Baudelaire, Charles, 168
Beerbohm, Max, 49
Bennett, Arnold, 49
Benton, Thomas Hart, 175
Bernanos, Georges, 92, 93
Blackmur, R. P., 80, 87, 88, 143

Born, Bertrans de, 87
Bouvard et Pécuchet (Flaubert), 44
"Brennbaum," 49
"Broken Mirrors, The" (Kenner), 81
Browning, Robert, 7, 8, 17, 28, 39, 87, 125, 158
Buchanan, Robert Williams, 48, 53

C

Campion, Thomas, 154
Camus, Albert, 92
Cantos, The, 1-8 *passim,* **11-16,** 23, 44, 52, 56, **57-63, 64-79, 87-96,** 160-162
   Chinese history in, 62-63, 64, 72, 94
   Chinese ideograms in, 58, 62-63, 95, 100, 102, 107, 109, 111, 121, 171-73
   and the *Divine Comedy* (Dante), 5, 64-65, 67-68, 90
   haiku imagery in, 126-28
   and *Hugh Selwyn Mauberley,* 36-40, 52, 56, 57, 61
   musical influences in, 135-41
   and the *Odyssey* myths, 5, 9, 11-12, 58-61, 64-79, 85
   Pisan Cantos, 2, 5, 8, 40, 44, 52*n*, 58, 62-63, 74-79, **80-86,** 90, 94, 126, 141, 175
   realism *vs.* nominalism in, 100-114

Cantos, The, (*continued*)
as *révolte* poetry, 91-97
Section: Rock Drill, 62-63, 175-76
speech rhythms in, 12-14
structure of, 58-63, 88, 138-41
Thrones, 63, 138, 152-53
vocabulary of, 12-13, 15
and Whitman, influence of,
163-77 *passim*
Yeats on, 3, 9-10
Carne-Ross, D. S., 81
Carruth, Hayden, 96
Cathay, 44 (*see also* titles of individual
poems)
Catullus, 60
Cavalcanti, Guido, 61, 71, 76, 95,
133-34
Céline, Louis-Ferdinand, 92, 93, 94,
95
Cézanne, Paul, 105-6
Chamber Music (Joyce), 44
Chinese history, in *The Cantos,* 62-63,
64, 72, 94
Chinese ideograms, in *The Cantos,* 58,
62-63, 95, 100, 102, 107, 109, 111,
121, 171-73
"Coming of War, The: Actaeon," 123
Confucius, Pound's translations of,
6, 7, 172
Corbière, Tristan, 45n, 47
Couperin, François, 136
Criticism, Pound's work in, 20-23,
157

D

Daniel, Arnaut, 21, 132, 133, 155
Dante Alighieri, 5, 64-65, 67-68, 90,
132, 155
Date Line, 21-22
Divine Comedy, The (Dante), and
The Cantos, 5, 64-65, 67-68, 90
Dolmetsch, Arnold, 136
"Donna mi prega" (Cavalcanti), 71,
76, 95, 133-34
Doolittle, Hilda (H.D.), 118, 121
Dubliners (Joyce), 44
"Dum Capitolium Scandet," 122

E

"Edward Wadsworth, Vorticist,"
118
*Elegy Written in a Country Church-
yard* (Gray), 85
Eliot, T. S., 2, 3-4, 7, 10, 17-25, 26-
27, 30, 37-38, 40, 42-43, 84, 88, 96-
97, 125, 132, 142-43, 144, 149,
150, 156-62 *passim*
Elliott, George P., 7
"Encounter, The," 125
"Envoi," 34-35, 50, 54, 160
"E. P. Ode Pour L'Election de son
Sepulchre," 45, 54, 148, 159
Evans, David W., 5

F

"Fan-Piece, for her Imperial Lord,"
124
Fascism, Pound's involvement with
(*see* Political and economic views)
Fenollosa, Ernest, 100, 121
Finnegans Wake (Joyce), 43
"Fish and Shadow," 125
Flaubert, Gustave, 7, 43, 46-47
Fletcher, John Gould, 128
Flint, F. S., 117, 121
Ford, Ford Madox, 7, 49-50
Four Quartets (Eliot), 42-43, 84
Frohock, W. M., 6
Frost, Robert, 2, 17, 20

G

Gaudier-Brzeska, Henri, 118
"Gentildonna," 45, 122
Gesell, Silvio, 7
"Ghost, The" (Lowell), 143
Gilbert, Stuart, 137-38
Giono, Jean, 93, 94
Gitanjali (Tagore), 131
Gladstone, William, 33, 48
Goethe, Johann Wolfgang von, 134
Gosse, Edmund, 53
Gourmont, Rémy de, 21
Gray, Thomas, 85

Great Digest (Confucius), 172
Guernica (Picasso), 109
Guide to Kulchur, 130, 139, 168, 169
Guinicelli, Guido, 155

H

"Had I the Heavens' embroidered cloths" (Yeats), 134
Haiku imagery, Pound's use of, 115-28
    in *The Cantos*, 126-28
Hawk's Well, The (Yeats), 17, 24
H.D. (*see* Doolittle, Hilda)
Hesiod, 73
"Hippopotamus, The" (Eliot), 159
"History of Imagism, The" (Flint), 117
Homage to Sextus Propertius, 4, 19, 23, 41, 44, 142-51
Homer, 160 (*see also Odyssey*, myths of)
Hugh Selwyn Mauberley, 1, 2, 4, 19, 27-36, 39-40, 41-56, 87, 88, 144-51 *passim*, 159-60
    and *The Cantos*, 36-40, 52, 56, 57, 61
    musical influences in, 134
Hulme, T. E., 19, 117

I

Iliad (Homer), 160
Imagism, 2, 6, 19-20, 105, 117-28, 172
"In a Station at the Metro," 120, 121
Interpretation of Music of the XVIIth and XVIIIth Centuries, The (Dolmetsch), 136
"Isolated Superiority" (Eliot), 37
It Was the Nightingale (Ford), 50

J

James, Henry, 21, 51, 91
Jefferson, Thomas, 7, 61, 94, 167
Johnson, Dr. Samuel, 50, 151

Journey to the End of the Night (Céline), 93, 95
Joyce, James, 2, 20, 43-44, 137-39

K

Kenner, Hugh, 4, 81, 96, 134, 157, 161
Koestler, Arthur, 85-86

L

Leaves of Grass (Whitman), 167
Leavis, F. R., 41-42
Lewis, C. Day, 10
Lewis, Wyndham, 20, 170
"Liu Ch'e," 123-24
Lowell, Amy, 20, 128
Lowell, Robert, 143
Lume Spento, A, 1
Lustra, 28-29, 44, 121, 133 (*see also* titles of individual poems)

M

Mace, Thomas, 136
Madame Bovary (Flaubert), 46
Make It New, 21, 91
Malatesta, Sigismondo, 7, 23, 60, 64, 94, 111, 170, 173, 174
Mallarmé, Stéphane, 21
Malraux, André, 92-93
Man's Fate (Malraux), 92-93
Masks, Pound's theory of, 1-2, 41, 43, 143-44, 146, 158-59
Mathews, Elkin, 1
"Mauberley," 125
Mauberley (*see Hugh Selwyn Mauberley*)
"Medallion," 54-55
Metamorphoses (Ovid), 68
Miles, Josephine, 154
Miner, Earl, 6
"Mr. Nixon," 34
Monet, Claude, 106
Monroe, Harriet, 2, 147, 167, 173
Montaigne, Michel de, 162, 164
Montherlant, Henri de, 93
More, Paul, 19

Moritake, 116-17
Morris, William, 27
Mozart, Wolfgang Amadeus,
 129
"Mr. Nixon," 34
Musical influences, in Pound's work,
 6, 129-41, 156
 in *The Cantos*, 135-41
Mussolini, Benito, 2, 7, 61, 62, 82,
 83

N

"Na Audiart," 133
"Near Perigord," 125
"Needle, The," 45

O

Odyssey (Homer), myths of, in
 The Cantos, 5, 9, 11-12, 58-61, 64-
 79, 85
"Out of the Cradle Endlessly Rocking"
 (Whitman), 165, 166-67
Ovid, 68

P

Packet for Ezra Pound, A (Yeats), 80
"Papyrus," 135
Pater, Walter, 156
"Patria Mia," 163
Pearce, Roy Harvey, 7
Personae, 1, 28, 132 (*see also*
 *Homage to Sextus Propertius; Hugh
 Selwyn Mauberley;* titles of indi-
 vidual poems)
 haiku imagery in, 121-25
Picasso, Pablo, 108, 109
Pindar, 47
Pisan Cantos, 2, 5, 8, 40, 44, 52*n*, 58,
 62-63, 74-79, **80-86**, 90, 94, 126,
 141, 175
Plarr, Victor, 49
Poe, Edgar Allan, 17
Poetry of Ezra Pound, The (Kenner),
 81, 96, 157, 161
Polite Essays, 150

Porteus, Hugh Gordon,
 62
*Portrait of the Artist as a Young Man,
 A* (Joyce), 20
Pound, Ezra:
 aestheticism of, 30-32, 34
 biographical information, 1-2, 18-
  19
 and Browning, Robert, 7, 8, 17, 28,
  39, 87, 125, 158
 contemporary reception of,
  2
 as a critic, 20-23, 157
 and Eliot, T. S., 2, 3-4, 7, 10, 17-
  25, 26-27, 30, 37-38, 40, 42-43,
  84, 88, 96-97, 125, 132, 142-43,
  144, 149, 150, 156-62 *passim*
 and Flaubert, 43, 44, 46-47
 and *haiku* imagery, use of, 115-28
 and Imagism, 2, 6, 19-20, 105,
  117-28, 172
 influence of, 19-24, 26-27, 37,
  142, 143
 and Joyce, James, 2, 20, 43-44,
  137-39
 masks, theory of, 1-2, 41, 43,
  143-44, 146, 158-59
 musical influences on, 6, **129-41,**
  156
 political and economic views, 2, 8,
  40, 61, 62-63, 80, 90, 94, 97,
  100-114, 149-50, 153
 and Provençal love poetry, 21, 28,
  87, 123, **130-134**
 rhythm, use of, 32, 134-37, 155
 speech idiom, use of, 12-14, 29
 as a translator, 1-2, 6, 87, 142,
  143
 and *vers libre* techniques, 135-36
 Victorian romanticism of, 27-28
 and Vorticism, 2, 6, 118-19, 120-
  121, 172
 and Whitman, Walt, 163-77 *passim*
 and Williams, William Carlos, 2, 3
 and Yeats, William Butler, 3, 9-10,
  17, 24, 27, 28, 29, 80, 87, 91, 97,
  120, 134, 138, 143, 158, 160,
  162

Pound, Ezra, works by:
POETRY
"Age Demanded, The," 36
"Alba," 122, 153-54
"April," 122
"Art, L', 1910," 121, 122
"Bath Tub, The," 123
Cantos, The, 1-8 *passim,* 11-16, 23,
   44, 52, 56, 57-63, 64-79, 87-96,
   160-162 (*see also* main entry)
Cathay, 44
"Coming of War, The: Actaeon,"
   123
"Brennbaum," 49
"Dum Capitolium Scandet,"
   122
"Encounter, The," 125
"Envoi," 34-35, 50, 54, 160
"E.P. Ode Pour L'Election de son
   Sepulchre," 45, 54, 148, 159
"Fan-Piece, for her Imperial Lord,"
   124
"Fish and Shadow," 125
"Gentildonna," 45, 122
Hommage to Sextus Propertius, 4,
   19, 23, 41, 44, 142-51
Hugh Selwyn Mauberley, 1, 2, 4,
   19, 27-36, 39-40, 41-56, 87, 88,
   144-51 *passim,* 159-60
"In a Station at the Metro," 120,
   121
"Liu Ch'e," 123-24
Lume Spento, A, 1
Lustra, 28-29, 44, 121, 133
"Mauberley," 125
"Medallion," 54-55
"Mr. Nixon," 34
"Na Audiart," 133
"Near Perigord," 125
"Needle, The," 45
"Papyrus," 135
"Patria Mia," 163
Personae, 1, 28, 132 (see also *Hugh
   Selwyn Mauberley; Homage to
   Sextus Propertius;* titles of
   individual poems)
"Provincia Deserta," 135
Ripostes, 121, 133

"River Merchant's Wife, The,"
   159
Seafarer, The, 44
"Sestina: Altaforte," 133
"Siena mi fe'; disfecemi Maremma,"
   33-34
"Shop Girl," 125
"Tame Cat," 125
"To Whistler, American," 118
"Winter is icummen in," 134
"Women Before a Shop," 121,
   122
"Yeux Glauques," 33, 48
PROSE
ABC of Reading, 164
Date Line, 21-22
"Edward Wadsworth, Vorticist,"
   118
Guide to Kulchur, 130, 139, 168,
   169
Make It New, 21, 91
Polite Essays, 150
Spirit of Romance, The, 157, 169
Stray Document, A, 21, 22
"Vorticism," 119
OPERA
Testament, Le, 129
Poussin, Nicolas, 106
Primer of Ezra Pound, A (Rosenthal),
   5
*Propertius (see Homage to Sextus
   Propertius)*
Proust, Marcel, 89
Provençal love poetry, Pound's
   interest in, 21, 28, 87, 123, 130-
   134
"Provincia Deserta," 135

R

Ransom, John Crowe, 167
Read, Forrest, 5
Realism vs. nominalism, in *The Cantos,*
   100-114
Remembrance of Things Past, The
   (Proust), 89
"Return, The" (Yeats), 160
Révolte poetry, *The Cantos* as, 91-97

Rhythm, Pound's use of, 32, 134-37, 155

Riethmuller, Richard Henry, 165

Rimbaud, Arthur, 92, 95

Ripostes, 121, 133 (*see also* titles of individual poems)

"River Merchant's Wife, The," 159

Robbins, Russell, 96

Rosenthal, M. L., 5

Rossetti, D. G., 33, 48

Rousseau, Jean-Jacques, 136

S

Sappho, 60

Schafer, Murray, 6

Schoenberg, Arnold, 131

Schubert, Franz, 131

Seafarer, The, 44

Season in Hell, A (Rimbaud), 92

Section: Rock Drill (Cantos), 62-63, 175-76

"Sestina: Altaforte," 133

"Shop Girl," 125

"Siena me fe'; disfecemi Maremma," 33-34

Sitwell, Edith, 133

Song for Simeon, A (Eliot), 30

Song of Myself (Whitman), 168

Speech idiom, Pound's use of, 12-14, 29

Speech rhythms, in *The Cantos,* 12-14

Spenser, Edmund, 155

Spirit of Romance, The, 157, 169

Stravinsky, Igor, 135, 136

Stray Document, A, 21, 22

Sullivan, J. P., 6

"Sweeney Among the Nightingales" (Eliot), 159

Swinburne, Algernon, 27, 48

T

Tagore, Rabindranath, 131

"Tame Cat," 125

Tarr (Lewis), 20

Tate, Allen, 88, 169

Testament, Le, 129

Theocritus, 166

Thirty Years View (Benton), 175

Thrones, 63, 138, 152-53

"To Whistler, American," 118

Tradition and Individual Talent (Eliot), 142-43

Translation, Pound's work in, 1-2, 6, 87, 142, 143

Troubadors (*see* Provençal love poetry)

T.S. Eliot Myth, The (Robbins), 96

U

Ulysses (Joyce), 43-44, 46, 137-38

Usura (*see* Political and economic views)

V

Valéry, Paul, 21, 24

"Vanity of Human Wishes, The" (Johnson), 151

Vers libre techniques, Pound's use of, 135-36

Victorian romanticism, in Pound's work, 27-28

Villon, François, 46, 131

Vivaldi, Antonio, 129

Vorticism, 1, 2, 6, 118-19, 120-121, 172

W

Waller, Edmund, 160

Waste Land, The (Eliot), 19, 26, 38-39, 96, 125, 132, 144, 149, 150

Watts, Harold H., 6

Whitman, Walt, 17, 20, 22, 23, 163-77 *passim*

Williams, William Carlos, 2, 3

"Winter is icummen in," 134

Winters, Yvor, 42

"Women Before a Shop," 121, 122

Works and Days (Hesiod), 73

Y

Yeats, William Butler, 3, 9-10, 17, 24, 27, 28, 29, 80, 87, 91, 120, 134, 138, 143, 158, 160, 162

"Yeux Glauques," 33, 48

PROUST

A Collection of Critical Essays
Edited by RENÉ GIRARD

A

Additions au journal (Saint-Simon),
49
Agostinelli, Albert, 86
Alain (*pseud.* Émile Chartier), 144
Arabian Nights, 169
Aristocarcy, values of, 48, 50, 69-87
passim
Art, theme of, 10, 26, 37, 48, 54-55,
56, 57, 109, 110, 114, 116-17, 118,
124, 131
Artist, theme of, 54, 56, 58, 105, 109,
114, 115, 118-19
Auden, W. H., 28
Augustine, St., 107
Aurevilly, J. Barbey d', 67

B

Balzac, Honoré de, 30, 31, 32, 33, 35,
41, 55, 56, 65, 109, 110, 111, 112,
118, 124
Barres, A. M., 40, 42, 59
Baudelaire, Charles, 34, 39, 55, 56,
57, 60, 67, 127, 172, 177
Beethoven, Ludwig van, 56, 61,
90
Bell, Clive, 28
Bergson, Henri, 34, 38, 39, 45, **122-29,**
133, 172, 173
Bibesco, Princess, 162
Bible of Amiens (Ruskin), 16, 53, 64,
66

Billy, Robert de, 16, 23
Blanche, Jacques-Emile, 60
Blarenberghe, Henri van, 23, 25
Boileau, Nicolas, 60
Bois, E. -J., 63
Bos, Charles du, 12, 148
Bosanquet, B., 108
Bossuet, Bishop, 47, 62
Boston Adventure (Stafford), 34
Botticelli, 110
Boulenger, Jacques, 44
Bourgeois values, 69, 71, 76
Bourget, Paul, 35, 59, 157
Brabant, Geneviève de, 88, 113,
152

C

Cabalists, 89
Cailleux, Roland, 33
Calmette, Gaston, 23
Captive, The (La Prisonnière), 29, 36,
67, 97
Carlyle, Thomas, 26
Carmina burana, 100
Cattaui, Georges, 11
Cézanne, Paul, 34, 40, 120
Chardin, J. B. S., 40, 64
Charpentier, Gustave, 98
Chateaubriand, F. R. de, 29, 40, 55
*Cities of the Plain (Sodome et Gomor-
rhe),* 11
Claudel, Paul, 38
Coleman, Elliott, 11

Coleridge, S. T., 39, 119
"Combray," 111, 112-15, 116
Comédie humaine (Balzac), 31
Compagnie des Chemins de Fer de l'Est, 23
Comte, Auguste, 38
Condillac, E. B. de, 150, 160
Contre Sainte-Beuve (on *Art and Literature*), 9, 57, 58n, 67, 111, 120
Corydon (Gide), 31
Crémieux, Benjamin, 104-5
Crime and Punishment (Dostoevsky), 9
Critical writings, 14, 53-68, 112
Curtius, Ernst Robert, 55

D

Dante, 11, 12, 121
Daudet, Léon, 16
Daudet, Lucien, 32
Débats, 22
Debussy, Claude, 34
Descartes, René, 38, 144, 150, 176, 177
Desgranges, J. C. L. P., 98
Desire, metaphysical, 2, 4, 8, 9, 126, 162
Dewey, John, 38
Dickens, Charles, 36, 41
Diderot, Denis, 34
Divine Comedy (Dante), 10
Don Quixote (Cervantes), 9
Données immédiates, Les (Time and Free Will), (Bergson), 39
Dostoevski, F., 5, 6, 9, 12, 30, 31, 37, 41, 55, 56, 65, 67
Dreyfus, Alfred, 14, 78

E

Education sentimentale, L' (Flaubert), 42
Einführung in der Metaphysik (Heidegger), 107
Einsame, Der (Rilke), 104
Eliot, George, 55

Eliot, T. S., 34
English Tribute, An, 28
Eroticism, theme of, 2, 6, 31, 85-87, 97, 114
Essays (Montaigne), 51
Europe, 34
Evolution Créatrice, L' (Creative Evolution) (Bergson), 39, 122
Eyeless in Gaza (Huxley), 28-29

F

Fallois, M., 67
Faubourg St. Germain, 31, 70-87 *passim*
Faulkner, William, 31
Fernandez, Ramon, 6
Figaro, Le, 9, 14, 22, 23, 24, 67
Finnegans Wake (Joyce), 115
Flaubert, Gustave, 9, 30, 35, 42, 44, 55, 57, 62, 65, 66, 67
Flers, Robert de, 25
Form, 10, 12, 96, 104-9, 111, 114-19, 176-77
Forster, E. M., 36
Foire sur la place (Rolland), 49
France, Anatole, 35, 47, 60
François le champi (Sand), 113, 115
Freud, Sigmund, 34, 38, 116

G

Gaigneron, Jean, 105
Galileo, 40
Genet, Jean, 30
Gerold, M., 102
Gide, André, 29, 31, 34
Gilbert le Mauvais, 106, 117
Gilson, Étienne, 39
Gnosticism, 89
Goethe, J. W. von, 89, 152
Gougenheim, M., 98
Gramont, Corisande, 18
Gramont, Duchesse de, 18
Grève des forgerons, 49
Guedella, Philip, 28

H

Haggada, 90
Hardy, Thomas, 56, 67, 118
Hegel, G. W. F., 38, 90, 107, 108
Heidegger, Martin, 107, 108
Hérodiade (Mallarmé), 49
Hopkins, G. M., 90
Hudson, Stephen, 31, 34
Hugo, Victor, 55, 60, 62, 168
Hume, David, 108
Humières, Robert d', 16
Husserl, Edmund, 119
Huxley, Aldous, 28

I

Illusions perdues, Les (Balzac), 110, 112
Imagery, 52, 54, 86, 96, 105, 107, 113, 118, 119, 120-21, 123, 152
  architectural, 107-8, 114, 120, 176
  floral, 92, 94-97, 114-15, 162-63, 165
  religious, 2, 6, 7, 11, 58, 88, 92-96, 97
Imagination, 39-40, 113, 117, 125, 165-67
Ingres, J. A. D., 60

J

James, Henry, 234
James, William, 116
Jammes, Francis, 55
Jean-Christophe (Rolland), 49
Jean Santeuil, 7-10, 62, 117
Jenseits des Lustprinzips (Freud), 116
Joubert, Joseph, 176
Joyce, James, 29, 34, 40

K

Kafka, Franz, 29, 32, 34
Kant, Immanuel, 107
Kepler, J., 40

Kierkegaard, Sören, 90, 106, 108, 130, 162
King Lear (Shakespeare), 109

L

La Bruyère, 32
Language, 36, 62, 63, 96, 98-103
Langue populaire dans le premier quart du XIXe siècle, La (Gougenheim), 98
Larousse du XXe siècle, 99
Lauris, Georges de, 25
Lawrence, D. H., 28
Lecture, Une (Cailleux), 33
Letters from Iceland (Auden and MacNeice), 28
Levin, Harry, 56
Littré, M. P. E., 132
Loti, Pierre, 157
Louise (Charpentier), 98
Love, theme of, 48, 109, 114, 116-17, 118, 122, 158

M

Mackenzie, Compton, 28
Macksey, Richard, 7
MacNeice, Louis, 28
Madame Bovary (Flaubert), 42
Madaule, Jacques, 90
Maeterlinck, Maurice, 35, 55, 62
Mallarmé, Stéphane, 34, 47, 49, 88, 155
Malraux, André, 66
Matière et mémoire (Matter and Memory) (Bergson), 38, 127
Matisse, Henri, 34
Maurois, André, 105
Mélanges litteraires (Paris), 99
Mémoires (Saint-Simon), 49, 51
Memory, centrality of, 6, 7, 11, 20, 22, 37, 38, 40, 51, 55, 58, 93, 106-7, 112, 115, 123-31 *passim*, 138-39, 144, 156-77
Meno (Plato), 128
Meredith, George, 143, 144, 146
Metamorphoses (Ovid), 89

Method, 35-38, 43-46, 80-84, 112-15
  repetition, 2, 3, 5, 7, 8, 35, 82,
    83, 84, 115, 126, 127, 128, 130,
    166
  paired opposites, 8, 49, 97, 105-21
    passim, 115-17, 119, 124
Michaud, Régis, 101*n*
Middlemarch (Eliot), 26
Montaigne, Michel de, 1, 29, 39, 49,
  52, 140
Montesquiou, Robert de, 15, 18, 20,
  21
Moore, George, 28, 40
Morand, Paul, 41
Mornand, Louisa de, 16, 19
Mortimer, Raymond, 37
Motifs, recurrent (*see also* Method),
  56, 64, 65, 67, 88
  enchanted garden, 4, 5, 7, 8
  hawthorns, 56, 92-93, 114-15,
    165
  madeleine, 4, 11, 54, 56, 93, 96,
    104, 114, 115, 125, 157
  petite phrase, 35, 36, 56, 95, 110,
    111, 116, 118-19, 166, 168
Murry, J. Middleton, 28
Musique au moyen âge, La (Gerold),
  102

N

Narrative devices, 35, 97-103, 107-12,
  147
Newman, John Cardinal, 138, 142,
  143, 144, 146
Newton, Isaac, 40
Nerval, G. de, 55, 89
Nietzsche, F., 5, 90, 108
"Night Watch" (Rembrandt), 30
Noailles, Comtesse Hélie de, 18
Noailles, Comtesse Mathieu de, 18, 19,
  20, 21
Nordlinger, Marie, 16, 17, 23
Nourritures terrestres, Les (Gide), 53

O

Olsen, Regina, 130

On Art and Literature, 9
"On Reading," 22
Orphism, 89
Ortega y Gasset, José, 41
Ovid, 89

P

Panofsky, Erwin, 111
Paris, Gaston, 99, 100
Parmenides (Plato), 128
Pascal, Blaise, 55, 90
*Past Recaptured, The (Le Temps re-
  trouvé),* 7, 9, 10, 11, 18, 35, 55, 68,
    105, 118, 126
Pater, Walter, 40
*Pensée et le mouvant, La (The Creative
  Mind)* (Bergson), 38, 39
Petit Dictionnaire du peuple
  (Desgranges), 98
Petites Vieilles, Les (Baudelaire),
  56
Peyre, Henri, 12
Phrases-types, 56, 64, 65, 67, 88
Pierre-Quint, Léon, 34, 54
Plato, 11, 34, 40, 57, 107, 128, 129
Pleasure, quest for, 69-70, 79-81, 84,
  111
*Pleasures and Regrets (Les Plaisirs et
  les jours),* 7, 47, 167, 174
Poe, E. A., 39
Poulet, Georges, 11, 12, 112, 113,
  120
Prelude (Wordsworth), 128
Propos de peintre (Blanche), 57, 60
Proudhon, P. J., 108
Proust, Madame (mother), 17, 18, 19
Proust, Marcel:
  and art, 55-58, 64-68, 96, 109, 116,
    120-21, 129-30
  biographical information, 1, 10, 13-
    27, 65-66, 145
  and Christianity, 2, 11-12, 14, 156
  critical response to, 28-33
  esthetics of, 35, 37, 41, 53-68 *pas-
    sim,* 85, 117
  and French literary tradition, 44-45,
    49-52, 135

Proust, Marcel: (*continued*)
  and homosexuality, 1, 14, 30
  literary criticism of, 14, 53-68,
    112
  literary influence of, 33-34, 45
  moral vision of, 12, 39, 87, 134,
    136-49
  psychological insight of, 37, 50,
    52, 119-21, 137-40 *passim*,
    147-49, 156-59
  and soul, idea of, 139-40
Proust, Marcel, works by:
  Contre Sainte-Beuve, 9, 57, 58*n*,
    67, 111, 120
  Jean Santeuil, 7-10, 62, 117
  "On Reading," 22
  *Pleasures and Regrets (Les Plaisirs et
    les jours)*, 7, 47, 167, 174
  *Remembrance of Things Past (A la
    Recherche du temps perdu)*, 1-12
    passim, 22, 27, 28, 34, 43, 52,
    54, 56, 62, 63, 67, 68, 77, 90, 92,
    96, 104, 111, 123, 134
  *Swann's Way (Du Côté de chez
    Swann)*, 29, 48, 63, 105, 109,
    115, 133
    "Combray," 111, 112-15, 116
    "Swann in Love," 111, 115-16
    133
  *Within a Budding Grove (A
    L'ombre des jeunes filles en
    fleurs)*, 31, 48
  *Cities of the Plain (Sodome et
    Gomorrhe)*, 11
  Captive, The (La prisonnière),
    29, 36, 67, 97
  *Past Recaptured, The (Le temps
    retrouvé)*, 7, 9, 10, 11, 18, 35,
    45, 63, 68, 105, 118, 126
Proust, Robert (brother), 17
Psychologie de l'art (Malraux),
  66

Q

*Quest for Time Lost (Remembrance
  of Things Past)*, 123, 126

R

Racine, 32, 44, 55, 60, 117
*Refrain in der französichen Chanson,
  Der* (Thurau), 99
Régnier, Henri de, 35
Regnard, J. F., 60
Rembrandt, 30, 64
Remembrance of Things Past, 1-12
  passim, 22, 27, 28, 34, 43, 52, 54,
  56, 62, 63, 67, 68, 77, 90, 92, 96,
  104, 111, 123, 134
*Renaissance politique, littéraire,
  artistique*, 62
Renan, J. E., 65
Renoir, P. A., 61
Ribot, T. A., 157
Rilke, Rainer Maria, 89, 104
Rimbaud, Arthur, 168
Rire, Le (Bergson), 38
Rivière, Jacques, 10, 12, 40, 104,
  116
Rolland, E., 100
Rolland, Romain, 49
Romanticism, 12, 39, 40, 45, 89, 90,
  125, 129, 177
Rosny, J. H., 60
Rougemont, Denis de, 88
Rousseau, Jean-Jacques, 39, 62, 108,
  160
Rozière, Madame de, 25
Ruskin, John, 1, 14, 16, 22, 26, 55,
  57, 63, 66, 105

S

Sainte-Beuve, C. A., 55, 56, 57, 67
Saint-Simon, Duc de, 32, 49, 50, 51,
  65
Samain, Albert, 35
Sand, Georges, 6, 67
Sartre, Jean-Paul, 34, 90, 106
Schiff, Sidney, 31
Schelling, F. W. J. von, 34
Schopenhauer, Arthur, 34, 40, 117,
  129
Sesame and Lilies (Ruskin), 22
Singleton, Charles S., 10

Smith, Logan Pearsall, 28
Snobbery, theme of, 2, 3, 4, 7, 8, 30, 76, 79, 106
Social ambition, theme of, 2-5, 32, 38, 69-76, 78-80, 85-87, 111
Socrates, 128
Sophist (Plato), 107
Souday, Paul, 31
Spinoza, B., 128-29
Stafford, Jean, 34
Stendhal, 42, 67, 117
Stevenson, R. L., 65
Straus, Madame E., 17, 18, 20, 21
Strauss, Walter, 121
"Structure de *Swann*" (Vigneron), 113*n*
Style, 50-52, 107, 132-35
"Swann in Love," 111, 115-16, 133
Swann's Way (Du Côté de chez Swann), 29, 48, 63, 105, 109, 115, 133
Symbolism, 12, 35, 43, 90, 92-96
Symons, Arthur, 28

T

Taine, Hippolyte, 157
Temps, 63
Tendres Stocks (Morand), 41, 60, 61
Themes, major, 54, 114
   art, 10, 26, 37, 48, 54-55, 56, 57, 109, 110, 114, 116-17, 118, 124, 131
   love, 48, 109, 114, 116-17, 118, 122, 158
   time, 2, 6, 44, 55, 58, 89, 92, 96, 104-21, 108, 115, 119, 122-31 *passim*, 133, 143-44, 150-77
Thibaudet, Albert, 12
Thousand and One Nights, 172

Thurau, G., 99, 100
Time, theme of, 2, 6, 44, 55, 58, 89, 92, 96, 104-21, 108, 115, 119, 122-31 *passim*, 133, 143-44, 150-77
Tolstoy, Leo, 41, 55
Traherne, Thomas, 114
True Story, A (Hudson), 34

V

Valéry, Paul, 38, 47, 48, 49, 88, 89, 150, 177
Vermeer, 54, 55, 64
Vigneron, Robert, 9, 113
Vingtième siècle (Michaud), 101*n*
Vogüé, C. J. M., Marquis de, 59
Voiture, 47
Voltaire, 51

W

Wagner, Richard, 35, 61, 124
Walküre, Die (Wagner), 61
Waugh, Alec, 28
Weil, Louis, 22
Weil, Simone, 10, 90
Wharton, Edith, 31
Widmer, Dr., 15, 17
Wilde, Oscar, 110
Wilson, Edmund, 35
Within a Budding Grove (A L'ombre des jeunes filles en fleurs), 31, 48
Wordsworth, William, 125

Y

Yeats, William Butler, 34
Yturri, Gabriel de, 15, 16

RESTORATION DRAMATISTS

A Collection of Critical Essays

Edited by EARL MINER

A

Absolom and Achitophel (Dryden),
5
Addison, Joseph, 61, 173
All for Love (Dryden), 14-15, 17, 37,
38, 47-48, 49, 51-62
Ambitious Stepmother, The (Rowe),
61
Annus Mirabilis (Dryden), 11, 35,
46
Antony and Cleopatra (Shakespeare),
17, 51-53, 55-56, 58, 60
Aristotle, 99, 140
Atheist, The (Otway), 120
Aureng-Zebe (Dryden), 14, 22-24,
27-30, 33, 34, 35, 37-49, 51-53, 59-
60, 140-141
Austen, Jane, 6

B

Barry, Elizabeth, 15, 16
Beaumont, Francis, 2
Beaux' Strategem, The (Farquhar),
4
Behn, Aphra, 10, 121
Booth, Barton, 14, 16
Boyle, Roger, Earl of Orrery, 19,
44
Buckingham, Duke of (*see* Villiers,
George)
Bunyan, John, 166
Burney, Fanny, 6

C

Calderón de la Barca, Pedro, 107
Cavendish, William, Duke of
Newcastle, 2
Charles I, 105
Charles II, 2, 174
Chaucer, Geoffrey, 4
Chekhov, Anton, 64, 76
Chrétien de Troyes, 109
Cibber, Colley, 13-16, 69, 106
Clifford, Martin, 20
Coleridge, Samuel Taylor, 156
Collier, Jeremy, 5, 61, 168
Comical Revenge, The (see *Love in a
Tub*)
Congreve, William, 1-4, 7, 13, 85, 123,
151-64, 165-74
and Addison, Joseph, 173
and Coleridge, Samuel Taylor, 156
and Dennis, John, 155
and Etherege, Sir George, 115, 122,
124, 161-62, 166, 171, 172
and Locke, John, 155
neoplatonism of, 155
and Pope, Alexander, 174
and Shakespeare, William, 151, 153
and Wycherley, William, 110,
116-17, 122, 153, 164
Congreve, William, works by:
Double-Dealer, The, 164, 173
Love for Love, 151-64, 165, 166
Old Batchelour, The, 7, 12-13, 115,
154, 157, 162-63, 165, 173

Congreve, William, works by:
(*continued*)
"To Doria," 157-58
Way of the World, The, 1, 9, 153,
164, **165-74**
Conquest of Granada, The (Dryden),
11, 13, 19-21, **23-27**, 30, 32-33, 34,
35, 39, 46, 57, 59, 60
Cooper, Anthony Ashley, Earl of
Shaftesbury, 143
Cooper's Hill (Denham), 44, 45
Corneille, Pierre, 39
Country Wife, The (Wycherley), 1, 5
106, **110-14**, 118, 121, 132
Crowne, John, 19, 120, 121

D

D'Avenant, Sir William, 45, 46
"Defense of an Essay of Dramatic
Poesie, A" (Dryden), 46
Denham, Sir John, 14, 45
Dennis, John, 155
Descartes, René, 140
Donne, John, 99-100
Don Quixote (Cervantes), 166
Don Sebastian (Dryden), 14-16
Double-Dealer, The (Congreve),
164, 173
Dryden, John, 1, 3-5, 7, 9, 11, 13-14,
16, 17, **19-35**, **37-49**, **51-62**, 135
and Corneille, Pierre, 39
and Etherege, Sir George, 83
and Otway, Thomas, 145
parody, use of, 26
religious beliefs, 21-22
rhyme, use of, **43-47**
scepticism of, **21-24**
and Shakespeare, William, 21, 34,
47, 51-53, 55-56, 58, 60
tragedy, theory of, 140-141
and Wycherley, William, 106
Dryden, John, works by:
Absolom and Achitophel, 5
All for Love, 14-15, 17, 37, 38, 47-
48, 49, **51-62**
Annus Mirabilis, 11, 35, 46
Aureng-Zebe, 14, 22-24, 27-30, 33,

34, 35, **37-49**, 51-53, 59-60,
140-41
Conquest of Granada, The, 11, 13,
19-21, **23-27**, 30, 32-33, 34, 35,
39, 46, 57, 59, 60
"Defense of an Essay of Dramatic
Poesie, A," 46
Don Sebastian, 14-16
Evening's Love, An, 109-10
Hind and the Panther, The,
22, 35
Indian Emperor, The, 21, 31-32,
34, 38, 40
Indian Queen, The (with Howard),
23, 34, 37
Mac-Flecknoe, 35
Marriage a-la-mode, 4, 12
Of Dramatic Poesie, 45
"Parallel of Poetry and Painting,
A," 51
Rival Ladies, The, 44-46
St. Cecelia Odes, The, 2
Secret Love, 106, 109
Sir Martin Mar-all (with Cavendish),
2
Spanish Friar, The, 12
State of Innocence, The, 22
Troilus and Cressida, 47, 48-49, 61,
140
Tyrannic Love, 21, 27, 30, 34

E

Etherege, Sir George, 2, 3, 5, 7, 45,
63-85, 123
Christianity of, 98-99, 101-2
comic theory of, **63-65**
and Congreve, William, 115, 122,
124, 161-62, 166, 171, 172
and Dryden, John, 83
and Hobbes, Thomas, 97, 98,
102
and Jonson, Ben, 46, 63
language, use of, 87-99, 102-3
and Machiavelli, Niccoló, 93, 97,
98, 102
and Middleton, Thomas, 63, 66
and Molière, 69

Etherege, Sir George, (*continued*)
  and Otway, Thomas, 121
  and Shadwell, Thomas, 105
  and Shakespeare, William, 64
  and Steele, Sir Richard, 85
  wit of, **99-102**
  and Wycherley, William, 105,
    106-8, 110, 111, 114-15, 116,
    118-22, 126
Etherege, Sir George, works by:
  Love in a Tub, 64, **65-70**, 73, 83,
    105, 106
  Man of Mode, The, 1, 7, 64, 68,
    70, **76-85**, **89-94**, 97-99, 101,
    102, 105, 110, 114-15, 116, 121,
    160, 171
  She Wou'd if She Cou'd, **70-76**,
    78, 83, **94-95**, 96, 101, 105, 110
Euripides, 61
Evelina (Burney), 6
Evelyn, John, 8
Evening's Love, An (Dryden), 109-10

F

Fair Penitent, The (Rowe), 15
False One, The (Fletcher and Massin-
  ger), 56
Farquhar, George, 2, 3, 4, 7
Fletcher, John, 2, 46, 56
Four New Plays (Howard), 41, 45
Freud, Sigmund, 99
Friendship in Fashion (Otway),
  120-21

G

Gentleman Dancing Master, The
  (Wycherley), 105, **107-10**, 115

H

Hamlet (Shakespeare), 153
Henry IV (Shakespeare),
  101, 132
Henry V (Boyle), 19
Hind and the Panther, The (Dryden),
  22, 35

*History of Charles the Eighth of
  France, The* (Crowne), 19
Hobbes, Thomas, 10, 97, 98,
  102
Horace, 16
Howard, Sir Robert, 34, 41, 45

I

Indian Emperor, The (Dryden), 21,
  31-32, 34, 38, 40
Indian Queen, The (Dryden and
  Howard), 23, 34, 37

J

Johnson, Samuel, 20, 37, 99, 156
Jonson, Ben, 2, 9, 46, 63, 64, 100
Juvenal, 124, 127-28, 136

K

Kierkegaard, Sören, 154
Kynaston, Edward, 4, 16

L

Lamb, Charles, 6
Lee, Nathaniel, 15, 16, 49, 120,
  121
Lives of the Poets (Cibber), 69
Locke, John, 155
Love for Love (Congreve), **151-64**,
  165, 166
Love in a Tub (Etherege), 64, **65-70**,
  73, 83, 105, 106
Love in a Wood (Wycherley), 105,
  106-7, 110, 165
Love's Labour's Lost
  (Shakespeare), 110

M

Mac-Flecknoe (Dryden), 35
Machiavelli, Niccoló, 93, 97, 98, 102,
  113-14
Maestro de Danzar, El (Calderón), 107

Mandragola, La (Machiavelli), 113

Man of Mode, The (Etherege), 1, 7, 64, 68, 70, 76-85, 89-94, 97-99, 101, 102, 105, 110, 114-15, 116, 160, 171

Marlowe, Christopher, 27, 61

Marriage a-la-mode (Dryden), 4, 12

Massinger, Philip, 56

Middleton, Thomas, 63, 66

Midsummer-Night's Dream, A (Shakespeare), 151

Milton, John, 17, 149

Misanthrope, The (Molière), 114, 117-18

Molière, 69, 114, 115, 117-18

Mustapha (Boyle), 19

N

Newcastle, Duke of (*see* Cavendish, William)

O

Oedipus (Lee), 15

Of Dramatic Poesie (Dryden), 45

Old Batchelour, The (Congreve), 7, 12-13, 115, 154, 157, 162-63, 165, 173

Oroonoko (Southerne), 10, 12

Orphan, The (Otway), 15

Orrery, Earl of (*see* Boyle, Roger)

Otway, Thomas, 2, 15, 16-17, 49, 120, 134-49

    and Cooper, Anthony Ashley, 143

    and Dryden, John, 145

    and Milton, John, 148-49

    morality of, 145

    Platonism of, 141

    and Shakespeare, William, 17, 149

    and Wycherley, William, 120

Otway, Thomas, works by:

    Atheist, The, 120

    Friendship in Fashion, 120-21

    Orphan, The, 15

    Soldier's Fortune, The, 121

Venice Preserv'd, 15, 139-49

Ovid, 46

P

Paradise Lost (Milton), 22

"Parallel of Poetry and Painting, A" (Dryden), 51

Pepys, Samuel, 2, 8, 65

Plain-Dealer, The (Wycherley), 10, 13, 106, 114-22, 123-38, 153, 164

Pope, Alexander, 103, 138, 174

Princess of Cleves (Lee), 120, 121, 122

Prynne, William, 166

Q

Quarles, Francis, 165

R

Recruiting-Officer, The (Farquhar), 2

Rehearsal, The (Villiers *et al.*), 17

Rival Ladies, The (Dryden), 44-46

Rochester, Earl of (*see* Wilmot, John)

Rowe, Nicholas, 15, 61

S

St. Cecelia Odes, The (Dryden), 2

Saintsbury, George, 21, 43

Samson Agonistes (Milton), 17, 54

"Satyr Against Mankind, A" (Wilmot), 119

Scroop, Sir Car, 7

Scudéry, Madelein de, 19

Secret Love (Dryden), 106, 109

Sedley, Sir Charles, 5

Shadwell, Thomas, 2, 7, 105, 115, 116

Shaftesbury, Earl of (*see* Cooper, Anthony Ashley)

Shakespeare, William, 2, 8, 15, 17, 21, 34, 100-101, 110

She Wou'd if She Cou'd (Etherege), 70-76, 78, 83, 94-95, 96, 101, 105, 107, 110

Shakespeare, William (*continued*)
  and Congreve, William, 151, 153
  and Dryden, John, 21, 47, 51-53,
    55-56, 58, 60
  and Etherege, Sir George, 64
  and Otway, Thomas, 17, 149
  and Wycherley, William, 107, 116,
    136-37
Shakespeare, William, works by:
  Antony and Cleopatra, 17, 51-53,
    55-56, 58, 60
  Hamlet, 153
  Henry IV, 101, 132
  Love's Labour, Lost, 110
  Midsummer-Night's Dream, A,
    151
  Taming of the Shrew, The,
    107
  Twelfth Night, 136-37
Sir Fopling Flutter (*see Man of Mode,*
  The)
Sir Martin Mar-all (Dryden and
  Cavendish), 2
Soldier's Fortune, The, (Otway),
  121
Sophocles, 61
Southerne, Thomas, 10, 120
Spanish Friar, The (Dryden), 12
Spectator (Steele), 85
State of Innocence, The (Dryden), 22
Steele, Sir Richard, 61, 85, 106
Suckling, Sir John, 166, 169
Sullen Lovers, The (Shadwell), 115
Swift, Jonathan, 103

T

Taming of the Shrew, The
  (Shakespeare), 107
Temple, Sir Richard, 174
"To Doris" (Congreve), 157-58
Tonson, Jacob, 174
Town Sparks, The (Crowne), 121
Troilus and Cressida (Dryden), 47,
  48-49, 61, 140
Twelfth Night (Shakespeare), 136-37
Tyrannic Love (Dryden), 21, 27, 30,
  34

U

"Upon Nothing" (Wilmot), 119

V

Vanbrugh, Sir John, 3, 9
Venice Preserv'd (Otway), 15, 139-49
Villiers, George, 5
Virgil, 46, 140
Virtuoso, The (Shadwell), 115
Voltaire, 114

W

Waller, Edmund, 44, 45
Way of The World, The (Congreve), 1,
  9, 153, 164, 165-74
Webster, John, 2
Widow Ranter, The (Behn), 10, 12
Wilmot, John, Earl of Rochester, 5, 83,
  85, 118, 122
Wycherley, William, 1, 3, 7, 10, 13, 14,
  105-22, 123-38
  and Calderón de la Barca, Pedro,
    107, 161
  and Cibber, Colley, 126
  and Congreve, William, 110, 116-17,
    122, 153, 164
  and Crowne, John, 120
  and Dryden, John, 106
  and Etherege, Sir George, 105,
    106-8, 110, 111, 114-115, 116,
    118-22, 126
  and Juvenal, 124, 127-28, 136
  and Lee, Nathaniel, 122
  and Machiavelli, Niccoló, 113-14
  and Molière, 114, 115, 117-18
  and Otway, Thomas, 120
  and Pope, Alexander, 138
  satire of, 123-38
  and Shadwell, Thomas, 115, 116
  and Shakespeare, William, 107, 116,
    136-37
  and Southerne, Thomas, 120
  and Steele, Sir Richard, 106
  and Wilmot, John,
    118

Wycherley, William,
  works by:
    Country Wife, The,
      1, 5, 106, **110-14,** 118,
      121, 132
    Gentlemen-Dancing Master,
      The, 105, **107-10,** 115

Love in a Wood, 105, 106-7,
  110, 165
Plain-Dealer, The,
  10, 13, 106, **114-22,**
  123-38, 153, 164

SAMUEL RICHARDSON

A Collection of Critical Essays

Edited by JOHN CARROLL

A

Abrams, M. H., 33
Addison, Joseph, 119
Advance of the English Novel, The
  (Phelps), 5
Age of Innocence, The (Wharton),
  39
Ambassadors, The (James), 1, 2
Amis, Kingsley, 11
Another Pamela (Sinclair), 11
*Apology for the Life of Mrs. Shamela
  Andrews, An* (Fielding), 5, 21, 116,
  120, 162
Aristotle, 119
Aspects of the Novel (Forster), 1
Atheist's Tragedy, The (Tourneur),
  122
Austen, Jane, 19, 136-37, 138, 147,
  161

B

Baker, E. A., 137
Beggars' Opera, The (Gay), 106, 114
Behn, Aphra, 93
Betterton, Thomas, 155
Birch, Thomas, 126
Black, Frank Gees, 140
Blake, William, 11, 23
Blanchard, F. T., 9
Boswell, James, 8, 116, 119, 127
Bradshaigh, Lady, 4, 6, 80, 105, 119,
  120, 164, 166, 175

Brinnin, John Malcolm, 11
British Recluse, The (Haywood),
  94
Brontë, Emily, 72
Brooke, Tucker, 45
Bunyan, John, 114
Burney, Fanny, 132, 147

C

Caesar, 173
Careless Husband, The (Cibber), 4
Catastrophe and Imagination (McCor-
  mick), 91
Cervantes, Miguel de, 140
Chaplin, Charlie, 122
Chapone, Sarah, 165
Characterization by style, 35-37, 95-
  101
Chase Richard, 64
Chaucer, Geoffrey, 41
Cheyne, George, 31
Cibber, Colley, 4, 110
Clarissa Harlowe, 1-19 *passim,* 21, 23,
  30, 33, 38, 39-48 *passim,* 49-66, 67-
  79, 92-101, 124, 128, 129, 131, 136,
  137, 138, 143, 144, 146, 147, 152-60
  passim, 161, 167-80 *passim*
  as myth, 53-66
  social milieu of, 102-133
  structure of, 80-91
"Clarissa Harlowe and Her Times"
  (Hill), 17

Class-interpenetration, theme of, 39-48
passim
Coleridge, S. T., 10, 82, 138
Conjectures (Young), 33
Conrad, Joseph, 55
Conscious Lovers, The (Steele),
125
Cooper, Maria Susannah, 135
Copernicus, 33
Correspondence of Samuel Richardson
(ed. Barbauld), 105, 107, 109, 119,
120, 132, 162, 163, 178

D

Daiches, David, 3, 162, 169
Defoe, Daniel, 42, 47, 115, 118
Demonic, theme of, 15-17, 87-88
Diana of the Crossways (Meredith),
42
Dickens, Charles, 166
Diderot, Denis, 8, 9, 75-76, 122-23,
134
Divided mind, theme of, 18, 146, 176
Divine Comedy (Dante), 41
Dobson, Austin, 10, 161
Dominance-submission, theme of,
164-80 *passim*
Dostoevsky, F., 161
Downs, Brian W., 155*n*
Dreiser, Theodore, 11
Duncombe, William, 128

E

Echlin, Lady, 4
Economic History Review, 103
Edwards, Thomas, 165
Éloge de Richardson (Diderot), 134
"English Landownership, 1680-1740"
(Habakkuk), 103
English Novel, The (Ford), 2
Epistolary form, 6, 10, 12-14, 21-22,
28-35, 49-53, 80, 88, 134, 139-51
antecedents of, 90-97
and point of view, 10, 12-13, 29-
30, 49, 144-46

F

Fable of the Bees, The (Mandeville),
106
Fair Penitent, The (Rowe), 100, 145
Falkland, Viscount, 124
*Familiar Letters on Important Occa-
sions*, 92-93
*Familiar Letters Written for Particular
Friends*, 115, 119
Familie in Puritanismus, Die (Schück-
ing), 116
Family relationships, theme of, 44-46,
61-63, 114-15
Farrell, William, 13
Faulkner, William, 161
Faux-Monnayeurs, Les (Gide), 140
Fiction and the Reading Public
(Leavis), 102
Fiedler, Leslie, 2, 8, 15, 86, 169
Fielding, Henry, 8, 9, 21, 28, 29, 34,
35, 38, 41, 44, 75, 83, 110, 112, 125,
134, 161, 162
Fielding the Novelist (Blanchard),
9
First Impressions (Austen), 137
Fitzgerald, F. Scott, 40
Five Masters (Krutch), 5
Ford, Ford Madox, 2, 7
Form, 7-8, 21-22, 49-51
Forster, E. M., 1
Freud, Sigmund, 75, 178
Freval, J. B. de, 7
"From Pamela to Clarissa" (Sale), 17

G

Garrick, David, 174
Gesture, importance of, 156-60
Giannone, 124
Gide, André, 11, 55-56, 140
Golden, Morris, 16
Grandison, Earl of, 124
Green, F. C., 62
Grove, Henry, 136
Gulliver's Travels (Swift),
106

H

Habakkuk, H. J., 102, 103, 105
Hamlet, 30
Hardy, Thomas, 14, 83
"Harlot's Progress, The" (Hogarth), 106
Haywood, Eliza, 93
Hazlitt, William, 10, 138
Hildesley, Bishop, 33
Hill, Aaron, 3, 6, 8, 80, 81
Hill, Christopher, 17
Hilles, Frederick, 14
History of English Literature (Taine), 5
History of Naples (Giannone), 124
History of the English Novel, The (Baker), 137
History of the English Stage (attrib. to Betterton), 155
Hobbes, Thomas, 122
Hogarth, William, 86
Horace, 34, 75, 90
Howells, William Dean, 39, 40
Hutcheson, Francis, 130

I

Imagery, 51-55, 64-65, 72-75, 90-91
Inquiry into the Original of Our Ideas of Beauty and Virtue (Hutcheson), 130
Introduction to the English Novel, An (Kettle), 107
Isle of Pines, The (Nevill), 114, 120
Isolation, theme of, 113-14, 143-45

J

James, Henry, 1, 2, 3, 7, 8, 39, 40, 42, 43
Johnson, Samuel, 5, 47, 65, 70, 85, 116, 174
Jonathan Wild (Fielding), 106, 111, 114, 173
Joseph Andrews (Fielding), 21, 112, 116

K

Kany, Charles E., 93
Kearney, A. M., 13
Kettle, Arnold, 107, 110, 120
King Lear (Shakespeare), 45
Kinkead-Weekes, M., 12, 14
Krutch, Joseph Wood, 5

L

Lamb, Charles, 138
Language, 24, 29-30, 92, 97-101
Lawrence, D. H., 161
Leavis, Q. D., 102, 107
Letters from a Lady of Quality, The (trans. Haywood), 94-95
Life of Johnson (Boswell), 116, 119
Literary Anecdotes of the 18th Century (Nichols), 110
Locke, John, 32, 114, 117
Loftus, Smyth, 80
Love and Death in the American Novel (Fiedler), 15
Lovejoy, Arthur O,, 164
Lubbock, Percy, 2, 3
Luther, Martin, 120, 121

M

Macauley, Thomas Babington, 9, 10
McCormick, John, 91
McKillop, A. D., 11, 12, 13, 18, 108, 169
Macpherson, P., 117
Mandeville, Bernard de, 41, 109, 110
Marlowe, Christopher, 122
"Marriage à la mode" (Hogarth), 106
"Marriage Settlements in the 18th Century" (Habakkuk), 102-3
Mencken, H. L., 41
Meredith, George, 39, 42, 133
Method, 2, 7, 22-27 *passim*, 29-31, 42-43, 49-53, 76-79, 127, 139-51, 152-60
Miller, Perry, 122

Milton, John, 30, 32, 87, 114, 115, 118, 120
Minuet (Green), 62
Molière, 3
Moll Flanders (Defoe), 52, 57, 115
Montagu, Lady Mary Wortley, 31

N

Narrative devices, 6-8, 10, 18, 37, 43, 50-53, 72, 82-85, 89-90, 128-29, 141-47, 150
Needham, G. B., 106, 118
Neveu de Rameau, Le (Diderot), 76
Nevill, Henry, 114, 120
New England Mind: From Colony to Province, The (Miller), 122
Newgate Calendar, The (anon.), 114
Nichols, J., 110
Notes and Queries, 110
Nouvelle Héloïse, La (Rousseau), 138

O

Oroonoko (Behn), 114

P

Pamela, or Virtue Rewarded, 1-19 passim, 20-27, 28-38, 39-48 passim, 69, 73, 80, 109, 110, 119, 138, 139, 142, 147, 149, 153-60 passim, 167-80 passim
Pamela's Daughters (Utter and Needham), 106
Paradise Lost (Milton), 87, 110, 113, 114
Paul, Saint, 118, 120
Perils of Pauline, The, 85
Persuasion (Austen), 137
Phelps, William Lyon, 5
Pilgrim's Progress (Bunyan), 115
Pilkington, Laetitia, 110
Pope, Alexander, 31
Post, Emily, 41
Praz, Mario, 8, 15, 72
Pride and Prejudice (Austen), 137

Property-marriage, theme of, 102-23 passim
Prose Works (Milton), 118
Puritanism, reflected in works, 21, 57-58, 60, 63, 67-79 passim, 102-23 passim

R

"Rake's Progress, The" (Hogarth), 106
Reid, B. L., 3, 8
Religious Courtship (Defoe), 115
Richardson (Downs), 55, 59
"Richardson and the Bold Young Men" (Golden), 16
Richardson, Samuel:
biographical information, 3-5, 20, 80-81, 106-7, 110, 126, 161-80 passim
critical response to, 7-8, 10-11
didactic purposes of, 5, 25, 32, 37-38, 69, 76, 119-20, 124, 130-31, 160
and eighteenth-century milieu, 17, 33, 39-43, 47, 61, 102-23
influence on later writers, 134-38
and modern novel, 40-42
moral vision of, 16-17, 25-27, 43, 74, 130
popularity of, 9-11, 20-21, 41, 64, 116, 119, 134, 138
psychological understanding of, 8-9, 12, 15-16, 21, 33, 73-75, 161
Richardson, Samuel, works by:
Familiar Letters on Important Occasions, 92-93
Familiar Letters Written for Particular Friends, 115, 119
Clarissa Harlowe, 1-19 passim, 21, 23, 30, 33, 38, 39-48 passim, 49-66, 67-79, 92-101, 124, 128, 129, 131, 136, 137, 138, 143, 144, 146, 147, 152-60 passim, 161, 167-80 passim
Pamela, or Virtue Rewarded, 1-19 passim, 20-27, 28-38, 39-48 passim, 69, 73, 80, 109, 110, 119, 138, 139, 142, 147, 149, 153-60

Richardson, Samuel, works by:
(*continued*)
   passim, 167-80 *passim*
   Sir Charles Grandison, 1, 3, 4, 12,
     17, 18, 25, 36, 45, 61, 80, **124-38**,
     144, 147, 149, 162, 166, 175,
     178
Richardson's Characters (Golden), 16
Rise of the Novel, The (Watt), 16
Robinson Crusoe (Defoe), 114
Romantic Agony, The (Praz), 15
Romanticism, 72, 121
Rousseau, J.-J., 114, 122, 164
Rowe, Nicholas, 100, 145
Roxana (Defoe), 115
Ruskin, John, 10

S

Sade, Marquis de, 9, 72
Sale, W. M., 11, 17
Samuel Richardson (Dobson), 161
Samuel Richardson (McKillop), 108
*Samuel Richardson: A Bibliographical
  Record* (Sale), 11
Sanditon (Austen), 137
Schücking, L. L., 116
Scott, John, 128
Scott, Sir Walter, 10
Selected Letters of Samuel Richardson
  (ed. Carroll), 2, 3, 4, 6, 8, 17, 31, 32,
  33, 34, 37
Sense and Sensibility (Austen), 137
Sentimentalism, 130-34
Sexual conflict, theme of, 15, 18, 26-
  27, 42-43, 49-51, 63-65, 67-79
  passim, 107-8, 167-69
Shakespeare, William, 43, 107
Shelley, Percy B., 121
Sherburn, George, 13
Sinclair, Upton, 11
Sir Charles Grandison, 1, 3, 4, 12, 17,
  18, 25, 36, 45, 61, 80, **124-38**, 144,
  147, 149, 162, 166, 175, 178
Smollett, Tobias, 41
"Social Bearings of Locke's Political
  Theory, The" (Macpherson), 117

Social class, importance of, 35, 37,
  39-40, 57-60, 112-13, 136-37
Sorrows of Young Werther, The
  (Goethe), 138
Sound and the Fury, The (Faulkner),
  39
Spectator, 130
Steel, Richard, 21, 125
Stein, Gertrude, 11
Stephen, Leslie, 10
Terne, Laurence, 8, 33, 127
Stinstra, John, 80, 82, 91, 162, 163
Structure, 14-15, 23-24, **28-38**, **80-91**,
  108, 127
Stuart, Lady Louisa, 138
Style, 13-14, 92-101, 132
Stylistic devices, 13, 19, 31-32, 88-89,
  92, 97-101
Swift, Jonathan, 31, 41, 47, 174

T

Taine, Hippolyte, 5
Taylor, Jeremy, 83
Thackerary, W. M., 9
Thomson, Clara, 10-11, 43, 80
Tom Jones (Fielding), 35, 44
Tourneur, Cyril, 122
Tristram Shandy (Sterne), 33
True Confessions, 54
True Detective Stories, 54
Twain, Mark, 127

U

Unfortunate Mistress, The (Haywood),
  94
Universal Magazine, 166
Utter, R. P., 106, 118

V

Van Ghent, Dorothy, 8, 15-17
Venice Preserved (Otway), 99
Vogue, 54
Voltaire, 147

EDWIN ARLINGTON ROBINSON

A Collection of Critical Essays

Edited by FRANCIS MURPHY

A

"Aaron Stark," 50*n*
Abelard, Peter, 56
Adams, Henry, 49
Adams, Oscar Fay, 104
Adler, Alfred, 93
AE (*see* Russell, George)
Aeschylus, 18
Aiken, Conrad, 5, 14, 123
Aldrich, T. B., 98
"Alice Doane's Appeal" (Hawthorne),
  148
Allen, James Lane, 168
Altar of the Dead, The (James), 15-17
  passim
Amaranth, 64, 99-100, 137
Ambassadors, The (James), 70
"Another Dark Lady," 59
Aquinas, St. Thomas, 55, 163
Arnold, Matthew, 40, 57, 150, 168,
  170
"Atherton's Gambit," 19
Auden, W. H., 101
Avon's Harvest, 15-17, 20, 22, 58,
  59, 86, 112, 114, 115, 141

B

"Ballade of Broken Flutes," 103-5,
  107
Ballades and Rondeaus (White),
  104
Barrett, William, 138

Bates, Esther Willard, 115
Baudelaire, Charles, 43
Bellow, Saul, 127
"Ben Jonson Entertains a Man from
  Stratford," 10, 12, 17, 21, 23, 121,
  132-33
Bergson, Henri, 162
Berthoff, Warner, 7
Bierce, Ambrose, 98
Blackmur, Richard, 5, 96*n*
Blake, William, 49
"Bokardo," 141
Boy's Will, A (Frost), 117
Bradley, Henry, 149
Braithwaite, W. S. B., 117
Bridges, Robert, 40, 57
Brooks, Van Wyck, 69
Browning, Robert, 1, 12, 21, 23, 85,
  107, 113, 116, 169
Bryant's Library of Poetry and Song,
  167
Bunner, H. C., 98
Burr, Aaron, 55
Burroughs, John, 149, 150-51,
  163
Byron, George Gordon, 108, 126

C

"Calverly's," 78-80
Cantos (Pound), 49
"Cap and Bells" (Keats), 16
Captain Craig, 2, 17, 19, 58, 121,
  125-27, 129-31, 132, 135, 140, 147

Carlyle, Thomas, 55
Carpenter, F. I., 153
"Cassandra," 54-55
Cavender's House, 50n, 123n, 141
Cawein, Richard, 98
"Charles Carville's Eyes,"
 125
Chekhov, Anton, 34
Children of the Night, The, 2, 3-4, 10,
 13, 18, 51, 58, 110, 118, 151, 154n,
 176
"Chills and Fever" (Ransom), 166
Chivers, Thomas H., 114
"Christmas Sonnet, A," 59
"Clerks, The," 58, 70-71, 106
"Cliff Klingenhagen," 125
"Clinging Vine, The," 59
Coleridge, Samuel Taylor, 110, 113,
 115
Collected Poems, 4, 6, 22, 82, 84
Columbus, Christopher, 56
"Comedian as the Letter C, The"
 (Stevens), 126
Conrad, Joseph, 32
Cooper, James Fenimore, 3
Cowley, Malcolm, 118, 120
Coxe, Louis, 6, 127, 166
Cozzens, James Gould, 127
Crabbe, George, 23, 31, 37
Crane, Hart, 48, 101
Crane, Stephen, 98
"Credo," 51, 106, 121
Critic, 107
Croce, Benedetto, 9
Crowder, Richard, 98
Cummings, E. E., 98
Cunningham, J. V., 4

D

"Dance, The" (Crane), 48
Dante Alighieri, 100
"Dark Hills," 59, 151
"Dear Friends," 111
De la Mare, Walter, 26, 98
"Demos," 54, 55
"Demos and Dionysus," 54,
 57

Dewey, John, 162
Dickey, James, 6, 7
Dickinson, Emily, 8-9, 98, 110
Dionysus in Doubt, 54, 56, 58,
 59
Discourses (Reynolds), 95
Divine Fire, The (Sinclair), 37
Dobson, Austin, 104
"Doctor of Billiards," 58
Donne, John, 5, 47n, 100, 106,
 167
"Dover Beach" (Arnold), 51
Dowson, Ernest C., 98
Dreiser, Theodore, 98
Dumas, Alexandre, 165
Dunbar, Paul Lawrence, 98

E

Eddy, Mary Baker, 149
Edwards, Jonathan, 53
Eliot, Charles W., 3
Eliot, T. S., 4, 5, 14, 61, 64, 75, 90,
 100-103, 106, 120, 122, 152, 163,
 166
Emerson, Ralph Waldo, 8-9, 44, 48,
 49, 52, 53, 55, 57, 58, 95, 107,
 121, 126, 137, 149, 151, 153
"End of the World" (MacLeish), 161
"En Passant," 50
"Envoi, L'," 112
"Eros Turannos," 12-13, 32, 42, 44,
 58, 61, **64-68**, 70, 71, 125, 139-40,
 151, 172
Essay on Man (Pope), 58

F

"False Gods, The," 99-100
Faulkner, William, 5, 127
Field, Eugene, 98
Fiske, John, 149, 153
"Flammonde," 53-54, 60, 120, 124,
 125, 140, **143-47**
Fletcher, J. G., 43
"For a Dead Lady," 25-26, 42, 44, 58,
 61, 64, 75

Forms of Discovery (Winters), 6
Four Quartets (Eliot), 103
Fowlers, F. G. and H. W., 46-47
Franklin, Benjamin, 49
"Free Man's Worship, A" (Russell), 152
Frost, Robert, 2, 3, 4, 10, 101, 110,
   114, 116, **117-27**, 163, 164, 170
Fussell, Edwin, 7

G

Galileo, 56
"George Crabbe," 58, 107
"Gift of God, The," 61, 62, 71-75,
   172
Gilder, Richard W., 98
Gledhill, Arthur, 159
Gould, Gerald, 13
"Growth of Lorraine," 58
Guiney, Louise Imogen, 1, 98, 110

H

Hagedorn, Hermann, 115-16, 131*n*
Hamilton, Alexander, 55
Hamlet (Shakespeare), 100
Hardy, Thomas, 17, 21, 23, 57, 79,
   85, 98, 101, 110, 117, 169
"Haunted House," 50*n*, 59
Hawthorne, Nathaniel, 5, 25, 117,
   148-49, 163, 168, 169
Hecht, Ben, 115
Hegel, G. W. F., 171-72
Hemingway, Ernest, 98
Hess, Jane, 124
"Hillcrest," 40-41, 42, 44, 57, 58,
   151
*History of the Warfare of Science with
   Theology in Christendom* (White),
   150
Hitler, Adolf, 55
Holmes, Oliver Wendell, 49
Hopkins, Gerard Manley, 87, 91
Horace, 119
"Horace to Leuconoë," 58
"House on the Hill, The," 3, 83-84,
   106, 118-19
Housman, A. E., 110

Hovey, Richard, 98
"How Annendale Went Out," 64
Hugh Selwyn Mauberley (Pound),
   126
Huxley, Aldous, 150

I

Ibsen, Henrik, 95
Iceman Cometh, The (O'Neill), 93,
   127
Ingersoll, Robert, 153
"Isaac and Archibald," 10, 17, 19,
   64, **88-90**, 131, 140, 151, 178-81
Is Life Worth Living? (James), 171,
   175

J

James, Henry, 5, 15, 23-25, 26, 28,
   30, 40, 61, 67
James, William, 7, 81, 133*n*, 149,
   150, 162, 163, 170, 171-73, 175,
   176, 181
Jeffers, Robinson, 31
"Jeu, Le" (Baudelaire), 43
"John Brown," 46
"John Evereldown," 17, 129
"John Gorham," 38, 59
Jude the Obscure (Hardy), 168

K

Kaplan, Estelle, 6, 150*n*, 171
"Karma," 59
Keats, John, 16, 85, 87
Kelly, Robert, 115
King Jasper, 33-39, 75, 122, 141, 151,
   154
Kipling, Rudyard, 98
Krutch, Joseph Wood, 150

L

Lancelot, 10, 16, 20, 22, 24, 26, 84,
   123*n*, 136, 137
Langer, Susanne K., 148, 157*n*, 161
Lanier, Sidney, 110, 117

Last Night, The (Dickinson), 9
Lawrence, D. H., 13
Leonard, William Ellery, 119
Levenson, J. C., 6-7
Light of Day, The (Burroughs), 150
Lincoln, Abraham, 31, 54, 55, 121
Long Day's Journey into Night (O'Neill), 127
Longfellow, Henry Wadsworth, 96, 124n
"Long Race, The," 59
"Lost Anchors," 46, 58
Louis XIV, of France, 57
Lowell, Amy, 2, 43, 98, 100, 118
Lowell, Robert, 127
Lucifer (Santayana), 119
"Luke Havergal," 3, 13, 17, 42, 44, 58, 106, 125
Luther, Martin, 33

M

McClure, Michael, 115
MacDowell, Mrs. Edward, 40
MacLeish, Archibald, 150, 161
Mallarmé, Stéphane, 49
Malory, Sir Thomas, 21, 24, 26, 27
Man Against the Sky, The, 16, 19, 20-23 *passim*, 40, 44, 51, 58, 59, **91-95**, 125, 151, **156-61**, 164-65
Mann, Thomas, 159n
Man Who Died Twice, The, 87, 123n, 140, 176
"Many Are Called," 46-47, 58
Markham, Edwin, 117
"Marquis of Grandvin" (Melville), 126
"Master, The," 54, 58, 121
Masters, Edgar Lee, 13, 64, 98, 100, 118
Matthias at the Door, 86, 123n
Mauriac, François, 79
Mead, George Herbert, 133n
Melville, Herman, 126
Mencken, H. L., 23
Merlin, 10-11, 16, 21, 22, 24, 26, 84, 123n

Mifflin, Lloyd, 98
Miles, Josephine, 7
"Mill, The," 50, 59
Miller, Henry, 127
Miller, Joaquin, 117
"Mills of the Kavanaughs" (Lowell), 127
Milton, John, 100, 106, 126, 168
Mind, Self, and Society (Mead), 133n
"Miniver Cheevey," 13, 58, 60, 151
"Mr. Flood's Party," 38-39, 42, 44, 59, 125
Modern Temper, The (Krutch), 150
"Momus," 107-9
"Monocle de Mon Oncle, Le" (Stevens), 14
Moody, William Vaughan, 98, 110 114, 115, 119
Moore, H. D., 14
Moore, Marianne, 14, 65
Morris, William, 26
Morris, Wright, 127
"Mortmain," 82
Moulton, Louise Chandler, 1, 98

N

"New England," 59, 151
Nicodemus, 58, 135, 136-37
Nietzsche, Freidrich, 149, 162
Norton, Charles Eliot, 171

O

"Octaves," 10, 13-14, 52, 61, 112
Ode on Intimations of Immortality (Wordsworth), 23, 106
"Oh for a Poet," 107
"Old King Cole," 45
"Old Man's Winter Night, An" (Frost), 10
"Old Trails," 70
On a Certain Blindness in Human Beings (James), 171-72
"On the Way," 54, 55
O'Neill, Eugene, 93, 127
O'Reilly, John Boyle, 117

P

Petrarch, 106
Philip II, of Spain, 57
Philosophy in a New Key (Langer),
     148
*Philosophy in the Poetry of Edwin
     Arlington Robinson* (Kaplan), 6, 171
"Pity of the Leaves, The," 111
Plato, 9
Poe, Edgar Allan, 14, 114, 115, 125
"Poems about God" (Ransom), 166
"Poor Relation, The," 42, 43-44, 58
Pope, Alexander, 58, 61
Popular Science Monthly, 149
Pound, Ezra, 4, 14, 36, 49, 101, 120,
     123, 126
Praed, W. M., 41, 45, 85
"Problem, The" (Emerson), 48
Proust, Marcel, 26

R

Ransom, John Crowe, 5, 64, 166
Ray, David, 115
Redman, Ben Ray, 114-15
Reese, Lizette Woodworth, 1, 98, 117
Rembrandt, 31, 131
"Rembrandt to Rembrandt," 46, 114,
     115, 121, **132-35**
"Reuben Bright," 17, 50*n*, 106
"Reunion," 59
"Revealer, The," 54
Reynolds, Sir Joshua, 95
"Richard Cory," 3, 17, 54, 60, 106,
     125, 129, 131, 172, 174-75
Richards, Laura, 159
Riley, James Whitcomb, 98, 117
Rimbaud, Arthur, 49
Robinson, Edwin Arlington:
     and Christian Science, 122, 149
     critical reception of, 5-7, 22, 60,
          98, 166
     early years of, 2-3, 30, 95-97,
          169
     and Eliot, T. S., their work com-
          pared, 100-103

and failure, as dramatic theme, 86-
     87,
first commercial publication, 107
and Gardiner, Maine, 2-3, 123, 131,
     135-36, 167
"greatest poems" of, according to
     Eliot, 58-59
and Frost, Robert, 33, 35-36,
     117-27
and Harvard University, 2-3, 95,
     170-72
and language, use of, 1, 19, 24,
     31-32, 46-47, 52, 67-69, 71, 91-
     92, 110-16, 123-24, 156
and MacDowell Colony, 4, 40
philosophical views of, 2, 7,
     149-52, 156, 161-62, 171
political poems of, 54-57
and Pulitzer Prize, 4, 78
religious consciousness of, 3, 51-
     53, 63, 122, 135-36, 153-55,
     158-59, 163, 175-76
and rhyme, use of, 68-69
and Roosevelt, Theodore, 3-4, 167
and Tilbury Town, 31, **128-32**,
     140, 144, 146
Robinson, Edwin Arlington, major
works of:
     Amaranth, 64, 99-100, 137
     Avon's Harvest, 15-17, 20, 22, 58,
          59, 86, 112, 114, 115, 141
     "Ben Jonson Entertains a Man from
          Stratford," 10, 12, 17, 21, 23,
          121, 132-33
     Captain Craig, 2, 17, 19, 58, 121,
          125-27, **129-31**, 132, 135, 140,
          147
     Cavender's House, 50*n*, 123*n*,
          141
     Children of the Night, The, 2, 3-4,
          10, 13, 18, 51, 58, 110, 118,
          151, 154*n*, 176
     Collected Poems, 4, 6, 22, 82, 84
     "Eros Turannos," 12-13, 32, 42,
          44, 58, 61, **64-68**, 70, 71, 125,
          139-40, 151, 172
     "Flammonde," 53-54, 60, 120,
          124, 125, 140, **143-47**

Robinson, Edwin Arlington, major
  works of (*continued*)
  "Isaac and Archibald," 10, 17, 19,
    64, **88-90**, 131, 140, 151, 178-81
  King Jasper, 33-39, 75, 122, 141,
    151, 154
  Lancelot, 10, 16, 20, 22, 24, 26,
    84, 123*n*, 136, 137
  Man Against the Sky, The, 16, 19,
    20-23 *passim*, 40, 44, 51, 58, 59,
    91-95, 125, 151, **156-61**, 164-65
  Man Who Died Twice, The, 87,
    123*n*, 140, 176
  Matthias at the Door, 86, 123*n*
  Merlin, 10-11, 16, 21, 22, 24, 26,
    84, 123*n*
  Nicodemus, 58, 135, 136-37
  Three Taverns, The, 13, 20, 22,
    46, 50, 58, 59, 135-36
  Torrent and the Night Before, The,
    107, 118, 129, 167
  Town Down the River, The, 2, 4,
    18, 25, 36, 58
  Tristram, 4, 26-27, 78, 112-14,
    115, 123*n*
  (*see also* titles of individual poems)
Robinson, W. R., 7
Robinson and William James
  (Stevick), 171
Roman Bartholow, 123*n*
Roosevelt, Theodore, 3-4, 54, 55, 167
Rossetti, D. G. 85, 106
Rothenberg, Jerome, 115
Royce, Josiah, 7, 149, 150, 162, 170,
  171-73, 175-77, 181
Russell, Bertrand, 152, 156, 163
Russell, George (AE), 98

S

"Sage, The," 53
Salinger, J. D., 127
Sandburg, Carl, 14, 100, 118
Santayana, George, 1, 2, 98, 119,
  149, 150
Schopenhauer, Arthur, 149, 162
Science and Health (Eddy), 149
Scott, W. T., 115, 166

Shakespeare, William, 12, 31, 47*n*, 81,
  95, 100, 106, 126, 131, 168
Shaw, George Bernard, 25
"Sheaves, The," 32, 39, 46, 47-48,
  58
Sherman, Frank D., 98
Sidney, Sir Philip, 47*n*
Sill, E. R., 1, 110, 114, 115, 117
Sinclair, May, 37
"Sisera," 141-42
Smith, Chard Powers, 6, 93
Smith, Harry de Forest, 3, 96*n*, 117,
  121
Snyder, Gary, 115
Socrates, 56
"Song of the Happy Shepherd"
  (Yeats), 105
"Sonnet," 52
Sonnets and Other Verses (Santayana),
  119
Sophocles, 18
"Souvenir," 59
Spencer, Herbert, 149, 162, 163
Spoon River Anthology, The
  (Masters), 13, 30
Sterling, George, 110, 114, 115
Stevens, Wallace, 10, 14, 101, 114,
  115, 118, 122, 123, 126
Stevick, Robert, 171
Stickney, Trumbull, 119
Stoddard, Elizabeth, 98
"Story of the Ashes and the Flames,
  The," 111
Styron, William, 127
Sullivan, Harry Stack, 93
Swift, Jonathan, 76
Swinburne, Algernon Charles, 26, 110,
  114, 126
Symons, Arthur, 26
Synge, John Millington, 98

T

Tabb, Father, 98, 117
Taft, William, 168
Talifer, 5
Tate, Allen, 5, 60-61, 97, 157*n*
"Tavern, The," 50*n*

Tennyson, Alfred, 10, 21, 26, 116, 126, 150, 168
Thomas, Edith Matilda, 98
"Three Quatrains," 111
"Three Taverns, The," 13, 20, 22, 46, 50, 58, 59, 135-36
Torrent and the Night Before, The, 107, 118, 129, 167
Town Down the River, The, 2, 4, 18, 25, 36, 58, 107, 123
Tristram, 4, 26-27, 78, 112-14, 115, 123n
Turn of the Screw, The (James), 15
Twain, Mark, 38
"Two Gardens in Linndale," 58

U

Unamuno, Miguel de, 128
Urban, W. M., 157n

V

"Vain Gratuities," 59
"Valley of the Shadows, The," 59
"Veteran Sirens," 42-43, 58, 63
"Vicar, The," (Praed), 45
"Voice of the Age, The," 59

W

Waggoner, Hyatt, 7
Wagner, Richard, 26
"Walt Whitman," 121
"Wandering Jew, The," 44-46, 58, 69, 135

Warren, Robert Penn, 127
Washington, George, 55-56
Watson, John B., 155
"Where Are the Pipes of Pan?" (Adams), 104
Where the Light Falls (Smith), 6
"Whip, The," 50, 64, 75
White, Andrew Dickson, 149-50
White, Gleeson, 104
Whitehead, Albert North, 155, 162
"White Lights, The," 58
Whitman, Walt, 1, 9, 13, 48, 64, 107, 116, 120, 149, 168
Wilde, Oscar, 110
"Wilderness, The," 3
Will to Believe, The (James), 171
Williams, William Carlos, 5, 115
Wilson, Edmund, 5
Wings of the Dove, The (James), 24
Winters, Yvor, 6, 7, 60, 75, 121, 124, 157n, 161, 166
"With Pipe and Flute," 104-5
Wordsworth, William, 23, 57, 84, 85, 95, 106, 107, 126, 164, 165, 167, 168, 178

Y

Yeats, W. B., 3, 5, 14, 30, 63, 98, 101, 105, 110, 113

Z

Zabel, Morton, 2, 84
"Zola," 31, 111, 141

SARTRE

A Collection of Critical Essays
Edited by EDITH KERN

A

Adler, Alfred, 149
Aeschylus, 85, 87
Age of Reason, The (L'Âge de raison),
7, **31-33**, 41, 44, 47, 48, 51-52
Alain (Émile Auguste Chartier), 123,
149
Alouette, L' (Anouilh), 68
Anderson, Maxwell, 76
"Ange du morbide," 32, 36
Anouilh, Jean, 68, 71n, 73, 77
Anthologie de l'humour noir (Breton),
42
Antigone (Anouilh), 68, 77
Artiste et la conscience, L' (Lebowitz),
129
Aspasia, 46
Aury, Mme. Dominique, 37

B

Bach, Johann Sebastian, 77
Bachelard, Gaston, 127, 133n,
149
Balzac, Honoré, 22, 36, 48, 90
Barres par lui-ême (Jeanson, ed.)., 125
Barrett, William, 48-49, 52
Barthes, Roland, 124, 125, 126
Bastide, Jules, 125
Baudelaire, Charles, 32, 39, 133, 134,
150, 154
Baudelaire, 122, 154
Beaufret, Jean, 10

Beauvoir, Simone de, 19, 152, 157
Bouches inutiles, Les, 74
Ethics of Ambiguity, The, 5, 11,
86n
and Sartre, 2-3, 6, 7, 12, 16
She Came to Stay, 33, 43-44
theatre of, 73, 74
Becque, Henry François, 77
Beguin, Albert, 125, 126, 128
*Being and Nothingness (L'Être et le
néant)*, 4, 7-8, 10, 16, 59, 83, 150,
161, 163, 168
and existential psychology, 58, 153,
157, 159
and God, concept of, 41, 42, 49
and love, theme of, 32, 82
and the "other," 1, 80
and phenomenology, 2-3, 142
Bentley, Eric, 69
Berdyaev, Nikolai Aleksandrovich,
4
Bergson, Henri, 28, 133
Bernanos, Georges, 165
Beyond Good and Evil (Nietzsche),
88
Binswanger, Ludwig, 156
Blake, William, 88
Blanchot, Maurice, 127
Blätter und Stein (Jünger), 60
Borel, Pétrus, 42, 44
Boss, Medard, 156
Bouches inutiles, Les (Beauvoir), 74
Bourget, Charles Joseph Paul, 36
Brecht, Bertolt, 13, 78

Brée, Germaine, 67
Breton, André, 42
Brock, Erich, 58
Brombert, Victor, 7

C

Caligula (Camus), 62, 65, 68
Camus, Albert, 3, 15, 16, 51, 62-72, 73, 152
Camus (Brée), 67
Céline, Louis Ferdinand, 36
Chamberlain, Neville, 34
"Chambre, La" (*see* "The Room")
Chapsal, Madeleine, 4, 13, 14
Chemins de la liberté, Les (*see Roads to Freedom*)
Cocteau, Jean, 17, 53, 68
Condemned of Altona, The (Les Séquestrés d'Altona), 14, 63-64, 71, 92-103, 165
Condition humaine, La (Malraux), 59, 64
Corbin, John, 6
Corneille, Pierre, 77, 78
Courteline, Georges, 34
Criticism of Dialectical Reasoning (Critique de la raison dialectique), 161-65
Critique (Dort), 126
Croce, Benedetto, 129, 130, 134

D

Daladier, Édourard, 34
Dead without Burial (Morts sans sépulture), 31n, 48, 68, 74-77, 113
Défaite, 35
Degré zéro de l'écriture, Le (Barthes), 124
Descartes, Réné, 4, 18, 40, 59
Devil and the Good Lord, The (Le Diable et le bon Dieu), 44, 46, 62-70 *passim,* 82, 84-91 *passim,* 135n
Diderot, Denis, 77
Dirty Hands (Les Mains sales), 7, 46, 62-65 *passim,* 68, 69, 70

Domenach, Jean Marie, 125
Dort, Bernard, 126
Dos Passos, John, 22, 26n, 33, 37, 38, 52
Dostoevsky, Fyodor, 22, 37, 56
Dreiser, Theodore, 37
Dumas, Alexandre, 68, 113

E

Eckhart, Meister, 83n
Écrivains de toujours (Jeanson, ed.), 125
Engels, Friedrich, 50, 162
Escape from Freedom (Fromm), 150-51
Esprit, 128
Essay on Phenomenological Ontology, 142 (*see also Being and Nothingness*)
État de siège, L' (Camus), 62, 64, 67, 68, 69, 71
Ethics of Ambiguity (Beauvoir), 5, 11
Étranger, L' (*see The Stranger*)
Être et le néant, L' (*see Being and Nothingness*)
Études sur le temps humain (Poulet), 127
Existence and Therapy (Sonnemann), 155
Existentialism, 2, 85n, 150
"Existentialism, 48
Existentialism: A New Trend in Philosophy (Kecskemeti), 49
Existentialisme est un humanism, L' (*see Existentialism*)
Existential Psychoanalysis, 153

F

Faulkner, William, 22, 37, 38, 77, 114
Faust (Goethe), 33
Fischer, Franz, 156
Flaubert, Gustave, 13, 38, 48, 104, 121, 124
Flies, The (Les Mouches), 1, 7, 31n, 33, 46, 52, 54-61, 64-68 *passim,* 73, 81, 82, 85, 91, 150, 163, 165, 167

France, Anatole, 48
Freud, Sigmund, 125, 149, 152, 153-54, 155
Fromm, Erich, 149-53, 154-55

G

Gautier, Théophile, 19
Gebsattel, V. E. von, 155
Genêt, Jean, 17, 91, 109, 121-23, 129, 134, 154
Giacometti, Paolo, 9
Gide, André, 35, 41, 71, 110
Giono, Jean, 36
Giraudoux, Jean, 26, 57, 63, 71
Goethe, Johann Wolfgang von, 11, 33, 35, 56
Grapes of Wrath, The (Steinbeck), 48-49
Grenier, Jean, 3
Gurvich, Aron, 4

H

Hardy, Thomas, 37
Hegel, G. W. F., 4, 5, 33, 137, 152, 168, 170
Heidegger, Martin, 30, 50, 137, 138, 139
    and *Dasein*, concept of, 5, 6, 9, 10, 12-13
    influence of, on Sartre, 2, 3, 7, 49, 123, 142, 144-46, 155, 158
    style of, 4, 5
Hemingway, Ernest, 37, 52
High Wind in Jamaica, A (Hughes), 150
Hobbes, Thomas, 170
Hopkins, Gerard, 31
Horace, 130
Horney, Karen, 149-50, 153-55
Hughes, Richard, 150
Hugo, Victor, 36, 77, 124
Huis-clos (see *No Exit*)
Husserl, Edmund, 9, 155
Huysmans, Joris Karl, 37
    37

I

Imaginaire, L', 134
Intellectual Hero, The (Brombert), 7
Invitée, L' (see *She Came to Stay*)

J

Janet, P. M. F., 149
Jaspers, Karl, 2, 137, 138, 139, 146, 155
Jean-Paul Sartre par lui-même (Jeanson), 125
Jean-Paul Sartre: Philosopher Without Faith (Marill-Albérès), 12
Jeanson, Francis, 125, 126
Johnson, Dr. Samuel, 33
Joyce, James, 13, 36, 37, 115
Jünger, Ernst, 60
Justes, Les (Camus), 62, 64, 65, 68

K

Kafka, Franz, 15, 23, 33, 128, 133*n*
Kant, Immanuel, 4, 11, 50, 86, 131, 134, 139, 142, 170
Kean, 7, 65, 68, 113
Kecskemeti, Paul, 49, 50
Kierkegaard, Sören, 3-5, 136, 137, 138, 170-71
Kleist, Heinrich von, 42
Koefoed, Oleg, 31
Kuhn, Roland, 156

L

Langer, Susanne K., 129
La Rouchefoucauld, Duc François de, 12
Last Chance, The, 47
Lautreamont, Comte de, 127-28, 133*n*
Lawrence, D. H., 21
Leibnitz, Gottfried Wilhelm, 169
Lettres françaises, Les, 37
Lettres nouvelles, Les (Vinaver), 126

Littérature et sensation (Richard), 127

Lonely Crowd, The (Riesman), 153

Lukács, Georgy, 168

Lutte avec l'ange, La (Malraux), 58

M

Maeterlinck, Maurice, 77

Magny, Claude-Edmonde, 11

Mains sales, Les (see *Dirty Hands*)

Malentendu, Le (Camus), 62, 67, 68, 69

Mallarmé, Stéphane, 6, 13, 36, 43, 129, 133

Malraux, André, 36, 37, 52, 71, 126, 165
   Condition humain, La, 64
   Voie royale, La, 58-59, 124

Man for Himself (Fromm), 150, 151

Manhattan Transfer (Dos Passos), 33

Mann, Heinrich, 37

Mann, Thomas, 38

Marcel, Gabriel, 2, 3, 4, 75-76, 83, 136-37, 139, 140, 167

Marill-Albérès, René, 12*n*

Maurras, Charles, 18

Marriage of Heaven and Hell, The (Blake), 88

Marx, Karl, 49-50, 51, 123, 125, 168

Maupassant, Guy de, 34, 37, 52

Mauriac, François, 21, 22, 35, 37

Meredith, George, 22

Merleau-Ponty, Maurice, 19

Meyerson, Émile, 29*n*

Michelet, Jules, 37, 124

Michelet par lui-même (Barthes), 126

Minkowski, Eugene, 155

Misfortune of the Bachelor, The (Kafka), 23

Modern Review, 49

Molière, 90

Montaigne par lui-même (Jeanson), 125

Montesquieu par lui-même (Jeanson, ed.), 125

Moravia, Alberto, 38

Morris, Charles, 129

Mort dans l'âme, La (see *Troubled Sleep*)

Morts sans sépulture (see *Dead without Burial*)

Mouches, Les (see *The Flies*)

"Mur, Le" (see "The Wall")

Musset, Alfred de, 77

Mystery of Being, The (Marcel), 139

N

Nausea (La Nausée), 1, 7, 8, 11, 14, 15, 22-30, 31, 36, 39-40, 64, 69, 86, 161, 165

Nekrassov, 62, 65, 68, 69

New Leader, 74

New Masses, 74

Nietzsche, Friedrich, 88, 167

No Exit (Huis-clos), 1, 7, 11, 14, 52, 62-67 *passim*, 69, 72-74, 77, 80, 91

Nouvelle Revue Française, 127

O

On Humanism (Heidegger), 10

Open City, 75

Oresteia (Aeschylus), 54, 85, 87

Orwell, George, 52

P

"Paris sous l'occupation," 35

Partisan Review, 52

Pascal, Blaise, 12, 15

Pascal par lui-même (Béguin), 126

Pavese, Cesare, 38

Peste, La (Camus), 69

Pétain, Henri Philippe, 50

Phenomenological Approach to Psychiatry (Van Den Berg), 156

Philosophie (Jaspers), 138, 139

"Philosophy in the Literary Work of Jean-Paul Sartre" (Brock), 58

Piaget, Jean, 149

Picasso, Pablo, 33

Picon, Gaetan, 125

Plato, 4, 22, 166
Poe, Edgar Allan, 43
Poesie, La (Croce), 130
Portrait of the Anti-Semite, 52
Poulet, Georges, 127
Pouillon, Jean, 126n
"Presentation," 49
Prévost, Jean, 123, 130
Prometheus Unbound (Shelley), 86
Proust, Marcel, 21, 25n, 37, 48, 123
Psychology of the Imagination, The (L'Imaginaire), 134
Putain respectueuse, La (see *The Respectful Prostitute*)

Q

Queneau, Raymond, 36
"Qu'est-ce que la littérature?" (*see* "What is Literature?")
Question of Method, 162 (*see also* *Criticism of Dialectical Reasoning*)

R

Rabelais, François, 18
Racine, Jean Baptiste, 77, 78, 90
Renan, Joseph Ernst, 35
Reprieve, The (Le Sursis), 8-9, 14, 31, 33-35, 46, 47, 117-18
Republic, The (Plato), 22
"République du silence, La, " 35
Respectful Prostitute, The (La Putain respectueuse), 31n, 65, 68, 74, 75
Richard, Jean Pierre, 127
Richards, I. A., 129
Roads to Freedom (Chemins de la liberté), 8, 31-38, 39, 40, 41, 46, 47, 69, 167 (*see also* titles for individual volumes of this work: *The Age of Reason, The Reprieve, Troubled Sleep,* and *The Last Chance*)
Romains, Jules, 20, 34, 36
"Room, The" ("La Chambre"), 22, 30, 45
Rousseau, Jean Jacques, 2

Roy, Claude, 125
Rubins, Jack L., 153
Russell, Bertrand, 138-39

S

Sacre du Printemps (Stravinsky), 77
Sade, Marquis de, 127
Sagan, Françoise, 20
Saint-Exupéry, Antoine de, 6, 9
Saint-Genêt, 84, 86, 87, 121-23, 126n, 134n
Saint-Simon, Duc de, 124, 125
Sane Society, The (Fromm), 150, 151, 153
Sartre, Jean-Paul:
  and *Dasein,* concept of, 5-6, 9, 10, 12, 18, 143
  and existentialism, 3-6, 15-20, 36-37, 47-53, 121-28, 130, 137-41, 142-48, 149-60, 166-68, 170-71
  and existential psychoanalysis, 110, 132-33, 149-60
  and Freudianism, 11, 125
  and in-itself and for-itself (*en soi* and *pour soi*), concept of, 4, 9-11, 13, 143-45, 147, 151
  and language, theories and use of, 13, 35-36, 104-20, 129
  and Marxism, 18, 49-50, 125, 126, 147, 161-65, 168
  novels of, 21-30, 31-38, 39-46, 47-53
  and the Other, theme of, 1, 3, 12, 13, 14, 39, 46, 80, 84
  and phenomenology, 2, 19, 123, 126, 133, 136-41, 142, 155-56, 159-60
  politics of, 12, 147, 161-65, 166-71
  and *salauds,* theme of, 22, 24, 27, 29, 30, 147
  style of, 104-20
  theatre works of, 54-61, 62-72, 73-79, 80-91, 92-103
Sartre, Jean-Paul, major literary works of:
  Age of Reason, The (L'Âge de

Sartre, Jean-Paul, major literary works
of (*Age of Reason, The*) (*continued*)
raison), 7, **31-33**, 41, 44, 47, 48,
51-52
Baudelaire, 122, 154
*Condemned of Altona, The (Les
Séquestrés d'Altona)*, 14, 63-64,
71, **92-103**, 165
*Dead without Burial (Morts sans
sépulture)*, 48, 68, 74-77, 113
Défaite, 36
*Devil and the Good Lord, The (Le
Diable et le bon Dieu)*, 44, 46,
62-70 *passim*, 82, 84-91 *passim*,
136n
Dirty Hands (Les Mains sales), 7,
46, 62-65 *passim*, 68, 69, 70
Flies, The (Les Mouches), 1, 7, 33,
46, 52, **54-61**, 64-68 *passim*, 73,
81, 82, 85, 91, 150, 163, 165,
167
Kean, 7, 65, 68, 113
Last Chance, The, 47
Nausea (La Nausée), 1, 7, 8, 11, 14,
15, **22-30**, 31, 36, 39-40, 64, 69,
86, 161, 165
Nekrassov, 62, 65, 68, 69
No Exit (Huit-clos), 1, 7, 11, 14,
52, 62-67 *passim*, 69, 73-74, 77,
80, 91
Reprieve, The (Le Sursis), 8-9, 14,
31, 33-35, 46, 47, 117-118
*Respectful Prostitute, The (La Pu-
tain respectueuse)*, 65, 68, 74,
75
*Roads to Freedom (Les Chemins de
la liberté)*, 8, 31-38, 39, 40, 41,
46, 47, 69, 167
"Room, The" ("La Chambre"), 22,
33, 45
Saint-Genêt, 84, 121-23, 126n,
134n
*Troubled Sleep (La Mort dans
l'âme)*, 11, 31, 35, 44, 47n
"Wall, The," ("Le Mur"), 1,
30n
Sartre, Jean-Paul, major philosophical
works of:

*Being and Nothingness (L'Être et le
néant) q.v.*, 1, 2, 3, 4, 7-8, 9, 32,
41, 42, 49, 58, 59, 80, 82, 83,
150, 153, 157, 159, 161, 163,
168
Criticism of Dialectical Reasoning,
161-65
*Essay on Phenomenological Ontol-
ogy*, 142
*Existentialism (L'Existentialisme
est un humanism)*, 2, 48, 150
Existential Psychoanalysis, 153
Portrait of the Anti-Semite, 52
*Psychology of the Imagination, The
(L'Imaginaire)*, 134
Situations, 35, 129
Transcendence of the Ego, The,
6-7, 10
"What Is Literature?" ("Qu'est-ce
que la littérature?"), 9, 13, 35,
129, 130, 134, 168-69
Schneider, Pierre, 124
Sein und Zeit (Heidegger), 137
Séquestrés d'Altona, Les (see *The
Condemned of Altona*)
Shakespeare, William, 64
She Came to Stay (Beauvoir), 16, 33,
43-44
Shelley, Percy Bysshe, 86, 88, 133n
Situations, 35, 129
Socrates, 86
Sonnemann, Ulrich, 155, 160n
Sophocles, 77
Spinoza, Baruch, 32
Starobinski, Jean, 125
Stekel, Wilhelm, 149
Steinbeck, John, 48, 77
Stendhal, 36
Stranger, The (Camus), 15, 69
Strauss, Erwin, 155
Stravinsky, Igor, 77
Strindberg, August, 69, 76
Sullivan, Harry Stack, 150
Sursis, Le (see *The Reprieve*)
Sutton, Eric, 48
Swift, Jonathan, 13, 42, 44
Swinburne, Algernon Charles,
134

T

Temps et roman (Pouillon), 126n
Temps modernes, Les, 3, 12, 49, 52, 53, 132
Thackeray, William Makepeace, 22
Theatre Arts, 38n, 74, 75, 77
Thibaudet, Albert, 123
Time, 74, 75
Tocqueville, Alexis de, 31n
Tolstoy, Count Leo, 36
Transcendence of the Ego, The, 6-7, 10
Troubled Sleep, 11, 31, 35, 44
Twain, Mark, 38

U

Über den Humanismus (*see on Humanism*)
Unglück des Junggesellen, Das (*see The Misfortune of the Bachelor*)
U.S.A. (Dos Passos), 33

V

Valéry, Paul, 41, 123, 129, 133n

Van Den Berg, J. H., 156-60
View, 77
Vinaver, Michel, 126
Visages, 80
Voie royale, La (Malraux), 58
Voix vive, La (Schneider), 124

W

Wahl, Jean, 4
"Wall, The" ("Le Mur"), 1, 30n
What is Existentialism? (Barrett), 48
"What is Literature?" ("Qu'est-ce que la littérature?"), 9, 13, 35, 124, 129, 130, 134, 168-69
Wind, Sand, and Stars (Saint-Exupéry), 6
Wordsworth, William, 36

Z

Zeno, 108
Zola, Émile, 78

SHAKESPEARE: THE COMEDIES

A Collection of Critical Essays

Edited by KENNETH MUIR

A

Aeschylus, 90, 107
Aesop, 164, 173
Alexander, Peter, 19
All's Well that Ends Well, 8, 56, 116, 119-32, 133-51
Amphitryon (Plautus), 4, 18
Andria (Terence), 24
Antony and Cleopatra, 2, 136
Apolonius and Silla (Riche), 75
Appearance *vs.* Reality, theme of, 6, 21-22, 47, 56, 67-68, 168-70, 173
Arcadia (Sidney), 19
Archer, William, 12
Ariosto, 4
Aristotle, 55, 84, 126, 127
Arthurian romances, 19, 89
As You Like It, 1, 3, 5, 6, 36, 58-71, 144

B

Bacon, Francis, 41, 69, 104, 121
Baldwin, T. W., 18, 19, 24
Bandello, Matteo, 74
Barber, C. L., 1
"Basis of Shakespearian Comedy, The," (Coghill) 60
Battenhouse, Roy, 8, 112
Beaumont, Francis, 9
Bethell, S. L., 2
Blake, William, 175

Boccaccio, 121
Book of Martyrs (Foxe), 93
Bradbrook, Muriel C., 4, 8, 9
Bradley, A. C., 1, 104, 107
Bridges, Robert, 8, 45
Brown, John, 1, 21, 22
Bullough, Geoffrey, 20

C

Calderon, P., 93, 101
Castle of Perseverance, The, 24
Chambers, Sir Edmund, 26, 31, 88-89, 102-3, 107
Chambers, R. W., 8
Chaplin, Charlie, 57
Chapman, George, 110, 123
Charlton, H. B., 1, 77
Chekhov, A., 165
Chesterton, G. K., 103
Child, Harold, 32
Christian Renaissance, The (Knight), 137
Chronicles (Holinshed), 9
Civile Conversation (Guazzo), 123
Clitherow, Ven. Margaret, 94
Coghill, Neville, 60-61
Coleridge, S. T., 8, 33, 54, 55, 100-101, 103
Colin Clout's Come Home Again (Spenser), 124
Collier, J., 75
Comedy of Errors, The, 3, 4, 11-25, 65, 73, 75

Condell, Henry, 98
Confidential Clerk, The (Eliot), 23
Convivio (Dante), 130, 131
Coriolanus, 12
Coulter, Cornelia, 19
Craig, Hardin, 16
Craik, T. W., 52
Cymbeline, 9, 10, 133, 165, 167

D

Dante, 90, 130, 131
Decameron (Boccaccio), 56
Dee, Dr. John, 169
Defence of Poetry (Shelley), 137, 138
De la Mare, Walter, 5
De Quincey, Thomas, 175
De Vere Nobilitate (Buonaccorso), 1, 23
Diana (Montemayor), 4
Dickens, Charles, 49
Discourse of Civil and Christian Nobility (Osorio), 126
Disguise, use of, 2-3, 67, 90
Doran, Madeleine, 19
Dramatic devices, 10, 11-13, 16-20, 24, 29, 37-40, 52, 54-55, 60-61, 69, 78, 80-83, 91, 102-3, 112, 120, 123, 136, 142-44, 152-54, 157
Draper, J. W., 2

E

Eastward Ho! (Chapman, Marston, and Jonson), 129
Eliot, T. S., 9, 169, 173
Elizabethan conventions, 18-19, 21, 27, 36, 49, 88, 90, 109-10, 118, 122-25, 156, 160, 167
Ellis-Fermor, Una, 8
Elyot, Sir Thomas, 69, 125, 127, 130
Erasmus, 23
Essay on Man (Pope), 138
Euripides, 110
Evans, Bertrand, 1, 2

F

Faerie Queene, The (Spenser), 19
Fate, theme of, 168-73, 175
Feeling and Form (Langer), 61
Fernandel, 57
Fletcher, John, 9
Florio, John, 4
Folklore, as source, 31, 33, 59, 65
Fontenelle, 164
Fool, use of the, 23, 69, 80-81, 84, 86
Forgiveness, theme of, 41, 92-94, 101, 103, 105-8, 113, 117, 165, 175
Foxe, John, 93
Fulgens and Lucres (Medwall), 123

G

Gascoigne, George, 4, 20
Gide, André, 173
Gittings, Robert, 4
Golding, M., 173
Gorboduc (Norton and Sackville), 110
Gordon, George, 1
Gosson, Stephen, 34
Gower, J., 20
Granville-Barker, Harvey, 5
Graves, Robert, 174
Greene, Graham, 111
Greene, Robert, 3, 20
Greenwood, Sir George, 95
Guazzo, Stefano, 123, 125-26

H

Halle, Edward, 109
Hamlet, 2, 33, 46, 107,
Hart, H. P., 113
Harvey, G., 4
Hazlitt, William, 32, 39, 95, 101
Heminge, John, 98
1 Henry IV, 55, 56
2 Henry IV, 116, 117
Henry VIII, 150, 173
Henslowe, Philip, 34
Heywood, Thomas, 9
Holinshed, R., 9

Homer, 90, 164, 173
Hotson, Leslie, 2, 72
Housman, A. E., 69, 104-5
Hunter, G. K., 3
Hunter, Joseph, 75

I

Identity, theme of, 13, 14, 21, 23,
    74
Imagery, 5, 6, 10, 22, 134, 137-38,
    143, 152-53, 159-61, 166-67, 172
Ingannati, Gl', 74-75
Inganni, Gl' (Secchi), 74-75
Ion, 23

J

Jenkins, Harold, 67
Jew, The, 34
James 1, 167
Johnson, Samuel, 26, 47-48, 51, 60,
    80
Jonson, Ben, 2, 61, 97, 110, 119, 123
Jouvet, 57
Jude the Obscure (Hardy), 110
Julius Caesar, 150

K

Kean, Edmund, 32
Keats, John, 9, 157
King John, 123
King Lear, 2, 60, 65, 116, 150
Kittredge, G. Lyman, 168-69
Knight, G. Wilson, 2, 5, 8, 9, 23, 109,
    113, 117, 135

L

Lamb, Charles, 84, 174
Langer, Suzanne, 61
Language, 47-50, 54-57, 131, 158
Lascelles, Mary, 2
Lawrence, W. W., 2, 8, 113
Leech, Clifford, 8
Lennox, Charlotte, 74, 80, 95

Lewis, C. S., 5
Linacre, T., 94
Lodge, Thomas, 6, 59-60
Love, theme of, 6-7, 21, 73-76, 120,
    136-50 *passim*
Love-madness, theme of, 27-29
Love's Labour's Lost, 1, 2, 4, 11, 61,
    63, 64, 69, 76, 139
Lyly, John, 3, 19, 23

M

Macauley, Rose, 94
Macbeth, 62, 110, 150
Magician (Calderon), 93
Manningham, John, 74, 83
Marlowe, Christopher, 119, 169
Masefield, John, 6
Maurice, François, 111
Maxwell, J. C., 8
Measure for Measure, 2, 8, 56, 61, **88-
    108, 109-118**, 121, 131, 138, 143,
    173
Menacchmi (Plautus), 3, 17, 18, 20
Menaphon (Greene), 20
Merchant of Venice, The, 2, 5, 6, 32-
    46, 61, 64, 69, 90, 116, 133
Merry Wives of Windsor, The,
    3, 5
Method, 2-3, 11-12, 32-46 *passim*,
    63, 73
Middleton, Thomas, 123
Midsummer-Night's Dream, A, 2, 5,
    26-31, 56, 61, 62, 64, 76, 138, 169
Milton, John, 59
Misunderstanding, theme of, 47, 51-57
    passim, 63-64, 67-68, 83-84, 90
Montemayor, J. de, 4
More, St. Thomas, 96
Mother Bombie (Lyly), 19
Mozart, W. A., 59
Much Ado About Nothing, 1, 2, 5, 6,
    36, 47-57, 64, 69, 122
Muir, Kenneth, 165, 168
Murray, Gilbert, 11
Murry, J. Middleton, 6, 8
Mutual Flame, The (Knight), 135, 137,
    138

N

Nennio, Il (Nenna), 126
New Cambridge Shakespeare, 34, 36, 40-41, 95
Nobility as virtue, theme of, 9, 121-32 *passim,* 133-36, 150

O

Oedipus Tyrannus (Sophocles), 103
Of Gentylness and Nobylyte (Rastell), 123
Order, theme of, 21-23, 31, 71, 131
Orsino, Virginio, 72
Ovid, 11, 22, 156, 173

P

Painter, William, 121
Parrott, T. M., 1, 8
Pastoral conventions, 58, 152-63 *passim*
Pater, Walter, 7
Penitence, theme of, 99-102, 152, 163
Perez, 4
Pericles, 9, 10, 143, 144, 165, 167
Pettet, E. C., 1, 8
Philebus (Plato), 53
Philoctetes (Sophocles), 97
Phoenix and the Turtle, The, 136, 137
Plato, 53
Plautus, 3, 17, 18, 19
Pope, Alexander, 32, 138
Pope, Elizabeth M., 8, 109, 110-12, 116-17
Promos and Cassandra (Whetstone), 88, 107, 121
Prouty, C. T., 2

Q

Quiller-Couch, Sir Arthur, 6, 42, 65-66, 90, 95, 103

R

Racine, 2
Raimu, 57
Raleigh, Sir Walter, 4, 90, 102, 106, 113
Rape of Lucrece, The, 11
Reconciliation, theme of, 10, 71, 131, 152-54, 163, 165, 166, 175
Relationship, theme of, 14-15, 20-23, 68, 144, 152, 154, 158
Religious references, 70-71, 92-93, 96-97, 101, 106, 108, 110-13, 131, 142, 162
"Renaissance Background of *Measure for Measure,* The" (Pope), 109
Richard III, 11, 33
Riche, Barnaby, 75
Rimbaud, Arthur, 173
Risk, theme of, 12, 14-15, 21
Robertson, J. M., 40
Romeo and Juliet, 31, 35
Rosalynde (Lodge), 59

S

Saint Joan (Shaw), 149
Scrutiny, 168
Self-knowledge, theme of, 47, 67-68, 73, 76-80, 83, 86
Seneca, 19, 110, 165
Sen Gupta, S. C., 1
Shakespeare, 8
Shakespeare, William:
  biographical information, 11, 107, 114, 119
  and contemporary writers, 3-4, 59-61, 74-75, 119, 171, 173
  and Elizabethan conventions, 18-19, 21, 27, 36, 49, 88, 90, 109-10, 118, 122-25, 156, 160, 167
  moral vision of, 62, 69-70, 104-6, 113, 137, 138
Shakespeare, William, works by:
  All's Well that Ends Well, 8, 56, 116, **119-32,** 133-51
  Antony and Cleopatra, 2, 136

Shakespeare, William, works by:
(*continued*)
As You Like It, 1, 3, 5, 6, 36, **58-71**, 144
Comedy of Errors, The, 3, 4, **11-25**, 65, 73, 75
Cymbeline, 9, 10, 133, 165, 167
Coriolanus, 12
Hamlet, 2, 33, 46, 107, 150
1 Henry IV, 55, 56
2 Henry IV, 116, 117
Henry VIII, 150, 173
Julius Caesar, 150
King John, 123
King Lear, 2, 60, 65, 116, 150
Love's Labour's Lost, 1, 2, 4, 11, 61, 63, 64, 69, 76, 139
Macbeth, 62, 110, 150
Measure for Measure, 2, 8, 56, 61, **88-108,** 109-18, 121, 131, 138, 143, 173
Merchant of Venice, The, 2, 5, 6, **32-46,** 61, 64, 69, 90, 116, 133
Merry Wives of Windsor, The, 3, 5
Midsummer-Night's Dream, A, 2, 5, **26-31,** 56, 61, 62, 64, 76, 138, 169
Much Ado about Nothing, 1, 2, 5, 6, 36, **47-57,** 64, 69, 122
Pericles, 9, 10, 143, 144, 165, 167
Phoenix and the Turtle, The, 136, 137
Rape of Lucrece, The, 11
Richard III, 11, 33
Romeo and Juliet, 31, 35
Taming of the Shrew, The, 2, 4, 11, 16, 21, 76, 140
Tempest, The, 3, 10, 31, 105, 106, 107, **164-75**
Timon of Athens, 137
Titus Andronicus, 2
Troilus and Cressida, 56, 110
Twelfth Night, 1, 2, 5, 6, 25, 26, 34, 63, **72-87,** 136
Two Gentlemen of Verona, The, 2, 4, 11, 16, 25, 63, 64, 73, 74, 76, 78, 79, 81, 133

Venus and Adonis, 11
Winter's Tale, The, 2, 10, 26, 134, 135, 145, 146, **152-63,** 165, 166, 168
Shakespeare and his Comedies (Brown), 1
Shakespeare and the Romance Tradition (Pettet), 1
Shakespeare and the Tragic Pattern (Muir), 2
Shakespeare Quarterly, 83
Shakespeare Survey, 8, 67
Shakespeare's Festive Comedy (Barber), 1
"Shakespeare's Final Period" (Strachey), 9
Shakespeare's Happy Comedies (Wilson), 2
Shakespeare's Predecessors (Symonds), 88
Shakespearian Comedy (Gordon), 1
Shaw, G. B., 9, 149
Shelley, P. B., 137, 138
Sheridan, R. B., 49
Sidney, Philip, 61
Silent Woman, The (Jonson), 2
Soliloquy, function of, 13-15
Song, importance in works, 3, 58-59, 78-79, 165, 170, 173, 175
Sonnets, 120, 134, 135, 136, 137, 138, 139
Sophocles, 90, 97, 103, 107
Sources (*see also* Folklore), 3-5, 7, 16-27, 31, 34, 59-60, 72-76, 88, 121
Spanish Tragedy, The (Kyd), 11
Spenser, Edmund, 124
Squire's Tale, The (Chaucer), 19
Steevens, G., 26, 27
Strachey, Lytton, 9
Structure, 11-25 *passim,* 52, 55, 63, 69, 118, 119-32 *passim,* 158, 165
Stylistic devices, 47-50, 77, 82, 110, 138, 147-49
Supposes (Gascoigne), 4, 20, 23
Swinburne, A. G., 100
Symbols, 52-53, 124-25, 129, 141, 157

Symonds, John Addington, 88

T

Tamburlaine (Marlowe), 116
Taming of the Shrew, The, 2, 4, 11, 16, 21, 76, 140
Tempest, The, 3, 10, 31, 105, 106, 107, **164-75**
Terence, 3, 19, 24
Tillyard, E. M. W., 2, 8, 9, 169
Time, theme of, 12-13, 22, 23, 152, 163
Timon of Athens, 137
Titus Andronicus, 2
Tragedy, 61-63
Tragedy of Darius (Stirling), 171
Traversi, Derek, 2, 168
Troilus and Cressida, 56, 110
Twelfth Night, 1, 2, 5, 6, 25, 26, 34, 63, **72-87**, 136
Two Gentlemen of Verona, The, 2, 4, 11, 16, 25, 63, 64, 73, 74, 76, 78, 79, 81, 133

V

Venus and Adonis, 11
Versification, 3, 5, 144, 147-48, 162

W

Wealth, theme of, 12-13, 15
Whetstone, George, 88
Winter's Tale, The, 2, 10, 26, 134, 135, 145, 146, **152-63**, 165, 166, 168
Wilson, F. P., 113
Wilson, J. Dover, 1, 2, 5, 29, 42-45, 88, 111
Wilson, Robert, 119
Woman Killed with Kindness, A (Heywood), 129
Women in the plays, 7, 82-83, 97-98, 107-8, 133-51 *passim*
Woodstock, 49

Y

Yates, Frances, 2, 4, 5

SHAKESPEARE: THE HISTORIES

A Collection of Critical Essays

Edited by EUGENE M. WAITH

A

Abridgement of the Chronicles of England, An (Grafton), 26
Aegidus Romanus, 163, 166
Aeneid (Virgil), 54, 162, 166, 167
Ainger, Alfred, 133, 137
Alexander, 28
Alphonsus, King of Arragon (Greene), 47
Ambrose, Saint, 155
Anabasis (Xenophon), 16
Anarchy, theme of, 55, 58, 60, 70, 104, 107, 110-11
André, Bernard, 15, 16
Antony and Cleopatra, 9, 129
Aristotle, 153
Ascham, Roger, 21, 22, 43
Asteley, Sir Robert, 21
Augustine, Saint, 39

B

Bacon, Francis, 13
Baker, George Pierce, 3
Baldwin, William, 42, 43, 44
Bale, John, 2, 19, 20, 21, 49, 50
Barber, C. L., 8
Barnes, Harry Elmer, 13
Battenhouse, R., 176
Beaumont, Francis, 169
Bernard of Clairvaux, 157
Berners, Lord, 19
Biblical references, 39, 156

Blake, William, 139
Boccaccio, 43, 176
Bolingbroke, Henry (later Henry IV), 25, 29
Bonjour, Adrien, 86n, 95
Book of Common Prayer, 156
Boswell-Stone, W. G., 55, 59, 61, 62
Bradley, A. C., 140, 144
Brooke, Tucker, 4
Bruni, Leonardo, 21
Butterfield, Herbert, 56

C

Caesar, 16, 28, 38
Calvin, J., 50, 176
Camden, William, 13
Campbell, Lily B., 4, 5, 6, 7, 8, 10, 89
Campion, E., 177
Caxton, William, 19
Chambers, R. W., 139
Charlton, H. B., 5, 132
Chelidonius, 154-55, 167
Chichele, Archbishop, 161
Christianity and History (Butterfield), 56
Chronicle (Fabyan), 137
Chronicle (Hardyng), 15, 23
Chronicles (Holinshed), 5, 27, 67
Churchill, Winston S., 164-65
Churchyard, Thomas, 42
Cicero, 19, 24, 27, 28, 30, 159

Cinthio, G. G., 47
Civil war, theme of, 41, 55-65 *passim*, 70-71, 103-8, 113-14
Civil Wars (Daniel), 25, 62, 152
Coleridge, S. T., 3, 10
Collingwood, R. G., 55-56
Complete Gentleman, The (Peacham), 36
Cooper, Thomas, 20
Copernicus, 163
Cranmer, Thomas, 49
Cromwell, Oliver, 49
Cymbeline, 10, 47

D

Daniel, Samuel, 25, 62, 147, 152
Davies, Sir John, 38-39
De Casibus (Boccaccio), 43, 174, 176
De Consideratione (Bernard of Clairvaux), 157
Defence of Poesie (Sidney), 30
De Seyssel, Claude, 15, 16
Discoveries (Jonson), 153
Divine retribution, theme of, 56, 67-68, 72, 78, 82-84, 103, 175-79
Donne, John, 156
Dorius, R. J., 9
Dramatic devices, 10, 119-20, 158-59, 173
  "asides," 80-82
  dreams, 72-74
  formal patterning, 68-70, 75, 96-100
  paradox, 69-70, 82-84
  soliloquy, 63, 107-8, 143
Drayton, M., 174
Dryden, John, 32
Dudley, Lord Robert, 25
Duthie, G. I., 83, 84

E

Ecclesiastical Polity (Hooker), 157, 158
Edward IV, 42, 174
Edward VI, 40

Eliot, T. S., 69, 72
Elizabeth I, 35, 45, 49, 52, 53
Elizabethan historiography, 4-7, 13-31, 43-44, 50-51, 56, 102
Elizabethan world order, 8, 32-41, 44-46, 83-84, 102-5, 152-67 *passim*, 172
Elizabethan World Picture, The (Tillyard), 6
Ellis, Sir Henry, 17
Elyot, Sir Thomas, 43, 63, 154
English Historical Literature in the Fifteenth Century (Kingsford), 13
Epicene (Jonson), 170
Erasmus, 19, 154, 162, 166, 167
Essay on the Dramatic Character of Sir John Falstaff (Morgann), 3
Euripides, 138
Eusebius, 16
Everyman, 48
Excess, theme of, 113-31 *passim*, 135

F

Fabyan, Robert, 19, 24, 25, 43, 137, 140
Faerie Queen (Spenser), 51
Fair Em (anon.), 47
Fall, theme of, 9-10, 119-20, 172-79
Falls of Princes (Lydgate), 43
Falstaff, function of, 110, 127-30, 132-51 *passim*, 162-63
Famous Historye of the life and death of Captaine Thomas Stukeley, The, 1
Farnham, Willard, 9, 174, 175
Ferrers, George, 42
Fletcher, John, 169, 170
Fortescue, Sir John, 33-34
Fortunes Fashion (Sampson), 174
Fortunes of Falstaff (Wilson), 5
Froissart, Jean, 19, 24
Fueter, E., 13, 21

G

Geoffrey of Monmouth, 18, 24, 51

Gildas, 24
Gorboduc (Norton and Sackville), 42, 50, 51-54, 62
Governour, The (Elyot), 63, 154
Grafton, Richard, 15, 23, 26, 27, 30
Granville-Barker, Harvey, 3
Greene, Robert, 2, 47
Grey, Lady Elizabeth, 174
Grynaeus, 19

H

Halle, Edward, 5-8, 17, 21, 23, 25, 26, 27, 30, 42, 43, 46, 47, 52, 53, 62, 64, 67, 83, 103, 157, 159, 161, 163, 165
Hamlet, 10, 116, 150
Hardyng, John, 15, 19, 23, 26
Hart, Alfred, 41
Hayward, Sir John, 35
Hazlitt, William, 141
Henry IV, 29
Henry IV, 3, 8, 9, 10, 47, 83, 104-9 *passim*, 113-31 *passim*, 132-51 *passim*
  1 Henry IV, 114, 125, 128, 132, 143, 144-50, 155, 158
    chivalry, theme of, 134, 142-51
    and Falstaff, 132-51
    ideal king, theme of, 104-5, 138, 143
    salvation, theme of, 134-35, 138-39
    vanity, theme of, 140-41
  2 Henry IV, 66, 104, 108, 110, 114-15, 130, 140, 142, 144, 145, 155, 158, 162, 164
    and Falstaff, 132-51
    ideal king, theme of, 104-5, 138, 143
    justice, theme of, 134
    salvation, theme of, 134-35, 138-39
    vanity, theme of, 140-41
Henry V, 3, 5, 8, 102-12 *passim*, 113-31 *passim*, 140, 141
  and contemporary view of history, 152-59
  as epic, 152-67 *passim*
  conversion, 140-41, 152, 155-59
  ideal king, theme of, 8, 105, 110, 113, 131, 152-67 *passim*
  order, theme of, 8, 110, 114
Henry VI, 55
Henry VI, 55-65
  anarchy, theme of, 55, 56-64
  order, theme of, 55, 56-57
    1 Henry VI, 1, 61
    2 Henry VI, 56-57, 59, 60, 62-63
    3 Henry VI, 2, 56-60, 63-65
Henry VII, 44
Henry VIII, 42, 49
Henry VIII, 1, 2, 3, 10, 113, **168-79**
Hexaemeron (Ambrose), 155
Heywood, Thomas, 2, 61
Higden, R., 14, 34
Historical drama, 1
  ancestry of, 7-8, 42-54
  contemporary popularity of, 1-2
  nature of, 3-4, 56, 83-84
History of Richard III, The (More), 21, 23
History of the World (Raleigh), 30
Hobbes, Thomas, 60
Holinshed, R., 5, 19, 27, 28-30, 57, 59, 60, 61, 67, 68, 103, 147, 157, 160, 161, 163, 177
Holy Living and Holy Dying (Taylor), 156-57
Homilies, 40, 44, 50, 52, 53
Honor, theme of, 85-101 *passim*
Hooker, Richard, 27, 156, 157, 158

I

Idea of History, The (Collingwood), 56
Imagery, 9, 114
  birth, 63-64
  fatness and disease, 9, 114-17, 120-22, 126, 128-31

Imagery (*continued*)
  garden, 7, 117-25
  husbandry, 114, 117, 120
  music, 32, 119
  nature, 62-63, 65, 93, 120-21,
    131
  night, 75-76
  time, 66, 91, 117-25, 129-30
Institutes (Calvin), 50
Institutio Principis (Erasmus), 154-55

J

Jewel, Bishop of Salisbury, 45
Johnson, Samuel, 3, 94, 146, 169
Jonson, Ben, 153, 169

K

Kabbala, 39
King Johan (Bale), 2, 49, 50
King John, 49
King John, 1, 69, 111
  opportunism, theme of, 85-101,
    129
King Lear, 1, 10, 61
Kingliness, ideal of, 63, 105-6, 108-9,
  113, 143, 155, 159-63, 166-67
Kingsford, C. L., 5, 13, 14, 17, 137,
  140
Knights, L. C., 8

L

*Laboryouse Journey and Serche of
  Johan Leylande for Englands An-
  tiquities* (Leland), 19
Language, 61, 68-69, 85, 113-31
  passim
Languet, 21
Leech, Clifford, 9
Leland, John, 19, 20, 27
Liber Metricus (Elmham),
  157
*Life and Death of Thomas Wolsey
  Cardinal* (Storer), 177
Life of Wolsey (Cavendish), 176

Livy, 16
Lollardy, 133, 137, 160
Lovejoy, A., 39
Lovesick King, The (anon.), 47
Lydgate, John, 43

M

Macbeth, 1, 10, 11, 12, 60
Machiavelli, N., 79-80
*Manuell of the Chronicles of England,
  A* (Grafton), 26
Marlowe, Christopher, 1, 54, 71, 82
Marriott, J. A. R., 4, 6
Mary, Queen of Scots, 45
Mary Tudor, 49
Matilda (Drayton), 174
Measure for Measure, 66
Melancthon, 28
Milton, John, 38, 39, 139
Mirror for Magistrates, A (Sackville
  et al.), 7, 8, 25, 42, 43, 44, 47, 51,
  53, 173, 174, 176, 177, 178
More, Sir Thomas, 13, 21, 22, 23, 25,
  26, 27, 46, 67
Morgann, Maurice, 3
Morris, Christopher, 6

N

Nashe, Thomas, 1
Natural History (Pliny), 155
Natural Theology (de Sebonde),
  36-37
Nelson, William, 15, 16
Newton, Isaac, 67
Norton, Thomas, 50, 53

O

*Of the Institution and firste beginning
  of Christian Princes* (Chelidonius),
  154-55
Oldcastle, Sir John, 133, 137
Orchestra (Davies), 38-39
Order, theme of, 6-7, 11, 32-34, 39,
  51

Order, theme of (*continued*)
  in *Henry IV*, 133-34, 140
  in *Henry VI*, 56-57
  in *King John*, 100-101
  in *Richard II*, 8, 103-6
Orff, Carl, 76

P

Paradise Regained (Milton), 139
Pastime of People (Rastell), 18
Paul, Saint, 157
Plato, 32, 38, 39
Plautus, 135
Pliny, 155
Political themes, predominance of,
  4-6, 8, 12, 113, 133-34
Polychronicon (Higden), 14, 34
Pope, Alexander, 34
Prayer for My Daughter, A (Yeats),
  77
Primaudaye, 176
Principe, Il (Machiavelli), 80
Prudence, theme of, 113-31 *passim*

R

Raleigh, Sir Walter, 13, 15, 27, 30,
  159, 175, 176
Rastell, John, 18
Reese, M. M., 7, 8
Revenge, theme of, 61, 77
Ribner, Irving, 8
Richard II, 11, 25, 29, 42
Richard II, 3, 5, 89, 102-12 *passim*,
  113-31 *passim*
  and allegory, 7
  and contemporary political thought,
    102-6
  expiation, theme of, 103-4
  imagery, 9, 114-15, 117-25
  negligence, theme of, 105-6, 117-25
  order, theme of, 8, 103-6
  waste, theme of, 104, 117-20,
    113-17
Richard III, 26, 29, 42, 44, 45, 55,
  67, 113
Richard III, 3, 5, 7, 10, 64-65, **66-84**

anarchy, theme of, 70-71
  humor, function of, 69-70, 72,
    78-82
  order, theme of, 11
  retribution, theme of, 8, 67-68,
    72-74
  soliloquy, function of, 59
  supernatural in, 72, 76-77, 92
Richardus Tertius (Legge), 2
Ridley, M. R., 79-80
Roderick, Richard, 168
Rosamund (Daniel), 174
Rossiter, A. P., 7, 10
Royal responsibility, theme of, 4-5, 8,
  12, 113
  in *Henry IV*, 108-9, 138, 143
  in *Henry V*, 165-67
  in *Henry VIII*, 172, 178-79
  in *King John*, 95

S

Sackville, Thomas, 42, 50
Sallust, 16
Schanzer, Ernest, 9
*Scottish History of James IV, slain at
  Flodden, The* (Greene), 47
Sebonde, M. de, 36-37
Self-interest, theme of, 85-101 *passim*
Seneca, 61, 69, 71, 72, 77, 78, 83
Sermon of Obedience, or *An Exhortation concerning good Ordre and
  Obedience to Rulers and Magistrates,*
  40
Shakespeare, William:
  biographical information, 1, 41
  civil war, experience of, 41
  and contemporary attitude to his-
    tory, 4-8, 13-29
  contemporary relevance of themes,
    1-2, 30, 103
  and Elizabethan world order, 32-34,
    36-37, 39-41
  and Holinshed, 5, 30, 57, 60, 67,
    103, 160-61, 177
  medieval mystery plays, influence
    of, 7-8
  and national unity, 4-5

Shakespeare, William (*continued*)
    political ideas of, 8
    popular success of, 1, 3
    stage experience of, 79
Shakespeare, William, works by: (*see*
    main entry for starred items*)
    Antony and Cleopatra, 9, 129
    Cymbeline, 10, 47
    Hamlet, 10, 116, 150
    Henry IV, * 3, 8, 9, 10, 47, 66, 83,
        104-9 *passim,* 113-31 *passim,*
        132-51 *passim,* 155, 158
    Henry V, * 3, 5, 8, 102-12 *passim,*
        113-31 *passim,* 140, 141, 152-67
    Henry VI, * 1, 2, 5, 55-65, 69, 70,
        73, 76, 78, 79, 120, 128, 164,
        166
    Henry VIII, 1, 2, 3, 10, 113, 168-79
    King John, * 1, 6, 9, 85-101, 111,
        129
    King Lear, 1, 10, 61
    Macbeth, 1, 10, 11, 12, 60
    Measure for Measure, 66
    Richard II, * 3, 5, 7, 8, 9, 89,
        102-12 *passim,* 113-31 *passim,*
        138, 143, 178
    Richard III, * 3, 5, 7, 10, 11, 59, 64,
        65, 66-84, 92, 158
    Tempest, The, 56
    Troilus and Cressida, 5, 6, 32
    Winter's Tale, The, 168, 171, 174
Shakespeare's History Plays (Tillyard),
    83
Shore, Jane, 42
Sidney, Sir Philip, 30, 45, 54, 148,
    153
Simpson, Richard, 55
Sophonisba (Murray), 174
Sources, 5-6, 8, 13-31 *passim,* 40-41,
    66-67, 85, 106-7, 150
Spenser, Edmund, 51, 146-47
Spurgeon, C., 173
Storer, Thomas, 177
Structure, 7, 9
    of *Henry IV,* 116-17
    of *Henry V,* 153
    of *King John,* 86
    of *Richard III,* 66-84

Stylistic devices, 9, 57
    echoes, 69, 74-75
    rhetorical patterns, 10, 11, 69-70,
        82-83, 115
Suetonius, 16
Supernatural, use of, 38, 72, 76-77,
    92
Surrey, Henry Howard, Earl of, 54

T

Tacitus, 16
Tamburlaine (Marlowe), 82
Taylor, Jeremy, 156
Tempest, The, 56
Tennyson, Alfred Lord, 169, 170
Terence, 135, 136, 138
Thomas Aquinas, 175
Thucydides, 16, 22, 28
Thyestes (Heywood), 61
Tillyard, E. M. W., 4, 5, 6, 7, 8, 83,
    84, 90, 92, 95, 152
*Tragicall History of the Life and
    Death of Doctor Faustus* (Marlowe),
    1
Troilus and Cressida, 5, 6, 32
Troublesome Raigne, The (anon.),
    85
Troyes, Treaty of, 166

U

*Union of the Two Noble and Illustrious
    Families of York and Lancaster, The*
    (Halle), 5
Usurpation, theme of, 6, 8, 70, 103,
    104, 106

V

Valerius Maximus, 16
Vegetius, 163
Vergil, Polydore, 13, 15, 16, 17, 18,
    19, 21, 25, 43, 46
Virgil, 159, 162, 166
Vita et Gesta Henrici Quinti (anon.),
    157-58

W

Wagner, Richard, 71
Walpole, Horace, 67
When you see me you know me
    (Rowley), 173
Wilson, F. P., 2
Wilson, J. Dover, 5, 7, 8, 83, 84, 102,
    152, 153, 159, 164, 165, 166
Winter's Tale, The, 168, 171, 174
Wolfe, Reginald, 27
Woodstock (anon.), 103
Works (Hooker), 156

Wright, Louis, 4

X

Xenophon, 15, 16

Y

Yeats, W. B., 77
Youth (anon.), 134

Z

Zeeveld, W. Gordon, 23

SHAKESPEARE: THE TRAGEDIES

A Collection of Critical Essays

Edited by ALFRED HARBAGE

A

Acts and Monuments (Foxe), 7
Aeschylus, 9, 18, 19, 23
Allegory:
  in *King Lear*, 113-14, 118, 120,
    122
  in *Othello*, 83-84
  in *Timon of Athens*, 149
Antony and Cleopatra, 8, 45, 151,
  152-68, 170, 171
  characterization in, 166
  imagery in, 153-54
  Dr. Johnson on, 152
  and *Julius Caesar*, 161
  and *Timon of Athens*, 151
  and *Troilus and Cressida*, 159
Apology for Actors (Heywood),
  4
Arcadia (Sidney), 120
Aristotle, 5-6, 9, 105-12, 148 (*see also*
  Poetics)

B

Baldwin, William, 4, 6
Beethoven, Ludwig van, 174
Bismarck, Otto von, 26
Blake, William, 96
Boccaccio, Giovanni, 4, 6
Bond of Association (1584), 61
Bowers, F. T., 66
Bradley, A. C., 1, 22, 45, 62-63, 64,
  67, 68, 70

Broglie, Duc de, 85

C

Canterbury Tales, The (Chaucer),
  3-4
Carlyle, Thomas, 139
Chapman, George, 7, 71
Characterization:
  in *Antony and Cleopatra*, 166
  in *King Lear*, 117-21, 142-44
  in *Othello*, 75-76, 80-81, 85-92
Chaucer, Geoffrey, 3-4
Chekhov, Anton, 123
Christian influences:
  in Elizabethan tragedy, 7, 11-12,
    112
  in *King Lear*, 115-16, 146
Cicero, 69
Cocktail Party, The (T. S. Eliot), 62
Coleridge, Samuel Taylor, 70, 74,
  165, 173
Comic relief:
  in *Hamlet*, 72
  in *King Lear*, 123-38
Contemptus mundi, concept of, in
  Elizabethan tragedy, 4-6, 21, 22
Contention of Ajax and Ulysses, The
  (Shirley), 4
Coriolan (T. S. Eliot), 174
Coriolanus, 8, 152, **169-75**
  imagery in, 172-73
  sources of, 170-71
Cromwell, Thomas, 7

Curry, W. C., 102

D

Dante Alighieri, 105
Death, theme of, in *Hamlet*, 71-74
De casibus forms, in Elizabethan
  tragedy, 5-7, 21
De Casibus Virorum Illustrium
  (Boccaccio), 4, 6
Declaration of Egregious Popishe
  Impostures (Harsnett), 114
Devereux, Robert, 169
Divine Comedy, The, (Dante), 105
Donatus, Aelius, 3, 6
Donne, John, 69
Dostoevsky, Fydor, 123, 136, 146
Drayton, Michael, 6
Duchess of Malfi, The (Webster),
  132

E

"East Coker" (T. S. Eliot), 57
Eliot, George, 73
Eliot, T. S., 45, 57, 62, 63, 73,
  145-46, 174
Elizabeth I, 4, 61, 170
Elizabethan Revenge Tragedy
  (Bowers), 66
Elizabethan tragedy:
  and Aristotle's *Poetics*, 105-12
  Christian influences on, 7, 11-12,
    112
  contemptus mundi, concept of, 4-
    6, 21, 22
  de casibus forms, 5-7, 21
  definitions of, 7
  development of, 3-9
  and Greek tragedy, 11, 12, 18, 23,
    66-67
  heroes in, 7-8, 146
  and medieval forms, 3-4, 8, 67
  revenge tragedy, 5
Emerson, Ralph Waldo, 114
Enemy of the People, An (Ibsen), 173
Essex, Earl of (*see* Devereux, Robert;
  Cromwell, Thomas)

Ethics (Aristotle), 105
Euripides, 9
Evil, theme of:
  in *King Lear*, 116-17, 120-21, 142
  in *Macbeth*, 93-95, 101-2

F

Faerie Queene, The (Spenser), 69,
  114
Fall of Princes, The (Lydgate), 4, 6
Fate, theme of, 3, 8, **10-11**
  in *Hamlet*, 54
  in *Romeo and Juliet*, 30-31, 33
Fortune (*see* Fate, theme of)
Foxe, John, 7
France, Anatole, 57
Freud, Sigmund, 113

G

Geoffrey of Monmouth, 114
Gladstone, William, 26
Goethe, J. W. von, 74
Granville-Barker, H., 14, 58, 68, 85,
  152, 153, 155, 156, 161
Greek tragedy, and Elizabethan
  tragedy, 11, 12, 18, 23, 66-67
Greene, Robert, 24, 25

H

Hamlet, 2, 8, 12, 13-14, 16, 19-20, 21,
  44-60, 61-70, 71-74, 140-41, 151,
  170, 171
  comic relief in, 72
  death, theme of, 71-74
  Fate, theme of, 54
  imagery in, 50-53
  Dr. Johnson, on, 62-64, 65, 67,
    70
  and *Julius Caesar*, 72
  and *King Lear*, 72, 140-41
  and *Macbeth*, 69
  mortality, theme of, 53-54, 59
  nineteenth-century criticism of, 2
  and *Othello*, 44-45, 68-69, 72
  puns and riddles in, 46-47

Hamlet (*continued*)
    reality vs. appearance, theme of,
      48-50, 53
    revenge, theme of, 56-59, 61
    and *Revenger's Tragedy, The*
      (Tourneur), 65-66
    and *Romeo and Juliet*, 72
    and *Spanish Tragedy, The* (Kyd),
      64-65, 66, 67, 70, 71
    and *Timon of Athens*, 151
    and *Titus Andronicus*, 65, 70
Harsnett, Samuel, 114
Hazlitt, William, 115, 117
Henry IV, Part I, 7-8, 87
Henry of Navarre, 61
Heroes, in Elizabethan tragedy, 7-8,
    146
Heywood, Thomas, 4
Higgins, John, 114
Historia Regum Britanniae (Geoffrey
    of Monmouth), 114
History of the World, The (Raleigh),
    65
Hobbes, Thomas, 97
Holinshed, Raphael, 114
Humanism, in Shakespeare's drama,
    14-17

I

Ibsen, Henrik, 173
Imagery:
    in *Antony and Cleopatra*, 153-54
    in *Coriolanus*, 172-73
    in *Hamlet*, 50-53
    in *King Lear*, 139-40, 144
    in *Macbeth*, 98-100
    in *Romeo and Juliet*, 30, 32

J

James I, 110
Johnson, Dr. Samuel:
    on *Antony and Cleopatra*,
      152
    on *Hamlet*, 62-64, 65, 67, 70
    on *King Lear*, 115
Jonson, Ben, 9

Joyce, James, 174
Julius Caesar, 8, **34-43**, 161, 170,
    171
    and *Antony and Cleopatra*, 161
    and *Hamlet*, 72

K

Keats, John, 115
King John, 87-88
King Lear, 1-2, 6, 8, 13, 14, 16, 20-21,
    45, 58, 68, 87, 94-97, 98, 113-22,
    123-38, 139-47, 168, 170, 171
    allegory in, 113-14, 118, 120, 122
    characterization in, 117-21, 142-44
    Christian influences on, 115-16,
      146
    comic relief in, 123-38
    evil, theme of, 116-17, 120-21, 142
    and *Hamlet*, 72, 140-41
    imagery in, 139-40, 144
    Dr. Johnson on, 115
    and *Macbeth*, 94-97, 98
    and *Merchant of Venice, The*, 113
    nineteenth-century criticism of, 1-2,
      115
    and *Othello*, 127, 139
    reality vs. appearance, theme of,
      119
    Senecan influences, 145-46
    sources of, 115
    subplot in, 131-34, 136
    and *Timon of Athens*, 127, 130-31,
      150, 151
    and *Titus Andronicus*, 24, 26, 132
    and *Troilus and Cressida*, 127-28,
      130
Knight, Wilson, 98
Kyd, Thomas, 25, 64-65, 66-67, 70,
    71

L

Lamb, Charles, 115, 117
Leviathan (Hobbes), 97
Lydgate, John, 4, 6
Lyly, John,
    24

M

Macbeth, 2, 8, 13, 14, 16, 19, 20, 21, 45, 58, 69, **93-104, 105-12,** 168, 170, 171
  and Aristotle's theories, 105-12
  evil, theme of, 93-95, 101-2
  and *Hamlet,* 69
  imagery in, 98-100
  and *King Lear,* 94-97, 98
  nineteenth-century criticism of, 2
  reality vs. appearance, theme of, 95-103
  structure of, 109-111
Madariaga, Salvador de, 45
Marlowe, Christopher, 24-25
Matilda (Drayton), 6
Merchant of Venice, The, 113
Middlemarch (G. Eliot), 73
Midsummer Night's Dream, A, 28-29, 78
Mirror for Magistrates, The (Baldwin and Higgins), 4, 6, 114
Mirror for Martyrs, The (Weever), 6
Monk's Tale, The (Chaucer), 3-4
Morality tradition (*see* Elizabethan tragedy, and medieval forms)
More, Sir Thomas, 7
Mortality, theme of, in *Hamlet,* 53-54, 59

N

Neale, Sir John, 61
Necessity (*see* Fate, theme of)
Niccols, Richard, 6-7
North, Sir Thomas, 171

O

Oedipus Rex (Sophocles), 105-6
Oldcastle, Sir John, 6, 7
Othello, 2, 8, 13-14, 16, 20-21, 57, 68-69, **75-84, 85-92,** 127, 139, 170, 174
  allegory in, 83-84

  characterization in, 75-76, 80-81, 85-92
  and *Hamlet,* 44-45, 68-69, 72
  and *King Lear,* 127, 139
  and *Midsummer Night's Dream, A,* 78
  nineteenth-century criticism of, 2
  structure of, 76
  symbolism in, 77-79
  and *Tempest, The,* 78

P

Paul, Henry N., 109, 110
Paul, Saint, 85
Peele, George, 24, 25
Phaedo (Plato), 69
Plato, 69, 175
Plutarch, Shakespeare's use of, 35, 36, 37, 42, 170-71, 174
Poetics (Aristotle), 6, 9, 148
  and *Macbeth,* 105-12
Political themes, in Shakespeare's drama, 26, 34-43 *passim*
Prefaces to Shakespeare (Granville-Barker), 152, 153, 155, 156, 161
Psychology (Aristotle), 105
Puns and riddles, in *Hamlet,* 46-47
Puttenham, Samuel, 5

R

Raleigh, Sir Walter, 65, 169
Rape of Lucrece, The, 6, 28, 98, 100
Reality vs. appearance, theme of:
  in *Hamlet,* 48-50, 53
  in *King Lear,* 119
  in *Macbeth,* 95, 103
Redemption and atonement, in Elizabethan tragedy, 7
Reinhardt, Max, 169
Revenge, theme of, 64-70
  in *Hamlet,* 56-59, 61
Revenge tragedy, forms of, 5
Revenger's Tragedy, The (Tourneur), 65-66

Richard II, 41, 43, 169
Richard III, 12, 19
Robert Duke of Normandy
  (Drayton), 6
Romeo and Juliet, 8, 28-33, 57
  Fate, theme of, 30-31, 33
  and Hamlet, 72
  imagery in, 30, 32
  and Midsummer Night's Dream, A,
    28-29
Royal Play of Macbeth, The (Paul),
  109

S

Seneca, 3, 4, 66, 72n
  influence of, in King Lear, 145-46
Shakespeare, William:
  and his contemporaries, 8-9, 24-25,
  humanism of, 14-17
  and Marlowe, Christopher, 24-25
  moral world of, 10-17 passim
  nineteenth-century criticism of, 1-2
  and Plutarch, use of, 35, 36, 37, 42,
    170-71, 174
  as a political dramatist, 26, 34-43
    passim
  and Seneca, 3, 4, 66, 72n
Shakespeare, William, works by: (see
  also main entry for starred items)
  Antony and Cleopatra,* 8, 45, 151,
    152-68, 170, 171
  Coriolanus,* 8, 152, 169-75
  Hamlet,* 2, 8, 12, 13-14, 16, 19-20,
    21, 44-60, 61-70, 140-41, 151,
    170, 171
  Henry IV, Part I, 7-8, 87
  Julius Caesar,* 8, 34-43, 161, 170,
    171
  King John, 87-88
  King Lear,* 1-2, 6, 8, 13, 14, 16,
    20-21, 45, 58, 68, 87, 94-97, 98,
    113-22, 123-38, 139-47, 168, 170,
    171
  Macbeth,* 2, 8, 13, 14, 16, 19, 20,
    21, 45, 58, 69, 93-104, 105-12,
    168, 170, 171
  Merchant of Venice, The, 113

Midsummer Night's Dream, A, 28-
  29, 78
Othello,* 2, 8, 13-14, 16, 20-21, 57,
  68-69, 75-84, 85-92, 127, 139,
  170, 174
Rape of Lucrece, The, 6, 28, 98,
  100
Richard II, 41, 43, 169
Richard III, 12, 19
Romeo and Juliet,* 8, 28-33, 57
Tempest, The, 78, 87
Timon of Athens,* 8, 127, 130-31,
  137, 148-51, 152, 171
Titus Andronicus,* 8, 24-27, 132,
  172
Troilus and Cressida,* 8, 127-28,
  130, 159
Shakespearean Tragedy (Bradley), 1,
  22, 45, 62-63, 64, 67, 68, 70
Shakespeare's Philosophical Patterns
  (Curry), 102
Shirley, James, 4
Sidney, Sir Philip, 5, 120
Sophocles, 9, 19, 105-6
Spanish Tragedy, The (Kyd), 64-65,
  66, 67, 70
  and Hamlet, 71
Spenser, Edmund, 69, 114
Spinoza, Baruch, 100
Spurgeon, Caroline, 50, 54
Structure:
  of Macbeth, 109-11
  of Othello, 76
Stuart, Mary, 61
Subplot, in King Lear, 131-34, 136
Symbolism, in Othello, 77-79

T

Tempest, The, 78, 87
Tillyard, E. M. W., 45, 46, 56, 58
Timon of Athens, 8, 127, 130-31, 137,
  148-51, 152, 171
  allegory in, 149
  and Antony and Cleopatra, 151
  and Hamlet, 151
  and King Lear, 127, 130-31, 137,
    150, 151

Titus Andronicus, 8, **24-27,** 132, 172
    and *Hamlet,* 65, 70
    and *King Lear,* 24, 26, 132
Tolstoy, Leo, 113
Tourneur, Cyril, 65-66
Tragedy (*see* Elizabethan tragedy)
Troilus and Cressida, 8, 127-28, 130,
    159
    and *Antony and Cleopatra,* 159
    and *King Lear,* 127-28, 130
*True Chronicle History of King Leir,
    The* (anon.), 114

W

Waste Land, The (T. S. Eliot),
    145
Webster, John, 132
Weever, John, 6
William the Silent, 61
Wilson, J. Dover, 62

Y

Yeats, William Butler, 60

G. B. SHAW
A Collection of Critical Essays
Edited by R. J. KAUFMANN

A

Adventures of the Black Girl in Her Search for God, The, 129
Aeschylus, 52, 146-49
Aesthetics, of Shaw, 43-51, 53, 170-78 *passim*
Albee, Edward, 12
Allegory, Shaw's use of, 45-47, 53-54
Androcles and the Lion, 37, 123, 127
Apple Cart, The, 11, 68, 78-85 *passim,* 121, 122-23, 128
Archer, William, 46, 59, 61, 67-68
Aristophanes, 3, 54, 119
Aristotle, 52, 54-55, 58, 59, 60, 144, 145, 149
Arms and the Man, 59, 62-63, 64, 106, 123, 138
Augier, Émile, 59-62

B

Bacchae, The, (Euripides), 94
Back to Methuselah, 8, 9, 53, 76n, 78-84 *passim,* 100, 108, 113, 120, 122, 124, 125, 128, **130-42,** 174
Badiali, Cesare, 24
Barker, Granville, 130-31, 139
Barzun, Jacques, 42, 53
Bassetto, Corno di (Shaw's *nom de plume* as music critic), 23
Bataille de Dames (Scribe), 59
Beethoven, Ludwig van, 44

Bellamy, Edward, 28
Blackmur, R. P., 44, 51, 52
Blake, William, 9, 44, 109, 170-78
Brecht, Bertolt, 5, 15-18
Brieux, Eugène, 169
Brooke, Stopford, 28
Brophy, Brigid, 12
Bunyan, John, 44, 119, 170
Buoyant Billions, 129
Burlador de Sevilla, El (Tirso de Molina), 108
Butler, Samuel, 30, 49, 102, 133, 135n
Byron, George Gordon, Lord, 123, 125, 127, 128

C

Caesar and Cleopatra, 7, 78-85 *passim,* 123, 126, 129, 172, 176
Campbell, Mrs. Patrick, 69
Candida, 69-72, 73, 112, 121, 122, 173
and *Doll's House, A* (Ibsen), 70-72
Captain Brassbound's Conversion, 7, 68, 80-85 *passim,* 120, 121, 126
Carlisle, Lady Rosalind Frances, Countess of, 89-90
Carlyle, Thomas, 30, 165
Carpenter, Edward, 43
Cashel Byron's Profession, 50
Ceinture dorée, La (Augier), 59
Chekhov, Anton, 30, 111, 115-16
Cherry Orchard, The (Chekhov), 115-16

Chesterton, G. K., 43, 44, 47, 48, 50, 53, 130n, 134n, 162
Coleridge, Samuel Taylor, 49
"Common Sense About the War," 29, 37
Condition of the Working Class in England in 1844, The (Engels), 45, 47
Congreve, William, 54, 112
Creditors (Strindberg), 86

D

Darwin, Charles, 28, 98, 102
Death of a Salesman (Miller), 146
Dekker, Thomas, 54
Devil's Disciple, The, 62, 106, 170
Dickens, Charles, 11, 30
Doctor's Dilemma, The, 9, 11, 121, 163-65, 166, 168
Doll's House, A (Ibsen), 70-72
Don Giovanni (Mozart-Da Ponte), 64, 108, 138
Don Juan (Byron), 128
"Don Juan in Hell" (*see Man and Superman*)
Drama:
    comic, 7, **51-56**, **57-75**, 104-5, 106-7, 110, 112, 117-18, 119, 132
    tragic, **51-56**, 104-5, 105n, **143-61**, **162-69**
    tragicomic, 7, 76-87, 107, 130-42 *passim*
Drama criticism, of Shaw, 4, 58, 76-77
Dramaturgy, 5, 12, 58-66
    of *Arms and the Man*, 62-63
    of *Man and Superman*, 64-66
    of *Widowers' Houses*, 59-62
Dream Play, The (Strindberg), 104, 140
Dumas, Alexandre (*fils*), 59, 62

E

Einstein, Albert, 101
Eliot, T. S., 9, 114, 143-61

Emerson, Ralph Waldo, 171
Engels, Friedrich, 45, 47
Erewhon (Butler), 133, 135n
Euripides, 44, 52, 91, 94
Everybody's Political What's What, 29, 103
Everyman (Anon.), 64, 153

F

Fabian Society, 4, 44, 98, 103-4
Facts for Fabians (Shaw, et al.), 44
Family Reunion, The (Eliot), 114, 147
Fanny's First Play, 11, 106
Farewell to Arms, A (Hemingway), 144, 145, 160
Father, The (Strindberg), 86
Fergusson, Francis, 44, 51-55, 88, 151
Flecker, James Elroy, 128
Forster, E. M., 91
Freud, Sigmund, 102
Frisch, Max, 11

G

Galsworthy, John, 114
George, Henry, 28
Getting Married, 104n, 121, 122, 123-24
Ghosts, (Ibsen), 145
Goethe, Johann Wolfgang von, 44, 119
Golden Journey to Samarkand, The, (Flecker), 128
Good King Charles's Golden Days, 121, 129
Gorky, Maxim, 30
Gounod, Charles, 24
Gurly, Walter, 45

H

Hamlet (Shakespeare), 144, 145, 148, 161
Hardy, Thomas, 43
Harris, Frank, 34-35, 67, 68, 71, 74

Heartbreak House, 8, 82-83, **113-18**,
   122, 124, 126, 128, 129, 132, 138,
   170
Hemingway, Ernest, 144, 146, 147,
   160
Henderson, Archibald, 45, 45*n*, 48*n*,
   50, 53, 76, 114
Hitler, Adolf, 11, 31
Hogarth, William, 170
Humor, Shaw's use of, 9, 21, 126-28,
   166-67
Hyndman, H. M., 107, 110

I

Ibsen, Henrik, 12, 30, 44, 46-47, 58,
   70-72, 91, 102, 104, 111, 115, 117,
   119, 123, 125, 126, 145, 147, 161,
   162, 169
Ice Man Cometh, The (O'Neill), 104
Idealism, in Shaw's works, 36-41, 46,
   100-118 *passim*, 135
Immaturity, 28
*Intelligent Woman's Guide to Social-
   ism and Capitalism, The*, 35
Ionesco, Eugène, 11

J

James, Henry, 43
Joad, Cyril, 50
John Bull's Other Island, 11, 35, 88-
   89, 122, 124, 127, 128, 129
Johnson, Samuel, 49
Jonson, Ben, 54, 62, 105
Joyce, James, 43, 145

K

Kant, Immanuel, 48
Keats, John, 10
King Lear (Shakespeare), 104, 165
Kopit, Arthur, 11
Kronenberger, Louis, 42

L

Lady Inger of Ostraat (Ibsen), 58

Lamarck, Jean Baptiste de, 119
Langer, Susanne, 44, 48, 49*n*
Lawrence, D. H., 86-87, 106
Liberalism, and Shaw, 88-99, 102
Literary style, of Shaw, 32-36, 39-41,
   47-50

M

Mailer, Norman, 146
Major Barbara, 7, 13, 72, 83-84, **88-99**,
   117, 120, 123, 137-38, 141, 173
Mallarmé, Stéphane, 48
Man and Superman, 6, 8, 13, 39-40,
   64-66, 74-75, 81, 88-89, 103, **108-13**,
   116, 120, 121, 122, 125, 127, 129,
   138, 170, 171, 172, 176
Man of Destiny, The, 122
Marx, Karl, 28, 30, 51, 104, 107, 110,
   119
Maupassant, Guy de, 72
Menander, 54
Michelangelo, 24, 44
Miller, Arthur, 105, 105*n*, 146
Milton, John, 144, 145, 155, 161
Misalliance, 120, 122, 124, 126, 127,
   128, 138
Miss Julie (Strindberg), 86
Molière, 11, 12, 30, 54, 62, 65, 89, 90,
   105, 173
Morris, William, 30, 43
Mourning Becomes Electra (O'Neill),
   146
Mozart, Wolfgang Amadeus, 12, 51,
   73
Mrs. Warren's Profession, 9, 11, 68, 72-
   73, 79-83 *passim*, 104*n*, 119, 163,
   165-66
Much Ado About Nothing (Shake-
   speare), 112
Murder in the Cathedral (Eliot), 9,
   143-61
Murray, Gilbert, 89, 90-91, 99, 150
Music, and Shaw, 4, 12, 23, 50-51,
   137-38
Mussolini, Benito, 11, 31, 32*n*
My Fair Lady (Lerner), 74
Myth, and Shaw, 47, 47*n*, 52-54, 109

N

Naked and the Dead, The (Mailer), 146
Nietzsche, Friedrich, 30, 71, 109, 110, 119, 123, 126, 127, 128
Nobel, Alfred, 94-95
Nobel Prize, 12

O

O'Casey, Sean, 128, 129, 162
Oedipus (Sophocles), 55, 104, 124, 144, 148, 149, 154-55, 156, 159, 161
O'Neill, Eugene, 104, 146-47
On the Rocks, 119, 120, 126, 127, 175
Othello (Shakespeare), 161
Overruled, 68, 106

P

Passion, Poison and Petrifaction, 11
Pater, Walter, 50
Pavlov, Ivan, 101
Peacock, Ronald, 55
Pearson, Hesketh, 28
Perfect Wagnerite, The, 46, 50-51
Phèdre (Racine), 144, 145
Philanderer, The, 106, 119, 121, 122
Philosophy, of Shaw, 37-41, 100-118, 120, 140-41
Pinter, Harold, 11
Pirandello, Luigi, 44, 52
Plato, 53-54, 133-34, 135, 136, 141
Plautus, 54, 62
Political criticism, of Shaw, 7-8, 30-31, 100-118 *passim,* 170-78 *passim*
Portrait of the Artist as a Young Man, A, (Joyce), 145
Pound, Ezra, 43, 49
Powys, John Cowper, 128
Pretenders, The (Ibsen), 127
Pygmalion, 7, 11, 73-74, 77-84 *passim,* 106

Q

Quintessence of Ibsenism, The, 39, 45-46, 46n, 100-101, 121, 135

R

Rabelais (Powys), 128
Racine, Jean, 144, 145
Rationalism, and Shaw, 52-54, 55
Read, Sir Herbert, 49
Realism, and Shaw, 39-41, 45-46, 65, 100-118 *passim,* 135
Realms of Being (Santyana), 146
Religion, and Shaw, 23, 25, 27, 37, 45, 105, 170-78 *passim*
"Religion of the Pianoforte, The," 46
Republic (Plato), 133-34, 136, 141
Revolutionist's Handbook, The, 33-34, 34n, 110, 120
Rhinegold (Archer), 59
Rilke, Rainer Maria, 47
Ring of the Nibelung, The (Wagner), 23, 45, 51
Rosmersholm (Ibsen), 104, 145, 147
Ruskin, John, 30

S

Sacred Wood, The (Eliot), 155
Saint Joan, 4, 9, 11, 13, 44, 72, 75, 103, 122, 124-25, 127, 128, **143-61**, 163, 166-68
Samson Agonistes (Milton), 144, 145, 155, 161
Santayana, George, 146
Sappho, 45
Sardou, Victorien, 58, 62
Schopenhauer, Arthur, 30, 109
Scott, Dixon, 48
Scribe, Eugène, 50, 58-60, 62, 63, 64, 65, 72, 73
Sexuality, and Shaw, 66-69, 80-87, 108-9, 111-12, **120-26**
Shakespeare, William, 1, 4, 10, 11, 12, 23, 24, 42, 48, 48n, 65, 67, 81, 101, 103, 104, 106, 112, 125, 126, 128,

Shakespeare, William (*continued*)
141*n*, 144, 145, 161, 165, 171,
172-73
Shavian personality, 1-13, 15-18, 19-
25, 26-41, 57, 100-118 *passim*,
170-78 *passim*
Shaw, G. B.:
  aesthetics of, 43-51, 53, 170-78
    passim
  and allegory, 45-47, 53-54
  and Blake, William, 9, 44, 109,
    170-78
  and Brecht, Bertolt, 5, 15-18
  and his characters, 2, 4-5, 6, 7, 9,
    10, 11, 16-17, 30, 39-40, 58, 60-
    61, 69-71, 110-13, 116-17, 120-29
    passim
  and Chekhov, Anton, 30, 111,
    115-16
  critical reputation of, 1-13, 42-56,
    118, 130, 130*n*
  and drama, comic, 7, 51-56, 57-75,
    104-5, 106-7, 110, 112, 117-18,
    119, 132
  and drama, tragic, 9, 51-56, 104-5,
    105*n*, 143-61, 162-69
  and drama, tragicomic, 7, 76-87,
    107, 130-42 *passim*
  and drama criticism, 4, 58, 76-77
  and drama settings, 128-29
  dramaturgy of, 5, 12, 58-66
  and Eliot, T. S., 9, 114, 143-61
  and his family, 21-23, 27-28
  and humor, 9, 21, 126-28, 166-67
  and Ibsen, Henrik, 12, 30, 44, 46-
    47, 58, 70-72, 91, 102, 104, 111,
    115, 117, 119, 123, 125, 126,
    161, 162, 169
  and idealism, 36-41, 46, 100-118
    passim, 135
  and imagery, 3, 135
  and Lawrence, D. H., 86-87, 106
  and liberalism, 88-99, 102
  life of, 4, 19-25, 27-28
  literary style of, 32-36, 39-41, 47-
    50, 171
  and Marx, Karl, 28, 30, 51, 104,
    107, 110, 119

  and Molière, 11, 12, 30, 54, 62, 65,
    89, 90, 105, 173
  and Mozart, 12, 51, 173
  and Murray, Gilbert, 89, 90-91, 99,
    150
  and music, 4, 12, 23, 50-51, 137-38
  and myth, 47, 47*n*, 52-54, 109
  and Nietzsche, 30, 71, 109, 110,
    119, 123, 126, 127, 128
  as novelist, 4, 20-21
  and parent-child relationship,
    78-80
  philosophy of, 37-41, 100-118,
    120, 140-41, 170-78 *passim*
  and Plato, 53-54, 133-34, 135, 136,
    141
  as poet, 43-50, 162
  and political criticism, 7-8, 30-31,
    100-118 *passim*, 170-78 *passim*
  and rationalism, 52-54, 55
  and realism, 39-41, 45-46, 65, 100-
    118 *passim*, 135
  and religion, 23, 25, 27, 37, 45,
    105, 170-78 *passim*
  and Scribe, Eugène, 50, 58-60, 62,
    63, 64, 65, 72, 73
  and sexuality, 66-69, 80-87, 108-9,
    111-12, 120-26
  and Shakespeare, 1, 4, 10, 11, 12,
    23, 24, 48, 48*n*, 65, 67, 81, 101,
    103, 104, 106, 112, 125, 126,
    128, 141*n*, 161, 165, 171, 172-73
  and the Shavian personality, 1-13,
    15-18, 19-25, 26-41, 57, 100-118
    passim, 170-78 *passim*
  and Shelley, 3, 43, 44, 46, 53
  and social criticism, 1-5, 6, 10-11,
    26-32, 37-41, 45-46, 76-77, 78,
    79, 100-118 *passim*, 119-21,
    170-78 *passim*
  and Socialism, 7, 24, 98, 107
  and Socrates, 2-3, 5, 89
  and Strindberg, August, 12, 71, 86-
    87, 104, 111, 118, 140
  and the theatre of the absurd, 11-12
  and Wagner, 23, 30, 44, 45-47, 50-
    51, 53, 119
  and Wilde, Oscar, 40, 43, 106, 110

and will, 76-87
and Yeats, 3, 49, 106, 118, 162
Shaw, G. B., works by:
DRAMA
  *Adventures of the Black Girl in Her
    Search for God, The,* 129
  Androcles and the Lion, 37, 123,
    127
  Apple Cart, The, 11, 68, 78-85
    passim, 121, 122-23, 129
  Arms and the Man, 59, 62-63, 64,
    106, 123, 138
  Back to Methuselah, 8, 9, 53, 76n,
    78-84 *passim,* 100, 108, 113, 120,
    122, 124, 125, 128, **130-42,** 174
  Buoyant Billions, 129
  Caesar and Cleopatra, 7, 78-85 *pas-
    sim,* 123, 126, 129, 172, 176
  Captain Brassbound's Conversion,
    7, 68, 80-85 *passim,* 120, 121,
    126
  Candida, 69-72, 73, 112, 121, 122,
    173
  Devil's Disciple, The, 62, 106,
    170
  Doctor's Dilemma, The, 9, 11, 121,
    163-65, 166, 168
  Fanny's First Play, 11, 106
  Getting Married, 104, 121, 122,
    123-24
  Good King Charles's Golden Days,
    121, 129
  Heartbreak House, 8, 82-83, **113-
    18,** 122, 124, 126, 128, 129, 132,
    138, 170
  John Bull's Other Island, 11, 35, 88-
    89, 122, 124, 127, 128, 129
  Major Barbara, 7, 13, 72, 83-84, **88-
    99,** 117, 120, 123, 137-38, 141,
    173
  Man and Superman, 6, 8, 13, 39-40,
    64-66, 74, 87, 88-89, 103, **108-13,**
    116, 120, 121, 122, 125, 127,
    129, 138, 170, 171, 172, 176
  Man of Destiny, The, 122
  Misalliance, 120, 122, 124, 126,
    127, 128, 138
  Mrs. Warren's Profession, 9, 11, 68,

  72-73, 79-83 *passim,* 104n, 119,
    163, 165-66
  On the Rocks, 119, 120, 126, 127,
    175
  Overruled, 68, 106
  Passion, Poison and Petrifaction,
    11
  Philanderer, The, 106, 119, 121,
    122
  Pygmalion, 7, 11, 72, 73-74, 77-84
    passim, 106
  Saint Joan, 4, 9, 11, 13, 44, 72, 75,
    103, 122, 124-25, 127, 128,
    143-61, 163, 166-68
  *Shewing-Up of Blanco Posnet,
    The,* 178
  *Simpleton of the Unexpected Isles,
    The,* 129, 177
  Too True to Be Good, 9, 29, 84,
    101-2, 112n, 122, 123, 127, 128
  Widowers' Houses, **59-62,** 72, 110,
    119
  You Can Never Tell, 106, 122
ESSAYS
  "Common Sense About the War,"
    29, 37
  Everybody's Political What's What,
    29, 103
  *Intelligent Woman's Guide to
    Socialism and Capitalism, The,* 35
  Perfect Wagnerite, The, 46, 50-51
  Quintessence of Ibsenism, The, 39,
    45-46, 46n, 100-101, 121, 135
  "Religion of the Pianoforte, The,"
    46
  Revolutionist's Handbook, The, 33-
    34, 34n, 110, 120
  Sixteen Self-Sketches, 44
  *What I Really Wrote About the
    War,* 29
FICTION
  Cashel Byron's Profession, 50
  Immaturity, 28
Shelley, Percy Bysshe, 3, 43, 44, 46,
  53
Shewing-Up of Blanco Posnet, The,
  178
Sidney, Sir Philip, 42

Simpleton of the Unexpected Isles, The, 129, 177
Sixteen Self-Sketches, 44
Social criticism, and Shaw, 1-5, 6, 10-11, **26-32, 37-41,** 45-46, 76-77, 78, 79, 100-118 *passim,* 119-21, 170-78 *passim*
Socialism, 7, 24, 98, 107
Socrates, 2-3, 5, 89
Sons and Lovers (Lawrence), 86
Sophocles, 52, 55, 104, 144, 148, 149, 154-55, 156, 159, 161
Stalin, Joseph, 11, 31
Streetcar Named Desire, A (Williams), 146
Strindberg, August, 12, 71, 86-87, 104, 111, 118, 140, 140*n*
Swift, Jonathan, 103, 104, 150, 165
Swinburne, Algernon Charles, 45
Synge, John Millington, 162

T

Tempest, The (Shakespeare), 161
Terence, 54
Terry, Ellen, 69
Theatre of the absurd, 11-12
Thus Spake Zarathustra (Nietzsche), 126, 128
Timon of Athens (Shakespeare), 165
Tirso de Molina, 108
Tolstoy, Leo, 5, 130
Too True to Be Good, 9, 29, 84, 101-2, 112*n*, 122, 123, 127, 128

Tree, Beerbohm, 12
Trotsky, Leon, 103
Turner, Joseph, 170

U

Uncle Vanya (Chekhov), 115

W

Wagner, Richard, 23, 30, 44, 45-47, 50-51, 53, 119
Walkley, A. B., 88
Way of the World, The (Congreve), 112
Webb, Beatrice and Sidney, 29, 44, 69
Wells, H. G., 3, 105, 110, 114
Wesimann, August, 101
What I Really Wrote About the War, 29
Who's Afraid of Virginia Woolf? (Albee), 12
Widowers' Houses, **59-62,** 72, 110, 119
Wild Duck, The (Ibsen), 72
Wilde, Oscar, 40, 43, 106, 110
Wilson, Edmund, 44, 54, 55, 130*n*, 134*n*, 140, 141
Winsten, Steven, 43, 47*n*
Women in Love (Lawrence), 86

Y

Yeats, William Butler, 3, 49, 106, 118, 162
You Can Never Tell, 106, 122
Yvette (Maupassant), 72

SHELLEY

A Collection of Critical Essays
Edited by GEORGE M. RIDENOUR

A

Adonais, 10-11, 28-29, 48, 61, **161-68**, 171
Alastor, 5, 6, 9, 10, 24-25, 31, 35, 43, 48, **51-68**, 148, 166, 171, 176
"Ancient Mariner, The" (Coleridge), 150
Aristophanes, 61
Arnold, Matthew, 47
"Assassins, The," 7
Astrophel (Spenser), 163
"Aziola, The," 35

B

Bagehot, Walter, 103
Barruel, Abbé, 127
Beach, Joseph Warren, 14
"Belle Dame sans Merci, La" (Keats), 62
Berkeley, Bishop George, 71, 72, 75, 81, 91
Blake, William, 170, 172, 176
Bradley, A. C., 21
Brailsford, H. N., 103
Brontë, Emily, 3
Brooke, Stopford, 56-57, 60
Browning, Robert, 3, 5, 154
Byron, George Gordon, Lord, 2, 149, 150, 154, 164, 165
"Byzantium" (Yeats), 150

C

Campi Phlegraei (Hamilton), 115
"Cave of Demogorgon, The," 119-20
Cenci, The, 104
Charles the First, 104
Chatterton, Thomas, 106
Chaucer, Geoffrey, 154
Cicero, 122
"Cloud, The," 15
Clutton-Brock, A., 103
Coleridge, Samuel Taylor, 148, 149, 150-51, 154, 175
Cooper, Lane, 61
Cooper's Hill (Denham), 69

D

"Daemon of the World, The," 33
Dante Alighieri, 19, 62, 168, 170, 172, 175
Darwin, Erasmus, 113
David Copperfield (Dickens), 3
Davy, Humphrey, 113, 119
Defence of Poetry, A, 15, 116, 142
De la Mare, Walter, 161
Denham, John, 69, 79, 80
De Rerum Natura (Lucretius), 51
Desire and Restraint in Shelley (Stovall), 57
"Destiny of Nations, The" (Coleridge), 148
Don Juan (Byron), 2, 154

Drummond, William, 71

E

Endymion (Keats), 161, 162, 163
Epipsyche, 51-68
Epipsychidion, 3, 39-41, 43, 45, 48, 61
"Essay on a Future Life," 82
"Essay on Life," 72, 80-81
Essay on Man (Pope), 11
"Essay on Morals," 73, 83
Euripides, 6
Excursion, The (Wordsworth), 55

F

Faerie Queene, The (Spenser), 113, 161
Fall of Hyperion, The (Keats), 168
Fogle, R. H., 9
Frye, Northrop, 163

G

Gingerich, S. F., 14, 103, 107
Goethe, Johann Wolfgang von, 148
Godwin, Mary *(see* Shelley, Mary)
Grabo, Carl, 14, 15, 113, 119, 120
Graves, Robert, 6
Grove, Harriet, 58

H

Hamilton, William, 114, 115, 118, 120-21, 122, 126, 130
Hardy, Thomas, 5
Havens, R. D., 52, 53
Hazlitt, William, 168, 169
Hellas, 32, 104, 105, 109-10, 125, 129
Hitchiner, Elizabeth, 8, 58, 62-63
Hobbes, Thomas, 71
Hoffman, H. L., 52, 55, 57, 65, 66
Hogg, T. S., 57, 58, 59-60, 64, 127
Holloway, John, 8

Hopkins, Gerard Manley, 154
Humboldt, Alexander von, 120, 124, 128-29
Hume, David, 71, 72, 74, 81, 82, 91
Hunt, Leigh, 161, 164
Hutton, James, 130
"Hymn of Apollo," 153-54, 156-58
"Hymn of Pan," 153, 154-55
"Hymn to Intellectual Beauty," 4, 5, 9, 16
Hyperion (Keats), 14, 162, 163

I

Idylls of the King (Tennyson), 154

J

Jack, A. A., 14
James, D. G., 124
James, Henry, 62
Julian and Maddalo, 108

K

King, Edward, 163
Knight, Wilson G., 21
"Kubla Khan" (Coleridge), 147, 148

L

"Lamia" (Keats), 62
Laon and Cythna, 104, 106
Lawrence, D. H., 48
Lea, F. A., 47, 48, 49
Lewis, C. S., 116, 136, 137
Locke, John, 71, 74
Lucretius, 51, 120
Lycidas (Milton), 162

M

Magic Plant, The (Grabo), 21
"Mask of Anarchy, The," 115
Medwin, Thomas, 52
Memoirs Illustrating the History of Jacobinism (Barreul), 127

Michell, John, 128
Midas (Mary Shelley), 153
Milton, John, 113, 120, 125, 149,
    162, 163, 170
Missionary, The (Morgan), 58
"Mont Blanc," 4, 9, **69-102**
    philosophy in, 69-98
    religious doctrine in, 98-102
Moore, Thomas, 164
"Motivation of Shelley's *Prometheus
    Unbound,* The" (Rajan), 119
Murry, Middleton, 48

N

"Numpholeptos" (Browning), 5

O

"Ode to a Nightingale" (Keats), 166
"Ode to Heaven," 17
"Ode to Liberty," 115
"Ode to Naples," 117
"Ode to the West Wind," **31-35**, 43, 45,
    124, 168, 169
"On Polytheism," 82

P

Paradise Lost (Milton), 136, 170
Peacock, Thomas Love, 52, 54, 55,
    63, 95, 112, 116, 126, 127
Peck, W. E., 52, 103-4
Personal Narrative (Humboldt),
    128-29
"Peter Bell" (Wordsworth), 148
Phaedrus (Plato), 61
Philosophical View of Reform, A,
    125
Plato, 61, 110
Pliny, 120, 122
Poe, Edgar Allan, 154
Pope, Alexander, 69
Pottle, Frederick A., 9
Powell, A. E., 14
Priestley, J. B., 113
Prince Athanase, 33
Prometheus Unbound, 2, **6-11**, 13-14, -

18-20, **25-28**, 34, 35, 44, 61, 67,
    105-6, 110, 111-13, 116, 120, **122-25,**
    130-31, **133-43, 145-48,** 151, 152,
    159
"Proposals for an Association of
    Philanthropists," 9
Purgatorio (Dante), 168, 170, 175

R

"Refutation of Deism, A," 82
Revolt of Islam, The, 31, 33, 34, 35,
    43, 61, 67, 116, 119, 120, 131, 148,
    150, 152
Romantic Theory of Poetry, The
    (Powell), 48-49
"Rosalind and Helen," 44
Rousseau, Jean-Jacques, 171, 172,
    173-74

S

Salt, Henry, 20
Seneca, 122
Shakespeare, William, 14, 57, 148,
    150, 151
Shelley, Elizabeth, 58
Shelley, Mary, 3, 52, 58-60, 62-63, 82,
    126, 153
Shelley, Percy Bysshe:
    abstractness of, 13-29
    and Berkeley, Bishop George, 75,
        91
    classicism of, 3
    and Coleridge, Samuel Taylor,
        148-49
    and Denham, John, 69, 79, 80
    and empiricism, 71
    evil, theory of, **103-10**
    and Hume, David, 82-83, 91
    and Keats, John, 18, 19, **161-68**
    love, theme of, **51-68**
    Platonism of, 14
    symbolism of, **20-29**
    volcanoes, theme of, **111-31**
Shelley, Percy Bysshe, works by:
    Adonais, 10-11, 28-29, 48, 61,
        161-68, 171

Shelley, Percy Bysshe, works by
(*continued*):
Alastor, 5, 6, 9, 10, 24-25, 31, 35,
43, 48, **51-68**, 148, 166, 171, 176
"Assassins, The," 7
"Aziola, The," 35
"Cave of Demogorgon, The,"
119-20
Cenci, The, 104
Charles the First, 104
"Cloud, The," 15
"Daemon of the World, The," 33
Epipsyche, 51-68
Epipsychidion, 3, 39-41, 43, 45,
48, 61
"Essay on a Future Life," 82
"Essay on Life," 72, 80-81
"Essay on Morals," 73, 83
Hellas, 32, 104, 105, 109-10, 125,
129
"Hymn of Apollo," 153-54, 156-58
"Hymn of Pan," 153, 154-55
"Hymn to Intellectual Beauty,"
4, 5, 9, 16
Julian and Maddalo, 108
Laon and Cythna, 104, 106
"Mask of Anarchy, The," 115
"Mont Blanc," 4, 9, **69-102**
"Ode to Heaven," 17
"Ode to Liberty," 115
"Ode to Naples," 117
"Ode to the West Wind," **31-35**,
43, 45, 124, 168, 169
"On Polytheism," 82
Philosophical View of Reform, A,
125
Prince Athanase, 33
Prometheus Unbound, 2, **6-11**, 13-
14, 18-20, **25-28**, 34, 35, 44, 61,
67, 105-6, 110, 111-13, 116, 120,
122-25, 130-31, **133-43**, **145-48**,
151, 152, 159
"Proposals for an Association of
Philanthropists," 9
"Refutation of Deism, A," 82
Revolt of Islam, The, 31, 33, 34,
35, 43, 61, 67, 116, 119, 120,
131, 148, 150, 152

"Rosalind and Helen," 44
Speculations on Morals, 104
"To Jane, The Recollection,"
41-44
"To a Skylark," 16-17, 35-39, 45
"Treatise on Morals," 76, 94, 100
Triumph of Life, The, 61, 104-5,
147, **168-76**
"Two Spirits: An Allegory,"
159-61
Witch of Atlas, The, 5, 6, **145-52**,
161
"Shelley's View of Poetry" (Bradley),
21
Sidney, Sir Philip, 162-63, 166
Socrates, 171
Solve, M. T., 14
Southey, Robert, 2
Speculations on Morals, 104
Spenser, Edmund, 113, 162-63
Spinoza, Baruch, 104-10
Stovall, Floyd, 52, 57
Strabo, 120
Strong, A. T., 14, 21, 25
Swinburne, A. C., 5
Symonds, J. A., 47
Symposium (Plato), 61, 66

T

"To Jane, The Recollection," **41-44**
"To a Skylark," 16-17, 35-39, 45
"Treatise on Morals," 76, 94, 100
Triumph of Life, The, 61, 104-5, 147,
168-76
Trollope, Anthony, 2
Trotsky, Leon, 8
Turner, Cornelia, 58
Twelfth Night (Shakespeare), 113
"Two Spirits: An Allegory," 159-61

W

Wasserman, Earl R., 9
Weaver, Bennett, 21
Westbrook, Harriet, 58
White, Newman Ivey, 21, 52

SOPHOCLES

A Collection of Critical Essays
Edited by THOMAS WOODARD

A

Addison, John, 124
Aeschylus, 3, 18-19, 20, 35, 72,
  125-26, 128, 153
Ahnfrau, Die (Grillparzer), 103
Ajax, 7, 21, **29-61**, 69, 155, 173
  plight of man, theme of, 52-61
  sword of Hector, symbolism of,
    45-46
  time and change, theme of, 31, 39-
    61
  traditional morality, theme of, 31-
    40, 48-61
Anaxagoras, 7, 84
Anecdota Graeca (ed. Cramer), 118-19
Anouilh, Jean, 2, 8
Antigone, 7, 9, 11, 14, 26, **62-100**,
  123, 149
  conflict in, 62-66, 68-73
  control of nature, theme of, 76-79
  death, theme of, 84-85
  and *deinon*, meaning of, 88-91
    94-98
  desecration of the human body,
    theme of, 82-83
  disaster, theme of, 98-100
  human essence, theme of, 84-85,
    87-100
  human relations, theme of, 72-75,
    78
  imagery of birds in, 75-76, 79
  law and justice, theme of, 64-66,
    72

man's relation to the gods, theme
  of, 66-69
man-woman dichotomy, theme of,
  69-73
masculine rationality, theme of,
  66-79
philosophy in, 62-63, 71-72
political aspects of, 83-85
prosody, 91-96
religious pollution, theme of,
  81-83
shelter, theme of, 79-81
and *technē*, meaning of, 96-98
yielding motif in, 73-75
Antigone (Anouilh), 2, 8
Antigone (Brecht), 3
Apology of Socrates (Plato),
  55
Archilochus, 32
Aristotle, 2, 10-11, 14, 24, 164
Aurispa, Giovanni, 174
Austen, Jane, 122

B

Baudelaire, Charles, 6
Beckett, Samuel, 15
Bias of Priene, 32, 56
Bowra, C. M., 24, 40-41
Brecht, Bertholt, 2-3

C

Caligula (Camus), 8

504

Sophocles

Camus, Albert, 8
Canterbury Tales (Chaucer), 123
Charmides (Plato), 112
Chaucer, Geoffry, 123
Cimon, 148
Cocteau, Jean, 2, 6, 15
Cornford, Francis, 3, 4
Cramer, J. A., 118-19
Cratylus (Plato), 112

D

Danse de Sophocle, La (Cocteau), 15
Dante, 23, 37
Democritus, 84
Dignity of Man (Pico), 174
Divina Commedia (Dante), 37

E

Elder Statesman, The (Eliot), 3
Electra, 3, 7, **122-45**, 146, 154, 171
    characterization, 122-24, 125-27,
        130-33, 137, 140-43, 144-45
    contrast of men and women, theme
        of, 127-30, 132-33
    imbalanced antithesis in, 127-28,
        138, 143-44
    language of characters in, 129-36,
        140-42
    logos and *ergon*, concepts of,
        128-45
    structure, 125-26, 129-30, 136-37
    the urn, symbolism of, 138-39
Eliot, T. S., 3, 13, 15
Empedocles, 7
Euclid, 20-21
Eumenides (Aeschylus), 35
Euripides, 10, 13, 36, 38, 146, 148,
    162

F

Faust (Goethe), 21
Fergusson, Francis, 4
Finley, Jr., J. H., 4
Fraser, James, 3

Freud, Sigmund, 4, 14

G

Gide, André, 2, 15
Goethe, Johann, 18, 21
Goheen, R. F., 12
Greek Tragedy (Kitto), 12
Grillparzer, Franz, 103
Guthrie, Tyrone, 3

H

Harrison, Jane, 3
Havelock, Eric, 4
Hegel, George, 14, 62, 64
Heidegger, Martin, 2
Heraclitus, 7
Heroic Temper, The (Knox),
    13
Hesiod, 121
Hippocrates, 84
Hippodamus of Miletus, 84
Hölderlin, Friedrich, 170
Homer, 50, 52, 54, 61, 148, 155, 162,
    171

I

Idea of a Theater, The (Fergusson),
    4
Iliad (Homer), 52, 148
Imagery of Sophocles' Antigone
    (Goheen), 12
Ismenias the Theban, 32

J

Jaeger, Werner, 4
Jebb, Sir R. C., 11
Jesus, 32-33
Joyce, James, 15

K

Keats, John, 13
King Lear (Shakespeare), 20-21

Kitto, H. D. F., 11-13, 30
Knox, Bernard, 2, 10, 13, 112

L

Lawrence, D. H., 15

M

Machine Infernale, La (Cocteau), 2
Mann, Thomas, 15
Memorabilia (Xenophon), 107
Mouches, Les (Sartre), 3
Murray, Gilbert, 13

N

Niccoli, Niccolo de', 174
Nietzsche, Friedrich, 2, 6

O

Odyssey (Homer), 50, 61, 148, 155
Oedipe Roi (Gide), 2
Oedipus at Colonus, 3, 10, 17-19, 25-28, 85, 121, 146-74
  action of, 146-47, 165
  birds, symbolism of, 157-58
  the curse, theme of, 167-68
  death, theme of, 171-72
  defilement, symbolism of, 156-57
  guilt, theme of, 159-63
  the heroic nature, theme of, 148, 150-51, 157, 162, 171-72
  historical aspects of, 147-48, 165-66
  inner and outer values, theme of, 158-62, 165-67, 171
  insight, symbolism of, 168-69
  man's value, symbolism of, 165-66
  moral independence, theme of, 155, 160-62, 166-70
  and *Philoctetes*, 161-63, 166, 168
  plot summary, 148-54
  political aspects of, 163-66
  and *Prometheus Bound* (Aeschylus), 18-19
  religious aspects of, 169-70

and the riddle of the Sphinx, purpose of, 27-28
  structure, 25-28
  symbolism in the prologue of, 149-50
  time, theme of, 146, 151-52, 154-56, 159, 169
Oedipus at Thebes (Knox), 13, 112
Oedipus Rex (*also Oedipus Tyrannus*), 3, 10, 14-15, 16-17, 24-28, 72, 81, 82, 101-21, 148-49, 154, 159
  human nature, theme of, 114-17, 120-21
  linguistic analysis of, 107-21
  plot summary, 101-2
  political aspects of, 117-18
  privacy, theme of, 107-13
  psychological aspects of, 103-4
  riddle of the Sphinx, meaning of, 27-28, 106-7, 114, 119-20
  structure, 24-28
  tyranny, concept of, 106-8, 111
Oedipus Rex (Brecht), 3
Oresteia (Aeschylus), 125

P

Parmenides, 7
Pausanias, 148
Perdiccas, 32
Periander, 32
Pericles, 2, 56, 83, 84
Pico della Mirandola, 174
Pindar, 32, 44, 50, 55
Pittacus, 32
Philoctetes, 10, 21, 146, 161-63, 166, 168
Philosophie der Weltgeschichte (Hegel), 105
Phoenissae (Euripides), 148, 162
Plato, 5, 32-33, 39, 55, 72, 112, 119
Plutarch, 112
Poetics (Aristotle), 10-11
Pound, Ezra, 3
Prometheus Bound (Aeschylus), 18-19, 72
Protagoras, 71-72, 84
Protagoras (Plato), 72
Proust, Marcel, 123

R

Reinhardt, Karl, 11, 63
Reinhardt, Max, 2
Rembrandt, 22
Republic (Plato), 32, 39

S

Sartre, Jean-Paul, 3
Schlegel, August Wilhelm von, 30
Seven Against Thebes (Aeschylus), 148
Shakespeare, William, 20-21
Simonides, 32, 158
Snell, Bruno, 4
Socrates, 7, 32, 39, 158
Solomon, 28
Solon, 32
Sons and Lovers (Lawrence), 15
Sophocles:
  and Aeschylus, 125-26
  and the clash of opposites, theme of, 7-8
  dialectical principles, in works of, 7-9, 128-45
  and the hero, concept of, 6-9, 148, 150-51, 157, 162, 171-72
  implied meaning, in works of, 24-28
  interpretations of, 3-15
  life of, 1-3
  morality of, 31-36, 159-61, 173
  philosophy of, 71-72, 84-85, 172-74
  politics of, 163-66
  symbolism, in works of, 4-9
Sophocles, works by:
  Ajax, 7, 21, **29-61**, 69, 155, 173
  Antigone, 7, 9, 11, 14, 26, **62-100**, 123, 149
  Electra, 3, 7, **122-45**, 146, 154, 171
  Oedipus at Colonus, 3, 10, 17-19, 25-28, 85, 121, **146-74**
  Oedipus Rex, 3, 10, 14-15, 16-17, 24-28, 72, 81, 82, **101-21**, 148-49, 154, 159
  Philoctetes, 10, 21, 146, 161-63, 166, 168
  Women of Trachis, 3, 7, 173

Sophocles (Whitman), 12
Sophokles (Reinhardt), 10
Spengler, Oswald, 6, 14
Suppliants (Aeschylus), 153
Symbolism:
  in *Ajax*, 45-46
  in *Antigone*, 75-76, 79
  in *Electra*, 138-39
  in *Oedipus at Colonus*, 149-50, 156-58, 165-66, 168-69
  of situations, in Greek drama, 21-22
  in Sophocles' works, 4-9

T

Tennyson, Alfred, 1
Theognis, 32, 38
Theogony (Hesiod), 121
Thucydides, 56, 83, 166
Time, theme of:
  in *Ajax*, 31, 39-61
  in *Oedipus at Colonus*, 146, 151-52, 154-56, 159, 169
Torquato Tasso (Goethe), 21
Tragedy, concept of, 20-22

V

Verrall, Arthur Woollgar, 25
Virgil, 37
Voltaire, 124

W

Waldock, A. J. A., 24-26
Weil, Simone, 14
Whitman, Cedric H., 2, 10-13, 63
Wilamowitz, Tycho von, 30
Women of Trachis, 3, 7, 173
Woolf, Virginia, 15

X

Xenophon, 107
Xerxes, 32

Y

Yeats, William Butler, 3, 13, 15

SPENSER

A Collection of Critical Essays
Edited by HARRY BERGER, JR.

A

Aeneid (Vergil), 63, 67
Alençon, Duc d', 27
Allegory, 1, 22-29, 34-39, 64-65, 69-72, 77-78, 133-34
Amoretti, 7, 10, 47, 49, 50, 52-53, 62, 102, 104, 107
Antiquites de Rome, Les (Bellay), 14, 15
Apollodorus, 109
Apuleius, 111
Arcadia (Sidney), 132, 142
Aristotle, 27, 94-95, 118, 121
Ars Amatoria (Ovid), 109, 112
Aspiration, theme of, 37-39
Astrophel, 13, 17-18
Auerbach, E., 2

B

Bacon, Francis, 9
Bellay, Joachim du, 14, 15, 16
Berger, Harry Jr., 91, 94, 95
Bion, 33
Bodin, Jean, 125, 126
Book of the Duchess, The (Chaucer), 17
Bruno, 9
Bryskett, Lodowick, 18
Burckhardt, J., 2
Burghley, Lord (William Cecil), 16, 18, 26, 27

C

Calvin, John, 120
Camden, W., 14, 16
Cassirer, Ernst, 2, 5
Castiglione, 24-25, 144
Cecil, William, Lord Burghley, 16, 18, 26, 27
Chaucer, Geoffrey, 3, 17, 19, 22, 36, 38, 67
Cheney, G., 173
Christianity, 32-39, 58-60, 88-96, 174-76
Ciris (anon.), 110, 111
Cloe Hunting (Prior), 104
Coleridge, S. T., 45
Colin Clout (Skelton), 26
Colin Clouts Come Home Againe, 8, 11, 17, 132
Comes, Natalis, 112, 121, 165
Complaints, 13, 14
Cortegiano, Il (Castiglione), 24-25, 144
Courtly love, tradition of, 107-8
Culex (*see Virgils Gnat*), 14
Curtius, E. R., 2
Cyropaedia (Elyot), 25

D

Daniel, Samuel, 19
Dante, 55, 57, 67, 118
Daphnaida, 13, 17

Decay and loss, theme of, 19, 21, 29,
    45-46
Defence of Good Women (Elyot), 120
Development, theme of, 10-12, 146-47
Dilthey, G. W., 2
Diodorus Siculus, 100, 109, 115
Donne, John, 2
Drayton, M., 32
Dreames, 16
Dudley family, 15, 16

E

Education of a Christian Prince
    (Erasmus), 26
Either/Or (Kierkegaard), 62
E. K., 16, 30, 31, 32, 34, 36, 37,
    39
Eliot, T. S., 2
Elizabeth I, 27-28, 36, 37, 39, 41, 78,
    111, 128, 133, 144
Elyot, Thomas, 25, 120
Envy, theme of, 20-21
Epithalamion, 7, 10, 40, 47-62, 142
    and *Amoretti,* 49-50
    envoy, function of, 47-49, 61-62
    imagery, 52-54, 56-58
    mythology, 54-62 *passim*
    number symbolism in, 47, 51
    structure, 58-61
    time, theme of, 49-55, 62
Erasmus, 10, 26, 27
"Essay on Allegorical Poetry"
    (Hughes), 42
Essex, Earl of, 18
Ethiopian History, An (Underdown),
    142

F

Faerie Queene, The, 1, 5, 8, 9, 10, 11,
    23, 27, 29, 39, 94, 102, 113, 115,
    123, 135, 144-45
    Book I, 63-87
        allegory, 64-65, 69-72, 77-78
        chivalric ethic, 75-76, 79-81, 84
        Christian references, 65, 69-70,
            78, 82, 123-25

    and contemporary events, 127-31
    golden age, theme of, 115-20
    holiness, theme of, 65-67
    imagery, 65-68, 70-76, 78
    justice, theme of, 115-31 *passim*
    quest, theme of, 65-66, 76-77
    nature of hero, theme of, 65-70,
        79, 82-83
    and pastoral convention, 63-64
    Proem, 63-64, **115-31**
    reconciliation, theme of, 75-76
    Book II, 88-96
        as Christian allegory, 88-96 *pas-
        sim*
        Palmer, function of, 88-94
        parallels with Book I, 95-96
        and reason, 89, 96
        redemption, theme of, 96
    Books III and IV,
        and classical myth, 97-114
            passim
        concord, theme of,
            103-4, 110-14
        and contemporary events, 111
        imagery, 105-7
        love, theme of, 101-3
        method, 100-105
        quest, theme of, 114
        and tradition of courtly love,
            107-8
    Book V, 151-53
    Book VI, 133
        allegory in, 133-34
        and contemporary events, 132-34
        and Elizabethan poetic conven-
            tions, 140-45
        escape from tedium, theme of,
            134-35
        freedom and discipline, theme
            of, 138-39, 142-45
        imagery, 134-35, 140
        method, 137-39, 142-44
        poetry as subject, 136
        structure, 133-36
Ficino, 9
Fourth Eclogue (Vergil), 32
Fowre Hymnes, 8, 10
Freud, Sigmund, 3

G

Gascoigne, George, 22
Gemistus Pletho, 9
Geoffrey of Monmouth, 116
Gombrich, Ernst, 5
Gorges, Sir Arthur, 17
Greene, Thomas, 52-53, 159, 173
Grey, Lord, 130
Guilpin, Edward, 30

H

Haeckel, Ernst, 146
Hamilton, A. C., 100
Hegel, G. W. F., 2, 6, 164
Henry V (Shakespeare), 25
Henry VIII, 83-84, 120
Herbert, George, 95
Hieatt, A. K., 47, 52
Homer, 99, 112, 154
Hooker, R. H., 96, 120
Hughes, John, 42
Humanist aesthetics, 51-52
Hymne of Love, An, 102,
  107

I

Iliad (Homer), 19
Image of Governaunce (Elyot),
  25
Imagery, 1, 5
  in *Amoretti*, 52-53
  in *Epithalamion*, 52-54, 52-58
  in *Faerie Queene*, 65-68, 70-76,
    78, 105-7, 134-35, 140
  in *Two Cantos of Mutability*,
    168-69
Ing, Catherine, 40

J

Jonson, Ben, 8

K

Kermode, Frank, 88, 91, 94

Kernodle, George, 5
Kierkegaard, Sören, 62
King Lear (Shakespeare), 20

L

Lament for Adonis (Bion), 33
Lee, Sir Sidney, 40
Legend of Artegall, 132
Leicester, Earl of, 15
Letter to Ralegh, 64, 134
Library of History (Diodorus),
  115
Lycidas (Milton), 39
Lyric Poetry, 6-8

M

McLuhan, Marshall, 5
Mad, 155
Marot, Clément, 104
Marsh, Edward, 40, 44
Mary Queen of Scots, 127-28, 130
Measure for Measure (Shakespeare),
  123-24, 127, 130
Merchant of Venice, The (Shakespeare), 124
Metamorphoses (Ovid), 110, 112,
  164
Middle Ages, 13
Milton, John, 31, 37, 39, 93
Mock-heroic, use of, 19, 164
Mother Hubberds Tale, 7, 13, 21-29
passim
  allegory in, 22-29
  and astronomy, 21
  and contemporary events, 27-29
  satire on Utopia, 22
  and true courtier versus false,
    24-25
Muiopotmos, 10, 11, 13, 29
  decay, theme of, 19-21
  metamorphosis in, 20
  and Vergil, 19-20
Musophilus (Daniel),
  19
Mythologiae (Comes),
  122, 165

N

Narrative poetry, 6-8
Nashe, Thomas, 30
Neoplatonism, 3, 4, 9, 105
Norton, Dan S., 40-41
Numerical devices, 17
    in *Daphnaida*, 17
    in *Epithalamion*, 17
    in *Ruines of Time*, 47

O

Ong, Walter, 5
Ovid, 16, 55, 77, 82, 109, 110, 160,
    164

P

Pageaunts, 16
Panofsky, Erwin, 5
Paracelsus, 9
Paradise Lost (Milton), 93, 96, 118
Parlement of Foules (Chaucer), 67
Pastoral, use of, 4, 31-35, 36, 39, 63-
    64, 159-61
Peasants' Revolt, 23
Pembroke, Countess of, 14, 17, 18
Petrarch, 13-14, 16
Pico della Mirandola, 9, 51
Plato, 48, 143, 144, 147
Plutarch, 111
Pope, Alexander, 19
Premature union and fulfillment,
    theme of, 10-11
Prior, Matthew, 104
Protestantism, 83-84
Prothalamion, 6
    allegory in, 44-45
    decay, theme of, 45-46
    mutability, theme of, 45-46
    refrain, function of, 40-46 *passim*
    structure, 41-45
Purgatorio (Dante), 55
Pythagorism, 51-52

R

Raleigh, Sir Walter, 64, 132

Rape of the Lock, The (Pope),
    19
Reformation, 36, 176
Renaissance, 3, 8, 13, 22, 24, 65, 82,
    102, 113, 176
Renaissance imagination, 2-6
Rich, Penelope, 18
Richard III (Shakespeare), 25-26
Ruines of Time, The, 14-17, 18,
    29
Ruskin, John, 69-70

S

Saintsbury, George, 40
Shakespeare, William, 15, 25, 82, 130
Shepheardes Calender, The, 7, 11, 30-
    39, 64, 132, 143
    allegory in, 34-39
    as antipastoral, 34-35, 36, 39
    aspiration, theme of, 37-39
    and Christianity, 32-39
    and contemporary events, 30-31,
        34
    didactic purpose, 31, 36-37
    pastoral form, 31-34
    quest theme, 33
    and role of poet, 38
    structure, 34-38
Sidney, Sir Philip, 4, 14, 15, 16, 31,
    133
Skelton, John, 26, 27
Skialetheia (Guilpin), 30
Smith, Hallett, 32
"Songe" (Bellay), 14, 16
Speak, Parrot (Skelton), 26
Spenser, Edmund
    and astronomy, 21
    biographical information, 18, 40,
        48-50, 62
    Christianity in works of, 32-39,
        58-60, 88-96, 174-76
    and contemporary literary conven-
        tions, 7, 22, 140-45
    and contemporary politics, 18, 27-
        29, 111, 133-34
    and Elizabethan Renaissance, 3, 22,
        36, 140-42

Spenser, Edmund: (*continued*)

and function of poetry, 8, 175-76
historical sense, 6, 8-12, 146-52
and New Criticism, 2
and poet's role, 38
and Sir Philip Sidney, 14-18
translations by, 14
and Vergil, 8, 19-20, 35
Spenser, Edmund, works by: (*see
main listings for starred items*)
Amoretti, 7, 10, 47, 49, 50, 52-53,
62, 102, 104, 107
Astrophel, 13, 17-18
Colin Clouts Come Home Againe,
8, 11, 17, 132
Complaints, 13, 14
Daphnaida, 13, 17
Dreames, 16
*Epithalamion,** 7, 10, 40, 47-62,
142
*Faerie Queene, The,** 1, 5, 8, 9, 10,
11, 23, 27, 29, 39, **63-87, 88-96,
97-114, 132-45**
Fowre Hymnes, 8, 10
Hymne of Love, An, 102, 107
Letter to Ralegh, 64, 134
*Mother Hubberds Tale,** 7, 13-21
passim
*Muiopotmos,** 10, 11, 13, 19-21,
29
Pageaunts, 16
*Prothalamion,** 6, **40-46**
Ruines of Time, The, 14-17, 18,
29
*Shepheardes Calender, The,** 7, 11,
30-39, 64, 132, 143
Teares of the Muses, The, 7, 18
*Two Cantos of Mutabilitie,** 137,
146-76
Virgils Gnat, 8, 14
"Standomi un giorno solo a la fenetra"
(Petrarch), 13
Statius, 112
Stones of Venice (Ruskin), 70
Style, 19, 64-65, 68, 71-73
Stylistic devices, 65
in *Faerie Queene,* 65-66, 71-77,

80-82, 129
in *Two Cantos of Mutabilitie,*
153-60, 169-71

T

Tasso, 9
Tate, Allen, 2
Teares of the Muses, The, 7
structure, 18
Tempest, The (Shakespeare), 176
Templar Knights, 45
*Theatre Wherein Be Represented as
Wel the Miseries and Calamities
That Follow the Voluptuous World-
lings, A* (ed. van der Noot), 14
Time, theme of, 14-17, 49-55, 62,
152-76 *passim*
Tuve, Rosemund, 5
Two Cantos of Mutabilitie, 137,
146-76
allusion, use of, 170-72
and Christianity, 174-76
and cyclical natural order, 162-67
imagery, 168-69
method, 148-69
mutability vs. nature, theme of,
152-76 *passim*
pastoral, use of, 159-61
and Spencer's historical viewpoint,
146-152

V

Valla, 10
Venus and Adonis (Shakespeare),
82
Vergil, 14, 19-20, 32, 35, 63, 104,
105, 110, 147
Vinci, Leonardo da, 4
Virgils Gnat (trans. Spenser),
8, 14

W

Watkins, W. B. C., 172
Warburg Institute, 2

Whetstone, George, 30
Whitaker, Vergil K., 93
Why Come Ye Not to Court?
    (Skelton), 25
Wild Man (Cheney), 173, 175
Wind, Edgar, 2, 5
Winter's Tale, The (Shakespeare),
    143
Wittkower, Rudolf, 5

Wolsey, Thomas Cardinal,
    26-27
Wyatt, Thomas, 3

X

Xenophon, 25

Y

Yates, Frances, 5

STEINBECK

A Collection of Critical Essays

Edited by ROBERT MURRAY DAVIS

A

Aesop, 152
Affaire Lettuceberg, L', 77, 81 (*see also Grapes of Wrath*)
After Many a Summer Dies the Swan (Huxley), 6
Agee, James, 114
Alcott, Bronson, 169
Aldrich, Bess Streeter, 12
Allee, W. C., 125
American Exodus: A Record of Human Erosion, An (Lange, Taylor) 78
American Literature, 2
Animal Aggregations (Allee), 125
Animal Farm (Orwell), 152
Asheim, Lester, 103, 104, 112, 119
Augustine, Saint, 73, 132
Avenging Conscience, The (Griffith), 106

B

Babbitt, Irving, 128
Bacon, Roger, 73
Barzun, Jacques, 34, 128
"Battle Hymn of the Republic" (Howe), 78, 94
Benét brothers, 2
Berlin, Isaiah, 130
Berry, Tony, 123, 124
Between Pacific Tides (Ricketts, Calvin), 122

"Big Two-Hearted River" (Hemingway), 137
Bleak House (Dickens), 16
Bluestone, George, 17, 101n
Bombs Away, 1, 3, 7
Bourke-White, Margaret, 78
Bowron, Bernard, 96n
Boys in the Back Room, The (Wilson), 102
Bradbrook, Muriel, 37-38, 39
Brighton Rock (Greene), 5
Bromfield, Louis, 12
Burke, Kenneth, 93
Burning Bright, 7, 147
Burns, Robert, 65
Burton, Thomas, 118

C

Caball, James Branch, 6
Caldwell, Erskine, 78, 99
Camus, Albert, 166
Cannery Row, 3, 4, 15, 26, **135-48**
  characterization, 11, 13, 27, 69, 140-41, 144
  ethical paradoxes, 8, 23, 132
  Marxism and class struggle, 27, 142
  non-teleologic philosophy, 31, 141-43
  optimism, 14, 171
Canterbury Tales, The (Chaucer), 150
Carradine, John, 120
Catch-22 (Heller), 11
Cerf, Bennett, 102, 103

Champney, Freeman, 17, 62
Chesterton, G. K., 133
"Chrysanthemums, The, " 15
Clark, Walter Van Tilburg, 104
Coleridge, Samuel Taylor, 150, 151, 157
Colletto, Tiny, 123, 124
Conrad, Joseph, 152
Cooper, James Fenimore, 168
Covici, Pascal, 78, 150, 171
Cowley, Malcolm, 118, 135
Crane, Stephen, 65
Cup of Gold, 63, 66, 83, 165

D

Dante, 151, 152, 157, 160
Darien, Frank, 120
Darwell, Jane, 120
Darwin, Charles, 30, 74, 130, 132
Death in the Afternoon (Hemingway), 29, 125
Death of a Salesman (Miller), 66
DeVoto, Bernard, 100
Dickens, Charles, 16, 134
Divine Comedy, The (Dante), 152, 157, 158
Dos Passos, John, 26, 90, 99, 163
Douglas, Norman, 123-24
Dreiser, Theodore, 142
"Dubious Battle in California," 75

E

East of Eden, 1, 4-5, 164-71 *passim,* 175
  allegory, role of, 9, 159, 170, 171
  characterization, 6, 10, 13, 170
Ecce Homo! (Lorentz), 90
Einstein, Albert, 74, 130
Emerson, Ralph Waldo, 82, 99, 127, 166, 168, 171, 173
Empson, William, 135, 136, 138-39, 147*n*
Enea, Sparky, 123, 124
"Epistle to Dr. Arbuthnot, An" (Pope), 16
Everyman (anon.), 149, 161

F

Fable, A (Faulkner), 152
Fabulators, The (Scholes), 9
Factories in the Field (McWilliams), 19, 24
Farewell to Arms, A (Hemingway), 71
Farm Security Administration, 114
Faulkner, William, 21, 134, 137, 141, 152, 163, 164, 172
Fitzgerald, F. Scott, 6, 67, 137
Flaherty, Robert, 114
"Flight," 15
Fonda, Henry, 120
Ford, John, 102, 103, 104, 114, 117, 118, 121
Forgotten Village, The, 7, 92-93, 123
Forsyte Saga, The (Galsworthy), 10
Francis, Saint, 38, 40, 45, 73, 130
Franklin, Benjamin, 11
French, Warren, 1, 9-10, 157, 160
Frost, Robert, 141

G

Galsworthy, John, 8, 10
Gassner, John, 114
Geismar, Maxwell, 150-51, 152
Gide, André, 60
"Gift, The," 70, 71
Gone with the Wind (Mitchell), 80
Grapes of Gladness (Hartranft), 79
Grapes of Wrath, 3, 6, 12, 15, 22, 24, 75-101, 132, 133, 158, 163, 165, 166, 167, 171, 172, 173
  Biblical analogies and allegory, 4, 63-64, 94-96, 149
  characterization, 8, 27, 28, 137, 169
  filming of, 1, **102-21**
  mysticism, 70, 73, 130
  non-teleologic philosophy, 5, 13, 32, 141
  structure, 83-87, 92, 94-96, 99-100
  symbolism, 86-87, 91, 94-95, 104-5, 111
Grapewin, Charlie, 120
Great Gatsby, The (Fitzgerald), 67

"Great Mountains, The," 70, 71, 74
Greene, Graham, 5, 166
Group Mind, The (McDougall), 125

H

Hardy, Thomas, 118
Harper's magazine, 26, 34
"Harvest Gypsies, The," 75
Hawthorne, Nathaniel, 166, 172
Heart of Darkness (Conrad), 152
Hegel, G. W. F., 130
Hemingway, Ernest, 1*n*, 11, 29, 32,
    70, 71, 72, 77-78, 90, 125, 137, 163
Highway 66 (Zanuck), 112
Hillmann, Sister Mary Vincent, 162
Historical Inevitability (Berlin), 130
Huckleberry Finn (Twain), 28, 167
Huxley, Aldous, 6
Hyman, Stanley Edgar, 81, 130

I

Index Translationum, 1
"Indian Camp" (Hemingway), 72
In Dubious Battle, 11, 15, **49-62**, 64,
    76, 77, 78, 87, 133, 173
    allegory, role of, 53, 57, 149
    characterization, 49-50, 57, 68
    "group-man" and collectivism, 13,
        26, 52-56, 58, 61, 126, 128, 131
    language and style, 158, 165, 172
    Marxism and communism, 22, 23,
        47-48, 60
    non-teleological philosophy, 31
    structure and organization, 51, 83,
        92, 100
Industrial Valley (McKenney), 79

J

James, Henry, 134, 166
Jeffers, Robinson, 20
Jefferson, Thomas, 82, 83
Jesus, 73, 130, 132
Johnson, Nunnally, 102, 104, 114,
    120, 121
John Steinbeck (French), 157

Joyce, James, 152
Jung, G. C., 142

K

Keats, John, 157
Kellogg, Robert, 9
Kelly, Walt, 152
Kronenberger, Louis, 36, 118
Krutch, Joseph Wood, 12

L

Land of the Free (MacLeish), 78, 114
Lange, Dorothea, 78
"Leader of the People, The," 70, 71,
    72, 86, 95
Leibniz, G. W., 127, 132
Lettuceberg, 77 (*see also Grapes of
    Wrath*)
Let Us Now Praise Famous Men (Agee),
    114
Lewis, R. W. B., 5, 15, 17
Lewis, Sinclair, 99, 137
Life magazine, 77, 80
Lindsay, Vachel, 106
Lisca, Peter, 2, 65, 125, 140, 147, 157
Log from the Sea of Cortez, The, 123
Long Valley, The, 22, 99, 149
Lorentz, Pare, 78, 90, 91, 102, 114
Lubbock, Percy, 83-84, 91

M

Macdonald, Dwight, 4, 8
McDougall, William, 125
McKenney, Ruth, 79
MacLeish, Archibald, 2, 78, 114
McWilliams, Carey, 19, 21
Magic Mountain, The (Mann), 152
Malory, Sir Thomas, **36-46**, 64
Malraux, André, 166
Manhattan Transfer (Dos Passos), 99
Man in the Gray Flannel Suit, The
    (Wilson), 121
Mann, Thomas, 152
Marvell, Andrew, 147-48

Medal for Benny, A, 123
Melville, Herman, 67, 118, 168, 175
Miller, Arthur, 66
Milton, John, 149, 159
Moby Dick (Melville), 67, 175
Modern Fiction Studies, 2
Moon Is Down, The, 1, 3, 13, 172
Moore, Harry T., 1-2, 10
Morte d'Arthur (Malory), 36-46

N

Nation, The, 75, 81
Nevius, Blake, 12
Newman, Alfred, 102
"Notes Left Over" (Whitman), 82
*Novels of John Steinbeck: A Critical
    First Study, The* (Moore), 1-2

O

Occident, 76
Of Mice and Men, 15, 23, **63-69,** 75,
    76, 82, 172, 173
    allegory and symbolism, 63-65, 87
    characterization, 3, 10, 68-69, 164
    filming of, 1, 117
    structure, 4, 83
Oklahoma, 77 (*see also Grapes of
    Wrath*)
"Open Boat, The" (Crane), 65
Orwell, George, 152

P

Paradise Lost (Milton), 149, 151
Paradiso (Dante), 157
Pastures of Heaven, The, 4, 10, 13, 15,
    42, 83, 149, 168
Pearl, The, 1, 4, 9, 15, 126, **149-62**
Pearl of the World, The, 150 (*see also
    Pearl, The*)
Peckham, Morse, 127
People, Yes, The (Sandburg), 90
Prilgrim's Progress (Bunyan), 89, 151
Plow That Broke the Plains, The
    (Lorentz), 78, 90
Pope, Alexander, 8, 16

Porter, Katherine Anne, 152
"Primer on the 30's, A," 7
"Promise, The," 70, 71, 72

R

Rahv, Philip, 9
"Raid, The," 22
Random House, 102
Red Pony, The, 1, 15, 63, 70-74, 173
Resettlement Administration, 114
Ricketts, Edward, 122-34 *passim,* 137,
    140
River, The (Lorentz), 78, 90
Romance of the Rose, The (Chaucer),
    150
Ross, Woodburn O., 136
Russian Journal, A, 9n

S

Sandburg, Carl, 2, 90
San Francisco News, 75, 76, 81, 83,
    96
Sea of Cortez, 6, 15, 26, 29, **122-34,**
    140, 141, 155
    non-teleological philosophy, 30,
        31, 35, 129-30, 131-32
    mysticism, 70, 73, 144
Shakespeare, William, 67, 137, 150,
    157
Ship of Fools (Porter), 152
Short Reign of Pippin IV, The, 6
Sidney, Sir Philip, 4, 137
Siren Land (Douglas), 124
Slochower, Harry, 95n, 99n
"Snake, The," 15
Some Versions of Pastoral (Empson),
    135
Spencer, Herbert, 125, 126, 130-31,
    133
Spenser, Edmund, 137, 150, 151
Statesman's Manual (Coleridge), 151
Steinbeck, John Ernst:
    and allegory, use of, 9, 53, 57, 67,
        149-62, 170-71
    and Arthurian legends, 36-46, 63-65
    and Biblical themes, use of, 13,

Steinbeck, John Ernst: (*continued*)
  63-64, 88-89, 90, 94-96, 98,
  169-71
  biological studies and theories of,
    29, 31-32, 35, 103-6, 108, 110,
    112, **122-34**, 141-42
  characterization in novels of, 10-11,
    12-13, 67-68, 93, 116, 165, 169
  and Christian imagery, use of, 36-
    40, 60, 95, 98, 107-8, 130,
    173-74
  comic and tragi-comic elements in
    works of, 43, 45, 67, 112, 136,
    147, 172
  and Darwin, Charles, 30, 74, 130,
    132
  and Emerson, Ralph Waldo, 70, 99,
    127, 168, 171, 173
  filming of novels of, 1, 17, 76, 80,
    102-21
  and "group-man" and concepts of
    organic collectivism, 13, 52-55,
    57, 61, 125-26, 128
  and language, use of, 61-62, 87-90,
    165, 172
  and Marxism, 22-23, 26, 47, 49-62
    passim, 81, 142
  and mysticism, 70, 73, 82, 120,
    138, 139-40, 142, 165
  and Nobel Prize, 1
  non-teleological philosophy of, 5,
    30-31, 35, 125, 129-32, 141, 143
  and pastoral themes, 135-48
  philosophical influences on, 122-34
  and Ricketts, Edward, 122-34
    passim, 137, 140
  and Spencer, Herbert, 125, 126,
    130-31, 133
  structural patterns in novels of, 4,
    70-74, 84-86, 93
  and symbolism, use of, 9, 70, 82,
    86-87, 94, 100, 146-47, 153, 156
Steinbeck, John Ernst, works by:
MAJOR WORKS
  Bombs Away, 1, 3, 7
  Burning Bright, 7, 147
  Cannery Row, 3, 4, 8, 11, 13, 14,
    15, 23, 26, 27, 31, 69, 132, 135-

  48, 171 (*see also* main entry)
Cup of Gold, 63, 66, 83, 165
East of Eden, 1, 4-5, 6, 9, 10, 13,
  159, 164-71 *passim*, 175 (*see also*
  main entry)
Forgotten Village, The, 7, 92-93,
  123
Grapes of Wrath, 1, 3, 4, 5, 6, 8, 12,
  13, 15, 22, 24, 27, 28, 32, 63-64,
  70, 73, **75-101**, 102-21, 130, 132,
  133, 137, 141, 149, 158, 163,
  165, 166, 167, 169, 171, 172,
  173 (*see also* main entry)
In Dubious Battle, 11, 13, 15, 22,
  23, 26, 31, **47-48**, **49-62**, 64, 68,
  76, 77, 78, 83, 87, 92, 100, 126,
  128, 131, 133, 149, 158, 165,
  172, 173 (*see also* main entry)
Log from the Sea of Cortez, The,
  123
Long Valley, The, 22, 99, 149
Medal for Benny, A, 123
Moon Is Down, The, 1, 3, 13, 172
Of Mice and Men, 1, 3, 4, 10, 15,
  23, **63-69**, 75, 76, 82, 83, 87,
  117, 164, 172, 173 (*see also* main
  entry)
Pastures of Heaven, The, 4, 10, 13,
  15, 42, 83, 149, 168
Pearl, The, 1, 4, 9, 15, 126, **149-62**
Red Pony, The, 1, 15, 63, **70-74**,
  173
Sea of Cortez, 6, 15, 26, 29, 30,
  31, 35, 70, 73, **122-34**, 140, 141,
  144, 155 (*see also* main entry)
Sweet Thursday, 171
To a God Unknown, 6, 13, 14, 15,
  82, 83, 87, 127, 128, 130, 165,
  167, 168-69 (*see also* main entry)
Tortilla Flat, 1, 2, 4, 11-12, 13, 15,
  19, 27, **36-46**, 63, 83, 87, 128,
  136, 168, 171 (*see also* main entry)
Travels with Charley, 3
Wayward Bus, The, 1, 3, 11, 15, 29,
  31, 32, 33, 34, 35, 69, 149, 159,
  161 (*see also* main entry)
Winter of Our Discontent, The, 2, 3,
  158, 161

Steinbeck, John Ernst, works by:
(*continued*)
    STORIES AND ARTICLES
        "Chrysanthemums, The," 15
        "Dubious Battle in California," 75
        "Flight," 15
        "Gift, The," 70, 71
        "Great Mountains, The," 70, 71, 74
        "Harvest Gypsies, The," 75
        "Leader of the People, The," 70,
            71, 72, 86, 95
        "Primer on the 30's, A," 7
        "Promise, The," 70, 71, 72
        "Raid, The," 22
        "Snake, The," 15
        "Their Blood Is Strong," 75n
        "White Quail, The," 12, 15, 32
Steinbeck Quarterly, 2
Sweet Thursday, 171

                T

Tarkington, Booth, 12
These Are Our Lives (WPA pub.), 78
Thoreau, Henry David, 71, 166, 167,
    168
To a God Unknown, 6, 15, 83, 87,
    128, 165, 167-69
    detachment, theme of, 13, 14
    mysticism and unity of being,
        theme of, 82, 127, 130
Toland, Gregg, 102, 114
Tortilla Flat, 1, 2, 11-12, 15, **36-46**,
    63, 128, 168
    Arthurian legends, based on, 36-46
    characterization, 13, 19, 27
    structure, 4, 38-39, 83
    style, 87, 136, 171

Travels with Charley, 3
Troilus and Criseyde (Chaucer), 150
*Truth about John Steinbeck and the
    Migrants, The* (Miron), 79, 80-81
Twain, Mark, 11, 28

                U

Ulysses (Joyce), 152
Uncle Tom's Cabin (Stowe), 80
U.S.A. (Dos Passos), 99

                W

Wace, Robert, 37
War and Peace (Tolstoy), 83, 84
Waugh, Evelyn, 2
Wayward Bus, The, 1, 3, 15, 31, 32,
    34, 35
    allegory, use of, 149, 159, 161
    characterization, 11, 29, 33, 69
Whipple, T. K., 8, 10
"White Quail, The," 12, 15, 32
Whitman, Walt, 72, 82, 90, 168
Whole Earth Catalog, 11
Wide World of John Steinbeck, The
    (Lisca), 149-50
Wilson, Edmund, 5, 6, 16, 102, 103-4,
    106, 110
Winter of Our Discontent, The, 2, 3,
    158, 161
Wolfe, Thomas, 163
Woman's Home Companion, 150
Wordsworth, William, 16

                Z

Zanuck, Darryl, 80, 102, 112, 121

STENDHAL

A Collection of Critical Essays
Edited by VICTOR BROMBERT

A

Abbesse de Castro, 95
Albérès, Francine, 97
Alienation, theme of, 4, 18-19, 40
Aminta (Tasso), 165
Amour peintre, L' (Molière), 54
"Ariostesco Stendhal, L." (Trompeo), 165
Ariosto, 9, 10, 165
Armance, 4, 6, 37, 110, 158, 164
Aubigné, T. A. d', 23
Auerbach, Erich, 3

B

Balzac, Honoré de, 1, 5, 44, 58, 71, 86, 88, 92, 126, 135, 158
Barrès, A. M., 7
Bentham, Jeremy, 106
Beyle, Chérubin (father), 115
Beyle, Henri (*pseud.* Stendhal), 38-39 (*see also* Stendhal)
Beyle, Pauline (sister), 102, 104, 115, 158
"Beylism," 4, 11, 101-13
Biran, Maine de, 111, 128, 142
Blum, Léon, 67, 78
Borgia, Lucretia, 149
Boucher, F., 137
Bourget, Paul, 7, 21, 111
Bouvard et Pécuchet (Flaubert), 52
Brantôme, Seigneur de, 23

Brombert, Victor, 72
Buffon, Comte G. L. L. de, 52
Bussière, Auguste, 107
Byron, George Gordon Lord, 71, 85, 94, 113, 158

C

Callot, Jacques, 54
Camus, Albert, 4, 19, 32, 73
Captive Mind, The (Milosz), 4
Casanova, 157
Causes Célèbres, 159
Cenci, 160-61
Cenci, Beatrice, 159
Cervantes, 54
Characterization, method of, 17-18, 19, 110-13
Chartreuse de Parme, La, 3, 10, 11, 12, 25, 37, 47, 48, 59, 79, 86, 87, 88, 90, 91, 93, **94-100,** 105, 130, 133, 138, 160, 163
Chateaubriand, F. R. de, 43, 52, 137, 138, 159
Chatterton, Thomas, 69
Chenier, André, 61
Chroniques du crime, 159
Chroniques italiennes, 12, 150
Cimarosa, 40, 163
Class Struggles in France (Marx), 86
Class war, theme of, 16, 17, 68, 73, 85
Code Civil, 113, 132
Comédie humaine (Balzac), 58

Comedy, 64-67, 70, 86, 93, 145-46
Condillac, E. B. de, 101, 102, 107,
    113, 164
Confessions (Rousseau), 6
Conrad, Joseph, 76, 77, 86
Constant, Benjamin, 14, 21
Constitutional, Le, 110
Corneille, 22, 108, 164
Corregio, 124
Cour d'assises, 159
Courrier anglais, 2, 159, 160
Critical realism, 3, 44, 69

D

Danton, G. J., 83
Daumier, H., 54
David, J. L., 137
De la France (Heine), 66
De l'Amour, 13, 112, 157-58, 165
Delille, J., 108
Diderot, Denis, 45
Dionysos, Apologie pour le théâtre
    (Touchard), 70
Discourses on Livy (Machiavelli), 88,
    89
Divan, 55
Dostoevski, F., 76, 77, 86
Du Barry, Madame, 149
Duclos, C. P., 110

E

Eighteenth-century influences, 127-28,
    146
Eléments d'idéologie (Tracy), 129
Encylopedists, 78, 80, 102
Energy, importance of, 11, 13, 19,
    39, 69, 79-80, 109, 150-51, 160
Enlightenment, 42, 45, 46, 76
Époques de la nature (Buffon),
    52
Ernestine ou la naissance de l'amour,
    164
Espagnolisme, 82, 91,
    108
Étranger, L' (Camus), 32,
    73

F

Facheux, Les (Molière), 50
Farnese, Alessandro, 95
Farnese, Vannozza, 48, 160
Father-search, theme of, 6
Father-son conflict, theme of, 2,
    115
Faux-pas (Blanchot), 127
Fielding, Henry, 42, 51, 52, 53, 54
Filosofia Nova, 143
Flaubert, Gustave, 19, 44, 79, 92,
    159
Fouché, Joseph, 114
Fourberies de Scapin, Les (Molière), 56
Fragonard, J. H., 137
Freedom, problem of, 3-5, 82-83, 84,
    87, 104, 114-19, 150-53
French Revolution, 1-2, 36, 38, 39,
    43, 45, 46, 68, 77, 78, 99, 108

G

Gautier, Théophile, 159
Gazette des Tribunaux, 159
Gaulthier, Madame Jules, 47
Gerusalemme liberata (Tasso), 9
Gide, André, 19, 28, 158
Gil Blas (Lesage), 57
Gobineau, 4
Goethe, J. W. von, 38, 113
Good European, idea of, 84, 115
Goldsmith, Oliver, 42
Gros, A. J., 137

H

Han d'Islande (Hugo), 160
Happiness as goal, 12-13, 44, 71, 97,
    100, 102-10 *passim,* 128, 154-56
Hauser, Arnold, 66, 80, 88
Haydn, F. J., 48
Heine, Heinrich, 65-66, 70
Helvétius, 101, 102, 106, 107, 108,
    164
Hemingway, Ernest, 159
Histoire de la peinture en Italie, 12,
    111

Hitler, 4
Howe, Irving, 3, 4
Hugo, Victor, 46, 160
Huxley, Aldous, 70
Hypocrisy, idea of, 4, 36, 72-74, 104-5, 120, 133

I

Identity-quest, theme of, 5-6
Idéologues, 7, 101, 130, 131, 134, 136, 140, 141-42, 164
Imagery, 3, 16-17, 32-33, 85, 97, 119, 164
Inaccessible, importance of the, 12
Individualism, 4, 19, 81
Ingres, J. A. D., 137
Interior monologue, use of, 56-57
Italy, influence of, 11, 12, 40, 72, 95

J

James, Henry, 76, 77
Jansenists, 37
Jefferson, Thomas, 83
Jesuits, 37, 79
Josephson, Matthew, 32n
Jouffroy, T., 111
Journal, 120
Journal des Faux-Monnayeurs (Gide), 28
July Monarchy, 64, 67, 69

K

Kafka, Franz, 100, 122

L

La Bruyère, 41, 51
Laclos, P. A. F. Choderlos de, 21, 25, 104
La Fayette, Madame de, 21
La Fontaine, 96
Lamennais, F. R. de, 54
Lamiel, 8, 47, 48, 49, 65, 81

Language, 7, 13, 27-31, 131, 140
La Rouchefoucauld, 106
Lauzun, Duc de, 110
Lesage, A. R., 42
Levin, Harry, 23
Liaisons dangereuses (Laclos), 25, 63, 104
Lingay, Joseph, 2
Logic (Condillac), 101
Logique (Tracy), 136
Love, 12, 13-14, 69, 107, 119, 135, 154-56, 158-66
Lucien Leuwen, 11, 37, 47-62, 63-75, 85, 86
  Chasseur vert, Le, 54, 61

M

Machiavelli, N., 86, 88, 89, 90, 94
Malraux, André, 5, 92, 159
Mareste, Baron de, 2
Marivaux, 54, 155, 164
Maroncelli, 3
Martineau, Henri, 2, 47, 55, 58, 66, 67, 69
Martyrs, Les (Chateaubriand), 52
Marx, Karl, 85-86
Mask, function of, 7, 72-73, 114-26 *passim*
Maurras, Charles, 10
Meinecke, F., 45
Mélanges de littérature, 72
Mélanges intimes, 48
Mérimée, Prosper, 101, 158, 159
Metamorphosis, 120-26
Method, 8-10, 18, 22, 50-62, 93-94, 140-43
Metternich, Prince, 39
Milosz, Czeslaw, 4
Molière, 15, 50, 54, 95, 98, 123
Montaigne, Michel de, 42
Montesquieu, Baron de la B. et de, 101, 110, 128
Montigny, Darles de, 157
Moral vision, 10, 11, 63-67, 101-10
Mounier, Edouard, 102
Mozart, W. A., 40
Musset, A. de, 56, 113

N

Napoleon, 1, 2, 3, 12, 19, 20, 23, 36,
    39, 40, 45, 46, 74, 80, 81, 83, 87,
    90, 95, 96, 113, 128
Narrative devices (*see also* Method),
    5, 7, 9-10, 25-27, 55-57, 93, 96, 99,
    141, 161-63
Naturel chez Stendhal, Le (Albérès),
    97
Neuville, Marie de, 69
Neveu de Rameau (Diderot), 45
New Monthly Magazine, 160
Nietzsche, F. W., 84, 91, 94, 103
Nouvelle, Héloïse, La (Rousseau), 13,
    63, 128

O

Oeuvre de Stendhal, L' (Martineau),
    19n
*Origine delle grandezze della famiglia
    Farnese,* 160
Orlando (Ariosto), 165

P

Palais de justice, 159
Parain, Brice, 4
Pellico, Silvio, 3
Point de lendemain (Vivant-Denon),
    157
Politics, theme of, 2-3, 12, 35-38, 57,
    77-94 *passim*
Position Sociale, Une, 56, 58, 62
Praz, Mario, 159
Prévost, A. F., 23, 42
Prince, The (Machiavelli), 89-90
Princess Casamassima, The (James),
    76
Princess d'Élide, La (Molière), 54
Prison, theme of, 12, 13, 14, 32, 97,
    119, 164
Privilèges du 10 avril 1840, Les, 48,
    120-25 *passim*
Promenades dans Rome, 12, 13, 160
Proust, Marcel, 14, 56, 100, 119, 139,
    140, 164

R

Racine, 27, 123, 164
Racine et Shakespeare, 64-65
Rambaud, Henri, 55
Regnard, J. F., 54, 56
Renunciation, theme of, 73, 164
Restoration, 1, 2, 35, 37, 45, 68, 74,
    85
Revue des Deux Mondes, 107
Richard, Jean-Pierre, 5, 70
Richardson, Samuel, 155
Rimbaud, Arthur, 126, 159
Rivière, Jacques, 22
Romanticism, 1, 19, 20, 27, 40, 43, 46,
    80-81, 108, 137, 158
Rome, Naples et Florence, 3, 12
Rossini, G. A., 54
Rouge et le noir, Le, 2, 11, 15-33, 34,
    47, 48, 49, 50-57, 61, 68, 69, 71, 79,
    84, 85, 89, 91, 138, 141, 143, 159,
    161
Rousseau, Jean-Jacques, 6, 12, 13, 23,
    36, 38, 40, 42, 45, 83, 108, 110,
    129, 164
Routrou, 99
Rue transnonain (Daumier), 54
Ruota, La, 165

S

Sade, Marquis de, 157, 158
Sainte-Beuve, C. A., 20, 157
Saint-Simon, Duc de, 42
Scarron, 54
Schiller, Friedrich von, 42, 71
Sénancour, E. P. de, 46
Self-esteem, theme of, 49, 153, 158
Self-knowledge, search for, 14, 20-21,
    23, 105, 151
Shakespeare, William, 40, 87, 101,
    108
Sharpe, Sutton, 79
Shelley, P. B., 159, 160, 161
Social disintegration, theme of, 78-79,
    85-86
Social History of Art (Hauser),
    66

Souvenirs d'Égotisme, 6, 14, 41, 43, 44, 65
Staël, Madame Germaine de, 136-37
Stalin, 4
Starobinski, Jean, 7
Stendhal (*pseud.* of Henri Beyle):
  biographical information, 1, 6, 8, 38-43, 114-16, 158-60
  comic, idea of, 66-67
  and the eighteenth century, 127-28, 146
  esthetics of, 110-11
  and Happy Few, 11, 79, 81, 93, 102, 116
  as journalist, 2-3
  modernism of, 2
  and moral values, 10, 11, 63-67, 101-10
  and painting, influence of, 130, 137-38
  and pseudonyms, use of, 114-26 *passim*
  theatrical experience of, 54, 144-45
  and women, 147-56 *passim*
  on writing, 136-37, 143
Stendhal, works by:
  Armance, 4, 6, 37, 110, 158, 164
  Cenci, 160-61
  Chartreuse de Parme, La, 3, 10, 11, 12, 25, 37, 47, 48, 59, 79, 86, 87, 88, 90, 91, 93, 94, 95-100, 105, 130, 133, 138, 160, 163
  Chroniques italiennes, 12, 150
  De l'Amour, 13, 112, 157-58, 165
  Ernestine ou la naissance de l'amour, 164
  Filosofia Nova, 143
  Histoire de la peinture en Italie, 12, 111
  Journal, 120
  Lamiel, 8, 47, 48, 49, 65, 81
  Lucien Leuwen, 11, 37, 47-62, 63-75, 85, 86
  Mélanges de littérature, 72
  Mélanges intimes, 48
  Privilèges du 10 avril 1840, Les, 48, 120-25 *passim*
  Promenades dans Rome, 12, 13, 160

Racine et Shakespeare, 64-65
Rome, Naples et Florence, 3, 12
Rouge et le noir, Le, 2, 11, 15-33, 34, 47, 48, 49, 50-57, 61, 68, 69, 71, 79, 84, 85, 89, 91, 138, 141, 143, 159, 161
Souvenirs d'égotisme, 6, 14, 41, 43, 44, 65
Vie de Henry Brulard, 6, 8, 11, 12, 13, 41, 43, 44, 65, 67, 68, 113, 129, 130
Vie de Rossini, 12
Vies de Haydn, Mozart et Métastase, 12
Stendhal et la voie oblique (Brombert), 73
Stendhal et le Beylism (Blum), 67
Stendhal or The Pursuit of Happiness (Josephson), 32
Stranger, theme of, 19-24, 32, 67, 85, 91, 95-96, 106
Structure, 49, 86, 143
Style, 28-31, 39, 44, 53, 61, 70, 83, 94, 127, 130-31
Suarès, André, 11
Swinburne, A. C., 159

T

Taine, Hippolyte, 7, 20, 111, 113, 164
Tartuffe (Molière), 20
Tasso, 9, 10, 157, 164
Tempest, The (Shakespeare), 87
Temps retrouvé, Le (Proust), 139
Tocqueville, Alexis de, 83
Tom Jones (Fielding), 51-52
Touchard, P. -A., 70
Toward Stendhal (Levin), 23
Tracy Destutt de, 101, 136, 164
Trompeo, Pietro-Paolo, 165
Turnell, Martin, 92

V

Valéry, Paul, 60-61, 75
Velasquez, 54
Vénus d'Ille (Mérimée), 136

Véritable saint Genest, Le (Routrou), 99

Vie de Henry Brulard, 6, 8, 11, 12, 13, 41, 43, 44, 65, 67, 68, 113, 129, 130

Vie de Rossini, 12

Vies de Haydn, Mozart et Métastase, 12

Vigny, Alfred de, 1

Vita Nuova (Dante), 157

Vivant-Denon, 157

Voltaire, 42, 44, 128

W

Walls, significance of, 15, 16, 17, 21, 99

Walpole, Horace, 70

Waterloo, 5, 79

Wilde, Oscar, 84

Will, importance of, 1-9, 105-6, 125

Will, The (Taine), 164

LAURENCE STERNE

A Collection of Critical Essays
Edited by JOHN TRAUGOTT

A

Absalom and Achitophel (Dryden),
44
Addison, Joseph, 31, 97
"Air and Angels" (Donne), 149
Alienation, theme of, 19, 55, 130, 132,
133, 135, 139, 142
Anatomy of Melancholy, The (Burton),
48, 155
Appearance versus reality, theme of,
2, 4, 5, 8, 11-13, 27, 31-33, 90-91,
113, 114, 115-19, 124, 128, 162-63,
169
Arbuthnot, John, 138
Aristotle, 7, 134, 152
Art of Sinking in Poetry, The (Pope),
150, 151-52
Association of ideas, 8, 9, 13, 14, 25,
30, 33, 53, 61, 92, 93, 94, 98, 102,
113, 115, 119, 132, 163
Austen, Jane, 22
Autobiography of Michel de Montaigne (ed. Loewenthal), 30

B

Bacon, Francis, 22
Bathurst, Lord, 138
Battle of the Books, The (Swift),
159
Beckett, Samuel, 14, 116, 119
Bergson, Henri, 44,
92

Berkeley, Bishop, 17, 128, 132, 133,
135, 139
Beroalde de Verville, 22, 41, 142
Blount, Thomas, 22
Boehme, Jacob, 125
Book of Snobs, The (Thackeray), 41
Booth, Wayne, 60
Boswell, James, 133
Bouchet, 22, 142
"Brothers Shandy, The" (Priestly),
132
Bradford, Gamaliel, 35
Brontë, Emily, 22-23
Browne, Sir Thomas, 154, 155
Bruscambille, 22, 41, 142
Burckhardt, Sigurd, 20
Burger, G. A., 123
Burton, Richard, 18, 22, 41, 48,
136, 142, 155, 173
Butler, Samuel, 41, 97

C

Candide (Voltaire), 42, 142
Cervantes, Miguel de, 19, 37, 40, 41,
56, 57, 59, 75, 77, 111
Chance, importance of, 10, 12, 24, 32,
35, 39-40, 49, 53, 56, 66-67, 71, 113,
119, 130, 160-63, 164, 165, 170
Characterization, methods of, 38-39,
45, 118-19, 165-66
Clarissa (Richardson), 55, 64
Coleridge, S. T., 1, 15, 34, 91, 107,
125

Compleat Angler, The (Walton), 154
"Composition" (Diderot), 106
Connolly, Cyril, 20
Conrad, Joseph, 101, 102, 105
Crane, R. S., 64
Crébillon, 108
Cross, Wilbur, 31, 35, 40, 60, 62,
163

D

Dante, 158
Dead Souls (Gogol), 68
Defoe, Daniel, 38, 64
Deguileville, G. de, 158
De Quincey, Thomas, 101
Descartes, 113, 149
Dickens, Charles, 41
Diderot, Denis, 106, 111, 112, 125
Digressions, use of, 7, 9, 26, 33, 49,
51, 52, 53, 57, 59, 66, 73-75, 82,
93, 97, 99, 101, 121, 137, 163
Discourse on Method (Descartes), 113
Donne, John, 18, 149, 153, 167
Don Quixote (Cervantes), 42, 69, 74
Draper, Eliza, 108
Dryden, John, 44, 153

E

Eighteenth-century milieu, influence
of, 3, 14, 17, 19, 25, 40, 49-51, 58,
61, 64, 114, 116-17, 137-41, 150
Eliot, George, 3
Eliot, T. S., 5, 56, 158
Emerson, R. W., 55
Encyclopédie, 106
Erasmus, 112, 136, 141
*Essay Concerning Human Understand-
ing, An* (Locke), 113, 128, 129, 132,
135, 137, 143, 144
"Essay on the Freedom of Wit and
Humour, An" (Shaftesbury), 51
Essays of Montaigne, 29, 30
"Evolution of *A Sentimental Journey*,
The" (Putney), 62

F

Faux-Monnayeurs, Les (Gide), 42,
43, 106
Ferriar, Dr. John, 22, 41, 142
Fielding, Henry, 3, 4, 12, 21, 22, 23,
25, 27, 34, 35, 37, 40, 41, 48, 57,
59, 64, 90, 91, 175
Finnegans Wake (Joyce), 120
Fontenelle, 31, 46
Ford, F. M., 102
Form, 3, 5-6, 21, 30-33, 56-58, 66-89,
100, 132, 135, 148-49, 159, 166
Formalists, 5
Forster, E. M., 3, 140, 148
Fourmantelle, Kitty, 108
France, Anatole, 31
Furetière, Antoine, 90

G

Galen, 151
Garden of Epicurus (France), 31
Garrick, David, 30, 176
Gesture, importance of, 7, 38-40, 52,
55, 71-72, 75, 114, 124, 170, 174,
176-77
Gide, André, 42, 101, 106, 107,
123
Gogol, N. V., 68, 76
Goldsmith, Oliver, 35, 127
Goncharov, I. A., 68
Greene, Graham, 148
Greuze, J. B., 111
Gulliver's Travels (Swift), 42, 141

H

Hall, Bishop Joseph, 22
Hartley, David, 125
Henry Esmond (Thackeray), 105
*History of a Good Warm Watch-Coat
(see also Political Romance, A)*, 36,
173
Hobbes, Thomas, 25
Hoffmann, H., 76
Hogarth, William, 174
Homer, 69

Hume, David, 17, 57, 58, 127, 132, 139, 140
Humphry Clinker (Smollett), 56, 60
Huxley, Aldous, 53, 101

I

Illustrations of Sterne (Ferriar), 41
Impotence, theme of, 83-86, 139
Ionesco, E., 112
It Was the Nightingale (Ford), 102

J

James, Henry, 107
James, William, 44
Jefferson, D. W., 18, 19
Johnson, Samuel, 2, 35, 132
Jonson, Ben, 18, 151, 153, 158
Joseph Conrad, a Personal Remembrance (Ford), 102
Journal des Faux-Monnayeurs (Gide), 43
Journal to Eliza, 62, 108
Joyce, James, 21, 24, 35, 52, 56, 57, 58, 107, 112, 115, 116, 120, 125

K

Kafka, Franz, 35
Kant, Immanuel, 152
Kater Murr (Hoffmann), 76
Keats, John, 44

L

La Bruyère, 117
Lamb, Charles, 148
Language, limitations of, 24, 53, 55, 56, 80, 90-92, 99-100, 111, 114, 125, 127, 130-33
"Laocoön" (Lessing), 106
"Laurence Sterne: Apostle of Laughter" (Putney), 62*n*
Laurence Sterne, sa Personne et ses Ouvrages (Stapfer), 31

Lawrence, D. H., 10, 108
Learned wit, tradition of, 18, 19, 37, 41, 42, 59, 129, 136, **148-67**
Lehman, Benjamin, 1, 3, 5, 6, 46
Lenore (Bürger), 123
Lessing, G. E., 106
Life and Opinions of Tristram Shandy, Gent., The, 1, 5, 6, 7, 8, 9, 14, 16, 21-33 *passim*, 36, 38, 41, 54-63 *passim*, 92, 93, 95-99, 101-11, 115, 118, 168, 173, 175
  and "learned wit," 148-67
  Locke's influence on, 126-47
  parody in, 66-89
Locke, John, 2, 3, 4, 12, 13, 14, 17, 25, 43, 44, 57, 92, 94, 113, 114, 115, 117, 120, 126-47, 149, 168
Lockridge, Ernest, 20
Loewenthal, Marvin, 30
"Lovers' Infiniteness" (Donne), 149
Love's Labour's Lost (Shakespeare), 157
Lumley, Elizabeth, 173

M

Mackenzie, Henry, 61, 63
McKillop, A. D., 16, 18
Magic Mountain, The (Mann), 1, 22
Mahomet, 31
Mann, Thomas, 21, 25
Man of Feeling, The (Mackenzie), 61
Marivaux, P. C. de C. de, 41
Marlborough, Duke of, 4, 14
Marvell, Andrew, 167
Mayoux, Jean-Jacques, 3, 8, 10, 11, 12, 19
Melville, Herman, 122
Memoirs of Martinus Scriblerus (Swift), 41, 128, 141, 150, 162
Mendilow, A. A., 8, 9, 10
Merchant of Venice, The (Shakespeare), 153
Method, 2-14 *passim*, 19-20, 26-30, 34, 39, 41-43, 45-65 *passim*, 68-89, 94-107, 130-35, 139-42, 165-67, 172-79
Mitford, Mary, 91

Moby Dick (Melville), 122
Montaigne, Michel de, 22, 30, 41, 136, 173
Muir, Edwin, 20

N

Narrative devices (*see also* Method), 8-10, 14, 55-58, 68-89 *passim*, 128, 136-43, 163, 172-79
Nest of Gentlefolk, The (Turgenev), 68
Newton, Isaac, 2, 4, 5, 25, 57, 149
Nicolson, Margaret, 46

O

Obscenity, question of, 10, 22, 108-11
Odyssey (Homer), 56
Of Solitariness (Montaigne), 30
Of the Vanitie of Words (Montaigne), 30

P

Pamela (Richardson), 1, 22
Paracelsus, 115
Parody, 3, 8, 14, **66-89**, 113, 115, 117, 120, 124, 157
Picasso, Pablo, 67
Political Romance, A (*see also History of a Good Warm Watch-Coat*), 36
Pons, E., 38
Pope, Alexander, 31, 114, 115, 138, 150, 152
Powys, John Cowper, 40-41
Priestley, J. B., 14, 20, 131-32
Prior, Matthew, 138
Proust, Marcel, 12, 21, 27, 35, 52, 98, 107, 114, 119, 168, 169
Pushkin, Alexander, 68
Putney, Rufus, 62

R

Rabelais, 3, 10, 18, 19, 22, 39, 41, 75,

109, 136, 141, 142, 150, 151, 153, 154, 156, 157, 162
Read, Sir Herbert, 15, 16, 20
Remembrance of Things Past, The (Proust), 1, 22, 26
Rhetoric (Aristotle), 134
Richardson, Samuel, 4, 19, 21, 22, 23, 25, 27, 34, 35, 37, 38, 40, 63, 64, 91, 97, 106
Richter, Jean Paul, 65
Ritual Songs of Spring (Anichkov), 79
Rousseau, Jean-Jacques, 112
Rowlandson, Thomas, 123

S

Saintsbury, G., 22
Scarron, 22
Scott, Sir Walter, 59
Sentimentalism, 4, 10, 11, 14, 15, 18, 19, 34, 37, 39, 40, 61, 62, 63, 108, 111, 112, 130, 166
Sentimental Journey through France and Italy, A, 7, 16, 23, 27, 32, 36, 42, 48, 60, 61, 62, 75, 76, 110, 168, 171, 173
Sermons of Mr. Yorick, The, 16, 41
Shaftesbury, Earl of, 51
Shakespeare, William, 18, 74
Shenstone, William, 61
Shklovsky, Viktor, 5, 6, 7, 10, 14
"Shot, The" (Pushkin), 68
"Shponka and His Aunt" (Gogol), 76
Silent Woman, The (Jonson), 153
Sir Charles Grandison (Richardson), 38, 97
Smith, Adam, 58
Social sympathy, 55, 111, 132-35, 140
Solipsism, 4, 45
Sophocles, 152
Spectator, 97n
Staël, Madame de, 97
Stapfer, Paul, 31, 46
Sterility, theme of, 139
Sterne, Laurence:
    biographical information, 35-36,

Sterne, Laurence (biographical information) (*continued*)
35-36, 59-60, 138, 168, 173
comic vision of, 19, 23, 115, 126-47
critical reception of, 1-2, 22-23, 34, 58-59, 108-10
and mock-heroic tradition, 37, 62
modernism of, 1-2, 5, 21, 52-53, 58, 91-93, 101, 107, 115-16, 125
moral vision, 4, 15-17, 18, 23-25, 29, 37-38, 115, 126-29, 165, 172-73
popular success of, 1, 36, 62
and Swift, 136-40
and theatre, influence of, 3, 175-78
Sterne, Laurence, works by:
History of a Good Warm Watch-Coat, 36, 173
Journal to Eliza, 62, 108
Life and Opinions of Tristram Shandy, Gent., The, 1, 5, 6, 7, 8, 9, 14, 16, 21-33 *passim*, 36, 38, 41, 54-63 *passim*, 66-89, 92, 93, 95-99, 101-11, 115, 118, 126-47, 148-67, 168, 173, 175
Sentimental Journey through France and Italy, A, 7, 16, 23, 27, 32, 36, 42, 48, 60, 61, 62, 75, 76, 110, 168, 171, 173
Sermons of Mr. Yorick, The, 16, 41
Smollett, Tobias, 34, 35, 40, 51, 60, 64
Stevenson, John Hall, 36, 108
Stout, Gardner, 16, 20
"Strider" (Tolstoy), 79
Style, 17, 19, 22, 23, 115, 172-73
Suard, J. B., 44, 94
Swift, Jonathan, 4, 18, 19, 22, 37, 38, 51, 79, 114, 115, 132, 136, 137, 138, 139, 140, 154, 158, 159, 164, 173

T

Table-Talk (Coleridge), 107n
Tale of a Tub, A (Swift), 19, 41, 137, 138, 139, 150, 153, 159

Terence, 44
Thackeray, W. M., 1, 14, 41, 108
Theatre, influence of, 3, 175-78
Tillotson, Geoffrey, 61
Time, treatment of, 7, 8, 9, 11, 25-27, 33, 46, 52, 67, 68, 74, 84, 92-107 *passim*, 115, 119-24, 176-79
Tolstoy, Leo, 72, 79
Tom Jones (Fielding), 23, 55, 56, 58
"Tom Thumb," 79
"Tradition and the Individual Talent" (Eliot), 5
Treatise of Human Nature, A (Hume), 17
"*Tristram Shandy*—a Parodying Novel" (Shklovsky), 6
Trivia, use of, 18, 19, 37, 38, 39, 49, 62, 116, 136, 137, 164
Turgenev, Ivan, 68

U

Ulysses (Joyce), 1, 22, 24, 56, 58, 115, 125
"Ulysses, Myth and Order" (Eliot), 56
Urquhart, Sir Thomas, 150

V

Vanity Fair (Thackeray), 105
Vigny, Alfred de, 123
Virgil, 91
Voltaire, 142
Vulgar Errors (Browne), 154

W

War and Peace (Tolstoy), 21
Warton, Thomas, 90
Watkins, W. B. C., 20, 46
West, Rebecca, 24
Whitehead, A. N., 154
"Woman's Constancy" (Donne), 153
Woolf, Virginia, 20, 107, 114
Work, J. A., 54, 58

WALLACE STEVENS

A Collection of Critical Essays

Edited by MARIE BORROFF

A

"Academic Discourse at Havana,"
44
Accent, 43
"Adagia," 100, 108
"Add This to Rhetoric," 17-18, 170
Adonais (Shelley), 84
Aeschylus, 174
"Anecdote of the Jar," 152
"Anecdote of the Prince of Peacocks,"
154
"Another Weeping Woman," 6, 144
"Anything Is Beautiful If You Say It
Is," 19, 22
"Apostrophe to Vincentine," 63-64
Aristotle, 63, 161, 162, 164, 171
Ash Wednesday (Eliot), 152
"Asides on the Oboe," 44, 45, 48-51,
52, 120, 172
Auden, W. H., 110, 152
Augustine, Saint, 153
"Autumn Refrain," 136
"Auroras of Autumn, The," 22, 57,
104, 106, 163
Auroras of Autumn, The, 1, 72,
158

B

"Bagatelles the Madrigals, The," 171
Bakst, L., 154
Baudelaire, Charles, 152
"Bed of Old John Zeller, The," 121

"Beginning, The," 21
Belief, problem of, 3-4, 9-10, 15-17,
35, 44, 46-47, 74-75, 93, 98-101,
114-17, 121-22, 158-59, 167-68
Bergson, Henri, 99
Blackmur, R. P., 102
Blake, William, 77, 79, 83, 86, 87, 93,
94, 176
"Blue Buildings in the Summer Air,
The," 99, 119
"Botanis on Alp (No. 1)," 117
"Bouquet, The," 8
"Bouquet of Belle Sçavoir,"
119
"Bouquet of Roses in Sunlight,"
54-55
Bridge, The (Crane), 30
Brinnin, John Malcolm, 65
Browning, Robert, 45
Burnshaw, Stanley, 139
Byron, George Gordon Lord, 84

C

"Cape Hatteras" (Crane), 30
"Carlos among the Candles," 64
Carlyle, Thomas, 171
"Celle qui fût Heaulmiette," 169
"Certain Phenomena of Sound," 56-57
Change, theme of, 10-13, 16-17, 23,
56, 62-64, **83-88**, 124-26
"Chanting the Square Deific" (Whit-
man), 32
Chapman, G., 45

Coleridge, S. T., 79, 84, 88, 94, 162
Collected Poems, 19, 23, 138, 167, 169
"Colloquy with a Polish Aunt," 44
Colum, Mary, 43, 45, 49, 50
"Comedian as the Letter C," 4, 41, 44, 77, 116, 117, 145, 152, 154, 158
"Connoisseur of Chaos," 44, 167
Consciousness, theme of, 1-5, 6, 12-17, 21, 78-79, 80, 97-101, 114, 135, 165
"Course of a Particular, The," 41
Cowley, Abraham, 50
Crane, Hart, 30, 154
Crashaw, Richard, 50
"Credences of Summer," 15, 84, 98, 101, 121, 145, 148, 166
Cummings, E. E., 152

D

Dante, 46
Death, theme of, 6, 10, 33, 36-37, 42, 86, 96-106, 168
"Democratic Vistas" (Whitman), 32, 34
"Depression before Spring," 11-12, 13
Descartes, René, 161
"Description without Place," 100, 105, 174
Dewey, John, 43
"Dezembrum," 119
Dickinson, Emily, 37, 143
"Dish of Peaches in Russia, A," 14
"Disillusionment at Ten O'Clock," 154
"Domination of Black," 113, 167
Don Juan (Byron), 84
Donne, John, 44, 45, 49, 50, 51, 52, 143, 144, 145
Donne Tradition, The (Williamson), 49
"Dove in the Belly, The," 169
"Duck for Dinner, A," 44
"Dwarf, The," 11

E

Ecclesiastes, 27, 29, 62
"Effects of Analogy," 60-61, 71
Eliot, T. S., 45, 49, 51, 64, 66, 112, 144, 151, 152, 154, 155, 161, 174-75
Ellmann, Richard, 103, 108
Emerson, Ralph Waldo, 31, 32, 34, 81, 173
"Emperor of Ice-Cream, The," 36, 114, 154
Enesco, Georges, 133
"Esthetique du Mal," 4, 5, 7, 36, 101, 102, 103, 109, 112, 120, 121, 126-30, 167
"Evening without Angels," 44
"Examination of the Hero in a Time of War," 44
"Extracts from Addresses to the Academy of Fine Ideas," 3-4, 120

F

"Fading of the Sun, A," 11, 136
Fairie Queene, The (Spenser), 19
Fall of Hyperion, The (Keats), 89, 94
"Farewell to Florida," 44, 117, 138
"Faune" (Mallarmé), 153
"Figure of the Youth as Virile Poet, The," 61, 65
"Final Soliloquy of the Interior Paramour," 84, 169
Finnegans Wake (Joyce), 108
Fitzgerald, F. Scott, 174
Form, 1, 12, 22, 51, 55, 124
Four Quartets, The (Eliot), 64, 66, 152
   "Burnt Norton," 152
   "East Coker," 152
Freud, Sigmund, 73, 74, 157, 168
"Frogs Eat Butterflies," 154
Frost, Robert, 110, 151
Frye, Northrop, 103
Future of an Illusion, The (Freud), 73

G

Gay Science, The (Nietzsche), 99

"Ghosts as Cocoons," 11, 21
"Girl in a Nightgown," 54
"God is Good. It Is a Beautiful Night."
  11
Goethe, J. W. von, 160
Golden Bowl, The (James), 132
"Golden Woman in a Silver Mirror,"
  1, 169
"Gray Stones and Gray Pigeons,"
  136
Gregory, Horace, 43, 44, 45, 49, 50
"Greenest Continent, The," 44, 48
Grierson, H. J. C., 49, 50
Gyres, The (Yeats), 76

H

Hamlet, 19
"Hand as Being, The," 8
Hardy, Thomas, 152, 174
Harmonium, 2, 5, 44, 72, 85, 91, 98,
  111, 112-17, 124, 133, 135, 137,
  141, 148, 151, 152, 156, 160, 165,
  166, 174, 176
Hegel, G. W. F., 32, 34
Herbert, George, 50
Herbert, Lord of Cherbury, 45
"Hermitage at the Center, The," 105
"High-toned Old Christian Woman, A,"
  13, 167
"Holiday in Reality," 59
Holy Sonnets (Donne), 143-45
Hopkins, G. M., 143, 144, 151, 152,
  153, 154, 157
"House Was Quiet and the World Was
  Calm, The," 11, 64
Housman, A. E., 174
"How to Live. What to Do." 100, 107
Hulme, T. E., 163
"Human Arrangement," 11
Humanists, 151

I

"Idea of Order at Key West, The," 9,
  42, 44, 117, 119, 125, 136, 142, 144,
  175
Ideas of Order, 44, 97, 117-20,

  136-38, 139, 158
Imagery, 10, 12-13, 16, 21, 36, 47,
  49-50, 85, 91-92, 96-110 *passim,*
  112, 120, 151-55, 167-69
Images, recurrent, 16, 22, 47, 96-98
Imagination, centrality of, 7-9, 14-16,
  21, 24-29, 33, 37, 41, 44, 47-49, 54-
  70 *passim,* 73-74, 77, 78-95, 97-105,
  111-32, 133-50, 155-56, **162-72**
Imagists, 52, 60, 151
"In a Bad Time," 107
"Infanta Marina," 125, 130, 168
"In the Clear Season of Grapes," 11
"Irish Cliffs of Moher, The," 105

J

"Jack-Rabbit, The," 167
James, Henry, 132, 153
James, William, 31, 43
Jarrell, Randall, 72, 96
Joyce, James, 99, 108
"July Mountain," 11
"Jumbo," 163
Jung, Carl, 141, 165

K

Kafka, Franz, 73
Keats, John, 80, 83, 84, 88, 89, 94
Kenyon Review, 30

L

"Lack of Repose, The," 130-31
"Landscape with Boat," 54, 119, 145
Language, 1-2, 9, 12-13, 22, 41, 68,
  115-16, 141-42
"Large Red Man Reading," 23, 54
"Last Looks at the Lilacs," 11
"Latest Freed Man, The," 44, 67
"Like Decorations in a Nigger Ceme-
  tery," 6
"Lions in Sweden," 44, 46, 117
Locke, John, 130
"Loneliness in Jersey City,"
  12
Lowell, Amy, 151

M

"Madame La Fleurie," 166
Mallarmé, Stéphane, 110, 152, 153, 154, 157
"Man Carrying Thing," 54
Manning, Bishop, 50
"Man on the Dump," 82, 167
"Man with the Blue Guitar, The," 11, 44, 47
Man with the Blue Guitar, The, 99, 118, 119, 138-39, 141-42
"Martial Cadenza," 16
Marvell, Andrew, 51, 150, 165
Marx, Karl, 130, 139
Mauron, Charles, 153
Mather, Cotton, 99
"Men Made Out of Words," 121
"Men That Are Falling," 99
Metamorphoses (Ovid), 56, 62
"Metamorphosis," 58
"Metaphor as Degeneration," 170
Metaphysical Lyrics and Poems of the Seventeenth Century (ed. Grierson), 51
Metaphysical poets, 45, 49, 50, 51, 52, 53
"Metaphysical Poets, The" (Eliot), 45
Method, 8-9, 16-20, 52-53, 85, 124, 127, 157
Milton (Blake), 83
Milton, John, 92, 165
"Monocle de mon Oncle, Le," 5-6, 10, 115, 116, 121
"Montrachet-le-Jardin," 44, 67
Moore, Marianne, 66, 155
Morse, Samuel French, 30, 138
"Motive for Metaphor, The," 57-58, 121
"Mozart, 1935," 117
"Mrs. Alfred Uruguay," 21
Muir, Edwin, 158-59
Munson, Gorham, 154-55
"Mystic Garden and Middling Beast," 46

N

"Native Element, The" (Morse), 30
Nature (Emerson), 173
Necessary Angel, The, 71, 101, 103, 105, 110, 157, 159, 161, 162, 163, 168, 169, 172, 174
"New England Verses," 154
"News and the Weather," 51
New York Times Book Review, The, 43
Nietzsche, F. W., 99
"Noble Rider, The," 134
"Notes toward a Supreme Fiction," 8, 11, 21, 44, 45, 58, 63, **76-95,** 111, 120, 121, 122-29, 145, 158, 175
    "It Must Be Abstract," **77-83,** 122
    "It Must Change," 11, **83-88,** 122, 124
    "It Must Give Pleasure," 83, 85, **88-95,** 122, 125
"Nuances of a Theme by Williams," 113

O

"Oak Leaves Are Hands," 68, 168
"Ode on a Grecian Urn" (Keats), 110
"Of Bright and Blue Birds and the Gala Sun," 15
"Of Modern Poetry," 44, 118, 143-44
"Old Woman and the Statue, The," 139
"On the Road Home," 44, 67, 70
Opus Posthumous, 2, 3, 7, 8, 23, 100, 105, 108, 136, 146
Order, search for, 2, 8, 13-15, 21, 40-41; 75, 76-95 *passim,* 97, 142, 162-65
"Ordinary Evening in New Haven, An," 16, 41, 57, 59, 69, 74, 75, 98
"Ordinary Woman, The," 167
"Out of the Cradle Endlessly Rocking" (Whitman), 37, 40
Ovid, 56, 62
"Owl in the Sarcophagus, The," 36-37, 103-4, 105, 168, 171-72
Owl's Clover, 44, 138, 139, 140-41, 142

P

Parts of a World, 43, 44, 58, 67, 118-20, 158, 170
"Passage to India" (Whitman), 32, 33
"Pastoral Nun," 65, 66
"Peter Quince at the Clavier," 6, 114, 169
"Phosphor Reading by his Own Light," 166
Picture of Little T. C. in a Prospect of Flowers (Marvell), 150
"Plain Sense of Things, The," 166
"Planet on the Table, The," 23
Plato, 42, 102, 157
Pleasure, theme of, 15, 29, 78, 88-95, 158
"Ploughing on Sunday," 154
"Plot Against the Giant, The," 154
"Poem as Icon, The," 107
"Poems of our Climate, The," 2, 12, 118
"Poem That Took the Place of a Mountain, The," 102, 109
"Poem with Rhythms," 44
"Poem Written at Morning," 17
"Poesie Abrutie," 13-14
"Poetry is a Destructive Force," 61-62, 167
Pope, Alexander, 164
Positivism, 73, 74
"Post-card from the Volcano, A," 57, 109
Pound, Ezra, 30, 45, 60
Poussin, N., 17
Prelude, The (Wordsworth), 79, 94
"Prologues to What Is possible," 8, 148, 172
Proust, Marcel, 72
"Puella Parvula," 19, 21, 22, 167
"Pure Good of Theory, The," 16, 171
Purgatory (Yeats), 76

Q

"Questions Are Remarks," 7

R

"Rabbit as King of the Ghosts, A," 66
"Reader, The," 166
Reality, nature of, 4, 10-11, 20-22, 24-29 *passim,* 33, 44, 54-70 *passim,* 75, 111-32 *passim,* 162-65
Reality and Process (Whitehead), 50
"Realm of Resemblance, The," 62, 63
Recluse, The (Wordsworth), 76, 94
Renoir, Auguste, 150
"Repetitions of a Young Captain," 18
Rilke, Rainer Maria, 89, 94, 108, 110, 152, 160, 167
Rimbaud, Arthur, 110
"River of Rivers in Connecticut," 168
Robinson, E. A., 151
"Rock, The," 102, 107, 109, 169
Rock, The, 22, 36, 95, 96-110, 176
Romanticism, 65, 73-74, 77, 79, 81, 82, 83, 87, 88, 89, 91, 93, 151, 163
Romney, George, 150

S

"Sad Strains of a Gay Waltz," 43-44, 117, 136
"Sailing after Lunch," 44, 137
"Sail of Ulysses, The," 105
"Sailing to Byzantium" (Yeats), 3
"St. Armorer's Church from the Outside," 109
Scales, François de, 146
Santayana, George, 22-23, 33, 37, 43, 45, 134-35
Scotus, Duns, 153
"Sea Surface Full of Clouds," 55, 113-14, 119
"Seventy Years Later," 106
Shakespeare, William, 19, 174
Shelley, P. B., 79, 83, 84, 86, 87, 160, 165
Signature, 25
"Sketch of the Ultimate Politician," 172
"Snow Man, The," 14

Socrates, 13, 126
"Solitude of Cataracts, The," 2
"Sombre Figuration," 54, 69
"Song of Myself" (Whitman), 33-34,
  38
"Somnabulisma," 85
"Song of Fixed Accord," 169, 175
"Spelt from Sibyl's Leaves" (Hopkins),
  153
Spenser, Edmund, 83, 84
"Statue at the World's End, The," 70,
  139
Stevens, Wallace:
  humanism of, 6-7, 44, 47-48, 78-95
    passim, 106-10, 115, 128, 137,
    151-60
  on metaphor, 24-29
  and Nature, 10, 15, 25-26, 31, 80,
    86, 93, 103-6, 133-34
  poetry, theory of, 24-29, 31, 41,
    54, 60-62, 71-75 *passim*, 89, 100-
    101, 118-20, 122-23, 132, 133-34,
    143-47, 155, 161-76 *passim*
  skepticism of, 2-4, 37, 42, 43-44,
    72-73
Stevens, Wallace, works by:
  "Academic Discourse at Havana,"
    44
  "Adagia," 100, 108
  "Add This to Rhetoric," 17-18, 170
  "Anecdote of the Jar," 152
  "Anecdote of the Prince of Pea-
    cocks," 154
  "Another Weeping Woman," 6, 44
  "Anything Is Beautiful If You Say
    It Is," 19, 22
  "Apostrophe to Vincentine," 63-64
  "Asides on the Oboe," 44, 45, 48-
    51, 52, 120, 172
  "Autumn Refrain," 136
  "Auroras of Autumn, The," 22, 57,
    104, 106, 163
  Auroras of Autumn, The, 1, 72,
    158
  "Bagatelles the Madrigals, The,"
    171
  "Bed of Old John Zeller, The,"
    121

"Beginning, The," 21
"Blue Buildings in the Summer Air,
  The," 99, 119
"Botanist on Alp (No. 1)," 117
"Bouquet, The," 8
"Bouquet of Belle Sçavoir," 119
"Bouquet of Roses in Sunlight,"
  54-55
"Carlos among the Candles,"
  64
"Celle qui fût Heaulmiette," 169
"Certain Phenomena of Sound,"
  56-57
Collected Poems, 19, 23, 138, 167,
  169
"Colloquy with a Polish Aunt," 44
"Comedian as the Letter C," 4, 41,
  44, 77, 116, 117, 145, 152, 154,
  158
"Connoisseur of Chaos," 44, 167
"Course of a Particular, The," 41
"Credences of Summer," 15, 84, 98,
  101, 121, 145, 148, 166
"Depression before Spring," 11-12,
  13
"Description without Place," 100,
  105, 174
"Dezembrum," 119
"Dish of Peaches in Russia, A," 14
"Disillusionment of Ten O'Clock,"
  153
"Domination of Black," 113, 167
"Dove in the Belly, The," 169
"Duck for Dinner, A," 44
"Dwarf, The," 11
"Effects of Analogy," 60-61, 71
"Emperor of Ice-Cream, The," 36,
  114, 154
"Esthetique du Mal," 4, 5, 7, 36,
  101, 102, 103, 109, 112, 120, 121,
  126-30, 167
"Evening without Angels," 44
"Examination of the Hero in a Time
  of War," 44
"Extract from Addresses to the
  Academy of Fine Ideas," 3-4, 120
"Fading of the Sun, A," 11, 136
"Farewell to Florida," 44, 117, 138

Stevens, Wallace, works by (*continued*)
"Figure of the Youth as Virile Poet,
The," 61, 65
"Final Soliloquy of the Interior
Paramour," 84, 167
"Frogs Eat Butterflies," 154
"Ghosts as Cocoons," 11, 21
"Girl in a Nightgown," 54
"God is Good. It Is a Beautiful
Night." 11
"Golden Woman in a Silver Mirror,"
169
"Gray Stones and Gray Pigeons,"
136
"Greenest Continent, The," 44,
48
"Hand as Being, The," 8
Harmonium, 2, 5, 44, 72, 85, 91,
98, 111, 112-17, 124, 133, 135,
137, 141, 148, 151, 152, 156,
160, 165, 166, 174, 176
"Hermitage at the Center, The,"
105
"High-toned Old Christian Woman,
A," 13, 167
"Holiday in Reality," 59
"House Was Quiet and the World
Was Calm, The," 11, 64
"How to Live. What to Do." 100,
107
"Human Arrangement," 11
"Idea of Order at Key West, The,"
9, 42, 44, 117, 119, 125, 136,
142, 144, 175
Ideas of Order, 44, 97, 117-20,
136-38, 139, 158
"In a Bad Time," 167
"Infanta Marina," 125, 130, 168
"In the Clear Season of Grapes,"
11
"Irish Cliffs of Moher, The," 105
"Jack-Rabbit, The," 167
"July Mountain," 11
"Jumbo," 163
"Lack of Repose, The," 130-31
"Landscape with Boat," 54, 119,
145
"Large Red Man Reading," 23, 54

"Last Looks at Lilacs," 11
"Latest Freed Man, The," 44, 67
"Like Decorations in a Nigger
Cemetery," 6
"Lions in Sweden," 44, 46, 117
"Loneliness in Jersey City,"
12
"Madame La Fleurie," 166
"Man Carrying Thing," 54
"Man on the Dump, The," 82, 167
"Man with the Blue Guitar, The,"
11, 44, 47
Man with the Blue Guitar, The, 99,
118, 119, 138-39, 141-42
"Martial Cadenza," 16
"Men Made Out of Words," 121
"Men That Are Falling," 99
"Metamorphosis," 58
"Metaphor as Degeneration,"
170
"Monocle de mon Oncle, Le," 5-6,
10, 115, 116, 121
"Montrachet-le-Jardin," 44, 67
"Motive for Metaphor, The," 57-58,
121
"Mozart, 1935," 117
"Mrs. Alfred Uruguay," 21
"Mystic Garden and Middling
Beast," 46
Necessary Angel, The, 71, 101, 103,
105, 110, 157, 159, 161, 162, 163,
168, 169, 172, 174
"New England Verses," 154
"News and the Weather, The," 51
"Noble Rider, The," 134
"Notes toward a Supreme Fiction,"
8, 11, 21, 44, 45, 58, 63, 76-95,
111, 120, 121, 122-29, 145, 158,
175 (*see also* main entry)
"Nuances of a Theme by Williams,"
113
"Oak Leaves Are Hands," 68, 168
"Of Bright and Blue Birds and the
Gala Sun," 15
"Of Modern Poetry," 44, 118,
143-44
"Old Woman and the Statue, The,"
139

Stevens, Wallace, works by (*continued*)
"On the Road Home," 44, 67, 170
Opus Posthumous, 2, 3, 7, 8, 23, 100, 105, 108, 136, 146
"Ordinary Evening in New Haven, An," 16, 41, 57, 59, 69, 74, 75, 98
"Ordinary Woman, The," 167
"Owl in the Sarcophagus, The," 36-37, 103-4, 105, 168, 171-72
Owl's Clover, 44, 138, 139, 140-41, 142
Parts of a World, 43, 44, 58, 67, 118-20, 158, 170
"Pastoral Nun," 65, 66
"Peter Quince at the Clavier," 6, 114, 169
"Phosphor Reading by his Own Light," 166
"Plain Sense of Things, The," 166
"Planet on the Table, The," 23
"Ploughing on Sunday," 154
"Plot Against the Giant, The," 154
"Poem as Icon, The," 107
"Poems of Our Climate, The," 2, 12, 118
"Poem That Took the Place of a Mountain," 102, 109
"Poem with Rhythms," 44
"Poem Written at Morning," 17
"Poesie Abrutie," 13-14
"Poetry Is a Destructive Force," 61-62, 167
"Post-card from the Volcano, A," 57, 109
"Prologues to What Is Possible," 8, 148, 172
"Puella Parvula," 19, 21, 22, 167
"Pure Good of Theory, The," 16, 171
"Questions Are Remarks," 7
"Rabbit as King of the Ghosts, A," 66
"Reader, The," 166
"Realm of Resemblance, The," 62, 63
"Repetitions of a Young Captain," 18

"River of Rivers in Connecticut, The," 168
"Rock, The," 102, 107, 109, 169
Rock, The, 22, 36, 95, 96-110, 176
"Sad Strains of a Gay Waltz," 43-44, 117, 136
"Sailing after Lunch," 44, 137
"Sail of Ulysses, The," 105
"St. Armorer's Church from the Outside," 109
"Sea Surface Full of Clouds," 55, 113-14, 119
"Seventy Years Later," 105
"Sketch of the Ultimate Politician," 172
"Snow Man, The," 14
"Solitude of Cataracts, The," 2
"Sombre Figuration," 54, 69
"Somnambulisma," 85
"Song of Fixed Accord," 169, 175
"Statue at the World's End, The," 70, 139
"Study of Two Pears," 14, 17, 54
"Sunday Morning," 4, 9, 34-36, 44, 69, 84, 85, 103, 114, 115, 116, 119, 121, 124, 125, 126, 130, 140, 143, 154, 158, 167
"Sun this March, The," 11
"Tea at the Palz of Hoon," 154, 166
"Things of August," 105, 166
"Thought Revolved, A," 44
"Thinking of a Relation between the Images of Metaphors," 172
"Thirteen Ways of Looking at a Blackbird," 154
"Three Academic Pieces," 54, 59-60
Three Travelers Watch a Sunrise, 168, 169
"To an Old Philosopher in Rome," 7, 22-23, 135
"To the One of Fictive Music," 40, 41, 115, 116, 121, 168, 175
Transport to Summer, 111, 112, 118, 120-22, 136, 158
"Two Disquisitions that the World Is What You Make It," 23

Stevens, Wallace, works by (*continued*)
  "Ultimate Poem Is Abstract, The,"
    171
  "Variations on a Summer Day,"
    51, 63, 119
  "Waving Adieu, Adieu, Adieu," 11
  "Weak Mind in the Mountains, A,"
    167
  "Winter Bells," 136
  "Woman Looking at a Vase of
    Flowers," 54, 55-56
  "Woman That Had More Babies
    Than That, The," 119
  "World as Meditation, The," 8,
    105, 106, 133-50
  "World without Peculiarity," 6-7
"Study of Two Pears," 14, 17, 54
Style, 2, 19, 22, 112, 133-35, 138-42,
  147-48, 151-60 *passim*
Stylistic devices, 2, 9-10, 12-21 *passim*,
  36-37, 49-51, 55-58, 85-87, 89, 95,
  96-99, 112-17, 128-30, 139-43, 149,
  151-52, 168-75
"Sunday Morning," 4, 9, 34-36, 44,
  69, 84, 103, 114, 115, 116, 119, 121,
  124, 125, 126, 130, 140, 143, 154,
  158, 167
"Sun this March, The," 11
Swinburne, A. C., 174
Symbolists, 30, 52-53
Symons, Julian, 152

T

"Tea at the Palz of Hoon," 154, 166
Tempest, The (Shakespeare), 110
Tennyson, Alfred Lord, 9, 45
"Things of August," 105, 166
"Thinking of a Relation between the
  Images of Metaphor," 172
"Thirteen Ways of Looking at a Black-
  bird," 154
Thomas Aquinas, 43, 44, 130, 153
Thomas, Dylan, 6, 151
"Thought Revolved, A," 44
"Three Academic Pieces," 54, 59-60
Three Travelers Watch a Sunrise,"
  168, 169

Tintern Abbey (Wordsworth), 81
"To an Old Philosopher in Rome," 7,
  22-23, 135
To Psyche (Keats), 89
"To the One of Fictive Music," 40, 44,
  115, 116, 121, 168, 175
Transport to Summer, 111, 112, 118,
  120-22, 136, 158
Triumph of Life, The (Shelley),
  84
"Two Disquisitions that the World Is
  What You Make It," 23

U

"Ultimate Poem Is Abstract, The,"
  171
"Under the Greenwood Tree"
  (Shakespeare), 19

V

Valéry, Paul, 71, 150, 152, 160,
  163
"Variations on a Summer Day," 51,
  63, 119
Vaughan, Henry, 50
Villon, François, 59
Voices, 65

W

Wagner, C. Roland, 99
Wardrop, James, 25
"Waving Adieu, Adieu, Adieu,"
  11
"Weak Mind in the Mountains, A,"
  167
"When Lilacs Last in the Dooryard
  Bloomed" (Whitman), 34
Whitman, Walt, 6, 30-42 *passim*
Whitehead, A. N., 43, 50
Williamson, George, 49-50, 51
"Windhover, The" (Hopkins), 153
"Winter Bells," 136
Winters, Yvor, 135-36

STRINDBERG

A Collection of Critical Essays

Edited by OTTO REINERT

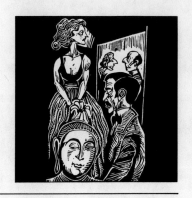

A

Advent, 15, 68, 76, 91, 117
Aeschylus, 42, 42*n*, 62
Afzelius, Arvid, 127
Agamemnon (Aeschylus), 42, 42*n*
Albee, Edward, 20
Alone, 9, 14
Antigone (Sophocles), 62
Antoine, André, 105
Aristophanes, 59
Artaud, Antonin, 24, 97
Atheist's Tragedy, The (Tourneur),
    43
Auerbach, Erich, 100

B

Bach, J. S., 12
Bäckström, Per Johan Edvard,
    127
Balzac, Honoré de, 12
Baudelaire, Charles, 35*n*, 73
Beckett, Samuel, 62
Becque, Henry François, 51
Beethoven, Ludwig van, 12
Bentley, Eric, 24, 25
Bernhein, Hippolyte-Marie, 83, 140
Björnson, Björnstjerne, 74
Black Banners, 7*n*, 13, 73*n*, 75
Black Glove, The, **152-63**
Blake, William, 157
Blavatsky, Helena Petrovna, 6
Blin, Roger, 97

Blue Books, The, 76, 81, 152, 154,
    157, 159, 160
Boccaccio, 130
Böcklin, Arnold, 100, 153
Bond, The, 2, 14*n*, 15, 43*n*, 68
Bonnier, Albert, 105, 107*n*
Bosse, Harriet (Strindberg's third wife),
    9-10, 35*n*, 36, 37*n*, 77-78
Brand (Ibsen), 28, 31, 32
Brandes, Georg, 18, 109, 115
Brecht, Bertolt, 104
Bridal Crown, The, 15, 24,
    Vienna production of, 101,
        102-4
Brustein, Robert, 3, 21-22, 23
Buckle, Henry Thomas, 5, 38, 128
"Building Program, The," 30, 157
Bullman, Joan, 129
Burned House, The, 16, 81-82,
    152-63
By the Open Sea, 13, 14, 75, 116

C

Charcot, Jean Martin, 83, 140
Charles XII, 12, 18, 128, 135
Chekhov, Anton, 13, 14, 112
"Child, The," 12
Choephori (Aeschylus), 42*n*
Chopin, Frédéric, 163
Comrades, 14*n*, 37, 41, 68, 101,
    110
Confessions of a Fool (*see Madman's
    Defense, A*)

Corneille, Pierre, 83, 108
Craig, Gordon, 19, 19n
Creditors, 8, 37, 40, 40n, 41, 43n,
  105, 106, 107, 110, 114
Crime and Crime, 15, 58

D

Dance of Death, The, 15, 20, 24, 47,
  50, 64, 66, 68, 72, 97-98, **118-24**,
  158, 162, 163
  danse macabre, theme of, 118-24
  male-female dichotomy in, 50, 98,
    119-24
  Paris production of, 97-98
  vampire figure in, 118-24
Darwin, Charles, 38, 39, 108, 115,
  140
Death of Tragedy, The (Steiner), 57,
  61
Debit and Credit, 67
Dickens, Charles, 12
Diebold, Bernhard, 137
"Doll's House, A," 12
Doll's House, A (Ibsen), 28-29, 42
Dostoevsky, Fedor, 11
Dramatic genres, in Strindberg's works,
  15
Dream Play, A, 11, 12, 15, 20, 22, 25,
  28, 32, 57, 63, **137-51**

E

Earl Birger of Bjälbo, 127, 136
Easter, 12, 15, 32, 101, 117
Edward III (anon.), 172
Emperor and Galilean (Ibsen), 31
Engelbrekt, 71, 135
Entry of the Bogars (Halvorsen),
  120
Erik XIV, 18, 125, 128, 129, 133, 134,
  136
"Esplanadsystemet" (*see* "Building
  Program, The")
Essen, Siri von (Strindberg's first wife),
  36, 38, 40n, 41, 42n, 109-10
Everyman (anon.),
  117

F

Falck, August, 19, 19n, 152, 160
Fantasie Impromptu (Chopin), 163
Father, The, 14, 15, 16, 22, 29n, 37,
  38, 39, 40, **41-47**, 50-51, 53, 62,
  66, 67, 68, 72, 98, 99, 104, 105,
  114
  allegory in, 43
  attitude towards women in, 45, 47
  and *Doll's House, A* (Ibsen), 42
  male-female dichotomy, theme of,
    42-47, 50-51, 62, 67, 72
  naturalism in, 41
Fergusson, Francis, 136
First Warning, The, 68
Five Years with Strindberg (Falck),
  152
Freethinker, The, 30
Freud, Sigmund, 49, 59, 83, 84, 85,
  140, 141, 145, 147, 148
Frisch, Max, 65
*From an Occult Diary: Marriage with
  Harriet Bosse*, 10
Fryxell, Anders, 127

G

Geijerstam, Gustaf af, 73, 73n, 91,
  107
Ghosts (Ibsen), 29, 29n, 32, 107
Ghost Sonata, The, 16, 17, 32, 55-56,
  57, 59, 63, 66, 96, 97, 100, **152-63**
  guilt, theme of, 55-56, 59
  Paris production of, 97, 100
  vampire figure in, 34n
Gide, André, 11
Goethe, Johann Wolfgang von, 4, 69,
  83
Gold, Käthe, 104
Goll, Ivan, 86, 87-88, 89
Gorboduc (Sackville and Norton),
  127
Granville-Barker, Harley, 112
Gravier, Maurice, 23, 24
Great Highway, The, 6-7
Gustafson, Alrik, 57
Gustav III, 135

Gustav Adolf, 18, 125, 135
Gustav Vasa, 16, 18, 71, 125, 129,
   131, 132-35, 136

H

Hall, Edward, 127
Halvorsen, Johan, 120
Hamlet (Shakespeare), 125, 152
Hartmann, Edouard von, 5, 68,
   140
Hasenclever, Walter, 79
Hauptmann, Gerhard, 102
Haydn, Franz Joseph, 12, 101
Heaven and Hell (Swedenborg),
   157
Hedda Gabler (Ibsen), 29, 39*n*
Hedén, Erik, 12
Heidenstam, Verner von, 4*n*, 115
Henry IV (Shakespeare), 132, 134
Henry V (Shakespeare), 127, 133, 134
Henry VI (Shakespeare), 129-32
Herrenmoral (Nietzsche), 5
Hesse, Hermann, 84
"Hidden One, The," 159
Holinshed, Raphael, 127

I

Ibsen, Henrik, 1-2, 14, 20, 21, 23, 27-
   36, 38, 39, 39*n*, 42, 45, 90*n*, 92-93,
   94, 96, 97, 98, 99, 100, 102, 107,
   111
Immortals, The (Goll), 86
Inferno, 8, 11, 13-14, 30*n*, 31-32, 34,
   35*n*, 58, 63, 69, 71, 160
Intimate Theatre, Stockholm, 16, 19,
   152, 153
Ionesco, Eugène, 65
Isle of the Dead (Böcklin), 100, 153
Isle of the Living (Böcklin), 153

J

Jacobsen, Jens Peter, 74
Janet, Pierre, 83
Johnson, Walter, 22, 24
Jonson, Ben, 18

Jung, C. G., 84, 85

K

Kafka, Franz, 11
Kant, Immanuel, 5
Kaufmann, R. J., 22-23
Kazan, Elia, 103
Keats, John, 62, 63
Kierkegaard, Sören, 5
King Lear (Shakespeare), 62, 125
King Nicolo (Wedekind), 79
Kleist, Heinrich von, 42
Kokoschka, Oskar, 79
Kornfeld, Paul, 79, 86-89
Kristina (see Queen Christina)

L

Lagerkvist, Pär, 23-24, 25, 29*n*
Lamm, Martin, 24
Last of the Knights, The, 136
Leech, Clifford, 125
Legends, 6, 11, 58
Life in the Skerries, 12
Linnaeus, 128

M

Macbeth (Shakespeare), 125
Machiavelli, Niccolò, 127
Madman's Defense, A, 6, 13, 36, 58,
   72, 110
Maeterlinck, Maurice, 19*n*, 103
Maladies de la personnalité, Les
   (Ribot), 108
Marauders (see Comrades)
Married, 6*n*, 12, 13, 71, 75
Marx, Karl, 140
Master Builder, The (Ibsen),
   29
Master Olof, 14, 18, 31, 67, 109,
   117
Maupassant, Guy de, 13, 74
Mendelssohn, Felix, 12
Metaphysics of the Love of the Sexes
   (Schopenhauer), 38
Mimesis (Auerbach), 100

Miss Julie, 15, 16, 18, 24, 30n, 37, 40, 40n, 41, 51-53, 62, 72, 79, 80, 89, **105-16,** 152
  male-female dichotomy, theme of, 52-53, 62
  naturalism in, 51-53, 105-14
  plot in, 110-11
  symbolism in, 107
Molander, Olof, 149
Molière, 18, 80, 81, 108
Motifs, in Strindberg's drama, 3, 15, 16-17, 22, 24, 54, 138, 155, 158, 160
  danse macabre, 22, 24, 118-24
  guilt, 16, 54-55, 59
  male-female dichotomy, 38, 40-41, 41-47, 49-51, 53, 72, 98, 101, 118-24
  vampire figures, 17, 34n, 118-24, 158
Munch, Edward, 65
"My Troll Castle," 145n

N

Natives of Hemsö, The (novel), 11, 12, 13
Natives of Hemsö, The (play), 12n
"Naturalisme au théâtre, Le" (Zola), 105
New Kingdom, The, 71
Nietzsche, Friedrich, 5, 24, 38-39, 40, 59, 67, 69, 115
No Exit (Sartre), 68

O

O'Neill, Eugene, 20, 99
"On Modern Drama and Modern Theatre," 38n, 108
"On Spiritual and Psychological Man" (Kornfeld), 86-87
Open Letters to the Intimate Theatre, 17, 18, 19, 81, 152, 158
Othello (Shakespeare), 42
Otto, Ted, 104
Outlaw, The, 30, 125

P

Pariah, 67
Pelican, The, 16, 34n, 82-83, **152-63**
Penthesilea (Kleist), 42
Phaedo (Plato), 152
Philosophy of the Unconscious (Hartmann), 5, 68
Pillars of Society, The (Ibsen), 28
Pinter, Harold, 62
Pirandello, Luigi, 18, 33
Pitoëff, Sacha, 97
Plato, 152
Playing with Fire, 61
Preface to *Miss Julie,* 18-19, 39, 49, 51-53, 58-59, 79-80, 82, 85, 95, 106, 108-9, 111, 112, 114, 115

Q

Queen Christina, 18, 127, 128, 135

R

Racine, Jean, 83, 97, 108
"Rebuilding," 144
Red Room, The, 11, 13, 71, 75
Ribot, Théodule, 83, 108, 140
Richard II (Shakespeare), 125, 133, 134, 136
Richard III (Shakespeare), 131
Road to Damascus, The (see *To Damascus*)
"Romantic Organist at Rånö, The," 144
Roofing Feast, The, 13, 14
Rosa Bernd (Hauptmann), 102
Rosmersholm (Ibsen), 99
Rothwell, Brian, 25
Rougon-Macquarts, Les (Zola), 114
Rousseau, Jean-Jacques, 30, 60, 75

S

Saga of the Folkungs, The, 6, 15, 125, 126, 127, 128, **129-32,** 133, 135, 136

Sagohävder (Afzelius), 127
Sartre, Jean-Paul, 68
Sayers, Dorothy, 99
Scapegoat, The, 11, 12, 13
Schiller, Friedrich, 83, 97
Schopenhauer, Arthur, 38, 140
Shakespeare, William, 3, 17-18, 23-24,
    42, 67, 81, 90*n*, 91, 109, 111,
    125-36, 152
Shaw, G. B., 20, 59
Simoon, 58
Sir Bengt's Wife, 14*n*
Son of a Servant, The, 2, 4, 6, 34, 58,
    59, 60, 64, 64*n*, 68, 69, 115
Sophocles, 62
Sorge, Reinhard Johannes, 79
Speech to the Swedish Nation, 71
Spengler, Oswald, 84
Sprigge, Elizabeth, 30*n*, 35*n*
Sprinchorn, Evert, 22, 25, 30*n*
Stanislavsky, K. S., 19, 103
Steene, Birgitta, 17, 24-25
Steiner, George, 57, 58, 60
Sternheim, Carl, 101
Storm, 14, 16, 81, 152-63
Streetscenes, 157
Strindberg, August:
    and allegory, 13, 15, 43
    and the chamber plays, 15-16, 92,
        152-63
    and his characters, 13, 18, 45, 59,
        62-63, 66-68, 72-73, 79-83, 85,
        88-89, 109-12, 142-43
    correspondence of, 1, 4*n*, 9, 10, 11,
        20, 30, 35*n*, 37*n*, 40, 41, 91, 105
    critical reputation of, 14, 20-25
    and Darwin, 38, 39, 108, 115,
        140
    dialogue of, 112-13
    dramatic career of, 14-20, 37-38
    dramaturgy of, 14, 15-20, 23-25,
        34, 42-43, 61-70, 79-89, 90-96,
        97-104, 105-16, 125-36, 137-51
        passim, 152-63
    dualism of, 21, 25, 34-37, 39
    and expressionism, 11, 13, 15, 18,
        20, 23-24, 27, 79, 83, 85, 88-89,
        90-95, 117

extraliterary activities of, 3-4, 7-8,
    27
and family relationship, 22, 34-36,
    40*n*, 76-77
and friendship, 2, 19*n*, 72-73, 73*n*
and the history plays, 15, 17-18,
    24-25, 91, 125-36
and humor, 58, 59
and Ibsen, 1-2, 14, 21, 23, 27-36,
    38, 39, 39*n*, 42, 45, 90*n*, 92-93,
    94, 96, 97, 98, 99, 100, 102, 107,
    111
ideologies of, 5-6, 6*n*, 27, 38-39, 67
and the Inferno crisis, 5-6, 6*n*, 15,
    22, 37, 76, 85, 89, 117, 128
and the Intimate Theatre, Stock-
    holm, 16, 19, 152, 153
life of, 1-11, 34-36, 71-78
literary contributions of, 4, 23-24,
    27-28, 53, 90-95, 117
and love, attitude towards, 25, 72,
    74, 78, 114
and the male-female dichotomy, 25,
    28, 34, 38, 40-47, 49-50, 53, 72,
    74-75, 76, 98, 101, 118-24
and marriage, attitude towards, 5,
    15, 36, 41, 72, 76-78, 119-24
and medieval drama, 117-18
and morality, 58, 117
and musical leitmotifs, use of, 12,
    101, 120, 163
and naturalism, 6*n*, 11, 14-15, 24,
    27, 33, 38, 38*n*, 40, 41, 51-53,
    74-75, 79, 85, 90, 92, 94, 95, 98,
    102, 105-16, 117
and Nietzsche, 5, 24, 38-39, 40, 59,
    67, 69, 115
as novelist, 11-13, 27
as occultist, 2, 6, 7, 8, 27, 31
and plot, use of, 16-17, 110-11
as poet, 12, 27, 30
psyche of, 1-25, 27-47, 57-70,
    71-78
radicalism of, 21, 30-34, 73
and realism, 13, 15, 25, 51, 71,
    102-3, 117, 128, 159
and religion, 5-6, 6*n*, 8, 9, 27, 30-
    33, 39, 75-76, 85, 102

Strindberg, August:
  (*continued*)
    as a Romantic, 22, 28, 30, 33-34,
      35, 58, **60-61**
    and science, 17*n*, 83
    and sex, attitude towards, 16-17,
      21-22, 25, 36-37, 37*n*, 38, 74-75
    and Shakespeare, 3, 17-18, 23-24,
      42, 67, 81, 90*n*, 91, 109, 111,
      125-36, 152
    and the short-story form, 12-13,
      27
    and Swedenborg, Emanuel, 6, 91,
      128, 134, 146, 156, 157, 159,
      160
    symbolism and imagery of, 15, 18,
      24, 25, 102-3, 107, **137-51**,
      157-59
    and tragedy, 15, 25, **48-56**, 60, 62
    and his wives, 9-10, 35*n*, 36, 37*n*,
      40*n*, 41, 43*n*, **77-78**, 109-10
    and women, attitude towards, 5, 6,
      11, 12, 28-29, **35-47**, 72, 75, 76-
      78
    and Zola, 41, 42, 74, 105, 106, 108,
      111, 112, 114
Strindberg, August, works by:
  AUTOBIOGRAPHICAL NOVELS
    Alone, 9, 14
    Inferno, 8, 11, 13-14, 30*n*, 31-32,
      34, 35*n*, 58, 63, 69, 71, 160
    Legends, 6, 8, 11, 58
    Madman's Defense, A, 6, 13, 36,
      58, 72, 110
    Roofing Feast, The, 13, 14
    Scapegoat, The, 11, 12, 13
    Son of a Servant, The, 2, 4, 6, 34,
      58, 59, 60 64, 64*n*, 68, 69, 115
  DRAMA (*see also* individual listings
  for plays marked by asterisk)
    Advent, 15, 68, 76, 91, 117
    Black Glove, The, **152-63**
    Bond, The, 2, 14*n*, 15, 43*n*, 68
    Bridal Crown, The, 15, 24, 101,
      102-4
    Burned House, The, 16, 81-82,
      152-63
    Charles XII, 12, 18, 128, 135

    Comrades, 14*n*, 37, 41, 68, 101,
      110
    Creditors, 8, 37, 40, 40*n*, 41, 43*n*,
      105, 106, 107, 110, 114
    Crime and Crime, 15, 58
    Dance of Death, The,* 15, 20, 24,
      47, 50, 64, 66, 68, 72, 97-98,
      118-24, 158, 162, 163
    Debit and Credit, 67
    Dream Play, A, 11, 12, 15, 20, 22,
      25, 28, 32, 57, 63, **137-51**
    Earl Birger of Bjälbo, 127, 136
    Easter, 12, 15, 32, 101, 117
    Engelbrekt, 71, 135
    Erik XIV, 18, 125, 128, 129, 133,
      134, 136
    Father, The,* 14, 15, 16, 22, 29*n*,
      37, 38, 39, 40, **41-47**, 50-51, 53,
      62, 66, 67, 68, 72, 98, 99, 104,
      105, 114
    First Warning, The, 68
    Freethinker, The, 30
    Ghost Sonata, The,* 16, 17, 32, 55-
      56, 57, 59, 63, 66, 96, 97, 100,
      152-63
    Great Highway, The, 6-7
    Gustav Adolf, 18, 125, 135
    Gustav III, 135
    Gustav Vasa, 16, 18, 71, 125, 129,
      131, **132-35**, 136
    Last of the Knights, The, 136
    Master Olof, 14, 18, 31, 67, 109, 117
    Miss Julie,* 15, 16, 18, 24, 30*n*,
      37, 40, 40*n*, 41, 51-53, 62, 72,
      79, 80, 89, **105-16**, 152
    Natives of Hemsö, The, 12*n*
    Outlaw, The, 30, 125
    Pariah, 67
    Pelican, The, 16, 34*n*, 82-83,
      152-63
    Playing with Fire, 61
    Queen Christina, 18, 127, 128,
      135
    Saga of the Folkungs, The, 6, 15,
      125, 126, 127, 128, **129-32**, 133,
      135, 136
    Simoon, 58
    Sir Bengt's Wife, 14*n*

Strindberg, August, works by
  (DRAMA) (*continued*)
    Storm, 14, 16, 81, **152-63**
    Stronger, The, 15, 68
    Swanwhite, 63, 72
    To Damascus,* 11, 12, 14n, 15, 30,
      30n, 31, 36, **53-55**, 59, 71, 91, 97,
      99-100, 117, 119, 139, 140, 141
    Toten-Insel, 152, 153
  MISCELLANEOUS
    Blue Books, The, 76, 81, 152, 154,
      157, 159, 160
    *From an Occult Diary: Marriage
      with Harriet Bosse*, 10
    New Kingdom, The, 71
    "On Modern Drama and Modern
      Theatre," 38n, 108
    *Open Letters to the Intimate
      Theatre*, 17, 18, 19, 81, 152, 158
    Preface to *Miss Julie*, 18-19, 39, 49,
      51-53, 58-59, 79-80, 82, 85, 95,
      106, 108-9, 111, 112, 114, 115
    Speech to the Swedish Nation, 71
    Streetscenes, 157
    Utopias, 71, 75
  NOVELS
    Black Banners, 7n, 13, 73n, 75
    By the Open Sea, 13, 14, 75, 116
    Natives of Hemsö, The, 11, 12, 13
    Red Room, The, 11, 13, 71, 75
  POETRY
    "Building Program, The," 30, 157
    "Hidden One, The," 159
    "My Troll Castle," 145n
  SHORT STORIES
    "Child, The," 12
    "Dance at the Tailor's," 12
    "Doll's House, A," 12
    Life in the Skerries, 12
    Married, 6n, 12, 13, 71, 75
    "Rebuilding," 144
    "Romantic Organist at Rånö, The,"
      144
Stronger, The, 15, 68
Svanberg, Victor, 23
Swanwhite, 63, 72
Swedenborg, Emanuel, 6, 91, 128,
  134, 146, 156, 157, 159, 160

T

Taine, Hippolyte Adolphe, 109
Tartuffe (Molière), 108
Tempest, The (Shakespeare), 152
Timaeus (Plato), 152
To Damascus, 11, 12, 14n, 15, 30,
  30n, 31, 36, **53-55**, 59, 71, 91, 97,
  99-100, 117, 119, 139, 140, 141
  guilt, theme of, 54-55, 59
  identity, theme of, 54
  Paris production of, 97, 99-100
Tolstoy, Leo, 63
Toten-Insel, 152, 153
Toulouse, Edouard, 83
Tourneur, Cyril, 43
Troublesome Reign of King John, The
  (anon.), 127

U

Uhl, Frida (Strindberg's second wife),
  36
Utopias, 71, 75

V

Viertel, Berthold, 102-4
Vilar, Jean, 97, 98
Vuillard, Edouard, 65, 66

W

Wagner, Richard, 100
Wedekind, Frank, 79, 96, 97, 100
Werfel, Franz, 83, 99
Who's Afraid of Virginia Woolf?
  (Albee), 20
Wild Duck, The (Ibsen), 29
Williams, Raymond, 22, 23, 25
Wrangel, Baron, 36, 40n, 43n

Y

Yeats, William Butler, 23, 63, 157

Z

Zola, Émile, 41, 42, 74, 105, 106, 108,
  111, 112, 114

SWIFT

A Collection of Critical Essays
Edited by ERNEST TUVESON

A

Allegory, Swift's use of, 95, 96
"Anal-Erotic Character Traits"
 (Jones), 52
Anal themes:
 in *Gulliver's Travels*, 31-54
  passim
 in *Tale of a Tub, A,* 31, 44-45
Anglicanism, 143-45, 154-55
Arbuthnot, Dr. John, 15, 51, 70
Argument Against Abolishing Christianity, An, 17-18, 99, 111, 142, 149
Aristophanes, 31

B

Bacon, Sir Francis, 163
Battle of the Books, The, 21, 96, 98-99, 121, 136
Blake, William, 140
Bolingbroke, Henry St. John, 7, 65
"Brobdingnag, A Voyage to" (*see Gulliver's Travels*)
Brown, Norman O., 4
Bury, J. B., 152, 163
Butler, Samuel, 128

C

"Cassinus and Peter," 31, 39-41
Cassirer, Ernst, 169
Chambers, R. W., 144,
 158

Circe (Gelli), and *Gulliver's Travels,*
 10-11
Civilization and Its Discontents
 (Freud), 39-40
Colie, Rosalie, 11, 128-29, 134
"Concerning that Universal Hatred
 which Prevails against the Clergy,"
 143
Conway, Lady Anne, 129
Cooper, Anthony Ashley (Earl of
 Shaftesbury), 7, 13, 105, 107
Crane, Ronald S., 128, 138
Cranmer, Thomas, 155
Cyrano de Bergerac, 130

D

Defence of Poesy (Sidney), 128
Defoe, Daniel, 16, 55-57, 161
Descartes, René, 134
"Digression Concerning . . . Madness,
 A," 22-28, 48-49, 132
Divine Dialogues (More), 102
Do What You Will (Huxley), 31-37
 passim
Drapier Letters, 99
Dunciad, The (Pope), 115, 121
"Duty of Mutual Subjection, The,"
 158

E

Eddy, W. A., 72-73

Ehrenpreis, Irvin, 5, 10, 11
Eighteenth Century Background, The
  (Willey), 63
Eliot, T. S., 140
Empson, William, 44-45, 47, 50
English Satire and Satirists (Walker),
  63
Erasmus, Desiderius, 148, 162
Essay Concerning Human Understand-
  ing (Locke), 125-26, 131-37
Essay on Man, An (Pope), 104
"Essay on the Fates of Clergymen,
  An," 158
"Evening Prayer, An," 103

F

Fictional techniques, in *Gulliver's*
  Travels, 55-59
Four Last Things (More), 151
Four Voyages (Vespucius), 160-61
Freud, Sigmund, 4, 32, 37, 39-40, 46-
  47, 48
Further Thoughts on Religion, 103,
  106

G

Gay, John, 15
Gelli, Giovanni, 10-11
Gibbon, Edward, 17
Gosse, Edmund, 3
Gulliver's Travels, 15-16, **55-70, 71-89**,
  101-3, 105-110, **111-14, 127-42**,
  143-44, **151-69**
  "Voyage to Lilliput, A," 8, 57-58,
    60, 75-76
  "Voyage to Brobdingnag, A," 8,
    57-58, 60, 106, 107, 108, 133,
    159
  "Voyage to Laputa . . ., A," 6-7,
    58-59, 60-61, 97, 143-44
  "Voyage to . . . the Houyhnhnms,
    A," 1-2, 7, **8-14**, 27, 28, 29,
    31, 32, 34, 41-43, 60, **61-70**, 72-
    74, **80-89**, 101-3, 105-110,
    127-42, 151-69
  anal themes in, 31-54 *passim*

and *Circe* (Gelli), 10-11
fictional techniques in, 55-59
humor, techniques of, 68-70
and *Histoire des oiseaux* (Cyrano),
  130
irony in, 77-78, 160, 165-66
myth in, 97
persona of Swift in, 72-89 *passim*,
  111, 113-14, 138-39, 145-46, 160,
  165-67
political satire in, 6-7, 156-60
religious beliefs in, 105-110
and *Robinson Crusoe* (Defoe), 16,
  55-56
and *Tale of a Tub, A*, 20, 22, 82
and *Utopia* (More), 145, 151-69

H

Hampshire, Stuart, 130-31, 132
Henry VIII, 143-45, 155, 158
Histoire des oiseaux (Cyrano de
  Bergerac), 130
Hobbes, Thomas, 97-98, 112
Horace, 73
Horrell, Joseph, 7, 9
"Houyhnhnms, A Voyage to the"
  (*see Gulliver's Travels*)
Hudibras (Butler), 128
Humor, techniques of, in *Gulliver's*
  Travels, 68-70
Huxley, Aldous, 31-37 *passim*, 53,
  139

I

Idea of Progress, The (Bury), 152,
  163
Ideology and Utopia (Mannheim), 63
"Instructions to Servants," 28
Irony, Swift's use of:
  in *Gulliver's Travels*, 77-78, 160,
    165-66
  in *Tale of a Tub, A*, 15-29

J

Johnson, Dr. Samuel, 20, 28, 63, 67

Jonathan Swift (Murry), 3, 5, 31-40
  passim
Jones, Ernest, 52
Juvenal, 73

K

Kautsky, Karl, 162
Kierkegaard, Sören, 140
King Lear (Shakespeare), 9

L

"Lady's Dressing Room, The," 31,
  40
Landa, Louis, 5, 140
"Laputa . . . , A Voyage to"
  (*see Gulliver's Travels*)
Lawrence, D. H., 33
Leavis, F. R., 3-4, 140
Letter of Advice to a Young Poet, A,
  34, 51
"Lilliput, A Voyage to" (*see
  Gulliver's Travels*)
Locke, John, 11, 125-26, 131-37
Lucretius, 56-57

M

Mannheim, Karl, 163
Marlborough, Duke of, 157
Marx, Karl, 140
"Mechanical Operation of the Spirit,
  The," 44-46, 49, 93, 96, 98-99
Memoirs of Martinus Scriblerus,
  51-52
Mind and Art of Jonathan Swift, The
  (Quintana), 32, 43, 72, 109
Misanthrope, Le (Molière), 142
Modest Proposal, A, 5, 17, 19, 92, 95-
  96, 99, 111, 125-27
Molière, 142
Montaigne, Michel de, 129, 130, 139
Moore, John B., 7
More, Henry, 102, 107
More, Sir Thomas, 143-69
Murry, John Middleton, 3, 5, 31-40
  passim, 57

Myth, Swift's use of, 97-98

N

Nietzsche, Friedrich, 38

O

"Of Original or Birth Sin," 104
"On the Martyrdom of King Charles I,"
  158
"On the Testimony of Conscience,"
  103
Orwell, George, 139

P

"Panegyrick on the Dean, A," 52-
  54
Parody, Swift's use of, 95-96
Partridge-Bickerstaff Papers, The,
  92
Perilous Balance (Watkins), 73
Personae, Swift's use of:
  in *Gulliver's Travels,* 72-89 *passim,*
    111, 113-14, 138-39, 145-46,
    160, 165-67
  in *Tale of a Tub, A,* 98-99
Phaedrus (Plato), 163, 165
Philebus (Plato), 153-54
Philosophical beliefs, in Swift's works,
  115-22
Plato, 153-54, 163, 165, 166
Platonic Renaissance in England
  (Cassirer), 169
Pliny, 139
Plutarch, 139
"Polite Conversation," 28
Political beliefs, in Swift's works,
  119-20, 156-60
Pope, Alexander, 11, 15, 26, 51, 65,
  69-70, 104, 105, 109, 121
"Praise of Folly, The" (Erasmus), 148
"Project for the Advancement of
  Religion, A," 27
Psychoanalytical views, of Swift's
  personality, 4, **31-54**

Q

Quintana, Ricardo, 5, 7, 14, 32, 43, 72, 109

R

Rabelais, François, 31
Read, Herbert, 16
Religious beliefs, in Swift's works, 103-4 (*see also* Anglicanism)
    in *Gulliver's Travels*, 105-10
"Remarks . . . on 'The Rights of the Christian Church'," 149
Republic, The (Plato), 163, 165, 166
Robinson Crusoe (Defoe), 16, 55-56
Ross, John, 13
Rousseau, Jean-Jacques, 7
Ruskin, John, 163

S

Satiric techniques, 7-8
    in *Gulliver's Travels*, 73-89, 156-60
    in *Tale of a Tub, A*, 22-28
Scott, Sir Walter, 1
"Sentiments of a Church of England Man," 149
Shaftesbury, Earl of (*see* Cooper, Anthony Ashley)
Shakespeare, William, 9
Sidney, Sir Philip, 128, 163-64
Stella, 5, 33
Stephen, Leslie, 71, 99
Stillingfleet, Edward, 134-36
Strachey, Lytton, 17
"Strephon and Chloe," 31, 39-41, 51
Swift, Jonathan:
    allegory, use of, 95, 96,
    Anglicanism of, 143-45, 154-55
    and Arbuthnot, Dr. John, 51, 70
    biographical information, 5, 35
    and Defoe, Daniel, 16, 55-57, 161
    and the eighteenth century, 7-8, 11
    and Gibbon, Edward, 17
    and Henry VIII, 143-45, 158

    and Hobbes, Thomas, 97-98, 112
    Huxley, Aldous, on, 31-37 *passim*, 53, 139
    irony, use of, 15-29, 77-78, 160, 165-66
    and Locke, John, 11, 125-26, 131-37
    "madness" of, 5, 33, 72
    "misanthropy" of, 2, 15, 88-89, 108, 121, 145
    and More, Sir Thomas, 143-69
    Murry, J. M., on, 31-40 *passim*, 57
    myth, use of, 97-98
    nineteenth-century views of, 1-2
    parody, use of, 95-96
    personae of, 72-89 *passim*, 98-99, 111, 113-14, 138-39, 145-46, 160, 165-67
    personality of, 2, 5, 35-36 (*see also* Psychoanalytical views)
    philosophical beliefs of, 115-22
    political beliefs of, 119-20, 156-60
    and Pope, Alexander, 11, 15, 26, 51, 65, 69-70, 104, 105, 109, 121
    psychoanalytical views of, 4, 31-54
    religious beliefs of, 103-4
    satiric techniques of, 7-8, 15-29, 73-89, 91-99, 115-22
    and Stella, 5, 33
    and Temple, Sir William, 130, 136
    Thackeray on, 1-2, 14, 15, 63, 71, 145
    and Vanessa, 33, 34
    and Varina, 33, 34, 35
Swift, Jonathan, works by: (*see also* titles of individual works)
PROSE
    Argument Against Abolishing Christianity, An, 17-18, 99, 111, 142, 149
    Battle of the Books, The, 21, 96, 98-99, 121, 136
    "Concerning that Universal Hatred which Prevails against the Clergy," 143
    Drapier Letters, 99

Swift, Jonathan, works by:
(PROSE) (*continued*)
   Further Thoughts on Religion,
     103, 106
   Gulliver's Travels (*see also* main
     entry), 15-16, **55-70**, **71-89**,
     101-3, 105-10, **111-14**, **127-42**,
     143-44, **151-69**
   "Instructions to Servants," 28
   *Letter of Advice to a Young Poet,
     A,* 34, 51
   Memoirs of Marinus Scriblerus,
     51-52
   Modest Proposal, A, 5, 17, 19, 92,
     95-96, 99, 111, 125-27
   Partridge-Bickerstaff Papers, The,
     92
   "Polite Conversation," 28
   "Project for the Advancement of
     Religion, A," 27
   Tale of a Tub, A (*see also* main
     entry), 3, 5, 8, 13-14, **19-29**, 44-
     47, 49-50, 92, 121, 122, 132-33,
     136
   *Writings on Religion and the
     Church,* 103-4, 149, 158
POETRY
   "Cassinus and Peter," 31, 39-41
   "Lady's Dressing Room, The," 31,
     40
   "Panegyrick on the Dean, A," 52-54
   "Strephon and Chloe," 31, 39-41,
     51

T

Tale of a Tub, A, 3, 5, 8, 13-14, **19-29**,

44-47, 48-50, 92, 121, 122, 132-33,
  136
  allegory in, 96
  anal themes in, 31, 44-45
  "Digression Concerning . . . Mad-
    ness, A," 22-28, 48-49, 132
  and *Gulliver's Travels,* 20, 22,
    82
  "Mechanical Operation of the
    Spirit, The," 44-46, 49, 93, 96,
    98-99
  myth in, 97
  persona of Swift in, 98-99
Temple, Sir William, 130, 136
Thackeray, W. M., on Swift, 1-2, 14,
  15, 63, 69, 71, 145
Thomas More and his Utopia
  (Kautsky), 62

V

Vanessa, 33, 34
Varina, 33, 34, 35
Vespucius, Americus, 160-61

W

Walker, Hugh, 63
Watkins, W. B. C., 73
Whibley, Charles, 15
Willey, Basil, 63
Williams, Kathleen M., 101
Wit and the Unconscious (Freud),
  38
Wordsworth, William, 2
Writings on Religion and the Church,
  103-4, 149, 158

THACKERAY

A Collection of Critical Essays

Edited by ALEXANDER WELSH

A

Addison, Joseph, 49-50, 122, 124
Adventures of Philip, The, 1-8 *passim,*
  18, 55, **161-77**
  author's commentary in, 5-7
  autobiographical elements in,
    166-77
  method, 4-6, 170-72
  mothers-in-law in, 55-64 *passim*
Agassiz, Louis, 7
Ainsworth, Harrison, 42-43, 66, 80
Ambition, theme of, 21
  in *Vanity Fair,* 22-24
Amelia (Fielding), 13, 33
Arcadia (Sannazaro), 106
Aristotle, 177
Arnold, Matthew, 54
Arnold, Thomas, 46
Austen, Jane, 9, 67

B

Bagehot, Walter, 98-99
Bedford, Duchess of, 44
Bleak House (Dickens), 10
Boileau, N., 114
Book of Snobs, The, 11, 15-16, 38-44,
  46, 50, 89, 163, 171, 174
Boucher, 110
Bowen, Elizabeth, 159
Brimley, George, 128, 141
Brogan, Howard O., 131, 132, 136,
  144-45

Brontë, Charlotte, 86, 104, 112
Brontë, Emily, 142
Brookfield, Jane, 45, 63, 127, 129,
  155
Brown, Mrs. John, 128
Brownell, W. C., 74, 79
Browning, Robert, 6
"Brown's Letters," 41-42
Bulwer-Lytton (*see* Lytton), 66, 161
Bunyan, John, 89, 90
Burne-Jones, Edward, 153
"Butler" (Johnson), 113-14
Butler, Samuel, 113

C

Capitalism and morality, 97-102
Catherine, 52, 107, 109, 161
Cato (Addison), 122
Cecil, Lord David, 144
Cervantes, Miguel de, 32, 113
"Charity and Humour," 32
Chartists, 123, 169
Civil War, 123
Chaucer, Geoffrey, 67, 80, 113
Clayhanger (Bennett), 148
Collins, Wilkie, 19
Congreve, William, 53
Coningsby (Disraeli), 151
Cooper, James Fenimore, 67
Cornhill Magazine, The, 61, 161,
  173
Craft of Fiction (Lubbock), 76
Cromwell, Oliver, 123

D

Denis Duval, 22, 62-63, 147
De Rerum Natura (Lucretius), 117
Devonshire, Duchess of, 44
Dickens, Charles, 9, 10, 12, 13, 15, 16, 19, 22, 25, 31, 35, 39, 46, 48, 73, 100, 156, 159
"Discourse Concerning Satire" (Dryden), 114
Disraeli, Benjamin, 46, 66, 67, 151, 158
Dobrée, Bonamy, 50
Dodds, John W., 137, 138, 143
Dombey and Son (Dickens), 101
Donne, John, 53
Dryden, John, 106, 114
Dunciad, The (Pope), 115, 116
Dundas, Lady Emily, 44

E

Ecclesiastes, 54
Economic Studies (Bagehot), 98
Edgar, Pelham, 130
Eliot, George, 10, 13, 75
Elwin, Whitwell, 148, 150, 158
English Humourists, The, 8, 49, 53
Ennis, Lambert, 55, 60
Ernest Maltravers (Bulwer-Lytton), 161
Ethics of the Dust (Ruskin), 13
Eugene Aram (Bulwer-Lytton), 66
Examiner, 154
"Example of Cervantes, The" (Levin), 105

F

Fielding, Henry, 2, 8, 13, 32, 33, 50, 84, 91, 96, 104, 121, 122
Fitzgerald, Edward, 44
Form, 20, 72-75, 104-20, 121-26, 143, 147-48
Forster, E. M., 10
Forster, Jack, 128

Fraser's 66, 69, 76, 161, 167, 169
Freud, Sigmund, 59

G

Gaskell, Mrs. Elizabeth, 87
Gay, John, 107
Gin Lane (Hogarth), 69
Glorious Revolution, 123
Goethe, J. W. von, 50
Good Samaritan, parable of, 171-76 *passim*
Gore, Mrs. C. G. F., 67
"Gossip on Romance, A" (Stevenson), 95
Granville, Lady, 44
Great Expectations (Dickens), 156
Great Hoggarty Diamond, The, 149, 151
Greene, Robert, 2, 47
Greuze, Jean-Baptiste, 110
Grieg, J. Y. T., 56
Grote, George, 46
Guardian, The, 106

H

Hard Times (Dickens), 159
History of Henry Esmond, The, 14, 20, 22, 28, 51, 52, 66, 113, 116, 155, 159, 167
    as historical novel, 121-26
    form, 121-26
    love, theme of, 127-46
    method, 28-29, 132-46 *passim*
    mortality, theme of, 52
    mothers-in-law in, 61-64 *passim*
History of Pendennis, The, 20, 22, 44, 51, 52-53, 54, 75, 90, 142, 158, 163, 176
    as sermon, 54
    incest, suggestion of, 57-59
    mortality, theme of, 52-53
    mothers-in-law in, 56-64 *passim*
    neoclassical conventions in, 104-20 *passim*
Hobbes, Thomas, 2
Hogarth, William, 69

Homer, 112-13, 118
Hudibras (Butler), 116

I

Iliad (Homer), 118
Imagery, 62-63, 110, 117-18, 120
Incestuous implications, 57-64, 145-
    46, 162-63
Industrial Revolution, 40
In Memoriam (Tennyson), 46
Irony and satire, 15-19, **30-37**, 54,
    66-73 *passim*, 79-80, 102-3, 104-20

J

Jack Sheppard (Ainsworth), 66
James, G. P. R., 67
James, Henry, 7, 10, 148, 149,
    156
Jane Eyre (Brontë), 128
Jeaffreson, Cordy, 38
Jeames's Diary, 46
Jerrold, Douglas, 39, 92
Johnson, Samuel, 107, 113, 114,
    115, 116
Jones, Mrs. George, 155
Jonson, Ben, 50
Journey from Cornhill to Grand Cairo,
    51
Jung, Carl, 62
Juvenal, 32

L

La Bruyère, 50
Language, 1-2, 97
Lansdowne, Lord, 44
Las Vergnes, M., 54
Lawrence, D. H., 9
Leavis, F. R., 10
Leech, John, 45
Lemprière, John, 112
*Letter and Private Papers of William
    Makepeace Thackeray, The* (ed. Ray),
    30, 39, 44-45, 47, 55, 63, 65, 67, 68,
    69, 83, 85, 98, 99, 128-29
Lever, Charles, 66, 67

Leviathan (Hobbes), 2
Levin, Harry, 105
Lewes, George Henry, 98
Logic (Mill), 46
Loofbourow, John, 8
Louis XIV, 122
Love, theme of, **127-46**, 155
Love and Friendship (Austen),
    67
Lovel the Widower, 56, 60
Lubbock, Percy, 7, 76
Luck, theme of, 166-69
Luck of Barry Lyndon, The, 163,
    165-66
Lucretius, 117
Luddites, 123
Luke, Gospel According to Saint,
    173
Lutrin, Le (Boileau), 114
Lyell, Sir Charles, 46
Lytton, E. G. E. L. Bulwer, 19, 66, 67,
    75, 80, 83, 148

M

Macauley, Thomas B., 9, 46, 50, 159
Macbeth (Shakespeare), 55
Mahratta War of 1803, 4
Man in society, emphasis on, 21, 27,
    74-75, 126, 151-52, 170-72
Manners, importance of, 21, 36, 45,
    122
Man of Property, The (Galsworthy),
    148
Market values, dominance of, 97-102
Marlborough, Duke of, 122, 134
Marriage market, theme of, 117-20,
    149, 153
Masks, uses of, 163-64
Method, 4-10, 15-19 *passim*, **20-29**,
    50-51, 67-69, 83-85, 132-46, 147-60,
    170-72
    retrospection, 22-23, 28-29, 84
    weaknesses of, 5, 17-18, 24-28
Middlemarch (Eliot), 10
Mill, J. S., 46
Milman, H. H., 46
Milnes, Monckton, 61

Mock-epic, use of, 111-20
  background, 113-15
Modern Painters (Ruskin), 46
Moral Essays (Pope), 106
Mortality, theme of, 52-53
Mothers, characterization of, 9
  in *Henry Esmond*, 61-64 *passim*
  in *Newcomes*, 55-64 *passim*
  in *Pendennis*, 52-64 *passim*
  in *Philip*, 55-64 *passim*
My Novel (Bulwer-Lytton), 148

N

Narrative devices, 5-6, 16-17, 25, 85,
  92-95, 130-34, 163
Neoclassical conventions, 104-20
  passim
    mock-epic, 111-20
    pastoral, 105-11
Newcomes, The, 2, 6, 7-8, 9-10, 12,
  20, 44, 55, 147-60
    author's commentary in, 148,
      158
    form, 147-49
    method, 9-10, 28, 159-60
    mothers-in-law in, 55-64 *passim*
    neoclassical conventions in, 104-20
      passim
Newman, John Cardinal, 46, 104, 177
New Monthly Magazine, 42-43
Nichomachaean Ethics (Aristotle),
  177
Northanger Abbey (Austen), 9

O

Odyssey (Homer), 112-13, 118
"On a medal of George IV," 51
"On a Pear-tree," 51
On Liberty (Mill), 150
"On Two Roundabout Papers which I
  intended to write," 51

P

Paris Sketchbook, The, 31
Parsons, Thomas, 43

Pastoral, use of, 105-11
  background, 106-8
Pater, Walter, 6
Peel, Sir Robert, 44, 87
Petronius, 114
Pickwick Papers (Dickens), 15
Pictures of Life and Character
  (Leech), 45
Plato, 176, 177
Political Economy (Mill), 46
Pope, Alexander, 106, 114-15, 116
Principles of Geology (Lyell), 46
"Psychological Aspects of the Mother
  Archetype" (Jung), 62
Punch, 38, 39, 41, 43, 44
Punch's Prize Novelists, 66-68
Pushkin, Alexander, 121

R

Rape of the Lock, The (Pope), 114,
  116
"Ravenswing, The," 57, 61
Ray, Gordon N., 10-12, 55, 129, 163
Reade, Charles, 19
Redgauntlet (Scott), 123
Reform Bill of 1832, 40
Respectability, theme of, 149-54
Ring and the Book, The (Browning),
  6-7
Ritchie, Lady A. I. T. (daughter), 127
Rob Roy (Scott), 123, 125
Romanticism, 104-5
Rothschild, Madame Lionel, 44
Rothschild, Sir Anthony, 44
Roundabout Papers, The, 41-42, 51,
  173
Ruskin, John, 13, 69
Russell, Lord John, 158

S

Saintsbury, George, 148, 159
Sannazaro, 106
Scott, Sir Walter, 8, 121, 123, 124,
  125
Sermons (Donne), 53
Sexual rivalry, theme of, 57-64

"Shabby Genteel Story, A," 162
Shaftesbury, Lord, 2
Shakespeare, William,
    113
Shawe, Mrs. (mother-in-law), 55, 63,
    64
Sir Thopas (Chaucer), 67
Smith, Horace, 33
Smollett, Tobias, 121
Snobbery, theme of, 11-12, 38-41,
    65
Snobs of England, The (*see The Book
    of Snobs*), 50
Sons and Lovers (Lawrence), 9
Spectator, The, 50, 124, 128
Spencer, Herbert, 13
Stanley, Lord of Alderney, 154
Steele, Richard, 106, 124, 139
Sterne, Laurence, 84, 85
Stevenson, R. L., 95
Structure, 66, 73, 121
Stuart Restoration, 123
Style, 17-18, 23-24, 68-69,
    121, 157-58
    in *Vanity Fair,* 87-103, 113
    weaknesses of, 2, 5-6, 90-92
Stylistic devices, 22-23, 90, 104-20,
    131-32, 143-44
Subjection of Women (Mill), 150
Sutcliff, Emerson Grant, 54
Swift, Jonathan, 32, 124
Swinburne, A. C., 18
Symbols, 57-58

T

Taine, Hippolyte, 50
Tennyson, Alfred Lord, 4
Thackeray, Isabella Shawe (wife),
    63
Thackeray, William Makepeace:
    and Addison, 49-50
    as preacher, 49-54, 66, 100
    as social critic, 11, 37, 38-48
        passim
    biographical information, 32, 43-46,
        55-56, 63-64, 65-66, 99, 127-29,
        149-50

and burlesque and parody, 8, 66-
    68, 97-98, 104-120
and charity, importance of, 13,
    156-57, 165
and Christianity, 12-13
commentary within works, 17, 25-
    26, 34, 36-37, 49-54, 82-85, 89-
    90, 148, 158
and contemporary ideal of gentle-
    man, 10-12, 38, 169-71
early journalism of, 8, 65-66,
    115-16, 147
early pseudonyms, 65
and the eighteenth century, 36,
    121-26 *passim*
and fiction as discovery, 7-8
and function of art, 30-31, 76
moral vision, 13-14, 33-35, 37,
    49-54, 65, 69, 76, 80-84, 156,
    163-64, 166-77
and novelistic conventions, 8-10,
    66-72
on human nature, 31-33, 75-76,
    103
on humour, 32-33
on mortality, 52-54
popular success of, 39, 44-46, 159
psychological insight of, 56-60, 124,
    164-65
and realism, 8, 31-33, 68-70, 73, 85,
    104-5, 121-22
and science, 7-8
social views of, 169-77
and writer's function, 31, 65-66,
    121-22
Thackeray, William Makepeace, works
by: (*see* main entries for starred
items)
    *Adventures of Philip, The,** 1-8
        passim, 18, 55-64 *passim,* **161-77**
    Book of Snobs, The, 11, 15-16, 38-
        44, 46, 50, 89, 163, 171, 174
    "Brown's Letters," 41-42
    Catherine, 52, 107, 109, 161
    "Charity and Humour," 32
    Denis Duval, 22, 62-63, 147
    English Humourists, The, 8, 49,
        53

Thackeray, William Makepeace,
works by (*continued*)
  Great Hoggarty Diamond, The,
    149, 151
  History of Henry Esmond, The,*
    14, 20, 22, 28-29, 51, 52, 61-64
    passim, 66, 112, 116, 121-46,
    155, 159, 162
  History of Pendennis, The,* 20, 22,
    44, 51, 52-64 *passim,* 75, 90, 104-
    20 *passim,* 142, 158, 163, 176
  Jeames's Diary, 46
  *Journey from Cornhill to Grand
    Cairo,* 51
  Lovel the Widower, 56, 60
  Luck of Barry Lyndon, The, 163,
    165-66
  Newcomes, The,* 2, 6, 7-8, 9-10,
    12, 20, 44, 55-64 *passim,* 104-120
    passim, 147-60
  "On a Medal of George IV," 51
  "On a Pear-tree," 51
  "On Two Roundabout Papers which
    I intended to write," 51
  Paris Sketchbook, The, 31
  Punch's Prize Novelists, 66-68
  "Ravenswing," 57, 61
  Roundabout Papers, The, 41-42,
    51, 173
  "Shabby Genteel Story, A,"
    162
  Vanity Fair,* 6, 7, 9, 20-27, 30,
    31, 33-37, 44, 46, 54, 65-86, 87-
    103, 122, 142, 148, 149, 151,
    160, 163
  Virginians, The, 57-58, 125
  Yellowplush Correspondence, The,
    46, 55, 62
Thackeray the Novelist (Tillotson), 95
Theocritus, 106
Three Musketeers, The (Dumas), 10
Tillotson, Geoffrey, 10, 95
Tolstoy, Leo, 125
Tono-Bungay (Wells), 148
Totem and Taboo (Freud), 59-60
Trollope, Anthony, 19, 66, 87-88, 90,
  139

Trollope, Mrs. Frances, 66

U

"Unspoken Dialogue" (Milnes), 61

V

Vanity Fair, 6, 7, 9, 20-21, 30, 31, 33,
  44, 46, 65-86, 122, 142, 148, 149,
  151, 160, 163
  as sermon, 54, 66, 100-102
  author's commentary in, 25-26,
    36-37, 66, 83-86, 89
  irony in, 33-36, 72-73, 77
  method, 22-27, 34-36, 65-86
  and neoclassical conventions, 104-20
    passim
  style, 87-103
Vergil, 5, 108, 114
Victorian middle-class standards, 9,
  46-48, 49-54, 117, 149-54
Virginians, The, 57-58, 125
Volume the First (Austen), 67

W

Waldegrave, Lady, 44
War and Peace (Tolstoy), 10
Waterloo, 77, 88
Waugh, Evelyn, 114
Waverley (Scott), 123
Wellington, Duke of, 4
Wharton, Edith, 159
Whately, Richard, 69
Whibley, Charles, 54
Wilhelm Meister (Goethe), 107
Wives and Daughters (Gaskell), 87

Y

Yellowplush Correspondence, The,
  46, 55, 62
Young, G. M., 46

Z

Zola, Émile 125

DYLAN THOMAS

A Collection of Critical Essays

Edited by CHARLES B. COX

A

Aberpennar, Davies, 122
Ackerman, John, 7
Adams, Robert M., 3, 8
Adventures in the Skin Trade, and other stories, 119n, 122
  "Adventure from a Work in Progress, An," 120, 124
  Adventures in the Skin Trade, 123, 127, 128, 129
  "After the Fair," 121n
  "Burning Baby, The," 120, 121, 121n
  "Dress, The," 120, 121n
  "Enemies, The," 120, 121, 121n, 127
  "Holy Six, The," 120, 121, 127
  "Horse's Ha, The," 120
  "In the Direction of the Beginning," 121, 124
  "Lemon, The," 120
  "Map of Love, The," 120
  "Mouse and the Woman, The," 119, 120, 121, 123
  "Orchards, The," 120, 121, 121n, 123, 127
  "Prologue to an Adventure," 118, 127
  "Prospect of the Sea, A," 120
  "Tree, The," 120, 121n
  "True Story, The," 118, 120, 121n
  "Vest, The," 118, 120, 121n
  "Visitor, The," 120, 121, 121n, 127

Agamemnon (Aeschylus), 33
Age of Anxiety, The (Auden), 166, 167
Amis, Kingsley, 122
Ancient Mariner, The (Coleridge), 164
Arnold, Matthew, 30, 33
Auden, W. H., 10, 26, 30, 37, 41, 87, 140, 143, 149, 153, 159, 164, 165, 166, 167, 171, 172

B

"Bateau Ivre" (Rimbaud), 164
Baudelaire, Charles, 59
Bayley, John, 4-5, 7, 8
Belloc, Hilaire, 167
Blake, William, 11, 39, 41, 66, 68, 86, 139, 142, 143, 178
Brinnin, John Malcolm, 74, 89
Burning Baby, The, 121

C

Camus, Albert, 80
Centuries of Meditation (Traherne), 42-43
Chamber Music (Joyce), 104
Chaplin, Charles, 179
Chaucer, Geoffrey, 30, 109
Chesterton, G. K., 167
Clare, John, 146

Cleveland, John, 130
Coleridge, Samuel Taylor, 30, 146,
147, 155, 157
Collected Poems, 7, 8, **9-13**, 26, 28,
37-38, 84, 85, 173
   "After the funeral," 165, 174
   "All all and all dry worlds lever,"
     124
   "Altarwise by owl-light," 20-21,
     42, **46-48**, 56-57, 69*n*, 85, 88,
     124, **135-39**, 161-63, 174
   "Among those Killed in the Dawn
     Raid," 174
   "And death shall have no
     dominion," 6, 17, 173
   "Author's Prologue," 28, 31, 54,
     81, 174
   "Ballad of the Long-legged Bait,"
     164, 174
   "Before I knocked," 16, 86-87
   "Ceremony After a Fire Raid," 17,
     54
   "Conversation of Prayer, The," 12-
     13, 163-64, 165
   "Do not go gentle into that good
     night," 6, 22, 174
   "Do you not father me," 173
   "Especially when the October
     wind," 155-56, 173
   "Fern Hill," 4, 22, 31, 32, 33, 43,
     85, 174
   "Force that through the green fuse
     drives the flower, The," 16, 87,
     173
   "From love's first fever to her
     plague," 165
   "Grief ago, A," 49-50, 173
   "Hand that signed the paper, The,"
     149, 160
   "How shall my animal," 174
   "Hunchback in the Park, The,"
     149, 174
   "I fellowed sleep," 157-58
   "If I were tickled by the rub of
     love," 41
   "'If my head hurt a hair's foot,'"
     1, 55
   "I, in my intricate image," 55-56,

     124, 152, 153-54, 156-57
   "In country sleep," 24, 79, 81-82,
     174
   "In my Craft or Sullen Art,"
     24
   "In the beginning," 55
   "In the white giant's thigh," 24, 79,
     82, 161
   "Into her Lying Down Head," 174
   "I see the boys of summer," 4, 17,
     173
   "It is the sinners' dust-tongued bell,"
     174
   "Light breaks where no sun shines,"
     8, 55, 175
   "Love in the Asylum," 5, 6
   "My world is pyramid," 124
   Note to, 28, 74, 176
   "Not from this anger," 174
   "Now," 86
   "Once it was the colour of saying,"
     12-13
   "On no work of words," 153
   "On the Marriage of a Virgin," 22,
     174
   "Out of the sighs," 149-51, 152,
     153, 156, 160
   "Over Sir John's hill," 4, 8, 22, 28,
     74-80, 81, 82-83, 174
   "Poem in October," 4, 10, 19, 22,
     23, 31, 43, 174
   "Poem on his birthday," 22, 28, 81,
     174
   "Process in the weather of the
     heart, A," 173
   "Refusal to Mourn the Death by
     Fire, of a Child in London, A,"
     6, 10-11, **17-20**, 22, 78, 142, 174
   Sonnets (*see* "Altarwise by owl-
     light")
   "Then was my neophyte," 173-74
   "There was a Saviour," 8, 42, **60-
     73**
   "This bread I break," 16, 18
   "This Side of the Truth," 149
   "Today, this insect," 21
   "Twenty-four years," 55, 161, 164,
     174, 180

Collected Poems (*continued*)
"Unluckily for a Death," 44
"Vision and Prayer," 22-23, 42, 56
"We lying by seasand," 149, 174
"When all my five and country senses see," 174
"When I Woke," 174
"When, like a running grave," 163, 173
"When once the twilight locks no longer," 54, 56
"Winter's Tale, A," 22, 174
Congreve, William, 167
Connolly, Cyril, 84
Conquest, Robert, 2-3
Cowley, Abraham, 130
Crashaw, Richard, 3, 8, 130-39

D

Dafydd ap Gwilym, 30, 172
Daiches, David, 7
Dali, Salvador, 133
Daphnaida (Spenser), 165
Davie, Donald, 3
Davies, W. H., 149
Death and Entrances, 44, 119
Deaths Duell (Donne), 41
Dickens, Charles, 167
Difficulties of a Statesman (Eliot), 111
Divine Comedy (Dante), 33
Divine Epigrams (Crashaw), 132-35, 137
Donne, John, 30, 41, 42, 130, 131, 136, 142, 143, 144, 151, 173
Doom on the Sun, 120-21
Dubliners (Joyce), 125, 125n, 126
Durrell, Lawrence, 121

E

18 Poems, 26, 44, 45, 119
Elements, of Thomas's poetry:
imagery, 2, 3-4, 5, 6, 8, 14-24 *passim*, 32, 41, 43, 65-73 *passim*, 77, 136, 142, 152-53, 154, 156, 163, 164, 175

language, 61-64, 136, **140-68**, 172-73, 174, 176
metaphor, 47-48, 68-73 *passim*, 77, 87, 142, 157, 158, 177
prosody, 3-4, 6, 12, 15-16, 18, 20, 21-23, 29, **31-34**, 60-73, 135, 172
symbolism, 41, **47-59**, 65-73 *passim*, 74, 77, 82, 83, 160-61, 171, 173, 174, 178
Eliot, T. S., 3, 10, 11, 16, 23n, 24, 26, 37, 41, 51, 62, 96, 111, 113, 153, 164, 171
Eluard, Paul, 119
Empson, William, 4, 6, 8, 12, 26, 143, 144
Europa Press, 121
Evans, Caradoc, 37

F

Façade (Sitwell), 179
Faust (Goethe), 96
Fraser, G. S., 122
Freud, Sigmund, 5, 25, 41, 48, 48n, 49, 68, 70, 72, 73, 123, 145, 173, 175
Fry, Christopher, 96

G

"Garden" (Marvell), 134
Goethe, Johann Wolfgang von, 96
Goodwin, Geraint, 34-35
Graves, Robert, 1, 10

H

Hamlet (Shakespeare), 167
Herbert, George, 42, 131, 172
Heyday in the Blood, The (Goodwin), 34-35
Hodgart, M. J. C., 1
Holbrook, David, 4, 8
Holy Sonnets (Donne), 42, 131
Hopkins, Gerard Manley, 12, 38, 140, 171, 172, 173, 177
Hughes, T. Rowland, 35
Huxley, Aldous, 173

Huysmans, Joris Karl, 118*n*

I

Ibsen, Henrik, 96
"In Country Heaven," 79, 80*n*

J

Janes, Alfred, 127
Johnson, Samuel, 86, 130, 131
Johnson Over Jordan (Priestley), 111
Jolas, Eugene, 123
Jones, Daniel, 89, 99
Jones, Glyn, 37
Jones, Gwyn, 33, 36-37
Jonson, Ben, 30, 102, 103, 115
Joyce, James, 8, 41, 69, 93-96, 100-116, 119, 125, 125*n*, 126, 167
Jung, Carl, 5, 48, 49, 119, 122-23, 145

K

Kafka, Franz, 41
Keats, John, 30, 48, 160
King Lear (Shakespeare), 96, 98
Kleinman, Hyman, 7
Koestler, Arthur, 145-46
Kubla Khan (Coleridge), 155

L

Laforgue, Jules, 146
Lawrence, D. H., 105, 115, 116, 178
Leavis, F. R., 146
Letters to Vernon Watkins, 67, 67*n*, 124-29 *passim*
Levy, Mervyn, 127
Lewis, Alun, 37, 40, 40*n*
Lewis, C. S., 74, 80
Life and Letters Today (magazine), 44
Life of Cowley (Johnson), 130
London Magazine, 14
Lost Girl, The (Lawrence), 115
Lycidas (Milton), 165

M

Machen, Arthur, 117-18, 118*n*
MacNeice, Louis, 45
Maeterlinck, Maurice, 162
Mallarmé, Stéphane, 157, 173
"Man Carrying Thing" (Stevens), 65-66
Map of Love, The, 50, 119, 121
Martin, J. H., 119
Marvell, Andrew, 134
Marx, Karl, 4
Maud, Ralph, 8, 64, 67, 119
Millay, Edna St. Vincent, 179
Miller, Henry, 121, 175
Milton, John, 165
Moore, Geoffrey, 7, 27
Morganwg, Iolo, 29
"Mountain Over Aberdare, The" (Lewis), 40, 40*n*

N

New Statesman, 8, 10
New Verse (magazine), 119
Notebooks (of Dylan Thomas), 117, 118, 119-20, 126, 128
   "Jasper, Melchior, and Balthazar," 120, 121*n*
   "Poem Written on the Death of a Very Dear Illusion," 117
"Notes on the Art of Poetry," 123
Nowottny, Winifred, 7-8

O

Obscurity, in Thomas's poetry, 1, 4-5, 8, 11, 21, 45, 46, 84, 86, 173
"Ode to a Nightingale" (Keats), 48
Olson, Elder, 7, 67, 69*n*, 164
"O Rose Thou art Sick" (Blake), 161
Owen, Wilfred, 146, 165

P

Parry, Thomas, 31
Pater, Walter, 118*n*

Peer Gynt (Ibsen), 96
"Pleasure Island" (Auden), 165
Pollock, Jackson, 138
Pope, Alexander, 1, 151, 159
Porteus, H. G., 45
Portrait of the Artist as a Young Dog,
    10, 122, 123, 124-27, 128, 129
    "Extraordinary Little Cough,"
        125
    "Just Like Little Dogs," 125, 126
    "Old Garbo," 125, 126
    "One Warm Saturday," 126, 127
    "Patricia, Edith and Arnold," 125
    "Peaches, The," 124, 125
    "Visit to Grandpa, A," 125
    "Where Tawe Flows," 126, 127
    "Who Do You Wish Was With Us,"
        125, 127
*Portrait of the Artist as a Young Man,
    A* (Joyce), 125*n*, 126
Pound, Ezra, 171
Powys, T. F., 101
Pratt, Annis, 8
Prelude, The (Wordsworth), 147-48
Priestley, J. B., 111
Prospect of the Sea, A, 122
Proust, Marcel, 41
Prys-Jones, A. G., 28-29, 41
"Psychology and Poetry" (Jung),
    119, 123

Q

Quite Early One Morning, 39-40, 79-
    80, 89
    "Answers to an Enquiry," 119, 123

R

Rabelais, François, 103
Raine, Kathleen, 86
Rank, Otto, 49
Read, Herbert, 9
Reavy, George, 121
"Relique, The" (Donne), 131
Renan, Ernest, 42
Rhys, Keidrych, 119
Riley, James Whitcomb, 172

Rimbaud, Arthur, 118, 140, 164, 173,
    177
Roussilat, Suzanne, 100
Ruskin, John, 157

S

Scrutiny (magazine), 10
"Second Coming, The" (Yeats), 171
Shakespeare, William, 59, 84, 96, 107,
    112, 142, 167
Shapiro, Karl, 7, 8, 26
Shaw, G. B., 59
Shelley, Percy Bysshe, 42, 146, 151,
    162
Sitwell, Edith, 1-2, 12, 46, 161, 162,
    163, 179
"Song for Simeon, A" (Eliot), 153
South Wales Daily Post, 119*n*
Spender, Stephen, 26, 37-38, 45
Spenser, Edmund, 30, 165
Spinoza, B., 51
Stanford, Derek, 118
Stevens, Wallace, 65-66
"Strange Meeting" (Owen), 165
Stravinsky, Igor, 173
Stuffed Owl, The (anthol.), 131
Sunday Referee, 87
Swinburne, Algernon Charles, 11, 117,
    142, 143
Symons, Arthur, 162
Symons, Julian, 160

T

Temple, The (Herbert), 42
Texas Quarterly, 123
Themes, in Thomas's poetry:
    birth, 21, 46, 54, 55, 165
    blood, 156
    childhood, 10, 41, 43
    death, 17, 18, 21, 41, 46, 54-55, 56-
        57, 77-79, 80-82, 165, 171
    genesis, 4, 55
    growth, 156
    human to animal to vegetable rela-
        tionship, 21, 55
    identity and unity, 16-20, 22, 30

Themes, in Thomas's poetry
(*continued*):
  interior geography of the body,
    55
  life, 54
  love, 54, 65, 173, 175
  madness of war, 6
  parent-child relationship, 21
  prenatal life, 21, 55
  procreation, 156
  religion, 10, 28-29, 40, 41-44, 60-
    73 *passim*, 74-76, 135-39
  Resurrection, 56, 137
  sex, 6, 10, 40, 41, 46, 65, 73, 165,
    174, 175, 176
  telescoping of existence, 163
  the viscera, 10
Thomas, Caitlin, 35
Thomas, Dylan:
  adolescence of, 117-18
  critical reputation of, 1-8, 9-13,
    14, 41, 45, 99, 122, 169-70
  death of, 14, 83, 83*n*, 169-70,
    177
  and drama, 85, 89-98, 99-116
  passim
  and film, 85-86

  Joyce's influence on, 8, 69, 93-96,
    100-16, 199, 125, 125*n*, 126
  personality of, 5-7, 14, 85-86
  and poetry (*see also* Elements, of
    Thomas's poetry; Obscurity, in
    Thomas's poetry; Themes, in
    Thomas's poetry), 1-8, 9-13, 14-
    24, 25-44, 45-59, 60-73, 74-83,
    84-88, 117-29 *passim*, 135-39,
    140-68, 169-80
  politics of, 87
  and prose, 6, 8, 89-98, 99-116,
    117-29, 166-68
  and religion, 34-36, 38-44, 80,
    174
  and sex, 6, 7, 10, 41, 175
  Welsh background of, 5, 7, 25-44
Thomas, Dylan, works by (*see also*
  individual listings for those works
  marked by asterisk):
  Adventures in the Skin Trade, and

  *Other Stories,** 119*n*, 122
  Burning Baby, The, 121
  *Collected Poems,** 7, 8, 9-13, 26,
    28, 37-38, 84, 85, 173
  Death and Entrances, 44, 119
  Doom on the Sun, 120-21
  18 Poems, 26, 44, 45, 119
  "In Country Heaven," 79, 80*n*
  Letters to Vernon Watkins, 67, 67*n*,
    124-29 *passim*
  Map of Love, The, 50, 119, 121
  *Notebooks,** 117, 118, 119-20,
    126, 128
  "Notes on the Art of Poetry," 123
  *Portrait of the Artist as a Young
    Dog,** 10, 122, 123, 124-27, 128,
    129
  Prospect of the Sea, A, 122
  *Quite Early One Morning,** 39-40,
    79-80, 89
  Twenty-Five Poems, 9, 26, 45,
    119
  Uncommon Genesis, 120-21
  *Under Milk Wood,** 8, 23, 23*n*, 24,
    26, 83, 85, 89-98, 99-116, 166-68
  World I Breathe, The, 121
Thomas, Edward, 38
Thomas, Gwyn, 39
Thomas, R. S., 37
Thomas, William, 36
Tindall, William York, 1, 4
"Tintern Abbey" (Wordsworth), 48
Traherne, Thomas, 41, 42-43, 172
transition (magazine), 5, 119, 123
Treece, Henry, 3, 154
Tuve, Rosamond, 143
Twenty-Five Poems, 9, 26, 45, 119

U

Ulysses (Joyce), 93-96, 100-116
Uncommon Genesis, 120-21
Under Milk Wood, 8, 23, 23*n*, 24, 26,
  83, 85, 89-98, 99-116, 166-68
  dialogue in, 91, 93, 106-11
  genesis of, 98-90
  humor in, 103-4, 108
  morality in, 103-4

Under Milk Wood (continued)
  narrative in, 90-92
  necrophilia in, 110
  reality in, 104
  song in, 91, 93
  structure of, 90, 97-98
  and *Ulysses* (Joyce), **93-96, 100-116**

V

Valéry, Paul, 142, 169
Vaughan, Henry, 41, 42, 172

W

Wain, John, 7
Wallenstein, Ruth, 134
Warren, Austin, 132, 134

Waste Land, The (Eliot), 113
Watkins, Vernon, 2, 27, 27n, 37, 43-
  44, 67, 67n, 116, 124
Welsh Review, 36
Weston, Jessie, 24
Whitman, Walt, 178, 180
Williams, Gwyn, 30
Williams, Raymond, 8
Women in Love (Lawrence), 116
Wordsworth, William, 42, 48, 84, 85,
  111, 146-48, 150, 154, 156
World I Breathe, The, 121

Y

Yeats, William Butler, 12, 43, 140,
  142, 156, 164, 169, 171, 172,
  178

THOREAU

A Collection of Critical Essays
Edited by SHERMAN PAUL

A

Alcott, Bronson, 24, 56, 96, 157, 162
"All Things Are Current Found," 138
American Notebook (Hawthorne),
 145
Areopagitica (Milton), 25
Autobiography (Franklin), 102
"Autumnal Tints," 49

B

Bacon, Francis, 29
Baudelaire, Charles, 133
Bergson, Henri, 15
Bernard, Saint, 135
"Big Two-Hearted River, The" (Hem-
 ingway), 26
"Biographical Sketch" (Emerson),
 175
Blake, William, 133, 137, 138
Brown, John, 11, 21, 22, 27, 29, 31,
 35-36, 124, 127-29, 162, 171
Brown Decades, The (Mumford), 2
Browne, Sir Thomas, 167
Byron, George Gordon, Lord, 132

C

Cape Cod, 63
Carlyle, Thomas, 59
Cartier, Jacques, 144
Champlain, Samuel de, 144
Channing, Ellery, 37, 38-39, 43, 56,
 57, 87, 142, 162

"Civil Disobedience," 1, 21, 24, 31,
 118-29
Civil disobedience, doctrine of, 4, 13,
 23-25, **118-30**
Clark, William, 144
"Cliffs and Springs, The," 139
"Cock-Crowing" (Vaughan), 136
Coleridge, S. T., 96
*Communitas: Means of Livelihood and
 Ways of Life* (Goodman and Good-
 man), 3
Confidence-Man, The (Melville),
 150-51
Cooper, James Fenimore, 149-50, 157
Corot, Jean Baptiste Camille, 138
Cowley, Malcolm, 26
Cowper, William, 137

D

Dante Alighieri, 135
Darwin, Charles, 15, 127
Debs, Eugene, 24
Democratic Vistas (Whitman), 92
De Quincey, Thomas, 61
Dickinson, Emily, 95, 131-32
Diogenes, 18, 49
"Dong, sounds the brass in the East,"
 139-40
Donne, John, 136

E

Emerson, Ralph Waldo, 4, 10, 11, 13-
 14, 15, 19-21, 23-24, 27, 30, 34, 36,

Emerson, Ralph Waldo (*continued*)
53-54, 56-57, 64, 74, 82, 93, 95-96,
99, 100, 106, 109, 113, 131-39
passim, 162, 167, 175

F

"Farewell," 36
Faulkner, William, 1, 26
"For Though the Caves Were
Rabitted," 140
Francis, Saint, 11
Franklin, Benjamin, 102
Freud, Sigmund, 98
Fuller, Margaret, 53

G

Gandhi, Mahatma, 2, 161
Garland, Hamlin, 13
Georgics (Virgil), 178
Glaspell, Susan, 13
Goethe, Johann Wolfgang von,
113
Goodman, Paul, 3
Goodman, Percival, 3

H

Hamilton, Alexander, 32
Harding, Walter, 1
Hawthorne, Nathaniel, 1, 25-26, 99,
143, 145, 148
Hedge, Frederic Henry, 39, 43
Hemingway, Ernest, 26, 55
Henry, Alexander, 144
Herbert, George, 137
"Higher Laws," 47
Holmes, Oliver Wendell, 99
Hopkins, Gerard Manley, 162, 167-70
Horace, 133, 134
Hulme, T. E., 55, 60

I

"I Am a Parcel of Vain Strivings Tied,"
137

"I Am the Autumnal Sun," 140
"I Am the Little Irish Boy," 140
"I Knew a Man by Sight," 137
Indian Notebooks, 142-43
"Inward Morning, The," 136

J

Jacob's Room (Woolf), 173
Jefferson, Thomas, 32, 119-20
James, Henry, 26, 34, 35, 174
Jerusalem Delivered (Tasso), 54
Jones, Samuel A., 1
Jonson, Ben, 133, 136
Journals, 26, 31, 33-35, 41, **44-51,** 53,
63-67, 69-70, 104, 127, 129, 142-43,
146-48, 150, **151-55,** 158-59, 168,
176
Joyce, James, 1, 35
Jung, Carl, 98

K

Keats, John, 60

L

"Lake Isle of Innisfree, The" (Yeats),
8
Landor, Walter Savage, 134
Lawrence, D. H., 2
Leatherstocking Tales (Cooper), 157
"Let such pure hate still underprop,"
134
Lewis, Meriwether, 144
"Life Without Principle," 27, 42
Lowell, James Russell, 12, 30, 35, 53,
54, 96, 131, 137

M

Macaulay, Thomas Babington, 29
MacKaye, Benton, 2, 18
Maine Woods, The, 143, 145
"Manhood," 134
Marble Faun, The (Hawthorne),
148

Marvell, Andrew, 136
Masters, Edgar Lee, 13
"May Morning," 138
Melville, Herman, 1, 26, 62, 149, 151, 152
Metamorphoses (Ovid), 106
Minott, George, 44, 45
Montaigne, Michel, 34
Morris, William, 21, 33
Mrs. Dalloway (Woolf), 174
Mumford, Lewis, 2
"Music," 139
"My Books I'd Fain Cast Off," 138
"My Boots," 140

N

Nature (Emerson), 101, 144
Naumburg, Margaret, 2
Niehardt, John G., 13
Nietzsche, Friedrich, 1, 6, 21
Note-Books (Hopkins), 168-70

O

"On Ponkawtasset," 136
Ovid, 106

P

Parkman, Francis, 148
Pascal, Blaise, 130
Pertaining to Thoreau (Jones), 1
Pindar, 132
Plato, 27, 29, 96, 134, 167-68
"Plea for Captain John Brown, A," 25, 33, 118, 123-24, 127-29,
Poe, Edgar Allan, 133
"Poverty," 136
Prescott, William, 148

R

Riesman, David, 3
Ripley, George, 40, 42
"River Swelleth More and More, The," 136

Romanticism, doctrines of, 1, 4-6, 19, 20, 95, 138, 145, 157
Rousseau, Jean-Jacques, 18, 122
"Rumors from an Aeolian Harp," 134
Ruskin, John, 121

S

Sacco, Nicola, 35
Schweitzer, Albert, 161
"Service, The," 38, 53-62
Shakespeare, William, 178
Shaw, G. B., 2
Simonides, 134
Skelton, John, 135
"Sketches from Memory" (Hawthorne), 143
"Slavery in Massachusetts," 28, 118, 123-24, 125-26, 128
"Sluggish Smoke Curls up from Some Deep Dell, The," 137
"Sound and Silence," 59

T

"Tall Ambrosia," 140
Tasso, Torquato, 54
Thomson, James, 133, 137
Thoreau (Canby), 1
Thoreau, Henry:
    and Alcott, Bronson, 24, 56, 96, 157, 162
    and Bergson, Henri, 15
    and Blake, William, 133, 137, 138
    and Brown, John, 11, 12, 22, 27, 29, 31, 35-36, 124, 127, 171
    and Browne, Sir Thomas, 167
    and Carlyle, Thomas, 59
    and Channing, Ellery, 37, 38-39, 43, 56, 57, 87, 142, 162
    and civil disobedience, doctrine of, 4, 13, 23-25, 118-30
    and Coleridge, S. T., 96
    and Cooper, James Fenimore, 149-50, 157
    critical reputation of, 1-7

Thoreau, Henry (*continued*):
  and Debs, Eugene, 24
  and De Quincey, Thomas, 61
  and Emerson, Ralph Waldo, 10, 11,
    15, 19-21, 23-24, 27, 30, 34, 36,
    54, 56-57, 64, 74, 82, 93, 95-96,
    99, 100, 113, 131-39 *passim*, 162,
    167, 175
  and Francis, Saint, 11
  and Goethe, Johann Wolfgang von,
    113
  and Gandhi, Mahatma, 2, 161
  and Goodman, Paul, 3
  and Goodman, Percival, 3
  and Hawthorne, Nathaniel, 25-26,
    99, 143, 145, 148
  and Hemingway, Ernest, 55
  and Hopkins, Gerard Manley,
    168-70
  influence of, 2-4, **117-30**
  and Jonson, Ben, 133, 136
  and Keats, John, 60
  life of, **9-12, 13-19,** 23, 32-38 *pas-
    sim*, 93-97, 100-16 *passim*,
    121-24, 148
  and Lowell, James Russell, 12,
    30, 35, 53, 54, 96, 131, 137
  and MacKaye, Benton, 2, 18
  and Melville, Herman, 26, 62, 149,
    151, 152
  and metaphysical poetry, 136-37
  and Morris, William, 21, 33
  and Naumburg, Margaret, 2
  and Ovid, 106
  poetry of, **131-41**
  and Plato, 27, 29, 96, 134,
    167-68
  and Riesman, David, 3
  and Ripley, George, 40, 42
  and Romanticism, doctrines of, 1,
    4-6, 19, 20, 95, 138, 145, 157
  and Rousseau, Jean-Jacques, 18,
    122
  and Ruskin, John, 121
  and transcendentalism, doctrines
    of, 4-6, 10, 19, 20-21, 29, 53, 95,
    138, 140, 162
  and Vaughan, Henry, 167

  and Whitman, Walt, 9, 11, 59, 92,
    95
  and Woolf, Virginia, 173-74, 178
  and Wordsworth, William, 15
  and Yeats, W. B., 140
Thoreau, Henry, works by:
  "All Things Are Current Found,"
    138
  "Autumnal Tints," 49
  Cape Cod, 63
  "Civil Disobedience," 1, 21, 24, 31,
    118-29
  "Cliffs and Springs, The," 139
  "Dong, sounds the brass in the
    East," 139-40
  "Farewell," 36
  "For Though the Caves Were Rabit-
    ted," 140
  "Higher Laws," 147
  "I Am a Parcel of Vain Strivings
    Tied," 137
  "I Am the Autumnal Sun," 140
  "I Am the Little Irish Boy," 140
  "I Knew a Man by Sight," 137
  Indian Notebooks, 142-43
  "Inward Morning, The," 136
  Journals, 26, 31, 33-35, 41, **44-51,**
    53, 63-67, 69-70, 104, 127, 129,
    142-43, 146-48, 150, **151-55,**
    158-59, 168, 176
  "Let such pure hate still under-
    prop," 134
  "Life Without Principle," 27, 42
  Maine Woods, The, 143, 145
  "Manhood," 134
  "May Morning," 138
  "Music," 139
  "My Books I'd Fain Cast Off,"
    138
  "My Boots," 140
  "On Ponkawtasset," 136
  "Plea for Captain John Brown, A,"
    25, 33, 118, 123-24, 127-29
  "Poverty," 136
  "River Swelleth More and More,
    The," 136
  "Rumors from an Aeolian Harp,
    134

Thoreau, Henry, works by
(*continued*)
  "Service, The," 38, **53-62**
  "Slavery in Massachusetts," 28, 118,
    123-24, 125-26, 128
  "Sluggish Smoke Curls up from
    Some Deep Dell, The," 137
  "Sound and Silence," 59
  "Tall Ambrosia," 140
  "Upon This Bank at Early Dawn,"
    136
  "Virgin, The," 135
  Walden, 1, 3, 11, 21-33 *passim*, 40-
    41, 44, 54, 58, 60, 63, 70, **71-91**,
    92-99 *passim*, **100-16**, 118, 121-
    22, 125, 142-53 *passim*, 161
  *Week on the Concord and the Merri-
    mack Rivers, A*, 1, 3, 59, **63-70**,
    71-72, 74-75, 100, 112, 143, 144,
    161
  "Where Gleaming Fields of Haze,"
    140
  "Wild Apples," 49
Thoreau, John, 46
Thoreau: A Century of Criticism
  (Harding), 1
Tocqueville, Alexis de, 14
Transcendentalism, doctrines of, 4-6,
  10, 19, 20-21, 29, 53, 95, 138, 140,
  162
Travels and Adventures (Henry), 144
Turner, Frederick Jackson, 156

Twain, Mark, 13, 26

U

"Upon This Bank at Early Dawn," 136

V

Vanzetti, Bartolomeo, 35
Vaughan, Henry, 137, 167
"Virgin, The," 135

W

Walden, 1, 3, 11, 21-33 *passim*, 40-41,
  44, 54, 58, 60, 63, 70, **71-91**, 92-99
  passim, **100-116**, 118, 121-22, 125,
  142-53 *passim*, 161
*Week on the Concord and the Merri-
  mack Rivers, A*, 1, 3, 59, **63-70**, 71-
  72, 74-75, 100, 112, 143, 144, 161
"Where Gleaming Fields of Haze," 140
Whitman, Walt, 9, 11, 59, 92, 95
"Wild Apples," 49
Woolf, Leonard, 178
Woolf, Virginia, 162, 164, 173-74, 178
Wordsworth, William, 15, 98, 132, 136
Writer's Diary, A (Woolf), 174

Y

Yeats, W. B., 8, 140

TOLSTOY

A Collection of Critical Essays

Edited by RALPH E. MATLAW

A

Adams, Henry, 12
Adolescence (see *Boyhood*), 32
Alexander I, Tsar, 41, 160*n*
Alexandrian School, 63
"Andrej Kolosov" (Turgenev), 76
Anna Karenina, 1-7 *passim*, 23-25, 38,
    41, 42, 44, 57-58, 67, 68, 76, 80, 83,
    86, 99, 100, 108, 160, 162
  autobiographical elements in,
    73-74
  capitalism, theme of, 88-89
  death, theme of, 136-45
  form, 72-75, 143-44
  manners, significance of, 129-45
    passim
  rebirth, theme of, 134-41
  sex, theme of, 122-26, 128
  structure, 23-24, 144-45
  technique, 74-75, **127-45**
Arakcheev, A. A., 160, 162
Aristotle, 48, 131, 132*n*, 157, 161
Arnold, Matthew, 1
"Art of Fiction, The" (James),
  147
Aspects of the Novel (Forster), 111
Augustine, Saint, 65, 168
Austen, Jane, 111, 129

B

Bacon, Francis, 48
Balzac, Honoré de, 84, 85, 86, 87

Beethoven, Ludwig van, 25
Behrs, Tatyana Andreyvna (*see*
  Kuzminskaya, T. A.), 95
Berlin, Isaiah, 1, 14
Blackmur, R. P., 113, 122-23
Boris Godunov (Pushkin), 40
Botkin, Vassili, 33
Bourget, C. J. P., 55
Boyhood, 11, 32, 65-67, 70
  autobiographical elements in, 11,
    65-67, 68
  narrative style of, 76-77
  structure, 68-69
Brahms, J., 55
Brothers Karamazov, The
  (Dostoevsky), 18
Buddenbrooks (Mann), 65
Buffon, G. L. L. de, 52
Byron, George Gordon Lord, 65

C

Cable, George W., 101
Capitalism, theme of, 88-94
Caravaggio, 113
Carlyle, Thomas, 31
Chance (Conrad), 155
Characterization, methods of, **56-64**,
  102-3
Chekhov, A., 110, 122
Childe Harold (Byron), 65
Childhood, 4, 11, 26, 32, 52, 65-67,
  70, 75

Childhood (*continued*)
  autobiographical elements in, 11,
    65-67, 68
  narrative style of, 75, 76-77
  structure, 68-69
Chopin, F., 39, 46
Cicero, 107
Cleopatra, 55
Cobbett, William, 31
Coleridge, S. T., 18
Comte, Auguste, 44
Confession, 53, 77, 99
Confessions (Augustine), 65
Confessions (Rousseau), 10, 65
Conrad, Joseph, 155
Conversion, theme of, 100-101,
  135
Cook, Albert, 2
Cooper, J. F., 84
Cossacks, The, 37-38, 41, 67, 69-70
  conception of society in, 88
Critique of Dogmatic Theology, A,
  18
Cromwell, Oliver, 84

D

Dante Alighieri, 29, 132, 137
David Copperfield (Dickens), 65
Death, theme of, 13, 22, 134-45
  passim, 157-72 *passim*
Death of Ivan Ilyich, The, 4, 5, 8, 22,
  38, 58-59, 85, 163
  author's intervention in, 146-51,
    155-56
  dehumanization, theme of, 89-90
  narrative devices, **146-56**, 158-59
  pursuit of pleasure, theme of,
    150-52, 153-54
  structure, 152-53
Defoe, Daniel, 83, 111
Dehumanization, theme of, 92
  in *Resurrection*, 90-91
  in *Death of Ivan Ilyich*, 89-90
Demosthenes, 107
Derzhavin, G. R., 46
Descartes, René, 167
Devil, The, 4, 98

Diary of a Madman, The, 157
  autobiographical elements in,
    159-63
Dichtung und Wahrheit (Goethe), 65,
  66
Dickens, Charles, 30, 65
Domestic Happiness (*see Family Happiness*), 21
Don Giovanni (Mozart), 40
Dostoevsky, F., 7, 15, 17, 18, 24, 25,
  38, 64, 102
Druzhinin, A. V., 54
Du Bos, Charles, 26

E

Ecclesiastes, 167
Eliot, T. S., 21, 27, 143
Émile (Rousseau), 47
Engels, F., 81
Enneads (Plotinus), 172
Epic form, 22-23, 65, 70-71, 79-85
  passim
Everyman, 22

F

Family Happiness, 8, 21, 41, 53
  autobiographical elements in, 21
Faulkner, William, 101, 148
Fet, A., 32, 33, 95
"First Love" (Turgenev), 76
Flaubert, Gustave, 27, 43, 82,
  155
Forged Coupon, The, 93
Form, 7, 53, 65-73 *passim*, 128
Formalists, 8, 22
Forster, E. M., 111
Franklin, Benjamin, 52

G

Goethe, J. W. von, 22, 25, 47, 65
Gogol, N., 46, 102, 161
Goldsmith, Oliver, 52
Goncharov, I. A., 32, 109
Gorky, M., 9, 12, 14, 20, 24, 92, 126

Grüne Heinrich, Der (Keller), 65
Gulliver's Travels (Swift), 8, 91

H

Hadji Murad, 7, 88
Hedgehog and the Fox, The (Berlin),
  1-2
Hegel, G. W. F., 31, 78, 81, 82
Heller, Erich, 25
Helvétius, 32, 43
Hemingway, Ernest, 27, 111
Herzen, T., 44
History of Russian Literature (Mirsky),
  98
History of Yesterday, A, 10
Homer, 22, 79, 84
Hume, David, 167
Huysmans, J. K., 55

I

Iliad (Homer), 23, 40, 63
Imagery, 2-4, 32, 116-19, 121-22,
  137-39
  as method of revelation, 3-4, 121-22

J

James, Henry, 4, 142, 147, 148, 149,
  154-55
Job, 29
Jung, Carl, 127

K

Kant, Immanuel, 37, 45, 48
Keats, John, 122
Keller, G., 65
Kreutzer Sonata, The, 7, 19, 20, 25,
  67, 92
  sex, theme of, 126
Kuzminskaya, Tatyana A., 95-101
  passim

L

Landowska, Wanda, 40

Language, 103-10
Laokoon (Lessing), 79
Lawrence, D. H., 11, 17, 21, 31
Lazursky, V., 53
Leavis, F. R., 111
Lenin, V. I., 15
Lermontov, Mikhail, 52
Leskov, N., 102
Lessing, G. E., 79
Lettres Persanes (Montesquieu),
  8
Light Shines in the Darkness, A,
  67
Living Corpse, The, 67, 93
Lord Jim (Conrad), 155
Love, theme of, 21, 53, 73
Lubbock, Percy, 6, 111, 113, 156
"Lucerne," 67
Lukács, G., 51n
Luther, Martin, 48, 49

M

Mably, Gabriel B. de, 36
Machiavelli, N., 29
Madame Bovary (Flaubert), 156
Mann, Thomas, 25, 65
Manners, significance of, 23-24,
  129-45 *passim*
Marlinsky (pseud. A. A. Bestuzhev),
  52
Marriage versus romantic love, theme
  of, 21
Marx, Karl, 41, 44
Master and Man, 4, 22, 163
  death as rebirth, theme of,
  163-72
Master and Servant (*see Master and
  Man*), 22
Maude, Aylmer, 105
Maude, Louise, 105
Maupassant, Guy de, 38, 42, 43, 46
Memoires (Gorky), 12
Merezhkovsky, D., 77
Method, 52, 56-64, 68-77, **80-94,**
  127-45 *passim,* **146-56**
Middle Years, The (James), 4
Mikhailovna, Marya, 96-97

Mikhailovsky, Nikolay, 15, 28, 41, 42, 47n
Mirsky, D. S., 98
Molière, 17
Montesquieu, Baron de La Brède et de, 8
"Morning after the Ball, The," 161
"Morning of a Landowner, The," 38, 67, 69, 70
Mozart, W. A., 39
Mussorgsky, 43

N

Napoleon, 12, 41, 103, 122
Napoleon III, 43
Narrative devices, 3, 6-7, 52-53, 56-64
  in Anna Karenina, 5, 7, 74-75, 127-45
  in Death of Ivan Ilyich, 5-6, 152-54
  in War and Peace, 7, 59-62
National destiny, theme of, 122
Nekrassov, N. A., 32, 33, 38, 75
Nero, 55
Nicholas I, 12, 162
Nietzsche, F. W., 15, 25
Ninth Symphony (Beethoven), 40
"Notes of a Billiard-Maker," 67

O

Odyssey (Homer), 23, 63
Orwell, George, 14

P

Panaev, I., 32
Pascal, Blaise, 18, 29
Paul, Saint, 63
Pestalozzi, 46
Phaedo (Plato), 157
Pisemsky, A. T., 32
Plato, 48, 157, 163
Plotinus, 170, 172
Populists, 43, 50
Portrait of a Lady, The (James), 154

Positivism, 44
Powers of Darkness, The, 25
Proudhon, Pierre-Joseph, 31
Proust, Marcel, 2
Psychology and Religion (Jung), 127
Pursuit of Pleasure, theme of, 150-52, 153-54
Pushkin, Alexander, 33, 39, 40, 46, 63, 64, 76, 109

Q

Quietism, 41-42

R

"Raid, The," 67, 68
Rebirth, theme of, 23, 112-22, 134-41, 163-72
Reminiscences (Lazursky), 53
Renan, J. E., 43
Repin, I. E., 43
Resurrection, 4, 8, 11, 25, 38, 44, 67, 68, 70, 80, 100, 126
  as tragedy of class society, 101
  conversion, theme of, 100-101
  dehumanization, theme of, 90-91
  expiation, theme of, 100
  sex, theme of, 126
"Right Hand and the Left Hand of Leo Tolstoy, The" (Mikhailovsky), 28
Rilke, Rainer Maria, 13, 19
Rimbaud, Arthur, 15
Robinson Crusoe (Defoe), 83
Romains, Jules, 71
Romanticism, 9, 41, 52-53
Rousseau, J.-J., 10, 16, 17, 29, 30, 36, 40, 41, 44, 47, 48, 52, 65
Russian Archive, 160

S

Saint-Pierre, Bernardin de, 52
Schopenhauer, Arthur, 40
Schorer, Mark, 155
"Sevastopol," 67, 70
Sevastopol in May, 9, 11

Sevastopol Sketches, 10, 32, 52
Sex, theme of, 24-25, 92
    in *Anna Karenina,* 122-26, 128
    in *Kreutzer Sonata,* 126
Shakespeare, William, 25, 26, 29,
    130, 143
Shklovsky, Victor, 8, 36*n*
Silentium (Tyutchev), 40
"Snowstorm, The," 67
Social change, theme of, 85-94
Socrates, 25
Sophocles, 132
Splendeur et Misère des Courtisanes
    (Balzac), 84
Srassov, V. V., 43
Stael, Madame G. de, 102
Stendhal, 52, 85, 86, 87, 111
Sterne, Laurence, 10, 52
Storm, Theodor, 75
Strakhev, F. A., 2
Strauss, Richard, 55
Structure, 2-3, 23-24, 71-74, 144-45
Style, 3, 4, 5-6, 32, 52-53, 75-76,
    102-10
Stylistic devices, 23, 75, 102-10
Swift, Jonathan, 91, 134

T

Tales of Sevastopol, The (see
    Sevastopol Sketches), 17
Tate, Allen, 156
Techniques, 1-2, 102, 156-57
    decentralization, 71-77
    gesture, use of, 11, 56-64, 102-3,
        111-13
    "making strange," 8-10
    psychological eavesdropping, 10-11
    repetition, 6, 23, 56, 102-8
Tolstoy, Alexandra (daughter), 95-96
Tolstoy, Leo:
    on art, function of, 42-43
    autobiographical elements in works,
        11, 21, 65-77 *passim,* 95-98,
        159-63
    biographical information, 32-37,
        53-55, 66-67, 95-101 *passim,* 126,
        158-62

and body as mirror of the soul,
    56-64
child, idealization of, 40-41
and condition of peasants, 33-34
and contemporary Russian intelli-
    gentsia, 29-30
conversion of, 45-46
and death, understanding of,
    157-72 *passim*
and didactic impulse, 3-5, 19, 21,
    146-56 *passim*
on education, 30-51 *passim*
and Enlightenment, sympathy with,
    16, 25, 29, 31-32, 36-37, 51, 52
and folk art, 53-55
and French language, influence of,
    108-9
on human nature, 15-16, 28, 30-31,
    37-38, 44-45, 103-4
and literary craftsmanship, 1-3, 22
and madness, fear of, 161-63
and milieu, significance in works,
    80-94 *passim*
modernity of, 75-76
moral vision of, 15-16, 23-24,
    28-30, 37-51 *passim,* 67-68,
    73-77, 92-94, **111-26**, 145-56
    passim, 157-72
and music, condemnation of, 25
and Nature, 13, 47, 83-84, 127
and nineteenth-century Realists,
    85-86
peasant, idealization of, 40-41, 69,
    99
and primitivism, 41, 54-55
quietism of, 41-42
and Realism, 26, 32, 52, **78-94**
religious quest of, 1, 14-16, 18-19,
    22, 41, 77, 172
and Rousseau, 30-31, 36-37, 41, 44-
    45, 47
as schoolmaster, 34-37, 54-55
and sense of evil, 25
social views of, 11-12, 14-15
and spiritual crises, 1, 11, 19, 52-55,
    77, 159-63
and truth, nature of, 39-43, 76-77
and truth versus invention, 38-39

Tolstoy, Leo, works by:
  Adolescence (*see Boyhood*)
  Anna Karenina, 1-7 *passim*, 23-25,
    38, 41, 42, 44, 57-58, 67, 68, 72-
    76, 80, 83, 86, 88-89, 99, 100,
    108, 122-26, 127-45, 160, 162
  Boyhood, 11, 32, 65-69, 70,
    76-77
  Childhood, 4, 11, 26, 32, 52, 65-
    69, 70, 75, 76-77
  Cossacks, The, 37-38, 41, 67, 69-
    70, 88
  Critique of Dogmatic Theology, A,
    18
  Death of Ivan Ilyich, The, 4, 5, 8,
    22, 38, 58-59, 85, 89-90, **146-56**,
    157-59, 163
  Devil, The, 4, 98
  Domestic Happiness (*see Family
    Happiness*), 21
  Family Happiness, 8, 21, 41, 53
  Hadji Murad, 7, 88
  History of Yesterday, A, 10
  Kreutzer Sonata, The, 7, 19, 20, 25,
    67, 92, 126
  Light Shines in Darkness, A, 67
  Master and Man, 4, 22, 163-72
  Powers of Darkness, The, 25
  Resurrection, 4, 8, 11, 25, 38, 44,
    67, 68, 70, 80, 90-91, 100-101,
    126
  Sevastopol in May, 9, 11
  Sevastopol Sketches, 10, 32, 52
  Tales of Sevastopol (*see Sevastopol
    Sketches*), 17
  Two Hussars, 8, 20
  War and Peace, 2, 4, 6-7, 19, 22-24,
    34, 38, 42, 44, 53, 59-62, 67, 68,
    69, 71-74, 75, 79-90, 95-99, 100,
    102-10, 111-22, 126, 160, 163-72
  What is Art?, 21, 41-42, 54-55
  Yasnaya Polyana, 34-35
  Youth, 11, 32, 36, 65-68, 70, 76-
    77
Tolstoy, Countess M. N. (wife), 76,
  77, 98
Tolstoy, Leo L. (Son), 77
Tolstoy, Sergei (brother), 96-97

Tolstoy as I Knew Him (Kuzminskaya),
  95
Töpfer, R., 52
Tragedy of Tolstoy, The (Tolstoy),
  97
Tristan (Mann), 25
Trollope, Anthony, 111
Turgenev, Ivan, 27, 32, 33, 38, 46,
  64, 75-76, 95, 102, 109
"Turgenev and Tolstoy" (James),
  149
Two Hussars, 8, 20
Tyutchev, F. I., 39, 40, 64

U

"Unity of *War and Peace*, The"
  (Cook), 2

V

Velasquez, 113
Vermeer, 113
Vinogradov, P. G., 109
Virgil, 132
Voguls, 55
Voltaire, 18

W

Wagner, R., 29, 55
War and Peace, 2, 4, 6-7, 19, 22, 24,
  34, 38, 42, 44, 53, 59-62, 67, 68,
  69, 71, 73, 74, 75, 87-90, 96, 102,
  111, 126, 160
  as epic, 22-23, 70-71, 79-85
    passim
  as idyll of nobility, 98-99, 100
  autobiographical elements in,
    95-98
  and decentralization, technique of,
    71-72
  form, 71-72
  manners, significance of, 23-24
  narrative devices, 7, 59-62
  national destiny, theme of,
    122

War and Peace
(*continued*)
   rebirth, theme of, 111-22 *passim*,
     163-72
   structure, 23-24, 71-74,
     116-22
   style, 102-10 *passim*
Waugh, Evelyn, 43
What is Art?, 21, 41-42, 54-55
"Who Should Teach Whom To
  Write: We the Peasant Children or
  the Peasant Children Us?", 54
"Wood Felling, The," 53, 67, 69

Y

Yasnaya Polyana, 14, 95, 99, 101
Yasnaya Polyana, 34-35
Youth, 11, 32, 36, 65-67, 70
   autobiographical elements in, 11,
     36, 65-67, 68
   narrative style of, 76-77
   structure, 68-69

Z

Zola, Émile, 55, 78

MARK TWAIN
A Collection of Critical Essays
Edited by HENRY NASH SMITH

A

Adams, Brooks, 173
Adams, Clover, 159
Adams, Henry, 9, 159-74 *passim*
Adams, John Quincy, 165
Adventure in Remote Seas, An,
  169
Adventures of Huckleberry Finn, The,
  6-8, 11, 12, 29, 31, 47-63, 64, 68,
  83-100, 101-16, 124, 127, 128,
  130-36, 146, 163
  and British culture, 113-16
  characterization, 92-94, 97-100
  dual perception of nature, theme of,
    58-60, 112-14
  morality, theme of, 88-93
  narrative technique of, 91-92
  and *Oliver Twist* (Dickens), 112-16
  plot development, 83-100, 101-6
  point of view in, 56-60, 95-97
  quest for freedom, theme of, 84-
    86, 96-97, 101-6
  racial stereotypes in, 101-11
  social values, theme of, 86-88
  style, 47-50, 55-60
  superstition, theme of, 101-8
  and *The Tragedy of Pudd'nhead
    Wilson*, 130-36
Adventures of Mark Twain, The
  (Allen), 67
Adventures of Tom Sawyer, The, 8,
  12, 31, 35-36, 48, 53-54, 60-61, 64-
  82, 101, 108, 146

autobiographical aspects of, 64-82
literary sources for, 71-82
Aldrich, Thomas Bailey, 76-78
Alger, Horatio, 79
Allen, Jerry, 67
America's Coming of Age (Brooks),
  3
Anderson, Sherwood, 41
"Appreciation" (Breton), 5
Aquinas, Saint Thomas, 172
Arnold, Matthew, 3, 4, 25, 120, 162
Asselineau, Roger, 5
Auden, W. H., 138

B

Bailey, James M., 78
Beecher, Henry Ward, 77
Bellamy, Edward, 118
Bellamy, Gladys, 120
"Benito Cereno" (Melville), 137
Benjamin, Judah P., 2
Benson, Ivan, 7
Blair, Walter, 7, 10, 11, 84, 121
Bostonians, The (James), 174
Bowen, Will, 66, 69
Boyesen, H. H., 43
Boy's Manuscript, 70, 76, 80
Brashear, Minnie M., 7, 11, 34
Breen, Henry, 72-73
Brooks, Van Wyck, 3-8 *passim*,
  10
Browne, Charles Farrar (pseud. Arte-
  mus Ward), 2, 13

Brownell, Francis, 109
Bryan, William Jennings, 169
Burdette, Robert J., 78
Burnham, Tom, 125
Byrd, William, 41, 44

C

Canby, Henry S., 5-6
Cannibalism in the Cars, 18
Carlyle, Thomas, 98
"Celebrated Jumping Frog of Calaveras
  County, and Other Sketches, The,"
  128
Cervantes, Miguel de, 32, 96
Chesterton, G. K., 138
"Christmas Fireside. For Good Little
  Girls and Boys, by Grandfather
  Twain, The," 78
Clark, Charles H., 74
Clemens, Jane, 75
Clemens, John Marshall, 165
Clemens, Orion, 19, 40-41, 124
Clemens, Samuel Langhorne (*pseud.*
  Mark Twain):
    and Adams, Henry, 159-74
    alienation of, 159-73
    and American culture, 3-6, 9-10,
      160-74
    autobiographical aspects, in works
      of, 64-82, 146-58
    and catastrophe, theme of, 149-53
    and commercial exploitation, 22-27
    and failure, 144-47
    and landscape description, problem
      of, 47-63
    life of, 32-35, 159-73
    and machines, obsession with,
      124-26, 163-65
    personality of, 40-46, 69-71
    and personal tragedy, effect of,
      140-58
    philosophy of, 147-48, 159-62,
      170-73
    politics of, 160-66, 172-74
    psychology of, 117-29, 140-58
    realism of, 29-37
    and Satan, perception of, 156-58

and satire, concept of, 19-20
and the stranger, in works of,
  128-29
and the voyage, image of, 166-70
and western humor, concept of,
  13-21, 38-39
and writing, function of, 143-45
Clemens, Samuel Langhorne, works
by: (*see* main entries for starred
items)
    Adventure in Remote Seas, An,
      169
    *Adventures of Huckleberry Finn,
      The*,* 6-8, 11, 12, 29, 31, 47-63,
      64, 68, 83-100, 101-16, 124, 127,
      128, 130-36, 146, 163
    Adventures of Tom Sawyer, The,*
      8, 12, 31, 35-36, 48, 53-54, 60-61,
      64-82, 101, 108, 146
    Boy's Manuscript, 70, 76, 80
    Cannibalism in the Cars, 18
    "Celebrated Jumping Frog of
      Calaveras County, and Other
      Sketches, The," 128
    "Christmas Fireside, The. For Good
      Little Girls and Boys, by Grand-
      father Twain," 78
    *Connecticut Yankee in King Arthur's
      Court, A*,* 3, 4, 9, 10, 25, 26, 34,
      99, 117-29, 141, 162
    "Cow, The" 80
    Curious Republic of Gondour, The,
      161
    Double-Barrelled Detective Story, A,
      4, 24
    Dutch Nick Massacre, The, 18
    Enchanted Sea Wilderness, The,
      169
    Following the Equator, 143
    Gilded Age, The, 79
    "Huck Finn and Tom Sawyer among
      the Indians," 85
    Innocents Abroad, The, 2, 4, 20, 25-
      26, 36, 40-42, 50, 68-69, 102, 122
    *Killing of Julius Caesar "Localized,"
      The*, 18
    Life on the Mississippi,* 48-58, 61,
      98-99, 163

Clemens, Samuel Langhorne, works by:
(*continued*)
  Lionizing Murderers, 18
  Mysterious Stranger, The, 8-9, 27,
    99, 128, 131, 156, 168, 171
  New Crime, A, 18
  "Old times on the Mississippi," 49-
    50, 53, 64-65, 67-68, 71, 79, 123
  *Personal Recollections of Joan of
    Arc*, 13
  Prince and the Pauper, The, 27, 34,
    136
  Roughing It,* 2, 10, 14, 31, 40-46,
    50, 68, 75, 123
  "Story of Mamie Grant, the Child-
    Missionary, The," 88
  "Story of the Bad Little Boy Who
    Did Not Come to Grief, The,"
    78
  "Story of the Good Little Boy
    Who Did Not Prosper, The,"
    78
  Tom Sawyer Abroad, 146
  Tom Sawyer, Detective, 132, 146
  *Tragedy of Pudd'nhead Wilson,
    The*,* 9, 31, 128, 130-39, 146
  Tramp Abroad, A, 23, 122, 173
  What Is Man?, 147-57 *passim*,
    171-72
  "Woman wid de Gold'n Arm, De,"
    109
Cleveland, Grover,
  165
*Connecticut Yankee in King Arthur's
  Court, A*, 3, 4, 9, 10, 25, 26, 34, 99,
  117-29, 141, 162
  machines, theme of, 124-26
  and the psychology of Mark Twain,
    117-29
Constantine the Great, 165
Cooper, James Fenimore, 9, 36, 42-43,
  85, 136
"Cow, The," 80
Cox, James M., 8, 10
Crane, Mrs. Theodore, 126
Crane, Theodore, 125
Curious Republic of Gondour, The,
  161

D

Davis, Jefferson, 2
DeVoto, Bernard, 4-10 *passim*, 37, 68,
  70, 80-81, 101, 169
Dickens, Charles, 21, 71, 74, 112-16,
  132
Diocletian, 165
Dividing Line (Byrd), 44
Don Quixote (Cervantes), 32, 96
Dostoevsky, Fyodor, 21
Double-Barrelled Detective Story, A,
  4, 24
Doyle, Arthur Conan, 138
Dreiser, Theodore, 30, 46
Dumas, Alexander, 73, 95
Dutch Nick Massacre, The, 18

E

Eddy, Mary Baker, 120
Education of Henry Adams, The
  (Adams), 160-63, 166, 170
Eggleston, Edward, 71-72
Ellison, Ralph, 106-7, 109-10
Emerson, Ralph Waldo, 168
Enchanted Sea Wilderness, The,
  169

F

Faraday, Michael, 171
Faulkner, William, 9, 132, 136-37
Ferguson, DeLancey, 7, 67
Fiedler, Leslie, 9, 10
Following the Equator, 143
Frank, Waldo, 3
French Revolution (Carlyle), 98-99
Freud, Sigmund, 18

G

George, Henry, 162
Georgia Scenes (Longstreet), 75
"Georgia Theatrics" (Longstreet), 75
Gilded Age, The, 79
"Gold Bug, The" (Poe), 74
Gould, Jay, 162

Grant, Ulysses S., 24-25, 33, 141, 146, 160, 166
Gray, Thomas, 73

H

Harris, George W., 11, 78
Harris, Joel Chandler, 109-10
Harte, Bret, 11, 13, 36, 43, 71-72
Hay, John, 172
Henry Adams: An Introduction and Interpretation (Hochfield), 160
History of the United States (Adams), 160-62, 170
Hochfield, George, 160
Hoffman, Daniel G., 11
Holland, Josiah G., 4
Holmes, Oliver Wendell, 72
Hoosier Schoolmaster, The (Eggleston), 71
"Horse-Swap, The" (Longstreet), 44
Howells, William Dean, 2, 7, 10, 21, 25-26, 43, 44, 53, 71, 76, 117-18, 127, 144, 172
"Huck Finn and Tom Sawyer among the Indians," 85
Hugo, Victor, 21

I

Ibsen, Henrik, 19
Innocents Abroad, The, 2, 4, 20, 25-26, 36, 40-42, 50, 68-69, 102, 122

J

Jackson, Andrew, 165
James, Henry, 173-74
James, William, 172
Jefferson, Thomas, 171
Joan of Arc, 74, 162, 165
Johnston, John D., 41

K

Kerr, Orpheus C., 13
Killing of Julius Caesar "Localized," The, 18

King, Clarence, 172

L

Langdon, Olivia, 70, 124
Law of Civilization and Decay, The (Adams), 173
Leary, Lewis, 5
Leathers, Jesse M., 1-2
Leaves of Grass (Whitman), 26
Le Breton, Maurice, 5
Lewis, Charles B., 78
Lewis, Sinclair, 46
Lewisohn, Ludwig, 24
Life and Sayings of Mrs. Partington (Shillaber), 75
Life of Albert Gallatin, The (Adams), 160
Life on the Mississippi, **48-58**, 61, 98-99, 163
  dual perception of nature, theme of, 49-52, 55, 58
  style, 49-55
Lincoln, Abraham, 2, 41
Lionizing Murderers, 18
Literary Reputation of Mark Twain, The (Asselineau), 5
Longstreet, Augustus, 44, 75
Looking Backward (Bellamy), 118
Luck of Roaring Camp and Other Sketches, The (Harte), 43, 71-72
Lynn, Kenneth, 10

M

Madison, James, 171
Mark Twain: A Biography (ed. Paine), 66, 109, 140, 147
Mark Twain: Man and Legend (Ferguson), 7
Mark Twain, Son of Missouri (Brashear), 7, 11
Mark Twain: The Man and His Work (Wagenknecht), 7
Mark Twain & Huck Finn (Blair), 11
Mark Twain and Southwestern Humor (Lynn), 10

Mark Twain at Work (DeVoto), 7-8
"Mark Twain Himself" (Canby), 5
Mark Twain's America (DeVoto), 4, 5, 7-8
Mark Twain's Burlesque Patterns (Rogers), 11
Mark Twain's Western Years (Benson), 7
Marx, Leo, 10
McKinley, William, 166
Melville, Herman, 4, 9, 46, 51-52, 117, 137
Milton, John, 73
Moby Dick (Melville), 52
Modern English Literature: Its Blemishes and Defects (Breen), 72-73
Molière, 73
Monroe, James, 171
Mrs. Partington's Knitting Work (Shillaber), 75
Mysterious Stranger, The, 8-9, 27, 99, 128, 131, 156, 168, 171

N

Nasby, Petroleum, 13
Native American Humor (Blair), 7
New Crime, A, 18

O

"Old Times on the Mississippi," 49-50, 53, 64-65, 67-68, 71, 79, 123
Oldtown Folks (Stowe), 71-72
Oliver Twist (Dickens), 112-16
Ordeal of Mark Twain, The (Brooks), 3, 4-5, 7
Outcasts of Poker Flat, The (Harte), 43

P

Paine, Albert B., 2, 7, 13-14, 17-18, 20, 24, 27-28, 65, 66, 70, 76, 81, 109, 140
Paine, Thomas, 34
Parrington, Vernon, 120, 174

Pearson, Karl, 168
Personal Memoirs (Grant), 24-25, 33, 141, 146
Personal Recollections of Joan of Arc, 13
Pierre (Melville), 117
"Pilot and the Passenger: Landscape Conventions and the Style, The" (Marx), 10
Poe, Edgar Allen, 74, 138
Pope, Alexander, 73
Porter, William T., 43
Prince and the Pauper, The, 27, 34, 136
Progress and Poverty (George), 162
Pudd'nhead Wilson (*see Tragedy of Pudd'nhead Wilson, The*)

R

Rogers, Franklin R., 11
Rogers, Henry, 126
Romeo and Juliet (Shakespeare), 108
Roughing It, 2, 10, 14, 31, 40-46, 50, 68, 75, 123
  social values in, 40-46
  violence, theme of, 43-45

S

Salomon, Roger, 10
Sam Lawson's Fireside Stories (Stowe), 71
Santayana, George, 4
Schmidt, Paul, 45
Scott, Walter, 36
Shakespeare, William, 73, 108, 136, 171
Shillaber, Benjamin P., 11, 75, 77-78
Smith, Henry Nash, 45
Sterne, Laurence, 38
Story of a Bad Boy, The (Aldrich), 76-77
"Story of Mamie Grant, the Child-Missionary, The," 78
"Story of the Bad Little Boy Who Did Not Come to Grief, The," 78

"Story of the Good Little Boy Who Did Not Prosper, The," 78
Stowe, Harriet Beecher, 36, 71-72, 122
Swift, Jonathan, 38
"Symbols of Despair, The" (DeVoto), 5

T

Tale of Two Cities, A (Dickens), 74
Tanner, Tony, 8-9
Tarkington, Booth, 68
Taylor, Annie, 79
Tennyson, Alfred, 4
Thackeray, William Makepeace, 11
Theory of the Leisure Class, The (Veblen), 174
Thoreau, Henry David, 41-42, 51-52, 127
Tilden, Samuel Jones, 171
Tocqueville, Alexis de, 46
Tom Sawyer Abroad, 146
Tom Sawyer, Detective, 132, 146
Tragedy of Pudd'nhead Wilson, The, 9, 31, 128, 130-39, 146
   and *The Adventures of Huckleberry Finn*, 130-36
   chivalry, theme of, 134-38
   freedom, theme of, 132-34
   miscegenation, theme of, 136-38
   symbolism of black and white in, 136-37

Tramp Abroad, A, 23, 122, 173
Tuckey, John S., 9
Turner, Frederick Jackson, 3, 4, 10
Twain, Mark (*see* Clemens, Samuel Langhorne)
Twain and the Image of History (Salomon), 10
Twichell, Joseph Hopkins, 143-44

V

Veblen, Thorstein, 174
Voltaire, 34

W

Wagenknecht, Edward, 7
Walden, or Life in the Woods (Thoreau), 41-42, 51-52
Ward, Artemus (*see* Browne, Charles Farrar)
Warner, Charles Dudley, 78
Washington, George, 79
Weaver, Raymond, 4
Webster, Charles L., 124
Wecter, Dixon, 69, 74
What Is Man?, 147-57 *passim*, 171-72
Whitman, Walt, 26, 41, 173
"Woman wid de Gold'n Arm, De," 109

Y

Young, Brigham, 40

VIRGIL

A Collection of Critical Essays
Edited by STEELE COMMAGER

A

Aeneid, 1, 4-13, 20, 41-61, **63-182**
  Allecto, concept of, 177-82
  awareness, theme of, 77-79
  characterization, 76-81
  and Chaucer, works of, 41-42
  cosmic symbolism in, 94-100,
    172-74
  death-journey, theme of, 149-51,
    154-62
  death-resurrection, theme of, 90-94
  and epic poetry, concept of, 54-61,
    180-82
  fate, theme of, 12-13, 83-87, 94-
    100, 112-22
  father-son relationship, theme of,
    147-49
  flame, imagery of, 138-40
  the golden bough, symbolism of,
    151-63
  the hero, concept of, 100-106
  historical aspects of, 109-23,
    145-48, 164-73
  horse as serpent, comparison of,
    129-31
  ideological aspects of, 92-96
  and the *Iliad* (Homer), 100-106,
    107-9, 112-13, 117, 174-82
  imagery and action in, 43-52,
    165-67
  inner experience, theme of, 143-56,
    160-63
  Laocoon passage, symbolism of,
    126-28
  magic, theme of, 156-60
  metaphorical parallels in, 124-28,
    130-32
  and the *Odyssey* (Homer), 65,
    68-72, 75-80, 89-106, 112-13,
    116-21, 174-82
  political aspects of, 71-74, 170-73
  problems of translation, 41-52
  psychological aspects of, 89-106
  rebirth, symbolism of, 137-41
  serpents, symbolism of, 124-42
  sleep, symbolism of, 131-33
  structure, 89-92, 96-97, 104-6,
    124-40, 143-58
  suffering, theme of, 117-22
  time and space, theme of, 63-64
  transition, theme of, 64-65
  Tree of Life, symbolism of, 158-60
  violence, symbolism of, 134-37
Aeneid, Die Dichtkunst Virgils
  Poeschl), 42
Aeneidea II (Henry), 126
Aeschylus, 142
Antony, Mark, 4, 10, 71, 114-15,
  171
Apollonius of Rhodes, 75, 164-65
Ars Poetica (Vida), 59
Augustus, Emperor, 2-3, 8, 10, 19, 31,
  36, 59, 68, 71, 86-87, 93, 103-4, 111,
  114-15, 117, 120, 146, 169,
  171-73

B

Baudelaire, Charles, 39
Belasco, David, 143
Beowulf, 54-55
Biblical references, 71-74
Bovie, Palmer, 3
Brutus, Lucius Junius, 86
Bukis of Eneados (Douglas), 45-46

C

Caesar, Julius, 2-4, 59, 68, 71-72, 86,
    93-94, 171
Callimachus, 16, 23
Camillus, Marcus Furius, 86
Camões, Luiz Vaz de, 59
Catiline, 71, 171, 176
Cato, 86, 171-72
Cato Minor (Plutarch), 171
Catullus, 132
Charlemagne, 58
Chaucer, Geoffrey, 41-42
Cicero, 38, 134, 171, 173
Cleopatra, 4, 9, 114-15
Conington, J., 129, 152
Coniuratio Catilinae (Sallust), 171
Cromwell, Oliver, 59

D

Dante Alighieri, 10, 46, 71, 177
Doré, Gustave, 39
Douglas, Gawin, 42, 45-46, 48
Dryden, John, 6, 10, 43, 45, 47

E

Eclogues, 1-2, 14-31, 89-94, 174-75
    death-resurrection, theme of, 90-
        94
    defeat of poetry, theme of, 28-30
    and Greek culture, 25-27
    and Homer, works of, 92-94
    myth and reality in, 14-26
    psychological aspects of, 89-94
    the soul, concept of, 22-23
    structure, 90-91
    and Theocritus' poetry, 17-22
Eliot, T. S., 45, 83
Ennius, 62-63, 75, 178, 180
Étude sur Virgile (Saint-Beuve), 174
Euripides, 179

F

Faustus, Perellius, 75
Fergusson, Francis, 48
Frazer, J. G., 152, 156-57

G

Gallus, 16-17, 21, 28-30
Georgics, 1-5, 10-11, **28-40,** 48, 73,
    89-94, 134, 138-41, 173-74
    death-resurrection, theme of, 90-94
    defeat of poetry, theme of, 28-31
    and Homer, works of, 92-94
    metaphorical parallels in, 138-41
    metaphysical aspects of, 38-40
    political aspects of, 35-38
    psychological aspects of, 89-94
    spiritual aspects of, 30-32
    structure, 90-91
    tragedy, symbolism of, 173-74
    work, theme of, 32-38
Giono, Jean, 38
Goethe, Johann, 71, 166, 174
Greene, Thomas, 5
Guinach, Kevin, 111

H

Hebbel, Friedrich, 166
Heinze, Richard, 177-78
Henry, J., 126, 131
Herodotus, 62
Heroides (Ovid), 132
Heyne, C. G., 152
Homer, 6, 8, 12-13, 17, 18, 20, 45-46,
    54-59, 62-67, 68-72, 75-81, 86, 89-
    106, 107-9, 112-20, 134, 150, 158,
    164, 168-69, 174-82 *passim*
Horace, 3, 5, 9, 18, 24, 28, 95, 171
House of Fame, The (Chaucer), 41-42

Humphries, Rolfe, 43, 49

I

Iliad (Homer), 13, 17, 20, 55, 62, 67, 75, 81, 89-106, 107-9, 112-13, 117, 164, 168, 174-82
Italicus, Silius, 139

J

James, Henry, 44, 47
Juvenal, 47

K

Kalevala, 55
Kapp, Ernst, 14
Knox, Bernard, 42
Kökeritz, Helge, 48

L

Layamon, 62
Lewis, C. Day, 43, 49, 51
Lucilius, 15
Lucretius, 33, 37, 75, 128

M

Macbeth (Shakespeare), 125
Mackail, J. W., 128-29
Macrobius, Ambrosius Theodosius, 11
Maecenas, 28, 36-37
Manlius (pseud. Torquatus), 86
Marcellus, Marcus Claudius, 86-87
Maximen und Reflexionen (Goethe), 166
Menander, 19
Milton, John, 47, 54-55, 59, 63
Mummius, Lucius, 86

N

Naevius, 62-63
Newman, Cardinal John Henry, 13

Norden, E., 152, 156-57, 178
"Notes on Elizabethan Classicists" (Pound), 46
Numa, Pompilius, 86

O

Octavian (*see* Augustus)
Odes (Horace), 5, 9, 18, 171
Odyssey (Homer), 6, 8, 13, 18, 20, 55, 65, 68-72, 75-80, 86, 89-106, 112-13, 116-21, 150, 158, 164, 174-82
Ovid, 132

P

Paradise Lost (Milton), 54
Paulus, Lucius Aemilius, 86
Pindar, 155
Piranesi, Giambattista, 39
Plato, 16, 71, 173
Plutarch, 171
Poeschl, Victor, 42
Pollio, 28
Polybius, 14, 17
Pompey, 86
Pound, Ezra, 42, 46-47
Poussin, Nicolas, 30
Propertius, 130
Punica (Italicus), 139

Q

Quintilius, 5

R

Robert of Gloucester, 62
Roland de La Platière, Jean Marie, 54-55, 57-58, 60
Rolland, Romain, 168
Rothstein, Max, 130
Rousseau, Jean-Jacques, 33

S

Sainte-Beuve, Charles Augustin, 69, 174

Sallust, 171
Schiller, Johann, 166, 181
Schlegel, August Wilhelm von, 181
Seneca, 33, 132-33
"Serpent and the Flame" (Knox), 42
Servius, 132, 152, 174
Shakespeare, William, 42, 125, 142
Shepherds of Arcadia (Poussin), 30
Song of Roland, 54-55
Stesichorus, 17-19
Sulla, 71
Symbolism:
    in the *Georgics,* 173-74
    in the *Aeneid,* 94-100, 124-42,
        151-63, 172-74

T

Tagebücher (Hebbel), 166
Tasso, Torquato, 59
Theocritus, 15-22, 175
Thucydides, 62, 171
Torquatus (*see* Manlius)
Troades (Seneca), 133
Tullus, Hostilius, 86

V

Varus, Alfenus, 28
Vida, Marco Girolamo, 59
Virgil:
    and allegory, development of,
        24-27, 171-72
    Arcadia, concept of, 14-27, 28-30

cosmic symbolism of, 94-100,
    172-74
epic poetry, concept of, 53-63,
    180-82
and Greek culture,
    25-27
the hero, concept of, 5-8, 57-61,
    92-94, 100-106
and Homer, 20-22, 55-59, 62-67,
    89-106, 107-9, 112-20, 174-82
and musical shepherds, development
    of, 17-22
philosophy of, 173-74
politics of, 2-5
and the psychological narrative,
    89-106
the soul, concept of, 22-24
spiritual outlook of, 28-32
themes, in works of, 1-5, 173-82
and Theocritus, 15-22
work, concept of, 32-38
Virgil, works by:
    Aeneid, 1, 4-13, 20, 41-61, 63-
        182
    Eclogues, 1-2, 14-31, 89-94,
        174-75
    Georgics, 1-5, 10-11, 28-40, 48, 73,
        89-94, 134, 173-74
Voss, Johann Heinrich, 15
Vraies Richesses (Giono), 38

W

Wolf, Friedrich, 181

VOLTAIRE

A Collection of Critical Essays
Edited by WILLIAM F. BOTTIGLIA

A

Agathocle, 127
Aiguillon, Duke and Duchess d', 44,
   115, 120
Aldenburg, Charlotte Sophie von, 52-
   53, 55
Alembert, Jean Le Rond d', 23, 27,
   47-48, 51-52, 54-55, 106, 108, 110,
   111, 113-14, 122
Ally, J. A. Honoré de Rochefort d',
   62
Anecdotes sur Fréron, 26, 29
Annales de l'Empire, 78, 79
Annet, Peter, 69-76 *passim*
Argence, M., 39
Argens, Marquis d', 20, 60-61
Argenson, M. P. de Voyer, Comte d',
   20, 116
Argental, M. d', 22, 37, 43, 44, 66,
   77, 109
Arouet, François Marie (*see* Voltaire)
Aumont, Duke d', 36, 44

B

Barre, Chevalier de la, 15, 22, 23
Baudelaire, Charles, 38
Bayle, Pierre, 67, 68, 72, 73, 108
Beaumarchais, P. A. Caron de,
   47
Beaumelle, M. La, 27
Bélisaire (Marmontel), 60
Bellessort, André, 151-52

Benedict XIV, 37
Bentinck, Countess (*see* Aldenburg,
   Charlotte Sophie von)
Berl, Emmanuel, 102-3
Bernis, Cardinal de, 24
Bible enfin expliquée, 68
Bigex, M., 54
Blet, Abbé, 58
Bolingbroke, Henry St. John, 71, 73,
   106-7
Bossuet, J. B., 85, 119
Boyer, Bishop, 19-20

C

Calas, Jean, 15, 22, 39, 117
Calmet, Dom, 68, 72
Candide, 32, **87-111**, 114, 154, 155
   conclusion of, 103-11
   evil, problem of, 88-92
   satire and parody in, 89
Carré, J.-R., 153
Castel, M., 67
Catherine II, 36, 39, 40, 47, 123,
   144
Ce qu'on ne fait pas–, 105
Chabanon de Maugris, 39, 61
Chalotais, General La, 115, 120
Charles XII, 81
Châtelet, Emilie du, 36, 40, **64-68**, 70,
   101, 102, 142
Chaussée, Nivelle de la, 66
Choiseul, Duke de, 118, 120, 121-22,
   143, 144

Christianity, Voltaire's views on, 20-
    25, 69-76, 107-8, 140-49 *passim*
Christianity as Old as Creation
    (Tindal), 70, 72
Christin, M., 54
Chubb, Thomas, 70, 71
Church *vs.* state, Voltaire's views on,
    133-34
Cicero, 33, 34, 67, 68
Cideville, M., 37, 53, 105
Clarke, Samuel, 66, 67, 68, 70, 142,
    144
Claudel, Paul, 39
Clement XIII, 37
Collins, Anthony, 70-76 *passim*
Condorcet, Marquis de, 84, 111, 122,
    129, 130
Constitutional absolutism, 8, 11,
    112-30
Copernican revolution, 9, 12
Corneille, Marie, 39, 53-54, 58
Corneille, Pierre, 66
Correspondance, 18-30 *passim*, 31-63,
    108
Cramer, Gabriel, 52
Crassy brothers, 15
Cromwell, Oliver, 81
Crouslé, Léon, 152

D

Damilaville, M. de, 18, 21, 39, 43,
    111, 115
Dangeau, Marquis de, 79
Deffand, Mme. du, 38, 39, 40, 43, 64,
    121, 143, 157
Deism, 9-10, 66, 67-68, 69-76, 140-49
    passim
Denis, Marie Louise, 48, 54, 56-60,
    62
Descartes, René, 9
Desfontaines, Abbé, 26, 29, 51
Destouches, Philippe, 66
Determinism (*see* Free will *vs.*
    determinism)
Dialogues entre A, B, C, 73, 155, 156,
    159

Diatribe à l'auteur des Ephémérides,
    129
Diatribe du docteur Akakia, 26
Dictionnaire philosophique, 18, 22, 32,
    71, 75, 79, 158-64 *passim*
Diderot, Denis, 19, 40, 106, 108, 110,
    118, 122, 145
Dîner du Comte de Boulainvilliers,
    21-22
Discours en vers sur l'homme, 103,
    164
Dorat, M., 61-62
Drama, Voltaire's work in, 66, 127
    (*see also* titles of individual plays)
Dryden, John, 72
Du Barry, Mme., 120
Du Pont de Nemours, M., 36
Dupuits family, 53-54, 59, 61
Duvernet, Abbé, 25

E

Eliot, T. S., 5
*Embellissements de la ville de Cache-
    mire*, 160
Encyclopaedists, 107-10, 157
Encyclopédie, 11, 101, 108-10
Erasmus, 33, 34
Essai sur les moeurs, 78, 81-82, 83,
    106
Eudoxie (Chabanon), 61
*Examen critique des apologistes de la
    religion chrétienne*, 68
*Examen critique du Nouveau Testa-
    ment*, 68
Examen de la Genèse (Châtelet),
    68
Examen de la religion, 68
*Examen important de milord Boling-
    broke*, 68, 73
*Extrait des sentiments de Jean
    Meslier*, 22, 73-74

F

Fabricius, J. A., 69-70, 72
Félicité des temps, La, 105

Fénelon, F. de La Mothe-, 145
Ferney, Voltaire's years at, 53-63
Flaubert, Gustave, 38, 103
Fleury, Duke de, 44, 72
Fontenelle, B. de, 36, 73, 140
France, Anatole, 140
Frederick II, 18, 26, 27, 36, 39, 40,
   42, 46-47, 53, 67, 68, 78, 101, 102,
   109, 142, 144, 159
Free will *vs.* determinism, Voltaire's
   views on, 10-11, 66-67, 101, 151
Fréron, Élie Catherine, 26

G

Gèvres, Duke de, 44
Gide, André, 39
Government, Voltaire's views on,
   132-33, 160-61
Graffigny, Mme. de, 64
Grafton, Duke of, 41
*Grounds and Reasons of the Christian
   Religion* (Collins), 70
Guénée, Abbé, 73
Guerre civile de Genève, La, 55-56,
   60
Gulliver's Travels (Swift), 106

H

Harpe, M. la, 54, 56, 60, 61
Havens, George R., 92
Helvétius, Claude Adrien, 39, 67,
   68
Hénault, C. J. F., 67, 118
Hennin, Pierre Michel, 60
Henri IV, 119
Henriade, La, 104
Hermenches, Constant d', 53
Histoire de Charles XII, 78, 79, 80,
   127
Histoire de Russie, 77-78, 79, 80
Histoire du Parlement de Paris, 78,
   118-20, 125
Historical writings, of Voltaire, 15-16,
   67, 77-86
History of Saint Paul (Annet), 71-72
Holbach, P. T. d', 70, 72

Homer, 162
Hornoy, M. d', 53, 58
Hume, David, 106, 110

I

Independent Whig, The, 72
Innate ideas, Voltaire's rejection of,
   10

J

James, Henry, 38
Jansenism, 103, 113-30 *passim,* 154,
   157
Jesuits, 113-30 *passim*
Joyce, James, 38

K

Koenig, M., 26

L

Labat, M., 53
La Bruyère, Jean de, 163
Laleu, M., 53
Lally, Comte de, 15
Lamartine, Louis de, 155
La Mettrie, J. O., de, 67, 68
La Rochefoucauld, Duke de,
   163
Law and legal procedures,
   Voltiare's views on, 26-27, 136-37,
   160
Lawrence, D. H., 39
Leblanc, Abbé, 64
Leibnitz, G. W. von, 67
Lemaître, Jules, 152
Lenclos, Ninon de, 35
Lenglet, M., 67
Leriche, F. L. H., 62
Lespinasse, Mlle. de, 40
*Lettre à l'auteur des Honnêtetés lit-
   téraires,* 80
Lettre de l'archevêque de Cantobéri,
   60

Lettre d'un Turc, 105
Lettres anglaises, 151
Lettres d'amour de Voltaire à sa nièce
   (Besterman), 48-49, 52
Lettres persanes (Montesquieu),
   19
Lettres philosophiques, 19, 106, 127
Lettres provinciales (Pascal), 113
Life of David (Annet), 71, 72, 75
Locke, John, 66, 67, 68, 70, 72, 142,
   144
Lois de Minos, Les, 127
Louis XI, 127
Louis XII, 127
Louis XIV, 80, 126, 127, 130
Louis XV, 114-30 *passim,* 137
Louis XVI, 129-30

M

Machault, J. B., 123
Mahomet, 20
Mairan, M., 42, 67
Malebranche, Nicolas de, 67, 68, 144
Mandeville, Bernard de, 6, 7, 68
Marmontel, Jean François, 60
Maupeou, René-Nicolas de, 117-30
   passim
Maupertuis, P. L. M. de, 25-26, 42, 67,
   101
Maurepas, Comte Jean Frédéric, 44
Mazarin, Cardinal, 119
Meslier, Jean, 68, 73-74
Middleton, Conyers, 67, 71-76
   passim
Mignot, Marie Louise (*see* Denis,
   Mme.)
Mondain, Le, 65, 104, 156
Montaigne, Michel de, 155, 162, 163
Montesquieu, Baron de, 19, 26, 67,
   84, 115-16, 131, 133, 161
Morality, Voltaire's views on, 14-15,
   162-65

N

Necker, Mme., 62
Neumann, Franz, 130

Newman, Frances, 25
Newton, Sir Isaac, 66, 67, 68, 70,
   142

O

Œdipe, 35, 141
Optimism (*see* Pessimism *vs.* optimism)

P

Palissot, Charles, 47
Panckoucke, André Joseph, 21
Pascal, Blaise, 27, 113, 153, 157,
   163
Père de la Tour, 19
Perrault, Nicolas, 73
Pessimism *vs.* optimism, in Voltaire's
   works, 11, 93, 101, 102-3, 151, 154
Peter the Great, 80, 81
Philosophy, Voltaire's interest and
   beliefs in, 66, 154-56
Piron, Alexis, 25
Poème sur la loi naturelle, 101, 104,
   164
Poème sur le désastre de Lisbonne,
   101, 107, 154
Politics, Voltaire's views on, 11-12,
   112-30
Pomaret, M. de, 29
Pomeau, René, 94, 95-96, 97, 99
Pompadour, Mme. de, 44, 121, 144
Pope, Alexander, 67, 68, 72
Progress, Voltaire's views on, 15-16
Proust, Marcel, 38, 39

Q

Questions sur l'Encyclopédie, 106,
   151

R

Racine, Jean, 66
Racle, M., 54
Religion chrétienne analysée, 68
Remarques sur Pascal, 151, 154, 156

Renan, Ernest, 34
Richelieu, Duke de, 58-59, 62, 81, 85, 119, 127
Rieu, Henri, 53, 56
Riggisberg, Erlach von, 55
Rome sauvée, 104
Rousseau, Jean-Jacques, 18-19, 22, 25, 26, 29, 40, 47, 82, 84, 101, 130, 131, 133, 145, 147, 161
Rousseau, Pierre, 54

S

Saint-Julien, Mme. de, 21
Saint-Pierre, Bernardin, 151
Sareil, Jean, 92
Satire, Voltaire's use of, 8 (*see also Candide*)
Saül, 72, 74
Saurin, M., 22
Scarmentado, 101
Scheme of the Literal Prophecy Considered (Collins), 70
Schlegel, A. W. von, 152
Science, Voltaire's interest in, 9, 12, 14, 67, 84, 142
Scienza Nuova (Vico), 86
Scythes, Les, 24
Séance de flagellation, 115-16, 117, 120
Sémiramis, 44
Sentiment des citoyens, 29
Sermon de J. Rossette, 148
Sermon des cinquante, 68, 73-74
Sévigné, Mme. de, 33, 34
Shakespeare, William, 66
Shaw, Bernard, 33, 34, 38-39
Siècle de Louis XIV, 21, 78, 79, 83
Siècle de Louis XV, 78
Sieyès, Abbé, 127
Sirven family, 22, 27, 39
Social reform, Voltaire's views on, 131-39, 158
Spinoza, Baruch, 9,
Staël, Mme. de, 62, 64
Suard, M., 36
Swift, Jonathan, 106

T

Tallentyre, S. G., 81
Taxation, Voltaire's views on, 134-35
Testament politique (Richelieu), 85
Thèse royale, 112-30 *passim*
Thieriot, M., 19, 20, 29, 37, 43, 104, 108
Tindal, Matthew, 70-76 *passim*
Tocqueville, Alexis de, 124
Toland, John, 69-70, 71, 72, 73
Torrey, Norman L., 101, 107, 110
Traité de métaphysique, 65, 103
Traité sur la tolérance, 27, 74, 75
Tronchin family, 52
Turgot, Anne-Robert-Jacques, 84, 123, 124, 128-30, 138, 161

V

Valéry, Paul, 63
Van Dale, M., 70, 71, 72
Végobre, Manoël de, 53
Vernes, Jacob, 63, 108
Vico, Giovanni Battista, 86
Villars, Duchess de, 44
Vinet, Alexandre, 152, 155, 156
Virgil, 162
Voltaire:
    anti-Christian views, 20-25, 69-76, 107-8, 140-49 *passim*
    biographical information, 34-35, 39, 41, 53-63, 65-66
    and Châtelet, Emilie du, 36, 40, **64-68**, 70, 101, 102, 142
    on Church *vs.* state, 133-34
    on constitutional absolutism, 8, 11, **112-30**
    critical approaches to, 4-6
    critical reputation of, 13-17, 50-51, 150-53
    and deism, 9-10, 66, 67-68, **69-76**, 140-49 *passim*
    and Denis, Mme. Marie Louise, 54, 56-60, 62
    as a dramatist, 66, 127

Voltaire (*continued*):
   and the Encyclopaedists, 107-10,
      157
   at Ferney, 53-63
   on free will *vs.* determinism, 10-11,
      66-67, 101, 151
   and Frederick II, 18, 26, 27, 36,
      39, 40, 42, 46-47, 53, 67, 68, 78,
      101, 102, 109, 142, 144, 159
   on government, 132-33, 160-61
   as an historian, 15-16, 67, **77-86**
   "hypocrisy" of, 18-30 *passim*
   and Jansenism, 103, 113-30 *passim*,
      154, 157
   on law and legal procedures, 26-27,
      136-37, 160
   as a moralist, 14-15, 162-65
   persecution of, 18-30
   personality of, 14, 17, 53-63
   pessimism *vs.* optimism, 11, 93,
      101, 102-3, 151, 154
   philosophical beliefs, 66, 154-56
   as a poet, 16
   political views, 11-12, **112-30**
   and progress, idea of, 15-16
   prose style of, 16-17
   and Rousseau, J.-J., 18-19, 22, 25,
      26, 29, 47, 131, 133, 145, 161
   satiric techniques, 8 (*see also*
      Candide)
   scientific interests of, 9, 12, 14, 67,
      84, 142
   and social reform, 131-39, 158
   on taxation, 134-35
Voltaire, works by:
   Agathocle, 127
   Anecdotes sur Fréron, 26, 29
   Annales de l'Empire, 78-79
   Bible enfin expliquée, 68
   Candide, 32, **87-111**, 114, 154, 155
   Ce qu'on ne fait pas—, 105
   Correspondance, 18-30 *passim*, 31-
      63, 108
   Dialogues entre A, B, C, 73, 155,
      156, 159
   Diatribe à l'auteur de Ehpémérides,
      129
   Diatribe du docteur Akakia, 26

Dictionnaire philosophique, 18,
   22, 32, 71, 75, 79, 158-64 *passim*
Dîner du Comte de Boulainvilliers,
   21-22
Discours en vers sur l'homme, 103,
   164
*Embellissements de la ville de
   Cachemire*, 160
Encyclopédie, 11, 101, 108-10
Essai sur les moeurs, 78, 81-82,
   83, 106
*Examen critique des apologistes de
   la religion chrétienne*, 68
*Examen critique du Nouveau Testa-
   ment*, 68
Examen de la religion, 68
*Examen important de milord
   Bolingbroke*, 68, 73
*Extrait des sentiments de
   Jean Meslier*, 22, 73-74
Félicité des temps, La, 105
Guerre civile de Genève, La, 55-56,
   60
Henriade, La, 104
Histoire de Charles XII, 78, 79,
   80, 127
Histoire de Russie, 77-78, 79, 80
Histoire du Parlement de Paris,
   78, 118-20, 125
*Lettre à l'auteur des Honnêtetés
   littéraires*, 80
Lettre de l'archevêque de Cantobéri,
   60
Lettre d'un Turc, 105
Lettres anglaises, 151
Lettres philosophiques, 19, 106,
   127
Lois de Minos, Les, 127
Mahomet, 20
Mondain, Le, 65, 104, 156
Œdipe, 35, 141
Poème sur la loi naturelle,
   101, 104, 164
Poème sur le désastre de Lisbonne,
   101, 107, 154
Questions sur l'Encyclopédie, 106,
   151
Religion chrétienne analysée, 68

Voltaire works by
(*continued*)
  Saül, 72, 74
  Scarmentado, 101
  Scythes, Les, 24
  Sémiramis, 44
  Sentiment des citoyens, 29
  Sermon de J. Rossette, 148
  Sermon des cinquante, 68, 73-74
  Siècle de Louis XIV, 21, 78, 79, 83
  Siècle de Louis XV, 78
  Traité de métaphysique, 65, 103
  Traité sur la tolérance, 27, 74, 75
  Zadig, 20, 101
  Zaïre, 145

Voltairomanie, 26
Voltariana, 29

W

Wagnière, Jean Louis, 21, 29, 54, 56-58, 59, 60
Walpole, Horace, 33, 34
Wolfe, Thomas, 39
Woolston, Thomas, 68, 70-76 *passim*
Wurtemberg, Duke de, 62

Z

Zadig, 20, 101
Zaïre, 145

NATHANAEL WEST

A Collection of Critical Essays
Edited by JAY MARTIN

A

Agee, James, 162
Alger, Horatio, 115, 119, 124-25,
  128, 129, 140, 166
Americana, 32
"Anywhere Out of This World"
  (Baudelaire), 102-9
Apollinaire, Guillaume, 29
Aragon, Louis, 20
Arp, Hans, 22
As I Lay Dying (Faulkner), 21-22,
  23
Augustine, Saint, 2

B

Baal (Brecht), 19
Balso Snell (*see Dream Life of Balso
  Snell, The*)
Balzac, Honoré de, 2
Baudelaire, Charles, 17, 47, 102-9
Benchley, Robert, 9
Bergson, Henri, 46
Big Money, The (Dos Passos), 142
"Bird and Bottle," 132-37
Bottom Dogs (Dahlberg), 21, 22, 23,
  162
Brecht, Bertolt, 19
Breton, André, 4, 20, 35
Broom, 21
Brounoff, George, 114
Bunyan, John, 77, 80, 81, 165
Burke, Kenneth, 168

C

Cabell, James Branch, 2
Cahan, Abraham, 124
Caldwell, Erskine, 112
Call It Sleep (Roth), 27
Candide (Voltaire), 7, 125, 140
Cartoon techniques:
  in *Cool Million, A*, 44-45
  in *Miss Lonelyhearts*, 6, 43-44,
    66-67, 103
Chagall, Marc, 1
Char, René, 68
Characterization, in *Miss Lonelyhearts*,
  69-70, 71
Chekhov, Anton, 2
Chirico, Giorgio de, 68
Christ dream, use of, in *Miss Lonely-
  hearts*, 6, 23, 36-38, 87-88, 89, 95-
  100
Christ in a Gas Mask (Grosz), 22
Coates, Robert M., 3-4, 126
Cocteau, Jean, 68
Cohen, Arthur, 74
Comic devices, West's use of, 9, 14,
  126-28 (*see also* Grotesque, West's
  use of the; Violence)
  in *Cool Million, A*, 126-28
Comic Tradition in America, The
  (Lynn), 41
Communist Party, 121, 162, 165, 166,
  167-68
Conroy, Jack, 41
Contact, 23

Gold, Mike, 115
Great American Novel, The (W. C. Williams), 128
Grosz, George, 22, 27
Grotesque, West's use of the, 2, 8, 43-44, 125-27, 151
Gulliver's Travels (Swift), 7, 125

H

Hamlet (Shakespeare), 149
Hawthorne, Nathaniel, 43
Hegel, Friedrich, 20
Hellman, Lillian, 1
Hemingway, Ernest, 17, 20, 25, 26, 101, 112
Herbst, Josephine, 40, 116-17, 124, 130, 163
Herrmann, John, 21, 22, 26, 130
Hitler, Adolf, 7, 120, 123
Hollis, C. C., 109
Hollywood, West's years in, 7, 26-28, 140-42
Howells, William Dean, 8, 128

I

Iceman Cometh, The (O'Neill), 93
It Can't Happen Here (Lewis), 27, 41, 126

J

James, Henry, 17, 117, 128
James, William, 37, 47, 67, 75-90 *passim*, 163-64, 165
Jarry, Alfred, 29
Jews Without Money (Gold), 115
Johnson, Dr. Samuel, 10
Jonson, Ben, 9
Josephson, Matthew, 2, 114, 124
Joyce, James, 3, 15, 17, 104
Justine (Sade), 152

K

Kafka, Franz, 125, 127

Kapstein, I. J., 116
Klee, Paul, 4
Ku Klux Klan, 121-22

L

Last Puritan, The (Santayana), 164
Last Tycoon, The (Fitzgerald), 142
Lautréamont, Comte de, 35-36, 103, 140
Lawrence, D. H., 21
Levin, Harry, 43
Levy, Melvin, 126
Lewis, Sinclair, 22, 27, 41, 126
Lieber, Maxim, 129
Light, James, 16-17, 23, 25, 54n, 74
Little Review, The, 21
Loyola, Saint Ignatius, 87
Lynn, Kenneth S., 41

M

McAlmon, Robert, 19
Machen, Arthur, 2
Magnasco, Alessandro, 8
Maldoror (Lautréamont), 35-36
Malraux, André, 24
Man's Fate (Malraux), 24
"Man That Was Used Up, The" (Poe), 127
Marxism (*see* Communist Party)
Masson, André, 35
Maupassant, Guy de, 2
Mein Kampf (Hitler), 7, 120, 123
Melville, Herman, 43, 94, 126, 127
Milburn, George, 9
Miss Lonelyhearts, 5-6, 7, 13-14, 15, 20-26 *passim,* 31-47 *passim,* 52-65, 68-73, 91-101, 110-13, 125, 130, 140, 142, 147-48, 154, 156-58, 160, 163-66
    and "Anywhere Out of This World" (Baudelaire), 102-9
    cartoon techniques in, 6, 43-44, 66-67, 103
    characterization in, 69-70, 71

Miss Lonelyhearts (*continued*)
  Christ dream in, 6, 23, 36-38, 87-
    88, 89, 95-100
  and *Cool Million, A*, 31-47 *passim*
  and *Day of the Locust, The*, 31-47
    passim
  "Notes" to, 74-75, 77, 84, 102,
    163-64
  religious experience in, 74-90, 95-
    100, 106-8
  revisions of, 23, 52-65
  and *Waste Land, The* (Eliot), 91-
    101
Moby Dick (Melville), 94
Mysticism, in West's works, 2, 84, 86-
  87

N

*Nathanael West: An Interpretive
  Study* (Light), 16-17, 23, 25, 54n,
  74
New Masses, 166, 167
"Next Time, The" (Henry James), 117
Nietzsche, Friedrich, 39
Notes from the Underground
  (Dostoevsky), 24, 38, 149

O

Olson, Floyd, 118, 119
O'Neill, Eugene, 93

P

Pair of Underdrawers, A (Sternheim),
  22
Pearce, Charles, 124, 129
Pecora, Ferdinand, 118
Pelley, William Dudley, 122-23
Penguin Island (France), 4, 125
Perelman, Laura, 1, 3, 26, 38
Perelman, S. J., 3, 5, 7, 11-12, 26, 40,
  124, 125, 126, 162, 166, 167, 169
Persius, 10
Pessimism, in West's work, 16, 92-93
Petronius, 2
Picasso, Pablo, 4

Pierre (Melville), 126, 127
Pilgrim's Progress, The (Bunyan), 77,
  80, 81, 165
Poe, Edgar Allan, 43, 66, 127
Politics, in West's works, 161-63,
  166-69
*Portrait of the Artist as a Young Man,
  A* (Joyce), 104
Poulaille, Henri, 68
Pound, Ezra, 2, 21
Pritchett, V. S., 108
Proust, Marcel, 4
Psychology of Religion (Starbuck),
  67, 75-76, 82-83, 163
Pushkin, Aleksander, 2

R

Rabelais, François, 10
Religious experience, in *Miss Lonely-
  hearts*, 74-90, 95-100, 106-8
Revolution in Revon (Schwitters),
  22
Ribemont-Dessaignes, Georges, 29,
  68
Rimbaud, Arthur, 36, 103, 140
Rise of David Levinsky, The (Cahan),
  124
Robber Barons, The (Josephson),
  114
Rockefeller, John D., Sr., 116, 124
Roosevelt, Franklin D., 115
Root, Wells, 130
Rosa, Salvator, 8
Roth, Henry, 27
Roussel, Raymond, 29

S

Sade, Marquis de, 4, 152
Sanctuary (Faulkner), 144-46
Santayana, George, 164
Satire, techniques of, in West's works,
  39-40, 46-47, 115, 149, 166-69
Schulberg, Budd, Jr., 142
Schwartz, E. G., 108, 109
Schwitters, Kurt, 4, 22, 30
Secession, 21

Shakespeare, William, 2, 149
Silone, Ignazio, 24
Smith, Gerald L. K., 122
Socialist realism, 24-25, 41, 51, 68-
   69, 162
Spiritual Exercises, The (Loyola),
   87
Starbuck, E. D., 67, 75-76, 82-83,
   163
Stein, Gertrude, 17, 163
Sternheim, Carl, 22
Stewart, Donald Ogden, 166
Success-ideal, in West's works, 2-3,
   7, 40-42, 115-31 *passim*, 115, 119,
   124, 129, 166
Suetonius, 2
Sullivan, Frank, 9
Sun Also Rises, The (Hemingway),
   101
Surrealist techniques, West's use of, 8,
   20, 29-30, 68 (*see also* Dadaism)
   in *Dream Life of Balso Snell, The,*
      35-36
Swift, Jonathan, 7, 38-39, 125

T

Thackeray, W. M., 2
This Quarter, 21
Those Who Perish (Dahlberg), 114
Tolstoy, Leo, 2, 9, 38, 77, 81, 165
transatlantic, 21
transition, 21
Turgenev, Ivan, 2
Twain, Mark, 115
Tzara, Tristan, 35

V

Varieties of Religious Experience
   (William James), 67, 75-90 *passim,*
   163-64, 165
Violence, West's use of, 2, 4, 7-8, 15,
   43-44, 46, 50-51, 127-28, 148-49
Voltaire, 7, 125, 140

W

War and Peace (Tolstoy), 38
Waste Land, The (Eliot), 77
   and *Cool Million, A,* 124-25
   and *Miss Lonelyhearts,*
      91-101
Weinstein, Max and Anna (father and
   mother), 1, 117
West, Nathanael:
   and Alger, Horatio, 115, 119,
      124-25, 129, 140, 166
   and Baudelaire, Charles, 102-9
   biographical information, 1-3, 7,
      25-26, 116, 117
   and contemporary illusions, 4-5, 6,
      36-39, 91-101
   comic devices, use of, 9, 14,
      126-28
   critical reputation of, 10, 31, 154,
      161-62
   and Dadaism, 18, 20, 22, 25-26,
      44, 68, 163, 167
   and Dahlberg, Edward, 21, 22, 23,
      25, 114, 162
   and Dostoevsky, Fydor, 17, 23-24,
      25, 37, 38, 43, 47, 68-69, 95,
      149, 155, 166
   dream life, use of, 4, 33, 95-100,
      147
   and Eliot, T. S., 91-101, 124-25
   and fascism in America, 41, 47,
      120-23, 126, 129
   and Faulkner, William, 21-22, 23,
      25, 112, 144-46
   and Fitzgerald, F. Scott, 7, 142-43,
      161, 163
   and French symbolism, 102-5
   and the grotesque, use of, 2, 8,
      43-44, 125-27, 151
   in Hollywood, 7, 26-28, 140-42
   and James, William, 37, 47, 67, 75-
      90 *passim,* 163-64, 165
   language and style of, 13, 14, 48-49,
      52-65 *passim*
   and left-wing politics, 161-63,
      166-69
   and mysticism, 2, 84, 86-87

West, Nathanael (*continued*)
and Perelman, S. J., 3, 5, 7, 11-12, 26, 40, 124, 126, 162, 167, 169
personality of, 3-4, 11-12, 17, 21, 110-11
pessimism of, 16, 92-93
satirical techniques, use of, 39-40, 46-47, 115, 149, 166-69
and Socialist realism, 24-25, 41, 51, 68-69, 162
and the success-ideal, 2-3, 7, 40-42, 115-31 *passim*, 115, 119, 124, 129, 166
surrealistic techniques, use of, 8, 20 29-30, 35-36, 68 (*see also* Dadaism)
and violence, use of, 2, 4, 7-8, 43-44, 46, 50-51, 127-28, 148-49
and Williams, William Carlos, 21, 37, 48-49, 66, 117, 128, 163
West, Nathanael, works by:
"Bird and Bottle," 132-37
Cool Million, A, 6-7, 21, 25, 27, 31-47, 103, 114-31, 140, 149, 151-52, 158, 166-69
Day of the Locust, The, 1, 8, 13, 14, 28, 31-47 *passim*, 103, 132-37, 138-39, 140-42, 144-46, 158-60
Dream Life of Balso Snell, The, 4-5, 13-15, 17, 19, 20, 29-30, 31-47, 68, 103-4, 116, 140, 154, 155-56, 157
Miss Lonelyhearts, 5-6, 7, 13-14, 15, 20-26 *passim*, 31-47 *passim*, 52-65, 68-73, 91-101, 110-13, 125, 130, 140, 142, 147-48, 154, 156-58, 160, 163-66
What Makes Sammy Run (Schulberg), 142
Williams, William Carlos, 21, 37, 47, 48-49, 66, 128, 163
Wilson, Edmund, 1, 103, 117, 163
Winrod, Gerard B., 122
Wolfe, Humbert, 115
Wolfe, Thomas, 9
Wylie, Philip, 3

Y

Yeats, W. B., 6

Z

Zola, Émile, 51

EDITH WHARTON

A Collection of Critical Essays
Edited by IRVING HOWE

A

Aeschylus, 17, 20
Age of Innocence, The, 3, 5, 9, 10, 12, 26, 27, 28, 29, 34, 37-38, 41, 42, 63, 65, 69, 71, 72, 82, 94, 122, 135, 151, 155-61, 162-71
   costs of innocence, theme of, 159, 168-69, 171
   method, 156, 170-71
   self-sacrifice, theme of, 157
   style, 8-9
   waste, theme of, 160-61
Ambassadors, The (James), 66, 76, 101
American, The (James), 7, 95, 164
American Tragedy, An (Dreiser), 25
Anderson, Sherwood, 175
"Angel at the Grave, The," 46
Arabian Nights, 23
Aristocracy vs. merchants, theme of, 91, 106-8, 122
Aristotle, 141
Artemis to Actaeon, 21
Art of Fiction, The (James), 134
Auchincloss, Louis, 10
Auden, W. H., 18
Austen, Jane, 75, 76, 80, 83, 85, 102, 163
"Autres temps . . . ," 87

B

Babbitt (Lewis), 24, 76, 175

Backward Glance, A, 29, 62, 75, 103, 163-64, 165, 173
Balzac, Honoré de, 96, 121, 134, 144, 167, 168
"Beast in the Jungle, The" (James), 169
Belchamber (Sturgis), 62, 99, 174
Bellow, Saul, 11
Bennett, Arnold, 28
Bérénice (Racine), 160
Berenson, Bernard, 62
Berry, Walter, 62, 135, 173, 175
Billy Budd, Foretopman (Melville), 137
Bookman, The, 99
Bos, Charles du, 170
Bostonians, The (James), 8, 75, 79
Bourget, Minnie, 62
Bourget, Paul, 19, 22, 29, 62
Boyle, Kay, 81
Brooks, Van Wyck, 81
Brothers Karamazov, The (Dostoevsky), 137
Brown, E. K., 7, 8
Buccaneers, The, 30, 42
Bulwer Lytton, E. G. E. L., 165
Bunner Sisters, The, 5, 25, 26, 69, 83, 86, 93, 133
Burden, Adèle, 41

C

Cabell, J. B., 100
Campton, John, 64

Canby, Henry Seidel, 126
Caricature, use of, 4, 24, 39
Carnegie, Andrew, 91
César Birotteau (Balzac), 168
Chanler, Margaret, 41
Children, The, 40, 99
Climbers, The (Fitch), 22
Conrad, Joseph, 3, 99, 156
Costs of innocence, theme of, 159, 168-69, 171
"Coward, A," 46
Cowley, Malcolm, 81
Craft of Fiction, The (Lubbock), 97
Crosby, Harry, 81
Crucial Instances, 68
"Cup of Cold Water, A," 133
Custom of the Country, The, 4-5, 8, 12, 23-24, 30, 34, 36-37, 42, 50-53, 57, 65, 69, 71, 72, 76, 79-80, 99, 122, 175
    caricature, use of, 4, 24
    method, 51-53
    satire, 8
    social disintegration, theme of, 79
    style, 8

D

Dana, R. H., 165
Dante, 30, 75
Decoration of Houses, The, 38
Descent of Man, The, 45
Dickens, Charles, 96, 144, 165
Dos Passos, John, 175
Dostoevsky, F., 144
Dreiser, Theodore, 25
Drew, Daniel, 91
Duchesse de Langeais (Balzac), 167

E

Education of Henry Adams, The (Adams), 81
Eliot, George, 76, 80, 83, 84, 85-86, 95, 96, 149
Emerson, R. W., 8

Ethan Frome, 5, 24-25, 26, 28, 53, 69, 72, 83, 84, 92, 98, 99, 100, 101, 130-36, 137-46, 155, 162, 168
    as drama of landscape, 54, 136
    form, 68
    frustrated love, theme of, 26
    limits of responsibility, theme of, 131-32
    method, 53-55, 98-99, 134-36
    point of view in, 133-34
    self-sacrifice, theme of, 131-32
    style, 135
    and tragedy, 140-42
    waste, theme of, 130-32
Ethics (Aristotle), 141
Eugénie Grandet (Balzac), 168
Eumenides, 20, 90, 115
Europeans, The (James), 26
Exile's Return (Cowley), 81
"Experience," 21

F

Failure as spiritual victory, theme of, 92-93, 108-9, 130
Fathers and Sons (Turgenev), 102
Faulkner, William, 3, 11, 12, 81, 144, 175
Federalists, 164
Fighting France, from Dunkerque to Belfort, 64
Fiske, Jim, 152-53
Fitch, Clyde, 22
Fitzgerald, F. Scott, 11, 41, 81, 161
Flaubert, Gustave, 3, 86, 96, 144
Flowering of New England, The (Brooks), 82
Forsyte Saga, The (Galsworthy), 79
Freud, Sigmund, 4, 16
Fruit of the Tree, The, 5, 17, 21, 24, 53, 66, 71, 83, 132, 163
Frustrated love, theme of, 15, 26, 122

G

Galsworthy, John, 79, 83
Girls (Fitch), 22
Gissing, George, 15

Glimpses of the Moon, The, 5, 28, 39, 40
Gods Arrive, The, 40, 65, 71
Goethe, J. W. von, 29
Golden Bowl, The (James), 75, 95, 101
Good Housekeeping, 73
Gould, Jay, 152
Goya, 110
"Grand Bretèche, La" (Balzac), 134
Grant, Ulysses S., 163
Greater Inclination, The, 68

H

Hamilton, Alexander, 164
Hardy, Thomas, 15, 20, 74, 84
Hawthorne, Nathaniel, 1, 161, 174, 175
Hemingway, Ernest, 144, 175
Hergesheimer, J., 97
Hermit and the Wild Woman, The, 69
Herrick, Robert, 93
Hobbes, Thomas, 143
House of Mirth, The, 2, 3, 4, 11, 12-13, 19, 21, 22, 24, 26, 27, 34, 35, 38, 42, 47-50, 51, 53-55, 62, 71, 75, 76-79, 80, 92, 98, **103-18**, **119-29**, 130, 155, 173
    cost of spontaneity, theme of, 120-21
    dialogue in, 98-99
    failure as spiritual victory, theme of, 92, 108-9
    frustrated love, theme of, 26, 122
    imagery, 115
    method, 8, 12, 50-51, 119-21
    money, predominance of, 108-10, 173
    point of view, 98
    society's victim, theme of, 49-50, 66, 99, 105-6
    waste, theme of, 3, 129
House with the Green Shutters, The (Douglas), 84
Howells, W. D., 91, 100, 138, 174, 175

Hudson River Bracketed, 39, 40, 65, 71, 98, 99, 136, 163, 165
Human Nature, 39
Humières, Robert d', 62
Huxley, Aldous, 81

I

Imagery, 59
    in *Ethan Frome*, 115
    in *House of Mirth*, 136, 139
In Morocco, 64
Irony and satire, 45, 71
    in *Age of Innocence*, 151, 156-60 *passim*
    in *Custom of the Country*, 80
    in *House of Mirth*, 77, 110, 127
Irving, Washington, 64, 165
Ivory Tower, The (James), 20

J

Java Head (Hergesheimer), 97
James, Henry, 1-18 *passim*, 19, 20, 26, 28, 29, 32-33, 38, 39, 62, 64, 67, 69, 70, 71, 74, 76, 79, 83, 85, 86, 89, 90, 92, 94, 95, 96-98, 100, 101, 102, 103, 104, 112, 113, 115, 119, 134, 147-50, 159, 164, 169, 172, 174, 175
James, Henry, Sr., 8
Jewett, Sarah Orne, 83, 100
Job, Book of, 145
Joyce, James, 144
Jude the Obscure (Hardy), 74
"Justice to Edith Wharton" (Wilson), 1, 84

K

Kazin, Alfred, 130

L

La Bruyère, 27, 29
Lafayette, Madame de, 167
Lapsley, Gaillard, 174
Leavis, Q. D., 7

Lenox, 93, 94
Lewis, Sinclair, 4, 24, 78, 85, 175
Lord Jim (Conrad), 99
Lovett, Robert Morss, 70, 101
Lubbock, Percy, 9, 97-98, 101,
 124-25, 136, 162, 172-76 *passim*
Lyautey, 64

M

Madame de Mauves (James), 7, 95
Madame de Treymes, 7, 39-40, 63, 95,
 99, 164
Main Street (Lewis), 24, 76
Male Characters, treatment of, 15, 26-
 27, 70, 124, 175-76
Manhattan Transfer (Dos Passos), 175
Manners, significance of, 4, 6-7, 12,
 48-49, 69, 101, 166
Mansfield, Katherine, 169
Mansfield Park (Austen), 102
Marxism, 106
Maupassant, Guy de, 20
Melville, Herman, 1, 3, 15, 131, 165
Mendel, G., 41
Method, 8, 12, 22-23, 45-47, 101
 dialogue, use of, 98-99
 inventory of furnishings, 22-23,
 38
Mill on the Floss, The (Eliot),
 76
"Mission of Jane," 46
Mitchell, S. Weir, 20, 173
Mitford, Nancy, 167
Mizener, Arthur, 41
Money, predominance of, 9-10, 35,
 80, 91-92, 108-10, 117, 121, 173
Month in the Country, A (Turgenev),
 102
"Moonrise over Tyringham," 21
Morris, William, 154
Mother's Recompense, The, 39, 41,
 67, 72, 95
"Moving Finger, The," 46

N

Nevius, Blake, 15

New Republic, 84
Norton, Charles Eliot, 30, 75, 90
Nouveaux riches, rise of, 10-12, 30,
 34-35, 37, 69, 106-8, 122

O

O'Hara, John, 11
Old Maid, The, 6, 165
Old New York, 28, 38, 65, 72, 82
Othello (Shakespeare), 115
"Other Two, The," 46

P

"Pelican, The," 46
Phillips, D. G., 93
Poe, E. A., 165
Point of view, 97-98
 in *Ethan Frome*, 133-34
Portrait of a Lady, The (James), 71,
 75
Portrait of Edith Wharton (Lubbock),
 172
Pretty Lady, The (Bennett), 28
Princess of Clèves, The (Lafayette),
 167
Proust, Marcel, 29, 35, 106
Puritanism, 24, 133, 151

R

Racine, 29, 33, 148, 150, 160
Ransom, John Crowe, 133-34
Realism, 5, 19, 83, 90, 160
"Recovery, The," 46
Reef, The, 4, 7, 23, 32-33, 55-59, 69,
 70, 72, 95, 98, 101, 132, 135, 136,
 147-50, 162
 Jamesian influence in, 7
 imagery, 59
 method, 55-59
 self-sacrifice, theme of, 131
"Rembrandt, The," 46
Reverberator, The (James), 26
Reynolds, Sir Joshua, 110, 111,
 164
Rieff, Philip, 16

Ring and the Book, The (Browning), 97
Romeo and Juliet (Shakespeare), 115
Romola (Eliot), 96
Roosevelt, Theodore, 101
Rossetti, Dante Gabriel, 30
Rudin (Turgenev), 102

S

Schiller, J. C. F. von, 29
Self-sacrifice, theme of, 15, 17
    in *Age of Innocence*, 38, 157
    in *Ethan Frome*, 131-32
    in *Reef*, 4
Shakespeare, William, 166
Shaw, G. B., 133
Silas Marner (Eliot), 84
Simmons, Ronald, 62
"Simple Heart, A" (Flaubert), 144
Sinclair, Upton, 93
Small Boy and Others, A (James), 81
Social disintegration, theme of, 29, 79, 80-81
Social mobility, theme of, 9-10, 30-31, 36-37, 65, 121
Society's power, theme of, 13, 16-17, 21, 99, 105-6, 113, 117, 168
Society's victim, theme of, 2, 3, 13, 16-17, 21, 26, 36-37, 53, 66, 89, 99, 105-6, 113, 125-26
Son at the Front, A, 28, 64, 99, 163
Stevens, General Ebenezer, 163
Strachey, Lytton, 40
Sturgis, Howard, 62, 99, 174
Style, 2-3, 5, 8, 39, 68-69, 80, 83, 127-28, 168
Summer, 5, 25-26, 27, 69, 83, 84, 86, 99, 101, 133, 136

T

Thackeray, William M., 40, 95, 102, 165
Titian, 110
Tolstoy, Leo, 55
Trilling, Lionel, 167

Trollope, Anthony, 75, 96
Truth, The (Fitch), 22
Turgenev, Ivan, 96, 102
Twain, Mark, 3, 15, 175
Twilight Sleep, 24, 28, 39, 40, 66, 80-81, 95, 98, 99

V

Valley of Decision, The, 47, 70, 96, 134
Vanderbilt, Commodore, 91, 152
Veronese, 110
Vesalius, 29

W

War and Peace (Tolstoy), 71
Washington Square (James), 95
Watteau, 110
Wells, H. G., 85
West, Nathanael, 4
Wharton, Edith:
    ancestry of, 64-65, 74, 104, 163
    as craftsman, 3-5, 8, 67-68, 71-72, 86, 94
    as social critic, 20, 26-27, 29, 101-2, 106, 165
    biographical information, 5-6, 13, 16-17, 25-26, 41, 62-67, 74-75, 89, 92-94, 101-2, 103-4, 135, 153-54, 162-65, 173-76
    and convention of double plot, 96
    critical neglect of, 1-2
    early work, 2, 20, 44, 68-69
    and George Eliot, 83-87, 95
    and Henry James, 6-9, 26, 32-33, 39, 69, 71, 75-76, 85-86, 89-90, 95-102 *passim*, 147-50, 175
    moral vision, 2, 14-18, 66-67, 96, 128-29
    and novel of manners, 12, 49, 69, 72, 166-67
    and "old New York," 9-14, 34-42, 48, 50, 65, 69, 71, 73, 77, 79, 94, 101-2, 106-7, 151, 162-63
    on art of writing, 67-68, 96-97
    sense of fatality, 15-18, 20-21, 90, 122, 126, 160

Wharton, Edith (*continued*)
social background, 8-14, 27, 34-35, 74-75, 176
treatment of sex, 112-13, 128
Wharton, Edith, works by:
Age of Innocence, The, 3, 5, 9, 10, 12, 26, 29, 34, 37-38, 41, 42, 63, 65, 69, 71, 72, 82, 94, 122, 135, 151, 155-61, **162-71**
"Angel at the Grave, The," 46
Artemis to Actaeon, 21
"Autres temps . . . ," 87
Backward Glance, A, 29, 62, 75, 103, 163, 164, 165, 173
Buccaneers, The, 30, 42
Bunner Sisters, The, 5, 25, 26, 69, 83, 86, 93, 133
Children, The, 40, 99
"Coward, A," 46
Crucial Instances, 68
"Cup of Cold Water, A," 133
Custom of the Country, The, 4-5, 8, 12, 23-24, 30, 34, 36-37, 42, 50-53, 57, 65, 69, 71, 72, 76, 79-80, 99, 122, 175
Decoration of Houses, The, 38
Descent of Man, The, 45
Ethan Frome, 5, 24-25, 26, 28, 53, 69, 72, 83, 84, 92, 98, 99, 100, 101, **130-36**, **137-46**, 155, 162, 168
"Experience," 21
Fighting France, from Dunkerque to Belfort, 64
Fruit of the Tree, The, 5, 17, 21, 24, 53, 66, 71, 83, 132, 163
Greater Inclination, The, 68
Gods Arrive, The, 40, 65, 71
Glimpses of the Moon, The, 5, 28, 39, 40
Hermit and the Wild Woman, The, 69
House of Mirth, The, 2, 3, 4, 11, 12-13, 19, 21, 22, 24, 26, 27, 34, 35, 38, 42, **47-50**, 51, **53-55**, 62, 66, 71, 75, 76-79, 80, 92, 98, 99, **103-18**, **119-29**, 130, 155, 173
Hudson River Bracketed, 39, 40, 65, 71, 98, 99, 136, 163, 165

Human Nature, 39
In Morocco, 64
Madame de Treymes, 7, 39-40, 63, 95, 99, 164
"Mission of Jane," 46
"Moonrise over Tyringham," 21
Mother's Recompense, The, 39, 41, 67, 72, 95
"Moving Finger, The," 46
Old Maid, The, 5, 165
Old New York, 28, 38, 65, 72, 82
"Other Two, The," 46
"Pelican, The," 46
"Recovery, The," 46
Reef, The, 4, 7, 23, 32-33, 55-59, 69, 70, 72, 95, 98, 101, 131, 132, 135, 136, **147-50**, 162
"Rembrandt, The," 46
Son at the Front, A, 28, 64, 99, 163
Summer, 5, 25-26, 27, 69, 83, 84, 86, 99, 101, 133, 136
Twilight Sleep, 24, 28, 39, 40, 66, 80-81, 95, 98, 99
Valley of Decision, The, 47, 70, 96, 134
Writing of Fiction, The, 29, 72, 167
Xingu, 25
Wharton, Edward (husband), 25-26, 62-63, 173
Whitman, Walt, 165
Wilkins, Mary, 83
Wilson, Edmund, 1, 4, 11, 17, 84
Wings of the Dove, The (James), 101
Woolf, Virginia, 85
Wordsworth, William, 86, 144
Writing of Fiction, The, 29, 72, 167
Wuthering Heights (Brontë), 84

X

Xingu, 25

Y

Yale University Library, 135, 176

Z

Zola, Émile, 40

WHITMAN
A Collection of Critical Essays
Edited by ROY HARVEY PEARCE

A

"Aboard at a Ship's Helm," 100
Abrams, M. H., 43
Adams, Henry, 72
Adams, John, 141
Adonais (Shelley), 84
"After Trying a Certain Book,"
  93n
Alcott, Bronson, 111
Alexander the Great, 108
Allen, Gay Wilson, 2-3, 46
American Primer, 32, 44-45, 55, 66,
  67, 68, 70, 75, 82, 92n
American Renaissance (Matthiessen),
  93n
American Whig Review, 94n
Anderson, Sherwood, 26
"Apostroph," 96
"Army Corps on the March, An,"
  128
Arnold, Matthew, 165, 168
Ash Wednesday (Eliot), 148
"As I Ebb'd with the Ocean of Life,"
  47, 57-58, 98n, 99, 100, 158
"As I Pondered in Silence," 61
Asselineau, Roger, 46, 133
Auden, W. H., 165
Aurelius, Marcus, 140

B

*Backward Glance O'er Travel'd Roads,
  A*, 1, 38, 41, 61, 93n, 101n, 103

Balzac, Honoré de, 114, 142
Bancroft, George, 143, 174
Barlow, Joel, 165, 171
"Base of All Metaphysics," 58
Baudelaire, Charles, 43, 67-68
Bhagavad-Gita, 74-89
Biographia Literaria (Coleridge),
  104
Blake, William, 40, 73, 94, 165, 173,
  174
"Boston Ballad, A," 29
Botticelli, Alessandro, 11
Boyle, Robert, 166
Bradstreet, Anne, 163, 166, 168-69
Bridge, The (Crane), 3-4, 25
"Broadway Pageant, A," 100
Brooklyn Daily Eagle, 26, 69, 104n
Brooks, Van Wyck, 158
Bryant, William Cullen, 105n
Bucke, R. M., 69, 71, 105, 111
"Burial," 51
Burns, Robert, 78, 146
Burroughs, John, 78, 107, 113
"By Blue Ontario's Shore," 34, 47, 62,
  95n, 96, 97, 100, 132-33
"By the Bivouac's Fitful Flame," 101

C

"Calamus," 16, 46, 50-51, 53, 56, 58,
  63, 82, 87, 94n, 96
Caesar, Augustus, 135, 140
Caesar, Julius, 135

"Cavalry Crossing a Ford," 98-99, 101, 127, 130
Carlyle, Thomas, 28, 35, 161-62
"Centenarian's Story, The," 97
Channing, W. E., 107
"Chants Democratic," 34, 37, 47, 53, 93, 96*n*
Chaplin, Charlie, 14
Chapman, John Gay, 4, 70
Chase, Richard, 26
Chaucer, Geoffrey, 152, 164
"Children of Adam" (*see* "Enfants d'Adam")
"Child's Amaze, A," 101
"Child's Reminiscence, A," 53
Chivers, Thomas Holly, 171
Claudel, Paul, 92
Coleridge, Samuel Taylor, 67, 104, 108, 119, 120, 168, 174
Columbus, Christopher, 108
Common Sense (Paine), 141
"Contemplations" (Bradstreet), 168-69
Cooper, James Fenimore, 142-43
"Cotton Boll, The" (Timrod), 170-71
Cowley, Malcolm, 26, 44
Crane, Hart, 3-4, 25, 163, 168, 174, 175
Cratylus, The (Plato), 108
Cromwell, Oliver, 153
"Crossing Brooklyn Ferry," 44, 51, 53, 72, 97, 117-18, 122-24, 130

D

Dante, 9, 30, 64, 114
Darwin, Charles, 141
Democratic Vistas, 38, 40, 60-61, 93*n*, 110, 117, 160, 161
Dialogues (Price), 135
Dickinson, Emily, 163, 173
"Dismantled Ship, The," 129-30
Divine Week (Du Bartas), 166
Donne, John, 164
Dostoevski, Fydor, 114
Drake, J. R., 165
Drum-Taps, 16, 63, 101, 102, 127-28, 133

Dryden, John, 30, 165
Du Bartas, Seigneur, 166
Dwight, Timothy, 165, 169

E

Eberhart, Richard, 163
Edwards, Jonathan, 109
"Eidolons," 105
Einstein, Albert, 150
Eliot, T. S., 3, 67-68, 115, 148-49, 150, 154, 163, 165, 174
Emerson, Ralph Waldo, 18, 28, 30, 42, 43, 45, 68, 69, 70-72, 74, 79, 87, 88, 89, 93*n*, 107-8, 111, 112, 120, 126, 163, 164
"Enfants d'Adam," 50, 51, 53, 56, 57, 69, 73, 82, 94*n*, 96, 109
Engels, Friedrich, 74
"Europe," 29, 50

F

"Faith Poem," 48
"Farm Picture, A," 101
Faulkner, William, 160, 174
Faust (Goethe), 33
Feuerbach, L. A., 74
Fichte, J. G., 73
Flaubert, Gustave, 20, 22
Fleurs du Mal, Les (Baudelaire), 67
Flint, R. W., 28
Four Quartets (Eliot), 3, 148-49, 168
Franklin, Benjamin, 141
Freneau, Philip, 165
Frost, Robert, 163, 165
Fry, Christopher, 151
"Full of Life Now," 50-51
Furness, Clifton J., 2

G

Galileo, 149
Georgics (Virgil), 165
Ginsberg, Allen, 37, 44
Goethe, J. W. von, 33, 42, 150
"Grand Is the Seen," 95

"Great Are the Myths," 47, 89, 95
"Greenfield Hill" (Dwight), 169

H

"Halcyon Days," 77
Halleck, F. G., 165
Hamlet (Shakespeare), 152
Hardy, Thomas, 165
Harris, Frank, 150
Hawthorne, Nathaniel, 18, 82-83, 87, 88, 116, 157
Hegel, G. W. F., 73, 116, 158
Henley, W. E., 20
Herbert, George, 164
Herrick, Robert, 164
History of the United States (Bancroft), 143
Holloway, Emory, 2-3, 101n, 104
Holloway, John, 42
Holmes, Oliver Wendell, 107, 109, 164
Homer, 9, 64, 110, 142, 143, 165, 167
Homer, Winslow, 127
Horace, 165, 166
Hulme, T. E., 168

I

"I Am He that Aches with Amorous Love," 12
"I Hear America Singing," 47
Imagination as a Means of Grace (Tuveson), 163
"Inscriptions," 61
"I Sing the Body Electric," 77, 100
"I Was Looking for a Long While," 47, 100-101

J

Jackson, Andrew, 28, 143
James, Henry, 111, 114, 148
Jefferson, Thomas, 141, 143, 147
Johnson, Dr. Samuel, 168
Jones, John Paul, 99

Jonson, Ben, 104
Joyce, James, 116

K

Kahler, Erich, 44
Kant, Emmanuel, 116
Keats, John, 52, 84, 174, 175
King, Edward, 84
Kinnaird, John, 5
"Kosmos," 51

L

Lardner, Ring, 77
Lawrence, D. H., 4-5, 57, 69, 159, 174
"Laws for Creation," 93n
"Leaf of Faces, A," 50
Leaves of Grass (*see* titles of individual poems)
"Leaves of Grass," 47, 53, 57
Lincoln, Abraham, 84, 85, 86, 129, 143
"Lines Suggested by a Visit to Washington" (Whittier), 171-73
Literature and the Irrational (Shumaker), 163
Locke, John, 108, 165, 166
Longfellow, Henry Wadsworth, 18
Lorca, Federico García, 51
Lucretius, 167
Lycidas (Milton), 84

M

MacLeish, Archibald, 134
Madison, James, 140, 141
"Mannahatta," 25, 28
Mather, Cotton, 139
Mathiessen, F. O., 93n, 95-96
Mays, Willie, 136
"Me Imperturbe," 47
Melville, Herman, 18, 23, 88, 110, 116, 157, 158
   Moby Dick, 11n, 13, 46
"Memories of President Lincoln," 63

Merton, Thomas, 154
"Messenger Leaves," 51, 53
Metamorphoses (Ovid), 166
Mill, John Stuart, 35
Miller, James, Jr., 5, 44
Miller, Perry, 163
Milton, John, 64, 152-53, 163, 165, 167
"Miracles," 48
Mirror and the Lamp, The (Abrams), 43
Moby Dick (Melville), 11n, 13, 46
"Modell of Christian Charity, A" (Winthrop), 138
Moore, Marianne, 173
More, Sir Thomas, 165
Murder in the Cathedral (Eliot), 148

N

Nevins, Allan, 142
Newton, Isaac, 166
Nietzsche, Friedrich, 34
"Night on the Prairies," 78, 95n, 105
Norton, Charles Eliot, 107
Notes and Fragments (Bucke), 105
November Boughs, 68, 78, 102

O

"Oda" (Lorca), 51
Ogden, 70
"One Hour of Madness and Joy," 100
O'Neill, Eugene, 174
"One's-Self I Sing," 61, 63
"On Journeys through the States," 173
"On the Beach at Night Alone," 100
"Open Road, The," 8
"Orchestra, The," (Williams), 124
"Our Old Feuillage," 116
Our Old Home (Hawthorne), 116
"Out of the Cradle Endlessly Rocking," 41, 50, 86, 96, 98n, 100, 121, 124-27
Ovid, 166

P

Paine, Thomas, 79, 141, 142, 150
Parsifal (Wagner), 149
"Passage to India," 38, 39, 64, 77, 87, 108, 115, 121, 124, 130
"Paumanok," 25, 29
Peri Bathous (Pope), 163
Pictures (Holloway), 101n
Pindar, 165, 167, 171, 175
Pisan Cantos (Pound), 3
Plato, 30, 42, 108
Pocahontas, 136-37
Poe, Edgar Allan, 18, 101-2
"Poem of Joys," 50, 53
"Poem of Many in One," 34, 95n
"Poem of the Daily Work of the Work-men and the Workwomen of These States," 99
"Poem of the Heart of the Son of Manhattan Island," 99
"Poem of the Last Explanation of Prudence," 99
"Poem of the Propositions of Naked-ness," 99
"Poem of the Sayers of the Words of the Earth," 92
"Poem of Walt Whitman, An Ameri-can," 99, 100, 120
"Poet, The" (Emerson), 42, 45, 71
"Poetry To-Day in America," 93n
"Poets to Come," 3, 37
Pope, Alexander, 163, 164, 165
Pound, Ezra, 3, 4-5, 45, 148, 151, 163, 168, 174
Price, Lucien, 132, 135
Princess, The (Tennyson), 93n
"Proto-Leaf," 47, 100
"Proud Music of the Storm," 64
Puritanism, 28, 137-39, 144, 167

Q

Quakerism, 28, 35, 73

R

Racine, Jean, 67

"Raven, The" (Poe), 102
"Reminiscence," 54
Representative Men (Emerson), 42
Richards, I. A., 70
"Rising of the Nations, The" (Chivers), 171
Robinson, E. A., 3
Roethke, Theodore, 174
Rourke, Constance, 31
"Runner, The," 101

S

Sainte-Beuve, Charles, 93
"Salut au Monde," 50, 53, 78, 116
Sand, George, 28
Sandburg, Carl, 32
"Sands at Seventy," 78
Sandys, George, 166
Santayana, George, 4, 159, 161-62
Sapir, Edward, 70
Satires (Horace), 165
"Says," 102
Scarlet Letter, The (Hawthorne), 18
Schlegel, Friedrich, 104
Schwob, Marcel, 10
Schyberg, Frederick, 46
Scott, Sir Walter, 141, 143
Seasons, The (Thomson), 165, 167-68
"Self-Reliance," 71
Shaftesbury, Earl of, 165
Shakespeare, 9, 42, 93n, 114, 151-53
Shapiro, Karl, 44, 163
Shelley, Percy Bysshe, 84, 94
"Ship, The," 101
Shumaker, Wayne, 163
"Sight in Camp in the Daybreak Gray and Dim, A," 128-29
Sigourney, Lydia, 165, 169-70
Skelton, John, 164
"Slang in America," 68
"Sleep Chasings," 51
"Sleeper, The," 24, 44, 51, 96
Smith, Alexander, 31
Smith, Captain John, 136-38
"So Long!," 52, 119
"Song for Occupations," 47, 75, 92, 97

"Song of Joys, A," 73, 96n
"Song of Myself," 7, 25, 27, 35-36, 44, 47, 71, 72, 82, 87, 89, 90, 91, 92, 93n, 94, 95, 97-98, 100, 101, 111, 112, 117, 120-22, 156, 157, 158, 160, 161, 173
"Song of Prudence," 48
"Song of the Answerer," 48, 105
"Song of the Banner at Daybreak," 70
"Song of the Broad Axe," 47
"Song of the Exposition," 62, 98, 156
"Song of the Open Road," 161
"Song of the Rolling Earth, A," 70, 83, 92, 100, 101n, 119
Specimen Days, 93, 105n, 161
Spenser, Edmund, 165, 167
Spirit of the Age, 110
"Spiritual Laws" (Emerson), 69
"Starting from Paumanok," 47, 61, 62, 82, 100, 119
Start with the Sun (Slote), 163
Sterling, John, 72
"Sun-Down Poem," 44, 122-23
"Supermarket in California, A" (Ginsberg), 37
"Supplement Hours," 104
Swedenborg, Emanuel, 42
Sylvester, Joshua, 165, 166, 167, 169

T

Tacitus, 140
Taylor, Edward, 165
Tennyson, Alfred, 93n, 175
Theocritus, 9, 10
"There Was a Child Went Forth," 48, 90
"This Compost," 48
Thomas, Dylan, 175
Thomson, James, 165, 167-68, 174
Thoreau, Henry David, 79
    Walden, 46, 109, 111
"Thou Mother with Thy Equal Brood," 99
Times (London), 134
Timrod, Henry, 170-71

Tocqueville, Alexis de, 108
"Tomb of a Young Friend" (Sigourney), 169-70
"Torch, The," 101
"To the Sunset Breeze," 9
"To Think of a Time," 51, 98
Tragabigzanda, Lady, 137
Traubel, Horace, 66, 75, 82, 106
"Trickle-Drops," 100
Trowbridge, J., T., 71
Trumbull, John, 165, 171
Tuveson, Ernest, 163
Twain, Mark, 35

V

Valéry, Paul, 104
Van Doren, Mark, 25
Vaughan, Henry, 164
Victorian Sage (Holloway), 42
Villon, François, 9
Virgil, 64, 165, 166

W

Wagner, Richard, 149
Walden (Thoreau), 46, 115
"Walt Whitman," 47, 53
Washington, George, 136
Waste Land, The (Eliot), 148, 168
Webster, Noah, 110
"When Lilacs Last in the Dooryard Bloom'd," 63, 84-86, 98n, 121, 124, 129, 133
"Whispers of Heavenly Death," 64
Whitehead, Alfred North, 132, 134, 135-37, 140, 143
Whitman, Walt:
    and America, theme of, 8-9, 19, 34, 35, 60-65, 68, 110-11, 132-45, 155-62
    and Blake, William, 40, 73, 94, 174
    and body, theme of, 27, 33, 72-73
    and death and immortality, theme of, 16-17, 23, 26, 51-53, 55, 84-86
    and democracy, theme of, 1, 2, 17, 23, 28, 34, 63, 64

    early days of, 25-26
    and Emerson, Ralph Waldo, 28, 30, 42, 45, 68, 69, 71-72, 74, 79, 93n, 107-8, 111, 120
    influence of, 3-4, 8-10, 148
    and language, 9, 29-30, 40, 42-45, 48, 55, 66-79, 82-83, 116, 147, 150-53
    and love, theme of, 12, 16, 19-20, 23, 31, 124
    and open road, theme of, 19-21, 122
    poetic forms of, 101, 106, 119-31
    and prophecy, 2, 8, 29, 31, 37-41, 43-44, 57, 59, 69, 161
    religious consciousness of, 37-38, 42, 52, 64, 109, 117, 129
    and rhythm, use of, 9, 27, 126
    and sexual themes, 15, 25-26, 50, 72-73
    and soul, theme of, 18, 23, 27-33, 35, 39, 54-55, 72-73, 117
    style of, 89-106, 119-31
Whitman, Walt, major works of (including those published separately and incorporated in later editions of *Leaves of Grass*):
    American Primer, 32, 44-45, 55, 66, 67, 68, 70, 75, 82, 92n
    Backward Glance O'er Travel'd Roads, A, 1, 38, 41, 61, 93n, 101n, 103
    Democratic Vistas, 38, 40, 60-61, 93n, 110, 117, 160, 161
    Drum Taps and Sequel, 16, 63, 101, 102, 127-28, 133
    Leaves of Grass (*see* titles of individual poems)
    November Boughs, 68, 78, 102
    "Passage to India," 38, 39, 64, 77, 87, 108, 115, 121, 124, 130
    Specimen Days, 93, 115n, 161
Whittier, John Greenleaf, 163, 171-73
Wilbur, Richard, 168
Wild Duck, The (Ibsen), 149
Williams, William Carlos, 4, 124
"Winter" (Thomson), 168

Winthrop, John, 138-39, 142, 143

"Woman Waits for Me, A," 76

Wood, Charles Erskine Scott, 163

"Word out of the Sea, A," 41, 48, 50, 52, 53-56, 59, 124 (*see also* "Out of the Cradle Endlessly Rocking")

Wordsworth, William, 30, 35, 94, 146

Y

"Years of Meteors," 98

Yeats, W. B., 10, 40

WILDE

A Collection of Critical Essays

Edited by RICHARD ELLMANN

A

Adey, More, 117
Aestheticism, 99-100 (*see also* Ruskin,
 John; Pater, Walter)
Albee, Edward, 8
Aldington, Richard, 50
America, Wilde's tour of, 120-21
Antimoralism, in Wilde's work, 3, 59,
 92, 146, 169-71
Arms and the Man (Shaw), 63
Arnold, Matthew, 122
Art criticism, Wilde's work in,
 86-88
Atta Troll (Heine), 74
Auden, W. H., 5, 7
"Aurora Leigh" (E. B. Browning),
 118

B

"Ballad of Reading Gaol, The," 1, 2,
 5-6, 105, 131, 134-35, 157, 163,
 165-68, 173
Balzac, Honoré de, 47, 53
Baudelaire, Charles, 47
Beardsley, Aubrey, 90, 100
Beckett, Samuel, 74
Behan, Brendan, 6
Bentley, Eric, 7
Betjeman, John, 6
Biblical parables, in Wilde's works,
 28-31
Bloy, Léon, 173

Borges, Jorge Luis, 8
Botticelli, Sandro, 86
Bridges, Robert, 118, 142
Broad, Lewis, 145
Browning, Elizabeth Barrett,
 118
Browning, Robert, 15, 65-66, 146
Burne-Jones, Sir Edward, 86
Byron, George Gordon, 47, 48, 138,
 139, 143, 144, 147

C

Candida (Shaw), 111
Cervantes, Miguel de, 129
Characterization:
 in *Importance of Being Earnest, The,*
  68-69
 in *Lady Windermere's Fan,* 66-67
 in *Woman of No Importance, A,*
  67-68
Chesterton, G. K., 174
Christ figure, Wilde as a, 6, 147-49
City of Dreadful Night, The
 (Thomson), 51
Comic devices, in *The Importance of
 Being Earnest,* 108-110
Congreve, William, 111
Conversation, Wilde's skill in, 9-10, 12-
 13, 15, 25-31, 34*n*, 35, 94-95, 117,
 119-20
Corydon (Gide), 4
Counterfeiters, The (Gide), 3
Crane, Hart, 6

Critic as Artist, The, 150, 173
Crown of Wild Olive, The (Ruskin),
    81

D

Dali, Salvador, 85
Dante, Alighieri, 139
"Dark Lady of the Sonnets, The"
    (Harris), 106
Daru, Pierre, 81
Davis, Jefferson, 121
Decay of Lying, The, 12
De l'Essence du Rire (Baudelaire),
    47
De Profundis, 5, 60, 80, 91, 105, 106,
    109, 123-24, 144, 145-46, 148, 157,
    161, 163, 173
De Quincey, Thomas, 50-51
Dialogue, in *The Importance of Being
    Earnest,* 112-14
Dickens, Charles, 51
Disraeli, Benjamin, 48, 50, 54
Divina Commedia (Dante), 139
Dixon, Canon, 118
"Doer of Good, The," 147
Don Juan (Byron), 139, 143
Doughty, Charles, 139
Douglas, Lord Alfred, 4-5, 7, 86,
    102-3, 106, 117, 122, **123-28,** 144,
    145, 149, 161
Dowden, Edward, 18
Dowson, Ernest, 118
Dramatic techniques, in *The Impor-
    tance of Being Earnest,* 61-63, 71
Duchess of Padua, The, 63-66
    and Shakespearean theater, 63-65

E

Evens, Lawrence, 86

F

"Fisherman and his Soul, The," 141,
    143
Flaubert, Gustave, 2, 15, 33, 53,
    74

Forbes, Archibald, 120
Fruits of the Earth, The (Gide), 4
Fullerton, Morton, 129

G

Gautier, Théophile, 2, 95
Genet, Jean, 3, 8
George, Stefan, 172
Gide, André, 2-4, **25-34**
Gilbert, Sir William S., 119, 120
Gosse, Edmund, 104
Gothic novel, and *The Picture
    of Dorian Gray,* 47-55
Green Child, The (Read), 139

H

Hankin, St. John, 7
"Happy Prince, The," 135, 141-42,
    145
"Harlot's House, The," 173
Harris, Frank, 122, 160
Hart-Davis, Rupert, 117
Heine, Heinrich, 73, 74
Henley, W. E., 9, 10, 13
Henry James (West), 172
Hérodiade (Mallarmé), 74
Histoire de la République de Venise
    (Daru), 81
Holland, Vyvyan, 124
Homosexuality, in Wilde's life, 4, 8,
    84, 97, 107, 117, **121-28** *passim,*
    136-37, 141, 144-45, 160-61
House of Pomegranates, The, 15, 60
Housman, A. E., 118
Housman, Laurence, 162
Hugo, Victor, 51
Huysmans, J. K., 73
Hymn in Honour of Beauty (Spenser),
    143

I

Ibsen, Henrik, 66, 70, 119
Ideal Husband, An, 62, 135
    social protest in, 157-59
Idealism in Wilde's works, 138-49

Immoralist, The (Gide), 3-4
Importance of Being Earnest, The,
    1, 7-8, 95-96, **111-15**, 131, 135-36,
    160
    characterization in, 68-69
    comic devices in, 108-10
    dialogue in, 112-14
    dramatic techniques in, 61-63, 71
In Excelsis (Douglas), 5
Intentions, 3, 35-36, 135
Irving, Washington, 121

J

James, Jesse, 121
Johnson, Lionel, 4, 17, 20, 172
Journal (Gide), 3
Joyce, James, 6, 56-60

K

King of the Great Clock Tower, The
    (Yeats), 2
Kipling, Rudyard, 118
Knight, G. Wilson, 6

L

Labouchère, Henry
Lady Windermere's Fan, 7, 57, 62,
    135, 156, 172
    characterization in, 66-67
Laforgue, Jules, 73
Land of Heart's Desire, The (Yeats),
    18
Langtry, Lily, 119
La Touche, Rose, 78-79, 82-83
Lautréamont, Comte de, 47, 49
Le Gallienne, Richard, 118
Letters of Oscar Wilde, The, 116-37
"Letter to the *Daily Chronicle,*" 147,
    163-65
Lever, Charles, 14
Leverson, Ada, 122, 130-31
Lewis, "Monk," 47
Life of Oscar Wilde, The (Pearson),
    138-49 *passim*

Literary influences, in Wilde's works,
    47-55
Lothair (Disraeli), 48
Lully, Raymond, 173
Lytton, Bulwer, 48, 54

M

Macbeth (Shakespeare), 139
Maeterlinck, Maurice, 74
McCarthy, n n n n n
Major Barbara (Shaw), 111
Mallarmé, Stéphane, 25, 73-74, 172
Mallock, W. H., 86
Mann, Thomas, 8
Marius the Epicurean (Pater), 89
Maturin, Charles Robert, 47-54
    passim
Mellor, Harold, 129
Melmoth the Wanderer (Maturin),
    47-49, 52, 53
Merchant of Venice, The
    (Shakespeare), 64
Meredith, George, 100, 111, 115
Meynell, Alice, 118
Miles, Frank, 119
Millais, John, 77, 86, 87
Milton, John, 139
Mirandola, Pica della, 84
Misérables, Les (Hugo), 51
Mocenigo, Tommaso, 81
Molière, 111
Moore, George, 2
Morality (*see* Antimoralism)
Morris, William, 118
Mystères de Paris, Les (Sue),
    51

N

Nietzsche, Friedrich, 8, 115, 142,
    145, 149, 169-71
Norton, Charles Eliot, 90

O

O'Connor, T. P., 98

Ollendorff, H. G., 74
O'Sullivan, Vincent, 148
Othello (Shakespeare), 139
Oxford Book of Modern Verse, The
   (Yeats, ed.), 2

P

Paradise Lost (Milton), 139
Pater, Walter, 4, 9, 15, 57, 75-76, 83-
   89
"Patience" (Gilbert and Sullivan), 119,
   120
Patmore, Coventry, 118
Pearson, Hesketh, 138-49 *passim*, 155,
   173
Peau de Chagrin, La (Balzac), 50
Pelham (Lytton), 48, 54
Pericles (Shakespeare), 139
Picture of Dorian Gray, The, 3, 4, 7,
   35-38, 101, 122, 135, 143, 148, 149,
   155, 173
   and the Gothic novel, 47-55
   influence of Ruskin and Pater, 88-
      89
   and *Intentions*, 35-36
Plato, 142, 170
Poe, Edgar Allan, 36, 38
Politics, Wilde's views on, 158-59
"Portrait of Mr. W. H., The," 135,
   144
Praz, Mario, 73, 74
Priest and the Acolyte, The (Wilde?),
   52
Prison, Wilde's experience in, 19-20,
   148, 161-68
Proust, Marcel, 4, 51-52, 91

Q

Queensbury, Marquis of, 16, 20, 34,
   58, 102, 103, 107, 123, 125, 126-27,
   160-61

R

Radcliffe, Ann, 47
Read, Herbert, 139

Redmond, Willie, 20
Rilke, Rainer Maria, 75
Roditi, Edouard, 7
Ross, Robert, 5, 47, 94, 101, 117,
   122, 160
Rossetti, D. G., 15, 118, 119
Ruskin, Effie, 77-78, 81-82
Ruskin, John, 57, 75-90 *passim*
Ruskin, Margaret, 81

S

"Sailing to Byzantium" (Yeats), 139
Salome (Heywood), 74-75
Salome, 2, 6, 7, 70-71, 73, 91, 122,
   135, 143-44
   and *The Picture of Dorian Gray*,
      89
School for Scandal, The (Sheridan),
   170
Sesame and Lilies (Ruskin), 78-79
Shakespeare, William, 64, 66, 139,
   142, 143
Shaw, G. B., 6, 7, 63, 70, **92-106**, 107,
   111-12, 119, 154-55
Sherard, Robert, 121
Sheridan, Thomas, 170
"Shropshire Lad, A" (Housman),
   118
Smithers, Leonard, 122, 131
Social reform, Wilde's views on,
   150-68
Soul of Man under Socialism, The,
   3, 89, 94, 135, 139, 146, **150-55**, 173
Soul's Tragedy, A (Browning), 65-66
Spenser, Edmund, 143
"Sphinx, The," 53, 172
"Star-Child, The," 141
Statue and the Bust, The (Browning),
   146
Stephen, Leslie, 173
Stevenson, R. A. M., 10-11
Stones of Venice, The (Ruskin), 77,
   78-80, 83-85
Strauss, Richard, 7
Studies in the History of the Renais-
   sance (Pater), 9, 76, 83
Sue, Eugène, 51

Sullivan, Sir Arthur, 119, 120
Swedenborg, Emanuel, 173
Swinburne, Algernon, 15, 118
Symons, Arthur, 2
"Symphony in Yellow," 173
Symposium, The (Plato), 142

T

Taylor, Alfred, 122, 136, 160
Testament of Beauty, The (Bridges), 142
Thomson, James, 51, 118
Thus Spake Zarathustra (Nietzsche), 142, 149
"To the Destroyer of a Soul" (Johnson), 4, 17
Tournour, Cyril, 65
Travels in Arabia Deserta (Doughty), 139
Tree, Beerbohm, 147
Tremaine (Ward), 54
Truth about Oscar Wilde, The (Broad), 145
Turner, Joseph, 86
Turner, Reginald, 117, 160
Tyler, Parker, 49

V

Valéry, Paul, 2
Vera or the Nihilist, 138-39, 140
Vereker, Hugh, 172
Verlaine, Paul, 127, 129
Veronese, Paolo, 82, 83
Villon, François, 129
Vinci, Leonardo da, 84, 85
Vivian Grey (Disraeli), 48, 50, 54

W

Wainwright, Thomas Griffiths, 3
Walpole, Horace, 47
Wanderings of Usheen, The (Yeats), 12
Ward, Robert Plumer, 54
Webster, John, 65
West, Rebecca, 172

Whistler, James MacNeil, 91, 96, 100 121
White, Gleeson, 21
Widowers' Houses (Shaw), 119
Wilde, Constance (wife), 121-22, 132, 133
Wilde, Lady (mother), 14, 19-20, 47, 48, 56-57, 93, 97, 138
Wilde, Oscar:
  aestheticism of, 99-100 (*see also* Ruskin, John; Pater, Walter)
  American tour, 120-21
  antimoralism of, 3, 59, 92, 146, 169-71
  art criticism of, 86-88
  Biblical parables of, 28-31
  and Byron, George Gordon, 138, 139, 144, 147
  as a Christ figure, 6, 147-49
  as a conversationalist, 9-10, 12-13, 15, 25-31, 34*n*, 35, 94-95, 117, 119-20
  and Douglas, Lord Alfred, 4-5, 7, 86, 102-3, 106, 117, 122, **123-28**, 144, 145, 149, 161
  early years of, 9-14, 25, 56-57, 75, 118-20
  and Gide, 2-4, 25-34
  and Henley, W. E., 9, 10, 13
  and homosexuality, 4, 8, 84, 97, 107, 117, **121-28,** *passim,* 136-37, 141, 144-45, 160-61
  and Ibsen, Henrik, 66, 70, 119
  idealism of, 138-49
  and Joyce, James, 6, 56-60
  last years of, 6, 58, 96, 104-6, 128-34
  literary influences on, 47-55
  literary interests of, 118-19
  and Lloyd, Constance (wife), 121-22, 132, 133
  and Mallarmé, Stéphane, 25, 73-74, 172
  and Maturin, Charles Robert, 47-54 *passim*
  and Nietzsche, Friedrich, 8, 115, 142, 145, 149, **169-71**
  and Pater, Walter, 4, 9, 15, 57,

Wilde, Oscar (and Pater, Walter)
    (*continued*)
    75-76, 83-89
    and Poe, Edgar Allan, 36, 38
    political views of, 158-59
    in prison, 19-20, 148, 161-68
    and Proust, 51-52, 91
    and Queensbury, Marquis of, 16,
        20, 34, 58, 102, 103, 107, 123,
        125, 126-27, 160-61
    and Ruskin, John, 75-90 *passim*
    and Shaw, G. B., 6, 7, 63, 70, **92-
        106**, 107, 111-12, 119, 154-55
    snobbery of, 98-99
    and social reform, 150-68
    trial of, 16-21, 34*n*, 42-43, 58, 101,
        121, 145, 161-62
    and the *Women's World,* 122
    and Yeats, William Butler, 2, **9-24,**
        74, 117, 118, 139, 158
Wilde, Oscar, works by:
FICTION
    "Fisherman and his Soul, The,"
        141, 143
    "Happy Prince, The," 135, 141-42,
        145
    House of Pomegranates, The, 15, 60
    Picture of Dorian Gray, The, 3, 4,
        7, **35-38,** 47-55, 88-89, 101, 122,
        135, 143, 148, 149, 155, 173
    "Star-Child, The," 141
    "Young King, The," 140-41
DRAMA
    Duchess of Padua, The, 63-66
    Ideal Husband, An, 62, 135, 157-59
    Importance of Being Earnest, The,
        1, 7-8, 61-63, 68-69, 71, 95-96,
        108-10, **111-15,** 131, 135-36,
        160
    Lady Windermere's Fan, 7, 57, 62,
        66-67, 135, 156, 172
    Salome, 2, 6, 7, 60, 70-71, **73-91,**
        122, 135, 143-44
    Vera, or the Nihilist, 138-39, 140

Woman of No Importance, A, 67-
    68, 135, 155-57
CRITICISM, PAMPHLETS, LETTERS
    Critic as Artist, The, 150, 173
    Decay of Lying, The, 12
    De Profundis, 5, 60, 80, 91, 105,
        106, 109, 123-24, 144, 145-46,
        148, 157, 161, 163, 173
    Intentions, 3, **35-36,** 135
    "Letter to the *Daily Chronicle,*"
        147, 163-65
    Letters of Oscar Wilde, The,
        116-37
    Soul of Man under Socialism, The,
        3, 89, 94, 135, 139, 146, **150-55,**
        173
POETRY
    "Ballad of Reading Gaol, The," 1, 2,
        5-6, 105, 131, 134-35, 157, 163,
        165-68, 173
    "Portrait of Mr. W. H., The," 135,
        144
    "Sphinx, The," 53, 172
Wilde, Sir William (father), 14, 93
Wilde, Willie (brother), 18-19, 20-21,
    105
Winckelmann, J. J., 84, 87
Woman of No Importance, A, 135
    characterization in, 67-68
    social protest in, 155-57
Women's World, Wilde's editorship of,
    122
Woodberry, George, 90
Woodcock, George, 6-7

Y

Yeats, William Butler, 2, **9-24,** 74, 117,
    118, 139, 158
"Young King, The," 140-41

Z

Zeno, Carlo, 81

WILLIAM CARLOS WILLIAMS

A Collection of Critical Essays
Edited by J. HILLIS MILLER

A

Adam and Eve and the City,
  146
Adams, Samuel, 124
Adolphe (Constant), 34
Adolphe (Rodker), 34
Adventures in the Arts (Hartley),
  26
Aeschylus, 32
Aesop, 60
"All the Fancy Things," 62
Al Que Quiere!, 41, 48, 59
American Background, The,
  121, 129-30
American Language, The (Mencken),
  127
"Approach to a City," 54
Aristotle, 32, 138
"Arrival," 67
"Asphodel, That Greeny Flower," 8,
  9, 58, 75, 102-3, 104, 147, 159
"At Kenneth Burke's Place," 54
"Attic Which I Desire, The," 63
*Autobiography of William Carlos
  Williams, The,* 12, 13, 76, 93, 140,
  141, 161

B

Bacon, Francis, 38
"Ballad of Faith," 129
Bard, Joseph, 35
"Bare Tree," 53

Barlow, Joel, 102
Bartram, William, 125
"Billy," 111
"Birds and Flowers," 44-45
Boone, Daniel, 78, 80, 87, 130, 145
Bouvard and Pécuchet (Flaubert),
  32
"Brilliant Sad Sun," 62
Brown, Norman O., 138
Browning, Robert, 126
Bryant, William Cullen, 124
"Bull, The," 55, 56, 62, 67
Burke, Edmund, 37
"Burning the Christmas Greens," 54,
  100-1, 121, 137
Burr, Aaron, 91, 125
Burroughs, John, 39
"By the road to the contagious hos-
  pital," 69, 158

C

"Catastrophic Birth," 147
Cantos, The (Pound), 82
Cathay (Pound), 69
"Catholic Bells, The," 154-55, 156
Cézanne, Paul, 19, 21, 24
Champlain, Samuel de, 79
Channing, Ellery, 124
Char, René, 6, 135, 136
Chaucer, Geoffrey, 126
"Cherry Blossoms at Evening," 61
"Choral: The Pink Church," 100-1
Cicero, 121

Clark, Herbert, 130
"Clouds, The," 58
"Cod Head, The," 55, 56, 62
Coffey, John, 146
Coleridge, Samuel Taylor, 142
Collected Earlier Poems, The, 1, 7, 8, 136, 141
Collected Later Poems, The, 1, 8, 53, 135, 136, 137, 138, 147
Collected Poems, 1921-1931, 55, 62-64
Collected Poems 1934, 2
Columbus, Christopher, 78, 79, 125, 130, 144
"Comedy Entombed," 122
"Complaint," 67, 69
Constant, Benjamin, 34
"Convivio," 122-23
"Coronal, A," 67, 126
Cortez, Hernando, 79, 80, 125
"Country Rain," 168
Crane, Hart, 108, 118
Creeley, Robert, 6, 165
"Crimson Cyclamen, The," 75, 146
Crèvecoeur, Michel, 125
Cromwell, Oliver, 114
"Crowd at the ball game, The," 68, 69
Curie, Marie, 130

D

"Dance, The," 147
"Danse Russe," 59, 97-98
Dante Alighieri, 104, 157
"Death," 98
"Dedication for a Plot of Ground," 126
"Dejection: An Ode" (Coleridge), 144
De Leon, Ponce, 79
"Delineaments of the Giants, The," 111
De Mundo (Aristotle), 138
Demuth, Charles, 75, 145, 146
"Descent, The," 172
"Descent of Winter," 67
"Desert Music, The," 8, 54, 78

De Soto, Hernando, 78
"Dog Injured in the Street," 172
Draft of XXX Cantos, A (Pound), 121-22
Drinkwater, John, 156
"Drunk and the Sailor, The," 172
Durkheim, Émile, 139

E

Early Martyr and Other Poems, An, 146
Einstein, Albert, 128, 138, 145
"Eleana," 130
"Elegy for D. H. Lawrence," 146
Eliot, T. S., 1, 6, 29, 32, 52, 59, 68, 71, 76-77, 94-95, 102, 103, 108, 109, 126, 130, 171
Emerson, Ralph Waldo, 29, 124
Essay on Rime (Shapiro), 117

F

"Farmers' Daughters, The," 164-70
Faulkner, William, 157
Flaubert, Gustave, 32
Ford, Ford Madox, 153
Four Quartets (Eliot), 6, 77, 103, 109, 172
Franklin, Benjamin, 52, 78, 125, 144
Freneau, Philip, 124, 125
Freud, Sigmund, 28
Frost, Robert, 1, 28, 154

G

"Gerontion" (Eliot), 158
Gide, André, 52
Goya, Francisco José de, 19
Great American Novel, The, 13, 34, 88-92, 125
"Great Figure, The," 50, 69
Greville, Fulke, 126
Gris, Juan, 18, 21, 136
Guillén, Jorge, 6

H

Hamilton, Alexander, 80, 82, 144
"Hard Core of Beauty, The," 55
Hardy, Thomas, 68, 118
Harmonium (Stevens), 56
Hartley, Marsden, 26
Hawthorne, Nathaniel, 124
Heidegger, Martin, 6
Hemingway, Ernest, 167
Henry, Patrick, 125
Herrick, Robert, 68
"High Talk" (Yeats), 6
"Hired Man, The" (Frost), 154
*History of the City of Paterson and
   the County of Passaic* (Nelson), 110,
   125
Holbein, Hans, 20
Homer, 42
Houston, Sam, 80
Hudson, W. H., 33, 36
"Hunter, The," 67, 69, 121
Husserl, Edmund, 6

I

Iliad, The (Homer), 32
Illuminations, Les (Rimbaud), 142
Imagism, doctrines of, 65
"Impromptu: The Suckers," 98
"Improvisations," 48
*Information to those who would re-
   move to America* (Franklin), 125
"Inquiry, The," 53
In the American Grain, 8-9, 13, 30, 35,
   78, 81, 86, 110, 121, 125, 130, 144,
   145, 161
I Wanted to Write a Poem, 143, 146

J

James, Henry, 35, 41, 88, 130
"January," 49
"January Morning," 41, 67
Jarrell, Randall, 116
Jefferson, Thomas, 125
Jones, John Paul, 78, 144
Journey to Love, 60

Joyce, James, 32, 36, 79
Joyce, Norah, 79

K

Kant, Immanuel, 129
Keats, John, 132, 140, 141
Knife of the Times, The, 146
Kora in Hell, 7, 8, 37-41, 92, 122,
   136, 140, 142, 145

L

Last Puritan, The (Santayana),
   111
Laughlin, James, 154
Lawrence, D. H., 145
Leaves of Grass (Whitman), 158
Lessing, Gotthold, 44, 64
"Library, The," 107
Life Along the Passaic River, 146
Lincoln, Abraham, 130
Lockridge, Ross, 89
"Locust Tree in Flower, The," 129
"Lonely Street, The," 67, 126
Longfellow, Henry Wadsworth, 87,
   156
Lowell, James Russell, 153
Lowell, Lawrence, 153
Lyrical Ballads (Coleridge and Words-
   worth), 2

M

Mallarmé, Stéphane, 5
Mann, Thomas, 52
Many Loves and Other Plays,
   10
Mather, Cotton, 78, 80, 125, 144
Maximus Poems (Olson), 165
"May 1st Tomorrow," 136
Melville, Herman, 124
Mencken, H. L., 124, 127
Merleau-Ponty, Maurice, 6
Miller, Henry, 154
Monet, Claude, 19
Montaigne, Michel, 32

Montezuma, 78, 80
Moore, Marianne, 1, 12, 25, 122, 135, 142, 158
"Music of Poetry" (Eliot), 102

N

"Nantucket," 99
Nelson, William, 110, 125
"News for the Delphic Oracle" (Yeats), 6
"Night Rider, The," 53
Notes toward the Definition of Culture (Eliot), 126
"Nuances of a Theme by Williams" (Stevens), 56

O

Olson, Charles, 6, 10, 165
"On the road to the contagious hospital," 68
"Ordinary Evening in New Haven, An" (Stevens), 6
Otis, James, 125

P

"Pastoral," 95-96
"Pastoral Letter" (Olson), 165
Paterson, 1, 3, 7, 13, 54, 55, 66, 70-87, 88, 94-95, 97, 99-100, 102, 104-6, 107-20, 121, 125, 127, 130, 134, 137, 146, 158, 172, 173
"Paterson: The Falls," 142
Phidias, 83
"Philomena Andronico," 148-52
Philosophical Investigations (Wittgenstein), 6
Picasso, Pablo, 65, 79
Pictures from Breughel, 1, 4, 8, 9, 13, 171
"Pink Confused with White," 69
Poe, Edgar Allan, 86-87, 161
"Poem," 57
"Poem for Norman McLeod," 66
Poems, 6

"Portrait of a Lady," 67
"Portrait of the Author," 41
"Pot of Flowers, The," 69
Pound, Ezra, 1, 41, 52, 68, 69, 71, 76, 77, 79, 81-84, 94, 97, 101, 103, 118, 120, 126, 143, 154
Prometheus Bound (Aeschylus), 32
Psalm of Life (Longfellow), 156

Q

"Queen-Ann's-Lace," 8, 99

R

"Raindrops on a Briar," 138
Raleigh, Sir Walter, 78, 79
"Raleigh Was Right," 121, 147
Ransom, John Crowe, 157, 158
"Red Wheelbarrow, The," 125
Rexroth, Kenneth, 124
"Ribh denounces Patrick" (Yeats), 3
Richard II (Shakespeare), 11
Rimbaud, Arthur, 31, 142
Robbe-Grillet, Alain, 6
Rock-Drill Cantos, The (Pound), 103-4
"Romance Moderne," 67

S

Sandburg, Carl, 38
Santayana, George, 111
Sarraute, Nathalie, 6
"Sea-Elephant, The," 68, 69
"Sea-Trout and Butterfish," 141
Selected Essays, 4, 10, 12, 13, 125, 134, 136, 142, 146
Selected Letters, 3, 7, 10, 122, 142
"Semblables, The," 157
Shakespeare, William, 23, 42, 68
Shapiro, Karl, 117, 157
Shipwreck in Europe (Bard), 35
Siegel, Eli, 124
Significance of the Frontier in American History, The (Turner), 124

Sitwell, Edith, 155
"Smell!", 98
"Sort of a Song, A," 102
Sour Grapes, 48, 69
"Sparrow, The," 60, 173
Spender, Stephen, 152
Spenser, Edmund, 156
Spinoza, Baruch, 49
Spring and All, 4, 6, 7, 10, 11, 13, 14,
  15-26, 68, 69, 97, 98, 134, 142,
  143-44, 173
"Spring is Here Again, Sir," 53-54
"Spring Strains," 99
Sterne, Laurence, 12
Stevens, Wallace, 1, 6, 14, 44, 46, 55,
  56, 57-58, 68, 96, 102, 122, 126,
  132, 148
Stein, Gertrude, 79
Stieglitz, Alfred, 125
Swinburne, A. C., 156

T

Tate, Allen, 158
Tempest, The (Shakespeare), 105
Tennyson, Alfred, Lord, 3, 155
Theocritus, 153
"These," 126, 129
"This Florida: 1924," 67
"This Is Just To Say," 129
"Thoughtful Lover, The," 53
"To," 57
"To All Gentlemen," 147
"To Daphne and Virginia," 102, 121,
  127-28
"To Mark Antony in Heaven,"
  67
"To Waken An Old Lady," 67, 69,
  121, 129
"Tract," 126
Traveller in Little Things (Hudson), 36
"Trees, The," 66
Turner, Frederick Jackson, 124, 133
"Two Pendants," 121, 130

U

Ulysses (Joyce), 34

V

Velásquez, Diego, 19
"Venus, The," 35
Voyage to Pagany, A, 33-35

W

Wagner, Richard, 58
"Waiting," 67
"Wanderer, The," 7, 60, 70, 141,
  145
Washington, George, 78, 125, 130
Waste Land, The (Eliot), 76, 77, 93,
  94-95
Wedge, The, 146, 147
Well-Beloved, The (Hardy), 118
Whitman, Walt, 88, 94, 118, 124, 127,
  130, 132
"Widow's Lament in Springtime, The,"
  67, 69, 98, 121, 129
Williams, William Carlos:
  and Crane, Hart, 108
  and Eliot, T. S., 1, 6, 71, 76-77, 94-
    95, 102, 103, 108, 126, 130
  and Frost, Robert, 1, 28
  and Hardy, Thomas, 68
  and Herrick, Robert, 68
  and Imagism, 65
  and James, Henry, 35
  life of, 1, 27-30, 50
  and Moore, Marianne, 1, 12, 25,
    122, 135, 142
  and Olson, Charles, 10
  and Pound, Ezra, 1, 69, 71, 76, 77,
    79, 81-84, 94, 97, 101, 103, 120,
    143
  and Stein, Gertrude, 12
  and Stevens, Wallace, 1, 6, 44, 46,
    55, 57-58, 68, 96, 122, 126, 132,
    148
  and Whitman, Walt, 94, 130, 132
  and Yeats, W. B., 6
  and Zukofsky, Louis, 1
Williams, William Carlos, works by:
  Adam and Eve and the City, 146
  "All the Fancy Things," 62
  Al Que Quiere!, 41, 48, 59

Williams, William Carlos, works by
  (*continued*):
  American Background, The, 121,
    129-30
  "Approach to a City," 54
  "Arrival," 67
  "Asphodel, That Greeny Flower,"
    8, 9, 58, 75, 102-3, 104, 147, 159
  "At Kenneth Burke's Place," 54
  "Attic Which I Desire, The," 63
  *Autobiography of William Carlos
    Williams, The*, 12, 13, 76, 93,
    140, 141, 161
  "Ballad of Faith," 129
  "Bare Tree," 53
  "Billy," 111
  "Birds and Flowers," 44-45
  "Brilliant Sad Sun," 62
  "Bull, The," 55, 56, 62, 67
  "Burning the Christmas Greens,"
    54, 100-101, 121, 137
  "By the road to the contagious
    hospital," 69, 158
  "Catastrophic Birth," 147
  "Catholic Bells, The," 154-55, 156
  "Cherry Blossoms at Evening," 61
  "Choral: The Pink Church,"
    100-101
  "Clouds, The," 58
  "Cod Head, The," 55, 56, 62
  Collected Earlier Poems, The, 1, 7,
    8, 136, 141
  Collected Later Poems, The, 1, 8,
    53, 135, 136, 137, 138, 147
  Collected Poems, 1921-1931, 55,
    62-64
  Collected Poems 1934, 2
  "Comedy Entombed,"
    122
  "Complaint," 67, 69
  "Convivio," 122-23
  "Coronal, A," 67, 126
  "Country Rain," 168
  "Crimson Cyclamen, The," 75,
    146
  "Crowd at the ball game, The,"
    68, 69
  "Dance, The," 147

"Danse Russe," 59, 97-98
"Death," 98
"Dedications for a Plot of Ground,"
  126
"Delineaments of the Giants, The,"
  111
"Descent, The," 172
"Descent of Winter," 67
"Desert Music, The," 8, 54, 78
"Dog Injured in the Street," 172
"Drunk and the Sailor, The," 172
Early Martyr and Other Poems, An,
  146
"Eleana," 130
"Elegy for D. H. Lawrence," 146
"Farmers' Daughters, The," 164-70
Great American Novel, The, 13, 34,
  88-92, 125
"Great Figure, The," 50, 69
"Hard Core of Beauty, The," 55
"Hunter, The," 67, 69, 121
"Impromptu: The Suckers," 98
"Improvisations," 48
"Injury, The," 53
In the American Grain, 8-9, 13, 30,
  35, 78, 81, 86, 110, 121, 125,
  130, 144, 145, 161
I Wanted to Write a Poem, 143,
  146
"January," 49
"January Morning," 41, 67
Journey to Love, 60
Knife of the Times, The, 146
Kora in Hell, 7, 8, 37-41, 92, 122,
  136, 140, 142, 145
"Library, The," 107
Life Along the Passaic River, 146
"Locust Tree in Flower, The," 129
"Lonely Street, The," 67, 126
Many Loves and Other Plays, 10
"May 1st Tomorrow," 136
"Nantucket," 99
"Night Riders, The," 53
"On the road to the contagious
  hospital," 68
"Pastoral," 95-96
Paterson, 1, 3, 7, 13, 54, 55, 66,
  70-87, 88, 94-95, 99-100, 102,

Williams, William Carlos, works by (*Paterson*), (*continued*):
104-6, **107-20**, 121, 125, 127, 130, 134, 137, 146, 158, 172, 173
"Paterson: the Falls," 142
"Philomena Andronico," 148-52
Pictures from Breughel, 1, 4, 8, 9, 13, 171
"Pink confused with white," 69
"Poem," 57
"Poem for Norman McLeod," 66
Poems, 6
"Portrait of a Lady," 67
"Portrait of the Author," 41
"Pot of Flowers, The," 69
"Queen-Ann's-Lace," 8, 99
"Raindrops on a Briar," 138
"Raleigh Was Right," 121, 147
"Red Wheelbarrow, The," 125
"Romance Moderne," 67
"Sea-Elephant, The," 68, 69
"Sea-Trout and Butterfish," 141
Selected Essays, 4, 10, 12, 13, 125, 134, 136, 142, 146
Selected Letters, 3, 7, 10, 122, 142
"Semblables, The," 157
"Smell!," 98
"Sort of a Song, A," 102
"Sour Grapes," 48, 69
"Sparrow, The," 60, 173
Spring and All, 4, 6, 7, 10, 11, 13, 14, **15-26**, 68, 69, 98, 134, 142, 143-44, 173
"Spring is Here Again, Sir," 53-54
"Spring Strains," 99
"These," 126, 129
"This Florida: 1924," 67
"This Is Just To Say," 129
"Thoughtful Lover, The," 53
"To," 57
"To All Gentlemen," 147
"To Daphne and Virginia," 102, 121, 127-28
"To Mark Antony in Heaven," 67

"To Waken An Old Lady," 67, 69, 121, 129
"Tract," 126
"Trees, The," 66
"Two Pendants," 121, 130
"Venus, The," 35
Voyage to Pagany, A, 33-35
"Waiting," 67
"Wanderer, The," 7, 60, 70, 141, 145
Wedge, The, 146, 147
"Widow's Lament in Springtime, The," 67, 69, 98, 121, 129
"Words Lying Idle, The," 53
"World Contracted to a Recognizable Image, The," 134
"Writers of the American Revolution, The," 121
"Young Housewife, The," 129
"Young Sycamore," 2, 4, 5, 7, 8, 9, 12, 13, 64, 99
Winters, Yvor, 158
Wolfe, Thomas, 89
"Wonders of the Invisible World" (Mather), 79
"Words Lying Idle, The," 53
Wordsworth, William, 108
"World Contracted to a Recognizable Image, The," 134
"Writers of the American Revolution, The," 121
Wyatt, Thomas, 126

Y

"Yachts, The," 121
Yeats, W. B., 3, 6, 130
"Young Housewife, The," 129
"Young Sycamore," 2, 4, 5, 7, 8, 9, 12, 13, 64, 99

Z

Zola, Émile, 33
Zukofsky, Louis, 1

VIRGINIA WOOLF

A Collection of Critical Essays

Edited by CLAIRE SPRAGUE

A

Addison, Joseph, 113
Aiken, Conrad, 36
Antony and Cleopatra (Shakespeare), 36
A rebours (Huysmans), 79
Arnold, Matthew, 158
Art (Bell), 160
"Art of Fiction, The" (James), 162-63
"Artist's Vision, The" (Fry), 160
Auden, W. H., 21
Auerbach, Erich, 5
Austen, Jane, 19, 30, 60, 153

B

Bach, J. S., 21
Balzac, Honoré de, 68, 78
Batchelor, J. B., 6, 12
Baudelaire, Charles, 36-37
Bell, Clive, 2, 159-60, 161, 162, 164
Bell, Julian, 3
Bell, Vanessa Stephen, 2, 136
Bennett, Arnold, 6, 14, 19, 26, 43, 133, 137
Bennett, Joan, 126
Benson, Stella, 137
Bergson, Henri, 1, 26
Between the Acts, 4, 10-11, 13, 18, 40, 41, 49-50, **145-54**, 177, 178
  art in, 150-51
  characterization in, 40, 41, 49-50

chronology in, 150, 154
criticism of, 145-46
as novel-drama, 147, 148, 151-52, 153-54
pageant as device in, 18, 148-49, 149n, 150-51, 152, 153-54
parody in, 148-49
the poetic in, 146-47, 151
reality in, 150
structure of, 145, 146, 148, 151-52
symbolism in, 147n, 148, 149, 149n, 152
unity of, 146, 151n, 152-53, 154
Birrel, Francis, 137
Blackstone, Bernard, 135, 171
Bleak House (Dickens), 153
Bloomsbury group, 2, 157, 159
"Blue Green," 20
Borges, Jorge Luis, 129
Bostetter, Edward, 117
Bouvard et Pécuchet (Flaubert), 85
Boyd, Elizabeth, 95n
Bradley, A. C., 162
Brewster, Dorothy, 118-19, 124
Brontë, Charlotte, 113
Brontë, Emily, 37
Brower, Ruben, 6
Buck, Pearl, 88
Buddenbrooks (Mann), 85, 133
Butler, Samuel, 133
Byron, George Gordon, Lord, 120

C

Cambridge, 2, 15, 21, 95n, 157
Captain's Death Bed, The, 43
Carlyle, Thomas, 164
Carrington, Dora, 137
Carroll, Lewis, 112, 113
Cézanne, Paul, 161
Chambers, R. W., 5
"Character in Fiction" (*see* "Mr. Bennett and Mrs. Brown")
Chekhov, Anton, 42
"Coeur simple, Un" (Flaubert), 159
Coleridge, Samuel Taylor, 36, 158, 162, 163, 164, 167
Common Reader, The, 14, 18, 42, 134, 155, 157, 166, 167
Constant, Benjamin, 65
Corydon (Gide), 90
Craft of Fiction, The (Lubbock), 159
"Criticism" (James), 168
Croce, Benedetto, 163-64
Cymbeline (Shakespeare), 51, 127

D

Dante, 85, 110
Davies, Margaret Llewellyn, 23
Death of the Moth, The, 118, 124-26
Delattre, Floris, 105, 128n
Dickens, Charles, 78, 153
Dickinson, G. Lowes, 137
Divine Comedy (Dante), 85, 110
Downhill All the Way (L. Woolf), 92
Dreadnought Hoax, The (Stephen), 15n
Dryden, John, 158
Du Côté de chez Swann (Proust), 83-84

E

Edel, Leon, 5, 6
Eliot, George, 26
Eliot, T. S., 11, 36, 149n, 156, 158, 163, 165, 167, 168

Elton, Charles Isaac, 95n
Emerson, Ralph Waldo, 163
Emma (Austen), 19, 60
"Essay in Aesthetics, An" (Fry), 160
"Evening Over Sussex," 124-26
Excursion, The (Wordsworth), 118

F

Faulkner, William, 3
Fielding, Henry, 60
Flaubert, Gustave, 29, 43, 45, 85, 87, 159, 161
Flush, 18
Forster, E. M., 2, 3, 5, 42, 44, 128n, 131, 142, 169, 171, 173
Forsythe Saga, The (Galsworthy), 133
France, Anatole, 164
Frazer, Sir James, 33
Friedman, Melvin, 146
Friedman, Norman, 92
"Frontiers of Criticism, The" (Eliot), 167
Fry Roger, 2, 2n, 137, 159-60, 161-62, 164
"Function of Criticism, The" (Eliot), 163

G

Galsworthy, John, 6, 43, 133, 137
Gide, André, 90
Goethe, Johann Wolfgang von, 78
Golden Bough, The (Frazer), 33
Granite and Rainbows, 92, 104, 115
Gruber, Ruth, 169, 171
Guiguet, Jean, 5
Gulliver's Travels (Swift), 111, 112, 113

H

Hafley, James, 5
Hamlet (Shakespeare), 144
Hamsun, Knut, 85
Hemingway, Ernest, 36

Hicks, Granville, 131
Hilton, Walter, 120
Hitler, Adolf, 3, 143
Hogarth Press, 3, 5
Holtby, Winifred, 170
Homer, 5, 81-82
"Hours in a Library," 156
"How It Strikes a Contemporary,"
165-66
"How One Should Read a Book" 157,
158, 159
Hulme, T. E., 163
Huxley, Aldous, 143
Huysmans, Joris Karl, 79
"Hymn to Intellectual Beauty"
(Shelley), 119

I

Intimations Ode (Wordsworth),
126, 128
Isherwood, Christopher, 21

J

Jacob's Room, 7, 8-9, 11, 16-17, 19,
31, 43-44, 46, 47, 50, 115, 131, 140,
147, 171, 178
characterization in, 19, 31, 43-44,
46, 47, 50
chronicle in, 31
imagery and symbolism in, 8-9, 31
narration in, 115
the poetic in, 31
sensibility in,
31
structure of, 31
James, Henry, 3, 3n, 20, 27, 28, 29,
30, 31, 60, 68, 161, 162-63, 167,
168
Jane Eyre (Brontë), 113
Johnson, Samuel, 155, 158
Jonstone, J. K., 161
Journey Not the Arrival Matters, The
(L. Woolf), 92
Joyce, James, 1, 2, 5, 30, 31, 35, 45n,
63, 64, 66-69, 80, 85, 86, 90n,
146

K

Keller, Gottfried, 78
"Kew Gardens," 16, 17, 31
Keynes, John Maynard, 2, 4, 143
King Lear (Shakespeare), 110, 111
Krieger, Murray, 163

L

Lamb, Charles, 20
Lawrence, D. H., 1-2, 3, 4, 8, 12,
91n
Leavis, F. R., 3, 145
Lehman, John, 4-5
Leonardo da Vinci, 101
"Leslie Stephen," 10n, 156-57
"Life of Gray" (Johnson), 155
Literary elements, in V. Woolf's
work:
art, 90, 92, 94, 95, 98-99
language, 35-39, **51-62**, 68
musical form, 17
mysticism, 119-21, 126, 129
pattern, 17, 18, 59
plot, 47
the poetic, 6, 17, 18, **19-20**, 27,
33-34, **51-62**, **63-69**, 90, 131,
146-47, 151
reality, 1, 5, 6, 11, 16, 18, 26, 28,
33, 46, 74-89 *passim,* 96, 103,
130, 131, 150, 157n, 158, 176
rhythm, 32-33, 52
sensibility, 26-39
sensory perception, 20-21
silence, 6-7, 8
structure (form), 29-35, 39, 59, 62,
66, 74-89 *passim,* 93-94, 95, 96-
97, 100, 145, 146, 148, 151-52,
157-58, 159-63
style, 16, 35-39, **77-89**, 102, 106,
116
Literary experimentation, in V. Woolf's
work, 6-7, 8, 9, 17, 22, 27, 102, 161
Literary output, of V. Woolf, 12
Literary techniques and devices, in V.
Woolf's work, 1-5, 6-7, 10, 90, 93
caricature, 101-5

Literary techniques and devices, in V. Woolf's work *(continued)*
    characterization, 7-8, **19-20, 27-29,** 30-31, 32-34, 35, 39, **40-50,** 74-89 *passim,* 90, 95, 98, 115
    chronicle (legend), 31, 33, 92, 132, 135
    chronology (time), 9, 9*n,* 66, **79-86,** 90, 97, 116, 132, 150, 154, 176
    dialogue and description, 10
    dualism, 6, 12
    fantasy, 105, 106-7, 110-14, 176
    imagery and symbolism, 1-2, 8, 22, 31, **32-39, 51-62,** 68, 87, 92, 95-97, 100, 139, 140, 147*n,* 148, 149, 149*n,* 152
    impressionism, 64, 73-89 *passim,* 90, 98*n,* 155-56, 161, 162, 163
    irony, 105-6, 111, 112
    memory, 92, 92*n,* 94, 99, 140-41
    mockery, 105-6
    multipersonal consciousness, 7-8, 79, 83, **86-87,** 116
    narration, 7-8, 33-35, 57-58, 73-89 *passim,* 103, 115-16, 128, 139-40, 141
    omniscience, 7, 9, 75-77, 115, 116
    parody, 106-10, 141, 142, 148-49
    repetition, 8, 52
    satire, 105, 176
    stream of consciousness (interior monologue), 1, 5, 7, 28-29, 35, 63, 68-69, 74-89 *passim,* 98, 98*n,* 115, 118
    subjectivism, 27, 33, **63-69,** 74-89 *passim,* 155-56, 162
Literary unity and direction, of V. Woolf, 5, 6
Lubbock, Percy, 159, 160-61, 162
"Luriana, Lurilee" (Elton), 95*n*

M

MacCarthy, Desmond, 2
McConnell, Frank, 6, 11
Madame Bovary (Flaubert), 19, 43, 45, 85
Mallarmé, Stéphane, 36

"Mark on the Wall, The," 16, 31, 69
Mann, Thomas, 85, 133
Mauron, Charles, 162
Mayoux, J. J., 94
Melville, Herman, 124
Meredith, George, 20, 78
Mérimée, Prosper, 88
Moby Dick (Melville), 124
"Modern Fiction," 11
Monday or Tuesday, 20, 31, 34
Moore, G. E., 2, 164
Moore, George, 68
Morris, William, 164
Moths, The (see Waves, The)
"Mr. Bennett and Mrs. Brown," 6, 7, 11, 16, 26, 30, 42-43, 104
Mrs. Dalloway, 7, 9, 11, 17, 19, 21, 23, 28, 29, 31-32, 37-38, 40, 41, 43-45, 45*n,* 46, **51-62,** 64, **66-69,** 91, 92, 94, 115, 118, 127, 131, 140, 141-42, 147, 174, 175, 177-78, 178-79
    characterization in, 19, 40, 43-45, 46, 60, 174
    chronology in, 9, 66
    narration in, 57-58, 115
    imagery and symbolism in, 31-32, 37-38, **51-62,** 68
    language in, **51-62,** 68
    pattern in, 59
    the poetic in, **52-62**
    repetition in, 52
    rhythm in, 32, 52
    stream of consciousness in, 68-69
    structure of, 59, 62, 66
    and *Ulysses* (Joyce), 66-69
Murray, John Middleton, 9
Music, in V. Woolf's work, 16
Mussolini, Benito, 138, 143
"My Early Beliefs" (Keynes), 4

N

"Narrow Bridge of Art, The," 116, 146
Naturalism, V. Woolf's attitude towards, 26
Nicolson, Sir Harold, 4, 95*n*
Nietzsche, Friedrich, 169

Night and Day, 8, 8n, 16, 17, 18, 30,
40, 41, 42, 63, 100, 131, 132, 144,
171, 173
   characterization in, 30, 40, 41, 42
   feminism in, 171, 173
   narration in, 9, 63

O

Ode to the West Wind (Shelley), 117
Odyssey (Homer), 81-82
O'Faolain, Sean, 155
Old Wives' Tale, The (Bennett), 19,
133
"On Re-reading Novels," 158, 159,
160
Orlando, 7, 9, 10, 11-12, 18, 22, 32-
33, 38, 48, **101-16**, 133, 134-35,
174-77
   as biography, 107-16, 133
   caricature in, 101-5
   characterization in, 48, 115
   as essay novel, 10
   fantasy in, 105, 106-7, 110-14,
    176
   feminism in, 22, 174-77
   irony in, 105-6, 111, 112
   mockery in, 105-6
   objects in, 134
   parody in, 106-10
   satire in, 105, 176
   stream of consciousness in, 115
Outline of History (Wells), 11, 149,
152, 153, 154

P

Passage to India, A (Forster), 128n
"Pastons and Chaucer," 157
Pater, Walter, 158, 163, 164-65
Pilgrimage (Richardson), 31
Plomer, William, 19
Pope, Alexander, 113, 119
Portrait of a Lady, The (James), 60
*Portrait of the Artist as a Young Man,
A* (Joyce), 63
Preface to *Life as we have known it*,
14, 23

Pride and Prejudice (Austen), 153
Priestley, J. B., 134
"Professions for Women," 172
Proust, Marcel, 1, 26, 27, 29-30, 63,
64, 68, 79, 83-84, 85, 90, 90n, 91-92,
95n, 96, 98, 100, 116

Q

Quack, Quack! (L. Woolf), 143

R

Racine, Jean, 91
Ransom, John Crowe, 164
Rape of the Lock, The (Pope), 119
"Reading," 157
Remembrance of Things Past (Proust),
90, 98
Renaissance, The (Pater), 164
Richards, I. A., 164
Richardson, Dorothy, 1, 31, 63, 65,
169
Richardson, Samuel, 29
Robbe-Grillet, Alain, 127, 128n,
129
"Robinson Crusoe," 100
Roger Fry, 18-19, 161
Room of One's Own, A, 14, 19, 22,
169, 171-73, 174, 175, 176, 177,
178
Ruskin, John, 164
Ryle, Gilbert, 126

S

Sackville-West, Victoria (Vita), 3, 4,
95n, 137n
Sackville-West family, 133
Sacred Wood, The (Eliot), 156, 158,
167
Sarraute, Nathalie, 91, 127
Sartre, Jean-Paul, 122, 122n, 127
Savage, D. S., 145
Saxon-Turner, Sydney, 2
Schaefer, Josephine O'Brien, 99n
"School of Giorgione, The" (Pater),
165

Shakespeare, William, 22, 36, 51, 52, 58, 61, 91, 110, 127, 144, 164
Shelley, Percy Bysshe, 117-18, 119, 126, 127, 169
Sinclair, May, 31
"Some Questions in Esthetics" (Fry), 161-62
Stephen, Adrian, 2, 15n
Stephen, Sir Leslie, 2, 3, 12, 93, 93n, 94, 96n, 100, 156-57, 158
Stephen, Thoby, 9, 121, 137n
Sterne, Laurence, 29, 43, 116
Strachey, Lytton, 2, 2n, 4, 95n, 137, 137n
Swift, Jonathan, 105-6, 111, 112, 113
Swinburne, Algernon Charles, 36
Symons, Arthur, 163

T

Teasdale, Sara, 38
Tempest, The (Shakespeare), 51, 52
Temple, Ruth, 6
Temps retrouvé, Le (Proust), 83
Thackeray, William Makepeace, 43, 45
Thakur, N. C., 119
Thoreau, Henry David, 163
"Thoughts on Criticism by a Critic" (Stephen), 158
Three Guineas, 19, 22, 169-71, 172, 174, 177, 178
Time Machine, The (Wells), 128n
"Tlön, Uqbar, Orbis Tertius" (Borges), 129
Tolstoy, Leo, 29, 43, 45
Tom Jones (Fielding), 60
To the Lighthouse, 2, 7, 9, 11, 12, 16, 17, 19, 28, 29, 32, 37, 40, 43-45, 46-47, 64, 66, **70-89, 90-100**, 103, 115, 131, 132, 133, 141, 142-43, 147, 149n, 150, 174, 178
art in, 90, 92, 94, 95, 98-99, 150
as autobiography, 93-94, 95, 97, 100
characterization in, 19, 32, 40, 43-45, 46-47, 74-89 *passim*, 95, 98
chronology in, 9, 66, **79-86**, 97
imagery and symbolism in, 32, 37, 87, 92, **95-97**, 100, 149n
as legend, 92
impressionism in, 74-79 *passim*
memory in, 92, 92n, 94, 99
multipersonal consciousness in, 79, 83, **86-87**
narration in, 73-89 *passim*, 115
omniscience in, 75-77
Proust's influence on, 90, 90n, 91-92, 94, 95n, 96, 98, 100
reality in, 74-89 *passim*, 96
sensibility in, 28, 29
stream of consciousness (interior monologue) in, 74-89 *passim*, 98, 98n
structure of, 32, 74-89 *passim*, 93-94, 95, 96-97, 100
style in, **77-89**
subjectivism in, 74-89 *passim*
Toynbee, Philip, 94
Tristam Shandy (Sterne), 43, 116
Tropisms (Sarraute), 91
Troy, William, 3, 6
Turgenev, Ivan, 29, 166

U

Ulysses (Joyce), 63, 66-69, 85, 87, 146

V

Vanity Fair (Thackeray), 43, 45
"Vision and Design" (Fry), 160
Voyage Out, The, 1, 6, 8, 8n, 16, 19, 27, 30, 40, 42, 48, 50, 63, 64, 92, 100, 115, 171, 173, 178
characterization in, 19, 30, 42, 48, 50
feminism in, 171, 173
impressionism in, 64
narration in, 9, 63-64
the poetic in, 64

W

Walpole, Hugh, 19, 134

War and Peace (Tolstoy), 43, 45
Waves, The, 4, 6, 7, 9, 10, 14, 17-18,
  19, 22, 24-25, 27, 28, 32-34, 35, 40,
  41, 46, **47-50**, 60, 97, 104, 115,
  116, **117-29**, 130, 131, 132, 133,
  134, 143, 147
    as an antinovel, 10
    characterization in, 19, 33-34, 40,
      41, 46, **47-50**
    chronicle in, 33
    gestalt in, 123, 125
    imagery and symbolism in, 9, 22,
      32-34, 38
    mysticism in, 119-21, 126, 129
    narration in, 115, 116, 128
    omniscience in, 116
    the poetic in, 33-34, 35, 38, 60
    reality in, 33
    sensibility in, 27, 28
    subjectivism in, 33
Way of All Flesh, The (Butler), 133
Webb, Sidney, 4
Wellek, René, 164
Wells, H. G., 6, 11, 26, 43, 112,
  128*n*
Wesley, John, 120
West, Rebecca, 27, 169
Whitman, Walt, 163
Wilde, Oscar, 163
Wilder, Thornton, 36
Wilkinson, Ann, 6
Winter's Tale, A (Shakespeare), 51
Women in Love (Lawrence), 8
Woolf, Leonard, 2, 3, 4, 8*n*, 11*n*, 92,
  95, 95*n*, 135, 135*n*, 143
Woolf, Virginia:
    achievement of, 25, 63, 64
    and her art, 4, 15-16, 64-65, 90,
      90*n*, 146-47, **155-68**
    and biography, 18-19, **107-16**
    and the Bloomsbury group, 2-3, 4,
      157, 159
    and her characters, 6, 27-29
    contemporary attitude towards,
      3-4
    critical reputation of, 1-2, 4, 14,
      25, 40, 92-93, 94, 118-19, 155-56
    as critic and essayist, 11, 18, 19,

      104, **155-68**, 169-79 *passim*
    and English culture, 3, 21-22
    as feminist, 2, 3, 11-12, 15, 19, 22-
      24, 165, **169-79**
    intellect of, 21-22
    interests of, 20-24
    and Joyce, James, 1-2, 5, 30, 31,
      35, 45*n*, 63, **66-69**, 80, 85, 86,
      90*n*
    and mental illness and suicide, 4,
      4*n*, 17
    and the novel, 4-13, **16-20, 26-39,
      40-50, 51-62, 63-69, 70-89, 90-
      100, 117-29, 130-44, 145-54,
      155-68** *passim,* **169-79** *passim*
    and her parents, 93, 93*n*, 94, 100,
      156-57
    personality of, 2, 3, 4, 11, 14, **20-25**
    personal legend of, 2-3, 14
    and Proust, 1, 26, 27, 29-30, 63,
      64, 68, 79, 83-84, 85, 90, 90*n*,
      91-92, 95*n*, 96, 98, 100
    and religion, 3, 16, 92, 149*n*
    and Richardson, Dorothy, 1, 31, 63,
      65
    self-criticism of, 11
    and Shakespeare, 51-52, 58, 61, 91
    and the short story, 16, 64
    social milieu of, 2-3, 27-28
    social outlook of, 23-24
Woolf, Virginia, works by (*see also*
  individual listings for works marked
  by asterisk):
BIOGRAPHY
    Flush, 18
    *Orlando,** 7, 9, 10, 11-12, 18, 22,
      32-33, 38, 48, **101-16**, 133,
      134-35, 174-77
    Roger Fry, 18-19, 161
DIARY
    Writer's Diary, A (ed. Leonard
      Woolf), 2-13 *passim,* 44, 47, 91-
      100 *passim,* 102-12 *passim,* 119,
      120, 130-44 *passim,* 166
ESSAYS
    Captain's Death Bed, The, 43
    "Character in Fiction" (*see* "Mr.
      Bennett and Mrs. Brown")

Woolf, Virginia, works by: (ESSAYS) (*continued*)

Common Reader, The, 14, 18, 42, 134, 155, 157, 166, 167

Death of the Moth, The, 118, 124-26

"Evening Over Sussex," 124-26

Granite and Rainbows, 92, 104, 115

"Hours in a Library," 156

"How It Strikes a Contemporary," 165-66

"How One Should Read a Book," 157, 158, 159

"Leslie Stephen," 10*n*, 156-57

"Modern Fiction," 11

"Mr. Bennett and Mrs. Brown," 6, 7, 11, 16, 26, 30, 42-43, 104

"Narrow Bridge of Art, The," 116, 146

"On Re-reading Novels," 158, 159, 160

"Pastons and Chaucer," 157

Preface to *Life as we have known it*, 14, 23

"Professions for Women," 172

"Reading," 157

"Robinson Crusoe," 100

FEMINIST BOOKS

Room of One's Own, A, 14, 19, 22, 169, 171-73, 174, 175, 176, 177, 178

Three Guineas, 19, 22, 169-71, 172, 174, 177, 178

NOVELS

Between the Acts,* 4, 10-11, 13, 18, 40, 41, 49-50, 145-54, 177, 178

Jacob's Room,* 7, 8-9, 11, 16-17, 19, 31, 43-44, 46, 47, 50, 115, 131, 140, 147, 171, 178

Mrs. Dalloway,* 7, 9, 11, 17, 19, 21, 23, 28, 29, 31-32, 37-38, 40, 41, 43-45, 45*n*, 46, **51-62**, 64, **66-69**, 91, 92, 94, 115, 118, 127, 131, 140, 141-42, 147, 174, 175, 177-78, 178-79

Night and Day,* 8, 8*n*, 16, 17, 18, 30, 40, 41, 42, 63, 100, 131, 132, 144, 171, 173

To the Lighthouse,* 2, 7, 9, 11, 12, 16, 17, 19, 28, 29, 32, 37, 40, 43-45, 46-47, 64, 66, **70-89, 90-100**, 103, 115, 131, 132, 133, 141, 142-43, 147, 149*n*, 150, 174, 178

Voyage Out, The,* 1, 6, 8, 8*n*, 16, 19, 27, 30, 40, 42, 48, 50, 63, 64, 92, 100, 115, 171, 173, 178

Waves, The,* 4, 6, 7, 9, 10, 14, 17-18, 19, 22, 24-25, 27, 28, 32-34, 35, 40, 41, 46, **47-50**, 60, 97, 104, 115, 116, **117-29**, 130, 131, 132, 133, 134, 143, 147

Years, The,* 7, 10, 18, 42, 48-50, **130-44**, 171, 175, 177, 178

STORIES AND SKETCHES

"Blue Green," 20

"Kew Gardens," 16, 17, 31

"Mark on the Wall, The," 16, 31

Monday or Tuesday, 20, 31, 34

Wordsworth, William, 118, 120, 124, 126, 128

Writer's Diary, A (ed. Leonard Woolf), 2-13 *passim*, 44, 47, 91 100 *passim*, 102-12 *passim*, 119, 120, 130-44 *passim*, 166

Wuthering Heights (Brontë), 37

Y

Years, The, 7, 10, 18, 42, 48-50, **130-44**, 171, 175, 177, 178

as autobiography, 135-37

characterization in, 42, 48-50

chronicle in, 132, 135

chronology in, 132

communication in, 139-40

death in, 137, 138-39, 140

deformity in, 139, 140

as essay novel, 134

memory in, 140-41

narration in, 139-40, 141

parody in, 141, 142

symbolism in, 139, 140

Yeats, William Butler, 37, 126

Z

Zola, Émile, 68, 78

YEATS

A Collection of Critical Essays

Edited by JOHN UNTERECKER

A

Abbey Theatre, 29, 62, 163, 165
"Acre of Grass, An," 165
"Adam's Curse," 4, 57
AE (*see* Russell, George)
After Life in Roman Paganism
(Cumont), 138
Age of Justinian and Theodora, The
(Holmes), 132
Aglavaine et Selysette (Maeterlinck),
44
"All Souls' Night," 11-12, 18
"Among School Children," 10-11, 53,
84, 88
Aphorisms of Yoga (Patanjali), 169
Apotheosis and the After Life
(Strong), 132, 138
"Apparitions, The," 68-69, 72
Aquinas, Saint Thomas, 151
Arnold, Matthew, 159
Art vs. life, theme of, in Yeats's works,
37-42
Ash Wednesday (Eliot), 77
At The Hawk's Well, 61, 91
Auden, W. H., 81
Autobiography, 39, 45, 48, 66, 72
"Autumn of the Body, The," 49
Axel (Villiers), 43, 46-47
Axel's Castle (Wilson), 43, 155

B

Battle, Mary, 26

Baudelaire, Charles, 46, 51
Beardsley, Aubrey, 67
Beardsley, Mabel, 17
"Beautiful Lofty Things," 25
Berkeley, Bishop George, 168
Blackmur, R. P., 4, 101
"Black Tower, The," 173
Blake, William, 3, 26, 33-34, 35, 40,
45, 46, 49, 77, 83, 111, 136, 161,
165
Blavatsky, Mme., 45-46, 47
Bleak House (Dickens), 55
Book of Images, A (Horton), 49
"Book of the Great Dhoul and Harra-
han the Red, The," 81
Bowra, C. M., 43
Bradford, Curtis, 3, 4
"Bronze Head, A," 27
Brooks, Cleanth, 157, 158, 162
Browning, Robert, 55
Burkitt, F. C., 132
Burne-Jones, Sir E. C., 134
Bury, J. B., 133
Byron, George Gordon, Lord, 18,
20
Byzantine Art (Dalton), 133
Byzantine culture, Yeats's interest in,
93-96, 132-38 *passim*, 156-57
"Byzantium," 12, 51-52, 84, 85-86,
109, 115, 135, 136, 162
imagery in, 137-38
sources of, 95-96
working drafts of,
116-30

C

Calvary, 154
Campion, Thomas, 57
Canterbury Tales (Chaucer), 18
"Cap and Bells, The," 51
Casement, Roger, 165
Cathleen ni Houlihan, 27
Celtic Twilight, The, 41
Characters, Yeats's use of, 81-82, 87
Chatterjee, Mohini, 144
Chaucer, Geoffrey, 18
"Chosen," 36
"Cimetière Marin, Le," (Valéry), 45
"Circus Animals' Desertion, The," 2, 24, 89-90, 165, 169
Cities of Italy (Symons), 134
Claudel, Paul, 44
Claudian (Wills), 134
Coleridge, S. T., 17, 40
"Collar-Bone of a Hare, The," 15
Collected Poems of W. B. Yeats, The, organization of, 1
Colloque Sentimentale (Verlaine), 43
"Colonus' Praise," 10-11
"Coole Park (1929)," 60
Countess Kathleen, The, 26, 50
"Crazy Jane" poems, 74-75, 88
"Crazy Jane and the Bishop," 83-84
"Crazy Jane Talks with the Bishop," 77-78, 83-84
Cromwell, Oliver, 165
Crowley, Aleister, 48
Cumont, Franz Valéry, 138
Cutting of an Agate, The, 93
Cyclical theory of history, in Yeats's works, 112, 148

D

Dalton, O. M., 133
D'Alviella, Goblet, 137
Dante Alighieri, 19, 61, 64, 66, 74, 75, 158-59
"Death," 67
Death of Cuchulain, The, 3, 169, 173

"Death of Cuchullin, The," 3
Decay of Lying, The (Wilde), 134
Deirdre, 160
"Delphic Oracle upon Plotinus, The," 52, 86
Dhoya, 81
"Dialogue of Self and Soul, A," 84
Dickens, Charles, 55
Discoveries, 93
Divagations (Mallarmé), 45
Divine Comedy, The (Dante), 19, 66, 158-59
"Double Vision of Michael Robartes, The," 18, 34, 51
Dowson, Ernest, 26, 37, 39
Drama, Yeats's work in, 60-61, 172-73 (see also titles of individual plays)
Dramatis Personae, 23, 27
Dreaming of the Bones, The, 61
"Dream of Death, A," 57

E

Early Eastern Christianity (Burkitt), 132
"Ego Dominus Tuus," 2, 18, 84
Eliade, Mircea, 91
Eliot, T. S., 4, 13, 33, 34, 35, 77, 78, 149, 151, 159, 161-62
Ellmann, Richard, 3, 11, 33, 91
Enneads (Plotinus), 159
Equal Love (Field), 134

F

Fall of Constantinople, The (Neale), 134
"Fergus and the Druid," 145
Field, Michael, 134
"Folly of Being Comforted, The," 57
"For Anne Gregory," 84
"Four Ages of Man, The," 173
French symbolism, 43-45, 49-50, 52-53, 155
Freud, Sigmund, 50-51
"Friends," 29
Full Moon in March, A, 13, 153

G

"Gerontion" (Eliot), 162
Gibbon, Edward, 131-32
Gods and Fighting Men (Gregory),
  145
Gonne, Iseult, 44
Gonne, Maud, 6, 12, 24, 25, 27-28, 29,
  44
Gordon, D. J., 3, 4
Green Helmet, The, 60
Gregory, Lady Augusta, 2, 14, 28, 93,
  132, 145
Gregory, Robert, 6, 14, 24, 25
"Grey Rock, The," 82
Guaita, Stanislas de, 45
"Gyres, The," 112
Gyres, theory of (*see* Mysticism)

H

Harris, Frank, 169
Harrison, Frederic, 134
Henley, W. E., 37
Heritage of Symbolism (Bowra),
  43
Herne's Egg, The, 172-73
Hérodiade (Mallarmé), 45
Higgins, F. R., 165
"High Talk," 170
History of the Later Roman Empire
  (Bury), 133
"Hollow Men, The" (Eliot), 149
Holmes, W. G., 132
Hone, Joseph, 24, 43
Horton, W. T., 49
"Host of the Air, The," 81-82
Huysmans, J. K., 46

I

Ibsen, Henrik, 44
Identity of Yeats, The (Ellmann), 11,
  33
"Image from a Past Life, A," 88
Imagery, in the "Byzantium" poems,
  137-38 (*see also* Symbolism)
Indian philosophy, Yeats's interest in,

36, 144-45, 168-69
"In Memory of Major Robert
  Gregory," 14, 126, 160
Intruse, L' (Maeterlinck), 44
Ireland, Yeats's involvement with, 19,
  27, 31, 163-64, 166-68
"Irish Airman Foresees His Death, An,"
  14-15, 17
Irish mythology, Yeats's use of, 2-3,
  19, 47, 58, 81, 87, 111n, 160

J

James, Henry, 37-38
Jarry, Alfred, 44
John of the Cross, Saint, 80
Johnson, Lionel, 26, 28, 37, 38-39
Joyce, James, 34, 35, 78, 174

K

Keats, John, 20
Kenner, Hugh, 1
King Lear (Shakespeare), 61, 77
King of the Great Clock Tower, The,
  83, 111n, 165, 166, 167, 169, 171-72

L

Land of Heart's Desire, The, 81-82,
  160
Lane, Hugh, 29
"Lapis Lazuli," 6
Last Poems, 24, 76, 87, 88-92 (*see also*
  titles of individual poems)
Lawrence, D. H., 34, 35, 166
Leavis, F. R., 13
Lecky, William E. H., 132
"Leda" (Lawrence), 34
"Leda and the Swan," 2, 10, 34, 36,
  52, 73-74, 157
Lesson of the Master, The (James),
  37-38
Lévi, Eliphas, 46, 47, 49,
  50
Lovelace, Richard, 57
"Lover's Song, The,"
  76

M

MacBride, Major John, 27
MacKenna, Stephan, 52
MacNeice, Louis, 156, 158
Maeterlinck, Maurice, 44, 46, 50
"Magic," 46
Mallarmé, Stéphane, 43, 45, 51, 52, 53
Mann, Thomas, 78
Mannin, Ethel, 165, 167, 168, 170, 172
"Man Who Dreamed of Faeryland, The," 149
Marius the Epicurean (Pater), 38
Masks, Yeats's theory of, 2, 30-32, 94, 109, 127, 164
Mathers, MacGregor, 26, 45, 46, 48
"Matrix" (Wellesley), 169
Mead, G. R. S., 133
Melchiori, Giorgio, 4, 134, 136
"Men Improve with Years," 13-14, 15
Michael Robartes and the Dancer, 83 (*see also* titles of individual poems)
"Michael Robartes and the Dancer," 84
Migration of Symbols, The (D'Alviella), 137
Milton, John, 52
Moore, George, 51
Moore, Sturge, 115
Moréas, Jean, 51
Morris, William, 58, 134, 166
"Municipal Gallery Revisited, The," 23, 29
"Mystic and Cavalier," 39
Mysticism, 26, 33-36, 45-53 *passim*, 89, 94, 137-38, 139-54
Mythology (*see* Irish mythology, Yeats's use of)

N

Neale, J. E., 134
New Poems (Lawrence), 34
"News for the Delphic Oracle," 86
Nicephorus (Harrison), 134

O

O'Connor, Frank, 163, 165
O'Duffy, General, 166, 167
O'Grady, Standish, 25
"Oil and Blood," 84
O'Leary, Ellen, 27
O'Leary, John, 25, 26, 27, 89, 96
Only Jealousy of Emer, The, 61, 82-83
On the Boiler, 164, 165, 166
"On Woman," 35-36
Order of the Golden Dawn, 45, 47, 48, 51, 137
Origin of Christian Church Art, The (Strzygowski), 132
Ossietsky, Carl von, 107
"Out of the Rose," 44, 49

P

Pages from a Diary Written in Nineteen Hundred and Thirty, 88
Parnell, Charles Stewart, 165
"Parnell's Funeral," 164
"Parting," 77
Patanjali, 169
Pater, Walter, 38
Paul the Silentiary, 135
"Peace," 57
Péguy, Charles, 44
Péladan, Sar, 134
Per Amica Silentia Lunae, 2, 41
"Phases of the Moon, The," 13, 21-22
Philosophy, Yeats's system of, 64-79, 139-54 (*see also Vision, A*)
"Philosophy of Shelley's Poetry, The," 2, 13
Physical vs. spiritual, theme of, in Yeats's works, 81-92
Plato, 84, 86, 87
Player Queen, The, 36
Plays for Dancers, 58, 61
Plotinus, 52, 86, 159
Plutarch, 53
"Poet Pleads with the Elemental Powers, The," 47
"Poetry and the Tradition," 41

Poetry of W. B. Yeats, The
  (MacNeice), 156, 158
"Politics," 88
Politics, Yeats's involvement in,
  166-68
Pollexfen, George, 24, 26, 27
Pound, Ezra, 3, 18, 19, 28, 89, 133,
  162
"Prayer for My Daughter, A," 126
"Prayer for Old Age, A," 88
Prelude, The (Wordsworth), 19
Prince de Byzance, Le (Péladan),
  134
Procopius, 135
Prometheus Unbound (Shelley), 47,
  172
Prophetic Books (Blake), Yeats's
  edition of, 49
Purgatory, 59, 60, 166
Purohit, Swami Shri, 36, 168-69
Pythagoras, 52, 53

R

Ravenna (Wilde), 134
Régnier, Henri de, 51
Responsibilities, 13, 57, 82 (*see also*
  titles of individual poems)
Reveries, 1
Rhyme, Yeats's use of, 107-8, 111,
  126
"Ribh Denounced Patrick," 84, 85
Rilke, Rainer Maria, 75
Rimbaud, Arthur, 46, 50
Romanticism, and Yeats's works, 18-
  20, 40-41, 88, 155-62
Ronsard, Pierre, 43
"Rosa Alchemica," 35, 44, 49,
  134-35
Rose, The, 48-49 (*see also* titles of
  individual poems)
Rosenkreutz, Father Christian,
  48
Rosicrucians, 45-46, 47, 53
Rossetti, Dante Gabriel, 58
Ruddock, Margot, 165
Russell, George (AE), 26, 81,
  147

S

Sacred Dance,The (Mead), 133
"Sailing to Byzantium," 11, 18, 53,
  78, 84, 85, 90, 130, 134
  imagery in, 137-38
  sources of, 94-95
  working drafts of, 96-116
"Saint and the Hunchback, The,"
  52
"Second Coming, The," 2, 162, 167
Secret Rose, The, 81
*Selected Poems of Dorothy Wellesley,
  The*, 76-77
Sexual themes, in Yeats's works,
  35-36, 85, 88, 90-91
Shadowy Waters, The, 4, 44, 49, 50,
  58, 87
Shakespear, Olivia, 3, 28, 29, 36, 94
Shakespeare, William, 3, 25, 56,
  60, 77, 165
Sharp, William, 44
Shaw, George Bernard, 62
Shelley, Percy Bysshe, 3, 45, 46, 49,
  172
"Shepherd and Goatherd," 17, 20
"Solomon and the Witch," 36, 85,
  88
"Solomon to Sheba," 36
"Song of the Wandering Aengus, The,"
  51, 91
Speckled Bird, The, 35
"Spur, The," 59, 89, 165
"Statues, The," 170
Steinach, Eugen, 165-66
Stephans, F. G., 134
Strong, Mrs. Arthur, 132, 138
Strzygowski, Josef, 132
Suckling, Sir John, 57
Summa Theologica (Aquinas), 151
"Supernatural Song," 153
"Swan" (Lawrence), 34
Swedenborg, Emanuel, 46
Swift, Jonathan, 74, 75, 77, 165
Swinburne, Algernon, 55
Symbolism, Yeats's use of, 1, 43-53,
  76-79, 137-38
"Symbolism in Painting," 49

"Symbolism of Poetry, The," 2, 45

Symbolist Movement in Literature (Symons), 43, 45

Symons, Arthur, 43, 45, 49, 134

Synge, John Millington, 27

T

Tate, Allen, 4

Theophano (Harrison), 134

Theosophical Society, 45

"Three Bushes, The," 13, 83

"Three Songs to the One Burden," 170

"Three Songs to the Same Tune," 167

Tindall, William York, 4

Toller, Ernst, 167

"To Some I have Talked with by the Fire," 47-48

"To the Rose upon the Rood of Time," 49

"Towards Break of Day," 88

Tower, The, 10-12, 18 (*see also* titles of individual poems)

"Tower, The," 20, 88

Trembling of the Veil, The, 19, 23

Turner, W. J. R., 169

"Two Kings, The," 82

"Two Songs from a Play," 13

Tynan, Katherine, 1, 50, 87, 149

U

Ubu Roi (Jarry), 44

Ulysses (Joyce), 34

"Under Ben Bulben," 21, 24, 70-72, 145

Unity of Being, Yeats's concept of, 35, 38, 49, 91-92, 94, 96, 130, 136, 148, 157, 166

Upanishads, 168, 169, 170

"Upon a Dying Lady," 17-18

"Upon a House Shaken by the Land Agitation," 51

V

"Vacillation," 89, 90-91

Vale (Moore), 51

Valéry, Paul, 44-45

Variorum Edition, 1

Verlaine, Paul, 43, 44

Villiers de l'Isle Adam, 43, 46-47, 50

Villon, François, 64, 66, 74, 75

Vision, A, 2, 3, 4, 12-13, 22, 33, 34-36, 39, 51-52, 64-65, 70, 72, 91, 93-94, 95-96, 133, 137, 139-54, 156-62 *passim,* 168, 170-72

Voltaire, 131

W

Wade, Allen, 24

Wanderings of Oisin, The, 4, 50, 81, 149, 160

Waves, The (Woolf), 34

W. B. Yeats (Hone), 43

Wellesley, Dorothy, 6, 28, 65, 70, 76-77, 156, 158, 165, 169

"Wild Old Wicked Man, The," 88, 165

Wild Swans at Coole, The, 13-18 (*see also* titles of individual poems)

"Wild Swans at Coole, The," 16-17, 18

Wind Among the Reeds, The, 45, 49-50, 82 (*see also* titles of individual poems)

Winding Stair and Other Poems, The, 59 (*see also* titles of individual poems)

Wheelwright, Philip, 69

"When You Are Old" (Ronsard-Yeats), 43, 57

Where There Is Nothing, 87

"Who Goes with Fergus?" 56

"Why Should Not Old Men Be Mad?" 165

Wilde, Oscar, 26, 37, 40, 134, 137

Wills, William Gorman, 134

Wilson, Edmund, 43, 155

"Wisdom," 94

"Woman Young and Old, A," 75-76

Woolf, Virginia, 34, 35

Words upon the Window Pane, The, 86

Wordsworth, William, 19-20

Y

Yeats, John Butler (father), 1, 24, 39-40, 147, 164
Yeats: The Man and the Masks (Ellmann), 91
Yeats, William Butler:
  and the Abbey Theatre, 29, 62, 163, 165
  and art vs. life, theme of, 37-42
  and Blake, William, 3, 26, 33-34, 35, 40, 45, 46, 49, 77, 83, 111, 136, 161, 165
  and Blavatsky, Mme., 45-46, 47
  and Byzantine culture, 93-96, 132-38 *passim*, 156-57
  characters, use of, 81-82, 87
  and his contemporaries, 37-39
  cyclical theory of history, 112, 148
  as a dramatic poet, 60-61, 172-73
  and the French symbolists, 43-45, 49-50, 52-53, 155
  and Gonne, Maud, 6, 12, 24, 25, 27-28, 29, 44
  and Gregory, Lady Augusta, 2, 14, 28, 93, 132, 145
  and Indian philosophy, 36, 144-45, 168-69
  and Ireland, 19, 27, 31, 163-64, 166-68
  Irish mythology, use of, 2-3, 19, 47, 58, 81, 87, 111*n*, 160
  last years of, 163-74
  masks, theory of, 2, **30-32**, 94, 109, 127, 164

  myticism of, 26, 33-36, 45-53 *passim*, 89, 94, 137-38, **139-54**
  philosophical system of, 64-79, 139-54 (*see also Vision, A*)
  physical vs. spiritual, theme of, 81-92
  poetic development of, 55-59
  political beliefs of, 166-68
  rhyme, use of, 107-8, 111, 126
  and Romanticism, 18-20, 40-41, 88, 155-62
  sexual themes in works of, 35-36, 85, 88, 90-91
  and Shakespeare, William, 3, 25, 56, 60, 77, 165
  and Shelley, Percy Bysshe, 3, 45, 46, 49, 172
  symbolism, use of, 1, **43-53**, 76-79, 137-38
  Unity of Being, concept of, 35, 38, 49, 91-92, 94, 96, 130, 136, 148, 157, 166
  and Wellesley, Dorothy, 6, 28, 65, 70, 76-77, 156, 158, 165, 169
  and Wordsworth, William, 19-20
  working methods of, 3, 4-5, **96-130**
  and Yeats, John Butler (father), 1, 24, 39-40, 147, 164
Yeats, William Butler, works by: (*see individual titles*)
Yellow Book, The, 37

Z

Zola, Émile, 44
Zoroaster, 48

INDEX
TO
CRITICS

AARON, DANIEL
 Emerson and the Progressive Tradition   12: 85-99
 Late Thoughts on Nathanael West
  94: 161-70

ACKERMAN, JOHN
 The Welsh Background   56: 25-44

ADAMS, HAZARD
 "The Crystal Cabinet" and "The
  Golden Net"   58: 79-87

ADAMS, ROBERT M.
 Crashaw and Dylan Thomas: Devotional Athletes   56: 130-39

AGUINAGA, CARLOS BLANCO
 Cervantes and the Picaresque Mode:
  Notes on Two Kinds of Realism
  89: 137-51

AIKEN, CONRAD
 Emily Dickinson   28: 9-15
 Three Reviews   91: 15-28
 William Faulkner: The Novel as
  Form   65: 46-52

ALBEE, EDWARD
 Which Theater Is the Absurd One?
  69: 170-76

ALDRIDGE, JOHN
 Fitzgerald: The Horror and the
  Vision of Paradise   17: 32-42

ALEXANDER, STANLEY
 Cannery Row: Steinbeck's Pastoral
  Poem   100: 135-48

ALONSO, DAMASO
 Lorca and the Expression of the
  Spanish Essence   14: 50-56

ALVAREZ, A.
 Jude the Obscure   25: 113-22

AMIS, KINGSLEY
 A. E. H.   83: 13
 What Became of Jane Austen?
  [Mansfield Park]   26: 141-44

ANDERS, GÜNTHER
 Being without Time: On Beckett's
  Play Waiting for Godot   51:
  140-51

ANDERSON, CHARLES R.
Words   28: 144-49

ANDERSON, QUENTIN
George Eliot in *Middlemarch*   90:
141-60

ANDERSON, SHERWOOD
Sinclair Lewis   6: 27-28

ANDERSON, WARREN D.
Homer and Stephen Crane   66:
146-49

ARENDT, HANNAH
The Poet Bertolt Brecht   11: 43-
50

ARROWSMITH, WILLIAM
Euripides' Theater of Ideas   76:
13-33
Review of *The Mills of the Kavanaughs*   79: 106-9

ARVIN, NEWTON
The House of Pain   12: 46-59
Mardi, Redburn, White-Jacket
13: 21-38

ASSELINEAU, ROGER
Whitman's Style: From Mysticism
to Art   5: 89-106

AUCHINCLOSS, LOUIS
Edith Wharton and Her New Yorks
20: 32-42

AUDEN, W. H.
A. E. Housman   83: 11
Dingley Dell & the Fleet   72: 68-
82
Huck and Oliver   30: 112-16
An Improbable Life   87: 116-37
In Memory of W. B. Yeats   32: 7-
9
The Ironic Hero: Some Reflections
on Don Quixote   89: 73-81
Jehovah Housman and Satan Hous-
man   83: 32-34
A Literary Transference   25:
135-42
The Shield of Achilles
15: 79-80
West's Disease   94: 147-53

AUDIBERTI, JACQUES
Poquelin and Chaplin   41: 170-72

AUERBACH, ERICH
The Aesthetic Dignity of the
Fleurs du mal   18: 149-69
The Brown Stocking   93: 70-89
The Enchanted Dulcinea   89:
98-122
In the Hôtel de la Mole   7: 34-46
Madame Bovary   42: 132-40
Odysseus' Scar   15: 19-37
The Survival and Transformation of
Dante's Vision of Reality   46:
9-13

BAKER, CARLOS
The Necessity of Love: *Alastor* and
the Epipsyche   49: 51-68
The Two African Stories   8:
118-26

BAKER, JOSEP E.
The Adventures of Philip   75:
161-77

BALUKHATY, L. D.
The Cherry Orchard: A Formalist
Approach   71: 136-46

BARISH, JONAS A.
The Double Plot in *Volpone*   22:
93-105
Introduction to *Ben Jonson: A Collection of Critical Essays*   22:
1-13

BARNES, HAZEL E.
Humanistic Existentialism and
Contemporary Psychoanalysis
21: 149-60

BASLER, ROY P.
The Interpretation of "Ligeia"
63: 51-63

BASSAN, MAURICE
Introduction to *Stephen Crane: A
Collection of Critical Essays*
66: 1-11

BATCHELOR, J. P.
Feminism in Virginia Woolf   93:
169-79

BATE, WALTER JACKSON
Introduction to *Keats: A Collection of Critical Essays* 43: 1-8
Negative Capability 43: 51-68
The Ode *To Autumn* 43: 155-60

BATESON, F. W.
The Poetry of Emphasis 83: 130-46

BATTENHOUSE, ROY W.
Tamburlaine's Passions 44: 57-68

BAUDELAIRE, CHARLES
Madame Bovary 42: 88-96

BAUM, S. V.
E. E. Cummings: The Technique of Immediacy 98: 104-20

BAUMBACH, JONATHAN
Nightmare of a Native Son: *Invisible Man,* by Ralph Ellison 97: 64-78

BAXANDALL, LEE
The Theater of Edward Albee 69: 80-98

BAYLEY, JOHN
Dylan Thomas 56: 140-68
Oliver Twist: "Things as They Really Are" 72: 83-96
W. H. Auden 38: 60-80

BECK, WARREN
William Faulkner's Style 65: 53-65

BECKETT, SAMUEL, and GEORGES DUTHUIT
Three Dialogues 41: 16-22

BEEBE, MAURICE
The Universe of Roderick Usher 63: 121-33

BEERBOHM, MAX
The Feast 53: 13-15
Jacobean and Shavian 34: 18-26

BEHAN, BRENDAN
Oscar Wilde 87: 175-76

BEISSNER, FRIEDRICH
Kafka the Artist 17: 15-31

BELOOF, ROBERT
Prosody and Tone: The "Mathe-matics" of Marianne Moore 86: 144-49

BENARDETE, SETH
Sophocles' *Oedipus Tyrannus* 54: 105-21

BÉNICHON, PAUL
The Anti-Bourgeois 41: 60-68

BENTLEY, ERIC
Henrik Ibsen: A Personal Statement 52: 11-17
The Importance of Being Earnest 87: 111-15
The Making of a Dramatist (1892-1903) 50: 57-75
On Brecht's *In the Swamp, A Man's a Man,* and *Saint Joan of the Stockyards* 11: 51-58
Sartre's Struggle for Existenz 21: 73-79
Strindberg, the One and the Many 95: 97-104
Trying to Like O'Neill 39: 89-98

BERDNIKOV, A.
Ivanov: An Analysis 71: 88-98

BERGER, HARRY, JR.
Introduction to *Spenser: A Collection of Critical Essays* 80: 1-12
The *Mutabilitie Cantos:* Archaism and Evolution in Retrospect 80: 146-76

BERLIN, ISAIAH
Tolstoy and Enlightenment 68: 28-51

BERRYMAN, JOHN
Crane's Art 66: 27-51
Despondency and Madness 79: 124-30

BERTHOFF, WARNER
The "New" Poetry: Robinson and Frost 91: 117-27

BESPALOFF, RACHEL
Helen 15: 100-104
The World of the Man Condemned to Death 1: 92-107

BESTERMAN, THEODORE
The Real Voltaire through His
Letters   78: 31-63

BETHELL, Ş. L.
Antony and Cleopatra   40:
152-68

BETJEMAN, JOHN
The Arrest of Oscar Wilde at the
Cadogan Hotel   87: 42-43

BEVINGTON, DAVID M.
The Jew of Malta   44: 144-58

BEWLEY, MARIUS
Melville and the Democratic Experi-
ence   13: 91-115
Scott Fitzgerald's Criticism of
America   27: 125-42

BISHOP, THOMAS
Pirandello's Influence on French
Drama   67: 43-65

BLACKBURN, SUSAN SMITH
Humor in the Plays of Federico
García Lorca   14: 155-66

BLACKHAM, H. J.
Anguished Responsibility   21:
166-71

BLACKMUR, R. P.
The Craft of Herman Melville: A
Putative Statement   13: 75-90
The Dialectic of Incarnation: Tol-
stoy's *Anna Karenina*   68:
127-45
Emily Dickinson's Notation   28:
78-87
In the Hope of Straightening
Things Out   2: 136-48
Irregular Metaphysics   2: 58-64
The Method of Marianne Moore
86: 66-86
Review of *50 Poems*   98: 75-78
Review of *Land of Unlikeliness*
79: 38-39
Utopia, or Uncle Tom's Cabin   6:
108-10
W. B. Yeats: Between Myth and
Philosophy   32: 64-79

BLACKSTONE, BERNARD
Guilt and Retribution in Byron's
Sea Poems   91: 31-41

BLAIR, WALTER
Tom Sawyer   30: 64-82

BLANCHOT, MAURICE
Gide and the Concept of Literature
as Adventure   88: 49-62
Time, Art, and the Museum   37:
147-60

BLAU, HERBERT
The Whole Man and the Real Witch
84: 122-29

BLOCH, ERNST
Odysseus Did Not Die In Ithaca
15: 81-85

BLÖCKER, GUNTER
William Faulkner   65: 122-25

BLOMFIELD, JOAN
The Style and Structure of *Beowulf*
82: 57-65

BLOOM, HAROLD
Notes toward a Supreme Fiction:
A Commentary   33: 76-95
The *Ode to Psyche* and the *Ode on
Melancholy*   43: 91-101
States of Being: *The Four Zoas*
58: 104-18
"The Two Spirits," *Adonais,* and
The Triumph of Life   49:
159-76

BLOOMFIELD, MORTON W.
Beowulf and Christian Allegory: An
Interpretation of Unferth   82:
68-75

BLUESTONE, GEORGE
The Grapes of Wrath   100: 102-21

BLUM, LEON
A Theoretical Outline of "Beylism"
7: 101-13

BLUME, BERNHARD
Aspects of Contradiction: On Recent Criticisms of Thomas Mann
36: 155-69

BLUNT, ANTHONY
The First Illuminated Books   58:
127-41

BOGAN, LOUISE
A Mystical Poet   28: 137-43

BOGARD, TRAVIS
Anna Christie: Her Fall and Rise
39: 62-71
The Comedy of Thornton Wilder
69: 52-69

BONE, ROBERT
Ralph Ellison and the Uses of
Imagination   97: 45-63

BOOTH, PHILIP
Letter from a Distant Land   10:
180-84

BORGES, JORGE LUIS
About Oscar Wilde   87: 172-74

BORROFF, MARIE
Introduction to *Wallace Stevens: A
Collection of Critical Essays*
33: 1-23

BOSTETTER, EDWARD E.
The Nightmare World of *The
Ancient Mariner*   70: 65-77

BOTTIGLIA, WILLIAM F.
Candide's Garden   78: 87-111
Introduction to *Voltaire: A Collec-
tion of Critical Essays*   78: 1-17

BOURNE, RANDOLPH
The Art of Theodore Dreiser   96:
81-86

BOWRA, C. M.
Some Characteristics of Literary
Epic   62: 53-61
"The Tragic Vision"   99: 10-28

BRADBROOK, M. C.
The *Jew of Malta* and *Edward II*
44: 128-37
Virtue Is the True Nobility: A
Study of the Structure of *All's
Well that Ends Well*   47: 119-32

BRADBURY, MALCOLM
Howards End   59: 128-43
Introduction to *Forster: A Collec-*

tion of Critical Essays   59: 1-
14

BRADFORD, CURTIS
Yeats's Byzantium Poems: A Study
of Their Development   23:
93-130

BRAY, RENÉ
The Actor   41: 14-19
World of Imagination   41: 54-59

BRECHT, BERTOLT
Ovation for Shaw   50: 15-18

BREDVOLD, LOUIS I.
The Intellectual Milieu of John
Dryden   32: 17-30

BRÉE, GERMAINE
The Counterfeiters   88: 112-28
The Inhuman World of Pleasure
4: 69-87
Introduction to *Camus: A Collec-
tion of Critical Essays*   1: 1-10

BRENAN, GERALD
Cervantes   89: 13-33

BRIDGES, ROBERT
The Oddities of Genius   57: 71-75

BROCKBANK, J. P.
The Damnation of Faustus   44:
112-19
The Frame of Disorder—*Henry VI*
45: 55-65

BROMBERT, VICTOR
L'Education Sentimentale: Profana-
tion and the Permanence of
Dreams   52: 154-76
Introduction to *Stendhal: A Collec-
tion of Critical Essays*   7: 1-14
Malraux: Passion and Intellect
37: 134-46
Stendhal, Analyst or Amorist?   7:
157-66

BRONSON, BERTRAND H.
Johnson Agonistes   48: 30-45

BROOKS, CLEANTH
Alfred Edward Housman   83: 62-
84
Auden's Imagery   38: 15-25

BROOKS, CLEANTH (*continued*)
History and the Sense of the Tragic: *Absalom, Absalom!* 65: 186-203
The Language of Paradox: "The Canonization" 19: 100-108

BROOKS, CLEANTH, and ROBERT PENN WARREN
The Discovery of Evil: An Analysis of "The Killers" 8: 114-17

BROOKS, HAROLD
Themes and Structure in *The Comedy of Errors* 47: 11-25

BROOKS, R. A.
Discolor Aura: Reflections on the Golden Bough 62: 143-63

BROOKS, VAN WYCK
Mark Twain's Humor 30: 13-28
The Pilgrimage I 34: 57-62

BROWER, REUBEN A.
An Allusion to Europe: Dryden and Poetic Tradition 32: 43-54
Light and Bright and Sparkling: Irony and Fiction in *Pride and Prejudice* 26: 62-75
Something Central Which Permeated: Virginia Woolf and "Mrs. Dalloway" 93: 51-62

BROWN, E. K.
Edith Wharton 20: 62-72
Edith Wharton: The Art of the Novel 20: 95-102
Rhythm in E. M. Forster's *A Passage to India* 59: 144-59

BROWN, JOHN RUSSELL
Dialogue in Pinter and Others 74: 122-43
Introduction to *Modern British Dramatists: A Collection of Critical Essays* 74: 1-14

BROWN, NORMAN O.
The Excremental Vision 35: 31-54

BROWN, STUART GERRY
Dr. Johnson and the Old Order 48: 158-71

BRUMFITT, J. H.
Voltaire: Historian 78: 77-86

BRUSTEIN, ROBERT
August Strindberg 97: 27-47
Bernard Shaw: The Face Behind the Mask 50: 100-118
The English Stage 74: 164-70
The Men-Taming Women of William Inge: *The Dark at the Top of the Stairs* 69: 70-79
Pirandello's Drama of Revolt 67: 103-33

BRYANT, JOSEPH ALLEN
Catiline and the Nature of Jonson's Tragic Fable 22: 147-59

BUBER, MARTIN
Kafka and Judaism 17: 157-62

BÜDEL, OSCAR
Contemporary Theater and Aesthetic Distance 11: 59-85

BUDGEN, FRANK
James Joyce: An Encounter with Homer 15: 156-57

BURKE, KENNETH
Likings of an Observationist 86: 125-33
Motives and Motifs in the Poetry of Marianne Moore 86: 87-100
William Carlos Williams: Two Judgments 61: 47-61

BURKHARDT, SIGURD
Poetry and the Language of Communion 57: 160-67

BURNAM, TOM
The Eyes of Dr. Eckleburg: A Reexamination of *The Great Gatsby* 27: 104-11

BURNETT, ANNE PIPPIN
The Virtues of Admetus 76: 51-69

BURRA, PETER
The Novels of E. M. Forster 59: 21-33

BUSH, DOUGLAS
Characters and Drama 60: 109-20

BUSH, DOUGLAS (*continued*)
Keats   43: 13-40

CALDERWOOD, JAMES L.
Commodity and Honour in *King John*   45: 85-101

CALLAN, EDWARD
Auden's New Year Letter: A New Style of Architecture   38: 152-59

CAMBON, GLAUCO
Introduction to *Pirandello: A Collection of Critical Essays*   67: 1-10

CAMPBELL, LILY B.
English History in the Sixteenth Century   45: 13-31

CAMPBELL, ROY
The Early Poems   14: 65-79

CAMUS, ALBERT
Hope and the Absurd in the World of Franz Kafka   17: 147-55

CANTWELL, ROBERT
Sinclair Lewis   6: 111-18

CARNE-ROSS, DONALD
The Two Voices of Translation   79: 152-72

CARROLL, DAVID R.
Felix Holt: Society as Protagonist   90: 124-40

CARROLL, JOHN
Introduction to *Samuel Richardson: A Collection of Critical Essays*   85: 1-19

CATHER, WILLA
When I Knew Stephen Crane   66: 12-17

CATTAUI, GEORGES
Images as Instruments   4: 88-91

CAVAFY, C. P.
Ithaka   15: 158-59

CHAMBERS, ROSS
Beckett's Brinkmanship   51: 152-68
Measure for Measure   47: 88-108

CHAMPIGNY, ROBERT
Comedien and Martyr   21: 80-91
Ethics and Aesthetics in *The Stranger*   1: 122-31
Proust, Bergson, and Other Philosophers   4: 122-31

CHAMPNEY, FREEMAN
John Steinbeck, California   100: 18-35

CHARLTON, H. B.
Humanism and Mystery   40: 10-17

CHASE, RICHARD
The Brontës: A Centennial Observance   92: 19-33
Introduction to *Melville: A Collection of Critical Essays*   13: 1-10
Melville and *Moby Dick*   13: 49-61
Walt Whitman as American Spokesman   5: 155-62

CHAYES, IRENE H.
Little Girls Lost: Problems of a Romantic Archetype   58: 65-78

CHENEY, DONALD
From "Plowman and Knight: The Hero's Duality"   80: 63-87

CHESTERTON, G. K.
The Method of Allusive Irrelevancy   75: 15-19

CHIAROMONTE, NICOLA
Albert Camus: In Memoriam   1: 11-15
Malraux and the Demons of Action   37: 96-116
Sartre *versus* Camus: A Political Quarrel   1: 31-37

CHIZHEVSKY, DMITRI
Chekhov in the Development of Russian Literature   71: 49-61
The Theme of the Double in Dostoevsky   16: 112-29

CHRISTIAN, R. F.
Style in *War and Peace*   68: 102-10

CLAUSEN, WENDELL
An Interpretation of the *Aeneid*   62: 75-88

CLEMEN, WOLFGANG
Edward II   44: 138-43

CLIFFORD, JAMES L.
A Survey of Johnsonian Studies, 1887-1950   48: 46-62

CLINE, PATRICIA BUCHANAN TAL-MASON
The Whole E. E. Cummings   98: 60-70

CLURMAN, HAROLD
Arthur Miller's Later Plays   84: 143-68

COBURN, KATHLEEN
Introduction to *Coleridge: A Collection of Critical Essays*   70: 1-11

COHN, RUBY
Philosophical Fragments in the Works of Samuel Beckett   51: 169-77

COLEMAN, ELLIOTT
Religious Imagery   4: 92-96

COLLINS, CARVEL
Nathanael West's *The Day of the Locust* and *Sanctuary*   94: 144-46

COLVERT, JAMES B.
Stephen Crane's Magic Mountain   66: 95-105

COMMAGER, STEELE
Introduction to *Virgil: A Collection of Critical Essays*   62: 1-13

CONNOLLY, CYRIL
A. E. Housman: A Controversy   83: 35-50

CONRAD, JOSEPH
An Appreciation   34: 11-17
His War Book   66: 123-27

CONTINI, GIANFRANCO
Introduction to Dante's *Rime*   46: 28-38

COOK, ALBERT
The Moral Vision: Tolstoy   68: 111-26

COOKE, M. G.
Introduction to *Modern Black Novelists: A Collection of Critical Essays*   97: 1-12

COOLIDGE, JOHN S.
Fielding and "Conservation of Character"   9: 158-76
Marvell and Horace   81: 85-100

COPEAN, JACQUES
On *Les Fourberies de Scapin*   41: 150-54

CORMAN, CID
The Farmers' Daughters: A True Story about People   61: 164-70

CORRIGAN, ROBERT W.
Introduction to *Arthur Miller: A Collection of Critical Essays*   84: 1-22

COWLEY, MALCOLM
Third Act and Epilogue   27: 64-69
The Case against Mr. Frost   3: 36-45
Introduction to *The Portable Faulkner*   65: 34-45
The Last Flight from Main Street   6: 143-46
Nightmare and Ritual in Hemingway   8: 40-51
Sister Carrie's Brother   96: 52-62

COX, C. B.
Introduction to *Dylan Thomas: A Collection of Critical Essays*   56: 1-8

COX, JAMES M.
A Connecticut Yankee: The Machinery of Self-Preservation   30: 117-29
Introduction to *Robert Frost: A Collection of Critical Essays*   3: 1-15

COXE, LOUIS O.
E. A. Robinson: The Lost Tradition   91: 60-76
What Edith Wharton Saw in Innocence   20: 155-61

CRAIG, G. ARMOUR
On the Style of *Vanity Fair* 75: 87-103

CRAMP, ROSEMARY
Beowulf and Archaeology 82: 114-40

CRANE, HART
C 33 87: 46

CREED, ROBERT P.
The Making of an Anglo-Saxon Poem 82: 141-53

CREEGER, GEORGE R.
An Interpretation of *Adam Bede* 90: 86-106
Introduction to *George Eliot: A Collection of Critical Essays* 90: 1-10

CREELEY, ROBERT
A Character for Love 61: 160-63

CREWS, FREDERICK C.
E. M. Forster's Comic Spirit 59: 96-105
The Logic of Compulsion in "Roger Malvin's Burial" 55: 111-22

CROFTS, J. E. V.
John Donne: A Reconsideration 19: 77-89

CROMPTON, LOUIS
Shaw's Challenge to Liberalism 50: 88-99

CUNNINGHAM, DOLORA
The Jonsonian Masque as a Literary Form 22: 160-74

CURLEY, DANIEL
Legate of the Ideal 53: 75-82

D'AGOSTINO, NEMI
The Later Hemingway 8: 152-60

DAICHES, DAVID
The Poetry of Dylan Thomas 56: 14-24

DANIEL, CARTER A.
West's Revisions of *Miss Lonelyhearts* 94: 52-65

DAVIDSON, DONALD
The Traditional Basis of Thomas Hardy's Fiction 25: 10-23

DAVIE, DONALD
T. S. Eliot: The End of an Era 2: 192-205

DAVIS, ROBERT MURRAY
Introduction to *Steinbeck: A Collection of Critical Essays* 100: 1-17

DAY, CYRUS
Amor Fati: O'Neill's Lazarus as Superman and Savior 39: 72-81

DAY LEWIS, C.
Nearing Again the Legendary Isle 15: 90

deBEAUVOIR, SIMONE
Stendhal, or The Romantic of Reality 7: 147-56

DE CASTRIS, A. L.
The Experimental Novelist 67: 91-102

DEER, IRVING
Ibsen's Brand: Paradox and the Symbolic Hero 52: 52-62

DELAY, JEAN
The Consultation 88: 129-51

DEL RIO, ANGEL
Lorca's Theater 14: 140-54

DEMETZ, PETER
Introduction to *Brecht: A Collection of Critical Essays* 11: 1-15

D'ENTREVES, ALLESANDRO PASSERIN
Civitas 46: 141-50

DeVOTO, BERNARD
The Symbol of Despair 30: 140-58

DEWEY, JOHN
Ralph Waldo Emerson 12: 24-30

DICKEY, JAMES
Edwin Arlington Robinson: The Many Truths 91: 77-94

DIGEON, AURELIEN
  Jonathan Wild   9: 69-80
DIMOCK, GEORGE E., JR.
  The Name of Odysseus   15:
    106-21
DOBRÉE, BONAMY
  The Tempest   47: 164-76
DODDS, JOHN W.
  Thackeray's Irony   75: 30-37
DONNER, H. W.
  Dr. Johnson as a Literary Critic
    48: 102-13
DONOGHUE, DENIS
  The Cocktail Party   2: 173-86
  For a Redeeming Language   61:
    121-31
  The Other Emily   92: 157-72
  The Proper Plenitude of Fact   86:
    165-71
DOOLITTLE, JAMES
  The Humanity of Móliere's *Don
    Juan*   41: 90-102
DORIUS, R. J.
  A Little More than a Little   45:
    113-31
DOUBROVSKI, SERGE
  Camus in America   1: 16-19
  The Ethics of Albert Camus   1:
    71-84
DOUGLAS, ALFRED
  The Dead Poet   87: 44
  Sonnet on Wilde   87: 45
DOUGLAS, KENNETH
  The Self-Inflicted Wound   21: 39-
    46
DOVER WILSON, J.
  Falstaff and the Prince   45:
    132-51
DRAKE, WILLIAM
  Walden   10: 71-91
  A Week on the Concord and Merri-
    mack Rivers   10: 63-70
DREW, PHILIP
  Charlotte Brontë as a Critic of
    Wuthering Heights   92: 44-58

DRIVER, TOM F.
  On the Late Plays of Eugene O'Neill
    39: 110-23
  Strength and Weakness in Arthur
    Miller   84: 59-67
  What's the Matter with Edward
    Albee?   69: 99-103
DU BOS, CHARLES
  The Chekhovian Sense of Life   71:
    184-94
  Meditation on the Life of Baudel-
    aire   18: 38-66
DULLIN, CHARLES
  On *L'Avare*   41: 155-59
DURAN, MANUEL
  Introduction to *Lorca: A Collection
    of Critical Essays*   14: 1-17
DYSON, A. E.
  The Great Gatsby: Thirty-six Years
    After   27: 112-24
  Look Back in Anger   74: 47-57

EBERHART, RICHARD
  Review of *Lord Weary's Castle*   79:
    48-52
EDEL, LEON
  The Art of Evasion   8: 169-71
  Introduction to *Henry James: A
    Collection of Critical Essays*
    34: 1-10
  The Novel as Poem   93: 63-69
  The Tales   34: 172-79
EDGAR, PELHAM
  The Essential Novelist?   34: 92-
    101
EDITORS OF *THE SEVEN ARTS*
  Henry David Thoreau (1817-1917)
    10: 9-12
EHRENPREIS, IRVIN
  The Age of Lowell   79: 74-98
  The Meaning of Gulliver's Last
    Voyage   35: 123-42
EIKHENBAUM, BORIS M.
  Chekhov at Large   71: 21-31
  On Tolstoy's Crises   68: 52-55

ELIOT, T. S.
Andrew Marvell   81: 18-28
Ben Jonson   22: 14-23
Christopher Marlowe   44: 12-17
Ezra Pound   29: 17-25
Introduction to *Selected Poems*
   86: 60-65
John Dryden   32: 8-16
Keats   43: 11-12
Marianne Moore (1923)   86: 48-
   51
A Note on the Verse of John Milton
   60: 12-18
A Prediction   34: 55-56
The *Vita Nuova*   46: 23-27
Yeats   23: 54-63

ELLIOTT, GEORGE P.
Poet of Many Voices   29: 152-62

ELLIS-FERMOR, UNA
The Equilibrium of Tragedy   44:
   108-12

ELLMANN, RICHARD
Introduction to *Oscar Wilde: A
   Collection of Critical Essays*
   87: 1-8
Overtures to *Salome*   87: 73-91
Reality   23: 163-74

EMPSON, WILLIAM
Collected Poems and *Under Milk
   Wood*   56: 84-88
Milton and Bentley: The Pastoral of
   the Innocence of Man and Na-
   ture   60: 19-39
The Style of the Master   2: 152-54
Tom Jones   9: 123-45
"A Valediction: Of Weeping"   19:
   52-60

ENGEL, MONROE
The Continuity of Lawrence's
   Short Novels   24: 93-100

ENTWISTLE, WILLIAM J.
Ocean of Story   89: 162-68

ERDMAN, DAVID V.
Blake's Vision of Slavery   58: 88-
   103

ERIKSON, ERIK

Biographic: G.B.S. (70) on George
   Bernard Shaw (20)   50: 19-25

ESSLIN, MARTIN
Brecht's Language and Its Sources
   11: 171-82
Godot and His Children: The Thea-
   tre of Samuel Beckett and
   Harold Pinter   74: 48-70
Introduction to *Samuel Beckett:
   A Collection of Critical Essays*
   51: 1-15

EULAU, HEINZ
Wayside Challenger: Some Remarks
   on the Politics of Henry David
   Thoreau   10: 117-30

EVANS, DAVID W.
Ezra Pound as Prison Poet   29:
   80-86

EVANS, MAURICE
The Fall of Guyon   80: 88-96

FABRE, MICHEL
Fathers and Sons in James Baldwin's *Go Tell It on the Mountain*
   97: 88-104

FAGLES, ROBERT
Epilogue: Homer and the Writers
   15: 160-72

FAIRLEY, BARKER
The Defeat of Convention
   73: 10-25

FARNHAM, WILLARD
The Tragic Qualm   40: 18-23

FARRELL, WILLIAM J.
The Style and the Action in *Clarissa*
   85: 92-101

FEIDELSON, CHARLES, JR.
Hawthorne as Symbolist   55: 64-
   71
Toward Melville: Some Versions of
   Emerson   12: 136-57
Whitman as Symbolist   5: 80-88

FERGUSSON, FRANCIS
Action as Theatrical: *Six Characters
   in Search of an Author*   67: 35-
   42

FERGUSSON, FRANCIS (*continued*)
Broadway   69: 104-10
The Cherry Orchard: A Theater
   Poem of the Suffering of Change
   71: 147-60
Don Perlimplin: Lorca's Theater-
   Poetry   14: 167-76
Ghosts: The Tragic Rhythm in a
   Small Figure   52: 109-19
Macbeth as the Imitation of an Ac-
   tion   40: 105-12

FERNANDEZ, RAMON
The Comedy of Will   41: 50-53
In Search of the Self   4: 136-49

FIEDLER, LESLIE
As Free as Any Cretur   30: 130-39
Dreiser and the Sentimental Novel
   96: 45-51
Men without Women   8: 86-92
Some Notes on F. Scott Fitzgerald
   27: 70-76

FINLEY, JOHN H., JR.
The Suppliants   99: 63-72

FISHER, PETER F.
Blake and the Druids   58: 156-78

FISKE, IRVING
Bernard Shaw and William Blake
   50: 170-78

FITZGERALD, ROBERT
Hellas   15: 105

FJELDE, ROLF
Introduction to *Ibsen: A Collection
   of Critical Essays*   52: 1-11

FLETCHER, IAN, and D. J. GORDON
Byzantium   23: 131-38

FLETCHER, JOHN
The Private Pain and the Whey of
   Words: A Survey of Beckett's
   Verse   51: 23-32

FLORES, ANGEL
Miss Lonelyhearts in the Haunted
   Castle   94: 68-69

FOERSTER, FORMAN
Emerson on the Organic Principle
   in Art   12: 108-20

FOGLE, RICHARD HARTER
The Abstractness of Shelley   49:
   13-29
"The Artist of the Beautiful"   55:
   99-110
"Benito Cereno"   13: 116-24
Synaesthetic Imagery in Keats
   43: 41-50

FONTENROSE, JOSEPH
Sea of Cortez   100: 122-34

FORD, FORD MADOX
Conrad on the Theory of Fiction
   53: 167-77
Dodsworth: 6: 100-101

FORD, GEORGE H.
The Poet and the Critics of Prob-
   ability   72: 58-67

FORSTER, E. M.
The Ambassadors   34: 72-78
Ibsen the Romantic   52: 174-78
Our Photography: Sinclair Lewis
   6: 95-99
Virginia Woolf   93: 14-25

FOSTER, KENELM, O. P.
The Mind in Love: Dante's Philosophy   46: 43-60

FOSTER, RICHARD
Criticism as Rage: D. H. Lawrence
   24: 151-61

FRADKIN, I.
On the Artistic Orginality of Bertolt
   Brecht's Drama   11: 97-105

FRANK, JOSEPH
André Malraux: The Image of Man
   37: 71-85

FRASER, G. S.
The Career of W. H. Auden   38:
   81-104

FRECCERO, JOHN
Introduction to *Dante: A Collection
   of Critical Essays*   46: 1-8

FRENCH, WARREN
End of a Dream   100: 63-69

FREUD, SIGMUND
Dostoevsky and Parricide   **16:**
98-111
Oedipus Rex   **54:** 101-4
FRIEDMAN, NORMAN
Introduction to *E. E. Cummings:*
A Collection of Critical Essays
98: 1-4
The Meaning of Cummings   **98:**
46-59
FROHOCK, W. M.
The Power and the Glory   **37:** 31-
60
The Revolt of Ezra Pound   **29:**
87-97
FROST, ROBERT
Introduction to *King Jasper*   **91:**
33-39
On Emerson   **12:** 12-17
FRY, DONALD K.
Introduction to *The Beowulf Poet:*
A Collection of Critical Essays
82: 1-7
FRYCKSTEDT, OLOV W.
Cosmic Pessimism in *The Red Badge*
of Courage   **66:** 141-45
FRYE, NORTHROP
Blake's Introduction to Experience
58: 23-31
Introduction to *Blake: A Collection*
of Critical Essays   **58:** 1-7
Poetry and Design in William Blake
58: 119-26
The Realistic Oriole: A Study of
Wallace Stevens   **33:** 161-76
FUJIMURA, THOMAS H.
Congreve's Last Play   **64:** 167-74
FUSSELL, EDWIN S.
Fitzgerald's Brave New World   **27:**
43-56
One Kind of Traditional Poet   **91:**
95-109
The Red Face of Man   **10:** 142-60

GALLOWAY, DAVID D.
A Picaresque Apprenticeship:
Nathanael West's *The Dream*
Life of Balso Snell and *A Cool*
Million   **94:** 31-47
GARDNER, HELEN
As You Like It   **47:** 58-71
Don Juan   **91:** 113-21
The Historical Approach: *Hamlet*
40: 61-70
Introduction to *John Donne: A Col-*
lection of Critical Essays   **19:**
1-12
The Religious Poetry of John Donne
19: 123-36
GARGANO, JAMES W.
The Question of Poe's Narrators
63: 164-71
GASSNER, JOHN
The Duality of Chekhov   **71:**
175-83
Introduction to *O'Neill: A Collec-*
tion of Critical Essays   **39:** 1-6
The Nature of O'Neill's Achieve-
ment: A Summary and Appraisal
39: 165-71
GAY, PETER
Voltaire's Politics: France and Con-
stitutional Absolutism   **78:**
112-30
GEISMAR, MAXWELL
The Land of Faery   **6:** 129-38
Origins of a Dynasty   **6:** 10-16
GERMAIN, GABRIEL
The Sirens and the Temptation of
Knowledge   **15:** 91-97
GIDE, ANDRÉ
In Dubious Battle   **100:** 47-48
In Memoriam   **87:** 25-34
Notes for a Preface to Fielding's
Tom Jones   **9:** 81-83
GIFFORD, HENRY
Two Philologists   **86:** 172-78
GILMAN, RICHARD
Arden's Unsteady Ground   **74:**
104-16
The Drama Is Coming Now   **69:**
155-69

GILSON, ÉTIENNE
Baudelaire and the Muse   18: 67-
85

GIRARD, ALAIN
The Role of the *Journal* in Gide's
Work   88: 152-64

GIRARD, RENÉ
Existentialism and Criticism   21:
121-28
Introduction to *Proust: A Collection of Critical Essays*   4: 1-12

GIRAUD, RAYMOND
Introduction to *Flaubert: A Collection of Critical Essays*   42: 1-12
Romantic Realism in *Lucien Leuwen*   7: 63-75

GLECKNER, ROBERT F.
Point of View and Context in
Blake's Songs   58: 8-14

GOHEEN, ROBERT F.
Aspects of Dramatic Symbolism:
Three Studies in the *Oresteia*
99: 106-23

GOLDEN, MORRIS
Richardson and the Bold Young
Men   85: 161-80

GOLDMAN, MARK
Virginia Woolf and the Critic as
Reader   93: 155-68

GOLDSMITH, ARNOLD L.
Thematic Rhythm in *The Red Pony*
100: 70-74

GOODMAN, PAUL
Comic Plots: *The Alchemist*   22:
106-20

GORDON, CAROLINE
Notes on Hemingway and Kafka
17: 75-83

GORDON, D. J., and IAN FLETCHER
Byzantium   23: 131-38

GORKY, MAXIM
Fragments from Reminiscences
71: 195-205

GOSSMAN, LIONEL
The Comic Hero and His Idols
41: 69-78

GRAHAM, JOHN
The "Caricature Value" of Parody
and Fantasy in *Orlando*   93:
101-16

GRANGE, KATHLEEN M.
Samuel Johnson's Account of Certain Psychoanalytic Concepts
48: 149-57

GRANT, JOHN E.
Interpreting Blake's "The Fly"
58: 32-55

GRAVES, ROBERT
The Authoress of the *Odyssey*
15: 148-51
Review of *i:Six Nonlectures*   98:
172-76
Ulysses   15: 139

GRAVIER, MAURICE
The Character and the Soul   95:
79-89

GRAY, RONALD
Introduction to *Kafka: A Collection
of Critical Essays*   17: 1-11
Kafka the Writer   17: 61-73
On Brecht's *The Caucasian Chalk
Circle*   11: 151-56

GREEN, PETER
Some Versions of Aeschylus: A
Study of Tradition and Method
in Translating Classical Poetry
99: 164-83

GREENE, DONALD J.
Introduction to *Samuel Johnson: A
Collection of Critical Essays*
48: 1-9
Jane Austen and the Peerage   26:
154-65

GREENE, GRAHAM
The Private Universe   34: 111-12

GREG, W. W.
The Damnation of Faustus   44:
92-107

GREGOR, IAN
Introduction to *The Brontës: A Collection of Critical Essays*   **92:** 1-6
GREIG, J. Y. T.
The Social Critic   **75:** 38-48
GRIERSON, HERBERT J. C.
Donne's Love Poetry   **19:** 23-35
GRODDOCK, GEORG
Peer Gynt   **52:** 63-79
GRONICKA, ANDRÉ VON
Myth plus Psychology: A Stylistic Analysis of *Death in Venice*   **36:** 46-61
GROSSMAN, LEONID
The Naturalism of Chekhov   **71:** 32-48
GRUBE, G. M. A.
Euripides and the Gods   **76:** 34-50
GUARDINI, ROMANO
Aesthetic-Theological Thoughts on "The Windhover"   **57:** 76-79
GUERARD, ALBERT J.
Introduction to *Hardy: A Collection of Critical Essays*   **25:** 1-9
On *The Nigger of the "Narcissus"*   **53:** 17-36
Le Voyage d'Urien   **88:** 63-72
The Women of the Novels   **25:** 63-70
GUICHARNAUD, JACQUES
Introduction to *Molière: A Collection of Critical Essays*   **41:** 1-13
Man and His Acts   **21:** 62-72
Those Years: Existentialism 1943-1945   **21:** 15-20
GUIGUET, JEAN
Characters and Human Relations   **93:** 40-50
GUNN, THOM
William Carlos Williams   **61:** 171-73
GUTHRIE, TYRONE
The World of Thornton Wilder   **69:** 45-51

HAECKER, THEODORE
Odysseus and Aeneas   **62:** 68-74
HAGAN, JOHN
Control of Sympathy in *Wuthering Heights*   **92:** 59-75
HAGSTRUM, JEAN H.
William Blake Rejects the Enlightenment   **58:** 142-55
HAINES, GEORGE, IV
::2:1 The World and E. E. Cummings   **98:** 15-30
HALL, DONALD
The Art of Poetry: Marianne Moore [Interview]   **86:** 20-45
HALL, H. GASTON
A Comic *Dom Juan*   **41:** 103-10
HALLIDAY, E. M.
Hemingway's Ambiguity: Symbolism and Irony   **8:** 52-71
HAMBURGER, KATE
Tolstoy's Art   **68:** 65-77
HAMILTON, A. C.
The Argument of Spenser's *Shepeardes Calender*   **80:** 30-39
HAMMOND, N. G. L.
Personal Freedom and Its Limitations in the *Oresteia*   **99:** 90-105
HANKIN, ST. JOHN
Wilde as a Dramatist   **87:** 61-72
HANNA, THOMAS L.
Albert Camus and the Christian Faith   **1:** 48-58
HARBAGE, ALFRED
Introduction to *Shakespeare: The Tragedies: A Collection of Critical Essays*   **40:** 1-9
King Lear: An Introduction   **40:** 113-22
HARDING, D. W.
"Little Gidding"   **2:** 125-28
The Mechanisms of Failure   **27:** 143-45

HARDING, D. W. (*continued*)
Regulated Hatred: An Aspect of
the Work of Jane Austen 26:
166-79
The Theme of "The Ancient Mariner" 70: 51-64
T. S. Eliot, 1925-1935 2: 104-9

HARDWICK, ELIZABETH
Faulkner and the South Today
65: 226-30

HARDY, BARBARA
The Change of Heart in Dickens'
Novels 72: 39-57
The Moment of Disenchantment in
George Eliot's Novels 90: 55-
65

HARRIS, WILSON
Tradition and the West Indian Novel
97: 30-44

HARTMAN, GEOFFREY H.
The Dialectic of Self-Perception
57: 117-30
Introduction to *Hopkins: A Collec-
tion of Critical Essays* 57: 1-
16
Marvell, St. Paul, and the Body of
Hope 81: 101-19
Milton's Counterplot 60: 100-
108
The Return from Hell 37: 61-70

HARTNER, WILLY
Goethe and the Natural Sciences
73: 145-60

HARVEY, JOHN
Imagination and Moral Theme in
E. M. Forster's *The Longest
Journey* 59: 117-27

HARVEY, W. J.
Chance and Design in *Bleak House*
72: 135-46

HATFIELD, HENRY
Introduction to *Thomas Mann: A
Collection of Critical Essays*
36: 1-6
Thomas Mann's *Buddenbrooks:*

The World of the Father 36:
10-21

HAUSER, DAVID R.
Otway Preserved: Theme and Form
in *Venice Preserv'd* 64: 139-49

HAVELOCK, ERIC A.
Watching the *Trojan Women* 76:
115-27

HAYES, RICHARD
Eugene O'Neill: The Tragic in Exile
39: 52-56

HAZEN, ALLEN T.
Johnson's Prefaces and Dedications
48: 172-78

HEARNE, JOHN
The Fugitive in the Forest: Four
Novels by Wilson Harris 97:
177-80

HEFFNER, RAY L., JR.
Unifying Symbols in the Comedy
of Ben Jonson 22: 133-46

HEIDEGGER, MARTIN
The Ode on Man in Sophocles'
Antigone 54: 86-101

HEILMAN, ROBERT B.
Charlotte Brontë's "New Gothic"
92: 96-109
Variations on Picaresque (*Felix
Krull*) 36: 133-54

HELLER, ERICH
Conversation on the Magic Moun-
tain 36: 62-95
On Goethe's *Faust* 73: 132-44
The World of Franz Kafka 17:
99-122

HENN, T. R.
The Shavian Machine 50: 162-67

HERBST, JOSEPHINE
Miss Lonelyhearts: An Allegory
94: 69-70
Nathanael West 94: 13-28

HERFORD, C. H.
Introduction to *Every Man Out of
His Humour* 22: 82-92

HERINGTON, C. J.
Aeschylus: The Last Phase   99: 148-63

HERMAN, WILLIAM
Pirandello and Possibility   67: 153-72

HEWITT, DOUGLAS
Lord Jim: Conrad and the "Few Simple Notions"   43: 55-62

HIGGINS, DAVID J. M.
Emily Dickinson's Prose   28: 162-78

HIGHET, GILBERT
The Poet and His Culture   31: 145-50

HILL, CHRISTOPHER
Clarissa Harlowe and Her Times   85: 102-23

HILLES, FREDERICK
The Plan of *Clarissa*   85: 80-91

HOEFER, JACQUELINE
Watt   51: 62-76

HOFFMAN, ARTHUR W.
Various John Dryden: All, All of a Piece Throughout   32: 165-80

HOFFMAN, DANIEL G.
The Confidence-Man: His Masquerade   13: 125-43
Crane and Poetic Tradition   66: 57-66
From "Black Magic—and White—in *Huckleberry Finn*"   30: 101-11

HOFMANNSTHAL, HUGO VON
Eugene O'Neill   39: 23-28

HOGGART, RICHARD
Introduction to Auden's Poetry   38: 105-24

HOLBROOK, DAVID
"A Place of Love": *Under Milk Wood*   56: 99-116

HOLLAND, NORMAN
Love for Love   64: 151-64

HOLLANDER, JOHN
Marvell's Commonwealth and

"The Empire of the Ear"   81: 29-41
The Odes to Music   32: 149-64

HOLLOWAY, JOHN
Hardy's Major Fiction   25: 52-62

HOLTHUSEN, HANS EGON
Brecht's Dramatic Theory   11: 106-16
The World without Transcendence   36: 123-32

HONIG, EDWIN
On the Interludes of Cervantes   89: 152-61
Triumph of Sensual Reality—Mature Verse   14: 80-99

HOOG, ARMAND
Malraux, Möllberg, and Frobenius   37: 86-95

HOOK, ANDREW D.
Charlotte Brontë, the Imagination, and *Villette*   92: 137-56

HOOKER, EDWARD N.
Dryden and the Atoms of Epicurus   32: 125-35

HORRELL, JOSEPH
What Gulliver Knew   35: 55-70

HOUGH, GRAHAM
Lawrence's Quarrel with Christianity: *The Man Who Died*   24: 101-11

HOUSE, HUMPHRY
The Poet of Adolescence   49: 47-49

HOUSE COMMITTEE ON UN-AMERICAN ACTIVITES
From the Testimony of Bertold Brecht   11: 30-42

HOWE, IRVING
Dostoevsky: The Politics of Salvation   16: 53-70
Dreiser and Tragedy: The Stature of Theodore Dreiser   96: 141-52
Introduction to *Edith Wharton: A Collection of Critical Essays*   20: 1-18

HOWE, IRVING (*continued*)
The Political Vocation   34:
156-71
A Reading of *The House of Mirth*
20: 119-29
Stendhal: The Politics of Survival
7: 76-94

HUBERT, JUDD D.
The Devaluation of Reality in the
Chartreuse de Parme   7: 95-
100
The Doctor's Curse   41: 160-69

HUMPHREYS, A. R.
Fielding's Irony: Its Methods and
Effects   9: 12-24

HUNT, ALBERT
Arden's Stagecraft   74: 98-103

HUXLEY, ALDOUS
From "Vulgarity in Literature"
63: 31-37

HYMAN, STANLEY EDGAR
Henry Thoreau in Our Time   10:
23-36

HYNES, SAMUEL
The Dynasts as an Example   25:
160-74

HYTIER, JEAN
The *Recits*   88: 73-92

ILSON, ROBERT
Benito Cereno from Melville to
Lowell   79: 135-42

IRELE, ABIOLA
Negritude: Literature and Ideology
97: 13-23

IRWIN, GEORGE
Dr. Johnson's Troubled Mind   48:
22-29

ISHERWOOD, CHRISTOPHER
Some Notes on Auden's Early
Poetry   38: 10-14

IZZO, CARL
The Poetry of W. H. Auden   38:
125-41

JACKSON, ROBERT LOUIS
Introduction to *Chekhov: A Collec-
tion of Critical Essays*   71: 1-20
The Seagull: The Empty Well, the
Dry Lake and the Cold Cave
71: 99-111

JAHN, JANHEINZ
Camara Laye: Another Interpretation   97: 142-46

JAMES, D. G.
The Two *Hyperions*   43: 161-69

JAMES, HENRY
Daniel Deronda: A Conversation
90: 161-66
On *The Reef*   20: 147-50

JAMES, WILLIAM
Address at the Emerson Centenary
in Concord   12: 18-23

JAMESON, FREDRIC
The Rhythm of Time   21: 104-20

JARRELL, RANDALL
From the Kingdom of Necessity
79: 40-47
Her Shield   86: 114-24
Texts from Housman   83: 51-61
To the Laodiceans   3: 83-104

JEFFERSON, D. W.
The Significance of Dryden's Heroic
Plays   64: 19-35
Tristram Shandy and the Tradition
of Learned Wit   77: 148-67

JENKINS, HAROLD
Shakespeare's *Twelfth Night*   47:
72-87

JOHN, S. BEYNON
Albert Camus: A British View   1:
85-91
Image and Symbol in the Work of
Albert Camus   1: 132-44

JOHNSON, GEORGE W.
Stephen Crane's Metaphor of
Decorum   66: 67-79

JOHNSON, LIONEL
The Destroyer of a Soul   87: 41

JOHNSON, LIONEL (*continued*)
In Honorem Doriani Creatorique
Eius **87**: 39-40

JOHNSON, THOMAS H.
The Poet and the Muse: Poetry as
Art **28**: 70-77

JOHNSON, WALTER
Strindberg and the Danse Macabre
95: 117-24

JOYCE, JAMES
Oscar Wilde: The Poet of *Salome*
87: 56-60

JULY, ROBERT W.
The African Personality in the
African Novel **97**: 105-21

JUMPER, WILL C.
Whom Seek Ye? A Note on Robert
Lowell's Poetry **79**: 53-62

KAFKA, FRANZ
The Silence of the Sirens **15**: 98-
99

KAHLER, ERICH
The Devil Secularized: Thomas
Mann's Faust **36**: 109-22

KAPLAN, SIDNEY
An Introduction to *Pym* **63**:
145-63

KAPROW, ALLAN
"Happenings" in the New York
Scene **69**: 121-30

KASKE, R. E.
Dante's *DXV* **46**: 122-40

KAUFMANN, F. W.
Ibsen's Conception of Truth **52**:
18-28

KAUFMANN, R. J.
Introduction to *G. B. Shaw: A Collection of Critical Essays* **50**:
1-14
On the Poetics of Terminal Tragedy:
Dryden's *All for Love* **32**: 86-
94
Strindberg: The Absence of Irony
95: 57-70

KAUL, A. N.
The Blithedale Romance **55**:
153-64
Introduction to *Hawthorne: A Collection of Critical Essays* **55**:
1-10

KAZIN, ALFRED
Edith Wharton **20**: 89-94
E. E. Cummings and His Fathers
[*i: Six Nonlectures*] **98**:
168-71
"Introduction" to *Moby-Dick*
13: 39-48
The New Realism: Sherwood Anderson and Sinclair Lewis **6**:
119-28
The Stature of Theodore Dreiser
96: 11-21
The Stillness of *Light in August*
65: 147-62

KEARNEY, A. M.
Richardson's *Pamela*: The Aesthetic
Case **85**: 28-38

KEITH, WILLIAM J.
The Complexities of Blake's "Sun-
flower": An Archetypal Specula-
tion **58**: 56-64

KENNER, HUGH
The Beckett Hero **51**: 52-61
Bradley **2**: 36-57
For Other Voices **2**: 187-91
Introduction to *T. S. Eliot: A Col-
lection of Critical Essays* **2**:
1-14
Mauberley **29**: 41-56
Meditation and Enactment **86**:
159-64
A Note on *The Great American
Novel* **61**: 88-92
The Sacred Book of the Arts **23**:
10-22
Supreme in Her Abnormality **86**:
139-43

KERMODE, FRANK
The Artist in Isolation **23**: 37-42
Mr. E. M. Forster as a Symbolist
59: 90-95

KERMODE, FRANK *(continued)*
What Is Shakespeare's *Henry VIII*
About?   45: 168-79

KERN, EDITH
Introduction to *Sartre: A Collection
of Critical Essays*   21: 1-14

KERNAN, ALVIN B.
The Attempted Dance: A Discussion of the Modern Theater
69: 12-33
Introduction to *The Modern American Theater: A Collection of
Critical Essays*   69: 1-11
Othello: An Introduction   40: 75-
84
Off-Broadway: Editor's Note   69:
111-12

KETTLE, ARNOLD
Emma   26: 112-23
Tom Jones   9: 84-88

KINKEAD-WEEKES, MARK
Pamela   85: 20-27
The Place of Love in *Jane Eyre* and
Wuthering Heights   92: 76-95

KINNAIRD, JOHN
Leaves of Grass and the American
Paradox   5: 24-36

KINNEY, ARTHUR F.
The Arthurian Cycle in *Tortilla Flat*
100: 36-46

KIRSCH, ARTHUR C.
The Significance of Dryden's
Aureng-Zebe   64: 37-49

KITCHIN, LAWRENCE
Drama with a Message: Arnold
Wesker   74: 71-82

KNECHT, LORING D.
A New Reading of Gide's *La Porte
étroite*   88: 93-111

KNIGHT, G. WILSON
Christ and Wilde   87: 138-49
Helena   47: 133-51
King Lear and the Comedy of the
Grotesque   40: 123-38

Shaw's Integral Theatre   50:
119-29
The Two Eternities   31: 15-30
The Witch of Atlas   49: 145-52

KNIGHTS, L. C.
Macbeth   40: 93-104
Tradition and Ben Jonson   22:
24-39

KNOEPFLMACHER, U. C.
George Eliot, Feuerbach, and the
Question of Criticism   90: 79-
85

KNOX, BERNARD M. W.
The *Ajax* of Sophocles   54: 39-61
The *Hippolytus* of Euripides   76:
90-114
The Serpent and the Flame: The
Imagery of the Second Book of
the *Aeneid*   62: 124-42

KOCHER, PAUL H.
Marlowe's Atheist Lecture   44:
159-66

KOHT, HALVDAN
Shakespeare and Ibsen   52: 41-51

KOLB, GWIN J., and JAMES H.
SLEDD
Johnson's *Dictionary* and Lexico-
graphical Tradition   48: 114-23

KONVITZ, MILTON R.
Introduction to *Emerson: A Collection of Critical Essays*   12: 1-11

KRIEGER, MURRAY
Dostoevsky's "Idiot": The Curse of
Saintliness   16: 39-52

KRUTCH, JOSEPH WOOD
Mr. Babbitt's Spiritual Guide   6:
36-38
The Philosophy of Composition
63: 15-30
Sinclair Lewis   6: 147-50

LAGERKVIST, PÄR
Strindberg and the Theater of
Tomorrow   95: 90-96

LAMM, MARTIN
Miss Julie   **95**: 105-16

LANG, H. J.
How Ambiguous Is Hawthorne?
55: 86-98

LANGE, VICTOR
Goethe's Craft of Fiction   **73**:
65-85
Introduction to *Goethe: A Collec-*
tion of Critical Essays
73: 1-9

LANSON, GUSTAVE
Molière and Farce   **41**: 20-28
The Voltairian Reformation of
France   **78**: 131-39

LAPP, JOHN C.
Art and Hallucination in Flaubert
42: 75-87

LATTIMORE, RICHMOND
Introduction to *The Oresteia*   **99**:
73-89

LAWRENCE, D. H.
The Argonauts   **15**: 173
Hardy's "Predilection d'artiste"
25: 46-51
Herman Melville's *Typee* and *Omoo*
13: 11-20
In Our Time: A Review
8: 93-94
Preface to Dostoevsky's *The Grand*
Inquisitor   **16**: 90-97
Sue Bridehead   **25**: 71-76
Whitman   **5**: 11-23

LAWSON, JOHN HOWARD
Eugene O'Neill   **39**: 42-51

LEAVIS, F. R.
Byron's Satire   **91**: 83-87
E. M. Forster   **59**: 34-47
Ezra Pound   **29**: 26-40
Gerard Manley Hopkins   **59**: 17-
36
The Irony of Swift   **35**: 15-29
Johnson as Critic   **48**: 70-88
T. S. Eliot's Later Poetry   **2**:
110-24
The Waste Land   **2**: 89-103

LEAVIS, Q. D.
Hawthorne as Poet   **55**: 25-63
Henry James's Heiress: The Importance of Edith Wharton   **20**:
73-88

LE BRETON, MAURICE
Mark Twain: An Appreciation   **30**:
29-39

LEECH, CLIFFORD
Introduction to *Marlowe: A Collec-*
tion of Critical Essays   **44**: 1-11
Marlowe's Humor   **44**: 167-78
The "Meaning" of *Measure for*
Measure   **47**: 109-18

LEGOUIS, PIERRE
The Dramatic Element in Donne's
Poetry   **19**: 36-51

LEHMAN, BENJAMIN H.
Of Time, Personality, and the
Author   **77**: 21-33

LEISHMAN, J. B.
Donne and Seventeenth Century
Poetry   **19**: 109-22

LEO, ULRICH
Pirandello between Fiction and
Drama   **67**: 83-90

LERNER, MAX
Thoreau: No Hermit   **10**: 20-22

LESTER, ELENORE
The Pass-the-Hat Theater Circuit
69: 113-20

LEVANT, HOWARD
The Unity of *In Dubious Battle:*
Violence and Dehumanization
100: 49-62

LEVENSON, J. C.
Robinson's Modernity   **91**: 164-81

LEVENTHAL, AL J.
The Beckett Hero   **51**: 37-51

LEVIN, HARRY
Coriolanus: An Introduction   **40**:
169-75
The Dead Shepherd   **44**: 18-35
The Example of Cervantes   **89**:
34-48

LEVIN, HARRY (*continued*)
Flaubert: Spleen and Ideal   **41:** 57-74
An Introduction to Ben Jonson **22:** 40-59
Observations on the Style of Ernest Hemingway   **8:** 72-85

LEVINE, GEORGE
Intelligence as Deception: *The Mill on the Floss*   **90:** 107-23

LEWIS, C. S.
Death in *Hamlet*   **40:** 71-74
Donne and Love Poetry in the Seventeenth Century   **19:** 90-99
A Note on Jane Austen   **26:** 25-34
The Style of Secondary Epic   **60:** 40-55
Virgil and the Subject of Secondary Epic   **62:** 62-67

LEWIS, R. W. B.
From *The American Adam*   **10:** 92-99
Introduction to *Malraux: A Collection of Critical Essays*   **37:** 1-11
John Steinbeck: The Fitful Daemon   **100:** 163-75
On Translating the *Aeneid:* Yif that I can   **62:** 4-52
The Return into Time: Hawthorne **55:** 72-86
William Faulkner: The Hero in the New World   **65:** 204-18

LEWIS, WYNDHAM
Early London Environment   **2:** 28-35

LIEBERT, HERMAN W.
Reflections on Samuel Johnson **48:** 15-21

LIEBLING, A. J.
The Dollars Damned Him   **66:** 18-26

LIPPMANN, WALTER
Sinclair Lewis   **6:** 84-94

LISCA, PETER
The Grapes of Wrath   **100:** 75-101

LITTLEJOHN, DAVID
Introduction to *Gide: A Collection of Critical Essays*   **88:** 1-14

LODGE, DAVID
Fire and Eyre: Charlotte Brontë's War of Earthly Elements   **92:** 110-36

LONGLEY, JOHN L., JR.
Joe Christmas: The Hero in the Modern World   **65:** 163-74

LOOFBOUROW, JOHN
Neoclassical Conventions: *Vanity Fair, Pendennis, The Newcomes* **75:** 104-20

LOPEZ-MORILLAS, JUAN
Lyrical Primitivism: García Lorca's *Romancero Gitano*   **14:** 130-39

LORD, ALBERT B.
Homer   **15:** 62-78

LORD, GEORGE deF.
From Contemplation to Action: Marvell's Poetical Career   **81:** 55-73
Introduction to *Andrew Marvell: A Collection of Critical Essays* **81:** 1-17

LOVETT, ROBERT MORSS
An Interpreter of American Life **6:** 32-35

LOWELL, ROBERT
On "Skunk Hour"   **79:** 131-34
William Carlos Williams   **61:** 153-59

LOWENTHAL, LEO
Henrik Ibsen: Motifs in the Realistic Plays   **52:** 139-57

LUBBOCK, PERCY
The Novels of Edith Wharton   **20:** 43-61
The Panoramic Method   **75:** 20-29
The Point of View [*The Ambassadors*]   **34:** 37-46

LUKÁCS, GEORG
Dostoevsky   16: 146-59
Henry Esmond as an Historical
   Novel   75: 121-26
Salammbô   42: 141-53
Tolstoy and the Development of
   Realism   68: 78-94
To Narrate or Describe?   15: 86-
   89
Wilhelm Meisters Lehrjahre   73:
   86-98

LUMIANSKY, P. M.
The Dramatic Audience in *Beowulf*
   82: 76-82

LYDENBERG, JOHN
Introduction to *Dreiser: A Col-
   lection of Critical Essays*   96:
   1-10
Theodore Dreiser: Ishmael in the
   Jungle   96: 22-36

LYNEN, JOHN F.
Frost as Modern Poet   3: 177-98

LYNN, KENNETH
Dreiser and the Success Dream
   96: 37-44
Roughing It   30: 40-46

LYTLE, ANDREW
Regeneration for the Man   65:
   231-37

MACAULAY, JEANNETTE
The Idea of Assimilation: Mongo
   Beti and Camara Laye   97:
   132-41

McCALL, MARSH H., JR.
Introduction to *Aeschylus: A Collection of Critical Essays*   99:
   1-9

McCARTHY, MARY
The Unimportance of Being Oscar
   87: 107-10

McCONNELL, FRANK D.
"Death among the Apple Trees":
   The Waves and the World of
   Things   93: 117-29

McDOWELL, FREDERICK P.
The Sea and the Mirror   38:
   142-51

MACK, MAYNARD
Gulliver's Travels   35: 111-14
Joseph Andrews and *Pamela*   9:
   52-58
The World of *Hamlet*   40: 44-60

McKIBBEN, ROBERT C.
The Image of the Book in *Wuthering Heights*   92: 34-43

McKILLOP, ALAN D.
Critical Realism in *Northanger
   Abbey*   26: 52-61
Epistolary Technique in Richard-
   son's Novels   85: 139-51
Laurence Sterne   77: 34-65
On *Sir Charles Grandison*   85:
   124-38

MACKSEY, RICHARD A.
Architecture of Time: Dialectics
   and Structure   4: 104-21
"A Certainty of Music": Williams'
   Changes   61: 132-47
Marianne (Craig) Moore: A Brief
   Chronology   86: 179-81

MacLEISH, ARCHIBALD
The Private World: Poems of Emily
   Dickinson   28: 150-61

McLUHAN, MARSHALL
The Analogical Mirrors   57: 80-88

MAGNY, CLAUDE-EDMONDE
The Duplicity of Being   21: 21-30
Faulkner, or Theological Inversion
   65: 66-78
Malraux the Fascinator   37:
   117-33

MAGOUN, FRANCIS P., JR.
Oral-Formulaic Character of Anglo-
   Saxon Narrative Poetry
   82: 83-113

MALRAUX, ANDRÉ
Reply to Trotsky   37: 20-24

MANN, THOMAS
Humor and Irony   36: 170-72

MANN, THOMAS (*continued*)
Voyage with *Don Quixote*   89:
49-72
Wilde and Nietzsche   87: 169-71

MANSELL, DARRELL, JR.
George Eliot's Conception of
"Form"   90: 66-78

MARCUS, STEVEN
Martin Chuzzlewit: The Self and the
World   72: 97-114

MARILL-ABÉRÈS, RENÉ
Neo-Marxism and *Criticism of Dialectical Reasoning*   21: 161-65

MAROWITZ, CHARLES
The Ascension of John Osborne
74: 117-21

MARTIN, JAY
The Black Hole of Calcoolidge
94: 114-31
Introduction to *Nathanael West:
A Collection of Critical Essays*
94: 1-10

MARTZ, LOUIS L.
Introduction to *Milton: Paradise
Lost: A Collection of Critical
Essays*   60: 1-11
John Donne in Meditation   19:
152-70
The Saint as Tragic Hero   50:
143-61
The Unicorn in Paterson: William
Carlos Williams   61: 70-87
Wallace Stevens: The World as
Meditation   33: 133-50

MARX, LEO
The Pilot and the Passenger   30:
47-63

MATTHEWS, G. M.
A Volcano's Voice in Shelley   49:
111-31

MATTHIESSEN, F. O.
Billy Budd, Foretopman   13:
156-68
"A Few Herbs and Apples"   12:
100-107

Hopkins and Whitman
57: 144-50
The House of the Seven Gables
55: 141-52
Only a Language Experiment   5:
66-79
What Music Shall We Have?   10:
53-62

MATLAW, RALPH E.
Introduction to *Tolstoy: A Collection of Critical Essays*
68: 1-13

MAUD, RALPH
Last Poems   56: 74-83

MAURER, ROBERT E.
E. E. Cummings' *Him*   98: 133-55
Latter-Day Notes on E. E. Cum-
mings' Language   98: 79-99

MAURIAC, FRANÇOIS
Charles Baudelaire, the Catholic
18: 30-37
The Death of André Gide   88:
19-29

MAYERSON, CAROLINE W.
Thematic Symbols in *Hedda Gabler*
52: 121-38

MAYOUX, JEAN-JACQUES
Laurence Sterne   77: 108-25
Samuel Beckett and the Universal
Parody   51: 77-91

MELCHIORI, GIORGIO
The Moment of Moments   23: 33-
36
Two Mannerists: James and Hopkins
57: 131-43

MENCKEN, H. L.
Consolation   6:   17-20
The Dreiser Bugaboo   96: 73-80
Portrait of an American Citizen
6: 20-22

MENDILOV, A. A.
The Revolt of Sterne   77: 90-107

MENNEMEIER, FRANZ NORBERT
Mother Courage and Her Children
11: 138-50

MEREZHKOVSKY, DMITRI
Tolstoy, Seer of the Flesh   68:
56-64

METMAN, EVA
Reflections on Samuel Beckett's
Plays   51: 117-39

MEYERHOLD, VSEVOLOD
Naturalistic Theater and Theater of
Mood   71: 62-68

MILES, JOSEPHINE
The Poetry of Praise   5: 163-76
Robinson's Inner Fire   91: 110-16

MILLER, JAMES E., JR.
A Gesture of Indefinite Revolt
27: 86-91
America's Epic   5: 60-65

MILLER, J. HILLIS
Introduction to *William Carlos
Williams: A Collection of Critical
Essays*   61: 1-14
Our Mutual Friend   72: 169-77
The Univocal Chiming   57: 89-
116

MILLER, PERRY
Emersonian Genius and the American Democracy   12: 72-84
The Shaping of the American Character   5: 132-45

MILLGATE, MICHAEL
The Sound and the Fury   65: 94-
108

MILLS, RALPH J., JR.
Wallace Stevens: The Image of the
Rock   33: 96-110

MILNE, TOM
The Hidden Face of Violence   74:
38-46

MINER, EARL
Introduction to *Restoration Dramatists: A Collection of Critical
Essays*   64: 1-18
The "Poetic Picture, Painted Poetry" of *The Last Instructions to
a Painter*   81: 165-74

Pound, *Haiku*, and the Image   29:
115-28
Some Characteristics of Dryden's
Use of Metaphor   32: 115-24

MIZENER, ARTHUR
Introduction to *F. Scott Fitzgerald:
A Collection of Critical Essays*
27: 1-10
The Maturity of Scott Fitzgerald
27: 57-68
To Meet Mr. Eliot   2: 15-27

MOERS, ELLEN
The Finesse of Dreiser   96: 153-62

MONTGOMERY, MARION
Robert Frost and His Use of Bar-
riers: Man *vs.* Nature toward God
3: 138-50

MOORE, GEOFFREY
Sinclair Lewis: A Lost Romantic
6: 151-66

MOORE, GERALD
Discovery   97: 147-61

MOORE, HARRY T.
The Plumed Serpent: Vision
and Language   24:
61-71

MOORE, MARIANNE
A Letter to Ezra Pound   86: 16-
19
Three Essays on Williams   61: 37-
46
W. H. Auden   38: 39-53

MOORE, WILL G.
Speech   41: 40-49

MORGAN, EDWIN
Dryden's Drudging   52: 55-70

MORGAN, MARGERY M.
Back to Methuselah: The Poet and
the City   50: 130-42

MORPURGO-TAGLIABUE, GUIDO
Literature and Poetry   21: 129-35

MORRIS, GEORGE L. K.
"Marie, Marie, Hold On Tight"
2: 86-88

MORRIS, WRIGHT
The Function of Nostalgia: F.
Scott Fitzgerald   **27**: 25-31

MOSER, THOMAS
Conrad's "Later Affirmation"   **53**:
145-65

MOTTRAM, ERIC
Arthur Miller: The Development of
a Political Dramatist in America
85: 23-57

MOYNAHAN, JULIAN
Lady Chatterley's Lover: The Deed
of Life   **24**: 72-92

MPHAHLELE, EZEKIAL
Roots   **97**: 24-29

MUCHNIC, HELEN
Circe's Swine: Plays by Gorky and
O'Neill   **39**: 99-109

MUDRICK, MARVIN
Introduction to *Conrad: A Collec-
tion of Critical Essays*
53: 1-11
Irony as Discrimination: *Pride and
Prejudice*   **26**: 76-97
The Originality of Conrad   **53**: 37-
44
The Originality of *The Rainbow*
24: 29-49

MUIR, EDWIN
Franz Kafka   **17**: 33-44
Telemachos Remembers   **15**: 38-
39
To Franz Kafka   **17**: 13

MUIR, KENNETH
Introduction to *Shakespeare: The
Comedies: A Collection of Criti-
cal Essays*   **47**: 1-10

MUMFORD, LEWIS
The America of Sinclair Lewis   **6**:
102-7
From *The Golden Day*   **10**: 13-19

MURCHLAND, BERNARD C., C.S.C.
Albert Camus: The Dark Night
before the Coming of Grace?
1: 59-64

MURPHY, FRANCIS
Introduction to *Edwin Arlington
Robinson: A Collection of Criti-
cal Essays*   **91**: 1-7

MURRAY, GILBERT
"The *Persae*"   **99**: 29-39

MURRAY, HENRY A.
"In Nomine Diaboli"   **13**: 62-74

MURRAY, ROBERT D., JR.
Thought and Structure in Sophoclean Tragedy   **55**: 23-28

MURRY, JOHN MIDDLETON
Baudelaire   **18**: 94-109
Fielding's "Sexual Ethic" in *Tom
Jones*   **9**: 89-97
Shakespeare's Method: *The Mer-
chant of Venice*   **47**: 32-46

MUSGROVE, S.
Eliot and Tennyson   **2**: 73-85

NADEAU, MAURICE
Samuel Beckett: Humor and the
Void   **51**: 33-36

NAPIER, JOHN T.
"A Momentary Stay against
Confusion"   **3**: 125-37

NARDI, BRUNO
Dante and Medieval Culture   **46**:
39-42

NAVES, RAYMOND
Voltaire's Wisdom   **78**: 150-66

NELSON, HUGH
The Homecoming: Kith and Kin
74: 145-63

NELSON, LOWRY, JR.
Introduction to *Cervantes: A Collection of Critical Essays*   **89**: 1-12

NELSON, ROBERT J.
The Unreconstructed Heroes of
Molière   **41**: 111-35

NELSON, WILLIAM
The Legend of Justice: The Idol and
the Crocodile   **80**: 115-31
The World's Vanity   **80**:
13-29

NEMEROV, HOWARD
A Few Bricks from Babel **86:** 134-38

NESTRICK, WILLIAM V.
The Virtuous and Gentle Discipline of Gentlemen and Poets **80:** 132-45

NEUSE, RICHARD
The Triumph over Hasty Accidents: A Note on the Symbolic Mode of the Epithalamion **80:** 47-62

NEVIUS, BLAKE
On *Ethan Frome* **10:** 130-36
On *The Age of Innocence* **30:** 162-71

NIETZSCHE, FRIEDRICH
Sophoclean Tragedy **54:** 16-19

NILSSON, NILS ÅKE
Intonation and Rhythm in Chekhov's Plays **71:** 161-74

NITCHIE, GEORGE W.
A Momentary Stay against Confusion **3:** 159-76

NORTHAM, JOHN
Ibsen's Search for the Hero **52:** 91-108

NOWOTTNY, WINIFRED
"There was a Saviour" **56:** 60-83

NURMI, MARTIN K.
Fact and Symbol in "The Chimney Sweeper" of Blake's *Songs of Innocence* **58:** 15-22

O'BRIEN, JUSTIN
Albert Camus: Militant **1:** 20-25

O'DONNELL, GEORGE MARION
Faulkner's Mythology **65:** 23-33

O'DONNELL, NORBERT F.
The Conflict of Wills in Shaw's Tragicomedy **50:** 76-87

O'DONNELL, W. G.
Robert Frost and New England: A Revaluation **3:** 46-57

O'FAOLAIN, SEAN
A Clean, Well-Lighted Place **8:** 112-13

OHMANN, RICHARD M.
Auden's Sacred Awe **38:** 172-78
Born to Set It Right: The Roots of Shaw's Style **50:** 26-41

O'LOUGHLIN, M. J. K.
This Sober Frame: A Reading of "Upon Appleton House" **81:** 120-42

OLSON, ELDER
The Universe of the Early Poems **56:** 45-59

ONG, WALTER J.
Sprung Rhythm and English Tradition **57:** 151-59

OSBORN, JAMES M.
The Medal of John Bayes **32:** 31-42

OTIS, BROOKS
The Odyssean *Aeneid* and the Iliadic *Aeneid* **62:** 89-106

PARIS, BERNARD J.
George Eliot's Religion of Humanity **90:** 11-36

PARK, BRUCE R.
A Mote in the Critic's Eye: Bernard Shaw and Comedy **50:** 42-56

PARKER, BRIAN
Point of View in Arthur Miller's *Death of a Salesman* **84:** 95-109

PARKER, HENRY B.
Emerson **12:** 121-35

PARKINSON, THOMAS
For the Union Dead **79:** 143-51
Introduction to *Robert Lowell: A Collection of Critical Essays* **79:** 1-11

PARRINGTON, VERNON L.
Our Literary Aristocrat **20:** 151-54
Sinclair Lewis: Our Own Diogenes **6:** 62-70

PARROT, LOUIS
A Poet Crazy about Color   14: 57-64

PARRY, ADAM
The Two Voices of Virgil's
Aeneid   62: 107-23

PARRY, BENITA
Passage to More than India   59:
160-74

PARRY, IDRIS
Kafka, Gogol, and Nathanael West
17: 85-90

PARTRIDGE, EDWARD B.
Epicene   22: 121-32

PASINETTI, P. M.
The "Jeanne Duval" Poems in *Les
Fleurs du mal*   18: 86-93

PATER, WALTER
A Novel by Mr. Oscar Wilde   87:
35-38

PATERSON, JOHN
The *Mayor of Casterbridge* as
Tragedy   25: 91-112

PAUL, SHERMAN
The Angle of Vision   12: 158-78
A Fable of the Renewal of Life
10: 100-116
Introduction to *Thoreau: A Collec-
tion of Critical Essays*   10: 1-7

PAULSON, RONALD
Introduction to *Fielding: A Collection of Critical Essays*   9: 1-11

PEACOCK, RONALD
Goethe's Version of Poetic Drama
73: 33-49

PEARCE, ROY HARVEY
Introduction to *Whitman: A Collec-
tion of Critical Essays*   5: 1-7
Marianne Moore   86: 150-58
Pound, Whitman, and the American
Epic   29: 163-77
Wallace Stevens: The Life of the
Imagination   33: 111-32
Whitman Justified: The Poet in
1860   5: 37-59

Williams and the "New Mode"   61:
93-106

PERELMAN, S. J.
Nathanael West: A Portrait   94:
11-12

PERKINS, DAVID
Hardy and the Poetry of Isolation
25: 143-59
Lamia   43: 143-53
The *Ode on a Nightingale*   43:
103-11

PEROSO, SERGIO
Naturalism and Impressionism in
Stephen Crane's Fiction   66:
80-94

PERRET, JACQUES
The *Georgics*   62: 28-40

PETER, JOHN
Murder in the Cathedral   2: 155-72

PEYRE, HENRI
Baudelaire, Romantic and Classical
18: 19-29
Camus the Pagan   1: 65-76
Introduction to *Baudelaire: A Col-
lection of Critical Essays*   18:
1-6
The Legacy of Proust   4: 28-41
Sartre's *Roads to Freedom*   21:
31-38

PFEIFFER, JOHANNES
"The Metamorphsis"   17: 53-59

PICKREL, PAUL
Great Expectations   72: 158-68

PICON, GAËTON
Exile and the Kingdom   1: 152-56
Malraux on Malraux   37: 161-73
Notes on *The Plague*   1: 145-51
The Presence of *André Gide*   88:
36-48

PINNEY, THOMAS
The Authority of the Past in George
Eliot's Novels   90: 37-54

PINTO, V. de S.
Poet without a Mask   24:
127-41

PIRANDELLO, LUIGI
The Poetry of Dante   46: 14-22

PIZER, DONALD
Stephen Crane's *Maggie* and
American Naturalism   66:
110-17

PODHORETZ, NORMAN
Nathanael West: A Particular Kind
of Joking   94: 154-60

POGGIOLI, RENATO
Paolo and Francesca   46: 61-77
Tolstoy as Man and Artist   68:
14-27

POMEAU, RENÉ
Voltaire's Religion   78: 140-49

POPKIN, HENRY
Camus as Dramatist   1: 170-72

PÖSCHL, VIKTOR
Basic Themes   62: 164-82

POTTLE, FREDERICK A.
The Role of Asia in the Dramatic
Action of Shelley's *Prometheus
Unbound*   49: 133-43

POUILLON, JEAN
Time and Destiny in Faulkner   65:
79-86

POULET, GEORGES
Baudelaire and Human Time   18:
132-48
Flaubert   42: 21-35
In Search of the Self   4: 150-78
The Metamorphoses of the Circle
46: 151-69

POUND, EZRA
A Brief Note   34: 27-30
Dr. Williams' Position   61: 27-36
Homer or Virgil?   15: 17-18
Marianne Moore and Mina Loy
86: 46-47
Mr. Eliot's Solid Merit   2: 149-51
Mr. Housman's Message   83: 12
Walt Whitman   5: 8-10

POWELL, JOCELYN
George Etherege and the Form of a
Comedy   64: 63-85

POWYS, JOHN COWPER
Preface to *Homer and the Aether*
15: 140-47

PRATT, ANNIS
Dylan Thomas's Prose   56: 117-29

PRAZ, MARIO
Donne's Relation to the Poetry of
His Time   19: 61-76
Metamorphoses of Satan   91: 42-49
Thackeray as Preacher   75: 49-54

PREVOST, JEAN
Baudelairean Themes: Death, Evil,
and Love   18: 170-78
Lucien Lutwin   7: 47-62

PRICE, H. T.
Construction in *Titus Andronicus*
40: 24-27

PRICE, MARTIN
Introduction to *Dickens: A Collection of Critical Essays*   72: 1-15

PRINCE, F. T.
Milton's Blank Verse: The Diction
60: 61-76

PRIOR, MOODY E.
Tragedy and the Heroic Play   32:
95-114

PRITCHETT, V. S.
Time Frozen: *A Fable*   65:
238-42

PROUST, MARCEL
Apropos of Baudelaire   18: 110-31
To the Reader   4: 179-80

PUCCIANI, ORESTE F.
Les Séquestrés d'Altona   21: 92-
103

QUILLIOT, ROGER
Albert Camus's Algeria   1: 38-47
An Ambiguous World   1: 157-69

QUINN, PATRICK F.
The French Response to Poe   63:
64-78

QUINN, SISTER M. BERNETTA
Metamorphosis in Wallace Stevens
33: 54-70

QUINN, SISTER M. BERNETTA
(*continued*)
On *Paterson*, Book One   61:
107-20

QUINTANA, RICHARDO
Situational Satire: A Commentary
on the Method of Swift   35:
91-99

RACEY, EDGAR F., JR.
Myth as Tragic Structure in *Desire
under the Elms*   39: 57-61

RADER, MELVIN M.
Shelley's Theory of Evil   49:
103-10

RAHV, PHILIP
Dostoevsky in *Crime and Punishment*   16: 16-38

RAJAN, B.
The Language of *Paradise Lost*
60: 56-60

RALEIGH, JOHN HENRY
Eugene O'Neill and the Escape from
the Château d'If   39: 7-22
F. Scott Fitzgerald's *The Great
Gatsby*   27: 99-103
O'Neill's *Long Day's Journey* into
Night and New England Irish
Catholicism   39: 124-41

RAMCHAND, KENNETH
The Road to *Banana Bottom*   97:
188-209

RANSOM, JOHN CROWE
Emily Dickinson: A Poet Restored
28: 88-100
On Being Modern with Distinction
86: 101-6

RAPHAEL, ROBERT
Illusion and the Self in *The Wild
Duck, Rosmersholm,* and *The
Lady from the Sea*   52: 120-30

RATNER, MARC L.
"Anywhere Out of This World":
Baudelaire and Nathanael West
94: 102-9

RAY, GORDON N.
The Newcomes   75: 147-60

READ, FORREST
A Man of No Fortune   29:
64-79

REESE, M. M.
Origins of the History Play   45:
42-54

REEVES, JAMES
Introduction to *Selected Poems of
Emily Dickinson*   28: 117-26

REGAN, ROBERT
Introduction to *Poe: A Collection
of Critical Essays*   63: 1-14

REID, STEPHEN A.
The "Unspeakable Rites" in Heart
of Darkness   53: 45-54

REINERT, OTTO
Introduction to *Strindberg: A Collection of Critical Essays*   95:
1-26

REINHARDT, KARL
Goethe and Antiquity: The Helen
Episode of Goethe's *Faust*   73:
99-109

REISS, H. S.
Recent Kafka Criticism (1944-
1955)—A Survey   17: 163-77

RENOIR, ALAIN
Point of View and Design for Terror
in *Beowulf*   82: 154-66

REXROTH, KENNETH
Classics Revisited—IV: *Beowulf*
82: 167-70

RICHARD, JOHN-PIERRE
The Creation of Form in Flaubert
42: 36-55
Knowledge and Tenderness in
Stendhal   7: 127-46

RICHARDS, I. A.
Coleridge: His Life and Work   70:
12-31
A Passage to Forster: Reflections on
a Novelist   59: 15-20

RICKS, CHRISTOPHER
Introduction to *A. E. Housman: A
Collection of Critical Essays*
83: 1-10
The Nature of Housman's
Poetry   83: 106-22

RIDDEL, JOSEPH N.
Walt Whitman and Wallace Stevens:
Functions of a "Literatus"
33: 30-42

RIDENOUR, GEORGE M.
Don Juan: "Carelessly I Sing"
31: 122-37
Introduction to *Shelley: A Collection of Critical Essays*   49: 1-
12

RIGHTER, ANNE
William Wycherley   64: 105-22

RILEY, E. C.
Literature and Life in *Don Quixote*
89: 123-36

RILKE, RAINER MARIA
Thomas Mann's *Buddenbrooks*
36: 7-9

RIZZO, GINO, and
LUIGI SQUARZINA
Directing Pirandello Today   67:
141-52

ROBBE-GRILLET, ALAIN
Samuel Beckett, or "Presence" in
the Theatre   51: 108-16

ROBINSON, W. R.
The Alienated Self   91: 128-47

ROBSON, W. W.
Byron as Improvisor   31: 88-95

RODITI, EDOUARD
Fiction as Allegory: *The Picture of
Dorian Gray*   87: 47-55

ROGERS, WINFIELD H.
Fielding's Early Aesthetic and
Technique   9: 25-44

ROGOFF, GORDON
The Juggernaut of Production
69: 131-54

ROHLEHR, GORDON
The Ironic Approach: The Novels
of V. S. Naipaul   97: 162-76

ROHRMOSER, GÜNTER
Brecht's *Galileo*   11: 117-26

ROPPOLO, JOSEPH PATRICK
Meaning and "The Masque of the
Red Death"   63: 134-44

ROSENFELD, PAUL
The Voyages [*Eimi*]   98: 156-67

ROSENMEYER, THOMAS G.
"*Seven Against Thebes:* The
Tragedy of War"   99: 40-62
Tragedy and Religion: *The Bacchae*
76: 150-70

ROSENTHAL, M. L.
The *Cantos*   29: 57-63
Robert Lowell and the Poetry of
Confession   79: 113-23

ROSS, JOHN F.
The Final Comedy of Lemuel Gulliver   35: 71-89

ROSS, LILLIAN
How Do You Like It Now, Gentlemen?   8: 17-39

ROSSITER, A. P.
Angel with Horns: The Unity of
Richard III   45: 66-84
Much Ado about Nothing   47:
47-57

ROTHWELL, BRIAN
The Chamber Plays   95: 152-63

ROURKE, CONSTANCE
Round Up   6: 29-31

ROUSSET, JEAN
Madame Bovary, or the Book about
Nothing   42: 112-31

RUSSELL, BERTRAND
Byron   31: 151-56

SAINTSBURY, GEORGE
John Donne   19: 13-22

SALE, ARTHUR
Introduction to *Every Man in His
Humour*   22: 75-81

SALE, WILLIAM M., JR.
From *Pamela* to *Clarissa*   85: 39-48

SALINAS, PEDRO
Lorca and the Poetry of Death
14: 100-107

SALZ, RICHARD
The Ritual Sacrifice in Lorca's
Poet in New York   14: 108-29

SAMUELS, CHARLES THOMAS
Mr. Trilling, Mr. Warren, and *An
American Tragedy*   96: 163-73

SANGER, C. P.
The Structure of *Wuthering Heights*
92: 7-18

SANTAYANA, GEORGE
Emerson   12: 31-38

SARTRE, JEAN-PAUL
An Explication of *The Stranger*
1: 108-21
Flaubert   42: 13-20
The Living Gide   88: 15-18
On *The Sound and the Fury:* Time
in the Works of Faulkner   65:
87-93
Tribute to Albert Camus   1:
173-75
Why the Trojan Women?   76:
128-31

SAVAGE, D. S.
E. M. Forster   59: 56-70
The Significance of F. Scott Fitz-
gerald   27: 146-56

SCHAEFER, JOSEPHINE O'BRIEN
The Vision Falters: *The Years,
1937*   93: 130-44

SCHAFER, MURRAY
Ezra Pound and Music   29:
129-41

SCHANZER, ERNEST
A Midsummer-Night's Dream
47: 26-31

SCHECHNER, RICHARD
The Unexpected Visitor in Ibsen's
Late Plays   52: 158-68

SCHILLING, BERNARD N.
Introduction to *Dryden: A Collection of Critical Essays*   32:
1-7

SCHLESINGER, EILHARD
On Euripides' *Medea*   76: 70-89

SCHORER, MARK
The Humiliation of Emma Wood-
house   26: 98-111
Introduction to *Sinclair Lewis: A
Collection of Critical Essays*
6: 1-9
Sinclair Lewis and the Method of
Half-Truths   6: 46-61
Women in Love and Death   24:
50-60

SCHUMACHER, ERNST
Piscator's Political Theater   11:
86-96

SCHWARTZ, DELMORE
Poetry and Belief in Thomas Hardy
25: 123-34

SEATON, ETHEL
Marlowe's Map   44: 36-56

SEGAL, CHARLES PAUL
Sophocles' Praise of Man and the
Conflicts of the *Antigone*   54:
62-85

SEGAL, ERICH
Introduction to *Euripides: A Collection of Critical Essays*   76:
1-12

SEIDEL, FREDERICK
Robert Lowell [Interview]   79:
12-35

SEIDLEN, OSKAR
Goethe's *Iphigenia* and the Humane Ideal   73: 50-64

SEWALL, RICHARD B.
Introduction to *Emily Dickinson:
A Collection of Critical Essays*
28: 1-8

SEWELL, ARTHUR
Character and Society in *King Lear*
40: 139-47

SEWELL, ELIZABETH
Lewis Carroll and T. S. Eliot as
Nonsense Poets   2: 65-72

SHAIN, CHARLES E.
This Side of Paradise   27: 77-79

SHAPIRO, KARL
Dylan Thomas   56: 169-80
Study of "Philomena Andronico"
61: 148-52

SHAW, GEORGE BERNARD
My Memories of Oscar Wilde
87: 92-106

SHAW, T. E.
Translator's Note   15: 153-55

SHEED, WILFRID
A Sober Conscience   1: 26-30

SHERBO, ARTHUR
Johnson as Editor of Shakespeare
48: 124-37

SHERBURN, GEORGE
Fielding's *Amelia:* An Interpreta-
tion   9: 146-57
"Writing to the Moment": One
Aspect   35: 152-60

SHERMAN, STUART P.
The Barbaric Naturalism of Mr.
Dreiser   96: 63-72

SHESTOV, LEO
The Last Judgment: Tolstoy's Last
Works   68: 157-72

SHKLOVSKY, VIKTOR
A Parodying Novel: Sterne's
Tristram Shandy   77: 66-89

SIMON, ALFRED
The Elementary Rites of Molière's
Comedy   41: 29-39
From Alceste to Scapin   41:
136-50

SIMONS, HI
The Genre of Wallace Stevens   33:
43-53

SIMPSON, EVELYN M.
The Literary Value of Donne's
Sermons   19: 137-51

SINGLETON, CHARLES S.
"In Exitu Israel de Aegypto"
46: 102-21

SINICROPI, GIOVANNI
The Later Phase: Towards Myth
67: 73-81

SKAFTZMOV, A.
Principles of Structure in Chekhov's
Plays   71: 69-86

SLEDD, JAMES H., and
GWIN J. KOLB
Johnson's *Dictionary* and Lexico-
graphical Tradition   48: 114-23

SMITH. A. J.
New Bearings in Donne: "Air and
Angels"   19: 171-79

SMITH, DAVID E.
The *Enormous Room* and The
Pilgrim's Progress   98: 121-32

SMITH, DAVID NICHOL
Johnson's Poems   48: 63-69

SMITH, H. A.
Forster's Humanism and the Nineteenth Century   59: 106-16

SMITH, HENRY NASH
Emerson's Problem of Vocation
12: 60-71
Introduction to *Mark Twain: A
Collection of Critical Essays*
30: 1-12
A Sound Heart and a Deformed
Conscience   30: 83-100

SMITH, MARCUS
Religious Experience in *Miss Lonelyhearts*   94: 74-90

SNELL, BRUNO
Arcadia: The Discovery of a
Spiritual Landscape   62:
14-27

SNODGRASS, W. D.
"Mêtis . . . Oûtis"   15: 152
A Rocking-Horse: The Symbol,
the Pattern, the Way to Live
24: 117-26

SOKEL, WALTER H.
Brecht's Split Characters and His
Sense of the Tragic   11: 127-37

SOLOMON, ERIC
The Crucible of Childhood   66:
165-76

SOUPAULT, PHILIPPE
Introduction to *Mademoiselle
Côuer-Brisé (Miss Lonelyhearts)*
94: 110-13

SPARROW, JOHN
The Housman Dilemma   83:
163-76

SPEARS, MONROE K.
For the Time Being   38: 160-71
Introduction to *Auden: A Collec-
tion of Critical Essays*   38: 1-9

SPENDER, STEPHEN
The Contemporary Subject   34:
102-10
Robert Lowell's Family Album
79: 110-12
W. H. Auden and His Poetry   38:
26-38

SPENGLER, OSWALD
Tragedy: Classical *vs.* Western   54:
20-22

SPILKA, MARK
Comic Resolution in Fielding's
Joseph Andrews   9: 59-68
The Death of Love in *The Sun Also
Rises*   8: 127-38
Introduction to *D. H. Lawrence: A
Collection of Critical Essays*
24: 1-14
Ritual Form in "The Blind Man"
24: 112-16

SPITZER, LEO
Intuition and Philology   4: 97-103
On the Significance of *Don Quijote*
89: 82-97
Speech and Language in *Inferno*
XIII   46: 78-101

SPIVACK, BERNARD
Iago Revisited   40:
85-92

SPOERRI, THEOPHIL
The Structure of Existence: *The
Flies*   21: 54-61

SPRAGUE, CLAIRE
Introduction to *Virginia Woolf: A
Collection of Critical Essays*
93: 1-13

SPRINCHORN, EVERT
The Logic of *A Dream Play*   95:
137-51

SQUARZINA, LUIGI, and
GINORIZZO
Directing Pirandello Today   67:
141-52

STALLMAN, R. W.
Notes Toward an Analysis of *The
Red Badge of Courage*   66:
128-40

STANFORD, W. B.
The Untypical Hero   15: 122-38

STAPLES, HUGH B.
"The Quaker Graveyard in Nantucket"   79: 63-73

STAPLETON, LAWRENCE
Introduction to *A Writer's Journal*
by Thoreau   10: 161-79

STAROBINSKI, JEAN
Truth in Masquerade   7: 114-26

STAUFFER, DONALD A.
The School of Love: *Romeo and
Juliet*   40: 28-33

STEENE, BIRGITTA
Shakespearean Elements in the
Historical Plays of Strindberg
95: 125-36

STEFFAN, GUY
The Devil a Bit of Our *Beppo*
91: 65-82
Don Juan: A Thousand Colors
91: 96-112

STEIN, ARNOLD
The War in Heaven   60: 148-55

STEIN, WILLIAM BYSSHE
"The Open Boat" and the Absurd
66: 150-53

STEINBERG, M. W.
Arthur Miller and the Idea of
Modern Tragedy   84: 81-93

STEINER, GEORGE
Introduction to *Homer: A Collection of Critical Essays*   15: 1-
14

STEVENS, WALLACE
About One of Marianne Moore's
Poems   86: 107-11
Three Academic Pieces: I   33: 24-
29
William Carlos Williams   61: 62-
65

STEWART, DONALD OGDEN
The Courtship of Miles Standish
27: 92-98

STILLINGER, JACK
The Hoodwinking of Madeline:
Skepticism in *The Eve of St.
Agnes*   43: 71-90

STIRLING, BRENTS
"Or Else Were This a Savage Specta-
cle" [Ritual in *Julius Caesar*]
40: 34-43

STOCK, A. G.
A Vision   23: 139-54

STOLLER, LEO
Thoreau's Doctrine of Simplicity
10: 37-52

STOVALL, FLOYD
The Conscious Art of Edgar Allan
Poe   63: 172-78

STRAUSS, WALTER A.
Criticism and Creation   4: 53-68

STROEVA, M. N.
The Three Sisters in the Production
of the Moscow Art Theater
71: 121-35

SULLIVAN, J. P.
"The Leading Classic of His Genera-
tion"   83: 146-52
Pound's *Homage to Propertius:*
The Structure of a Mask   29:
142-51

SUMMERS, JOSEPH H.
The Final Vision   60: 183-206
Marvell's "Nature"   81: 42-54

SUPREME SACRED CONGREGA-
TION OF THE HOLY OFFICE
Condemnation of the Works of
André Gide   88: 30-35

SUTTON, JULIET
Thackeray's Mothers-in-Law   75:
55-65

SUTTON, WALTER
Introduction to *Ezra Pound: A Collection of Critical Essays*   29:
1-8
Whitman's Poetic Ensembles   5:
119-32

SVANBERG, VICTOR
The Strindberg Cult   95: 71-78

SVENDSEN, PAULUS
Emperor and Galilean   52: 80-90

SYPHER, WYLIE
Cubist Drama   67: 67-71

TANNER, TONY
The Lost America—The Despair of
Henry Adams and Mark Twain
30: 159-74

TATE, ALLEN
E. E. Cummings [*ViVa*]   98: 71-74
Emily Dickinson   28: 16-27
Introduction to *Land of Unlikeness*
79: 36-37
Johnson on the Metaphysical Poets
48: 89-101
On *Ash-Wednesday*   2: 129-35
Our Cousin, Mr. Poe   63: 38-50
Yeats' Romanticism   23: 155-62

TAYLOR, JOHN RUSSELL
The Early Fifties   74: 15-25
John Arden   74: 83-97

TEMPLE, RUTH Z.
Never Say "I": *To the Lighthouse*
as Vision and Confession   93:
90-100

TENNANT, P. F. D.
  Ibsen as a Stage Craftsman   52:
    29-40

THACKREY, DONALD E.
  The Communication of the Word
    28: 51-69

THIBAUDET, ALBERT
  Faces of Proust   4: 47-52

THOMSON, GEORGE
  Prometheia   99: 124-47

THOMPSON, LAWRANCE
  Mirror Analogues in *The Sound and
    the Fury*   65: 109-21
  Robert Frost's Theory of Poetry
    3: 16-35

TIBBLE, ANNE
  Chinua Achebe   97: 122-31

TILFORD, JOHN E., JR.
  The Love Theme of *Henry Esmond*
    75: 127-46

TILGHER, ADRIANO
  Life *versus* Form   67: 19-34

TILLOTSON, KATHLEEN
  Dombey and Son   72: 115-34
  Vanity Fair   75: 65-87

TILLYARD, E. M. W.
  The Crisis of *Paradise Lost*   60:
    156-82
  The Elizabethan World Order   45:
    32-41
  Ode on Anne Killigrew   32:
    136-48
  The Secret Agent Reconsidered
    53: 103-10

TINDALL, WILLIAM YORK
  The Symbolism of W. B. Yeats
    23: 43-53

TINTNER, ADELINE
  The Museum World
    34: 139-55

TOLIVER, HAROLD E.
  Marvell's "Definition of Love" and
    Poetry of Self-Explanation
    81: 74-84

TOLKIEN, J. R. R.
  Beowulf: The Monsters and the
    Critics   82: 8-56

TOLSTOY, LEO
  Homer and Shakespeare   15: 15-
    16

TOMLINSON, CHARLES
  Introduction to *Marianne Moore: A
    Collection of Critical Essays*
    86: 1-15

TORREY, NORMAN L.
  Duplicity and Protective Lying
    78: 18-30
  Voltaire and the English Deists
    78: 69-76

TRAUGOTT, JOHN
  Introduction to *Laurence Sterne: A
    Collection of Critical Essays*
    77: 1-20
  The Shandean Comic Vision of
    Locke   77: 126-47
  A Voyage to Nowhere with Thomas
    More and Jonathan Swift: *Utopia*
    and *The Voyage to the Houyhn-
    hnms*   35: 143-69

TRAVERSI, DEREK
  Dostoevsky   16: 159-72
  The Historical Pattern from *Richard
    II* to *Henry V*   45: 102-12
  The Winter's Tale   47: 152-63

TREND, J. B.
  Lorca   14: 27-49

TRETIAKOV, SERGEY
  Bert Brecht   11: 16-29

TRILLING, DIANA
  The House of Mirth Revisited   10:
    103-18

TRILLING, LIONEL
  Forster and the Liberal Imagination
    59: 71-80
  Little Dorrit   72: 147-57
  Mansfield Park   26: 124-40
  The Morality of Inertia   20:
    137-46
  Reality in America: Part II   96:
    87-95

TRILLING, LIONEL (*continued*)
A Speech on Robert Frost: A Cultural Episode   3: 151-58

TROTSKY, LEON
The Strangled Revolution   37: 12-19

TROY, WILLIAM
The New Generation   34: 79-91
Scott Fitzgerald—The Authority of Failure   27: 20-24
Virginia Woolf: The Novel of Sensibility   93: 26-39

TURNELL, MARTIN
Le Rouge et le noir   7: 15-33

TUVESON, ERNEST
Introduction to *Swift: A Collection of Critical Essays*   35: 1-14
Swift: The Dean as Satirist   35: 101-10

TYNAN, KENNETH
American Blues: The Plays of Arthur Miller and Tennessee Williams   69: 34-44

UNDERWOOD, DALE
The Comic Language   64: 87-103

UNTERECKER, JOHN
Faces and False Faces   23: 23-32
Introduction to *Yeats: A Collection of Critical Essays*   23: 1-6

VALÉRY, PAUL
The Position of Baudelaire   18: 7-18

VAN DOREN, MARK
Joseph and His Brothers: A Comedy in Four Parts   36: 96-108
The Scarlet Letter   55: 129-40
Timon of Athens   40: 148-51

VAN GHENT, DOROTHY
The Dickens World: A View from Todger's   72: 24-38
On *Clarissa Harlowe*   85: 49-66
On *Sons and Lovers*   24: 15-28
On *Tess of the D'Urbervilles*   25: 77-90

VICKERY, OLGA
Crime and Punishment: *Sanctuary*   65: 127-36

VIETOR, KARL
La Maladie du Siècle   73: 26-32

VIGNERON, ROBERT
Creative Agony   4: 13-27

VILLIERS, ANDRÉ
Dom Juan Revisited   41: 79-89

VIVANTE, LEONE
Shelley and the Creative Principle   49: 31-45

VIVAS, ELISEO
Kafka's Distorted Mask   17: 133-46
The Two Dimensions of Reality in *The Brothers Karamazov*   16: 71-89

VOLPE, EDMUND L.
The Wasteland of Nathanael West   94: 91-101

WADE, IRA O.
Voltaire and Madame du Chatelet   78: 64-68

WAGGONER, HYATT H.
E. A. Robinson: The Cosmic Chill   91: 148-63
The Marble Faun   55: 164-76
Notes on the Use of Coincidence in the Novels of E. M. Forster   59: 81-89
Past as Present: *Absalom, Absalom!*   65: 175-85

WAGNER, C. ROLAND
A Central Poetry   33: 71-75

WAIN, JOHN
Dylan Thomas: A Review of His Collected Poems   56: 9-13
Housman   83: 26-31
An Idiom of Desperation   57: 57-70
The Search for Identity   31: 157-70

WAITH, EUGENE M.
  All for Love   64: 51-62
  Eugene O'Neill: An Exercise in
    Unmasking   39: 29-41
  Introduction to *Shakespeare: The
    Histories: A Collection of
    Critical Essays*   45: 1-12
  Tamburlaine   44: 69-91

WALCUTT, CHARLES CHILD
  Theodore Dreiser and the Divided
    Stream   96: 104-28

WALDCOCK, A. J. A.
  Satan and the Technique of Degra-
    dation   60: 77-99

WALDMEIR, JOSEPH
  Confiteor Hominen: Ernest Heming-
    way's Religion of Man   8:
    161-68

WALLACE, JOHN M.
  Andrew Marvell and Cromwell's
    Kingship: "The First Anni-
    versary"   81: 143-64

WALTER, J. H.
  Introduction to *Henry V*   45:
    152-67

WANNING, ANDREWS
  Fitzgerald and His Brethren   27:
    57-63

WARREN, AUSTIN
  E. M. Forster   59: 48-55
  Emily Dickinson   28: 101-16
  Franz Kafka   17: 123-32
  Instress of Inscape   57: 168-77
  Symbolic Imagery   34: 123-38

WARREN, ROBERT PENN
  An American Tragedy   96: 129-40
  Faulkner: The South, the Negro,
    and Time   65: 251-71
  Introduction to *Faulkner: A Collec-
    tion of Critical Essays*   65: 1-
    22
  Melville the Poet   13: 114-55

WARREN, ROBERT PENN, and
CLEANTH BROOKS
  The Discovery of Evil: An Analysis

of "The Killers"   8: 114-17

WARSHOW, ROBERT
  The Liberal Conscience in *The
    Crucible*   84: 111-21

WASIOLEK, EDWARD
  Tolstoy's "The Death of Ivan Ilytch"
    and Jamesian Fictional Impera-
    tives   68: 146-56

WASSERMAN, EARL R.
  Dryden: Epistle to Charleton   32:
    71-85
  "Mont Blanc"   49: 69-102
  The *Ode on a Grecian Urn*   43:
    113-41

WATERMAN, ARTHUR E.
  The Plays of D. H. Lawrence   24:
    142-50

WATKINS, W. B. C.
  Creation   60: 121-47
  From "Yorick Revisited"   77:
    168-79

WATSON, BARBARA
  The Dangers of Security: E. E. Cum-
    mings' Revolt against the Future
    98: 31-45

WATT, IAN
  Clarissa and Lovelace   85: 76-79
  Introduction to *Jane Austen: A
    Collection of Critical Essays*
    26: 1-14
  On *Sense and Sensibility*   26:
    41-51
  Shamela   9: 45-51
  Tom Jones and *Clarissa*   9: 98-122

WATTS, HAROLD H.
  Reckoning   29: 98-114
  Robert Frost and the Interrupted
    Dialogue   3: 105-22

WEALES, GERALD
  Arthur Miller's Shifting Image of
    Man   84: 131-42

WEBER, JEAN-PAUL
  Edgar Poe, or The Theme of the
    Clock   63: 79-97

WEEKS, ROBERT P.
Introduction to *Hemingway: A Collection of Critical Essays* **8:** 1-16

WEIGAND, HERMANN J.
Thomas Mann's *Royal Highness* as Symbolic Autobiography **36:** 35-45

WEISS, AURÉLIU
The Technique of the Unseizable **67:** 135-39

WEISS, DANIEL
"The Blue Hotel": A Psychoanalytic Study **66:** 154-64

WELLEK, RENÉ
Introduction to *Dostoevsky: A Collection of Critical Essays* **16:** 1-15

WELLS, HENRY W.
An Evaluation of Thoreau's Poetry **10:** 131-41
Romantic Sensibility **28:** 45-50

WELLUSHOFF, DIETER
Failure of an Attempt at De-Mythologization: Samuel Beckett's Novels **51:** 92-107

WELSH, ALEXANDER
Introduction to *Thackeray: A Collection of Critical Essays* **75:** 1-14

WEST, NATHANAEL
Bird and Bottle **94:** 132-37
Some Notes on Miss L **94:** 66-67
Some Notes on Violence **94:** 50-51
Through a Hole in the Mundane Millstone **94:** 29-30

WEST, PAUL
Introduction to *Byron: A Collection of Critical Essays* **31:** 1-14
The Plays [of Byron] **31:** 50-64

WEST, RAY B., JR.
The Biological Trap **8:** 139-51

WEST, REBECCA
Babbitt **6:** 23-26

Sinclair Lewis Introduces Elmer Gantry **6:** 39-45

WHALLEY, GEORGE
The Mariner and the Albatross **70:** 32-50

WHARTON, EDITH
The Man of Letters **34:** 31-36

WHICHER, GEORGE F.
American Humor **28:** 41-44

WHICHER, STEPHEN E.
Emerson's Tragic Sense **12:** 39-45
The World of Ibsen **52:** 169-73

WHIPPLE, T. K.
Sinclair Lewis **6:** 71-83

WHITMAN, CEDRIC H.
Apocalypse: *Oedipus at Colonus* **54:** 146-74
Fire and Other Elements **15:** 40-61

WHITMAN, ROBERT F.
O'Neill's Search for a "Language of the Theatre" **39:** 142-64

WIDMER, KINGSLEY
Black Existentialism: Richard Wright **97:** 79-87

WILBUR, RICHARD
Beowulf **82:** 66-67
The House of Poe **63:** 98-120
Round About a Poem of Housman's **83:** 85-105
"Sumptuous Destitution" **28:** 127-36

WILD, JOHN D.
Existentialism as a Philosophy **21:** 142-48
The New Empiricism **21:** 136-41

WILEY, PAUL L.
Conrad's Solitaries **53:** 63-73

WILKINSON, ANN Y.
A Principle of Unity in *Between the Acts* **93:** 145-54

WILKINSON, ELIZABETH M.
Goethe's Conception of Form **73:** 110-31

WILKINSON, ELIZABETH M. (*continued*)
Tonio Krüger: An Interpretation
36: 22-34

WILLEN, GERALD
Dreiser's Moral Seriousness   96: 96-103

WILLETT, JOHN
Brecht: The Music   11: 157-70

WILLIAMS, CHARLES
The Recollection of the Way   46: 170-77

WILLIAMS, KATHLEEN
Conclusion to *Jonathan Swift and the Age of Compromise*   36: 115-22

WILLIAMS, RAYMOND
Dylan Thomas's Play for Voices   56: 89-98
Lawrence's Social Writings   24: 162-74
New English Drama   74: 26-37
Private Tragedy: Strindberg   95: 48-56
The Realism of Arthur Miller   84: 69-79

WILLIAMS, WILLIAM CARLOS
The Day of the Locust   94: 138-39
An Essay on *Leaves of Grass*   5: 146-54
Excerpts from a Critical Sketch: *A Draft of XXX Cantos* by Ezra Pound   29: 11-16
Federico García Lorca   14: 18-26
In a Mood of Tragedy: *The Mills of the Kavanaughs*   79: 104-5
Lower Case Cummings   98: 100-103
Marianne Moore (1925)   86: 52-59
A New American Writer   94: 48-49
Prose from *Spring and All*   61: 15-26
Sordid? Good God!   94: 70-73

WILLOUGHBY, LEONARD A.
Unity and Continuity in Goethe   73: 161-78

WILSON, ANGUS
The Heroes and Heroines of Dickens   72: 16-23

WILSON, EDMUND
A. E. Housman   83: 14-25
André Malraux   37: 25-30
The Boys in the Back Room   94: 140-43
Byron in the Twenties   31: 138-44
A Dissenting Opinion on Kafka   17: 91-97
Edith Wharton: A Memoir by an English Friend   20: 172-76
F. Scott Fitzgerald   27: 80-85
Jean-Paul Sartre: The Novelist and the Existentialist   31: 47-53
Justice to Edith Wharton   20: 19-31
A Long Talk about Jane Austen   26: 35-40
Morose Ben Jonson   22: 60-74
The Original of Tolstoy's Natasha   68: 95-101
The Pilgrimage II   34: 63-71
Reëxamining Dr. Johnson   48: 11-14
Salute to an Old Landmark: Sinclair Lewis   6: 139-42
W. H. Auden in America   38: 54-59
William Faulkner's Reply to the Civil-Rights Program   65: 219-25

WILSON, F. P.
The Massacre at Paris and Edward II   44: 128-37

WILSON, MILTON
"Hymns of Pan and Apollo"   49: 153-58

WIMSATT, W. K., JR.
Scientific Imagery in *The Rambler*   48: 138-48

WINE, M. L.
Spenser's "Sweete *Themmes*": Of Time and the River 80: 40-46

WINKLER, R. O. C.
The Novels 17: 45-51

WINTERS, YVOR
A Cool Master 91: 8-14
Emily Dickinson and the Limits of Judgment 28: 28-40
Gerard Manley Hopkins 57: 37-56
Maule's Curse, or Hawthorne and the Problem of Allegory 55: 11-24
Poetry of Feeling 61: 66-69
Robert Frost, or the Spiritual Drifter as Poet 3: 58-82
The Shorter Poems 91: 40-59

WOLFF, CHRISTIAN
Orestes 76: 132-49

WOODARD, THOMAS
The Electra of Sophocles 54: 125-45
Introduction to *Sophocles: A Collection of Critical Essays* 54: 1-15

WOODCOCK, GEORGE
The Social Rebel 87: 150-68

WOOLF, VIRGINIA
The Ghost Stories 34: 47-54
Jane Austen 26: 15-24
On Sophocles' *Electra* 54: 122-24

WRIGHT, ANDREW H.
Persuasion 26: 145-53

WRIGHT, DAVID
Canons Ashby 32: 181

YEATS, WILLIAM BUTLER
The Catastrophe 87: 16-21
Ezra Pound 29: 9-10
The Lake Isle of Innisfree 10: 8

My First Meeting with Oscar Wilde 87: 9-15
Wilde in Phase 19 87: 22-24

YERMILOV, V.
Uncle Vanya: The Play's Movement 71: 112-20

YOUNG, PHILIP
Adventures of Nick Adams 8: 95-111
Crane and Hemingway 66: 52-56
A Defense 8: 172-74

YOUNG, STARK
Eugene O'Neill's New Play [*Mourning Becomes Electra*] 39: 82-88
The Pirandello Play 67: 11-13
Pirandello's Commedia 67: 15-18

ZABEL, MORTON DAUWEN
Hardy in Defense of His Art 25: 24-45
Introduction to *Under Western Eyes* 53: 111-44
Robinson in America 91: 29-32
Wallace Stevens and the Image of Man 33: 151-60

ZENKOVSKY, V. V.
Dostoevsky's Religous and Philosophical Views 16: 130-45

ZIFF, LARZER
The Ethical Dimension of "The Custom House" 55: 123-29
Outstripping the Event: Crane's *Maggie* 66: 106-9

ZIMBARDO, ROSE A.
The Satiric Design in *The Plain Dealer* 64: 123-38

ZWERDLING, ALEX
W. B. Yeats: Variations on the Visionary Quest 23: 80-92

1	CAMUS	51	SAMUEL BECKETT
2	T. S. ELIOT	52	IBSEN
3	ROBERT FROST	53	CONRAD
4	PROUST	54	SOPHOCLES
5	WHITMAN	55	HAWTHORNE
6	SINCLAIR LEWIS	56	DYLAN THOMAS
7	STENDHAL	57	HOPKINS
8	HEMINGWAY	58	BLAKE
9	FIELDING	59	FORSTER
10	THOREAU	60	MILTON: PARADISE LOST
11	BRECHT	61	WILLIAM CARLOS WILLIAMS
12	EMERSON	62	VIRGIL
13	MELVILLE	63	POE
14	LORCA	64	RESTORATION DRAMATISTS
15	HOMER	65	FAULKNER
16	DOSTOEVSKY	66	STEPHEN CRANE
17	KAFKA	67	PIRANDELLO
18	BAUDELAIRE	68	TOLSTOY
19	JOHN DONNE	69	THE MODERN AMERICAN
20	EDITH WHARTON		THEATER
21	SARTRE	70	COLERIDGE
22	BEN JONSON	71	CHEKHOV
23	YEATS	72	DICKENS
24	D. H. LAWRENCE	73	GOETHE
25	HARDY	74	MODERN BRITISH
26	JANE AUSTEN		DRAMATISTS
27	F. SCOTT FITZGERALD	75	THACKERAY
28	EMILY DICKINSON	76	EURIPIDES
29	EZRA POUND	77	LAURENCE STERNE
30	MARK TWAIN	78	VOLTAIRE
31	BYRON	79	ROBERT LOWELL
32	DRYDEN	80	SPENSER
33	WALLACE STEVENS	81	ANDREW MARVELL
34	HENRY JAMES	82	THE BEOWULF POET
35	SWIFT	83	A. E. HOUSMAN
36	THOMAS MANN	84	ARTHUR MILLER
37	MALRAUX	85	SAMUEL RICHARDSON
38	AUDEN	86	MARIANNE MOORE
39	O'NEILL	87	OSCAR WILDE
40	SHAKESPEARE:	88	GIDE
	THE TRAGEDIES	89	CERVANTES
41	MOLIERE	90	GEORGE ELIOT
42	FLAUBERT	91	EDWIN ARLINGTON
43	KEATS		ROBINSON
44	MARLOWE	92	THE BRONTËS
45	SHAKESPEARE:	93	VIRGINIA WOOLF
	THE TRAGEDIES	94	NATHANAEL WEST
46	DANTE	95	STRINDBERG
47	SHAKESPEARE:	96	DREISER
	THE COMEDIES	97	MODERN BLACK NOVELISTS
48	SAMUEL JOHNSON	98	E. E. CUMMINGS
49	SHELLEY	99	AESCHYLUS
50	G. B. SHAW	100	STEINBECK